S0-AJI-606

Eighth Edition

Understanding
PSYCHOLOGY

Charles G. Morris
Albert A. Maisto

Prentice Hall Upper Saddle River, NJ 07458

NOTICE:
This work is protected by U.S. copyright laws and is provided solely for the use of college instructors in reviewing course materials for classroom use. Dissemination or sale of this work, or any part (including on the World Wide Web) is not permitted. Complimentary examination copies of Pearson Education college textbooks that will not be adopted for course use can be returned to the publisher by using the pre-paid mailing label that is available on our website at www.prenhall.com/returnlabel.

Editorial Director: Leah Jewell
Executive Editor: Jessica Mosher
Editorial Assistant: Jessica Kupetz
Editor-in Chief, Development: Rochelle Diogenes
Developmental Editor: Susan Moss
Director, Media and Assessment: Shannon Gattens
Media Editor: Brian Hyland
Managing Supplements Editor: Ginny Livsey
Assessment Editor: Kerri Scott
Director of Marketing: Brandy Dawson
Senior Marketing Manager: Jeanette Moyer
Assistant Marketing Manager: Billy Grieco
Marketing Assistant: Laura Kennedy
Director of Operation/Associate Director of Production: Barbara Kittle
Senior Managing Editor: Joanne Riker

Assistant Managing Editor, Production: Maureen Richardson
Project Manager, Production: Kathy Sleys
Manufacturing Manager: Nick Sklitsis
Manufacturing Buyer: Sherry Lewis
Creative Design Director: Leslie Osher
Interior/Cover Designer: Nancy Wells
Cover Illustration/Photo: Chip Simons / Science Faction / Getty Images, Inc
Director Image Resource Center: Melinda Reo
Manager, Rights and Permissions: Zina Arabia
Image Permission Coordinator: Michelina Viscusi
Manager, Visual Research: Beth Brenzel
Photo Researcher: Diane Austin
Composition/Full-Service Project Management: Preparé, Inc.
Printer/Binder: Courier Companies
Cover Printer: Phoenix Color Corp.

Credits and acknowledgments borrowed from other sources and reproduced, with permission, in this textbook appear on appropriate page within text (or on page PC-1).

Copyright © 2008, 2006, 2003, 2001, 1999 by Pearson Education, Inc., Upper Saddle River, New Jersey, 07458. All rights reserved. Printed in the United States of America. This publication is protected by Copyright and permission should be obtained from the publisher prior to any prohibited reproduction, storage in a retrieval system, or transmission in any form or by any means, electronic, mechanical, photocopying, recording, or likewise. For information regarding permission(s), write to: Rights and Permissions Department.

Pearson Prentice Hall™ is a trademark of Pearson Education, Inc.
Pearson® is a registered trademark of Pearson plc
Prentice Hall® is a registered trademark of Pearson Education, Inc.

Pearson Education Ltd.
Pearson Education Australia PTY, Ltd.
Pearson Education Singapore, Pte. Ltd.
Pearson Education North Asia Ltd
Pearson Education, Canada, Ltd.

Pearson Educación de Mexico, S.A. de C.V.
Pearson Education–Japan
Pearson Education Malaysia, Pte. Ltd.
Pearson Education, Upper Saddle River NJ

10 9 8 7 6 5 4 3 2 1
ISBN 0-13- 234341-X
978-0-13-234341-1

Brief Contents

Contents

Preface

This has been an unusually challenging revision because we have combined two related textbooks into one. Starting with *Understanding Psychology*, 7th edition, we incorporated some of the best additional material from the companion text *Introduction to Psychology*, 12th edition. The decision to join the two came about as we sifted through reviews for the new edition of each text. Response from our readers indicated that both our books are valued for "getting it right" and for paring down the voluminous psychological literature to present only the most important research and topics. So many similarities existed between the two texts that we decided to glean the best from each. Extensive editing resulted in a seamless integration of the two books. This 8th edition text is supported and enhanced by an improved art program that contains new figures and new photos. The result is an exciting "new" book that truly retains the best of both worlds and includes an entirely new Appendix entitled "Psychology Applied to Work."

Continued Focus on Basic Unifying Concepts

Despite the changes, our original goals for this book remain the same. We wanted to present a scientific, accurate, and thorough overview of the essential concepts of psychology; to use engaging language that students can easily comprehend; to be current without being trendy; and to write clearly and accessibly about psychology and its concrete, real-life applications—without being condescending to the introductory-level student. In this new book, we continue to focus on three unifying, basic concepts, which have been woven throughout every edition of our texts:

1. **Psychology is a science that is rapidly evolving.** From the thousands of articles that have appeared during the past several years, we selected more than1,000 new references for this edition, of which two-thirds are from 2004 to 2007. We have added more than a dozen **new** "Cutting Edge" boxes that describe recent, progressive research in the field of psychology. These featured discussions not only serve to inform but to challenge our current understanding of such phenomena as sleep deprivation, the effect of playing violent video games, the way we store emotional experiences, the evolution of language, and virtual therapy.

2. **Human behavior and thought are diverse, varied, and affected by culture.** Increased attention to diversity is found in every chapter, from the expanded discussion of human diversity and research (Chapter 1) to language, thought, and culture (Chapter 7) to cultural differences in psychological disorders (Chapter 12).

3. **The study of psychology involves active thinking, questioning, and problem solving.** We have added dozens of **new** "Thinking Critically About" exercises. The topics encourage the reader to engage in genuine critical thinking by questioning the methods used to gather data, considering possible alternative explanations for findings, and imagining further research that might shed additional light on the phenomenon under study.

Increased Attention to Enduring Issues

We believe that an important part of active learning is for students to recognize recurring themes that run through the material they are reading. In Chapter 1 we introduce a set of five **Enduring Issues** that cut across and unite all subfields of psychology (see pages 7–8):

- **Person–Situation:** To what extent is behavior caused by processes that occur inside the person, such as thoughts, emotions, and genes? In contrast, to what extent is behavior caused or triggered by factors outside the person, such as incentives, cues in the environment, and the presence of other people?
- **Nature–Nurture:** Is the person we become a product of innate, inborn tendencies, or a reflection of experience and upbringing?
- **Stability–Change:** Are the characteristics we develop in childhood more or less permanent and fixed, or do we change in predictable (and unpredictable) ways over the course of our lives?
- **Diversity–Universality:** Because we are all human, each person is like every other person. But in some respects, each person is only like certain other people. And in other respects, each of us is like no other person. Thus, anywhere humans exist there will be both similarity and diversity.
- **Mind–Body:** How are mind and body connected? Many psychologists are fascinated by the relationship between what we experience, such as thoughts and feelings, and biological processes, such as activity in the nervous system.

These five issues represent enduring themes in the history of psychology. Depending on the events and intellectual climate of a given time period, one or another of these issues has assumed special prominence, For example, at the beginning of the 21st century the role of genetics (heredity) is receiving much greater attention than it has in the past. Diversity is also an issue of much greater concern, as is the role of biological processes.

Throughout this book, we will highlight the importance of these matters. Each chapter opens with a **new** section highlighting the enduring issues to be encountered in that chapter. Several times in each chapter we will call your attention to the way in which the topic under consideration—whether it be new discoveries about communication within the nervous system, research into how we learn, or the reason that people abuse drugs—reflects one of these issues. In this way, we will show the surprising unity and coherence of the diverse and exciting science of psychology.

New To This Edition

Each chapter of our text begins with an opening vignette. Reviewers have often commented on how useful it is to have the vignette woven throughout the chapter to help students understand and apply information. In addition to the streamlining content, updating more than 1,000 new references, the inclusion of numerous new photographs and figures within each chapter, following is a list of the most significant chapter-by-chapter changes.

CHAPTER 1   THE SCIENCE OF PSYCHOLOGY
- Updated chapter-opening vignette about Brooke Ellison
- Three new "Thinking Critically About" boxes
- New "Cutting Edge" box on prescription privileges
- Expanded discussion of "Human Diversity and Research"
- 53 new references

CHAPTER 2   THE BIOLOGICAL BASIS OF BEHAVIOR
- New chapter-opening vignette about brain plasticity
- Three new "Enduring Issues"
- Two new "Thinking Critically About" boxes
- New section on long-term potentiation
- New discussion of handedness
- Substantial updating and editing of genetics discussion
- New "Cutting Edge" on mirror neurons (includes critical thinking exercise)
- Three new figures, including one on the relation among genes, chromosomes, and DNA
- 101 new references

CHAPTER 3   SENSATION AND PERCEPTION
- New chapter-opening vignette
- Three new "Enduring Issues"
- Two new "Thinking Critically About" boxes
- New "Cutting Edge" box on pheromones
- Modest expansion of coverage of ESP
- New section on color vision in other species
- New introduction to the section on hearing
- Virtually all-new discussion of pain
- New discussion of proximal and distal stimuli
- 47 new references

CHAPTER 4   STATES OF CONSCIOUSNESS
- New chapter-opening vignette
- Four new "Enduring Issues"
- Three new "Thinking Critically" boxes
- New "Cutting Edge" on sleep deprivation (includes critical thinking exercise)
- Expanded and updated discussion of hypnosis
- Greatly revised discussion of binge drinking on college campuses
- Updated drug use data
- Four updated figures and one new figure: a new graph showing alcohol usage over time
- 101 new sources

CHAPTER 5   LEARNING
- Two new chapter-opening vignettes
- Four new "Enduring Issues"
- Three new "Thinking Critically" boxes
- New "Cutting Edge" box on violent video games (includes critical thinking exercise)
- New section on cognitive learning in nonhumans
- New material on "over imitating" among children
- Two new figures: response acquisition and extinction/spontaneous recovery in classical conditioning
- 39 new references

CHAPTER 6   MEMORY
- New chapter-opening vignette
- Three new "Enduring Issues"
- Three new "Thinking Critically" boxes
- New "Cutting Edge" box on storing emotional experiences
- New section on tip-of-the-tongue phenomenon
- New section on extraordinary memory
- New information on hormones and long-term memory
- New information on the effect of stress on recall
- New figure depicting the progression of Alzheimer's disease in the brain over time
- 62 new references

CHAPTER 7   COGNITION AND MENTAL ABILITIES
- Four new "Enduring Issues"
- Five new "Thinking Critically About" boxes
- New "Cutting Edge" box on biological measures of intelligence
- Greatly expanded discussion of language, thought, and culture
- New section on gender stereotyping and language.
- New section on nonhuman thought and language
- Greatly revised discussion of cultural differences in abilities
- 75 new references

CHAPTER 8   MOTIVATION AND EMOTION
- Four new "Enduring Issues"
- Four new "Thinking Critically About" boxes
- New "Cutting Edge" box on interpreting facial expressions
- Updated statistics on eating disorders and incidence of violent crimes
- Expanded discussion of sexuality and sexual orientation
- Four new figures: one on physiological factors regulating appetite and body weight, a graph on rising obesity in American youth, a chart on body mass index (BMI), and a graph on sexual behavior around the world
- 100 new references

CHAPTER 9   LIFE-SPAN DEVELOPMENT
- New chapter-opening vignette
- Two new "Thinking Critically About" boxes
- New "Cutting Edge" box on evolution of language
- Updated statistics on women in the work force, dual-career families, and population age structure
- One updated figure on infant mortality and one new figure on synaptic density in the human brain from infancy to adulthood
- 116 new references

CHAPTER 10 PERSONALITY

* Four new "Enduring Issues"
* Three new "Thinking Critically About" boxes
* New "Cutting Edge" box on genetic basis of personality
* Significant updating and expansion of Big Five theory of personality
* 34 new references

CHAPTER 11 STRESS AND HEALTH PSYCHOLOGY

* New chapter-opening vignette
* Three new "Enduring Issues"
* Three new "Thinking Critically About" boxes
* New "Cutting Edge" box on "tend and befriend"
* New material on road rage, Type D personality, effect of divorce on children, and adversity as an impetus for positive growth
* Greatly expanded discussion of posttraumatic stress disorder (PTSD)
* 78 new references

CHAPTER 12 PSYCHOLOGICAL DISORDERS

* Four new "Enduring Issues"
* Three new "Thinking Critically About" boxes
* New "Cutting Edge" box on "the neuroscience revolution"
* Expanded coverage of depression, sexual disorders, autism, gender, and cultural differences in psychological disorders
* Significant revision of passages on mental illness and the law and causes of ADHD
* One new graph on gender and racial differences in the suicide rate across the life span
* 87 new references

CHAPTER 13 THERAPIES

* Two new "Enduring Issues"
* Two new "Thinking Critically About" boxes
* New "Cutting Edge" box on Virtual Therapy
* New material on *Consumer Reports* survey
* Greatly expanded discussion of the effectiveness of psychotherapy
* Significant revision of short-term therapy and therapeutic use of modeling
* 64 new references

CHAPTER 14 SOCIAL PSYCHOLOGY

* Three new "Enduring Issues"
* Three new "Thinking Critically About" boxes
* New "Cutting Edge" box on beauty and privilege
* Significant revision of discussion of conformity
* Relocation of I/O psychology to new Appendix
* 81 new references

APPENDIX A MEASUREMENT AND STATISTICAL METHODS

* New section on meta-analysis
* New section on bimodal distributions

* Four new figures, including two graphs on bimodal distributions, one on meta-analysis, and one illustrating correlations.

APPENDIX B PSYCHOLOGY APPLIED TO WORK

* Entirely new I/O appendix written specifically for this new edition
* New information on matching people to jobs (job analysis and predicting job performance)
* New information on measuring job performance
* New information on fairness in employment
* New information on behavior within organizations (training and motivating employees)
* New information on organizational culture (teams, teamwork, leadership)
* New information on organizational attitudes (job satisfaction, organizational justice)
* New graphic exemplifying a BARS performance evaluation
* 59 new references

Enhanced Supplements Package

It is increasingly true today that, as valuable as a good textbook is, it is one element of a comprehensive learning package. We have made every effort to provide high-quality instructor and student supplements that will save you preparation time and will enhance the classroom experience

FOR ACCESS TO ALL INSTRUCTOR SUPPLEMENTS FOR MORRIS/MAISTO *UNDERSTANDING PSYCHOLOGY* 8/E AND ANY OTHER PEARSON TEXT SIMPLY GO TO http://prenhall.com/irc and follow the directions to register (or login if you already have a user name and password). Once you have registered and your status as an instructor is verified, you will be emailed a login name and password. Use your login name and password to access the catalogue. Click on the "online catalog" link, click on "Psychology" followed by "Introductory Psychology" and then the "Morris/Maisto *Understanding Psychology*, 8/e" text. Under the description of each supplement is a link that allows you to download and save the supplement to your desktop.

Hard copies of the supplements can be requested through your Prentice Hall sales representative. If you do not know your sales representative, go to http://prenhall.com/replocator/ and follow the directions to locate your sales representative.

For technical support for any of your Prentice Hall products, you and your students can contact http://247.prenhall.com/ or call customer technical support at 1-800-677-6337.

SUPPLEMENTS FOR INSTRUCTORS

TEST ITEM FILE (0-13-233517-4): One of the most respected test banks on the market today, developed by Gary Piggrem of DeVry University, this test file contains over 4,000 multiple-choice, true/false, and essay questions. To facilitate your selection of items, each question is page referenced to the textbook. A two-page Total Assessment Guide chapter overview makes creating tests easier by listing all of the test items in an easy-to-reference grid. The Total Assessment Guide organizes all test items by text section and question type/level of difficulty. All multiple-choice questions are categorized as either factual, conceptual, or applied. Many of the items also include statistics indicating how many students answered that question correctly in class-testing at both 2-year and 4-year schools. In addition, the text author, Charles Morris, has carefully reviewed the test file and has indicated a number of "Author's Choice" questions because of their challenging nature or interesting focus.

PRENTICE HALL'S TESTGEN (0-13-13233515-8): Available on one dual-platform CD-ROM, this computerized test generator program provides instructors "best in class" features in an easy-to-use program. Create tests using the TestGen Wizard and easily select questions with drag-and-drop or point-and-click functionality. Add or modify test questions using the built-in Question Editor. TestGen also offers algorithmic functionality, which allows for the creation of unlimited versions of a single test. The Quiz Master feature allows for online test delivery. Complete with an instructor grade book and full technical support. Available online through the Instructor's Resources Center or on the Instructor Resource CD-ROM.

ALSO AVAILABLE, PRENTICE HALL'S NEW TESTING PLATFORM *MYTEST* is an alternative program to TestGen. A powerful assessment generation program that helps instructors easily create and print quizzes, tests, exams, as well as homework or practice handouts. Questions, assessments, or assignments can all be authored online, allowing instructors ultimate flexibility and the ability to efficiently manage assessments at anytime, from anywhere. Contact your local Prentice Hall representative for more information.

POWERPOINT PRESENTATION AND CLASSROOM RESPONSE QUESTIONS (on Instructor's CD-ROM or online at http://prenhall. com): A completely redesigned PowerPoint presentation by Darrell Rudmann (Shawnee State University), created especially for the 8th edition, incorporating the text art and outlining the key points for each text chapter. Also available, Classroom Response questions ("clicker" questions) created for *Understanding Psychology*, Eighth Edition and designed to promote in-class discussion. For more on Classroom Response Systems see the next section.

CLASSROOM RESPONSE SYSTEMS (http://www.prenhall.com/crs) Pearson Education is pleased to offer the benefits of our partnerships with two of the leading classroom response systems on the market. Customers using a Prentice Hall Classroom Response System with their text are entitled to student and department savings exclusively from Pearson Education. Whether you are considering a system for the first time or are interested in expanding a program department-wide, we can help you select the best system for your needs. For more information about classroom response systems and our partnerships, please visit our Web site at http://www.prenhall.com/crs.

INSTRUCTOR'S RESOURCE MANUAL (0-13-233519-0): In this abundant collection of resources, for each chapter, you'll find activities, exercises, assignments, handouts, and demos for in-class use, as well as guidelines for integrating the many Morris media resources into your classroom and syllabus. The material for each chapter is organized in an easy-to-use Chapter Lecture Outline.

This resource saves prep work and helps you make maximum use of your classroom time.

PH COLOR TRANSPARENCIES (0-13-192699-3): A set of full-color transparencies is designed to be used in large lecture settings. Available on the Instructor Resource Center online at http://prenhall.com/irc or on CD-ROM, as well as in acetate format. Lecture notes to accompany the transparencies for easy use in the classroom are also available online.

INSTRUCTOR'S CD-ROM (0-13-233519-0): Bringing all of the 8th edition's instructor resources together in one place, the Instructor's Resource CD-ROM offers the PowerPoint presentations, the electronic files for the Instructor's Resource Manual materials, and the Test Item File to help you customize your lecture notes. (Note that all of these resources can be downloaded from the Instructor Resource Center online by following the directions at http://prenhall.com/irc.

COLLEGE TEACHING TIPS (0-13-614317-2) This guide by Fred W. Whitford helps new instructors or graduate teaching assistants manage the myriad complex tasks required to teach an introductory course effectively. The author has used his own teaching experiences over the last 25 years to help illustrate some of the types of problems that a new instructor may expect to face. The guide has been completely revised and updated from the former *Teaching Psychology: A Guide for the New Instructor*, Fourth Edition to include content applicable to a number of disciplines with introductory courses.

MOVIES AS ILLUSTRATIONS FOR INTRODUCTORY PSYCHOLOGY (0-13-145510-9) This teaching guide suggests 45 different movie scenes, several for each chapter of a typical introductory psychology textbook, which can be used to spark discussion and clarify concepts covered in class. Includes scene notes, which summarize the scenes and provide context; topic notes, which tie in the movie scenes to topics likely covered in introductory psychology classes, and discussion questions, which suggest ways of engaging the class in conversation about the scene.

MEDIA AND ONLINE RESOURCES FOR INSTRUCTORS AND STUDENTS

VANGONOTES (http://www.vangonotes.com): With VangoNotes students can study "in between" all the other things they need to get done. Students download chapter reviews from their text and listen to them on any MP3 player. VangoNotes gives students the confidence needed to succeed in the classroom. They're **flexible**; just download and go. And, they're **efficient**. Use them in the car, at the gym, walking to class, wherever; for more information or to download go to www.vangonotes.com

NEW *MYPSYCHLAB* FOR UNDERSTANDING PSYCHOLOGY, 8/E (http://www.mypsychlab.com) Continual feedback is an important component to successful student progress. New to this edition is Prentice Hall's *MyPsychLab*, an

easy-to-use online resource that allows instructors to assess student progress and adapt course material to meet the specific needs of the class. *MyPsychLab* enables students to judge their progress by completing online self-assessment tests. The tests have a large base of questions, distinct from the test bank and other supplementary materials. A variety of question types are used for the pre- and posttests, including multiple choice, text match, ranking, fill in the blank, and drag and drop.

Based on the results of the pretest, each student is provided with a customized study plan that includes a variety of tools to help them fully master the material such as e-book exercises, simulations, and activities. Students can use the activities to study key content areas and they can also continue to quiz themselves by taking the posttest as many times as they want. Pre- and posttests are randomized, so if students opt to take the posttest again, they have exposure to additional questions for the same content area.

MyPsychLab records the pretest, study plan, and posttest results as individual student grades and provides an aggregate report of class progress. Based on these data, the instructor can adapt course material to suit the needs of individual students or the class as a whole. Having instructor course materials, such as extra lecture notes, PowerPoint slides, and activities available in *MyPsychLab* saves valuable planning time. Based on the results of the pretests, instructors can choose to use only those resources , that are relevant to their students' areas of difficulty.

MyPsychLab provides a more compelling classroom experience by allowing students to better assess their own progress and by providing instructors the materials specific to the needs of their class. *MyPsychLab* saves instructors time by cataloguing student progress and providing tools to help students achieve success in their introductory psychology class. Students access *MyPsychLab* through an access code packaged with their text, or purchased online at www.mypsychlab.com. Contact your local Prentice Hall representative for an instructor's code and for more information.

 LIVE!PSYCH MEDIA LIBRARY: (http://www.prenhall.com/livepsych): The *Live!Psych* media library is a series of experiments, simulations, and activities developed to offer students an interactive way to master the major concepts presented in introductory psychology and to reinforce the scientific nature of the discipline. These media activities were created in consultation with psychology instructors and carefully reviewed by a board of experts to ensure accuracy and pedagogical effectiveness. They were designed to stimulate student interaction with the material and to appeal to different learning styles, For the development of the *Live!Psych* experiments, a special thank you goes to Linda Lockwood, Metro State College, the content author, and to the members of our *Live!Psych* review board. The *Live!Psych* media library is available through *MyPsychLab* or on a CD-ROM (0131947745). Contact your local Prentice Hall representative for more information.

 **RESEARCH NAVIGATOR™** (http://www.research navigator.com): Research Navigator helps students find, cite, and conduct research with three exclusive databases: EBSCO's ContentSelect Academic Journal Database; The *New York Times* Search-by-Subject Archive; and Best of the Web Link Library.

Available through *MyPsychLab* or packaged with the text, Prentice Hall representative for ordering information.

VIDEO CLASSICS IN PSYCHOLOGY CD-ROM (0-13-189154-5): Using the power of video to clarify key concepts in the text, this CD-ROM offers original footage of some of the best-known classic experiments in psychology, including Milgram's obedience study, Watson's Little Albert, Bandura's BoBo doll, Pavlov's dog, Harlow's monkey, and others. In addition, students can see interviews with renowned contributors to the field like B. F. Skinner, Carl Rogers, Erik Erickson, Carl Jung, and others. Each video is preceded by background information on the importance of the experiment or researcher to the field and is followed by questions that connect the video to concepts presented in the text. Contact your local sales representative for the package ISBN of the text and CD-ROM.

 SAFARIX WEBBOOK (http://www.SafariX.com): Students can buy an online subscription to *Understanding Psychology*, Eighth Edition at a 50% savings. With the SafariX WebBook, students can search the text, make notes online, print out reading assignments that incorporate lecture notes, and bookmark important passages. Ask your local Prentice Hall representative for details or visit www.safarix.com

COMPANION WEB SITE (http://www.prenhall.com/morris): Visit the Prentice Hall Introductory Psychology Web site, your guide to exploring the fascinating and diverse world of psychology. On this site you can find information about psychology and gain an understanding of its history. The Web site presents examples of the types of research done in the major fields of psychology, links to useful sites in the major areas of psychology, news links to current real-world issues in psychology, and online quizzes that provide immediate scoring and feedback. The Prentice Hall Introductory Psychology Web site for Morris is an open-access site available to all.

VIDEO RESOURCES FOR INSTRUCTORS

Prentice Hall is proud to present you with the following video packages, available exclusively to qualified adopters of the Morris/Maisto text.

INTRODUCTORY PSYCHOLOGY TEACHING FILMS BOXED SET (0-13-192687-X) This package provides an easy-to-use multi-DVD set of videos, organized by chapter topics, to incorporate into your introductory psychology course. This resource offers approximately 100 short video clips of 5–15 minutes in length from many of the most popular video sources for psychology content, such as *ABC News*; the *Films for the Humanities* series; PBS, and more. Available to qualified adopters, contact your local Prentice Hall representative for more information.

PRENTICE HALL LECTURE LAUNCHER VIDEO FOR INTRODUCTORY PSYCHOLOGY (0-13048640-X) Adopters can receive this video, which is ideal for launching lecture topics. It includes short clips covering all major topics in introductory psychology. The clips have been carefully selected from the Films for Humanities and Sciences library and edited to provide brief and compelling video content for enhancing your lectures. Contact your local representative for a full list of video clips on this tape.

FILMS FOR HUMANITIES AND SCIENCES VIDEO LIBRARY (http://www.films.com) Qualified adopters can select videos on various topics in psychology from the extensive library of Films for the Humanities and Sciences. Contact your local sales representative for a list of videos and ISBNs.

Other video series are available. Ask your Prentice Hall sales representative for more details.

SUPPLEMENTARY TEXTS

Contact your Prentice Hall representative to package any of the following supplementary texts with *Understanding Psychology*, Eighth Edition (note a package ISBN is required for your bookstore order):

UNDERSTANDING PSYCHOLOGY, EIGHTH EDITION STUDENT STUDY GUIDE (0-13-233530-1): The eighth edition study guide contains material to help reinforce students' understanding of the concepts covered in the text. Each chapter provides an overview to introduce students to the chapter; learning objective exercises to test students' understanding of the main themes; multiple-choice pre- and posttests for gauging students' progress. Contact your local Prentice Hall sales representative for a package ISBN of the text and study guide.

CURRENT DIRECTIONS IN INTRODUCTORY PSYCHOLOGY: READINGS FROM THE AMERICAN PSYCHOLOGICAL SOCIETY (0-13-152367-8) This exciting reader includes over 20 articles carefully selected for the undergraduate audience, and taken from the very accessible *Current Directions in Psychological Science* journal. These timely, cutting-edge articles allow instructors to bring their students real-world perspective about today's most current and pressing issues in psychology.

TIME SPECIAL EDITION: PSYCHOLOGY (0-13-109024-0) Prentice Hall and *Time* magazine are pleased to offer you and your students a chance to examine today's most current and compelling psychology issues in an exciting and new way. *Time* Special Edition: *Psychology* offers a selection of 15 *Time* articles on today's most current issues and debates in the field of psychology, perfect for discussion groups, in-class debates, or research assignments.

Forty Studies That Changed Psychology, **Fifth Edition** (0131147293) by Roger Hock (Mendocino College). Presenting the seminal research studies that have shaped modern psychological study, this brief supplement provides an overview of the environment that gave rise to each study, its experimental design, its findings, and its impact on current thinking in the discipline.

The Psychology Student Writer's Manual, 2/E (0130413828) by Jill M. Scott, (University of Central Oklahoma), Russell Koch (University of Central Oklahoma), Gregory M. Scott (University of Central Oklahoma), Stephen M. Garrison (University of Central Oklahoma). This manual is ideal as either a companion or a stand-alone text for any psychology course that requires students to write papers. This clear and functional handbook shows how to research and write in the discipline and to improve one's overall writing ability, as well. Every fundamental aspect of writing is covered, ranging from content to form, grammar, tracking sources of information, and citing sources. The manual assists students in preparing two specific types of papers: research reports and term papers.

The Psychology Major: Careers and Strategies for Success, **3rd edition (0131987518)** by Eric Landrum (Idaho State University) and Stephen Davis (Emporia State University) This paperback text provides valuable information about career options available to psychology majors, as well as tips for improving academic performance, and a guide to the APA style of research reporting.

How to Think Like a Psychologist: Critical Thinking in Psychology, **Second Edition (0130150460)** by Donald McBurney (University of Pittsburgh). This unique supplementary text uses a question and answer format to explore some of the most common questions students ask about psychology.

Acknowledgements

We are grateful for the assistance we received from those who reviewed the previous edition and suggested improvements for this edition. Their thoughtful comments helped greatly to identify areas in need of special attention.

Jack Harnett   Virginia Commonwealth University

Joseph Lao, Borough of Manhattan Community College

Jennifer Peluso, Mercer University

Cheryl Bluestone, Queensborough Community College

Dixon A. Bramblett, Lindenwood University

Terry Pettijohn, Ohio State University

Joe Grisham, Indian River Community College

Joy Easton, DeVry University

Tom Frangicetto, Northampton Community College

Jason Kaufman, Ph.D, Inver Hills Community College

Gregory Manley, University of Texas, San Antonio

Karen Tinsley, Guilford College

Jim Dalton, Sanford-Brown College

Carolyn Tremblay, Orlando Culinary Academy

Daniel Dickman, Ivy Tech

Stephen Colarelli, Central Michigan University

Christian Fossa-Anderson, DeVry University South Florida

Fred Whitford, Montana State University

Stephen M. Colarelli, Central Michigan University

Michael Durnam, Montana State University, Bozeman

Kelly Charlton , University of North Carolina, Pembroke

John Lindsay, Georgia College and State University

Blaine Weller, Baker College

Dr. B. Hannon, University of Texas, San Antonio

Leslie Reeder, Wallace Community College

Jason Kaufman, Ph.D, Inver Hills Community College

Dr. Gary J. Springer, Texas State University, San Marcos

Dr. Sharon Sawatzky, Butler County Community College

Dr. Dan Muhwezi, Butler County Community College

Layton Seth Curl, Ph.D., Metropolitan State College of Denver

David Copeland, University of Southern Mississippi

Karen Tinsley , Guilford College

Gregory G. Manley, PhD, University of Texas, San Antonio

Jason Kaufman, Ph.D., Inver Hills Community College

We would like to extend a special thank you to Wendy Dunn (Coe College) for her content expertise and many contributions to the Industrial Organization Appendix. Thank you as well to Sara Farrell (Coe College) and John Gambon (Ozarks Technical College) for their insights. Thank you to Vera Dunwoody, Chaffey College, for her contributions to the student study skills section.

Special thanks go to our superb Development Editor, Susan Moss, who worked hand-in-glove with us from the first draft of Chapter 1 through the last draft of Appendix B. Her incisive comments and meticulous editing have helped immeasurably to improve the resulting book. Mary Marshall lent her considerable creative talents to the new chapter-opening vignettes.

We continue to be immensely grateful to our outstanding colleagues at Prentice Hall, without whose assistance this book simply would not exist. Jessica Mosher, Executive Editor, Psychology, provided valuable advice and counsel from day one. Her Editorial Assistant, Jessica Kupetz, superbly handled the many administrative details that inevitably arise as a book evolves. Rochelle Diogenes, Editor-in-Chief of Development, helped greatly to keep the revision on track and on schedule during the crucial development phase. The production of the eighth edition was managed by Preparè and expertly supervised by Caterina Melara. Thanks also to manufacturing buyer, Sherry Lewis and project manager, Kathy sleys for making sure that this book got done on time. Art Director Nancy Wells did a splendid design for both the interior and the cover. Finally, our sincere thanks to the Prentice Hall sales staff for their enthusiastic support of our text and for the excellent service they provide to our adopters.

Charles G. Morris
Albert A. Maisto

To the Student

Welcome to Psychology!

How does the brain command a finger to move? Do our dreams mean anything? What do genes have to do with intelligence? How do babies learn to talk? What is love? In this book, you will learn about the full range of human behavior, how psychologists go about trying to answer the preceding questions, and so much more. You will also learn about learning itself. Do you know how *you* learn? How many times have you sat down to read your textbook and found your mind wandering off? You know that your eyes have picked up every word on the page, but by the end of the page, you have no memory of reading anything! Remember this saying by Thomas Alva Edison: "I have not failed. I've just found 10,000 ways that won't work." You are about to learn some ways of studying that *do* work, techniques that are based on what psychologists know about learning and memory.

Knowing how you learn—your personal "learning style"—is the first step. Your learning style has nothing to do with how intelligent you are. There is no "good" or "bad" learning style—there are simply different ways of learning. For example, some people are best at remembering information they hear. Other people are better at remembering information that they see. Your preferred learning style is simply the way you learn best. Once you know your preferred learning style, you can use that knowledge to your advantage to make your studying more efficient and effective. You will remember more information in a shorter amount of time, thus paving the way for you to do better in all of your classes

Analyze Your Learning Style

Psychologists have identified a number of learning styles (Suskie, 2003).We will mention just four of them here. To understand thesestyles, think about how you usually carry out a new task—say, putting together a piece of furniture for which the dreaded "some assembly is required." The furniture comes with a printed set of directions with words and pictures. Do you read the directions word for word and go through the steps in an orderly way? If so, you are probably a *visual/verbal learner*. Or are you the type of learner who just looks at the pictures and doesn't need the written instructions? If so, you are most likely a *visual/nonverbal learner*. How about those of you who prefer to read the instructions out loud or have a friend read them to you while you work on the piece of furniture? You are most likely an *auditory learner* who learns best when you hear something. Finally, how about those of you who don't need directions at all—you study the pieces and then just start putting the furniture together? Chances are that you are a *tactile/kinesthetic learner* who learns best by "doing" a hands-on task. Now think about some of the classes you have had in the past.

You may have had some classes in which the material made perfect sense and was easy to remember. In those classes, it is likely that the teaching style and your learning style were well matched. Then there may have been other classes in which you tried and tried to remember the material, but nothing seemed to work—you proba-

bly had difficulty staying interested and perhaps had difficulty even staying awake! In those instances, most likely your learning style and the teaching style did not match. The sooner you can figure out your own "best" learning style, the easier your studying and learning will become because you will be able to adapt any information you are given to your optimal learning style.

One of the simplest ways to assess your preferred learning style is online (and it's free!). Simply point your Web browser to http://www.metamath.com/lsweb/dvclearn.htm. You will find much more information about these four learning styles. At the bottom of the page you can click on **"Learning Styles Survey"** to assess your preferred style and to learn about study techniques that are particularly appropriate for that style. If you click on **"Four Learning Styles"** you can discover much more about the four learning styles and their respective learning strategies.

Arousal and Optimal Learning

Do you ever get drowsy just as you start to study, or during class or during an exam? It may have something to do with your sleep habits. But it may also be that you are not getting the stimulation you need to concentrate. The traditional study method is to sit in a quiet place and just read. This works well for some people but not all. You may find that you need some "noise" in the background to study and remember effectively. This could be noise from a television program in the background, the chatter in a local coffeehouse, or music that you are listening to. If you need noise rather than quiet to help you concentrate, then use it! While you are studying, listen to your CD player with headphones. Or turn on the television or the radio. Experiment a little to find your optimum level of stimulation for learning. (For more information on optimal levels of arousal, see Chapter 8, "Motivation and Emotion.")

Reading the Text and Actually Remembering It!

Psychologists have found one tried-and-true method that helps students to remember concepts from printed material. It is called the SQ3R Method: *Survey, Question, Read, Recite,* and *Review.* This text has been prepared with a number of tools that will help you use this effective method of studying printed material. You can make use of your knowledge of your preferred learning style to make the SQ3R method more effective for you.

SURVEY: Surveying, or previewing, prepares your brain to receive information in an organized way. Properly done, it will help you read faster and comprehend better. Before you begin a chapter, survey its topics by reading the **Overview** on the chapter title page. If you are a visual/verbal learner (the most traditional learning style), reading the overview while thinking about what the topics mean should work just fine. However, if you are primarily an auditory learner, you may want to read the overview aloud and ask yourself questions about what each section of the chapter might be about.

Visual/nonverbal learners should read the overview, perhaps highlighting the key concepts or writing questions in the margin in bright colors, and looking over the illustrations in the chapter while surveying the material. The tactile/kinesthetic learner might walk around with the textbook and read it, maybe even reading out loud while walking. If possible, write out questions about the chapter topics in your text or on a separate piece of paper while you read. Yes, you really need to get used to writing in your textbooks! Those wide margins are there for a reason—notes, stars, marks, doodles . . . just about anything can be written there to help you to remember the material.

QUESTION: Be sure to read the **Questions** that appear in color at the beginning of each major section in the chapter. These opening questions indicate key ideas you should be looking for as you read that section. Again, the same learning-style techniques used in surveying will help here. Compare those opening questions to the questions you thought up when you were surveying the chapter. If you think that writing information down or typing it out helps you to remember, then write down or type out these questions as well. They help you to identify what is especially important in each chapter.

READ: As you read each section, keep the opening question in mind and actively look for answers to it. The key terms in the margins provide clear definitions of the most important terms in the text, so study them, too, as you go along, rather than waiting until you have finished reading the chapter. Now you know that "to study" means *to use the techniques for your primary learning style* . . . don't just sit there passively and let your eyes touch the words while nothing goes into your brain! Figures and photos will help you visualize concepts that are described in the text, and summary tables will aid in organizing the information for you.

RECITE: After each main section, be sure to take the **Check Your Understanding** and **Apply Your Understanding** quizzes. These brief quizzes will help you process the material you just read, making it more likely that you will understand it fully and remember it later. The quiz questions are typical of the questions that are likely to appear on multiple-choice and fill-in-the-blank exams. Think of them as mini pretests.

REVIEW: At the end of each chapter is a **Key Term** list with page references. Review each term carefully and refer back to the appropriate page if there are any such terms you can't recall. Use your preferred learning method to help ensure that you remember the meaning of these terms. Next, read through the detailed **Chapter Review**, which summarizes the key concepts in the chapter. Again, reviewing and reading passively while sitting in a quiet room works for some students but not all. During your review, you need to use the methods that are most effective for your learning style. If you know you study well with another person, then these key terms and the chapter review are perfect for reviewing with your "study buddy."

Improving Your Memory and Recall (Also Known as "Getting to the Exam With Your Memory Intact!")

Are there ways you can actually improve your memory and recall for material presented in class and in the text? Absolutely! Knowing your learning style, being aware of how much "noise" you need for optimal stimulation, and using the SQ3R method will all help to improve your memory for course material. However, there are other effective steps you can take.

Perhaps you have noticed that you remember the material discussed in class more easily than the material in the text. If so, it is probably because you build multiple retrieval cues for the class material. Here is how it works: You hear the material, you may also see it (if the instructor writes on the board or puts it into an electronic presentation); you think about it and decide it is important; you write it down when you take notes; and you probably are given examples of the concept or are asked to come up with some examples in class. All of those actions provide you with cues for retrieving the material later when you need it. In contrast, if you passively read the text, assuming the information ever gets into long-term memory, you have few if any cues for retrieving it later. Thus, the mystery has been solved: You need to build *multiple* retrieval cues for material you want to remember. This can be done in a number of ways, some of which we have already mentioned. Here is a new one: Have you ever tried reading the textbook out loud into a mirror? Actors often use this technique to learn their lines. It may work for you, too. You will see the information when you read it, you will hear it when you speak it, and you will probably also have a mental picture of yourself reading while looking in the mirror. You will be amazed how well this simple technique works to provide those retrieval cues! (See Chapter 6, "Memory," for much more information on the importance of retrieval cues.)

Take a look at the techniques for improving your memory in Chapter 6 (p. 207). The most important step you can take to improve your memory is to make connections between new material and other information already stored in your long-term memory. Using examples, discussing things you want to remember, and applying the material to real-life events help to form bonds between new and old information in long-term memory. Special memory techniques called *mnemonics* (pronounced ni-MON-iks) work in the same way. Some of the simplest mnemonic techniques are rhymes and jingles that we use for remembering dates. For example, "Thirty days hath September, . . . April, June, and November . . ." helps us to recall how many days are in a month. Also, forming mental images or making up a story using the material to be remembered really can help. Similarly, making up a story (rather than writing out a list) that uses the items you need to remember at the market can help your memory by providing retrieval cues as you are shopping.

Insider Tips on Note Taking During Class and on Test Taking

You will be able to take notes more efficiently if you have an idea of what will be covered in class on a particular day. Always check the date of the class for the topic and chapter(s) to be covered. Then read at least the chapter objectives and summary for the day's lesson if you don't have time to read the full chapter. Be sure to bring all of your favorite note-taking tools to class, such as different-color pens, highlighter markers, and note cards. Try to get to class early. Relax a little and get yourself ready to learn. To get in the mood for learning, it may help to review your notes from the previous class. Other tips that will help with note taking and remembering the material include sitting close to the front of the class where there will be fewer distractions. Also, try to be active in class. Take part in demonstrations, join the class discussions, and ask questions. Try to relate the topic being discussed to an interest of yours or to an event that happened to you or to a friend. Be on the lookout for clues to what is important (for example, when the instructor repeats something several times or say "The important point is . . ."). Other clues to particularly important information are summary statements, information written on the board, and information in handouts. If you miss a few key words while taking lecture notes, just leave a blank space and ask the instructor or teaching assistant after class to help you fill in the missing material.

Well before your first exam, ask about testing procedures if you are not clear about them. Is it possible to ask questions during the exam? Are any notes allowed? Is the test timed? When you first receive the quiz or exam, read the directions carefully. Then reread them! When actually starting the test, you may not want to complete the questions in the order they are presented in the exam. You may want to read through all the questions once and then skip around and answer first the easiest, shortest questions and the ones that you know for sure. Then move on to the questions you are a little less sure of. By using this technique, you won't get stuck in one area of the exam if you don't remember that particular material. Use your memory techniques when you're stuck and don't dwell on any one question too long. Be sure to watch your time if the quiz or exam must be completed in a specified period. Budget your time on the basis of how many points each question or section is worth. Here are a few more words to the wise: If you are having trouble with a particular question, look for helpful clues in other test questions. A term, name, date, or other fact that you can't seem to remember might appear in the test itself. Or something in another question might serve as a retrieval cue and trigger your memory for the missing information. Also think back to the quizzes in the textbook and on the Web site—it's possible that they contained a similar question (that is another reason to use those resources). More **Tips on Test Taking** can be found in the preface of the student study guide that accompanies this text.

MORE INSIDER INFORMATION: GENERAL STUDY TECHNIQUES FOR ANY COLLEGE CLASS

You should plan at least 2 hours of study time for every hour you spend in class. Using the knowledge and techniques associated with your primary learning style will make this time more effective for you. First study the subjects that you find boring or difficult. Take short breaks as you study: Long study sessions can make you overly tired, and your attention will go downhill fast! Be aware of your best time of the day or night for studying. Cramming right before an exam is not a good study method. You do need some sleep after you study and before you take an exam. As you will see in Chapter 4, "States of Consciousness", sleeping and dreaming help to solidify new memories.

If you find that studying with other people helps you, then, by all means, start a study group. Look for other dedicated students who share your academic goals as well as your time schedule. You might ask your instructor for help in forming these groups, or just write a note on the board before class saying that you want to start a study group. Limit the group to about five or six people. People of similar learning styles seem to work best together, so you may want to ask about the other students' learning styles. Initially, plan a one-time-only study session. If that works out, then plan additional sessions. Some activities for your study group can be found in the student study guide for this text and on the companion Web site.

How to Have an "A" College Student Attitude

Optimism helps! Approach your studying with an optimistic, positive, "can-do" attitude. If you get a low grade on an exam, put it behind you and set about doing better next time. A famous cartoon figure, Ziggy, says, "You can complain because roses have thorns, or you can rejoice because thorns have roses." Optimists do the latter. An optimistic attitude helps you to meet challenges head-on and conquer just about any task! In the world of academia, you are playing the part of the student. Are you playing the part of an "A" student or a failing student? Here are some tips on playing the part of an "A" student both inside and outside of the classroom: While in class, make eye contact with the instructor—often. Don't be afraid to ask questions in class (if that is permitted) or during office hours. Take notes and nod your head in approval when the instructor says something interesting or helpful (as you will see in Chapter 5, "Learning," this may actually increase the amount of interesting and helpful material the instructor provides). Don't engage in distracting side conversations with other students. Outside of the classroom, be well organized. Get a calendar that you can write in and carry with you. You need to have a clear idea of due dates and exam dates. Your handouts and notes should be organized by class and date. Get a three-ring binder for a class notebook that has pockets for handouts; if it doesn't, use a three-hole punch to put handouts where they belong. Always bring the handouts from the previous class with you unless otherwise instructed. Early in the term, go through the course syllabus carefully. Highlight sections that give you specific instructions about assignments such as term papers, quizzes, and exams. Also, make a note indicating how to get in touch with your instructor if you have questions outside of class. The instructor's email address or phone number is usually on the syllabus. If your class has an accompanying Web site, use it! If you don't have Internet access at home, use the computer facility at your college or local library. And whatever you do, make one or more backup copies of any work you do on the computer. There seems to be an unwritten law that if a computer is going to crash, or a disk is going to become unreadable, it will happen the night before something important is due!

Getting to know your professor or teaching assistant is also important, and they also should get to know you and understand that you are an interested and highly motivated student. Letting them get to know you can be quite challenging if you are in a large class. So introduce yourself during posted office hours and let this important person know that you are eager to do well in the class. If he or she doesn't have office hours, send an email or introduce yourself after class.

Most students do not think they need tutoring until after they do poorly on an exam or paper. The "A" students know how to get tutoring *before* they do poorly! Tutoring serves multiple goals. First, it will give you insight into what is important in the course and perhaps what is important for an exam, paper, or other assignment. Second, it will make the subject matter more real and personal, and we already know that this alone will help your recall. Last, but not least, when you show up for tutoring, you are reinforcing the message that you are motivated to do well.

Closing the Deal: Learning What You Need to Know and Getting an "A"

After reading the information in this introductory section you may be feeling more overwhelmed than helped! There is so much more to being a good learner and knowledgeable person than meets the eye. Sitting passively listening to a lecture and regurgitating information back onto a test is just not enough anymore, if it ever was. You should now feel very well equipped with new techniques and tools to reach your goals in school as well as in life. Just knowing your preferred style of learning and using even a few of the techniques presented here will work wonders for you. Now that you have the tools and techniques, match them with your optimistic attitude and you will greatly increase your chances of being successful.

Once again, ***Welcome to psychology!***

More Study Tools Available for You

CHECK OUT THE FOLLOWING STUDY TOOLS ONLINE AT www.myPearsonstore.com

VANGONOTES Study on the go with VangoNotes. Just download chapter reviews from your text and listen to them on any MP3 player. Now wherever you are—whatever you're

doing—you can study by listening to the following for each chapter of your textbook:

- **Big Ideas:** Your "need to know" for each chapter
- **Practice Test:** A gut check for the Big Ideas—tells you if you need to keep studying
- **Key Terms:** Audio "flashcards" to help you review key concepts and terms
- **Rapid Review:** A quick drill session—use it right before your test

VangoNotes are **flexible**; download all the material directly to your player, or only the chapters you need. And they're **efficient**. Use them in your car, at the gym, walking to class, wherever. So get yours today. And get studying. Check it out at http://www.VangoNotes.com.

NEW *MYPSYCHLAB* FOR *UNDERSTANDING PSYCHOLOGY*, 8/E Prentice Hall's *MyPsychLab* is an easy-to-use online resource that helps you assess how you are doing in your class. The program contains multiple quizzes tied to your textbook. Based on the results of a content pretest, you are provided with your own customized study plan. The study plan contains a variety of activities such as e-book exercises, simulations, and activities that help you master key content. You can continue to quiz yourself by taking the posttest as many times as you want. Pre- and posttests are randomized, so if you opt to take the posttest again, you have access to additional questions for the same content area. Find out more at http://www.mypsychlab.com.

COMPANION WEB SITE (http://www.prenhall.com/morris): Visit the Prentice Hall Introductory Psychology Web site, your guide to exploring the fascinating and diverse world of psychology. On this site you can find information on psychology and gain an understanding of the history of the discipline. Here you can view examples of the types of research done in the major fields of psychology; access links to useful sites in the major areas of psychology; connect with news links to current real-world issues in psychology; take online quizzes that provide immediate scores and feedback. The Prentice Hall Introductory Psychology Web site for Morris is an open-access site available to all.

***UNDERSTANDING PSYCHOLOGY*, 8/E, STUDENT STUDY GUIDE** (0-13-233530-1): This updated study guide contains material to help reinforce your understanding of the concepts covered in the text. Each chapter provides an overview to introduce you to the chapter; learning-objective exercises to test your understanding of the main themes; and multiple-choice pre- and posttests for gauging your progress. You can purchase a copy of the study guide through your school bookstore or at http://www.mypearsonstore.com.

SAFARIX WEBBOOK: If you want to purchase a text book at a 50% savings, check out *SafariX* WebBook where you can buy an online subscription. With the SafariX WebBook, you can search the text, make notes online, print out reading assignments that incorporate lecture notes, and bookmark important passages. Find out more at http://www.safarix.com

Understanding
PSYCHOLOGY

1 The Science of Psychology

OVERVIEW

To this day Brooke Ellison has no recollection of the moment that changed her life when she was 11 years old. While walking home from her first day at junior high school, she darted across a busy highway and was hit by an oncoming car. Brooke was hurled 100 feet, and the impact of her landing severely damaged her spinal cord. A day and a half later, she awoke in an intensive care unit, with no idea of where she was or what had happened to her. As she struggled to sit up, she came to a horrifying realization. Try as she might, she could not flex even a single muscle below her head. Her body simply would not obey her brain. She felt as if she had been decapitated and had no body at all. Brooke tried to call for help, but no words came out of her mouth. Slowly it dawned on her that the noisy machine next to her bed must be a respirator that was pumping air into and out of her lungs. Her injuries were so severe that she could not even breathe on her own, and with no air passing over her vocal cords, speech was no longer possible. Brooke was terrified.

Fortunately, with the help of a special valve to redirect her exhaled air, Brooke was eventually able to speak again. But after 6 weeks in the hospital and 9 months at a rehabilitation center, it was clear that she was permanently paralyzed from her head down and would always need a respirator to breathe. Nevertheless, she went home determined to pick up the pieces of her life and enroll in regular junior high classes. Many people doubted that she would succeed, given her physical condition. Not Brooke. Accompanied by her mother, to attend to her nursing needs, and with a special education aide to take notes for her in class, Brooke began a challenging eighth-grade honors program. She never listened to the naysayers and seldom dwelled on what might have been. By her senior year in high school, she had an A+ average and such high SAT scores that she was readily accepted at Harvard for the following fall.

With her mother again accompanying her, Brooke tackled the new challenge of life at a top-ranking college. She obtained a wheelchair controlled by a tongue-operated device to get her around campus. Most of her exams would be taken orally, and all of her writing would have to be done with a voice-activated computer. Despite her severe handicaps, Brooke made many friends, inspiring everyone she met. Four years later, she graduated magna cum laude—the highest honors possible—with a major in cognitive neuroscience (a combined major of psychology and biology). Since then, she has coauthored a book about her experiences, worked on a movie of her life, earned a master's degree in public policy from Harvard's Kennedy School of Government, enrolled in a PhD program in political science, and run for a seat in the New York State senate. She also finds time to travel widely as a motivational speaker. Audience members feel they can do anything after learning about the obstacles that Brooke has overcome.

What Is Psychology?

"Most psychologists study mental and emotional problems and work as psychotherapists." Is this statement true or false?

Why have we chosen the story of Brooke Ellison to introduce you to the subject of psychology? It is because this story raises so many fascinating questions about human beings. What motivates a person to persevere against all odds and overcome enormous challenges? Do certain personality traits give such people unusual resilience to hardship? Or could anyone, investing enough effort, accomplish what Brooke has done? Many people in Brooke's situation would have succumbed to depression and given up trying to achieve. Why does this happen to some people, but not to others?

These are the same kinds of questions that psychologists also ask. Psychology is not confined to investigating abnormal behavior, as many people mistakenly assume. **Psychology** is the scientific study of behavior and mental processes in all their many facets. As such, viewed from a wealth of different perspectives, it encompasses every aspect of human thoughts, feelings, and actions. In fact, with new research technologies, new areas of inquiry to explore, and more collaboration with other sciences, psychology is continually redefining itself more broadly (R. B. Evans, 1999). One way to grasp the breadth and depth of topics in psychology is to look at the major subfields within it. These are shown in **Table 1–1** and we discuss several key areas next.

Brooke Ellison, paralyzed since a car hit her at age 11, has not allowed physical limitations to limit her achievements.

psychology The scientific study of behavior and mental processes.

table 1–1   AMERICAN PSYCHOLOGICAL ASSOCIATION DIVISIONS (2006)

The two major organizations of psychologists in the United States are the American Psychological Association (APA), founded over 100 years ago, and the Association for Psychological Science (APS), founded in 1988. Members of both groups work in a wide variety of areas. The following list of divisions of the APA reflects the enormous diversity of the field of psychology:

Division*

1. Society for General Psychology
2. Society for the Teaching of Psychology
3. Experimental Psychology
5. Evaluation, Measurement, and Statistics
6. Behavioral Neuroscience and Comparative Psychology
7. Developmental Psychology
8. Society for Personality and Social Psychology
9. Society for the Psychological Study of Social Issues (SPSSI)
10. Psychology and the Arts
12. Society of Clinical Psychology
13. Society of Consulting Psychology
14. Society for Industrial and Organizational Psychology
15. Educational Psychology
16. School Psychology
17. Counseling Psychology
18. Psychologists in Public Service
19. Military Psychology
20. Adult Development and Aging
21. Applied Experimental and Engineering Psychology
22. Rehabilitation Psychology
23. Society for Consumer Psychology
24. Theoretical and Philosophical Psychology
25. Behavior Analysis
26. History of Psychology
27. Society for Community Research and Action: Division of Community Psychology
28. Psychopharmacology and Substance Abuse
29. Psychotherapy

30. Society of Psychological Hypnosis
31. State Psychological Association Affairs
32. Humanistic Psychology
33. Mental Retardation and Developmental Disabilities
34. Population and Environmental Psychology
35. Society for the Psychology of Women
36. Psychology of Religion
37. Child, Youth, and Family Services
38. Health Psychology
39. Psychoanalysis
40. Clinical Neuropsychology
41. American Psychology—Law Society
42. Psychologists in Independent Practice
43. Family Psychology
44. Society for the Psychological Study of Lesbian, Gay, and Bisexual Issues
45. Society for the Psychological Study of Ethnic Minority Issues
46. Media Psychology
47. Exercise and Sport Psychology
48. Society for the Study of Peace, Conflict, and Violence: Peace Psychology Division
49. Group Psychology and Group Psychotherapy
50. Addictions
51. Society for the Psychological Study of Men and Masculinity
52. International Psychology
53. Society of Clinical Child and Adolescent Psychology
54. Society of Pediatric Psychology
55. American Society for the Advancement of Pharmacotherapy
56. Trauma Psychology

* There are no divisions 4 or 11.

For information on a division, e-mail the APA at *division@apa.org*, or locate them on the Internet at *http://www.apa.org/about/division.html*

Source: American Psychological Association (2006). Divisions of the American Psychological Association. Retrieved October 9, 2006, from *http://www.apa.org/about/division.html*

THE FIELDS OF PSYCHOLOGY

Psychology is not so much a single, unified field of study as it is an umbrella concept for a loose amalgamation of different subfields (R. B. Evans, 1999). The American Psychological Association (APA) has no fewer than 54 divisions, each representing a specialized area of research and interest. Here, we introduce you to seven of the largest subfields in psychology.

DEVELOPMENTAL PSYCHOLOGY *Developmental psychologists* study all aspects of human growth and change—physical, mental, social, and emotional—from the prenatal period through old age. Most specialize in a particular stage of human development. *Child psychologists* focus on infants and children, concerning themselves with such issues as whether babies are born with distinct temperaments, how infants become attached to their care-givers, at what age sex differences in behavior emerge, and what changes occur in the meaning and importance of friendship during childhood. *Adolescent psychologists*, who specialize in the often-difficult teenage years, look largely at how puberty affects a whole range of developmental phenomena, from relationships with peers and parents to the search for a personal identity. Finally, *life-span psychologists* focus on the challenges and changes of adulthood, from marrying and having children, to meeting demands at work, to facing the transitions related to aging and eventual death.

Developmental psychologists would be very interested in Brooke Ellison's story. They would want to know how Brooke, despite her physical handicaps, managed to negotiate the challenges of adolescence so well. As Brooke herself discovered, teenagers often have difficulty interacting with a person with a serious disability. It is as if the individual with the disability makes them painfully aware of their own vulnerability. Hence, they shy away from peers with physical handicaps or interact with them only in superficial ways. Consequently, the teenage years are particularly lonely for adolescents with disabilities. Although Brooke experienced some of this loneliness after her accident, she was able to retain a remarkable sense of optimism and hope that helped to pull her through her bleakest hours. For her senior thesis at Harvard, Brooke decided to research how a positive and hopeful outlook fosters psychological resiliency in adolescents like her who face very difficult challenges. This topic is tailor-made for developmental psychologists.

PHYSIOLOGICAL PSYCHOLOGY *Physiological psychologists* investigate the biological basis of human behavior, thoughts, and emotions. Among these, *neuropsychologists* are interested in the workings of the brain and nervous system. How does the brain enable us to perceive the world through our senses? How does it allow us to think, speak, sleep, move our bodies, and feel emotions such as anger, sadness, and joy? Neuropsychologists help to answer these and many other fundamental questions about how thoughts, feelings, and behaviors are controlled. Their colleagues known as *biological psychologists* study the body's biochemistry and the ways that hormones, psychoactive medications, and "social drugs" affect us. They investigate such topics as how the hormones of puberty are related to mood swings or how alcohol consumption by a pregnant woman impairs the development of her unborn child. *Behavioral geneticists* add yet another dimension: They explore the impact of heredity on both normal and abnormal behavior. To what degree is individual intelligence hereditary? Do illnesses such as alcoholism and depression have a genetic component? What about differences in the ways that men and women think, act, and feel? Behavioral geneticists focus on finding answers to questions like these.

Physiological psychologists have much to tell us about spinal cord injuries that cause paralysis of the body, such as the injury Brooke Ellison suffered. In Brooke's case, the damage prevents any messages from being passed between Brooke's brain and body. Her body can still send signals up her spinal cord, but her brain can no longer receive them. Although her brain can still give orders for actions to her limbs, those orders never reach her body. Brooke's mind is essentially cut off from the body below her head. In Chapter 2, you will learn how recent research in the field of physiological psychology may someday help people like Brooke move again.

EXPERIMENTAL PSYCHOLOGY *Experimental psychologists* conduct research on basic psychological processes, including learning, memory, sensation, perception, thinking, motivation, and emotion. How do people remember information; and what makes them forget? How do they go about making decisions and solving various kinds of problems? Is there a difference in the way men and women solve complex problems? Why are some people more achievement motivated than others, constantly striving for excellence in athletics, scholarship, or the arts? Experimental psychologists search for answers to questions like these.

An experimental psychologist would certainly be interested in the intellectual talents that enabled Brooke Ellison to read, analyze, and remember thousands of pages of text, while also absorbing very demanding lectures and participating in challenging seminars. Some experimental psychologists would want to discover whether or not a student such as Brooke processes information differently from the ways other people do. Does she have an unusually good memory, and, if so, how does she organize data to facilitate retention?

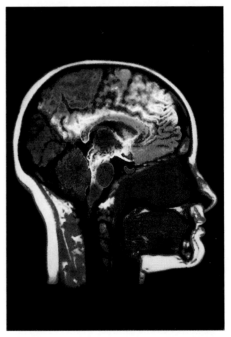

Recent advances in neuroimaging techniques enable physiological psychologists to investigate how specific regions of the brain are involved in complex behaviors and mental processes.

Does she excel at forming connections between facts, helping her to both remember and analyze information? Other experimental psychologists would want to investigate Brooke's remarkable motivation to achieve in a rigorous academic environment. They might explore the validity of Brooke's mother's theory that Brooke became driven to excel intellectually when success at physical pursuits became unachievable.

PERSONALITY PSYCHOLOGY *Personality psychologists* study the differences among individuals in such traits as sociability, conscientiousness, emotional stability, self-esteem, agreeableness, aggressive inclinations, and openness to new experiences. Psychologists in this field attempt to determine what causes some people to be optimists and others to be pessimists, why some people are outgoing and friendly, whereas others are shy and reserved, as well as whether there are consistent differences in the personality characteristics of males and females.

Brooke Ellison undoubtedly would rate high on personality tests of extraversion, conscientiousness, emotional stability, optimism, and openness to new experiences. She would also rate high in terms of personal sensitivity. In an essay she wrote in high school, she described herself this way: "I am a lover of all things beautiful: nature, art, friendship, a kind word. I love music, all kinds of music . . . anything that will stir my soul" (Ellison & Ellison, 2001, p. 131). In addition, Brooke clearly has a healthy level of self-esteem. Personality psychologists would want to know where these characteristics came from. Was Brooke born destined to have the personality she possesses, or are her traits more a product of the experiences she has had from early childhood onward? And if her personality characteristics have been largely shaped by her experiences, how stable are they in the long run? Is the Brooke Ellison of today the Brooke of yesterday and also the Brooke of tomorrow?

CLINICAL AND COUNSELING PSYCHOLOGY When asked to describe a psychologist, most people think of a therapist who sees troubled patients in an office, clinic, or hospital. This popular view is half correct. About 50% of psychologists specialize in clinical or counseling psychology, both of which seek to help people deal more successfully with their lives. The two areas also differ, however. *Clinical psychologists* are interested primarily in the diagnosis, causes, and treatment of psychological disorders, such as depression or acute anxiety. *Counseling psychologists*, in contrast, are concerned mainly with the "normal" everyday problems of adjustment that most of us face at some point in life, such as making a difficult career choice or coping with a troubled relationship. Clinical and counseling psychologists often divide their time between treating patients and conducting research on the causes of psychological disorders and the effectiveness of different types of therapy.

For a person like Brooke Ellison, who has suffered severe spinal cord damage, the rehabilitation team often includes a counseling psychologist who seeks to understand how the injured person is thinking and feeling, helping him or her to cope successfully with the traumatic situation. Some people who suffer traumas comparable to Brooke's lapse into serious depression, requiring treatment by a clinical psychologist. Brooke, fortunately, escaped major depression. Brooke's older sister Kysten, however, suffered from depression as a result of Brooke's accident more than Brooke herself did. She lost her appetite and had trouble eating; she refused to return to the dance school that she had been attending with Brooke; she even found it unbearable to visit Brooke in the rehab center. A clinical psychologist could help a person like Kysten overcome her feelings of depression and put her life back on track.

SOCIAL PSYCHOLOGY *Social psychologists* start with the assumption that a person's personality characteristics are insufficient to predict that person's thoughts, feelings, and behaviors. This is because, like it or not, we are all greatly influenced by other people. Social psychology is the scientific study of how these social influences are exerted and the effects they have. Social psychologists investigate such issues as interpersonal attraction, persuasive communications and attitude formation, obedience to authority, conformity to group norms, and how people often behave differently in crowds.

What aspects of Brooke Ellison's story would interest social psychologists? They would certainly be interested in the stereotyped attitudes that people often hold toward people with handicaps. These preconceived attitudes are frequently based on little firsthand experience, but are instead the product of shared ideas and assumptions that are part of a society's culture. In Brooke's case, stereotyped attitudes toward her in high school sometimes caused teachers to underestimate her abilities and classmates to avoid her as a friend. In response to these reactions, Brooke formed a powerful attitude of her own—the conviction that people should be accepted for whom they are, rather than be judged by how they look. Yet, oddly enough, when Brooke was in college and a handsome classmate asked her to a formal dance, Brooke at first refused him. In so doing, she kept him from acting in accordance with the very attitude that she professed to hold. This obvious discrepancy between her attitude and her action made Brooke feel uncomfortable. Social psychologists have extensively studied situations like this one, in which an attitude conflicts with an action. In Chapter 14, "Social Psychology," you will learn how people resolve such dilemmas, known as *cognitive dissonance*.

INDUSTRIAL AND ORGANIZATIONAL (I/O) PSYCHOLOGY *Industrial and organizational (I/O) psychologists* apply the principles of psychology to the workplace. They are concerned with such practical issues as selecting and training personnel, improving productivity and working conditions, and the impact of computerization and automation on workers. I/O psychologists seek to determine in advance who will be effective as a salesperson, as an airline pilot, or in any other career. They ask whether organizations tend to operate differently under female versus male leadership and, if so, what the drawbacks or benefits of each might be. And because research shows that high morale fosters more productive workers, I/O psychologists also search for specific strategies that managers can use to improve group morale. Hence, I/O psychology plays an important role in the modern world of work. Wherever you, Brooke Ellison, or anyone else might eventually find a job, that workplace will probably have been shaped to some extent by the efforts of I/O psychologists.

ENDURING ISSUES

Given this broad range of careers and interests, what unifies the field of psychology?

What do psychologists who study organizations, psychological disorders, memory and cognition, behavioral genetics, or attachment in infants have in common? All psychologists share a common interest in five enduring issues that override their areas of specialization and that cut to the core of what it means to be human. As we list them here, recall that these unifying themes are reflected in many of the various questions psychologists in different fields would have about Brook Ellison.

PERSON–SITUATION To what extent is behavior caused by such internal processes as thoughts, emotions, motives, attitudes, values, personality, and genes? In contrast, to what extent is behavior caused or triggered by such external factors as incentives, environmental cues, and the presence of other people? Put another way, are we masters of our fate or victims of circumstances? We will encounter these questions most directly in our consideration of behavior genetics, learning, emotion and motivation, personality, and social psychology.

NATURE–NURTURE Is the person we become a product of innate, inborn tendencies, or a reflection of experiences and upbringing? This is the famous "nature versus nurture" debate. For decades, psychologists have argued about the relative influence of heredity (genes) versus environment (experience) on thought and behavior. To what degree is each responsible? This issue surfaces in our discussions of behavior genetics, intelligence, development, personality, and abnormal psychology; and it will arise elsewhere as well.

STABILITY–CHANGE Are the characteristics we develop in childhood more or less permanent and fixed, or do we change in predictable (and unpredictable) ways over the course of our lives? Is the self a cognitive construct, a "fictional character" we create to maintain a sense of inner continuity in the face of varied, sometimes unpredictable experiences? Developmental psychologists are especially interested in these and other questions, as are psychologists who specialize in personality, adjustment, abnormal psychology, and therapy.

"I told my parents that if grades were so important they should have paid for a smarter egg donor."

© *The New Yorker Collection,* 1999. Donald Reilly from *www.cartoonbank.com.* All Rights Reserved.

To understand human behavior, we must appreciate the rich diversity of culture throughout the world.

DIVERSITY–UNIVERSALITY Because we are all human, each person is like every other person. But in some respects, each person is only like certain other people. And in other respects, each of us is like no other person. Thus, anywhere humans exist there will be both similarity and diversity. Because people differ in how they look, feel, and behave (Kwantes, Bergeron, & Kaushal, 2005), human diversity is necessarily a central concern for psychologists. Throughout this book, we will encounter these questions: Does our understanding of human behavior apply equally well to every human being? Does it apply only to men or just to women, or only to particular racial or ethnic groups or particular societies (especially our own)? Do we perhaps need "different psychologies" to account for the wide diversity of human behaviors?

MIND–BODY Finally, how are mind and body connected? Many psychologists are fascinated by the relationship between what we experience (such as thoughts and feelings) and what our biological processes are (such as activity in the nervous system). This mind–body issue will arise most clearly in our discussions of the biological basis of behavior, sensation and perception, altered states of consciousness, emotion and motivation, adjustment and health psychology, and disorders and therapy.

These five issues represent enduring themes in the history of psychology. Depending on the events and intellectual climate of a given time period, one or another of these issues has assumed special prominence in the history of psychology. For example, at the beginning of the 21st century the role of genetics (heredity) is receiving much greater attention than in the past. Diversity is also an issue of much greater concern, as is the role of biological processes. Even within a particular time period, psychologists in one field or one school within a field may emphasize the person or the situation, heredity or environment, stability or change, diversity or universality, or subjective experience or biological processes. Philosophers have pondered these issues for centuries; in contrast, psychologists look at these topics through a scientific lens.

Throughout this book, we will highlight the importance of these matters. Several times in each chapter we will call your attention to the way in which the topic under consideration—whether it is new discoveries about communication within the nervous system, research into how we learn, or the reason that people abuse drugs—reflects one of these issues. In this way, we will show the surprising unity and coherence of the diverse and exciting science of psychology.

PSYCHOLOGY AS SCIENCE

What does psychology have in common with other sciences?

Earlier we defined psychology as the science of behavior and mental processes. The key word in this definition is *science*. Psychologists rely on the **scientific method** when seeking

scientific method An approach to knowledge that relies on collecting data, generating a theory to explain the data, producing testable hypotheses based on the theory, and testing those hypotheses empirically.

to answer questions. They collect data through careful, systematic observation; attempt to explain what they have observed by developing theories; make new predictions based on those theories; and then systematically test those predictions through additional observations and experiments to determine whether they are correct. Thus, like all scientists, psychologists use the scientific method to describe, understand, predict, and, eventually, achieve some measure of control over what they study.

For example, consider the issue of males, females, and aggression. Many people believe that males are naturally more aggressive than females. Others contend that boys learn to be aggressive because our society and culture encourage—indeed, require—males to be combative, even violent. How would psychologists approach the issue? First, they would want to find out whether men and women actually differ in aggressive behavior. A number of research studies have addressed this question; and the evidence seems conclusive: Males are more aggressive than females, particularly as regards physical aggression (G. P. Knight, Fabes, & Higgins, 1996; Zimmer-Gembeck, Geiger, & Crick, 2005). Perhaps girls and women make nasty remarks or yell (Ostrov & Keating, 2004; M. K. Underwood, 2003), but boys and men are far more likely to fight physically. Once psychologists have established that there are sex differences in physical aggression and have described those differences, the next step is to explain them. A number of explanations are possible.

Let's say you are a psychologist with an interest in sex differences in physical aggression. If you are a physiological psychologist, you will probably ascribe these differences to genetics or body chemistry; if you are a developmental psychologist, you might look to the ways a child is taught to behave "like a boy" or "like a girl"; and if you are a social psychologist, you might explain the differences in terms of cultural norms, which require males to "stand up for themselves" and hold that physical aggression isn't "feminine."

Each of these explanations stands as a **theory** about the causes of sex differences in aggression; each attempts to distill a few principles from a large number of facts. And each theory allows you to make a number of new **hypotheses**, or predictions, about the phenomenon in question. If gender differences in aggression arise because males have higher levels of testosterone than females do, then you would predict that extremely violent men should have higher levels of testosterone than do men who are generally nonviolent. If sex differences in aggression stem from early training, then you would predict that there should be fewer sex differences in aggression in families where parents did not stress gender differences. Finally, if sex differences in aggression reflect cultural norms, then you would predict that within societies that do not prohibit girls and women from fighting, or in those that consider physical aggression abnormal or improper for both sexes, the difference in aggression across the sexes should be small.

Each of these predictions or hypotheses can be tested through research, and the results should indicate whether one theory is better than another at accounting for known facts and predicting new facts. If one or more of the theories is supported by research evidence, it should be possible to control aggressive behavior to a greater degree than was possible before. For example, if cultural norms are part of the reason for differences in aggression, then these differences should be smaller in situations in which individuals do not feel that they are being evaluated in terms of their masculinity or femininity. One research team tested this hypothesis with a computer war game (Lightdale & Prentice, 1994). When the researcher introduced participants in a way that made clear who was male or female,

Males seem to be more physically aggressive than females. Different schools of psychology have different explanations for why this is the case.

theory Systematic explanation of a phenomenon; it organizes known facts, allows us to predict new facts, and permits us to exercise a degree of control over the phenomenon.

hypotheses Specific, testable predictions derived from a theory.

women played less aggressively than men; when women were told that they were anonymous to the researchers and other participants, however, women played just as aggressively as men did.

CRITICAL THINKING: THINKING LIKE A SCIENTIST

We have seen how psychologists might shed light on the question of whether men are naturally more aggressive than women. Now consider the following statements:

- Gifted children are less well adjusted than other children.
- Opposites attract.
- Subliminal messages on self-help audiotapes have beneficial effects.

Do you agree with these statements? Many people answer yes without a moment's hesitation on the grounds that "Everybody knows that." Critical thinkers, however, question common knowledge, and learning to use critical thinking is one of the "fringe benefits" of studying psychology. (See "Applying Psychology: The Benefits of Studying Psychology.")

What exactly is critical thinking? It is the process of examining the information we have and then, based on this inquiry, making judgments and decisions. When we think critically, we define problems, examine evidence, analyze assumptions, consider alternatives and, ultimately, find reasons to support or reject an argument. To think critically, you must adopt a state of mind that is characterized by objectivity, caution, a willingness to challenge other people's opinions, and—perhaps most difficult of all—a willingness to subject your deepest beliefs to scrutiny. In other words, you must think like a scientist.

Psychologists use a number of strategies in questioning assumptions and examining data. Here, we use the rules of psychological investigation to judge whether the previously mentioned assertion that "opposites attract" is correct:

- *Define the problem or the question you are investigating.* Do opposites attract each other?
- *Suggest a theory or a reasonable explanation for the problem.* People who are dissimilar balance each other in a relationship.
- *Collect and examine all the available evidence.* In doing so, be skeptical of people's self-reports, as they may be subjectively biased. If data conflict, try to find more evidence. Research on attraction yields no support for the idea that opposites attract, whereas many studies confirm that people of similar looks, interests, age, family background, religion, values, and attitudes seek each other.
- *Analyze assumptions.* Because balancing different people's strengths and weaknesses is a good way to form a group, you might assume it is a good basis for personal relationships as well, which would explain why people of opposite temperaments are naturally attracted to each other. Yet research evidence shows that such an assumption is false. Why should people of similar temperaments attract each other? One important reason is that they often belong to the same social circles. Research suggests proximity is a big factor in attraction.
- *Avoid oversimplifying.* Don't overlook the evidence that people of similar temperaments find living together rather difficult in some ways. For example, living with someone who is as tense as you are may be harder than living with someone of calm temperament—your opposite.
- *Draw conclusions carefully.* It seems safe to conclude that, in general, opposites don't attract, but there are specific exceptions to this general rule.
- *Consider every alternative interpretation.* People may cite cases that conflict with your conclusion. Remember, however, that their arguments are likely to be based on subjective observations and a far narrower database than researchers have used when studying this question.

APPLYING PSYCHOLOGY

THE BENEFITS OF STUDYING PSYCHOLOGY

We know that many students take psychology classes in order to fulfill a requirement for their degree, rather than out of a compelling interest in the subject. Those students, and even some who are keenly interested in psychology, may wonder, "What am I going to gain from taking this course?" There are several benefits that you can gain from studying psychology:

- *Self-understanding.* Almost all of us want to understand ourselves and others better. In our daily lives, we often look for answers by relying on our own experience, knowledge, and assumptions. But, as you will see, that barely scratches the surface. As a psychology student, you will be challenged to go beyond the superficial in your life and to confront what really lies behind your most basic actions. You will learn to look deeply into human behavior and to ask complex and precise questions. In the process, you will not only achieve a better understanding of yourself and your fellow human beings, but also come to realize that much of what we consider "just plain common sense about people" doesn't hold up under close scrutiny.
- *Critical thinking skills.* In addition to greater understanding of yourself and others, by studying psychology you will also have an opportunity to

acquire some specific skills. One of those skills is the ability to think critically about psychological issues: to clearly define issues, to examine the evidence bearing on them, to become more aware of hidden assumptions, to resist the temptation to oversimplify, to draw conclusions carefully, and above all to realize the relevance of empirical research to understanding psychological issues. As a result of practicing critical thinking, you will become a more sophisticated consumer of the information that is available to you in the mass media. You will also become more cautious about too quickly accepting what looks like "common sense."

- *Study skills.* You will also have the opportunity to acquire better study skills that will serve you well in all your courses. In addition to the study tips provided at the beginning of this text (see "To the Student"), you will find an entire chapter on human memory (Chapter 6) containing excellent information about making the most of your study time. But you will also find information about the relation between sleep and learning and the effects of drugs on memory (Chapter 4), about the nature of intelligence and its relation to success in school and in later life (Chapter 7), about the effects of motivation and

arousal on the ability to learn and to perform (Chapter 8), and about age differences in the ability to learn and remember (Chapter 9).
- *Job skills.* Finally, you may acquire some skills that will help you find a job. This chapter lists many career possibilities for students who earn degrees in psychology. In addition, many careers outside psychology draw on a person's knowledge of psychology. For example, personnel administrators deal with employee relations; vocational rehabilitation counselors help people with disabilities to find employment; directors of volunteer services recruit and train volunteers; probation officers work with parolees; and supervisors of day-care centers oversee the care of preschool children of working parents. Indeed, employers in areas such as business and finance seek out psychology majors because of their knowledge of the principles of human behavior and their skills in experimental design and data collection and analysis.

Of course, all of these benefits are much more likely to accrue to students who regularly attend class, study, and try to apply what they learn to their own lives. As with many other opportunities, the benefits you receive are, in large part, up to you.

- *Recognize the relevance of research to events and situations.* Let's say you have been thinking of dating someone whose temperament seems quite different from yours. You may decide, based on what you now know, not to rush into things but to go more slowly, testing your own observations against your knowledge of research findings.

By the way, psychological research has demonstrated that the statements about gifted children and subliminal messages at the beginning of this discussion are also false.

CHECK YOUR UNDERSTANDING

1. Indicate whether each of the following statements is true (T) or false (F):

   a. _____ Psychologists collect data through careful, systematic observation.

   b. _____ Psychologists try to explain their observations by developing theories.

   c. _____ Psychologists form hypotheses or predictions on the basis of theories.

   d. _____ Psychologists appeal to common sense in their arguments.

   e. _____ Psychologists systematically test hypotheses.

   f. _____ Psychologists base their conclusions on widely shared values.

Answers: see note elsewhere regarding punctuaction with T/F answers. a. (T); b. (T); c. (T); d. (F); e. (T); f. (F).

APPLY YOUR UNDERSTANDING

1. Caroline is interested in the question of whether our personality characteristics are determined for life by genetics or if they can be changed as a result of the experiences of our lives. Which of the enduring issues discussed in this chapter best describes Caroline's interests?

   a. mind–body

   b. diversity–universality

   c. nature–nurture

   d. tastes great–less filling.

2. Dakota spends most of his work time in his office helping clients with adjustment problems, such as troubled marriages, and coping with career changes, such as retirement. Dakota is most likely a(n) _____ psychologist.

   a. industrial

   b. organizational

   c. clinical

   d. counseling

Answers: 1. c. 2. d.

The Growth of Psychology

"Psychology has a long past, but a short history." What does that mean?

In the West, since the time of Plato and Aristotle, people have wondered and written about human behavior and mental processes. But not until the late 1800s did they begin to apply the scientific method to questions that had puzzled philosophers for centuries. Only then did psychology come into being as a formal, scientific discipline separate from philosophy. The history of psychology can be divided into three main stages: the emergence of a science of the mind, the behaviorist decades, and the "cognitive revolution."

THE "NEW PSYCHOLOGY": A SCIENCE OF THE MIND

How did Wundt help to define psychology as a science of the mind?

Why did James think that sensation and perception alone couldn't explain behavior?

Why was Freud's theory of the unconscious shocking at the turn of the 20th century?

At the beginning of the 20th century, most university psychology programs were located in philosophy departments. But the foundations of the "new psychology"—the science of psychology—had been laid.

WILHELM WUNDT AND EDWARD BRADFORD TITCHENER: VOLUNTARISM AND STRUC-TURALISM Most psychologists agree that psychology was born in 1879, the year that Wilhelm Wundt founded the first psychological laboratory at the University of Leipzig in

Germany. In the public eye, a laboratory identified a field of inquiry as "science" (Benjamin, 2000). At the outset, Wundt did not attract much attention; only four students attended his first lecture. By the mid-1890s, however, his classes were filled to capacity.

Wundt attempted to explain immediate experience and to develop ways to study it scientifically, though he also believed that some mental processes could not be studied through scientific experiments (Blumenthal, 1975). Wundt was primarily interested in memory (S. K. Carpenter, 2005) and *selective attention*—the process by which we determine what we are going to attend to at any given moment. Wundt used the term *voluntarism* to describe his view of psychology. He believed that attention is actively controlled by intentions and motives; and that this sets human attention apart from attention in other organisms. In turn, attention controls such other psychological processes as perceptions, thoughts, and memories. We will examine the role of attention more closely in Chapter 4 ("States of Consciousness") and Chapter 6 ("Memory"), but for the moment it is sufficient to note that, in establishing a laboratory and insisting on measurement and experimentation, Wundt moved psychology out of the realm of philosophy and into the world of science (Benjamin, 2000).

One important product of the Leipzig lab was its students who carried the new science of psychology to universities in other countries, including the United States: G. Stanley Hall (who established the first American psychology laboratory at Johns Hopkins University in 1883), J. M. Cattell (a professor at the University of Pennsylvania in 1888, who was the first American to be called a "professor of psychology"), and British-born Edward Bradford Titchener, who went to Cornell University. Titchener's ideas differed sharply in many respects from those of his mentor (Zehr, 2000). Titchener was impressed by recent advances in chemistry and physics, achieved by analyzing complex compounds (molecules) in terms of their basic elements (atoms). Similarly, Titchener reasoned, psychologists should analyze complex experiences in terms of their simplest components. For example, when people look at a banana they immediately think, "Here is a fruit, something to peel and eat." But this perception is based on associations with past experience; what are the most fundamental elements, or "atoms," of thought?

Titchener broke down consciousness into three basic elements: physical sensations (what we see), feelings (such as liking or disliking bananas), and images (memories of other bananas). Even the most complex thoughts and feelings, he argued, can be reduced to these simple elements. Titchener saw psychology's role as identifying these elements and showing how they can be combined and integrated—an approach known as **structuralism**. Although the structuralist school of psychology was relatively short-lived and has had little long-term effect, the study of perception and sensation continues to be very much a part of contemporary psychology, as you will see in Chapter 3, "Sensation and Perception."

WILLIAM JAMES: FUNCTIONALISM One of the first academics to challenge structuralism was an American, William James (son of the transcendentalist philosopher Henry James, Sr., and brother of novelist Henry James). As a young man, James earned a degree in physiology and also studied philosophy on his own, unable to decide which interested him more. In psychology, he found the link between the two. In 1875, James offered a class in psychology at Harvard. He later commented that the first lecture he ever heard on the subject was his own.

James argued that Titchener's "atoms of experience"—pure sensations without associations—simply do not exist in real-life experience. Our minds are constantly weaving associations, revising experience, starting, stopping, and jumping back and forth in time. Perceptions, emotions, and images cannot be separated, James argued; consciousness flows in a continuous stream. If we could not recognize a banana, we would have to figure out what it was each time we saw one. Mental associations allow us to benefit from previous experience. When we get up in the morning, get dressed, open the door, and walk down the street, we don't have to think about what we are doing: We act out of habit. James suggested that when we repeat something, our nervous systems are changed so that each repetition is easier than the last.

James developed a **functionalist theory** that focused on how individuals use their perceptual abilities to adapt and function in their environment. This theory raised questions about learning, the complexities of mental life, the impact of experience on the brain, and humankind's place in the natural world that still seem current today. Although impatient

Wilhelm Wundt

William James

structuralism School of psychology that stresses the basic units of experience and the combinations in which they occur.

functionalist theory Theory of mental life and behavior that is concerned with how an organism uses its perceptual abilities to function in its environment.

with experiments, James shared Wundt and Titchener's belief that the goal of psychology was to analyze experience. Wundt, however, was not impressed. After reading James's *The Principles of Psychology* (1890), he commented, "It is literature, it is beautiful, but it is not psychology" (M. Hunt, 1994, p. 139).

SIGMUND FREUD: PSYCHODYNAMIC PSYCHOLOGY Of all psychology's pioneers, Sigmund Freud is by far the best known—and the most controversial. A medical doctor, unlike the other figures we have introduced, Freud was fascinated by the central nervous system. He spent many years conducting research in the physiology laboratory of the University of Vienna and only reluctantly became a practicing physician. After a trip to Paris, where he studied with a neurologist who was using hypnosis to treat nervous disorders, Freud established a private practice in Vienna in 1886. His work with patients convinced him that many nervous ailments are psychological, rather than physiological in origin. Freud's clinical observations led him to develop a comprehensive theory of mental life that differed radically from the views of his predecessors.

Freud held that human beings are not as rational as they imagine and that "free will," which was so important to Wundt, is largely an illusion. Rather, we are motivated by unconscious instincts and urges that are not available to the rational, conscious part of our mind. Other psychologists had referred to the unconscious, in passing, as a dusty warehouse of old experiences and information we could retrieve as needed. In contrast, Freud saw the unconscious as a dynamic cauldron of primitive sexual and aggressive drives, forbidden desires, nameless fears and wishes, and traumatic childhood memories. Although repressed (or hidden from awareness), unconscious impulses press on the conscious mind and find expression in disguised or altered form, including dreams, mannerisms, slips of the tongue, and symptoms of mental illness, as well as in socially acceptable pursuits such as art and literature. To uncover the unconscious, Freud developed the technique of *free association*, in which the patient lies on a couch, recounts dreams, and says whatever comes to mind.

Freud's psychodynamic theory was as controversial at the turn of the century as Darwin's theory of evolution had been 25 years earlier. Many of Freud's Victorian contemporaries were shocked, not only by his emphasis on sexuality, but also by his suggestion that we are often unaware of our true motives and thus are not entirely in control of our thoughts and behavior. Conversely, members of the medical community in Vienna at that time generally held Freud's new theory in high regard, nominating him for the position of Professor Extraordinarious at the University of Vienna (Esterson, 2002). Freud's lectures and writings attracted considerable attention in the United States as well as in Europe; he had a profound impact on the arts and philosophy, as well as on psychology. However, Freud's theories and methods continue to inspire heated debate.

Psychodynamic theory, as expanded and revised by Freud's colleagues and successors, laid the foundation for the study of personality and psychological disorders, which we will discuss in Chapters 10, 12, and 13. His revolutionary notion of the unconscious and his portrayal of human beings as constantly at war with themselves are taken for granted today, at least in literary and artistic circles. Freud's theories were never totally accepted by mainstream psychology, however; and in recent decades his influence on clinical psychology and psychotherapy has declined (R. W. Robins, Gosling, & Craik, 1999; see also Westen, 1998).

REDEFINING PSYCHOLOGY: THE STUDY OF BEHAVIOR

How was Watson's approach to human behavior different from that of Freud?

How did Skinner expand behaviorism?

Until the beginning of the 20th century, psychology was defined as the study of mental processes. The primary method of collecting data was introspection or self-observation, which occurred in a laboratory or on an analyst's couch. At the beginning of the 20th century, however, a new generation of psychologists rebelled against this "soft" approach. The leader of the challenge was the American psychologist John B. Watson.

JOHN B. WATSON: BEHAVIORISM While Sigmund Freud explored unconscious forces in Vienna, across the ocean, John B. Watson argued that the whole idea of mental life was

Sigmund Freud

John B. Watson

psychodynamic theories Personality theories contending that behavior results from psychological factors that interact within the individual, often outside conscious awareness.

superstition, a relic left over from the Middle Ages. In "Psychology as a Behaviorist Views It" (1913), Watson contended that you cannot see or even define consciousness any more than you can observe a soul. And if you cannot locate or measure something, it cannot be the object of scientific study. For Watson, psychology was the study of observable, measurable behavior—and nothing more.

Watson's view of psychology, known as **behaviorism**, was based on the work of the Russian physiologist Ivan Pavlov, who had won a Nobel Prize for his research on digestion. In the course of his experiments, Pavlov noticed that the dogs in his laboratory began to salivate as soon as they heard their feeder coming, even before they could see their dinner. He decided to find out whether salivation, an automatic reflex, could be shaped by learning. He began by repeatedly pairing the sound of a buzzer with the presence of food. The next step was to observe what happened when the buzzer was sounded without introducing food. This experiment clearly demonstrated what Pavlov had noticed incidentally: After repeated pairings, the dogs salivated in response to the buzzer alone. Pavlov called this simple form of training *conditioning*. Thus a new school of psychology was inspired by a casual observation—followed by rigorous experiments. We will learn more about the findings of this approach in Chapter 5, "Learning."

Watson came to believe that all mental experiences—thinking, feeling, awareness of self—are nothing more than physiological changes in response to accumulated experiences of conditioning. An infant, he argued, is a *tabula rasa* (Latin for "blank slate") on which experience may write virtually anything:

> Give me a dozen healthy infants, well-formed, and my own specialized world to bring them up in, and I'll guarantee to take any one at random and train him to become any type of specialist I might select—doctor, lawyer, artist, merchant chief and, yes, even beggar man, and thief, regardless of his talents, penchants, tendencies, abilities, vocations, and race. (J. B. Watson, 1924, p. 104)

Watson attempted to demonstrate that all psychological phenomena—even Freud's unconscious motivations—are the result of conditioning (Rilling, 2000). In one of the most infamous experiments in psychology's history, Watson attempted to create a conditioned fear response in an 11-month-old boy. "Little Albert" was a secure, happy baby who enjoyed new places and experiences. On his first visit to Watson's laboratory, Albert was delighted by a tame, furry white rat, but he became visibly frightened when Watson banged a steel bar with a hammer just behind the infant's head. On his second visit, Watson placed the rat near Albert, and the moment the baby reached out and touched the rat, Watson banged the hammer. After half a dozen pairings, little Albert began crying the instant the rat was introduced, without any banging. Further experiments found that Alfred was frightened by anything white and furry—a rabbit, a dog, a sealskin coat, cotton wool, and Watson wearing a Santa Claus mask (J. B. Watson & Rayner, 1920). Freud had labeled the transfer of emotions from one person or object to another "displacement," a neurotic response that he traced to the unconscious. Drawing on Pavlov, Watson called the same phenomenon "generalization," a simple matter of conditioning (Rilling, 2000). As far as Watson was concerned, psychodynamic theory and psychoanalysis were "voodooism."

Watson was also interested in showing that fears could be eliminated by conditioning. Mary Cover Jones (M. C. Jones, 1924), one of his graduate students, successfully reconditioned a boy who showed a fear of rabbits (not caused by laboratory conditioning) to overcome this fear. Her technique, which involved presenting the rabbit at a great distance and then gradually bringing it closer while the child was eating, is similar to conditioning techniques used by psychologists today.

B. F. SKINNER: BEHAVIORISM REVISITED Following in the footsteps of Pavlov and Watson, B. F. Skinner became one of the leaders of the behaviorist school of psychology in the mid-20th century. Like Watson, Skinner fervently believed that psychologists should study only observable and measurable behavior (J. Moore, 2005; B. F. Skinner, 1938, 1987, 1989, 1990). He, too, was primarily interested in changing behavior through conditioning—and in discovering natural laws of behavior in the process. But Skinner added a new element to the behaviorist repertoire: reinforcement. He rewarded his subjects for behaving the way he wanted them to behave.

behaviorism School of psychology that studies only observable and measurable behavior.

Mary Cover Jones

B. F. Skinner

Gestalt psychology School of psychology that studies how people perceive and experience objects as whole patterns.

humanistic psychology School of psychology that emphasizes nonverbal experience and altered states of consciousness as a means of realizing one's full human potential.

For example, an animal (rats and pigeons were Skinner's favorite subjects) was put into a special cage and allowed to explore it. Eventually, the animal reached up and pressed a lever or pecked at a disk on the wall, whereupon a food pellet dropped into the box. Gradually, the animal learned that pressing the bar or pecking at the disk always brought food. Why did the animal learn this? It learned because it was *reinforced*, or rewarded, for doing so. Skinner thus made the animal an active agent in its own conditioning.

Behaviorism dominated academic psychology in the United States well into the 1960s. One unintended and, at the time, largely unnoticed consequence was that psychology developed an *environmental bias*: Virtually every aspect of human behavior was attributed to learning and experience. Investigating evolutionary influences on behavior or studying hereditary, genetic influences on individual and group differences was considered taboo (R. B. Evans, 1999).

THE COGNITIVE REVOLUTION

How did Gestalt psychologists influence the way we think about perception?

What aspects of life do humanistic psychologists stress?

In the late 1960s, behaviorism began to loosen its grip on the field. On the one hand, research on perception, personality, child development, interpersonal relations, and other topics that behaviorists had ignored raised questions they couldn't readily explain. On the other hand, research in other fields (especially anthropology, linguistics, neurobiology, and computer science) was beginning to shed new light on the workings of the mind. Psychologists came to view behaviorism not as an all-encompassing theory or paradigm, but as only one piece of the puzzle (R. W. Robins et al., 1999; W. Tryon, 2002). They began to look into the "black box" of the human mind, and put more emphasis on humans (and other animals) as *sentient*—conscious, perceptive, and alert—beings, that is, as active learners, rather than passive recipients of life's lessons.

THE PRECURSORS: GESTALT AND HUMANISTIC PSYCHOLOGY Even during the period that behaviorism dominated American psychology, not all psychologists had accepted behaviorist doctrines. Two schools that paved the way for the cognitive revolution were Gestalt psychology and humanistic psychology.

In Germany, psychologists Max Wertheimer, Wolfgang Köhler, and Kurt Koffka were all interested in perception, particularly in certain tricks that the mind plays on itself. For example, when we see a series of still pictures flashed at a constant rate (for example, movies or "moving" neon signs), why do the pictures seem to move? Phenomena like these launched a new school of thought, **Gestalt psychology**. Roughly translated from German, *Gestalt* means "whole" or "form." When applied to perception, it refers to our tendency to see patterns, to distinguish an object from its background, to complete a picture from a few cues. Like William James, the Gestalt psychologists rejected the structuralists' attempt to break down perception and thought into their elements. When we look at a tree, we see just that, a tree, rather than a series of isolated leaves and branches. We'll see in Chapter 3 that Gestalt psychology paved the way for the modern study of perception.

During the same period, the American psychologist Abraham Maslow, who studied under Gestalt psychologist Max Wertheimer and anthropologist Ruth Benedict, developed a more holistic approach to psychology, in which feelings and yearnings play a key role. Maslow referred to **humanistic psychology** as the "third force"—beyond Freudian theory and behaviorism. Humanistic psychologists emphasize human potential and the importance of love, belonging, self-esteem and self-expression, peak experiences (when one becomes so involved in an activity that self-consciousness fades), and self-actualization (the spontaneity and creativity that result from focusing on problems outside oneself and looking beyond the boundaries of social conventions). These psychologists focus on mental health and well-being, on self-understanding and self-improvement, rather than on mental illness.

Humanistic psychology has made important contributions to the study of motivation and emotions (see Chapter 8), as well as to the subfields of personality and psychotherapy (Chapters 10 and 13). But this doctrine has never been totally accepted by mainstream psychology. Because humanistic psychology is interested in questions of meaning, values, and ethics, many people—including its own members—see this school of psychology more as a cultural and spiritual movement than as a branch of science. In recent years, however, positive psychologists (whom we discuss further later in this chapter) have begun to reinvestigate some of the questions that humanistic psychologists raised a half century ago (Bohart & Greening, 2001; Froh, 2004).

THE RISE OF COGNITIVE PSYCHOLOGY As behaviorism fell out of favor in the late 1960s, psychology began to come full circle in what can be described as a *cognitive revolution*—a shift away from a limited focus on behavior toward a broad interest in such mental processes as memory, decision making, and information processing. The field evolved from a period in which consciousness was considered inaccessible to scientific inquiry to one in which researchers resumed investigating and theorizing about the mind—but now with new research methods and behaviorism's commitment to objective, empirical research. As a result of this shift in focus, even the definition of psychology changed. Psychology is still the study of human behavior, but psychologists' concept of "behavior" has been expanded to include thoughts, feelings, and states of consciousness.

This new focus applies to existing fields of psychology as well as to new subfields. In developmental psychology, for example, the idea that a child is a blank slate, whose development is shaped entirely by his or her environment, was replaced by a new view of babies and children as aware, competent, social beings. In this new view, children actively seek to learn about and make sense of their world. Moreover, all healthy children are "equipped" with such distinctively human characteristics as the ability to acquire language through exposure, without formal education. Developmental psychology is one of several subfields contributing to and benefiting from the emergence of cognitive psychology.

Cognitive psychology is the study of our mental processes in the broadest sense: thinking, feeling, learning, remembering, making decisions and judgments, and so on. If the behaviorist model of learning resembled an old-fashioned telephone switchboard (a call or a stimulus comes in, is relayed along various circuits in the brain, and an answer or a response goes out), the cognitive model resembles a high-powered, modern computer. Cognitive psychologists are interested in the ways in which people acquire information, process or transform that information using their cognitive "hardware" and "software," and use the results to make sense out of the world, to solve problems, and so on.

In contrast to behaviorists, cognitive psychologists believe that mental processes can and should be studied scientifically. Although we cannot observe memories or thoughts directly, we can observe behavior and make inferences about the kinds of cognitive processes that underlie that behavior. For example, we can read a lengthy story to people and then observe the kinds of things that they remember from that story, the ways in which their recollections change over time, and the sorts of errors in recall that they are prone to make. On the basis of systematic research of this kind, we can gain insight into the cognitive processes underlying human memory (which we discuss in Chapter 6, "Memory"). Moreover, with the advent of new brain-imaging techniques (described in Chapter 2), cognitive psychologists have begun to address questions about the neurological mechanisms that underlie such cognitive processes as learning, memory, intelligence, and emotion, giving rise to the rapidly expanding field of *cognitive neuroscience* (D'Esposito, Zarahn, & Aguirre, 1999; Rosenzweig, Breedlove, & Watson, 2005).

In just a short time, cognitive psychology has had an enormous impact on almost every area of psychology (Sperry, 1988, 1995) and has become the most prominent school in contemporary scientific psychology (Johnson & Erneling, 1997; Robins et al., 1999).

NEW DIRECTIONS

Where do evolutionary psychologists look for the roots of human behavior?

What new focus is positive psychology bringing to the study of human behavior?

Is there a single perspective dominating psychology today?

During much of the 20th century, psychology was divided into competing theoretical schools. Crossing theoretical lines was considered intellectual heresy. In the 21st century, by contrast, psychologists are more flexible in considering the merits of new approaches,

cognitive psychology School of psychology devoted to the study of mental processes in the broadest sense.

evolutionary psychology An approach to, and subfield of, psychology that is concerned with the evolutionary origins of behaviors and mental processes, their adaptive value, and the purposes they continue to serve.

positive psychology An emerging field of psychology that focuses on positive experiences, including subjective well-being, self-determination, the relationship between positive emotions and physical health, and the factors that allow individuals, communities, and societies to flourish.

combining elements of different perspectives as their interests or research findings dictate. As a result, new theories and initiatives are emerging.

EVOLUTIONARY PSYCHOLOGY As the name indicates, **evolutionary psychology** focuses on the origins of behavior patterns and mental processes, the adaptive value they have or had, and the functions they serve or served in our emergence as a distinct species (Buss, 2005). All of the theoretical views we have discussed so far seek to explain modern humans, or *Homo sapiens*. In contrast, evolutionary psychologists ask, how did human beings get to be the way we are? In what ways might the roots of behavior serve to promote the survival of the species? For example, men the world over tend to prefer women with a waist-to-hip ratio of 0.7 (Streeter & McBurney, 2003). And a small waist-to-hip ratio is associated with a female's reproductive age and overall health (D. Singh, 1993). Since these preferences appear to be universal, rather than the product of any particular society, might they be "built in" since they have been adaptive for humans in the past?

Evolutionary psychologists study such diverse topics as perception, language, helping others (altruism), parenting, happiness, sexual attraction and mate selection, jealousy, and violence (Bernhard & Penton-Voak, 2002; Buss, 2000a, 2000b; Caporael, 2001; Rhodes, 2006; G. Miller, 2000). By studying such phenomena in different species, different habitats, different cultures, and in males and females, evolutionary psychologists seek to understand the basic programs that guide thinking and behavior (R. W. Byrne, 2002; J. Cartwright, 2000).

We have said that cognitive psychologists tend to see the human mind as a "general purpose" computer that requires software (experience) to process information. In contrast, many evolutionary psychologists see the mind as "hardwired," suggesting that human beings are predisposed to think and act in certain ways (Cosmides, Tooby, & Barkow, 1992; Goode, 2000b; Siegert & Ward, 2002). Further, they contend that these fixed programs evolved hundreds of thousands of years ago when our ancestors lived as hunter–gatherers, although the problem-solving strategies that benefited early humans may or may not be adaptive in the modern era. Whether evolutionary psychology finds a place among the major fields of psychology or stays on the sidelines remains to be seen (see Bering & Shackelford, 2005; Bjorklund, 2003; Buller, 2005; Buss & Reeve, 2003; C. B. Crawford, 2003; Krebs, 2003; Lickliter & Honeycutt, 2003a, 2003b; Tooby, Cosmides, & Barrett, 2003).

POSITIVE PSYCHOLOGY Another emerging perspective is **positive psychology** which, as we mentioned earlier, traces its roots back to humanistic psychology. According to this view, psychology should devote more attention to "the good life": the study of subjective feelings of happiness and well-being; the development of such individual traits as intimacy, integrity, leadership, altruism, and wisdom; and the kinds of families, work settings, and communities that encourage individuals to flourish (Gable & Haidt, 2005; M. E. P. Seligman & Csikszentmihalyi, 2000; M. E. P. Seligman, Steen, & Park, 2005). As mentioned earlier, the roots of positive psychology can be traced back to the humanistic perspective.

Positive psychologists argue that psychologists have learned a great deal about the origins,

THINKING CRITICALLY ABOUT . . .

Autonomy

The first edition of the journal *American Psychologist* in the new millennium was dedicated to positive psychology. The issue included two articles on autonomy, or self-determination (January, 2000).

In one, the authors (Ryan & Deci, 2000) concluded that autonomy—freedom to make one's own decisions—is essential to motivation and personal growth. Without options, they argue, people become passive. In the other, the author (B. Schwartz, 2000) argued that too much freedom of choice is debilitating. Without strong cultural guidelines, people have no way of evaluating their choices and so are more vulnerable to depression.

- Which conclusion do you support? How did you arrive at this view? From personal experience, or from experience in other cultures?

- Play "devil's advocate" in the sense of developing arguments for the view you oppose. What does this exercise teach you?

- In the United States, Americans tend to assume that everyone should have freedom of choice, and we espouse this view for everyone, in every culture and society. Is our view culturally biased? What kind of research evidence would you need to determine whether your view is in fact correct?

Suggestion: In debating this question with yourself and others, we urge you to read the original articles:

Ryan, R. M., & Deci, E. L. (2000). Self-determination theory and the facilitation of intrinsic motivation, social development, and well-being. *American Psychologist, 55,* 68–78.

Schwartz, B. (2000). Self-determination: The tyranny of freedom. *American Psychologist, 55,* 79–88.

diagnosis, and treatment of mental illness but relatively little about the origins and nurturance of mental wellness. In recent decades, for example, psychologists have made great strides in understanding the neurology of depression, schizophrenia, and other disorders. We have come to understand a lot about how individuals survive and endure under conditions of extreme adversity, but far less about ordinary human strengths and virtues (Sheldon & King, 2001). We know more about intelligence than about wisdom; more about conformity than originality; and more about stress than about tranquility. There have been many studies of prejudice and intergroup hostility, for example, but very few about tolerance and intergroup harmony.

Today's positivists do not argue that psychologists should abandon their role in the science of healing. To the contrary, they support efforts to promote better, more widespread use of what psychologists have learned. But they argue that psychology has reached a point where building positive qualities should receive as much emphasis as repairing damage (Duckworth, Steen, & Seligman, 2005).

Positive psychology seeks to understand more about ordinary human strengths and virtues such as altruism, tolerance, happiness, philanthropy and wisdom. For instance, what factors lead to the self-sacrifice and volunteerism displayed here by Nelson Pedro, a firefighter who volunteered to help evacuate families from the New Orleans Superdome in the aftermath of Hurricane Katrina?

MULTIPLE PERSPECTIVES OF PSYCHOLOGY TODAY As we've seen, contemporary psychologists tend to see different perspectives as complementary, with each perspective contributing to our understanding of human behavior. When they study aggression, for example, psychologists no longer limit their explanations to the behavioral view (aggressive behavior is learned as a consequence of reward and punishment) or the Freudian perspective (aggression is an expression of unconscious hostility toward a parent). Instead, most contemporary psychologists trace aggression to a number of factors, including long-standing adaptations to the environment (evolutionary psychology) and the influences of culture, gender, and socioeconomic status on the way people perceive and interpret events—"That guy is making fun of me" or "She's asking for it"—(cognitive psychology). Similarly, physiological psychologists no longer limit themselves to identifying the genetic and biochemical roots of aggression. Instead, they study how heredity and the environment interact to elicit aggressive behavior.

Sometimes these theoretical perspectives mesh and enhance each other beautifully; at other times, adherents of one approach challenge their peers, arguing for one viewpoint over all the others. But all psychologists agree that the field advances only when new evidence is added to support or challenge existing theories.

WHERE ARE THE WOMEN?

During psychology's early years, why were relatively few women accepted in the field?

As you read the brief history of modern psychology, you may have concluded that the founders of the new discipline were all men. But did psychology really have only fathers and no mothers? If there were women pioneers in the field, why are their names and accomplishments missing from historical accounts?

In fact, women have contributed to psychology from its beginnings. In the United States, women presented papers and joined the national professional association as soon as it was formed in 1892. Often, however, they faced discrimination. Some colleges and universities did not grant degrees to women; professional journals were reluctant to publish their work; and teaching positions were often closed to them (Kite et al., 2001; Minton, 2002). Despite these barriers, a number of early women psychologists made important contributions and were acknowledged by some of the men in the growing discipline of psychology.

In 1906, James McKeen Cattell published *American Men of Science*, which, despite its title, included a number of women, among them 22 female psychologists. Cattell rated 3 of these women as among the 1,000 most distinguished scientists in the country: Mary Whiton Calkins (1863–1930), for her analysis of how we learn verbal material and her contributions to self-psychology; Christine Ladd-Franklin (1847–1930), for her work in color vision; and Margaret Floy Washburn (1871–1939) for her pioneering research examining the role of imagery in thought processes. In addition, Mary Whiton Calkins was elected and served as the first female

Margaret Floy Washburn

Elizabeth Loftus's research on the memory of eyewitnesses is helping us understand more about cognitive processes.

president of the American Psychological Association (APA) in 1905, a position also held by Margaret Floy Washburn in 1921. However, because the doors to an academic career remained closed, other early female psychologists found positions in therapeutic and other nonacademic settings; pursued careers in allied professions, such as child development and education, which were considered acceptable fields for women; or gained recognition by collaborating on research projects and books with their spouses (R. B. Evans, 1999).

In recent decades, the situation has changed dramatically. The number of women who receive PhDs in psychology has grown by leaps and bounds. (See **Figure 1–1**.) Indeed, women have begun to outnumber men in psychology. In 1999 through 2000, women received three fourths of the baccalaureate degrees awarded in psychology (National Science Foundation, 2001). In the same period, women represented just under three fourths of all psychology graduate students (Pate, 2001), and in 1999 women earned two out of three doctorate degrees awarded in psychology (National Science Foundation, 2002). Since female psychologists perform key research in all of the psychology subfields, you will find their work referred to throughout this text. For example, Terry Amabile has studied creativity, in particular the positive effects that exposure to creative role models can have on people. Elizabeth Loftus's research on memory has uncovered how unreliable eyewitness accounts of a crime can be. Carol Nagy Jaklin has studied the role that parents' expectations can play in girls' (and boys') perceptions of the value of mathematics. Judith Rodin's research examines eating behavior, in particular bulimia and obesity. Eleanor Maccoby, Alice Eagly, and Jacqueline Eccles are prominent among the growing number of women and men who are studying sex differences in a variety of areas, such as emotionality, math and verbal ability, and helping behavior. Throughout the text, we look at this work to see what part biology and society play in differences in the behavior of women and men.

The relative absence of women from the history of psychology is only one aspect of a much bigger and more troubling concern: the relative inattention to human diversity that characterized psychology through most of the 20th century. Only recently have psychologists looked closely at the ways in which culture, gender, race, and ethnicity can affect virtually all aspects of human behavior. In the next section, we begin our examination of this important topic.

CHECK YOUR UNDERSTANDING

1. It was not until the late _____ that psychology came into its own as a separate discipline.

Answers: 1. 1800s or 19th century.

APPLY YOUR UNDERSTANDING

1. Gregory believes that most of human behavior can be explained by examining our unconscious impulses. Gregory takes a _____ view of psychology.
   a. psychodynamic
   b. behavioral
   c. Gestalt
   d. structuralist

2. As a contestant on the television show *Jeopardy!*, you are delighted that you took a psychology course when you read the clue, "Founder of the first psychological laboratory," and you know that the correct answer (phrased in the form of a question, as required by the show) is, "Who was _____?"
   a. B. F. Skinner
   b. John B. Watson
   c. William James
   d. Wilhelm Wundt

Answers: 1. a. 2. d.

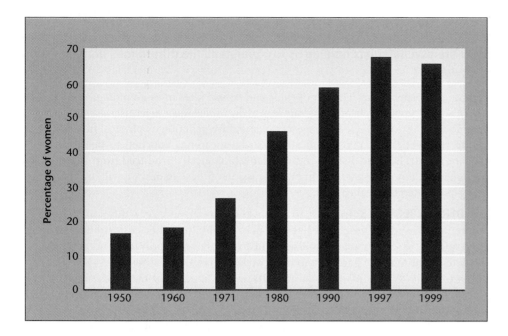

Figure 1–1

Percentage of women recipients of PhDs in psychology, 1950–1999.

Source: Summary Report: Doctorate Recipients from United States Universities (Selected Years). National Research Council. Figure compiled by the APA Research Office. Copyright © 2000. 1999 data from the National Science Foundation, 2002.

Human Diversity

Why should you learn about human diversity?

In the early 20th century, psychology was a White male profession with a distinctly American accent (Strickland, 2000). The great majority of research studies were conducted by White male professors at American universities, using White male American college students as participants. This arrangement was not a conscious or deliberate decision to study just one particular group. As in the medical community and in other sciences and prestigious professions in Europe and North America, psychology took for granted that what was true of White Western males would be true for other people as well. One critical history of psychology during this period was entitled *Even the Rat Was White!* (R. Guthrie, 1976).

For students like you, however—who will be tomorrow's citizens of the world—understanding human diversity is essential. The reason for that urgency is all around you. Our major cities are home to people from diverse backgrounds, with diverse values and goals, living side by side. But proximity does not always produce harmony; sometimes it leads to aggression, prejudice, and conflict. Understanding cultural, racial, ethnic, and gender differences in thinking and behavior gives us the tools to reduce some of these interpersonal tensions. Looking at human diversity from a scientific perspective will allow you to separate fact from fiction in your daily interactions with people. Moreover, once you understand how and why groups differ in their values, behaviors, approaches to the world, thought processes, and responses to situations, you will be better able to savor the diversity around you. Finally, the more you comprehend human diversity, the more you will appreciate the many universal features of humanity.

The process of examining and overcoming past assumptions and biases has been slow and uneven, but a new appreciation of human diversity is taking shape (Enns & Sinacore, 2005; Ocampo et al., 2003; Tucker & Herman, 2002). Psychologists have begun to question assumptions that are explicitly based on gender, race, and culture. Are women more likely than men to help a person in distress? Are African Americans more vulnerable to certain types of mental illness than are European Americans, or vice versa? Do the Japanese view children's ability to learn in the same way Americans do? Do homosexuals have different motives and emotions than heterosexuals? Research indicates that the answer to such questions often is "no."

Despite stereotypes of fathers as distant from their children, many fathers today take a very active role in parenting.

Carol Gilligan

---

gender The psychological and social meanings attached to being biologically male or female.

feminist theory Feminist theories offer a wide variety of views on the social roles of women and men, the problems and rewards of those roles, and prescriptions for changing those roles.

GENDER

How are psychologists helping us to understand the differences between men and women?

Gender has many layers. The words *male* and *female* refer to one's biological makeup, the physical and genetic facts of being one sex or the other. Some scientists use the term *sex* to refer exclusively to biological differences in anatomy, genetics, or physical functioning, and **gender** to refer to the psychological and social meanings attached to being biologically male or female. Because distinguishing what is biologically produced from what is socially influenced is almost impossible, in our discussion of these issues, we will use the terms *sex* and *gender* interchangeably.

GENDER STEREOTYPES In the past, men and women led very different lives. Today, women in many societies are as likely as men to obtain higher education; to work full-time, pursue careers, start businesses; and to be active in politics. And men are more likely to be more active parents and homemakers than their fathers were. Yet, stereotypes about how the "typical male" looks and acts or the "accepted social roles" for females still lead to confusion and misunderstandings between the sexes. In general, our culture promotes the idea that men are dominant, strong, and aggressive, whereas women are accommodating, emotional, and affectionate. As a result, many boys learn to hide their emotions, to deny feelings of weakness even to themselves, and to fight. Many girls, by contrast, learn to hide their ambitions, to deny their talents and strengths even to themselves, and perhaps to give in. Stereotypes are rarely benign. As we will see in Chapter 9, "Life-Span Development," the negative effects of these particular stereotypes on both boys and girls are significant and lasting.

Beyond our stereotypes about what males and females "typically" are like, we have general beliefs about gender roles—that is, cultural expectations regarding acceptable behavior and activities for males and females, respectively. As a rule, cultural norms change more slowly than behavior patterns. Although most modern American families depend on two salaries, the assumption that the husband should be the chief breadwinner and the wife should put her home and children first remains powerful. Working wives and mothers work a "second shift" (keeping house and caring for children) at home—as much because they feel that doing so is their responsibility and area of expertise, as because their husbands still expect them to so (Hochschild & Machung, 1989; Kroska, 2003; Powers & Reiser, 2005).

The study of gender similarities and differences has become part of mainstream psychology. Psychologists in virtually every subfield conduct research to determine whether their findings apply equally to males and females, and if not, why not. As we will see, **feminist theory** is not for women only.

FEMINIST PSYCHOLOGY As the number of female psychologists has grown in recent decades (see **Figure 1–1**), so have their concerns about traditional psychological theories, research, and clinical practices (Denmark, Rabinowitz, & Sechzer, 2000; Minton, 2002). Feminist psychologists such as Carol Gilligan make three main points. As we have noted, much of the research supporting key psychological theories, such as moral development, was based on all-male samples. Measured against "universal male" standards, females often were found "lacking." Second, reports of gender differences tend to focus on the extremes, exaggerating small differences and ignoring much greater similarities (Hyde, 2005a; Spelke, 2005). Third, the questions that psychologists ask and the topics that they study reflect what they consider to be important; male and female psychologists differ to some extent in that regard.

Beyond research and theory, contemporary feminist psychology has begun to influence every facet of psychological practice by seeking mechanisms to empower women in the community, by advocating action to establish policies that advance equality and social justice, and by increasing women's representation in global leadership. Feminists also took the lead in urging other psychologists to recognize sexual orientation as simply another aspect of human diversity.

As psychologists study the origins of homosexuality, gay couples seek social acceptance as parents.

SEXUAL ORIENTATION The term **sexual orientation** refers to whether a person is sexually attracted to members of the opposite sex (heterosexuality), the same sex (homosexuality), or both sexes (bisexuality). Division 44 of the American Psychological Association, "Society for the Psychological Study of Lesbian, Gay, and Bisexual Issues," was founded in 1985 to promote research and education regarding sexual orientation, for psychologists as well as the general public. Psychologists have only just begun to investigate the many sensitive issues associated with this dimension of human diversity—including such topics as the origins of sexual orientation (Hyde, 2005b; LeVay & Hamer, 1994), brain differences between heterosexual and homosexual men (Swaab & Hoffman, 1995), and the ethical issues that may arise if specific genes are identified that influence sexual orientation (Hyde, 2005b).

RACE AND ETHNICITY

Why are psychologists interested in racial and ethnic differences?

One of the first things we notice about someone (along with their sex) is that person's race or ethnicity (Omi & Winant, 1994). **Race** is a biological term used to refer to a subpopulation whose members have reproduced exclusively among themselves and therefore are genetically similar and distinct from other members of the same species (Betancourt & López, 1993; Diamond, 1994;). Most people simply take for granted the idea that the human species can be divided into a number of distinct races (Asians, Africans, Caucasians, Native Americans, and so on). However, human beings have migrated, intermarried, and commingled so frequently over time that it is impossible to identify biologically separate races (V. O. Wang & Sue, 2005). To a greater or lesser degree, all humans are "racial hybrids." Moreover, the criteria people use to differentiate among different races are arbitrary. In the United States, we assign people to different races primarily on the basis of skin color and facial features. In central Africa, members of the Tutsi and Hutu tribes see themselves as different races, although they are similar in skin color and facial features. In spite of these different definitions, most people continue to believe that racial categories are meaningful; and as a result, race shapes people's social identities, their sense of self, their experiences in their own and other societies, and even their health.

Whereas racial categories are based on physical differences, **ethnicity** is based on cultural characteristics. An *ethnic group* is a category of people who have migrated to another country, but still identify themselves—and are perceived by others—as distinctive because of a common homeland and history, language, religion, or traditional cultural beliefs and social practices. For example, Hispanic Americans may be Black, White, or any shade in between. What unites them is their language and culture. By the mid-1980s, there was

sexual orientation Refers to the direction of one's sexual interest toward members of the same sex, the other sex, or both sexes.

race A subpopulation of a species, defined according to an identifiable characteristic (that is, geographic location, skin color, hair texture, genes, facial features, and so forth).

ethnicity A common cultural heritage—including religion, language, or ancestry—that is shared by a group of individuals.

Kenneth Clark's research on the effects of segregation influenced the Supreme Court to outlaw segregated schools in *Brown v. Board of Education*.

sufficient interest among psychologists in ethnicity that the APA created a new division (Division 45), devoted to the psychological study of ethnic minority issues. Increasing numbers of psychologists are now studying why ethnicity is so important both in our country and in others and how individuals select or create an ethnic identity and respond to ethnic stereotypes.

RACIAL AND ETHNIC MINORITIES IN PSYCHOLOGY Most ethnic minorities are still underrepresented among the ranks of American psychologists. According to the APA, ethnic-minority students account for almost 25% of college entrants, but represent only 16% of graduates who major in psychology, 14% of those who enroll in graduate school in psychology, 12% of those who receive master's degrees in psychology, and 9% of those who earn doctorates (Sleek, 1999). Why? One possibility is that when Black, Hispanic American, Native American, and other students look at the history of psychology or the psychology faculties of modern universities, they find few role models; likewise, when they look at psychological research, they find little about themselves and their realities (Strickland, 2000). One survey of psychology journals found that less than 2% of the articles focused on U.S. racial and ethnic minorities (Iwamasa & Smith, 1996). Nonetheless, their small numbers have not prevented them from achieving prominence and making significant contributions to the field (see Pickren, 2004). For example, the late Kenneth Clark (1914–2005), a former president of the American Psychological Association, received national recognition for the important work he and his wife, the late Mamie Clark (1917–1983), did on the effects of segregation on Black children (Lal, 2002). This research was cited by the Supreme Court in the *Brown v. Board of Education* decision of 1954 that outlawed segregated schools in the United States (Keppel, 2002).

In an effort to remedy the underrepresentation of ethnic minorities, the APA's Office of Ethnic Minority Affairs is sponsoring programs to attract ethnic-minority students to psychology (Townsend, 2004; Rabasca, 2000a). This initiative includes summer programs for high school students, recruitment at the high school and college levels, mentor and other guidance programs, and a clearinghouse for college students who meet the requirements for graduate programs.

Psychologists are also working to uncover and overcome biases in psychological research that are related to gender, race, and ethnicity. The field of psychology is broadening its scope to probe the full range and richness of human diversity, and this text mirrors that expansive and inclusive approach. We will consider the problem of bias in psychological research more fully later in the chapter.

THINKING CRITICALLY ABOUT . . .

Psychology and Minority Students

In the text, we cited Strickland's conclusion that members of minority groups are underrepresented among psychology majors and in psychology postgraduate programs because a majority of their instructors and professors are White, and because so many of the research studies they read about in introductory psychology are based on White-only participants (Strickland, 2000).

- Do you agree with Strickland? Why or why not?

- What other reasons might explain why Whites are more likely than people of color to choose psychology as their main area of study and future career?

- How might you go about determining whether those various explanations are valid? What kind of research evidence would lead you to favor one explanation over another?

CULTURE

How does culture contribute to human diversity?

A classic definition of **culture** is a people's "design for living" (Kluckhohn, 1949). A culture provides modes of thinking, acting, and communicating; ideas about how the world works and why people behave as they do; beliefs and ideals that shape our individual dreams and desires; information about how to use and improve technology; and, perhaps most important, criteria for evaluating what natural events, human actions, and life itself mean. All large, complex modern societies also include subcultures—groups whose values, attitudes, behavior, and vocabulary or accent distinguish them from the cultural mainstream. Most Americans participate in a number of subcultures as well as in mainstream culture.

Many of the traits we think of as defining us as human—especially language, morals, and technology—are elements of culture. Even one's sense of self is dependent on culture

culture The tangible goods and the values, attitudes, behaviors, and beliefs that are passed from one generation to another.

and subculture (Bruner, 2005: Segall, Lonner, & Berry, 1998). Thus, psychology must take cultural influences into account. In **cross-cultural research**, psychologists examine the way these influences affect behavior. For example, cross-cultural research on motivation and emotions, personality, and self-esteem has called attention to a broad distinction between *individualistic cultures* (which value independence and personal achievement) and *collectivist cultures* (which value interdependence, fitting in, and harmonious relationships) (Fujimoto & Härtel, 2004; Kagitcibasi, 1997). Moreover, cross-cultural studies have had a significant impact on the study of gender. Anthropologist Margaret Mead's classic work, *Sex and Temperament in Three Primitive Societies* (1935), is still cited by feminists and others as showing that definitions of masculinity and femininity are not biological givens, but are instead created by cultures and learned by their members along with other cultural norms, which makes them subject to change. Finally, in our increasingly multicultural society, psychologists are now dealing with diverse clients, research participants, and students (Loner, 2005; C. C. I. Hall, 1997; Laungani, 2004; Woldt & Toman, 2005). To meet this challenge, psychology has begun working to educate and train "culturally competent" professionals.

Within the dominant culture, members of subcultures share values, attitudes, rituals, and often styles of dress.

Throughout this book, we will explore similarities and differences among individuals and groups of people. For example, we will examine differences in personality characteristics, intelligence, and levels of motivation; also, we will look at similarities in biological functioning and developmental stages. In most chapters we will examine research on males and females, members of different racial and ethnic groups, and cross-cultural studies.

CHECK YOUR UNDERSTANDING

1. A _____ is a group within a larger society that shares a certain set of values, beliefs, outlooks, and norms of behavior.
2. People who have ancestors from the same region of the world and who share a common language, religion, and set of social traditions are said to be part of the same _____ group.
3. "Minority groups are seriously underrepresented among psychologists." Is this statement true (T) or false (F)?

Answers: 1. subculture. 2. ethnic. 3. (T).

APPLY YOUR UNDERSTANDING

1. Which of the following is NOT a reason you should study human diversity?
   a. _____ because our society is made up of so many different kinds of people
   b. _____ as a way of helping to solve interpersonal tensions based on misunderstandings of other people
   c. _____ to help define what humans have in common
   d. _____ because diversity psychology is one of the major subdivisions of psychology
2. Which of the following subcultures has been historically overrepresented in psychological research?
   a. _____ African Americans
   b. _____ homosexual men and women
   c. _____ White males
   d. _____ the homeless

Answers: 1. d. 2. c.

cross-cultural research Research involving the exploration of the extent to which people differ from one culture to another.

Research Methods in Psychology

What are some of the research methods that psychologists use in their work?

All sciences—including psychology, sociology, economics, political science, biology, medicine, and physics—require evidence based on careful observation and experimentation. To collect data systematically and objectively, psychologists use a variety of research methods, including naturalistic observation, case studies, surveys, correlational research, and experimental research.

NATURALISTIC OBSERVATION

Why is a natural setting sometimes better than a laboratory for observing behavior?

The world-famous primatologist Jane Goodall has spent most of her adult life observing chimpanzees in their natural environment in Africa.

Psychologists use **naturalistic observation** to study human or animal behavior in its natural context. One psychologist with this real-life orientation might observe behavior in a school or a factory; another might actually join a family to study the behavior of its members; still another might observe monkeys in the wild rather than viewing them in captivity. The primary advantage of naturalistic observation is that the behavior observed in everyday life is likely to be more natural, spontaneous, and varied than that observed in a laboratory.

For example, researchers used naturalistic observation in a recent study (Hammen, Gitlin, & Altshuler, 2000) designed to understand why some patients with bipolar disorder (a mental disorder discussed more fully in Chapter 12, "Psychological Disorders") are more likely to adjust successfully to the workplace than others. By carefully studying 52 people over a 2-year period in their natural settings, these investigators found that the people who displayed the most successful work adjustment were those who also had strong supportive personal relationships with other people. Surprisingly, stressful life events did not seem to play an important role in how well these people adjusted to work. Because simulating a genuine workplace environment in a laboratory would have been extremely difficult (especially over an extended period of time), naturalistic observation provided a practical alternative with which to explore this issue.

Naturalistic observation is not without its drawbacks. Psychologists using naturalistic observation have to take behavior as it comes. They cannot suddenly yell, "Freeze!" when they want to study in more detail what is going on. Nor can psychologists tell people to stop what they are doing because it is not what the psychologists are interested in researching. Moreover, simply describing one's impressions of "a day in the life" of a particular group or the way that different people behave in the same setting is not science. Observers must measure behavior in a systematic way, for example, by devising a form that enables them to check what people are doing at planned timed intervals.

The main drawback in naturalistic observation is **observer bias**. As we will see in Chapter 6, "Memory," eyewitnesses to a crime are often very unreliable sources of information. Even psychologists who are trained observers may subtly distort what they see to make it conform to what they were hoping to see. For this reason, contemporary researchers often use videotapes that can be analyzed and scored by other researchers who do not know what the study is designed to find out. Another potential problem is that psychologists may not observe or record behavior that seems to be irrelevant. Therefore, many observational studies employ a team of trained observers who pool their notes. This strategy often generates a more complete picture than one observer could draw alone.

Unlike laboratory experiments that can be repeated, each natural situation is a one-time-only occurrence. Therefore, psychologists prefer not to make general statements

naturalistic observation Research method involving the systematic study of animal or human behavior in natural settings rather than in the laboratory.

observer bias Expectations or biases of the observer that might distort or influence his or her interpretation of what was actually observed.

based solely on information from naturalistic studies. Rather, they must test the information from naturalistic observation under controlled laboratory conditions before they draw generalizations.

Despite these disadvantages, naturalistic observation is a valuable tool. After all, real-life behavior is what psychology is all about. Naturalistic observation often provides new ideas and suggests new theories, which can then be studied more systematically and in more detail in the laboratory. This method also helps researchers maintain their perspective by reminding them of the larger world outside the lab.

case study Intensive description and analysis of a single individual or just a few individuals.

CASE STUDIES

When can a case study be most useful?

A second research method is the **case study**: a detailed description of one person or a few individuals. Although in some ways this method is similar to naturalistic observation, the researcher here uses a variety of methods to collect information that yields a detailed, in-depth portrait of the individual. A case study usually includes real-life observation, interviews, scores on various psychological tests, and whatever other measures the researcher considers revealing. For example, the Swiss psychologist Jean Piaget developed a comprehensive theory of cognitive development by carefully studying each of his three children as they grew and changed during childhood. Other researchers have tested Piaget's theory with experiments involving larger numbers of children, both in our own culture and in others. (See Chapter 9, "Life-Span Development.")

Like naturalistic observation, case studies can provide valuable insights but they also can have significant drawbacks. Observer bias is as much a problem here as it is with naturalistic observation. Moreover, because each person is unique, we cannot confidently draw general conclusions from a single case. Nevertheless, case studies figure prominently in psychological research. For example, the famous case of Phineas Gage, who suffered severe and unusual brain damage, led researchers to identify the front portion of the brain as important for the control of emotions and the ability to plan and carry out complex tasks. (See Chapter 2, "The Biological Basis of Behavior.") The case study of another brain-damaged patient (Milner, 1959) called "H. M.," who could remember events that preceded his injury but nothing that happened after it, prompted psychologists to suggest that we have several distinct kinds of memory. (See Chapter 6, "Memory.")

Jean Piaget based his theory of cognitive development on case studies of children.

SURVEYS

What are some of the benefits of survey research?

In some respects, surveys address the shortcomings of naturalistic observation and case studies. In **survey research**, a carefully selected group of people is asked a set of predetermined questions in face-to-face interviews or in questionnaires. Surveys, even those with a low-response rate, can generate a great deal of interesting and useful information at relatively low cost, but for results to be accurate, researchers must pay close attention to the survey questions (Tourangeau, Rips, & Rasinski, 2000). In addition, the people surveyed must be selected with great care and be motivated to respond to the survey thoughtfully and carefully (Krosnick, 1999; Visser, Krosnick, & Lavrakas, 2000). For example, asking parents, "Do you ever use physical punishment to discipline your children?" may elicit the socially correct answer, "No." Asking "When was the last time you spanked your child?" or "In what situations do you feel it is necessary to hit your child?" is more likely to elicit honest responses, because the questions are specific and imply that most parents use physical punishment—the researcher is merely asking when and why. At the same time, survey researchers must be careful not to ask leading questions, such as "Most Americans approve of physical punishment; do you?" Guaranteeing anonymity to participants in a survey can also be important.

Naturalistic observations, case studies, and surveys can provide a rich set of raw data that describes behaviors, beliefs, opinions, and attitudes. But these research methods are not ideal for making predictions, explaining, or determining the causes of behavior. For these purposes, psychologists use more powerful research methods, as we will see in the next two sections.

CORRELATIONAL RESEARCH

What is the difference between correlation and cause and effect?

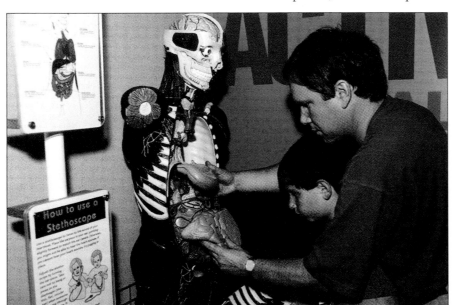

Can the experiences we have as children actually increase intelligence? Researchers might want to study the relationship between stimulating activities, such as frequent visits to science museums, and children's IQ scores. The relationship between the two may show a correlation, but researchers would not conclude from a correlational study that such experiences alone would cause a change in a child's IQ.

A psychologist, under contract to the U.S. Air Force, is asked to predict which applicants for a pilot-training program will make good pilots. An excellent approach to this problem would be **correlational research**. The psychologist might select several hundred trainees, give them a variety of aptitude and personality tests, and then compare the results with their performance in training school. This approach would tell him whether some characteristic or set of characteristics is closely related to, or correlated with, eventual success as a pilot.

Suppose that the psychologist finds that the most successful trainees score higher than the unsuccessful trainees on mechanical aptitude tests and that they are also cautious people who do not like to take unnecessary risks. The psychologist has discovered that there is a *correlation*, or relation, between these traits and success as a pilot trainee: High scores on tests of mechanical aptitude and caution predict success as a pilot trainee. If these correlations are confirmed in new groups of trainees, then the psychologist could recommend with some confidence that the Air Force consider using these tests to select future trainees.

Correlational data are useful for many purposes, but they do not permit the researcher to explain cause and effect. This important distinction is often overlooked. Correlation means that two phenomena seem to be related: When one goes up, the other goes up (or down). For example, young people with high IQ scores usually earn higher grades in school than do students with average or below-average scores. Such a correlation allows researchers to predict that children with high IQ scores will do well on tests and other academic work. But correlation does not identify the direction of influence. A high IQ might cause or enable a child to be a good student. But the reverse might also be true: Working hard in school might cause chil-

survey research Research technique in which questionnaires or interviews are administered to a selected group of people.

correlational research Research technique based on the naturally occurring relationship between two or more variables.

dren to score higher on IQ tests. Or a third, unidentified factor might intervene. For example, growing up in a middle-class family that places a high value on education might cause both higher IQ scores and higher school grades. (See Appendix A for more on correlation.)

This is illustrated with our pilot trainee example. The psychologist has *described a relation* between skill as a pilot and two other characteristics; and as a result he is able to use those relationships to predict with some accuracy which trainees will and will not become skilled pilots. But he has no basis for drawing conclusions about cause and effect. Does the tendency to shy away from taking risks make a trainee a good pilot? Or is it the other way around: Learning to be a skillful pilot makes people cautious? Or is there some unknown factor that causes people to be both cautious and capable of acquiring the different skills needed in the cockpit? The psychologist does not know.

Despite limitations, correlational research often sheds light on important psychological phenomena. In this book, you will come across many examples of correlational research: People who are experiencing severe stress are more prone to develop physical illnesses than people who are not stressed; children whose parent(s) have schizophrenia are more likely to develop this disorder than are other children; and when someone needs help, the more bystanders there are, the less likely it is that any one of them will come forward to offer help. These interesting findings allow us to make some predictions, but psychologists want to move beyond simply making predictions. To explain the causes of psychological phenomena, psychologists most often use experimental research.

EXPERIMENTAL RESEARCH

What kinds of research questions are best studied by experimental research?

A psychology instructor notices that on Monday mornings, most students in her class do not remember materials as well as they do later in the week. She has discovered a correlation between the day of the week and memory for course-related material. On the basis of this correlation, she could predict that next Monday and every Monday thereafter, the students in her class will not absorb material as well as on other days. But she wants to go beyond simply predicting her students' behavior. She wants to understand or explain why their memories are poorer on Mondays than on other days of the week.

As a result of her own experiences and some informal interviews with students, she suspects that students stay up late on weekends and that their difficulty remembering facts and ideas presented on Mondays is due to lack of sleep. This hypothesis appears to make sense, but the psychologist wants to prove that it is correct. To gather evidence that lack of sleep actually causes memory deficits, she turns to the **experimental method**.

Her first step is to select **participants**, people whom she can observe to find out whether her hypothesis is correct. She decides to use student volunteers. To keep her results from being influenced by sex differences or intelligence levels, she chooses a group made up of equal numbers of men and women, all of whom scored between 520 and 550 on the verbal section of their college board exams.

The psychologist then needs to know which participants are sleep deprived. Simply asking people whether they have slept well is not ideal: Some may say "no," so that they will have an excuse for doing poorly on the test, and others may say "yes," because they do not want a psychologist to think that they are so unstable that they cannot sleep. And two people who both say they "slept well" may not mean the same thing by that phrase. So the psychologist decides to intervene—that is, to *control* the situation more closely—to determine which participants have sleep deficits. Everyone in the experiment, she decides, will spend the night in the same dormitory. They will be kept awake until 4:00 A.M. and then awakened at 7:00 A.M. sharp. She and her colleagues will patrol the halls to make sure that no one falls asleep ahead of schedule. By manipulating the amount of time the participants sleep, the psychologist is introducing and controlling an essential element of the experimental method: an independent variable.

Next, she needs to know how well the students remember new information after they are deprived of sleep. For this, she designs a memory task. She needs something that none of her participants will know in advance. If she chooses a chapter in a history book, for example, she runs the risk that some of her participants are history buffs.

experimental method Research technique in which an investigator deliberately manipulates selected events or circumstances and then measures the effects of those manipulations on subsequent behavior.

participants Individuals whose reactions or responses are observed in an experiment.

Given the various possibilities, the psychologist decides to print a page of geometric shapes, each labeled with a nonsense word. Circles are "glucks," triangles are "rogs," and so on. She gives students half an hour to learn the names from this page, then takes it away and asks them to assign those same labels to geometric shapes on a new page. The psychologist believes that the students' ability to learn and remember labels for geometric shapes will depend on their having had a good night's sleep. Performance on the memory task (the number of correct answers) thus becomes the dependent variable. According to the psychologist's hypothesis, changing the **independent variable** (the amount of sleep) should also change the **dependent variable** (performance on the memory task). Her prediction is that this group of participants, who get no more than 3 hours of sleep, should do quite poorly on the memory test.

At this point, the experimenter begins looking for loopholes in her experimental design. How can she be sure that poor test results mean that the participants did less well than they would have done if they had more sleep? For example, their poor performance could simply be the result of knowing that they were being closely observed. To be sure that her experiment measures only the effects of inadequate sleep, the experimenter creates two groups, containing equal numbers of males and females of the same ages and with the same college board scores. One of the groups, the **experimental group**, will be kept awake, as described, until 4:00 A.M. That is, they will be subjected to the experimenter's manipulation of the independent variable—amount of sleep. Members of the other group, the **control group**, will be allowed to go to sleep whenever they please. If the only consistent difference between the two groups is the amount of sleep they get, the experimenter can be much more confident that if the groups differ in their test performance, the difference is due to the length of time they slept the night before.

Finally, the psychologist questions her own objectivity. Because she believes that lack of sleep inhibits students' learning and memory, she does not want to prejudice the results of her experiment; that is, she wants to avoid **experimenter bias**. So she decides to ask a neutral person, someone who does not know which participants did or did not sleep all night, to score the tests.

The experimental method is a powerful tool, but it, too, has limitations. First, many intriguing psychological variables, such as love, hatred, or grief, do not readily lend themselves to experimental manipulation. And even if it were possible to induce such strong emotions as part of a psychological experiment, this treatment would raise serious ethical questions. In some cases, psychologists may use animals rather than humans for experiments. But some subjects, such as the emergence of language in children or the expression of emotions, cannot be studied with other species. Second, because experiments are conducted in an artificial setting, participants—whether human or nonhuman animals—may behave differently than they would in real life.

The accompanying **Summary Table** groups the main advantages and disadvantages of each of the research methods we have discussed. Because each method has drawbacks, psychologists often use more than one method to study a single problem.

MULTIMETHOD RESEARCH

What does multimethod research allow psychologists to do?

Suppose that a psychologist were interested in studying creativity. She would probably combine several of the methods we have described. She might begin her research by giving a group of college students a creativity test that she had invented to measure their capacity to discover or produce something new, and look for *correlations* among the students' scores on her test, their grades, and their scores on commonly used intelligence tests. Then, she would spend several weeks *observing* a college class and *interviewing* teachers, students, and parents to correlate classroom behavior and the interview data with the students' scores on the creativity test. She would go on to test some of her ideas with an *experiment* by using a group of students as participants. Her findings at any point in this research program might prompt her to revise her creativity test or her hypotheses. Eventually, her research might be able to give the general public new insights into creativity.

---

independent variable In an experiment, the variable that is manipulated to test its effects on the other, dependent variables.

dependent variable In an experiment, the variable that is measured to see how it is changed by manipulations in the independent variable.

experimental group In a controlled experiment, the group subjected to a change in the independent variable.

control group In a controlled experiment, the group not subjected to a change in the independent variable; used for comparison with the experimental group.

experimenter bias Expectations by the experimenter that might influence the results of an experiment or its interpretation.

SUMMARY TABLE

BASIC METHODS OF RESEARCH

	Research Method	Advantages	Limitations
Naturalistic Observation	Behavior is observed in the environment in which it occurs naturally.	Provides a great deal of firsthand behavioral information that is more likely to be accurate than reports after the fact. The participant's behavior is more natural, spontaneous, and varied than behaviors taking place in the laboratory. A rich source of hypotheses as well.	The presence of an observer may alter the participants' behavior; the observer's recording of the behavior may reflect a preexisting bias; and it is often unclear whether the observations can be generalized to other settings and other people.
Case Studies	Behavior of one person or a few people is studied in depth.	Yields a great deal of detailed descriptive information. Useful for forming hypotheses.	The case(s) studied may not be a representative sample. This method can be time consuming and expensive. Observer bias is a potential problem.
Surveys	A large number of participants are asked a standard set of questions.	Enables an immense amount of data to be gathered quickly and inexpensively.	Sampling biases can skew results. Poorly constructed questions can result in answers that are ambiguous, so data are not clear. Accuracy depends on ability and willingness of participants to answer questions honestly.
Correlational Research	This approach employs statistical methods to examine the relationship between two or more variables.	May clarify relationships between variables that cannot be examined by other research methods. Allows prediction of behavior.	This method does not permit researchers to draw conclusions regarding cause-and-effect relationships.
Experimental Research	One or more variables are systematically manipulated, and the effect of that manipulation on other variables is studied.	Because of strict control of variables, offers researchers the opportunity to draw conclusions about cause-and-effect relationships.	The artificiality of the lab setting may influence subjects' behavior; unexpected and uncontrolled variables may confound results; many variables cannot be controlled and manipulated.

THE IMPORTANCE OF SAMPLING

How can sampling affect the results of a research study?

One obvious drawback to every form of research is that it is usually impossible, or at least impractical, to measure every single occurrence of a characteristic. No one could expect to measure the memory of every human being, to study the responses of all individuals who suffer from the irrational fears known as phobias, or to record the maternal behavior of all female monkeys. No matter what research method is used, whenever researchers conduct a study, they examine only a relatively small number of people or animals of the population they seek to understand. In other words, researchers almost always study a small **sample**, or subset of the population, and then use the results of that limited study to generalize about larger populations. For example, the psychology instructor who studied the effect of lack of sleep on memory assumed that her results would apply to other students in her classes (past and future), as well as to students in other classes and at other colleges.

How realistic are these assumptions? How confident can researchers be that the results of research conducted on a relatively small sample of people apply to the much larger population from which the sample was drawn? (See "Applying Psychology: Internet Users— A Flawed Study?") By reducing *sampling errors* social scientists have developed several techniques to improve the generalizability of their results. One is to select participants at random from the larger population. For example, the researcher studying pilot trainees might begin with an alphabetical list of all trainees and then select every third name or every fifth name on the list to be in his study. These participants would constitute a

sample A subgroup of a population.

APPLYING PSYCHOLOGY

INTERNET USERS: A FLAWED STUDY?

"Sad, Lonely World Discovered in Cyberspace"
"Isolation Increases with Internet Use"
"Online and Bummed Out"

What's behind these headlines that appeared in various publications during the fall of 1998 while the Internet was still relatively new in our culture? Researchers had found that—as these publications phrased it—"using the Internet can cause isolation, loneliness, and depression"; "the Internet is actually bad for some people's psychological well-being"; and "greater use of the Internet leads to shrinking social support and happiness" (Kraut et al., 1998).

As a critical thinker, you would ask a number of questions about these headlines. Who was studied? How did the researchers determine Internet use? How did they measure such things as isolation, loneliness, depression, social support, and happiness? Did the researchers actually conduct a genuine experiment, manipulating the independent variable of Internet use and observing its effect on the dependent variables, or did they use some other, less powerful research design? If the latter, how do they know that Internet use caused any changes they might have observed?

The answers should motivate you to be far more cautious than the headline writers about what the research actually showed. To begin with, the researchers studied 256 people from only 93 families in Pittsburgh, and 20 of the families and 87 of the people dropped out before the study was completed. The families were selected either because they had teenagers enrolled in high school journalism classes or because an adult was on the board of directors of a community development organization. Households with preexisting Internet connections were excluded.

Thus, for most of the households, this was their first experience with a home computer. Would you consider that a representative sample of the population? Are you confident that the results from this sample can be generalized as broadly as the mass media did? Is it possible that the Internet users were already unusually lonely or isolated or depressed? If so, how might Internet use affect these individuals?

Going further, the researchers actually tracked Internet use through software on the computer. To measure social involvement and psychological well-being, however, they relied entirely on *self-report measures;* that is, the participants themselves supplied all the relevant data. The participants were asked to estimate the amount of time they spent communicating with other family members, as well as the number of people they socialized with, talked to, or visited during an average month. In addition, they filled out questionnaires on social support, loneliness, stress, and depression in their lives.

Does this reliance on self-reports cause you to be cautious about the results of the research? How do we know whether these reports were accurate? For example, did loneliness actually increase as a result of Internet use, or did people simply become more willing to *say* that they were lonely as time went on? Did actual depression increase, or did people's *reports* of being depressed increase? Does Internet use "cause isolation, loneliness, and depression," or does it cause people to *say* that they are more "isolated, lonely, and depressed"?

WILEY@NON-SEQUITUR.NET   DIST. BY UNIVERSAL PRESS SYND.   WWW.NON-SEQUITUR.NET

If you relied solely on the headlines, you might conclude that the study found dramatic differences between Internet users and nonusers. In fact, the changes in the dependent variable were *not* very large. The most that could be said is that heavier users of the Internet showed very slight declines in some aspects of social involvement and only slight increases in self-reported feelings of loneliness and depression. Moreover, even those slight negative effects disappeared over time (Kraut et al., 2002). And more recent research indicates that greater Internet use is associated with various positive outcomes (B. Bower, 2002; Kraut & Kiesler, 2003).

Finally, you might ask whether anything happened during the period from March 1995 to March 1997 that might have increased Internet use and also have caused people to report more loneliness, isolation, and depression. For example, some of the participants were adolescents. Is it possible that they made greater use of the Internet and also withdrew somewhat from their families simply as part of growing up? In other words, could another variable have caused *both* greater Internet use and increased social withdrawal? We don't know the answer to this question, but it should be explored.

These are the kinds of questions you should ask yourself when you read accounts of psychological research in the mass media. And in fairness, they are among the questions the researchers themselves raised in their article, although later reporters in the popular media did not.

About Internet Users

1. What other questions about this research would you add to the ones already mentioned?

2. If you read sensationalistic headlines about another research topic, such as obesity and social activity, or parenting and juvenile crime, how would you go about learning the details of the research, so you could answer your own critical-thinking questions?

random sample from the larger group of trainees, because every trainee had an equal chance of being chosen for the study.

Another way to make sure that conclusions apply to the larger population is to pick a **representative sample** of the population being studied. For example, researchers looking for a representative cross section of Americans would want to ensure that the proportion of males and females in the study matched the national proportion, that the number of participants from each state matched the national population distribution, and so on. Even with these precautions, however, unintended bias may influence psychological research. This issue has received a great deal of attention recently, particularly in relation to women and African Americans, as we discussed earlier.

random sample Sample in which each potential participant has an equal chance of being selected.

representative sample Sample carefully chosen so that the characteristics of the participants correspond closely to the characteristics of the larger population.

HUMAN DIVERSITY AND RESEARCH

Can we generalize about research findings from one group to another?

As we noted earlier, psychologists have recently begun to question early assumptions that the results of research conducted with White male participants would also apply to women, to people of other racial and ethnic groups, and to people of different cultures. In fact, research indicates that people's gender, race, ethnic background, and culture often have a profound effect on their behavior. Studies have found consistent cultural or gender differences, for instance, in aggression (Bergeron & Schneider, 2005; Eagly & Steffen, 1986; Haskell, 2003), memory (Heath & Gant, 2005; Piefke, Weiss, & Markowitsch, 2005; Q. Wang & Ross, 2005), certain aspects of emotional behavior and temperament (Else-Quest, Hyde, & Goldsmith, 2006; Sarlo, Palomba, & Buodo, 2005), and some mental disorders (R. Bradley, Conklin, & Westen, 2005; S. M. Marcus et al., 2005).

UNINTENDED BIASES IN RESEARCH The gender, race, or ethnicity of the experimenter may also introduce subtle, unintended biases. For example, some early research concluded that women were more likely than men to conform to social pressure in the laboratory (e.g., Crutchfield, 1955). Later research revealed no gender differences, however, when the experimenter is female (Eagly & Carli, 1981). More recent studies continue to demonstrate that the gender of the experimenter may produce different results when testing male versus female participants (Lundström &Olsson, 2005).

Similarly, evidence suggests that the results of research with African American participants may be significantly affected by the race of the experimenter (Graham, 1992; Weisse, Foster, & Fisher, 2005). Data on race and IQ scores have been widely misinterpreted as "demonstrating" innate racial inferiority. Advocates of this view (of innate racial inferiority) rarely noted that African Americans score higher on IQ and other tests when the person administering the test is also an African American (Graham, 1992). Similarly, do feminist theories, developed by and tested primarily with White, college-educated women, apply to women of color (Roth, 2004)?

CHECK YOUR UNDERSTANDING

1. A method of research known as _____ allows psychologists to study behavior as it occurs in real-life settings.

2. Psychologists use _____ research to examine relationships between two or more variables without manipulating any variable.

3. The method of research best suited to explaining behavior is _____ research.

4. The _____ variable in an experiment is manipulated to see how it affects a second variable; the _____ variable is the one observed for any possible effects.

5. To ensure that the results of a particular study apply to a larger population, researchers use _____ or _____ samples

Answers: 1. naturalistic observation. 2. correlational. 3. experimental. 4. independent, dependent. 5. random, representative.

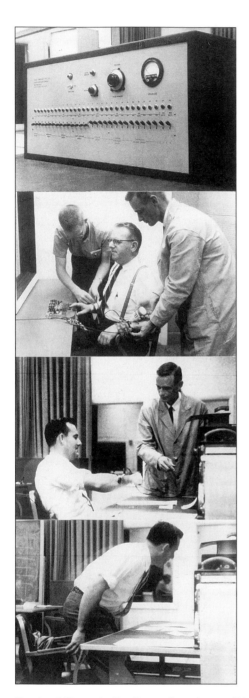

Stanley Milgram's Obedience Experiment. (A) The shock generator used in the experiment. (B) With electrodes attached to his wrists, the learner provides answers by pressing switches that light up on an answer box. (C) The subject administers a shock to the learner. (D) The subject breaks off the experiment. Milgram's study yielded interesting results, but it also raised serious questions about the ethics of such experimentation.

APPLY YOUR UNDERSTANDING

1. Proper use of the experimental method is associated with all of the following, EXCEPT
   a. hypotheses
   b. variables
   c. experimenter bias
   d. subjects or participants
2. Margaret would like to be able to apply her research results to college sophomores as a whole. Which of the following would be the LEAST appropriate method for her to use?
   a. experiments that use college sophomores
   b. a case study of a college sophomore
   c. surveys of college sophomores
   d. interviews with college sophomores

Answers: 1. c. 2. b.

Ethics and Psychology:
Research on Humans and Animals

Are there ethical guidelines for conducting psychological research?

What objections have been raised regarding research on animal subjects?

If the college or university you attend has a research facility, it is likely that you will have a chance to become a participant in an experiment in your psychology department. You will probably be offered a small sum of money or class credit to participate. But you may not learn the true purpose of the experiment until after it's over. Is this deception necessary to the success of psychology experiments? And what if the experiment causes you discomfort, as it did for Little Albert in Watson and Rayner's research mentioned earlier? Before answering, consider the ethical debate that flared up in 1963 when Stanley Milgram published the results of several experiments he had conducted.

Milgram hired people to participate in what he said was a learning experiment. In a typical session, a young man would arrive at the laboratory to participate. He was met by a stern-faced researcher in a lab coat; another man in street clothes was sitting in the waiting room. The researcher explained that he was studying the effects of punishment on learning. When the two men drew slips out of the hat, the participant's slip said "teacher." The teacher watched as the "learner" was strapped into a chair and an electrode attached to his wrist. Then the teacher was taken into an adjacent room and seated at an impressive-looking "shock generator" with switches from 15 to 450 volts (V), labeled "Slight Shock," "Very Strong Shock," up to "Danger: Severe Shock," and, finally, "XXX." The teacher's job was to read a list of paired words, which the learner would attempt to memorize and repeat. The teacher was instructed to deliver a shock whenever the learner gave a wrong answer and to increase the intensity of the shock each time the learner made a mistake. At 90 V, the learner began to grunt; at 120 V, he shouted, "Hey, this really hurts!" At 150 V, he demanded to be released, and at 270 V, his protests became screams of agony. Beyond 330 V, the learner appeared to pass out. If the teacher became concerned and asked whether he could stop, the experimenter politely but firmly replied that he was expected to continue, that this experiment was being conducted in the interests of science.

In reality, Milgram was studying obedience, not learning. He wanted to find out whether ordinary people would obey orders to cause another person pain. As part of his research, Milgram (1974) described the experiment to 110 psychiatrists, college students, and middle-class adults, and he asked them at what point they thought participants would stop. Members of all three groups guessed that most people would refuse to continue beyond 130 V and that no one would go beyond 300 V. The psychiatrists estimated that only one in a thousand people would continue to the XXX shock panel. Astonishingly, 65% of Milgram's participants administered the highest level of shock, even though many worried aloud that the shocks might be causing serious damage to the learners.

To find out what he wanted to know, Milgram had to deceive his participants. The stated purpose of the experiment—to test learning—was a lie. The "learners" were Milgram's accomplices, who had been trained to act as though they were being hurt; the machines were fake; and the learners received no shocks at all (Milgram, 1963). But, critics argued, the "teachers"—the real subjects of the study—were hurt. Not only did most voice concern, but also they showed clear signs of stress: They sweated, bit their lips, trembled, stuttered, or in a few cases, broke into uncontrollable nervous laughter. Critics also worried about the effect of the experiment on the participants' self-esteem. How would you like to be compared with the people who ran the death camps in Nazi Germany?

Although the design of this experiment was not typical of the vast majority of psychological experiments, it sparked such a public uproar that the APA reassessed its ethical guidelines, which were first published in 1953. A new code of ethics on psychological experimentation was approved. The code is assessed each year and periodically revised to ensure that it adequately protects participants in research studies. In addition to outlining the ethical principles guiding research and teaching, the code spells out a set of ethical standards for psychologists who offer therapy and other professional services, such as psychological testing.

The APA code of ethics requires that researchers obtain informed consent from participants and stipulates the following:

- Participants must be informed of the nature of research in clearly understandable language.
- Informed consent must be documented.
- Risks, possible adverse effects, and limitations on confidentiality must be spelled out in advance.
- If participation is a condition of course credit, equitable alternative activities must be offered.
- Participants cannot be deceived about aspects of the research that would affect their willingness to participate, such as risks or unpleasant emotional experiences.
- Deception about the goals of the research can be used only when absolutely necessary to the integrity of the research.

In addition, psychological researchers are required to follow the U.S. government's Code of Federal Regulations, which includes an extensive set of regulations concerning the protection of human participants in all kinds of research. Failure to abide by these federal regulations may result in the termination of federal funding for the researcher and penalties for the research institution.

Despite these formal ethical and legal guidelines, controversy still rages about the ethics of psychological research on humans. Some people contend that research procedures should never be emotionally or physically distressing. Others assert that ethical guidelines that are too strict may undermine the scientific value of research or cripple future research. Still others maintain that psychology, as a science, should base its ethical code on documented evidence about the effects of research procedures on participants, not on conjecture about what is "probably" a good way to conduct research. Yet another view is that developing the explanations necessary to produce informed consent may help researchers themselves get a better understanding of the goals and methods of research.

ANIMAL RESEARCH

In recent years, questions have also been raised about the ethics of using animals in psychological research (Herzog, 2005). Psychologists study animal behavior to shed light on human behavior. Crowding mice into small cages, for example, has yielded valuable insights into the effects of overcrowding on humans. Animals are used in experiments in which it would be clearly unethical to use human participants—such as studies involving brain lesions (requiring cutting into the brain) or electric stimulation of parts of the brain. In fact, much of what we know about sensation, perception, drugs, emotional attachment, and the neural basis of behavior is derived from animal research (Carroll & Overmier, 2001; Dess & Foltin, 2005). Yet, animal protectionists and others question whether it is ethical to use nonhuman animals, which cannot give their consent to serve as subjects, in psychological research.

Their opponents contend that the goals of scientific research—in essence, to reduce or eliminate human suffering—justify the means, even though they agree that animals should be made to suffer as little as possible (M. A. Novak, 1991). They argue that procedures now in place, including the use of anesthesia in many experiments, already minimize animal suffering.

The APA has addressed this issue in its ethical guidelines, noting that psychologists using animals in research must ensure "appropriate consideration of [the animal's] comfort, health, and humane treatment" (APA, 1992, 2003).

CHECK YOUR UNDERSTANDING

Are the following statements true (T) or false (F)?

1. _____ Controversy over ethical standards in psychology has almost disappeared.
2. _____ The APA code of ethics used today is unchanged since 1953.
3. _____ Researchers who fail to follow the Federal Code of Regulations are subject to penalties.

Answers: 1. (F). 2. (F). 3. (T).

APPLY YOUR UNDERSTANDING

1. Your classmate Jared says he does not need to be concerned about ethical standards for his naturalistic observation study. On the basis of what you have learned from this chapter, your reply should be
   a. "You're right, because there are only ethical guidelines for the protection of animals."
   b. "You're right. Only laboratory experiments must conform to ethics standards."
   c. "That's incorrect. All psychological research is subject to ethical guidelines."
   d. "That's incorrect. Actually, naturalistic observation is the only kind of research subject to ethics rules."

2. Before they agree to be in her experiment, Yolanda gives the participants a short description of what they will be asked to do in the study, the reasons she is conducting the study, and any risks or discomfort that they might face. Yolanda is
   a. getting informed consent from her participants.
   b. mollycoddling her participants.
   c. deceiving her participants.
   d. not adhering to ethical guidelines for the treatment of human research participants.

Answers: 1. c. 2. a.

Careers in Psychology

What can you do with a background in psychology or with an advanced degree?

Some readers may be studying psychology out of general interest; others may be considering careers in psychology. What kinds of careers are open to psychology graduates? Community college graduates with associates degrees in psychology are well qualified for paraprofessional positions in state hospitals, mental health centers, and other human service settings. Job responsibilities may include screening and evaluating new patients, record keeping, and assisting in consultation sessions.

Graduates with bachelor's degrees in psychology may find jobs assisting psychologists in mental health centers, vocational rehabilitation facilities, and correctional centers. They may also take positions as research assistants, teach psychology in high school, or find jobs in government or business.

For those who pursue advanced degrees in psychology—a master's degree or a doctorate—career opportunities span a wide range. Many doctoral psychologists join the faculties of colleges and universities. Others work in applied fields such as school, health, industrial, commercial, and educational psychology. Nearly half of doctoral psychologists are clinicians or counselors who treat people experiencing mental, emotional, or adaptational problems. Master's degree graduates in psychology often work as researchers, collecting and analyzing data, at universities; in government; or for private companies. Students with a master's degree in industrial/organizational psychology are particularly sought by large corporations to work in personnel and human resource departments, while doctoral graduates in industrial/organizational psychology are hired into management or consulting positions in industry (B. Murray, 2002). Others work in health, industry, and education. APA standards require that master's degree graduates who work in clinical, counseling, school, or testing and measurement settings be supervised by a doctoral-level psychologist.

Many students who major in psychology want to become therapists. For these students, there are five main career paths:

About one third of psychologists work in colleges and universities. Here, Al Maisto, coauthor of this text, talks with a student at the University of North Carolina, Charlotte, NC.

- A *psychiatrist* is a medical doctor who, in addition to 4 years of medical training, has completed 3 years of residency training in psychiatry, most of which is spent in supervised clinical practice. Psychiatrists specialize in the diagnosis and treatment of abnormal behavior. In addition to providing psychotherapy, in most states, psychiatrists are the only mental health professionals who are licensed to prescribe medications, although some states are beginning to grant prescription privileges to psychologists. (See "On the Cutting Edge: Prescription Privileges for Clinical Psychologists.")

ON THE CUTTING EDGE

PRESCRIPTION PRIVILEGES FOR CLINICAL PSYCHOLOGISTS

In February 2005, New Mexico and Louisiana became the first two states to implement legislation providing prescription privileges to clinical psychologists who have appropriate training in pharmacology (Meyers, 2005). Previously, only medical doctors, principally psychiatrists, could prescribe drugs for patients with mental disorders (Daw, 2002; Long, 2005). Some psychologists in these two states now have the ability to prescribe medications used to treat mental disorders, much like dentists and optometrists are limited to prescribing medications relevant to the body parts they treat.

At a time when prescription medications have become increasingly important in the treatment of mental disorders, this change dramatically increases the range of treatment options available to psychologists. As we will see in Chapter 13, ("Therapies") prescription medications are commonly used today to treat a wide range of mental disorders including depression, schizophrenia, bipolar disorder, and attention deficit disorder. Prescription medications have been shown to be particularly effective when combined with the more traditional forms of psychotherapy offered by psychologists. In addition, research has shown that when medication and psychotherapy are provided by the same professional, quality care is more cost effective than when split between two providers (Goldman et al., 1998).

To gain prescription privileges, New Mexico law requires that clinical psychologists first complete 400 hours of coursework, undergo supervised training, and pass a national exam. Afterwards, they receive a 2-year license to prescribe medication under the supervision of a medical doctor. If approved by the medical supervisor and an oversight board, after the 2-year period, psychologists may apply to prescribe medication independently. Similar to the standards established in New Mexico, Louisiana also monitors and restricts the prescription privileges of psychologists.

Advocates of this legislation believe it may set an important precedent for other states to follow. Currently, at least 4 other states (Georgia, Illinois, Hawaii, and Tennessee) have pending legislation that would provide limited prescription privileges for psychologists; and 31 states have task forces lobbying for legislation. Although some psychiatrists and psychologists have misgivings about this new legislation, a carefully designed Department of Defense study has shown that psychologists with appropriate training can use prescription privileges to provide safe and high quality care to patients (see APA Practice, 2003).

- A *psychoanalyst* is a psychiatrist (or psychologist) who has received additional specialized training in psychoanalytic theory and practice, usually at a psychoanalytic institute that requires him or her to undergo psychoanalysis before practicing.
- *Clinical psychologists* assess and treat mental, emotional, and behavioral disorders, ranging from short-term crises to chronic disorders such as schizophrenia. They hold advanced degrees in psychology (a PhD or PsyD)—the result of a 4- to 6-year graduate program, plus a 1-year internship in psychological assessment and psychotherapy and at least 1 more year of supervised practice.
- *Counseling psychologists* help people cope with situational problems, such as adjusting to college, choosing a vocation, resolving marital problems, or dealing with the death of a loved one.
- Finally, *social workers* may also treat psychological problems. Typically they have a master's degree (MSW) or a doctorate (DSW). Social workers often work under psychiatrists or clinical psychologists, although in some states they may be licensed to practice independently.

A free booklet, *Psychology: Scientific Problem Solvers, Careers for the Twenty-First Century*, is available by calling the Order Department of the American Psychological Association at 1-800-374-2721. The APA also maintains a Web site, *http://www.apa.org/*, which provides up-to-date information about employment opportunities, as well as a vast array of related material of interest to psychology students.

CHECK YOUR UNDERSTANDING

Is each of the following statements true (T) or false (F)?

1. _____ Careers in psychology are largely limited to people with PhDs.
2. _____ Almost all the careers related to a knowledge of psychology are in the mental health field.

Answers: 1. (F). 2. (F).

APPLY YOUR UNDERSTANDING

1. KeShawn is a medical doctor who specializes in diagnosing and treating people suffering from psychological disorders. He is a
   a. _____ psychiatrist.
   b. _____ counseling psychologist.
   c. _____ clinical psychologist.
   d. _____ social worker.
2. Psychologists can be found working in which of the following settings?
   a. _____ research laboratories
   b. _____ schools
   c. _____ government and corporations
   d. _____ all of the above

Answers: 1. a. 2. d.

CHAPTER REVIEW

What Is Psychology?

"Most psychologists study mental and emotional problems and work as psychotherapists." Is this statement true or false?
Psychology is the scientific study of behavior and mental processes. Through its many subdivisions its proponents seek to describe and explain human thought, feelings, perceptions, and actions.

Developmental psychologists are concerned with processes of growth and change over the life course, from the prenatal period through old age and death. *Neuropsychologists and physiological psychologists* focus on the body's neural and chemical systems, studying how these affect thought and behavior. *Behavioral geneticists* explore how genetics influence behavior. *Experimental psychologists* investigate basic psychological processes, such as learning, memory, sensation, perception, cognition, motivation, and emotion. *Personality psychologists* look at the differences among people in such traits as sociability, anxiety, aggressiveness, and self-esteem. *Clinical* and *counseling psychologists* specialize in the diagnoses and treament of psychological disorders, whereas *social psychologists* focus on how people influence one another's thoughts and actions. *Industrial and organizational psychologists* study problems in the workplace and other settings.

Given the broad range of careers and interests, what holds the subfields of psychology together as a distinct scientific discipline? Five enduring issues or fundamental themes unify the various subfields of psychology:

- Person–Situation: Is behavior caused more by inner traits or by external situations?
- Nature–Nurture: How do genes and experiences interact to influence people?
- Stability–Change: How much do we stay the same as we develop and how much do we change?
- Diversity–Universality: In what ways do people differ in how they think and act?

- Mind–Body: What is the relationship between our internal experiences and our biological processes?

What does psychology have in common with other sciences? Like the other sciences, psychology relies on the **scientific method** to find answers to questions. This method involves careful observation and collection of data, the development of **theories** about relationships and causes, and the systematic testing of **hypotheses** (or predictions) to disprove invalid theories.

The Growth of Psychology

"Psychology has a long past, but a short history." What does that mean? Psychology has a long tradition because humans have wondered about behavior and mental processes since ancient times. As a scientific discipline, however, psychology's history is short, dating back only to the late 19th century.

How did Wundt help to define psychology as a science of the mind? Why did James think that sensation and perception alone couldn't explain behavior? Why was Freud's theory of the unconscious shocking at the turn of the 20th century? Wilhelm Wundt established the first psychology laboratory in 1879 at the University of Leipzig in Germany. His use of experiment and measurement marked the beginnings of psychology as a science. One of his students, Edward Titchener, established a perspective called **structuralism**, which was based on the belief that psychology's role was to identify the basic elements of experience and how they combine.

In his perspective known as **functionalism**, American psychologist William James criticized structuralism, arguing that sensations cannot be separated from the mental associations that allow us to benefit from past experiences. James believed that our rich storehouse of ideas and memories is what enables us to function in our environment.

The **psychodynamic theories** of Sigmund Freud, his colleagues, and successors added another new dimension to psychology: the idea that much of our behavior is governed by unconscious conflicts, motives, and desires.

How was Watson's approach to human behavior different from that of Freud? How did Skinner expand behaviorism? John B. Watson, a spokesman for **behaviorism**, argued that psychology should concern itself only with observable, measurable behavior. Watson based much of his work on the conditioning experiments of Ivan Pavlov.

B. F. Skinner's beliefs were similar to those of Watson, but he added the concept of reinforcement or reward. In this way, he made the learner an active agent in the learning process. Skinner's views dominated American psychology into the 1960s.

How did Gestalt psychologists influence the way we think about perception? What aspects of life do humanistic psychologists stress? According to **Gestalt psychology**, perception depends on the human tendency to see patterns, to distinguish objects from their backgrounds, and to complete pictures from a few clues. In this emphasis on wholeness, the Gestalt school differed radically from structuralism.

Humanistic psychology, with its focus on meaning, values, and ethics, emphasizes the goal of reaching one's fullest potential. **Cognitive psychology** is the study of mental processes in the broadest sense, focusing on how people perceive, interpret, store, and retrieve information. Unlike behaviorists, cognitive psychologists believe that mental processes can and should be studied scientifically. This view has dramatically changed American psychology from its previous behaviorist focus.

Where do evolutionary psychologists look for the roots of human behavior? What new focus is positive psychology bringing to the study of human behavior? Is there a single perspective dominating psychology today? **Evolutionary psychology** focuses on the functions and adaptive value of various human behaviors and the study of how those behaviors have evolved. **Positive psychology** studies subjective feelings of happiness and well-being; the development of individual traits such as integrity and leadership; and the settings that encourage individuals to flourish. In this way, it seeks to add a new dimension to psychological research. Most contemporary psychologists do not adhere to a single school of thought. They believe that different theories can often complement one another and together enrich our understanding of human behavior.

During psychology's early years, why were relatively few women accepted in the field? Although psychology has profited from the contributions of women from its beginnings, women often faced discrimination: Some colleges and universities did not grant degrees to women, professional journals were often reluctant to publish their work, and teaching positions were often closed to them.

Human Diversity

Why should you learn about human diversity? A rich diversity of behavior and thought exists in the human species, among individuals and groups. Being attuned to this diversity can help reduce the

tensions that arise when people misunderstand one another. It can also help us to define what humans have in common.

How are psychologists helping us to understand the differences between men and women? **Feminist theory** explores the differences and similarities in thought and behavior between the two sexes or **genders**. Culturally generated beliefs regarding these differences are called *gender stereotypes*. Psychologists are trying to determine the hereditary and cultural causes of gender differences as well as the origins of sexual orientation.

Why are psychologists interested in racial and ethnic differences? **Race**, a biological term, refers to subpopulations who are genetically similar. **Ethnicity** involves a shared cultural heritage based on common ancestry, which can affect norms of behavior.

How does culture contribute to human diversity? The intangible aspects of **culture**—the beliefs, values, traditions, and norms of behavior that a particular people share—make an important contribution to human diversity. Because many subcultural groups exist, psychology must take both inter- and cross-cultural influences into account.

Research Methods in Psychology

What are some of the research methods that psychologists use in their work? Psychologists use naturalistic observation, case studies, surveys, correlational research, and experiments to study behavior and mental processes.

Why is a natural setting sometimes better than a laboratory for observing behavior? Psychologists use **naturalistic observation** to study behavior in natural settings. Because there is minimal interference from the researcher, the behavior observed is likely to be more accurate, spontaneous, and varied than behavior studied in a laboratory. Researchers using this method must be careful to avoid **observer bias**.

When can a case study be most useful? Researchers conduct a **case study** to investigate in depth the behavior of one person or a few persons. This method can yield a great deal of detailed, descriptive information that is useful for forming hypotheses, but is vulnerable to observer bias and overgeneralization of results.

What are some of the benefits of survey research? **Survey research** generates a large amount of data quickly and inexpensively by asking a standard set of questions of a large number of people. Great care must be taken, however, in the wording of questions and in the selection of respondents.

What is the difference between correlation and cause and effect? **Correlational research** investigates the relation, or correlation, between two or more variables. Although two variables may be *related* to each other, that does not imply that one *causes* the other.

What kinds of research questions are best studied by experimental research? An **experiment** is called for when a researcher wants to draw conclusions about cause and effect. In an experiment, the impact of one factor can be studied while all other factors are held constant. The factor whose effects are being studied is called the **independent variable**, since the researcher is free to manipulate it at will. The factor on which there is apt to be an impact is called the **dependent variable**. Usually an experiment includes both an **experimental group** of **participants** and a **control group** for comparison purposes. Often a neutral person records data and scores results, so **experimenter bias** doesn't creep in.

What does multimethod research allow psychologists to do? Many psychologists overcome the limitations of using a single research method by using multiple methods to study a single problem.

How can sampling affect the results of a research study? Regardless of the research method used, psychologists usually study a small **sample** of subjects and then generalize their results to larger populations. Proper sampling is critical to ensure that results have broader application. **Random samples**, in which each potential participant has an equal chance of being chosen, and **representative samples**, in which subjects are chosen to reflect the general characteristics of the population as a whole, are two ways of doing this.

Can we generalize about research findings from one group to another? Because of differences among people based on age, sex, ethnic background, culture, and so forth, findings from studies that use White, male, American college students as participants cannot always be generalized to other groups. In addition, the gender, race, and ethnic background of a psychologist can have a biasing impact on the outcome of research.

Ethics and Psychology: Research on Humans and Animals

Are there ethical guidelines for conducting psychological research? What objections have been raised regarding research on animal subjects? The APA has a code of ethics for conducting research involving human participants or animal subjects. Researchers must obtain informed consent from study participants. Participants must be told in advance about the nature and possible risks of the research. People should not be pressured to participate.

Although much of what we know about certain areas of psychology has come from animal research, the practice of experimenting on animals has strong opponents because of the pain and suffering that are sometimes involved. Although APA and the federal government have issued guidelines for the humane treatment of laboratory animals, many animal rights advocates argue that the only ethical research on animals is naturalistic observation.

Careers in Psychology

What can you do with a background in psychology or with an advanced degree? A background in psychology is useful in a wide array of fields because so many jobs involve a basic understanding of people. Careers for those with advanced degrees in psychology include teaching, research, jobs in government and private business, and occupations in the mental health field. Opportunities in the mental health field depend on one's degree of training. Practice in psychiatry requires medical training; practice in clinical psychology, requires a doctoral degree. Positions in counseling psychology and social work are additional career options.

2 The Biological Basis of Behavior

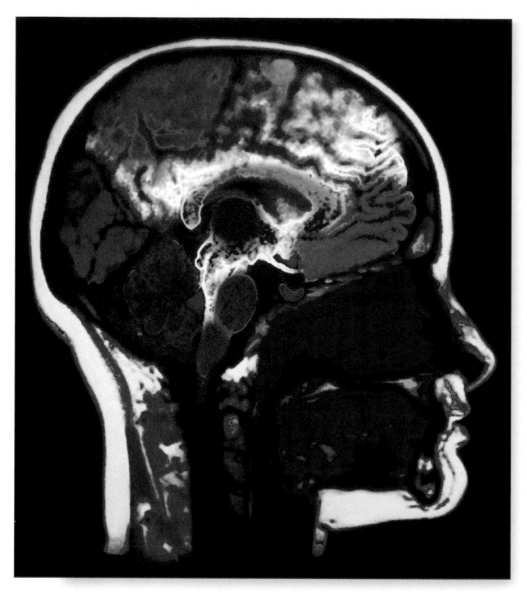

OVERVIEW

If you observed 5-year-old Nico, you would never guess how different he is from other children. People are enchanted by his infectious smile and friendly conversation. He shows an aptitude for creating computer graphics and his ability to use language is well above average. His vocabulary is rich; talking with him is never dull. Nico also interacts well with other children. In fact, the only thing unusual about him is a slight limp and some difficulty in using his left arm. This is amazing, because inside, Nico is not at all like other children. Nico, you see, has only half a brain (Battro, 2000).

He was not born with this condition. What Nico was born with is a left *hemiplegia*, or partial paralysis on the left side of his body. Despite this, he learned to walk at $1^1/_2$, . But as he approached his second birthday, he began to suffer epileptic seizures. Over time the seizures became much worse and Nico would frequently lose consciousness during them. Tests revealed an area on the right side of his brain where the seizures started and spread. Medications were useless in calming this area's erratic electrical activity; so when Nico was age $3^1/_2$, his parents authorized surgical removal of the afflicted region. After this treatment failed, his desperate parents reluctantly agreed to a much more radical procedure—removal of the entire right half of Nico's brain.

Wouldn't the impact of this surgery be devastating, adversely affecting all of Nico's thinking and behavior? Remarkably, it was not. Nico's epileptic seizures immediately stopped and he fully retained his ability to speak. Within a few days he was up and walking, displaying his typical good humor. How could this be when removing half a brain entails removing about 50 billion brain cells? The answer lies in some extraordinary traits possessed by the human brain: its complexity and plasticity.

The human brain is enormously complex. Its 100 billion cells, on average, interconnect to form a multitude of pathways and networks. These pathways overlap to a great extent and have numerous backup systems, giving most of us far more "mental equipment" than we really need. In addition, although the two sides of the brain constantly work together, they are not symmetrical in terms of their specialized tasks. For example, in most people the left side of the brain houses language abilities while the right side excels at certain nonverbal skills, especially spatial ones like those needed to assemble a puzzle. This is why removal of Nico's right brain had virtually no effect on his use of language.

But most important of all to Nico's recovery is the fact that the brain of a very young child is remarkably adaptable, or *plastic*. The left side of Nico's brain readily took over most of the functions that the right side was designed to perform. This shift probably began even before his operation and intensified after the right half of his brain was removed, demonstrating that although the brain is the command center of the body, it also responds to sensory and environmental feedback. As a result, for Nico, half a brain is enough.

The journey through the brain that you will take in this chapter is part of the branch of psychology known as **psychobiology**. Since this field deals with the biological bases of behavior and mental processes, it is related to virtually every other topic in this book—from learning and memory, to thinking and problem solving, to emotion, motivation, personality, and psychological disorders. Psychobiology overlaps with a much larger interdisciplinary field of study called **neuroscience**, which specifically focuses on the study of the brain and the nervous system. Many psychobiologists who study the brain's influence on behavior call themselves *neuropsychologists*.

We begin by looking at the basic building blocks of the brain and *nervous system*: the cells known as neurons. The electrical and chemical messages that neurons transmit are what allow you to react with such speed and complexity to events around you. But neurons are only part of the story of how human behavior is controlled and coordinated. Next, we consider the *endocrine system* of glands that secrete chemical messages called hormones into the blood. Finally, we examine the influence of heredity and evolution on human behavior.

ENDURING ISSUES IN THE BIOLOGICAL BASIS OF BEHAVIOR ●●

As you read through this chapter, you will encounter all five "Enduring Issues" introduced in chapter 1. To what extent is behavior caused by internal processes, as opposed to environmental factors (*Person–Situation*)? The core of this chapter—the notion that biological processes affect thoughts, emotions, and behavior—directly addresses this question. The chapter also sheds light on the connection between what we experience and our biological

psychobiology The area of psychology that focuses on the biological foundations of behavior and mental processes.

neuroscience The study of the brain and the nervous system.

processes (*Mind–Body*) and on the extent to which heredity affects behavior (*Nature–Nurture*). In addition, you may be surprised to learn that the nervous system changes permanently as a result of experience (*Stability–Change*). Finally, you will learn that there are significant differences between men and women in the way that the brain works (*Diversity–Universality*).

Mind–Body Window on the Mind

In the mind–body debate, neuropsychologists stand at the crossroad, where our sense of self intersects with advances in scientific knowledge. How does the organ we call the brain create the experience of what we call the mind? Until recently this question seemed unanswerable (A. R. Damasio, 1999, 2003). After all, the body and brain are observable, physical entities. Whether looking at how a person behaves or studying a brain scan, different observers see the same things. In contrast, the mind is a subjective entity, private and unique, and observable only to its owner.

In the 1990s—called the Decade of the Brain—neuropsychologists learned more about the brain than during the entire previous history of psychology. New technology enabled researchers to identify—in a normal, living person—which areas of the brain were active during such different activities as naming an object or studying a face. A number of neuropsychologists believe that in the near future we will be able to describe and explain the mind and even complex social behaviors such as empathy in biological terms (Cacioppo & Berntson, 2005; A. R. Damasio, 2003). ●●

Neurons: The Messengers

What types of cells are found in the nervous system?

The brain of an average human being contains as many as 100 billion nerve cells, or **neurons**. Billions more neurons are found in other parts of the nervous system. Neurons vary widely in size and shape, but they are all specialized to receive and transmit information. A typical neuron is shown in **Figure 2–1**. Like other cells, the neuron's cell body is made up of a nucleus, which contains a complete set of chromosomes and genes; cytoplasm, which keeps the cell alive; and a cell membrane, which encloses the whole cell. What makes a neuron different from other cells is the tiny fibers that extend out from the cell body, enabling a neuron to perform its special job, receiving and transmitting messages. The short fibers branching out around the cell body are **dendrites**. Their role is to pick up incoming messages from other neurons and transmit them to the cell body. The single long fiber extending from the cell body is an **axon**. The axon's job is to carry outgoing messages to neighboring neurons or to a muscle or gland. Axons vary in length from 1 or 2 millimeters (about the length of the word "or" in this sentence) to 3 feet. (In adults, a single axon may run from the brain to the base of the spinal cord or from the spinal cord to the tip of the thumb.) Although a neuron has only one axon, near its end the axon splits into many terminal branches. When we talk about a **nerve** (or **tract**), we are referring to a group of axons bundled together like wires in an electrical cable. *Terminal buttons* at the end of each axon release chemical substances called *neurotransmitters*. We will examine this process in the next section.

The axon in **Figure 2–1** is surrounded by a white, fatty covering called a **myelin sheath**. The myelin sheath is "pinched" at intervals, making the axon resemble a string of microscopic sausages. Not all axons have this covering, but myelinated axons are found in all parts of the body. (Because of this white covering, tissues made up primarily of myelinated axons are known as "white matter," whereas tissues made up primarily of unmyelinated axons are called "gray matter.") The myelin sheath has two functions:

neurons Individual cells that are the smallest unit of the nervous system.

dendrites Short fibers that branch out from the cell body and pick up incoming messages.

axon Single long fiber extending from the cell body; it carries outgoing messages.

nerve (or tract) Group of axons bundled together.

myelin sheath White fatty covering found on some axons.

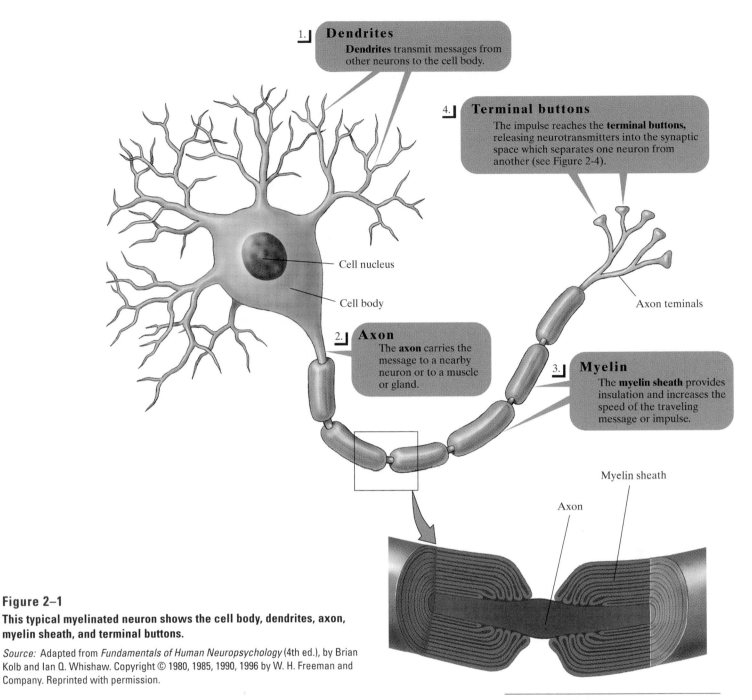

1. **Dendrites**
Dendrites transmit messages from other neurons to the cell body.

4. **Terminal buttons**
The impulse reaches the **terminal buttons,** releasing neurotransmitters into the synaptic space which separates one neuron from another (see Figure 2-4).

Cell nucleus

Cell body

Axon teminals

2. **Axon**
The **axon** carries the message to a nearby neuron or to a muscle or gland.

3. **Myelin**
The **myelin sheath** provides insulation and increases the speed of the traveling message or impulse.

Myelin sheath

Axon

Figure 2–1

This typical myelinated neuron shows the cell body, dendrites, axon, myelin sheath, and terminal buttons.

Source: Adapted from *Fundamentals of Human Neuropsychology* (4th ed.), by Brian Kolb and Ian Q. Whishaw. Copyright © 1980, 1985, 1990, 1996 by W. H. Freeman and Company. Reprinted with permission.

First, it provides insulation, so that signals from adjacent neurons do not interfere with each other; second, it increases the speed at which signals are transmitted.

Neurons that collect messages from sense organs and carry those messages to the spinal cord or the brain are called **sensory** (or **afferent**) **neurons**. Neurons that carry messages from the spinal cord or the brain to the muscles and glands are called **motor** (or **efferent**) **neurons**. And neurons that carry messages from one neuron to another are called **interneurons** (or **association neurons**).

The nervous system also contains a vast number of **glial cells** (or **glia** the word *glia* means "glue"). Glial cells hold the neurons in place, provide nourishment, and remove waste products, prevent harmful substances from passing from the bloodstream into the brain, and form the myelin sheath that insulates and protects neurons. Recent evidence suggests that glial cells may play an important role in learning and memory, enhance communication between neurons, and thereby may affect the brain's response to new experiences (Cambras, López, & Arias, 2005; Featherstone, Fleming, & Ivy, 2000).

sensory (or afferent) neurons Neurons that carry messages from sense organs to the spinal cord or brain.

motor (or efferent) neurons Neurons that carry messages from the spinal cord or brain to the muscles and glands.

interneurons (or association neurons) Neurons that carry messages from one neuron to another.

glial cells (or glia) Cells that insulate and support neurons by holding them together, provide nourishment and remove waste products, prevent harmful substances from passing into the brain, and form the myelin sheath.

ions Electrically charged particles found both inside and outside the neuron.

resting potential Electrical charge across a neuron membrane resulting from more positive ions concentrated on the outside and more negative ions on the inside.

polarization The condition of a neuron when the inside is negatively charged relative to the outside; for example, when the neuron is at rest.

THE NEURAL IMPULSE

What "language" do neurons speak?

How do neurons "talk" to one another? What form do their messages take? Neurons speak in a language that all cells in the body understand: simple "yes–no," "on–off" electrochemical impulses.

When a neuron is at rest, the membrane surrounding the cell forms a partial barrier between the fluids that are inside and outside the neuron. Both solutions contain electrically charged particles, or **ions**. (See **Figure 2–2A**.) Because there are more negative ions inside the neuron than outside, there is a small electrical charge (called the **resting potential**) across the cell membrane. Thus, the resting neuron is said to be in a state of **polarization**. A resting, or polarized, neuron is like a spring that has been compressed or a guitar string that has been pulled, but not released. All that is needed to generate a neuron's signal is the release of this tension.

When a small area on the cell membrane is adequately stimulated by an incoming message, pores (or channels) in the membrane at the stimulated area open, allowing a sudden inflow of positively charged sodium ions. (See **Figure 2–2B**.) This process is called *depolarization*; now the inside of the neuron is positively charged relative to the outside. Depolarization sets off a chain reaction. When the membrane allows sodium to enter the neuron at one point, the next point on the membrane opens. More sodium ions flow into the neuron at the second spot and depolarize this part of the neuron, and so on, along the

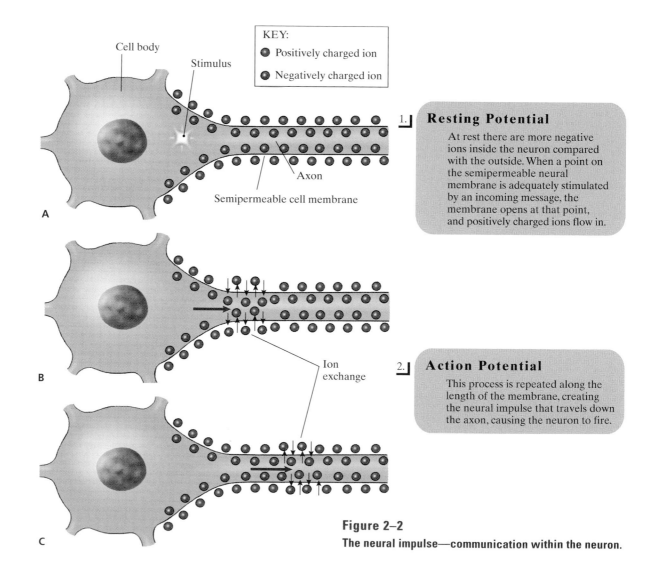

KEY:
● Positively charged ion
● Negatively charged ion

Cell body
Stimulus
Axon
Semipermeable cell membrane
A

1. **Resting Potential**
At rest there are more negative ions inside the neuron compared with the outside. When a point on the semipermeable neural membrane is adequately stimulated by an incoming message, the membrane opens at that point, and positively charged ions flow in.

B
Ion exchange

2. **Action Potential**
This process is repeated along the length of the membrane, creating the neural impulse that travels down the axon, causing the neuron to fire.

C

Figure 2–2
The neural impulse—communication within the neuron.

entire length of the neuron. As a result, an electrical charge, called a **neural impulse** (or **action potential**), travels down the axon, much like a fuse burning from one end to the other. (See **Figure 2–2C**.) When this happens, we say that the neuron has "fired." The speed at which neurons carry impulses varies widely, from as fast as nearly 400 feet per second on largely myelinated axons to as slow as about 3 feet per second on those with no myelin.

A single neuron may have many hundreds of dendrites and its axon may branch out in numerous directions, so that it is in touch with hundreds or thousands of other cells at both its input end (dendrites) and its output end (axon). At any given moment, a neuron may be receiving messages from other neurons, some of which are primarily excitatory (telling it to "fire"), and from others, primarily inhibitory (telling it to "rest"). The constant interplay of excitation and inhibition determines whether the neuron is likely to fire or not.

As a rule, single impulses received from neighboring neurons do not make a neuron fire. The incoming message causes a small, temporary shift in the electrical charge, called a **graded potential**, which is transmitted along the cell membrane and may simply fade away, leaving the neuron in its normal polarized state. For a neuron to fire, graded potentials caused by impulses from many neighboring neurons—or from one neuron firing repeatedly—must exceed a certain minimum **threshold of excitation**. Just as a light switch requires a minimum amount of pressure to be turned on, an incoming message must be above the minimum threshold to make a neuron fire.

Either neurons fire or they do not, and every firing of a particular neuron produces an impulse of the same strength. This is called the **all-or-none law**. However, the neuron is likely to fire *more often* when stimulated by a strong signal. The result is rapid neural firing that communicates the message "There's a very strong stimulus out here!" Immediately after firing, the neuron goes through an *absolute refractory period:* For about a thousandth of a second, the neuron will not fire again, no matter how strong the incoming messages may be. Following that is a *relative refractory period*, when the cell is returning to the resting state. During this period, the neuron will fire, but only if the incoming message is considerably stronger than is normally necessary to make it fire. Finally, the neuron returns to its resting state, ready to fire again, as shown in **Figure 2–3**.

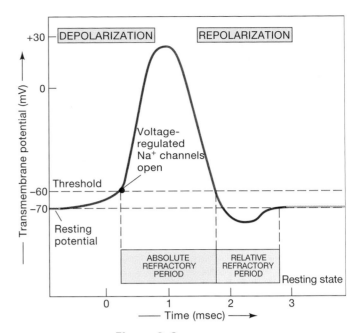

Figure 2–3

Electrical changes during the action potential.

The incoming message must be above a certain threshold to cause a neuron to fire. After it fires, the neuron is returned to its resting state. This process happens very quickly; and within a few thousandths of a second (msec), the neuron is ready to fire again.

THE SYNAPSE

What happens as information moves from one neuron to the next?

Neurons are not directly connected like links in a chain. Rather, they are separated by a tiny gap, called a **synaptic space**, or **synaptic cleft**, where the axon terminals of one neuron *almost* touch the dendrites or cell body of other neurons. The entire area composed of the axon terminals of one neuron, the synaptic space, and the dendrites and cell body of the next neuron is called the **synapse**. (See **Figure 2–4**.)

For the neural impulse to move on to the next neuron, it must somehow cross the synaptic space. It is tempting to imagine that the neural impulse simply leaps across the gap like an electrical spark, but in reality the transfer is made by chemicals. What actually

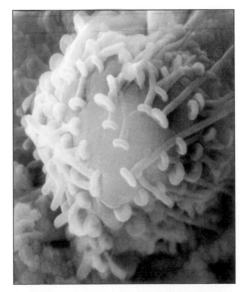

A photograph taken with a scanning electron microscope, showing the synaptic knobs at the ends of axons. Inside the knobs are the vesicles that contain neurotransmitters.

neural impulse (or action potential) The firing of a nerve cell.

graded potential A shift in the electrical charge in a tiny area of a neuron.

threshold of excitation The level an impulse must exceed to cause a neuron to fire.

all-or-none law Principle that the action potential in a neuron does not vary in strength; either the neuron fires at full strength, or it does not fire at all.

synaptic space (or synaptic cleft) Tiny gap between the axon terminal of one neuron and the dendrites or cell body of the next neuron.

synapse Area composed of the axon terminal of one neuron, the synaptic space, and the dendrite or cell body of the next neuron.

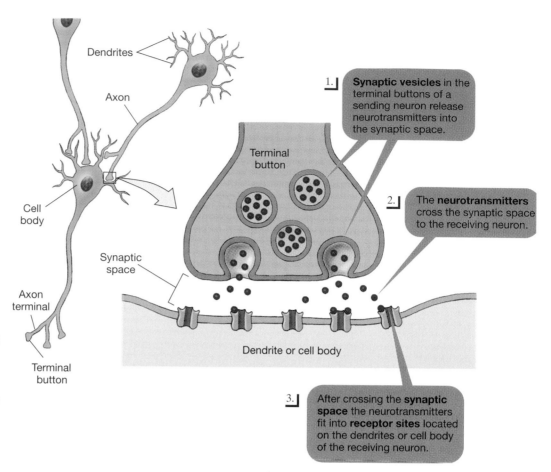

Figure 2–4

Synaptic transmission—communication between neurons.
When a neural impulse reaches the end of an axon, tiny oval sacs, called synaptic vesicles, at the end of most axons release varying amounts of chemical substances called neurotransmitters. These substances travel across the synaptic space and affect the next neuron.

terminal button (or synaptic knob) Structure at the end of an axon terminal branch.

synaptic vesicles Tiny sacs in a terminal button that release chemicals into the synapse.

neurotransmitters Chemicals released by the synaptic vesicles that travel across the synaptic space and affect adjacent neurons.

receptor sites Locations on a receptor neuron into which a specific neurotransmitter fits like a key into a lock.

happens is this: When a neuron fires, an impulse travels down the axon, out through the axon terminals, into a tiny swelling called a **terminal button**, or **synaptic knob**. Most terminal buttons contain a number of tiny oval sacs called **synaptic vesicles**. (See **Figure 2–4**.) When the neural impulse reaches the end of the terminals, it causes these vesicles to release varying amounts of chemicals called **neurotransmitters** into the synaptic space. Each neurotransmitter has specific matching **receptor sites** on the other side of the synaptic space. Neurotransmitters fit into their corresponding receptor sites just as a key fits into a lock. This lock-and-key system ensures that neurotransmitters do not randomly stimulate other neurons, but follow orderly pathways.

Once their job is complete, neurotransmitters detach from the receptor site. In most cases, they are either reabsorbed into the axon terminals to be used again, broken down and recycled to make new neurotransmitters, or disposed of by the body as waste. The synapse is cleared and returned to its normal state.

NEUROTRANSMITTERS In recent decades, neuroscientists have identified hundreds of neurotransmitters; their exact functions are still being studied. (See "**Summary Table**: Major Neurotransmitters and Their Effects.") However, a few brain chemicals are well known.

Acetylcholine (ACh) acts where neurons meet skeletal muscles. It also appears to play a critical role in arousal, attention, memory, and motivation (Gold, 2003; Pych, Chang, & Colon-Rivera, 2005). Alzheimer's disease, which involves loss of memory and severe language problems, has been linked to degeneration of the brain cells that produce and respond to ACh (Froelich & Hoyer, 2002; Kihara & Shimohama, 2004).

Dopamine generally affects neurons associated with voluntary movement, learning, memory, and emotions. The symptoms of Parkinson's disease—tremors, muscle spasms, and increasing muscular rigidity—have been traced to loss of the brain cells that produce dopamine (A. Costa et al., 2003).

SUMMARY TABLE

MAJOR NEUROTRANSMITTERS AND THEIR EFFECTS

Acetylcholine (ACh)	Distributed widely throughout the central nervous system, where it is involved in arousal, attention, memory, motivation, and movement. Involved in muscle action through presence at neuromuscular junctions (specialized type of synapse where neurons connect to muscle cells). Degeneration of neurons that produce ACh has been linked to Alzheimer's disease. Too much ACh can lead to spasms and tremors; too little, to paralysis or torpor.
Dopamine	Involved in a wide variety of behaviors and emotions, including pleasure. Implicated in schizophrenia and Parkinson's disease.
Serotonin	Involved in the regulation of sleep, dreaming, mood, eating, pain, and aggressive behavior. Implicated in depression.
Norepinephrine	Affects arousal, wakefulness, learning, memory, and mood.
Endorphins	Involved in the inhibition of pain. Released during strenuous exercise. May be responsible for "runner's high."

Serotonin is popularly known as "the mood molecule" because it is often involved in emotional experiences. Serotonin is an example of a neurotransmitter that has widespread effects. Serotonin is like a master key that opens many locks—that is, it attaches to as many as a dozen receptor sites (Mintun et al., 2004; Thierry et al., 2004).

Other brain chemicals regulate the sensitivity of large numbers of synapses, in effect "turning up" or "turning down" the activity level of whole portions of the nervous system. *Endorphins*, for example, appear to reduce pain by inhibiting, or "turning down," the neurons that transmit pain messages in the brain.

Endorphins were discovered in the early 1970s. Researchers Candace Pert and Solomon Snyder (1973) were attempting to explain the effects of *opiates*—painkilling drugs such as morphine and heroin that are derived from the poppy plant—when they discovered that the central nervous system contained receptor sites for these substances. They reasoned that these receptor sites would not exist unless the body produced its own natural painkillers. Not long after, researchers discovered the endorphins. Morphine and other narcotics lock into the receptors for endorphins and have the same painkilling effects. Research on endorphins has provided clues to why people become addicted to morphine, heroin, and, in some cases, even alcohol (Modesto-Lowe & Fritz, 2005). When a person takes one of these drugs repeatedly, the body's production of *natural* painkillers slows down. As a result, an addict needs more of the artificial drug to feel "normal."

Imbalances in neurotransmitters appear to contribute to many types of mental illness. Schizophrenia, for example, has been associated with an overabundance of, or hypersensitivity to, dopamine (Silver, Goodman, Isakov, Knoll, & Modai, 2005). An undersupply of serotonin and norepinephrine has been linked to depression and other disorders. As in the case of endorphins, the design and testing of drugs has helped neuroscientists to identify the functions of neurotransmitters. (For more on the relationship between drugs and behavior, see **"Applying Psychology."**)

Endorphins, which are released into the brain and body during exercise, are neurotransmitters that act as natural painkillers.

NEURAL PLASTICITY AND NEUROGENESIS

How does experience change the brain? Can the brain and the nervous system repair themselves?

 ENDURING ISSUES

Stability–Change   Neural Plasticity

The brain is the one organ in the body that is unique to each individual. From the beginning, your brain has been encoding experience, developing the patterns of emotion and thought that make you who you are. At the same time, your brain is continually changing

neural plasticity The ability of the brain to change in response to experience.

as you learn new information and skills and adjust to changing conditions. How do neurons perform this intricate balancing act, maintaining stability while adapting to change? Even more remarkably, how does the brain recover from injury or reorganize itself after surgery (as in the example at the beginning of the chapter)? The answer lies in *neural plasticity*, the ability of the brain to be changed structurally and chemically by experience. ●●

In a classic series of experiments, M. R. Rosenzweig (1984) demonstrated the importance of experience to neural development. In the laboratory, Rosenzweig assigned baby rats into two groups. Members of one group were raised in an impoverished environment, isolated in barren cages. Members of the second group were raised in an enriched environment; they lived in cages with other rats and a variety of toys that offered opportunities for exploration, manipulation, and social interaction. Rosenzweig found that the rats raised in enriched environments had larger neurons with more synaptic connections than those raised in impoverished environments. (See **Figure 2–5.**) In more recent experiments, Rosenzweig (1996) and others (Ruifang & Danling, 2005) have shown that similar changes occur in rats of any age. Other researchers have found that rats raised in stimulating environments perform better on a variety of problem-solving tests and develop more synapses when required to perform complex tasks (Kleim, Vij, Ballard, & Greenough, 1997). These combined results suggest that the brain changes in response to the organism's experiences, a principle called **neural plasticity**. Furthermore, they demonstrate that neural plasticity is

APPLYING PSYCHOLOGY

DRUGS AND BEHAVIOR

Understanding how neurotransmitters work can also help you understand how chemical substances, including some common ones that you may use, affect your brain. You have already seen in this chapter how such opiates as morphine and heroin work because they fit into the same receptors as naturally occurring endorphins. Other psychoactive drugs as well as many toxins (or poisons) also work by either blocking or enhancing the transmission of chemicals across synapses. Consider the following examples:

- *Botulism* (produced by the bacteria in improperly canned or frozen food) prevents the release of acetylcholine (Ach), which carries signals to the muscles. The result is paralysis and, sometimes, rapid death.
- *Curare*, a poison that some native people of South America traditionally used to tip their arrows, instantly stuns and sometimes kills their prey or enemies. Curare blocks the ACh *receptors*—that is, it has the same

effect as botulism, but acts at the other side of the synapse.

- The poison of the *black widow spider* produces the opposite effect. It causes ACh to spew into the synapses of the nervous system. As a result, neurons fire repeatedly, causing spasms and tremors.
- Antipsychotic medications *chlorpromazine* (trade name Thorazine) and *clozapine* prevent dopamine from binding to receptor sites; this reduction in stimulation apparently reduces schizophrenic hallucinations.
- *Caffeine* works in a slightly more complex way. It blocks the action of adenosine, a transmitter that inhibits the release of other neurotransmitters such as epinephrine (Cauli & Morelli, 2005). Without the restraining effects of adenosine, more of these other excitatory, arousing neurotransmitters are released. Two or three cups of coffee contain enough caffeine to block half the adenosine

receptors for several hours, producing a high state of arousal and, in some cases, anxiety and insomnia.

- *Cocaine* works in yet another way. It prevents dopamine from being reabsorbed from the synapse after it has done its job of stimulating the next neuron. As a result, excess amounts of dopamine accumulate in the synapses, producing heightened arousal of the entire nervous system (Freeman et al., 2002; Szucs, Frankel, McMahon, & Cunningham, 2005).
- Some *antidepressant medications* also work by preventing or slowing the removal of neurotransmitters from the synapse. We will say more about these "miracle drugs" that help reduce the hopelessness of severe depression in Chapter 12, "Psychological Disorders," and Chapter 13, "Therapies."

We will have much more to say about drugs and their effects in Chapter 4, "States of Consciousness."

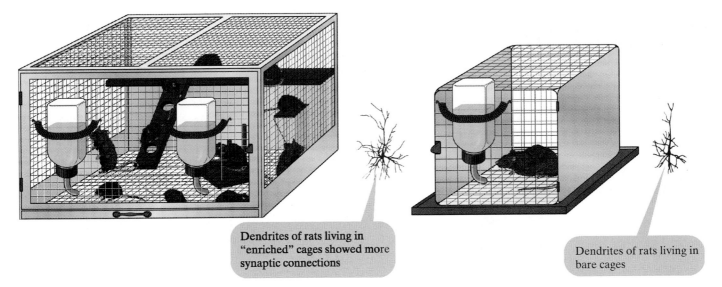

Dendrites of rats living in "enriched" cages showed more synaptic connections

Dendrites of rats living in bare cages

Figure 2–5

Brain growth and experience.

In Rosenzweig's experiment, young rats lived in two kinds of cages: "impoverished," with nothing to manipulate or explore, or "enriched," with a variety of objects. When Rosenzweig examined the rats' brains, he found that the enriched group had larger neurons with more synaptic connections (shown as dendrites in the drawing) than the rats that lived in the bare cages. Experience, then, can actually affect the structure of the brain.

Source: From "Brain changes in response to experience" by M. R. Rosenzweig, E. L. Bennett, and M. C. Diamond. Copyright © 1972, Scientific American, Inc. All rights reserved. Adapted with permission of the estate of Bunji Tagawa.

a feedback loop: Experience leads to changes in the brain, which, in turn, facilitate new learning, which leads to further neural change, and so on (D. L. Nelson, 1999; also see Doyon & Benali, 2005).

As we saw in the story of Nico at the beginning of the chapter, reorganization of the brain as a result of experience is not limited to rats (B. Kolb, Gibb, & Robinson, 2003). For example, violinists, cellists, and other string musicians spend years developing precise left-hand sensitivity and dexterity. Researchers have found that the area of the musicians' brains associated with left-hand sensation is larger than the area that represents the right hand (which string musicians use for bowing), and larger than the left-hand area in nonmusicians (Elbert, Pantev, Wienbruch, Rockstroh, & Taub, 1995). Moreover, plasticity in the brain is not just limited to changes that affect motor behaviors. The brains of female mammals apparently change in response to hormonal changes that occur during pregnancy (Kinsley & Lambert, 2006). Plasticity also permits changes in the way our nervous system responds to sensation. For example, studies with adult primates have shown that the auditory cortex changes in response to vocal experience (Cheung, Nagarajan, & Schreiner, 2005). And, perhaps most remarkably, in deaf people an area of the brain usually responsible for hearing rewires itself to read lips and sign language (Bosworth & Dobkins, 1999). Moreover, in blind people, the portion of the brain normally responsible for vision reorganizes to respond to touch and hearing (Amedi, Merabet, Bermpohl, & Pascual-Leone, 2005).

Experience also causes changes in the *strength* of communication across synapses. Stimulating the left hand of string musicians resulted in a strong increase in neural activity, but a comparatively weak response in nonmusicians (Elbert et al., 1995). Interestingly, this effect was most pronounced for musicians who began playing a string instrument before age 12. Other researchers have studied this phenomenon at the cellular level (Taufiq et al., 2005). When neurons in the hippocampus (a brain structure involved in forming memories in humans and other animals) are stimulated by an electrical pulse, the initial response in nearby neurons is very weak. But repeated stimulation of the same pathway causes the

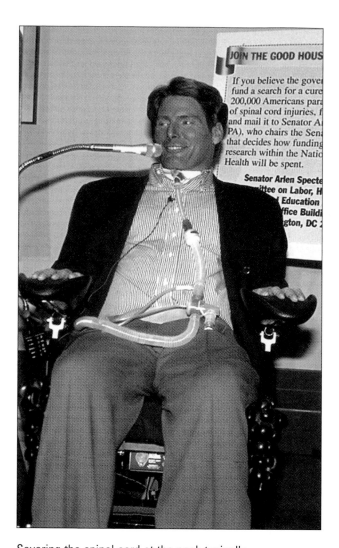

Severing the spinal cord at the neck typically causes paralysis of everything below the head because nerves connecting to the body's muscles no longer have a cable to the brain. The late actor Christopher Reeve suffered from paralysis of everything below the head when his spinal cord was severed after he was thrown from a horse and the nerves connected to his body's muscles no longer had a cable to the brain. Others with similar injuries may someday benefit from research on neurogenesis.

neurogenesis The growth of new neurons.

nearby neurons to respond vigorously, an effect that lasts weeks after the stimulation was stopped. *Long-term potentiation* (LTP), as this is called, appears to help the brain learn and store new information (Bliss, Collingridge, & Morris, 2004).

We have seen that experience can lead to dramatic changes in the number and complexity of synaptic connections in the brain—that is, in the connections between neurons. Might experience also produce new neurons? For many years, psychologists believed that organisms are born with all the brain cells they will ever have. New research however, has overturned this traditional view by showing that adult brains are capable of **neurogenesis**, the production of new brain cells (Gage, 2003; Mohapel, Leanza, Kokaia, & Lindvall, 2006; Prickaerts, Koopmans, Blokland, & Scheepens, 2004).

The discovery of lifelong neurogenesis has widespread implications for treating neurological disorders. Traditionally, injuries to the brain and spinal cord have been considered permanent; treatment was limited to stabilizing the patient to prevent further damage, treating related infections, and using rehabilitation to maximize remaining capabilities (McDonald, 1999). Some individuals with brain damage recovered over time, but they were the exception. However, the discovery of adult neurogenesis raises new possibilities (Van Praag, Zhao, & Gage, 2004).

One of these possibilities, the use of fetal stem cells, has been the focus of recent debate in Congress and the media. Scientists have long known that embryos contain large numbers of stem cells: undifferentiated, precursor cells or "precells" that, under the right conditions, can give rise to any specialized cell in the body—liver, kidney, blood, heart, or neurons (Bjornson, Rietze, Reynolds, Magli, & Vescovi, 1999). Remarkably, in tests with animals, stem cells transplanted into a brain or spinal cord spontaneously migrated to damaged areas and began to generate specialized neurons for replacement (Kokaia & Lindvall, 2003; Nowakowski & Hayes, 2004). It was as if stem cells moved through the brain, going from one neuron to the next looking for damage. If damage was found, the stem cells began to divide and produce specialized neurons appropriate for that area of the brain.

In clinical trials with patients suffering from Parkinson's disease, fetal nerve cell transplants have improved motor control for periods of 5 to 10 years (Barinaga, 2000). But the supply of fetal tissue is limited, and its harvest and use raise ethical questions (Check, 2005; Patenaude, Guttmacher, & Collins, 2002).

Another potential use of new research findings is to stimulate the brain's own stem cells to provide "self-repair." Once the chemicals that regulate neurogenesis are understood more fully, it may be possible to increase the amounts of these substances in areas of the central nervous system where neural growth needs to occur (Gage, 2000). Some researchers have already begun to identify substances and environmental conditions that show promise of stimulating neural regrowth (Auvergne et al., 2002; Keilhoff, Bernstein, Becker, Grecksch, & Wolf, 2004; Mirescu, Peters, & Gould, 2004; Rasika, Alvarez-Buylla, & Nottebohm, 1999). One substance in particular, inosine, has been shown in rats to stimulate undamaged nerve fibers to grow new connections and restore motor functioning following strokes (Chen, Goldberg, Kolb, Lanser, & Benowitz, 2002).

To translate this discovery into treatment, scientists need to learn more about what causes (or blocks) the production of adult stem cells and what causes their "daughter cells" to become mature, specialized neurons and to migrate to different areas of the brain (Gage, 2000; Van Praag & Gage, 2002). Specific treatments may take years to develop, but people suffering from such neurological disorders as Parkinson's and Alzheimer's diseases, as well as victims of spinal cord injuries and stroke, now have hope (Barinaga, 2000; Gage, 2000; McMillan, Robertson, & Wilson, 1999; Van Praag & Gage, 2002).

CHECK YOUR UNDERSTANDING

Match each term with the appropriate definition.

1. ___ neuron
2. ___ neural plasticity
3. ___ dendrites
4. ___ axons
5. ___ neural impulse
6. ___ resting potential
7. ___ absolute refractory period
8. ___ neurogenesis
9. ___ synapse
10. ___ neurotransmitters
11. ___ dopamine
12. ___ serotonin
13. ___ all-or-none law

a. growth of new neurons
b. long, cellular fibers carrying outgoing messages
c. when a nerve cell cannot fire again
d. neurotransmitter that affects emotions, arousal, and sleep
e. cell that transmits information
f. when experience changes the brain
g. chemicals that carry messages across synapses
h. short, cellular fibers that pick up incoming messages
i. neurotransmitter with a role in schizophrenia and Parkinson's disease
j. action potential
k. a neuron either fires at full strength or not at all
l. terminal button, synaptic space, and dendrite of neighboring neuron
m. electrical imbalance across a neural membrane at rest

Answers: 1. e. 2. f. 3. h. 4. b. 5. j. 6. m. 7. c. 8. a. 9. l. 10. g. 11. i. 12. d. 13. k.

APPLY YOUR UNDERSTANDING

1. You return from a day at the beach to find you have developed a severe sunburn. Which neurons are sending messages from your burned skin to your brain informing you of the pain from the burn?

   a. afferent neurons
   b. efferent neurons
   c. interaction neurons
   d. motor neurons

2. John is a 75-year-old male who is in the early stages of Alzheimer's disease. The cause of his disorder is most likely a deficiency of

   a. acetylcholine
   b. dopamine
   c. serotonin
   d. norepinephrine

Answers: 1. a. 2. a.

The Central Nervous System

THE ORGANIZATION OF THE NERVOUS SYSTEM

How is the nervous system organized?

Every part of the nervous system is connected to every other part. To understand its anatomy and functions, however, it is useful to analyze the nervous system in terms of the divisions and subdivisions shown in **Figure 2–6**. The **central nervous system** includes the brain and spinal cord, which together contain more than 90% of the body's neurons. The **peripheral nervous system** consists of nerves that connect the brain and spinal cord to every other part of the body, carrying messages back and forth between the central nervous

central nervous system (CNS) Division of the nervous system that consists of the brain and spinal cord.

peripheral nervous system (PNS) Division of the nervous system that connects the central nervous system to the rest of the body.

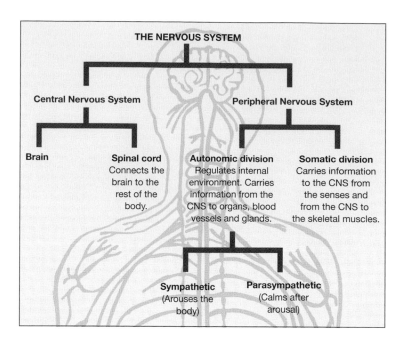

THE NERVOUS SYSTEM

Central Nervous System

Peripheral Nervous System

Brain

Spinal cord
Connects the brain to the rest of the body.

Autonomic division
Regulates internal environment. Carries information from the CNS to organs, blood vessels and glands.

Somatic division
Carries information to the CNS from the senses and from the CNS to the skeletal muscles.

Sympathetic
(Arouses the body)

Parasympathetic
(Calms after arousal)

Figure 2–6
A schematic diagram of the divisions of the nervous system and their various subparts.

hindbrain Area containing the medulla, pons, and cerebellum.

medulla Structure in the hindbrain that controls essential life support functions including breathing, heart rate and blood pressure.

system and the sense organs, muscles, and glands. The peripheral nervous system is subdivided into the *somatic nervous system*, which transmits information about body movements and the external environment, and the *autonomic nervous system*, which transmits information to and from the internal organs and glands. (We will discuss the endocrine system, which works hand in hand with the nervous system, later in the chapter.)

THE BRAIN

What are the major structures and areas of the brain, and what functions do they serve?

The brain is the seat of awareness and reason, the place where learning, memory, and emotions are centered. It is the part of us that decides what to do and whether that decision was right or wrong, and it imagines how things might have turned out if we had acted differently.

The human brain—our "crowning glory"—is the product of millions of years of evolution. As new, more complex structures were added, older structures were retained. One way to understand the brain is to look at three layers that evolved in different stages of evolution: (1) the primitive *central core*; (2) the *limbic system*, which evolved later; and (3) the *cerebral hemispheres*, which are in charge of higher mental processes such as problem solving and language. (See **Figure 2–7**.) We will use these three basic divisions to describe the parts of the brain, what they do, and how they interact to influence our behavior. (See "**Summary Table**: Parts of the Brain and Their Functions.")

THE CENTRAL CORE At the point where the spinal cord enters the skull, it becomes the hindbrain. Because the **hindbrain** is found in even the most primitive vertebrates, it is believed to have been the earliest part of the brain to evolve. The part of the hindbrain nearest to the spinal cord is the **medulla**, a narrow structure about 1.5 inches long. The medulla controls such bodily functions as breathing, heart rate, and blood pressure. The

SUMMARY TABLE

PARTS OF THE BRAIN AND THEIR FUNCTIONS

Central Core	Medulla	Regulates respiration, heart rate, blood pressure.
	Pons	Regulates sleep–wake cycles.
	Cerebellum	Regulates reflexes and balance; coordinates movement.
	Reticular formation	Regulates attention and alertness.
	Thalamus	Major sensory relay center; regulates higher brain centers and peripheral nervous system.
	Hypothalamus	Influences emotion and motivation; governs stress reactions.
Limbic System	Hippocampus	Regulates formation of new memories.
	Amygdala	Governs emotions related to self-preservation.
Cerebral Cortex	Frontal lobe	Goal-directed behavior; concentration; emotional control and temperament; voluntary movements; coordinates messages from other lobes; complex problem solving; involved in many aspects of personality.
	Parietal lobe	Receives sensory information; visual/spatial abilities.
	Occipital lobe	Receives and processes visual information.
	Temporal lobe	Smell and hearing; balance and equilibrium; emotion and motivation; some language comprehension; complex visual processing and face recognition.

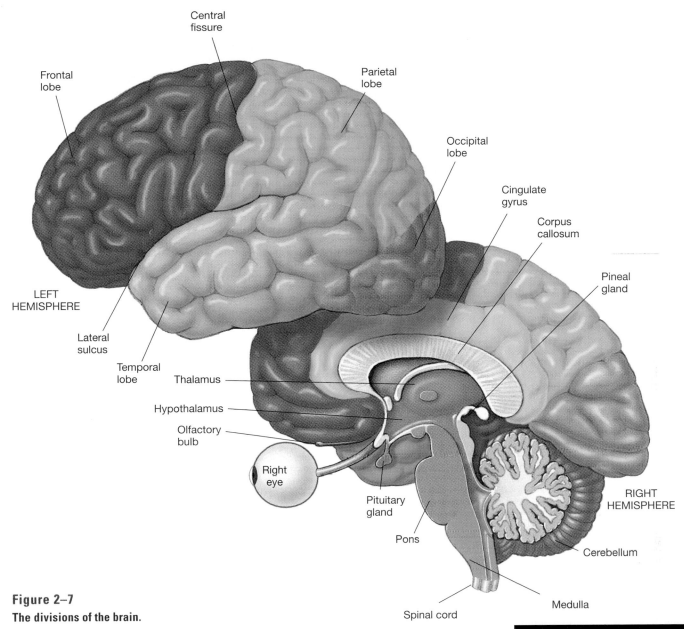

Figure 2–7
The divisions of the brain.

medulla is also the point at which many of the nerves from the body cross over on their way to and from the higher brain centers; nerves from the left part of the body cross to the right side of the brain and vice versa (a topic to which we will return). Near the medulla lies the **pons**, which produces chemicals that help maintain our sleep–wake cycle. (See Chapter 4, "States of Consciousness.") Both the medulla and the pons transmit messages to the upper areas of the brain.

The part of the hindbrain at the top and back of the brain stem is the **cerebellum**. The cerebellum is sometimes called the "little brain," but in this case, appearances are deceiving. Though the cerebellum takes up only a small space, its surface area is almost two-thirds that of the much larger cerebral cortex. It also contains more neurons than the rest of the brain. Traditionally, it has been thought that the cerebellum is simply responsible for our sense of balance and for coordinating the body's actions to ensure that movements go together in efficient sequences. Damage to the cerebellum in adults does indeed cause severe problems in movement, such as jerky motions and stumbling. Recent research suggests, however, that the cerebellum is also involved in many more psychological processes,

The human brain, viewed from the top. Its relatively small size belies its enormous complexity.

pons Structure in the midbrain that regulates sleep and wake cycles.

cerebellum Structure in the hindbrain that controls certain reflexes and coordinates the body's movements.

including emotional control, attention, memory, and coordinating sensory information (J. M. Bower & Parsons, 2003; Highstein & Thatch, 2002). In addition, recent studies have indicated that a number of mental disorders such as autism, schizophrenia, and attention deficit disorder may be associated with cerebellar dysfunction (Tamminga & Vogel, 2005).

Above the cerebellum, the brain stem widens to form the **midbrain**. The midbrain is especially important for hearing and sight. It is also one of several places in the brain where pain is registered.

More or less directly over the brain stem are the two egg-shaped structures that make up the **thalamus**. The thalamus is often described as a relay station: Almost all sensory information passes through the thalamus on the way to higher levels of the brain, where it is translated and routed to the appropriate brain location. Directly below the thalamus is the smaller **hypothalamus**, which exerts an enormous influence on many kinds of motivation. Portions of the hypothalamus govern hunger, thirst, sexual drive, and body temperature (Sewards & Sewards, 2003; Winn, 1995) and are directly involved in emotional behavior such as experiencing rage, terror, or pleasure.

The **reticular formation (RF)** is a netlike system of neurons that weaves through all of these structures. Its main job is to send "Alert!" signals to the higher parts of the brain in response to incoming messages. The RF can be subdued, however; during sleep, the RF is turned down. Anesthetics work largely by temporarily shutting this system off, and permanent damage to the RF can even induce a coma.

THE CEREBRAL CORTEX Ballooning out over and around the central core, virtually hiding it, is the *cerebrum*. The cerebrum is divided into two hemispheres and covered by a thin layer of gray matter (unmyelinated cells) called the **cerebral cortex**. This is what most people think of first when they talk about "the brain"; it is the part of the brain that processes thought, vision, language, memory, and emotions. The cerebral cortex takes up most of the room inside the skull, accounting for about 80% of the weight of the human brain and containing about 70% of the neurons in the central nervous system.

The cerebral cortex, which is the most recently evolved part of the nervous system, is more highly developed in humans than in any other animal. Spread out, the human cortex would cover 2 to 3 square feet and be about as thick as the letter "T." To fit inside the skull, in humans the cerebral cortex has developed intricate folds—hills and valleys called *convolutions*. In each person, these convolutions form a pattern that is as unique as a fingerprint.

A number of landmarks on the cortex allow us to identify distinct areas each with different functions. The first is a deep cleft, running from front to back, that divides the brain into *right* and *left* hemispheres. As seen in **Figure 2–7**, each of these hemispheres can be divided into four *lobes* (described below), which are separated from one another by crevices, or fissures, such as the *central fissure*. In addition, there are large areas on the cortex of all four lobes called **association areas** that integrate information from diverse parts of the cortex and are involved in mental processes such as learning, thinking, and remembering.

The different lobes of the cerebral hemispheres are specialized for different functions. (See **Figure 2–8**). The **frontal lobe**, located just behind the forehead, accounts for about half the volume of the human brain, yet it remains the most mysterious part of the brain. The frontal lobe receives and coordinates messages from the other three lobes of the cortex and seems to keep track of previous and future movements of the body. This ability to monitor and integrate the complex tasks that are going on in the rest of the brain has led some investigators to hypothesize that the frontal lobe serves as an "executive control center" for the brain (Dubois & Levy, 2004; E. Goldberg, 2001; Waltz et al., 1999) and is involved in a wide range of problem-solving tasks, including answering both verbal and spatial IQ-test questions (Duncan et al., 2000). The section of the frontal lobe known as the **primary motor cortex** plays a key role in voluntary action. The frontal lobe also seems to play a key role in the behaviors we associate with personality, including motivation, persistence, affect (emotional responses), character, and even moral decision making (J. Greene & Haidt, 2002; Jackson et al., 2003).

Until recently, our knowledge of the frontal lobes was based on research with nonhuman animals, whose frontal lobes are relatively undeveloped, and on studies of rare cases of

---

midbrain Region between the hindbrain and the forebrain; it is important for hearing and sight, and it is one of several places in the brain where pain is registered.

thalamus Forebrain region that relays and translates incoming messages from the sense receptors, except those for smell.

hypothalamus Forebrain region that governs motivation and emotional responses.

reticular formation (RF) Network of neurons in the hindbrain, the midbrain, and part of the forebrain, whose primary function is to alert and arouse the higher parts of the brain.

cerebral cortex The outer surface of the two cerebral hemispheres that regulates most complex behavior.

association areas Areas of the cerebral cortex where incoming messages from the separate senses are combined into meaningful impressions and outgoing messages from the motor areas are integrated.

frontal lobe Part of the cerebral cortex that is responsible for voluntary movement; it is also important for attention, goal-directed behavior, and appropriate emotional experiences.

primary motor cortex The section of the frontal lobe responsible for voluntary movement.

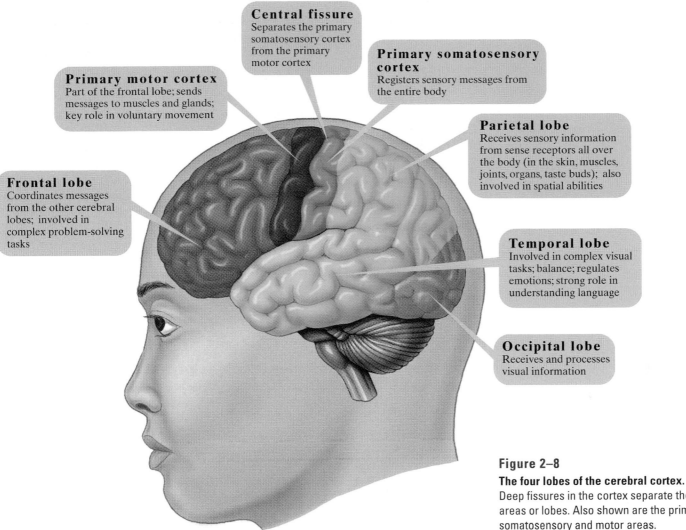

Central fissure
Separates the primary somatosensory cortex from the primary motor cortex

Primary motor cortex
Part of the frontal lobe; sends messages to muscles and glands; key role in voluntary movement

Primary somatosensory cortex
Registers sensory messages from the entire body

Frontal lobe
Coordinates messages from the other cerebral lobes; involved in complex problem-solving tasks

Parietal lobe
Receives sensory information from sense receptors all over the body (in the skin, muscles, joints, organs, taste buds); also involved in spatial abilities

Temporal lobe
Involved in complex visual tasks; balance; regulates emotions; strong role in understanding language

Occipital lobe
Receives and processes visual information

Figure 2–8
The four lobes of the cerebral cortex.
Deep fissures in the cortex separate these areas or lobes. Also shown are the primary somatosensory and motor areas.

people with frontal lobe damage. One famous case, involving a bizarre accident, was reported in 1848. Phineas Gage, the foreman of a railroad construction gang, made a mistake while using some blasting powder. The explosion blew a nearly 4-foot-long tamping iron more than an inch thick into his cheek and all the way through the top of his head, severely damaging his frontal lobes. To the amazement of those who witnessed the accident, Gage remained conscious, walked part of the way to a doctor, and suffered few physical aftereffects. He did, however, suffer lasting psychological changes, including difficulty reasoning and making decisions, as well as difficulty controlling his emotions. These changes were so radical that, in the view of his friends, he was no longer the same man. (See Macmillan, 2000; Wagar & Thagard, 2004.)

A century later, most neuroscientists agree that personality change—especially loss of motivation and ability to concentrate—is the major outcome of frontal lobe damage. The frontal lobes are involved in goal-directed behavior and the ability to lead a mature emotional life (Rule, 2001). So, when adults suffer strokes or other traumas to the prefrontal cortex, their ability to make judgments and control their emotions is often seriously impaired (H. Damasio, Grabowski, Galaburda, & Damasio, 2005).

Much more research needs to be done before psychologists can understand how this part of the cortex contributes to such a wide and subtle range of mental activities. (See "**Summary Table**: Parts of the Brain and Their Functions.")

The **occipital lobe**, located at the very back of the cerebral hemispheres, receives and processes visual information. Damage to the occipital lobe can produce blindness or visual hallucinations (Beniczky et al., 2002). (See **Figure 2–8**.)

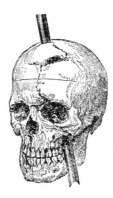

The skull of Phineas Gage, showing where the tamping iron passed through it, severely damaging his frontal lobes.

occipital lobe Part of the cerebral hemisphere that receives and interprets visual information.

parietal lobe Part of the cerebral cortex that receives sensory information from throughout the body.

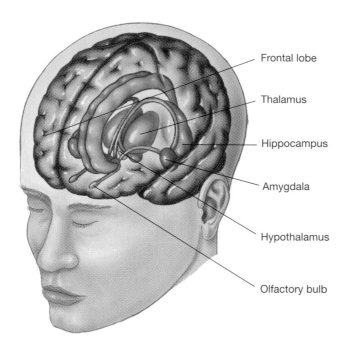

Figure 2–9
The limbic system.
A system of brain structures, including the thalamus, hippocampus, amygdala, hypothalamus, and olfactory bulb. This system is primarily involved in regulating behaviors having to do with motivation and emotion.

Frontal lobe

Thalamus

Hippocampus

Amygdala

Hypothalamus

Olfactory bulb

primary somatosensory cortex Area of the parietal lobe where messages from the sense receptors are registered.

temporal lobe Part of the cerebral hemisphere that helps regulate hearing, balance and equilibrium, and certain emotions and motivations.

limbic system Ring of structures that plays a role in learning and emotional behavior.

corpus callosum A thick band of nerve fibers connecting the left and right cerebral hemispheres.

The **parietal lobe** occupies the top back half of each hemisphere. This lobe receives sensory information from all over the body—from sense receptors in the skin, muscles, joints, internal organs, and taste buds. Messages from these sense receptors are registered in the **primary somatosensory cortex**. The parietal lobe also seems to oversee spatial abilities, such as the ability to follow a map or to tell someone how to get from one place to another (Chafee, Crowe, Averbeck, & Georgopoulos, 2005).

The **temporal lobe**, located in front of the occipital lobe, roughly behind the temples, plays an important role in complex visual tasks such as recognizing faces and interpreting the facial emotions of others (Holdstock, 2005; Yamada et al., 2005). The temporal lobe also receives and processes information from the ears, contributes to balance and equilibrium, and regulates emotions and motivations such as anxiety, pleasure, and anger. In addition, researchers believe the ability to understand and comprehend language is concentrated primarily in the rear portion of the temporal lobes, though some language comprehension may also occur in the parietal and frontal lobes (Crinion, Lambon-Ralph, & Warburton, 2003; Hutsler, 2003).

THE LIMBIC SYSTEM The **limbic system** is a ring of loosely connected structures located between the central core and the cerebral hemispheres. (See **Figure 2–9**.) In evolutionary terms, the limbic system is more recent than the central core and is fully developed only in mammals.

The limbic system plays a central role in times of stress, coordinating and integrating the activity of the nervous system. One part of the limbic system, the *hippocampus*, plays an essential role in the formation of new memories. People with severe damage to this area can still remember names, faces, and events that they recorded in memory before they were injured, but they cannot remember anything new. Another structure, the *amygdala* (working together with the hippocampus) is involved in governing and regulating emotions and in establishing emotional memories (R. J. Davidson, Jackson, & Kalin, 2002; Hamann, Ely, Hoffman, & Kilts, 2002), particularly those related to fear and self-preservation (Donley, Schulkin, & Rosen, 2005). In aggressive nonhuman animals, when portions of these structures are damaged or removed the animals become tame and docile. In contrast, stimulation of some portions of these structures causes animals to exhibit signs of fear and panic, whereas stimulation of other portions triggers unprovoked attacks.

Other limbic structures are involved in the experience of pleasure. Given the opportunity to press a bar that electrically stimulates one such region, animals do so endlessly, ignoring food and water. Humans also experience pleasure when some areas of the limbic system are electrically stimulated, though apparently not as intensely (Olds & Forbes, 1981). Even our ability to read the facial expressions of emotion in other people (such as smiling or frowning) is registered in the limbic system (L. Carr, Iacoboni, Dubeau, Mazziotta, & Lenzi, 2005; Lange et al., 2003). (We will return to the limbic system in Chapter 8, "Motivation and Emotion.")

HEMISPHERIC SPECIALIZATION

How are the left and right hemispheres specialized for different functions?

The cerebrum, as noted earlier, consists of two separate cerebral hemispheres. Quite literally, humans have a "right half-brain" and a "left half-brain." The primary connection between the left and the right hemispheres is a thick, ribbonlike band of nerve fibers under the cortex called the **corpus callosum**. (See **Figure 2–10**.)

Under normal conditions, the left and right cerebral hemispheres are in close communication through the corpus callosum and work together as a coordinated unit (Banich, 1998; Saint-Amour, Lepore, Lassonde, & Guillemot, 2004). But research suggests that the cerebral hemispheres are not really equivalent. (See **Figure 2–10**.)

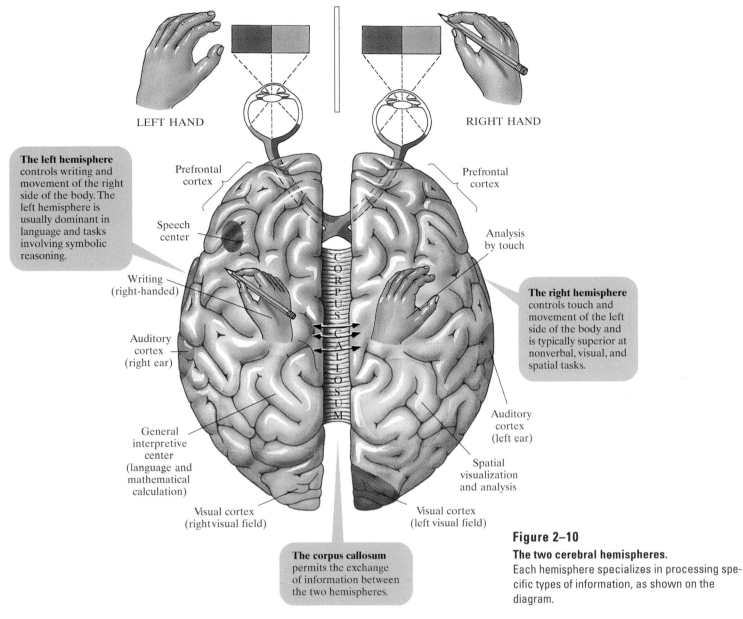

LEFT HAND

RIGHT HAND

The left hemisphere controls writing and movement of the right side of the body. The left hemisphere is usually dominant in language and tasks involving symbolic reasoning.

Prefrontal cortex

Speech center

Writing (right-handed)

Auditory cortex (right ear)

General interpretive center (language and mathematical calculation)

Visual cortex (right visual field)

Prefrontal cortex

Analysis by touch

The right hemisphere controls touch and movement of the left side of the body and is typically superior at nonverbal, visual, and spatial tasks.

Auditory cortex (left ear)

Spatial visualization and analysis

Visual cortex (left visual field)

CORPUS CALLOSUM

The corpus callosum permits the exchange of information between the two hemispheres.

Figure 2–10

The two cerebral hemispheres.
Each hemisphere specializes in processing specific types of information, as shown on the diagram.

The most dramatic evidence comes from "split-brain" patients. In some cases of severe epilepsy, surgeons cut the corpus callosum to stop the spread of epileptic seizures from one hemisphere to the other. In general, this procedure is successful: The patients' seizures are reduced and sometimes eliminated. But their two hemispheres are functionally isolated; in effect, their right brain doesn't know what their left brain is doing (and vice versa). Since sensory information typically is sent to both hemispheres, in everyday life, split-brain patients function quite normally. However, a series of ingenious experiments revealed what happens when the two hemispheres cannot communicate (Gazzaniga, 2005; Sperry, 1964, 1968, 1970).

In one such experiment, split-brain patients were asked to stare at a spot on a projection screen. When pictures of various objects were projected to the *right* of that spot, they could name the objects. And, with their right hands, they could pick them out of a group of hidden objects. (See **Figure 2–11A.**) However, when pictures of objects were shown on the *left* side of the screen, something changed. Patients could pick out the objects by feeling them with their left hands, but they couldn't say what the objects were! In fact, when asked what objects they saw on the left side of the screen, split-brain patients usually said "nothing." (See **Figure 2–11B.**)

Figure 2–11

The split-brain experiment.
(A) When split-brain patients stare at the "X" in the center of the screen, visual information projected on the right side of the screen goes to the patient's left hemisphere, which controls language. When asked what they see, patients can reply correctly. (B) When split-brain patients stare at the "X" in the center of the screen, visual information projected on the left side of the screen goes to the patient's right hemisphere, which does not control language. When asked what they see, patients cannot name the object, but can pick it out by touch with the left hand.

Source: Adapted from Carol Ward, © 1987, Discover Publications.

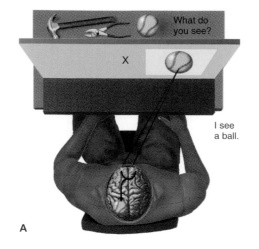
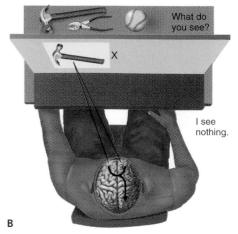

The explanation for these unusual results is found in the way each hemisphere of the brain operates. When the corpus callosum is cut, the *left hemisphere* receives information only from the right side of the body and the right half of the visual field. As a result, it can match an object shown in the right visual field with information received by touch from the right hand, but it is unaware of (and thus unable to identify) objects shown in the left visual field or touched by the left hand. Conversely, the *right hemisphere* receives information only from the left side of the visual field and the left side of the body. Consequently, the right hemisphere can match an object shown in the left visual field with information received by touch from the left hand, but it is unaware of any objects shown in the right visual field or touched with the right hand.

But why can't the right hemisphere verbally identify an object that is shown in the left visual field? The answer is that for the great majority of people (even for most left-handers), in the process of learning to read, language ability becomes concentrated primarily in the *left* hemisphere (Hellige, 1993; Turkeltaub, Gareau, Flowers, Zeffiro, & Eden, 2003). As a result, when an object is in the left visual field, the nonverbal right hemisphere can see the object, but can't name it. The verbal left hemisphere, in contrast, can't see an object in this location, so when asked what it sees, it answers that nothing is on the screen.

Does the left hemisphere specialize in any other tasks besides language? Some researchers think that it may also operate more analytically, logically, rationally, and sequentially than the right hemisphere does (Kingstone, Enns, Mangun, & Gazzaniga, 1995). In contrast, the right hemisphere excels at visual and spatial tasks—nonverbal imagery, including music, face recognition, and the perception of emotions (Buklina, 2005; Steinke, 2003). Put another way, the left hemisphere specializes in analyzing sequences and details, whereas the right hemisphere specializes in holistic processing (Reuter-Lorenz & Miller, 1998), in solving problems that require *insight* or creative solutions (Bowden & Jung-Beeman, 2003), and in preserving one's sense of personal identity or "self" (B. Bower, 2006; Feinberg & Keenan, 2005; Uddin, Kaplan, Molnar-Szakacs, Zaidel, & Iacoboni, 2005). The right hemisphere is also more likely than the left hemisphere to respond emotionally to spoken words, interpreting whether a message conveys happiness, sadness, or anger (Hagemann, Hewig, Naumann, Seifert, & Bartussek, 2005; Vingerhoets, Berckmoes, & Stroobant, 2003).

The frontal lobes of the two hemispheres may also influence temperament in distinctive ways. People whose left frontal lobe is more active than the right tend to be more cheerful, sociable, ebullient, and self-confident, whereas people with more right frontal lobe activity are more easily stressed, frightened, and upset by unpleasant things. They also tend to be more suspicious and depressed than people with predominantly left frontal lobe activity (Rotenberg, 2004; Shankman et al., 2005).

Although such research is fascinating and fun to speculate about, be cautious in interpreting it. First, not everyone shows the same pattern of differences between the left and right hemispheres. In particular, the differences between the hemispheres may be greater in men than in women (Mucci et al., 2005). Second, it is easy to oversimplify and exaggerate differences between the two sides of the brain. Split-brain research has given rise to several popular but misguided books that classify people as "right-brain" or "left-brain" thinkers. It is important to remember that under normal conditions, the right and left hemispheres are in close communication through the corpus callosum and so work together in a coordinated, integrated way (Gazzaniga, 2005). Furthermore, as we saw in the story of Nico at the beginning of the chapter, the plasticity of the brain means that both hemispheres have the potential to perform a range of tasks.

LANGUAGE The notion that human language is controlled primarily by the left cerebral hemisphere was first set forth in the 1860s by a French physician named Paul Broca. Broca's ideas were modified a decade later by the scientist Karl Wernicke. Thus, it should come as no surprise that the two major language areas in the brain have traditionally been called *Broca's area* and *Wernicke's area*. (See **Figure 2–12**.)

Wernicke's area lies toward the back of the temporal lobe. This area is crucial in processing and understanding what others are saying. By contrast, Broca's area, found in the frontal lobe, is considered to be essential to our ability to talk. To oversimplify a bit, Wernicke's area seems to be important for listening, and Broca's area seems to be important for talking. Support for these distinctions comes from patients who have suffered left-hemisphere strokes and resulting brain damage. Such strokes often produce predictable language problems, called **aphasias**. If the brain damage primarily affects Broca's area, the aphasia tends to be "expressive." That is, the patients' language difficulties lie predominantly in sequencing and producing language (talking). If the damage primarily affects Wernicke's area, the aphasia tends to be "receptive," and patients generally have profound difficulties understanding language (listening). Neuroimaging studies of people without brain damage confirm the role of Broca's and Wernicke's areas in language production and reception (Gernsbacher & Kaschak, 2003), as well as in the auditory hallucinations that torment people suffering from schizophrenia (Hoffman et al., 2003).

HANDEDNESS A common misconception is that hemispheric specialization is related to handedness. In particular, many people mistakenly believe that in left-handed people the right hemisphere governs language, analytic, and sequential tasks, whereas the left hemisphere dominates in visual, spatial, and nonverbal tasks. The fact is that speech is most often localized in the left hemisphere for both right- and left-handed people. However, in a small percentage of left-handed individuals, language functions are concentrated in the right hemisphere (Knecht et al., 2000; Toga & Thompson, 2003).

Nevertheless, psychologists have uncovered a number of interesting facts about handedness. Approximately 90% of humans are right-handed, with slightly more males than females showing a tendency toward left-handedness. Though research has not fully explained why some people are left-handed and others are right-handed, like most human traits it appears to involve an interaction of genetics, environment, and prenatal development. Whatever the reason for handedness, the tendency toward right-handedness appears to be a trait humans have possessed for quite some time, as anthropological studies of prehistoric cave drawing, tools, and human skeletons have shown (Steele, 2000). Interestingly, nonhuman primates also show a strong tendency toward right-handedness (Hopkins et al., 2005a), especially in those animals that use their hands to communicate (Corballis, 2003; Hopkins et al., 2005b).

Some research has shown a slightly higher incidence of such health problems as high blood pressure, epilepsy (Bryden, Bruyn, & Fletcher, 2005), asthma and allergies (Andreou, Krommydas, Gourgoulianis, Karapetsas, & Molyvdas, 2002) among left-handed people, though a clear explanation for this relationship has yet to emerge.

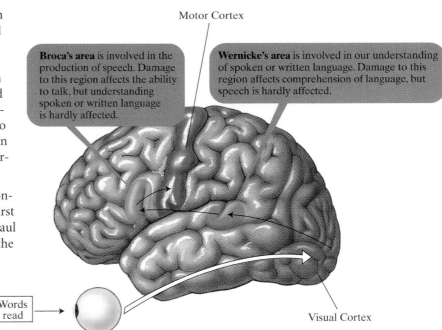

Broca's area is involved in the production of speech. Damage to this region affects the ability to talk, but understanding spoken or written language is hardly affected.

Wernicke's area is involved in our understanding of spoken or written language. Damage to this region affects comprehension of language, but speech is hardly affected.

Motor Cortex

Visual Cortex

Words read

Figure 2–12
Processing of speech and language.
Broca's and Wernicke's areas, generally found only on the left side of the brain, work together, enabling us to produce and understand speech and language.

aphasias Impairments of the ability to use (expressive aphasia) or understand (receptive aphasia) language that usually results from brain damage.

TOOLS FOR STUDYING THE BRAIN

What methods have been developed to study the brain?

For centuries, our understanding of the brain depended entirely on observing patients who had suffered brain injury or from examining the brains of cadavers. Another approach—that is still in use—is to remove or damage the brains of nonhuman animals and study the effects. But the human cerebral cortex is far more complicated than that of any other animal. How can scientists study the living, fully functioning human brain? Contemporary neuroscientists have four basic techniques—microelectrodes, macroelectrodes, structural imaging, and functional imaging. New, more accurate techniques have been developed almost every year and are used for both diagnosis and research. (The "**Summary Table**: Tools for Studying the Nervous System" reviews these techniques and their uses.)

MICROELECTRODE TECHNIQUES *Microelectrode* recording techniques are used to study the functions of single neurons. A microelectrode is a tiny glass or quartz pipette or tube (smaller in diameter than a human hair) that is filled with a conducting liquid. When technicians place the tip of this electrode inside a neuron, they can study changes in the electrical conditions of that neuron. Microelectrode techniques have been used to understand action potentials, the effects of drugs or toxins on neurons, and even processes that occur in the neural membrane.

MACROELECTRODE TECHNIQUES *Macroelectrode* recording techniques are used to obtain an overall picture of the activity in particular regions of the brain, which may contain millions of neurons. The first such device—the *electroencephalograph* (EEG)—is still in use today. Flat electrodes, taped to the scalp, are linked by wires to a device that translates electrical activity into lines on a moving roll of paper (or, more recently, images on a computer screen). This graph of so-called brain waves provides an index of both the strength and the rhythm of neural activity. As we will see in Chapter 4, "States of Consciousness," this technique has given researchers valuable insights into changes in brain waves during sleep and dreaming.

SUMMARY TABLE

TOOLS FOR STUDYING THE NERVOUS SYSTEM

Microelectrode Techniques	Used to study the functions of individual neurons.
Macroelectrode Techniques	Used to obtain a picture of the activity in a particular region of the brain. The EEG is one such technique.
Structural Imaging	Family of techniques used to map structures in a living brain.
Computerized axial tomography (CAT or CT)	Permits three-dimensional imaging of a living human brain.
Magnetic resonance imaging (MRI)	Produces pictures of inner brain structures.
Functional Imaging Techniques	Family of techniques that can image activity in the brain as it responds to various stimuli.
EEG imaging	Measures brain activity on a millisecond-by-millisecond basis.
Magnetoencephalography (MEG)	Two procedures that are similar to EEG imaging but have greater accuracy.
Magnetic source imaging (MSI)	
Positron emission tomography (PET) scanning	Three techniques that use radioactive energy to map exact regions of brain activity.
Radioactive PET	
Single photon emission computed tomography (SPECT)	
Functional magnetic resonance imaging (fMRI)	Measures the movement of blood molecules in the brain, pinpointing specific sites and details of neuronal activity.

The macroelectrode technique enables researchers to "listen" to what is going on in the brain, but it does not allow them to *look* through the skull and see what is happening. Some newer techniques, however, do just that.

STRUCTURAL IMAGING When researchers want to map the structures in a living human brain, they turn to two newer techniques. *Computerized axial tomography* (CAT or CT) *scanning* allows scientists to create three-dimensional images of a human brain without performing surgery. To produce a CAT scan, an X-ray photography unit rotates around the person, moving from the top of the head to the bottom; a computer then combines the resulting images. *Magnetic resonance imaging* (MRI) is even more successful at producing pictures of the inner regions of the brain, with its ridges, folds, and fissures. With MRI the person's head is surrounded by a magnetic field and the brain is exposed to radio waves, which causes hydrogen atoms in the brain to release energy. The energy released by different structures in the brain generates an image that appears on a computer screen.

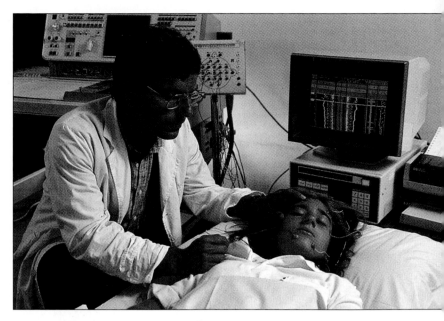

In an EEG, electrodes attached to the scalp are used to create a picture of neural activity in the brain.

Recent advances in MRI technology now enable scientists to compare precise three-dimensional images obtained over extended periods. This permits tracking of progressive structural changes in the brain that accompany slow neurodegenerative disorders like Alzheimer's disease. One study, for example, was able to compare the nerve tissue loss in patients with Alzheimer's disease with that in elderly people without the disorder. Alzheimer's patients showed an average of 5% loss of brain tissue, compared to a 0.5% loss for the healthy people (Thompson et al., 2003).

FUNCTIONAL IMAGING In many cases, researchers are interested in more than structure; they want to look at the brain's *activity* as it actually reacts to sensory stimuli such as pain, tones, and words. Such is the goal of several *functional imaging* methods. EEG imaging measures brain activity "on a millisecond-by-millisecond basis" (Fischman, 1985, p. 18). In this technique, more than two dozen electrodes are placed at important locations on the scalp. These electrodes record brain activities, which are then converted by a computer into colored images on a television screen. The technique has been extremely useful in detecting abnormal cortical activity such as that observed during epileptic seizures, like those suffered by Nico, the boy described at the beginning of the chapter.

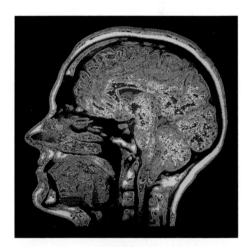

MRI image of the human head.

Two related techniques, called *magnetoencephalography* (MEG) and *magnetic source imaging* (MSI), take the procedure a step further. In standard EEG, electrical signals are distorted as they pass through the skull; and their exact source is difficult to determine. However, those same electrical signals create magnetic fields that are unaffected by bone. Both MEG and MSI measure the strength of the magnetic field and identify its source with considerable accuracy. By using these procedures, neuroscientists have begun to determine exactly which parts of the brain do most of the work in such psychological processes as memory (Campo et al., 2005) language processing (Valaki, Maestu, Ortiz, Papanicolaou, & Simos, 2004,), and reading. In turn, this research is beginning to shed new light on such disorders as amnesia and dyslexia (a reading disorder that is neurological in origin).

Another family of functional imaging techniques—including *positron emission tomography* (PET) *scanning*—uses radioactive energy to map brain activity. In these techniques, a person first receives an injection of a radioactive substance. Brain structures that are especially active immediately after the injection absorb most of the substance. When the substance starts to decay, it releases subatomic particles. By studying where most of the particles come from, researchers can determine exactly which portions of the brain are most active. Some of the findings produced by these techniques have been surprising. For example, one study found that, in general, the brains of people with higher IQ scores are *less* active than those of people with lower IQ scores, perhaps because they process information more efficiently (Haier, 1993; Sternberg, Loutrey, & Lubart, 2003). Progress has also

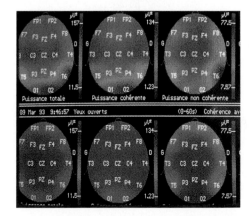

EEG imaging of one person's alpha brain waves (looking down on the brain, front of the head toward the top of the page). Red and yellow colors indicate greater alpha-wave activity.

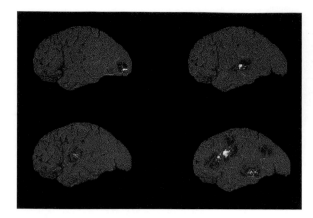

PET scans of a person at rest (top) and using language (bottom). The "hot" colors (red and yellow) indicate greater brain activity. These scans show that language activity is located primarily, but not exclusively, in the brain's left hemisphere.

been made in locating the damaged brain region in Parkinson's disease (Pinto et al., 2004). Other researchers have used these techniques to investigate how our memory for words and images is stored in the brain (Cabeza & Nyberg, 2000; Craik et al., 1999). These techniques also increase our knowledge of the effects of psychoactive drugs, such as antidepressants.

One of the newest and most powerful techniques for recording activity in the brain is called *functional magnetic resonance imaging* (fMRI). Functional MRI measures the movement of blood molecules (which is related to neuron activity) in the brain, permitting neuroscientists to pinpoint specific sites and details of neuronal activity. By comparing brain activity in normal learners with brain activity in children with learning problems, researchers have begun to identify the biological origins of attention-deficit hyperactivity disorder (ADHD) (Sowell et al., 2003); dyslexia (J. Ackerman, 2004; Shaywitz et al., 1998); and disorders that involve difficulties in controlling emotions (Heinzel et al., 2005). With fMRI it is even possible to determine with some accuracy what a person is thinking about and whether he or she is lying (P. Ross, 2003). Because fMRI enables us to collect extremely precise images rapidly and is noninvasive in that it does not require the injection of radioactive chemicals, it is especially promising as a new research tool (D'Esposito, Zarahn, & Aguirre, 1999; C. A. Nelson et al., 2000).

By combining these various techniques, neuroscientists can simultaneously observe anatomical structures (from CAT and MRI), sites of energy use (PET and MEG), blood and water movement (fMRI), and areas of electrical activity in the brain (EEG). As a result, scientists have begun to study the impact of drugs on the brain, the formation of memories (Craik et al., 1999), and the sites of many other mental activities (Blood & Zatorre, 2001; Sarter, Berntson, & Cacioppo, 1996). They are also gaining insights into the role of the brain in disorders such as schizophrenia (P. M. Thompson et al., 2001) and Tourette syndrome, a neurological disorder characterized by involuntary movements and vocalizations (Gates et al., 2004).

THE SPINAL CORD

What does the spinal cord do? How does it work with the brain to sense events and act on them?

We talk of the brain and the spinal cord as two distinct structures, but in fact, there is no clear boundary between them; at its upper end, the spinal cord enlarges into the brain stem. (See **Figure 2–13**.)

The **spinal cord** is our communications superhighway, connecting the brain to most of the rest of the body. Without it, we would be literally helpless. More than 400,000 Americans are partially or fully paralyzed—about half as a result of sudden traumas to the spinal cord (most often due to car crashes, gunshot wounds, falls, or sports injuries); and half as a result of tumors, infections, and such disorders as multiple sclerosis (McDonald, 1999; P. J. O'Connor, 2006). When the spinal cord is severed, parts of the body are literally disconnected from the brain. These victims lose all sensations from the parts of the body that can no longer send information to higher brain areas, and they can no longer control the movements of those body parts.

The spinal cord is made up of soft, jellylike bundles of long axons, wrapped in insulating myelin (white matter) and surrounded and protected by the bones in the spine. There are two major neural pathways in the spinal cord. One consists of motor neurons, descending from the brain, that control internal organs and muscles and help to regulate the autonomic nervous system (described later). The other consists of ascending, sensory neurons that carry information from the extremities and internal organs to the brain. In addition, the spinal cord contains neural circuits that produce reflex movements (and control some aspects of walking). These circuits do not require input from the brain.

To understand how the spinal cord works, consider the simple act of burning your finger on a hot pan. (See **Figure 2–14**.) You pull your hand away without thinking, but that quick response was the last event in a series of reactions in your nervous system. First,

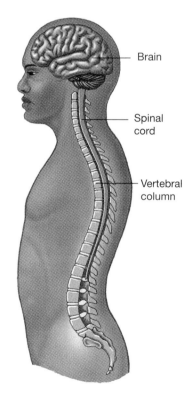

Figure 2–13
Brain and spinal cord.

Source: Human Physiology, An Integrated Approach by A. C. Silverthorn, © 1989. Reprinted by permission of Pearson Education, Inc., Upper Saddle River, NJ.

spinal cord Complex cable of neurons that runs down the spine, connecting the brain to most of the rest of the body.

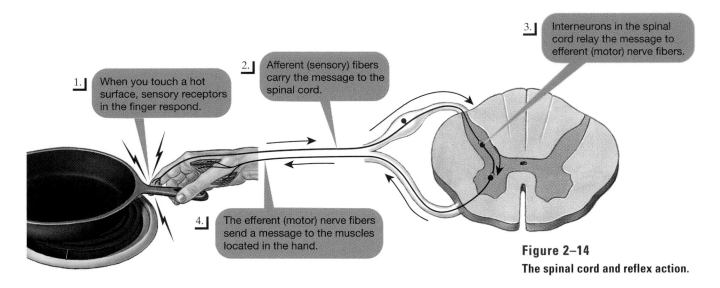

Figure 2–14
The spinal cord and reflex action.

special sensory cells pick up the message that your finger is burned. They pass this information along to *interneurons* located in the spinal cord. The interneurons, in turn, connect to motor neurons, triggering a quick withdrawal of your hand. (A similar reaction occurs when the doctor taps your knee with a rubber mallet.) At the same time, the message is being sent to other parts of your nervous system. Your body goes on "emergency alert": You breathe faster, your heart pounds, your entire body (including the endocrine system) mobilizes itself against the wound. Meanwhile, your brain is interpreting the messages it receives: You feel pain, you look at the burn, and you run cold water over your hand. A simple, small burn, then, triggers a complex, coordinated sequence of activities.

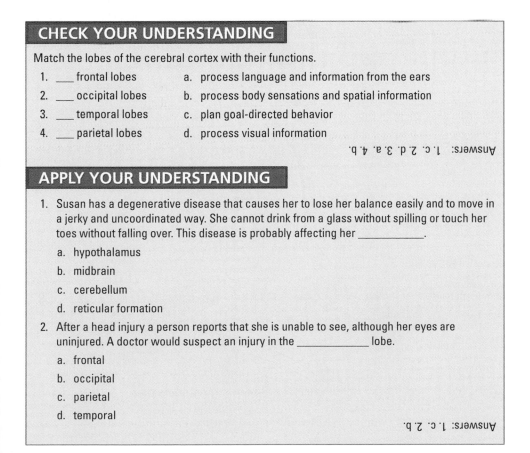

CHECK YOUR UNDERSTANDING

Match the lobes of the cerebral cortex with their functions.

1. ___ frontal lobes   a. process language and information from the ears
2. ___ occipital lobes   b. process body sensations and spatial information
3. ___ temporal lobes   c. plan goal-directed behavior
4. ___ parietal lobes   d. process visual information

Answers: 1. c. 2. d. 3. a. 4. b.

APPLY YOUR UNDERSTANDING

1. Susan has a degenerative disease that causes her to lose her balance easily and to move in a jerky and uncoordinated way. She cannot drink from a glass without spilling or touch her toes without falling over. This disease is probably affecting her _____.
   a. hypothalamus
   b. midbrain
   c. cerebellum
   d. reticular formation
2. After a head injury a person reports that she is unable to see, although her eyes are uninjured. A doctor would suspect an injury in the _____ lobe.
   a. frontal
   b. occipital
   c. parietal
   d. temporal

Answers: 1. c. 2. b.

afferent neurons Neurons that carry messages from sense organs to the spinal cord or brain.

efferent neurons Neurons that carry messages from the spinal cord or brain to the muscles and glands.

somatic nervous system The part of the peripheral nervous system that carries messages from the senses to the central nervous system and between the central nervous system and the skeletal muscles.

autonomic nervous system The part of the peripheral nervous system that carries messages between the central nervous system and the internal organs.

The Peripheral Nervous System

How does the brain communicate with the rest of the body? How is the autonomic branch of the peripheral nervous system involved in controlling emotions?

The origins of the quick response your body makes to touching a hot pan are in your peripheral nervous system. The peripheral nervous system (PNS) links the brain and spinal cord to the rest of the body, including the sensory receptors, glands, internal organs, and skeletal muscles. (See **Figure 2–6**.) It consists of both **afferent neurons**, which carry messages *to* the central nervous system (CNS), and **efferent neurons**, which carry messages *from* the CNS. The afferent neurons carry sensory information. All the things that register through your senses—sights, sounds, smells, temperature, pressure, and so on—travel to your brain via afferent neurons. The efferent neurons carry signals from the brain to the body's muscles and glands.

Some neurons belong to a part of the PNS called the **somatic nervous system**. Neurons in this system are involved in making voluntary movements of the skeletal muscles. Every deliberate action you make, from pedaling a bike to scratching a toe, involves neurons in the somatic nervous system. Other neurons belong to a part of the PNS called the autonomic nervous system. Neurons in the **autonomic nervous system** govern involuntary activities of your internal organs, from the beating of your heart to the hormone secretions of your glands.

The autonomic nervous system is of special interest to psychologists because it is involved not only in vital body functions, such as breathing and blood flow, but also in important emotions as well. To understand the workings of the autonomic nervous system, you must know about the system's two parts: the *sympathetic* and the *parasympathetic* divisions. (See **Figure 2–15**.)

Figure 2–15

The sympathetic and parasympathetic divisions of the autonomic nervous system. The sympathetic division generally acts to arouse the body, preparing it for "fight or flight." The parasympathetic follows with messages to relax.

Source: Adapted from *General Biology*, revised edition, 1st edition by Willis Johnson, Richard A. Laubengayer, and Louis E. Delanney, Copyright © 1961. Reprinted with permission of Brooks/Cole, an imprint of the Wadsworth Group, a division of Thomson Learning.

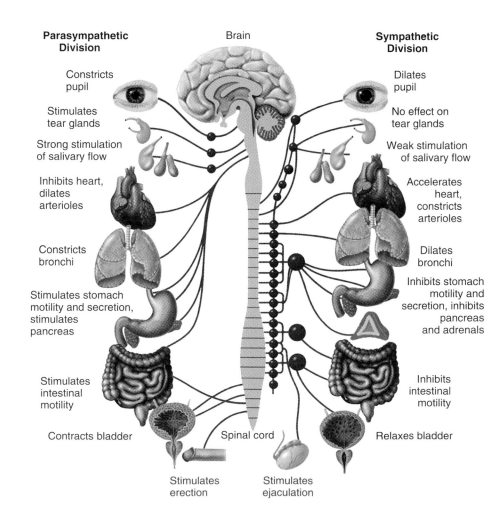

Parasympathetic Division
Constricts pupil
Stimulates tear glands
Strong stimulation of salivary flow
Inhibits heart, dilates arterioles
Constricts bronchi
Stimulates stomach motility and secretion, stimulates pancreas
Stimulates intestinal motility
Contracts bladder
Stimulates erection

Brain

Sympathetic Division
Dilates pupil
No effect on tear glands
Weak stimulation of salivary flow
Accelerates heart, constricts arterioles
Dilates bronchi
Inhibits stomach motility and secretion, inhibits pancreas and adrenals
Inhibits intestinal motility
Relaxes bladder
Stimulates ejaculation

Spinal cord

The nerve fibers of the **sympathetic division** are busiest when you are intensely aroused, such as being enraged or very frightened. For example, if you were hiking through the woods and suddenly encountered a large, growling bear, your sympathetic division would be instantaneously triggered. In response to messages from it, your heart would begin to pound, your breathing would quicken, your pupils would enlarge, and your digestion would stop. All these changes would help direct your energy and attention to the emergency you faced, giving you the keen senses, stamina, and strength needed to flee from the danger or to stand and fight it. Your sympathetic division would also tell your glands to start pumping hormones into your blood to further strengthen your body's reactions. Sympathetic nerve fibers connect to every internal organ—a fact that explains why the body's response to sudden danger is so widespread.

Although sympathetic reactions are often sustained even after danger is passed, eventually even the most intense sympathetic division reaction fades and the body calms down, returning to normal. The heart then goes back to beating at its regular rate, the stomach muscles relax, digestion resumes, breathing slows down, and the pupils contract. This calming effect is promoted by the **parasympathetic division** of the autonomic nervous system. Parasympathetic nerve fibers connect to the same organs as sympathetic nerve fibers do, but they cause the opposite reaction. So, whereas the sympathetic division arouses the body's organs in response to danger and stress, the parasympathetic division calms them once the threat has passed.

Traditionally, the autonomic nervous system was regarded as the "automatic" part of the body's response mechanism (hence its name). You could not, it was believed, tell your own autonomic nervous system when to speed up or slow down your heartbeat or when to stop or start your digestive processes. However, studies in the 1960s and 1970s showed that humans (and animals) have some control over the autonomic nervous system. For example, people can learn to moderate the severity of high blood pressure (Buist, 2002) or migraine headaches (Hermann & Blanchard, 2002), and even to regulate their own heart rate and brain waves (Monastra, Monastra, & George, 2002) through *biofeedback*, a subject we will look at more closely in Chapter 5, "Learning."

When you are in a frightening situation, such as being confronted with an angry bear, the sympathetic division of the autonomic nervous system triggers a number of responses within your body. These responses give you the strength and stamina to either fight the danger or flee from it.

CHECK YOUR UNDERSTANDING

Indicate whether each function is associated with the sympathetic (S) or the parasympathetic (P) division of the autonomic nervous system.

1. ___ heartbeat increases
2. ___ stomach starts digesting food
3. ___ breathing speeds up
4. ___ body recovers from an emergency situation

Answers: 1. (S). 2. (P). 3. (S). 4. (P).

APPLY YOUR UNDERSTANDING

1. The heavy footsteps on the stairs get closer and closer. Slowly, the door to the bedroom creaks open. As a stranger lunges in, you let out an ear-piercing scream. Which of the following most accurately describes your nervous system at this point?
   a. Your sympathetic nervous system is more active than your parasympathetic nervous system.
   b. Your parasympathetic nervous system is more active than your sympathetic nervous system.
   c. Both your sympathetic and your parasympathetic nervous systems are extremely active.
   d. Neither your sympathetic nor your parasympathetic nervous systems are unusually active.

2. John started jogging to lose weight. The first day he ran two miles. The next morning, as he lay in bed relaxing and trying to recover, the nerves of his _____ nervous system made him painfully aware that he had overexercised.
   a. parasympathetic
   b. somatic
   c. autonomic
   d. sympathetic

Answers: 1. a. 2. b.

---

sympathetic division Branch of the autonomic nervous system; it prepares the body for quick action in an emergency.

parasympathetic division Branch of the autonomic nervous system; it calms and relaxes the body.

The Endocrine System

Why are psychologists interested in hormones?

The nervous system is not the only mechanism that regulates the functioning of our bodies. The endocrine system plays a key role in helping to coordinate and integrate complex psychological reactions. In fact, as we've noted throughout this chapter, the nervous system and the endocrine system work together in a constant chemical conversation. The **endocrine glands** release chemical substances called **hormones** that are carried throughout your body by the bloodstream. Hormones serve a similar function to neurotransmitters: They carry messages. Indeed, the same substance—for example, norepinephrine—may serve both as a neurotransmitter and as a hormone. A main difference between the nervous and the endocrine systems is speed. A nerve impulse may travel through the body in a few hundredths of a second. Traveling through the bloodstream is a slower process: Hormones may take seconds, even minutes, to reach their target.

Hormones interest psychologists for two reasons. First, at certain stages of development, hormones *organize* the nervous system and body tissues. At puberty, for example, hormone surges trigger the development of secondary sex characteristics, including breasts in females, a deeper voice in males, and pubic and underarm hair in both sexes. Second, hormones *activate* behaviors. They affect such things as alertness or sleepiness, excitability, sexual behavior, ability to concentrate, aggressiveness, reactions to stress, even desire for companionship. Hormones can also have dramatic effects on mood, emotional reactivity, ability to learn, and ability to resist disease. Radical changes in some hormones may also contribute to serious psychological disorders, such as depression. The locations of the endocrine glands are shown in **Figure 2–16**. Here, we focus on those glands whose functions are best understood and that have the most impact on behavior and mental processes.

The **pituitary gland**, which is located on the underside of the brain, is connected to the hypothalamus. The pituitary produces the largest number of different hormones and thus has the widest range of effects on the body's functions. In fact, it is often called the "master gland" because of its influential role in regulating other endocrine glands. The pituitary influences blood pressure, thirst, contractions of the uterus during childbirth, milk production, sexual behavior and interest, body growth, the amount of water in the body's cells, and other functions as well.

The pea-sized **pineal gland** is located in the middle of the brain. It secretes the hormone *melatonin*, which helps to regulate sleep–wake cycles. Disturbances in melatonin are responsible, in part, for "jet lag." We will discuss the biological clock in greater detail in Chapter 4, "States of Consciousness."

The **thyroid gland** is located just below the larynx, or voice box. It produces one primary hormone, *thyroxin*, which regulates the body's rate of metabolism and, thus, how alert and energetic people are and how fat or thin they tend to be. An overactive thyroid can produce a variety of symptoms: overexcitability, insomnia, reduced attention span, fatigue, agitation, acting out of character, and making snap decisions, as well as reduced concentration and difficulty focusing on a task. Too little thyroxin leads to the other extreme: constantly feeling tired and wanting to sleep and sleep. It is not surprising that thyroid problems are often misdiagnosed as depression or simply as "problems in living."

Embedded in the thyroid gland are the **parathyroids**—four tiny organs that control and balance the levels of calcium and phosphate in the body, which in turn influence levels of excitability.

The **pancreas** lies in a curve between the stomach and the small intestine. The pancreas controls the level of sugar in the blood by secreting two regulating hormones: *insulin* and *glucagon*. These two hormones work against each other to keep the blood-sugar level properly balanced. Underproduction of insulin leads to *diabetes mellitus*, a chronic disorder characterized by too much sugar in the blood and urine; oversecretion of insulin leads to the chronic fatigue of *hypoglycemia*, a condition in which there is too little sugar in the blood.

The two **adrenal glands** are located just above the kidneys. Each adrenal gland has two parts: an inner core, called the *adrenal medulla*, and an outer layer, called the *adrenal cortex*. Both the adrenal cortex and the adrenal medulla affect the body's reaction to stress.

---

endocrine glands Glands of the endocrine system that release hormones into the bloodstream.

hormones Chemical substances released by the endocrine glands; they help regulate bodily activities.

pituitary gland Gland located on the underside of the brain; it produces the largest number of the body's hormones.

pineal gland A gland located roughly in the center of the brain that appears to regulate activity levels over the course of a day.

thyroid gland Endocrine gland located below the voice box; it produces the hormone thyroxin.

parathyroids Four tiny glands embedded in the thyroid.

pancreas Organ lying between the stomach and small intestine; it secretes insulin and glucagon to regulate blood-sugar levels.

adrenal glands Two endocrine glands located just above the kidneys.

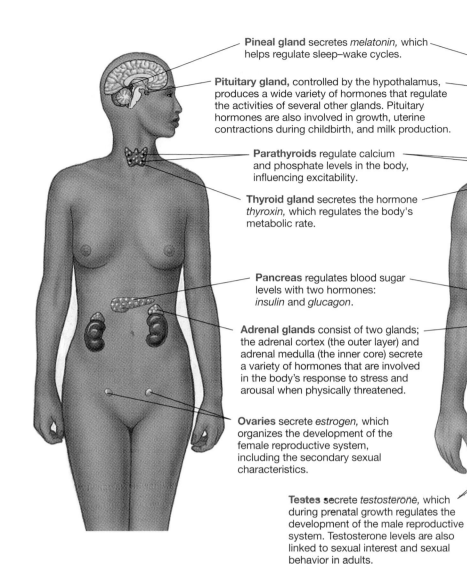

Pineal gland secretes *melatonin,* which helps regulate sleep–wake cycles.

Pituitary gland, controlled by the hypothalamus, produces a wide variety of hormones that regulate the activities of several other glands. Pituitary hormones are also involved in growth, uterine contractions during childbirth, and milk production.

Parathyroids regulate calcium and phosphate levels in the body, influencing excitability.

Thyroid gland secretes the hormone *thyroxin,* which regulates the body's metabolic rate.

Pancreas regulates blood sugar levels with two hormones: *insulin* and *glucagon.*

Adrenal glands consist of two glands; the adrenal cortex (the outer layer) and adrenal medulla (the inner core) secrete a variety of hormones that are involved in the body's response to stress and arousal when physically threatened.

Ovaries secrete *estrogen,* which organizes the development of the female reproductive system, including the secondary sexual characteristics.

Testes secrete *testosterone,* which during prenatal growth regulates the development of the male reproductive system. Testosterone levels are also linked to sexual interest and sexual behavior in adults.

Figure 2–16
The glands of the endocrine system.
Endocrine glands secrete hormones that produce widespread effects on the body.

Stimulated by the autonomic nervous system, the adrenal cortex pours several hormones into the bloodstream. One, *epinephrine,* activates the sympathetic nervous system. Another hormone, *norepinephrine* (also a neurotransmitter), not only raises blood pressure by causing the blood vessels to become constricted, but also is carried by the bloodstream to the anterior pituitary, where it triggers the release of still more hormones, thus prolonging the response to stress. This process is why it takes time for the body to return to normal after extreme emotional excitement. (We will see other examples of this interaction in Chapter 8, "Motivation and Emotion.")

The **gonads**—the *testes* in males and the *ovaries* in females—secrete hormones that have traditionally been classified as masculine (the *androgens*) and feminine (the *estrogens*). (Both sexes produce both types of hormone, but androgens predominate in males, whereas estrogens predominate in females.) These hormones play a number of important organizing roles in human development. For example, in humans, if the hormone *testosterone* is present during the 3rd and 4th month after conception, the fetus will develop as a male; otherwise, it will develop as a female (Kalat, 2001; Knickmeyer et al., 2005).

Testosterone has long been linked to aggressive behavior. For example, violence is greatest among males between the ages of 15 and 25, the years when testosterone levels are highest. However, recent studies suggest that estrogen also may be linked to aggressive behavior in both males and females. For example, male mice that are genetically engineered to lack estrogen receptors are much less aggressive than normal male mice (Ogawa, Lubahn, Korach, & Pfaff, 1997), and in humans, men who have low levels of testosterone report feeling aggressive and irritable before they receive replacement testosterone (Angier, 1995).

gonads The reproductive glands—testes in males and ovaries in females.

Sex hormones may also be linked to a boost in cognitive abilities. Women do better at some cognitive tasks, such as tests of manual dexterity, verbal skills, and perceptual speed, during the ovulatory phase of their menstrual cycles, when estrogen levels are high. Post-menopausal women often show improvement in them when they undergo hormone replacement therapy (Aveleyra, Carranza-Lira, Ulloa-Aguirre, & Ostrosky-Solís, 2005; Kimura & Hampson, 1994), though the long-term impact of hormone replacement therapy on cognition is mixed (O'Hara et al., 2005). Studies with elderly men have also shown that the higher their testosterone levels, the better their performance on cognitive tasks (Yaffe, Yung, Zmuda, & Cauley, 2002).

Interestingly, testosterone levels also appear to differ between married and unmarried men, as well as between married men who have children and those who do not. Research has shown that married men have lower testosterone levels than unmarried men; and this difference is even larger for married men with children (P. B. Gray, Kahlenberg, Barrett, Lipson, & Ellison, 2002). For example, fathers of newborns have a 33% lower testosterone level when compared with father-to-be (Berg & Wynne-Edwards, 2001). Evolutionary psychologists suggest these variations in testosterone level may be associated with a physiological response of the male body that increases the nurturing capacity of men who become fathers and husbands. Further research is necessary, however, to confirm this provocative hypothesis.

CHECK YOUR UNDERSTANDING

1. Communication in the endocrine system depends on _____, which are chemicals secreted directly into the bloodstream.

2. Match each gland with its major function.

___ thyroid gland	a. balance calcium and phosphate in the body
___ parathyroid glands	b. controls sugar level in the blood
___ pineal gland	c. involved in stress response
___ pancreas	d. produce androgens and estrogens
___ pituitary gland	e. regulates rate of metabolism
___ gonads	f. controls other endocrine glands
___ adrenal glands	g. controls daily cycle of activity levels

Answers: 1. hormones. 2. thyroid gland (e); parathyroid glands (a); pineal gland (g); pancreas (b); pituitary gland (f); gonads (d); adrenal glands (c).

APPLY YOUR UNDERSTANDING

1. A clinical psychologist refers a new client to a medical doctor because the client's psychological symptoms could indicate an overactive thyroid gland. What symptoms might the psychologist be responding to?

   a. The client is having trouble getting to sleep and staying asleep.

   b. The client, who in the past was usually careful and thoughtful, is now making careless "snap decisions."

   c. The client finds it increasingly difficult to concentrate and to focus on tasks.

   d. All of the above could be symptoms of an overactive thyroid gland.

2. Mary has been under a great deal of stress lately. Her blood pressure has increased, she has lost her appetite, and her heart is beating faster than usual. These changes are most likely the result of

   a. increased activity in the pineal gland.

   b. reduced activity in the pancreas.

   c. increased activity in the adrenal glands.

   d. reduced activity in the thyroid gland.

Answers: 1. d. 2. c.

Genes, Evolution, and Behavior

Our brain, nervous system, and endocrine system keep us aware of what is happening outside (and inside) our bodies; enable us to use language, think, and solve problems; affect our emotions; and thus guide our behavior. To understand why they function as they do, we need to look at our genetic heritage, as individuals and as members of the human species.

Heredity–Environment   The Pendulum Swings

Try asking a dozen people, "Why are some individuals more intelligent than others?" The chances are most will say "heredity"; intelligence is inborn or innate. If you had asked the same question 25 years ago, in all probability most people would have answered that intelligence is a result of upbringing (that is, of parents who encouraged learning, good schools, and so on). This shift in popular opinion parallels changes in scientific thinking.

For many years, scientists were divided by the so-called "nature versus nurture" debate. Psychologists in one camp emphasized genes and heredity (or nature). Psychologists in the other camp emphasized the environment and experience (or nurture). Most contemporary psychologists view this debate as artificial: Both genes and environment shape human behavior. As described in our section on neural plasticity, researchers have made great strides in understanding how these two forces interact. Nonetheless, strong disagreement still exists regarding the relative influence of heredity and environment on our thoughts, abilities, personalities, and behaviors.

Two different but related fields address the influence of heredity on human behavior. **Behavior genetics** focuses on the extent to which heredity accounts for individual differences in behavior and thinking. **Evolutionary psychology** studies the evolutionary roots of behaviors and mental processes that all human beings share. To understand the contributions of these fields, we must first understand the process of inheritance. ●●

GENETICS

How are traits passed from one generation to the next?

Genetics is the study of how living things pass on traits from one generation to the next. Offspring are not carbon copies or "clones" of their parents, yet some traits reappear from generation to generation in predictable patterns. Around the beginning of the 20th century, scientists named the basic units of inheritance **genes**. But they did not know what genes were or how they were transmitted. Today, however, we know much more about genes and the way they work. To understand more about these blueprints for development, let's take a look at some cellular components.

As shown in **Figure 2–17**, the nucleus of each cell contains **chromosomes**, tiny threadlike bodies that carry genes—the basic units of heredity. Each chromosome contains hundreds or thousands of genes in fixed locations. Chromosomes vary in size and shape, and usually come in pairs. Each species has a constant number: Mice have 20 pairs, monkeys have 27, and peas have 7. Human beings have 23 pairs of chromosomes in every normal cell, except the sex cells (eggs and sperm), which have only half a set of chromosomes. At fertilization, the chromosomes from the father's sperm link to the chromosomes from the mother's egg, creating a new cell called a *zygote*. That single cell and all of the billions of body cells that develop from it (except sperm and eggs) contain 46 chromosomes, arranged as 23 pairs.

Genes are composed primarily of **deoxyribonucleic acid (DNA)**, a complex organic molecule that looks like two chains twisted around each other in a double-helix pattern. Amazingly, a six-foot strand of DNA is crammed into the nucleus of every cell of your body

behavior genetics Study of the relationship between heredity and behavior.

evolutionary psychology A subfield of psychology concerned with the origins of behaviors and mental processes, their adaptive value, and the purposes they continue to serve.

genetics Study of how traits are transmitted from one generation to the next.

genes Elements that control the transmission of traits; they are found on the chromosomes.

chromosomes Pairs of threadlike bodies within the cell nucleus that contain the genes.

deoxyribonucleic acid (DNA) Complex molecule in a double-helix configuration that is the main ingredient of chromosomes and genes and that forms the code for all genetic information.

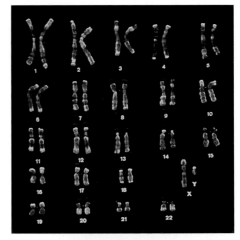

(*Above*) The 23 pairs of chromosomes found in every normal human cell. The two members of 22 of these pairs look exactly alike. The two members of the 23rd pair, the sex chromosomes, may or may not look alike. Females have equivalent X chromosomes, while males have one X and one Y chromosome, which look very different. (*Below*) The chromosome pattern that causes Down syndrome: the presence of three chromosomes in pair 21.

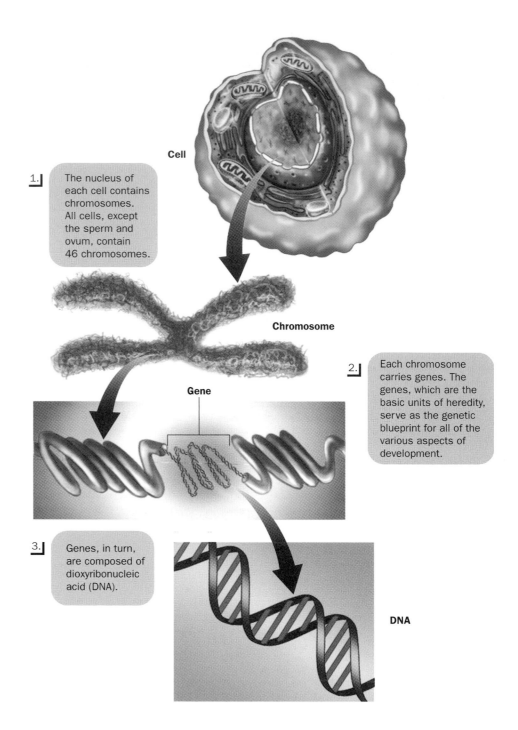

Cell

1. The nucleus of each cell contains chromosomes. All cells, except the sperm and ovum, contain 46 chromosomes.

Chromosome

2. Each chromosome carries genes. The genes, which are the basic units of heredity, serve as the genetic blueprint for all of the various aspects of development.

Gene

3. Genes, in turn, are composed of dioxyribonucleic acid (DNA).

DNA

Figure 2–17

The relation among chromosomes, genes, and DNA.

dominant gene Member of a gene pair that controls the appearance of a certain trait.

recessive gene Member of a gene pair that can control the appearance of a certain trait only if it is paired with another recessive gene.

(Travis, 2004). DNA is the only known molecule that can replicate or reproduce itself, which happens each time a cell divides.

Genes, like chromosomes, occur in pairs. In some cases, such as eye color, one may be a **dominant gene** (B for brown eyes) and the other a **recessive gene** (b for blue eyes). A child who inherits the gene for blue eyes from both parents (bb) will have blue eyes. (See **Figure 2–18**.) A sibling who inherits the gene for brown eyes from both parents (BB) will have brown eyes. And, because the brown-eye gene dominates, so will a sibling who inherits the gene for brown eyes from one parent and the gene for blue eyes from the other (Bb or bB).

POLYGENIC INHERITANCE Thus far, we have been talking about single-gene inheritance: We have said that a gene is a small segment of DNA that carries directions for a particular trait or group of traits. Examples of a single gene that controls a single trait are rare, however. In **polygenic inheritance**, multiple genes contribute to a particular trait. Weight, height, skin pigmentation, intelligence and countless other characteristics are polygenic. Just as each of the instruments in a symphony orchestra contributes separate notes to the sound that reaches the audience, each of the genes in a polygenic system contributes separately to the total effect.

Your own unique genetic "blueprint" is internally coded on your 46 matched chromosomes and is called your **genotype**. Except for reproductive cells, your genotype is contained in every cell in your body. But heredity need not be immediately or fully apparent. Even identical twins, who have the same genotype, differ in small ways that allow family members to tell them apart. In some cases, expression of a trait is delayed until later in life. For example, many men inherit "male-pattern baldness" that does not show up until middle age. Moreover, quite often genes may predispose a person to developing a particular trait, but full expression of the characteristic depends on environmental factors. Given the same environment, for example, a person who inherits "tall" genes will be tall, and a person who inherits "short" genes, short. But if the first person is malnourished in childhood and the second person is well nourished as a child, they may be the same height as adults. Since an individual's genotype does not always obviously correspond directly to what is expressed, we use the term **phenotype** when referring to the *outward expression* of a trait. For example, people with an inherited tendency to gain weight (genotype) may or may not become obese (phenotype), depending on their diet, exercise program, and overall health.

We have seen that physical characteristics can reflect the interaction of more than one gene and that environmental factors can have an impact on genetic expression. But how many genes do we have? We'll learn about this in the next section.

THE HUMAN GENOME The term *genome* refers to the full complement of an organism's genetic material (all the genes and all the chromosomes). Thus, the genome for any particular organism contains a complete blueprint for building all the structures and directing all the living processes for the lifetime of that organism. The **human genome**, the sum total of all the genes necessary to build a human being, is approximately 20,000 to 25,000 genes, located on the 23 pairs of chromosomes that make up human DNA. At first that seems like

polygenic inheritance Process by which several genes interact to produce a certain trait; responsible for our most important traits.

genotype An organism's entire unique genetic makeup.

phenotype The characteristics of an organism; determined by both genetics and experience.

human genome The full complement of genes within a human cell.

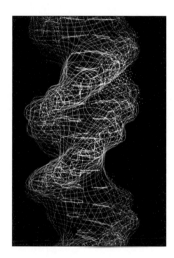

The twisted chain of the long DNA molecule contains the genetic code.

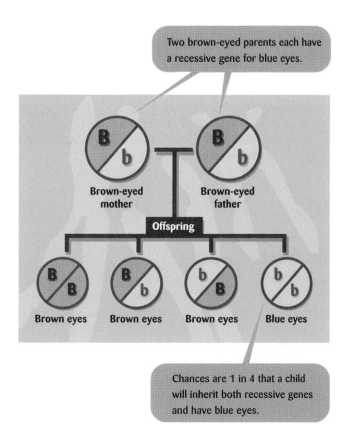

Two brown-eyed parents each have a recessive gene for blue eyes.

Brown-eyed mother

Brown-eyed father

Offspring

Brown eyes

Brown eyes

Brown eyes

Blue eyes

Chances are 1 in 4 that a child will inherit both recessive genes and have blue eyes.

Figure 2–18

Transmission of eye color by dominant (B) and recessive (b) genes.
This figure represents the four possible combinations of eye-color genes in these parents' offspring. Because three out of the four combinations result in brown-eyed children, the chance that any child will have brown eyes is 75%.

a surprisingly small number for our species (Lincoln, 2004) since these genes, contained within every cell of our body, distinguish us from other forms of life. However, only very small variations in the genetic code distinguish humans from other organisms. For instance, humans share 98.7% of their genes with chimpanzees (Olson & Varki, 2003). Even smaller variations in the human genome are responsible for the individual differences we see in the world's 6 billion people. Experts believe that the average variation in the human genetic code for any two different people (such as Hillary Rodham Clinton and Britney Spears) is much less than 1%.

In June 2000, researchers working on the *Human Genome Project* announced the first rough map of the entire human genome. The results of this project have already led researchers to identify genes on specific chromosomes that are associated with Alzheimer's disease (Papassotiropoulos et al., 2002), alcoholism (Kim et al., 2004), schizophrenia (Fan & Sklar, 2005; Kendler et al., 2000), suicide (Abbar et al., 2001; Du et al., 1999), cognitive functioning (Gécz & Mulley, 2000; T. E. Goldberg & Weinberger, 2004), intelligence (Plomin & Spinath, 2004), and even mathematical ability (Kovas, Harlaar, Petrill, & Plomin, 2005). By using these genetic markers, researchers expect not only to prevent or reverse some genetic diseases, but also to understand better the role of heredity in even the most complex behaviors (Kelsoe, 2004; Plomin & Asbury, 2005; Plomin, DeFries, Craig, & McGuffin, 2003). Moreover, in forensic science, application of advances in genetics have already begun to play a important role in identifying potential suspects based on DNA left at the scene of a crime, and exonerating the wrongly accused, sometimes after years of wrongful imprisonment (Lazer, 2004).

Although rich with promise, the Human Genome Project raises many social and ethical questions (N. B. Anderson & Nickerson, 2005; Kissell, 2002). For example, will predicting the likelihood of cancer in an individual lead to discrimination from potential employers and insurers? Will the knowledge that a person has a 25% chance of producing a child with Parkinson's disease affect their choices about having children? How will the products of the Human Genome Project, such as medicines and diagnostic techniques, be patented, commercialized, and shared by the international community? Fortunately, committees made up of ethicists, physicians, researchers, and other concerned professionals have already begun to confront many of these issues. As our understanding of human genetic inheritance continues to grow, it will not, we hope, outpace our understanding of how to apply this knowledge in ways that are both effective and socially responsible.

In this section, we've discussed mechanisms of heredity and dramatic advances in genetics that may someday lead to functional improvements in a variety of medical arenas. For the most part, we have used physical characteristics as examples. Behavior geneticists apply the same principles to *psychological* characteristics.

BEHAVIOR GENETICS

What methods do psychologists use to study the effects of genes on behavior?

Behavior geneticists study the topics that interest all psychologists—perception, learning and memory, motivation and emotions, personality, and psychological disorders—but from a genetic perspective. Their goal is to identify what genes contribute to intelligence, temperament, talents, and other characteristics, as well as genetic predispositions to psychological and neurological disorders (Cunningham, 2003; DiLalla, 2004; Plomin, 1999; Spinath, Harlaar, Ronald, & Plomin, 2004). Of course, genes do not directly cause behavior. Rather, they affect both the development and operation of the nervous system and the endocrine system, which, in turn,

People clearly do inherit physical traits from their parents. Whether—and to what extent—they also inherit behavioral traits remains uncertain.

influence the likelihood that a certain behavior will occur under certain circumstances (Moffitt, 2005; Wahlsten, 1999).

In the remainder of this chapter, we will look at some of the methods used by behavior geneticists as well as some of their more interesting discoveries. We will start with methods appropriate for animal studies and then examine the techniques used to study behavior genetics in humans.

ANIMAL BEHAVIOR GENETICS Much of what we know about behavior genetics comes from studies of nonhuman animals. Mice are favorite subjects because they breed quickly and have relatively complex behavior patterns. In **strain studies**, close relatives, such as siblings, are intensively inbred over many generations to create strains of animals that are genetically similar to one another, but different from other strains. When animals from different strains are raised together in the same environment, differences between them largely reflect genetic differences in the strains. This method has shown that performance on learning tasks, as well as sense of smell and susceptibility to seizures, are affected by heredity.

Selection studies are another way to assess *heritability*, the degree to which a trait is inherited. If a trait is closely regulated by genes, when animals with the trait are interbred, more of their offspring should have the trait than one would find in the general population. Humans have practiced selective breeding for thousands of years to create breeds of dogs and other domesticated animals that have desirable traits—both physical and psychological. Today, with more than 400 breeds, dogs are more variable in size and shape than any other species, with the possible exception of humans.

HUMAN BEHAVIOR GENETICS For obvious reasons, scientists cannot conduct strain or selection studies with human beings. But there are a number of ways to study behavioral techniques indirectly (Faith, 2005; Hutchison, Stallings, McGeary, & Bryan, 2004).

strain studies Studies of the heritability of behavioral traits using animals that have been inbred to produce strains that are genetically similar to one another.

selection studies Studies that estimate the heritability of a trait by breeding animals with other animals that have the same trait.

ON THE CUTTING EDGE

MIRROR NEURONS: SEEING OURSELVES IN OTHERS

Have you ever been at an exciting sporting event and noticed the person sitting next to you moving as though he was actually participating in the game? Or perhaps during a scary scene in a movie—when the hero was creeping closer to danger—you noticed your own leg muscles tensing as if you were in the actor's place? It turns out that there are specialized neurons whose function is to cause us to mimic what others are doing.

Just over a decade ago, a team of Italian neuroscientists led by Giacomo Rizzolatti discovered special neurons that fired in a monkey's brain when it grabbed an object. Interestingly, the same neurons fired when the animal witnessed another monkey grab an object. Subsequently, scientists found that these special cells, or *mirror neurons*, exist in other primates as well (Fadiga, Fogassi, Pavesi, & Rizzolatti, 1995). Initially these findings did not attract much attention. What's more, scientists were puzzled about the purpose of such neurons. However, one prominent neuroscientist later hailed this finding as one of the most important discoveries of the decade, predicting this discovery "will do for psychology what DNA did for biology" (Ramachandran, 2005; see also Winerman, 2005). Scientists now believe that mirror neurons allow a primate's brain to mimic the sensations and feelings experienced by other related animals and, thus, to identify and empathize with them (Rizzolatti, 2005).

Mirror neurons are especially prevalent in humans (Rizzolatti, Fadiga, Fogassi, Gallese, 2002) and, not surprisingly, humans also reflexively mimic the behavior of others. For example, scientists have shown that when people were exposed to a noxious odor, mirror neurons that fired up when they wrinkled their noses in disgust also reacted when participants viewed a short film of an actor wrinkling *his* nose (Wicker et al., 2003). Such research suggests that mirror neurons allow humans to mimic not only other humans' actions but also their emotions. Interestingly, fewer active mirror neurons are present in humans diagnosed with autism, a mental disorder characterized by a limited capacity for imitation, empathy, and other crucial social abilities (Oberman et al., 2005).

The tendency for primates to identify with the behaviors and emotions of others is obviously of central importance to the development of learning by imitation, understanding the behavior of others, the development of language, and many other social skills (Rizzolatti & Craighero, 2004). Indeed, mirror neurons may provide a clue to why humans and many of our closest primate relatives have developed such remarkably sophisticated social systems (Rizzolatti, Gallese, & Keysers, 2004). Realizing that others are fundamentally like us is at the heart of all social interaction and the foundation of all social systems.

family studies Studies of heritability in humans based on the assumption that if genes influence a certain trait, close relatives should be more similar on that trait than distant relatives.

twin studies Studies of identical and fraternal twins to determine the relative influence of heredity and environment on human behavior.

identical twins Twins developed from a single fertilized ovum and therefore identical in genetic makeup at the time of conception.

fraternal twins Twins developed from two separate fertilized ova and therefore different in genetic makeup.

Family studies are based on the assumption that if genes influence a trait, close relatives should share that trait more often than distant relatives, because close relatives have more genes in common. For example, overall, schizophrenia occurs in only 1 to 2% of the general population (N. L. Nixon & Doody, 2005; L. N. Robins & Regier, 1991). Siblings of people with schizophrenia, however, are about 8 times more likely (and children of schizophrenic parents about 10 times more likely) to develop the disorder than someone chosen randomly from the general population. Unfortunately, because family members share not only some genes but also similar environments, family studies alone cannot clearly distinguish the effects of heredity and environment.

To obtain a clearer picture of the influences of heredity and environment, psychologists often use **twin studies**. **Identical twins** develop from a single fertilized ovum and are therefore identical in genetic makeup at conception. Any differences between them must be due to their experiences. **Fraternal twins**, however, develop from two separate fertilized egg cells and are no more similar genetically than are other brothers and sisters. If twin pairs grow up in similar environments and if identical twins are no more alike in a particular characteristic than fraternal twins, then heredity cannot be very important for that trait.

Twin studies suggest that heredity plays a crucial role in schizophrenia. When one identical twin develops schizophrenia, the chances that the other twin will develop the disorder are about 50%. For fraternal twins, the chances are about 15% (Gottesman, 1991). Such studies have also provided evidence for the heritability of a wide variety of other behaviors, including verbal skills (Viding et al., 2004), mild intellectual impairment (Spinath, Harlaar, Ronald, & Plomin, 2004), aggressiveness (Eley, Lichenstein, & Stevenson, 1999), compulsive gambling (Shah, Eisen, Xianj, & Potenza, 2005), depression, anxiety, and eating disorders (Eley & Stevenson, 1999; O'Connor, McGuire, Reiss, Hetherington, & Plomin, 1998; Silberg & Bulik, 2005). Identical twins are also very similar in the traits they value when selecting a friend or a spouse (Rushton & Bons, 2005).

Identical twins develop from a single ovum and consequently start out with the same genetic material.

Similarities between twins, even identical twins, cannot automatically be attributed to genes, however; twins nearly always grow up together. Parents and others may treat them alike—or try to emphasize their differences, so that they grow up as separate individuals. In either case, the data for heritability may be biased. To avoid this problem, researchers attempt to locate identical twins who were separated at birth or in very early childhood and then raised in different homes. A University of Minnesota team led by Thomas Bouchard followed separated twins for more than 10 years (Bouchard, 1984, 1996; Bouchard et al., 1990; Johnson, Bouchard, Segal, & Samuel, 2005). They confirmed that genetics plays a major role in mental retardation, schizophrenia, depression, reading skill, and intelligence. Bouchard and his colleagues have also found that complex personality traits, interests, and talents, and even the structure of brain waves, are guided by genetics.

Studies of twins separated shortly after birth have also drawn criticism. For example, the environment in the uterus may be more traumatic for one twin than the other (Foley, Neale, & Kendler, 2000; J. A. Phelps, Davis, & Schartz, 1997). Also, since adoption agencies usually try to place twins in similar families, their environments may not be much different (B. D. Ford, 1993; Wyatt, 1993). Finally, the number of twin pairs separated at birth is fairly small. For these reasons, scientists sometimes rely on other types of studies to investigate the influence of heredity.

THINKING CRITICALLY ABOUT . . .

Mirror Neurons

1. Assuming that mirror neurons cause us to mimic the behavior of others, does it follow that they also allow us to mimic the sensations and feelings of others? Can you design an experiment showing whether that is true? Alternatively, what kind of evidence would you need before you would be willing to conclude that mirror neurons allow us to mimic the sensations and emotions of others?

2. Going one step further, what kind of evidence would you need before you would be willing to conclude that, in fact, the ability to identify and empathize with others depends on the activity of mirror neurons?

3. Do you agree that the ability to empathize with others is "at the heart of all social interaction and the foundation of all social systems?" Why or why not? Are other abilities also essential?

Adoption studies focus on children who were adopted at birth and brought up by parents not genetically related to them. Adoption studies provide additional evidence for the heritability of intelligence and some forms of mental illness (Kato & Pedersen, 2005; Scarr & Weinberg, 1983) and the role of genetics in behavior previously thought to be solely determined by environmental influences, even smoking (Kendler, Thornton, & Pedersen, 2000).

By combining the results of *twin, adoption*, and *family* studies, psychologists have obtained a clearer picture of the role of heredity in many human characteristics, including schizophrenia. As shown in **Figure 2–19**, the average risk of schizophrenia steadily increases in direct relation to the closeness of one's biological relationship to an individual with the disorder.

SOCIAL IMPLICATIONS

What are some of the ethical issues that arise as society gains more control over genetics?

Science is not simply a process that takes place in a laboratory; it can also have widespread effects on society at large. To the extent that we can trace individual differences in human behavior to chromosomes and genes, we have a potential, biologically, to control people's lives. This potential raises new ethical issues.

Modern techniques of prenatal screening now make it possible to detect many genetic defects even before a baby is born. *Chorionic villus sampling* and *amniocentesis* are two procedures for obtaining samples of cells from fetuses in order to analyze their genes. In the first, the cells are taken from membranes surrounding the fetus; in the second, the cells are harvested from the fluid in which the fetus grows. Using these procedures, genetic problems are detected in about 2% of pregnancies. Does the child in these cases nonetheless have a right to live? Do the parents have a right to abort the fetus? Should society protect all life, no matter how imperfect it is in the eyes of some? If not, which defects are so unacceptable that abortion is justified? Most of these questions have a long history, but recent progress in behavior genetics and medicine has given them a new urgency. We are reaching the point at which we will be able to intervene in a fetus's development by replacing some of its genes with others. For which traits might this procedure be considered justified, and who has the right to make those decisions? If in tampering with genes we significantly change our society's gene pool, are future generations harmed or benefited? Such questions pose major ethical dilemmas, and it is important that we all think critically about them (Barinaga, 2000; Patenaude, 2005; Patenaude, Guttmacher, & Collins, 2002; Pelletier & Dorval, 2004).

Another concern is one that centers on the difficulty in understanding the complex new genetic technologies and their implications. Although scientists are careful to report their research findings accurately and to use appropriate caution in suggesting how results might be applied, the mass media often report these findings in overly simplified, "either–or" sound bites ("scientists have discovered a gene for x"). As a result, the pendulum of popular opinion seems to have swung from an environmental (or a nurture) position, which holds that all people have significant potential, to a genetic (or nature) position, which

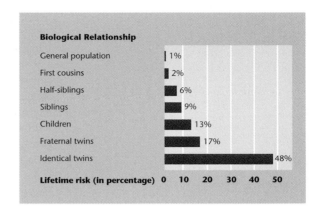

Figure 2–19

Average risk of schizophrenia among biological relatives of people with schizophrenia.

Source: Gill, M. (2004, October). Genetic approaches to the understanding of mental illness. Paper presented at the 12th World Congress on Psychiatric Genetics, Dublin, Ireland. Retrieved March 10, 2006, from *http://www.tcd.ie/Psychiatry/Neuropsychiatry/ Genes&MentalHealth.pdf*

adoption studies Research carried out on children, adopted at birth by parents not related to them, to determine the relative influence of heredity and environment on human behavior.

THINKING CRITICALLY ABOUT . . .

Media Accounts of Research

What is wrong with this headline?

"Scientists Find Gene for Intelligence"

Robert Plomin (1998) compared genetic data on 50 children whose SAT scores were equivalent to IQ scores of 160 or higher to a control group. He found that a variant of a particular gene was twice as common in children with ultra-high IQs as in children with average IQs (scores of 100). Scientists estimate that about 50% of the variation in IQ scores is due to heredity. The gene had a small effect, accounting for about 2% of the variance among individuals, or 4 IQ points, but the researchers made an important first step in uniting biological technology with behavioral genetics.

What rules of critical thinking did this headline ignore? How would you rewrite this headline?

Hints: Consider the size of the sample, the danger of focusing on extremes, and what "heritability" means.

holds that intelligence, temperament, and other qualities are inborn (DeWaal, 1999). Again, it is important to think critically about research, and to remember that human behavior is the result of the complex interplay of *both* heredity and environment.

So far, we have been talking about the environment as if it were something *out there*, something that happens *to* people, over which they have little control. But individuals also shape their environments. The genes and predispositions individuals inherit alter the environment in several ways (Plomin, DeFries, Craig, & McGuffin, 2003). For example, people tend to seek environments in which they feel comfortable. A shy child might prefer a quieter play group than would a child who is more outgoing. In addition, our own behavior causes others to respond in particular ways. A teacher's approach to correcting the behavior of a sensitive child might be quite different from how a more energetic child would be treated. Because genes and environments interact in so many intricate ways, trying to separate and isolate the effects of heredity and environment—nature and nurture—is artificial (Collins, Maccoby, Steinberg, Hetherington & Bornstein, 2000, 2001; Plomin & Asbury, 2005). The interaction of genes and environment is also a key element in evolutionary psychology.

The study of behavior genetics and that of evolutionary psychology, which we will consider next, makes many people uneasy. Some fear that it may lead to the conclusion that who we are is written in some kind of permanent ink before we are born. Some people also fear that research in these fields could be used to undermine movements toward social equality. But far from finding human behavior to be genetically predetermined, recent work in behavior genetics shows just how important the environment is in determining which genetic predispositions come to be expressed and which do not (Rutter, 1997). In other words, we may inherit predispositions, but we do not inherit destinies. The emerging picture confirms that both heredity and environment (nature and nurture) together shape most significant behaviors and traits (Plomin, DeFries, Craig, & McGuffin, 2003; Plomin & Asbury, 2005).

EVOLUTIONARY PSYCHOLOGY

How might the process of natural selection influence human social behaviors?

Much as behavior geneticists try to explain the individual differences in human behavior, evolutionary psychologists try to explain the behavioral traits that people have in common. The key to these shared characteristics, they feel, is the process of evolution by **natural selection**, first described by Charles Darwin in *On the Origin of Species* (1859).

According to the principle of natural selection, those organisms that are best adapted to their environments are most likely to survive and reproduce. If the traits that give them a survival advantage are genetically based, those same genetic characteristics are passed on to their offspring. Organisms that do not possess the adaptive traits tend to die off before they reproduce, and hence, the less-adaptive traits do not get passed along to future generations.

Natural selection, therefore, promotes the survival and reproduction of individuals who are genetically well adapted to their particular environment. If the environment changes or the individual moves into a new environment, the survival and reproductive value of inherited characteristics may also change, and so eventually may the frequency of genes in the population's gene pool.

As described in Chapter 1, evolutionary psychologists study the origins of behaviors and mental processes, emphasizing the adaptive or survival value of such traits. Rather than focusing on the *structural* changes in organisms, as evolutionary biologists do, evolutionary psychologists look at the role that natural selection might have played in selecting for adaptive *behaviors*, especially during the long period that our ancestors lived as hunter–gatherers. They argue that, just as our hands and upright posture are products of natural selection, so are our brains. As a result, our brains are "prewired" to learn some things more easily than others, to analyze problems in certain ways, and to communicate in distinctively human ways.

Evolutionary psychologists cite language as a prime example (Crow, 2004; Pinker, 1994, 1997, 2002). As we will see in Chapter 9, "Life-Span Development," all normal

natural selection The mechanism proposed by Darwin in his theory of evolution, which states that organisms best adapted to their environment tend to survive, transmitting their genetic characteristics to succeeding generations, whereas organisms with less adaptive characteristics tend to vanish from the earth.

children acquire language without specific instruction; children in different cultures acquire language at about the same ages and in predictable stages; and the underlying structure of all human languages (nouns and verbs, subjects and objects, questions and conditional phrases, and so on) is basically the same. Taken as a whole, evolutionary psychologists argue, the evidence strongly suggests that our human brains have a built-in "program" for language. In support of this notion, scientists recently identified a specific gene, distinct to humans, which may have played a pivotal role in stimulating the emergence of language among our early ancestors (Enard et al., 2002).

Evolutionary psychologists cite mate selection as another example. In choosing a partner, males and females tend to pursue different strategies. Why? Evolutionary psychologists answer this way: Human females usually have only one child at a time. Women also invest more in each child than men do—going through pregnancy, caretaking, and providing nourishment. It would seem to be most adaptive for females to look for males who will provide the best genes, resources, and long-term parental care. Males, on the other hand, are limited only by the number of prospective mates they can attract, because sperm are plentiful and quickly replaced. It may be most adaptive for males to seek to mate with as many females as they can and to compete with other males for access to females. Studies analyzing human behaviors associated with sexual selection have found that men and women do indeed take different approaches to sexuality, mate choice, and aggression, as predicted by evolutionary psychology (Buss, 2000b, 2004; Callahan, 2000; Chuang, 2002; Pawloski, Dunbar, & Lipowicz, 2000). In comparing evolutionary explanations with more traditional social-learning explanations of sex differences in social behavior, it appears that evolutionary psychology does a much better job of accounting for overall patterns (Archer, 1996).

Evolutionary psychology is not without its critics (Siegert & Ward, 2002). Some opponents argue that science is being used to justify perpetuating unjust social policies. These critics claim that simply by saying a trait is adaptive implies that it is both genetically determined and good. In the past, racists and fascists have misused biological theories to promote social injustices. In Nazi Germany, for example, Jews were considered genetically inferior, a view that was used to justify their extermination. Similarly, the evolutionary theory of male–female differences in mate selection could be seen as endorsing male promiscuity, since it is biologically adaptive. In response, evolutionary psychologists are quick to point out that their aim is not to shape social policy, but to understand the origins of human behavior. They argue further that behaviors that may have contributed to our adaptive success during the early years of human evolution may no longer be adaptive in our current environment and therefore should not be viewed as good and right simply because at one time they may have once served an important adaptive function (Pinker, 2002).

Other critics chide evolutionary psychologists for too hastily explaining behaviors from an evolutionary perspective, rather than investigating other plausible origins of them. They argue that, just because a behavior occurs to some degree across a wide variety of cultures, it does not necessarily mean that it has evolutionary roots. Evolutionary psychologists answer that their goal is not to propose evolutionary theories that exclude all other possible explanations; instead, their aim is to offer an evolutionary perspective that may complement other points of view.

As a relatively new approach in psychology, the evolutionary perspective has yet to take its place among psychology's most respected theoretical paradigms. Only the results of empirical research, which compares evolutionary explanations with competing theoretical explanations of behavior, will determine the fate of this provocative and intriguing new perspective.

THINKING CRITICALLY ABOUT...

Depression

We have touched on depression a number of times in this chapter: in our discussion of neuropharmacology, hormones, hemispheric specialization, behavioral genetics, and, here, evolutionary psychology. Based on what you have read:

- Is depression inherited (nature), acquired (nurture), or both?
- Are these different perspectives on depression mutually exclusive or complementary?
- Do psychologists know what causes depression?

Hints: Avoid either/or thinking, confusing correlation with cause and effect, and jumping to conclusions. Look for alternative explanations, for example, the possibility that there are different forms of depression, with different origins.

CHECK YOUR UNDERSTANDING

Are the following statements true (T) or false (F)?

1. ___ "Individual differences in intelligence, emotional reactivity, and susceptibility to schizophrenia and depression may all be influenced by genes."

2. ___ *Neuropsychology* is the study of how traits are passed from one generation to another.

Answers: 1. (T). 2. (F).

APPLY YOUR UNDERSTANDING

1. A woman exhibits a recessive characteristic such as blue eyes. Her children _____ exhibit the same trait.

   a. definitely will

   b. may or may not

   c. will definitely *not*

2. Imagine that psychologists document a long history of criminal behavior in a family: children, their parents, their grandparents, and even their great-grandparents have long lists of convictions for crimes. Knowing only this, the most reasonable conclusion you can draw is that criminal behavior is most likely due to

   a. genetic factors.

   b. environmental factors.

   c. a combination of genetic and environmental factors.

Answers: 1. b. 2. c.

KEY TERMS

psychobiology, *p. 43*
neuroscience, *p. 43*

Neurons: The Messengers

neurons, *p. 44*
dendrites, *p. 44*
axon, *p. 44*
nerve (or tract), *p. 44*
myelin sheath, *p. 44*
sensory (or afferent)
  neurons, *p. 45*
motor (or efferent)
  neurons, *p. 45*
interneurons (or association
  neurons), *p. 45*
glial cells (or glia), *p. 45*
ions, *p. 46*
resting potential, *p. 46*
polarization, *p. 46*
neural impulse (or action
  potential), *p. 47*
graded potential, *p. 47*
threshold of excitation, *p. 47*
all-or-none law, *p. 47*
synaptic space (or synaptic
  cleft, *p. 47*

synapse, *p. 47*
terminal button (or synaptic
  knob), *p. 48*
synaptic vesicles, *p. 48*
neurotransmitters, *p. 48*
receptor sites, *p. 48*
neural plasticity, *p. 50*
neurogenesis, *p. 52*

The Central Nervous System

central nervous system
  (CNS), *p. 53*
peripheral nervous system
  (PNS), *p. 53*
hindbrain, *p. 54*
medulla, *p. 54*
pons, *p. 55*
cerebellum, *p. 55*
midbrain, *p. 56*
thalamus, *p. 56*
hypothalamus, *p. 56*
reticular formation (RF), *p. 56*
cerebral cortex, *p. 56*
association areas, *p. 56*
frontal lobe, *p. 56*
primary motor cortex, *p. 56*

occipital lobe, *p. 57*
parietal lobe, *p. 57*
primary somatosensory
  cortex, *p. 58*
temporal lobe, *p. 58*
limbic system, *p. 58*
corpus callosum, *p. 58*
aphasias, *p. 61*
spinal cord, *p. 64*

The Peripheral Nervous System

afferent neurons, *p. 66*
efferent neurons, *p. 66*
somatic nervous system, *p. 66*
autonomic nervous
  system, *p. 66*
sympathetic division, *p. 67*
parasympathetic division, *p. 67*

The Endocrine System

endocrine glands, *p. 68*
hormones, *p. 68*
pituitary gland, *p. 68*
pineal gland, *p. 68*
thyroid gland, *p. 68*
parathyroids, *p. 68*

pancreas, *p. 68*
adrenal glands, *p. 68*
gonads, *p. 69*

Genes, Evolution, and Behavior

behavior genetics, *p. 71*
evolutionary psychology, *p. 71*
genetics, *p. 71*
genes, *p. 71*
chromosomes, *p. 71*
deoxyribonucleic acid
  (DNA), *p. 71*
dominant gene, *p. 72*
recessive gene, *p. 72*
polygenic inheritance, *p. 73*
genotype, *p. 73*
phenotype, *p. 73*
human genome, *p. 73*
strain studies, *p. 75*
selection studies, *p. 75*
family studies, *p. 76*
twin studies, *p. 76*
identical twins, *p. 76*
fraternal twins, *p. 76*
adoption studies, *p. 77*
natural selection, *p. 78*

CHAPTER REVIEW

Biological processes are the basis of our thoughts, feelings, and actions. All of our behaviors are kept in tune with our surroundings and coordinated with one another through the work of two interacting systems: the nervous system and the endocrine system.

Neurons: The Messengers

What types of cells are found in the nervous system? The basic building block of the nervous system is the **neuron**, or nerve cell. Neurons have several characteristics that distinguish them from other cells. Neurons receive messages from other neurons through short fibers called **dendrites**. A longer fiber, called an **axon**, carries outgoing messages from the cell. A group of axons bundled together forms a **nerve** or **tract**. Some axons are covered with a fatty **myelin sheath** made up of **glial cells**; this increases neuron efficiency and provides insulation.

What "language" do neurons speak? When a neuron is at rest (a state called the **resting potential**), there is a slightly higher concentration of negatively charged **ions** inside its membrane than there is outside. The membrane is said to be **polarized**—that is, the electrical charge inside it is negative relative to its outside. When an incoming message is strong enough, this electrical imbalance abruptly changes (the membrane is depolarized), and an **action potential** (**neural impulse**) is generated. Incoming messages cause **graded potentials**, which, when combined, may exceed the minimum **threshold of excitation** and make the neuron "fire." After firing, the neuron briefly goes through the **absolute refractory period**, when it will not fire again, and then through the **relative refractory period**, when firing will occur only if the incoming message is much stronger than usual. According to the **all-or-none law**, every firing of a particular neuron produces an impulse of equal strength. More rapid firing of neurons is what communicates the strength of a message.

What happens as information moves from one neuron to the next? **Neurotransmitter** molecules, released by **synaptic** vesicles, cross the tiny **synaptic space** (or **cleft**) between an **axon terminal** (or **terminal button**) of a sending neuron and a dendrite of a receiving neuron. Here they latch on to **receptor sites**, much as keys fit into locks, and pass on their excitatory or inhibitory messages. Psychologists need to understand how **synapses** function because neurotransmitters affect an enormous range of physical and emotional responses.

How does experience change the brain? Can the brain and the nervous system repair themselves? Research demonstrates that experiences in our environments can produce changes in the brain, a principle called **neural plasticity**. Human brains also are capable of **neurogenesis**—the production of new brain cells. The study of neurogenesis may help treat neurological disorders, but also raises ethical questions.

The Central Nervous System

How is the nervous system organized? The nervous system is organized into two parts: the **central nervous system (CNS)**, which consists of the brain and spinal cord, and the **peripheral nervous system (PNS)**, made up of nerves that radiate throughout the body, linking all of the body's parts to the CNS.

What are the major structures and areas of the brain, and what functions do they serve? Physically, the brain has three more-or-less distinct areas: the central core, the limbic system, and the cerebral hemispheres.

The central core consists of the hindbrain, cerebellum, midbrain, thalamus and hypothalamus, and reticular formation. The **hindbrain** is made up of the **medulla**, a narrow structure nearest the spinal cord that controls breathing, heart rate, and blood pressure, and the **pons**, which produces chemicals that maintain our sleep–wake cycle. The medulla is the point at which many of the nerves from the left part of the body cross to the right side of the brain and vice versa. The **cerebellum** controls the sense of balance and coordinates the body's actions. The **midbrain**, which is above the cerebellum, is important for hearing and sight and is one of the places in which pain is registered. The **thalamus** is a relay station that integrates and shapes incoming sensory signals before transmitting them to the higher levels of the brain. The **hypothalamus** is important to motivation, drives, and emotional behavior. The **reticular formation**, which is woven through all of these structures, alerts the higher parts of the brain to incoming messages.

The cerebrum takes up most of the room inside the skull. The outer covering of the cerebral hemispheres is known as the **cerebral cortex**. They are the most recently evolved portion of the brain, and they regulate the most complex behavior. Each cerebral hemisphere is divided into four lobes, delineated by deep fissures on the surface of the brain. The **occipital lobe** of the cortex, located at the back of the head, receives and processes visual information. The **temporal lobe**, located roughly behind the temples, helps us perform complex visual tasks, such as recognizing faces. The **parietal lobe**, which sits on top of the temporal and occipital lobes, receives sensory information from all over the body and oversees spatial abilities. Messages from sensory receptors are registered in the **primary somatosensory cortex**. The **frontal lobe** receives and coordinates messages from the other lobes and keeps track of past and future body movement. It is primarily responsible for goal-directed behavior and is key to the ability to lead a mature emotional life. The **primary motor cortex** is responsible for voluntary movement. The **association areas**—areas that are free to process all kinds of information—make up most of the cerebral cortex and enable the brain to produce behaviors requiring the coordination of many brain areas.

The **limbic system**, a ring of structures located between the central core and the cerebral hemispheres, is a more recent evolutionary development than the central core. It includes the hippocampus, which is essential to the formation of new memories, and the amygdala, which, together with the hippocampus, governs emotions related to self-preservation. Other portions of the limbic system heighten the experience of pleasure. In times of stress, the limbic system coordinates and integrates the nervous system's response.

How are the left and right hemispheres specialized for different functions? The two cerebral hemispheres are linked by the **corpus callosum**, through which they communicate and coordinate their activities. Nevertheless, each hemisphere appears to specialize in certain tasks (although they also have overlapping functions). The right hemisphere excels at visual and spatial tasks, nonverbal imagery, and the perception of emotion, whereas the left hemisphere excels at language and perhaps analytical thinking, too. The right hemisphere controls the left side of the body, and the left hemisphere controls the right side.

What methods have been developed to study the brain? An increasingly sophisticated technology exists for investigating the brain. Among the most important tools are microelectrode techniques, macroelectrode techniques (EEG), structural imaging (CT scanning and MRI), and functional imaging (EEG imaging, MEG, and MSI). Two new functional imaging techniques, PET scanning and fMRI, allow us to observe not only the structure, but also the functioning of parts of the brain. Scientists often combine these techniques to study brain activity in unprecedented detail—information that can help in the treatment of medical and psychological disorders.

What does the spinal cord do? How does it work with the brain to sense events and act on them? The **spinal cord** is a complex cable of nerves that connects the brain to most of the rest of the body. It is made up of bundles of long nerve fibers and has two basic functions: to permit some reflex movements and to carry messages to and from the brain. When a break in the cord disrupts the flow of impulses from the brain below that point, paralysis occurs.

The Peripheral Nervous System

How does the brain communicate with the rest of the body? How is the autonomic branch of the peripheral nervous system involved in controlling emotions? The peripheral nervous system (PNS) contains two types of neurons: **afferent neurons**, which carry sensory messages *to* the central nervous system, and **efferent neurons**, which carry messages *from* the CNS. Neurons involved in making voluntary movements of the skeletal muscles belong to a part of the PNS called the **somatic nervous system**, whereas neurons involved in governing the actions of internal organs belong to a part of the PNS called the autonomic nervous system. The **autonomic nervous system** is itself divided into two parts: the **sympathetic division**, which acts primarily to arouse the body when it is faced with threat, and the **parasympathetic division**, which acts to calm the body down, restoring it to normal levels of arousal.

The Endocrine System

Why are psychologists interested in hormones? The endocrine system is the other communication system in the body. It is made up of **endocrine glands** that produce **hormones**, chemical substances released into the bloodstream to either *trigger* developmental changes in the body or to activate certain behavioral responses.

The **thyroid gland** secretes thyroxin, a hormone involved in regulating the body's rate of metabolism. Symptoms of an overactive thyroid are agitation and tension, whereas an underactive thyroid produces lethargy. The **parathyroids** control and balance the levels of calcium and phosphate in the blood and tissue fluids. This process in turn affects the excitability of the nervous system. The **pineal gland** regulates activity levels over the course of the day and also regulates the sleep–wake cycle. The **pancreas** controls the level of sugar in the blood by secreting insulin and glucagon. When the pancreas secretes too much insulin, the person can suffer *hypoglycemia*. Too little insulin can result in *diabetes mellitus*. Of all the endocrine glands, the **pituitary gland** regulates the largest number of different activities in the body. It affects blood pressure, thirst, uterine contractions in childbirth, milk production, sexual behavior and interest, and the amount and timing of body growth, among other functions. Because of its influences on other glands, it is often called the "master gland." The **gonads**—the testes in males and the ovaries in females—secrete hormones called androgens (including testosterone) and estrogens. Testosterone has long been linked to aggressive behavior, and recent research suggests that estrogen may also play a role in aggression, as well as cognitive ability. Each of the two **adrenal glands** has two parts: an outer covering, the *adrenal cortex*, and an inner core, the *adrenal medulla*. Both affect our response to stress, although the adrenal cortex affects other body functions, too. One stress-related hormone of the adrenal medulla is epinephrine, which amplifies the effects of the sympathetic nervous system.

Genes, Evolution, and Behavior

How are traits passed from one generation to the next? The related fields of **behavior genetics** and **evolutionary psychology** explore the influences of heredity on human behavior. Both are helping to settle the nature-versus-nurture debate over the relative contributions of genes and the environment to human similarities and differences. **Genetics** is the study of how traits are passed on from one generation to the next via genes. This process is called heredity. Each **gene**, or basic unit of inheritance, is lined up on tiny threadlike bodies called **chromosomes**, which in turn are made up predominantly of a complex molecule called **deoxyribonucleic acid (DNA)**. The **human genome** is the full complement of genes necessary to build a human body—approximately 20,000 to 25,000 genes. The Human Genome Project has produced a rough map of the genes on the 23 pairs of human chromosomes. Each member of a gene pair can be either **dominant** or **recessive**. In **polygenic inheritance** a number of genes interact to produce a trait.

What methods do psychologists use to study the effects of genes on behavior? Psychologists use a variety of methods to study *heritability*—that is, the contribution of genes in determining variations in certain traits. **Strain studies** approach the problem by observing strains of highly inbred, genetically similar animals, whereas **selection studies** try to determine the extent to which an animal's traits can be passed on from one generation to another. In the study of humans, **family studies** tackle heritability by looking for similarities in traits as a function of biological closeness. Also useful in studying human heritability are **twin studies** and **adoption studies**.

How might the process of natural selection influence human social behaviors? The theory of evolution by **natural selection** states that organisms best adapted to their environment tend to survive, transmitting their genetic characteristics to succeeding generations, whereas organisms with fewer adaptive characteristics tend to die off. **Evolutionary psychology** analyzes human behavioral tendencies by examining their adaptive value from an evolutionary perspective. While not without its critics, it has proved useful in helping to explain some of the commonalities in human behavior that occur across cultures.

What are some of the ethical issues that arise as society gains more control over genetics? Manipulating human genes in an effort to change how people develop is a new technology that makes many people uneasy, but their concerns may be exaggerated because genes are not all-powerful. Both heredity and environment play a part in shaping most significant human behaviors and traits.

3 Sensation and Perception

OVERVIEW

Enduring Issues in Sensation and Perception

The Nature of Sensation
- Sensory Thresholds
- Subliminal Perception

Vision
- The Visual System
- Color Vision

Hearing
- Sound
- The Ear
- Theories of Hearing

The Other Senses
- Smell
- Taste
- Kinesthetic and Vestibular Senses
- The Skin Senses
- Pain

Perception
- Perceptual Organization
- Perceptual Constancies
- Perception of Distance and Depth
- Perception of Movement
- Visual Illusions
- Observer Characteristics

Smell is sometimes considered the "dispensable" sense—the one we could easily live without if necessary. After all, we enter odorless environments all the time and are not handicapped by the absence of aromas. We are not like dogs, who depend on a keen sense of smell to navigate through the world. Since we use the senses of sight and sound so extensively, how bad could an absence of a sense of smell really be? *Surprisingly devastating,* according to people who suffer a loss of this sensation.

Anita Chang, who lost her sense of smell when hit by an SUV as she was crossing the street, is one of them. When she was thrown backwards by the collision, her head hit the pavement and her brain rebounded forward, smashing into the front of her skull. The front of the brain contains the delicate nerves of the olfactory system; and hers were severely damaged. The smells associated with that traumatic moment are the last ones she ever experienced (Chang, 2006).

For Anita the world has become strangely sterile, as though encased in an impenetrable film of plastic wrap. Odors simply don't get through to her brain. Walking into a bakery is the same as entering a restroom, which is no different than walking through a hyacinth garden in spring. Friends joke that at least she now avoids the unpleasant odors of the city, but Anita does not see it that way. She longs for the aroma of freshly ground coffee, the fragrance of hand creams, and the unmistakable scent of newly mown grass. Thanksgiving is not the same without the smell of turkey roasting in the oven; and Christmas has lost some of its joy without the aromas of pine, bayberry, and cinnamon. Even worse, Anita often feels anxious: Is her stove leaking gas? Has the milk for her cereal gone sour? And what about the noisier-than-usual toaster oven? Might it be starting an electrical fire? Without a sense of smell, it is very hard for Anita to say.

Smell is just one of the senses giving us a window on the world. Evolution has provided us with many others—vision, hearing, taste, touch, pain, pressure, warmth, cold, and the kinetic senses—that combine into a rich mosaic of awareness forming the basis of consciousness. Without sensations, the human mind would be in limbo. It is sensations that give us connections both to our own selves and to our surroundings.

We are constantly being bombarded by bits of sensory information, all competing for attention like vibrant pieces of a jigsaw puzzle, but this is only a starting point. To be meaningful, this kaleidoscope of sensory input must be organized and interpreted. *Perception* is the mental process of sorting, identifying, and arranging these bits of raw data into coherent patterns. For example, seeing flashes of brilliant red and hearing loud, repetitive bursts of sound are both sensory experiences. But when the brain unifies these sensations into the awareness of a speeding fire truck, perception occurs.

We begin this chapter by looking at the basic principles of sensation—how we acquire information from the external (and internal) world. We examine the body's various sense organs to see how each converts physical stimuli, such as light waves, sound waves, or chemical molecules, into nerve impulses. But sensation is only half the story. Our eyes register only light, dark, and color; but our brains "perceive" distinctive visual objects—a tree, a branch, a leaf, a shimmering drop of rain—in three-dimensional space. Our ears are designed to detect the movement of vibrating air molecules, yet we distinguish between a baby's cry and a Bach concerto. We explore these phenomena in the last section of this chapter, which deals with perception.

ENDURING ISSUES IN SENSATION AND PERCEPTION ••

Two key questions we address in this chapter concern the extent to which our perceptual experiences accurately reflect what is in the outside world (*Person–Situation*) and the ways in which our experiences depend on biological processes (*Mind–Body*). We will also examine the extent to which people around the world perceive events in the same way (*Diversity–Universality*) and the ways that our experience of the outside world changes as a result of experience over the course of our lives (*Stability–Change* and *Nature–Nurture*).

The Nature of Sensation

What causes sensory experiences? How is energy, such as light or sound, converted into a message to the brain?

Sensation begins when energy, either from an external source or from inside the body, stimulates a receptor cell in one of the sense organs, such as the eye or the ear. Each **receptor cell** responds to one particular form of energy—light waves (in the case of vision) or vibration of air molecules (in the case of hearing). When there is sufficient energy, the receptor cell "fires" and sends to the brain a coded signal that varies according to the characteristics of the stimulus. The process of converting physical energy, such as light or sound, into electrochemical codes is called **transduction**. For instance, a very bright light might be coded by the rapid firing of a set of nerve cells, but a dim light would set off a much slower firing sequence. The neural signal is coded still further as it passes along the sensory nerves to the central nervous system, so the message that reaches the brain is precise and detailed. The coded signal that the brain receives from a flashing red light differs significantly from the message signaling a soft yellow haze. And both of these signals are coded in a much different way from a loud, piercing noise. The specific sensation produced, then, depends on *how many* neurons fire, *which* neurons fire, and *how rapidly* these neurons fire.

Each sensory experience—the color of a flower or the sound of a fire engine—is an illusion created in the brain by patterns of neural signals. The brain, isolated inside the skull, is bombarded by "impulses," or "firings," of coded neural signals arriving on millions of nerve fibers. The impulses on the optic nerve reliably produce an experience we call vision, just as impulses moving along an auditory nerve produce the experience we call hearing, or audition. The one-to-one relationship between stimulation of a specific nerve and the resulting sensory experience is known as the *doctrine of specific nerve energies*. Even if the impulses on the optic nerve are caused by something other than light, the result is still a visual experience. Gentle pressure on an eye, for instance, results in signals from the optic nerve that the brain interprets as visual patterns—the visual pattern of "seeing stars" when we're hit in the eye is so familiar that even cartoons depict it.

SENSORY THRESHOLDS

What are the limits on our ability to sense stimuli in our environment?

To produce any sensation at all, the physical energy reaching a receptor cell must achieve a minimum intensity, or **absolute threshold**. Any stimulation below the absolute threshold will not be experienced. But how much sensory stimulation is enough? How loud must a sound be, for example, for a person to hear it? How bright does a blip on a radar screen have to be for the operator to see it?

To answer such questions, psychologists present a stimulus at different intensities and ask people whether they sense anything. You might expect that there would come a point at which people would suddenly say, "Now I see the flash" or "Now I hear a sound." But actually, there is a range of intensities over which a person sometimes—but not always—can sense a stimulus. The absolute threshold is defined as the point at which a person can detect the stimulus 50 % of the time that it is presented. (See **Figure 3–1**.)

Although there are differences among people—and even from moment to moment for the same person—the absolute threshold for each of our senses is remarkably low. The approximate absolute thresholds under ideal circumstances are as follows (McBurney & Collings, 1984):

- Hearing: The tick of a watch from 6 m (20 feet) in very quiet conditions
- Vision: A candle flame seen from 50 km (30 miles) on a clear, dark night
- Taste: 1 g (0.0356 ounces) of table salt in 500 L (529 quarts) of water
- Smell: One drop of perfume diffused throughout a three-room apartment
- Touch: The wing of a bee falling on the cheek from a height of 1 cm (0.39 inches)

sensation The experience of sensory stimulation.

receptor cell A specialized cell that responds to a particular type of energy.

transduction The conversion of physical energy into coded neural signals.

absolute threshold The least amount of energy that can be detected as a stimulation 50% of the time.

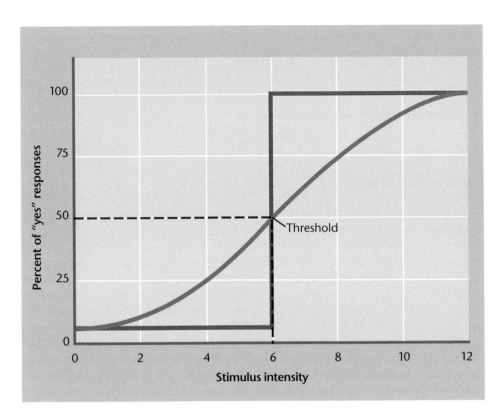

Figure 3–1
Determining a sensory threshold.
The red line represents an ideal case: At all intensities below the threshold, the person reports no sensation or no change in intensity; at all intensities above the threshold, the person reports a sensation or a change in intensity. In reality, however, we never come close to the ideal of the red line. The blue line shows the actual responses of a typical person. The threshold is taken as the point where a person reports a sensation or a change in intensity 50% of the time.

Under normal conditions, absolute thresholds vary according to the level and nature of ongoing sensory stimulation. For example, your threshold for the taste of salt would be considerably higher after you ate salted peanuts; and your vision threshold would be much higher in the middle of a sunny day than at midnight on a moonless night. In both cases, the absolute threshold would rise because of sensory **adaptation**, in which our senses automatically adjust to the overall average level of stimulation in a particular setting. When confronted by a great deal of stimulation, they become much less sensitive than when the overall level of stimulation is low. Similarly, when the level of stimulation drops, our sensory apparatus becomes much more sensitive than under conditions of high stimulation. This process of adaptation allows all of our senses to be keenly attuned to a multitude of environmental cues without getting overloaded. We can hear the breathing of a sleeping baby when we enter a quiet room, but if we are on a city street during rush hour, the traffic noise would be deafening if our ears did not become less sensitive to stimulation. Similarly, adaptation lets us go from a dark room into bright sunshine without experiencing great pain. (Later in this chapter, we look more closely at adaptation.)

Adding one pound to this barbell would not produce a noticeable difference because one pound would fall below the difference threshold for this amount of weight.

Imagine now that you can hear a particular sound. How much stronger must the sound become before you notice that it has grown louder? The smallest change in stimulation that you can detect 50% of the time is called the **difference threshold**, or the **just-noticeable difference (jnd)**. Like the absolute threshold, the difference threshold varies from person to person and from moment to moment for the same person. And, like absolute thresholds, difference thresholds tell us something about the flexibility of sensory systems. For example, adding 1 pound to a 5-pound load will certainly be noticed, so we might assume that the difference threshold must be considerably less than 1 pound. Yet adding 1 pound to a 100-pound load probably would not make much of a difference, so we might conclude that the difference threshold must be considerably more than 1 pound. But how can the difference threshold (jnd) be both less than and greater than 1 pound? It turns out that the difference threshold varies according to the strength or intensity of the original stimulus. The greater the stimulus, the greater the change necessary to produce a jnd.

adaptation An adjustment of the senses to the level of stimulation they are receiving.

difference threshold or just-noticeable difference (jnd) The smallest change in stimulation that can be detected 50% of the time.

Weber's law The principle that the jnd for any given sense is a constant fraction or proportion of the stimulation being judged.

In the 1830s, Ernst Weber concluded that the difference threshold is a constant *fraction or proportion* of the original stimulus; this is a theory known as **Weber's law**. It is important to note that the values of these fractions vary significantly for the different senses. Hearing, for example, is very sensitive: We can detect a change in sound of 0.3% (one-third of 1%). By contrast, producing a jnd in taste requires a 20% change. To return to our earlier example of weight, a change in weight of 2% is necessary to produce a jnd. So adding 1 pound to a 50-pound load would produce a noticeable difference half of the time; adding 1 pound to a 100-pound load would not.

SUBLIMINAL PERCEPTION

Under what circumstances might messages outside our awareness affect our behavior?

The idea of an absolute threshold implies that some events occur *subliminally*—below our level of awareness. Can subliminal messages used in advertisements and self-help tapes, for example, change people's behavior? For decades, the story has circulated that refreshment sales increased dramatically when a movie theater in New Jersey flashed subliminal messages telling people to "Drink Coca-Cola" and "Eat Popcorn." In fact, sales of Coke and popcorn did not change (Dijksterhuis, Aarts, & Smith, 2005).

Similarly, audiotapes with subliminal self-help messages often promise more than they deliver. In one series of studies, volunteers used such tapes for several weeks. About half said they had improved as a result of listening to the tapes, but objective tests detected no measurable change. Moreover, the perceived improvement had more to do with the label on the tape than its subliminal content: About half the people who received a tape labeled "Improve Memory" said that their memory had improved even though many of them had actually received a tape intended to boost self-esteem, and about one-third of the people who listened to tapes labeled "Increase Self-Esteem" said that their self-esteem had gone up, though many of them had actually been listening to tapes designed to improve memory (Greenwald, Spangenberg, Pratkanis, & Eskenazi, 1991).

Nevertheless, there is some evidence that under carefully controlled conditions, people can be influenced by information outside their awareness. In one study, for example, a group of people was shown a list of words related to competition, whereas a second group was exposed to a list of neutral words. Later, when playing a game, participants who had been shown the subliminal list of words with competitive overtones became especially competitive. In another study, one group of people was subliminally exposed to words conveying honesty (a positive trait), whereas other people were subliminally exposed to words conveying hostility (a negative trait). Subsequently, all the participants read a description of a woman whose behavior could be looked at as either honest or hostile. When asked to assess various personality characteristics of the woman, the people who had been subliminally exposed to "honest" words rated her as more honest, and those who had been subliminally exposed to "hostile" words judged her as being hostile (Erdley & D'Agostino, 1988).

THINKING CRITICALLY ABOUT . . .

Advertising and Subconscious Messages

TV ads do not contain hidden, subliminal messages, but they do attempt to make viewers associate products with idealized images and lifestyles. For example, luxury sedans are shown in front of mansions and opera houses; sports utility vehicles are shown in remote canyons. Ads also play on our senses. Visual cues (the models, the setting, the cuts from one scene to another) and auditory cues (the voice-over, the musical background, the sounds of nature) are the most obvious examples. But tactile cues (a car's leather interior) and kinesthetic cues (the feeling of a test drive created by placing the camera inside a moving car) are also common.

1. Analyze a series of ads for sensory content. Choose a specific category, such as ads for vacations or pain medications. What sensory cues are the advertisers using to hold your attention? to create conscious or subconscious associations?
   (**Hint:** Try turning off the sound to focus on visual cues; close your eyes to analyze auditory cues.)

2. What is the underlying message—that is, the associations beyond the specific information the ad conveys?

NOTE: This exercise is not designed to make you more skeptical of advertising (although this may be one outcome), but rather to make you as aware of sensory communication as advertisers are!

These studies and others like them (Ferguson, Bargh, & Nayak, 2005; Mussweiler & Englich, 2005) indicate that, *in a controlled laboratory setting*, people can process and respond to information outside of awareness. But this does *not* mean that people automatically or mindlessly "obey" subliminal messages in advertisements, rock music, self-help tapes, or any other form. To the contrary, independent scientific studies show that hidden messages *outside* the laboratory have no significant effect on behavior (Dijksterhuis, Aarts, & Smith, 2005).

Questions about subliminal perception inevitably lead to questions about extrasensory perception. Do some individuals have special powers of perception? Psychologists continue to debate and research this issue.

EXTRASENSORY PERCEPTION Some people claim to have an extra power of perception, one beyond those of the normal senses. This unusual power, known as *extrasensory perception*, or *ESP*, refers to the ability to perceive or acquire information without using the ordinary senses. ESP refers to a variety of phenomena, including *clairvoyance*—awareness of an unknown object or event; *telepathy*—knowledge of someone else's thoughts or feelings; and *precognition*—foreknowledge of future events. The operation of ESP and other psychic phenomena is the focus of a field of study called *parapsychology*.

Much of the research into ESP has been criticized for poor experimental design, failure to control for dishonesty, or selective reporting of results. Even carefully designed experiments have failed to produce consistent results (Milton & Wiseman, 1999, 2002; Palmer, 2003; Storm & Ertel, 2001). Thus, despite decades of research, experimentation has not yet provided clear scientific support for the existence of ESP.

So far, we have been talking about the general characteristics of sensation, but each of the body's sensory systems works a little differently. Individual sensory systems contain receptor cells that specialize in converting a particular kind of energy into neural signals. The threshold at which this conversion occurs varies from system to system. So do the mechanisms by which sensory data are sent to the brain for additional processing. We now turn to the unique features of each of the major sensory systems.

Subliminal advertising. Advertisers have tried to use subliminal messages, which occur below our level of awareness, to encourage people to buy products such as refreshments at the movie theatre. The use of subliminal messages reached a new low in their suspected application in the 2000 U.S. presidential campaign. A storm of controversy brewed over the word "RATS" allegedly superimposed over the image of a presidential contender.

CHECK YOUR UNDERSTANDING

1. A _____ _____ converts energy into a neural signal.
2. Perception of sensory information that is below the threshold of awareness is called _____ perception.

Answers: 1. receptor cell. 2. subliminal.

APPLY YOUR UNDERSTANDING

1. A psychologist who asked you to make a series of judgments to determine whether or not a light was present in an unlighted room would be trying to assess your _____ for perceiving light.
   a. psychometric function
   b. just-noticeable difference (jnd)
   c. response bias
   d. absolute threshold
2. According to Weber's law, in order for a person to detect a change in the weight of an object, the weight must change by at least 2%. If you are lifting a 50-pound weight, how much must the weight change before you will notice that it is lighter or heavier?
   a. 1 ounce
   b. 8 ounces
   c. 1 pound
   d. 2 pounds

Answers: 1. d. 2. c.

cornea The transparent protective coating over the front part of the eye.

pupil A small opening in the iris through which light enters the eye.

iris The colored part of the eye that regulates the size of the pupil.

lens The transparent part of the eye behind the pupil that focuses light onto the retina.

retina The lining of the eye containing receptor cells that are sensitive to light.

fovea The area of the retina that is the center of the visual field.

Vision

Why have psychologists studied vision more than any other sense?

Different animal species depend more on some senses than on others. Dogs rely heavily on the sense of smell, bats on hearing, and some fish on taste. But for humans, vision is the most important sense; hence, it has received the most attention from psychologists. To understand vision, we need to look first at the parts of the visual system, beginning with the structure of the eye.

THE VISUAL SYSTEM

How does light create a neural impulse?

The structure of the human eye, including the cellular path to the brain, is shown in **Figure 3–2**. Light enters the eye through the **cornea**, the transparent protective coating over the front part of the eye. It then passes through the **pupil**, the opening in the center of the **iris**, the colored part of the eye. In very bright light, the muscles in the iris contract to make the pupil smaller and thus protect the eye from damage. This contraction also helps us to see better in bright light. In dim light, the muscles relax to open the pupil wider and let in as much light as possible.

Inside the pupil, light moves through the **lens**, which focuses it onto the **retina**, the light-sensitive inner lining of the back of the eyeball. Normally, the lens is focused on a middle distance, and it changes shape to focus on objects that are closer or farther away. To focus on a very close object, tiny muscles contract and make the lens rounder. To focus on something far away, the muscles flatten the lens. Directly behind the lens is a depressed spot in the retina called the **fovea**. (See **Figure 3–3**.) The fovea occupies the center of the visual field, and images that pass through the lens are in sharpest focus here. Thus, the words you are now reading are hitting the fovea, while the rest of what you see—a desk, walls, or whatever—is striking other areas of the retina.

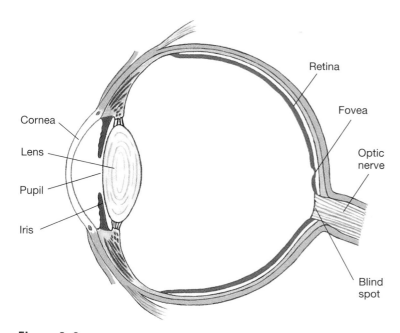

Figure 3–2

A cross section of the human eye.

Light enters the eye through the cornea, passes through the pupil, and is focused by the lens onto the retina.

Source: Adapted from Hubel, 1963.

Figure 3–3

The retina.

View of the retina through an ophthalmoscope, an instrument used to inspect blood vessels in the eye. The small dark spot is the fovea. The yellow circle marks the blind spot, where the optic nerve leaves the eye.

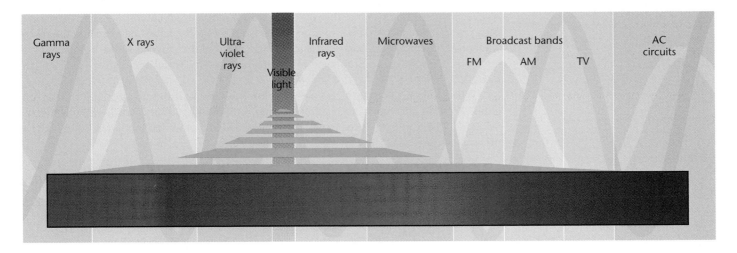

Figure 3–4
The electromagnetic spectrum.
The eye is sensitive to only a very small segment of the spectrum, known as visible light.

THE RECEPTOR CELLS The retina contains the receptor cells responsible for vision. These cells are sensitive to electromagnetic energy. (See **Figure 3–4**.) Energies in the electromagnetic spectrum are referred to by their **wavelength**. Although we receive light waves from the full spectrum, only a portion of it is *visible light* to us; the rest is other energies. The shortest wavelengths that we can see are experienced as violet–blue colors; the longest appear as reds.

There are two kinds of receptor cells in the retina—**rods** and **cones**—named for their characteristic shapes. (See **Figure 3–5**.) About 120 million rods and 8 million cones are present in the retina of each eye. Rods and cones differ from each other in a number of ways, as listed in "**Summary Table:** Rods and Cones." Rods, chiefly responsible for *night vision*, respond only to varying degrees or intensities of light and dark. Cones, in contrast, allow us to see colors. Operating chiefly in daylight, cones are also less sensitive to light than rods are (Hadjikhani & Tootell, 2000; MacLeod, 1978). In this regard, cones, like color film, work best in relatively bright light. The more sensitive rods, like black-and-white film, respond to much lower levels of illumination.

Cones are found mainly, but not exclusively, in the fovea, which contains no rods. The greatest density of cones is in the very center of the fovea, which is where images are projected onto the retina in sharpest focus. Rods predominate just outside the fovea. The greater the distance from the fovea, the sparser both rods and cones become, until, at the extreme edges of the retina, there are almost no cones and only a few rods.

Rods and cones also differ in the ways that they connect to the nerve cells leading to the brain. Both rods and cones connect to specialized neurons called **bipolar cells**, which have only one axon and one dendrite. (See **Figure 3–6**.) In the fovea, cones generally connect with only one bipolar cell—a sort of "private line" arrangement. In contrast, it is normal for several rods to share a single bipolar cell.

Also, outside the fovea, the number of rods and cones that connect to a single bipolar cell increases, and **visual acuity**—the ability visually to distinguish fine details—decreases. As a result, our peripheral vision is somewhat blurred.

The one-to-one connection between cones and bipolar cells in the fovea allows for maximum visual acuity. To see it for yourself, hold this book about 18 inches from your eyes and look at the "X" in the center of the following line:

This is a test to show how visual **X** acuity varies across the retina.

Your fovea picks up the "X" and about four letters to each side. This is the area of greatest visual acuity. Notice how your vision drops off for words and letters toward the left or right end of the line.

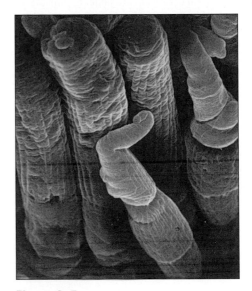

Figure 3–5
Rods and cones.
As you can see from this photomicrograph, the rods and cones are named for their shape.

Source: E. R. Lewis, Y. Y. Zeevi, & F. S. Werblin (1969). Scanning electron microscopy of vertebrate receptors. *Brain Research, 15,* 559–562.

wavelengths The different energies represented in the electromagnetic spectrum.

rods Receptor cells in the retina responsible for night vision and perception of brightness.

cones Receptor cells in the retina responsible for color vision.

bipolar cells Neurons that have only one axon and one dendrite; in the eye, these neurons connect the receptors on the retina to the ganglion cells.

visual acuity The ability to distinguish fine details visually.

In the dark, however, the fovea is almost useless because it contains no light-sensitive rods. To see an object, we have to look to one side so that the image falls outside the fovea where rods are present. Also, because rods normally pool their signals to the bipolar cells, a less-detailed message is sent to the brain. Outside the fovea, visual acuity drops by as much as 50%.

When we want to examine something closely, we move it into the sunlight or under a lamp. For activities such as reading, sewing, and writing, the more light, the better: Stronger light stimulates more cones, increasing the likelihood that bipolar cells will start a message to the brain.

Figure 3–6

A close-up of the layers of the retina.
Light must pass between the ganglion cells and the bipolar cells to reach the rods and cones. The sensory messages then travel back out from the receptor cells, via the bipolar cells, to the ganglion cells. The axons of the ganglion cells gather together to form the optic nerve, which carries the messages from both eyes to the brain. (See **Figure 3–2**.)

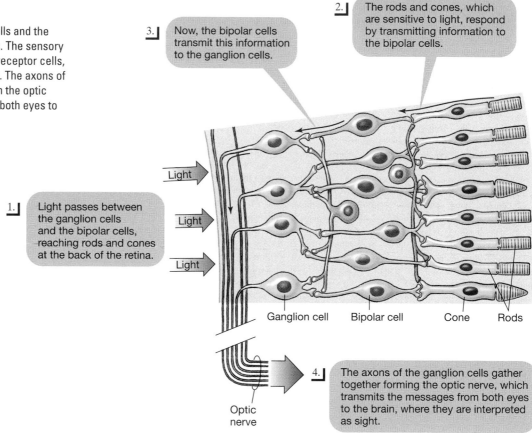

3. Now, the bipolar cells transmit this information to the ganglion cells.

2. The rods and cones, which are sensitive to light, respond by transmitting information to the bipolar cells.

1. Light passes between the ganglion cells and the bipolar cells, reaching rods and cones at the back of the retina.

Ganglion cell   Bipolar cell   Cone   Rods

Optic nerve

4. The axons of the ganglion cells gather together forming the optic nerve, which transmits the messages from both eyes to the brain, where they are interpreted as sight.

SUMMARY TABLE

RODS AND CONES

Type of Receptor Cell	Features and Functions	Location	Connections
Rods	• Highly sensitive to light • Responsible for night vision • Responsible for perception of brightness	• Missing from the fovea • Concentrated just outside the fovea	Typically, many rods connect to a single bipolar cell.
Cones	• Moderately sensitive to light • Most useful in daylight • Responsible for color vision	• Located mainly in the fovea • Concentrated in the center of the fovea	In the fovea, typically, only a single cone connects to a single bipolar cell.

ADAPTATION Earlier in the chapter, we introduced the term *adaptation*, the process by which our senses adjust to different levels of stimulation. In the case of vision, adaptation occurs as the sensitivity of rods and cones changes according to how much light is available. When you go from bright sunlight into a dimly lit theater, your cones and rods are initially fairly insensitive to light, and you can see little as you look for a seat. Over a period of about 30 minutes, first the cones and then the rods slowly adapt until they reach their maximum sensitivity. There is usually not enough energy in very dim light, however, to stimulate many cones, so you see the world in only black, white, and gray. The process by which rods and cones become more sensitive to light in response to lowered levels of illumination is called **dark adaptation.**

Problems with dark adaptation account in part for the much greater incidence of highway accidents at night. When people drive at night, their eyes shift from the darkened interior of the car, to the road area illuminated by headlights, to the darker areas at the side of the road. Unlike the situation in a darkened movie theater, these changing night-driving conditions do not permit complete adaptation to the rapidly changing light conditions.

In the reverse process, **light adaptation**, the rods and cones become less sensitive to light. By the time you leave a movie theater, your rods and cones have grown very sensitive, and all the neurons fire at once when you go into bright outdoor light. You squint and shield your eyes, and your irises contract—all of which reduces the amount of light entering your pupils and striking your retinas. As light adaptation proceeds, the rods and cones become less sensitive to stimulation by light. Within about a minute, both rods and cones are fully adapted to the light, and you no longer need to shield your eyes.

Dark and light adaptation can cause an **afterimage,** as shown in **Figure 3–7**. The gray-and-white afterimage appears because the part of the retina that was exposed to the dark stripes of the upper square became more sensitive. (It becomes adapted to the dark.) The area exposed to the white part of the upper square became less sensitive. (It becomes adapted to the light.) When you shifted your eyes to the lower square, the less sensitive parts of the retina produced the sensation of gray rather than white. This afterimage fades within a minute as the retina adapts again, this time to the solid white square.

These examples show how visual adaptation is a partial back-and-forth process. In the real world, our eyes do not adapt completely, because light stimulation is rarely focused on the same receptor cells long enough for them to become totally insensitive. Rather, small involuntary eye movements keep the image moving slightly on the retina, so the receptor cells never have time to adapt completely.

FROM EYE TO BRAIN We have so far directed our attention to the eye, but messages from the eye must travel to the brain in order for a visual experience to occur. (See **Figure 3–6.**) To begin with, rods and cones are connected to bipolar cells in many different numbers and combinations. In addition, sets of neurons called *interneurons* link receptor cells to one another and bipolar cells to one another. Eventually, these bipolar cells hook up with the **ganglion cells**, leading out of the eye. The axons of the ganglion cells join to form the **optic nerve**, which carries messages from each eye to the brain. The place on the retina where the axons of all the ganglion cells join to form the optic nerve is called the **blind spot**. This area contains no receptor cells. Hence, even when light from a small object is focused directly on the blind spot, the object will not be seen. (See **Figure 3–8.**)

dark adaptation Increased sensitivity of rods and cones in darkness.

light adaptation Decreased sensitivity of rods and cones in bright light.

afterimage Sense experience that occurs after a visual stimulus has been removed.

ganglion cells Neurons that connect the bipolar cells in the eyes to the brain.

optic nerve The bundle of axons of ganglion cells that carries neural messages from each eye to the brain.

blind spot The place on the retina where the axons of all the ganglion cells leave the eye and where there are no receptors.

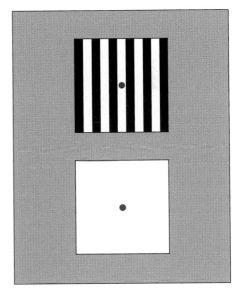

Figure 3–7
An afterimage.
First stare continuously at the center of the upper square for about 20 seconds, then look at the dot in the lower square. Within a moment, a gray-and-white afterimage should appear inside the lower square.

Figure 3–8
Finding your blind spot.
To locate your blind spot, hold the book about a foot away from your eyes. Then close your right eye, stare at the "X," and slowly move the book toward you and away from you until the red dot disappears.

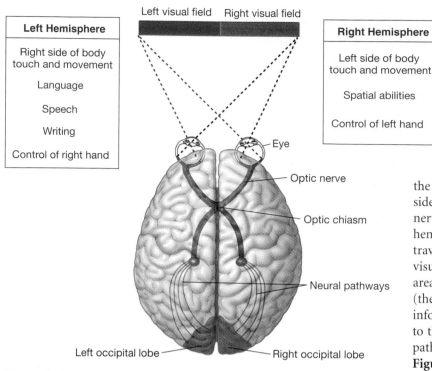

Left Hemisphere
Right side of body touch and movement
Language
Speech
Writing
Control of right hand

Right Hemisphere
Left side of body touch and movement
Spatial abilities
Control of left hand

Left visual field   Right visual field

Eye
Optic nerve
Optic chiasm
Neural pathways
Left occipital lobe
Right occipital lobe

Figure 3–9

The neural connections of the visual system.
Messages about the red-colored area in the left visual field of each eye travel to the right occipital lobe; information about the blue area in the right visual field of each eye goes to the left occipital lobe. The crossover point is the optic chiasm.

Source: Adapted from "The Split Brain in Man," by Michael S. Gazzaniga. Copyright © 1967. Adapted with permission.

Although there are more than 125 million rods and cones in each retina, there are only about 1 million ganglion cells in the optic nerve. The information collected by the 125 million receptor cells must be combined and reduced to fit the mere 1 million "wires" that lead from each eye to the brain. Research indicates that most of this consolidation takes place in the interconnection between receptors and ganglion cells (H. Kolb, 2003; Solomon, Lee, White, Rüttiger, & Martin, 2005).

After the nerve fibers that make up the optic nerves leave the eyes, they separate, and some of them cross to the other side of the head at the **optic chiasm**. (See **Figure 3–9**) The nerve fibers from the right side of each eye travel to the right hemisphere of the brain; those from the left side of each eye travel to the left hemisphere. Thus, as shown in **Figure 3–9**, visual information about any object in the left visual field, the area to the left of the viewer, will go to the right hemisphere (the pathway traced by the red line in **Figure 3–9**). Similarly, information about any object in the right visual field, the area to the right of the viewer, will go to the left hemisphere (the pathway traced by the blue line). (You can refer back to **Figures 2–9** and **2–10** in Chapter 2, "The Biological Basis of Behavior," to recall how researchers took advantage of the split processing of the two visual fields to study split-brain patients.)

The optic nerves carry their messages to various parts of the brain. Some messages reach the area of the brain that controls the reflex movements that adjust the size of the pupil. Others go to the region that directs the eye muscles to change the shape of the lens. Still others appear to go to lower brain centers, rather than the visual cortex. As a result, some people who are temporarily or permanently blind nonetheless can describe various visual stimuli around them even though they say they "saw" nothing (Boyer, Harrison, & Ro, 2005). But the main destinations for messages from the retina are the visual projection areas of the cerebral cortex, that is, the occipital lobe(see **Figure 2–8**, **The four lobes of the cerebral cortex**, p. 57), where the complex coded messages from the retina are registered and interpreted.

How does the brain register and interpret these signals, "translating" light into visual images? In research for which they received a Nobel Prize, David H. Hubel and Torsten N. Wiesel (1959, 1979) found that certain brain cells—called **feature detectors**—are highly specialized to detect particular elements of the visual field, such as horizontal or vertical lines. Other feature-detector cells register more complex information, with some being sensitive to movement, others to depth, and still others to color. These different types of feature detectors send messages to specific, but nearby, regions of the cortex. Visual experience, then, depends on the brain's ability to combine these pieces of information into a meaningful image.

COLOR VISION

How do we see color?

Humans, like many—but not all—other animals see in color, at least during the day. Color vision is highly adaptive for an animal that needs to know when fruit is ripe or how to avoid poisonous plants and berries (which tend to be brightly hued), as our ancestors did. There are different ideas, however, about how it is that we are able to see colors.

PROPERTIES OF COLOR Look at the color solid in **Figure 3–10**. What do you see? Most people report that they see some oranges, some yellows, some reds—a number of different colors. We call these different colors **hues**, and to a great extent, the hues you see depend on the wavelength of the light reaching your eyes. (See **Figure 3–4**.)

optic chiasm The point near the base of the brain where some fibers in the optic nerve from each eye cross to the other side of the brain.

feature detectors Specialized brain cells that only respond to particular elements in the visual field such as movement or lines of specific orientation.

hues The aspects of color that correspond to names such as red, green, and blue.

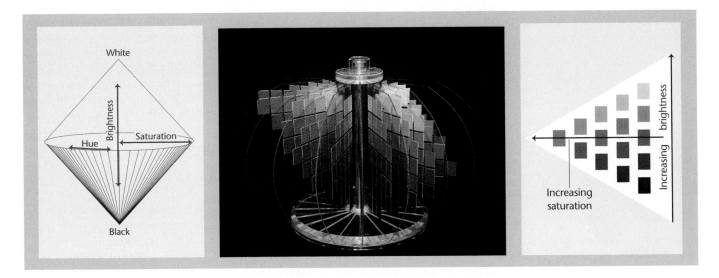

Now look at the triangle of green colors on the right side of **Figure 3–10**. Although each color patch on the triangle is the same hue, the green color is deepest or richest toward the left side of the triangle. The vividness or richness of a hue is its **saturation**.

Finally, notice that the colors near the top of the color patches are almost white, whereas those close to the bottom are almost black. This is the dimension of **brightness**, which depends largely on the strength of the light entering your eyes. If you squint and look at the color solid, you will reduce the apparent brightness of all the colors in the solid, and many of them will appear to become black.

Hue, saturation, and brightness are three separate aspects of our experience of color. Although people can distinguish only about 150 hues (Coren, Porac, & Ward, 1984), gradations of saturation and brightness within those 150 hues allow us to see more than 2 million different colors (Travis, 2003). Some of this variety is captured in **Figure 3–10**.

THEORIES OF COLOR VISION If you look closely at a color television screen, you will see that the picture is actually made up of tiny red, green, and blue dots that blend together to give all possible hues. The same principle is at work in our own ability to see thousands of colors.

For centuries, scientists have known that they could produce all of the basic hues humans can see by mixing together only a few lights of different colors. (See **Figure 3–11**.)

Figure 3–10
The color solid.
In the center portion of the figure, known as a color solid, the dimension of hue is represented around the circumference. *Saturation* ranges along the radius from the inside to the outside of the solid. *Brightness* varies along the vertical axis. The drawing at the left illustrates this arrangement schematically. The illustration at the right shows changes in saturation and brightness for the same hue.

saturation The vividness or richness of a hue.

brightness The nearness of a color to white as opposed to black.

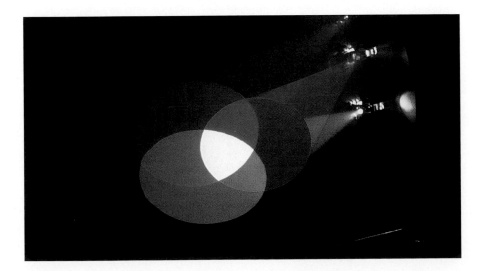

Figure 3–11
Additive color mixing.
Mixing light waves is an additive process. When red and green lights are combined, the resulting hue is yellow. Adding blue light to the other two yields white light.

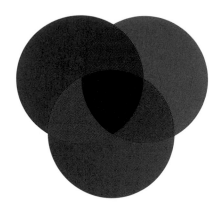

Figure 3–12

Subtractive color mixing.
The process of mixing paint pigments rather than lights is a subtractive process, because the pigments absorb some wavelengths and reflect others. A mixture of the three primary pigments (red, yellow, and blue) absorbs all wavelengths, producing black.

---

additive color mixing The process of mixing lights of different wavelengths to create new hues.

subtractive color mixing The process of mixing pigments, each of which absorbs some wavelengths of light and reflects others.

trichromatic (or three-color) theory The theory of color vision that holds that all color perception derives from three different color receptors in the retina (usually red, green, and blue receptors).

trichromats People (and animals) that have normal color vision.

color blindness Partial or total inability to perceive hues.

dichromats People (and animals) that are blind to either red–green or yellow–blue.

monochromats Organisms that are totally color blind.

opponent-process theory Theory of color vision that holds that three sets of color receptors (yellow–blue, red–green, black–white) respond to determine the color you experience.

Specifically, red, green, and blue lights—the primary colors for light mixtures—can be combined to create any hue. For example, red and green lights combine to give yellow; red and blue lights combine to make magenta. Combining red, green, and blue lights in equal intensities produces white. The process of mixing lights of different wavelengths is called **additive color mixing**, because each light adds additional wavelengths to the overall mix.

Color mixing with paint follows different rules than does color mixing with light. With light, different wavelengths add together, but the color of paint depends not on which wavelengths are *present*, but rather on which are *absorbed* and which are *reflected*. For example, red paint absorbs light from the blue end of the spectrum and reflects light from the red end. Since paint mixing depends on what colors are absorbed, or subtracted, the process is called **subtractive color mixing**. (See **Figure 3–12**.)

In the early 1800s, the German physiologist Hermann von Helmholtz proposed a theory of color vision based on additive color mixing. Helmholtz reasoned that, since there are three primary colors of light, the eye must contain three types of cones: some that are sensitive to red light, others that pick up green, and still others that respond most strongly to blue–violet. According to this view, color experiences come from mixing the signals from the three receptors. Helmholtz's explanation of color vision is known as **trichromatic (or three-color) theory**.

Trichromatic theory explains how three primary colors can be combined to produce any other hue. In fact, people with normal color vision are called **trichromats**. Trichromats perceive all hues by combining the three primary colors. However, approximately 10% of men and 1% of women display some form of **color blindness**, which is not well explained by trichromatic theory. People with the two most common forms of color blindness are called **dichromats**, since they see the world in terms of only reds and greens (the red–green dichromats) or of blues and yellows (the blue–yellow dichromats). (See **Figure 3–13**.) Among humans, **monochromats**, who see no color at all, but respond only to shades of light and dark, are extremely rare.

Trichromatic theory does not, however, explain some aspects of normal color vision. Why, for example, don't people with normal color vision ever see a light or a pigment that can be described as "reddish green" or "yellowish blue"? And what accounts for *color afterimages*? (See **Figure 3–14**.)

In the later 19th century, another German scientist, Edward Hering, proposed an alternative theory of color vision that can explain these phenomena. Hering proposed the existence of three *pairs* of color receptors: a yellow–blue pair and a red–green pair that determine the hue you see; and a black–white pair that determines the brightness of the colors you see. The yellow–blue pair can relay messages about yellow *or* blue, but not messages about yellow *and* blue light at the same time; the same is true for red–green receptors. Thus, the members of each pair work in opposition to each other, which explains why we never see yellowish blue or reddish green. Hering's theory is now known as the **opponent-process theory**.

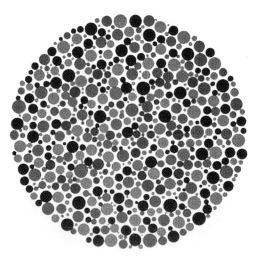

Figure 3–13

Experiencing color blindness.
Perceiving the number 96 embedded in the mass of green circles is easy, except for people who have red–green color blindness.

Source: Ishihara, Test for Color Deficiency. Courtesy of the Isshinkai Foundation founded by Prof. Ishihara, Tokyo, Japan.

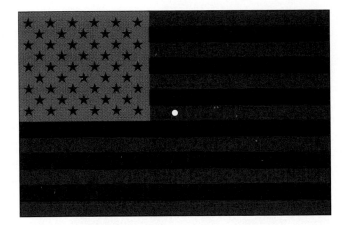

Figure 3–14
Afterimage.
Stare at the white spot in the center of the flag for about 30 seconds. Then look at a blank piece of white paper, and you will see an afterimage in complementary colors. Although the flag is printed in green, yellow, and black, its afterimage will appear in red, blue, and white.

Opponent-process theory also explains color afterimages. While you were looking at the green stripes in **Figure 3–14**, the red–green receptors were sending "green" messages to your brain, but they were also adapting to the stimulation by becoming less sensitive to green light. When you later looked at the white page (made up of light from all parts of the spectrum), the red–green receptors responded vigorously to wavelengths in the red portion of the spectrum, so you saw red stripes instead of green. Hering's opponent-process theory also explains the color experiences of dichromats. If the red–green system fails, then all that is left is the yellow–blue system and vice versa.

Trichromatic and opponent-process theories are summarized in the "**Summary Table**: Theories of Color Vision." Today, psychologists believe that both the trichromatic and opponent-process theories are valid, but at different stages of the visual process. As trichromatic theory asserts, there are three kinds of cones for color. (Some are most sensitive to violet–blue light, others are most responsive to green light, and still others are most sensitive to yellow light—not red light, as Helmholtz contended.) Thus, trichromatic theory corresponds fairly closely to the types of color receptors that actually exist in the retina. The opponent-process theory closely reflects what happens along the neural pathways that connect the eye and the brain. Together, trichromatic theory and opponent-process theory account for most color phenomena.

COLOR VISION IN OTHER SPECIES Most of us assume that color is "out there," in the environment; our eyes simply take it in. But studies of other species show, that to a great extent, color is in the eye of the beholder. Humans and most other primates are trichromats; we perceive a wide range of colors. Most other mammals are dichromats—they experience the world only in reds and greens or blues and yellows (Abramov & Gordon, 1994; Travis, 2003). Hamsters, rats, squirrels, and other rodents are completely color blind, or monochromats. So are owls, nocturnal birds of prey that have only rods in their eyes. At the same time, however, some animals can see colors that we can't. Bees and some birds, for example, see ultraviolet light (Ackerman, 1995; Travis, 2003). To a bee's eyes, flowers with white petals that look drab to us flash like neon signs pointing the way to nectar. Birds, bats, and moths find red flowers irresistible, but bees pass them by.

SUMMARY TABLE

THEORIES OF COLOR VISION

Theory	Developed By	Main Ideas
Trichromatic theory	Helmholtz	Three kinds of receptors in the retina (red, green, blue)
Opponent-process theory	Hering	Three pairs of receptors in the retina (yellow–blue, red–green, black–white)

CHECK YOUR UNDERSTANDING

Match the terms with the appropriate definitions.

1. _____ cornea
2. _____ pupil
3. _____ iris
4. _____ lens
5. _____ fovea
6. _____ retina

a. colored part of the eye
b. center of the visual field
c. opening in the iris through which light enters
d. protective layer over front part of the eye
e. part that contains the receptor cells that respond to light
f. part that focuses light onto the retina

Answers: 1. d. 2. c. 3. a. 4. f. 5. b. 6. e.

APPLY YOUR UNDERSTANDING

1. Imagine that you are wearing a multicolored shirt when you go out for a short walk on a dark night. During the walk you look down and notice that the colors all look like patches of gray. The reason that you no longer see the colors as different hues is that

   a. you are seeing primarily with the cones.

   b. you are seeing primarily with the rods.

   c. the image of your shirt is falling on your blind spot.

   d. the colors have become saturated.

2. Your six-year-old nephew asks you to use crayons to draw a green car and a red fire truck, but you have no green crayon. He says "My teacher says yellow and blue make green. Can you do that?" You realize your nephew understands the basics of _____ better than you do.

   a. additive color mixing

   b. subtractive color mixing

   c. the trichromatic theory of color vision

   d. the opponent-process theory of color vision

Answers: 1. b. 2. b.

Hearing

If a tree falls in the forest and no one is there, does the tree make a sound?

If you had to make a choice, would you give up your sight or your hearing? Presented with this hypothetical choice, most people say they would give up hearing first. But the great teacher and activist Helen Keller, who was both blind and deaf from infancy, regretted her inability to hear more than anything else.

> I am just as deaf as I am blind. The problems of deafness are deeper and more complex, if not more important than those of blindness. Deafness is a much worse misfortune. For it means the loss of the most vital stimulus—the sound of the voice that brings language, sets thoughts astir and keeps us in the intellectual company of man. (Keller, 1948; quoted in D. Ackerman, 1995, pp. 191–192)

For some animals, hearing is the most acute sense. For example, bats, dolphins, porpoises, and whales are not blind but they "see" more with their ears than with their eyes. They emit steady streams of high-pitched chirps that bounce off nearby objects. Neurons in their auditory systems extract an extraordinary amount of information from these echoes, a process known as *echolocation* (Perkins, 2005). Remarkably, if a flying insect is nearby, a bat can determine exactly where it is, how far away it is, how fast it is flying, its size, characteristics of its wing beats, and its general features. Still, no other species use sound to create meanings, in music as well as language, as extensively as humans do.

SOUND

How do the characteristics of sound waves cause us to hear different sounds?

The sensation we call **sound** is our brain's interpretation of the ebb and flow of air molecules pounding on our eardrums. When something in the environment moves, pressure is caused as molecules of air or fluid collide with one another and then move apart again. This pressure transmits energy at every collision, creating **sound waves**. The simplest sound wave—what we hear as a pure tone—can be pictured as the sine wave shown in **Figure 3–15**. The tuning fork vibrates, causing the molecules of air first to contract and then to expand. The **frequency** of the waves is measured in cycles per second, expressed in a unit called **hertz (Hz)**. Frequency primarily determines the **pitch** of the sound—how high or how low it is. The human ear responds to frequencies from approximately 20 Hz to 20,000 Hz. Cats can hear noises as high as 64,000 Hz and mice apparently can hear sounds (and sing "songs") up to 100,000 Hz. A double bass can reach down to about 50 Hz; a piano can reach as high as 5000 Hz.

The height of the sound wave represents its **amplitude** (**Figure 3–15**), which, together with frequency, determines the perceived loudness of a sound. Sound intensity is measured by a unit called **decibel**. (See **Figure 3–16**.) As we grow older, we lose some of our ability to hear soft sounds, but we can hear loud sounds as well as ever.

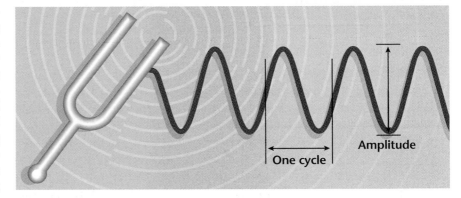

Figure 3–15
Sound waves.
As the tuning fork vibrates, it alternately compresses and expands the molecules of air, creating a sound wave.

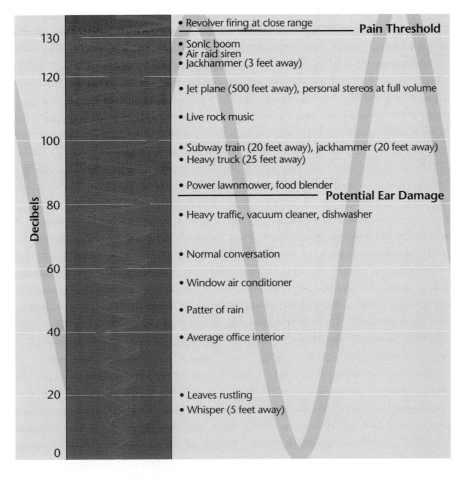

Figure 3–16

A decibel scale for several common sounds.
Prolonged exposure to sounds above 85 decibels can cause permanent damage to the ears, as can even brief exposure to sounds near the pain threshold.

Source: Adapted from T. Dunkle (1982, April). The sound of silence. *Science '82*, 30–33.

sound A psychological experience created by the brain in response to changes in air pressure that are received by the auditory system.

sound waves Changes in pressure caused when molecules of air or fluid collide with one another and then move apart again.

frequency The number of cycles per second in a wave; in sound, the primary determinant of pitch.

hertz (Hz) Cycles per second; unit of measurement for the frequency of sound waves.

pitch Auditory experience corresponding primarily to frequency of sound vibrations, resulting in a higher or lower tone.

amplitude The magnitude of a wave; in sound, the primary determinant of loudness.

decibel Unit of measurement for the loudness of sounds.

THINKING CRITICALLY ABOUT . . .

An Ancient Question

At one time or another, everyone has debated the ancient question, "If a tree falls in the forest and no one is there, does the tree make a sound?"

- How would a psychologist answer this question?

Hints: Think about one of the major themes of this chapter: sights, sounds, and other sensations are psychological experiences created by the brain in response to stimulation. Put another way, psychologists distinguish between what happens in the environment (e.g., sound waves) and what we perceive (e.g., sounds).

The sounds that we hear seldom result from pure tones. Unlike a tuning fork, which can produce a tone that is almost pure, musical instruments produce **overtones**—accompanying sound waves that are different multiples of the frequency of the basic tone. This complex pattern of overtones determines the **timbre**, or texture, of the sound. A note played on the piano sounds different from the same note played on a violin because of the differing overtones of the two instruments. Music synthesizers can mimic different instruments electronically because they produce not only pure tones, but also the overtones that produce the timbre of different musical instruments.

Like our other senses, hearing undergoes adaptation and can function optimally under a wide variety of conditions. City residents enjoying a weekend in the country, for example, may be struck at first by how quiet everything seems. But after a while they may find that the country starts to sound very noisy because they have adapted to the quieter environment.

THE EAR

What path does sound follow from the ear to the brain?

Hearing begins when sound waves are gathered by the *outer* ear and passed along to the eardrum (see **Figure 3–17**) causing it to vibrate. The quivering of the eardrum prompts three tiny bones in the *middle* ear—the *hammer*, the *anvil*, and the *stirrup*—to hit each other in sequence and thus carry the vibrations to the *inner* ear. The last of these three bones, the stirrup, is attached to a membrane called the **oval window**. Vibrations of the oval window, in turn, are transmitted to the fluid inside a snail-shaped structure called the **cochlea**. The cochlea is divided lengthwise by the **basilar membrane**, which is stiff near the oval window but gradually becomes more flexible toward its other end. When the fluid in the cochlea begins to move, the basilar membrane ripples in response.

Lying on top of the basilar membrane and moving in sync with it is the **organ of Corti**. Here the messages from the sound waves finally reach the receptor cells for the sense of hearing: thousands of tiny hair cells that are embedded in the organ of Corti (Fridberger et al., 2004; Spoendlin & Schrott, 1989). As you can see in **Figure 3–18**, each hair cell is topped by a bundle of fibers. These fibers are pushed and pulled by the vibrations of the basilar membrane. When these fibers move, the receptor cells send a signal through afferent nerve endings that join to form the **auditory nerve** to the brain. The brain pools the information from thousands of hair cells to create sounds.

NEURAL CONNECTIONS The sense of hearing is truly bilateral: Each ear sends messages to both cerebral hemispheres. The switching station where the nerve fibers from the ears cross over is in the medulla, part of the brain stem. (See **Figure 2–6**.) From the medulla, other nerve fibers carry the messages from the ears to the higher parts of the brain. Some messages go to the brain centers that coordinate the movements of the eyes, head, and ears. Others travel through the reticular formation (which we examined in Chapter 2). But the primary destinations for these auditory messages are the auditory areas in the temporal lobes of the two cerebral hemispheres. (See **Figure 2–8**.) En route to the temporal lobes, auditory messages pass through at least four lower brain centers where auditory information becomes more precisely coded.

---

overtones Tones that result from sound waves that are multiples of the basic tone; primary determinant of timbre.

timbre The quality or texture of sound; caused by overtones.

oval window Membrane across the opening between the middle ear and inner ear that conducts vibrations to the cochlea.

cochlea Part of the inner ear containing fluid that vibrates, which in turn causes the basilar membrane to vibrate.

basilar membrane Vibrating membrane in the cochlea of the inner ear; it contains sense receptors for sound.

organ of Corti Structure on the surface of the basilar membrane that contains the receptor cells for hearing.

auditory nerve The bundle of axons that carries signals from each ear to the brain.

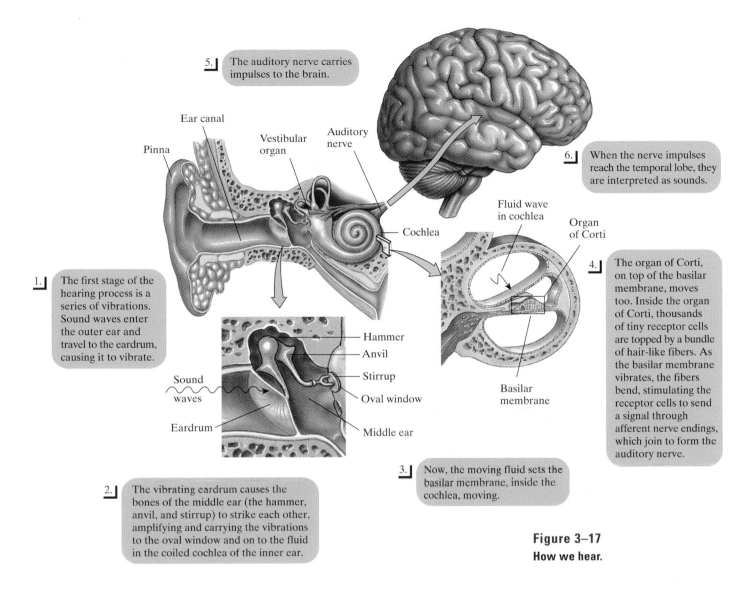

5. The auditory nerve carries impulses to the brain.

6. When the nerve impulses reach the temporal lobe, they are interpreted as sounds.

Ear canal

Pinna

Vestibular organ

Auditory nerve

Cochlea

Fluid wave in cochlea

Organ of Corti

Basilar membrane

1. The first stage of the hearing process is a series of vibrations. Sound waves enter the outer ear and travel to the eardrum, causing it to vibrate.

Hammer
Anvil
Stirrup
Oval window
Middle ear

Sound waves

Eardrum

4. The organ of Corti, on top of the basilar membrane, moves too. Inside the organ of Corti, thousands of tiny receptor cells are topped by a bundle of hair-like fibers. As the basilar membrane vibrates, the fibers bend, stimulating the receptor cells to send a signal through afferent nerve endings, which join to form the auditory nerve.

3. Now, the moving fluid sets the basilar membrane, inside the cochlea, moving.

2. The vibrating eardrum causes the bones of the middle ear (the hammer, anvil, and stirrup) to strike each other, amplifying and carrying the vibrations to the oval window and on to the fluid in the coiled cochlea of the inner ear.

Figure 3–17
How we hear.

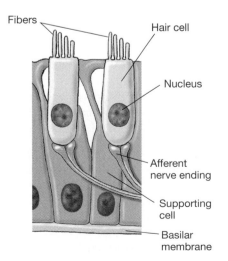

Fibers

Hair cell

Nucleus

Afferent nerve ending

Supporting cell

Basilar membrane

Figure 3–18

A detailed drawing of a hair cell.
At the top of each hair cell is a bundle of fibers. If the fibers bend as much as 100 trillionths of a meter, the receptor cells transmit a sensory message to the brain.

Source: Adapted from "The Hair Cells of the Inner Ear," by A. J. Hudspeth, © 1983. Illustrated by Bunji Tagawa for *Scientific American*. Adapted with permission from the Estate of Bunji Tagawa.

place theory Theory that pitch is determined by the location of greatest vibration on the basilar membrane.

frequency theory Theory that pitch is determined by the frequency with which hair cells in the cochlea fire.

volley principle Refinement of frequency theory; it suggests that receptors in the ear fire in sequence, with one group responding, then a second, then a third, and so on, so that the complete pattern of firing corresponds to the frequency of the sound wave.

THEORIES OF HEARING

How do we distinguish low-frequency and high-frequency sounds?

Thousands of tiny hair cells send messages about the infinite variations in the frequency, amplitude, and overtones of sound waves. But how are the different sound-wave patterns coded into neural messages? One aspect of sound—loudness—seems to depend primarily on how many neurons are activated: The more cells that fire, the louder the sound seems to be. The coding of messages regarding pitch is more complicated. There are two basic views of pitch discrimination: place theory and frequency theory. (See "**Summary Table**: Theories of Pitch Discrimination.") According to **place theory**, the brain determines pitch by noting the place on the basilar membrane at which the message is strongest. High-frequency sounds cause the greatest vibration at the stiff base of the basilar membrane; low-frequency sounds resonate most strongly at the opposite end (Zwislocki, 1981). The brain detects the location of the most intense nerve-cell activity and uses this to determine the pitch of a sound.

The **frequency theory** of pitch discrimination holds that the frequency of vibrations of the basilar membrane as a whole—not just parts of it—is translated into an equivalent frequency of nerve impulses. Thus, if a hair bundle is pulled or pushed rapidly, its hair cell fires rapidly, sending a rush of signals to the brain. Because neurons cannot fire as rapidly as the frequency of the highest pitched sound that can be heard, however, theorists have modified the frequency theory to include a **volley principle**. According to this view, auditory neurons can fire in sequence: One neuron fires, then a second one, and then a third. By then, the first neuron has had time to recover and can fire again. In this way, a set of neurons together, firing in sequence, can send a more rapid series of impulses to the brain than any single neuron could send by itself.

Because neither place theory nor frequency theory alone fully explains pitch discrimination, some combination of the two is necessary. Frequency theory appears to account for the ear's responses to frequencies up to about 4000 Hz; above that, place theory provides a better explanation of what is happening.

HEARING DISORDERS Since the mechanisms that allow us to hear are so complicated, the potential is great for a large number of possible problems that may interfere with hearing. Deafness, one of the most common concerns, may result from defects in the middle ear—for instance, the eardrum may be damaged, or the small bones of the middle ear may not work properly. Deafness may also occur because of damage to the basilar membrane, the hair cells, or the auditory nerve, caused by disease, infections, and even long-term exposure to loud noise. Of the 28 million Americans with hearing loss, about 10 million are victims of exposure to noise. The chief culprits are leaf blowers, chain saws, snowmobiles, jet planes, and personal stereo systems. (See **Figure 3–16**; Biassoni et al., 2005; E. B. Goldstein, 1999; W. E. Leary, 1990.)

For people with irreversible hearing loss, a number of remedies are available. New digital technology has made hearing aids, which simply amplify sound, more precise by enhancing speech perception and reducing background noise. Surgery can help people

Loud music can cause damage to the sensitive structures of the ears, leading to hearing loss.

SUMMARY TABLE

THEORIES OF PITCH DISCRIMINATION

Place theory	Pitch is determined by the place on the basilar membrane where vibration is greatest.
Frequency theory	Pitch is determined by the overall rate of firing of neurons in the cochlea. Groups of neurons can "volley" their firing to increase the overall rate of the group.

with conductive hearing loss due to a stiffening of the connections between the bones (hammer, anvil, and stirrup) of the middle ear.

Implants offer hope to people who suffer from deafness due to cochlear damage (G. M. Clark, 1998; Fischetti, 2003; Shallop, Jin, Driscoll, & Tribisar, 2004). One or more platinum electrodes are inserted into the cochlea of one ear. The electrodes bypass the damaged hair cells and convey electrical signals from a miniature sound synthesizer directly to the auditory nerve, which conveys an auditory message to the brain. Many of the people who receive cochlear implants are children. Not surprisingly, the younger a hearing-impaired child is when he or she receives cochlear implants, the more the child's speech recognition and language development are improved, prompting many experts to recommend the surgery be performed during the first three years of life (Kileny, Zwolan, & Ashbaugh, 2001).

ENDURING ISSUES

Diversity–Universality   Deaf Culture

Should doctors do everything possible to restore hearing in children who are born deaf or become deaf at an early age? Surprisingly perhaps, The National Association of the Deaf argues no. Many of these procedures only partially restore hearing. As a result, the association argues, children are left in limbo. On the one hand, they are denied access to sign language and to the deaf subculture; on the other, they are pushed into a hearing culture that labels them "disabled," reducing self-esteem (Ladd, 2003). The association holds that sign language is a legitimate language (Burch, 2004; Emmorey, 1994) and should be recognized as such. (See Chapter 7, "Cognition and Mental Abilities.") Children who learn sign language as their native language function quite well, often better than children who struggle to understand spoken language they can barely hear.

Underlying this position is the view that deafness is not a disability; indeed, it can lead to a sharpening of the other senses (Clay, 1997). Rather, deafness is a variation on the common human pattern, a form of human diversity. ●●

Far from not hearing enough sound, some people hear too much of the wrong kind of sound and suffer greatly because of it (Eggermont & Roberts, 2004). Almost everybody has at some time heard a steady, high-pitched hum that persists even in the quietest room. This sound, which seems to come from inside the head, is called *tinnitus*. Problems from tinnitus are estimated to afflict approximately one out of every eight persons (Johansson & Arlinger, 2003). In some people, it becomes unbearably loud—like the screeching of subway brakes—and does not go away. In most cases, tinnitus results from irritation or damage to the hair cells. Prolonged exposure to loud sound or toxins, certain medical conditions, and even some antibiotics can cause permanent damage to the hair cells. In many cases, drug therapies, implants that create "white noise" (or sound blockage), and biofeedback can provide relief.

CHECK YOUR UNDERSTANDING

In which order would a sound wave reach the following structures when traveling from the outer ear to the inner ear? Number the following terms in the correct order.

1. _____ oval window
2. _____ anvil
3. _____ cochlea
4. _____ auditory nerve
5. _____ eardrum

Answers: 1. 3rd. 2. 2nd. 3. 4th. 4. 5th. 5. 1st.

olfactory bulb The smell center in the brain.

APPLY YOUR UNDERSTANDING

1. As you sit in front of a sound generator, the frequency of the sound is gradually increased. You are most likely to notice an increase in
    a. pitch.
    b. loudness.
    c. saturation.
    d. overtones.

2. A friend says, "I hear this loud ringing in my ears. Sometimes it's so loud I have trouble sleeping. It's driving me crazy!" Your friend is most likely describing
    a. cochlear degeneration.
    b. timbre.
    c. rippling of the basilar membrane.
    d. tinnitus.

Answers: 1. a. 2. d.

The Other Senses

What are the chemical senses?

Researchers have focused most of their attention on vision and hearing because humans rely primarily on these two senses to gather information about their environment. Our other senses—including smell, taste, balance, motion, pressure, temperature, and pain— are also at play, even when we are less conscious of them. We turn first to the chemical senses: smell and taste.

SMELL

What activates the sense of smell?

Although the sense of smell in humans is much weaker than in most animals (Travis, 2003), it is still about 10,000 times as acute as that of taste. Like our other senses, smell undergoes adaptation, so that odors that seem strong at first gradually become less noticeable.

Research has unlocked many of the mysteries of our other senses, but exactly how we smell is still an open question (A. Keller & Vosshall, 2004). Our sense of smell for common odors is activated by a complex protein produced in a nasal gland. As we breathe, a fine mist of this protein, called *odorant binding protein* (OBP), is sprayed through a duct in the tip of the nose. The protein binds with tiny airborne molecules that then activate roughly 1,000 different types of receptor cells for this sense, located high in each nasal cavity (Buck & Axel, 1991). (See **Figure 3–19**.) The axons from millions of these receptors go directly to the **olfactory bulb**, where some recoding takes place. Then messages are routed to the brain, resulting in our ability to recognize and remember about 10,000 different smells.

Odor sensitivity is related to gender. Numerous studies confirm that women generally have a better sense of smell than do men (Dalton, Doolittle, & Breslin, 2002). Age also makes a difference: Generally, the ability to smell is sharpest during the early adult years (ages 20 to 40); (Doty, 1989; Schiffman, 1997). Of the people tested by Doty and his colleagues, one-quarter of those over the age of 65 and half of those over the age of 80 had completely lost their ability to smell. Anosmia, the complete loss of smell described in the opening of this chapter, can be devastating. In contrast, dogs have extraordinarily sharp senses of smell, in large part because they have more than 200 million smell receptors (compared with only 10 million receptors in humans). And recent evidence indicates that rats smell in

Certain animal species rely more on their sense of smell than humans do. This dog has been trained to use its keen sense of smell to help security forces at the airport.

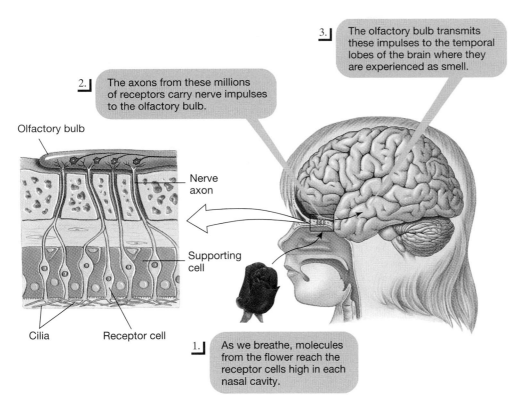

Figure 3–19

The human olfactory system.

The sense of smell is triggered when odor molecules in the air reach the olfactory receptors located inside the top of the nose. Inhaling and exhaling odor molecules from food does much to give food its flavorful "taste."

Source: Human Anatomy and Physiology by Anthony J. Gaudin and Kenneth C. Jones. Copyright © 1989. Reprinted by permission.

stereo, which allows them to locate the source of an odor with just one or two sniffs (Rajan, Clement, & Bhalla, 2006).

Most mammals, including humans, have a second sensory system devoted to the sense of smell—which some animals use for communicating sexual, aggressive, or territorial signals. Receptors located in the roof of the nasal cavity detect chemicals called **pheromones**, which can have quite specific and powerful effects on behavior. (See "On The Cutting Edge: Pheromones.")

TASTE

How do we detect the basic tastes?

To understand taste, we must distinguish it from flavor—a complex interaction of taste and smell. Try holding your nose when you eat. You will notice that most of the food's flavor will disappear, and you will experience only the basic taste qualities: *sweet, sour, salty, bitter,* and *umami* (umami accounts for our sensitivity to monosodium glutamate—MSG—and related proteins). Like Anita Chang (described at the beginning of this chapter) who lost her sense of smell, you get the taste, but not the flavor.

The receptor cells for the sense of taste are housed in the **taste buds**, most of which are found on the tip, sides, and back of the tongue. The tip of the tongue is most sensitive to sweetness and saltiness; the back, to bitterness; and the sides, to sourness (see **Figure 3–20**), although each area can distinguish all taste qualities to some degree (Bartoshuk & Beauchamp, 1994). Because the number of taste buds decreases with age, older people often lose interest in food—they simply cannot taste it as well as they used to.

The taste buds are embedded in the tongue's *papillae*, bumps that you can see if you look at your tongue in the mirror. When we eat something, the chemical substances in the food dissolve in saliva and go into the crevices between the papillae, where they come into contact with the taste buds. In turn, the taste buds release a neurotransmitter that causes adjacent neurons to fire (Finger et al., 2005), sending a nerve impulse to the parietal lobe of the brain and to the limbic system.

Taste, like the other senses, experiences adaptation. When you first start eating salted peanuts or potato chips, the saltiness is quite strong, but after a while it becomes less

pheromones Chemicals that communicate information to other organisms through smell.

taste buds Structures on the tongue that contain the receptor cells for taste.

ON THE CUTTING EDGE

PHEROMONES

"Something in the Way She Smells: Pheromones Enhance Females' Sexual Attractiveness to Males" (ABC News, 3/21/02)

"Pheromones Act as Sexual Magnet" (*http://www.sfsu.edu/~news/2002/19.htm*)

"Got Pheromones? Get Affection." WebMD (*my.webmd.com/content/article/25/2953_971*)

With headlines like those, it's no wonder that pheromones have triggered a lot of interest among researchers and nonresearchers alike! What are the facts?

It is true that many animals are capable of smelling pheromones. They also use those smells in daily living for such important things as marking their territory, identifying sexually receptive mates, and recognizing members of their group. Humans also have receptors for pheromones (Mateo, 2002; Takami, Getchell, Chen, Monti-Bloch, & Berliner, 1993) and, like other mammals, secrete and detect hormones (Benson, 2002; Doty, 2001; Thorne, Neave, Scholey,

Moss, & Fink, 2002). For example, studies have demonstrated that pheromones can affect the menstrual cycles in women (McClintock, 1999; K. Stern & McClintock, 1998). Researchers have also shown that when males are exposed to a natural female pheromone, their general mood is elevated and their ratings of the *sexual attractiveness* of females described in a story are enhanced. Similarly, when females and gay men are exposed to a natural male pheromone, their general mood is also elevated, as are their ratings of male *sexual attractiveness* (Savic, Berglund, & Lindstrom, 2005; Scholey, Bosworth, & Dimitrakaki, 1999; Thorne, Neave, Scholey, Moss, & Fink, 2002; Thorne, Scholey, & Neave, 2000). One recent study of three dozen female university students showed that women who used a perfume laced with a synthetic pheromone engaged in significantly more heterosexual behavior, although they were not approached more often by men nor did they have more informal dates when compared with women who

used the same perfume, but without the pheromone (McCoy & Pitino, 2002). Similar findings were reported in an earlier study of 17 heterosexual men (W. B. Cutler, Friedmann, & McCoy, 1998).

Thinking Critically About

Pheromones

1. After reading the summaries of research, what is your evaluation of the headlines at the top of this box? Is one headline more justified than the other? Why do you think so?

2. A search of the Internet by entering the word "pheromones" will reveal many vendors claiming that buying their pheromone products will enhance customers' sex lives. What additional evidence or information would you need in order to fully evaluate these claims?

3. Do you think that the preceding research findings would apply to everyone? Can you think of people or situations or cultures where the conclusions probably would not apply (i.e., "exceptions to the rule")?

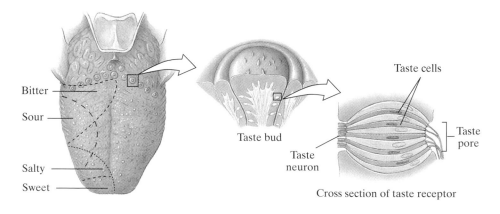

Figure 3–20
The structure of a taste bud.
The sensory receptors for taste are found primarily on the tongue. Taste cells can detect only sweet, sour, salty, bitter, and umami qualities. All other tastes result from different combinations of these taste sensations.

1. Different areas on the tongue are slightly more sensitive to different tastes.

2. When we eat, chemicals in the food dissolve in saliva and come into contact with the taste cells (receptors) within the taste buds.

3. Now, adjacent neurons fire, sending nerve impulses to the brain's parietal lobe, where the messages are perceived as taste.

noticeable. Furthermore, exposure to one quality of taste can modify other taste sensations—after brushing your teeth in the morning, for instance, you may notice that your orange juice has lost its sweetness.

KINESTHETIC AND VESTIBULAR SENSES

How do we know which way is up and whether we are moving or standing still?

The **kinesthetic senses** provide information about the speed and direction of our movement in space (Carello & Turvey, 2004). More specifically, they relay information about muscle movement, changes in posture, and strain on muscles and joints. Specialized nerve endings called **stretch receptors** are attached to muscle fibers, and different nerve endings called **Golgi tendon organs** are attached to the tendons, which connect muscle to bones. Together these two types of receptors provide constant feedback from the stretching and contraction of individual muscles. The information from these receptors travels via the spinal cord to the cortex of the parietal lobes, the same brain area that perceives the sense of touch.

The **vestibular senses** provide information about our orientation or position in space (Bottini et al., 2001). We use this information to determine which way is up and which way is down. Birds and fish also rely on these senses to determine in which direction they are heading when they cannot see well. Like hearing, the vestibular senses originate in the inner ear, where hair cells serve as the sense organs. There are actually two kinds of vestibular sensation. The first one, which relays messages about the speed and direction of body rotation, arises in the three *semicircular canals* of the inner ear. As in the cochlea, each canal is filled with fluid that shifts hair bundles, which in turn stimulate hair cells, sending a message to the brain about the speed and direction of body rotation.

The second vestibular sense gives us information about gravitation and movement forward and backward, up and down. This sense arises from the two *vestibular sacs* that lie between the semicircular canals and the cochlea. Both sacs are filled with a jellylike fluid that contains millions of tiny crystals. When the body moves horizontally or vertically, the crystals bend hair bundles, prompting a sensory message.

The nerve impulses from both vestibular organs travel to the brain along the auditory nerve, but their ultimate destinations in the brain are still something of a mystery. Certain messages from the vestibular system go to the cerebellum, which controls many of the reflexes involved in coordinated movement. Others reach the areas that regulate the internal body organs, and some find their way to the parietal lobe of the cerebral cortex for analysis and response.

Perhaps we are most acutely aware of our vestibular senses when we experience *motion sickness*. Certain kinds of motion, such as riding in ships, cars, airplanes, even on camels and elephants, trigger strong reactions in some people. According to one theory, motion sickness stems from discrepancies between visual information and vestibular sensations (Bubka & Bonato, 2003; R. M. Stern & Koch, 1996). In other words, our eyes and our body are sending our brain contradictory information. The same thing occurs when we watch an automobile chase scene that was filmed from inside a moving car: Our eyes tell our brain that we are moving, but the organs in our inner ear insist that we are sitting still. Susceptibility to motion sickness appears to be related to both race and genetics: People of Asian ancestry are particularly susceptible to motion sickness (Muth, Stern, Uijtdehaage, & Koch, 1994).

THE SKIN SENSES

What types of sensory messages are sent from the skin to the brain?

Our skin is our largest sense organ—a person 6 feet tall has about 21 square feet of skin. Skin protects us from the environment, holds in body fluids, regulates our internal temperature, and contains receptors for our sense of touch, which plays an important role in human interaction and emotion. In most societies, hellos and good-byes are accompanied by shaking hands, hugging, and other gestures involving touch. And in most cultures, lovers express their affection by kissing, holding hands, and caressing. Touching and being touched by

kinesthetic senses Senses of muscle movement, posture, and strain on muscles and joints.

stretch receptors Receptors that sense muscle stretch and contraction.

Golgi tendon organs Receptors that sense movement of the tendons, which connect muscle to bone.

vestibular senses The senses of equilibrium and body position in space.

This dancer is utilizing information provided by both her kinesthetic and her vestibular senses. Her kinesthetic senses are relaying messages pertaining to muscle strain and movements; her vestibular senses are supplying feedback about her body position in space.

others bridges, at least momentarily, our isolation. Of all our senses, then, touch may be the most comforting. In fact, as described in the "Applying Psychology" feature, some kinds of touch may even be medically beneficial.

The skin's numerous nerve receptors, distributed in varying concentrations throughout its surface, send nerve fibers to the brain by two routes. Some information goes through the medulla and the thalamus and from there to the sensory cortex in the parietal lobe of the brain—which is presumably where our experiences of touch, pressure, and so on arise. (See **Figure 2–8**.) Other information goes through the thalamus and then on to the reticular formation, which, as we saw in Chapter 2, is responsible for arousing the nervous system or quieting it down.

Skin receptors give rise to sensations of pressure, temperature, and pain, but the relationship between the receptors and our sensory experiences is a subtle one. Researchers believe that our brains draw on complex information about the patterns of activity received from many different receptors to detect and discriminate among skin sensations. For example, our skin has "cold fibers" that increase their firing rate as the skin cools down and that slow their firing when the skin heats up. Conversely, we have "warm fibers" that accelerate their firing rate when the skin gets warm and that slow down when the skin cools. The

APPLYING PSYCHOLOGY

MASSAGE: RUBBING PEOPLE THE RIGHT WAY?

Therapeutic massage is one of the most ancient practices related to medicine. The first book on the subject was written in China approximately 3000 B.C. For some time, however, the reputation of massage suffered, and it came to be regarded as something of an unproven, "alternative" practice. Recently, however, medical and psychological researchers have started taking another look at some of the benefits of a "hands-on" approach. Recent research indicates that massage therapy can

- *Help babies grow.* In a now-famous study, researchers compared premature infants who were massaged three times a day for 15 minutes at a time with a control group that was left untouched in their incubators (Field, 1986). The researchers found that the massaged babies were subsequently more responsive to faces and rattles and were generally more active than the other babies. Because of their comparatively rapid growth, the massaged infants were discharged from the hospital an average of 6 days earlier than the nonmassaged infants were. What's more, 8 months later,

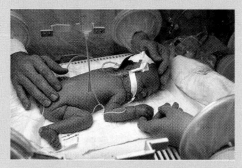

The human response to touch may sometimes be therapeutic. Gentle massage tends to calm agitated premature babies, and by regularly massaging them, their growth rate can be increased. These findings agree with the common belief that touch is among our most comforting senses.

the massaged infants maintained their weight advantage while performing better on tests of motor and mental ability. These results have had significant effects on the way parents and hospital staff care for premature infants (Dieter, Field, Hernandez, Emory, & Redzepi, 2003).

- *Reduce pain.* Adults also benefit from touching (Field, 2001). A study of 129 patients suffering from long-term musculoskeletal pain also found

that massage therapy was effective in reducing pain. A 3-month follow-up of these patients revealed, however, that their symptoms reappeared after the therapy had been discontinued (Hasson, Ametz, Jelveus, & Edelstam, 2004). Thus, the long-term benefits of massage therapy are still open to question.

- *Alleviate anxiety and depression.* One review of 37 studies evaluating massage therapy for adults with anxiety and depression (Moyer, Rounds, & Hannum, 2004) found that a single massage therapy session could effectively reduce immediate feelings of anxiety. Multiple sessions were effective at reducing long-term anxiety and depression, as well as for alleviating pain. The authors of this study concluded that multiple applications of massage therapy produced benefits similar to those of psychotherapy when used to treat anxiety and depression. Although additional research is needed before the benefits of massage therapy are fully understood and begin to gain widespread acceptance among therapists, results like these show promise.

brain may use the combined information from these two sets of fibers as the basis for determining skin temperature. If both sets are activated at once, the brain may read their combined pattern of firings as "hot" (Susser, Sprecher, & Yarnitsky, 1999). Thus, you might sometimes think that you are touching something hot when you are really touching something warm and something cool at the same time, a phenomenon known as *paradoxical heat*. (See **Figure 3–21**.)

The skin senses are remarkably sensitive. For example, skin displacement of as little as 0.00004 of an inch can result in a sensation of pressure. Moreover, various parts of the body differ greatly in their sensitivity to pressure: Your face and fingertips are extremely sensitive, whereas your legs, feet, and back are much less so. This remarkable sensitivity in our fingertips makes possible Braille touch reading, which requires identifying patterns of tiny raised dots distributed over a very small area.

Like other senses, the skin senses undergo various kinds of sensory adaptation. When we first get into a bath, it may be uncomfortably hot; but in a few minutes we adapt to the heat, just as our eyes adapt to darkness. Skin senses are also influenced by our expectations. When someone tickles us, our skin senses respond with excitement, but tickling ourselves produces no effect. Clearly, the brain draws on many sources of information in interpreting the sense of touch.

PAIN

What differences among people have an effect on the degree of pain they experience?

More people visit doctors for relief of pain than for any other reason. The economic impact of pain is nearly $100 billion a year in the United States alone (Mackey, 2005). Congress declared the first decade of the new millennium the "Decade of Pain Control and Research." Yet, to a great extent, pain remains a puzzle. What is the purpose of pain? An old adage holds that pain is nature's way of telling you that something is wrong; and it does seem reasonable to assume that damage to the body causes pain. But in many cases, actual physical injury is not accompanied by pain. Athletes injured during a game often feel no pain until the excitement of competition has passed. One researcher found that only 25 % of soldiers wounded during battle requested pain medication, whereas more than 80 % of surgical patients asked for painkillers for comparable "wounds" (Beecher, 1972).

Conversely, some people feel pain without having been injured or long after an injury has healed (Watkins & Maier, 2003). One of the most perplexing examples of this is the *phantom limb phenomenon* (Sherman, 1996), which occurs in about 85 % of amputees. After amputation of an arm or a leg, a patient often continues to feel the missing limb is still there. The site of the missing limb may itch, tickle, cramp, or be a source of considerable pain; the patient may even forget that the limb is gone and try to move it. As the brain slowly reorganizes the neurons associated with the amputated limb, the pain often subsides with time (Flor, Elbert, Knecht, Weinbruch, & Pantev, 1995), demonstrating the force of neural plasticity (see Chapter 2).

GATE-CONTROL THEORY The sensation of pain in many ways remains mysterious, but some progress has been made in understanding why and how pain occurs. For example, although we can reasonably assume that pain occurs when a pain receptor is stimulated, it turns out that there is no simple relationship between pain receptors and the experience of pain. In fact, scientists have had great difficulty even finding pain receptors. However, research indicates that free nerve endings may be involved (Dubner & Gold, 1998). When body tissue is damaged, information from these receptors travels to the spinal cord where, according to the **gate-control theory** of pain, a "neurological gate" in the spinal cord controls the transmission of pain impulses to the brain (Melzack, 1980; Melzack, & Katz, 2004). If the gate is open, we experience more pain than when it is closed. Whether the gate is closed or open depends on a complex competition between two different types of sensory nerve fibers—large fibers that "close the gate" and small fibers that "open the gate" when they are stimulated, enabling transmission of pain messages to the brain.

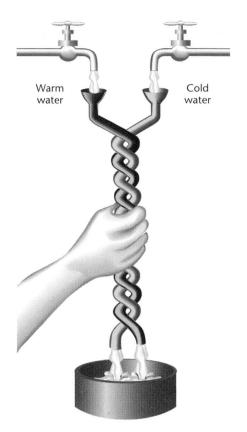

Figure 3–21
Paradoxical heat.
Touching a warm pipe and a cold pipe at the same time causes two sets of skin receptors to signal at once to the brain. The brain reads their combined pattern of firings as "hot," a phenomenon known as paradoxical heat.

gate-control theory The theory that a "neurological gate" in the spinal cord controls the transmission of pain messages to the brain.

biopsychosocial theory The theory that the interaction of biological, psychological, and cultural factors influences the intensity and duration of pain.

When pain messages reach the brain, a complex series of reactions begins. As we saw in Chapter 2, the sympathetic nervous system springs into action. The nervous system and endocrine system go on alert to help deal with the crisis. Meanwhile, chemicals to reduce or stop the pain messages may be released both in the brain and in the spinal cord. Certain areas of the brain stem may also reduce the flow of incoming pain information by sending signals to fibers in the spinal cord to partially or completely close the "gate." These processes account for the fact that, despite an injury, little or no pain may be experienced.

Individuals vary widely both in their *pain threshold* (the amount of stimulation required to feel pain) and their *pain tolerance* (the amount of pain with which they can cope). Most people do experience pain, but there is no absolute correspondence between the perception of pain and the amount of tissue damage sustained. How, then, do psychologists explain why the experience of pain differs among individuals? According to the gate control theory, these differences are governed primarily by the number of small and large sensory nerve fibers a person has. Also, some people may have faulty neurological gates, resulting in a greater or lesser experience of pain than others. To the extent that these differences are hereditary, it follows that some people may be born with greater pain sensitivity than other people.

BIOPSYCHOSOCIAL THEORY Some psychologists believe that the gate-control theory oversimplifies the complex experience we call pain. According to **biopsychosocial theory**, pain sensations involve three interrelated phenomena: biological mechanisms, psychological mechanisms, and social mechanisms.

Biological mechanisms involve the degree to which tissue is injured (as discussed above) and our pain pathways have adapted. For example, chronic pain can alter pathways in the nervous system. As a result, the nerves in the spinal cord can become hypersensitive. Let's say you break a bone in your foot and don't get medical attention until pain prevents you from walking. Even after the break heals, a mild blow to your foot may be painful.

Genetics also appears to play a role. Scientists have recently identified a small genetic variation that accounts partially for individual differences in the experience of pain. Not surprisingly, this gene produces an enzyme involved in the production of endorphins in the brain, which, as we saw in Chapter 2, are implicated in regulating pain and mood (Zubieta et al., 2003).

Psychological mechanisms—our thoughts, beliefs, and emotions—also can affect our experience of pain. In a recent study in which heat pulses were administered to the lower right leg, participants who expected only moderate pain reported much less pain when the stimulus was actually severe. Moreover, there was much lower activity in pain-related brain areas; and participants' expectations of lower pain were almost as effective as morphine in relieving physical pain (Koyama, McHaffie, Laurienti, & Coghill, 2005).

Some people make an active effort to cope with pain: Confident that they can overcome pain, they avoid negative feelings ("I'll get better"), engage in diverting activities, and refuse to let pain interfere with their daily lives. By contrast, others with the same injuries or disorders are overwhelmed: They feel "victimized," that their pain is beyond their control, that it is ruling their life, and that no one understands. Studies indicate that believing in one's ability to cope may actually cause higher brain centers to reduce or block pain signals (Padhi, 2005; Wall & Melzack, 1996). And even temporary psychological states can have an impact; researchers have found that distracting people with sounds or pleasant aromas can reduce not only the sensation of pain, but also activity in portions of the brain that respond to pain (Villemure & Bushnell, 2002; Villemure, Slotnick, & Bushnell, 2003).

Social mechanisms, such as the degree of family support, can also influence the experience and management of pain. In one large study of chronic pain patients, those who described their families as being supportive reported significantly less pain intensity, less reliance on medication, and greater activity levels than patients who reported family disharmony and limited support (Jamison & Virts, 1990). Subsequent research has produced similar results with a variety of painful disorders (Evers, Kraaimaat, Geenen, Jacobs, & Bijlsma, 2003; Holtzman, Newth, & Delongis, 2004). Cultural expectations can also affect the experience of pain as well as ways of coping with pain. (Bonham, 2001; M. Sullivan, 2004; Weissman, Gordon, & Biedar-

Glowing coals smolder under the feet of these participants in an annual ritual at Mt. Takao, Japan. How do they do it? Is it mind over matter—the human ability to sometimes "turn off" pain sensations? The secret in this case may actually lie more in the coals than in the men. Because wood is a poor conductor of heat, walking over wood coals quickly may not be that painful after all.

Sielaff, 2002). For example, one study of the difference in reported pain between Hispanics and Caucasians with serious health problems demonstrated that Hispanics were more likely to report higher levels of pain than Caucasians (Hernandez & Sachs-Ericsson, 2006).

ALTERNATIVE TREATMENTS Increasingly, Americans are turning to so-called alternative medicine to treat chronic pain. Are people who use these approaches fooling themselves? Many studies have shown that if you give pain sufferers a chemically inert pill, or *placebo*, but tell them that it is an effective pain reducer, they often report some relief. No doubt many home remedies and secret cures rely on the **placebo effect**. Research indicates that both placebos and acupuncture, which involves the insertion of thin needles into parts of the body, work in part through the release of endorphins, the pain-blocking neurotransmitters that we examined in Chapter 2 (Zubieta et al., 2005). But recent research shows that even for placebos and acupuncture, endorphin release alone does not account for pain reduction (Kong et al., 2006; Matre, Casey, & Knardahl, 2006). Moreover, some other pain-reduction techniques—such as hypnosis or related concentration exercises (as in the Lamaze birth technique)—appear to have nothing at all to do with endorphins, but rely on some other means of reducing the pain sensation (deCharms et al., 2005). As you can see, much more research is needed before we will fully understand the sensation of pain.

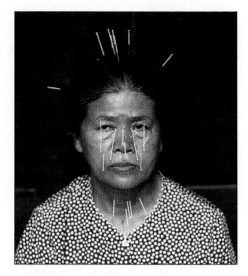

Traditional Asian medicine has used acupuncture to reduce or eliminate pain. Studies indicate that acupuncture works by releasing endorphins into the body.

CHECK YOUR UNDERSTANDING

1. The basic tastes are _____, _____, _____, _____, and _____.
2. Skin senses include sensations of _____, _____, and _____.
3. Our _____ sense provides awareness of our body's position.

Answers: 1. sweet, sour, salty, bitter and umami. 2. pressure, temperature, and pain. 3. kinesthetic.

APPLY YOUR UNDERSTANDING

1. A seven-year-old is asked to eat something that he would rather not eat. He holds his nose, eats it, and says, "Ha! I couldn't taste it!" You remember what you have learned in this course, and you decide to correct him: "Actually, you have only gotten rid of
   a. the flavor, not the taste."
   b. the taste, not the flavor."
   c. the smell, not the taste or flavor."
   d. the papillae, not the taste."

2. George suffers from chronic back pain. His doctor suggests that he try a form of therapy in which electrical stimulation is applied to his back. You recognize that this therapy is based on the idea that stimulating large sensory nerves in the spinal cord can prevent the sensation of pain, and that it is an application of the _____ theory of pain.
   a. gate-control
   b. contra-stimulation
   c. free nerve ending
   d. patterned-firing

Answers: 1. a. 2. a.

Perception

How is perception different from sensation?

Our senses provide us with raw data about the external world. But unless we interpret this raw information, it is nothing more than what William James (1890) called a "booming, buzzing confusion." The eye records patterns of lightness and darkness, but it does not "see" a bird flittering from branch to branch. The eardrum vibrates in a particular fashion,

placebo effect Pain relief that occurs when a person believes a pill or procedure will reduce pain. The actual cause of the relief seems to come from endorphins.

Figure 3–22
Perception transforms sensation into a meaningful whole.
(Left) Closeup of a pointillist painting. *(Right)* The painting in its entirety.

Source: Signac, Paul (1893-1935), "Saint-Tropez, in a thunderstorm." Musee de l'Annonciade, St. Tropez, France. Reunion des Musees Nationaux/Art Resource, NY. © ARS, NY.

perception The brain's interpretation of sensory information so as to give it meaning.

but it does not "hear" a symphony. Deciphering *meaningful* patterns in the jumble of sensory information is what we mean by perception. But how does perception differ from sensation?

Perception is the brain's process of organizing and making sense of sensory information. Using sensory information as raw material, the brain creates perceptual experiences that go beyond what is sensed directly. The close up of the painting in **Figure 3–22** corresponds to sensation: discrete "blips" of color. Viewed as a whole, however, these units of color become a picture. Another graphic illustration of the way perception transforms mere sensations into a meaningful whole can be seen in **Figure 3–23**. Although we tend to perceive a white triangle in the center of the pattern, the sensory input consists only of three circles from which "pie slices" have been cut and three 60-degree angles. Or consider **Figure 3–24**. At first glance most people see only an assortment of black blotches. However, when you are told that the blotches represent a person riding a horse, suddenly your perceptual experience changes. What was meaningless sensory information now takes shape as a horse and rider.

How do we see objects and shapes? Psychologists assume that perception begins with some real-world object with real-world properties "out there." Psychologists call that object, along with its important perceptual properties, the *distal stimulus*. We never experience the distal stimulus directly, however. Energy from it (or in the case of our chemical

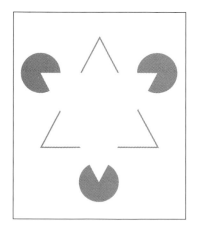

Figure 3–23
An illusory triangle.
When sensory information is incomplete, we tend to create a complete perception by supplying the missing details. In this figure we fill in the lines that let us perceive a white triangle in the center of the pattern.

Figure 3–24
Perceiving a pattern.
Knowing beforehand that the black blotches in this figure represent a person riding a horse changes our perception of it.

senses, molecules from it) must activate our sensory system. We call the information that reaches our sensory receptors the *proximal* stimulus. Although the distal stimulus and the proximal stimulus are never the same thing, our perception of the distal stimulus is usually very accurate.

Sometimes, as in certain optical illusions, you perceive things that could not possibly exist. The trident shown in **Figure 3–25** exemplifies such an "impossible" figure; on closer inspection, you discover that the object that you "recognized" is not really there. In all these cases, the brain actively creates and organizes perceptual experiences out of raw sensory data—sometimes even from data we are not aware of receiving. We now explore how perceptual processes organize sensory experience.

PERCEPTUAL ORGANIZATION

How do we organize our perceptual experiences?

Early in the 20th century, a group of German psychologists, calling themselves *Gestalt psychologists*, set out to discover the principles through which we interpret sensory information. The German word *Gestalt* has no exact English equivalent, but essentially it means "whole," "form," or "pattern." The Gestalt psychologists believed that the brain creates a coherent perceptual experience that is more than simply the sum of the available sensory information and that it does so in predictable ways.

In one important facet of the perceptual process, we distinguish *figures* from the *ground* against which they appear. A colorfully upholstered chair stands out from the bare walls of a room. A marble statue is perceived as a whole figure separate from the red brick wall behind it. The figure–ground distinction pertains to all of our senses, not just vision. We can distinguish a violin solo against the ground of a symphony orchestra, a single voice amid cocktail-party chatter, and the smell of roses in a florist's shop. In all these instances, we perceive some objects as "figures" and other sensory information as "background."

Sometimes, however, there are not enough cues in a pattern to permit us to easily distinguish a figure from its ground. The horse and rider in **Figure 3–24** illustrate this problem, as does **Figure 3–26**, which shows a spotted dog investigating shadowy

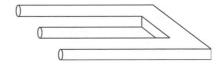

Figure 3–25
An optical illusion.
In the case of the trident, we go beyond what is sensed (blue lines on flat white paper) to perceive a three-dimensional object that isn't really there.

Figure 3–26
Random dots or something more?
This pattern does not give us enough cues to allow us to easily distinguish the figure of the Dalmatian dog from the ground behind it.
Source: Gregory, 1970.

It's not what it looks like.

Source: © *The New Yorker Collection*, 2000.
John O'Brien from *www.cartoonbank.com*.
All rights reserved.

surroundings. It is hard to distinguish the dog because it has few visible contours of its own, and as a result, it seems to have no more form than the background. This is the principle behind camouflage: to make a figure blend into its background.

Sometimes a figure with clear contours can be perceived in two very different ways because it is unclear which part of the stimulus is the figure and which is the ground. (See **Figures 3–27** and **3–28**.) At first glance, you perceive figures against a specific background, but as you stare at the illustrations, you will discover that the figures and the ground reverse, making for two very different perceptions of the same illustration. The artwork or stimulus hasn't changed, but your perception has changed (Adelson, 2002; Vecera, Vogel, & Woodman, 2002).

Figure 3–29 demonstrates some other important principles of perceptual organization. As these figures demonstrate, we use sensory information to create a perception that is more than just the sum of the parts. Although sometimes this process can cause problems, the perceptual tendency to "fill in the blanks" usually broadens our understanding of the world. In its search for meaning, our brain tries to fill in missing information, to group various objects together, to see whole objects, and to hear meaningful sounds, rather than just random bits and pieces of raw, sensory data (Shermer, 2005).

Figure 3–27

The reversible figure and ground in this M. C. Escher woodcut cause us first to see black devils and then to see white angels in each of the rings.

Source: M. C. Escher's "Circle Limit IV" © 2003, Cordon Art B. V. Baarn, Holland. All rights reserved.

Figure 3–28

Figure–ground relationship . . . How do you perceive this figure?

Do you see a goblet or the silhouettes of a man and a woman? Both interpretations are possible, but not at the same time in reversible figures like this work because it is unclear which part of the stimulus is the figure and which is the neutral ground against which the figure is perceived.

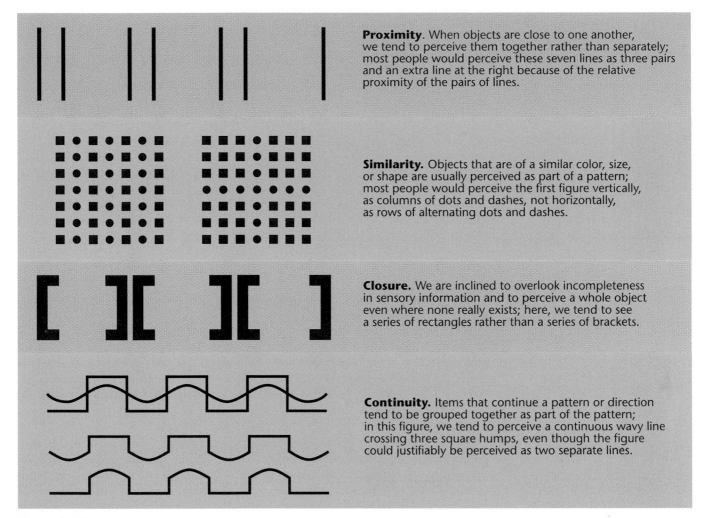

Proximity. When objects are close to one another, we tend to perceive them together rather than separately; most people would perceive these seven lines as three pairs and an extra line at the right because of the relative proximity of the pairs of lines.

Similarity. Objects that are of a similar color, size, or shape are usually perceived as part of a pattern; most people would perceive the first figure vertically, as columns of dots and dashes, not horizontally, as rows of alternating dots and dashes.

Closure. We are inclined to overlook incompleteness in sensory information and to perceive a whole object even where none really exists; here, we tend to see a series of rectangles rather than a series of brackets.

Continuity. Items that continue a pattern or direction tend to be grouped together as part of the pattern; in this figure, we tend to perceive a continuous wavy line crossing three square humps, even though the figure could justifiably be perceived as two separate lines.

Figure 3–29
Gestalt principles of perceptual organization.

PERCEPTUAL CONSTANCIES

How do we perceive things as unchanging despite changing sensory information?

When anthropologist Colin Turnbull (1961) studied the Mbuti pygmies of Zaire, most of them had never left the dense Ituri rain forest and had rarely encountered objects that were more than a few feet away. On one occasion, Turnbull took a pygmy guide named Kenge on a trip onto the African plains. When Kenge looked across the plain and saw a distant herd of buffalo, he asked what kind of insects they were. He refused to believe that the tiny black spots he saw were buffalo. As he and Turnbull drove toward the herd, Kenge believed that magic was making the animals grow larger. Because he had no experience of distant objects, he could not perceive the buffalo as having constant size.

Perceptual constancy refers to the tendency to perceive objects as relatively stable and unchanging despite changing sensory information. Once we have formed a stable perception of an object, we can recognize it from almost any position, at almost any distance, under almost any illumination. A white house looks like a white house by day or by night and from any angle. We see it as the same house. The sensory information may change as illumination and perspective change, but the object is perceived as constant. Without this ability, we would find the world very confusing (as Kenge did).

perceptual constancy A tendency to perceive objects as stable and unchanging despite changes in sensory stimulation.

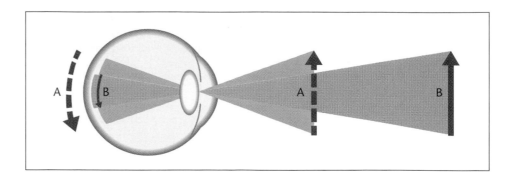

Figure 3–30

The relationship between distance and the size of the retinal image.
Object A and object B are the same size, but A, being much closer to the eye, casts a much larger image on the retina.

We tend to perceive familiar objects at their true size regardless of the size of the image that they cast on the retina. As **Figure 3–30** shows, the farther away an object is from the lens of the eye, the smaller the retinal image it casts. We might guess that a woman some distance away is 5 feet 4 inches tall when she is really 5 feet 8 inches, but hardly anyone would perceive her as being 3 feet tall, no matter how far away she is. We know from experience that adults are seldom that short. **Size constancy** depends partly on experience—information about the relative sizes of objects stored in memory—and partly on distance cues.

Familiar objects also tend to be seen as having a constant shape, even though the retinal images they cast change as they are viewed from different angles. This is called **shape constancy**. A dinner plate is perceived as a circle even when it is tilted and the retinal image is oval. A rectangular door will project a rectangular image on the retina only when it is viewed directly from the front. From any other angle, it casts a trapezoidal image on the retina, but it is not perceived as having suddenly become a trapezoidal door. (See **Figure 3–31**.)

Similarly, we tend to perceive familiar objects as keeping their colors, regardless of information that reaches the eye. If you own a red automobile, you will see it as red whether it is on a brightly lit street or in a dark garage, where the low light may send your eye a message that it is closer to brown or black than red. But **color constancy** does not always hold true. When objects are unfamiliar or there are no customary color cues to guide us, color constancy may be distorted—as when you buy a sweater in a brightly lit store, only to discover that in ordinary daylight, it is not the shade you thought it was.

Brightness constancy means that even though the amount of light available to our eyes varies greatly over the course of a day, the perceived brightness of familiar objects hardly varies at all. We perceive a sheet of white paper as brighter than a piece of coal whether we see these objects in candlelight or under bright sunlight. Brightness constancy occurs because an object reflects the same percentage of the light falling on it whether that light is from a candle or the sun. Rather than basing our judgment of brightness on the absolute amount of light that the object reflects, we assess how the relative reflection compares with the surrounding objects.

size constancy The perception of an object as the same size regardless of the distance from which it is viewed.

shape constancy A tendency to see an object as the same shape no matter what angle it is viewed from.

color constancy An inclination to perceive familiar objects as retaining their color despite changes in sensory information.

brightness constancy The perception of brightness as the same, even though the amount of light reaching the retina changes.

Figure 3–31

Examples of shape constancy.
Even though the image of the door on the retina changes greatly as the door opens, we still perceive the door as being rectangular.

Source: From *Foundations of Psychology* by E. G. Boring, H. S. Langfeld, H. P. & Weld (1976). Reprinted by permission of John Wiley & Sons.

Memory and experience play important roles in perceptual constancy. Look at **Figure 3–32**. If you see former President Clinton and Vice President Gore, look again! Clinton's face has been superimposed over Gore's. Because we focus on the perceptual cues of head shape, hair style, and context (the microphones and the president are standing in front of the vice president, as protocol requires) we perceive the more likely image of the president and vice president standing together.

PERCEPTION OF DISTANCE AND DEPTH

How do we know how far away something is?

We are constantly judging the distance between ourselves and other objects. When we walk through a classroom, our perception of distance helps us to avoid bumping into desks or tripping over the wastebasket. If we reach out to pick up a pencil, we automatically judge how far to extend our hand. We also assess the depth of objects—how much total space they occupy. We use many cues to determine the distance and the depth of objects. Some of these cues depend on visual messages that one eye alone can transmit; these are called **monocular cues**. Others, known as **binocular cues**, require the use of both eyes. Having two eyes allows us to make more accurate judgments about distance and depth, particularly when objects are relatively close. But monocular cues alone are often sufficient to allow us to judge distance and depth quite accurately, as we see in the next section.

MONOCULAR CUES One important monocular distance cue that provides us with information about relative position is called interposition. **Interposition** occurs when one object partly blocks a second object. The first object is perceived as being closer, the second as more distant. (See **Figure 3–33**.)

As art students learn, there are several ways in which perspective can help in estimating distance and depth. In **linear perspective**, two parallel lines that extend into the distance seem to come together at some point on the horizon. In **aerial perspective**, distant objects have a hazy appearance and a somewhat blurred outline. On a clear day, mountains often seem to be much closer than on a hazy day, when their outlines become blurred. The **elevation** of an object also serves as a perspective cue to depth: An object that is on a higher horizontal plane seems to be farther away than one on a lower plane. (See **Figure 3–34**.)

Another useful monocular cue to distance and depth is **texture gradient**. An object that is close seems to have a rough or detailed texture. As distance increases, the texture becomes finer, until finally the original texture cannot be distinguished clearly, if at all. For

Figure 3–32
Look again!
Context, hair style, and head shape lead us to believe that this is a picture of former President Clinton and former Vice President Gore when, in reality, Clinton's face is superimposed over the face of Gore.

Source: APA Monitor, 1997.

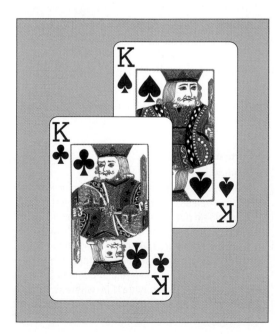

Figure 3–33
Interposition.
Because the King of Clubs appears to have been superimposed on the King of Spades, we perceive it to be closer to us.

monocular cues Visual cues requiring the use of one eye.

binocular cues Visual cues requiring the use of both eyes.

interposition Monocular distance cue in which one object, by partly blocking a second object, is perceived as being closer.

linear perspective Monocular cue to distance and depth based on the fact that two parallel lines seem to come together at the horizon.

aerial perspective Monocular cue to distance and depth based on the fact that more distant objects are likely to appear hazy and blurred.

elevation Monocular cue to distance and depth based on the fact that the higher on the horizontal plane an object is, the farther away it appears.

texture gradient Monocular cue to distance and depth based on the fact that objects seen at greater distances appear to be smoother and less textured.

Figure 3–34
Elevation as a visual cue.
Because of the higher elevation and the suggestion of depth provided by the road, the tree on the right is perceived as being more distant and about the same size as the tree at lower left. Actually, it is appreciably smaller, as you can see if you measure the heights of the two drawings.

example, when standing on a pebbly beach, you can distinguish among the gray stones and the gravel in front of your feet. As you look down the beach, however, the stones appear to become smaller and finer until eventually you cannot make out individual stones at all (See **Figure 3–36**). **Shadowing**, another important cue to the distance, depth, and solidity of an object, is illustrated in **Figure 3–35**.

Bus or train passengers often notice that nearby trees or telephone poles seem to flash past the windows, whereas buildings and other objects farther away seem to move slowly. These differences in the speeds of movement of images across the retina as you move give an important cue to distance and depth. You can observe the same effect if you stand still and move your head from side to side as you focus your gaze on something in the middle distance: Objects close to you seem to move in the direction opposite to the direction in which your head is moving, whereas objects far away seem to move in the same direction as your head. This distance cue is known as **motion parallax**.

BINOCULAR CUES All the visual cues examined so far depend on the action of only one eye. Many animals—such as horses, deer, and fish—rely entirely on monocular cues. Although they have two eyes, the two visual fields do not overlap, because their eyes are located on the sides of the head rather than in front. Humans, apes, and many predatory animals—such as lions, tigers, and wolves—have a distinct physical advantage over these other animals. Because both eyes are set in the front of the head, the visual fields overlap. The **stereoscopic vision** derived from combining the two retinal images—one from each eye—makes the perception of depth and distance more accurate.

Because our eyes are set approximately $2\frac{1}{2}$ inches apart, each one has a slightly different view of things. The difference between the two images that the eyes receive is known as **retinal disparity**. The left eye receives more information about the left side of an object,

shadowing Monocular cue to distance and depth based on the fact that shadows often appear on the parts of objects that are more distant.

motion parallax Monocular distance cue in which objects closer than the point of visual focus seem to move in the direction opposite to the viewer's moving head, and objects beyond the focus point appear to move in the same direction as the viewer's head.

stereoscopic vision Combination of two retinal images to give a three-dimensional perceptual experience.

retinal disparity Binocular distance cue based on the difference between the images cast on the two retinas when both eyes are focused on the same object.

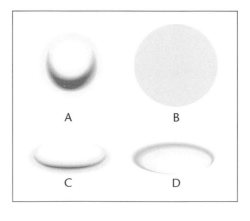

Figure 3–35
Shadowing.
Shadowing on the outer edges of a spherical object, such as a ball or globe, gives it a three-dimensional quality (A). Without shadowing (B), it might be perceived as a flat disk. Shadowing can also affect our perception of the direction of depth. In the absence of other cues, we tend to assume overhead lighting, so image C appears to be a bump because its top edge is lit, whereas image D appears to be a dent. If you turn the book upside down, the direction of depth is reversed.

Figure 3–36
Texture gradient.
Note how the nearby pebbles on this beach appear larger and clearer than the distant ones.

and the right eye receives more information about the right side. You can easily prove that each of your eyes receives a different image. Close one eye and line up a finger with some vertical line, like the edge of a door. Then open that eye and close the other one. Your finger will appear to have moved a great distance. When you look at the finger with both eyes, however, the two different images become one.

An important binocular cue to distance comes from the muscles that control the **convergence** of the eyes. When we look at objects that are fairly close to us, our eyes tend to converge—to turn slightly inward toward each other. The sensations from the muscles that control the movement of the eyes thus provide a cue to distance. If the object is very close, such as at the end of the nose, the eyes cannot converge, and two separate images are perceived. If the object is more than a few yards (meters) away, the sight lines of the eyes are more or less parallel, and there is no convergence.

LOCATION OF SOUNDS Just as we use monocular and binocular cues to establish visual depth and distance, we draw on **monaural** (single-ear) and **binaural** (two-ear) **cues** to locate the source of sounds. (See **Figure 3–37**.) In one monaural cue, loud sounds are perceived as closer than faint sounds, with changes in loudness translating into changes in distance. Binaural cues work on the principle that because sounds off to one side of the head reach one ear slightly ahead of the other (in the range of 1/1000th of a second), the time difference between sound waves reaching the two ears registers in the brain and helps us to make accurate judgments of location.

In a second binaural cue, sound signals arriving from a source off to one side of you are slightly louder in the nearer ear than in the ear farther from the source. The slight difference occurs because your head, in effect, blocks the sound, reducing the intensity of sound in the opposite ear. This relative loudness difference between signals heard separately by the two ears is enough for the brain to locate the sound source and to judge its distance. When sound engineers record your favorite musical group, they may place microphones at many different locations. On playback, the two speakers or headphones project sounds at slightly different instants to mimic the sound patterns you would hear if you were actually listening to the group perform right in front of you.

Most of us rely so heavily on visual cues that we seldom pay much attention to the rich array of auditory information available around us. Blind people, who often compensate for their lack of vision by sharpening their awareness of sounds (Morgan, 1999), can figure out where obstacles lie in their paths by listening to the echoes from a cane, their own footsteps, and their own voices. Many blind people can judge the size and distance of one object in

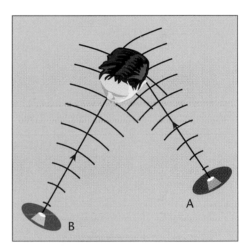

Figure 3–37
Cues used in sound localization.
Sound waves coming from source B will reach both ears simultaneously. A sound wave from source A reaches the left ear first, where it is also louder. The head casts a "shadow" over the other ear, thus reducing the intensity of the delayed sound in that ear.

Source: From *Foundations of Psychology* by E. G. Boring, H. S. Langfeld, H. P., & Weld, (1976). Reprinted by permission of John Wiley & Sons

convergence A visual depth cue that comes from muscles controlling eye movement as the eyes turn inward to view a nearby stimulus.

monaural cues Cues to sound location that require just one ear.

binaural cues Cues to sound location that involve both ears working together.

autokinetic illusion The perception that a stationary object is actually moving.

stroboscopic motion Apparent movement that results from flashing a series of still pictures in rapid succession, as in a motion picture.

phi phenomenon Apparent movement caused by flashing lights in sequence, as on theater marquees.

relation to another by using nothing more than sound cues. They can also discriminate between contrasting surfaces, such as glass and fabric, by listening to the difference in the echo produced when sound strikes them.

PERCEPTION OF MOVEMENT

How do we perceive movement?

The perception of movement is a complicated process involving both visual information from the retina and messages from the muscles around the eyes as they follow an object. On occasion, our perceptual processes play tricks on us, and we think we perceive movement when the objects that we are looking at are in fact stationary. We must distinguish, therefore, between real and apparent movement.

Real movement refers to the physical displacement of an object from one position to another. The perception of real movement depends only in part on movement of images across the retina of the eye. If you stand still and move your head to look around you, the images of all the objects in the room will pass across your retina. Yet you will probably perceive all of the objects as stationary. Even if you hold your head still and move only your eyes, the images will continue to pass across your retina. But the messages from the eye muscles seem to counteract those from the retina, so the objects in the room will be perceived as motionless.

The perception of real movement seems to be determined less by images moving across the retina than by how the position of objects changes in relation to a background that is perceived as stationary. When we perceive a car moving along a street, for example, we see the street, the buildings, and the sidewalk as a stationary background and the car as a moving object.

Apparent movement occurs when we perceive movement in objects that are actually standing still. One form of apparent movement is referred to as the **autokinetic illusion**—the perceived motion created by the absence of visual cues surrounding a single stationary object. If you stand in a room that is absolutely dark except for one tiny spot of light and stare at the light for a few seconds, you will begin to see the light drift. In the darkened room, your eyes have no visible framework; there are no cues telling you that the light is really stationary. The slight movements of the eye muscles, which go unnoticed most of the time, make the light appear to move.

Another form of apparent movement is **stroboscopic motion**—the apparent motion created by a rapid series of still images. This form of apparent movement is illustrated best by a motion picture, which is not in motion at all. The film consists of a series of still pictures showing people and objects in slightly different positions. When the separate images are projected sequentially onto a screen at a specific rate of speed, the people and objects seem to be moving because of the rapid change from one still picture to the next.

Another common perceptual illusion, known as the **phi phenomenon**, occurs as a result of stroboscopic motion. When a light is flashed on at a certain point in a darkened room, then flashed off, and a second light is flashed on a split second later at a point a short distance away, most people will perceive these two separate lights as a single spot of light

When we look at an electronic marquee such as this one, we see motion, even though the sign consists of stationary lights that are flashed on and off.

moving from one point to another. This perceptual process causes us to see motion in neon signs or theater marquees, where words appear to move across the sign, from one side to the other, as the different combinations of stationary lights are flashed on and off.

VISUAL ILLUSIONS

What causes visual illusions?

Visual illusions graphically demonstrate the ways in which we use a variety of sensory cues to create perceptual experiences that may (or may not) correspond to what is out there in the real world. By understanding how we are fooled into "seeing" something that isn't there, psychologists can figure out how perceptual processes work in the everyday world and under normal circumstances.

Psychologists generally distinguish between physical and perceptual illusions. One example of a *physical illusion* is the bent appearance of a stick when it is placed in water—an illusion easily understood because the water acts like a prism, bending the light waves before they reach our eyes. *Perceptual illusions* occur because the stimulus contains misleading cues that give rise to inaccurate or impossible perceptions.

The illusions in **Figure 3–38** and **Figure 3–39** result from false and misleading depth cues (Spehar & Gillam, 2002). For example, in **Figure 3–39C**, both monsters cast the same size image on the retina in our eyes. But the depth cues in the tunnel suggest that we are looking at a three-dimensional scene and that therefore the top monster is much farther away. In the real world, this perception would mean that the top monster is actually much larger than the bottom monster. Therefore we "correct" for the distance and actually perceive the top monster as larger, despite other cues to the contrary. We know that the image is actually two dimensional, but we still respond to it as if it were three dimensional.

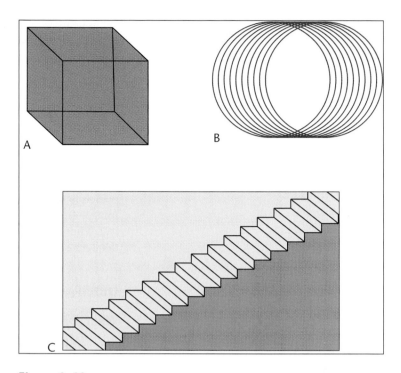

Figure 3–38
Reversible figures.
Images A, B, and C are examples of reversible figures—drawings that we can perceive two different ways, but not at the same time.

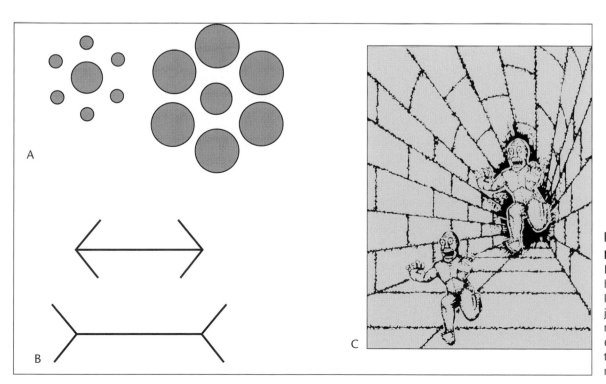

Figure 3–39
Misleading depth cues.
Images A, B, and C show how, through the use of misleading depth cues, we misjudge the size of objects. The middle circles in image A are exactly the same size, as are the lines in Image B and the monsters in Image C.

There are also "real-world" illusions that illustrate how perceptual processes work, such as the illusion of *induced movement*. When you are sitting in a stationary train and the train next to you begins to move forward, you seem to be moving backward. Because you have no reference point by which to tell whether you are standing still, you are confused as to which train is actually moving. However, if you look down at the ground, you can establish an unambiguous frame of reference and make the situation clear to yourself.

Artists rely on many of these perceptual phenomena both to represent reality accurately and to distort it deliberately. In paintings and sketches drawn on a two-dimensional surface, it is almost always necessary to distort objects for them to be perceived correctly by viewers. For example, in representational art, the railroad tracks, sidewalks, and tunnels are always drawn closer together in the distance. Three-dimensional movies also work on the principle that the brain can be deceived into seeing three dimensions if slightly different images are presented to the left and right eyes (working on the principle of retinal disparity). Thus, our understanding of perceptual illusion enables us to manipulate images for deliberate effect—and to delight in the results.

OBSERVER CHARACTERISTICS

What personal factors influence our perceptions?

We clearly draw on past experience and learning when it comes to perception, but our own motivations, values, expectations, cognitive style, and cultural preconceptions can also affect our perceptual experiences. Although the focus of this section is on differences among individuals, consider how a person's sensory and perceptual experiences are affected by race, culture, and gender.

Diversity–Universality   How Does Ethnicity Influence Perception?

All normal human beings have the same sense organs and perceptual capacity. Yet our individuality—our motivations, values, expectations, cognitive style, and cultural preconceptions—influences what we perceive. We focus on individual differences in this section. But as you read, think about the degree to which people's sensory and perceptual experiences differ depending on their race, culture, or gender. ●●

MOTIVATION Our desires and needs shape our perceptions. People in need are likely to perceive something that they think will satisfy that need. The best known example of this, at least in fiction, is a *mirage*: People lost in the desert have visual fantasies of an oasis over the next dune. Research has found that when people have not eaten (16 hours seems to be a cutoff point) they perceive vague images or ambiguous pictures related to food (McClelland & Atkinson, 1948; Sanford, 1937).

VALUES In an experiment that revealed how strongly perceptions can be affected by a person's values, nursery, school-children were shown a poker chip. Each child was asked to compare the size of the chip with the size of an adjustable circle of light until the child said that the chip and the circle of light were the same size. The children were then brought to a machine with a crank that, when turned, produced a poker chip that could be exchanged for candy. Thus, the children were taught to value the poker chips more highly than they had before. After the children had been rewarded with candy for the poker chips, they were again asked to compare the size of the chips with a circle of light. This time the chips seemed larger to the children (W. W. Lambert, Solomon, & Watson, 1949).

EXPECTATIONS Preconceptions about what we are supposed to perceive can influence perception by causing us to delete, insert, transpose, or otherwise modify what we see (S. J. Lachman, 1996). S. J. Lachman (1984) demonstrated this phenomenon by asking people to copy a group of stimuli similar to this one:

PARIS
IN THE
THE SPRING

Often, people tended to omit the "extra" words and to report seeing more familiar (and more normal) expressions, such as PARIS IN THE SPRING. This phenomenon reflects a strong tendency to see what we *expect* to see, even if our expectation conflicts with external reality.

COGNITIVE STYLE As we mature, we develop a cognitive style—our own way of dealing with the environment—that also affects how we see the world. Some psychologists distinguish between two general approaches that people use in perceiving the world (Witkin et al., 1962; Zhang, 1995). People taking the *field-dependent approach* tend to perceive the environment as a whole and do not clearly delineate in their minds the shape, color, size, or other qualities of individual items. If field-dependent people are asked to draw a human figure, they generally draw it so that it blends into the background. By contrast, people who are *field independent* are more likely to perceive the elements of the environment as separate and distinct from one another and to draw each element as standing out from the background.

Cognitive styles can also be viewed from the perspective of "levelers" and "sharpeners"—those who level out the distinctions among objects and those who magnify them. To investigate the differences between these two cognitive styles, G. S. Klein (1951) showed people sets of squares of varying sizes and asked them to estimate the size of each one. One group, the levelers, failed to perceive any differences in the size of the squares. The sharpeners, however, picked up the differences in the size of the squares and made their size estimates accordingly.

EXPERIENCE AND CULTURE Cultural background also influences people's perceptions (Kitayama, Duffy, Kawamura, & Larsen, 2003). As we will see in Chapter 7, "Cognition and Mental Abilities," the language that people speak affects the ways in which they perceive their surroundings. Cultural differences in people's experiences can also influence how people use perceptual cues. For example, East African Masai, who depend on herding animals for their living, are more perceptive about the characteristics of individual animals in their herd than are Westerners. Similarly, professional dog breeders see championship qualities in a pup that most people would not recognize. And wine experts can distinguish subtle differences in the flavor of different vintages that most of us could not detect.

PERSONALITY A number of researchers have shown that our individual personalities influence perception. (For a review of the research, see Greenwald, 1992.) For example, one study compared clinically depressed college students to students with eating disorders in terms of their ability to identify words related to depression and food (von Hippel, Hawkins, & Narayan, 1994). The students saw a series of words very quickly (for less than one-tenth of a second each). In general, students with an eating disorder were faster at identifying words that referred to foods that they commonly thought about than they were at identifying foods that they rarely thought about. Similarly, depressed students were faster at identifying adjectives describing personality traits that they commonly thought about (such as "quiet," "withdrawn," "hesitant," and "timid") than adjectives that described traits that they rarely thought about (such as "extroverted," "lively," and "bold"). These findings suggest that personality—along with the other factors explored in this chapter—may influence perception.

ENDURING ISSUES

Person–Situation   Do Perceptual Experiences Reflect the Outside World?

After reading this chapter, have your ideas changed about the relative importance of processes that occur inside the individual (thoughts, emotions, motives, attitudes, values, personalities) as opposed to objects and events in the real world? If someone were to ask you whether perceptual experiences match more closely the image on the retina or the outside world, what would you say? What examples would you select from the chapter to make your point most effectively? ●●

CHECK YOUR UNDERSTANDING

Match the following principles of perception with the appropriate definitions.

1. _____ similarity
2. _____ continuity
3. _____ proximity
4. _____ closure

a. tendency to perceive a whole object even where none exists

b. elements that continue a pattern are likely to be seen as part of the pattern

c. objects that are like one another tending to be grouped together

d. elements found close together tending to be perceived as a unit

Answers: 1. c. 2. b. 3. d. 4. a.

APPLY YOUR UNDERSTANDING

1. You are seated at a small table talking to a friend opposite you who is drinking coffee. As she lifts the cup off the saucer and raises it to her mouth, the image made on your retina by the cup actually changes shape, but you still "see" it as being a cup. This is due to

   a. good continuation

   b. motion parallax

   c. perceptual constancy

   d. the phi phenomenon

2. As you study a painting, you notice that a pathway in the painting is made up of stones that become smaller and smaller as you look "down the lane." The artist has used which one of the following distance cues to create the impression of depth?

   a. interposition

   b. texture gradient

   c. elevation

   d. shadowing

Answers: 1. c. 2. b.

KEY TERMS

The Nature of Sensation
sensation, *p. 86*
receptor cell, *p. 86*
transduction, *p. 86*
absolute threshold, *p. 86*
adaptation, *p. 87*
difference threshold or just-
  noticeable difference
  (jnd), *p. 87*

Weber's law, *p. 87*

Vision
cornea, *p. 90*
pupil, *p. 90*
iris, *p. 90*
lens, *p. 90*
retina, *p. 90*
fovea, *p. 90*

wavelengths, *p. 91*
rods, *p. 91*
cones, *p. 91*
bipolar cells, *p. 91*
visual acuity, *p. 91*
dark adaptation, *p. 93*
light adaptation, *p. 93*
afterimage, *p. 93*
ganglion cells, *p. 93*

optic nerve, *p. 93*
blind spot, *p. 93*
optic chiasm, *p. 94*
feature detectors, *p. 94*
hues, *p. 94*
saturation, *p. 95*
brightness, *p. 95*
additive color mixing, *p. 96*
subtractive color mixing, *p. 96*

CHAPTER REVIEW

The Nature of Sensation

What causes sensory experiences? Humans have sensory experiences of sight, hearing, smell, taste, touch, pain, and balance, which are known as **sensations**. These experiences begin when the body's sensory receptors are stimulated. In each case, some form of physical energy is converted into neural impulses that are carried to the brain.

How is energy, such as light or sound, converted into a message to the brain? The process of sending a sensory message to the brain begins when energy stimulates **receptor cells** in one of the sense organs. Through the process of **transduction**, receptor cells convert the stimulation into coded signals that vary according to the characteristics of the stimulus. Further coding occurs as the signal passes along sensory nerve fibers, so that the message finally reaching the brain is very detailed and precise.

What are the limits on our ability to sense stimuli in our environment? The amount of physical energy that reaches sensory receptors must be of a minimal intensity to produce a detectable sensation. The least amount of energy needed to produce a sensation 50% of the time is called the **absolute threshold**. For hearing, the absolute threshold is roughly the tick of a watch from 6 m (20 feet) away in a very quiet room, and for vision, it is a candle flame seen from 50 km (30 miles) on a clear, dark night. Absolute thresholds vary according to the intensity of the stimulus present at any given time—a process called **adaptation**. Also, we are very sensitive to *changes* in the stimulus intensity. The **difference threshold** or the **just-noticeable difference (jnd)** is the smallest change in stimulation that can be detected 50% of the time.

Under what circumstances might messages outside our awareness affect our behavior? When people respond to sensory messages that are below their threshold level of awareness, they are said to be responding subliminally. Such subliminal processing can

occur in controlled laboratory settings, but there is no scientific evidence that subliminal messages have any effect in everyday life.

Vision

Why have psychologists studied vision more than any other sense? Different animal species depend more on some senses than others. In bats and dogs, hearing and sense of smell, respectively, are particularly important. In humans, vision is paramount, which is why it has received the most research attention.

How does light create a neural impulse? Light enters an eye through the **cornea** (a transparent protective coating) and passes through the **pupil** (the opening in the **iris**) as well as through the **lens**, which focuses it onto the eye's light-sensitive inner lining called the **retina**. Neural impulses are generated in the retina by receptor cells known as **rods** and **cones**. The rods and cones connect to nerve cells called **bipolar cells**, which in turn connect to **ganglion cells**. The axons of ganglion cells converge to form the **optic nerve**, which carries to the brain the neural impulses triggered in the retina. **Light** and **dark adaptation** occur as the sensitivity of rods and cones changes with the availability of light.

How do we see color? The **trichromatic theory** of color vision is based on the principles of **additive color mixing**. It holds that the eyes contain three different kinds of color receptors, one of which is most responsive to red, another to green, and another to blue. By combining signals from these three types of receptors, the brain can detect a wide range of shades. In contrast, the **opponent-process theory** of color vision maintains that receptors in the eyes are specialized to respond to one member of three basic color pairs: red–green, yellow–blue, and black–white (or light–dark). Research gives some support for both these theories. There are indeed three kinds of color receptors in the retinas, but the messages they initiate are coded by other neurons into opponent-process form. **Hue**, **saturation**, and **brightness** are properties of color vision.

Hearing

If a tree falls in the forest and no one is there, does the tree make a sound? Our ability to hear **sound** is important as it permits us to understand language and communicate with other people. Some animals such as bats, whales, porpoises, and dolphins use echolocation to locate objects with great accuracy.

How do the characteristics of sound waves cause us to hear different sounds? The physical stimuli for the sense of hearing are **sound waves**, which produce vibration in the eardrums. **Frequency**, the number of cycles per second in a sound wave, is the primary determinant of **pitch** (how high or low the tones seems to be). The complex patterns of **overtones** which accompany real world sounds determine the **timbre** or texture of a sound. **Amplitude**, or loudness refers to the magnitude of a sound wave, and is measured using a **decibel** scale.

What path does sound follow from the ear to the brain? When sound waves strike an eardrum and cause it to vibrate, three bones in the middle ear—the hammer, the anvil, and the stirrup—are stimulated to vibrate in sequence. These vibrations are magnified in their passage through the middle ear and into the inner ear beyond it. In the inner ear, movement of the **basilar membrane** stimulates sensory receptors in the **organ of Corti**. This stimulation of the hair cells produces auditory signals that travel to the brain through the **auditory nerve**.

How do we distinguish low-frequency and high-frequency sounds? The **place theory** holds that the brain distinguishes low-frequency sounds from high-frequency sounds by noting the place on the basilar membrane at which the greatest stimulation is occurring. For high-frequency sounds, this is the base of the basilar membrane; for low-frequency sounds, it is the membrane's opposite end. According to the **frequency theory** of pitch discrimination, the frequency of vibrations on the basilar membrane as a whole is translated into an equivalent frequency of nerve impulses that travel to the brain. This theory, with its associated **volley principle**, can account for pitch detection up to frequencies of about 4000 Hz. Above that, the place theory seems to provide a better explanation.

The Other Senses

What are the chemical senses? Two senses—smell and taste—are designed to detect the presence of various chemical substances in the air and in food.

What activates the sense of smell? Substances carried by airborne molecules into the nasal cavities activate highly specialized receptors for smell. From here, messages are carried directly to the **olfactory bulb** in the brain, where they are sent to the brain's temporal lobe, resulting in our awareness of smell. **Pheromones** are chemicals produced by organisms to communicate using their sense of smell.

How do we detect the basic tastes? Flavor is a complex blend of taste and smell. There are five basic ones—sweet, sour, salty, bitter and umami—and other tastes derive from combinations of these.

The five receptors for taste are housed in the **taste buds** on the tongue. When these receptors are activated by the chemical substances in food, their adjacent neurons fire, sending nerve impulses to the brain.

How do we know which way is up and whether we are moving or standing still? The **vestibular senses** provide information about our orientation or position in space, such as whether we are right side up or upside down. The receptors for these senses are in two vestibular organs in the inner ear—the semicircular canals and the vestibular sacs. The vestibular organs are responsible for motion sickness. This queasy feeling may be triggered by discrepancies between visual information and vestibular sensations. The kinesthetic senses provide information about the speed and direction of our movements. They rely on feedback from two sets of specialized nerve endings—**stretch receptors**, which are attached to muscle fibers, and **Golgi tendon organs**, which are attached to the tendons that connect muscle to bone.

What types of sensory messages are sent from the skin to the brain? The skin is the largest sense organ, and sensations that arise from the receptors embedded in it produce our sensation of touch, which includes pressure, temperature, and pain. Research has not yet established a simple, direct connection between these three sensations and the various types of skin receptors whose nerve fibers lead to the brain.

What differences among people have an effect on the degree of pain they experience? People have varying degrees of sensitivity to pain based on their physiological makeup, their current mental and emotional state, their expectations, and their cultural beliefs and values. One commonly accepted explanation of pain is the **gate-control theory**, which holds that a "neurological gate" in the spinal cord controls the transmission of pain messages to the brain. **Biopsychosocial theory** proposes that pain results from the interaction of biological, psychological, and social mechanisms. As pain reducers, placebos and acupuncture work in part through the release of pain-blocking neurotransmitters called endorphins.

Perception

How is perception different from sensation? Sensation refers to the raw sensory data that the brain receives from the senses of sight, hearing, smell, taste, balance, touch, and pain. **Perception**, which takes place in the brain, is the process of organizing, interpreting, and giving meaning to those data.

How do we organize our perceptual experiences? Twentieth-century Gestalt psychologists believed the brain creates a coherent perceptual experience that is more than simply the sum of the available sensory data. The brain imposes order on the data it receives partly by distinguishing patterns such as figure and ground, proximity, similarity, closure, and continuity.

How do we perceive things as unchanging despite changing sensory information? **Perceptual constancy** is our tendency to perceive objects as unchanging even given many changes in sensory stimulation. Once we have formed a stable perception of something, we see it as essentially the same regardless of differences in viewing angle, distance, lighting, and so forth. These **size**, **shape**, **brightness**, and **color constancies** help us better to understand and relate to the world.

How do we know how far away something is? We perceive distance and depth through both **monocular cues** (received even by one eye alone) and **binocular cues** (requiring the interaction of both eyes). Examples of monocular cues are **interposition** (in which one object partly covers another), **linear perspective**, **elevation** (or closeness of something to the horizon), **texture gradient** (from coarser to finer depending on distance), **shadowing**, and **motion parallax** (differences in the relative movement of close and distant objects as we change position). An important binocular cue is **stereoscopic vision**, which is derived from combining our two retinal images to produce a 3-D effect. Two other binocular cues are **retinal disparity** (the difference between the two separate images received by the eyes) and **convergence** of the eyes as viewing distance decreases. Just as we use monocular and binocular cues to sense depth and distance, we use **monaural** (one-ear) and **binaural** (two-ear) cues to locate the source of sounds.

How do we perceive movement? Perception of movement is a complicated process involving both visual messages from the retina and messages from the muscles around the eyes as they shift to follow a moving object. At times our perceptual processes trick us into believing that an object is moving when in fact it is not. There is a difference, then, between real movement and apparent movement. Examples of apparent movement are the **autokinetic illusion** (caused by the absence of visual cues surrounding a stationary object), **stroboscopic motion** (produced by rapidly flashing a series of pictures), and the **phi phenomenon** (produced by a pattern of flashing lights).

What causes visual illusions? Visual illusions occur when we use a variety of sensory cues to create perceptual experiences that do not actually exist. Some are *physical illusions*, such as the bent appearance of a stick in water. Others are *perceptual illusions*, which occur because a stimulus contains misleading cues that lead to inaccurate perceptions.

What personal factors influence our perceptions? In addition to past experience and learning, our perceptions are also influenced by our motivation, values, expectations, cognitive style, experience and culture, and personality.

4 States of Consciousness

OVERVIEW

As a student, you probably know what extreme tiredness is like. When studying for final exams far into the night, a dusty cloud seems to gradually envelop your brain. Awareness dulls as you struggle to keep your focus, gluing your eyes to words on the page that begin to blur together. It is as if a murky haze is replacing your normal state of awareness.

Now transfer this same state of fatigue to the wards of a large hospital, where resident doctors in training are sometimes expected to work shifts lasting as long as 36 nonstop hours. One physician, looking back on his days as a resident, recalls how he once assisted a team of neurosurgeons in a complicated operation after working 30 consecutive hours. His mind was bleary and unfocused as he stood behind the performing surgeon, dutifully holding the retractors as the minutes ticked monotonously by. A mental fuzziness slowly descended; and then his state of utter exhaustion slipped quietly into slumber. The next moment he was asleep on the surgeon's shoulder, snoring softly in his ear.

Although this story is amusing, the problem it highlights is no laughing matter. Compared with residents who have shifts of 16 hours or less, those who are "on-call" for more than 24 hours every other day experience twice as many failures of attention while working at night. They make over one-third of serious medical errors regarding patients, including five times as many serious diagnostic mistakes that could be life-threatening (Landrigan et al., 2004; Landrigan, 2005). In one survey, over 85% of surgical residents reported having fallen asleep while driving home from an all-night shift (Worth, 1999). To put the state of exhaustion into further perspective, residents working heavy schedules perform similarly on cognitive tasks to people with blood alcohol levels between 0.04% and 0.05%—the level reached when an average-sized man consumes three beers in a single hour (Arnedt, Owens, Crouch, Stahl, & Carskadon, 2005).

Extreme fatigue is just one of many states of consciousness. Psychologists define **consciousness** as a person's awareness of mental processes. These include concentrating, making decisions, planning, remembering, daydreaming, reflecting, sleeping, and dreaming, to name a few. Our range of qualitative states of consciousness is remarkably broad. One familiar state is normal **waking consciousness**—all the different thoughts, feelings, and perceptions occupying the mind when we are awake and reasonably alert (Baruss, 2003). Waking consciousness is usually action- or plan-oriented and tuned in to what is going on around us. This is the state of consciousness we associate with writing a paper, programming a computer, or skiing down an icy slope. During normal waking consciousness, awareness is fully engaged.

Other forms of consciousness, to varying degrees, are more detached from the external world. These are known as **altered states of consciousness**. Some—such as fatigue, sleep, and daydreaming—occur spontaneously during the course of a day. Others are intentionally induced. When you drink a margarita, take a Ritalin, or calm your mind through yoga, you are purposely undertaking to change your state of consciousness.

In this chapter we explore the fascinating variations of human consciousness, beginning with the normal waking state. Next, we see what psychologists know about sleep and dreaming. We then turn to the various ways in which people seek out altered states of awareness. One centuries-old method is taking psychoactive drugs. We look at many of the recreational drugs used today—from depressants like alcohol, to stimulants such as cocaine, to hallucinogenic drugs like marijuana. Finally, we consider meditation and hypnosis—two altered states of consciousness that are induced without the use of drugs.

ENDURING ISSUES IN STATES OF CONSCIOUSNESS ●●

In this chapter, you will quickly recognize several of the "Enduring Issues" that were introduced in Chapter 1. The mind–body relation is central to this entire chapter since we will be exploring the ways in which psychological states can affect biological processes and, conversely, the ways in which biological changes can profoundly affect psychological experiences. In addition, we will discover that that there are significant differences among people in their susceptibility to various altered states of consciousness (diversity–universality) and that the settings in which consciousness altering substances are taken can greatly alter their effects (person–situation).

consciousness Our awareness of various cognitive processes, such as sleeping, dreaming, concentrating, and making decisions.

waking consciousness Mental state that encompasses the thoughts, feelings, and perceptions that occur when we are awake and reasonably alert.

altered states of consciousness Mental states that differ noticeably from normal waking consciousness.

Conscious Experience

What problems could arise if we were constantly aware of all external and internal sensations?

Even when we are fully awake and alert, we are usually conscious of only a small portion of what is going on around us. At any given moment, we are exposed to a great variety of sounds, sights, and odors from the outside world. At the same time, we experience all sorts of internal sensations, such as heat and cold, touch, pressure, pain, and equilibrium, as well as an array of thoughts, memories, emotions, and needs. Normally, however, we are not aware of all these competing stimuli. To make sense of our environment, we must select only the most important information to attend to and then filter out everything else. At times we pay such close attention to what we are doing that we are oblivious to what is going on around us. How the process of attention works is examined at some length in Chapter 6, "Memory." Here, it is enough to note that the hallmark of normal waking consciousness is the highly selective nature of attention.

The selective nature of attention can be seen in the number of processes that occur without eliciting our conscious attention. We are rarely attuned to such vital bodily processes as blood pressure and respiration, for example; and we can walk down the street or ride a bicycle without consciously thinking about every movement. In fact, we carry out certain tasks, such as signing our name, better when we are *not* consciously aware of performing each movement. Similarly, when we drive or walk along a familiar route that we always take to work or school, the process may be so automatic that we remain largely unaware of our surroundings.

Many psychologists believe that certain key mental processes, such as recognizing a word or a friend's face, also happen outside of normal waking consciousness. As we learned in Chapter 1, Sigmund Freud thought that many of the most important influences on our behavior—such as erotic feelings for our parents—are screened from our consciousness and may be accessible only through states such as dreaming. We explore the notion of unconscious mental processes as we consider various altered states of consciousness, beginning with natural ones such as daydreaming, and we return to them when we discuss behavioral disorders in Chapter 12.

DAYDREAMING AND FANTASY

Do daydreams serve any useful function?

In James Thurber's classic short story, *The Secret Life of Walter Mitty* (Thurber, 1942), the meek, painfully shy central character spends much of his time weaving elaborate fantasies in which he stars as a bold, dashing adventurer. Daydreams are his reality—and his waking-conscious experience is something of a nightmare. Few people live in their imaginations to the extent that Walter Mitty does. Thurber deliberately used exaggeration to explore the secret life that all of us share, but that few of us discuss: our fantasies. Everyone has **daydreams**: apparently effortless, spontaneous shifts in attention away from the here and now into a private world of make-believe.

The urge to daydream seems to come in waves, surging about every 90 minutes and peaking between noon and 2 P.M. (Ford-Mitchell, 1997). According to some estimates, the average person spends almost half of his or her waking hours fantasizing, though this proportion varies from person to person and situation to situation. Typically, we daydream when we would rather be somewhere else or be doing something else, so daydreaming is a momentary escape.

Are daydreams random paths that your mind travels? Not at all. Studies show that most daydreams are variations on a central theme: thoughts and images of unfulfilled goals and wishes, accompanied by emotions arising from an appraisal of where we are now compared with where we want to be (Singer, 2006). Daydreams, and daydreamers, fall into distinct categories: positive, negative, scattered, and purposeful (Langens & Schmalt, 2002; Singer, 1975). Some people—"happy daydreamers"—imagine pleasant, playful, entertain-

daydreams Apparently effortless shifts in attention away from the here and now into a private world of make-believe.

ing scenarios, uncomplicated by guilt or worry. By contrast, people who are extremely oriented to achieve tend to experience recurring themes of frustration, guilt, fear of failure, and hostility, reflecting the self-doubt and competitive envy that accompany great ambition. People who score high on measures of anxiety often have fleeting, loosely connected, worrisome daydreams, which give them little pleasure. Finally, people with high levels of curiosity tend to use daydreams to solve problems, think ahead, and develop insights.

Does daydreaming serve any useful function? Some psychologists view daydreaming as nothing more than a retreat from the real world, especially when that world is not meeting our needs. As such, daydreaming can interfere with productive activities and make those problems worse (the "Walter Mitty" syndrome). Although most daydreaming is quite normal, it is considered maladaptive when it involves extensive fantasizing, replacing human interaction, and interfering with vocational or academic success (Somer, 2002). Clearly, people who have difficulty distinguishing between fantasy and reality and who begin replacing real-life relationships with imaginary family and friends need professional help.

Other psychologists stress the positive value of daydreaming and fantasy (Langens & Schmalt, 2002). Daydreams may provide a refreshing break from a stressful day and serve to remind us of neglected personal needs. Freudian theorists tend to view daydreams as a harmless way of working through hostile feelings or satisfying guilty desires. Cognitive psychologists emphasize that daydreaming can build problem-solving and interpersonal skills, as well as encourage creativity. Moreover, daydreaming helps people endure difficult situations: Prisoners of war have used fantasies to survive torture and deprivation. Daydreaming and fantasy, then, may provide welcome relief from unpleasant reality and reduce internal tension and external aggression.

"Harry lives inside a beltway all his own."

Source: © The New Yorker Collection, 1993. Dana Fradon from www.cartoonbank.com. All rights reserved.

Sleep

How do evolutionary psychologists explain the need for sleep?

Human beings spend about one-third of their lives in the altered state of consciousness known as sleep: a natural state of rest characterized by a reduction in voluntary body movement and decreased awareness of the surroundings. No one who has tried to stay awake longer than 20 hours at a time could doubt the necessity of sleep. Some people claim they never sleep, but when observed under laboratory conditions, they actually sleep soundly without being aware of it. When people are deprived of sleep, they crave sleep just as strongly as they would food or water after a period of deprivation. Merely resting doesn't satisfy us.

All birds and mammals sleep; and although scientists are not sure about reptiles, frogs, fish, and even insects go into "rest states" similar to sleep. Indeed, Drosophila fruit flies, a favorite subject for genetic studies because they reproduce rapidly, are remarkably like us: They are active during the day and somnolent at night; when deprived of sleep, they need long naps to recover. Caffeine keeps them awake, whereas antihistamines make them drowsy (Hendricks & Sehgal, 2004; Shaw, Cirelli, Greenspan, & Tononi, 2000). How long organisms sleep, where, in what positions, and other details vary from species to species (J. M. Siegel, 2005). In general, large animals sleep less than small animals, perhaps because eating enough to support their size requires more time awake.

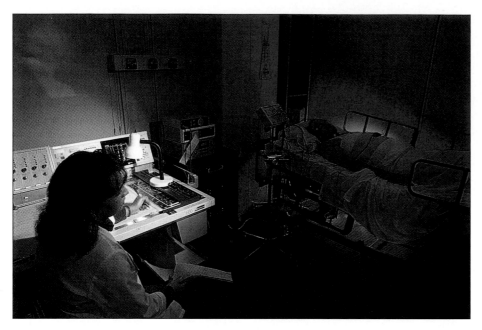

Sleep researchers monitor volunteers' brain waves, muscle tension, and other physiological changes during sleep.

Nobody knows exactly why we need to sleep, although evidence has begun to accumulate that sleep may play an important restorative function, both physically and mentally (Walker & Stickgold, 2006). For instance, one study has shown that getting adequate sleep boosts our immune response, making us less susceptible to disease (T. Lange, Perras, Fehm, & Born, 2003). In addition, recent research has revealed that when people are presented with complex problems and are permitted to sleep prior to solving them, they are more likely to generate insightful solutions than if they are kept from sleeping (U. Wagner, Gais, Haider, Verleger, & Born, 2004). This latter finding supports the idea that creativity and problem-solving skills may be enhanced by getting adequate sleep. Evolutionary psychologists see sleep as an adaptive mechanism that evolved to allow organisms to conserve and restore energy (P. McNamara, 2004). In support of this theory, researchers have shown that people use less energy when they are asleep than when they are awake (Madsen, 1993).

The naturally occurring chemical, adenosine, appears to trigger sleepiness (Porkka-Heiskanen et al., 1997; Thakkar, Winston, & McCarley, 2003). In one group of studies, cats kept awake an abnormally long time were found to have elevated levels of adenosine in their brains during wakefulness. When the cats were finally permitted to sleep, the adenosine levels dropped. To determine whether the adenosine buildup actually caused the sleepiness, the investigators injected adenosine into well-rested cats. These cats immediately became sleepy and began to exhibit the EEG patterns typical of drowsiness. Exactly why a high level of adenosine appears to trigger sleepiness is not known, but additional research along this line may soon provide us with a better understanding of the neurological processes underlying the need for sleep (Lindberg et al., 2002; Strecker et al., 2002).

CIRCADIAN CYCLES: THE BIOLOGICAL CLOCK

What is the biological clock and what does it have to do with jet lag?

Like many other biological functions, sleep and waking follow a daily, or circadian, cycle (from the Latin expression *circa diem*, meaning "about a day") (Saper, Scammell, & Lu, 2005). **Circadian rhythms** are an ancient and fundamental adaptation to the 24-hour solar cycle of light and dark, found not only in humans and other animals, but also in plants and even one-celled organisms (R. Y. Moore, 1999; Refinetti, 2000). The human *biological clock* is largely governed by a tiny cluster of neurons just above the optic chiasm in the lower region of the hypothalamus (see **Figures 2–7** and **3–9**) known as the **suprachiasmatic nucleus (SCN)** (C. M. Novak & Albers, 2002). The SCN receives information about the daily light and dark cycles via a direct pathway from the retina of the eye (Zisapel, 2001). In response to the light and dark cycles detected by the eye, the SCN releases specific neurotransmitters that control our body's temperature, metabolism, blood pressure, hormone levels, and hunger, which vary predictably through the course of the day. For example, the level of the hormone epinephrine (which causes the body to go on alert) reaches a peak in the late morning hours and then steadily declines until around midnight, when it suddenly drops to a very low level and remains there until morning. By contrast, levels of melatonin (which promotes sleep) surge at night and drop off during the day. Animal studies have shown that the SCN even responds to seasonal variations in the length of the day, regulating the production of various hormones and behaviors like mating, which are linked to seasonal changes in many species (Sumova, Sladek, & Jac, 2002).

circadian rhythm A regular biological rhythm with a period of approximately 24 hours.

suprachiasmatic nucleus (SCN) A cluster of neurons in the hypothalamus that receives input from the retina regarding light and dark cycles and is involved in regulating the biological clock.

However, the SCN is not the only determinant of circadian rhythms, because the biological clock can continue to function even in the absence of external cues to the cycle of day and night (Refinetti, 2000). For example, Czeisler, Duffy, and Shanahan (1999) studied 24 people who volunteered to live in an artificial environment for 3 weeks. The only time cues that participants had were a weak cycle of light and dark set at 28 hours and a bedtime signal. Even in this misleading environment, their body temperatures, hormone levels, and other biological processes showed that their bodies continued to function according to their own internal 24-hour cycle.

We rarely notice circadian rhythms until they are disturbed. Jet lag is a familiar example. Travelers who cross several time zones in one day often feel "out of it" for several days. The reason for jet lag is not so much lack of sleep as *desynchronization*. Sleep-and-wake cycles adapt quickly, but hormones, body temperature, and digestive cycles change more slowly. As a result, bodily functions are out of synch. Likewise, shift workers often lose weight and suffer from irritability, insomnia, and extreme drowsiness for some time after changing to a new shift (Basner, 2005).

Researchers may have found a way to adjust our biological clocks. Light inhibits the production of melatonin, which goes up as the sun goes down. A small dose of melatonin taken in the morning (the time when the hormone is usually tapering off) sets back or slows down the biological clock (Liu et al., 1997). Taken in the evening, melatonin speeds up the biological clock, making the person fall asleep earlier than usual (Lewy, Ahmed, Latham, & Sack, 1992; Zemlan et al, 2005). Applying this knowledge, melatonin has been successfully used as an aid to persons with blindness, who sometimes are unable to sense dark–light cycles, causing insomnia or daytime sleepiness. Carefully timed doses of melatonin seem to "reset" the biological clocks of such people, enabling them to sleep better at night and remain alert during the day (Sack, Brandes, Kendall, & Lewy, 2001). A low dose of melatonin added to evening milk has also been shown to be useful in improving sleep quality in elderly persons, thus increasing their daytime activity and improving cognitive functioning (Peck, LeGoff, Ahmed, & Goebert, 2004; Valtonen, Niskanen, Kangas, & Koskinen, 2005). However, there is little evidence that melatonin is an effective cure for sleep disorders such as chronic insomnia (Buscemi et al., 2006) (see discussion of insomnia, below).

Travel, especially across many time zones, can disrupt people's circadian rhythms, leaving them groggy and tired—a feeling known as jet lag.

THE RHYTHMS OF SLEEP

What physical changes mark the rhythms of sleep?

To say that psychologists know more about sleep than about waking consciousness would be only a slight exaggeration. Over the years, researchers have accumulated a large body of observations about what happens in our bodies and brains during sleep. In a typical study, researchers recruit volunteers who spend one or more nights in a "sleep lab." With electrodes painlessly attached to their skulls, the volunteers sleep comfortably as their brain waves, eye movements, muscle tension, and other physiological functions are monitored. Data from such studies show that, although there are significant individual differences in sleep behavior, almost everyone goes through the same stages of sleep. Each stage is marked by characteristic patterns of brain waves, muscular activity, blood pressure, and body temperature (N. R. Carlson, 2000). **Figure 4–1** illustrates the electrical activity related to the brain, heart, and facial muscles at each stage.

"Going to sleep" means losing awareness and failing to respond to a stimulus that would produce a response in the waking state. As measured by an EEG, brain waves during this "twilight" state

Figure 4–1
Waves of sleep.
This series of printouts illustrates electrical activity in the brain, heart, and facial muscles during the various stages of sleep. Note the characteristic delta waves that begin to appear during Stage 3 and become more pronounced during Stage 4.

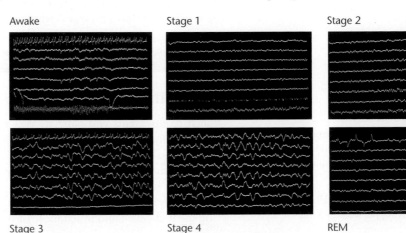

are characterized by irregular, low-voltage alpha waves. This brain-wave pattern mirrors the sense of relaxed wakefulness that we experience while lying on a beach or in a hammock or when resting after a big meal. In this twilight state with the eyes closed, people often report seeing flashing lights and colors, geometric patterns, and visions of landscapes. Sometimes they also experience a floating or falling sensation, followed by a quick jolt back to consciousness.

After this initial twilight phase, the sleeper enters *Stage 1* of sleep. Stage-1 brain waves are tight and of very low amplitude (height), resembling those recorded when a person is alert or excited. But, in contrast to normal waking consciousness, Stage 1 of the sleep cycle is marked by a slowing of the pulse, muscle relaxation, and side-to-side rolling movements of the eyes—the last being the most reliable indication of this first stage of sleep (Dement, 1974). Stage 1 usually lasts only a few moments. The sleeper is easily aroused at this stage and, once awake, may be unaware of having slept at all.

Stages 2 and *3* are characterized by progressively deeper sleep. During Stage 2, short rhythmic bursts of brain-wave activity called *sleep spindles* periodically appear. In Stage 3, *delta waves*—slow waves with very high peaks—begin to emerge. During these stages, the sleeper is hard to awaken and does not respond to stimuli such as noises or lights. Heart rate, blood pressure, and temperature continue to drop.

In *Stage 4* sleep, the brain emits very slow delta waves. Heart rate, breathing rate, blood pressure, and body temperature are as low as they will get during the night. In young adults, delta sleep occurs in 15- to 20-minute segments—interspersed with lighter sleep—mostly during the first half of the night. Delta sleep time lessens with age, but continues to be the first sleep to be made up after sleep has been lost.

About an hour after falling asleep, the sleeper begins to ascend from Stage 4 sleep to Stage 3, Stage 2, and back to Stage 1—a process that takes about 40 minutes. The brain waves return to the low-amplitude, saw-toothed shape characteristic of Stage 1 sleep and waking alertness. Heart rate and blood pressure also increase, yet the muscles are more relaxed than at any other point in the sleep cycle, and the person is very difficult to awaken. The eyes move rapidly under closed eyelids. This **rapid-eye movement (REM) sleep** stage is distinguished from all other stages of sleep (called **non-REM** or **NREM**) that precede and follow it.

REM sleep is also called **paradoxical sleep**, because although measures of brain activity, heart rate, blood pressure, and other physiological functions closely resemble those recorded during waking consciousness, the person in this stage appears to be deeply asleep and is incapable of moving; the body's voluntary muscles are essentially paralyzed. Some research suggests that REM sleep is also the stage when most dreaming occurs, though dreams also take place during NREM sleep. In addition, different brain mechanisms appear to be responsible for controlling REM sleep and dreaming, suggesting they may be unrelated processes (Solms, 2003). The first Stage 1–REM period lasts about 10 minutes and is followed by Stages 2, 3, and 4 of NREM sleep. This sequence of sleep stages repeats itself all night, averaging 90 minutes from Stage 1–REM to Stage 4 and back again. Normally, a night's sleep consists of 4 to 5 sleep cycles of this sort. But the pattern of sleep changes as the night progresses. At first, Stages 3 and 4 dominate; but as time passes, the Stage 1–REM periods gradually become longer, and Stages 3 and 4 become shorter, eventually disappearing altogether. Over the course of a night, then, about 45 to 50% of the sleeper's time is spent in Stage 2, whereas REM sleep takes up another 20 to 25% of the total.

ENDURING ISSUES

Diversity–Universality   Individual Differences in Sleep

Sleep requirements and patterns vary considerably from person to person. Some adults need hardly any sleep. Researchers have documented the case of a Stanford University professor who slept for only 3 to 4 hours a night over the course of 50 years and that of a woman who lived a healthy life on only 1 hour of sleep per night (Rosenzweig & Leiman, 1982). As shown in **Figure 4–2**, sleep patterns also change with age (Philip et al., 2004; Sadeh, Raviv, & Gruber, 2000). Infants sleep much longer than adults—13 to 16 hours during the first year—and much more of their sleep is REM sleep. (See **Figure 4–3**.)

Rapid-eye movement (REM) or paradoxical sleep Sleep stage characterized by rapid-eye movements and increased dreaming.

non-REM (NREM) sleep Non-rapid-eye-movement stages of sleep that alternate with REM stages during the sleep cycle.

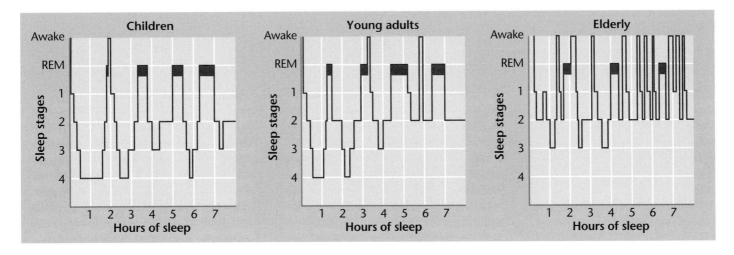

Figure 4–2

A night's sleep across the life span.
Sleep patterns change from childhood to young adulthood to old age. The red areas represent REM sleep, the stage of sleep that varies most dramatically across age groups.

Source: Adapted by permission of *The New England Journal of Medicine, 290,* p. 487, 1974. Copyright © 1974 Massachusetts Medical Society. All rights reserved.

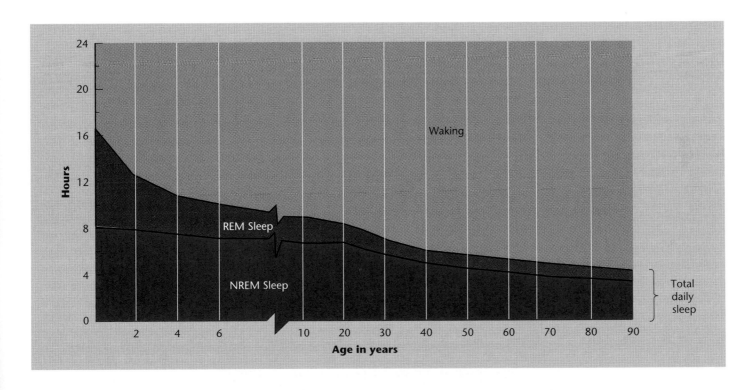

Figure 4–3

Changes in REM and NREM sleep.
The amount of REM sleep people need declines sharply during the first few years of life. Newborns spend about 8 hours, or almost half of their total sleep time in REM sleep, whereas older children and adults spend just 1 to 2 hours or about 20 to 25% of their total sleep time in REM sleep.

Source: Adapted with permission from H. P. Roffwarg, "Ontogenetic Development of the Human Sleep-Dream Cycle," *Science, 152,* p. 604. Copyright © 1966 by the American Association for the Advancement of Science.

ON THE CUTTING EDGE

MOST OF US NEED MORE SLEEP THAN WE GET

Inadequate sleep has become a "national epidemic" in the United States. Between one-third and one-half of all adults regularly fail to get enough sleep. High school students report that they fall asleep in class about once a week (Acebo & Carskadon, 2002; Maas, 1998). Inadequate sleep and poor sleep patterns among adolescents have even been associated with an increased tendency to engage in risky behaviors and suicide (X. Liu, 2004; E. M. O'Brien & Mindell, 2005).

Despite common beliefs, people do not adapt to chronic sleep loss (Hébert, 2003; Van Dongen, Maislin, Mullington, & Dinges, 2003). Extensive research shows that losing an hour or two of sleep every night, week after week, month after month, makes it more difficult for people to pay attention (especially to monotonous tasks) and to remember things (Johnsen, Laberg, Eid, & Hugdahl, 2002). Reaction time slows down, behavior becomes unpredictable, logical reasoning is impaired, and accidents and errors in judgment increase, while productivity and the ability to make decisions decline (Babkoff, Caspy, Mikulincer, & Sing, 1991; Blagrove & Akehurst, 2000, 2001; J. P. R. Scott, McNaughton, & Polman, 2006). These findings have important implications. For example, experts estimate that sleep loss is a contributing factor in between 200,000 and 400,000 automobile accidents each year, resulting in approximately 1,500 deaths and 71,000 injuries (Carskadon, 2002). Research suggests that driving while sleepy is just as dangerous as driving while drunk (Eoh, Chung, & Kim, 2005; Otmani, Pebayle, Roge, & Muzet, 2005; N. B. Powell et al., 2001). Combining sleep deprivation with drinking, even moderate drinking, is especially dangerous (Horne, Reyner, & Barrett, 2003).

Sleep deprivation may also routinely affect the performance of people in high-risk positions such as nuclear power plant operators, who often have to make critical decisions on short notice. In 1979, there was an accident at the nuclear power plant at Three Mile Island, Pennsylvania, in which human error transformed a minor mishap into a major nuclear disaster. And, as we saw at the start of this chapter, hospital residents who work long hours without rest make a disproportionate number of serious medical errors compared to residents who work shorter shifts.

Awareness of the relationship between sleep deprivation and accidents has led to changes in the working patterns of people whose jobs can have life-and-death consequences. The Accreditation Council for Graduate Medical Education (2003) has developed common duty hour standards that set a cap of 80 hours per week and that limit continuous duty time to 24 hours for physicians in training. The "Patient and Physician Safety and Protection Act of 2005," under consideration in Congress, would make those limits a matter of federal law. Similarly, the number of hours a pilot can fly or a truck driver can drive without having time off to sleep has come under federal regulation.

Sleep deprivation is also clearly related to depression in high school and college students. According to Mary Alice Carskadon, a leading researcher in the area of sleep among college students, "Every study we have ever done over the past decade on high school and college students shows the less sleep they get the more depressed mood they report" (Markel, 2003, p. D6).

Unfortunately, people do not always know when they are not getting enough sleep. Most truck drivers involved in accidents that resulted from their falling asleep at the wheel claimed that they felt rested at the time (Wald, 1997). In a laboratory study, one group of healthy college students who were getting 7 to 8 hours of sleep a night showed no apparent signs of sleep deprivation. Yet 20% of them fell asleep immediately when they were put into a dark room, a symptom of chronic sleep loss. Another group for a period of time went to bed 60 to 90 minutes earlier than their normal bedtime. These students reported that they felt much more vigorous and alert—indeed, they performed significantly better on tests of psychological and mental acuity (Carskadon, Acebo, & Jenni, 2004; Carskadon & Dement, 1982). One experiment with rats demonstrated that sleep deprivation influenced neurogenesis (see Chapter 2, "The Biological Basis of Behavior") in the hippocampus, the area of the brain involved in the formation of new memories (Guzman-Marin et al., 2005).

According to a well-known sleep researcher, Dr. William Dement, one way to reduce your sleep debt is to take short naps. Even a 20-minute nap can increase alertness, reduce irritability, and improve efficiency, while 1-hour naps lead to more marked increases in performance (S. C. Mednick et al., 2002). In many cultures midafternoon is seen as siesta time. In America, this is unfortunately not the case and we often reach for a cup of coffee or other caffeinated beverage to keep us going.

SLEEP DISORDERS

Are prescription medicines the best way to treat occasional insomnia?

At any given time, at least 50 million Americans suffer from chronic, long-term sleep disorders; and 20 million other Americans experience occasional sleep problems. Also, there is a link between sleep and a large number of diseases, including asthma and stroke (National

Institute of Neurological Disorders and Stroke, 2003). A recent study of 72,000 female nurses found that women who sleep either too much (more than 9 hours) or too little (less than 5 hours) have an increased risk for heart disease. Although researchers could not determine exactly why this relationship was present, they suggested the tendency to sleep too much or too little might be indicative of underlying medical conditions (Ayas et al., 2003). The scientific study of typical sleep patterns has yielded further insights into several sleep disorders, including the ones we discuss next: sleeptalking and sleepwalking, nightmares and night terrors, insomnia, apnea, and narcolepsy.

THINKING CRITICALLY ABOUT...

Sleep Deprivation

1. The Accreditation Council for Graduate Medical Education (2003) (ACGME) duty standards are intended to reduce serious errors and improve patient care. Do you know whether research confirms that they have such a beneficial effect? If not, how might you go about determining whether indeed they have the desired effect?

2. One study cited above concluded that even a brief nap can "increase alertness, reduce irritability, and improve efficiency." But many people report that they feel more tired after taking a brief nap than they did before! How might you explain the apparent contradiction between these two facts?

SLEEPTALKING, SLEEPWALKING, AND NIGHT TERRORS *Sleeptalking* and *sleepwalking* usually occur during Stage 4. Both are more common among children than adults: About 20% of children have at least one episode of either sleepwalking or sleeptalking. Boys are more likely to walk in their sleep than girls. Contrary to popular belief, waking a sleepwalker is not dangerous (in fact it may be more dangerous *not* to wake the person), but because sleepwalking commonly takes place during a very deep stage of sleep, waking a sleepwalker is not easy (National Sleep Foundation, 2005).

Sometimes sleep can be frightening, when people experience nightmares or night terrors, also known as sleep terrors. Although both these phenomena are bad dreams, they are very different (Mindell & Owens, 2003; Zadra & Donderi, 2000). **Nightmares** occur during REM sleep and we can remember them in the morning. These frightening dreams are also very common; virtually everyone has them occasionally. **Night terrors**, a form of nocturnal fright that makes the dreamer suddenly sit up in bed—often screaming out in fear—occur during NREM sleep. People generally cannot be awakened from night terrors and will push away anyone trying to comfort them. Unlike nightmares, night terrors cannot be recalled the next morning. Night terrors are fairly rare, occurring in fewer than 10% of children, although they occur more often if the person is very tired.

Although nightmares and night terrors are more common in children, adults can have them during times of stress (Muris, Merckelbach, Gadet, & Moulaert, 2000). Neither nightmares nor night terrors alone indicate psychological problems. Anxious people have no more nightmares than other people do. People whose nightmares stem from a traumatic experience, however, may be plagued by terrifying nighttime episodes for years.

INSOMNIA, APNEA, AND NARCOLEPSY Insomnia, the inability to fall or remain asleep, afflicts as many as 35 million Americans. Most episodes of insomnia grow out of stressful events and are temporary (see "Applying Psychology: Are You Getting Enough Sleep?") and many cases of insomnia yield to drug therapy or behavioral therapy (Irwin, Cole, & Nicassio, 2006; M. T. Smith & Perlis, 2006). But for some sufferers, insomnia is a persistent disruption. Treatments can create problems as well. Some prescription medications for insomnia can cause anxiety, memory loss, hallucinations, and violent behavior (Gathchel & Oordt, 2003; Morin, Bastien, Brink, & Brown, 2003).

The causes of insomnia vary for different individuals (Lichstein, Wilson, & Johnson, 2000). For some people, insomnia is part of a larger psychological problem such as depression, so its cure requires treating the underlying disorder. Research even indicates that interpersonal difficulties, such as loneliness, can contribute to difficulty sleeping (Cacioppo et al., 2002). For others, insomnia results from an overaroused biological system. A physical predisposition to insomnia may combine with anxiety over chronic sleeplessness to create a cycle in which biological and emotional factors reinforce one another. People may worry so much about not sleeping that even simple "good sleep hygiene" bedtime rituals may unwittingly usher in anxiety, rather than set the stage for relaxation. Furthermore, bad sleep habits—such as varying bedtimes—and distracting sleep settings may aggravate or even cause insomnia.

nightmares Frightening dreams that occur during REM sleep and are remembered.

night terrors Frightening, often terrifying dreams that occur during NREM sleep from which a person is difficult to awaken and doesn't remember the content.

insomnia Sleep disorder characterized by difficulty in falling asleep or remaining asleep throughout the night.

APPLYING PSYCHOLOGY

ARE YOU GETTING ENOUGH SLEEP?

Sleep is sometimes elusive. The ancient Greeks believed that sleep was a gift of the god *Morpheus,* who granted or refused it to mortals. Like most people, you probably have had at least a few nights when you found it difficult to fall asleep. Episodes of even temporary or occasional insomnia can impair your ability to function during the day. So what can you do if you suddenly find yourself going through a period when you are unable to get a good night's sleep? Here are some tips that may help:

- Maintain regular bedtime hours; don't sleep late on weekends.
- Establish a regular, relaxing bedtime routine that you follow each night before retiring, such as a warm bath, followed by a little reading or making an entry into a journal.
- Abstain from drugs, including alcohol, caffeine, and nicotine, as well as the routine use of sleeping pills. Tryptophan, a substance that promotes sleep, may be taken as a sleep aid in the form of warm milk, confirming a folk remedy for sleeplessness.
- Adjust the temperature of the room if it is too cold or too warm.
- Avoid foods that may cause sleeplessness, such as chocolate.
- Establish a regular exercise program during the day, but never exercise within several hours of bedtime.

- Avoid anxious thoughts while in bed. Set aside regular times during the day—well before bedtime—to mull over your worries. This technique may be supplemented by relaxation training, using such methods as biofeedback, self-hypnosis, or meditation (Gathchel & Oordt, 2003).
- Don't fight insomnia when it occurs. The old saying "If I can't sleep, I mop the kitchen floor" makes sense to sleep researchers, who counsel their clients to get out of bed and engage in a relaxing activity for an hour or so until they feel sleepy again.

Sleep quiz: Are you getting enough sleep? Test yourself.

According to surveys, millions of Americans simply don't get enough sleep. The problem is particularly acute among adolescents and young adults, who feel pressured to work, be successful in school, and remain socially active. At the end of the day, something has to give, and all too often, it is sleep. Ironically, not getting enough sleep often interferes with the very activities that keep us awake, reducing one's effectiveness at work, school, and in interpersonal relationships. Take the following sleep quiz and see if you need more sleep.

Answer yes or no to the following questions.

_____ Do you often fall asleep while watching TV?

_____ Is it common for you to fall asleep after large meals or while relaxing after dinner?

_____ Do you often fall asleep or fear nodding off during boring lectures, tedious activities, or in warm rooms?

_____ Do you need an alarm clock to wake up in the morning?

_____ Do you often press the snooze button on your alarm clock to get more sleep?

_____ Do you struggle to get out of bed in the morning?

_____ Do you often feel tired, irritable, or stressed out during the day?

_____ Do you have trouble concentrating or remembering?

_____ Are you easily distracted or feel slow while performing tasks that require thinking, problem solving, or creativity?

_____ Do you sometimes feel drowsy or fear nodding off while driving?

_____ Do you need a nap to help you get through the day?

According to sleep researcher James Maas, if you answered yes to three or more of these questions you may need more sleep than you are getting.

Source: Adapted from: Maas, J. B. (1999). *Power sleep: The revolutionary program that prepares your mind for peak performance.* New York: Harper Collins.

Another sleep disorder, obstructive sleep **apnea**, affects 10 to 12 million Americans, many of whom have inherited the condition (Kadotani et al., 2001). Apnea is associated with breathing difficulties at night: In severe cases, the victim actually stops breathing after falling asleep. When the level of carbon dioxide in the blood rises to a certain point, apnea sufferers are spurred to a state of arousal just short of waking consciousness. Because this process may happen hundreds of times a night, apnea patients typically feel exhausted and fall asleep repeatedly the next day. They may also complain of depression, sexual dysfunction, difficulty concentrating, and headaches (El-Ad & Lavie, 2005; Strollo & Davé, 2005). Moreover, sleep-related breathing disorders have been shown to be related to hyperactivity, conduct disorders, and aggressiveness among children and adolescents (Chervin, Killion, Archbold, & Ruzicka,

apnea Sleep disorder characterized by breathing difficulty during the night and feelings of exhaustion during the day.

2003). Depending on its severity, sleep apnea can also double or triple the risk of having a stroke or dying (Yaggi et al., 2005).

People suffering from insomnia and apnea may envy those who have no trouble sleeping. But too much sleep has serious repercussions as well. **Narcolepsy** is a hereditary disorder whose victims nod off without warning in the middle of a conversation or other alert activity. People with narcolepsy often experience a sudden loss of muscle tone upon expression of any sort of emotion. A joke, anger, sexual stimulation—all bring on the muscle paralysis associated with deep sleep. Suddenly, without warning, they collapse. The sudden onset and similarity of symptoms of narcolepsy to epilepsy occasionally leads to misdiagnosis in young children (Macleod, Ferrie, & Zuberi, 2005). Another symptom of the disorder is immediate entry into REM sleep, which produces frightening hallucinations that are, in fact, dreams that the person is experiencing while still partly awake. Narcolepsy is believed to arise from a defect in the central nervous system (Scammell, 2003).

Dreams

What are dreams?

Every culture, including our own, attributes meaning to dreams. In some cultures, people believe that dreams contain messages from their gods or that dreams predict the future. Psychologists define **dreams** as visual and auditory experiences that our minds create during sleep. The average person has four or five dreams a night, accounting for about one to two hours of the total time spent sleeping. People awakened during REM sleep report graphic dreams about 80 to 85% of the time (Domhoff, 2003). Less striking dreamlike experiences that resemble normal wakeful consciousness are reported about 50% of the time during NREM sleep.

Most dreams last about as long as the events would in real life; they do not flash on your mental screen just before waking, as was once believed. Generally, dreams consist of a sequential story or a series of stories. Stimuli, both external (such as a train whistle or a low-flying airplane) and internal (such as hunger pangs), may modify an ongoing dream, but they do not initiate dreams. Often, dreams are so vivid that it is difficult to distinguish them from reality (Domhoff, 2005).

WHY DO WE DREAM?

Psychologists have long been fascinated by dream activity and the contents of dreams, and a number of explanations have been proposed.

DREAMS AS UNCONSCIOUS WISHES Sigmund Freud (1900), the first modern theorist to investigate this topic, called dreams the "royal road to the unconscious." Believing that dreams represent unfulfilled wishes, he asserted that people's dreams reflect the motives guiding their behavior—motives of which they may not be consciously aware. Freud distinguished between the *manifest,* or surface, *content* of dreams and their *latent content*—the hidden, unconscious thoughts or desires that he believed were expressed indirectly through dreams.

THINKING CRITICALLY ABOUT . . .

Sleep Loss and Illness

"Too little sleep—or too much—may raise the risk of developing heart disease."

That headline referred to a study of more than 70,000 nurses conducted over more than a decade in which it was shown that those who slept less than 5 hours a night were almost 40% more likely to develop heart disease than those who averaged the normal 8 hours of sleep (Ayas et al., 2003).

1. The headline implies that the findings from this study apply universally—to women who are not nurses, to men, and to people around the world. Do you agree or disagree? Why or why not?

2. Note that the headline says that too little sleep "may" raise the risk of developing heart disease. Can you think of other factors that might cause both sleep loss and increase the risk of heart disease, and thus account for the relationship between the two?

3. The research depended on self-report of sleep: In other words, those who *said* they slept little were also those who were at greater risk of developing heart disease. Does that fact change your interpretation of the research results and your answers to the first two questions above?

4. Interestingly, the study also showed that *too much* sleep is also associated with a higher risk of heart disease. Nurses who said they slept more than 9 hours a night on average were 37% more likely to develop heart disease than those who said they slept the normal 8 hours. Does this additional piece of information change your thinking about this issue? How might you explain the relationship between self-reports of too much sleep and risk of developing heart disease?

---

narcolepsy Hereditary sleep disorder characterized by sudden nodding off during the day and sudden loss of muscle tone following moments of emotional excitement.

dreams Vivid visual and auditory experiences that occur primarily during REM periods of sleep.

The fanciful images of Marc Chagall's paintings capture the quality of many of our dreams. Is a dream of an entwined man and woman floating high above a city symbolic of some subconscious sexual desire, as Freud would have suggested? Or is it just an illogical image caused by random brain-cell activity during sleep? As yet, psychologists have no conclusive answer. Perhaps both views have merit.

Source: Marc Chagall (Russian, 1887–1985), "Above the City." Tretyakov Gallery, Moscow, Russia. Super-Stock, Inc.© Artists Rights Society (ARS), New York.

In dreams, according to Freud, people permit themselves to express primitive desires that are relatively free of moral controls. For example, someone who is not consciously aware of hostile feelings toward a sister may dream about murdering her. However, even in a dream, such hostile feelings may be censored and transformed into a symbolic form. For example, the desire to do away with one's sister (the dream's latent content) may be recast into the dream image of seeing her off at a train "terminal" (the dream's manifest content). According to Freud, this process of censorship and symbolic transformation accounts for the highly illogical nature of many dreams. Deciphering the disguised meanings of dreams is one of the principal tasks of psychoanalysts (C. E. Hill et al., 2000; Mazzoni, Lombardo, Malvagia, & Loftus, 1999). Freud's pioneering work, focused on exploring the meaning of dreams, paved the way for contemporary investigations of dream content (Marinelli & Mayer, 2003).

DREAMS AND INFORMATION PROCESSING A completely different explanation for dreaming emerged in the later part of the 20th century with the advent of *information processing theory* (see Chapter 6, "Memory"). This view holds that in our dreams, we reprocess information gathered during the day as a way of strengthening memories of information that is crucial to survival (Carpenter, 2001; Winson, 1990). During our waking hours, our brains are bombarded with sensory data. We need a "time out" to decide what information is valuable, whether it should be filed in long-term memory, where it should be filed (with which older memories, ideas, desires, and anxieties), and what information should be erased so that it doesn't clutter neural pathways (Crick & Mitchison, 1995; Payne & Nadel, 2004). According to this view, dreams seem illogical because the brain is rapidly scanning old files and comparing them with new, unsorted "clippings."

In support of this view, research has demonstrated that both humans and nonhumans spend more time in REM sleep after learning difficult material; furthermore, interfering with REM sleep immediately after learning severely disrupts the memory for the newly learned material (C. T. Smith, Nixon, & Nader, 2004; Wetzel, Wagner, & Balschun, 2003). Brain-imaging studies have also demonstrated that the specific area of the brain most active while learning new material is also active during subsequent REM sleep (Maquet et al., 2000).

Other psychologists see dreams as a form of emotional processing. In dreams, emotionally significant events may be integrated with previous experiences (Farthing, 1992). For example, children's first experience of a carnival or an amusement park is usually a blend of terror and excitement. Later in life, whenever they have experiences that are exciting, but also somewhat frightening, carnival rides or images may dominate their dreams. Some psychologists (R. D. Cartwright, 1996) have suggested that we work through problems in our dreams—indeed, that dreams are part of the healing process after a divorce, the death of a loved one, or other emotional crises. But critics argue that these breakthroughs may be more the result of foresight or hindsight than of dreams themselves (Domhoff, 2003).

DREAMS AND WAKING LIFE Still another theory maintains that dreams are an extension of the conscious concerns of daily life in altered (but not disguised) form (Domhoff, 2003). Research has shown that what people dream about is generally similar to what they think about and do while awake, though some recent research shows that consciously trying *not* to think of someone actually increases the likelihood that they will appear in your dreams (Wegner, Wenzlaff, & Kozak, 2004). Most often, dream content reflects an individual's unique conceptions, interests, and concerns. For example, a parent who's having problems with a child may dream about childhood confrontations with his or her own parents.

Dream content is also related to where you are in your sleep cycle, what you've been doing before you sleep, your gender, your age, and even your socioeconomic status. For example, although the dreams of men and women have become more similar over the last several decades, men more often dream about weapons, unfamiliar characters, male characters, aggressive interactions, and failure outcomes, whereas women are more likely to dream about being the victims of aggression (Bursik, 1998; Domhoff, 1996; Kolchakian & Hill, 2002). Dream content also appears to be relatively "consistent" for most individuals, displaying similar themes across years and even decades (Domhoff, 2003). Moreover, many of our dreams seem realistic and coherent while they are occurring and even after we are awake (Squier & Domhoff, 1998).

DREAMS AND NEURAL ACTIVITY New research using advanced brain-imaging techniques has indicated that the limbic system, which is involved with emotions, motivations, and memories, is "wildly" active during dreams; so, to a lesser extent, are the visual and auditory areas of the forebrain that process sensory information. However, areas of the forebrain involved in working memory, attention, logic, and self-monitoring are relatively inactive during dreams (Braun et al., 1998; Occhionero, 2004). This fact might explain the highly emotional texture of dreams, as well as the bizarre imagery and the loss of critical insight, logic, and self-reflection. This uncensored mixture of desires, fears, and memories comes very close to the psychoanalytic concept of unconscious wishes, suggesting that Freud may have come closer to the meaning of dreams than many contemporary psychologists have acknowledged.

Dreams are the most common alteration of normal consciousness; and as we have seen, they occur naturally under normal conditions. Altered states of consciousness can also be induced by drugs, a topic to which we next turn our attention.

CHECK YOUR UNDERSTANDING

1. Our awareness of the mental processes of our everyday life is called _____.
2. Technological innovations such as _____ (_____) enable scientists to study brain activity during various states of consciousness.
3. The major characteristic of waking consciousness is _____.
4. In humans, sleeping and waking follow a _____ cycle.
5. Most vivid dreaming takes place during the _____ stage of sleep.
6. We normally spend about _____ hours each night dreaming.
7. Freud distinguished between the _____ and _____ content of dreams.

Answers: 1.consciousness. 2.electroencephalography (EEG). 3.selective attention. 4.circadian. 5.REM. 6.two. 7.manifest, latent.

APPLY YOUR UNDERSTANDING

1. You are a psychologist studying an elderly person's sleep cycle. Compared with a younger person, you would expect to find that this person spends _____ time in Stage 3 and Stage 4 sleep.
   a. less
   b. more
   c. about the same
2. Recently, your sister has found it difficult to stay awake during the day. In the middle of a conversation, she will suddenly nod off. At night when she goes to bed, she often describes frightening hallucinations. Your sister is probably suffering from
   a. sleep apnea.
   b. REM deprivation.
   c. narcolepsy.
   d. insomnia.

Answers: 1. a. 2. c.

Drug-Altered Consciousness

How is today's drug problem different from the drug use in other societies and times?

In Chapter 2, "TheBiological Basis of Behavior," we examined how various drugs affect the function of the nervous system by fitting into the same receptor sites as naturally occurring chemicals or by blocking or enhancing transmission across the synapse. Here we will address the impact drugs have on behavior and consciousness.

The use of **psychoactive drugs**—substances that change people's moods, perceptions, mental functioning, or behavior—is almost universal. In nearly every known culture throughout history, people have sought ways to alter waking consciousness. Many legal and illegal drugs currently available have been used for thousands of years. For example, marijuana is mentioned in the herbal recipe book of a Chinese emperor, dating from 2737 B.C. Natives of the Andes Mountains in South America chew leaves of the cocaine-containing coca plant as a stimulant—a custom dating back at least to the Inca Empire of the 15th century.

In the 19th century, Europeans began adding coca to wine, tea, and lozenges (Karch, 2006). Following this trend, in 1886, an Atlanta pharmacist combined crushed coca leaves from the Andes, caffeine-rich cola nuts from West Africa, cane sugar syrup, and carbonated water in a patent medicine he called "Coca-Cola." *Laudanum*—opium dissolved in alcohol—was also popular in the United States at that time and was used as a main ingredient in numerous over-the-counter (or patent) medicines.

Of all psychoactive substances, alcohol has the longest history of widespread use. Archaeological evidence suggests that Late-Stone-Age groups began producing mead (fermented honey flavored with sap or fruit) about 10,000 years ago. The Egyptians, Babylonians, Greeks, and Romans viewed wine as a "gift from the gods." Wine is frequently praised in the Bible, and drinking water is hardly mentioned. In the Middle Ages, alcohol earned the title *aqua vitae*, the "water of life," with good reason (Vallee, 1998). Wherever people settled, water supplies quickly became contaminated with waste products. As recently as the 19th century, most people in Western civilizations drank alcohol with every meal (including breakfast) and between meals, as a "pick-me-up," as well as on social and religious occasions.

Is today's drug problem different from the drug use in other societies and times? In many ways, the answer is yes. First, motives for using psychoactive drugs have changed. In most cultures, psychoactive substances have been used as part of religious rituals, as medicines and tonics, as nutrient beverages, or as culturally approved stimulants (much as we drink coffee). By contrast, the use of alcohol and other drugs in contemporary society is primarily recreational. For the most part, people do not raise their glasses in praise of God or inhale hallucinogens to get in touch with the spirit world, but to relax, have fun with friends (and strangers), and get high. The French often drink wine with dinner, the Spanish are renowned not only for bullfights but for *tapas* bars, the British have their pubs, and Greeks have their festivals. Americans most often imbibe and inhale in settings specifically designed for recreation and inebriation: bars, clubs, beer parties, cocktail parties, "raves" (large, all-night dance parties), and so-called crack houses. In addition, people use and abuse drugs privately and secretly in their homes, sometimes without the knowledge of their family and friends—leading to hidden addiction. Whether social or solitary, the use of psychoactive substances today is largely divorced from religious and family traditions.

Second, the drugs themselves have changed. Modern psychoactive substances often are stronger than those used in other cultures and times. For most of Western history, wine (12% alcohol) was often diluted with water. Hard liquor (40% to 75% alcohol) appeared only in the 10th century A.D., and the heroin available on the streets today is stronger and more addictive than that available in the 1930s and 1940s.

In addition, new, synthetic drugs appear regularly, with unpredictable consequences. In the 1990s, the National Institute for Drug Abuse created a new category, "Club Drugs," for increasingly popular psychoactive substances manufactured in small laboratories or even home kitchens (from recipes available on the Internet). Because the source, the psychoactive ingredients, and any possible contaminants are unknown, the symptoms, toxicity, and short- or long-term consequences are also unknown—making these drugs

---

psychoactive drugs Chemical substances that change moods and perceptions.

especially dangerous. The fact that they are often consumed with alcohol multiplies the risks. Examples include "Ecstasy" (methylene-dioxymethamphetamine [MDMA]), a combination of the stimulant amphetamine and a hallucinogen; "Grievous Bodily Harm" (gammahydroxybutyrate [GHB]), a combination of sedatives and growth hormone stimulant; "Special K" (ketamine), an anesthetic approved for veterinary use that induces dreamlike states and hallucinations in humans; and "Roofies" (flunitrazepam), a tasteless, odorless sedative/anesthesia that can cause temporary amnesia, which is why it is also known as the "Forget-Me Pill" and is associated with sexual assault.

Finally, scientists and the public know more about the effects of psychoactive drugs than in the past. Nicotine is an obvious example. The Surgeon General's Report issued in 1964 confirmed a direct link between smoking and heart disease, as well as lung cancer. Subsequent research establishing that cigarettes are harmful not only to smokers, but also to people around them (as a result of secondhand smoke), as well as to their unborn babies (Ness et al., 1999; Schick & Glantz, 2005), transformed a personal health decision into a moral issue. Nonetheless, tens of millions of Americans still smoke, and millions of others use drugs they know to be harmful.

THINKING CRITICALLY ABOUT . . .

Mental Illness and Substance Abuse

The relationship between substance abuse and mental illness is called *comorbidity*. The question is, which comes first? Or are both problems the result of some other factor(s)? Does substance abuse lead to psychological disorders, for example, by triggering panic attacks, episodes of depression, and in some cases symptoms of severe disorder (psychosis)? Or do people who suffer from persistent emotional problems, such as social phobia, generalized anxiety, or posttraumatic stress, use psychoactive drugs in an attempt to medicate themselves? Or does something else entirely predispose people to both mental illness and substance abuse?

1. Which explanation do you think is most plausible? Why do you think so?

2. What kind of research evidence would convince you that your position is correct?

3. What kind of research evidence would convince you that your position is incorrect and that another explanation is better?

SUBSTANCE USE, ABUSE, AND DEPENDENCE

How can we tell whether someone is dependent on a psychoactive substance?

If we define drugs broadly, as we did earlier, to include caffeine, tobacco, and alcohol, then most people throughout the world use some type of drug on an occasional or a regular basis. Most of these people use such drugs in moderation and do not suffer ill effects. But for some, substance use escalates into **substance abuse**—a pattern of drug use that diminishes a person's ability to fulfill responsibilities, that results in repeated use of the drug in dangerous situations, or that leads to legal difficulties related to drug use. For example, people whose drinking causes ill health and problems within their families or on their jobs are abusing alcohol (D. Smith, 2001). Substance abuse is America's leading health problem (S. Martin, 2001).

The ongoing abuse of drugs, including alcohol, may lead to compulsive use of the substance, or **substance dependence**, which is also known as *addiction*. (See **Table 4–1**.) Although not everyone who abuses a substance develops dependence, dependence usually follows a period of abuse. Dependence often includes *tolerance*, the phenomenon whereby higher doses of the drug are required to produce its original effects or to prevent *withdrawal symptoms*, the unpleasant physical or psychological effects following discontinuance of the substance. Many organizations publicize self-tests based on these and other elements in the definition of substance abuse. For example, a self-test from the National Council on alcoholism includes the questions, "Can you handle more alcohol now than when you first started to drink?" and "When drinking with other people, do you try to have a few extra drinks the others won't know about?"

The causes of substance abuse and dependence are a complex combination of biological, psychological, and social factors that varies for each individual and for each substance. Also, the development of substance dependence does not follow an established timetable. One person might drink socially for years before abusing alcohol, whereas someone else

---

substance abuse A pattern of drug use that diminishes the ability to fulfill responsibilities at home, work, or school that results in repeated use of a drug in dangerous situations or that leads to legal difficulties related to drug use.

substance dependence A pattern of compulsive drug taking that results in tolerance, withdrawal symptoms, or other specific symptoms for at least a year.

table 4–1	SIGNS OF SUBSTANCE DEPENDENCE

The most recent clinical definition of dependence (American Psychiatric Association, 2000; Anthony & Helzer, 2002) describes a broad pattern of drug-related behaviors characterized by at least three of the following seven symptoms over a 12-month period:

1. Developing tolerance, that is, needing increasing amounts of the substance to gain the desired effect or experiencing a diminished effect when using the same amount of the substance. For example, the person might have to drink an entire six-pack to get the same effect formerly experienced after drinking just one or two beers.
2. Experiencing withdrawal symptoms, which are physical and psychological problems that occur if the person tries to stop using the substance. Withdrawal symptoms range from anxiety and nausea to convulsions and hallucinations.
3. Using the substance for a longer period or in greater quantities than intended.
4. Having a persistent desire or making repeated efforts to cut back on the use of the substance.
5. Devoting a great deal of time to obtaining or using the substance.
6. Giving up or reducing social, occupational, or recreational activities as a result of drug use.
7. Continuing to use the substance even in the face of ongoing or recurring physical or psychological problems likely to be caused or made worse by the use of the substance.

might become addicted to cocaine in a matter of days. Before we examine specific drugs and their effects, we first look at how psychologists study drug-related behaviors.

HOW DRUG EFFECTS ARE STUDIED The effects of particular drugs are studied under carefully controlled scientific conditions. In most cases, experimenters compare people's behavior before the administration of the drug with their behavior afterward, taking special precautions to ensure that any observed changes in behavior are due to the drug alone.

To eliminate research errors based on subject or researcher expectations, most drug experiments use the **double-blind procedure**, in which some participants receive the active drug while others take a neutral, inactive substance called a **placebo**. Neither the researchers nor the participants know who is taking the active drug and who is taking the placebo. If the behavior of the participants who actually received the drug differs from the behavior of those who got the placebo, the cause is likely to be the active ingredient in the drug.

Studying drug-altered consciousness is complicated by the fact that most drugs not only affect different people in different ways, but also produce different effects in the same person at different times or in different settings (S. Siegel, 2005). For example, some people are powerfully affected by even small amounts of alcohol, whereas others are not. And drinking alcohol in a convivial family setting usually produces somewhat different effects than does consuming alcohol under the watchful eyes of a scientist.

Recently, sophisticated neuroimaging procedures have proved useful for studying drug effects. Techniques such as PET imaging have enabled researchers to isolate specific differences between the brains of addicted and nonaddicted people. For example, the "addicted brain" has been found to differ qualitatively from the nonaddicted brain in a variety of ways, including metabolically and in responsiveness to environmental cues. Investigators have also focused on the role played by neurotransmitters in the addictive process (see Chapter 2, "The Biological Basis of Behavior")—noting that every addictive drug causes dopamine levels in the brain to increase (Addolorato, Leggio, Abenavoli, & Gasbarrini, 2005). Results like these may lead not only to better understanding of the biological basis of addiction, but also to a more effective treatments.

In analyzing drugs and drug use, it is convenient to group psychoactive substances into three categories: depressants, stimulants, and hallucinogens. (See "**Summary Table**: Drugs: Characteristics and Effects.") (We will look at a fourth category of psychoactive drugs, medications used in the treatment of mental illness, in Chapter 13, "Therapies.") These categories are not rigid, as the same drug may have multiple effects or different effects on different users, but this division helps organize our knowledge about drugs.

double-blind procedure Experimental design useful in studies of the effects of drugs, in which neither the subject nor the researcher knows at the time of administration which subjects are receiving an active drug and which are receiving an inactive substance.

placebo Chemically inactive substance used for comparison with active drugs in experiments on the effects of drugs.

SUMMARY TABLE

DRUGS: CHARACTERISTICS AND EFFECTS

	Typical Effects	Effects of Overdose	Tolerance/Dependence
Depressants			
Alcohol	Biphasic; tension-reduction "high," followed by depressed physical and psychological functioning.	Disorientation, loss of consciousness, death at extremely high blood-alcohol levels.	Tolerance; physical and psychological dependence, withdrawal symptoms.
Barbiturates Tranquilizers	Depressed reflexes and impaired motor functioning, tension reductions.	Shallow respiration, clammy skin, dilated pupils, weak and rapid pulse, coma, possible death.	Tolerance; high psychological and physical dependence on barbiturates, low to moderate physical dependence on such tranquilizers as Valium, although high psychological dependence; withdrawal symptoms.
Opiates	Euphoria, drowsiness, "rush" of pleasure, little impairment of psychological functions.	Slow, shallow breathing, clammy skin, nausea, vomiting, pinpoint pupils, convulsions, coma, possible death.	High tolerance; physical and psychological dependence; severe withdrawal symptoms.
Stimulants			
Amphetamines Cocaine Caffeine Nicotine	Increased alertness, excitation, euphoria, increased pulse rate and blood pressure, sleeplessness.	For amphetamines and cocaine: agitation and, with chronic high doses, hallucinations (e.g., "cocaine bugs"), paranoid delusions, convulsions, death. For caffeine and nicotine: restlessness, insomnia, rambling thoughts, heart arrhythmia, possible circulatory failure. For nicotine: increased blood pressure.	For amphetamines, cocaine, and nicotine: tolerance, psychological and physical dependence. For caffeine: physical and psychological dependence; withdrawal symptoms.
Hallucinogens			
LSD	Illusions, hallucinations, distortions in time perception, loss of contact with reality.	Psychotic reactions.	No physical dependence for LSD; degree of psychological dependence unknown for LSD.
Marijuana	Euphoria, relaxed inhibitions, increased appetite, possible disorientation.	Fatigue, disoriented behavior, possible psychosis.	Psychological dependence.

DEPRESSANTS: ALCOHOL, BARBITURATES, AND THE OPIATES

Why does alcohol, a depressant, lead to higher rates of violence?

Depressants are chemicals that retard behavior and thinking by either speeding up or slowing down nerve impulses. Generally speaking, alcohol, barbiturates, and the opiates have depressant effects. People take depressants to reduce tension, to forget their troubles, or to relieve feelings of inadequacy, loneliness, or boredom.

ALCOHOL The most frequently used psychoactive drug in Western societies is **alcohol**. The effects of alcohol depend on the individual, the social setting, and cultural attitudes, as well as on how much a person consumes and how fast.

In spite of, or perhaps because of, the fact that it is legal and socially approved, alcohol is America's number-one drug problem. More than 30% of high school seniors say that they get drunk; and alcohol is also a significant problem among middle-school students. (See **Figure 4–4**.) Alcohol is a highly addictive drug with potentially devastating long-term

depressants Chemicals that slow down behavior or cognitive processes.

alcohol Depressant that is the intoxicating ingredient in whiskey, beer, wine, and other fermented or distilled liquors.

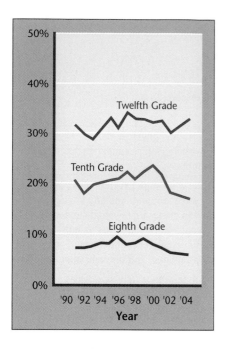

Figure 4–4

Teenage use of alcohol (% drunk in past 30 days).

A national survey found that use of alcohol by American teenagers has remained relatively steady since 1990. Approximately 30% to 35% of 12th graders report getting drunk during the past 30 days.

Source: L. D. Johnston, P. M. O'Malley, J. G. Bachman, & J. E. Schulenberg. (2005). Monitoring the Future national results on adolescent drug use: Overview of key findings, 2004. (NIH Publication No. 05-5726). Bethesda, MD: National Institute on Drug Abuse.

effects. At least 14 million Americans (more than 7% of the population ages 18 and older) have problems with drinking, including more than 8 million alcoholics, who are addicted to alcohol. Three times as many men as women are problem drinkers. For both sexes, alcohol abuse and addiction is highest in the 18- to 29-year-old age group (Hingson, Heeren, Winter, & Wechsler, 2005; National Institute on Alcohol Abuse and Alcoholism, 2003).

Excessive, chronic alcohol use can harm virtually every organ in the body, beginning with the brain, and is associated with impairments in perceptual–motor skills, visual–spatial processing, problem solving, and abstract reasoning (S. J. Nixon, 1999). Alcohol is the leading cause of liver disease and kidney damage, is a major factor in cardiovascular disease, increases the risk of certain cancers, and can lead to sexual dysfunction and infertility. Alcohol is particularly damaging to the nervous system during the teenage years. Areas of the brain that are not fully developed until age 21 are especially susceptible to damage from high levels of alcohol intoxication (Ballie, 2001; Tapert & Schweinsburg, 2005). The cost of alcohol abuse and dependence in America is high; estimated at $100 billion annually and 100,000 deaths (Enoch, 1998).

The social costs of abusing alcohol are high as well. Alcohol is involved in a substantial proportion of violent and accidental deaths, including suicides, which makes it the leading contributor (after AIDS) to death among young people. Alcohol is implicated in more than two-thirds of all fatal automobile accidents, two-thirds of all murders, two-thirds of all spouse beatings, and more than half of all cases of violent child abuse. Moreover, the use of alcohol during pregnancy has been linked to a variety of birth defects, the most notable being fetal alcohol syndrome. (See Chapter 8, "Life Span Development.") More than 40% of all heavy drinkers die before the age of 65 (compared with less than 20% of nondrinkers). In addition, there is the untold cost in psychological trauma suffered by the nearly 30 million children of alcohol abusers.

What makes alcohol so powerful? Alcohol first affects the frontal lobes of the brain (K. Adams & Johnson-Greene, 1995; Noël, et al., 2001), which figure prominently in inhibitions, impulse control, reasoning, and judgment. As consumption continues, alcohol impairs functions of the cerebellum, the center of motor control and balance (Manto & Jacquy, 2002). Eventually, alcohol consumption affects the spinal cord and medulla, which regulate such involuntary functions as breathing, body temperature, and heart rate. A blood-alcohol level of 0.25% or more may cause this part of the nervous system to shut down and may severely impair functioning; slightly higher levels can cause death from alcohol poisoning. (See **Table 4–2**.)

table 4–2	THE BEHAVIORAL EFFECTS OF BLOOD-ALCOHOL LEVELS
Levels of Alcohol in the Blood	**Behavioral Effects**
0.05%	Feels good; less alert; reduced inhibitions
0.10%	Is slower to react; less cautious; slurred speech
0.15%	Reaction time is much slower
0.20%	Sensory–motor abilities are suppressed
0.25%	Is staggering (motor abilities severely impaired); perception is limited as well
0.30%	Is in semistupor; confused
0.35%	Is at level for anesthesia; death is possible
0.40%	Stupor
0.50%	Coma
0.60%	Respiratory paralysis and death

Source: Data from *Drugs, Society, and Human Behavior*, 10th ed., by Oakley Ray, 2003, New York: McGraw-Hill; U.S. National Library of Medicine. (2006). *Alcohol use.* Retrieved March 16, 2006, from *http://www.nlm.nih.gov/medlineplus/ency/article/001944.htm.*

Even in moderate quantities, alcohol affects perception, motor processes, memory, and judgment. It diminishes the ability to see clearly, to perceive depth, and to distinguish the differences between bright lights and colors, and it generally affects spatial–cognitive functioning—all clearly necessary for driving a car safely. Alcohol interferes with memory storage: Heavy drinkers may also experience *blackouts*, which make them unable to remember anything that occurred while they were drinking; but even long-term alcoholics show improvements in memory, attention, balance, and neurological functioning after three months of sobriety (E. V. Sullivan, Rosenbloom, Lim, & Pfefferbaum, 2000).

Heavy drinkers have difficulty focusing on relevant information and ignoring inaccurate, irrelevant information, thus leading to poor judgments (S. J. Nixon, 1999). Dozens of studies demonstrate that alcohol use is correlated with increases in aggression, hostility, violence, and abusive behavior (Aviles, Earleywine, Pollock, Stratton, & Miller , 2005; Grekin, Sher, & Larkins, 2004; M. P. Thompson & Kingree, 2006) . Thus, intoxication makes people less aware of and less concerned about the negative consequences of their actions, increasing their likelihood to engage in risky behavior (S. George, Rogers, & Duka, 2005). The same principle applies to potential victims. For instance, when women are intoxicated, their ability to accurately evaluate a dangerous situation with a potential male aggressor is diminished, so that their risk of being sexually assaulted increases (Testa, Livingston, & Collins, 2000). Similarly, people who are intoxicated are more likely to engage in unprotected sex than if they were sober (MacDonald, Fong, Zanna, & Martineau, 2000; MacDonald, MacDonald, Zanna, & Fong, 2000; M. Stein et al., 2005).

ENDURING ISSUES

Diversity–Universality   Women and Alcohol

Women are especially vulnerable to the effects of alcohol (National Institute on Alcohol Abuse and Alcoholism [NIAAA], 2003). Because women generally weigh less than men, the same dose of alcohol has a stronger effect on the average woman than on the average man (NIAAA, 2003). Most women have lower levels of the stomach enzyme that regulates alcohol metabolism. The less of this enzyme in the stomach, the greater the amount of alcohol that passes into the bloodstream and spreads through the body. (This is the reason why drinking on an empty stomach has more pronounced effects than drinking with meals.) In addition, neuroimaging studies reveal that women's brains may also be more vulnerable to damage from alcohol consumption than male brains (K. Mann et al., 2005). As a rough measure, one drink is likely to have the same effects on a woman as two drinks have on a man. ●●

The dangers of alcohol notwithstanding, alcohol continues to be popular because of its short-term effects. As a depressant, it calms the nervous system, much like a general anesthetic (McKim, 2007). Thus, people consume alcohol to relax or to enhance their mood. It is often experienced as a stimulant because it inhibits centers in the brain that govern critical judgment and impulsive behavior. Alcohol makes people feel more courageous, less inhibited, more spontaneous, and more entertaining. To drinkers, the long-term negative consequences of alcoholism pale beside these short-term positive consequences.

The good news is that since 1977, the overall consumption of alcohol is generally down with only a slight increase in the recent decade due largely to increased consumption of wine (See **Figure 4-5**) (Nekisha, Gerald, Hsiao-ye, & Michael, 2005) . Alcohol-related traffic deaths, while still too common, are also declining (Yi, Williams, & Dufour, 2002). (See **Figure 4–6**). The alarming news is that drinking in high school (and earlier) is still common: More than 30% of high school seniors say they have gotten drunk in the previous 30 days, and binge drinking has become a dangerous "tradition" on college campuses.

BINGE DRINKING ON COLLEGE CAMPUSES One of the few places today where drunkenness is tolerated, and often expected, is the American college campus. National surveys of colleges, universities, and persons between the age of 18 and 20 found that almost half of

Excessive drinking and public drunkenness have been widely frowned on in many cultures. In this etching, *Gin Lane*, by the 18th-century English artist William Hogarth, a baby slips carelessly from the arms of a drunken mother.

Source: William Hogarth (1697–1765), *Gin Lane*. The Metropolitan Museum of Art, Harris Brisbane Dick Fund, 1932. © The Metropolitan Museum of Art

Figure 4–5

Per capita annual alcohol consumption in the United States, 1977–2003

Source:
http://pubs.niaaa.nih.gov/publications/
surveillance73/CONS03.htm#fig1

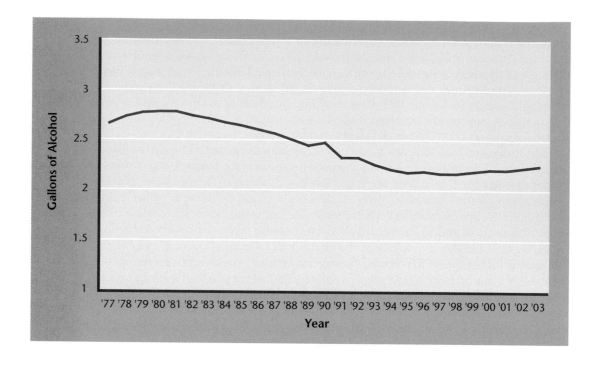

college students engage in "binge drinking," defined as five or more drinks in a row for men, four or more drinks for women (Serdula, Brewer, Gillespie, Denny, & Mokdad, 2004; Wechsler, Dowdall, Davenport, & DeJong, 2000). The extent of binge drinking at different schools ranged from 1% percent to 70%, indicating that the campus environment is an important influence on drinking patterns.

About half of binge drinkers—one in five students overall—had gone on binges three or more times during the two weeks before the survey and been intoxicated three or more times over the past month. Most of these students cited getting drunk as their main reason for drinking. Regardless of how much they drank, very few (less than 1%) considered themselves "problem drinkers."

It is not surprising that frequent binge drinkers had more problems, and more serious problems, than other students. Many had missed classes, fallen behind in schoolwork, engaged in unplanned—and unprotected—sex, gotten in trouble with campus police, engaged in vandalism or violence, or been hurt or injured. Bingers were more likely than other students to have used other drugs, especially cigarettes and marijuana (R. D. Brewer & Swahn, 2005; Pirkle & Richter, 2006). They were ten times more likely to have driven a

Figure 4–6

Persons killed in alcohol-related traffic crashes.
Deaths in alcohol-related traffic accidents have generally declined since the 1980s, although the total number for the most recent year is still tragically high.

Source: http://www-nrd.nhtsa.dot.gov/pdf/nrd-30/NCSA/TSFAnn/TSF2004.pdf

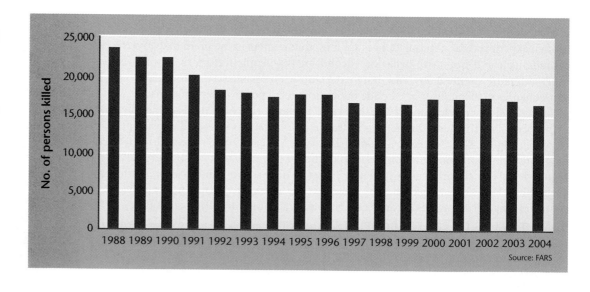

car after drinking and more than 15 times more likely to have ridden with a driver who was drunk or high.

The effects of binge drinking are not limited to students who participate. At schools with high binge rates, a majority of students report that they have been unable to study or sleep because of binge drinking. Many sober students have cared for drunken friends, endured drunken insults, and fended off unwanted sexual advances. Yet most are reluctant to report these problems to campus or other authorities.

Researchers emphasize that the majority of students at 4-year institutions—56% nationally—abstain or drink in moderation, a strong foundation for change (Wechsler et al., 2000). Nevertheless, binge drinking is an extremely serious problem that not only interferes with education but also carries a high risk of disease, injury, and death.

BARBITURATES **Barbiturates**, commonly known as "downers," include such medications as Amytal, Nembutal, Seconal, and phenobarbital. Discovered about a century ago, this class of depressants was first prescribed for its sedative and anticonvulsant qualities. But after researchers recognized in the 1950s that barbiturates had potentially deadly effects— particularly in combination with alcohol—their use declined, though they are still sometimes prescribed to treat such diverse conditions as insomnia, anxiety, epilepsy, arthritis, and bed-wetting (Alvarez, 1998; Reinisch & Sanders, 1982). Though barbiturates are often prescribed to help people sleep, they actually disrupt the body's natural sleep patterns and cause dependence when used for long periods.

The general effects of barbiturates are strikingly similar to those of alcohol: Taken on an empty stomach, a small dose causes light-headedness, silliness, and poor motor coordination (McKim, 2007), whereas larger doses may bring on slurred speech, loss of inhibition, and increases in aggression (Aston, 1972). When taken during pregnancy, barbiturates, like alcohol, produce such birth defects as a cleft palate and malformations of the heart, skeleton, and central nervous system (Olney, Wozniak, Farber, Jevtovic-Todorovic, & Bittigau, 2002; Wilder & Bruni, 1981).

OPIATES Psychoactive substances derived from, or resembling, sap taken from the seedpod of the opium poppy, **opiates** have a long history of use—though not always abuse. A Sumerian tablet from 4000 B.C. refers to the "joy plant." Originating in Turkey, opium spread west around the Mediterranean and east through India into China, where it was used in pill or liquid form in folk medicines for thousands of years. But changes in the way opium and its derivative, morphine, were used opened the door to abuse. In the mid-17th century, when the emperor of China banned tobacco and the Chinese began to smoke opium, addiction quickly followed. During the American Civil War, physicians used a new invention, the hypodermic needle, to administer morphine, a much-needed painkiller for soldiers. In this form, morphine was far more addictive than smoking opium. Heroin—introduced in 1898 as a cure for morphine addiction—created an even stronger dependency.

Morphine compounds are still used in painkillers and other medications, such as codeine cough syrups. The nonmedicinal distribution of opiates was banned early in the 20th century. After that, a black market for heroin developed. In the public mind, the heroin addict became synonymous with the "dope fiend," the embodiment of social evil.

Heroin and other opiates resemble endorphins, the natural painkillers produced by the body, and occupy many of the same nerve-receptor sites. (See Chapter 2, "The Biological Basis of Behavior.") Heroin users report a surge of euphoria soon after taking the drug, followed by a period of "nodding off" and clouded mental functioning. Regular use leads to tolerance; tolerance may lead to physical dependence. In advanced stages of addiction, heroin becomes primarily a painkiller to stave off withdrawal symptoms. These symptoms, which may begin within hours of the last dose, include profuse sweating; alternating hot flashes and chills with goose bumps resembling the texture of a plucked turkey (hence the term *cold turkey*); severe cramps, vomiting, and diarrhea; and convulsive shaking and kicking (as in "kicking the habit").

Heroin abuse is associated with serious health conditions, including fatal overdose, spontaneous abortion, collapsed veins, pulmonary problems, and infectious diseases, especially HIV/AIDS and hepatitis, as a result of sharing needles (Bourgeois, 1999;

Nineteenth-century immigrants to the United States are shown gambling and smoking opium pipes at a clubhouse in New York's Chinatown. Problems associated with abuse of this drug led to it being banned for nonmedical use early in the 20th century.

barbiturates Potentially deadly depressants, first used for their sedative and anticonvulsant properties, now used only to treat such conditions as epilepsy and arthritis.

opiates Drugs, such as opium and heroin, derived from the opium poppy, that dull the senses and induce feelings of euphoria, well-being, and relaxation. Synthetic drugs resembling opium derivatives are also classified as opiates.

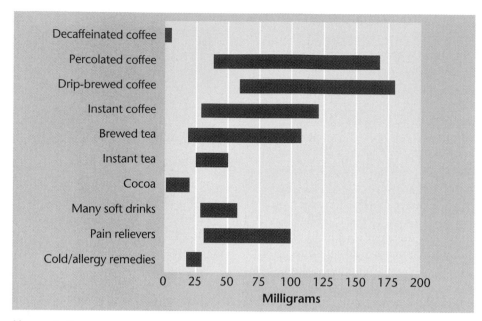

Figure 4–7

The amount of caffeine in some common preparations.
Caffeine occurs in varying amounts in coffee, tea, soft drinks, and many nonprescription medications. On average, Americans consume about 200 mg of caffeine each day.

Source: August 7, 1991, by the *New York Times.*

Supermodel Christie Turlington posed for a series of antismoking ads after her father died of lung cancer.

Source:www.smokingisugly.com. Reprinted by permission of Christy Turlington.

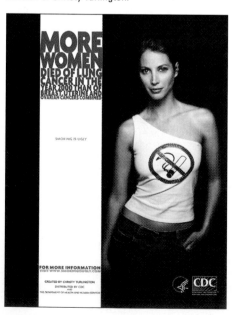

McCurdy, Williams, Kilonzo, Ross, & Leshabari, 2005). The mortality rate of heroin users is almost 15 times higher than that of nonusers (Inciardi & Harrison, 1998). No longer an inner-city problem, its use is growing in suburbs and among young people and women, who often inhale or smoke heroin in the mistaken belief that it is not dangerous in this form (National Institute on Drug Abuse, 2005b).

STIMULANTS: CAFFEINE, NICOTINE, AMPHETAMINES, AND COCAINE

How do people tend to feel after a stimulant wears off?

The drugs classified as **stimulants**—caffeine, nicotine, amphetamines, and cocaine—have legitimate uses, but because they produce feelings of optimism and boundless energy, the potential for abuse is high.

CAFFEINE Caffeine, which occurs naturally in coffee, tea, and cocoa, belongs to a class of drugs known as *xanthine stimulants*. The primary ingredient in over-the-counter stimulants, caffeine is popularly believed to maintain wakefulness and alertness, but many of its stimulant effects are illusory. In one study, research participants performing motor and perceptual tasks thought they were doing better when they were on caffeine, but their actual performance was no better than without it. In terms of wakefulness, caffeine reduces the total number of sleep minutes and increases the time it takes to fall asleep. It is the only stimulant that does not appear to alter sleep stages or cause REM rebound, making it much safer than amphetamines.

Caffeine is found in many beverages and nonprescription medications, including pain relievers and cold and allergy remedies. (See **Figure 4–7.**) It is generally considered a benign drug, although large doses—more than five or six cups of strong coffee per day, for example—may cause caffeinism, or "coffee nerves": anxiety, headaches, heart palpitations, insomnia, and diarrhea. Caffeine interferes with prescribed medications, such as tranquilizers and sedatives, and appears to aggravate the symptoms of many psychiatric disorders. It is not clear what percentage of coffee drinkers are dependent on caffeine. Those who are dependent experience tolerance, difficulty in giving it up, and physical and psychological distress, such as headaches, lethargy, and depression, whether the caffeine is in soda, coffee, or tea (Juliano & Griffiths, 2004).

NICOTINE Nicotine, the psychoactive ingredient in tobacco, is probably the most dangerous and addictive stimulant in use today. Recent studies have found that the neurochemical properties of nicotine are similar to those of cocaine, amphetamines, and morphine (Fredrickson, Boules, Lin, & Richelson, 2005). When smoked, nicotine tends to arrive at the brain all at once following each puff—a rush similar to the "high" experienced by heroin users. The smoker's heart rate increases and blood vessels constrict, causing dull skin and cold hands and accelerating the process of wrinkling and aging. Nicotine affects levels of several neurotransmitters, including norepinephrine, dopamine, and serotonin. Depending on the time, the amount smoked, and other factors, it may have sedating or stimulating effects. Symptoms of withdrawal from nicotine include nervousness, difficulty concentrating, both insomnia and drowsiness, headaches, irritability, and intense craving, which continue for weeks and may recur months or even years after a smoker has quit (Haro & Drucker-Colín, 2004).

Despite well-known health risks and strong social pressures (Edwards, 2004), millions of Americans continue to smoke, either for the pleasure of the combined stimulant-sedative effects or to prevent cravings and withdrawal symptoms. Particularly worrisome is that the number of teenagers who start smoking each year has hardly changed. Youth aged 12 to 17 who smoke are about 12 times more likely to use illicit drugs, and 16 times more likely to drink heavily, than their nonsmoking peers and have an increased risk of depression (National Household Survey on Drug Abuse, 1998; D. Smith, 2001).

AMPHETAMINES Amphetamines are powerful synthetic stimulants, first marketed in the 1930s as a nasal spray to relieve symptoms of asthma. At the chemical level, **amphetamines** resemble epinephrine, a hormone that stimulates the sympathetic nervous system. (See Chapter 2, "The Biological Basis of Behavior.") During World War II, the military routinely gave soldiers amphetamines in pill form to relieve fatigue. After the war, the demand for "pep pills" grew among night workers, truck drivers, students, and athletes. Because amphetamines tend to suppress the appetite, they were widely prescribed as "diet pills." Today, the only legitimate medical uses for amphetamines are to treat narcolepsy and attention deficit disorder. (Paradoxically, amphetamines have a calming effect on hyperactive children.) They are, however, widely used for nonmedical, "recreational" reasons.

Amphetamines not only increase alertness, but also produce feelings of competence and well-being. People who inject them intravenously report a "rush" of euphoria. After the drug's effects wear off, however, users may "crash" into a state of exhaustion and depression. Amphetamines are habit forming: Users may come to believe that they cannot function without them. High doses can cause sweating, tremors, heart palpitations, anxiety, and insomnia—which may lead people to take barbiturates or drugs to counteract these effects. Excessive use of amphetamines may cause personality changes, including paranoia, homicidal and suicidal thoughts, and aggressive, violent behavior (Baker & Dawe, 2005). Chronic users may develop *amphetamine psychosis,* which resembles paranoid schizophrenia and is characterized by delusions, hallucinations, and paranoia. The label "dope fiend" more accurately describes the behavior of amphetamine addicts than that of heroin addicts!

Methamphetamine—known on the street as "speed" and "fire," or in a crystal, smokable form as "ice," "crystal," and "crank"—is easily produced in clandestine laboratories from ingredients available over the counter. A variation that was briefly popular around the turn of the 21st century, Ecstasy (methylenedioxymethamphetamine, or MDMA), acts as both a stimulant and a hallucinogen. The name "Ecstasy" reflects the users' belief that the drug makes people love and trust one another, puts them in touch with their own emotions, and heightens sexual pleasure.

Short-term physical effects include involuntary teeth clenching (which is why users often wear baby pacifiers around their neck or suck lollipops), faintness, and chills or sweating. Although early research on Ecstasy with primates suggested that even short-term recreational use could have long-term harmful consequences, more recent studies have not verified evidence of permanent damage from short-term use (Navarro & Maldonado, 2004; Ricaurte, Yuan, Hatzidimitriou, Cord, & McCann, 2003; Sumnall, Jerome, Doblin, & Mithoefer, 2004). There is still some reason to be concerned, however, especially by heavy use. Animal research going back more than 20 years shows that high doses of methamphetamine damage the axon terminals of dopamine- and serotonin-containing neurons (National Institute on Drug Abuse, 2005a). Increased aggression in rats has been observed following a single low dose administration of methamphetamine (Kirilly et al., 2006). One study also found that the recreational use of Ecstasy may lead to a decrease in intelligence test scores (Gouzoulis-Mayfrank et al., 2000), and heavy use of MDMA has been associated with a decline in visual memory (Back-Madruga et al., 2003). Moreover, the use of Ecstasy during pregnancy has been associated with birth defects (McElhatton, Bateman, Evans, Pughe, & Thomas, 1999). Increased public awareness of the potential dangers associated with Ecstasy explains in part the very recent and sharp decline in its usage (L. D. Johnston, O'Malley, Bachman, & Schulenberg, 2005). (See **Figure 4–8.**)

COCAINE First isolated from cocoa leaves in 1885, **cocaine** came to be used widely as a topical anesthetic for minor surgery (and still is, for example, in the dental anesthetic Novocain). Around the turn of the century, many physicians believed that cocaine was beneficial as a general stimulant, as well as a cure for excessive use of alcohol and morphine addiction.

stimulants Drugs, including amphetamines and cocaine, that stimulate the sympathetic nervous system and produce feelings of optimism and boundless energy.

amphetamines Stimulant drugs that initially produce "rushes" of euphoria often followed by sudden "crashes" and, sometimes, severe depression.

cocaine Drug derived from the coca plant that, although producing a sense of euphoria by stimulating the sympathetic nervous system, also leads to anxiety, depression, and addictive cravings.

Figure 4–8
Teenage use of Ecstacy.
Teenage use of Ecstacy has dropped sharply in recent years, after rising steadily after 1998.

Source: L. D. Johnston, P. M. O'Malley, J. G. Bachman, & J. E. Schulenberg. (2005). Monitoring the Future national results on adolescent drug use: Overview of key findings, 2004. (NIH Publication No. 05-5726). Bethesda, MD: National Institute on Drug Abuse.

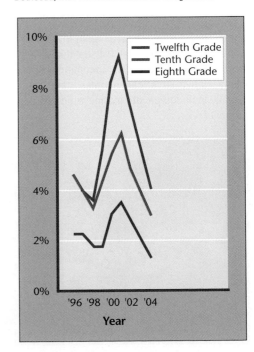

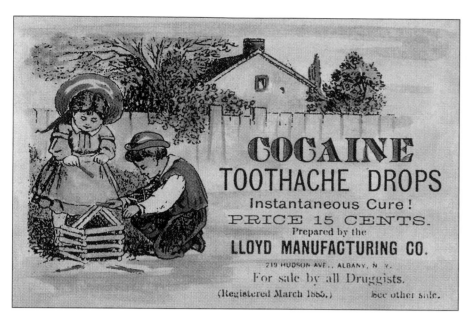

An 1885 American advertisement for Cocaine Toothache Drops, obviously intended for young children, as well as adults. The addition of cocaine to everyday products, including Coca-Cola, was quite common in the 19th century.

---

hallucinogens Any of a number of drugs, such as LSD and mescaline, that distort visual and auditory perception.

lysergic acid diethylamide (LSD) Hallucinogenic or "psychedelic" drug that produces hallucinations and delusions similar to those occurring in a psychotic state.

These Native American women in Mexico are grinding dry peyote that will be mixed with water and drunk during an upcoming festival. Many Native American peoples have traditionally included peyote in their religious ceremonies.

Among the more famous cocaine users was Sigmund Freud. When he discovered how addictive cocaine was, Freud campaigned against it, as did many of his contemporaries, and ingesting the drug fell into disrepute.

Cocaine made a comeback in the 1970s in such unlikely places as Wall Street, among investment bankers who found that the drug not only made them high, but also allowed them to wheel and deal around the clock with little sleep (Califano, 1999). In the white-powdered form that is snorted (street names include "coke" and "snow"), it became a status drug, the amphetamine of the wealthy. In the 1980s, a cheaper, smokable, crystallized form known as "crack" (made from the by-products of cocaine extraction) appeared in inner-city neighborhoods. Crack reaches the brain in less than 10 seconds, producing a high that lasts from 5 to 20 minutes, followed by a swift and equally intense depression. Users report that crack leads to almost instantaneous addiction. Addiction to powdered cocaine, which has longer effects, is not inevitable, but is likely. Babies born to women addicted to crack and cocaine often are premature or have low-birth weight, may have withdrawal symptoms, and enter school with subtle deficits in intelligence and language skills (Inciardi, Surratt, & Saum, 1997; S. Nelson, Lerner, Needlman, Salvator & Singer, 2004).

On the biochemical level, cocaine blocks the reabsorption of the neurotransmitter dopamine, which is associated with awareness, motivation, and, most significantly, pleasure (Bressan & Crippa, 2005). From an evolutionary perspective, dopamine rewards such survival-related activities as eating, drinking, and engaging in sex. Excess dopamine intensifies and prolongs feelings of pleasure—hence the cocaine user's feelings of euphoria. Normally, dopamine is reabsorbed, leading to feelings of satiety or satisfaction; dopamine reabsorption tells the body, "That's enough." But cocaine short-circuits this feeling of satisfaction, in effect telling the body, "More!" The addictive potential of cocaine may be related to the fact that it damages the brain cells that produce dopamine, thus increasing the amount of cocaine needed to get the same high in the future (Little, Krowlewski, Zhang, & Cassin, 2003).

HALLUCINOGENS AND MARIJUANA

How does marijuana affect memory?

Certain natural or synthetic drugs can cause striking shifts in perception of the outside world or, in some cases, can cause their users to experience imaginary landscapes, settings, and beings that may seem more real than the outside world. Because such experiences resemble hallucinations; the drugs causing them are known as **hallucinogens**. The hallucinogens include lysergic acid diethylamide (LSD, also known as "acid"), mescaline, peyote, and psilocybin. Marijuana is sometimes included in this group, although its effects are normally less powerful. In large enough doses, many other drugs bring on hallucinatory or delusional experiences, mimicking those that occur in severe mental illnesses; hallucinogens do so in small doses, usually without toxic effects. How many cultural groups have used hallucinogens is not known. Historians believe that Native Americans have used mescaline, a psychedelic substance found in the mushroom-shaped tops or "buttons" of peyote cactus, for at least 8,000 years.

By contrast, the story of **lysergic acid diethylamide (LSD)**, the drug that triggered the current interest in the hallucinogens, begins in the 20th century. In 1943, an American pharmacologist synthesized LSD, and after ingesting it, he reported experiencing "an uninterrupted stream of fantastic pictures and extraordinary shapes with an intense, kaleidoscopic play of colors." His report led others to experiment with LSD as an artificial form of psychosis, a painkiller for terminal cancer patients, and a cure for alcoholism in the 1950s (Ashley, 1975). LSD came to public attention in the 1960s, when Harvard psychologist Timothy Leary, after trying the related hallucinogen psilocybin, began spreading the "Turn On, Tune In, Drop Out" gospel of the hippie movement. Use of LSD and marijuana declined steadily in the 1970s, but became popular once again in the 1990s, especially with high school and college students (Janofsky, 1994).

About an hour after ingesting LSD, people begin to experience an intensification of sensory perception, loss of control over their thoughts and emotions, and feelings of depersonalization and detachment, as if they were watching themselves from a distance. Some LSD users say that things never looked or sounded or smelled so beautiful; others have terrifying, nightmarish visions. Some users experience a sense of extraordinary mental lucidity; others become so confused that they fear they are losing their minds. The effects of LSD are highly variable, even for the same person on different occasions.

"Bad trips," or unpleasant experiences, may be set off by a change in dosage or an alteration in setting or mood. During a bad trip, the user may not realize that the experiences are being caused by the drug and thus may panic. Flashbacks, or recurrences of hallucinations, may occur weeks after ingesting LSD. Other consequences of frequent use may include memory loss, paranoia, panic attacks, nightmares, and aggression (Pechnick & Ungerleider, 2004).

Unlike depressants and stimulants, LSD and the other hallucinogens do not appear to produce withdrawal effects. If LSD is taken repeatedly, tolerance builds up rapidly: After a few days, no amount of the drug will produce its usual effects, until its use is suspended for about a week (McKim, 2007). This effect acts as a built-in deterrent to continuous use, which helps explain why LSD is generally taken episodically, rather than habitually. After a time, users seem to get tired of the experience and so decrease or discontinue their use of the drug, at least for a period of time.

MARIJUANA Marijuana is a mixture of dried, shredded flowers and leaves of the hemp plant *Cannabis sativa* (which is also a source of fiber for rope and fabrics). Unlike LSD, marijuana usage has a long history. In China, cannabis has been cultivated for at least 5,000 years. The ancient Greeks knew about its psychoactive effects; and it has been used as an intoxicant in India for centuries. But only in the 20th century did marijuana become popular in the United States. Today, marijuana is the most frequently used illegal drug in the United States and the fourth most popular drug among students, after alcohol, caffeine, and nicotine (Treaster, 1994). **Figure 4–9** shows the trend in marijuana use by adolescents in recent years (L. D. Johnston, O'Malley, Bachman, & Schulenberg, 2005).

Although the active ingredient in marijuana, *tetrahydrocannabinol* (THC), shares some chemical properties with hallucinogens like LSD, it is far less potent. Marijuana smokers report feelings of relaxation; heightened enjoyment of food, music, and sex; a loss of awareness of time; and on occasion, dreamlike experiences. As with LSD, experiences are varied. Many users experience a sense of well-being, and some feel euphoric, but others become suspicious, anxious, and depressed.

Marijuana has direct physiological effects, including dilation of the blood vessels in the eyes, making the eyes appear bloodshot; a dry mouth and coughing (because it is generally smoked); increased thirst and hunger; and mild muscular weakness, often in the form of drooping eyelids (Donatelle, 2004). The major physiological dangers of marijuana are potential respiratory and cardiovascular damage, including triggering heart attacks (National Institute on Drug Abuse, 2004a). Among the drug's psychological effects is a distortion of time, which appears to be related to the impact marijuana has on specific regions of the brain (D. S. O'Leary et al., 2003): Feelings that minutes occur in slow motion or that hours flash by in seconds are common. In addition, marijuana may produce alterations in short-term memory and attention (S. D. Lane, Cherek, Lieving, & Tcheremissine, 2005).

While under the influence of marijuana, people often lose the ability to remember and coordinate information, a phenomenon known as *temporal disintegration*. For instance, someone who is "high" on marijuana may forget what he or she was talking about in midsentence. Such memory lapses may trigger anxiety and panic (Leccese, 1991). While

marijuana A mild hallucinogen that produces a "high" often characterized by feelings of euphoria, a sense of well-being, and swings in mood from gaiety to relaxation; may also cause feelings of anxiety and paranoia.

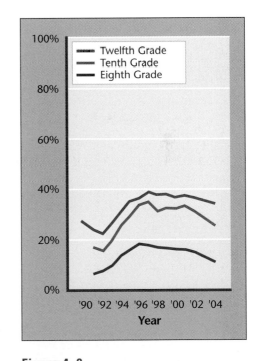

Figure 4–9

Teenage use of marijuana in past year.
A national survey found that use of marijuana by American teenagers leveled off in 1995 and has begun to show a recent decline.

Source: L. D. Johnston, P. M. O'Malley, J. G. Bachman, & J. E. Schulenberg. (2005). Monitoring the Future national results on adolescent drug use: Overview of key findings, 2004. (NIH Publication No. 05-5726). Bethesda, MD: National Institute on Drug Abuse.

THINKING CRITICALLY ABOUT . . .

Teenage Use of Marijuana

According to the National Institute on Drug Abuse (2000a): Longitudinal research on marijuana use among young people below college age indicates those who used marijuana have lower achievement than the nonusers, more acceptance of deviant behavior, more delinquent behavior and aggression, greater rebelliousness, poorer relationships with parents, and more associations with delinquent and drug-using friends.

1. Write down as many possible explanations for the relationship between using marijuana and other behaviors mentioned as you can think of—the more, the better.

2. Now decide which of these explanations you consider most likely and why. How might you go about determining whether those explanations are, in fact, correct?

3. Examine the assumptions underlying your decisions, or exchange your list with classmates and evaluate each other's assumptions.

high, marijuana users have shortened attention spans and delayed reactions, which contribute to concerns about their ability to drive a car or to study or work effectively (National Institute on Drug Abuse, 2004b).

Is marijuana a "dangerous" drug? This question is the subject of much debate in scientific circles as well as public forums. On the one hand are those who contend that marijuana can be psychologically if not physiologically addictive (Haney et al., 2004; Levin et al., 2004); that frequent, long-term use has a negative impact on learning and motivation; and that legal prohibitions against marijuana should be continued. The evidence for cognitive or psychological damage is mixed. One study of college students showed that critical skills related to attention, memory, and learning are impaired among people who use marijuana heavily, even after discontinuing its use for at least 24 hours (National Institute on Drug Abuse, 2004a). On the other hand are those who maintain that marijuana is less harmful than the legal drugs, alcohol and nicotine. They argue that the criminalization of marijuana forces people to buy unregulated cannabis from illegal sources, which means that they might smoke "pot" contaminated with more harmful substances. Moreover, some evidence indicates that marijuana can relieve some of the unpleasant side effects of chemotherapy and can reduce suffering among terminal cancer patients. Scientists have recently begun to develop new medicines modeled on the psychoactive ingredient in marijuana (THC) to allow patients to achieve similar positive medical effects without using marijuana (Kathuria et al., 2003; Piomelli, 2001). In short, the jury is still out, and the debate over marijuana is likely to continue (J. Stein, 2002).

So far, we have been talking about the effects of individual drugs. In reality, most people who abuse drugs abuse more than one, and most addicts are polyaddicted (Califano, 2000). As a rule, young people who use "club drugs" also drink and smoke; likewise, college binge drinkers typically smoke cigarettes and marijuana as well. The same behavior is true of older drug abusers. In addition, people who use one drug (say, the stimulants amphetamine or cocaine) often use another drug (such depressants as alcohol, barbiturates, or minor tranquilizers) to counteract the effects of the first drug. This practice not only multiplies their risks as individuals, but also makes efforts to diagnose and treat drug problems more difficult.

EXPLAINING ABUSE AND ADDICTION

What combination of factors makes it more likely that someone will abuse drugs?

Some people drink socially and never develop a problem with alcohol, whereas others become dependent or addicted. Some experiment with crack, which is known to be almost instantly addictive, or use "club drugs," which are known to be dangerous, whereas others "just say no." Each year, millions of Americans stop smoking cigarettes. Given the known hazards of smoking, why do a significant number of them relapse after months, even years, of not smoking?

The causes of substance abuse and dependence are complex, the result of a combination of biological, psychological, social, and cultural factors that varies from person to person, and depend on what psychoactive drug or drugs are used. There is no "one-size-fits-all" explanation. But psychologists have identified a number of factors that, especially in combination, make it more likely that a person will abuse drugs.

BIOLOGICAL FACTORS Are some individuals biologically vulnerable to drug abuse because of hereditary factors? There is evidence of a genetic basis for alcohol abuse. People whose biological parents have alcohol-abuse problems are more likely to abuse alcohol—even if they are adopted and are raised by people who do not abuse alcohol. Identical twins are far more likely to have similar patterns relating to alcohol, tobacco, and marijuana use than are fraternal twins (Gordis, 1996; C. Lerman, et al., 1999; J. C. Liu et al., 2004; National Institute on Drug Abuse, 2004a).

Psychologists have not reached consensus on the exact role that heredity plays in a predisposition for alcoholism (or abuse of other substances). Some psychologists point to hereditary differences in levels of the stomach enzyme mentioned earlier, deducing that people born with higher levels of the enzyme have to drink more alcohol to achieve the same psychological effects as those with lower levels of the enzyme. People also appear to differ genetically in their tolerance for alcohol in the blood and in the ways they react to alcohol (D. Ball, 2004).

Is addiction a disease, like diabetes or high blood pressure? Alcoholics Anonymous (AA), the oldest and probably the most successful self-help organization in this country, has long endorsed this view. According to the disease model, alcoholism is not a moral issue, but a medical one; and rather than being a sign of character flaws, alcohol abuse is a symptom of a physiological condition. An important aspect of the disease model is that, regardless of the initial source of the addiction, addictive substances dramatically change the brain. Those changes can take months or years to reverse and, during that time, cravings to use the drug can be intense (Nestler & Malenka, 2004; Vastag, 2003).

The disease model has been applied to many addictions. For example, a new organization called Nicotine Anonymous, dedicated to helping smokers quit, now operates over 450 active groups nationwide (Lichtenstein, 1999). To some degree, the disease model has become part of conventional wisdom: Many Americans view substance abuse as a biological problem, often the result of "bad" genes, that requires medical treatment. Not all psychologists agree, however. Problems with alcohol are better described as a continuum, ranging from mild to severe dependence with many stages in between. The either/or view tends to discourage people from seeking help until their problems have become severe and are more difficult to overcome, and to stigmatize those who go through cycles of sobriety and relapse as weak and contemptible, emphasizing their setbacks rather than their success. It may be best to consider addiction to have a physical basis but important psychological, social, and cultural implications as well.

PSYCHOLOGICAL, SOCIAL, AND CULTURAL FACTORS Whether a person uses a psychoactive drug and what effects that drug has also depend on the person's expectations, the social setting, and cultural beliefs and values.

A number of studies have shown that people use or abuse alcohol because they expect that drinking will help them to feel better (M. L. Cooper, Frone, Russell, & Mudar, 1995). During the 1960s and 1970s, members of the counterculture held similar expectations for marijuana, as do a significant number of young people today.

ENDURING ISSUES

Person/Situation   Factors Affecting Drug Effects

The setting in which drugs are taken is another powerful determinant of their effects (S. Siegel, 2005). Every year thousands of hospital patients are given opiate-based painkillers before and after surgery. They may have experiences that a heroin or cocaine user would label as a "high," but they are more likely to consider them confusing than pleasant. In this setting, psychoactive substances are defined as medicine, dosage is supervised by physicians, and patients take them to get well, not to get high. In contrast, at teenage raves, college beer parties, and all-night clubs, people drink specifically to get drunk and take other drugs to get high. But even in these settings, some individuals participate without using or abusing drugs, and motives for using drugs vary. People who drink or smoke marijuana because they think that they need a drug to overcome social inhibitions and to be accepted are more likely to slip into abuse than people who use the same substances in the same amounts because they want to have more fun. ●●

The family in which a child grows up also shapes attitudes and beliefs about drugs. For example, children whose parents do not use alcohol tend to abstain or to drink only moderately; children whose parents abuse alcohol tend to drink heavily (Chassin, Pitts, Delucia, & Todd, 1999; Chassin, Flora, & King, 2004). Such children are most likely to abuse alcohol if their family tolerates deviance in general or encourages excitement and pleasure seeking (Finn, Sharkansky, Brandt, & Turcotte, 2000). Moreover, adolescents who have been physically assaulted or sexually abused in their homes are at increased risk for drug abuse (Kilpatrick et al., 2000). Parents are not the only family influence; some research indicates that siblings' and peers' attitudes and behavior have as much or more impact on young people than parents do (Ary, Duncan, Duncan, & Hops, 1999; J. R. Harris, 1998).

Culture, too, may steer people toward or away from alcoholism. Parents and spouses may introduce people by example to a pattern of heavy drinking. Alcohol is also more acceptable in some ethnic cultures than in others—for example, many religions frown on the excessive use of alcohol, and Muslims, Mormons, conservative Baptists, and Seventh-Day Adventists prohibit it.

Many researchers believe that a full understanding of the causes of alcoholism and other drug addictions will not be achieved unless we take account of a wide variety of factors: heredity, personality, social setting, and culture (Jacob, Waterman, & Heath, 2003).

As we have seen, a wide variety of psychoactive drugs may alter consciousness, often with negative consequences such as abuse and addiction. In the next section we will look at meditation and hypnosis, two procedures that have been used for centuries to promote positive outcomes through altered states of consciousness.

CHECK YOUR UNDERSTANDING

Indicate whether the following statements are true (T) or false (F):

1. _____ Alcohol is implicated in more than two-thirds of all automobile accidents.
2. _____ Caffeine is not addictive.
3. _____ Many users become dependent on crack cocaine almost immediately after beginning to use it.
4. _____ Recurring hallucinations are common among users of hallucinogens.
5. _____ Marijuana interferes with short-term memory.

Answers: 1. (T), 2. (F), 3. (T), 4. (T), 5. (T).

APPLY YOUR UNDERSTANDING

1. Although you know that alcohol is a central nervous system depressant, your friend says it is actually a stimulant because he does things that he wouldn't otherwise do after having a couple of drinks. He also feels less inhibited, more spontaneous, and more entertaining. The reason your friend experiences alcohol as a stimulant is that

   a. alcohol has the same effect on the nervous system as amphetamines.

   b. alcohol has a strong placebo effect.

   c. the effects of alcohol depend almost entirely on the expectations of the user.

   d. alcohol depresses areas in the brain responsible for critical judgment and impulsiveness.

2. John drinks five or six cups of strong coffee each day. Which of the following symptoms is he most likely to report?

   a. nausea, loss of appetite, cold hands, and chills

   b. feelings of euphoria and well being

   c. anxiety, headaches, insomnia, and diarrhea

   d. time distortion and reduced emotional sensitivity

Answers: 1. d. 2. c.

Meditation and Hypnosis

Can hypnosis help you overcome a problem, such as smoking or overeating?

At one time, Western scientists viewed meditation and hypnosis with great skepticism. However, research has shown that both techniques can produce alterations in consciousness that can be measured through such sophisticated methods as brain imaging.

MEDITATION

What are the effects of meditation?

For centuries, people have used various forms of **meditation** to experience an alteration in consciousness (Benson, 1975). Each form of meditation focuses the meditator's attention in a slightly different way. *Zen meditation* concentrates on respiration, for example, whereas *Sufism* relies on frenzied dancing and prayer. In *transcendental meditation* (TM), practitioners intone a mantra, which is a sound, specially selected for each person, to keep all other images and problems at bay and to allow the meditator to relax more deeply. The fact that mediation may take many different forms presents one of the challenges facing psychologists who study meditation (Caspi & Burleson, 2005). Generally speaking, the goal of meditation is to attain a restful, yet fully alert state that enables the self-regulation of one's emotions.

Meditation can help relieve anxiety and promote peace of mind and a sense of well-being.

In all its forms, meditation suppresses the activity of the sympathetic nervous system which, as we noted in Chapter 2, is the part of the nervous system that prepares the body for strenuous activity during an emergency (Davidson et al., 2003). Meditation also lowers the rate of metabolism, reduces heart and respiratory rates, and decreases blood lactate, a chemical linked to stress. Alpha brain waves (which accompany relaxed wakefulness) increase noticeably during meditation. Not surprisingly, brain-imagining studies indicate that practicing meditation activates brain centers involved in attention and regulation of the autonomic nervous system activity (Cahn & Polich, 2006; Lazar et al., 2000).

Meditation has been used to treat certain medical problems, especially so-called functional complaints (those for which no physical cause can be found). For example, stress often leads to muscle tension and, sometimes, to pressure on nerves—and pain. In other cases, pain leads to muscle tension, which makes the pain worse. Relaxation techniques such as meditation may bring relief of such physical symptoms (Blanchard et al., 1990; Moriconi, 2004). Recent evidence suggests that meditation may even be useful in treating children diagnosed with attention-deficit hyperactive disorder, and in helping their parents manage the additional stress often placed on their families (Harrison, Manocha, & Rubia, 2004). Several studies have also found that people stopped using drugs after taking up meditation (Alexander, Robinson, & Rainforth, 1994). Finally, some recent evidence indicates that meditation may increase the effectiveness of the immune system (Davidson et al., 2003).

Besides physiological benefits, people who regularly practice some form of meditation report emotional and even spiritual gains, including increased sensory awareness and a sense of timelessness, well-being, and being at peace with oneself and the universe (Hameroff, Kaszniak, & Scott, 1996; Kumar & Ali, 2003; Lantz, Buchalter, & McBee, 1997).

HYPNOSIS

What clinical uses have been found for hypnosis?

In mid-18th-century Europe, Anton Mesmer, a Viennese physician, fascinated audiences by putting patients into trances to cure their illnesses. Mesmerism—now known as **hypnosis**—was initially discredited by a French commission chaired by Benjamin Franklin (Forrest, 2002). But some respectable 19th-century physicians revived interest in hypnosis

meditation Any of the various methods of concentration, reflection, or focusing of thoughts undertaken to suppress the activity of the sympathetic nervous system.

hypnosis Trancelike state in which a person responds readily to suggestions.

when they discovered that it could be used to treat certain forms of mental illness. Nevertheless, even today considerable disagreement persists about how to define hypnosis.

One reason for the controversy is that from a behavioral standpoint, there is no simple definition of exactly what it means to be hypnotized (Hasegawa & Jamieson, 2002; Kirsch & Braffman, 2001). Different people who are believed to have undergone hypnosis describe their experiences in very different ways. Similarly, some researchers who study hypnosis still debate whether or not it should be characterized as a state of altered consciousness (S. Lynn & Kirsch, 2006c). Other researchers stress that studying the phenomena that characterize a hypnotic state, such as the social interactions and the neurophysiological changes (Gruzelier, 2005), is of more importance than reaching a consensus on whether hypnosis is an altered state (Kihlström, 2005; Lynn, Fassler, & Knox, 2005).

THE PROCESS OF HYPNOSIS The Society of Psychological Hypnosis (Division 30 of the APA) states that

> Hypnosis typically involves an introduction to the procedure during which the subject is told that suggestions for imaginative experiences will be presented. . . . When using hypnosis, one person (the subject) is guided by another (the hypnotist) to respond to suggestions for changes in subjective experience, alterations in perception, sensation, emotion, thought or behavior (American Psychological Association, 2005).

Although the specifics of the procedure may vary depending on the hypnotist and the purpose for the hypnosis, most hypnotic induction procedures involve a suggestion to relax. Some people learn to administer hypnotic procedures to themselves, in which case it is referred to as *self-hypnosis*.

HYPNOTIC SUGGESTIONS Individuals also vary in their susceptibility to hypnosis. Several studies have shown that although susceptibility to hypnosis is not related to personal characteristics such as trust, gullibility, submissiveness, and social compliance, it is related to the ability of an individual to become absorbed in reading, music and daydreaming. (See Nash, 2001.)

One measure of susceptibility is whether people respond to hypnotic suggestion. Some people who are told that they cannot move their arms or that their pain has vanished do, in fact, experience paralysis or anesthesia; if told that they are hearing a certain piece of music or are unable to hear anything, they may hallucinate or become deaf temporarily (Montgomery, DuHamel, & Redd, 2000). When hypnotized subjects are told, "You will remember nothing that happened under hypnosis until I tell you," some people do experience amnesia. But, contrary to rumors, hypnotic suggestion cannot force people to do something foolish and embarrassing—or dangerous—against their will.

Another measure of the success of hypnosis is whether people respond to *posthypnotic commands*. For example, under hypnosis, a person suffering from back pain may be instructed that when he feels a twinge, he will imagine that he is floating on a cloud, his body is weightless, and the pain will stop—a technique also called "imaging." A runner may be told that when she pulls on her ear, she will block out the noise of the crowd and the runners on either side of her to heighten her concentration—a form of self-hypnosis. As the last example suggests, hypnosis has become increasingly popular among professional athletes and their weekend counterparts (Edgette & Rowan, 2003; Liggett, 2000).

Susceptibility to hypnosis varies from person to person, but many people have found it useful in a variety of medical and counseling situations.

ENDURING ISSUES

Mind–Body   Clinical Applications of Hypnosis

Because hypnotic susceptibility varies significantly from one person to another, its value in clinical and therapeutic settings is difficult to assess. Nevertheless, hypnosis is used in a variety of medical and counseling situations. (See Rhue, Lynn, & Kirsch, 1993; also see Nash, 2004.) Some research indicates that it can enhance the effectiveness of traditional forms of psychotherapy (Chapman, 2006; Kirsch, Montgomery, & Sapirstein, 1995), especially when it is used to treat anxiety disorders (Lynn & Kirsch, 2006a), and posttraumatic stress disorder (Lynn & Kirsch, 2006b). Hypnosis has been shown to be effective in controlling various types of physical pain (Lynn, Kirsch, & Koby, 2006; D. R. Patterson & Jensen, 2003; D. R. Patterson & Ptacek, 1997). Dentists have used it as an anesthetic for years. Hypnosis has also been used to alleviate pain in children with leukemia who have to undergo repeated bone-marrow biopsies (Hilgard, Hilgard, & Kaufmann, 1983). Moreover, it also has a role in treating some medical conditions, such as irritable bowel syndrome (Gonsalkorale, Miller, Afzal, & Whorwell, 2003).

Can hypnosis make someone change or eliminate bad habits? In some cases, posthypnotic commands temporarily diminish a person's desire to smoke or overeat (Elkins & Rajab, 2004; Green & Lynn, 2000; Lynn & Kirsch, 2006d). But even certified hypnotists agree that this treatment is effective only if people are motivated to change their behavior. Hypnosis may shore up their will, but so might joining a support group, such as Nicotine Anonymous or Weight Watchers. ●●

CHECK YOUR UNDERSTANDING

Match the following terms with the appropriate description:

1. _____ meditation
2. _____ hypnosis
3. _____ hypnotic susceptibility
   a. varies tremendously over time
   b. is a controversial altered state of consciousness
   c. suppresses sympathetic nervous system

Answers: 1. c. 2. b. 3. a.

APPLY YOUR UNDERSTANDING

1. Marie is a professional athlete involved in competitive sports. She regularly practices transcendental meditation as part of her training. The most likely reason she finds this practice beneficial is that meditation
   a. increases the rate of metabolism
   b. increases the activity of the sympathetic nervous system
   c. produces deep relaxation
   d. increases the respiratory rate
2. You overhear some people discussing the effects of hypnosis. On the basis of what you have learned in this chapter, you agree with everything they say EXCEPT
   a. "Some people can easily be hypnotized and some people can't."
   b. "If you tell someone under hypnosis to forget everything that happens, some people will actually do that."
   c. "Under hypnosis, people can be forced to do foolish or embarrassing things against their will."
   d. "Hypnosis can actually be used to control some kinds of pain."

Answers: 1. c. 2. c.

KEY TERMS

CHAPTER REVIEW

Conscious Experience

What problems could arise if we were constantly aware of all external and internal sensations? **Consciousness** is our awareness of various cognitive processes that operate in our daily lives such as sleeping, dreaming, concentrating, and making decisions. To make sense of our complex environment, we selectively choose which stimuli to absorb and we filter out the rest. This process applies to such external stimuli as sounds, sights, and smells. It also applies to such internal sensations as heat, cold, pressure, and pain, and to such phenomena as thoughts, memories, emotions, and needs. We perform familiar tasks, such as signing our names, without deliberate attention. Psychologists divide consciousness into two broad areas: **waking consciousness**, which includes thoughts, feelings, and perceptions that arise when we are awake and reasonably alert; and **altered states of consciousness**, during which our mental state differs noticeably from normal waking consciousness.

Do daydreams serve any useful function? The temporary escape offered by **daydreaming** occurs without effort when we spontaneously shift our attention away from the demands of the real world. Some psychologists see no positive or practical value in this activity. Others contend daydreams let us process hidden desires without guilt or anxiety. Daydreams may also build cognitive and creative skills that help us survive difficult situations or to relieve tension.

Sleep

How do evolutionary psychologists explain the need for sleep? Evolutionary psychologists see sleep as an adaptation allowing organisms to conserve and restore energy.

What is the biological clock and what does it have to do with jet lag? Like many other biological functions, sleep and waking follow a daily biological cycle known as a **circadian rhythm**. The human *biological clock* is governed by a tiny cluster of neurons in the brain known as the **suprachiasmatic nucleus (SCN)** that regulates proteins related to metabolism and alertness. Normally, the rhythms and chemistry of the body's cycles interact smoothly; but when we cross several time zones in one day, hormonal, temperature, and digestive cycles become desynchronized.

What physical changes mark the rhythms of sleep? Normal sleep consists of several stages. During *Stage 1*, the pulse slows, muscles relax, and the eyes move from side to side. The sleeper is easily awakened from Stage 1 sleep. In *Stages 2 and 3*, the sleeper is hard to awaken and does not respond to noise or light. Heart rate, blood pressure, and temperature continue to drop. During *Stage 4* sleep, heart and breathing rates, blood pressure, and body temperature are at their lowest points of the night. About an hour after first falling asleep, the sleeper begins to ascend through the stages back to Stage 1—a process that takes about 40 minutes. At this stage in the sleep cycle, heart rate and blood pressure increase, the muscles become more relaxed than at any other time in the cycle, and the eyes move rapidly under closed eyelids. This stage of sleep is known as **rapid-eye movement (REM)** or **paradoxical sleep**.

Are prescription medicines the best way to treat occasional insomnia? Sleep disorders include sleeptalking, sleepwalking, night terrors, insomnia, apnea, and narcolepsy. Most episodes of sleeptalking and sleepwalking occur during a deep stage of sleep. Unlike **nightmares,** frightening dreams that most often occur during REM sleep and are remembered, **night terrors** are more common among children than adults, prove difficult to be awakened from, and are rarely remembered the next morning. **Insomnia** is characterized by difficulty in falling asleep or remaining asleep throughout the night. Some prescription medicines can cause anxiety, memory loss, hallucinations, and violent behavior. **Apnea** is marked by breathing difficulties during the night and feelings of exhaustion during the day. **Narcolepsy** is a hereditary sleep disorder characterized by sudden nodding off during the day and sudden loss of muscle tone following moments of emotional excitement.

Dreams

What are dreams? **Dreams** are visual or auditory experiences that occur primarily during REM periods of sleep. Less vivid experiences that resemble conscious thinking tend to occur during **NREM** sleep.

Why do we dream? Several theories have been developed to explain the nature and content of dreams. According to Freud, dreams have two kinds of contents: manifest (the surface content of the dream itself) and latent (the disguised, unconscious meaning of the dream). According to a more recent hypothesis, dreams arise out of the mind's . reprocessing of daytime information that is important to the survival of the organism. With this hypothesis, dreaming thus strengthens our memories of important information.

Drug-Altered Consciousness

How is today's drug problem different from drug use in other societies and times? Chemical substances that change moods and perceptions are known as **psychoactive drugs**. Although many of the psychoactive drugs available today have been used for thousands of years, the motivation for using drugs is different today. Traditionally, these drugs were used in religious rituals, as nutrient beverages, or as culturally approved stimulants. Today, most psychoactive drug use is recreational, divorced from religious or family traditions.

How can we tell whether someone is dependent on a psychoactive substance? **Substance abuse** is a pattern of drug use that diminishes the person's ability to fulfill responsibilities at home, work, or school and that results in repeated use of a drug in dangerous situations or that leads to legal difficulties related to drug use. Continued abuse over time can lead to **substance dependence**, a pattern of compulsive drug taking that is much more serious than substance abuse. It is often marked by tolerance, the need to take higher doses of a drug to produce its original effects or to prevent withdrawal symptoms. Withdrawal symptoms are the unpleasant physical or psychological effects that follow discontinuance of the psychoactive substance. When studying drug effects, most researchers use the **double-blind procedure** in which some participants receive the active drug while others take a neutral, inactive substance called a **placebo**.

Why does alcohol, a depressant, lead to higher rates of violence? **Depressants** are chemicals that slow down behavior or cognitive processes. **Alcohol** calms down the nervous system, working like a general anesthetic. It is often experienced subjectively as a stimulant because it inhibits centers in the brain that govern critical judgment and impulsive behavior. This accounts for its involvement in a substantial proportion of violent and accidental deaths. **Barbituates** are potentially deadly depressants, first used for their sedative and anticonvulsant properties, but today their use is limited to the treatment of such conditions as epilepsy and arthritis. The **opiates** are highly addictive drugs such as opium, morphine, and heroin that dull the senses and induce feelings of euphoria, well-being, and relaxation. Morphine and heroin are derivatives of opium.

How do people tend to feel after a stimulant wears off? **Stimulants** are drugs that stimulate the sympathetic nervous system and produce feelings of optimism and boundless energy, making the potential for their abuse significant. Caffeine occurs naturally in coffee, tea, and cocoa. Considered a benign drug, in large doses caffeine can cause anxiety, insomnia, and other unpleasant conditions. Nicotine occurs naturally only in tobacco. Although it is a stimulant, it acts like a depressant when taken in large doses. **Amphetamines** are stimulants that initially produce "rushes" of euphoria often followed by sudden "crashes" and, sometimes, depression. **Cocaine** brings on a sense of euphoria by stimulating the sympathetic nervous system, but it can also cause anxiety, depression, and addictive cravings. Its crystalline form—crack—is highly addictive.

How does marijuana affect memory? **Hallucinogens** include drugs such as **LSD**, psilocybin, and mescaline that distort visual and auditory perception. **Marijuana** is a mild hallucinogen capable of producing feelings of euphoria, a sense of well-being, and swings in mood from gaiety to relaxation to paranoia. Though similar to hallucinogens in certain respects, marijuana is far less potent, and its effects on consciousness are far less profound. Marijuana can disrupt memory, causing people to forget what they are talking about in midsentence.

What combination of factors makes it more likely that someone will abuse drugs? A possible genetic predisposition, the person's expectations, the social setting, and cultural beliefs and values make drug abuse more likely.

Meditation and Hypnosis

What are the effects of meditation? **Meditation** refers to any of several methods of concentration, reflection, or focusing of thoughts intended to suppress the activity of the sympathetic nervous system. Meditation not only lowers the metabolic rate but also reduces heart and respiratory rates. Brain activity during meditation resembles that experienced during relaxed wakefulness; and the accompanying decrease in blood lactate reduces stress.

What clinical uses have been found for hypnosis? **Hypnosis** is a trancelike state in which the hypnotized person responds readily to suggestions. Susceptibility to hypnosis depends on how easily people can become absorbed in concentration. Hypnosis can ease the pain of certain medical conditions and can help people stop smoking and break other habits.

5 Learning

OVERVIEW

What do the following anecdotes have in common?

- In Mozambique, a giant pouched rat the size of a cat scurries across a field, pauses, sniffs the air, turns, sniffs again, and then begins to scratch at the ground with her forepaws. She has discovered yet another land mine buried a few inches underground. After a brief break for a bit of banana and a pat or two from her handler, she scurries off again to find more land mines.

- In the middle of a winter night, Adrian Cole—four years old and three feet tall—put on his jacket and boots and drove his mother's car to a nearby video store. When he found the store closed, he drove back home. Since he was driving very slowly with the lights off and was also weaving a bit, he understandably attracted the attention of police officers who followed him. When he got home, he collided with two parked cars and then backed into the police cruiser! When the police asked him how he learned to drive, he explained that his mother would put him on her lap while she drove and he just watched what she did.

- While driving along a congested boulevard, a middle-aged man glances at a park bench and, for a moment, his heart pounds as he experiences a warm feeling throughout his body. At first, he can't understand why passing this spot has evoked such a strong emotion. Then he remembers: It was the meeting place he once shared with his high school sweetheart over 20 years ago.

The common element in all these stories—and the topic of this chapter—is learning. Although most people associate learning with classrooms and studying for tests, psychologists define it more broadly. To them, **learning** occurs whenever experience or practice results in a relatively permanent change in behavior or in potential behavior. This definition includes all the examples previously mentioned, plus a great many more. When you remember which way to put the key into your front-door lock, when you recall how to park a car, or where the library water fountain is, you are showing a tiny part of your enormous capacity for learning.

Human life would be impossible without learning; it is involved in virtually everything we do. You could not communicate with other people, recognize yourself as human, or even know what substances are appropriate to eat if you were unable to learn. In this chapter, we explore several kinds of learning. One type is learning to associate one event with another. When rats associate the smell of TNT and receiving food or when a person associates a certain place and a certain strong emotion, they are engaging in two forms of learning called *operant* and *classical conditioning*. Because psychologists have studied these forms of learning so extensively, much of this chapter is devoted to them. But making associations isn't all there is to human learning. Our learning also involves the formation of concepts, theories, ideas, and other mental abstractions. Psychologists call it *cognitive learning*, and we discuss it at the end of this chapter.

Our tour of learning begins in another time and place: the laboratory of a Nobel Prize–winning Russian scientist at the turn of the 20th century. His name is Ivan Pavlov, and his work is helping to revolutionize the study of learning. He has discovered classical conditioning.

ENDURING ISSUES IN LEARNING ••

This chapter addresses how humans and other animals acquire new behaviors as a result of their experiences. Thus it bears directly on the enduring issue of Stability versus Change (the extent to which organisms change over the course of their lives). The events that shape learning not only vary among different individuals (diversity–universality) but also are influenced by an organism's inborn characteristics (nature–nurture). Finally, some types of learning can affect our physical health by influencing how our body responds to disease (mind–body).

learning The process by which experience or practice results in a relatively permanent change in behavior or potential behavior.

classical (or Pavlovian) conditioning The type of learning in which a response naturally elicited by one stimulus comes to be elicited by a different, formerly neutral, stimulus.

unconditioned stimulus (US) A stimulus that invariably causes an organism to respond in a specific way.

unconditioned response (UR) A response that takes place in an organism whenever an unconditioned stimulus occurs.

conditioned stimulus (CS) An originally neutral stimulus that is paired with an unconditioned stimulus and eventually produces the desired response in an organism when presented alone.

Classical Conditioning

How did Pavlov discover classical conditioning?

The Russian physiologist, Ivan Pavlov (1849–1936) discovered **classical (or Pavlovian) conditioning**, a form of learning in which a response elicited by a stimulus becomes elicited by a previously neutral stimulus, almost by accident. He was studying digestion, which begins when saliva mixes with food in the mouth. While measuring how much saliva dogs produce when given food, he noticed that they began to salivate even before they tasted the food. The mere sight of food made them drool. In fact, they even drooled at the sound of the experimenter's footsteps. This aroused Pavlov's curiosity. What was causing these responses? How had the dogs learned to salivate to sights and sounds?

To answer this question, Pavlov sounded a bell just before presenting his dogs with food. A ringing bell does not usually make a dog's mouth water, but after hearing the bell many times right before getting fed, Pavlov's dogs began to salivate as soon as the bell rang. It was as if they had learned that the bell signaled the appearance of food; and their mouths watered on cue even if no food followed. The dogs had been *conditioned* to salivate in response to a new stimulus: the bell, which normally would not prompt salivation (Pavlov, 1927). **Figure 5–1** shows one of Pavlov's procedures in which the bell has been replaced by a touch to the dog's leg just before food is given.

ELEMENTS OF CLASSICAL CONDITIONING

How might you classically condition a pet?

Figure 5–2 diagrams the four basic elements in classical conditioning: the unconditioned stimulus, the unconditioned response, the conditioned stimulus, and the conditioned response. The **unconditioned stimulus (US)** is an event that automatically elicits a certain reflex reaction, which is the **unconditioned response (UR)**. In Pavlov's studies, food in the mouth was the unconditioned stimulus, and salivation to it was the unconditioned response. The third element in classical conditioning, the **conditioned stimulus (CS)**, is an

Figure 5–1

Pavlov's apparatus for classically conditioning a dog to salivate.
The experimenter sits behind a one-way mirror and controls the presentation of the conditioned stimulus (touch applied to the leg) and the unconditioned stimulus (food). A tube runs from the dog's salivary glands to a vial, where the drops of saliva are collected as a way of measuring the strength of the dog's response.

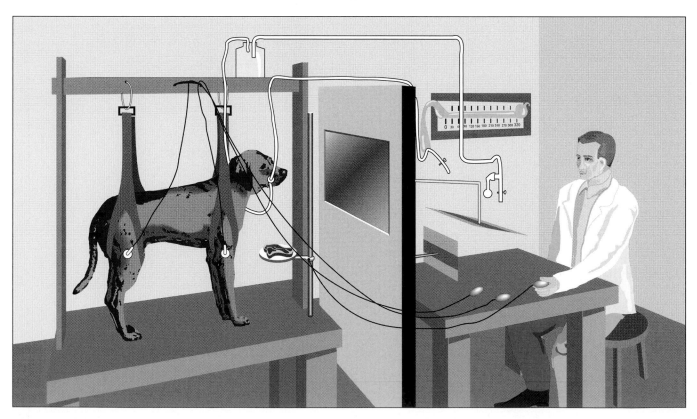

event that is repeatedly paired with the unconditioned stimulus. For a conditioned stimulus, Pavlov often used a bell. At first, the conditioned stimulus does not elicit the desired response. But eventually, after repeatedly being paired with the unconditioned stimulus, the conditioned stimulus alone comes to trigger a reaction similar to the unconditioned response. This learned reaction is the **conditioned response (CR)**.

Classical conditioning has been demonstrated in virtually every animal species, even cockroaches, bees, squid, and spiders (Abramson & Aquino, 2002; Hidehiro & Makato, 2006; Krasne & Glanzman, 1995; Watanabe, Kobayashi, Sakura, Matsumoto, & Mizunami, 2003). You yourself may have inadvertently classically conditioned one of your pets. For instance, you may have noticed that your cat begins to purr when it hears the sound of the electric can opener running. For a cat, the taste and smell of food are unconditioned stimuli for a purring response. By repeatedly pairing the can opener whirring with the delivery of food, you have turned this sound into a conditioned stimulus that triggers a conditioned response.

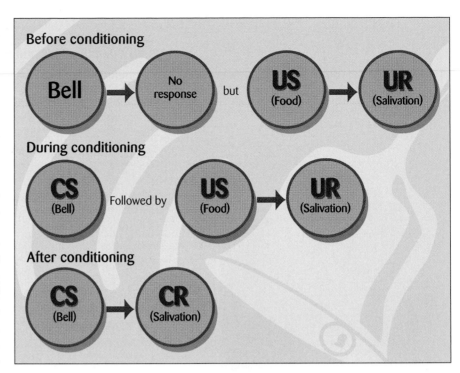

Figure 5–2
A model of the classical conditioning process.

ESTABLISHING A CLASSICALLY CONDITIONED RESPONSE

If you once burned your finger on a match while listening to a certain song, why doesn't that song now make you reflexively jerk your hand away?

As shown in **Figure 5–3**, it generally takes repeated pairings of an unconditioned stimulus and a cue before the unconditioned response eventually becomes a conditioned response. The likelihood or strength of the conditioned response increases each time these two stimuli are paired. This learning, however, eventually reaches a point of diminishing returns. The amount of each increase gradually becomes smaller, until finally no further learning occurs. The conditioned response is now fully established.

It is fortunate that repeated pairings are usually needed for classical conditioning to take place (B. Schwartz, 1989). There are always a lot of environmental stimuli present whenever an unconditioned stimulus triggers an unconditioned response. If conditioning occurred on the basis of single pairings, all these usually irrelevant stimuli would generate some type of CR. Soon we would be overwhelmed by learned associations. Because a number of pairings are usually needed to produce a conditioned response, only a cue consistently related to the unconditioned stimulus typically becomes a conditioned stimulus.

The spacing of pairings is also important in establishing a classically conditioned response. If pairings of the CS and US follow each other very rapidly, or if they are very far apart, learning the association is slower. If the spacing of pairings is moderate—neither too far apart nor too close together—learning occurs more quickly. It is also important that the CS and US rarely, if ever, occur alone. Pairing the CS and US only once in a while, called **intermittent pairing**, reduces both the rate of learning and the final strength of the learned response.

conditioned response (CR) After conditioning, the response an organism produces when a conditioned stimulus is presented.

intermittent pairing Pairing the conditioned stimulus and the unconditioned stimulus on only a portion of the learning trials.

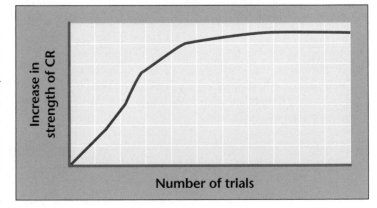

Figure 5–3
Response acquisition.
At first, each pairing of the US and CS increases the strength of the response. After a number of trials, learning begins to level off; and eventually it reaches a point of diminishing returns.

CLASSICAL CONDITIONING IN HUMANS

What is an example of classical conditioning in your own life?

Classical conditioning is as common in humans as it is in other animals. The story at the beginning of the chapter about the sight of a park bench triggering strong emotions is an example of classical conditioning. Some people learn phobias through classical conditioning. *Phobias* are intense, irrational fears of particular things or situations, such as spiders, snakes, flying, or being in enclosed places (claustrophobia). In Chapter 1, we discussed the study in which John Watson and his assistant, Rosalie Rayner, used classical conditioning to instill a phobia of white rats in a 1-year-old baby named Little Albert (J. B. Watson & Rayner, 1920). They started by showing Albert a white rat, which he happily tried to play with. But every time he approached the rat, the experimenters made a loud noise by striking a steel bar behind the baby's head. After a few attempts at pairing the rat and the frightening noise, Albert would cry in fear at the sight of the rat alone. By being paired with the unconditioned stimulus of the loud noise, the rat had become a conditioned stimulus for a conditioned fear response.

Several years later, psychologist Mary Cover Jones demonstrated a way that fears can be unlearned by means of classical conditioning (M. C. Jones, 1924). Her subject was a three-year-old boy named Peter who, like Albert, had a fear of white rats. Jones paired the sight of a rat with an intrinsically pleasant experience—eating candy. While Peter sat alone in a room, a caged white rat was brought in and placed far enough away so that the boy would not be frightened. At this point, Peter was given plenty of candy to eat. On each successive day, the cage was moved closer to Peter, after which, he was given candy. Eventually, he showed no fear of the rat, even without any candy. By being repeatedly paired with a stimulus that evoked a pleasant emotional response, the rat had become a conditioned stimulus for pleasure.

In more recent times, psychiatrist Joseph Wolpe (1915–1997) adapted Jones's method to the treatment of certain kinds of anxiety (Wolpe, 1973, 1990). Wolpe reasoned that because irrational fears are learned (conditioned), they could also be unlearned through conditioning. He noted that it is not possible to be both fearful and relaxed at the same time. Therefore, if people could be taught to relax in fearful or anxious situations, their anxiety should disappear. Wolpe's **desensitization therapy** begins by teaching a system of deep-muscle relaxation. Then the person constructs a list of situations that prompt various degrees of fear or anxiety, from intensely frightening to only mildly so. A person with a fear of heights, for example, might construct a list that begins with standing on the edge of the Grand Canyon and ends with climbing two rungs on a ladder. While deeply relaxed, the person imagines the least distressing situation on the list first. If he or she succeeds in remaining relaxed, the person proceeds to the next item on the list, and so on until no anxiety is felt, even when imagining the most frightening situation. In this way, classical conditioning is used to change an undesired reaction: A fear-arousing thought is repeatedly paired with a muscular state that produces calmness until eventually the formerly fearful thought no longer triggers anxiety. Desensitization therapy has been used successfully to treat a variety of disorders such as phobias and posttraumatic stress disorder (Everly & Lating, 2004; Travis, 2004), a topic we will turn our attention to again in Chapter 13, "Therapies."

Desensitization therapy is based on the belief that we can overcome fears by learning to remain calm in the face of increasingly fear-arousing situations. Here people being desensitized to a fear of heights are able to swing high above the ground without panicking.

ENDURING ISSUES

Mind–Body   Classical Conditioning and the Immune System

In another example of classical conditioning in humans, researchers have devised a novel way to treat autoimmune disorders, which cause the immune system to attack healthy organs or tissues. Although powerful drugs can be used to suppress the immune system and thus reduce the impact of the autoimmune disorder, these drugs often have dangerous side effects, so they must be administered sparingly. The challenge, then, was to find a treatment that could suppress the immune system without damaging vital organs. Researchers

desensitization therapy A conditioning technique designed to gradually reduce anxiety about a particular object or situation.

discovered that they could use formerly neutral stimuli either to increase or to suppress the activity of the immune system (Hollis, 1997; Markovic, Dimitrijevic, & Jankovic, 1993). Here's how it works: As US, the researchers use immune-suppressing drugs and pair them with a specific CS, such as a distinctive smell or taste. After only a few pairings of the drug (US) with the smell or taste (CS), the CS alone suppresses the immune system (the CR) without any dangerous side effects! In this case, classical conditioning works on the mind but ultimately affects the body. While the use of classical conditioning to treat autoimmune disorders shows promise, additional research is still necessary to validate its effectiveness and evaluate its potential application as a therapy to treat these disorders (Bovbjerg, 2003; G. E. Miller & Cohen, 2001). ●●

CLASSICAL CONDITIONING IS SELECTIVE

Why are people more likely to develop a phobia of snakes than of flowers?

If people can develop phobias through classical conditioning, as Little Albert did, why don't we acquire phobias of virtually everything that is paired with harm? For example, many people get shocks from electric sockets, but almost no one develops a socket phobia. Why should this be the case? Why shouldn't most carpenters have phobias of hammers due to accidentally pounding their fingers with them?

Psychologist Martin Seligman (1971) has offered an answer: The key, he says, lies in the concept of **preparedness**. Some things readily become conditioned stimuli for fear responses because we are biologically prepared to learn those associations. Among the common objects of phobias are heights, snakes, and the dark. In our evolutionary past, fear of these potential dangers probably offered a survival advantage, and so a readiness to form such fears may have become "wired into" our species.

ENDURING ISSUES

Nature–Nurture   The Evolutionary Basis of Fear

To what extent does our evolutionary heritage condition our fears; and to what extent are fears the result of our experiences? Recent studies suggest that the two work in tandem (Mineka & Oehman, 2002). For example, some stimuli unrelated to human survival through evolution, but which we have learned to associate with danger, can serve as CSs for fear responses. Pictures of handguns and butcher knives, for example, are as effective as pictures of snakes and spiders in conditioning fear in some people (Lovibond, Siddle, & Bond, 1993). These studies suggest that preparedness may be the result of learning rather than evolution. Other studies have shown that people who do not suffer from phobias can rather quickly unlearn fear responses to spiders and snakes if those stimuli appear repeatedly without painful or threatening USs (Honeybourne, Matchett, & Davey, 1993). Thus even if humans are prepared to fear these things, that fear can be overcome through conditioning. In other words, our evolutionary history and our personal learning histories interact to increase or decrease the likelihood that certain kinds of conditioning will occur. ●●

Seligman's theory of preparedness argues that we are biologically prepared to associate certain stimuli, such as heights, the dark, and snakes, with fear responses. In our evolutionary past, fear of these potential dangers probably offered a survival advantage.

Preparedness also underlies **conditioned taste aversion**, a learned association between the taste of a certain food and a feeling of nausea and revulsion. Conditioned taste aversions are acquired very quickly. It usually takes only one pairing of a distinctive flavor and subsequent illness to develop a learned aversion to the taste of that food. Seligman calls this aversion the "sauce béarnaise effect," because he once suffered severe nausea after eating sauce béarnaise and ever since has abhorred the flavor. In one study, more than half the college students surveyed reported at least one such conditioned taste aversion (Logue, Ophir, & Strauss, 1981). Readily learning connections between distinctive flavors and illness has clear benefits. If we can quickly learn which foods are poisonous and avoid those foods in

preparedness A biological readiness to learn certain associations because of their survival advantages.

conditioned taste aversion Conditioned avoidance of certain foods even if there is only one pairing of conditioned and unconditioned stimuli.

A bird's nervous system is adapted to remember sight–illness combinations, such as the distinctive color of a certain berry and subsequent food poisoning. In mammals, by contrast, taste–illness combinations are quickly and powerfully learned.

the future, we greatly increase our chances of survival. Other animals with a well-developed sense of taste, such as rats and mice, also readily develop conditioned taste aversions, just as humans do (Brooks, Bowker, Anderson, & Palmatier, 2003; Chester, Lumeng, Li, & Grahame, 2003; Cross-Mellor, Kavaliers, & Ossenkopp, 2004).

Even knowing that a certain food paired with nausea wasn't the cause of the illness doesn't spare us from developing a conditioned taste aversion. Seligman knew that his nausea was due to stomach flu, not to something he ate, but he acquired an aversion to sauce béarnaise just the same. Similarly, cancer patients often develop strong taste aversions to foods eaten right before nausea-inducing chemotherapy, even though they know that it is the drug that triggered their nauseous reaction. These patients can't prevent themselves from automatically learning a connection that they are biologically prepared to learn (Jacobsen, Bovbjerg, Schwartz, & Andrykowski, 1994).

CHECK YOUR UNDERSTANDING

1. The simplest type of learning is called _____ _____. It refers to the establishment of fairly predictable behavior in the presence of well-defined stimuli.

2. Match the following in Pavlov's experiment with dogs:

   ___ unconditioned stimulus   a. bell

   ___ unconditioned response   b. food

   ___ conditioned stimulus   c. salivating to bell

   ___ conditioned response   d. salivating to food

3. The intense, irrational fears that we call phobias can be learned through classical conditioning. Is this statement true (T) or false (F)?

4. A learned association between the taste of a certain food and a feeling of nausea is called _____ _____ _____.

5. Teaching someone to relax even when he or she encounters a distressing situation is called _____ _____.

6. In the experiment with Little Albert, the unconditioned stimulus was _____ _____.

Answers: 1. classical conditioning. 2. unconditioned stimulus—b; unconditioned response—d; conditioned stimulus—a; conditioned response—c. 3. T. 4. conditioned taste aversion. 5. desensitization therapy. 6. loud noises.

APPLY YOUR UNDERSTANDING

1. Which of the following are examples of classical conditioning?

   a. eating when not hungry just because we know it is lunchtime

   b. a specific smell triggering a bad memory

   c. a cat running into the kitchen to the sound of a can opener

   d. All of the above are examples of classical conditioning.

2. You feel nauseated when you read about sea scallops on a restaurant menu, because you once had a bad episode with some scallops that made you sick. For you in this situation, the menu description of the scallops is the

   a. US

   b. CS

   c. CR

Answers: 1. d. 2. b.

Operant Conditioning

How are operant behaviors different from the responses involved in classical conditioning?

Around the turn of the 20th century, while Pavlov was busy with his dogs, the American psychologist Edward Lee Thorndike (1874–1949) was using a "puzzle box," or simple

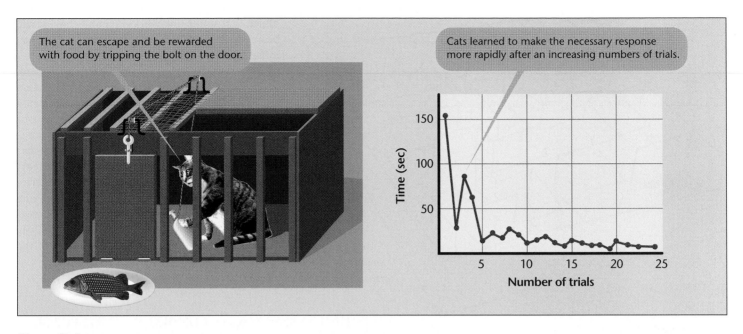

Figure 5–4
A cat in a Thorndike "puzzle box."
The cat can escape and be rewarded with food by tripping the bolt on the door. As the graph shows,
Thorndike's cats learned to make the necessary response more rapidly after an increasing number of trials.

wooden cage, to study how cats learn (Thorndike, 1898). As illustrated in **Figure 5–4**, Thorndike confined a hungry cat in the puzzle box, with food just outside where the cat could see and smell it. To get to the food, the cat had to figure out how to open the latch on the box door, a process that Thorndike timed. In the beginning, it took the cat quite a while to discover how to open the door. But on each trial, it took the cat less time, until eventually it could escape from the box in almost no time at all. Thorndike was a pioneer in studying the kind of learning that involves making a certain response due to the consequences it brings. This form of learning has come to be called **operant** or **instrumental conditioning**. The pouched rat described at the opening of this chapter learned to find land mines through operant conditioning.

ELEMENTS OF OPERANT CONDITIONING

What two essential elements are involved in operant conditioning?

One essential element in operant conditioning is *emitted behavior*. This is one way in which operant conditioning is different from classical conditioning. In classical conditioning, a response is automatically triggered by some stimulus. Food in the mouth automatically triggers salivation; a loud noise automatically triggers fear. In this sense, classical conditioning is passive in that the behaviors are elicited by stimuli. However, this process is not true of the behaviors involved in operant conditioning. Thorndike's cats *spontaneously* tried to undo the latch on the door of the box. You *spontaneously* wave your hand to signal a taxi or bus to stop. You study your teacher's assignments *by choice* in an effort to earn a good grade. You *voluntarily* put money into machines to obtain food, sodas, entertainment, or a chance to win a prize. These and similar actions are called **operant behaviors** because they involve "operating" on the environment.

A second essential element in operant conditioning is a *consequence* following a behavior. Thorndike's cats gained freedom and a piece of fish for escaping from the puzzle boxes; your dog may receive a food treat for sitting on command; a child may receive praise or a chance to watch television for helping to clear the table; the land mine-sniffing rat received a bit of banana and a few pats after discovering a hidden mine. Consequences like these,

operant (or instrumental) conditioning The type of learning in which behaviors are emitted (in the presence of specific stimuli) to earn rewards or avoid punishments.

operant behaviors Behaviors designed to operate on the environment in a way that will gain something desired or avoid something unpleasant.

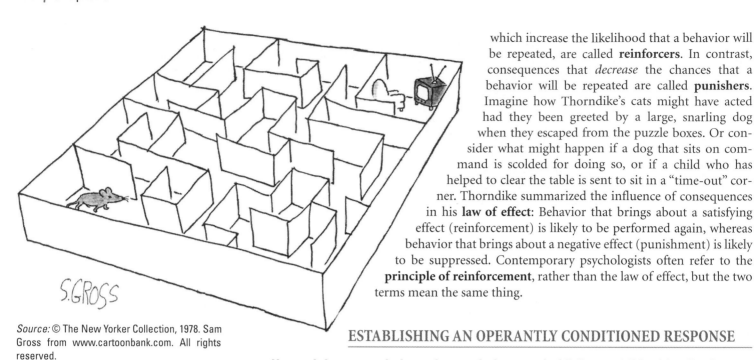

Source: © The New Yorker Collection, 1978. Sam Gross from www.cartoonbank.com. All rights reserved.

reinforcers A stimuli that follows a behavior and increases the likelihood that the behavior will be repeated.

punishers Stimuli that follows a behavior and decreases the likelihood that the behavior will be repeated.

Figure 5–5
A rat in a Skinner box.
By pressing the bar, the rat releases food pellets into the box; this procedure reinforces its bar-pressing behavior.

which increase the likelihood that a behavior will be repeated, are called **reinforcers**. In contrast, consequences that *decrease* the chances that a behavior will be repeated are called **punishers**. Imagine how Thorndike's cats might have acted had they been greeted by a large, snarling dog when they escaped from the puzzle boxes. Or consider what might happen if a dog that sits on command is scolded for doing so, or if a child who has helped to clear the table is sent to sit in a "time-out" corner. Thorndike summarized the influence of consequences in his **law of effect**: Behavior that brings about a satisfying effect (reinforcement) is likely to be performed again, whereas behavior that brings about a negative effect (punishment) is likely to be suppressed. Contemporary psychologists often refer to the **principle of reinforcement**, rather than the law of effect, but the two terms mean the same thing.

ESTABLISHING AN OPERANTLY CONDITIONED RESPONSE

How might a speech therapist teach the sound of "s" to a child with a lisp?

Because the behaviors involved in operant conditioning are voluntary ones, it is not always easy to establish an operantly conditioned response. The desired behavior must first be performed spontaneously in order for it to be rewarded and strengthened. Sometimes you can simply wait for this action to happen. Thorndike, for example, waited for his cats to trip the latch that opened the door to his puzzle boxes. Then he rewarded them with fish.

But when there are many opportunities for making irrelevant responses, waiting can be slow and tedious. If you were an animal trainer for a circus, imagine how long you would have to wait for a tiger to decide to jump through a flaming hoop so you could reward it. One way to speed up the process is to increase motivation, as Thorndike did by allowing his cats to become hungry and by placing a piece of fish outside the box. Even without food in sight, a hungry animal is more active than a well-fed one and so is more likely, just by chance, to make the response you're looking for. Another strategy is to reduce opportunities for irrelevant responses, as Thorndike did by making his puzzle boxes small and bare. Many researchers do the same thing by using Skinner boxes to train small animals in. A **Skinner box** (named after B. F. Skinner, another pioneer in the study of operant conditioning), is a small cage with solid walls that is relatively empty, except for a food cup and an activating device, such as a bar or a button. (See **Figure 5–5**.) In this simple environment, it doesn't take long for an active, hungry rat or pigeon to press the bar or peck the button that releases food into the cup, thereby reinforcing the behavior.

Usually, however, the environment cannot be controlled so easily; hence a different approach is called for. Another way to speed up operant conditioning is to reinforce successive approximations of the desired behavior. This approach is called **shaping**. In a Skinner box, for example, we might first reward a rat for turning toward the bar, then for moving toward it, then for touching the bar with its paw, and so on until it performs the desired behavior. The circus is a wonderful place to see the results of shaping. To teach a tiger to jump through a flaming hoop, the trainer might first reinforce the animal simply for jumping up on a pedestal. After that behavior has been learned, the tiger might be reinforced only for leaping from that pedestal to another. Next, the tiger might be required to jump through a hoop between the pedestals to gain a reward. And finally, the hoop is set on fire, and the tiger must leap through it to be rewarded. In much the same way, a speech therapist might reward a child with a lisp for closer and closer approximations of the correct sound of "s."

As in classical conditioning, the learning of an operantly conditioned response eventually reaches a point of diminishing returns. If you look back at **Figure 5–4**, you'll see that the first few reinforcements produced quite large improvements in performance, as indicated by the rapid drop in time required to escape from the puzzle box. But each successive reinforcement produced less of an effect until, eventually, continued reinforcement brought no evidence of further learning. After 25 trials, for instance, Thorndike's cats were escaping from the box no more quickly than they had been after 15 trials. The operantly conditioned response had then been fully established. Can operant conditioning influence human behavior? See "Applying Psychology: Modifying Your Behavior," page 170, to learn about how you can use operant conditioning to modify your own behavior.

law of effect (principle of reinforcement) Thorndike's theory that behavior consistently rewarded will be "stamped in" as learned behavior, and behavior that brings about discomfort will be "stamped out."

Skinner box A box often used in operant conditioning of animals; it limits the available responses and thus increases the likelihood that the desired response will occur.

shaping Reinforcing successive approximations to a desired behavior.

APPLYING PSYCHOLOGY

MODIFYING YOUR OWN BEHAVIOR

Can you modify your own undesirable behaviors by using operant conditioning techniques? Yes, but first you must observe your own actions, think about their implications, and plan a strategy of intervention.

1. Begin by identifying the behavior you want to acquire: This is called the "target" behavior. You will be more successful if you focus on acquiring a new behavior rather than on eliminating an existing one. For example, instead of setting a target of being less shy, you might define the target behavior as becoming more outgoing or more sociable. Other possible target behaviors might include behaving more assertively, studying more, and getting along better with your roommates. In each case, you have spotlighted the behavior that you want to acquire rather than the behavior that you want to eliminate.

2. The next step is defining the target behavior precisely: What exactly do you mean by "assertive" or "sociable"? Imagine situations in which the target behavior could be performed. Then describe in writing the way in which you now respond to these situations. For example, in the case of

shyness, you might write, "When I am sitting in a lecture hall, waiting for class to begin, I don't talk to the people around me." Next, write down how you would rather act in that situation: "In a lecture hall before class, I want to talk to at least one other person. I might ask the person sitting next to me how he or she likes the class or the professor or simply comment on some aspect of the course."

3. The third step is monitoring your present behavior: You may do so by keeping a daily log of activities related to the target behavior. This will establish your current "base rate" and give you something concrete against which to gauge improvements. At the same time, try to figure out whether your present, undesirable behavior is being reinforced in some way. For example, if you find yourself unable to study, record what you do instead (Get a snack? Watch television?) and determine whether you are inadvertently rewarding your failure to study.

4. The next step—the basic principle of self-modification—is providing yourself with a positive reinforcer that is contingent on specific improvements in the target behavior: You may be able

to use the same reinforcer that now maintains your undesirable behavior, or you may want to pick a new reinforcer. For example, if you want to increase the amount of time you spend studying, you might reward yourself with a token for each 30 minutes of study. Then, if your favorite pastime is watching movies, you might charge yourself three tokens for an hour of television, whereas the privilege of going to a movie might cost six.

Remember that the new, more desirable behavior need not be learned all at once. You can use shaping or successive approximations to change your behavior bit by bit. A person who wants to become more sociable might start by giving rewards just for sitting next to another person in a classroom rather than picking an isolated seat. The person could then work up to rewarding increasingly sociable behaviors, such as first saying hello to another person, then striking up a conversation.

If you would like to try a program of self-improvement, a book by David Watson and Roland Tharp, *Self-Directed Behavior: Self-Modification for Personal Adjustment* (1997), is a good place to start. It contains step-by-step instructions and exercises that provide a useful guide.

A CLOSER LOOK AT REINFORCEMENT

What is the difference between positive and negative reinforcement? What are some of the unintentional effects that reinforcement can have?

We have been talking about reinforcement as if all reinforcers are alike, but in fact this is not the case. Think about the kinds of consequences that would encourage you to perform some behavior. Certainly these include consequences that give you something positive, like praise, recognition, or money. But the removal of some negative stimulus is also a good reinforcer of behavior. When new parents discover that rocking a baby will stop the infant's persistent crying, they sit down and rock the baby deep into the night; the removal of the infant's crying is a powerful reinforcer.

These examples show that there are two kinds of reinforcers. **Positive reinforcers,** such as food, praise, or money, add something rewarding to a situation, whereas **negative reinforcers,** such as stopping an aversive noise, subtract something unpleasant. Animals will learn to press bars and open doors not only to obtain food and water (positive reinforcement), but also to turn off a loud buzzer or to avoid an electric shock (negative reinforcement).

Both positive and negative reinforcement results in the learning of new behaviors or the strengthening of existing ones. Remember, in everyday conversation when we say that we have "reinforced" something, we mean that we have strengthened it. "Reinforced concrete" is strengthened by the addition of steel rods or steel mesh; generals strengthen armies by sending in "reinforcements"; arguments are strengthened by being "reinforced" with facts. Similarly, in operant conditioning, reinforcement—whether positive or negative—always strengthens or encourages a behavior. A child might practice the piano because she or he receives praise for practicing (positive reinforcement) or because it gives her or him a break from doing tedious homework (negative reinforcement), but in either case the end result is a higher incidence of piano playing.

But what if a particular behavior is just *accidentally* reinforced because it happens by chance to be followed by some rewarding incident? Will the behavior still be more likely to occur again? B. F. Skinner (1948) showed that the answer is yes. He put a pigeon in a Skinner box and at random intervals dropped a few grains of food into the food cup. The pigeon began repeating whatever it had been doing just before the food was given: standing on one foot, hopping around, or strutting with its neck stretched out. None of these actions had anything to do with getting the food, of course. But still the bird repeated them over and over again. Skinner called the bird's behavior *superstitious,* because it was learned in a way that is similar to how some human superstitions are learned (Aeschleman, Rosen, & Williams, 2003). If you happen to be wearing an Albert Einstein T-shirt when you get your first A on an exam, you may come to believe that wearing this shirt was a factor. Even though the connection was pure coincidence, you may keep on wearing your "lucky" shirt to every test thereafter.

In the case of forming superstitions, reinforcement has an illogical effect on behavior, but that effect is generally harmless. Some psychologists believe that reinforcement can also lead inadvertently to negative results. They believe that offering certain kinds of reinforcers (candy, money, play time) for a task that could be intrinsically rewarding (that is, reinforcing in and of itself) can undermine the intrinsic motivation to perform it. People may begin to think that they are working only for the reward and lose enthusiasm for what they are doing. They may no longer see their work as an intrinsically interesting challenge in which to invest creative effort and strive for excellence. Instead, they may see work as a chore that must be done to earn some tangible payoff. This warning can be applied to many situations, such as offering tangible rewards to students for their work in the classroom, or giving employees a "pay for performance" incentive to meet company goals (Kohn, 1993; Rynes, Gerhart, & Parks, 2005).

Other psychologists, however, suggest that this concern about tangible reinforcers may be exaggerated. Although the use of rewards may sometimes produce negative outcomes, this is not always the case (Cameron, Banko, & Pierce, 2001). In fact, one extensive review of more than 100 studies showed that when used appropriately, rewards do not compro-

positive reinforcers Events whose presence increases the likelihood that ongoing behavior will recur.

negative reinforcers Events whose reduction or termination increases the likelihood that ongoing behavior will recur.

mise intrinsic motivation, and under some circumstances, they may even help to encourage creativity (Eisenberg & Cameron, 1996; Eisenberg & Shanock, 2003). For example, research has shown that rewarding highly creative behavior on one task often enhances subsequent creativity on other tasks (Eisenberg & Rhoades, 2001).

punishment Any event whose presence decreases the likelihood that ongoing behavior will recur.

PUNISHMENT

What problems can punishment create?

Although we all hate to be subjected to it, **punishment** is a powerful controller of behavior. After receiving a heavy fine for failing to report extra income to the IRS, we are less likely to make that mistake again. After being rudely turned down when we ask someone for a favor, we are less likely to ask that person for another favor. In both cases, an unpleasant consequence reduces the likelihood that we will repeat a behavior. This is the definition of punishment.

Punishment is different from negative reinforcement. Reinforcement of whatever kind *strengthens* (reinforces) behavior. Negative reinforcement strengthens behavior by removing something unpleasant from the environment. In contrast, punishment adds something unpleasant to the environment; and as a result, it tends to *weaken* the behavior that caused it. If going skiing during the weekend rather than studying for a test results in getting an F, the F is an unpleasant consequence (a punisher) that makes you less likely to skip homework for ski time again.

Is punishment effective? We can all think of instances when it doesn't seem to work. Children often continue to misbehave even after they have been punished repeatedly for that particular misbehavior. Some drivers persist in driving recklessly despite repeated fines. The family dog may sleep on the couch at night despite being punished for being on the couch every morning. Why are there these seeming exceptions to the law of effect? Why, in these cases, isn't punishment having the result it is supposed to?

For punishment to be effective, it must be imposed properly (Gershoff, 2002). First, punishment should be *swift*. If it is delayed, it doesn't work as well. Sending a misbehaving child immediately to a time-out seat (even when it is not convenient to do so) is much more effective than waiting for a "better" time to punish. Punishment should also be *sufficient* without being cruel. If a parent briefly scolds a child for hitting other children, the effect will probably be less pronounced than if the child is sent to his or her room for the day. At the same time, punishment should be *consistent*. It should be imposed for all infractions of a rule, not just for some. If parents allow some acts of aggression to go unpunished, hitting and bullying other children are likely to persist.

Punishment is particularly useful in situations in which a behavior is dangerous and must be changed quickly. A child who likes to poke things into electric outlets must be stopped immediately, so punishment may be the best course of action. Similarly, punishment may be called for to stop severely disturbed children from repeatedly banging their heads against walls or hitting themselves in the face with their fists. Once this self-destructive behavior is under control, other forms of therapy can be more effective. But even in situations like these, punishment has drawbacks (Gershoff, 2002; B. F. Skinner, 1953).

PUNISHMENT CANNOT UNTEACH UNWANTED BEHAVIORS. First, it only *suppresses* the undesired behavior; it doesn't prompt someone to "unlearn" the behavior, and it doesn't teach a more desirable one. If the threat of punishment is removed, the negative behavior is likely to recur. This result is apparent on the highway. Speeders slow down when they see a police car (the threat of punishment), but speed up again as soon as the threat is passed. Punishment, then, rarely works when long-term changes in behavior are wanted (Pogarsky & Piquero, 2003).

PUNISHMENT CAN BACKFIRE. Second, punishment often stirs up negative feelings (frustration, resentment, self-doubt), which can impede the learning of new, more desirable behaviors. For example, when a child who is learning to read is scolded for every mispronounced word, the child may become very frustrated and hesitant. This frustration and doubt about

The use of punishment has potential drawbacks. It cannot "unteach" unwanted behavior, only suppress it. Punishment may also stir up negative feelings in the person who is punished or inadvertently provide a model of aggressive behavior.

THINKING CRITICALLY ABOUT...

Corporal Punishment

Some school systems still use some form of corporal punishment, such as paddling, for students who misbehave. The justification is that it is an effective method of changing undesirable behavior, it develops a sense of personal responsibility, it teaches self-discipline, and it helps develop moral character.

Based on what you now know about operant conditioning,

1. under what circumstances (if any) should corporal punishment be used in schools?

2. what factors, besides the student's immediate actions, should adults consider before using corporal punishment?

3. what unintended consequences might arise from the use of corporal punishment?

ability can prompt more mispronunciations, which lead to more scolding. In time, the negative feelings that punishment has caused can become so unpleasant that the child may avoid reading altogether. In addition, some studies have shown that children who frequently experience corporal punishment have a higher incidence of depression, antisocial behavior, decreased self-control, and increased difficulty relating to their peers (Matta, 2002; Slessareva & Muraven, 2004). In contrast, other research has shown that parents who are authoritative, loving, and communicative are likely to have well-adjusted children even if they occasionally spank them (Baumrind, 2001; Baumrind, Larzelere, & Cowen, 2002; Larzelere, 2000).

PUNISHMENT CAN TEACH AGGRESSION. A third drawback of punishment, when it is harsh, is the unintended lesson that it teaches: Harsh punishment may encourage the learner to copy that same harsh and aggressive behavior toward other people (Gershoff, 2002). In laboratory studies, monkeys that are harshly punished tend to attack other monkeys, pigeons other pigeons, and so on (B. Schwartz, 1989). In addition, punishment often makes people angry, and angry people frequently become more aggressive and hostile (Lansford et al., 2005).

Because of these drawbacks, punishment should be used carefully, and always together with reinforcement of desirable behavior. Once a more desirable response is established, punishment should be removed to reinforce negatively that new behavior. Positive reinforcement (praise, rewards) should also be used to strengthen the desired behavior. This approach is more productive than punishment alone, because it teaches an alternative behavior to replace the punished one. Positive reinforcement also makes the learning environment less threatening.

Sometimes, after punishment has been administered a few times, it needn't be continued, because the mere threat of punishment is enough to induce the desired behavior. Psychologists call it **avoidance training**, because the person is learning to avoid the possibility of a punishing consequence. Avoidance training is responsible for many everyday behaviors. It has taught you to carry an umbrella when it looks like rain to avoid the punishment of getting wet and to keep your hand away from a hot iron to avoid the punishment of a burn. Avoidance training, however, doesn't always work in our favor. For instance, a child who has been repeatedly criticized for poor performance in math may learn to shun difficult math problems in order to avoid further punishment. Unfortunately, because of this avoidance, the child fails to develop math skills and therefore fails to improve any innate capabilities, and so a vicious cycle has set in. The avoidance must be unlearned through some positive experiences with math in order for this cycle to be broken.

ENDURING ISSUES

Diversity–Universality   What Is Punishment?

We do not know whether something is reinforcing or punishing until we see whether it increases or decreases the occurrence of a response. We might assume that candy, for example, is a reinforcer for children, but some children don't like candy. We might also assume that having to work alone, rather than in a group of peers would be punishing, but some children prefer to work alone. Teachers must understand the children in their classes as individuals before they decide how to reward or punish them. Similarly, what is reinforcing for men may not be reinforcing for women, and what is reinforcing for people in one culture might not have the same effect for people in other cultures.

avoidance training Learning a desirable behavior to prevent the occurrence of something unpleasant, such as punishment.

In addition, an event or object might not be consistently rewarding or punishing over time. So even if candy is initially reinforcing for some children, if they eat large amounts of it, it can become neutral or even punishing. We must therefore be very careful in labeling items or events as "reinforcers" or "punishers." ●●

LEARNED HELPLESSNESS

In what ways do some college students exhibit learned helplessness?

Have you ever met someone who has decided he will never be good at science, or perhaps never find someone to fall in love with? We have said that through avoidance training, people learn to prevent themselves from being punished, but what happens when such avoidance of punishment isn't possible? The answer is often a "giving-up" response that can generalize to other situations. This response is known as **learned helplessness**.

Martin Seligman and his colleagues first studied learned helplessness in experiments with dogs (M. E. P. Seligman & Maier, 1967). They placed two groups of dogs in chambers that delivered a series of electric shocks to the dogs' feet at random intervals. The dogs in the control group could turn off (escape) the shock by pushing a panel with their nose. The dogs in the experimental group could not turn off the shock—they were, in effect, helpless. Next, both the experimental and the control animals were placed in a different situation, one in which they could escape shock by jumping over a hurdle. A warning light always came on 10 seconds before each 50-second shock was given. The dogs in the control group quickly learned to jump the hurdle as soon as the warning light flashed, but the dogs in the experimental group didn't. These dogs, which had previously experienced unavoidable shocks, didn't even jump the hurdle *after* the shock started. They just lay there and accepted the shocks. Also, many of these dogs were generally listless, suffered loss of appetite, and displayed other symptoms associated with depression.

Many subsequent studies have shown that learned helplessness can occur both in animals and in humans (G. W. Evans & Stecker, 2004; C. Peterson, Maier, & Seligman, 1993b; Overmier, 2002). Once established, the condition generalizes to new situations and can be very persistent, even given evidence that an unpleasant circumstance can now be avoided (C. Peterson, Maier, & Seligman, 1993a). For example, when faced with a series of unsolvable problems, a college student may eventually give up trying and make only halfhearted efforts to solve new problems, even when the new problems are solvable. Moreover, success in solving new problems has little effect on the person's behavior. He or she continues to make only halfhearted tries, as if never expecting *any* success at all. Similarly, children raised in an abusive family, where punishment is unrelated to behavior, often develop a feeling of helplessness (C. Peterson & Bossio, 1989). Even in relatively normal settings outside their home, they often appear listless, passive, and indifferent. They make little attempt either to seek rewards or to avoid discomfort. In recent years, researchers have begun to explore the biochemical and neurological mechanisms that underlie learned helplessness and depression (Minor & Hunter, 2002; Saade, Balleine, Bernard, & Minor, 2003; Shumake & Gonzalez-Lima, 2003) and to devise effective therapies to help people overcome it (Cemalcilar, Canbeyli, & Sunar, 2003; Flannery, 2002).

SHAPING BEHAVIORAL CHANGE THROUGH BIOFEEDBACK

How can operant conditioning be used to control biological functions?

Patrick, an eight-year-old third grader, was diagnosed with *attention-deficit disorder (ADD)*. He was unable to attend to what was going on around him, was restless, and was unable to concentrate. An EEG showed increased numbers of slow brain waves. After a course of 40 training sessions using special computer equipment that allowed Patrick to *monitor* his brain-wave activities, he learned how to produce more of the fast waves that are associated with being calm and alert. As a result, Patrick became much more "clued in" to what was going on around him and much less likely to become frustrated when things didn't go his way (Fitzgerald, 1999; Fuchs, Birbaumer, Lutzenberger, Gruzelier, & Kaiser, 2003; Rossiter, 2002).

learned helplessness Failure to take steps to avoid or escape from an unpleasant or aversive stimulus that occurs as a result of previous exposure to unavoidable painful stimuli.

THINKING CRITICALLY ABOUT...

Biofeedback and Neurofeedback

*A*ssume for the moment that you are skeptical about the benefits of biofeedback and neurofeedback. What questions would you ask about research studies that claim to show they are beneficial? To get started, refer back to Chapter 1 and the section on "Critical Thinking."

1. What kind of evidence would you look for to support your skeptical position? What kind of evidence would cause you to rethink your position? Are you swayed by reports of single cases (such as Patrick) or would you be more influenced by studies of large numbers of people? Would you be interested in short-term effects, or would you want to see results over a much longer period of time?

2. What assumptions would you need to watch out for? How would you know whether biofeedback or neurofeedback really worked? (Remember that you should be skeptical of self-reports.)

3. Might there be alternative explanations for the results of the research you find? In other words, is it possible that something quite apart from biofeedback or neurofeedback could explain the results?

4. Once you have formulated your position on the benefits of biofeedback or neurofeedback, how would you avoid oversimplifying your conclusions?

When operant conditioning is used to control certain biological functions, such as blood pressure, skin temperature or heart rate, it is referred to as **biofeedback**. Instruments are used to measure particular biological responses—muscle contractions, blood pressure, heart rate, brain waves. Variations in the strength of the response are reflected in the form of a light, a tone, or some other signal. By using the signal—the tone or light—the person can learn to control the response through shaping. For example, Patrick learned to control his brain waves by controlling the movement of a Superman icon on a computer screen. When biofeedback is used to monitor and control brain waves, as in Patrick's case, it is referred to as **neurofeedback** (Butnik, 2005).

Biofeedback and neurofeedback have become well-established treatments for a number of medical problems, including migraine headaches (Kropp, Siniatchkin, & Gerber, 2005), hypertension (Rau, Buehrer, & Weitkunat, 2003), asthma, irritable bowel conditions, and panic attacks (Meuret, Wilhelm, & Roth, 2004). Biofeedback has also been used by athletes, musicians, and other performers to control the anxiety that can interfere with their performance. Marathon runners use it to help overcome the tight shoulders and shallow breathing that can prevent them from finishing races. Biofeedback has even been used in space: NASA has used biofeedback as part of a program to reduce the motion sickness astronauts experience at zero gravity.

Biofeedback treatment does have some drawbacks. Learning the technique takes considerable time, effort, patience, and discipline. And it does not work for everyone. But it gives many patients control of their treatment, a major advantage over other treatment options, and it has achieved impressive results in alleviating certain medical problems (Olton & Noonberg, 1980).

biofeedback A technique that uses monitoring devices to provide precise information about internal physiological processes, such as heart rate or blood pressure, to teach people to gain voluntary control over these functions.

neurofeedback A biofeedback technique that monitors brain waves with the use of an EEG to teach people to gain voluntary control over their brain wave activity.

CHECK YOUR UNDERSTANDING

1. An event whose reduction or termination increases the likelihood that ongoing behavior will recur is called _____ reinforcement, whereas any event whose presence increases the likelihood that ongoing behavior will recur is called _____ reinforcement.

2. A type of learning that involves reinforcing the desired response is known as _____ _____.

3. When a threat of punishment induces a change to more desirable behavior, it is called _____ _____.

4. Superstitious behavior can result when a behavior is rewarded by pure _____.

5. Any stimulus that follows a behavior and decreases the likelihood that the behavior will be repeated is called a _____.

6. Which of the following problems may result from avoidance training?

   a. A person may continue to avoid something that no longer needs to be avoided.

   b. The effects of avoidance training tend to last for only a short time.

   c. Avoidance training may produce latent learning.

   d. Avoidance training tends to take effect when it is too late to make a difference in avoiding the problem situation.

Answers: 1. negative; positive. 2. operant conditioning. 3. avoidance training. 4. coincidence. 5. punishment. 6. a.

APPLY YOUR UNDERSTANDING

1. Imagine that you want to teach a child to make his or her bed. What kind of reinforcement could you use to do that?

   a. punishment

   b. positive reinforcement

   c. negative reinforcement

   d. both (b) and (c) would work

2. You are hired to make a commercial for a company that manufactures dog food. They want you to get a dog to run from a hallway closet, under a coffee table, around a sofa, leap over a wagon, rush to the kitchen and devour a bowl of dog food. The most effective way to accomplish this task would be to

   a. wait for this chain of events to happen and then use a reinforcer to increase the likelihood that the behavior will occur again on demand.

   b. use shaping.

   c. teach the dog to discriminate between the various landmarks on its way to the food.

   d. hire a smart dog.

Answers: 1. d. 2. b.

Factors Shared by Classical and Operant Conditioning

Can you think of any similarities between classical and operant conditioning?

Despite the differences between classical and operant conditioning, these two forms of learning have many things in common. First, they both involve the learning of associations. In classical conditioning, it is a learned association between one stimulus and another (between food and a bell, for instance), whereas in operant conditioning, it is a learned association between some action and a consequence. Second, the responses in both classical and operant conditioning are under the control of stimuli in the environment. A classically conditioned fear might be triggered by the sight of a white rat; an operantly conditioned jump might be cued by the flash of a red light. In both cases, moreover, the learned responses to a cue can generalize to similar stimuli. Third, neither classically nor operantly conditioned responses will last forever if they aren't periodically renewed. This doesn't necessarily mean that they are totally forgotten, however. Even after you think that these responses have long vanished, either one can suddenly reappear in the right situation. And fourth, in both kinds of learning—classical *and* operant conditioning—new behaviors can build on previously established ones.

THE IMPORTANCE OF CONTINGENCIES

How can changes in the timing of a conditioned stimulus lead to unexpected learning? Why does intermittent reinforcement result in such persistent behavior?

Because classical and operant conditioning are both forms of associative learning, they both involve perceived contingencies. A **contingency** is a relationship in which one event *depends* on another. Graduating from college is *contingent* on passing a certain number of courses. Earning a paycheck is *contingent* on having a job. In both classical and operant conditioning, perceived contingencies are very important.

CONTINGENCIES IN CLASSICAL CONDITIONING In classical conditioning, a contingency is perceived between the CS and the US. The CS comes to be viewed as a signal that the US is about to happen. This is why, in classical conditioning, the CS not only must occur in

contingency A reliable "if–then" relationship between two events, such as a CS and a US.

close proximity to the US, but also should precede the US and provide predictive information about it (Rescorla, 1966, 1967, 1988).

Imagine an experiment in which animals are exposed to a tone (the CS) and a mild electric shock (the US). One group always hears the tone a fraction of a second before it is shocked. Another group sometimes hears the tone first, but other times the tone sounds a fraction of a second *after* the shock, and still other times the tone and shock occur together. Soon the first group will show a fear response upon hearing the tone alone, but the second group will not. This is because the first group has learned a contingency between the tone and the shock: The tone has always preceded the shock, so it has come to mean that the shock is about to be given. For the second group, in contrast, the tone has signaled little or nothing about the shock. Sometimes the tone has meant that a shock is coming, sometimes it has meant that the shock is here, and sometimes it has meant that the shock is over and "the coast is clear." Because the meaning of the tone has been ambiguous for the members of this group, they have not developed a conditioned fear response to it.

Although scientists once believed that no conditioning would occur if the CS *followed* the US, this belief turns out not to be true. The explanation again lies in contingency learning. Imagine a situation in which a tone (the CS) always follows a shock (the US). This process is called *backward conditioning*. After a while, when the tone is sounded alone, the learner will not show a conditioned fear response to it. After all, the tone has never predicted that a shock is about to be given. But what the learner *does* show is a conditioned *relaxation* response to the sound of the tone, because the tone has served as a signal that the shock is over and will not occur again for some time. Again, we see the importance of contingency learning: The learner responds to the tone on the basis of the information that it gives about what will happen next.

Other studies similarly show that predictive information is crucial in establishing a classically conditioned response. In one experiment with rats, for instance, a noise was repeatedly paired with a brief electric shock until the noise soon became a conditioned stimulus for a conditioned fear response (Kamin, 1969). Then a second stimulus—a light—was added right before the noise. You might expect that the rat came to show a fear of the light as well, because it, too, preceded the shock. But this is not what happened. Apparently, the noise–shock contingency that the rat had already learned had a **blocking** effect on learning that the light also predicted shock. Once the rat had learned that the noise signaled the onset of shock, adding yet another cue (a light) provided no new predictive information about the shock's arrival, and so the rat learned to ignore the light (Kruschke, 2003). Classical conditioning, then, occurs only when a stimulus tells the learner something *new* or *additional* about the likelihood that a US will occur.

CONTINGENCIES IN OPERANT CONDITIONING Contingencies also figure prominently in operant conditioning. The learner must come to perceive a connection between performing a certain voluntary action and receiving a certain reward or punishment. If no contingency is perceived, there is no reason to increase or decrease the behavior.

But once a contingency is perceived, does it matter how often a consequence is actually delivered? When it comes to rewards, the answer is yes. Fewer rewards are often better than more. In the language of operant conditioning, *partial* or *intermittent reinforcement* results in behavior that will persist longer than behavior learned by *continuous reinforcement.* Why would this be the case? The answer has to do with expectations. When people receive only occasional reinforcement, they learn not to expect reinforcement with every response, so they continue responding in the hopes that eventually they will gain the desired reward. Vending machines and slot machines illustrate these different effects of continuous versus partial reinforcement. A vending machine offers continuous reinforcement. Each time you put in the right amount of money, you get something desired in return (reinforcement). If a vending machine is broken and you receive nothing for your coins, you are unlikely to put more money in it. In contrast, a casino slot machine pays off intermittently; only occasionally do you get something back for your investment. This intermittent payoff has a compelling effect on behavior. You might continue putting coins into a slot machine for a very long time even though you are getting nothing in return.

blocking A process whereby prior conditioning prevents conditioning to a second stimulus even when the two stimuli are presented simultaneously.

Psychologists refer to a pattern of reward payoffs as a **schedule of reinforcement**. Partial or intermittent reinforcement schedules are either fixed or variable, and they may be based on either the number of correct responses or the time elapsed between correct responses. **Table 5–1** gives some everyday examples of different reinforcement schedules.

On a **fixed-interval schedule**, learners are reinforced for the first response after a certain amount of time has passed since that response was previously rewarded. That is, they have to wait for a set period before they will be reinforced again. With a fixed-interval schedule, performance tends to fall off immediately after each reinforcement and then tends to pick up again as the time for the next reinforcement draws near. For example, when exams are given at fixed intervals—like midterms and finals—students tend to decrease their studying right after one test is over and then increase studying as the next test approaches. (See **Figure 5–6**.)

A **variable-interval schedule** reinforces correct responses after varying lengths of time following the last reinforcement. One reinforcement might be given after 6 minutes, the next after 4 minutes, the next after 5 minutes, and the next after 3 minutes. The learner typically gives a slow, steady pattern of responses, being careful not to be so slow as to miss all the rewards. For example, if exams are given during a semester at unpredictable intervals, students have to keep studying at a steady rate, because on any given day there might be a test.

On a **fixed-ratio schedule**, a certain number of correct responses must occur before reinforcement is provided, resulting in a high response rate, since making many responses in a short

Table 5–1	EXAMPLES OF REINFORCEMENT IN EVERYDAY LIFE
Continuous reinforcement (reinforcement every time the response is made)	Putting money in a parking meter to avoid getting a ticket. Putting coins in a vending machine to get candy or soda.
Fixed-ratio schedule (reinforcement after a fixed number of responses)	Being paid on a piecework basis. In the garment industry, for example, workers may be paid a fee per 100 dresses sewn.
Variable-ratio schedule (reinforcement after a varying number of responses)	Playing a slot machine. The machine is programmed to pay off after a certain number of responses have been made, but that number keeps changing. This type of schedule creates a steady rate of responding, because players know that if they play long enough, they will win. Sales commissions. You have to talk to many customers before you make a sale, and you never know whether the next one will buy. The number of sales calls you make, not how much time passes, will determine when you are reinforced by a sale, and the number of sales calls will vary.
Fixed-interval schedule (reinforcement of first response after a fixed amount of time has passed)	You have an exam coming up, and as time goes by and you haven't studied, you have to make up for it all by a certain time, and that means cramming. Picking up a salary check, which you receive every week or every two weeks.
Variable-interval response (reinforcement of first response after varying amounts of time)	Surprise quizzes in a course cause a steady rate of studying because you never know when they'll occur; you have to be prepared all the time. Watching a football game; waiting for a touchdown. It could happen anytime. If you leave the room, you may miss it, so you have to keep watching continuously.

Source: From Landy, 1987, p. 212. Adapted by permission.

schedule of reinforcement In operant conditioning, the rule for determining when and how often reinforcers will be delivered.

fixed-interval schedule A reinforcement schedule in which the correct response is reinforced after a fixed length of time since the last reinforcement.

variable-interval schedule A reinforcement schedule in which the correct response is reinforced after varying lengths of time following the last reinforcement.

fixed-ratio schedule A reinforcement schedule in which the correct response is reinforced after a fixed number of correct responses.

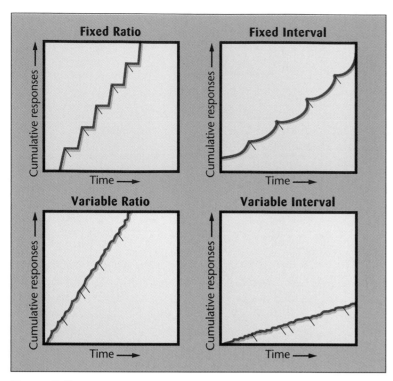

Figure 5–6

Response patterns to schedules of reinforcement.

On a fixed-interval schedule, as the time for reinforcement approaches, the number of responses increases, and the slope becomes steeper. On a variable-interval schedule, the response rate is moderate and relatively constant. Notice that each tick mark on the graph represents one reinforcement. The fixed-ratio schedule is characterized by a high rate of response and a pause after each reinforcement. A variable-ratio schedule produces a high rate of response with little or no pause after each reinforcement.

---

variable-ratio schedule A reinforcement schedule in which a varying number of correct responses must occur before reinforcement is presented.

extinction A decrease in the strength or frequency, or stopping, of a learned response because of failure to continue pairing the US and CS (classical conditioning) or withholding of reinforcement (operant conditioning).

spontaneous recovery The reappearance of an extinguished response after the passage of time, without training.

time yields more rewards. Being paid on a piecework basis is an example of a fixed-ratio schedule. Farm workers might get $3 for every 10 baskets of cherries they pick. The more they pick, the more money they make. Under a fixed-ratio schedule, a brief pause after reinforcement is followed by a rapid and steady response rate until the next reinforcement. (See **Figure 5–6**.)

On a **variable-ratio schedule**, the number of correct responses needed to gain reinforcement is not constant. The casino slot machine is a good example of a variable-ratio schedule. It will eventually pay off, but you have no idea when. Because there is always a chance of hitting the jackpot, the temptation to keep playing is great. Learners on a variable-ratio schedule tend not to pause after reinforcement and have a high rate of response over a long period of time. Because they never know when reinforcement may come, they keep on testing for a reward.

EXTINCTION AND SPONTANEOUS RECOVERY

Can you ever get rid of a conditioned response? Under what circumstances might old learned associations suddenly reappear?

Another factor shared by classical and operant conditioning is that learned responses sometimes weaken and may even disappear. If a CS and a US are never paired again or if a consequence always stops following a certain behavior, the learned association will begin to fade until eventually the effects of prior learning are no longer seen. This outcome is called **extinction** of a conditioned response.

EXTINCTION AND SPONTANEOUS RECOVERY IN CLASSICAL CONDITIONING For an example of extinction in classical conditioning, let's go back to Pavlov's dogs, which had learned to salivate upon hearing a bell. What would you predict happened over time when the dogs heard the bell (the CS), but food (the US) was no longer given? The conditioned response to the bell—salivation—gradually decreased until eventually it stopped altogether. The dogs no longer salivated when they heard the bell. **Extinction** had taken place. Extinction of classically conditioned responses also occurs in your own life. If scary

The slot machine is a classic example of a variable-ratio schedule of reinforcement. The machine eventually pays off, but always after a variable number of plays. Because people keep hoping that the next play will be rewarded, they maintain a high rate of response over a long period of time.

music in films (a CS) is no longer paired with frightening events on the screen (a US), you will eventually stop becoming tense and anxious (a CR) when you hear that kind of music. Your classically conditioned response to the music has undergone extinction.

Once such a response has been extinguished, is the learning gone forever? Pavlov trained his dogs to salivate when they heard a bell, then extinguished this conditioned response. A few days later, the dogs were exposed to the bell again in the laboratory setting. As soon as they heard it, their mouths began to water. The response that had been learned and then extinguished reappeared on its own with no retraining. This phenomenon is known as **spontaneous recovery**. The dogs' response was now only about half as strong as it had been before extinction, and it was very easy to extinguish a second time. Nevertheless, the fact that the response occurred at all indicated that the original learning was not completely forgotten (see **Figure 5–7**). Similarly, if you stop going to the movies for a while, you may find that the next time you go, the scary music once again makes you tense and anxious. A response that was extinguished has returned spontaneously after the passage of time.

How can extinguished behavior disappear and then reappear later? According to Mark Bouton (1993, 1994, 2002), the explanation is that extinction does not erase learning. Rather, extinction occurs because new learning interferes with a previously learned response. New stimuli in other settings come to be paired with the conditioned stimulus; and these new stimuli may elicit responses different from (and sometimes incompatible with) the original conditioned response. For example, if you take a break from watching the latest horror movies in theaters and instead watch reruns of classic horror films on television, these classic films may seem so amateurish that they make you laugh rather than scare you. Here you are learning to associate the scary music in such films with laughter, which in effect opposes your original fear response. The result is interference and extinction. Spontaneous recovery consists of overcoming this interference. For instance, if you return to the theater to see the latest Stephen King movie, the conditioned response of fear to the scary music may suddenly reappear. It is as if the unconditioned stimulus of watching "up-to-date" horror acts as a reminder of your earlier learning and renews your previous classically conditioned response. Such "reminder" stimuli work particularly well when presented in the original conditioning setting.

EXTINCTION AND SPONTANEOUS RECOVERY IN OPERANT CONDITIONING Extinction and spontaneous recovery also occur in operant conditioning. In operant conditioning, extinction happens as a result of withholding reinforcement. The effect usually isn't immediate. In fact, when reinforcement is first discontinued, there is often a brief *increase* in the strength or frequency of responding before a decline sets in. For instance, if you put coins in a vending machine and it fails to deliver the goods, you may pull the lever more forcefully and in rapid succession before you finally give up.

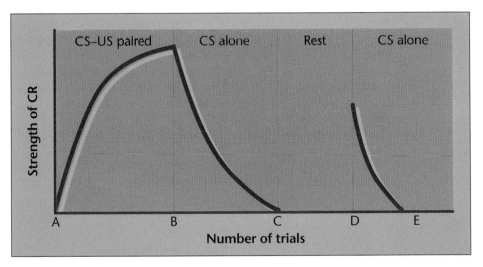
THINKING CRITICALLY ABOUT...
Reinforcement Schedules
Think about how you could apply the principles of behavioral learning to

1. design the ideal slot machine—one that would keep people playing over and over again, even though they won very little money.
2. design a reward system for a fifth-grade class that would result in both effort at schoolwork and in good behavior.
3. design an ideal lottery or mail-in contest.
4. design an ideal payment system for salespeople (you may include both salary and commission).

For each type of reward system, think about what the reinforcers should be, what contingencies are operating, and what behaviors you want to elicit. Also think about how you would demonstrate to a skeptic that your procedures have actually resulted in a change in the desired direction.

Figure 5–7

Response acquisition and extinction in classical conditioning.
From point A to point B, the conditioned stimulus and the unconditioned stimulus were paired; and learning increased steadily. From B to C, however, the conditioned stimulus was presented alone. By point C, the response had been extinguished. After a rest period from C to D, spontaneous recovery occurred—the learned response reappeared at about half the strength that it had at point B. When the conditioned stimulus was again presented alone, the response extinguished rapidly (point E).

Just as in classical conditioning, extinction in operant conditioning doesn't completely erase what has been learned. Even though much time has passed since a behavior was last rewarded and the behavior seems extinguished, it may suddenly reappear. This spontaneous recovery may again be understood in terms of interference from new behaviors. If a rat is no longer reinforced for pressing a lever, it will start to engage in other behaviors—turning away from the lever, biting at the corners of the Skinner box, attempting to escape, and so on. These new behaviors will interfere with the operant response of lever pressing, causing it to extinguish. Spontaneous recovery is a brief victory of the original learning over interfering responses. The rat decides to give the previous "reward" lever one more try, as if testing again for a reward.

The difficulty of extinguishing an operantly conditioned response depends on a number of factors:

- *Strength of the original learning.* The stronger the original learning, the longer it takes the response to extinguish. If you spend many hours training a puppy to sit on command, you will not need to reinforce this behavior very often once the dog grows up.
- *Pattern of reinforcement.* As you learned earlier, responses that were reinforced only occasionally when acquired are usually more resistant to extinction than responses that were reinforced every time they occurred.
- *Variety of settings in which the original learning took place.* The greater the variety of settings, the harder it is to extinguish the response. Rats trained to run several different types of alleys in order to reach a food reward will keep running longer after food is withdrawn than will rats trained in a single alley.
- *Complexity of the behavior.* Complex behavior is much more difficult to extinguish than simple behavior is. Complex behavior consists of many actions put together, and each of those actions must be extinguished in order for the whole to be extinguished.
- *Learning through punishment versus reinforcement.* Behaviors learned through punishment rather than reinforcement are especially hard to extinguish. If you avoid jogging down a particular street because a vicious dog there attacked you, you may never venture down that street again, so your avoidance of the street may never extinguish.

One way to speed up the extinction of an operantly conditioned response is to put the learner in a situation that is different from the one in which the response was originally learned. The response is likely to be weaker in the new situation, and therefore it will extinguish more quickly. Of course, when the learner is returned to the original learning setting after extinction has occurred elsewhere, the response may undergo spontaneous recovery, just as in classical conditioning. But now the response is likely to be weaker than it was initially, and it should be relatively easy to extinguish once and for all. You may have experienced this phenomenon yourself when you returned home for the holidays after your first semester in college. A habit that you thought you had outgrown at school may have suddenly reappeared. The home setting worked as a "reminder" stimulus, encouraging the response, just as we mentioned when discussing classical conditioning. Because you have already extinguished the habit in another setting, however, extinguishing it at home shouldn't be difficult.

STIMULUS CONTROL, GENERALIZATION, AND DISCRIMINATION

How can anxiety about math in grade school affect a college student? Why do people often slap the wrong card when playing a game of slapjack?

The home setting acting as a "reminder" stimulus is just one example of how conditioned responses are influenced by surrounding cues in the environment. This outcome is called **stimulus control**, and it occurs in both classical and operant conditioning. In classical conditioning, the conditioned response (CR) is under the control of the conditioned stimulus (CS) that triggers it. Salivation, for example, might be controlled by the sound of a bell. In

When reinforcement has been frequent, a learned behavior tends to be retained even after reinforcement is reduced. A dog "shaking hands" is an excellent example. Many previous rewards for this response tend to keep the dog offering people its paw even when no reward follows.

stimulus control Control of conditioned responses by cues or stimuli in the environment.

operant conditioning, the learned response is under the control of whatever stimuli come to be associated with delivery of reward or punishment. A leap to avoid electric shock might come under the control of a flashing light, for instance. In both classical and operant conditioning, moreover, the learner may respond to cues that are merely similar (but not identical) to the ones that prevailed during the original learning. This tendency to respond to similar cues is known as **stimulus generalization**.

GENERALIZATION AND DISCRIMINATION IN CLASSICAL CONDITIONING There are many examples of stimulus generalization in classical conditioning. One example is the case of Little Albert, who was conditioned to fear white rats. When the experimenters later showed him a white rabbit, he cried and tried to crawl away, even though he had not been taught to fear rabbits. He also showed fear of other white, furry objects—cotton balls, a fur coat, even a bearded Santa Claus mask. Similarly, Pavlov noticed that after his dogs had been conditioned to salivate when they heard a bell, their mouths would often water when they heard a buzzer or the ticking of a metronome. Both Pavlov's dogs and Albert had generalized their learned reactions from rats and bells to similar stimuli. In much the same way, a person who learned to feel anxious over math tests in grade school might come to feel anxious about any task involving numbers, even balancing a checkbook.

Stimulus generalization is not inevitable, however. Through a process called **stimulus discrimination**, learners can be trained not to generalize, but rather to make a conditioned response only to a single specific stimulus. This process involves presenting several similar stimuli, only one of which is followed by the unconditioned stimulus. For instance, Albert might have been shown a rat, a rabbit, cotton balls, and other white, furry objects, but only the rat would be followed by a loud noise (the US). Given this procedure, Albert would have learned to discriminate the white rat from the other objects, and the fear response would not have generalized as it did.

Learning to discriminate is essential in everyday life. We prefer for children to learn not to fear *every* loud noise, *every* insect, *every* dog, and so forth, but only those that are potentially harmful. Through stimulus discrimination, behavior becomes more finely tuned to the demands of our environment.

GENERALIZATION AND DISCRIMINATION IN OPERANT CONDITIONING Stimulus generalization also occurs in operant conditioning. A baby who is hugged and kissed for saying "Mama" when he sees his mother may begin to call everyone "Mama"—males and females alike. Although the person whom the baby sees—the stimulus—changes, he responds with the same word. Similarly, the skills you learn when playing tennis may be generalized to badminton, Ping-Pong, and squash.

In operant conditioning, responses, too, can be generalized, not just stimuli. For example, the baby who calls everyone "Mama" may also call people "Nana." His learning has generalized to other sounds that are similar to the correct response, "Mama." This is called **response generalization**. Response generalization doesn't occur in classical conditioning. If a dog is taught to salivate when it hears a high-pitched tone, it will salivate less when it hears a low-pitched tone, but the response is still salivation.

Just as discrimination is useful in classical conditioning, it is also useful in operant conditioning. Learning *what* to do has little value if you do not know *when* to do it. Learning that a response is triggered is pointless if you do not know which response is right. Discrimination training in operant conditioning consists of reinforcing *only* a specific, desired response and *only* in the presence of a specific stimulus. With this procedure, pigeons have been trained to peck at a red disk, but not at a green one. First they are taught to peck at a disk. Then they are presented with two disks, one red and one green. They get food when they peck at the red one, but not when they peck at the green. Eventually they learn to discriminate between the two colors, pecking only at the red. In much the same way, children learn to listen to exactly what the teacher is asking before they raise their hands.

The skills a person learns in playing tennis may also be utilized in such sports as Ping-Pong, squash, and badminton. This is an example of stimulus generalization in operant conditioning.

stimulus generalization The transfer of a learned response to different but similar stimuli.

stimulus discrimination Learning to respond to only one stimulus and to inhibit the response to all other stimuli.

response generalization Giving a response that is somewhat different from the response originally learned to that stimulus.

NEW LEARNING BASED ON ORIGINAL LEARNING

How might you build on a conditioned response to make an even more complex form of learning? Why is money such a good reinforcer for most people?

There are other ways, besides stimulus generalization and discrimination, that original learning can serve as the basis for new learning. In classical conditioning, an existing conditioned stimulus can be paired with a new stimulus to produce a new conditioned response. This is called **higher order conditioning**. In operant conditioning, objects that have no intrinsic value can nevertheless become reinforcers because of their association with other, more basic reinforcers. These learned reinforcers are called *secondary reinforcers*.

HIGHER ORDER CONDITIONING Pavlov demonstrated higher-order conditioning with his dogs. After the dogs had learned to salivate when they heard a bell, Pavlov used the bell (*without* food) to teach the dogs to salivate at the sight of a black square. Instead of showing them the square and following it with food, he showed them the square and followed it with the bell until the dogs learned to salivate when they saw the square alone. In effect, the bell served as a substitute unconditioned stimulus, and the black square became a new conditioned stimulus. This procedure is known as *higher order conditioning* not because it is more complex than other types of conditioning or because it incorporates any new principles, but simply because it is conditioning based on previous learning.

Higher order conditioning is difficult to achieve because it is battling against extinction of the original conditioned response. The unconditioned stimulus no longer follows the original conditioned stimulus and that is precisely the way to extinguish a classically conditioned response. During higher order conditioning, Pavlov's dogs were exposed to the square followed by the bell, but no food was given. Thus, the square became a signal that the bell would not precede food, and soon all salivation stopped. For higher order conditioning to succeed, the unconditioned stimulus must be occasionally reintroduced. Food must be given once in a while after the bell sounds so that the dogs will continue to salivate when they hear the bell.

SECONDARY REINFORCERS Some reinforcers, such as food, water, and sex, are intrinsically rewarding in and of themselves. These are called **primary reinforcers**. No prior learning is required to make them reinforcing. Other reinforcers have no intrinsic value. They have acquired value only through association with primary reinforcers. These are the **secondary reinforcers** we mentioned earlier. They are called secondary not because they are less important, but because prior learning is needed before they will function as reinforcers. Suppose a rat learns to get food by pressing a bar; then a buzzer is sounded every time food drops into the dish. Even if the rat stops getting the food, it will continue to press the bar for a while just to hear the buzzer. Although the buzzer by itself has no intrinsic value to the rat, it has become a secondary reinforcer through association with food, a primary reinforcer.

Note how, in creating a secondary reinforcer, classical conditioning is involved. Because it has been paired with an intrinsically pleasurable stimulus, a formerly neutral stimulus comes to elicit pleasure, too. This stimulus can then serve as a reinforcer to establish an operantly conditioned response.

For humans, money is one of the best examples of a secondary reinforcer. Although money is just paper or metal, through its exchange value for food, clothing, and other primary reinforcers, it becomes a powerful reinforcer. Children come to value money only after they learn that it will buy such things as candy (a primary reinforcer). Then the money becomes a secondary reinforcer. And through the principles of higher order conditioning, stimuli paired with a secondary reinforcer can acquire reinforcing properties. Checks and credit cards, for example, are one step removed from money, but they can also be highly reinforcing.

SUMMING UP

Does operant conditioning ever look like classical conditioning?

Classical and operant conditioning both entail forming associations between stimuli and responses, and perceiving contingencies between one event and another. Both are

higher order conditioning Conditioning based on previous learning; the conditioned stimulus serves as an unconditioned stimulus for further training.

primary reinforcers Reinforcers that are rewarding in themselves, such as food, water, or sex.

secondary reinforcers Reinforcers whose value is acquired through association with other primary or secondary reinforcers.

ON THE CUTTING EDGE

VIOLENT VIDEO GAMES AND AGGRESSION

The great majority of video games contain violence—often extreme violence directed toward other game characters (Dill, Gentile, Richter, & Dill, 2005). Almost all American children play video games (on average more than 9 hours a week) (C. A. Anderson, Gentile, & Buckley, 2006). During the course of the games, players not only observe violence but are often rewarded with extra points for behaving violently. Does rewarding violent behavior in video games increase aggressive feelings, thoughts, and behaviors? If violent behavior is punished, do aggressive feelings, thoughts, and behaviors decrease?

Nicholas Carnagey and Craig Anderson of Iowa State University explored these questions in a series of three studies in which the participants played the car-race video game *Carmageddon 2* (2005). In one version of the game, killing pedestrians and other drivers was rewarded with extra points. In a second version, killing pedestrians and drivers was punished with a loss of points. And in the third version, it wasn't possible to kill pedestrians or other drivers. In all three studies, they found that participants who were rewarded for killing pedestrians and other drivers did so far more often than those who were punished or who played the nonviolent version of the game. That should be no surprise to you after reading this far in the chapter. But they were surprised to find that both those who were rewarded and those who were punished for violent behavior reported feeling more hostile and aggressive than those who played the nonviolent game. In other words, simply playing a violent video game increased aggressive feelings regardless of rewards or punishments. They also found that rewarding violent behavior in the video game led not only to more aggressive and violent thoughts but also to more aggressive behavior toward others after the game was over. They concluded that ". . . people who play a video game in which violent actions are rewarded exhibit increased aggressive behavior, compared with people who play versions of the same competitive game in which violence is punished or does not occur." (p. 887)

---

subject to extinction and spontaneous recovery, as well as to stimulus control, generalization, and discrimination. The main difference between the two is that in classical conditioning, the learner is passive and the behavior involved is usually involuntary, whereas in operant conditioning, the learner is active and the behavior involved is usually voluntary.

Some psychologists downplay these differences, however, suggesting that classical and operant conditioning are simply two different ways of bringing about the same kind of learning. For example, classical conditioning can be used to shape voluntary movements (P. L. Brown & Jenkins, 1968; Vossel & Rossman, 1986), and operant conditioning can be used to shape involuntary responses such as heart rate, blood pressure, and brain waves (Fultz, 2002; Violani & Lombardo, 2003.) In addition, once an operant response becomes linked to a stimulus, it looks very much like a conditioned response in classical conditioning. If you have been reinforced repeatedly for stepping on the brake when a traffic light turns red, the red light comes to elicit braking just as the sound of a bell elicited salivation in Pavlov's dogs. Classical and operant conditioning, then, may simply be two different procedures for achieving the same end. If so, psychologists may have overstressed the differences between them and paid too little attention to what they have in common.

THINKING CRITICALLY ABOUT...

Violent Video Games

1. Carnagey & Anderson studied college undergraduates in the United States. Do you think that the same results would be found with young children or older adults? What about countries other than the United States? Why or why not?

2. The researchers measured aggressive behavior immediately after the participants played the video game. Do you think they would have obtained the same results if they had waited for an hour, a day or a week before taking the measurements? Does your answer to that question affect the conclusions you are willing to draw from this research about long-term effects of violent video games?

3. Do you think that the results might have been the same if they had studied the effects of repeated exposure to many violent video games over a period of weeks or months? How might you conduct an experiment to determine whether frequently playing violent video games has any long-lasting effects on aggressive emotions, thoughts, or behavior?

CHECK YOUR UNDERSTANDING

1. After extinction and a period of rest, a conditioned response may suddenly reappear. This phenomenon is called _____ _____.

2. The process by which a learned response to a specific stimulus comes to be associated with different, but similar stimuli is known as _____ _____.

3. Classify the following as primary (P) or secondary (S) reinforcers.
    a. food _____
    b. money _____
    c. college diploma _____
    d. sex _____

Answers: 1. spontaneous recovery. 2. stimulus generalization. 3. a. (P); b. (S); c. (S); d. (P).

APPLY YOUR UNDERSTANDING

1. On the first day of class, your instructor tells you that there will be unscheduled quizzes *on average* about every 2 weeks throughout the term, but not exactly every 2 weeks. This is an example of a _____ reinforcement schedule.
    a. continuous
    b. fixed-interval
    c. fixed-ratio
    d. variable-interval

2. In the situation in question 1, what study pattern is the instructor most likely trying to encourage?
    a. slow, steady rates of studying
    b. cramming the night before quizzes
    c. studying a lot right before quizzes, then stopping for a while right after them

Answers: 1. d. 2. a.

Cognitive Learning

How would you study the kind of learning that occurs when you memorize the layout of a chessboard?

Some psychologists insist that because classical and operant conditioning can be *observed* and *measured*, they are the only legitimate kinds of learning to study scientifically. But others contend that mental activities are crucial to learning and so can't be ignored. How do you grasp the layout of a building from someone else's description of it? How do you know how to hold a tennis racket just from watching a game of tennis being played? How do you enter into memory abstract concepts like *conditioning* and *reinforcement*? You do all these things and many others through **cognitive learning**—the mental processes that go on inside us when we learn. Cognitive learning is impossible to observe and measure directly, but it can be *inferred* from behavior, and so it is also a legitimate topic for scientific study.

LATENT LEARNING AND COGNITIVE MAPS

Did you learn your way around campus solely through operant conditioning (rewards for correct turns, punishments for wrong ones), or was something more involved?

Interest in cognitive learning began shortly after the earliest work in classical and operant conditioning (Eichenbaum & Cohen, 2001). In the 1930s, Edward Chace Tolman, one of the pioneers in the study of cognitive learning, argued that we do not need to show our learning in order for learning to have occurred. Tolman called learning that isn't apparent because it is not yet demonstrated **latent learning**.

cognitive learning Learning that depends on mental processes that are not directly observable.

latent learning Learning that is not immediately reflected in a behavior change.

Tolman studied latent learning in a famous experiment (Tolman & Honzik, 1930). Two groups of hungry rats were placed in a maze and allowed to find their way from a start box to an end box. The first group found food pellets (a reward) in the end box; the second group found nothing there. According to the principles of operant conditioning, the first group would learn the maze better than the second group—which is, indeed, what happened. But when Tolman took some of the rats from the second, unreinforced group and started to give them food at the goal box, almost immediately they ran the maze as well as the rats in the first group. (See **Figure 5–8**.) Tolman argued that the unrewarded rats had actually learned a great deal about the maze as they wandered around inside it. In fact, they may have even learned *more* about it than the rats that had been trained with food rewards, but their learning was *latent*—stored internally, but not yet reflected in their behavior. It was not until they were given a motivation to run the maze that they put their latent learning to use.

Since Tolman's time, much work has been done on the nature of latent learning regarding spatial layouts and relationships. From studies of how animals or humans find their way around a maze, a building, or a neighborhood with many available routes, psychologists have proposed that this kind of learning is stored in the form of a mental image, or **cognitive map**. When the proper time comes, the learner can call up the stored image and put it to use.

In response to Tolman's theory of latent learning, Thorndike proposed an experiment to test whether a rat could learn to run a maze and store a cognitive image of the maze without experiencing the maze firsthand. He envisioned researchers carrying each rat through the maze in a small wire-mesh container and then rewarding the rat at the end of each trial as if it had run the maze itself. He predicted that the rat would show little or no evidence of learning as compared with rats that had learned the same maze on their own through trial and error. Neither he nor Tolman ever conducted the experiment.

Two decades later, however, researchers at the University of Kansas did carry out Thorndike's idea (McNamara, Long, & Wike, 1956). But instead of taking the passive rats through the "correct" path, they carried them over the same path that a free-running rat had taken in that maze. Contrary to Thorndike's prediction, the passenger rats learned the maze just as well as the free-running rats. They did, however, need visual cues to learn the maze's layout. If carried through the maze only in the dark, they later showed little latent learning.

More recent research confirms this picture of cognitive spatial learning. Animals show a great deal more flexibility in solving problems like mazes than can be explained by simple conditioning (Collett & Graham, 2004). In experiments using rats in a radial maze, rats are able to recall which arms of the maze contain food, even when scent cues are removed (Grandchamp & Schenk, 2006). Moreover, when the configuration of the maze is repeatedly changed, the rats not only quickly adapt but also remember previous maze configurations (Tremblay & Cohen, 2005). Studies such as these suggest that the rats develop a cognitive map of the maze's layout (Save & Poucet, 2005). Even in rats, learning involves more than just a new behavior "stamped in" through reinforcement. It also involves the formation of new mental images and constructs that may be reflected in future behavior.

INSIGHT AND LEARNING SETS

Do you have a learning set for writing a term paper?

During World War I, the German Gestalt psychologist Wolfgang Köhler conducted a classic series of studies into another aspect of cognitive learning: sudden **insight** into a problem's

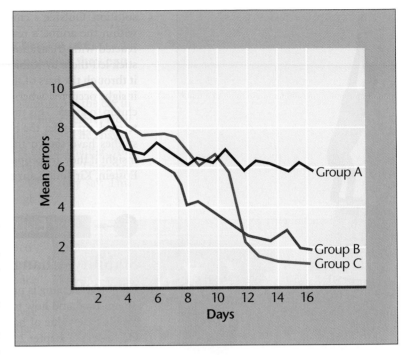

Figure 5–8

Graph showing the results of the Tolman and Honzik study.

The results of the classic Tolman and Honzik study are revealed in the graph. Group A never received a food reward. Group B was rewarded each day. Group C was not rewarded until the 11th day, but note the significant change in the rats' behavior on Day 12. The results suggest that Group C had been learning all along, although this learning was not reflected in their performance until they were rewarded with food for demonstrating the desired behaviors.

Source: Tolman & Honzik, 1930.

cognitive map A learned mental image of a spatial environment that may be called on to solve problems when stimuli in the environment change.

insight Learning that occurs rapidly as a result of understanding all the elements of a problem.

rats. Chimpanzees learn to use long sticks to fish for termites by watching their mothers (Lonsdorf, 2005). At least the females do. Males tend to play instead of watch and as a result their learning is delayed by several years! And some female dolphins in Australia cover their sensitive beaks with sponges when foraging for food on the sea floor, a skill they apparently learn by imitating their mothers (Krützen et al., 2005). These surprising results, along with reports that animals as diverse as chickens and octopi, whales and bumblebees learn by watching others, further support the notion that nonhuman animals do indeed learn in ways that reflect the cognitive theory of learning. In Chapter 7, "Cognition and Mental Abilities," we will revisit this topic, examining in more detail some of the intriguing new procedures scientists have used to explore the cognitive abilities of other animals (e.g., Boysen & Himes, 1999).

Use of sponges as tools among some dolphins. Dolphins have been observed using sponges to protect their snouts as they probe the sea floor searching for fish. Researchers believe mother dolphins teach this sponge-tool technique to their young. See http://dsc.discovery.com/news/briefs/20050606/dolphin.html

CHECK YOUR UNDERSTANDING

Match the following terms with the appropriate definition.

1. ___ latent learning
2. ___ insight
3. ___ observational learning

a. new, suddenly occurring idea to solve a problem
b. learning by watching a model
c. learning that has not yet been demonstrated in behavior

Are the following statements true (T) or false (F)?

4. _____ "Social learning theory broadens our understanding of how people learn skills and gain abilities by emphasizing expectations, insight, information, self-satisfaction, and self-criticism."

5. _____ "Social learning theory supports spanking as an effective way to teach children not to hit."

Answers: 1. (b). 2. (a). 3. (c). 4. (T). 5. (F).

APPLY YOUR UNDERSTANDING

1. An ape examines a problem and the tools available for solving it. Suddenly the animal leaps up and quickly executes a successful solution. This is an example of
   a. insight.
   b. operant conditioning.
   c. trial-and-error learning.

2. Before Junior got his driver's license, he rode along whenever his older sister had driving lessons, watching and listening carefully, especially when she had trouble learning to parallel park and another driver yelled at her for denting his fender. When Junior's turn to drive came, he was especially careful never to bump other cars when parallel parking. Junior learned to avoid parallel parking collisions as a result of
   a. insight.
   b. vicarious punishment.
   c. trial-and-error learning.
   d. higher order conditioning.

Answers: 1. a. 2. b.

KEY TERMS

learning, p. 163

Classical Conditioning

classical (or Pavlovian)
   conditioning, p. 164
unconditioned stimulus (US),
   p. 164
unconditioned response (UR),
   p. 164
conditioned stimulus (CS),
   p. 164
conditioned response (CR),
   p. 165
intermittent pairing, p. 165
desensitization therapy, p. 166
preparedness, p. 167
conditioned taste aversion,
   p. 167

Operant Conditioning

operant (or instrumental)
   conditioning, p. 169
operant behaviors, p. 169
reinforcers, p. 170
punishers, p. 170
law of effect (principle of
   reinforcement), p. 171
Skinner box, p. 171
shaping, p. 171
positive reinforcers, p. 172
negative reinforcers, p. 172
punishment, p. 173
avoidance training, p. 174
learned helplessness, p. 175

**Factors Shared by Classical
and Operant Conditioning**

biofeedback, p. 176
neurofeedback, p. 176
contingency, p. 177
blocking, p. 178
schedule of reinforcement,
   p. 179
fixed-interval schedule, p. 179
variable-interval schedule,
   p. 179
fixed-ratio schedule, p. 179
variable-ratio schedule, p. 180
extinction, p. 180
spontaneous recovery, p. 180
stimulus control, p. 182
stimulus generalization, p. 183

stimulus discrimination, p. 183
response generalization, p. 183
higher order conditioning,
   p. 184
primary reinforcers, p. 184
secondary reinforcers, p. 184

Cognitive Learning

cognitive learning, p. 186
latent learning, p. 186
cognitive map, p. 187
insight, p. 187
learning set, p. 188
observational (or vicarious)
   learning, p. 189
social learning theorists, p. 189
vicarious reinforcement
   (or punishment), p. 189

CHAPTER REVIEW

Classical Conditioning

How did Pavlov discover classical conditioning? **Learning** is the process by which experience or practice produces a relatively permanent change in behavior or potential behavior. One basic form of learning involves learning to associate one event with another. **Classical conditioning** is a type of associative learning that Pavlov discovered while studying digestion. Pavlov trained a dog to salivate at the sound of a bell when he rang the bell just before food was given. The dog learned to associate the bell with food and began to salivate at the sound of the bell alone.

How might you classically condition a pet? Suppose you wanted to classically condition salivation in your own dog. You know that food is an **unconditioned stimulus (US)** that automatically evokes the **unconditioned response (UR)** of salivation. By repeatedly pairing food with a second, initially neutral stimulus (such as a bell), the second stimulus would eventually become a **conditioned stimulus (CS)** eliciting a **conditioned response (CR)** of salivation.

If you once burned your finger on a match while listening to a certain song, why doesn't that song now make you reflexively jerk your hand away? Establishing a classically conditioned response usually is easier if the US and CS are paired with each other repeatedly, rather than a single time or even once in a while (**intermittent pairing**). That is why a single burn to your finger is not usually enough to produce a classically conditioned response. It is also important that the spacing of pairings be neither too far apart nor too close together.

What is an example of classical conditioning in your own life? In the case of Little Albert, Watson conditioned a child to fear white rats by always pairing a loud, frightening noise with a rat. Perhaps you have acquired a classically conditioned fear or anxiety (to the

sound of a dentist's drill, for instance) in much the same way; or perhaps you have also unlearned a conditioned fear by repeatedly pairing the feared object with something pleasant. Mary Cover Jones paired the sight of a feared rat (at gradually decreasing distances) with a child's pleasant experience of eating candy. This procedure was the precursor to **desensitization therapy**.

Why are people more likely to develop a phobia of snakes than of flowers? The concept of **preparedness** accounts for the fact that certain conditioned responses are acquired very easily. The ease with which we develop **conditioned taste aversions** illustrates preparedness. Because animals are biologically prepared to learn them, conditioned taste aversions can occur with only one pairing of the taste of a tainted food and later illness, even when there is a lengthy interval between eating the food and becoming ill. A fear of snakes may also be something that humans are prepared to learn.

Operant Conditioning

How are operant behaviors different from the responses involved in classical conditioning? **Operant** or **instrumental conditioning** is learning to make or withhold a certain response because of its consequences. **Operant behaviors** are different from the responses involved in classical conditioning because they are voluntarily emitted, whereas those involved in classical conditioning are elicited by stimuli.

What two essential elements are involved in operant conditioning? One essential element in operant conditioning is an operant behavior, or a behavior performed by one's own volition while "operating" on the environment. The second essential element is a consequence associated with that operant behavior. When a consequence increases the likelihood of an operant behavior's being emitted, it is called a **reinforcer**. When a consequence decreases the likelihood of

6 Memory

OVERVIEW

Enduring Issues in Memory

The Sensory Registers

- Visual and Auditory Registers
- Attention

Short-Term Memory

- Capacity of STM
- Encoding in STM
- Maintaining STM

Long-Term Memory

- Capacity of LTM
- Encoding in LTM
- Serial Position Effect
- Maintaining LTM
- Types of LTM
- Explicit and Implicit Memory

The Biology of Memory

- Where Are Memories Stored?

Forgetting

- The Biology of Forgetting
- Experience and Forgetting

Special Topics in Memory

- Cultural Influences
- Autobiographical Memory
- Extraordinary Memory
- Flashbulb Memories
- Eyewitness Testimony
- Recovered Memories

Rajan Mahadevan, an Indian psychologist, has always had a knack for remembering numbers. At age 5 he became intrigued by the license plate numbers on the cars of some 50 guests at a party given by his parents. Quickly memorizing all the plates, he flabbergasted everyone by reciting the numbers in the order in which the cars were parked. Similarly, in fourth grade Rajan astonished his teacher with a long list of memorized statistics on railroad accidents in India during the previous decade. His teacher had insisted Indian railways were safe; and Rajan wanted to prove him incorrect (Thompson, Cowan, & Frieman, 1993).

But what landed Rajan in the *Guinness Book of World Records* was his memorization of *pi*. In 1981, at the age of 24, he recited from memory the value of *pi* to 31,810 decimal places. This gave him the world record for memorized numbers, a distinction he held for the next six years until Hideaki Tomoyori, a memory whiz from Japan, topped him by reciting 40,000 *pi* digits. Yet even when superseded, Rajan's performance was still in some ways more impressive than that of his rival. Whereas Tomoyori required 13 hours and 6 minutes to accomplish his feat, averaging 0.85 digits per second, Rajan raced through nearly 32,000 numbers in a mere 21/2 hours, averaging 3.5 digits a second over his entire performance and an amazing 4.9 digits per second for the first 10,000 decimal places. Today, he is so familiar with the first 2,000 digits of pi that he can rocket through them at the astounding rate of nearly 7 digits a second, which is faster than most people can read them (Thompson et al., 1993).

How does Rajan do it? Basically, he divides the numbers into groups of 10 and learns the groups as units, which he then strings together. Unlike most other memory virtuosos, he learns each 10-digit unit largely by rote memorization. Occasionally he attaches meaning to a 3- or 4-digit string of numbers, enabling him to recall that string as a single chunk. For example, he remembers the string 312 as the area code for Chicago and the string 1865 as the year Lincoln died. But for Rajan this strategy is only incidental. Primarily his recall of each digit is cued merely by its numerical location in the overall sequence. This is very different from what his Japanese rival Tomoyori does. In Japanese each word for a digit also has a second meaning, so Tomoyori uses these second meanings to create a story line. He then recalls the story to bring the digits to mind (Thompson et al., 1993).

You may wonder if people like Rajan and Tomoyori are born with their extraordinary talent for memorization, or whether their feats are more a matter of learned strategies and effort. Some insights come from a study in which a college student named Steve Faloon enormously improved his memory for strings of random digits presented to him at a rate of 1 digit per second (Ericsson, Chase, & Faloon, 1980). At first Faloon could recall strings of only 7 digits, which is an average score. But after being paid to practice for 20 months, he could rattle off 80-digit strings without error. His performance breakthrough came when he began using his knowledge of long-distance running to "chunk" groups of digits as running times. However, when the researchers suddenly switched to presenting letters instead of digits, this recall strategy failed and Faloon's memory span fell back down to 7. In much the same way, when Rajan was tested for retention of material to which his digit strategy did not apply, such as recalling a complex story or reproducing from memory an intricate geometric design, his performance also fell to average (Thompson et al., 1993).

In this chapter we look at human memory as an extremely capable information-processing system that all people possess. This system is composed of several parts, including sensory registers that input data, a short-term storage bin for actively processing information, and a long-term file containing everything that has been stockpiled for possible future use. We also consider how these various components of memory are wired into the brain and what accounts for the all-too-common experience of forgetting. Finally, we conclude with some fascinating special topics in the study of memory, such as why we don't recall events from our earliest childhood, and whether memories recovered through procedures like hypnosis are real or imagined.

Accounts of people with extraordinary memories raise many questions about the nature of **memory** itself: Why are some people so much better at remembering things than others? Are they simply born with this ability, or could any of us learn to remember as much as they do? And why is it that remembering may sometimes be so simple (think how effortlessly baseball fans remember the batting averages of their favorite players) and other times so difficult (as when we grope for answers on an exam)? Why do older adults often find it so hard to remember something that happened only a few months back, yet, we can recall in vivid detail some other event that happened 10, 20, even 30 years ago? Just how does memory work, and what makes it fail?

Among the first to seek scientific answers to these questions was the 19th-century German psychologist Hermann Ebbinghaus. Using himself as a subject, Ebbinghaus composed lists of "nonsense syllables," meaningless combinations of letters, such as PIB, WOL, or TEB. He memorized lists of 13 nonsense syllables each. Then, after varying amounts of time, he

"Hold on a second, Bob. I'm putting you on a stickie."

Source: © *The New Yorker Collection*, 1997. Arnie Levin from *www.cartoonbank.com*. All Rights Reserved.

For those who take an interest in military history, these three chunks (which are dates of important battles) will be much easier to remember than 12 unrelated digits. In the same way, Steve Faloon chunked groups of digits as long-distance running times with which he was already familiar. And Rajan was able to remember the string 312 as the area code for Chicago and the string 1865 as the year Lincoln died.

By chunking words into sentences or sentence fragments, we can process an even greater amount of information in STM (Baddeley, 1994; T. Carter, Hardy, & Hardy, 2001). For example, suppose that you want to remember the following list of words: *tree, song, hat, sparrow, box, lilac, cat*. One strategy would be to cluster as many of them as possible into phrases or sentences: "The sparrow in the tree sings a song"; "a lilac hat in the box"; "the cat in the hat." You may remember that Tomoyori, whose remarkable memory was described at the start of this chapter, used this technique to create a story line from a long string of digits. But isn't there a limit to this strategy? Would five sentences be as easy to remember for a short time as five single words? No. As the size of any individual chunk increases, the number of chunks that can be held in STM declines (Simon, 1974). STM can easily handle five unrelated letters or words at once, but five unrelated sentences are much harder to remember.

Keep in mind that STM usually has to perform more than one task at a time (Jonides, Lacey, & Nee, 2005). During the brief moments you spent memorizing the preceding rows of letters, you probably gave them your full attention. But normally you have to attend to new incoming information while you work on whatever is already present in short-term memory. Competition between these two tasks for the limited work space in STM means that neither task will be done as well as it could be. Try counting backward from 100 while trying to learn the rows of letters in our earlier example. What happens?

Now turn on some music and try to learn the rows of letters. You'll find that the music doesn't interfere much, if at all, with learning the letters. Interestingly, when two memory tasks are presented in different sensory modalities (for instance, visual and auditory), they are less likely to interfere with each other than if they are in the same modality (Cocchini, Logie, Sala, MacPherson, & Baddeley, 2002). This suggests the existence of *domain-specific* working memory systems that can operate at the same time with very little interference.

ENCODING IN STM

Do we store material in short-term memory as it sounds or as it looks?

We encode verbal information for storage in STM *phonologically*—that is, according to how it sounds. This is the case even if we see the word, letter, or number on a page, rather than hear it spoken (Inhoff, Connine, Eiter, Radach, & Heller, 2004; Vallar, 2006). We know this because numerous experiments have shown that when people try to retrieve material from STM, they generally mix up items that sound alike (Sperling, 1960). A list of words such as *mad, man, mat, cap* is harder for most people to recall accurately than is a list such as *pit, day, cow, bar* (Baddeley, 1986).

But not all material in short-term memory is stored phonologically. At least some material is stored in visual form, and other information is retained on the basis of its meaning (R. G. Morrison, 2005). For example, we don't have to convert visual data such as maps, diagrams, and paintings into sound before we can code them into STM and think about them. Moreover, research has shown that memory for images is generally better than memory for words because we often store images both phonologically and as images, while words are usually stored only phonologically (Paivio, 1986). The *dual coding* of images accounts for the reason it is sometimes helpful to form a mental picture of something you are trying to learn (Sadoski & Paivio, 2001; Sadoski, 2005).

MAINTAINING STM

How can we hold information in STM?

As we have said, short-term memories are fleeting, generally lasting a matter of seconds. However, we can hold information in STM for longer periods through rote rehearsal, also called *maintenance rehearsal*. **Rote rehearsal** consists of repeating information over and over, silently or out loud. Although it may not be the most efficient way to remember something permanently, it can be quite effective for a short time.

While remembering a small amount of information for a short period of time is important, our ability to store vast quantities of information for indefinite periods of time is essential if we are to master complex skills, acquire an education, or remember the personal experiences that contribute to our identity. In the next section we will explore how memories that often last a lifetime are stored.

CHECK YOUR UNDERSTANDING

1. ____ memory is what we are thinking about at any given moment. Its function is to briefly store new information and to work on that and other information.

2. ____ enables us to group items into meaningful units.

3. Strings of letters and numbers are encoded ____ in short-term memory.

4. ____ rehearsal, or simply repeating information over and over, is an effective way of retaining information for just a minute or two.

Answers: 1. short-term. 2. chunking. 3. phonologically. 4. rote.

APPLY YOUR UNDERSTANDING

1. You try to remember the letters CNOXNPEHFOBSN, but despite your best efforts you can't seem to remember more than half of them. Then you are told that the letters can be rearranged as CNN FOX HBO ESPN (four TV channels). After that, you are able to remember all the letters even weeks later. Rearranging the letters into groups that are easier to retain in memory is known as

   a. shadowing.
   b. chunking.
   c. rote rehearsal.
   d. cueing.

2. Your sister looks up a phone number in the phone book, but then can't find the phone. By the time she finds the phone, she has forgotten the number. While she was looking for the phone, she apparently failed to engage in

   a. rote rehearsal.
   b. parallel processing.
   c. phonological coding.
   d. categorizing.

Answers: 1. b. 2. a.

Long-Term Memory

What types of information are retained in long-term memory?

Everything that we learn is stored in **long-term memory (LTM)**: the words to a popular song; the results of the last election; the meaning of *justice*; how to roller skate or draw a face; your enjoyment of opera or your disgust at the sight of raw oysters; and what you are supposed to be doing tomorrow at 4:00 P.M.

rote rehearsal Retaining information in memory simply by repeating it over and over.

long-term memory (LTM) The portion of memory that is more or less permanent, corresponding to everything we "know."

Looking into a bakery window, perhaps smelling the aromas of the cakes inside, may prime the memory, triggering distinct memories associated with those sights and smells, formed many years ago.

THE TIP-OF-THE-TONGUE PHENOMENON Everyone has had the experience of knowing a word but not quite being able to recall it. This is called the **tip-of-the-tongue phenomenon** (or **TOT**) (R. Brown & McNeil, 1966; Hamberger & Seidel, 2003; B. L. Schwartz, 2002; Widner, Otani, & Winkelman, 2005). Although everyone experiences TOTs, these experiences become more frequent during stressful situations and as people get older (B. L. Schwartz & Frazier, 2005; K. K. White & Abrams, 2002). Moreover, other words—usually with a sound or meaning similar to the word you are seeking—occur to you while you are in the TOT state and these words interfere with and sabotage your attempt to recall the desired word. The harder you try, the worse the TOT state gets. The best way to recall a blocked word, then, is to stop trying to recall it! Most of the time, the word you were searching for will pop into your head, minutes or even hours after you stopped consciously searching for it (B. L. Schwartz, 2002). (If you want to experience TOT yourself, try naming Snow White's seven dwarfs.)

The distinction between explicit and implicit memories means that some knowledge is literally unconscious. Moreover, as we shall soon see, explicit and implicit memories also seem to involve different neural structures and pathways. However, memories typically work together. When we remember going to a Chinese restaurant, we recall not only when and where we ate and whom we were with (episodic memory), but also the nature of the food we ate (semantic memory), the skills we learned such as eating with chopsticks (procedural memory), and the embarrassment we felt when we spilled the tea (emotional memory). When we recall events, we typically do not experience these kinds of memories as distinct and separate; rather, they are integrally connected, just as the original experiences were. Whether we will continue to remember the experiences accurately in the future depends to a large extent on what happens in our brain, as we will see in the next section.

CHECK YOUR UNDERSTANDING

1. The primacy effect accounts for why we remember items at the _____ of a list, while the recency effect accounts for why we remember items at the _____ of the list.

2. If information is learned through repetition, this process is _____ rehearsal; if it is learned by linking it to other memories, this process is _____ rehearsal.

3. A schema is a framework in memory into which new information is fit. Is this statement true (T) or false (F)?

4. Implicit memories consist of _____ and _____ memories, whereas explicit memories consist of _____ and _____ memories.

Answers: 1. beginning; end. 2. rote; elaborative. 3. (T). 4. procedural and emotional; episodic and semantic.

APPLY YOUR UNDERSTANDING

1. You run into an old friend who gives you his phone number and asks you to call. You want to be sure to remember the phone number, so you relate the number to things that you already know. "555" is the same as the combination to your bicycle lock. "12" is your brother's age. And "34" is the size of your belt. This technique for getting information into long-term memory is called

   a. rote rehearsal.   c. elaborative rehearsal.

   b. relational rehearsal.   d. episodic rehearsal.

2. *He:* "We've been to this restaurant before."

   She: "I don't think so."

   He: "Didn't we eat here last summer with your brother?"

   She: "That was a different restaurant, and I think it was last fall, not last summer."

   This couple is trying to remember an event they shared and, obviously, their memories differ. The information they are seeking is most likely stored in

   a. procedural memory.   c. semantic memory.

   b. emotional memory.   d. episodic memory.

Answers: 1. c. 2. d.

tip-of-the-tongue phenomenon (or TOT)
Knowing a word, but not being able to immediately recall it.

The Biology of Memory

What role do neurons play in memory?

Research on the biology of memory focuses mainly on the question, *How and where are memories stored?* Simple as the question is, it has proved enormously difficult to answer and our answers are still not entirely complete.

Current research indicates that memories consist of changes in the synaptic connections among neurons (Kandel, 2001; Squire & Kandel, 1999). When we learn new things, new connections are formed in the brain; when we review or practice previously learned things, old connections are strengthened. These chemical and structural changes can continue over a period of months or years (Gold & Greenough, 2001), during which the number of connections among neurons increases as does the likelihood that cells will excite one another through electrical discharges, a process known as **long-term potentiation (LTP)** .

Although learning takes place in the brain, it is also influenced by events occurring elsewhere in the body. Two hormones in particular, epinephrine and cortisol, affect long-term retention. A number of studies with rats, monkeys, and humans, have shown, for example, that epinephrine can enhance the recall of exposure to stimuli associated with unpleasant experiences, such as exposure to shock (Liang, 2001).

ENDURING ISSUES

Mind–Body   Effects of Stress on Body and Brain

Epinephrine secretion is part of the "fight or flight" syndrome (see Chapter 11, "Stress and Health Psychology"), and has the effect of arousing the organism to action. However, the effect on memory of epinephrine and other stress-related hormones is not merely the result of general arousal. Apparently these hormones indirectly act on specific brain centers, such as the hippocampus and the amygdala, that are critical for memory formation (Vermetten & Bremner, 2002). Increased blood levels of epinephrine probably also explain improved performance in humans under conditions of mild stress (L. Cahill & Alkire, 2003). Extreme stress, however often interferes with both the learning and later recall of specific information. For example, research has demonstrated that when people are exposed to highly stressful events, their memory for the emotional aspect of the event may be enhanced but their ability to recall the nonemotional aspects of the event is disrupted (Payne et al., 2006). If you are studying for an exam, then, a little anxiety will probably improve your performance, but a high level of anxiety will work against you. ●●

WHERE ARE MEMORIES STORED?

Are STM and LTM found in the same parts of the brain?

Not all memories are stored in one place (J. B. Brewer, Zhao, Desmond, Glover, & Gabriel, 1998). However, this characteristic does not mean that memories are randomly distributed throughout the brain. In fact, different parts of the brain are specialized for the storage of memories (See **Figure 6–4**; Rolls, 2000).

Short-term memories, for example, seem to be located primarily in the prefrontal cortex and temporal lobe (Rainer & Miller, 2002; Rolls, Tovee, & Panzeri, 1999; Scheibel & Levin, 2004; Szatkowska, Grabowska, & Szymanska, 2001). Long-term semantic memories seem to be located primarily in the frontal and temporal lobes of the cortex, which interestingly, also play a prominent role in consciousness and awareness. Research shows increased activity in a particular area of the left temporal lobe—for example, when people are asked to recall the names of people. A nearby area shows increased activity when they are asked to recall the names of animals, and another neighboring area becomes active when they are asked to recall the names of tools (H. Damasio, Grabowski, Tranel, Hichawa, & Damasio, 1996).

long-term potentiation (LTP)   A long-lasting change in the structure or function of a synapse that increases the efficiency of neural transmission and is thought to be related to how information is stored by neurons.

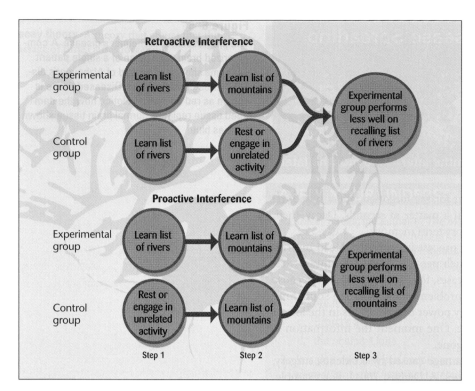

Figure 6-7

Diagram of experiments measuring retroactive and proactive interference.

In retroactive interference, the experimental group usually does not perform as well on tests of recall as those in the control group, who experience no retroactive interference from a list of words in Step 2. In proactive interference, people in the experimental group suffer the effects of proactive interference from the list in Step 1. When asked to recall the list from Step 2, they perform less well than those in the control group.

---

retroactive interference The process by which new information interferes with information already in memory.

proactive interference The process by which information already in memory interferes with new information.

becomes harder to remember. Such forgetting is said to be due to *interference*. As portrayed in **Figure 6-7**, there are two kinds of interference. In **retroactive interference**, new material interferes with information already in long-term memory. Retroactive interference occurs every day. For example, once you learn a new telephone number, you may find it difficult to recall your old number, even though you used that old number for years.

In the second kind of interference, **proactive interference**, old material interferes with new material being learned. Like retroactive interference, proactive interference is an everyday phenomenon. Suppose you always park your car in the lot behind the building where you work, but one day all those spaces are full, so you have to park across the street. When you leave for the day, you are likely to head for the lot behind the building—and may even be surprised at first that your car is not there. Learning to look for your car behind the building has interfered with your memory that today you parked the car across the street.

The most important factor in determining the degree of interference is the similarity of the competing items. Learning to swing a golf club may interfere with your ability to hit a baseball, but probably won't affect your ability to make a free throw on the basketball courts. The more dissimilar something is from other things that you have already learned, the less likely it will be to mingle and interfere with other material in memory (G. H. Bower & Mann, 1992).

SITUATIONAL FACTORS Whenever we try to memorize something, we are also unintentionally picking up information about the context in which the learning is taking place. That information becomes useful when we later try to retrieve the corresponding information from LTM. If those environmental cues are absent when we try to recall what we learned, the effort to remember is often unsuccessful. Context-dependent memory effects tend to be small, so studying in the same classroom where you are scheduled to take an exam will probably not do too much to improve your grade. Nevertheless, contextual cues are occasionally used by police who sometimes take witnesses back to the scene of a crime in the hope that they will recall crucial details that can be used to solve the crime.

Our ability to accurately recall information is also affected by internal cues, a phenomenon known as *state-dependent memory*. Researchers have found that people who learn material in a particular physiological state tend to recall that material better if they return to the same state they were in during learning (de-l'Etoile, 2002; Kelemen & Creeley, 2003; Riccio, Millin, & Gisquet-Verrier, 2003). For example, if people learn material while under the influence of caffeine, recall of the material is slightly improved when they are again under the influence of caffeine (Keleman & Creeley, 2003). Similarly, if you discovered a bakery with scrumptious pastries on a day when you were really hungry, finding your way there again may be easier when you're hungry than when you are full.

THE RECONSTRUCTIVE PROCESS Forgetting also occurs because of what is called the "reconstructive" nature of remembering. Earlier, we talked about how schemata are used in storing information in long-term memory. Bartlett proposed that people also use schemata to "reconstruct" memories (Bartlett, 1932; Schacter, Norman, & Koutstaal, 1998). This reconstructive process can lead to huge errors. Indeed, we are sometimes more likely to recall events that never happened than events that actually took place (Brainerd & Reyna, 1998)! The original memory is not destroyed; instead, people are sometimes unable to tell the difference between what actually happened and what they merely heard about or imagined (Garry & Polaschek, 2000; S. R. Schmidt, 2004; S. E. Taylor, Pham, Rivkin, & Armor, 1998). In other words, sometimes people combine the elements of both real and imagined events (Henkel, Franklin, & Johnson, 2000). People also unknowingly "rewrite" past events to fit their current image or their desired image of themselves and their past decisions (Mather, Shafir, & Johnson, 2000).

We may also reconstruct memories for social reasons or personal self-defense (Feeney & Cassidy, 2003). Each time you tell someone the story of an incident, you may unconsciously make subtle changes in the details of the story. Consequently, these changes become part of your memory of the event. When an experience doesn't fit our view of the world or ourselves, we tend, unconsciously, to adjust it or to blot it out of memory altogether (Bremner & Marmar, 1998). Such distortions of memory become critically important in criminal trials, in which a person's guilt or innocence may depend on the testimony of an eyewitness—a topic we will return to later in this chapter.

CHECK YOUR UNDERSTANDING

Match the following terms with their appropriate definitions:

1. ___ retrograde amnesia
2. ___ retroactive interference
3. ___ proactive interference

a. forgetting because new information makes it harder to remember information already in memory

b. forgetting because old information in memory makes it harder to learn new information

c. can result from head injury or electroconvulsive therapy

Answers: 1. c. 2. a. 3. b.

APPLY YOUR UNDERSTANDING

1. You are trying to explain to someone that "forgetting" sometimes occurs because of the reconstructive nature of long-term memory. Which of the following would be an example that you might use to support your position?

   a. People can distinguish between real and fictional accounts in narratives.

   b. People who learn material in a particular setting tend to recall that material better if they return to that same setting.

   c. Rote rehearsal with no intention to remember has little effect on long-term memory.

   d. People often rewrite their memories of past events to fit their current view or desired view of themselves.

2. You are given a chance to earn $10 if you can correctly learn a list of 20 words. You have 5 minutes to learn the entire list. At the end of that time, you can recite the list perfectly. But before you are given a chance to show what you have learned, you are required to learn a second list of similar words. When it comes time to show how well you learned the first list, to your dismay, you discover that you have forgotten half the words that you once knew perfectly! What is the most likely cause of your forgetting the words on the first list?

   a. negative transfer

   b. retroactive interference

   c. retroactive facilitation

   d. proactive interference

Answers: 1. d. 2. b

Special Topics in Memory

What factors can influence how well you remember a specific incident?

Now that we have reviewed the various types of memory and how our memory for different events is stored in the brain, we will turn our attention to some special factors that affect memory. For example, what effect does culture have on memory? Do people from different cultures remember things in the same way? Is there a unique memory system that enables us to retain our personal experiences—the events, places, people, and emotions that shape our lives? Do some memories go away, only to return years later? Under what

Look carefully at these cows and try to notice significant distinguishing characteristics of each animal. Is this task difficult for you? It probably is, unless you have been working closely with cattle all your life, as these two people have.

circumstances can we really trust our memory? Why do we have difficulty remembering events from our early childhood? Conversely, why are some of our memories particularly vivid, and why do some people seem to have extraordinarily good memories?

CULTURAL INFLUENCES

Are the memory tasks in Western schools different from those in cultures that pass on traditions orally?

Remembering has practical consequences for our daily life and takes place within a particular context. It's not surprising, then, that many researchers believe that the values and customs of a given culture have a profound effect on what and how easily people remember (Confino & Fritzsche, 2002; Mistry & Rogoff, 1994). In many Western cultures, for example, being able to recite a long list of words or numbers, to repeat the details of a scene, and to provide facts and figures about historical events are all signs of a "good memory." In fact, tasks such as these are often used to test people's memory abilities. However, these kinds of memory tasks do not necessarily reflect the type of learning, memorization, and categorization skills taught in non-Western schools. Members of other cultures often perform poorly on such memory tests because the exercises seem so odd to them.

In contrast, consider the memory skills of a person living in a society in which cultural information is passed on from one generation to the next through a rich oral tradition. Such an individual may be able to recite the deeds of the culture's heroes in verse or rattle off the lines of descent of families, larger lineage groups, and elders. Or perhaps the individual has a storehouse of information about the migration of animals or the life cycles of plants that help people to obtain food and to know when to harvest crops.

ENDURING ISSUES

Diversity–Universality   Memory and Culture

Frederic Bartlett, whose work on memory was discussed earlier in this chapter, anticipated the intertwining of memory and culture long ago. Bartlett (1932) related a tale of a Swazi cowherd who had a prodigious memory for facts and figures about cattle. The cowherd could recite, with virtually no error, the selling price, type of cattle bought, and circumstances of the sale for purchases dating back several years. These skills are not surprising when you know that in Swazi culture the care and keeping of cattle are very important in daily life, and many cultural practices focus on the economic and social importance of cattle. In contrast, Bartlett reported, Swazi children did no better than his young European participants in recalling a 25-word message. Stripped of its cultural significance, their memory performance was not exceptional. More recent research showed that college students in Ghana, a culture with a strong oral tradition, were much better than college students in New York at remembering a short story they had heard (Matsumoto, 2000). ●●

AUTOBIOGRAPHICAL MEMORY

What kinds of events are most likely to be remembered?

Why do we have so few memories from the first 2 years of life?

Autobiographical memory refers to our recollection of events that happened in our life and when those events took place (Koriat, Goldsmith, & Pansky, 2000; K. Nelson & Fivush, 2004); as such, it is a form of episodic memory. Autobiographical memories are of fundamental importance. Indeed, M. A. Conway (1996, p. 295) contends that "autobiographical memory is central to self, to identity, to emotional experience, and to all those attributes that define an individual."

In general, recent life events are, of course, easier to recall than earlier ones. In a classic study of autobiographical memory, researchers asked young adults to report the earliest personal memory that came to mind when they saw each of 20 words and then to estimate how long ago each event had occurred. The words were all common nouns, such as *hall* and *oven*, for which people can easily create images. In general, most personal memories concerned relatively recent events: The longer ago an event occurred, the less likely people were to report it (Crovitz & Schiffman, 1974). Other research, however, shows that people over age 50 are more likely than younger people to recall events from relatively early in life, probably because many of the most critical choices we make in our lives occur in late adolescence and early adulthood (Janssen, Chessa, & Murre, 2005; Mackavey, Malley, & Stewart, 1991).

Exactly how the vast amount of autobiographical information stored in memory is organized is not fully understood, but research in this area has supported two interesting theories. It may be that we store autobiographical information according to important events in our lives, such as beginning college, getting married, or experiencing the death of a loved one. This view explains why we can usually remember when events occurred relative to these major landmarks in our lives (Shum, 1998). We may also store autobiographical memories in *event clusters*, which are groups of memories on a related theme or that take place close together in time (N. R. Brown, 2005; N. R. Brown & Schopflocher, 1998).

ENDURING ISSUES

Stability–Change Childhood Amnesia

Despite the richness of our autobiographical memories, research shows that people rarely if ever recall events that occurred before they were 2 years old (Howe, 2003). This phenomenon is sometimes called **childhood amnesia**, or *infantile amnesia*.

Exactly why people have difficulty remembering events from their first years of life is not well understood, although several explanations have been advanced (Q. Wang, 2003). One hypothesis holds that childhood amnesia is a result of the child's brain not being fully developed at birth. An immature brain structure, such as the prefrontal cortex, may be incapable of efficiently processing and storing information in memory. In fact, the hippocampus, which is so important in the formation of episodic and semantic memories, is not fully formed until about age 2 (W. J. Jacobs & Nadel, 1997).

Childhood amnesia may also occur because young children lack a clear sense of self (Wheeler et al., 1997). According to this theory, without a sense of one's self, very young children find it difficult to organize and integrate their experiences into a coherent autobiographical memory scheme. However, with the emergence of self-concept and self-awareness near the end of the second year, childhood amnesia would be expected to lessen—which it does (Howe & Courage, 1993). Childhood amnesia may also be linked to language skills: Young children do not have the language skills necessary to strengthen and consolidate early experiences (Hudson & Sheffield, 1998; Simcock & Hayne, 2002). Other research suggests that age-related changes in encoding, retention, and retrieval processes that accompany the transition from infancy to early childhood account for childhood amnesia (Hayne, 2004).

In a twist on these theories, Patricia Bauer (1996) has shown that infants as young as 13 months can construct and maintain memories of specific events. Bauer contends that appropriate cues and repetition are the primary influences on efficient recall, not age. Childhood amnesia has to do with the inability of *adults* to remember early experiences, especially before the age of 2. And that, argue many psychologists, is a real phenomenon that needs to be explained (Eacott, 1999; Newcombe, Drummey, Fox, Lie, & Ottinger-Alberts, 2000). ●●

childhood amnesia The difficulty adults have remembering experiences from their first two years of life.

EXTRAORDINARY MEMORY

What is photographic memory?

As you saw at the beginning of this chapter, some people are able to perform truly amazing feats of memory. From time to time, the newspaper will carry a report of a person with a "photographic memory." Such people can apparently create unusually sharp and detailed visual images of something they have seen—a picture, a scene, a page of text. This phenomenon, called **eidetic imagery**, enables people to see the features of an image in minute detail, sometimes even to recite an entire page of a book they read only once.

One study screened 500 elementary schoolchildren before finding 20 with eidetic imagery (Haber, 1969). The children were told to scan a picture for 30 seconds, moving their eyes to see all its various parts. The picture was then removed, and the children were told to look at a blank easel and report what they saw in an eidetic image. They needed at least 3 to 5 seconds of scanning to produce an image, even when the picture was familiar. In addition, the quality of eidetic imagery seemed to vary from child to child. One girl in this study could move and reverse images and recall them several weeks later. Three children could produce eidetic images of three-dimensional objects; and some could superimpose an eidetic image of one picture onto another and form a new picture. However, the children with eidetic imagery performed no better than their noneidetic classmates on other tests of memory.

One of the most famous documented cases of extraordinary memory comes from the work of the distinguished psychologist Alexander Luria (Luria & Solotaroff, 1987). For over 20 years, Luria studied a Russian newspaper reporter named Shereshevskii ("S"). In *The Mind of a Mnemonist* (1968), Luria described how "S" could recall masses of senseless trivia as well as detailed mathematical formulas and complex arrays of numbers. He could easily repeat lists of up to 70 words or numbers after having heard or seen them only once.

"S" and other people with exceptional memories were not born with a special gift for remembering things. Rather, they have carefully developed memory techniques using certain principles. For example, Luria discovered that when "S" studied long lists of words, he would form a graphic image for every item. When reading a long and random list of words, for example, "S" might visualize a well-known street, specifically associating each word with some object along the way. When asked to recite the lists of words, he would take an imaginary walk down that street, recalling each object and the word associated with it. By organizing his data in a way that was meaningful to him, he could more easily link them to existing material in his long-term memory. In turn, this connection provided him with many more retrieval cues than he would have had for isolated, meaningless facts.

Developing an exceptional memory takes time and effort (Ericsson & Charness, 1994, Wilding & Valentine, 1997). **Mnemonists** (pronounced nee-MON-ists), people who are highly skilled at using memory techniques, frequently have compelling reasons for developing their memories. "S" used his memory skills to his advantage as a newspaper reporter. As we will see in the next chapter, chess masters also sometimes display astonishing recall of meaningful chessboard configurations (Bédard & Chi, 1992; Haberlandt, 1997). For example, some master chess players are able to recall the position of every single piece on the board after only a five-second exposure to a particular pattern. Yet when these same masters view a totally random and meaningless array of chess pieces, their recall is no better than yours or mine (Ericsson & Chase, 1982).

FLASHBULB MEMORIES

Are flashbulb memories always accurate?

"We were on the phone together when the first building fell, and the two of us were just screaming—oh my god, oh my god, oh my god."
"The images of the towers burning and crashing—and the most bizarre thing is that this woman who I went to her house, just had a baby. And the baby's crib was right next to the

---

eidetic imagery The ability to reproduce unusually sharp and detailed images of something one has seen.

mnemonists People with highly developed memory skills.

television. Just to see the devastation of what was happening in New York, and to see this baby completely innocent laying right next to the television and completely oblivious, asleep to the history that was happening, it was one of the most surreal moments I've ever lived through in my life."

"I don't want to see another image of the plane going into that building. I've seen it enough in my nightmares . . . ."

From PRI, Public Radio International, Gray Matters, Produced in Association with the Dana Alliance for Brain Initiatives. http://www.dana.org/books/radiotv/gm_1001.cfm

A **flashbulb memory** is the experience of remembering vividly a certain event and the incidents surrounding it even after a long time has passed. We often remember events that are shocking or otherwise highly significant in this way (P. S. R. Davidson & Glisky, 2002; Wooffitt, 2005). The death of a close relative, a birth, a graduation, or a wedding day may all elicit flashbulb memories. So can dramatic events in which we were not personally involved, such as the attacks on the World Trade Center and the Pentagon on September 11, 2001 (Edery & Nachson, 2004; Talarico & Rubin, 2003): 97% of Americans surveyed 1 year after the September 11 attacks claimed they could remember exactly where they were and what they were doing when they first heard about the attacks (Pew Research Center for the People and the Press, 2002).

Millions of people will forever have a vivid flashbulb memory of planes flying into the twin towers of the World Trade Center in New York City on September 11, 2001.

The assumptions that flashbulb memories are accurate, that they form at the time of an event, and that we remember them better because of their highly emotional content have all been questioned (Talarico & Rubin, 2003). First, flashbulb memories are certainly not always accurate. Although this is a difficult contention to test, let's consider just one case. Psychologist Ulric Neisser vividly recalled what he was doing on the day in 1941 when the Japanese bombed Pearl Harbor. He clearly remembered that he was listening to a professional baseball game on the radio, which was interrupted by the shocking announcement. But professional baseball is not played in December, when the attack took place, so this sharp flashbulb memory was simply incorrect (Neisser, 1982).

Even if an event is registered accurately, it may undergo periodic revision, just like other long-term memories (Schmolck, Buffalo, & Squire, 2000). We are bound to discuss and rethink a major event many times, and we probably also hear a great deal of additional information about that event in the weeks and months after it occurs. As a result, the flashbulb memory may undergo reconstruction and become less accurate over the years until it sometimes bears little or no resemblance to what actually happened.

EYEWITNESS TESTIMONY

How much can we trust eyewitness testimony?

I know what I saw! When an eyewitness to a crime gives evidence in court, that testimony often overwhelms evidence to the contrary. Faced with conflicting or ambiguous testimony, jurors tend to put their faith in people who saw an event with their own eyes. However, there is now compelling evidence that this faith in eyewitnesses is often misplaced (Brodsky, 1999; Wells & Olsen, 2003). Whereas eyewitness accounts are essential to courtroom testimony, studies clearly show that people who say, "I know what I saw," often don't know.

For more than 20 years, Elizabeth Loftus (1993; Loftus & Hoffman, 1989; Loftus & Pickrell, 1995) has been the most influential researcher into eyewitness memory. In a classic study, Loftus and Palmer (1974) showed experimental participants a film depicting a traffic accident. Some of the participants were asked, "About how fast were the cars going when they hit each other?" Other participants were asked the same question, but with the words *smashed into*, *collided with*, *bumped into*, or *contacted* in place of *hit*. The researchers discovered that people's reports of the cars' speed depended on which word was inserted in the question. Those asked about cars that "smashed into" each other reported that the cars were going faster than those who were asked about cars that "contacted" each other. In another experiment, the participants were also shown a film of a collision and then were asked either "How fast were the cars going when they hit each other?" or "How fast were the cars going when they smashed into each

flashbulb memory A vivid memory of a certain event and the incidents surrounding it even after a long time has passed.

other?" One week later, they were asked some additional questions about the accident that they had seen on film the week before. One of the questions was "Did you see any broken glass?" More of the participants who had been asked about cars that had "smashed into" each other reported that they had seen broken glass than did participants who had been asked the speed of cars that "hit" each other. These findings illustrate how police, lawyers, and other investigators may, often unconsciously, sway witnesses and influence subsequent eyewitness accounts. On the basis of experiments like these, Loftus and Palmer concluded that eyewitness testimony is unreliable.

Why do eyewitnesses make mistakes? Some research suggests that the problem may be *source error*: People are sometimes unable to tell the difference between what they witnessed and what they merely heard about or imagined (Garry & Polaschek, 2000; Hekkanen & McEvoy, 2005; Reyna & Titcomb, 1997; S. E. Taylor, Pham, Rivkin, & Armor, 1998). This is especially true for young children (T. F. Shapiro, 2002; K. L. Thierry & Spence, 2002). We all know what it is like to imagine an event in a particularly vivid way and then later to have difficulty remembering whether the event really happened or we simply imagined it. Indeed, studies have shown that imagining an event sometimes makes people believe it actually happened (Garry & Polaschek, 2000; Henkel, Franklin, & Johnson, 2000; Mazzoni & Memon, 2003). Similarly, if you hear information about an event you witnessed, you might later confuse your memory of that information with your memory of the original event. For instance, studies have shown that if an eyewitness receives confirming feedback after picking a suspect out of a police lineup, the feedback often increases the reported *certainty* of their recognition (Neuschatz et al., 2005; Wells & Bradfield, 1999). Other studies have shown that simply describing the perpetrator shortly after the incident occurs actually interferes with memories of what the person actually looked like, thus making it more difficult for the eyewitness to pick the correct person out of a lineup at a later date (B. Bower, 2003a; Fiore & Schooler, 2002).

Even more disturbing, positive feedback following a lineup has been shown to change subsequent statements by witnesses with regard to "how good their view was" or "how much attention they paid to the crime" (Neuschatz et al., 2005; Wells & Bradfield, 1998, 1999). The impact of subsequent information seems to be particularly strong when it is repeated several times (Zaragoza & Mitchell, 1996), as is often the case with extensive media coverage, or when it comes from an authority figure such as a police officer (Roper & Shewan, 2002). On the basis of this research, many psychologists (Hekkanen & McEvoy, 2005; Zaragoza, Lane, Ackil, & Chambers, 1997) contend that if people paid more attention to the source of their memories, eyewitness accounts would be more reliable.

Whatever the reason for eyewitness errors, there is good evidence that such mistakes can send innocent people to jail (Kassin, Tubb, Hosch, & Memon, 2001). For example, based almost entirely on the eyewitness identification testimony of a single individual, Steven Avery was convicted of brutally attacking, raping, and nearly killing a woman in 1985 and was sentenced to 32 years in prison. Although Avery offered alibis from 14 witnesses and documentation showing he wasn't at the scene of the crime, it took repeated legal challenges and new advances in DNA testing for him to overcome the conviction. Finally, on September 11, 2003, Mr. Avery was exonerated of all charges and released from prison. Increasingly, courts are recognizing the limits of eyewitness testimony (Kassin et al., 2001). For example, judges instruct juries to be skeptical about eyewitness testimony and to evaluate it critically. But we still have a long way to go as shown in the "Thinking Critically" box.

RECOVERED MEMORIES

Can people be persuaded to "create" new memories about events that never occurred?

In recent years, a controversy has raged, both within the academic community and in society at large, about the validity of *recovered memories* (Cerri, 2005; Gerkens, 2005; McNally, 2003a, 2003b). The idea is that people experience an event, then lose all memory of it, and then later recall it, often in the course of psychotherapy or under hypnosis. Frequently, the recovered memories concern physical or sexual abuse during childhood. The issue is important not only for theoretical reasons, but also because of the fact that people have been imprisoned for abuse solely on the basis of the recovered memories of their "victims." No one denies the reality of childhood abuse or the damage that such experiences cause. But are the recovered memories real? Did the remembered abuse really occur?

The answer is by no means obvious. There is ample evidence that people can be induced to "remember" events that never happened (S. M. Smith et al, 2003). For example, when Loftus and her colleagues told people that relatives had mentioned an event in their lives, a fourth of the participants "remembered" the events even though they had never actually happened (Loftus, Coan, & Pickrell, 1996; Loftus & Pickrell, 1995). And as we have seen, simply imagining that something happened can increase the likelihood that people will "remember" that the event actually happened (Garry & Polaschek, 2000; Mazzoni & Memon, 2003). Other research confirms that it is relatively easy to implant memories of an experience merely by asking about it. The more times that people are asked about the event, the more likely they are to "remember" it. Sometimes these memories become quite real to the participant. In one experiment, 25% of adults "remembered" fictitious events by the third time they were interviewed about them. One of the fictitious events involved knocking over a punch bowl onto the parents of the bride

THINKING CRITICALLY ABOUT...

Eyewitness Testimony

T. R. Benton, Ross, Bradshaw, Thomas, & Bradshaw (2006) studied 111 jurors drawn from a jury pool in Hamilton County, Tennessee. Using a questionnaire with 30 statements about eyewitness testimony (Kassin et al., 2001), they found that jurors significantly disagreed with eyewitness experts on more than 85% of the items. For example, 98% of the experts agreed that "Police instructions can affect an eyewitness's willingness to make an identification" but only 41% of the jurors agreed. 81% of the experts agreed that "Eyewitnesses sometimes identify as a culprit someone they have seen in another situation or context;" only 30% of the jurors agreed. And 91% of the experts agreed that "Hypnosis increases suggestibility to leading and misleading questions," only 24% of the jurors agreed with that statement. The authors concluded that jurors "exhibit important limitations in their knowledge of eyewitness issues; their knowledge diverges significantly from expert opinion, and it is not high in overall accuracy" (p. 126).

1. What questions might you raise about the authors' conclusion? For example, do you think that their sample of jurors is representative of jurors throughout the United States? If so, why do you think so? If not, in what ways do you think it differed significantly and how do you think that might have affected their results?

2. The authors note that "... it is not surprising to find numerous and varied reasons offered by courts across the country for excluding testimony from eyewitness experts. One of the most commonly cited reasons is that eyewitness memory is common sense to jurors, and thus an eyewitness expert is simply not necessary."

3. Do you agree that testimony from eyewitness experts "is simply not necessary"? Why or why not? Are there some circumstances when such testimony might be more valuable than others? How might you go about determining whether, in fact, expert testimony is valuable at least sometimes?

at a wedding reception. At the first interview, one participant said that she had no recollection whatsoever of the event; by the second interview, she "remembered" that the reception was outdoors and that she had knocked over the bowl while running around. Some people even "remembered" details about the event, such as what people looked like and what they wore. Yet, the researchers documented that these events never happened (Hyman, Husband, & Billings, 1995). Other research shows that people can even become convinced that they remember experiences from infancy that never happened (Spanos, 1996; Spanos, Burgess, Burgess, Samuels, & Blois, 1997).

The implication of this and similar research is that it is quite possible for people to "remember" abusive experiences that never happened. And some people who have "recovered" abuse memories have later realized that the events never occurred. Some of these people have brought suit against the therapists who, they came to believe, implanted the memories. In one case, a woman won such a suit and was awarded $850,000 (Imrie, 1999).

However, there is reason to believe that not all recovered memories are merely the products of suggestion. There are numerous case studies of people who have lived through traumatic experiences, including natural disasters, accidents, combat, assault, and rape, who then apparently forgot these events for many years, but who later remembered them (Arrigo & Pezdek, 1997). For example, Wilbur J. Scott, a sociologist, claimed to remember nothing of his tour of duty in Vietnam during 1968–1969, but during a divorce in 1983, he discovered his medals and souvenirs from Vietnam, and the memories then came back to him (Arrigo & Pezdek, 1997).

What is needed is a reliable way of separating real memories from false ones, but so far no such test is available (Gleaves, Smith, Butler, & Spiegel, 2004). The sincerity and conviction of the person who "remembers" long-forgotten childhood abuse is no indication of the reality of that abuse. We are left with the conclusion that recovered memories are not, in themselves, sufficiently trustworthy to justify criminal convictions. There must also be corroborative evidence, since without corroboration, there is no way that even the most experienced examiner can separate real memories from false ones (Loftus, 1997).

CHECK YOUR UNDERSTANDING

Is each of the following statements true (T) or false (F)?

1. Retrograde amnesia is the phenomenon that we seldom remember events that occurred before our second birthday.

2. A long-lasting and vivid memory for a certain event and the incidents surrounding it is called a flashbulb memory.

3. Research demonstrates that it is nearly impossible to change a person's memory once that memory has been stored.

Answers: 1. (F), 2. (T), 3. (F).

APPLY YOUR UNDERSTANDING

1. You are talking with someone from a different culture who is not very good at remembering long lists of random words or numbers, but who can recite from memory all of his ancestors going back hundreds of years. What is the most likely explanation for this difference in memory skills?

   a. The values and customs of a given culture have a profound effect on what people remember.

   b. The person's autobiographical memory is stronger than his semantic memory.

   c. The list of his ancestors has been stored in flashbulb memory.

   d. The list of his ancestors is an example of a "recovered memory."

2. Your mother is reminiscing about your first birthday party and asks you, "Do you remember when Aunt Mary dropped her piece of cake in your lap?" Try as you might, you can't recall that incident. This is most likely an example of

   a. memory decay.

   b. retrograde amnesia.

   c. infantile amnesia.

   d. proactive interference.

Answers: 1. a. 2. c.

KEY TERMS

CHAPTER REVIEW

The Sensory Registers

What is the role of sensory registers? Many psychologists view **memory** as a series of steps in which we encode, store, and retrieve information, much as a computer does. This is called the **information-processing** model of memory. The first step in the model is inputting data through our senses into temporary holding bins, called **sensory registers**. These registers give us a brief moment to decide whether something deserves our attention.

What would happen if auditory information faded as quickly as visual information fades? Information entering a sensory register disappears very quickly if it isn't processed further. Information in the visual register lasts for only about a quarter of a second before it is replaced by new information. If sounds faded from our auditory register as rapidly as this, spoken language would be more difficult to understand. Luckily, information in the auditory register can linger for several seconds.

Why does some information capture our attention, while other information goes unnoticed? The next step in the memory process is **attention**—selectively looking at, listening to, smelling, tasting, or feeling what we deem to be important. The nervous system seems automatically to filter out peripheral information, allowing us to zero in on what is essential at a particular time. Unattended information receives at least some processing, however, so that we can quickly shift attention to it if it suddenly strikes us as significant.

Short-Term Memory

What are the two primary tasks of short-term memory? How much information can be held in short-term memory? **Short-term memory** (STM), also called *working memory*, holds whatever information we are actively attending to at any given time. Its two primary tasks are to store new information briefly and to "work" on information that we currently have in mind. We can process more information in STM by grouping it into larger meaningful units, a process called **chunking**.

Do we store material in short-term memory as it sounds or as it looks? Information can be stored in STM according to the way it sounds, the way it looks, or its meaning. Verbal information is encoded by sound, even if it is written rather than heard. The capacity for visual encoding in STM is greater than for encoding by sound.

How can we hold information in STM? Through **rote rehearsal**, or maintenance rehearsal, we retain information in STM for a minute or two by repeating it over and over again. However, rote memorization does not promote long-term memory.

Long-Term Memory

What types of information are retained in long-term memory? **Long-term memory** (LTM) stores everything we learn.

What is the limit of LTM? Long-term memory can store a vast amount of information for many years.

How are most memories encoded in LTM? Most of the information in LTM seems to be encoded according to its meaning.

Which items in a list are hardest to remember? Short- and long-term memory work together to explain the **serial position effect**, in which people tend to recall the first and last items in a list better than items in the middle. The *recency effect* explains that items at the end are still held in STM, whereas the *primacy effect* describes the extra LTM rehearsal given to items early in the list.

What three processes are used to hold information in LTM? The way in which we encode material for storage in LTM affects the ease with which we can retrieve it later on. Rote rehearsal is particularly useful for holding conceptually meaningless material, such as phone numbers, in LTM. Through the deeper and more meaningful mechanism of **elaborative rehearsal**, we extract the meaning of information and link it to as much material as possible that is already in LTM. Memory techniques such as **mnemonics** rely on elaborative processing.

A **schema** is a mental representation of an object or event that is stored in memory. Schemata provide a framework into which incoming information is fitted. They may prompt the formation of stereotypes and the drawing of inferences.

How do types of LTM differ? Episodic memories are personal memories for events experienced in a specific time and place. **Semantic memories** are facts and concepts not linked to a particular time. **Procedural memories** are motor skills and habits. **Emotional memories** are learned emotional responses to various stimuli.

What are the differences between implicit and explicit memories? Explicit memory refers to memories we are aware of, including episodic and semantic memories. **Implicit memory** refers to memories for information that either was not intentionally committed to LTM or is retrieved unintentionally from LTM, including procedural and emotional memories. This distinction is illustrated by research on *priming*, in which people are more likely to complete fragments of stimuli with items seen earlier than with other, equally plausible items.

The Biology of Memory

What role do neurons play in memory? Memories consist of changes in the chemistry and structure of neurons. The process by which these changes occur is called **long-term potentiation (LTP)**.

Are STM and LTM found in the same parts of the brain? Different parts of the brain are specialized for the storage of memories. Short-term memories seem to be located primarily in the prefrontal cortex and temporal lobe. Long-term memories seem to involve both subcortical and cortical structures. Semantic and episodic memories seem to be located primarily in the frontal and temporal lobes of the cortex, and procedural memories appear to be located primarily in the cerebellum and motor cortex. The hippocampus seems especially important in the formation of semantic, episodic, and procedural memories. Emotional memories are dependent on the amygdala.

Forgetting

What factors explain why we sometimes forget? Both biological and experiential factors can contribute to our inability to recall information.

How does the deterioration of the brain help to explain forgetting? According to the **decay theory**, memories deteriorate because of the passage of time. Severe memory loss can be traced to brain damage caused by accidents, surgery, poor diet, or disease. Head injuries can cause **retrograde amnesia**, the inability of people to remember what happened shortly before their accident. The hippocampus may have a role in long-term memory formation. Below-normal levels of the neurotransmitter acetylcholine may be implicated in memory loss seen in Alzheimer's disease.

What environmental factors contribute to our inability to remember? To the extent that information is apparently lost from LTM, researchers attribute the cause to inadequate learning or to interference from competing information. Interference may come from two directions: In **retroactive interference**, new information interferes with old information already in LTM; **proactive interference** refers to the process by which old information already in LTM interferes with new information.

When environmental cues present during learning are absent during recall, context-dependent forgetting may occur. The ability to recall information is also affected by one's physiological state when the material was learned; this process is known *as state-dependent memory.*

Sometimes we "reconstruct" memories for social or personal self-defense. Research on long-term memory and on forgetting offers ideas for a number of steps that can be taken to improve recall.

Special Topics in Memory

What factors can influence how well you remember a specific incident? Cultural values and customs profoundly affect what people remember and how easily they recall it. So do the emotions we attach to a memory, with some emotion-laden events being remembered for life. Also affecting how well we remember are the strategies we use to store and retrieve information.

Are the memory tasks in Western schools different from those in cultures that pass on traditions orally? Many Western schools stress being able to recall long lists of words, facts, and figures that are divorced from everyday life. In contrast, societies in which cultural information is passed on through a rich oral tradition may instead emphasize memory for events that directly affect people's lives.

What kinds of events are most likely to be remembered? *Autobiographical memory* refers to recollection of events from one's life. Not all of these events are recalled with equal clarity, of course, and some are not recalled at all. Autobiographical memories are typically strongest for events that had a major impact on our lives or that aroused strong emotion.

Why do we have so few memories from the first 2 years of life? People generally cannot remember events that occurred before age 2, a phenomenon called **childhood amnesia**. Childhood amnesia may result from the incomplete development of brain structures before age 2, from the infants' lack of a clear sense of self, or from the lack of language skills used to consolidate early experience. Research also suggests it may be related to an adult's inability to recall memories that were, in fact, stored during the first two years.

What is a photographic memory? People with exceptional memories have carefully developed memory techniques. **Mnemonists** are individuals who are highly skilled at using those techniques. A phenomenon called **eidetic imagery** enables some people to see features of an image in minute detail.

Are flashbulb memories always accurate? Years after a dramatic or significant event occurs, people often report having vivid memories of that event as well as the incidents surrounding it. These memories are known as **flashbulb memories**. Recent research has challenged the assumptions that flashbulb memories are accurate and stable.

How much can we trust eyewitness testimony? Jurors tend to put their faith in witnesses who saw an event with their own eyes. However, some evidence suggests that eyewitnesses sometimes are unable to tell the difference between what they witnessed and what they merely heard about or imagined.

Can people be persuaded to "create" new memories about events that never occurred? There are many cases of people who experience a traumatic event, lose all memory of it, but then later recall it. Such recovered memories are highly controversial, since research shows that people can be induced to "remember" events that never happened. So far there is no clear way to distinguish real recovered memories from false ones.

7 Cognition and Mental Abilities

OVERVIEW

"At the Braefield School for the Deaf, I met Joseph, a boy of 11 who had just entered school for the first time—an 11-year-old with no language whatever. He had been born deaf, but this had not been realized until he was in his fourth year. His failure to talk, or understand speech, at the normal age was put down to 'retardation,' then to 'autism,' and these diagnoses had clung to him. When his deafness finally became apparent he was seen as 'deaf and dumb,' dumb not only literally, but metaphorically, and there was never any attempt to teach him language.

"Joseph longed to communicate, but could not. Neither speaking nor writing nor signing was available to him, only gestures and pantomimes, and a marked ability to draw. What has happened to him? I kept asking myself. What is going on inside, how has he come to such a pass? He looked alive and animated, but profoundly baffled: His eyes were attracted to speaking mouths and signing hands—they darted to our mouths and hands, inquisitively, uncomprehendingly, and, it seemed to me, yearningly. He perceived that something was 'going on' between us, but he could not comprehend what it was—he had, as yet, almost no idea of symbolic communication, of what it was to have a symbolic currency, to exchange meaning. . . .

"Joseph was unable, for example, to communicate how he had spent the weekend. . . . It was not only language that was missing: there was not, it was evident, a clear sense of the past,

of 'a day ago' as distinct from 'a year ago.' There was a strange lack of historical sense, the feeling of a life that lacked autobiographical and historical dimension, . . . a life that only existed in the moment, in the present. . . .

"Joseph saw, distinguished, categorized, used; he had no problems with perceptual categorization or generalization, but he could not, it seemed, go much beyond this, hold abstract ideas in mind, reflect, play, plan. He seemed completely literal—unable to juggle images or hypotheses or possibilities, unable to enter an imaginative or figurative realm. And yet, one still felt, he was of normal intelligence, despite the manifest limitations of intellectual functioning. It was not that he lacked a mind, but that he was not using his mind fully. . . . " (Sacks, 2000, pp. 32–34)

As Sacks suggests, language and thought are intertwined. We find it difficult to imagine one without the other, and we consider both part of what it means to be human. Psychologists use the term **cognition** to refer to all the processes that we use to acquire and apply information. We have already considered the cognitive processes of perception, learning, and memory. In later chapters, we examine cognition's crucial relation to coping and adjustment, abnormal behavior, and interpersonal relations. In this chapter, we focus on three cognitive processes that we think of as characteristically human: thinking, problem solving, and decision making. We also discuss two mental abilities that psychologists have tried to measure: intelligence and creativity.

ENDURING ISSUES IN COGNITION AND MENTAL ABILITIES ••

The "Enduring Issues" in this chapter are highlighted in four prominent places. We will encounter the diversity–universality theme when we explore the differences and similarities in the way people process information and again when we discuss exceptional abilities. We make two additional references to the enduring issues as we discuss the stability–change of intelligence test scores over time and again when we explore how measures of intelligence and performance sometimes vary as a function of expectations and situations (person–situation).

Building Blocks of Thought

What are the three most important building blocks of thought?

When you think about a close friend, you may have in mind complex statements about her, such as "I'd like to talk to her soon" or "I wish I could be more like her." You may also have an image of her—probably her face, but perhaps the sound of her voice as well. Or you may think of your friend by using various concepts or categories such as *woman, kind, strong, dynamic,* and *gentle*. When we think, we make use of all these things—language, images, and concepts—often simultaneously. These are the three most important building blocks of thought.

cognition The processes whereby we acquire and use knowledge.

LANGUAGE

What steps do we go through to turn a thought into a statement?

Human **language** is a flexible system of symbols that enables us to communicate our ideas, thoughts, and feelings. Joseph, the deaf boy described at the beginning of this chapter, had great difficulty communicating because he knew no languages. Language is a unique human ability that sets us apart from other animals (MacWhinney, 2005). Although all animals communicate with each other, human language is a far more complex system. Chimpanzees—our closest relatives in the animal kingdom—use some three dozen different vocalizations plus an array of gestures, postures, and facial expressions to communicate, a system that is far simpler than the speech of a normal 3-year-old child.

One way to understand the uniquely human system of language is to consider its basic structure. Spoken language is based on units of sound called **phonemes**. The sounds of *t*, *th*, and *k*, for instance, are all phonemes in English. There are about 45 phonemes in the English language and as many as 85 in some other languages. By themselves, phonemes are meaningless and seldom play an important role in helping us to think. The sound *b*, for example, has no inherent meaning. But phonemes can be grouped together to form words, prefixes (such as *un-* and *pre-*), and suffixes (such as *-ed* and *-ing*). These meaningful combinations of phonemes are known as **morphemes**—the smallest meaningful units in a language. Morphemes play a key role in human thought. They can represent important ideas such as "red" or "calm" or "hot." The suffix *-ed* captures the idea of "in the past" (as in *visited* or *liked*). The prefix *pre-* conveys the idea of "before" or "prior to" (as in *preview* or *predetermined*).

We can combine morphemes to create words that represent quite complex ideas, such as *pre-exist-ing, un-excell-ed, psycho-logy*. In turn, words can be joined into even more complex thoughts. Just as there are rules for combining phonemes and morphemes, there are also rules for structuring sentences and their meaning. These rules are what linguists call **grammar**. The two major components of grammar are *syntax* and *semantics*. *Syntax* is the system of rules that governs how we combine words to form meaningful phrases and sentences. For example, in English and many other languages, the meaning of a sentence is often determined by word order. "Sally hit the car" means one thing; "The car hit Sally" means something quite different; and "Hit Sally car the" is meaningless.

Semantics describes how we assign meaning to morphemes, words, phrases, and sentences—in other words, the content of language. When we are thinking about something—say, the ocean—our ideas usually consist of phrases and sentences, such as "The ocean is unusually calm tonight." Sentences have both a *surface structure*—the particular words and phrases—and a *deep structure*—the underlying meaning. The same deep structure can be conveyed by different surface structures:

> The ocean is unusually calm tonight.
> Tonight the ocean is particularly calm.
> Compared with most other nights, tonight the ocean is calm.

Alternatively, the same surface structure can convey different meanings or deep structures, but a knowledge of language permits one to know what is meant within a given context:

Surface Structure	Might mean... Or...
Flying planes can be dangerous.	An airborne plane... The Profession of pilot...
Visiting relatives can be a nuisance.	Relatives who are visiting... The obligation to visit relatives...
The chicken is ready to eat.	Food has been cooked sufficiently... The Bird is hungry...

Syntax and semantics enable speakers and listeners to perform what linguist Noam Chomsky calls *transformations* between the surface structure and the deep structure. According to Chomsky (1957; Chomsky, Place, & Schoneberger, 2000), when you want to communicate an idea, you start with a thought, then choose words and phrases that will express the idea,

---

language A flexible system of communication that uses sounds, rules, gestures, or symbols to convey information.

phonemes The basic sounds that make up any language.

morphemes The smallest meaningful units of speech, such as simple words, prefixes, and suffixes.

grammar The language rules that determine how sounds and words can be combined and used to communicate meaning within a language.

and finally, produce the speech sounds that make up those words and phrases, as shown by the left arrow in **Figure 7–1**. When you want to understand a sentence, your task is reversed. You must start with speech sounds and work your way up to the meaning of those sounds, as represented by the right arrow in **Figure 7–1**.

IMAGES

What role do images play in thinking?

Think for a moment about Abraham Lincoln. Now imagine being outside in a summer thunderstorm. Your thoughts of Lincoln may have included such phrases as "wrote the Gettysburg Address," "president during the Civil War," and "assassinated by John Wilkes Booth." You probably also had some mental images about him: bearded face, lanky body, or log cabin. When you thought about the thunderstorm, you probably formed mental images of wind, rain, and lightning—perhaps even the smell of wet leaves and earth. An **image** is a mental representation of some sensory experience; and it can be used to think about things. We can visualize the Statue of Liberty; we can smell Thanksgiving dinner or the scent of a Christmas tree; we can hear Martin Luther King, Jr., saying, "I have a dream!" In short, we can think by using images.

Images allow us to think about things in nonverbal ways. Albert Einstein relied heavily on his powers of visualization to understand phenomena he would later describe by using complex mathematical formulas. This great thinker believed his extraordinary genius resulted in part from his skill in visualizing possibilities (Kosslyn, 2002). Like Einstein, we all use images to think about and solve problems. We have all seen an instructor clarifying a difficult concept by drawing a simple sketch on a chalkboard. Many times, when words make a tangled knot of an issue, a graphic image straightens out the confusion. Images also allow us to use concrete forms to represent complex and abstract ideas, as when newspapers use pie charts and graphs to illustrate how people voted in an election (Yang, Chen, & Hong, 2003; Stylianou, 2002).

Experiments using the brain-imaging techniques described in Chapter 2 have shown that we often use the same brain centers for thinking about images as we do for visual perception (Kreiman, Koch, & Freid, 2000). This research supports the idea that we do not simply remember images; rather, we also think pictorially.

CONCEPTS

How do concepts help us to think more efficiently?

Concepts are mental categories for classifying specific people, things, or events. *Dogs, books,* and *mountains* are concepts for classifying things, whereas *fast, beautiful,* and *interesting* can classify things, events, or people. When you think about a specific thing—say, Mt. Everest—you usually think of the concepts that apply to it, such as *highest* and *dangerous to climb.* Concepts can also be used to create and organize hierarchies or groups of subordinate categories. For example, the general concept of *plants* can be broken down into the subordinate categories of *trees, bushes,* and *grasses,* just as the subordinate concept of *trees* can be further subdivided into *oaks, maples,* and *pines* (Reed, 2003). If we could not form concepts, we would need a different name for every object. Thus, concepts help us to think efficiently about things and how they relate to one another.

Concepts also give meaning to new experiences. We do not stop and form a new concept for every new experience that we have. Instead, we draw upon existing concepts and place the new event into the appropriate category. As we do so, we may modify some of our concepts to

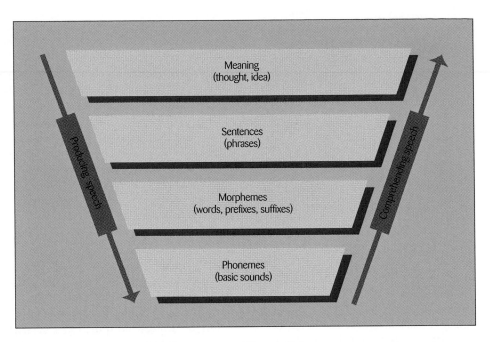

Figure 7–1

The direction of movement in speech production and comprehension.
Producing a sentence involves movement from thoughts and ideas to basic sounds; comprehending a sentence requires movement from basic sounds back to the underlying thoughts and ideas.

"Well, you don't look like an experimental psychologist to me."

Source: © *The New Yorker Collection,* 1994. Sam Gross from *www.cartoonbank.com.* All Rights Reserved.

image A mental representation of a sensory experience.

concepts Mental categories for classifying objects, people, or experiences.

Pablo Picasso, the great 20th-century artist, developed a style of painting known as Cubism. In paintings such as *Nude with Bunch of Irises and Mirror*, 1934, shown here, he re-formed objects into basic geometric shapes. We recognize the figure in this painting as a woman because its shapes represent the "concept" of a female.

better match our experiences. Consider a job interview. You probably have some concept of this process even before your first interview, but your concept will probably change somewhat after it. Once you have formed a concept of *job interview*, you will not have to respond to each interview as a totally new experience; you will know what to expect and how you are expected to behave. Conceptualizing thus is a way of organizing experiences.

Although it is tempting to think of concepts as simple and clear-cut, most of the concepts that we use are rather "fuzzy": They overlap one another and are often poorly defined. For example, most people can tell a mouse from a rat, but listing the critical differences between the two would be difficult (Rosch, 1973, 2002).

If we cannot explain the difference between mouse and rat, how can we use these *fuzzy concepts* in our thinking? We may construct a model, or **prototype (or model)**, of a representative mouse and one of a representative rat, and then use those prototypes in our thinking (Rosch, 1978, 1998, 2002). Our concept of bird, for example, does not consist of a list of a bird's key attributes, like *feathered, winged, two-footed*, and *lives in trees*. Instead, most of us have a model bird, or prototype, in mind—such as a robin or a sparrow—that captures for us the essence of *bird*. When we encounter new objects, we compare them with this prototype to determine whether they are, in fact, birds. And when we think about birds, we usually think about our prototypical bird.

Concepts, then, like words and images, help us to formulate thoughts. But human cognition involves more than just passively thinking about things. It also involves actively using words, images, and concepts to fashion an understanding of the world, to solve problems, and to make decisions. In the next three sections, we see how this is done.

CHECK YOUR UNDERSTANDING

1. _____, _____, and _____ are the three most important building blocks of thought.

2. In language, units of sound, called _____, are combined to form the smallest units of meaning, called _____. These smallest meaningful units can then be combined to create words, which in turn can be used to build phrases and whole _____.

3. Language rules that specify how sounds and words can be combined into meaningful sentences are called rules of _____.

4. Indicate whether the following statements are true (T) or false (F).

   a. ____ Images help us to think about things because images use concrete forms to represent complex ideas.

   b. ____ People decide which objects belong to a concept by comparing the object's features to a model or prototype of the concept.

   c. ____ Concepts help us give meaning to new experiences.

Answers: 1. language, images, concepts. 2. phonemes, morphemes, sentences. 3. grammar. 4. a. (T); b. (T); c. (T).

APPLY YOUR UNDERSTANDING

1. "I will spend tonight studying." "Tonight I will be studying." These two sentences exhibit the same

   a. surface structure.

   b. syntax.

   c. phonology.

   d. deep structure.

2. Harry cannot list the essential differences between dogs and cats, but he has no trouble thinking about dogs and cats. This is most likely due to the fact that he

   a. has a prototype of a representative dog and another of a representative cat.

   b. has developed a morpheme for a dog and another morpheme for a cat.

   c. is exhibiting functional fixedness.

   d. is using heuristics.

Answers: 1. d. 2. a.

prototype (or model) According to Rosch, a mental model containing the most typical features of a concept.

Language, Thought, and Culture

How do language, thought, and culture influence each other?

ENDURING ISSUES

Diversity–Universality Do We All Think Alike?

For at least 100 years, psychologists and philosophers assumed the basic processes of human cognition are universal. They accepted that cultural differences affect thought—thus Masai elders in the Serengeti count their wealth in heads of cattle, whereas Wall Street bankers measure theirs in stocks and bonds. But habits of thought—the ways people process information—were assumed to be the same everywhere. The tendency to categorize objects and experiences, the ability to reason logically, and the desire to understand situations in terms of cause and effect were thought to be part of human nature, regardless of cultural setting (Goode, 2000a). In this section, we will examine the validity of these viewpoints. ●●

Do people from different cultures perceive and think about the world in different ways? A series of controlled experiments suggests they do. In one experiment (Nisbett, Peng, Choi, & Norenzayan, 2001), American and Japanese students were shown an underwater scene and asked to describe what they saw. Most Japanese participants described the scene as a whole, beginning with the background; by contrast, most American participants described the biggest, brightest, fastest fish. (In psychological terms, the Japanese were "field dependent" and the Americans, "field independent"; see Chapter 3, "Sensation and Perception"). Other experiments revealed a similar difference in attitude regarding contexts with respect to social perceptions, as well as differing styles of reasoning.

Nisbett and his colleagues concluded these studies reflect fundamental, qualitative differences in how Easterners and Westerners perceive and think about the world. They also emphasized that the origin of these differences is cultural rather than genetic, because the cognitive approach of U.S.-born Asian Americans is indistinguishable from that of European Americans (Peng & Nisbett, 1999; Nisbett et al., 2001; Nisbett & Norenzayan, 2002).

Language, too, is closely tied to the expression and understanding of thoughts. Words—such as *friend*, *family*, *airplane*, and *love*—correspond to concepts. By combining words into sentences, we can link concepts and express complex ideas. Joseph, described at the beginning of this chapter, was judged as mentally retarded because he could not express his thoughts in language.

Can language also influence how we think and what we can think about? Benjamin Whorf (1956) strongly believed that it does. According to Whorf's **linguistic relativity hypothesis**, the language we speak determines the pattern of our thinking and our view of the world—a position known more generally as **linguistic determinism**. For Whorf, if a language lacks a particular expression, the corresponding thought will probably not occur to speakers of that language. For example, the Hopi of the southwestern United States have only two nouns for things that fly. One noun refers to birds; the other is used for everything else. A plane and a dragonfly, for instance, are both referred to with the same noun. According to Whorf, Hopi speakers would not see as great a difference between planes and dragonflies as we do, because their language labels the two similarly.

The linguistic relativity hypothesis has intuitive appeal—it makes sense to think that limits of language will produce limits in thinking. However, researchers have found several flaws in Whorf's theory. For example, the Dani of New Guinea have only two words for colors—dark and light—yet they see and can easily learn to label other basic colors like red, yellow, and green. They also judge the similarity of colors much as English-speaking people do (E. R. Heider & Oliver, 1972). Thus, the ability to think about colors is quite similar across cultures, even when these cultures have quite different color terms in their languages (Roberson, Davies, & Jules, 2000; P. E. Ross, 2004). Language may indeed influence

linguistic relativity hypothesis Whorf's idea that patterns of thinking are determined by the specific language one speaks.

linguistic determinism The belief that thought and experience are determined by language.

The Dani of New Guinea can perceive and remember the many colors of their world just as readily as you can, even though their language has only two color terms—*light* and *dark*. Human thought is not limited to the words in a person's language. Language may indeed influence thought, but it doesn't seem to restrict thought to the extent that Whorf believed.

thought, but it doesn't seem to restrict thought to the extent that some linguistic determinists believed.

Moreover, experience and thought actually influence language. For example, English-speaking skiers, realizing that different textures of snow can affect their downhill run, refer to snow as *powder, corn*, and *ice*. The growth of personal computers and the Internet has inspired a vocabulary of its own, such as *RAM*, *gigabyte*, *online*, *CPU*, and *blogs*. In short, people create new words when they need them. If the Hopi had been subjected to air raids, they probably would have created words to distinguish a butterfly from a bomber!

Psychologists have not dismissed the Whorf hypothesis altogether, but rather have softened it, recognizing that language, thought, and culture are intertwined (Giovanni, 2003; Matsumoto, 1996). In short, people create words to capture important aspects of their experiences; and to some extent, words shape how people think and what they think about. But people also can think about things for which they have no words. Experience shapes language; and language, in turn, affects subsequent experience. This realization has caused us to examine our use of language more carefully, as we will see in the next section.

IS LANGUAGE MALE DOMINATED?

Does language contribute to gender stereotyping?

The English language has traditionally used masculine terms such as *man* and *he* to refer to all people—female as well as male. Several studies suggest that this affects the way English speakers think. Hyde (1984) discovered that the use of "he" or "she" to describe a factory worker who made "wudges" (imaginary plastic parts for video games) affected how children assessed the performance of male and female workers. Children who heard wudgemakers described by the masculine pronoun "he" rated female wudgemakers poorly; those who heard wudgemakers identified by the pronoun "she" judged female wudgemakers most positively; and the ratings of children who heard gender-neutral descriptions of wudgemakers fell in between those of the two other groups. All the groups of children, however, viewed male wudgemakers equally positively.

More recent research has focused on the unconscious, automatic nature of gender stereotyping and language (Palomares, 2004: Parks & Roberton, 2004). In an experiment requiring men and women to respond rapidly to gender-neutral and gender-specific pronouns, both sexes responded more quickly to stimuli containing traditional gender stereotypes (e.g., nurse/she) than to stimuli containing nontraditional ones (e.g., nurse/he). This occurred even among participants who were explicitly opposed to gender stereotyping (Banaji & Hardin, 1996).

Therefore, it appears that referring to doctors, college professors, bankers, and executives by the generic "he" contributes to the gender stereotyping of these respected occupations as appropriate for men but not for women. In contrast, referring to secretaries and housekeepers as "she" reinforces the stereotype that those occupations are appropriate for women but not for men (Christie, 2003).

As we have seen, language, cognition, and culture are interrelated in a complex fashion, each contributing to how people, communicate, think, and behave. Although human language is far more complex and flexible than the communication observed in other species, other animals obviously do communicate with one another. This observation has prompted some psychologists to explore the nature of communication and cognition in nonhuman animals, a topic to which we will now turn.

CHECK YOUR UNDERSTANDING

1. According to Whorf's _____ _____ hypothesis, the language we speak shapes our thinking.

2. Indicate whether the following statements are true (T) or false (F).

   a. ___ Many words in our language correspond to concepts.

   b. ___ Experience shapes language.

   c. ___ Thoughts are limited to the words in the language that a person speaks.

Answers: 1. linguistic relativity. 2. a. (T); b. (T); c. (F).

APPLY YOUR UNDERSTANDING

1. Cross-cultural studies indicate that people from different cultures with very different languages nonetheless perceive and are able to think about such things as colors in very similar ways even if their language contains no words for these things. These data _____ Whorf's theory.

   a. support

   b. contradict

   c. neither support nor contradict

Answer: 1. b.

Nonhuman Thought and Language

Can scientists learn what is on an animal's mind?

Can animals think? Pet owners almost certainly will answer yes—and regale you with stories about a cat who jumped out of a car miles from home yet found the way back, a dog that saved its owner's life, and other amazing feats. From someone who does not own or like pets, however, you may well get a sarcastic reply such as, "Does a bullfrog have wings?" Ask a psychologist, and the most likely response will be a thoughtful pause, and then, "That's a difficult question."

In evaluating research on nonhuman animals, scientists seek to avoid *anthropomorphism*—the attribution of human characteristics to nonhuman animals (Wynne, 2004)—and *anthropocentrism*—the viewing of our own species as unique (G. Myers, 2002). Psychologists have only recently developed scientific techniques for learning how other animals use their brains and for identifying the similarities and differences between human and nonhuman thought (Bolhuis & Giraldeau, 2005).

ANIMAL COGNITION

Do some animals think like humans?

Numerous studies indicate that other animals have some humanlike cognitive capacities. Parrots, for example, are exceptionally good vocal mimics. But do parrots know what they are saying? According to Irene Pepperberg (2000, 2002, 2006), Alex, an African gray parrot, does. Alex can count to 6; identify more than 50 different objects; and classify objects according to color, shape, material, and relative size. Pepperberg contends that rather than demonstrating simple mimicry, the parrot's actions reflect reasoning, choice, and, to some extent, thinking.

Other researchers have taught dolphins to select which of two objects is identical to a sample object—the basis of the concepts *same* and *different* (Harley, Roitblat, & Nachtigall, 1996; Roitblat, Penner, & Nachtigall, 1990)—and to respond accurately to numerical concepts such as *more* and *less* (Jaakkola, Fellner, Erb, Rodriguez, & Guarino, 2005). What's more, rhesus monkeys can learn the concept of *numeration*, or the capacity to use numbers, and *serialization*, or the ability to place objects in a specific order based on a concept (Brannon & Terrace, 1998; Terrace, Son, & Brannon, 2003). In short, humans are not unique in their ability to form concepts.

The great apes—chimpanzees, gorillas, and orangutans—are of special interest. Sharing 97 to 99% of our genes, they are our closest kin and are the most likely to think as we do. In fact, apes have demonstrated sophisticated problem-solving skills. Recall from Chapter 5, ("Learning,") that chimpanzees figured out various ways to retrieve a bunch of bananas out of their reach. In other studies, chimpanzees have learned to use computer keyboards to make and respond to complex requests (Premack, 1971, 1976), to identify and categorize objects, and to place objects in order (Kawai & Matsuzawa, 2000).

But do chimps, dolphins, and parrots know what they know? Do nonhuman animals have a *sense of self* (L. M. Herman, 2002)? George Gallup (1985, 1998) noticed that after a few days' exposure, captive chimpanzees began making faces in front of a mirror and used it to examine and groom parts of their bodies they had never seen before. To test whether the animals understood that they were seeing themselves, Gallup anesthetized them and painted a bright red mark above the eyebrow ridge and on the top of one ear. The first time the chimps looked at the mirror after awakening, they reached up and touched the red marks, presumably recognizing themselves.

Hundreds of researchers have used the mirror test, with many other animals, for three decades. Only two nonhuman species—chimpanzees and orangutans—consistently show signs of self-awareness, even after extended exposure to mirrors (Boysen & Himes, 1999; Gallup, 1985; Vauclair, 1996). For that matter, even human infants do not demonstrate mirror-recognition until 18 to 24 months of age.

If chimpanzees possess self-awareness, do they understand that others have information, thoughts, and emotions that may differ from their own? Observational studies suggest they do have at least a limited sense of other-awareness (Goodall, 1971; Parr, 2003; Savage-Rumbaugh & Fields, 2000). One measure of other-awareness is *deception*. For example, if a chimpanzee discovers a hidden store of food and another chimpanzee happens along, the first may begin idly grooming himself. Presumably, the first chimpanzee recognizes that the second (a) is equally interested in food, and (b) will interpret the grooming behavior as meaning there is nothing interesting nearby. Both in the wild and in captive colonies, chimpanzees frequently practice deception in matters of food, receptive females, and power or dominance.

THE QUESTION OF LANGUAGE

What kind of communication and language do other animals use?

Although the forms of animal communication vary widely, all animals communicate. Birds do it, bees do it, whales and chimpanzees do it (to paraphrase Cole Porter). Honeybees enact an intricate waggle dance that tells their hive mates not only exactly where to find pollen, but also the quality of that pollen (Biesmeijer & Seeley, 2005). Humpback whales perform long, haunting solos ranging from deep bass rumblings to high soprano squeaks. The technical term for such messages is **signs**, general or global statements about the animal's *current* state.

Human beings also use signs. We scream "Help! or exclaim "Cool!"—which are not much different from a chimpanzee's *waaaa* (for danger) or *hoot* (for excitement)—and use body language to supplement or substitute for words. But fixed, stereotyped signals are far from equivalent to the complexities of language. The distinguishing features of language are *meaningfulness* (or semantics), *displacement* (talking or thinking about the past or the future), and *productivity* (the ability to produce and understand new and unique words and expressions such as slang terms). Using these criteria, as far as we know, no other species has its own language.

For more than two decades, however, Francine Patterson (Bonvillian & Patterson, 1997; F. G. Patterson, 1981) has used American Sign Language with a lowland gorilla named Koko. By age 5, Koko had a working vocabulary of 500 signs—similar to a 5-year-old deaf child using sign

signs Stereotyped communications about an animal's current state.

language, though far lower than a hearing, speaking child's vocabulary of 1,000 to 5,000 words (F. G. Patterson & Cohn, 1990). Now in her mid-20s, Koko reportedly signs about her own and her companions' happy, sad, or angry emotions. Most interesting, Koko refers to the past and the future (displacement). Using signs *before* and *later, yesterday* and *tomorrow* appropriately, she mourned the death of her pet kitten and expressed a desire to become a mother.

Critics suggest that researchers such as Patterson may be reading meaning and intentions into simple gestures. To reduce the ambiguity of hand signs, other researchers have used computer keyboards to teach and record communications with apes (Rumbaugh, 1977; Rumbaugh & Savage-Rumbaugh, 1978); to document behavior with and without humans on camera; to use double-blind procedures; and also to study another ape species, bonobos (for-

Professor Sue Savage-Rumbaugh and Kanzi. Savage-Rumbaugh continued Kanzi's naturalistic education through social interaction during walks outside. Kanzi now understands spoken English and more than 200 keyboard symbols. He responds to completely new vocal and keyboard requests and uses the keyboard to make requests, comment on his surroundings, state his intentions, and—sometimes—indicate what he is thinking about.

merly called "pygmy chimpanzees"). Most impressive—and surprising—was a bonobo named Kanzi (Savage-Rumbaugh & Lewin, 1994). Initially in the lab, Kanzi was adopted by an older female who lacked keyboard skills. Some months later, Kanzi, who had been accompanying his "mother" to lessons but who was not receiving formal training, was learning keyboard symbols and spoken English on his own—much as children do.

That apes can learn signs without intensive training or rewards from human trainers is clear. Whether they can grasp the deep structure of language is less clear (Blumberg & Wasserman, 1995). Moreover, at best, apes have reached the linguistic level of a 2- to 2-1/2-year-old child. Critics see this as evidence of severe limitations, whereas others view it as an extraordinary accomplishment.

Ultimately, research on nonhuman language raises as many questions as it answers. Are humans and great apes separated by an unbridgeable divide, or are the differences between us a matter of degree? If, as many scientists believe, humans and great apes are descended from a common ancestor—and if, as some scientists conclude, great apes have at least a rudimentary capacity for symbolic communication—why didn't they develop a language of their own? Equally significant, why did we?

So far, we have been talking about *what* humans and nonhumans think about. As we will see in the next section, cognitive psychologists are equally interested in *how* people use thinking to solve problems and make decisions.

CHECK YOUR UNDERSTANDING

1. Chimpanzees and orangutans are the only two nonhuman species to consistently show
   a. self-awareness.
   b. problem-solving ability.
   c. numeration comprehension.
2. Humans use language to communicate. What is the nonhuman animal equivalent of language?
   a. grunts   b. squeaks   c. signs

Answers: 1. a. 2. c.

APPLY YOUR UNDERSTANDING

1. When someone refers to their pet as "being sad," they are exhibiting:
   a. anthropomorphism.
   b. anthropocentrism.
   c. displacement.

Answer: 1. a.

Figure 7–2
Figure for Problem 1

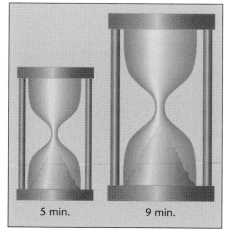

Figure 7–3
Figure for Problems 2 and 4

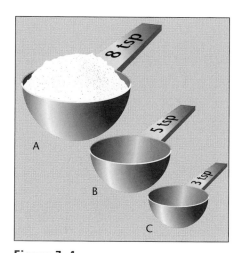

Figure 7–4
Figure for Problem 3

Problem Solving

What are three general aspects of the problem-solving process?

Solve the following problems:

PROBLEM 1 You have three measuring spoons. (See **Figure 7–2**) One is filled with 8 teaspoons of salt; the other two are empty, but have a capacity of 2 teaspoons each. Divide the salt among the spoons so that only 4 teaspoons of salt remain in the largest spoon.

PROBLEM 2 You have a 5-minute hourglass and a 9-minute hourglass. (See **Figure 7–3**.) How can you use them to time a 14-minute barbecue? (Adapted from Sternberg, 1986.)

Most people find these problems very easy. But now try solving more elaborate versions of them (the answers to all of the problems are at the end of this chapter):

PROBLEM 3 You have three measuring spoons. (See **Figure 7–4**.) One (spoon A) is filled with 8 teaspoons of salt. The second and third spoons are both empty. The second spoon (spoon B) can hold 5 teaspoons, and the third (spoon C) can hold 3 teaspoons. Divide the salt among the spoons so that spoon A and spoon B each have exactly 4 teaspoons of salt and spoon C is empty.

PROBLEM 4 You have a 5-minute hourglass and a 9-minute hourglass. (See **Figure 7–3**.) How can you use them to time a 13-minute barbecue? (Adapted from Sternberg, 1986.)

Most people find problems 3 and 4 much more difficult than the first two. Why? The answer lies in interpretation, strategy, and evaluation. Problems 1 and 2 are considered trivial because it's so easy to interpret what is needed, the strategies for solving them are simple, and you can effortlessly verify that each step you take moves you closer to a solution. Problems 3 and 4, in contrast, require some thought to interpret what is needed; the strategies for solving them are not immediately apparent; and it is harder to evaluate whether any given step has actually made progress toward your goal. These three aspects of problem solving—interpretation, strategy, and evaluation—provide a useful framework for investigating this topic.

INTERPRETING PROBLEMS

Why is representing the problem so important to finding an effective solution?

The first step in solving a problem is called **problem representation**, which means interpreting or defining the problem. It is tempting to leap ahead and try to solve a problem just as it is presented, but this impulse often leads to poor solutions. For example, if your business is losing money, you might define the problem as deciphering how to cut costs. But by defining the problem so narrowly, you have ruled out other options. A better representation of this problem would be to figure out ways to boost profits—by cutting costs, by increasing income, or both. Problems that have no single correct solution and that require a flexible, inventive approach call for **divergent thinking**—or thinking that involves generating many different possible answers. In contrast, **convergent thinking** is thinking that narrows its focus in a particular direction, assuming that there is only one solution, or at most a limited number of right solutions.

To see the importance of problem representation, consider the next two problems:

PROBLEM 5 You have four pieces of chain, each of which is made up of three links. (See **Figure 7–5**.) All links are closed at the beginning of the problem. It costs 2 cents to open a link and 3 cents to close a link. How can you join all 12 links together into a single, continuous circle without paying more than 15 cents?

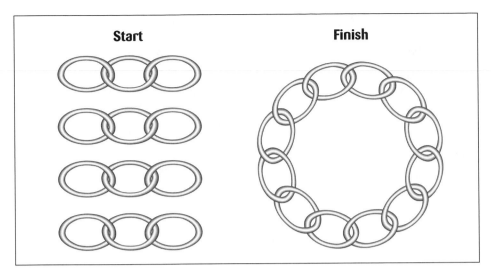

Figure 7–5
Figure for Problem 5

PROBLEM 6 You have six kitchen matches. (See **Figure 7–6**.) Arrange these matches into four equilateral triangles. Each side of every triangle must be only one match in length.

Problems 5 and 6 problems are difficult because people tend to represent them in ways that impede solutions. For example, in Problem 5, most people assume that the best way to proceed is to open and close the end links on the pieces of chain. As long as they persist with this "conceptual block," they will be unable to solve the problem. If the problem is represented differently, the solution is obvious almost immediately. Similarly, for the kitchen match problem, most people assume that they can work only in two dimensions—that is, that the triangles must lie flat on a surface—or that one match cannot serve as the side of two triangles. When the problem is represented differently, the solution becomes much easier. (The solutions to both of these problems appear at the end of this chapter.)

If you have successfully interpreted Problems 5 and 6, give Problem 7 a try:

PROBLEM 7 A monk wishes to get to a retreat at the top of a mountain. He starts climbing the mountain at sunrise and arrives at the top at sunset of the same day. During the course of his ascent, he travels at various speeds and stops often to rest. He spends the night engaged in meditation. The next day, he starts his descent at sunrise, following the same narrow path that he used to climb the mountain. As before, he travels at various speeds and stops often to rest. Because he takes great care not to trip and fall on the way down, the descent takes as long as the ascent, and he does not arrive at the bottom until sunset. Prove that there is one place on the path that the monk passes at exactly the same time of day on the ascent and on the descent.

This problem is extremely difficult to solve if it is represented verbally or mathematically. It is considerably easier to solve if it is represented visually, as you can see from the explanation that appears at the end of this chapter.

Another aspect of successfully representing a problem is deciding to which category the problem belongs. Properly categorizing a problem can provide clues about how to solve it. In fact, once a problem has been properly categorized, its solution may be very easy. Quite often, people who seem to have a knack for solving problems are actually just very skilled at categorizing them in effective ways. Star chess players, for example, can readily categorize a game situation by comparing it with various standard situations stored in their long-term memories (Huffman, Matthews, & Gagne, 2001; Waters, Gobet, & Leyden, 2002). This strategy helps them interpret the current pattern of chess pieces with greater speed and precision than the novice chess player can. Similarly, a seasoned football coach may quickly call for a particular play because the coach has interpreted a situation on the field in terms of familiar categories. Gaining expertise in any field, from football to physics, consists primarily of increasing your ability to represent and categorize problems so that they can be solved quickly and effectively (Tanaka Curran, & Sheinberg, 2005).

Figure 7–6
The six-match problem.
Arrange the six matches so that they form four equilateral triangles. The solution is given in **Figure 7–12**.

problem representation The first step in solving a problem; it involves interpreting or defining the problem.

divergent thinking Thinking that meets the criteria of originality, inventiveness, and flexibility.

convergent thinking Thinking that is directed toward one correct solution to a problem.

IMPLEMENTING STRATEGIES AND EVALUATING PROGRESS

Why are heuristics usually better for solving problems than is trial and error?

Once you have properly interpreted a problem, the next steps are to select a solution strategy and evaluate progress toward your goal. A solution strategy can be anything from simple trial and error, to information retrieval based on similar problems, to a set of step-by-step procedures guaranteed to work (called an algorithm), to rule-of-thumb approaches known as heuristics.

TRIAL AND ERROR Trial and error is a strategy that works best when choices are limited. For example, if you have only three or four keys to choose from, trial and error is the best way to find out which one unlocks your friend's front door. In most cases, however, trial and error wastes time because there are so many different options to test. It is better to eliminate unproductive approaches and to zero in on a more functional one. Let's consider some alternative strategies.

INFORMATION RETRIEVAL One approach is to retrieve information from long-term memory about how such a problem was solved in the past. Information retrieval is an especially important option when a solution is needed quickly. For example, pilots simply memorize the slowest speed at which a particular airplane can fly before it stalls.

ALGORITHMS Complex problems require complex strategies. An **algorithm** is a problem-solving method that guarantees a solution if it is appropriate for the problem and is properly carried out. For example, to calculate the product of 323 and 546, we multiply the numbers according to the rules of multiplication (the algorithm). If we do it accurately, we are guaranteed to get the right answer. Similarly, to convert temperatures from Fahrenheit to Celsius, we use the algorithm $C = 5/9 (F - 32)$.

HEURISTICS Because we don't have algorithms for every kind of problem, we often turn to **heuristics**, or rules of thumb. Heuristics do not guarantee a solution, but they may bring it within reach. Part of problem solving is to decide which heuristic is most appropriate for a given problem.

A very simple heuristic is **hill climbing**: We try to move continually closer to our goal without going backward. At each step, we evaluate how far "up the hill" we have come, how far we still have to go, and precisely what the next step should be. On a multiple-choice test, for example, one useful hill-climbing strategy is first to eliminate the alternatives that are obviously incorrect. Or imagine taking a long road trip—say from Los Angeles to New York. You'll be implementing a hill-climbing strategy if, whenever you come to a fork in the road, you always choose to take the road that goes more directly east.

Another problem-solving heuristic is to create **subgoals**, which involves breaking a problem into smaller, more manageable pieces that are easier to solve individually than the problem as a whole (Nunokawa, 2001; Reed, 2003). Consider the problem of the Hobbits and the Orcs:

PROBLEM 8 Three Hobbits and three Orcs are on the bank of a river. They all want to get to the other side, but their boat will carry only two creatures at a time. Moreover, if at any time the Orcs outnumber the Hobbits, the Orcs will attack the Hobbits. How can all the creatures get across the river without danger to the Hobbits?

You can find the solution to this problem by thinking of it in terms of a series of subgoals. What has to be done to get just one or two creatures across the river safely, temporarily leaving aside the main goal of getting everyone across? We could first send two of the Orcs across and have one of them return. That gets one Orc across the river. Now we can think about the next trip. It's clear that we can't then send a single Hobbit across with an Orc, because the Hobbit would be outnumbered as soon as the boat landed. Therefore, we have to send either two Hobbits or two Orcs. By working on the problem in this fashion—concentrating on subgoals—we can eventually get everyone across.

Once you have solved Problem 8, try Problem 9, which is considerably more difficult (the answers to both problems are at the end of the chapter):

algorithm A step-by-step method of problem solving that guarantees a correct solution.

heuristics Rules of thumb that help in simplifying and solving problems, although they do not guarantee a correct solution.

hill climbing A heuristic, problem-solving strategy in which each step moves you progressively closer to the final goal.

subgoals Intermediate, more manageable goals used in one heuristic strategy to make it easier to reach the final goal.

PROBLEM 9 This problem is identical to Problem 8, except that there are five Hobbits and five Orcs, and the boat can carry only three creatures at a time.

Subgoals are often helpful in solving a variety of everyday problems. According to Henry Ford, who invented assembly-line manufacturing of affordable automobiles in the early 1900s, "Nothing is particularly hard if you divide it into small steps." For example, a student whose goal is to write a term paper might set subgoals by breaking the project into a series of separate tasks: choosing a topic, doing research and taking notes, preparing an outline, writing the first draft, editing, rewriting, and so on. Even the subgoals can sometimes be broken down into separate tasks: Writing the first draft of the paper might break down into the subgoals of writing the introduction, describing the position to be taken, supporting the position with evidence, drawing conclusions, writing a summary, and writing a bibliography. Subgoals make problem solving more manageable because they free us from the burden of having to "get to the other side of the river" all at once. Although the overall purpose of setting subgoals is still to solve the larger problem, this tactic allows us to set our sights on closer, more manageable objectives.

One of the most frequently used heuristics, called **means-end analysis**, combines hill climbing and subgoals. Like hill climbing, means-end analysis involves analyzing the difference between the current situation and the desired end, and then doing something to reduce that difference. But in contrast to hill climbing—which does not permit detours away from the final goal in order to solve the problem—means-end analysis takes into account the entire problem situation. It formulates subgoals in such a way as to allow us temporarily to take a step that appears to be backward in order to reach our goal in the end. One example is the pitcher's strategy in a baseball game when confronted with the best batter in the league. The pitcher might opt to walk this batter intentionally even though doing so moves away from the major subgoal of keeping runners off base. Intentional walking might enable the pitcher to keep a run from scoring and so contribute to the ultimate goal of winning the game. This flexibility in thinking is a major benefit of means-end analysis.

But means-end analysis also poses the danger of straying so far from the end goal that the goal disappears altogether. One way of avoiding this situation is to use the heuristic of **working backward**. With this strategy, the search for a solution begins at the goal and works backward toward the "givens." Working backward is often used when the goal has more information than the givens and when the operations involved can work in two directions. For example, if you wanted to spend exactly $100 on clothing, it would be difficult to reach that goal simply by buying some items and hoping that they totaled exactly $100. A better strategy would be to buy one item, subtract its cost from $100 to determine how much money you have left, then purchase another item, subtract its cost, and so on, until you have spent $100.

OBSTACLES TO SOLVING PROBLEMS

How can a "mental set" both help and hinder problem solving?

In everyday life, many factors can either help or hinder problem solving. One factor is a person's level of motivation, or emotional arousal. Generally, we must generate a certain surge of excitement to motivate ourselves to solve a problem, yet too much arousal can hamper our ability to find a solution. (See Chapter 8, "Motivation and Emotion.")

Another factor that can either help or hinder problem solving is **mental set**—our tendency to perceive and to approach problems in certain ways. Set determines which information we tend to retrieve from memory to help us find a solution. Set can be helpful if we have learned operations that we can apply to the present situation. Much of our formal education involves learning sets and ways to solve problems (that is, learning heuristics and algorithms). But sets can also create obstacles, especially when a novel approach is needed. The most successful problem solvers can choose from many different sets and can judge when to change sets or when to abandon them entirely. Great ideas and inventions come out of such flexibility.

means-end analysis A heuristic strategy that aims to reduce the discrepancy between the current situation and the desired goal at a number of intermediate points.

working backward A heuristic strategy in which one works backward from the desired goal to the given conditions.

mental set The tendency to perceive and to approach problems in certain ways.

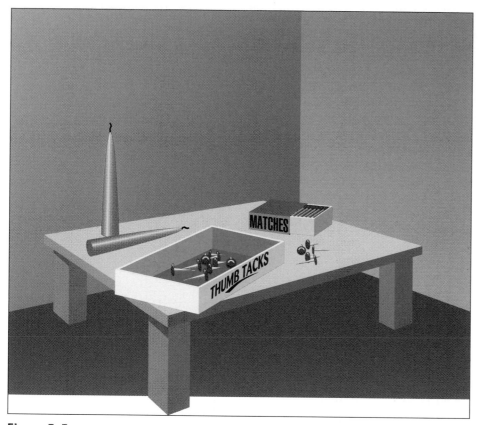

Figure 7–7
To test the effects of functional fixedness, participants might be given the items shown on the table and asked to mount a candle on the wall. See **Figure 7–15** for a solution.

One type of set that can seriously hinder problem solving is called **functional fixedness**. Consider **Figure 7–7**. Do you see a way to mount the candle on the wall? If not, you are probably stymied by functional fixedness. (The solution to this problem appears at the end of the chapter.) The more you use an object in only one way, the harder it is to see new uses for it, because you have "assigned" the object to a fixed function. To some extent, part of the learning process is to assign correct functions to objects—this is how we form concepts. But we need to be open to seeing that an object can be used for an entirely different function. See, Applying Psychology, "Becoming a More Skillful Problem Solver" for techniques that will improve your problem-solving skills.

Because creative problem solving requires generating original ideas, deliberate strategies don't always help. Solutions to many problems rely on insight, often a seemingly arbitrary flash "out of the blue." (See Chapter 5, "Learning.") Psychologists have only recently begun to investigate such spontaneous and unplanned problem-solving processes as insight and intuition (Gilhooly & Murphy, 2005; Novick & Sherman, 2003; Sinclair & Ashkanasy, 2005).

The value of looking for new ways to represent a difficult problem cannot be overstressed.

APPLYING PSYCHOLOGY

BECOMING A MORE SKILLFUL PROBLEM SOLVER

Even the best problem solvers occasionally get stumped, but you can do some things that will help you find a solution. These tactics encourage you to discard unproductive approaches and find strategies that are more effective.

1. **Eliminate poor choices.** When we are surer of what won't work than what will, the *tactic of elimination* can be very helpful. First, list all the possible solutions you can think of, and then discard all the solutions that seem to lead in the wrong direction. Now, examine the list more closely. Some solutions seem to be ineffective but may turn out to be good on closer examination.

2. **Visualize a solution.** If you are stumped by a problem, try using a basic building block of thought: visual images. *Visualizing* often involves diagramming courses of action (J. L. Adams, 1980). For example, in the Hobbit and Orc problems draw a picture of the river, and show the Hobbits and Orcs at each stage of the solution as they are ferried across. Drawing a diagram can help you grasp what a problem calls for. You also can visualize mentally.

3. **Develop expertise.** We get stumped on problems because we lack the knowledge to find a quick solution.

Experts not only know more about a particular subject but also organize their information in larger "chunks" that are extensively interconnected, much like a cross-referencing system in a library.

4. **Think flexibly.** Striving to be more flexible and creative is an excellent tactic for becoming a better problem solver. This will help you avoid *functional fixedness* or a *mental set* from standing in the way of solving a problem. Many problems require some original thinking. For example, how many unusual uses can you think of for a brick?

Ask yourself, "What is the real problem here? Can the problem be interpreted in other ways?" Also, be open to potential solutions that at first seem unproductive. The solution may turn out to be more effective, or it may suggest related solutions that will work. This is the rationale behind the technique called **brainstorming**: When solving a problem, generate a lot of ideas before you review and evaluate them (McGlynn, McGurk, Effland, Johll, & Harding, 2004; Park-Gates, 2002).

THINKING CRITICALLY ABOUT . . .

Solving Problems

Think for a moment of the last time you were confronted with a difficult problem.

1. What types of thinking or reasoning did you use to deal with that problem?
2. Having read this portion of the chapter, would you respond differently if you were faced with a similar problem? If so, what would you do differently?
3. You are headed for Mount Rushmore, and you can see it from a distance. You have no map. What is the best problem-solving strategy you can use to get there, and why?

CHECK YOUR UNDERSTANDING

1. Match each problem-solving strategy with the appropriate definition.

   ___ algorithm

   ___ heuristic

   ___ hill climbing

   ___ means-end analysis

   ___ working backward

   ___ subgoal creation

   a. rule-of-thumb approach that helps in simplifying and solving problems, although it doesn't guarantee a correct solution

   b. strategy in which each step moves you closer to a solution

   c. step-by-step method that guarantees a solution

   d. strategy in which one moves from the goal to the starting point

   e. strategy that aims to reduce the discrepancy between the current situation and the desired goal at a number of intermediate points

   f. breaking down the solution to a larger problem into a set of smaller, more manageable steps

2. Match each form of thinking with its definition and the kind of problems to which it is suited.

   ___ divergent thinking

   ___ convergent thinking

   a. suited to problems for which there is one correct solution or a limited number of solutions

   b. thinking that involves generating many different ideas

   c. suited to problems that have no one right solution and require an inventive approach

   d. thinking that limits its focus to a particular direction

Answers: 1. Algorithm—c. heuristic—a. hill climbing—b. means-end analysis—e. working backward—d. subgoal creation—f. 2. divergent thinking—b. and c. convergent thinking—a. and d.

APPLY YOUR UNDERSTANDING

1. Your car is not operating correctly. The mechanic opens the hood and says, "We've been seeing lots of cars recently with fouled plugs or dirty fuel filters. Let's start there and see if that's your problem, too." The mechanic is using a(n)

   a. heuristic.

   b. algorithm.

   c. compensatory decision model.

   d. noncompensatory decision model.

2. You are at a football game when it begins to rain heavily. As you get soaked, you see the people next to you pull folded plastic garbage bags out of their pockets to use as a temporary "raincoat." Your failure to realize that the garbage bag might also be used as rain protection is an example of

   a. an algorithm.

   b. a heuristic.

   c. means-end analysis.

   d. functional fixedness.

Answers: 1. a. 2. d.

functional fixedness The tendency to perceive only a limited number of uses for an object, thus interfering with the process of problem solving.

brainstorming A problem-solving strategy in which an individual or a group produces numerous ideas and evaluates them only after all ideas have been collected.

compensatory model A rational decision-making model in which choices are systematically evaluated on various criteria.

Decision Making

How does decision making differ from problem solving?

Decision making is a special kind of problem solving in which we already know all the possible solutions or choices. The task is not to come up with new solutions, but rather to identify the best available one based on whatever criteria we are using. This process might sound fairly simple, but sometimes we have to juggle a large and complex set of criteria as well as many possible options. For example, suppose that you are looking for an apartment among hundreds available. A reasonable rent is important to you, but so are good neighbors, a good location, a low noise level, and cleanliness. If you find an inexpensive, noisy apartment with undesirable neighbors, should you take it? Is it a better choice than a more expensive, less noisy apartment in a better location? How can you weigh your various criteria and make the best choice?

COMPENSATORY DECISION MAKING

How would you go about making a truly logical decision?

The logical way to make a decision is to rate each of the available choices on all the criteria you are using, arriving at some overall measure of the extent to which each choice matches your criteria. For each choice, the attractive features can offset or compensate for the unattractive features. This approach to decision making is therefore called a **compensatory model**.

Table 7–1 illustrates one of the most useful compensatory models applied to a car-buying decision. The buyer's three criteria are weighted in terms of importance: price (not weighted heavily), gas mileage, and service record (both weighted more heavily). Next, each car is rated from 1 (poor) to 5 (excellent) on each of the criteria. Car 1 has an excellent price (5) but relatively poor gas mileage (2) and service record (1); and Car 2 has a less desirable price but fairly good mileage and service record. Each rating is then multiplied by the weight for that criterion (e.g., for Car 1, the price rating of 5 is multiplied by the weight of 4, and the result is put in parentheses next to the rating). Finally, ratings are totaled for each car. Clearly, Car 2 is the better choice: It is more expensive, but that disadvantage is offset by its better mileage and service record; and these two criteria are more important than price to this particular buyer.

Although most people would agree that using such a table is a good way to decide which car to buy, at times people will abandon the compensatory decision-making process in the face of more vivid anecdotal information. For example, if a friend had previously bought Car 2 and found it to be a lemon, many people will choose Car 1 despite Car 2's well-thought out advantages. Moreover, as we will see in the next section, it is often not possible or desirable to rate every choice on all criteria. In such situations people typically use heuristics that have worked well in the past to simplify decision making, even though they may lead to less-than-optimal decision making (Dhami, 2003).

table 7–1 COMPENSATORY DECISION TABLE FOR PURCHASE OF A NEW CAR			
	Price (weight = 4)	Gas mileage (weight = 8)	Service record (weight = 10)	Weighted Total
Car 1	5 (20)	2 (16)	1 (10)	(46)
Car 2	1 (4)	4 (32)	4 (40)	(76)
Ratings: 5 = excellent; 1 = poor			

DECISION-MAKING HEURISTICS

How can heuristic approaches lead us to make bad decisions?

Research has identified a number of common heuristics that people use to make decisions. We use the **representativeness** heuristic whenever we make a decision on the basis of certain information that matches our model of the typical member of a category. For example, if every time you went shopping you bought the least expensive items and if all of these items turned out to be poorly made, you might eventually decide not to buy anything that seems typical of the category "very cheap." Another common heuristic is **availability** (N. Schwarz & Vaughn, 2002). In the absence of full and accurate information, we often base decisions on whatever information is most readily available to memory, even though this information may not be accurate.

A familiar example of the availability heuristic is the so-called *subway effect* (Gilovich, 1991). It seems to be a law of nature that if you are waiting at a subway station, one train after another will come along headed in the opposite direction from the direction that you want to go. Similarly, if you need a taxi in a hurry, inevitably an unusually long string of occupied or off-duty taxis will pass by. The problem here is that by the time a subway train or a taxi does come along, we have already left the scene, so we never get to see the opposite situation: several subway trains going in our direction before one comes the other way, or a long string of empty taxis. As a result, we tend to assume that those situations seldom or never occur, and so we make our decisions accordingly.

Another heuristic, closely related to availability, is **confirmation bias**—the tendency to notice and remember evidence that supports our beliefs and to ignore evidence that contradicts them (Nickerson, 1998). For example, individuals who believe that AIDS is something that happens to "other people" (homosexual men and intravenous drug users, not middle-class heterosexuals) are more likely to remember articles about rates of HIV infection in these groups or in third-world countries than articles about AIDS cases among people like themselves (Fischhoff & Downs, 1997). Convinced that HIV is not something that they personally need to worry about, they ignore evidence to the contrary.

A related phenomenon is our tendency to see *connections* or *patterns of cause and effect* where none exist (Kahneman & Tversky, 1996; Rottenstreich & Tversky, 1997). For example, many people still believe that chocolate causes acne to flare up in susceptible teenagers, yet this myth was disproved almost half a century ago. Many parents strongly believe that sugar may cause hyperactivity in children and that arthritis pain is related to weather—despite research evidence to the contrary. The list of commonsense beliefs that persist in the face of contrary evidence is long (Redelmeier & Tversky, 2004).

EXPLAINING OUR DECISIONS

How do we explain to ourselves the decisions we make?

FRAMING For the most part, people are reasonably satisfied with the decisions they make in the real world. However, these decisions can be intentionally or inadvertently swayed by the way the information provided to make the decision is presented, or *framed*. Psychologists use the term **framing** to refer to the perspective or phrasing of information that is used to make a decision. Numerous studies have shown that subtle changes in the way information is presented can dramatically affect the final decision (L. W. Jones, Sinclair, & Courneya, 2003; LeBoeuf & Shafir, 2003; Mann, Sherman, & Updegraff, 2004). A classic study (McNeil, Pauker, Sox, & Tversky, 1982) illustrates how framing may influence a medical decision. In this study, experimental participants were asked to choose between surgery and radiation therapy to treat lung cancer. However, the framing of information provided to make this choice was manipulated. In the *survival frame*, participants were given the statistical outcomes of both procedures in the form of survival statistics, thus emphasizing the 1- and 5-year *survival* rates after treatment. In the *mortality frame*, the participants were given the same information, presented (or framed) according to *death* rates after 1 year and after 5 years. Although the

representativeness A heuristic by which a new situation is judged on the basis of its resemblance to a stereotypical model.

availability A heuristic by which a judgment or decision is based on information that is most easily retrieved from memory.

confirmation bias The tendency to look for evidence in support of a belief and to ignore evidence that would disprove a belief.

framing The perspective from which we interpret information before making a decision.

hindsight bias The tendency to see outcomes as inevitable and predictable after we know the outcome.

counterfactual thinking Thinking about alternative realities and things that never happened.

actual number of deaths and survivors associated with each procedure was identical in both the survival and mortality frames, the percentage of participants who chose one procedure over another varied dramatically *depending on how the information was framed.* Probably most surprising was that this framing effect was found even when 424 experienced radiologists served as the experimental participants!

HINDSIGHT Whether a choice is exceptionally good, extraordinarily foolish, or somewhere in between, most people think about their decisions after the fact. The term **hindsight bias** refers to the tendency to view outcomes as inevitable and predictable after we know the outcome, and to believe that we could have predicted what happened, or perhaps that we did (Hoffrage & Pohl, 2003; Pohl, Schwarz, Sczesny, & Stahlberg, 2003). For example, physicians remember being more confident about their diagnoses when they learn that they were correct than they were at the time of the actual diagnoses.

Psychologists have long viewed the hindsight bias as a cognitive flaw—a way of explaining away bad decisions and maintaining our confidence (Louie, Curren, & Harich, 2000). A team of researchers in Berlin, however, argues that the hindsight bias serves a useful function (Hoffrage, Hertwig, & Gigerenzer, 2000). "Correcting" memory is a quick and efficient way to replace misinformation or faulty assumptions, so that our future decisions and judgments will be closer to the mark. In a sense, hindsight functions like the "find and replace" function in a word processing program, eliminating extra, time-consuming keystrokes and mental effort.

"IF ONLY" At times, everyone imagines alternatives to reality and mentally plays out the consequences. Psychologists refer to such thoughts about things that never happened as **counterfactual thinking**—in which thoughts are counter to the facts (Roese, 1997; Segura & McCloy, 2003; Walchle & Landman, 2003). Counterfactual thinking often takes the form of "If only" constructions, in which we mentally revise the events or actions that led to a particular outcome: "If only I had studied harder"; "If only I had said no"; "If only I had driven straight home." Research shows that counterfactual thinking usually centers around a small number of themes: reversing a course of events that led to a negative experience; explaining unusual events by assigning responsibility to someone or something; and regaining a sense of personal control (Roese, 1997).

Any discussion of cognition, problem solving, or decision making inevitably raises the question of how individuals differ in these skills. The next section of the chapter addresses intelligence, where the question of individual differences in reasoning and problem solving is of central importance.

CHECK YOUR UNDERSTANDING

1. Match each decision-making heuristic with the appropriate definition.

    ___ representativeness heuristic

    ___ availability heuristic

    ___ confirmation bias

    a. making judgments on the basis of whatever information can be most readily retrieved from memory

    b. attending to evidence that supports your existing beliefs and ignoring other evidence

    c. making decisions on the basis of information that matches your model of what is "typical" of a certain category

2. The way a question is framed usually will not affect its answer. Is this statement true (T) or false (F)?

3. Julio's girlfriend gets a speeding ticket, and he blames himself, saying, "If only I hadn't let her borrow my car." His thinking is an example of _____ _____.

Answers: 1. representativeness heuristic—c. availability heuristic—a. confirmation bias—b. 2. (F) 3. hindsight bias.

APPLY YOUR UNDERSTANDING

1. In deciding where to go on vacation, you decide you want a place where you can relax, a place that is warm, and a place that you can reach inexpensively. But you will not consider any place that is more than 1,000 miles away. What kind of decision-making model are you using?

   a. visualization

   b. brainstorming

   c. noncompensatory

   d. compensatory

2. You are driving down the highway at the posted speed limit. After a while you mention to your passenger, "It sure looks like everyone is either going slower or faster than the speed limit. Hardly anyone seems to be going the same speed as I am." In fact, most of the cars on the highway are also traveling at the speed limit. Your erroneous conclusion is most likely due to

   a. framing.

   b. hindsight bias.

   c. mental set.

   d. the availability heuristic.

Answers: 1. c. 2. d.

Intelligence and Mental Abilities

What types of questions are used to measure intelligence?

In many societies, one of the nicest things you can say is "You're smart"; and one of the most insulting is "You're stupid." Intelligence is so basic to our view of human nature that any characterization of a person that neglects to mention that person's intelligence is considered incomplete. Our mental capabilities affect our success in school, the kind of work we do, the kinds of recreation we enjoy, and even our choice of friends.

Psychologists have studied intelligence almost since psychology emerged as a science, yet still struggle to understand this complex and elusive concept. In the next few sections, you may come to appreciate the difficulty of their task. Toward that end, we begin by asking you some questions intended to measure intelligence:

1. Describe the difference between *laziness* and *idleness*.
2. Which direction would you have to face so that your right ear would be facing north?
3. What does *obliterate* mean?
4. In what way are an hour and a week alike?
5. Choose the lettered block that best completes the pattern in the following figure.

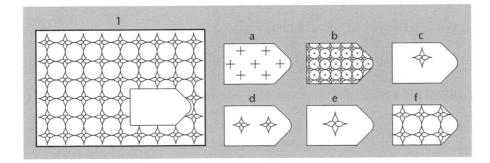

6. If three pencils cost 25 cents, how many pencils can you buy for 75 cents?

7. Select the lettered pair that best expresses a relationship similar to that expressed in the original pair:

CRUTCH: LOCOMOTION::

  a. paddle: canoe   b. hero: worship

  c. horse: carriage   d. spectacles: vision

  e. statement: contention

8. Decide how the first two items in the following figure are related to each other. Then find the one item at the right that goes with the third item in the same way that the second item goes with the first.

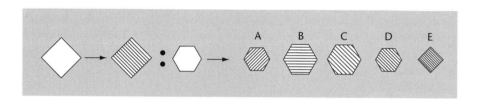

9. For each item in the following figure, decide whether it can be completely covered by using some or all of the given pieces without overlapping any.

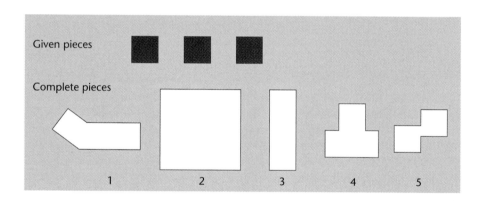

These questions were taken from various tests of **intelligence**, or general mental ability. (The answers appear at the end of the chapter.) We will discuss intelligence tests later in this chapter. But first, let's consider some historical and contemporary theories of intelligence.

THEORIES OF INTELLIGENCE

What are some of the major theories of intelligence?

For more than a century, psychologists have argued about what constitutes general intelligence—or even if "general" intelligence actually exists. One of their most basic questions is whether intelligence is a single, general mental ability or whether it is composed of many separate abilities (Lubinski, 2000).

EARLY THEORISTS Charles Spearman, an early 20th-century British psychologist, maintained that intelligence is quite general—a kind of well or spring of mental energy that flows through every action. Spearman believed that people who are bright in one area are often bright in other areas as well. The American psychologist L. L. Thurstone disagreed with Spearman. Thurstone argued that intelligence is composed of seven distinct kinds of mental abilities (Thurstone, 1938): *spatial ability, memory, perceptual speed, word fluency, numerical ability, reasoning,* and *verbal meaning.* Unlike Spearman, Thurstone believed that these abilities are relatively independent of one another. Thus, a person with exceptional

intelligence A general term referring to the ability or abilities involved in learning and adaptive behavior.

triarchic theory of intelligence Sternberg's theory that intelligence involves mental skills (analytical intelligence), insight and creative adaptability (creative intelligence), and environmental responsiveness (practical intelligence).

theory of multiple intelligences Howard Gardner's theory that there is not one intelligence, but rather many intelligences, each of which is relatively independent of the others.

emotional intelligence According to Goleman, a form of intelligence that refers to how effectively people perceive and understand their own emotions and the emotions of others, and can regulate and manage their emotional behavior.

spatial ability (the ability to perceive distance, recognize shapes, and so on) might lack word fluency.

CONTEMPORARY THEORISTS Contemporary psychologists have considerably broadened the concept of intelligence and how it can best be measured (Benson, 2003). For example, Robert Sternberg (1986, 2003) has proposed a **triarchic theory of intelligence**. Sternberg argues that human intelligence encompasses a broad variety of skills that are just as important as the more limited skills assessed by traditional intelligence tests. *Analytical intelligence* refers to the mental processes emphasized by most theories of intelligence, such as the ability to learn how to do things, acquire new knowledge, solve problems, and carry out tasks effectively. According to Sternberg, this is the aspect of intelligence assessed by most intelligence tests. *Creative intelligence* is the ability to adjust to new tasks, use new concepts, respond effectively in new situations, gain insight, and adapt creatively. Practical *intelligence* is the ability to find solutions to practical and personal problems.

Mariel Zagunis, the first U.S. woman to ever win an Olympic gold medal for fencing, possesses an abundance of what Howard Gardner calls bodily-kinesthetic intelligence.

Another contemporary theory of intelligence is the **theory of multiple intelligences** advanced by Howard Gardner and his associates at Harvard (J.-Q. Chen & Gardner, 2005; Gardner, 1983, 2004). Gardner, like Thurstone, believes that intelligence is made up of several distinct abilities, each of which is relatively independent of the others. Precisely how many separate intelligences might exist is difficult to determine, but Gardner lists eight: *logical–mathematical, linguistic, spatial, musical, bodily-kinesthetic, interpersonal, intrapersonal, and naturalistic.* The first four are self-explanatory. Bodily-kinesthetic intelligence is the ability to manipulate one's body in space; a skilled athlete shows high levels of this kind of intelligence. People who are extraordinarily talented at understanding and communicating with others, such as exceptional teachers and parents, have strong interpersonal intelligence. Intrapersonal intelligence reflects the ancient adage, "Know thyself." People who understand themselves and who use this knowledge effectively to attain their goals rank high in intrapersonal intelligence. Finally, naturalistic intelligence reflects an individual's ability to understand, relate to, and interact with the world of nature.

Gardner's approach has become quite influential, largely because he emphasizes the unique abilities that each person possesses. Gardner also notes that the different forms of intelligence often have different values placed on them by different cultures. For example, many traditional Native American cultures place a much higher value on naturalistic intelligence than does contemporary mainstream American culture. Because we have unique patterns of strengths and weaknesses in separate abilities, Gardner believes that education should be designed to suit the profile of abilities demonstrated by each child.

Finally, Daniel Goleman (1997) has proposed a theory of **emotional intelligence**, which refers to how effectively people perceive and understand their own emotions and the emotions of others and can manage their emotional behavior. Goleman contends that one of the reasons IQ tests sometimes fail to predict success accurately is that they do not take into account an individual's emotional competence. Five traits are generally recognized as contributing to emotional intelligence (Goleman, 1997; Goleman, Boyatzis, & McKee, 2002):

- *Knowing one's own emotions.* The ability to monitor and recognize our own feelings. This is of central importance to self-awareness and all other dimensions of emotional intelligence.

THINKING CRITICALLY ABOUT . . .

Multiple Intelligences

Gardner's theory clearly includes abilities not normally included under the heading of intelligence.

1. We earlier defined intelligence as general intellectual or mental ability. Do you agree that all of Gardner's facets of intelligence fit that definition? Should some be excluded? Or should the definition of intelligence perhaps be modified to include them? What might such a modified definition look like?

2. Some people have excellent "color sense"—they seem to know which colors go well together. Should this ability be included as one aspect of intelligence? What about rhyming ability?

3. In answering the first two questions, what criteria did you use for deciding which abilities to include as aspects of intelligence and which to exclude? Do other people share your viewpoint, or do their criteria differ? How might you go about deciding which viewpoints have most merit?

SUMMARY TABLE

COMPARING GARDNER'S, STERNBERG'S, AND GOLEMAN'S THEORIES OF INTELLIGENCE

Gardener's multiple intelligences	Sternberg's triarchic intelligences	Goleman's emotional intelligence
Logical-mathematical Linguistic	Analytical	
Spatial Musical Bodily-kinesthetic	Creative	
Interpersonal		Recognizing emotions in others and managing relationships
Intrapersonal	Practical	Knowing yourself and motivating yourself with emotions
Naturalistic		

- *Managing one's emotions.* The ability to control impulses, to cope effectively with sadness, depression, and minor setbacks, as well as to control how long emotions last.
- *Using emotions to motivate oneself.* The capacity to marshal emotions toward achieving personal goals.
- *Recognizing the emotions of other people.* The ability to read subtle, nonverbal cues that reveal what other people really want and need.
- *Managing relationships.* The ability to accurately acknowledge and display one's own emotions, as well as being sensitive to the emotions of others.

The concept of emotional intelligence is relatively new; and researchers have only begun to evaluate its measurement (Austin, Saklofske, Huang, & McKenney, 2004; Salovey, Mayer, Caruso, & Lopes, 2003; Sotres, Velasquez, & Cruz, 2002) and its scientific merit (Bar-On & Parker, 2000; G. Matthews, Zeidner, & Roberts, 2002). Some studies have shown promising results (Bar-On, Handley, & Fund, 2006). For example, Mayer and Geher (1996) found that the ability to identify emotions accurately in other people does correlate with SAT scores. As you might expect, the ability to manage and regulate one's emotions in the workplace and in other relationships also appears to be important (Cherniss & Goleman, 2001; Druskat, Sala, & Mount, 2006; Grandey, 2000).

Some investigators, however, remain skeptical, arguing that emotional intelligence is no different from traits that are already assessed by more traditional measures of intelligence and personality (Davies, Stankov, & Roberts, 1998). Despite these criticisms however, the theory of emotional intelligence continues to gain support from psychological research. In addition, it has captured the attention of managers and others responsible for hiring, promoting, and predicting the performance of people in the workplace (Salovey, 2006).

The **"Summary Table"** reviews the contemporary theories described here. These theories shape the content of intelligence tests and other measures that evaluate the abilities of millions of people. We consider these next.

INTELLIGENCE TESTS

What kinds of intelligence tests are in use today?

THE STANFORD–BINET INTELLIGENCE SCALE The first test developed to measure intelligence was designed by two Frenchmen, Alfred Binet and Théodore Simon. The test, first used in Paris in 1905, was designed to identify children who might have difficulty in school.

The first *Binet–Simon Scale* consisted of 30 tests arranged in order of increasing difficulty. With each child, the examiner started with the easiest tests and worked down the list until the child could no longer answer questions. A well-known adaptation of the *Binet–Simon Scale*, the *Stanford–Binet Intelligence Scale*, was prepared at Stanford University by L. M. Terman, first published in 1916 and updated repeatedly since then. The current Stanford–Binet Intelligence Scale is designed to measure four virtually universal abilities related to traditional views of intelligence: *verbal reasoning, abstract/visual reasoning, quantitative reasoning,* and *short-term memory*. The Stanford–Binet test is given individually by a trained examiner. It is best suited for children, adolescents, and very young adults. Questions 1 and 2 on page 247 were drawn from an early version of the Stanford-Binet.

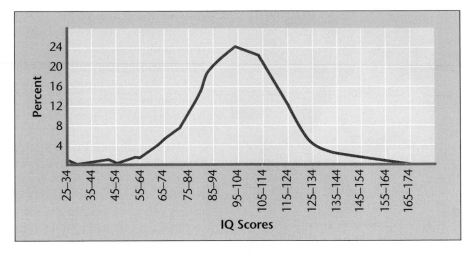

Figure 7–8

The approximate distribution of IQ scores in the population.
Note that the greatest percentage of scores fall around 100. Very low percentages of people score at the two extremes of the curve.

Terman also introduced the now famous term **intelligence quotient (IQ)** to establish a numerical value of intelligence, setting the score of 100 for a person of average intelligence. **Figure 7–8** shows an approximate distribution of IQ scores in the population.

THE WECHSLER INTELLIGENCE SCALES The most commonly used individual test of intelligence for adults is the **Wechsler Adult Intelligence Scale—Third Edition (WAIS-III)**, originally developed in the late 1930s by psychologist David Wechsler. The Stanford–Binet emphasizes verbal skills, but Wechsler believed adult intelligence consists more of the ability to handle life situations than to solve verbal and abstract problems.

The WAIS-III is divided into two parts, one stressing verbal skills, the other performance skills. The verbal scale includes tests of information, simple arithmetic, and comprehension. The performance scale measures routine tasks such as asking people to "find the missing part" (buttonholes in a coat, for example), to copy patterns, and to arrange three to five pictures so that they tell a story.

Although the content of the WAIS-III is somewhat more sophisticated than that of the Stanford–Binet, Wechsler's chief innovation was in scoring. His test gives separate verbal and performance scores as well as an overall IQ score. Moreover, on some items one or two extra points can be earned, depending on the complexity of the answer given. This unique scoring system gives credit for the reflective qualities that we expect to find in intelligent adults. Finally, on some questions both speed and accuracy affect the score. Questions 3 and 4 on page 247 resemble questions on the WAIS III.

Wechsler also developed a similar intelligence test for use with school-age children. Like the WAIS-III, the **Wechsler Intelligence Scale for Children–Third Edition (WISC-III)** yields separate verbal and performance scores as well as an overall IQ score.

GROUP TESTS With the Stanford–Binet, the WAIS-III, and the WISC-III, an examiner takes a single person to an isolated room, spreads the materials on a table, and spends from 30 to 90 minutes administering the test. The examiner may then take another hour or so to score the test according to detailed instructions in the manual. This is a time-consuming, costly operation; and under some circumstances the examiner's behavior can influence the score. For these reasons, test makers have devised **group tests**, which a single examiner can administer to many people at once. Instead of sitting across the table from a person who asks you questions, you receive a test booklet that contains questions for you to answer in writing within a certain amount of time.

Group tests have some distinct advantages over individualized tests. They eliminate bias on the part of the examiner, answer sheets can be scored quickly and objectively, and it is possible to collect data from large numbers of test takers. But group tests also have some distinct disadvantages. The examiner is less likely to notice whether a person is tired, ill, or confused by the directions. People who are not used to being tested tend to do less well on group tests than on individual tests. Finally, emotionally disturbed

intelligence quotient (IQ) A numerical value given to intelligence that is determined from the scores on an intelligence test on the basis of a score of 100 for average intelligence.

Wechsler Adult Intelligence Scale—Third Edition (WAIS-III) An individual intelligence test developed especially for adults; measures both verbal and performance abilities.

Wechsler Intelligence Scale for Children—Third Edition (WISC-III) An individual intelligence test developed especially for school-aged children; measures verbal and performance abilities and also yields an overall IQ score.

group tests Written intelligence tests administered by one examiner to many people at one time.

The Wechsler Intelligence Scales, developed by David Wechsler, are individual intelligence tests administered to one person at a time. There are versions of the Wechsler Scales for both adults and children. Here, a child is being asked to copy a pattern using blocks.

children and children with learning disabilities often do better on individual tests than on group tests (Anastasi & Urbina, 1997). Questions 5-14 on pages 247–8 are drawn from group tests.

PERFORMANCE AND CULTURE-FAIR TESTS To perform well on the intelligence tests that we have discussed, people must be adept at the language in which the test is given. How, then, can we test non-native English speakers in English-speaking countries? Psychologists have designed two general forms of tests for such situations: performance tests and culture-fair tests.

Performance tests consist of problems that minimize or eliminate the use of words. One of the earliest performance tests, the *Seguin Form Board*, is essentially a puzzle. The examiner removes specifically designed cutouts, stacks them in a predetermined order, and asks the person to replace them as quickly as possible. A more recent performance test, the *Porteus Maze*, consists of a series of increasingly difficult printed mazes. People trace their way through the maze without lifting the pencil from the paper. Such tests require the test taker to pay close attention to a task for an extended period and continuously to plan ahead in order to make the correct choices.

Culture-fair tests, like performance tests, minimize or eliminate the use of language (Ortiz & Dynda, 2005). But they also try to downplay skills and values—such as the need for speed—that vary from culture to culture. In the *Goodenough–Harris Drawing Test*, for example, people are asked to draw the best picture of a person that they can. Drawings are scored for proportions, correct and complete representation of the parts of the body, detail in clothing, and so on. An example of a culture-fair item from the *Progressive Matrices* is Question 5 on page 247. This test consists of 60 designs, each with a missing part. The person is given six to eight possible choices to replace the part.

ON THE CUTTING EDGE

BIOLOGICAL MEASURES OF INTELLIGENCE

Thus far we have considered psychological measures of intelligence. However, numerous efforts have been made to assess intelligence through biological measures (Haier, 2003; Stelmack, Knott, & Beauchamp, 1993; Vernon, 1993, 2000). Beginning early in the 20th century, psychologists attempted to correlate brain size with intelligence. The correlations were very weak but always positive, suggesting a slight relation between the two. More recently, investigators have compared the sizes and metabolic functioning of such brain structures as the cerebellum and hippocampus, revealing small but significant differences among the brains of people with different forms of mental retardation (Lawrence, Lott, & Haier, 2005). Other researchers have found modest relationships between intelligence and the electrical response of brain cells to stimulation (Stelmack et al., 2003).

Researchers have also studied glucose metabolism, or how much energy the brain uses when solving a problem (Haier, 1993). Results suggest that highly intelligent people focus their brain resources, using smaller regions that are essential to problem solving. As a result, they use less glucose when performing an intellectual task (Neubauer, 2000), suggesting their brains work more efficiently.

Another promising line of research has shown that the brains of extremely intelligent people may mature differently, particularly during childhood and adolescence. One study, which involved successive neuroimaging of average and highly intelligent children, revealed that regions of the frontal cortex thicken and then become thinner at varying rates in children with different IQs (P. Shaw et al., 2006). Peak cortical thickness for children with average

intelligence was generally reached by age 7 or 8, while in children with extremely high IQs peak thickness did not occur until age 13 and was followed by a rapid thinning. It appeared as though the cortexes of highly intelligent children were especially *plastic* (see Chapter 2), or able to change with experience, in that a prolonged period of thickening was followed by an equally vigorous period of thinning during early adolescence. This dynamic cortical sculpting in highly intelligent children may involve a pruning of redundant neural connections, again increasing operational efficiency.

To date, no known biological measure of intelligence approaches the accuracy of psychological tests, but findings like these show promise that measures of intelligence may someday involve a biological component.

WHAT MAKES A GOOD TEST?

What are some important characteristics of a good test?

How can we tell whether intelligence tests will produce consistent results no matter when they are given? And how can we tell whether they really measure what they claim to measure? Psychologists address these questions by referring to a test's reliability and validity. Issues of reliability and validity apply equally to all psychological tests, not just to tests of mental abilities. In Chapter 10, for example, we reexamine these issues as they apply to personality assessment.

RELIABILITY By **reliability**, psychologists mean the dependability and consistency of the scores that a test yields. If your alarm clock is set for 8:15 A.M. and it goes off at that time every morning, it is reliable. But if it is set for 8:15 and rings at 8:00 one morning and 8:40 the next, you cannot depend on it; it is unreliable. Similarly, a test has reliability when it yields consistent results.

How do we know whether a test is reliable? The simplest way to find out is to give the test to a group and then, after a short time, to give the same people the same test again. If they obtain similar scores each time, the test is said to have high *test-retest reliability*. For example, **Table 7–2** shows the IQ scores of eight people tested one year apart using the same test. Although the scores did change slightly, none changed by more than six points.

There is a drawback, however. How do we know that people have not simply remembered the answers from the first testing and repeated them the second time around? To avoid this possibility, psychologists prefer to give two equivalent tests, both designed to measure the same thing. If people score the same on both forms, the tests are considered reliable. One way to create alternate forms is to split a single test into two parts—for example, to assign odd-numbered items to one part and even-numbered items to the other. If scores on the two halves agree, the test has **split-half reliability**. Most intelligence tests do, in fact, have alternate equivalent forms, just as each college admission test often has many versions.

ENDURING ISSUES

Stability–Change   Test Reliability and Changes in Intelligence

If a person takes an intelligence test on Monday and obtains an IQ score of 90, and then retakes the test on Tuesday and scores 130, clearly something is amiss. But what? Is the test at fault, or do the differences in scores accurately reflect changes in performance?

People vary from moment to moment and day to day. Changes in health and motivation can affect test results even with the most reliable tests. And although IQ scores tend to be remarkably stable after the age of 5 or 6, intellectual ability does sometimes change dramatically—for better or worse. One person's mental ability may decline substantially after a mild head injury; another person's scores on intelligence tests may rise after years of diligent intellectual study.

Since scores on even the best tests vary somewhat from one day to the next, many testing services now report a person's score along with a range of scores that allows for variations. For example, a score of 110 might be reported with a range of 104–116. This implies that the true score is most likely within a few points of 110, but almost certainly does not fall lower than 104 or higher than 116. ●●

These methods of testing reliability can be very effective. But psychological science demands more precise descriptions than "very reliable" or "fairly reliable." Psychologists express reliability in terms of **correlation coefficients**, which measure the relation between two sets of scores (see Appendix A for a discussion of correlation coefficients). If test scores on one occasion are absolutely consistent with those on another occasion, the correlation coefficient is 1.0. If there is no relationship between the scores, the correlation coefficient is zero. In **Table 7–2**, where there is a very close, but not perfect, relationship between the two sets of scores, the correlation coefficient is .96.

table 7–2	IQ SCORES ON THE SAME TEST GIVEN 1 YEAR APART	
Person	**First Testing**	**Second Testing**
A	130	127
B	123	127
C	121	119
D	116	122
E	109	108
F	107	112
G	95	93
H	89	94

performance tests Intelligence tests that minimize the use of language.

culture-fair tests Intelligence tests designed to eliminate cultural bias by minimizing skills and values that vary from one culture to another.

reliability Ability of a test to produce consistent and stable scores.

split-half reliability A method of determining test reliability by dividing the test into two parts and checking the agreement of scores on both parts.

correlation coefficients Statistical measures of the degree of association between two variables.

How reliable are intelligence tests? In general, people's IQ scores on most intelligence tests are quite stable (G. J. Meyer et al., 2001). Performance and culture-fair tests are somewhat less reliable. However, as we've discussed, scores on even the best tests vary somewhat from one day to another.

VALIDITY Generally, intelligence tests are quite reliable, but do these tests really measure "intelligence"? When psychologists ask this question, they are concerned with test validity. **Validity** refers to a test's ability to measure what it has been designed to measure. How do we know whether a given test actually measures what it claims to measure?

One measure of validity is known as **content validity**—whether the test contains an adequate sample of the skills or knowledge that it is supposed to measure. Most widely used intelligence tests, such as those from which the questions at the beginning of this chapter were taken, seem to measure at least some of the mental abilities that we think of as part of intelligence. These include planning, memory, understanding, reasoning, concentration, and the use of language. Although they may not adequately sample all aspects of intelligence equally well, they at least seem to have some content validity.

Another way to measure a test's validity is to see whether a person's score on that test closely matches his or her score on another test designed to measure the same thing. The two different scores should be very similar if they are both measures of the same ability. Various intelligence tests seem to show this kind of validity as well. Despite differences in test content, people who score high on one test tend to score high on others.

Still, this outcome doesn't necessarily mean that the two tests measure intelligence. Conceivably, they could both be measuring the same thing, but that thing is not necessarily intelligence. To demonstrate that the tests are valid, we need an independent measure of intelligence against which to compare intelligence test scores. Determining test validity in this way is called **criterion-related validity**. Ever since Binet invented the intelligence test, the main criterion against which intelligence test scores have been compared has been school achievement. Even the strongest critics agree that IQ tests predict school achievement well (Aiken & Groth-Marnat, 2005; Anastasi & Urbina, 1997).

CRITICISMS OF IQ TESTS What is it about IQ tests, then, that makes them controversial? One major criticism concerns the narrowness of their content. Many critics believe that intelligence tests assess only a very limited set of skills: passive verbal understanding, the ability to follow instructions, common sense, and, at best, scholastic aptitude (Sattler, 1992). One critic observes, "Intelligence tests measure how quickly people can solve relatively unimportant problems making as few errors as possible, rather than measuring how people grapple with relatively important problems, making as many productive errors as necessary with no time factor" (Blum, 1979, p. 83). A test score is also a very simplistic way of summing up an extremely complex set of abilities. Maloney and Ward (1976) point out that we do not describe a person's personality with a two- or three-digit number. Why, then, they ask, should we try to sum up something as complex as intelligence by labeling someone "90" or "110"?

If there is one thing that all intelligence tests measure, it is the ability to take tests. This fact could explain why people who do well on one IQ test also tend to do well on other tests. And it could also explain why intelligence test scores correlate so closely with school performance: Academic grades also depend heavily on test-taking ability. However, an IQ is not the same thing as intelligence. Tests measure our ability level at a certain point in time. Test scores do not tell us why someone performs poorly or well. Moreover, as we have seen, most psychologists today believe that intelligence is not a single entity but rather a combination of abilities required for living effectively in the real world (J.-Q. Chen & Gardner, 2005; Sternberg, 2005).

However, another major criticism of IQ tests is that their content and administration do not take into account cultural variations and, in fact, discriminate against minorities. High scores on most IQ tests require considerable mastery of standard English, thus biasing the tests in favor of middle- and upper-class White people (Ortiz & Dynda, 2005). Moreover, White middle-class examiners may not be familiar with the speech patterns of lower income African American children or children from homes in which English is not the primary language, a complication that may hamper good test performance (Sattler, 2005). In addition, certain questions may have very different meanings for children of different social

validity Ability of a test to measure what it has been designed to measure.

content validity Refers to a test's having an adequate sample of questions measuring the skills or knowledge it is supposed to measure.

criterion-related validity Validity of a test as measured by a comparison of the test score and independent measures of what the test is designed to measure.

classes. The WISC-III, for instance, asks, "What are you supposed to do if a child younger than you hits you?" The "correct" answer is "Walk away." But for a child who lives in an environment where survival depends on being tough, the "correct" answer might be "Hit him back." This answer, however, receives zero credit.

ENDURING ISSUES

Person–Situation   Tracking the Future

Tracking, the practice of assigning students who "test low" to special classes for slow learners, can work to the student's disadvantage if the test results do not reflect the student's true abilities. However, the opposite mistake may sometimes work to the student's advantage: A student of mediocre ability who is identified early on as above average may receive special attention, encouragement, and tutoring that would otherwise have been considered "wasted effort" on the part of teachers. Thus, intelligence test scores can set up a self-fulfilling prophecy, so that students defined as slow become slow, and those defined as quick become quick. In this way, intelligence tests may not only predict achievement but also help determine it (Rosenthal, 2002b). ●●

Although some investigators argue that the most widely used and thoroughly studied tests are not unfairly biased against minorities (Damas, 2002; Herrnstein & Murray, 1994), others contend a proper study of cultural bias in testing has yet to be made (R. J. Gregory, 2004). The issue of whether tests are unfair to minorities will be with us for some time. If IQ tests were used only for obscure research purposes, their results would not matter much; but because they are used for so many significant purposes, it is critical that we understand their strengths and their weaknesses.

IQ AND SUCCESS As we've seen, IQ scores predict success in school with some accuracy. In many ways, it isn't surprising that scores on these tests correlate well with academic achievement, since both of these involve intellectual activity and stress verbal ability. Moreover, both academic achievement and high IQ scores require similar kinds of motivation, attention, perseverance, and test-taking ability.

IQ tests also tend to predict success after people finish their schooling. People with high IQ scores tend to enter high-status occupations: Physicians and lawyers tend to have higher IQs than truck drivers and janitors. Critics point out, however, that this pattern can be explained in various ways. For one thing, because people with higher IQs tend to do better in school, they stay in school longer and earn advanced degrees, thereby opening the door to high-status jobs. Moreover, children from wealthy families generally grow up in environments that encourage academic success and reward good performance on tests (Blum, 1979; Ceci & Williams, 1997). In addition, they are more likely to have financial resources for postgraduate education or advanced occupational training, as well as family connections that pave the way to occupational success. Still, higher grades and intelligence test scores do predict occupational success and performance on the job (Barret & Depinet, 1991; Kuncel, Hezlett, & Ones, 2004; Ree & Earles, 1992).

Psychologists continue to look for ways to better predict academic and job success. Although there is much more research to be done, it seems reasonable that abilities beyond those measured by intelligence tests contribute to success on the job and to success in school. For example, job performance may be better predicted by tests of tacit knowledge—the kind of practical knowledge that people need to be able to perform their jobs effectively. One approach to expanding the usefulness of intelligence testing in schools is to use IQ scores in conjunction with other kinds of information that help interpret what these scores mean. One such approach is the System of Multicultural Pluralistic Adjustment (SOMPA), which involves collecting a wide range of data on a child, such as overall health status and socioeconomic background. This information on the student's characteristics and his or her environment is used to provide a context within which intelligence test scores can be interpreted.

CHECK YOUR UNDERSTANDING

1. Indicate whether the following statements are true (T) or false (F).
   a. ___ Intelligence is synonymous with problem-solving ability.
   b. ___The early American psychologist L. L. Thurstone, maintained that intelligence was quite general and should not be thought of as several distinct abilities.
   c. ___ Intrapersonal intelligence reflects the adage, "Know thyself."
   d. ___ Sternberg's and Gardner's theories of intelligence both emphasize practical abilities.

2. In 1916, the Stanford psychologist L. M. Terman introduced the term _____ _____ , or _____, and set the score of _____ for a person of average intelligence.

3. _____ tests eliminate or minimize the use of words in assessing mental abilities. Like these tests, _____-_____ tests minimize the use of language, but they also include questions that minimize skills and values that vary across cultures.

Answers: 1. a. (F), b. (F), c. (T), d. (T). 2. intelligence quotient, I.Q., 100. 3. Performance, culture-fair.

APPLY YOUR UNDERSTANDING

1. Margaret is trying to create a 10-item intelligence test. She compares scores from her test to scores on the Stanford–Binet test in an attempt to determine her test's
   a. reliability.
   b. validity.
   c. standard scores.
   d. standard deviation.

2. A friend of yours says, "Everyone has different talents and abilities. Some people are really good at math but just kind of average at everything else. Other people are really good at music or athletics or dancing but can't add two numbers to save their lives. Because you have an ability in one area doesn't mean you're talented at other things." Your friend's view of abilities most closely matches which of the following theorists discussed in this section of the chapter?
   a. Spearman
   b. Gardner
   c. Thurstone
   d. Binet

Answers: 1. b. 2. b.

Heredity, Environment, and Intelligence

What determines individual differences in intelligence?

Is intelligence inherited, or is it the product of the environment? Sorting out the importance of each factor as it contributes to intelligence is a complex task.

HEREDITY

Why are twin studies useful in studying intelligence?

As we saw in Chapter 2, "The Biological Basis of Behavior," scientists can use studies of identical twins to measure the effects of heredity in humans. Twin studies of intelligence begin by comparing the IQ scores of identical twins who have been raised together. As **Figure 7–9** shows, the correlation between their IQ scores is very high. In addition to identical genes, however, these twins grew up in very similar environments: They shared parents, home, teachers, vacations, and probably friends, too. These common experiences could explain their similar IQ scores. To check this possibility, researchers have tested identical twins who were separated early in life—generally before they were 6 months old—and raised in different families. As **Figure 7–9** shows, even when identical twins are raised in different families, they tend to have very similar test scores; in fact, the similarity is much greater than that between nontwin siblings who grow up in the *same* environment.

These findings make a strong case for the heritability of intelligence. Although, for reasons identified in Chapter 2, twin studies do not constitute "final proof"; other evidence also demonstrates the role of heredity. For example, adopted children have been found to have IQ scores that are more similar to those of their *biological* mothers than to those of the mothers who are raising them. Researcher John Loehlin finds these results particularly interesting because "[they] reflect genetic resemblance in the absence of shared environment: These birth mothers had no contact with their children after the first few days of life" (Loehlin, Horn, & Willerman, 1997, p. 113). Do psychologists, then, conclude that intelligence is an inherited trait and that environment plays little, if any, role?

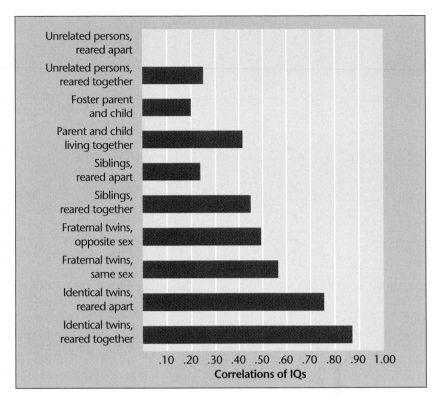

Figure 7–9

Correlations of IQ scores and family relationships. Identical twins who grow up in the same household have IQ scores that are almost identical to each other. Even when they are reared apart, their scores are highly correlated.

Source: Adapted from "Genetics and intelligence: A review," by L. Erienmeyer–Kimling and L. F. Jarvik 1963, *Science, 142,* pp. 1477–79. Copyright © 1963 by the American Association for the Advancement of Science. Reprinted with permission of the author.

ENVIRONMENT

What have we learned from early intervention programs about the influence of the environment on intellectual development?

Probably no psychologist denies that genes play a role in determining intelligence, but many believe that genes provide a base or starting point (Garlick, 2003). Each of us inherits a certain body build from our parents, but our actual weight is greatly determined by what we eat and how much we exercise. Similarly, although we inherit certain mental capacities, their development depends on what we see around us as infants, how our parents respond to our first attempts to talk, what schools we attend, which books we read, which television programs we watch—even what we eat (Sternberg & Grigorenko, 2001). Moreover, recent evidence indicates that the role of heredity varies with social economic status: In impoverished families, it appears to have little or no bearing on intelligence; in affluent families, its influence appears to be stronger (Turkheimer, Haley, Waldron, D'Onofrio, & Gottesman, 2003).

Environment affects children even before birth, such as through prenatal nutrition (Sigman, 2000). In one study of economically deprived pregnant women, half were given a dietary supplement and half were given placebos. At ages 3 and 4, the children of the mothers who had taken the supplement scored significantly higher on intelligence tests than the other children (Harrell, Woodyard, & Gates, 1955). During infancy, malnutrition can lower IQ scores by an average of 20 points (Stock & Smythe, 1963). Conversely, vitamin supplements can increase young children's IQ scores, possibly even among well-nourished children (Benton & Roberts, 1988; Schoenthaler et al., 1991).

Quite by chance, psychologist H. M. Skeels found evidence in the 1930s that IQ scores among children also depend on environmental stimulation. While investigating orphanages for the state of Iowa, Skeels observed that the children lived in very overcrowded wards and that the few adults there had almost no time to play with the children, to talk to them, or to read them stories. Many of these children were classified as "subnormal" in intelligence. Skeels followed the cases of two girls who, after 18 months in an orphanage, were

Individual differences in intelligence can be partly explained by differences in environmental stimulation and encouragement. The specific forms of stimulation given vary from culture to culture. Because our culture assigns importance to developing academic skills, the stimulation of reading and exploring information in books can give children an edge over those who are not so encouraged.

sent to a ward for women with severe retardation. Originally, the girls' IQs were in the range of retardation, but after a year on the adult ward, as if by magic, their IQs had risen to normal (Skeels, 1938). Skeels regarded this fact as quite remarkable—after all, the women with whom the girls had lived were themselves severely retarded. When he placed 13 other "slow" children as houseguests in such adult wards, within 18 months their mean IQ rose from 64 to 92 (within the normal range)—all because they had had someone (even someone of below-normal intelligence) to play with them, to read to them, to cheer them on when they took their first steps, and to encourage them to talk (Skeels, 1942). During the same period, the mean IQ of a group of children who had been left in orphanages dropped from were self-supporting, their occupations ranging from waiting on tables to real-estate sales. Of the contrasting group, half were unemployed, four were still in institutions, and all of those who had jobs were dishwashers (Skeels, 1966).

Later studies have reinforced Skeels's findings on the importance of intellectually stimulating surroundings as well as the importance of good nutrition (Capron & Duyme, 1989). The researchers found that the socioeconomic status (SES) of adoptive parents had an effect on their adopted children's IQs. Regardless of the socioeconomic status of the child's biological parents, children adopted by high-SES parents had higher IQs than did those adopted by low-SES parents, because high-SES families tend to provide children with better nutrition and heightened stimulation. Do such findings mean that intervention programs that enhance the environments of impoverished children can have a positive impact on their IQ?

INTERVENTION PROGRAMS: HOW MUCH CAN WE BOOST IQ? In 1961, the Milwaukee Project set out to learn whether intervening in a child's family life could offset the negative effects of cultural and socioeconomic deprivation on IQ scores (Garber & Heber, 1982; Heber, Garber, Harrington, & Hoffman, 1972). The average score of the 40 pregnant women in the study was less than 75 on the Wechsler scale. Women in the control group received no special education or training; those in the experimental group were sent to school, given job training, and instructed in child care, household management, and personal relationships.

After the babies were born, the research team shifted their focus to them. For 6 years, the children whose mothers received special training spent most of each day in an infant-education center, where they were fed, taught, and cared for by paraprofessionals who behaved like affluent mothers not working outside the home. The children whose mothers received no special training did not attend the center. Ultimately the children in the experimental group achieved an average IQ score of 126: 51 points higher than their mothers' average scores. In contrast, the average score of the children in the control group was 94. Thus, this study supported the notion that intervention may indeed counter the negative effects of cultural and socioeconomic deprivation on IQ scores.

Head Start, the nation's largest intervention program, began in 1965. Today, it provides comprehensive services for over 906,000 children, lasting at least half a day up to 2 years (Head Start Bureau, 2006). Focusing on preschoolers between the ages of 3 and 5 from low-income families, the program has two key goals: to provide children with educational and social skills before they go to school, and to provide information about nutrition and health to both the children and their families. Head Start involves parents in all its aspects, from daily activities to administration of the program itself. This parental involvement has been crucial to Head Start's success (Cronan, Walen, & Cruz, 1994; Mendez & Martha, 2001).

Several studies evaluating the long-term effects of Head Start have found that it boosts cognitive and language abilities (W. S. Barnett, 1998; Wasik, Bond, & Hindman, 2006; Zigler, 1998; Zigler & Styfco, 2001), but some experts are concerned that these improvements may be modest or short term. Nevertheless, children leaving Head Start are in a better position to profit from schooling than they would be otherwise (Zigler & Styfco, 1994). Studies following Head Start graduates until age 27 revealed higher academic achievement and lower delinquency level. Graduates also tended to stay in school longer and were more likely to graduate from college. Thus, even if the mental ability gains due to Head Start are not long lasting, the program still seems to provide long-term, practical benefits (Zigler & Styfco, 2001; Zigler, 2003).

Head Start is a program designed to do just what its name implies: to give children from disadvantaged environments a head start in acquiring the skills and attitudes needed for success in school. Although researchers debate whether Head Start produces significant and lasting boosts in IQ, it does have many school-related benefits for those who participate in it.

Overall, the effectiveness of early intervention appears to depend on the quality of the particular program (S. L. Ramey, 1999; C. T. Ramey, Ramey, & Lanzi, 2001; Zigler & Styfco, 1993). Intervention programs that have clearly defined goals; that explicitly teach such basic skills as counting, naming colors, and writing the alphabet; and that take into account the broad context of human development, including health care and other social services, achieve the biggest and most durable gains. Also, interventions that begin in the preschool years and include a high degree of parental involvement (to ensure continuity after the official program ends) are generally more successful (Zigler, Finn-Stevenson, & Hall, 2002).

THE IQ DEBATE: A USEFUL MODEL

How can the study of plants help us to understand the relationship between heredity and environment?

Both heredity and environment have important effects on individual differences in intelligence, but is one of these factors more important than the other? The answer depends on the IQs that you are comparing. A useful analogy comes from studies of plants (Turkheimer, 1991). Suppose that you grow one group of randomly assigned plants in enriched soil, and another group in poor soil. The enriched group will grow to be taller and stronger than the nonenriched group; the difference between the two groups in this case is due entirely to differences in their environment. *Within* each group of plants, however, differences among individual plants are likely to be primarily due to genetics, because all plants in the same group share essentially the same environment. Thus, the height and strength of any single plant reflects both heredity *and* environment.

Similarly, group differences in IQ scores might be due to environmental factors, but differences among people *within* groups could be due primarily to genetics. At the same time, the IQ scores of particular people would reflect the effects of both heredity *and* environment. Robert Plomin, an influential researcher in the field of human intelligence, concludes that "the world's literature suggests that about half of the total variance in IQ scores can be accounted for by genetic variance" (Plomin, 1997, p. 89). This finding means that environment accounts for the other half. Heredity and environment both contribute to human differences.

THE FLYNN EFFECT An interesting side note to this discussion is the fact that IQ scores have *gone up* in the population as a whole (Daley, Whaley, Sigman, Espinosa, & Neumann, 2003; Neisser et al., 1996; Neisser, 1998; Resing & Nijland, 2002). Because James Flynn (Flynn, 1984, 1987) of the University of Otago in New Zealand was the first to report this finding, it is often called the *Flynn Effect*. In his original research, Professor Flynn gathered evidence showing that, between 1932 and 1978, intelligence test scores rose about three points per decade. More recently, by pulling together data from five nations (Britain, Netherlands, Israel, Norway, and Belgium) Flynn (1999) has shown that the average increase in IQ may be as high as six points per decade. Consistent with this result is a finding by Flieller (1999) that children today between the ages of 10 and 15 years display significant cognitive advancement compared with children of the same age tested 20 and 30 years ago. And, as Neisser (1998) points out, accompanying this general increase in IQ scores is a decrease in the difference in intelligence scores between Blacks and Whites.

Although this finding has many possible explanations, none of them seem to account entirely for the magnitude of the effect (Flynn, 1999; Rowe & Rodgers, 2002). Rather than getting smarter, maybe people are simply getting better at taking tests. Environmental factors, such as improved nutrition and health care, may also contribute to this trend (Lynn, 1989; Teasdale & Owen, 2005). Some psychologists have suggested that the sheer complexity of the modern world is responsible (Schooler, 1998). For example, the proliferation of televisions, computers, and video games could be contributing to the rise in IQ scores (Greenfield, 1998; Neisser, 1998). Continued research on the Flynn Effect will undoubtedly shed more light on our understanding of the nature of intelligence and the factors that influence its development (Kanaya, 2004).

THINKING CRITICALLY ABOUT . . .

The Flynn Effect

Flynn and others have found that IQ scores are rising, but what does this really mean? As Flynn (1999) points out, it is hard to see how genes could account for so rapid an increase in IQ. Clearly, some aspect of the environment must account for most or all of the increase in IQ scores.

1. Of the possible explanations mentioned in the text, which seem to you to be most likely? Why? How might you go about determining whether one explanation is better than another?

2. Do you think IQ scores will continue to rise? Is your position on that question related to your answer to the first question?

3. Does a rise in IQ test scores necessarily mean that there has been a comparable increase in intelligence? Why or why not?

MENTAL ABILITIES AND HUMAN DIVERSITY: GENDER AND CULTURE

Do culture and gender influence mental abilities?

Are there differences in mental abilities between males and females or among people from different cultures? Many people assume, for example, that males are naturally better at mathematics and that females excel in verbal skills. Others believe that the sexes are basically alike in mental abilities. Similarly, how do we account for the superior academic performance by students from certain countries and certain cultural backgrounds? Research offers some interesting insights into these controversial issues.

GENDER Many occupations are dominated by one gender or the other. Engineering, for example, has traditionally been almost exclusively a male domain. Is it possible that this occupational difference and others like it reflect underlying gender differences in mental abilities?

In 1974, psychologists Eleanor Maccoby and Carol Jacklin published a review of psychological research on gender differences. They found no differences at all between males and females in most of the studies they examined. However, a few differences did appear in cognitive abilities: Girls tended to display greater verbal ability, and boys tended to exhibit stronger spatial and mathematical abilities. Largely as a result of this research, gender differences in verbal, spatial, and mathematical abilities became so widely accepted that they were often cited as one of the established facts of psychological research (Hyde, Fennema, & Lamon, 1990; Hyde & Linn, 1988).

Yet, a closer examination of the research literature, including more recent work, indicates that gender differences in math and verbal ability may be virtually nonexistent. For example, Janet Shibley Hyde and her colleagues analyzed 165 research studies, involving more than a million people, in which gender differences in verbal ability were examined. They concluded that "there are no gender differences in verbal ability, at least at this time, in American culture, in the standard ways that verbal ability has been measured" (Hyde & Linn, 1988, p. 62). In a similar analysis of studies examining mathematical ability, Hyde and her colleagues concluded that "females outperformed males by only a negligible amount. . . . Females are superior in computation, there are no gender differences in understanding of mathematical concepts, and gender differences favoring males do not emerge until the high school years" (Hyde et al., 1990, pp. 139, 151).

Males apparently do have an advantage over females in *spatial ability*, however (J. Choi & Silverman, 2003; Halpern, 1992, 1997; Voyer, Voyer, & Bryden, 1995). Spatial tasks include mentally rotating an object and estimating horizontal and vertical dimensions. These skills are particularly useful in solving certain engineering, architecture, and geometry problems. They are also handy in deciding how to arrange furniture in your new apartment or how to fit all those suitcases into the trunk of your car!

Men also differ from women in another way: They are much more likely than women to fall at the extremes of the intelligence range (N. Brody, 2000; Halpern, 1997). In one review of several large studies, Hedges and Nowell (1995) found that males accounted for seven out of eight people

Research shows there are only negligible differences between men and women in mathematical ability.

with extremely high IQ scores. These authors also reported that males represented an almost equally large proportion of the IQ scores within the range of mental retardation.

What should we conclude from these findings? First, the cognitive differences between males and females appear to be restricted to specific cognitive skills (Stumpf & Stanley, 1998). Scores on tests such as the Stanford–Binet or the WAIS reveal no gender differences in general intelligence (Halpern, 1992). Second, gender differences in specific cognitive abilities typically are small and in some cases appear to be diminishing—even when studied cross-culturally (Skaalvik & Rankin, 1994). Finally, we do not know whether the differences that do exist are a result of biological or cultural factors (Hyde & Mezulis, 2002).

Considerable research has identified several factors that discourage females from pursuing careers in mathematics and science. For example, one study found that women avoid careers in math and science partly because of *mathematics anxiety*. Girls and college women are more likely than males to agree with the statement "I dread mathematics class" (Chipman, Krantz, & Silver, 1992). Findings like these suggest that occupational and career differences may simply be an outgrowth of the ways that boys and girls are brought up.

CULTURE For years, U.S. media have been reporting an achievement gap, especially in math, between American and Asian students. Recent media reports suggest even broader differences. According to one report, "The United States is now behind, or has lost ground, on several important education measures among countries in the OECD, an economic- and social-policy organization of 30 industrialized countries" (Gehring, 2001).

Psychological research tells us something about the causes of these achievement gaps. Two decades ago, a team of researchers led by the late Harold Stevenson began to study the performance of first- and fifth-grade children in American, Chinese, and Japanese elementary schools (Stevenson, Lee, & Stigler, 1986). At that time, the American students at both grade levels lagged far behind the other two countries in math and came in second in reading. A decade later, when the study was repeated with a new group of fifth-graders, the researchers discovered that the American students performed even worse than they had earlier. In 1990, the research team also studied the original first-graders from all three cultures, now in the eleventh grade. The result? The American students retained their low standing in mathematics compared with the Asian students (Stevenson, 1992, 1993; Stevenson, Chen, & Lee, 1993).

The next question was, Why? Stevenson's team wondered whether cultural attitudes toward ability and effort might, in part, explain the differences. To test this hypothesis, the researchers asked students, their parents, and their teachers in all three countries whether they thought effort or ability had a greater impact on academic performance. From first through eleventh-grade, American students on the whole disagreed with the statement that "everyone in my class has about the same natural ability in math." In other words, the Americans thought that "studying hard" has little to do with performance. Their responses appear to reflect a belief that mathematical skill is primarily a function of innate ability. American mothers expressed a similar view. Moreover, 41% of the American eleventh-grade teachers thought "innate intelligence" is the most important factor in mathematics performance. By contrast, Asian students, parents, and teachers believed that effort and "studying hard" determine success in math.

Such culturally influenced views of the relative importance of effort and innate ability may have profound consequences for the way that children, their parents, and their teachers approach the task of learning. Students who believe that learning is based on natural ability see little value in working hard to learn a difficult subject. By contrast, students who believe that academic success comes from studying are more likely to work hard. Indeed, even the brightest students will not get far without making an effort. Although many Americans no doubt believe in the value of effort and hard work, our widespread perception that innate ability is the key to academic success may be affecting the performance of U.S. students (Stevenson, Lee, & Mu, 2000).

In short, while Stevenson's research confirms the existence of significant differences in student performance across various cultures, the evidence suggests that these differences reflect cultural attitudes toward the importance of ability and effort, rather than an underlying difference in intelligence across the cultures.

THINKING CRITICALLY ABOUT . . .

International Comparisons of School Achievement

1. Do you agree or disagree with the conclusions of Stevenson and his colleagues that cultural attitudes may account for some of the academic performance differences between American students and students from other countries? What additional evidence might provide support for your position?

2. If you were to research this topic today, would you do things differently than Stevenson's team did? Are there any other factors that might account for the differences in achievement that you would investigate? What specific questions would you ask of the parents, students, and teachers? What additional information about the school systems would you collect?

3. Given the results of this research, what specific steps would you take to improve the academic performance of American children?

mental retardation Condition of significantly subaverage intelligence combined with deficiencies in adaptive behavior.

EXTREMES OF INTELLIGENCE

What do psychologists know about the two extremes of human intelligence: very high and very low?

The average IQ score on intelligence tests is 100. Nearly 70% of all people have IQs between 85 and 115, and all but 5% of the population have IQs between 70 and 130. In this section, we focus on people who score at the two extremes of intelligence—those with mental retardation and those who are intellectually gifted.

MENTAL RETARDATION Mental retardation encompasses a vast array of mental deficits with a wide variety of causes, treatments, and outcomes. The American Psychiatric Association (1994) defines mental retardation as "significantly subaverage general intellectual functioning . . . that is accompanied by significant limitations in adaptive functioning" and that appears before the age of 21 (p. 39). There are also various degrees of mental retardation. Mild retardation corresponds to Stanford–Binet IQ scores ranging from a high of about 70 to a low near 50. Moderate retardation corresponds to IQ scores from the low 50s to the middle 30s. People with IQ scores between the middle 30s and 20 are considered severely retarded, and the profoundly retarded are those whose scores are below 20. (See **Table 7–3**.)

But a low IQ is not in itself sufficient for diagnosing mental retardation. The person must also be unable to perform the daily tasks needed to function independently (Rust & Wallace, 2004) A person who is able to live independently, for example, is not considered to have mental retardation even if his or her IQ may be extremely low. To fully assess individuals and to place them in appropriate treatment and educational programs, mental health professionals need information on physical health and on emotional and social adjustment.

Moreover, people with mental retardation sometimes display exceptional skills in areas other than general intelligence. Probably the most dramatic and intriguing examples involve *savant performance* (Boelte, Uhlig, & Poustka, 2002; L. K. Miller, 2005). Some people with mental retardation (or other mental handicaps) exhibit remarkable abilities in highly specialized areas, such as numerical computation, memory, art, or music (L. K. Miller, 1999; Treffert & Wallace, 2002). Savant performances include mentally calculating large numbers almost

table 7–3	LEVELS OF MENTAL RETARDATION	
Type of Retardation	**IQ Range**	**Attainable Skill Level**
Mild retardation	Low 50s to low 70s	People may be able to function adequately in society and learn skills comparable to a sixth-grader, but they need special help at times of unusual stress.
Moderate retardation	Mid-30s to low 50s	People profit from vocational training and may be able to travel alone. They learn on a second-grade level and perform skilled work in a sheltered workshop under supervision.
Severe retardation	Low 20s to mid-30s	People do not learn to talk or to practice basic hygiene until after age 6. They cannot learn vocational skills but can perform simple tasks under supervision.
Profound retardation	Below 20 or 25	Constant care is needed. Usually, people have a diagnosed neurological disorder.

Source: Based on APA, *DSM-IV*, 1994.

instantly, determining the day of the week for any date over many centuries, and playing back a long musical composition after hearing it played only once.

What causes mental retardation? In most cases, the causes are unknown (Beirne-Smith, Patton, & Ittenbach, 1994; Glidden, 2004)—especially in cases of mild retardation, which account for nearly 90% of all retardation. When causes can be identified, most often they stem from a wide variety of genetic, environmental, social, nutritional, and other risk factors (Baumeister & Baumeister, 2000).

About 25% of cases—especially the more severe forms of retardation—appear to involve genetic or biological disorders. Scientists have identified more than 100 forms of mental retardation caused by single defective genes (Plomin, 1997). One is the genetically based disease *phenylketonuria*, or *PKU*, which occurs in about one person out of 25,000. In people suffering from PKU, the liver fails to produce an enzyme necessary for early brain development. Fortunately, placing a PKU baby on a special diet can prevent mental retardation from developing (Merrick, Aspler, & Schwarz, 2005). Another form of hereditary mental retardation is *fragile-X syndrome* (Hagerman & Hagerman, 2002), which affects about 1 in every 1,250 males and 1 in every 2,500 females. A defect in the X chromosome, passed on between generations, seems to be caused by a specific gene (Visootsak, Warren, & Anido, 2005). In the disorder known as *Down syndrome*, which affects 1 in 600 newborns, an extra 21st chromosome is the cause. Down syndrome, named for the physician who first described its symptoms, is marked by moderate to severe mental retardation.

Biologically caused mental retardation can be moderated through education and training (Ramey, Ramey, & Lanzi, 2001). The prognosis for those with no underlying physical causes is even better. People whose retardation is due to a history of social and educational deprivation may respond dramatically to appropriate interventions. Today, the majority of children with physical or mental disabilities are educated in local school systems (Lipsky & Gartner, 1996), in *inclusion* arrangements (Kavale, 2002) (previously known as *mainstreaming*), which help these students to socialize with their nondisabled peers. The principle of mainstreaming has also been applied to adults with mental retardation, by taking them out of large, impersonal institutions and placing them in smaller community homes that provide more normal life experiences (Conroy, 1996; Maisto & Hughes, 1995; Stancliffe, 1997). Although the benefits of inclusion are debatable, most psychologists and educators support the effort (Doré, Wagner, & Doré, 2002; Zigler & Hodapp, 1991).

Down syndrome is a common biological cause of mental retardation, affecting one in 600 newborns. The prognosis for Down syndrome children today is much better than it was in the past. With adequate support, many children with the affliction can participate in regular classrooms and other childhood activities.

GIFTEDNESS At the other extreme of the intelligence scale are "the gifted"—those with exceptional mental abilities, as measured by scores on standard intelligence tests. As with mental retardation, the causes of **giftedness** are largely unknown.

The first and now-classic study of giftedness was begun by Lewis Terman and his colleagues in the early 1920s. They defined giftedness in terms of academic talent and measured it by an IQ score in the top 2 percentile (Terman, 1925). More recently, some experts have sought to broaden the definition of giftedness beyond that of simply high IQ (L. J. Coleman & Cross, 2001; Csikszentmihalyi, Rathunde, & Whalen, 1993; Subotnik & Arnold, 1994). One view is that giftedness is often an interaction of above-average general intelligence, exceptional creativity, and high levels of commitment (Renzulli, 1978). Various criteria can identify gifted students, including scores on intelligence tests, teacher recommendations, and achievement test results. School systems generally use diagnostic testing, interviews, and evaluation of academic and creative work (Sattler, 1992). These selection methods can identify students with a broad range of talent, but they can miss students with specific abilities, such as a talent for mathematics or music. This is an important factor because research suggests that most gifted individuals display special abilities in only a few areas. "Globally" gifted people are rare (Achter, Lubinski, & Benbow, 1996; Lubinski & Benbow, 2000; Olzewski-Kubilius, 2003; Winner, 1998, 2000).

A common view of gifted people is that they have poor social skills and are emotionally maladjusted. However, research does not support this stereotype (Richards, Encel, & Shute, 2003; A. Robinson & Clinkenbeard, 1998). Indeed, one review (Janos & Robinson, 1985) concluded that "being intellectually gifted, at least at moderate levels of ability, is clearly an asset in terms of psychosocial adjustment in most situations" (p. 181). Nevertheless, children who are exceptionally gifted sometimes do experience difficulty "fitting in" with their peers.

giftedness Refers to superior IQ combined with demonstrated or potential ability in such areas as academic aptitude, creativity, and leadership.

ENDURING ISSUES

Diversity–Universality   Not Everyone Wants to Be Special

Because gifted children sometimes become bored and socially isolated in regular classrooms, some experts recommend that they be offered special programs (Olzewski-Kubilius, 2003). Special classes for the gifted would seem to be something the gifted themselves would want, but this is not always the case. Special classes and, even more, special schools, can separate gifted students from their friends and neighbors. And stereotypes about the gifted may mean that, once identified as gifted, the student is less likely to be invited to participate in certain school activities, such as dances, plays, and sports. Gifted students also sometimes object to being set apart, labeled "brains," and pressured to perform beyond the ordinary. Many but not all gifted students welcome the opportunities offered by special programs. ●●

Any discussion of giftedness inevitably leads to the topic of creativity. The two topics are, indeed, closely related, as we shall see in the next section.

CHECK YOUR UNDERSTANDING

1. Indicate whether the following statements are true (T) or false (F):
   a. ___ When identical twins are raised apart, their IQ scores are not highly correlated.
   b. ___ Environmental stimulation has little, if any, effect on IQ.
   c. ___ Head Start graduates are more likely than their peers to graduate from college.
2. As psychologists learn more about giftedness, the definition of it has become (broader/narrower) _____.

Answers: 1. a. (F), b. (F), c. (T). 2. broader.

APPLY YOUR UNDERSTANDING

1. Imagine that an adoption agency separates identical twins at birth and places them randomly in very different kinds of homes. Thirty years later, a researcher discovers that the pairs of twins have almost identical scores on IQ tests. Which of the following conclusions is most consistent with that finding?
   a. Heredity has a significant effect on intelligence.
   b. Environment has a significant effect on intelligence.
   c. Heredity provides a starting point, but environment determines our ultimate intelligence.
   d. Because the twins were placed in very different environments, it's not possible to draw any conclusions.
2. Ten-year-old John has an IQ score of 60 on the Wechsler Intelligence Scale for Children. Which of the following would you need to know before you could determine whether John is mildly retarded?
   a. whether his score on the Stanford–Binet Intelligence Scale is also below 70
   b. whether he can perform the daily tasks needed to function independently
   c. whether he has a genetic defect in the X chromosome
   d. whether he suffered from malnutrition before birth

Answers: 1. a. 2. b.

Creativity

What is creativity?

Creativity is the ability to produce novel and socially valued ideas or objects ranging from philosophy to painting, from music to mousetraps (Mumford & Gustafson, 1988; Runco, 2004; Sternberg, 2001). Sternberg included creativity and insight as important elements in human intelligence. Most IQ tests, however, do not measure creativity, and many

creativity The ability to produce novel and socially valued ideas or objects.

researchers would argue that intelligence and creativity are not the same thing. What, then, is the relationship between intelligence and creativity? Are people who score high on IQ tests likely to be more creative than those who score low?

INTELLIGENCE AND CREATIVITY

How is creativity related to intelligence?

Early studies typically found little or no relationship between creativity and intelligence (for example, Getzels & Jackson, 1962; Wing, 1969), but these studies were concerned only with bright students. Perhaps creativity and intelligence are indeed linked, but only until IQ reaches a certain threshold level, after which higher intelligence isn't associated with higher creativity. There is considerable evidence for this threshold theory (Barron, 1963; Yamamoto & Chimbidis, 1966). All the research supporting it, however, has relied heavily on tests of creativity, and perhaps real-life creativity isn't the same as what these tests measure. Still, it makes sense that a certain minimum level of intelligence might be needed for creativity to develop, but that other factors underlie creativity as well.

Creative people are often perceived as being more intelligent than less creative people who have equivalent IQ scores. Perhaps some characteristic that creative people share—possibly "effectiveness" or some quality of social competence—conveys the impression of intelligence even though it is not measured by intelligence tests (Barron & Harrington, 1981).

In general, creative people are *problem finders* as well as problem solvers (Getzels, 1975). The more creative people are, the more they like to work on problems that they have set for themselves. Creative scientists (such as Charles Darwin and Albert Einstein) often work for years on a problem that has sprung from their own curiosity (Gruber & Wallace, 2001). Also, "greatness" rests not just on "talent" or "genius"; such people also have intense dedication, ambition, and perseverance (Stokes, 2006).

CREATIVITY TESTS

Can creativity be measured?

Measuring creativity poses special problems (Naglieri & Kaufman, 2001). Because creativity involves original responses to situations, questions that can be answered *true* or *false* or *a* or *b* are not good measures. More open-ended tests are better. Instead of asking for one predetermined answer to a problem, the examiner asks the test takers to let their imaginations run free. Scores are based on the originality of a person's answers and often on the number of responses, too.

In one such test, the *Torrance Test of Creative Thinking*, people must explain what is happening in a picture, how the scene came about, and what its consequences are likely to be. In the *Christensen–Guilford Test*, they are to list as many words containing a given letter as possible, to name things belonging to a certain category (such as liquids that will burn), and to write four-word sentences beginning with the letters RDLS—"Rainy days look sad, Red dogs like soup, Renaissance dramas lack symmetry," and so on. One of the most widely used creativity tests, S. A. Mednick's (1962) *Remote Associates Test (RAT)*, asks people to relate three apparently unrelated words. For example, the three stimulus words might be *poke, go,* and *molasses,* and one response is to relate them through the word *slow:* "Slowpoke, go slow, slow as molasses." In the newer *Wallach and Kogan Creative Battery*, people form associative groupings. For instance, children are asked to "name all the round things you can think of" and to find similarities between objects, such as between a potato and a carrot.

Although people who do not have high IQs can score well on the Wallach and Kogan test, the Torrance test seems to require a reasonably high IQ for adequate performance. This finding raises the question of which of these tests is a valid measure of creativity. In general, current tests of creativity do not show a high degree of validity (Clapham, 2004; Feldhusen & Goh, 1995), so measurements derived from them must be interpreted with caution.

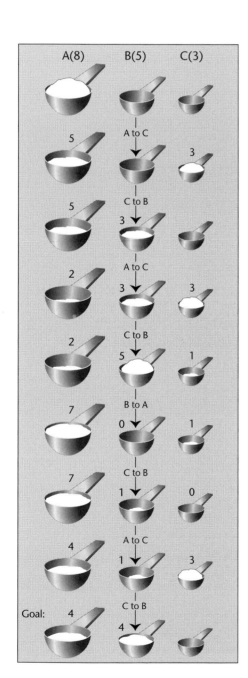

Figure 7–10
Answer to Problem 3.

CHECK YOUR UNDERSTANDING

1. The ability to produce novel and unique ideas or objects, ranging from philosophy to painting, from music to mousetraps, is termed _____.

2. Two important features of creative people are that they
   a. take risks and like to work on problems that they invent themselves.
   b. are perceived as less intelligent and more irresponsible than other people.
   c. excel at art but are poor at science.

3. _____-_____ tests are the best type for measuring creativity.

Answers: 1. creativity. 2. a. 3. Open-ended.

APPLY YOUR UNDERSTANDING

1. You are discussing creativity and intelligence with a friend who says, "Those are two different things. There's no relationship between being intelligent and being creative." Based on what you have learned in this chapter, which of the following would be the most accurate reply?
   a. "You're right. There is no evidence of a relationship between creativity and intelligence."
   b. "You're wrong. The higher a person's intelligence, the more creative he or she is likely to be."
   c. "That's apparently true only among very bright people. For most people, creativity and intelligence tend to go together."
   d. "That's true for people with IQ scores below about 100, but above that point, intelligence and creativity tend to go together."

Answers: 1. c.

Answers to Problems in the Chapter

PROBLEM 1 Fill each of the smaller spoons with salt from the larger spoon. That step will require 4 teaspoons of salt, leaving exactly 4 teaspoons of salt in the larger spoon.

PROBLEM 2 Turn the 5-minute hourglass over; when it runs out, turn over the 9-minute hourglass. When it runs out, 14 minutes have passed.

PROBLEM 3 As shown in **Figure 7–10**, fill spoon C with the salt from spoon A (now A has 5 teaspoons of salt and C has 3). Pour the salt from spoon C into spoon B (now A has 5 teaspoons of salt, and B has 3). Again fill spoon C with the salt from spoon A. (This leaves A with only 2 teaspoons of salt, while B and C each have 3.) Fill spoon B with the salt from spoon C. (This step leaves 1 teaspoon of salt in spoon C, while B has 5 teaspoons, and A has only 2.) Pour all of the salt from spoon B into spoon A. (Now A has 7 teaspoons of salt, and C has 1.) Pour all of the salt from spoon C into spoon B, and then fill spoon C from spoon A. (This step leaves 4 teaspoons of salt in A, 1 teaspoon in B, and 3 teaspoons in C.) Finally, pour all of the salt from spoon C into spoon B. (This step leaves 4 teaspoons of salt in spoons A and B, which is the solution.)

PROBLEM 4 Start both hourglasses. When the 5-minute hourglass runs out, turn it over to start it again. When the 9-minute hourglass runs out, turn over the 5-minute hourglass. Because there is 1 minute left in the 5-minute hourglass when you turn it over, it will run for only 4 minutes. Those 4 minutes, together with the original 9 minutes, add up to the required 13 minutes for the barbecue.

PROBLEM 5 Take one of the short pieces of chain shown in **Figure 7–11**, and open all three links. (This step costs 6 cents.) Use those three links to connect the remaining three pieces of chain. (Hence, closing the three links costs 9 cents.)

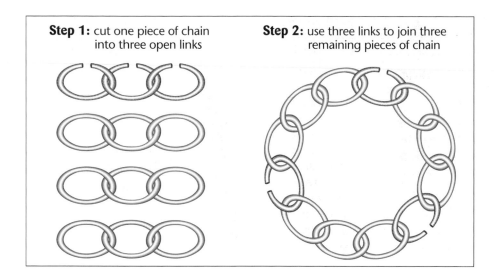

Step 1: cut one piece of chain into three open links

Step 2: use three links to join three remaining pieces of chain

Figure 7–11
Answer to Problem 5.

Figure 7–12
Answer to Problem 6.

PROBLEM 6 Join the matches to form a pyramid as shown in **Figure 7–12**.

PROBLEM 7 One way to solve this problem is to draw a diagram of the ascent and the descent, as in **Figure 7–13**. From this drawing, you can see that indeed there is a point that the monk passes at exactly the same time on both days. Another way to approach this problem is to imagine that there are two monks on the mountain; one starts ascending at 7 A.M., while the other starts descending at 7 A.M. on the same day. Clearly, sometime during the day the monks must meet somewhere along the route.

PROBLEM 8 This problem has four possible solutions, one of which is shown in **Figure 7–14**.

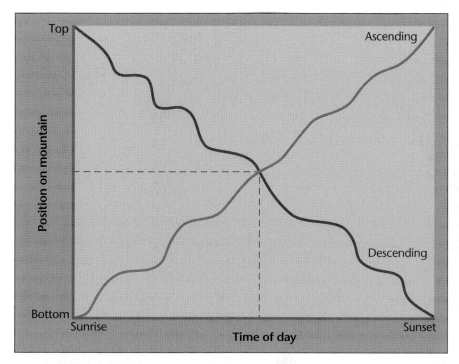

Figure 7–13
Answer to Problem 7.

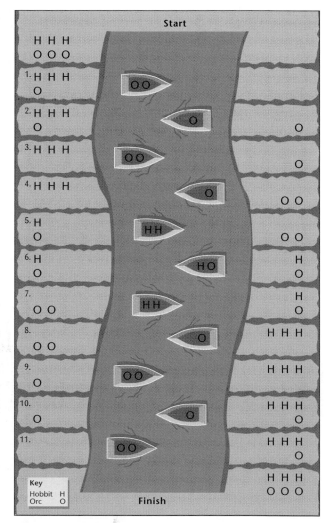

Figure 7–14
Answer to Problem 8.

Figure 7–15
Solution to Figure 7–7.
In solving the problem given in **Figure 7–7**, many people have trouble realizing that the box of tacks can also be used as a candleholder, as shown here.

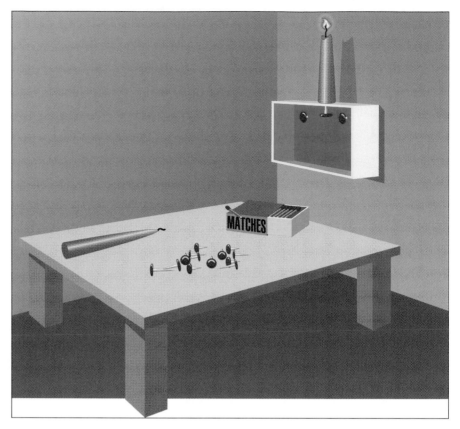

PROBLEM 9 There are 15 possible solutions to this problem, of which this is one: First, one Hobbit and one Orc cross the river in the boat; the Orc remains on the opposite side while the Hobbit rows back. Next, three Orcs cross the river; two of those Orcs remain on the other side (making a total of three Orcs on the opposite bank) while one Orc rows back. Now three Hobbits and one Orc row the boat back. Again, three Hobbits row across the river, at which point all five Hobbits are on the opposite bank with only two Orcs. Then, one of the Orcs rows back and forth across the river twice to transport the remaining Orcs to the opposite side.

Answers to Intelligence Test Questions

1. *Idleness* refers to the state of being inactive, not busy, unoccupied; *laziness* means an unwillingness or a reluctance to work. Laziness is one possible cause of idleness, but not the only cause.

2. If you face west, your right ear will face north.

3. *Obliterate* means to erase or destroy something completely.

4. Both an hour and a week are measures of time.

5. Alternative (f) is the correct pattern.

6. Seventy-five cents will buy nine pencils.

7. Alternative (d) is correct. A crutch is used to help someone who has difficulty with locomotion; spectacles are used to help someone who has difficulty with vision.

8. Alternative D is correct. The second figure is the same shape and size but with diagonal cross-hatching from upper left to lower right.

9. Figures 3, 4, and 5 can all be completely covered by using some or all of the given pieces.

CHAPTER REVIEW

Building Blocks of Thought

What are the three most important building blocks of thought? The three most important building blocks of thought are language, images, and concepts. As we think, we use words, sensory "snapshots," and categories that classify things.

What steps do we go through to turn a thought into a statement? **Language** is a flexible system of symbols that allows us to communicate ideas to others. When we express thoughts as statements, we must conform to our language's rules. Every language has rules indicating which sounds (or **phonemes**) are part of that particular language, how those sounds can be combined into meaningful units (or **morphemes**), and how those meaningful units can be ordered into phrases and sentences (rules of **grammar**). To communicate an idea, we start with a thought and then choose sounds, words, and phrases that will express the idea clearly. To understand the speech of others, the task is reversed.

What role do images play in thinking? **Images** are mental representations of sensory experiences. Visual images in particular can be powerful aids in thinking about the relationships between things. Picturing things in our mind's eye can sometimes help us solve problems.

How do concepts help us to think more efficiently? **Concepts** are categories for classifying objects, people, and experiences based on their common elements. Without the ability to form concepts, we would need a different name for every new thing we encounter. We draw on concepts to anticipate what new experiences will be like. Many concepts are "fuzzy," lacking clear-cut boundaries. Therefore we often use **prototypes**, mental models of the most typical examples of a concept, to classify new objects.

Language, Thought, and Culture

How do language, thought, and culture influence each other? According to Benjamin Whorf's **linguistic relativity hypothesis**, thought is greatly influenced by language. But critics contend that thought and experience can shape and change a language as much as a language can shape and change thought.

Is language male dominated? Some evidence indicates that the use of "man" and "he" to refer to all people affects the way that English speakers think. Referring to doctors, college professors, bankers, and executives by the generic "he" may contribute to the gender stereotyping of these respected occupations as appropriate for men but not for women. In contrast, referring to secretaries and housekeepers as "she" may reinforce the sterotype that those occupations are appropriate for women, not men.

Nonhuman Thought and Language

Can scientists learn what is on an animal's mind? Research indicates that some animals have humanlike cognitive capacities, such as the ability to form concepts and to reason. Apes have demonstrated sophisticated problem-solving skills. However, only chimpanzees and orangutans consistently show signs of self-awareness. Nonhuman animals communicate primarily though **signs**: general or global statements about the animal's current state. Using the distinguishing features of language, which include semantics, displacement, and productivity as criteria, no other species has its own language, athough chimpanzees have been taught to use American Sign Language.

Problem Solving

What are three general aspects of the problem-solving process? Interpreting a problem, formulating a strategy, and evaluating progress toward a solution are three general aspects of the problem-solving process. Each in its own way is critical to success at the task.

Why is representing the problem so important to finding an effective solution? **Problem representation**—defining or interpreting the problem—is the first step in problem solving. We must decide whether to view the problem verbally, mathematically, or visually; and to get clues about how to solve it we must categorize it. Some problems require **convergent thinking**, or searching for a single correct solution, while others call for **divergent thinking**, or generating many possible solutions. Representing a problem in an unproductive way can block progress completely.

Why are heuristics usually better for solving problems than is trial and error? Selecting a solution strategy and evaluating progress toward the goal are also important steps in the problem-solving process. A solution strategy can range from trial and error, to information retrieval based on similar problems, to a set of step-by-step procedures guaranteed to work (an **algorithm**), to rule-of-thumb approaches known as **heuristics**. An algorithm is often preferable over trial and error because it guarantees a solution and does not waste time. But because we lack algorithms for so many things, heuristics are vital to human problem solving. Some useful heuristics are **hill climbing**, creating **subgoals**, **means-end analysis**, and **working backward**.

How can a "mental set" both help and hinder problem solving? A **mental set** is a tendency to perceive and approach a problem in a certain way. Although sets can enable us to draw on past experience to help solve problems, a strong set can also prevent us from using essential new approaches. One set that can seriously hamper problem solving is **functional fixedness**—the tendency to perceive only traditional uses for an object. One way to minimize mental sets is the technique of **brainstorming** in which an individual or group collects numerous ideas and evaluates them only after all possible ideas have been collected.

Decision Making

How does decision making differ from problem solving? Decision making is a special kind of problem solving in which all possible solutions or choices are known. The task is not to come up with new solutions, but rather to identify the best one available based on whatever criteria are being used.

How would you go about making a truly logical decision? The logical way to make a decision is to rate each available choice in terms of weighted criteria and then to total the ratings for each choice. This approach is called a **compensatory model** because heavily weighted attractive features can compensate for lightly weighted unattractive ones.

How can heuristic approaches lead us to make bad decisions? Heuristics can save a great deal of time and effort, but they do not always result in the best choices. Errors in judgment may occur based on the **representativeness** heuristic, which involves making decisions based on information that matches our model of the "typical" member of a category. Other examples are overreliance on the **availability** heuristic (making choices based on whatever information we can most easily retrieve from memory, even though it may not be accurate) and the **confirmation bias** (the tendency to seek evidence in support of our existing beliefs and to ignore evidence that contradicts them).

How do we explain to ourselves the decisions we make? **Framing**, or perspective in which a problem is presented, can also affect the outcome of a decision. And regardless of whether a decision proves to be good or bad, we often use **hindsight bias**, which refers to our tendency to view outcomes as inevitable or predictable after we know the outcome to "correct" our memories so that the decision seems to be a good one. **Counterfactual thinking** involves revisiting our decisions by considering "what if" alternatives.

Intelligence and Mental Abilities

What types of questions are used to measure intelligence? Psychologists who study **intelligence** ask what intelligence entails and how it can be measured. To accomplish this, they use a variety of questions to assess general knowledge, vocabulary, arithmetic reasoning, and spatial manipulation.

What are some of the major theories of intelligence? Intelligence theories fall into two categories: those that argue in favor of a "general intelligence" that affects all aspects of cognitive functioning, and those that say intelligence is composed of many separate abilities, in which a person will not necessarily score high in all. Spearman's theory of intelligence is an example of the first category. Thurstone's theory is an example of the second category, as are Sternberg's **triarchic theory of intelligence** and Gardner's **theory of multiple intelligences**. Goleman's theory of **emotional intelligence** emphasizes skill in social relationships and awareness of others' and one's own emotions.

What kinds of intelligence tests are in use today? The *Binet–Simon Scale*, developed in France by Alfred Binet and Theodore Simon, was adapted by Stanford University's L. M. Terman to create a test that yields an **intelligence quotient (IQ)**, the *Stanford–Binet Intelligence Scale*. **The Wechsler Adult Intelligence Scale** and the **Wechsler Intelligence Scale for Children** were the first intelligence tests to yield both a verbal and performance IQ score as well as an overall IQ score. In contrast to these individual intelligence tests, **group tests** of intelligence are administered by one examiner to many people at a time. Alternatives to traditional IQ tests include **performance tests** of mental abilities that exclude the use of language and **culture-fair tests** that reduce cultural bias in a variety of ways.

What are some important characteristics of a good test? **Reliability**, refers to the ability of a test to produce consistent and stable scores. Psychologists express reliability in terms of **correlation coefficients**, which measure the relationship between two sets of scores. **Validity** is the ability of a test to measure what it has been designed to measure. **Content validity** exists if a test contains an adequate sample of questions relating to the skills or knowledge it is supposed to measure. **Criterion-related** validity refers to the relationship between test scores and whatever the test is designed to measure. In the case of intelligence, the most common independent measure is academic achievement. Although the reliability of IQ tests is seldom questioned, their validity is questioned. Critics charge that these tests assess a very limited set of mental skills and that some tests may be unfairly biased against minority groups. Also, poor school performance may be *the result of*, rather than caused by, low test scores. Finally, although IQ tests tend to predict occupational success and performance on the job after college, they are not ideally suited to that important task. New tests are being developed to address these concerns.

Heredity, Environment, and Intelligence

What determines individual differences in intelligence? Why are twin studies useful in studying intelligence? Although there has been extended debate about the extent to which heredity and environment contribute to IQ, studies comparing the IQ scores of identical and fraternal twins raised in the same and different families indicate that approximately 50% of differences in intelligence are due to genetics and the other half due to differences in environment, including education.

What have we learned from early intervention programs about the influence of the environment on intellectual development? With such a sizable percentage of the differences in IQ scores being attributable to the environment and education, many psychologists are strongly in favor of compensatory education programs for young children from disadvantaged homes. Two such programs are the Milwaukee Project and Head Start. Although they may not boost IQ scores greatly in the long run, such programs do seem to have significant educational benefits.

How can the study of plants help us to understand the relationship between heredity and environment? Plants grown in rich soil under ideal environmental conditions generally do better than plants grown in poor soil under less than ideal conditions, thus showing the importance of environment. But differences between plants grown under the same environmental conditions demonstrate the importance of heredity. Similarly, individual differences in human intelligence reflect both the genetic and environmental factors. However, psychologists cannot yet account for the fact that IQ scores on the whole are increasing (the Flynn Effect).

Do culture and gender influence mental abilities? Many people believe males and females are innately different in verbal and mathematical abilities. Others believe that people from certain cultures have a natural tendency to excel at academic skills. Neither belief holds up under scientific scrutiny.

What do psychologists know about the two extremes of human intelligence: very high and very low? The IQs of nearly 70% of the population fall between 85 and 115; and all but 5% have IQs between 70 and 130. **Mental retardation** and **giftedness** are the two extremes of intelligence. About 25% of cases of mental retardation can be traced to biological causes, including Down syndrome, but causes of the remaining 75% are not fully understood; nor are the causes of giftedness. Gifted people do not necessarily excel in all mental abilities.

Creativity

What is creativity? **Creativity** is the ability to produce novel and socially valued ideas or objects.

How is creativity related to intelligence? The threshold theory holds that a minimum level of intelligence is needed for creativity, but above that threshold level, higher intelligence doesn't necessarily make for greater creativity. Apparently factors other than intelligence contribute to creativity.

Can creativity be measured? Creativity tests are scored on the originality of answers and, frequently, on the number of responses (demonstrating divergent thinking). Some psychologists question how valid these tests are, however.

8 Motivation and Emotion

OVERVIEW

Classic detective stories are usually studies of motivation and emotion. At the beginning, all we know is that a murder has been committed: After eating dinner with her family, sweet old Amanda Jones collapses and dies of strychnine poisoning. "Now, why would anyone do a thing like that?" everybody wonders. The police ask the same question, in different terms: "Who had a motive for killing Miss Jones?" In a good mystery, the answer is "Practically everybody."

There is, for example, the younger sister—although she is 75 years old, she still bristles when she thinks of that tragic day 50 years ago when Amanda stole her sweetheart. And there is the next-door neighbor, who was heard saying that if Miss Jones's poodle trampled his peonies one more time, there would be consequences. Then there is the spendthrift nephew who stands to inherit a fortune from the deceased. Finally, the parlor maid has a guilty secret that Miss Jones knew and had threatened to reveal. All four suspects were in the house on the night of the murder, had access to the poison (which was used to kill rats in the basement), and had strong feelings about Amanda Jones. All of them had a motive for killing her.

In this story, motivation and emotion are so closely intertwined that drawing distinctions between them is difficult. However, psychologists do try to separate them. A **motive** is a specific need or desire that arouses the organism and directs its behavior toward a goal. All motives are triggered by some kind of stimulus: a bodily condition, such as low levels of blood sugar or dehydration; a cue in the environment, such as a Sale sign; or a feeling, such as loneliness, guilt, or anger. When a stimulus induces goal-directed behavior, we say that it has motivated the person.

Emotion refers to the experience of feelings such as fear, joy, surprise, and anger. Like motives, emotions also activate and affect behavior, but it is more difficult to predict the kind of behavior that a particular emotion will prompt. If a man is hungry, we can be reasonably sure that he will seek food. If, however, this same man experiences a feeling of joy or surprise, we cannot know with certainty how he will act.

The important thing to remember about both motives and emotions is that they push us to take some kind of action—from an act as drastic as murder to a habit as mundane as drumming our fingers on a table when we are nervous. Motivation occurs whether or not we are aware of it. We do not need to think about feeling hungry to make a beeline for the refrigerator or to focus on our need for achievement to study for an exam. Similarly, we do not have to recognize consciously that we are afraid before stepping back from a growling dog or to know that we are angry before raising our voice at someone. Moreover, the same motivation or emotion may produce different behaviors in different people. Ambition might motivate one person to go to law school and another to join a crime ring. Feeling sad might lead one person to cry alone and another to seek out a friend. On the other hand, the same behavior might arise from different motives or emotions: You may go to a movie because you are happy, bored, or lonely. In short, the workings of motives and emotions are very complex.

In this chapter, we will first look at some specific motives that play important roles in human behavior. Then we will turn our attention to emotions and the various ways they are expressed. We begin our discussion of motivation with a few general concepts.

ENDURING ISSUES IN MOTIVATION AND EMOTION ●●

The heart of this chapter concerns the ways in which motives and emotions affect behavior and are affected by the external environment (person–situation). While discussing those key issues, we will explore the question of whether motives and emotions are inborn or acquired (nature–nurture) and whether they change significantly over the life span (stability–change). We will also consider the extent to which individuals differ in their motives and emotions (diversity–universality) and the ways in which motives and emotions arise from and, in turn, affect biological processes (mind–body).

Perspectives on Motivation

How can you use intrinsic and extrinsic motivation to help you succeed in college?

INSTINCTS

Early in the 20th century, psychologists generally attributed behavior to **instincts**—specific, inborn behavior patterns characteristic of an entire species. Just as instincts motivate salmon

motive Specific need or desire, such as hunger, thirst, or achievement, that prompts goal-directed behavior.

emotion Feeling, such as fear, joy, or surprise, that underlies behavior.

instincts Inborn, inflexible, goal-directed behaviors that is characteristic of an entire species.

THINKING CRITICALLY ABOUT . . .

Primary Drives

Primary drives (hunger, thirst, sex) are, by definition, unlearned. But learning clearly affects how these drives are expressed. We learn how and what to eat and drink, and how to pursue interpersonal relationships.

1. Given that information, how might you design a research study to determine what aspects of a given drive, say hunger, are learned and which are not?

2. What steps would you take to increase the likelihood that your results apply to people in general and not just to a small sample of people?

3. Would you have to rely on self-reports or could you directly observe behavior?

to swim upstream to spawn and spiders to spin webs, instincts were thought to explain much of human behavior. In 1890, William James compiled a list of human instincts that included hunting, rivalry, fear, curiosity, shyness, love, shame, and resentment. But by the 1920s, instinct theory began to fall out of favor as an explanation of human behavior for three reasons: (1) Most important human behavior is learned; (2) human behavior is rarely rigid, inflexible, unchanging, and found throughout the species, as is the case with instincts; and (3) ascribing every conceivable human behavior to a corresponding instinct explains nothing (calling a person's propensity to be alone an "antisocial instinct," for example, merely names the behavior without pinpointing its origins). After World War I, psychologists started looking for more credible explanations of human behavior.

DRIVE-REDUCTION THEORY

An alternative view of motivation holds that bodily needs (such as the need for food or the need for water) create a state of tension or arousal called a **drive** (such as hunger or thirst). According to **drive-reduction theory**, motivated behavior is an attempt to reduce this unpleasant state of tension in the body and to return the body to a state of **homeostasis**, or balance. When we are hungry, we look for food to reduce the hunger drive. When we are tired, we find a place to rest. When we are thirsty, we find something to drink. In each of these cases, behavior is directed toward reducing a state of bodily tension or arousal.

According to drive-reduction theory, drives can generally be divided into two categories. **Primary drives** are unlearned, are found in all animals (including humans), and motivate behavior that is vital to the survival of the individual or species. Primary drives include hunger, thirst, and sex.

Not all motivation stems from the need to reduce or satisfy primary drives, however. Humans, in particular, are also motivated by **secondary drives**, drives that are acquired through learning. For instance, no one is born with a drive to acquire great wealth, yet many people are motivated by money. Other secondary drives include getting good grades in school and career success.

AROUSAL THEORY

Drive-reduction theory is appealing, but it cannot explain all kinds of behavior. It implies, for example, that, if able, people would spend as much time as possible at rest. They would seek food when hungry, water when thirsty, and so on, but once the active drives were satisfied, they would do little. They would literally have no motivation. Yet this is obviously not the case. People work, play, chat with one another, and do many things for which there is no known biological need that they are striving to satisfy.

Some psychologists suggest that motivation might have to do with arousal or state of alertness. The level of arousal at any given moment falls along a continuum from extreme alertness to sleep.

Arousal theory suggests that each of us has an optimum level of arousal that varies over the course of the day from one situation to another. According to the theory, behavior is motivated by the desire to maintain the optimum level of arousal for a given moment. Sometimes behavior seems to be motivated by a desire to reduce the state of arousal. For example, when you are sleepy, you are likely to turn off the television and turn off the light. Other times, behavior appears to be motivated by a desire to increase the state of arousal. For example, when you are bored, you may turn on the television, take a walk, or call a friend.

drive State of tension or arousal that motivates behavior.

drive-reduction theory States that motivated behavior is aimed at reducing a state of bodily tension or arousal and returning the organism to homeostasis.

homeostasis State of balance and stability in which the organism functions effectively.

primary drives Unlearned drive, such as hunger, that are based on a physiological state.

secondary drives Learned drives, such as ambition, that are not based on a physiological state.

arousal theory Theory of motivation that proposes that organisms seek an optimal level of arousal.

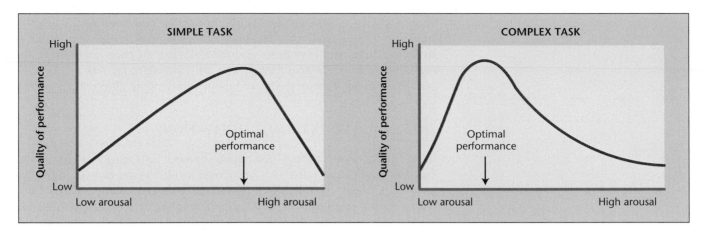

Not surprisingly, individuals' arousal level also affects their performance in different situations. Psychologists agree that there is no "best" level of arousal necessary to perform all tasks (J. R. Gray, Braver, & Raichle, 2002). Rather, it is largely a question of degree—of both the level of arousal and the complexity of the task. The **Yerkes–Dodson law** puts it this way: The more complex the task, the lower the level of arousal that can be tolerated without interfering with performance. Thus, higher levels of arousal are optimal when one is required to perform simple tasks, and relatively lower levels of arousal are best when performing complex tasks. (See **Figure 8–1**.) For example, most of us have been in situations where we failed to perform optimally on a difficult task, such as taking a college entrance exam, because emotions disrupted our concentration.

Arousal theory has some advantages over drive-reduction theory, but neither one can readily account for some kinds of behavior. For example, many people today participate in activities that are stimulating in the extreme: rock climbing, skydiving, bungee jumping, and hang gliding. Such thrill-seeking activities do not seem to be drive-reducing and do not seem to be done in pursuit of an optimal level of arousal. Zuckerman (1979, 1994, 2000) accounts for such activities by suggesting that *sensation seeking* is itself a basic motivation, at least some aspects of which are inherited and neurologically based (Arnaut, 2006; Zuckerman, 2005). In general, high sensation seekers, compared to low sensation seekers, are more likely to

- Prefer dangerous sports like skydiving, bungee jumping, surfing, and mountain climbing (Diehm & Armatas, 2004; Eachus, 2004);
- choose vocations that involve an element of risk and excitement like firefighting, rescue work, or a career in emergency medicine;
- smoke, drink heavily, gamble, and use illicit drugs (D'Silva, Grant–Harrington, Palmgreen, Donohew, & Pugzles-Lorch, 2001; Nower, Derevensky, & Gupta, 2004);
- engage in unsafe driving (high sensation seekers also report being more likely to fall asleep at the wheel on a monotonous, straight highway than are low sensation seekers) (Thiffault & Bergeron, 2003);
- have more sexual partners and engage in more varied sexual activities; and
- be classified in school as delinquent or hyperactive (though not more aggressive) (Ang & Woo, 2003).

ENDURING ISSUES

Nature–Nurture The Evolutionary Basis of Arousal Seeking

Some evolutionary theorists argue that the drive to seek high arousal states may have an evolutionary basis. For example, Cosmides and Tooby (2000) propose that risk-taking behavior may have played an important adaptive role for our ancestors by providing them with opportunities for limited exposure to potentially dangerous situations, and giving

Figure 8–1
The Yerkes–Dodson law.
A certain amount of arousal is needed to perform most tasks, but a very high level of arousal interferes with the performance of complicated activities. That is, the level of arousal that can be tolerated is higher for a simple task than for a complex one.

Source: After Hebb, 1955.

Yerkes–Dodson law States that there is an optimal level of arousal for the best performance of any task; the more complex the task, the lower the level of arousal that can be tolerated before performance deteriorates.

them a chance to develop successful strategies to deal with such dangers. Thus, early humans who took risks were potentially better equipped to cope with danger and turmoil in their environment than those who did not—making them more likely to survive and reproduce. This might help explain why some people today seek out high-risk activities such as skydiving, extreme skiing, and mountain climbing (Tooby & Cosmides, 2005). ●●

INTRINSIC AND EXTRINSIC MOTIVATION

Some psychologists further distinguish between intrinsic and extrinsic motivation. **Intrinsic motivation** refers to motivation provided by an activity itself. Play is a good example. Children typically climb trees, finger paint, and play games for no other reason than the fun they get from the activity itself. In the same way, many adults solve crossword puzzles, play golf, and tinker in a workshop largely for the enjoyment they get from the activity. **Extrinsic motivation** refers to motivation that derives from the consequences of an activity. For example, a child may do chores not because he enjoys them but because doing so earns an allowance, and an adult who hates golf may play a round with a client because doing so may help close a sale.

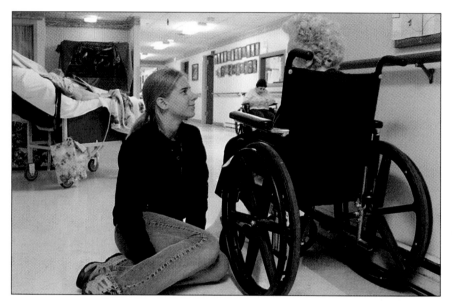

The same activity might be motivated intrinsically, just for the pleasure of doing it, or extrinsically, by rewards unrelated to the activity itself.

Whether behavior is intrinsically or extrinsically motivated can have important consequences. For example, if parents offer a reward to their young daughter for writing to her grandparents, the likelihood of her writing to them when rewards are no longer available may actually decrease. One recent analysis of some 128 studies that examined the effect of extrinsic rewards on the behavior of children, adolescents, and adults found that when extrinsic rewards are offered for a behavior, intrinsic motivation and sense of personal responsibility for that behavior are likely to decrease, at least for a short time (Deci, Koestner, & Ryan, 1999, 2001). However, unexpected (as opposed to contractual) rewards do not necessarily reduce intrinsic motivation, and positive feedback (including praise) may actually increase intrinsic motivation (P. Chance, 1992; Deci et al., 1999; Reiss, 2005).

intrinsic motivation A desire to perform a behavior that stems from the enjoyment derived from the behavior itself.

extrinsic motivation A desire to perform a behavior to obtain an external reward or avoid punishment.

hierarchy of needs A theory of motivation advanced by Maslow holding that higher order motives involving social and personal growth only emerge after lower level motives related to survival have been satisfied.

A HIERARCHY OF MOTIVES

Humanistic psychologist Abraham Maslow (1954) arranged motives in a hierarchy, from lower to higher. The lower motives spring from physiological needs that must be satisfied. As we move higher in Maslow's **hierarchy of needs**, the motives have more subtle origins: the desire to live as safely as possible, to connect meaningfully with other human beings, and to make the best possible impression on others. Maslow believed that the highest motive in the hierarchy is self-actualization—the drive to realize one's full potential. Maslow's hierarchy of motives is illustrated in **Figure 8–2**.

According to Maslow's theory, higher motives emerge only after the more basic ones have been largely satisfied: A person who is starving doesn't care what people think of her table manners.

Maslow's model offers an appealing way to organize a wide range of motives into a coherent structure. But recent research challenges the universality of his views. Maslow based his hierarchical model on observations of historical figures, famous living individuals, and even friends whom he admired greatly. However, the majority of these people were White males living in Western society. In many simpler societies, people often live on the very edge of survival, yet they form strong and meaningful social ties and possess a firm sense of self-esteem (Neher, 1991; Wubbolding, 2005). In fact, difficulty in meeting basic needs can actually foster the satisfaction of higher needs: A couple struggling financially to raise a family may grow closer as a result of the experience. In our discussion of development during adolescence and early adulthood (Chapter 9, "Life-Span Development"), we will examine some research indicating that males must have a firm sense of their own identity (and thus a degree of self-esteem) before they can successfully establish the kinds of close relationships with others that satisfy the need for belonging. As a result of such research findings, many psychologists now view Maslow's model with a measure of skepticism although it continues to be a convenient way to think of the wide range of human motives.

We have reviewed some basic concepts about motivation. With these concepts in mind, we now turn our attention to specific motives.

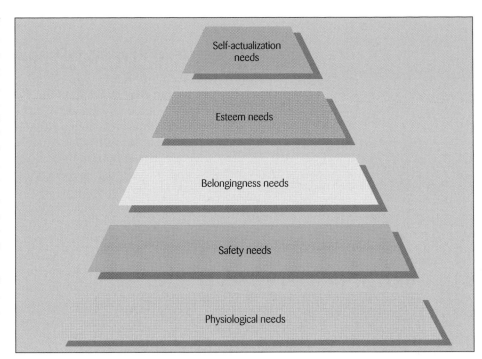

Figure 8–2

A pyramid representing Maslow's hierarchy of needs.

From bottom to top, the stages correspond to how fundamental the motive is for survival and how early it appears in both the evolution of the species and the development of the individual. According to Maslow, the more basic needs must largely be satisfied before higher motives can emerge.

Source: After Maslow, 1954.

CHECK YOUR UNDERSTANDING

Match the following terms with the appropriate definition.

1. ___ drive
2. ___ drive reduction
3. ___ homeostasis
4. ___ self-actualization
5. ___ intrinsic motivation
6. ___ extrinsic motivation

a. The drive to realize one's full potential

b. state of balance in which the organism functions effectively

c. theory that motivated behavior is focused on reducing bodily tension

d. tending to perform behavior to receive some external reward or avoid punishment

e. state of tension brought on by biological needs

f. motivation arising from behavior itself

Answers: 1. e. 2. c. 3. b. 4. a. 5. f. 6. d.

APPLY YOUR UNDERSTANDING

1. You are home alone and have nothing to do. You find yourself walking around. You look for something to read, but nothing seems quite right. Then you check to see if anything interesting is on TV, but again nothing seems worth watching. Finally, you decide to go jogging. This kind of motivated behavior that increases the state of arousal is a problem for

   a. the instinct theory of motivation.

   b. any theory of motivation.

   c. the drive-reduction theory of motivation.

   d. the Yerkes–Dodson law.

2. While you are working on a complex task, your boss stops by your desk and says, "You've only got 10 more minutes to finish that up. It's really important that it be done right. I know you can do it and I'm depending on you." When you complain that he's making you nervous and your performance will suffer, he replies, "I'm just trying to motivate you." Which of the following does your boss apparently not understand?

   a. drive-reduction theory

   b. homeostasis

   c. extrinsic motivation

   d. the Yerkes–Dodson law

Answers: 1. c. 2. d.

Hunger and Thirst

Why do people usually get hungry at mealtime?

When you are hungry, you eat. If you don't eat, your need for food will continue to increase, but your hunger may not. Suppose that you decide to skip lunch to study at the library. Your need for food will increase throughout the day, but your hunger will come and go. You will probably be hungry around lunchtime; then your hunger will likely abate while you are at the library. By dinnertime, no concern will seem as pressing as eating. The psychological state of hunger, then, is not the same as the biological need for food, although that need often sets the psychological state in motion.

Like hunger, *thirst* is stimulated by both internal and external cues. Internally, thirst is controlled by two regulators that monitor the level of fluids inside and outside the cells. Both of these regulators stimulate thirst when fluid levels are too low. Just as we become hungry in response to external cues, the experience of thirst can also be affected by environmental factors (W. G. Hall, Arnold, & Myers, 2000; Rowland, 2002). We may get thirsty when we see a TV commercial featuring people savoring tall, cool drinks in a lush, tropical setting. Seasonal customs and weather conditions also affect our thirst-quenching habits: Ice-cold lemonade is a summer staple, whereas hot chocolate warms cold winter nights.

BIOLOGICAL AND EMOTIONAL FACTORS

How can external cues influence our desire to eat?

Early research established the importance of the hypothalamus as the brain center involved in hunger and eating. Initially, researchers identified two regions in the hypothalamus as controlling our experience of hunger and satiety (being full to satisfaction). One of these centers appeared to act as the feeding center because when it was stimulated, animals began to eat; and when it was destroyed the animals stopped eating to the point of starvation. Another area of the hypothalamus was thought to be the satiety center: When it was stimulated, animals stopped eating; when it was destroyed, animals ate to the point of extreme obesity. The hypothalamus seemed to be a kind of "switch" that turned eating on or off, at least in rats.

However, recent studies have challenged this simple "on–off" explanation for the control of eating by showing that a number of other areas of the brain are also involved (Hinton et al., 2004). A third center in the hypothalamus appears to influence the drive to eat specific foods. Studies have also shown that regions of the cortex and spinal cord play an important role in regulating food intake. Moreover, the connections among brain centers that control hunger are now known to be considerably more complex than were once thought—involving more than a dozen different neurotransmitters (Flier & Maratos-Flier, 1998; Woods, Seeley, Porte, & Schwartz, 1998). Some of these neurotransmitters act to increase the consumption of specific foods such as carbohydrates or fats, whereas others suppress the appetite for these foods (Blundell & Halford, 1998; Volkow et al., 2003).

How do these various areas of the brain know when to stimulate hunger? It turns out that the brain monitors the blood levels of **glucose** (a simple sugar used by the body for energy), fats, carbohydrates, and the hormone *insulin* (which as we saw in Chapter 2, "The Biological Basis of Behavior", is involved in keeping glucose levels in the blood balanced). (See **Figure 8–3**.) Changes in the blood levels of these substances signal the need for food (Seeley & Schwartz, 1997). The presence of a particular hormone **leptin** also influences our desire to eat (Holtkamp et al., 2003; Leroy et al., 1996; Monteleone, DiLieto, Castaldo, & Maj, 2004; Ravussin et al., 1997). Fat cells within our body produce leptin, which travels in the bloodstream and is sensed by the hypothalamus. High levels of leptin signal the brain to reduce appetite, or to increase the rate at which fat is burned.

glucose A simple sugar used by the body for energy.

leptin A hormone released by fat cells that reduces appetite.

The brain also monitors the amount of food that you have eaten. Specialized cells in the stomach and the upper part of the small intestine sense the volume of food in the digestive system. When only a small quantity of food is present, these cells release a hormone called **ghrelin** into the bloodstream, which travels to the brain where it stimulates appetite and focuses our thoughts and imagination on food (Schmid et al., 2005).

But, as we noted earlier, a biological need for food does not always result in hunger. The sensation of hunger is the product not only of things going on in the body, but also of things going on outside the body. The smell of a cake baking in the oven, for example, may trigger the desire to eat whether the body needs fuel or not. Sometimes just looking at the clock and realizing that it is dinnertime can make us feel hungry. And recent research shows that people tend to eat more when they are with other people, especially if those other people are eating a lot (Herman, Roth, & Polivy, 2003). One intriguing line of research suggests that such external cues may set off internal biological processes that mimic those associated with the need for food. For example, the mere sight, smell, or thought of food causes an increase in insulin production, which, in turn, lowers glucose levels in the body's cells, mirroring the body's response to a physical need for food (Logue, 2000). Thus, the aroma from a nearby restaurant may serve as more than an **incentive** to eat; it may actually trigger an apparent need for food.

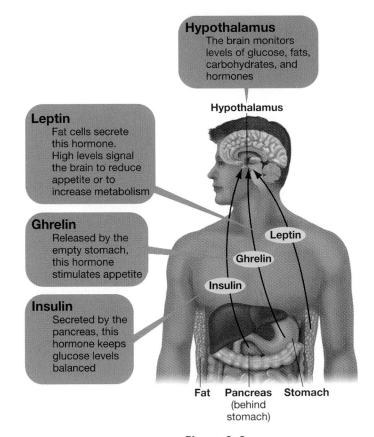

Hypothalamus
The brain monitors levels of glucose, fats, carbohydrates, and hormones

Hypothalamus

Leptin
Fat cells secrete this hormone. High levels signal the brain to reduce appetite or to increase metabolism

Ghrelin
Released by the empty stomach, this hormone stimulates appetite

Insulin
Secreted by the pancreas, this hormone keeps glucose levels balanced

Leptin
Ghrelin
Insulin

Fat Pancreas Stomach
(behind stomach)

Figure 8–3
Physiological factors regulating appetite and body weight.
A variety of chemical messengers interact to stimulate and suppress appetite. Among these are insulin, leptin, and ghrelin.

ENDURING ISSUES

Diversity–Universality   The Hunger Drive

The hunger drive is tied to emotions in complex ways. Some people head for the refrigerator whenever they are depressed, bored, anxious, or angry. Others lose all interest in food at these times and complain that they are "too upset to eat." One student studying for an important exam spends as much time eating as reading; another student studying for the same exam lives on coffee until the exam is over. Under emotionally arousing conditions, what one person craves may turn another person's stomach. ●●

CULTURAL AND SOCIAL FACTORS

How can the culture you were raised in influence your desire to eat?

How you respond when you are hungry will vary according to your experiences with food, which are mostly governed by learning and social conditioning. The majority of Americans eat three meals a day at regular intervals. A typical American family eats breakfast at 7 A.M., lunch around noon, and dinner about 6 P.M. But in Europe, people often have dinner much later in the evening. Italians, for example, rarely eat dinner before 9 P.M. Numerous studies with both humans and animals have shown that regularly eating at particular times during the day leads to the release at those times of the hormones and neurotransmitters that cause hunger (Woods, Schwartz, Baskin, & Seeley, 2000). In other words, we get hungry around noon partly because the body "learns" that if it's noon, it's time to eat.

ghrelin A hormone produced in the stomach and small intestines that increases appetite.

incentive External stimulus that prompts goal-directed behavior.

Social situations also affect our motivation to eat. Say that you are at lunch right after finishing an important exam. You may not feel very hungry, even though it is an hour past your usual lunchtime. Conversely, social situations may prompt you to eat even when you are not hungry. Imagine that on a day when you have slept late and eaten a large breakfast, you visit friends. When you arrive, you discover that a wonderful meal is being served in a few minutes. Although you are not at all hungry, you may decide to eat merely out of courtesy.

Culture influences what we choose to eat and how much. Although most Americans will not eat horsemeat, it is very popular in several European countries. Yet many Americans consume pork, which violates both Islamic and Jewish dietary laws. So, although hunger is basically a biological drive, it is not merely an internal state that we satisfy when our body tells us to. Hunger is the product of the complex interaction of both environmental and biological forces.

EATING DISORDERS AND OBESITY

How can you tell if someone is suffering from anorexia nervosa or bulimia?

ANOREXIA NERVOSA AND BULIMIA NERVOSA "When people told me I looked like someone from Auschwitz [the Nazi concentration camp], I thought that was the highest compliment anyone could give me." This confession comes from a young woman who as a teenager suffered from a serious eating disorder known as **anorexia nervosa**. She was 18 years old, 5 feet 3 inches tall, and weighed 68 pounds. This young woman was lucky. She managed to overcome the disorder and has since maintained normal body weight. Many others are less fortunate. In fact, Canadian researchers found recently that over 10% of the young women with anorexia nervosa between 1981 and 2000 died as a result of the disorder, suggesting it has one of the highest fatality rates for psychiatric disorders affecting young females (Birmingham, Su, Hlynsky, Goldner, & Gao, 2005; Derman & Szabo, 2006).

People with anorexia nervosa perceive themselves as overweight and strive to lose weight, usually by severely limiting their intake of food. Even after they become very thin, they constantly worry about weight gain. The following four symptoms are used in the diagnosis of anorexia nervosa (American Psychiatric Association, 2000; Bulik, Reba, Siega-Riz, & Reichborn-Kjennerud, 2005):

How and when you satisfy hunger and thirst depends on social, psychological, environmental, and cultural influences as well as on physiological needs. For example, the Japanese tea ceremony (*above*) is concerned more with restoring inner harmony than with satisfying thirst. Do you think the office worker (*below*) is drinking coffee because she is thirsty?

1. Intense fear of becoming obese, which does not diminish as weight loss progresses.
2. Disturbance of body image (for example, claiming to "feel fat" even when emaciated).
3. Refusal to maintain body weight at or above a minimal normal weight for age and height.
4. In females, the absence of at least three consecutive menstrual cycles.

Approximately 1% of all adolescents suffer from anorexia nervosa; about 90% of these are White upper- or middle-class females (Bulik, Sullivan, Tozzi, et al., 2006; Rosenvinge, Borgen, & Boerresen, 1999). Generally, people suffering from anorexia enjoy an otherwise normal childhood and adolescence. They are usually successful students and cooperative, well-behaved children. They have an intense interest in food, but view eating with disgust. They also have a very distorted view of their own body (Grant, Kim, & Eckert, 2002), although this characteristic is less prevalent among African American woman with this disorder (M. A. White, Kohlmaier, Varnado, & Williamson, 2003).

Anorexia is frequently compounded by another eating disorder known as **bulimia nervosa** (O'Brien & Vincent, 2003). The following criteria are used for its diagnosis (American Psychiatric Association, 2000):

1. Recurrent episodes of binge eating (rapid consumption of a large amount of food, usually in less than 2 hours).

anorexia nervosa A serious eating disorder that is associated with an intense fear of weight gain and a distorted body image.

bulimia nervosa An eating disorder characterized by binges of eating followed by self-induced vomiting.

2. Recurrent inappropriate behaviors to try to prevent weight gain, such as self-induced vomiting.

3. Binge eating and compensatory behaviors occurring at least twice a week for three months.

4. Body shape and weight excessively influencing the person's self-image.

5. Occurrence of the just-mentioned behaviors at least sometimes in the absence of anorexia.

Approximately 1 to 2% of all adolescent females suffer from bulimia nervosa, though recent evidence suggests this number may be decreasing (Keel, Heatherton, Dorer, Joiner, & Zalta, 2006). The binge-eating behavior usually begins at about age 18, when adolescents are facing the challenge of new life situations. Not surprisingly, residence on a college campus is associated with a higher incidence of bulimia (Gleaves, Miller, Williams, & Summers, 2000). The socioeconomic group at high risk for bulimia—again, primarily upper-middle- and upper-class women—is highly represented on college campuses.

Although anorexia and bulimia are much more prevalent among females than males (S. Turnbull, Ward, Treasure, Jick, & Derby, 1996; Gleaves et al., 2000), many more men are affected by these disorders than was once suspected (Al Dawi et al, 2002; Gila, Castro, & Cesena, 2005). For example, in a survey of people who had graduated from Harvard University in 1982, reported cases of eating disorders had dropped by half for women over the decade, but had doubled for men (Seligman, Rogers, & Annin, 1994). Interestingly, a related phenomenon called *muscle dysmorphia* appears to be on the increase among young men (H. G. Pope, 2000). Muscle dysmorphia is an obsessive concern with one's muscle size. Men with muscle dysmorphia, many of whom are well-muscled, are distressed at their perceived puniness, and spend an inordinate amount of time fretting over their diet and exercising to increase their muscle mass (Leit, Gray, & Pope, 2002; C. G. Pope, Pope, & Menard, 2005).

Because studies of eating disorders have focused almost entirely on females, we know very little about what might predispose an adolescent male to develop such a disorder (Crosscope-Happel, 2005). Among adolescent women, several factors appear likely (Bruch, 2001; Favaro, Tenconi, & Santonastaso, 2006; Garner & Magana, 2006). On one hand, mass media promote the idea that a woman must be thin to be attractive. In addition, psychological factors also contribute to the risk of eating disorders (Zonnevylle-Bender et al,, 2004). Women with bulimia commonly have low self-esteem, are hypersensitive to social interactions, and are more likely to come from families where negative comments are often made about weight (Crowther, Kichler, Sherwood, & Kuhnert, 2002; Viñuales-Mas, Fernández-Aranda, Jiménez-Murcia, Turón-Gil, & Vallejo-Ruiloba, 2001). Many also display clinical depression or obsessive–compulsive disorder (see Chapter 12, "Psychological Disorders") and have engaged in self-injurious behaviors such as cutting themselves (Milos, Spindler, Ruggiero, Klaghofer, & Schnyder., 2002; T. Paul, Schroeter, Dahme, & Nutzinger, 2002; T. D. Wade, Bulik, Neale, & Kendler, 2000). Feelings of vulnerability and helplessness apparently dispose many people to adopt inappropriate strategies for one area where they can exercise control—their own eating habits.

Finally, there is growing evidence that genetics plays a role in both anorexia nervosa and bulimia nervosa, although the two eating disorders may have a very different genetic basis (Jacobi, Hayward, de Zwaan, Kraemer, & Agras, 2004; Keel & Klump, 2003).

Anorexia and bulimia are notoriously hard to treat, and there is considerable disagreement on the most effective approach to therapy (BenTovim, 2003; Fairburn, Cooper, & Shafran, 2003; J. Russell, 2004). In fact, some psychologists doubt that we can ever eliminate eating disorders in a culture bombarded with the message that "thin is in." Regrettably, in many developing countries such as Taiwan, Singapore, and China, where dieting is becoming a fad, eating disorders, once little known, are now becoming a serious problem (Hsu, 1996; S. Lee, Chan, & Hsu, 2003).

Does the American obsession with superslimness lead adolescents to become anorexic?

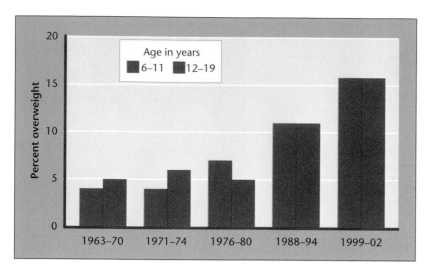

Figure 8–4

Rising obesity among American youth.

The number of overweight children and adolescents has increased sharply in recent years. From 1980 to 2002, the percentage of overweight adolescents tripled. This trend is particularly disturbing since overweight children and adolescents are likely to become overweight adults, placing them at increased risk for cardiovascular disease, hypertension, and diabetes.

Source: CDC/NCHS, NHES and NHANES.

Notes: Excludes pregnant women starting with 1971–74. Pregnancy status not available for 1963–65 and 1966–70. Data for 1963–65 are for children 6–11 years of age; data for 1966–70 are for adolescents 12–17 years of age, not 12–19 years.

BMI	Weight Status
Below 18.5	Underweight
18.5 – 24.9	Normal
25.0 – 29.9	Overweight
30.0 and above	Obese

Figure 8–5

Body Mass Index
The standard weight status categories associated with BMI ranges for adults.

body mass index (BMI) A numerical index calculated from a person's height and weight that is used to indicate health status and predict disease risk.

OBESITY AND WEIGHT CONTROL According to the U.S. Surgeon General, obesity is the most pressing health problem in America (P. J. Johnson, 2003). *Obesity* refers to an excess of body fat in relation to lean body mass, while *overweight* refers to weighing more than a desirable standard, whether from high amounts of fat or being very muscular. Obesity has increased by more than 50% during the past decade, with more than two-thirds of Americans being either overweight or obese. In contrast to anorexia nervosa and bulimia nervosa, obesity is more prevalent among poor Black women than among White women with higher incomes (M. A. White, Kohlmaier, Varnado, & Williamson, 2003).

Even more disturbing, the rate of obesity among young people has more tripled since 1980, with over 9 million overweight adolescents in America today. (See **Figure 8-4**). This problem is particularly serious since overweight children and adolescents are more likely to become overweight adults who are at an increased risk for serious diseases like hypertension, cardiovascular disease, diabetes, and sleep apnea (Nishimura et al., 2003).

Many factors contribute to overeating and obesity (Fairburn & Brownell, 2002). Some people inherit a tendency to be overweight (Bulik, Sullivan, & Kendler, 2003; Yanovski & Yanovski, 2002). Children born to two obese parents are seven times more likely to become obese than children born to parents of normal weight. A sedentary lifestyle contributes to the problem. Children in the United States today are more likely to watch television and play video games than to play soccer or hockey; and many adults lack adequate physical activity, too. Abundant opportunities and encouragement to overeat in American culture are also factors. Portion size has increased in recent years, as has the constant availability of food from vending machines and fast-food restaurants.

Adding to the medical difficulties accompanying obesity, overweight people often face ridicule and discrimination resulting in significant economic, social, and educational loss (D. Carr & Friedman, 2005; Maranto & Stenoien, 2000). Despite federal laws prohibiting employment bias against overweight people, studies show they are discriminated against in school and in the workplace. For example, overweight women have reported lowered self-confidence owing to victimization in school and at work because of their weight (C. Johnson, 2002; Rothblum, Brand, Miller, & Oetjen, 1990). And obese male lawyers earn less than male lawyers of normal weight (Saporta & Halpern, 2002). Even children who are overweight display increased rates of behavior problems, including aggression, lack of discipline, immaturity, anxiety, and depression when compared with their normal-weight peers (Q. Yang & Chen, 2001).

One screening tool used to identify weight problems is **body mass index (BMI)**, a numerical index calculated from a person's height and weight that is used to indicate health status and predict disease risk (see **Figure 8–5**). Body mass index is correlated with body fat, although variations exist by sex, race, and age. Elevated BMI is associated with increased risk for hypertension, stroke, coronary heart disease, Type II diabetes, and sleep apnea, among other conditions. You can calculate your BMI by using the following formula:

$$BMI = 703 \times weight(lb) / height(in)^2$$

BMI is not applicable to everyone, however. For example, competitive athletes often have a high BMI owing to their large proportion of muscle mass.

With all of the problems associated with being overweight, many people are constantly trying to lose weight. There are no quick fixes to weight loss, but the suggestions in Applying Psychology, "The Slow (but Lasting) Fix for Weight Gain," can help people lose weight and keep it off.

APPLYING PSYCHOLOGY

THE SLOW (BUT LASTING) FIX FOR WEIGHT GAIN

The study of hunger and eating has led to some compelling insights into the problem of weight control. It appears that our bodies are genetically "set" to maintain a certain weight (G. W. Wade, 2004; Hallschmid, Benedict, Born, Fehm, & Kern, 2004). According to this **set point theory**, if you consume more calories than you need for that weight, your metabolic rate will increase;, and you will feel an increase in energy that will prompt you to be more active, thereby burning more calories. If, however, you eat fewer calories than are needed to maintain your weight, your metabolic rate will decrease; and you will feel tired and become less active, thereby burning fewer calories. This mechanism was no doubt helpful during the thousands of years that our species lived literally hand to mouth, but it is less helpful where food is abundant, as in modern industrialized nations.

An implication of our current understanding of hunger and weight regulation is that a successful weight-control program must be long term and must work with, rather than against, the body's normal tendency to maintain weight. It should be undertaken only after consultation with a doctor. On the basis of studies of the hunger drive and the relationship between eating and body weight, here is our formula for weight control:

1. First, check with your doctor before you start. People want quick fixes, so they often go overboard on dieting or exercise, sometimes with disastrous consequences. Make sure your weight loss program will be safe.

2. Increase your body's metabolism through regular exercise. The most effective metabolism booster is 20–30 minutes of moderate activity several times a week. Although only about 200–300 calories are burned off during each exercise session, the exercise increases the resting metabolic rate. This means that you burn more calories when not exercising. Thus, exercise is an important part of a weight reduction program (Sarwer, Allison, & Berkowitz, 2004; Wadden, Crerand, & Brock, 2005).

3. Modify your diet. A moderate reduction in calories is beneficial. Also, reduce your consumption of fats (particularly saturated fats) and sugars. Sugars trigger an increase in the body's level of insulin; and high levels of fat and insulin in the blood stimulate hunger.

4. Reduce external cues that encourage you to eat undesirable foods. The mere sight or smell of food can increase the amount of insulin in the body, thus triggering hunger. Many people find that if they do their grocery shopping on a full stomach, it is easier to resist the temptation to buy junk foods.

5. Set realistic goals. Focus at least as much on preventing weight gain as on losing weight. If you must lose weight, try to shed just one pound a week for 2 or 3 months. After that, concentrate on maintaining that new, lower weight for several months before moving on to further weight loss.

6. Reward yourself—in ways unrelated to food—for small improvements. Use some of the behavior-modification techniques described in Chapter 5: Reward yourself not only for each pound of weight lost but also for each day or week that you maintain that weight loss. And remember, the only way you can keep the weight off is by continuing to adhere to a reasonable diet and exercise plan (Abdel, 2003; M. T. McGuire, Wing, Klem, Lang, & Hill, 1999).

To learn more about weight control, visit our Web site at www.prenhall.com/morris.

CHECK YOUR UNDERSTANDING

1. The level of _____ in the blood signals hunger.
2. Hunger can be stimulated by both _____ and _____ cues.

Match the following terms with the appropriate definition.

3. ___ hypothalamus
4. ___ anorexia nervosa
5. ___ bulimia nervosa

   a.   recurrent episodes of binge eating, followed by vomiting, taking laxatives, or excessively exercising

   b.   contains both a hunger center and a satiety center

   c.   intense fear of obesity, disturbance of body image, and very little intake of food, with resulting weight well below normal minimums

Answers: 1. glucose. 2. internal, external. 3. b. 4. c. 5. a.

set point theory A theory that our bodies are genetically predisposed to maintaining a certain weight by changing our metabolic rate and activity level in response to caloric intake.

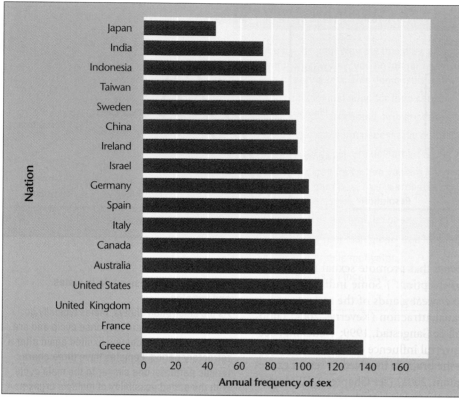

Figure 8–7

Frequency (annual) of sexual behavior around the world.

A global survey of reported sexual activity indicates the frequency that couples have sex varies dramatically by country.

Source: http://www.durex.com/cm/gss2005result.pdf

sex varies dramatically around the world (Durex Global Sex Survey, 2005). This survey also revealed that the frequency of sexual activity varies by age, with 35- to 44-year-olds reporting to have sex an average of 112 times a year, 25- to 34-year-olds having sex an average of 108 times per year, and 16- to 20-year-olds having sex 90 times annually.

Just as society dictates standards for sexual conduct, culture guides our views of sexual attractiveness. Culture and experience may influence the extent to which we find particular articles of clothing or body shapes sexually arousing (Furnham, McClelland, & Omar, 2003). In some cultures, most men prefer women with very large breasts, but in other cultures, small and delicate breasts are preferred. Among some African cultures, elongated earlobes are considered very attractive. In our own culture, what we find attractive often depends on the styles of the time.

PATTERNS OF SEXUAL BEHAVIOR AMONG AMERICANS

Contrary to media portrayals of sexual behavior in publications like *Playboy* or TV shows like *Sex in the City*, which depict Americans as oversexed and unwilling to commit to long-term relationships, research indicates that most people are far more conservative in their sex lives. One carefully designed study (Michael, Gagnon, Laumann, & Kolata, 1994) of 3,432 randomly selected people between the ages of 18 and 59 revealed the following patterns in the sexual activity of American men and women:

Do his elongated ear lobes and other bodily adornments enhance this young man's sexual attractiveness? It all depends on your cultural point of view. In the Samburu society of Kenya in which he lives, these particular adornments are considered highly attractive.

- About one-third of those sampled had sex twice a week or more, one-third a few times a month, and the remaining third a few times a year or not at all.
- The overwhelming majority of respondents did not engage in kinky sex. Instead, vaginal intercourse was the preferred form of sex for over 90% of those sampled. Watching their partner undress was ranked second, and oral sex, third.
- Married couples reported having sex more often—and being more satisfied with their sex lives—than did unmarried persons (see also Waite & Joyner, 2001).
- The average duration of sexual intercourse reported by most people was approximately 15 minutes.
- The median number of partners over the lifetime for males was 6 and for females 2 (17% of the men and 3% of the women reported having sex with over 20 partners).
- About 25% of the men and 15% of the women had committed adultery.

Extensive research has also documented at least four significant differences in sexuality between American men and women: Men are more interested in sex than are women; women are more likely than men to link sex to a close, committed relationship; aggression, power, dominance, and assertiveness are more closely linked to sex among men than among women; and women's sexuality is more malleable (more open to change over time and more closely associated with such things as level of education and religion) (Peplau, 2003).

SEXUAL ORIENTATION

What are the arguments for and against a biological explanation of homosexuality?

Sexual orientation refers to the direction of an individual's sexual interest. People with a *heterosexual orientation* are sexually attracted to members of the opposite sex; those with a *homosexual orientation* are sexually attracted to members of their own sex; and *bisexuals* are attracted to members of both sexes. Recent studies indicate that about 3% of males and just under 2% of females have a homosexual orientation (Laumann, Gagnon, Michael, & Michaels, 1994; L. Ellis, Robb, & Burke, 2005).

What determines sexual orientation? This issue has been argued for decades in the form of the classic nature-versus-nurture debate. Those on the nature side hold that sexual orientation is rooted in biology and is primarily influenced by genetics. They point out that homosexual men and women generally know before puberty that they are "different" and often remain "in the closet" regarding their sexual orientation for fear of recrimination (Lippa, 2005). Evidence from family and twin studies shows a higher incidence of male homosexuality in families with other gay men (Camperio-Ciani, Corna, & Capiluppi, 2004), and a higher rate of homosexuality among men with a homosexual twin even when the twins were raised separately (LeVay & Hamer, 1994). Despite these results from family and twin studies suggesting there is a genetic basis to sexual orientation, researchers have yet to identify a specific gene that predisposes people to different sexual orientation (Rahman & Wilson, 2003). Nevertheless, they contend if homosexuality were the result of early learning and socialization, children raised by gay or lesbian parents would be more likely to become homosexual. Research, however, has clearly demonstrated that this is not the case (C. J. Patterson, 2000). The nature position also derives support from studies revealing anatomical and physiological differences between the brains of homosexual and heterosexual men (L. S. Allen & Gorski, 1992; Hines, 2004; Kinnunen, Moltz, Metz, & Cooper, 2004; LeVay, 1991; Swaab & Hoffman, 1995).

Among other animals, homosexual activity occurs with some degree of regularity. For instance, among pygmy chimpanzees, about 50% of all observed sexual activity is between members of the same sex. Even male giraffes commonly entwine their necks until both become sexually stimulated. And among some birds, such as greylag geese, homosexual unions have been found to last up to 15 years (Bagemihl, 2000).

Those on the nurture side argue that sexual orientation is primarily a learned behavior, influenced by early experience and largely is under voluntary control. They criticize research supporting the biological position as methodologically flawed—sometimes confusing what causes homosexuality with what results from homosexuality (Byne, 1994). Also, they contend that early socialization determines sexual orientation. Moreover, they find support for their position from cross-cultural studies that show sexual orientations occurring at different frequencies in various cultures.

To date, neither the biological nor the socialization theory has provided a completely satisfactory explanation for the origin of sexual orientation. As with most complex behaviors, a more likely explanation probably involves a combination of these two positions (Garnets, 2002; Hammack, 2005).

Finally, although surveys indicate that most people are opposed to discriminating on the basis of sexual orientation (Herek, 2002), negative attitudes toward homosexuality are

Homosexual activity is common among animals. For example, male giraffes often engage in extreme necking, entwining, and rubbing, becoming sexually aroused as they do.

sexual orientation Refers to the direction of one's sexual interest toward members of the same sex, the other sex, or both sexes.

Positive family attitudes and social support for people with different sexual orientations reduce the risk of suicide, depression and substance abuse among homosexuals and bisexuals.

still common in the United States and elsewhere. Although societal prejudice and harassment increase the risk for depression, substance abuse, and suicide among homosexuals and bisexuals, recent evidence indicates these risks are reduced in the presence of positive family attitudes and a strong social support system (Cochran & Mays, 2006; D'Augelli, 2006; S. T. Russell, 2006).

CHECK YOUR UNDERSTANDING

1. The sex drive is necessary for the survival of the (individual/species).
2. The four stages of the sexual response cycle are _____, _____, _____, and _____.

Match the following terms with the appropriate definitions.

3. ___ pheromones
4. ___ testosterone
5. ___ the limbic system

a. brain center involved in sexual excitement
b. hormone that influences some aspects of sexual development
c. scents that may cause sexual attraction

Answers: 1. species. 2. excitement, plateau, orgasm, and resolution. 3. c. 4. b. 5. a.

APPLY YOUR UNDERSTANDING

1. Barbie has just "come out" to her friend Ken, telling him that she is a lesbian. She says she has known since she was a child that she was different from other girls because she was never attracted to boys, and she has concluded that this is just the way she is meant to be. Ken's reaction, however, is negative. He suggests that Barbie just isn't trying hard enough and that counseling could help her learn new patterns of attraction. Barbie is expressing the _____ view of homosexual orientation, while Ken's response demonstrates the _____ view.

   a. interventionist; interactionist
   b. interactionist; interventionist
   c. nurture; nature
   d. nature; nurture

2. You are reading an article in the newspaper when you come across the following statement: "The extent to which a male is interested in sex is determined by the level of the hormone testosterone at that moment." Which of the following would be an accurate response, based on what you have learned in this chapter?

   a. "That would be true only for adolescent and young adult males, not older adults."
   b. "Actually there is very little relationship between moment-to-moment levels of testosterone and sex drive in males."
   c. "That's true, but testosterone is a pheromone, not a hormone."
   d. "That's true, but only during the excitement phase of the sexual response cycle."

Answers: 1. d. 2. b.

Other Important Motives

How are stimulus motives different from primary drives?

So far, we have moved from motives that depend on biological needs (hunger and thirst) to a motive that is far more sensitive to external cues—sex. Next, we consider motives that are even more responsive to environmental stimuli. These motives, called **stimulus motives**, include *exploration, curiosity, manipulation,* and *contact.* They push us to investigate and often to change our environment. Finally, we will turn our attention to the motives of *aggression, achievement* and *affiliation.*

stimulus motives Unlearned motives, such as curiosity or contact, that prompts us to explore or change the world around us.

EXPLORATION AND CURIOSITY

What motives cause people to explore and change their environment?

Where does that road go? What is in that dark little shop? How does a television set work? Answering these questions has no obvious benefit: You do not expect the road to take you anywhere you need to go or the shop to contain anything you really want. Nor are you about to start a TV repair service. You just want to know. Exploration and curiosity are motives sparked by the new and unknown and are directed toward no more specific goal than "finding out." They are not unique to humans. The family dog will run around a new house, sniffing and checking things out, before it settles down to eat its dinner. Even rats, when given a choice, will opt to explore an unknown maze rather than run through a familiar one. But although curiosity is not uniquely human, it is perhaps particularly characteristic of humans.

Psychologists disagree about the nature of curiosity, its causes, and even how to measure it (Litman, Collins, & Spielberger, 2005; Loewenstein, 1994). William James viewed it as an emotion; Freud considered it a socially acceptable expression of the sex drive. Others have seen it as a response to the unexpected and as evidence of a human need to find meaning in life. We might assume that curiosity is a key component of intelligence, but studies attempting to establish a positive correlation between the two have been inconclusive. However, curiosity has been linked to creativity (Kashdan & Fincham, 2002).

Curiosity can also vary according to our familiarity with events and circumstances. As we continually explore and learn from our environment, we raise our threshold for the new and complex; and in turn our explorations and our curiosity become much more ambitious. In this respect, curiosity is linked to cognition. A gap in our understanding may stimulate our curiosity. But as our curiosity is satisfied and the unfamiliar becomes familiar, we tend to become bored. This outcome, in turn, prompts us to explore our surroundings further (Loewenstein, 1994).

MANIPULATION AND CONTACT

Is the human need for contact universal?

Why do museums have "Do Not Touch" signs everywhere? It is because the staff knows from experience that the urge to touch is almost irresistible. Unlike curiosity and exploration, manipulation focuses on a specific object that must be touched, handled, played with, and felt before we are satisfied. Manipulation is a motive limited to primates, who have agile fingers and toes. In contrast, the need for *contact* is more universal than the need for manipulation. Furthermore, it is not limited to touching with the fingers—it may involve the whole body. Manipulation is an active process, but contact may be passive.

In a classic series of experiments, Harry Harlow demonstrated the importance of the need for contact (Harlow, 1958; Harlow & Zimmerman, 1959). Newborn baby monkeys were separated from their mothers and given two "surrogate mothers." Both surrogate mothers were the same shape, but one was made of wire mesh and had no soft surfaces. The other was cuddly—layered with foam rubber and covered with terry cloth. Both surrogate mothers were warmed by means of an electric light placed inside them, but only the wire-mesh mother was equipped with a nursing bottle. Thus, the wire-mesh mother fulfilled two physiological needs for the infant monkeys: the need for food and the need for warmth. But baby monkeys most often gravitated to the terry-cloth mother, which did not provide food. When they were frightened, they would run and cling to it as they would to a real mother. Because both surrogate mothers were warm, the researchers concluded that the need for closeness goes deeper than a need for mere warmth. As described in Chapter 3, "Sensation and Perception," the importance of contact has also been demonstrated with premature infants. Low-birth-weight babies who are held and massaged gain weight faster, are calmer, and display more advanced sensory and motor skills at 1 year than those who are seldom touched (Field, 1986; S. J. Weiss, Wilson, & Morrison, 2004).

This toddler is exhibiting curiosity, a stimulus motive.

An infant monkey with Harlow's surrogate "mothers"—one made of bare wire, the other covered with soft terry cloth. The baby monkey clings to the terry-cloth mother, even though the wire mother is heated and dispenses food. Apparently, there is contact comfort in the cuddly terry cloth that the bare wire mother can't provide.

THINKING CRITICALLY ABOUT . . .

Culture and Aggression

The United States has one of the world's highest living standards and sends more young people to college than most other industrialized nations. Yet we have a very high incidence of violent crime.

1. Why do you think violence is so prevalent in U.S. culture? Can you design a research study to test your ideas?

2. How might the problem of widespread violence be reduced? What kind of evidence would be required to show that your ideas in fact work?

3. This critical-thinking exercise begins with several assertions about living standards, college attendance, and violent crime. However, no sources were cited to support those claims. Did you ask yourself whether there is any evidence to support them and, if so, whether the evidence is clear? What kinds of data would you want to see in order to determine if those assertions are correct?

---

aggression Behavior aimed at doing harm to others; also, the motive to behave aggressively.

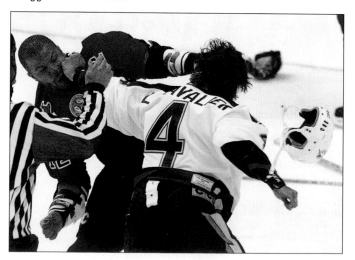

Some psychologists believe that aggression is largely a learned behavior. Professional athletes in contact sports often serve as models of aggressive behavior.

AGGRESSION

Is aggression a biological response or a learned one?

Human **aggression** encompasses all behavior that is intended to inflict physical or psychological harm on others. Intent is a key element of aggression. Accidentally hitting a pedestrian with your car is not an act of aggression—whereas deliberately running down a person would be.

Judging from the statistics (which often reflect underreporting of certain types of crimes), aggression is disturbingly common in this country. According to the *FBI's Uniform Crime Reports*, nearly 1.4 million violent crimes were reported in the United States in 2005. These crimes included more than 16,000 murders, nearly 94,000 forcible rapes, 417,000 robberies, and more than 860,000 aggravated assaults (Federal Bureau of Investigation, 2006). Family life also has a violent underside: One-quarter of families experience some form of violence. Some 3 to 4 million women are battered by their partners each year; more than 25% of these battered women seek medical attention for their injuries. In addition, more than 750,000 cases of child abuse were confirmed in 2004, with an estimated 1,500 children dying as a result of abuse. Children younger than 1 year accounted for 45% of the fatalities (National Clearing House on Child Abuse and Neglect, 2006).

Why are people aggressive? Freud considered aggression an innate drive, similar to hunger and thirst, that builds up until it is released. In his view, one important function of society is to channel the aggressive drive into constructive and socially acceptable avenues, such as sports, debate, and other forms of competition. If Freud's analysis is correct, then expressing aggression should reduce the aggressive drive. Research shows, however, that under some circumstances, venting one's anger is more likely to increase than to reduce future aggression (Bushman, 2002; Bushman, Baumeister, & Stack, 1999).

According to another view, aggression is a vestige of our evolutionary past (Mohl, 2006) that is triggered by pain or frustration (Lorenz, 1968). Some evidence shows that pain can prompt aggressive behavior. In one experiment, for example, when a pair of rats received electric shocks through the grid floor of their cage, they immediately attacked each other. As the frequency and intensity of the shocks increased, so did the fighting (Ulrich & Azrin, 1962).

Frustration also plays a role in aggression. However, frustration does not always produce aggression. For example, if frustration doesn't generate anger, aggression is unlikely (Berkowitz & Harmon-Jones, 2004). Moreover, people react to frustration in different ways: some seek help and support, others withdraw from the source of frustration, some become aggressive, and some choose to escape into drugs or alcohol. Finally, there is some evidence that frustration is most likely to cause aggression in people who have learned to be aggressive as a means of coping with unpleasant situations (R. E. Tremblay, Hartup, & Archer, 2005).

One way we learn aggression is by observing aggressive models, especially those who get what they want (and avoid punishment) when they behave aggressively. For example, in contact sports, we often applaud acts of aggression (C. J. Rowe, 1998). In professional hockey, fistfights between players may elicit as much fan fervor as does goal scoring.

But what if the aggressive model does not come out ahead or is even punished for aggressive actions? The ancient custom of public executions and painful punishments such as flogging and the stocks arose from the notion that punishing a person for aggressive acts would deter others from committing those acts. Observers usually will avoid imitating a model's behavior if it has negative consequences. However, as we saw in Chapter 5, "Learning," children who viewed aggressive behavior learned aggressive behavior, regardless of whether the aggressive model was rewarded or punished. The same results were obtained in a study in which children were shown films of aggressive behavior. Children who saw the aggressive model being punished were less aggressive than those who saw the aggressive model rewarded, but both groups of children were more aggressive than those who saw no aggressive model at all. These data are consistent with research showing that exposure to cinematic violence of any sort causes a small to moderate increase in aggressive behavior among children and adolescents (W. Wood, Wong, & Chachere, 1991). So, simply seeing an aggressive model seems to increase aggression among children, even if the model is punished; it also makes little difference whether the model is live or shown on film (C. A. Anderson, 1997). Children who grow up in homes where aggression and violence are prevalent are at particular risk (Feldman et al., 1995; Onyskiw, 2000).

AGGRESSION AND CULTURE Cultural variations exist in the handling of aggression (Triandis, 1994). For example, cultures as diverse as the Semai of the Malaysian rain forest, the Tahitian Islanders of the Pacific, the Zuni and Blackfoot nations in North America, the Pygmies of Africa, and the residents of Japan and the Scandinavian nations place a premium on resolving conflicts peacefully. They tend to withdraw from confrontations rather than risk open conflict. In contrast, cultures such as the Yanomanö of South America, the Truk Islanders of Micronesia, and the Simbu of New Guinea encourage aggressive behavior, particularly among males. Actually, we need not travel to exotic, far-away lands to find such diversity. Within the United States, such subcultures as Quakers, the Amish, the Mennonites, and the Hutterites have traditionally valued nonviolence and peaceful coexistence. This outlook contrasts markedly with attitudes and practices in mainstream American culture.

Cultural differences in aggressiveness are reflected in statistics on violent crimes. In the United States, violent-crime rates are shockingly high compared with those of other nations. The murder rate in Norway, for example, is less than 1 per 100,000 people; in England and Wales, it is 1.5; and in France it is 1.6. In contrast, in the United States, the 2004 murder rate was 5.5 per 100,000 people (Federal Bureau of Investigation, 2005). Indeed, the murder rate in the United States is the highest among the industrialized nations of the world (Geen, 1998). The United States also reports higher rates of rape and vandalism.

These striking cultural differences in aggressive behavior suggest that aggression is very much influenced by the learning that takes place within a particular cultural context and by cultural norms and values. Consider the relatively nonaggressive cultures we just mentioned. Most of them are *collectivist* societies that emphasize the good of the group over the desires of the individual. Members of collectivist societies are more likely to seek compromise or to withdraw from a threatening interaction because of their concern for maintaining group harmony. In contrast, members of *individualist* societies are more likely to follow the adage "Stand up for yourself."

GENDER AND AGGRESSION Across cultures and at every age, males are more likely than females to behave aggressively. In particular, men are more likely than women to murder, to use force to achieve their goals, and to prefer aggressive sports such as hockey, football, and boxing. Indeed, some acts of aggression, such as rape, are almost exclusively committed by males.

Three studies that reviewed more than 100 studies of aggression concluded that males are more aggressive than females both verbally (i.e., with taunts, insults, and threats) and, in particular, physically (i.e., with hitting, kicking, and fighting) (Bettencourt & Miller, 1996; Eagly & Steffen, 1986; Hyde, 1986). These gender differences tend to be greater in

Are males naturally more aggressive than females? Research suggests that both biology and culture encourage aggression in boys more than in girls. Adults often look the other way when two boys are fighting, sending the message that violence is an acceptable way to settle disputes.

natural settings than in controlled laboratory settings (Hyde, 2005a) and appear to be remarkably stable (Arsenio, 2004; Knight, Fabes, & Higgins, 1996). Indeed, even historical data that go back to 16th-century Europe show that males committed more than three times as many violent crimes as females (L. Ellis & Coontz, 1990).

Is the origin of gender difference in aggression biological or social? The answer is not simple. On the one hand, certain biological factors appear to contribute to aggressive behavior. As we saw in Chapter 2, "The Biological Basis of Behavior," low levels of testosterone and high levels of estrogen in both males and females are associated with aggressiveness and irritability. Moreover, exposure to high levels of testosterone during prenatal development is associated with increased aggressiveness (Reinisch, Ziemba-Davis, & Sanders, 1991). Other research suggests that human aggression has its roots in evolution and can be traced to defensive behaviors characteristic of our ancestors (Archer, & Côté, 2005).

At the same time, our society clearly tolerates and even encourages greater aggressiveness in boys than in girls (Sommers-Flanagan, Sommers-Flanagan, & Davis, 1993). For example, we are more likely to give boys toy guns and to reward them for behaving aggressively; girls are more likely than boys to be taught to feel guilty for behaving aggressively or to expect parental disapproval for their aggressive behavior (Perry, Perry, & Weiss, 1989). Perhaps the most accurate conclusion is that both biological and social factors contribute to gender differences in aggressive behavior. Like most of the complex behaviors that we have reviewed, aggression undoubtedly depends on the interaction of nature and nurture (Geen, 1998; Verona, Joiner, Johnson, & Bender, 2006).

ACHIEVEMENT

Is being highly competitive important to high achievement?

Climbing Mount Everest, sending rockets into space, making the dean's list, rising to the top of a giant corporation—all these actions may have mixed underlying motives. But in all of them there is a desire to excel, "to overcome obstacles, to exercise power, to strive to do something difficult as well and as quickly as possible" (H. A. Murray, 1938, pp. 80–81). It is this desire for achievement for its own sake that leads psychologists to suggest that there is a separate **achievement motive**.

Using a self-report questionnaire called the Work and Family Orientation scale (WOFO) to study achievement motivation, researchers discovered three separate but interrelated aspects of achievement-oriented behavior: *work orientation*, the desire to work hard and do a good job; *mastery*, the preference for difficult or challenging feats, with an emphasis on improving one's past performance; and *competitiveness*, the enjoyment of pitting one's skills against those of other people (Helmreich & Spence, 1978).

How do individual differences in the three aspects of achievement motivation relate to people's attainment of goals? In fact, excessive competitiveness may actually interfere with achievement. In one study, students' grade-point averages (GPAs) were compared with their WOFO scores. As you might expect, students who scored low in work, mastery, and competitiveness had lower GPAs. But students who scored high in all three areas did

achievement motive The need to excel, to overcome obstacles.

not have the highest GPAs. It turned out that the students with the highest grades were those who had high work and mastery scores, but low competitiveness scores. The counterproductive effect of competitiveness curbs achievement in others as well, including businesspeople, elementary-school students, and scientists (Morrone & Pintrich, 2006). What accounts for this phenomenon? Some researchers speculate that highly competitive people alienate the very people who would otherwise help them achieve their goals; others suggest that preoccupation with winning distracts them from taking the actions necessary to attain their goals.

From psychological tests and personal histories, psychologists have developed a profile of people with high achievement motivation. These people are fast learners. They relish the opportunity to develop new strategies for unique and challenging tasks, whereas people with a low need for achievement rarely deviate from methods that worked for them in the past. Driven less by the desire for fame or fortune than by the need to live up to a high, self-imposed standard of performance (M. Carr, Borkowski, & Maxwell, 1991), they are self-confident, willingly take on responsibility, and do not readily bow to outside social pressures. Although they are energetic and allow few things to stand in the way of their goals, they are also apt to be tense and to suffer from stress-related ailments, such as headaches. They may also feel like impostors even—or especially—when they achieve their goals.

AFFILIATION

How do psychologists explain the human need to be with other people?

Generally, people have a need for affiliation—to be with other people. If they are isolated from social contact for a long time, they may become anxious. Why do human beings seek one another out?

For one thing, the **affiliation motive** is aroused when people feel threatened. Cues that signal danger, such as illness or catastrophe, appear to increase our desire to be with others (Rofe, 1984). *Esprit de corps*—the feeling of being part of a sympathetic group—is critical among troops going into a battle, just as a football coach's pregame pep talk fuels team spirit. Both are designed to make people feel they are working for a common cause or against a common foe.

Fear and anxiety may also be closely tied to the affiliation motive. When rats, monkeys, or humans are placed in anxiety-producing situations, the presence of a member of the same species who remains calm will reduce the fear experienced by the anxious ones. Patients with critical illnesses tend to prefer being with healthy people, rather than with other seriously ill patients or by themselves (Rofe, Hoffman, & Lewin, 1985). In the same way, if you are nervous on a plane during a bumpy flight, you may strike up a conversation with the calm-looking woman sitting next to you.

On the basis of these facts, some theorists have argued that our need for affiliation has an evolutionary basis. (See Ainsworth, 1989; R. F. Baumeister & Leary, 2000; Buss, 1990, 1991.) In this view, forming and maintaining social bonds provided our ancestors with both survival and reproductive benefits. Social groups can share resources such as food and shelter, provide opportunities for reproduction, and assist in the care of offspring. Children who chose to stay with adults were probably more likely to survive (and ultimately reproduce) than those who wandered away from their groups. Thus, it is understandable that people in general tend to seek out other people.

In any given case, affiliation behavior (like most behavior) usually stems from a subtle interplay of biological and environmental factors. Whether you strike up a conversation with the person sitting next to you on a bumpy airplane flight depends on how friendly you normally are, what is considered proper behavior in your culture, as well as on how scared you feel at the moment, how calm your neighbor appears to be, and how turbulent the flight is.

affiliation motive The need to be with others.

CHECK YOUR UNDERSTANDING

1. A high degree of _____ may interfere with achievement.

2. A person who is willing to contend with the high risks of a career in sales is probably motivated by a high _____ motive.

3. Indicate whether the following statements are true (T) or false (F).

    a. ___ Curiosity has been linked to creativity.

    b. ___ Research shows that low-birth-weight babies gain weight faster with frequent physical contact.

    c. ___ Aggression may be a learned response to numerous stimuli.

Answers: 1. competitiveness. 2. achievement. 3. a. (T). b. (T). c. (T).

APPLY YOUR UNDERSTANDING

1. Susan scores high on tests of achievement motivation. Which of the following would you LEAST expect to be true of her?

    a. She is a fast learner who willingly takes on responsibility.

    b. She seldom deviates from methods that have worked for her in the past.

    c. She has a strong desire to live up to high, self-imposed standards of excellence.

    d. She is self-confident and resists outside social pressures.

2. You are watching a children's TV show in which the "bad guys" eventually are punished for their aggressive behavior. Your friend says, "It's a good thing the bad guys always lose. Otherwise, kids would learn to be aggressive from watching TV shows like this." You think about that for a minute and then, on the basis of what you have learned in this chapter, you reply,

    a. "Actually, seeing an aggressor punished for his or her actions leads to more aggression than seeing no aggression at all."

    b. "You're right. Seeing aggressors punished for their actions is a good way to reduce the amount of aggressiveness in children."

    c. "Aggression is an instinctual response to frustration, so it really doesn't matter what children see on TV. If they are frustrated, they will respond with aggression."

Answers: 1. b. 2. a.

Emotions

How many basic emotions are there?

Ancient Greek rationalists thought that emotions, if not held in check, would wreak havoc on higher mental abilities such as rational thought and decision making (Cacioppo & Gardner, 1999). In the past, psychologists, too, often viewed emotions as a "base instinct"—a vestige of our evolutionary heritage that needed to be repressed. Not surprisingly, emotions received very little attention from researchers (Mayne & Bonanno, 2001).

More recently, however, scientists have begun to see emotions in a more positive light. Today, they are considered essential to survival and a major source of personal enrichment and resilience (National Advisory Mental Health Council, 1995; Tugade & Fredrickson, 2004). Emotions are linked to variations in immune function and, thereby, to disease (S. Cohen, Doyle, Turner, Alper, & Skoner, 2003a; Segerstrom & Miller, 2004) (see Chapter 11, "Stress and Health Psychology"). As we saw in Chapter 7, "Cognition and Mental Abilities," emotions may also influence how successful we are (Goleman, 1997; Goleman, Boyatzis, & McKee, 2002). It is clear, then, that if we would understand human behavior, we must understand emotions. Unfortunately, that task is easier said than done. As you will soon see, even identifying how many emotions there are is difficult.

BASIC EMOTIONS

Are there basic emotions that all people experience regardless of their culture?

Many people have attempted to identify and describe the basic emotions experienced by humans (Cornelius, 1996; Schimmack & Crites, 2005). Some years ago, Robert Plutchik (1980), for example, proposed that there are eight basic emotions: *fear, surprise, sadness, disgust, anger, anticipation, joy,* and *acceptance.* Each of these emotions helps us adjust to the demands of our environment, although in different ways. Fear, for example, underlies flight, which helps protect animals from their enemies; anger propels animals to attack or destroy.

Emotions adjacent to each other on Plutchik's emotion "circle" (see **Figure 8–8**) are more alike than those situated opposite each other or that are farther away from each other. Surprise is more closely related to fear than to anger; joy and acceptance are more similar to each other than either is to disgust. Moreover, according to Plutchik's model, different emotions may combine to produce an even wider and richer spectrum of experience. Occurring together, anticipation and joy, for example, yield optimism; joy and acceptance fuse into love; and surprise and sadness make for disappointment. Within any of Plutchik's eight categories, emotions vary in intensity.

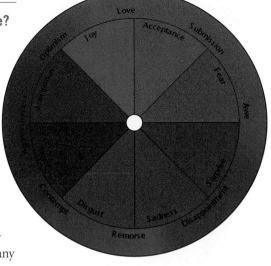

Figure 8–8
Plutchik's eight basic categories of emotion.
Source: Plutchik, 1980.

> → ENDURING ISSUES ← ←

Diversity–Universality   Are Emotions Universal?

Some scientists challenge Plutchik's model, noting that it may apply only to the emotional experience of English-speaking people. Anthropologists report enormous differences in the ways that other cultures view and categorize emotions. Some languages, in fact, do not even have a word for "emotion." Languages also differ in the number of words that they have to name emotions. English includes over 2,000 words to describe emotional experiences, but Taiwanese Chinese has only 750 such descriptive words. One tribal language has only 7 words that could be translated into categories of emotion. Some cultures lack words for "anxiety" or "depression" or "guilt." Samoans have 1 word encompassing love, sympathy, pity, and liking—all distinct emotions in our own culture (Frijda, Markam, & Sato, 1995; J. A. Russell, 1991). ●●

Figure 8–9

Display of anger in animal and human.
Compare the facial expressions. The human face is that of a Kabuki player who is simulating anger. Note how the actor bares his teeth, copying the mandrill's display of emotion.

Of interest is that words used to name or describe an emotion may influence how that emotion is experienced. For example, the Tahitian language has no direct translation for the concept of sadness. Instead, Tahitians experience sadness in terms of physical illness. The sadness we feel over the departure of a close friend would be experienced by a Tahitian as, say, exhaustion.

Because of the differences in emotions from one culture to another, the tendency now is to distinguish between primary and secondary emotions. Primary emotions are those shared by people throughout the world, regardless of culture. They include, at a minimum, fear, anger, and pleasure, but may also include sadness, disgust, surprise, and other emotions. Most researchers use four criteria to identify primary emotions (see Plutchick, 1994): The emotion must (1) be evident in all cultures, (2) contribute to survival, (3) be associated with a distinct facial expression, and (4) be evident in non-human primates. (See **Figure 8–9.**) As yet no consensus exists about what emotions qualify as

Figure 8–10

Name That Face.

Dr. Paul Ekman believes that facial expressions are distinct, predictable, and easy to read for someone who has studied them. His research involved breaking the expressions down into their specific muscular components and developing programs to help train people to become more accurate observers of the feelings that flit briefly across others' faces. Here, he demonstrates six emotional states. How many of them can you match to the pictures? The answers are below.

a. fear
b. neutral (no emotion)
c. sadness
d. anger
e. surprise
f. disgust

Source: New York Times, 2003.

Answers:
1. b (neutral)
2. f (disgust)
3. e (surprise)
4. a (fear)
5. d (anger)
6. c (sadness).

James–Lange theory States that stimuli cause physiological changes in our bodies, and emotions result from those physiological changes.

primary, but the number is small, very likely no more than a dozen.

Secondary emotions are those that are not found in all cultures. They may be thought of as subtle amalgamations of the primary emotions. There are many more secondary emotions than primary emotions, but there is, again, no consensus about what those emotions are or how many they number.

Attempts to identify primary emotions have generally used cross-cultural studies (Ekman et al., 1987; Izard, 1994; Yrizarry, Matsumoto, Imai, Kookenm, & Takeuchi, 2001). For example, one group of researchers asked participants from 10 countries to interpret photographs depicting various facial expressions of emotions (Ekman et al., 1987). The percentage of participants from each country who correctly identified the emotions ranged from 60% to 98%. (See **Figure 8–10**.) The researchers used this and other evidence to argue for the existence of six primary emotions—*happiness*, *surprise*, *sadness*, *fear*, *disgust*, and *anger*. Notice that love is not included in this list. Although Ekman did not find a universally recognized facial expression for love, many psychologists nevertheless hold that love is a primary emotion (C. Hendrick & Hendrick, 2003; Sabini & Silver, 2005). Its outward expression, however, may owe much to the stereotypes promoted by a culture's media (Fehr, 1994). In one study in which American college students were asked to display a facial expression for love, the participants mimicked the conventional "Hollywood" prototypes such as sighing deeply, gazing skyward, and holding their hand over their heart (Cornelius, 1996).

THEORIES OF EMOTION

What is the relationship among emotions, biological reactions, and thoughts?

In the 1880s, the American psychologist William James formulated the first modern theory of emotion; and the Danish psychologist Carl Lange reached the same conclusions. According to the **James–Lange theory**, stimuli in the environment (say, seeing a large growling dog running toward us) cause physiological changes in our bodies (accelerated heart rate, enlarged pupils, deeper or shallower breathing, increased perspiration, and goose bumps), and emotions arise from those physiological changes. The emotion of *fear*, then, would simply be the almost instantaneous and automatic awareness of physiological changes.

There has been some supporting evidence for this theory (R. J. Davidson, 1992; Levenson, 1992; McGeer & McGeer, 1980; Prinz, 2005), but if you think back to the biology of the nervous system (Chapter 2), you should be able to identify a major flaw in the James–Lange theory. Recall that sensory information about bodily changes flows to the brain through the spinal cord. If bodily changes are the source of emotions, then people with severe spinal cord injuries should experience fewer and less intense emotions, but this is not the case (Chwalisz, Diener, & Gallagher, 1988). Moreover, most emotions are accompanied by very similar physiological changes. Bodily changes, then, do not cause specific emotions and may not even be necessary for emotional experience.

Recognizing these facts, the **Cannon–Bard theory** holds that we mentally process emotions and physically respond simultaneously, not one after another. When you see the dog, you feel afraid *and* your heart races at the same time.

COGNITIVE THEORIES OF EMOTION Cognitive psychologists have taken Cannon–Bard's theory a step further. They argue that our emotional experience depends on our perception of a situation (Ellsworth, 2002; Lazarus, 1991a, 1991b, 1991c; Scherer, Schorr, & Johnstone, 2001). According to the **cognitive theory** of emotion, the situation gives us clues as to how we should interpret our state of arousal. One of the first theories of emotion that took into account cognitive processes was advanced by Stanley Schachter and Jerome Singer (1962; 2001). According to Schachter and Singer's *Two-Factor Theory of Emotion*, when we see a bear, there are indeed bodily changes; but we then use information about the situation to tell us how to respond to those changes. Only when we *cognitively* recognize that we are in danger do we experience those bodily changes as fear. (See **Figure 8–11** for a comparison of these three theories of emotion.)

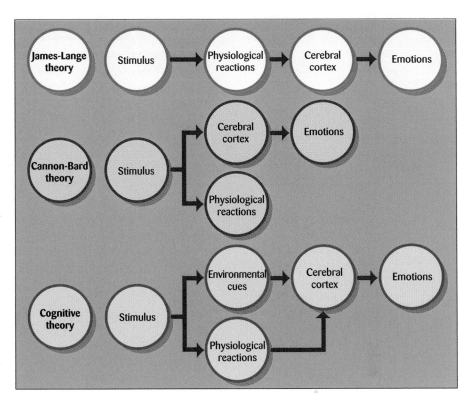

Figure 8–11

The three major theories of emotion.
According to the James–Lange theory, the body first responds physiologically to a stimulus, and then the cerebral cortex determines which emotion is being experienced. The Cannon–Bard theory holds that impulses are sent simultaneously to the cerebral cortex and the peripheral nervous system; thus, the response to the stimulus and the processing of the emotion are experienced at the same time, but independently. Cognitive theorists assert that the cerebral cortex interprets physiological changes in the light of information about the situation to determine which emotions we feel.

CHALLENGES TO COGNITIVE THEORY Although a cognitive theory of emotion makes a lot of sense, some critics reject the idea that feelings always stem from cognitions. Quoting the poet e. e. cummings, Zajonc (pronounced *ZY-unz*) argues that "feelings come first." Human infants, he points out, can imitate emotional expressions at 12 days of age, well before they acquire language. We have the ability to respond instantaneously to situations without taking time to interpret and evaluate them. But some emotional responses are not clear-cut. When we feel jittery, a cross between nervous and excited, we ask ourselves, "What's going on?" Zajonc (1984) believes that we invent explanations to label feelings: In his view, cognition follows emotion.

Another direct challenge to the cognitive theory claims that emotions can be experienced without the intervention of cognition (Izard, 1971, 1994). According to this view, a situation such as separation or pain provokes a unique pattern of unlearned facial movements and body postures that may be completely independent of conscious thought. When information about our facial expressions and posture reaches the brain, we automatically experience the corresponding emotion. According to Carroll Izard, then, the James–Lange theory was essentially right in suggesting that emotional experience arises from bodily reactions. But Izard's theory stresses facial expression and body posture as crucial to the experience of emotion, whereas the James–Lange theory emphasized muscles, skin, and internal organs.

Considerable evidence supports Izard's view that facial expressions influence emotions (Ekman, 2003; Ekman & Davidson, 1993; Soussignan, 2002). If further research bolsters Izard's theory, we will be able to say with certainty that a key element in determining our emotional experience is our own expressive behavior, the topic we turn to now.

CHECK YOUR UNDERSTANDING

1. Robert Plutchik asserts that emotions vary in _____ a fact that accounts in part for the great range of emotions we experience.

Answer: 1. intensity.

Cannon–Bard theory States that the experience of emotion occurs simultaneously with biological changes.

cognitive theory States that emotional experience depends on one's perception or judgment of a situation.

APPLY YOUR UNDERSTANDING

1. Ralph believes that if you're feeling depressed, you should smile a lot and your depression will fade away. His view is most consistent with

   a. Izard's theory.

   b. the Schachter–Singer theory.

   c. the James–Lange theory.

   d. the Cannon–Bard theory.

2. You are on a camping trip when you encounter a bear. You get butterflies in your stomach, your heart starts racing, your mouth gets dry, and you start to perspire. A psychologist who takes the cognitive perspective on emotion would say,

   a. "Seeing the bear caused the physical changes, which in turn caused you to experience fear."

   b. "Seeing the bear caused you to experience fear, which in turn caused all those physical changes."

   c. "Seeing the bear caused the physical changes. When you realized they were caused by the bear, you experienced fear."

   d. "Seeing the bear caused the physical changes and the emotion of fear at the same time."

Answers: 1. a. 2. c.

Communicating Emotion

What is the most obvious signal of emotion?

Sometimes you are vaguely aware that a person makes you feel uncomfortable. When pressed to be more precise, you might say, "You never know what she is thinking." But you do not mean that you never know her opinion of a film or what she thought about the last election. It would probably be more accurate to say that you do not know what she is feeling. Almost all of us conceal our emotions to some extent, but usually people can tell what we are feeling. Although emotions can often be expressed in words, much of the time we communicate our feelings nonverbally. We do so through, among other things, voice quality, facial expression, body language, personal space, and explicit acts.

THINKING CRITICALLY ABOUT . . .

Nonverbal Communication of Emotion

Some people are clearly better than others at reading and sending emotional messages. The question is, why? How might you determine:

1. if differences in these skills are learned or inherited?

2. the kinds of learning experiences that produce high skills?

3. whether it is possible to teach the skills?

VOICE QUALITY AND FACIAL EXPRESSION

What role can voice and facial expression play in expressing emotion?

If your roommate is washing the dishes and says acidly, "I *hope* you're enjoying your novel," the literal meaning of his words is quite clear, but you probably know very well that he is not expressing a concern about your reading pleasure. He is really saying, "I am annoyed that you are not helping to clean up." Similarly, if you receive a phone call from someone who has had very good or very bad news, you will probably know how she feels before she has told you what happened. In the same way, we can literally hear fear in a person's voice, as we do when we listen to a nervous student give an oral report. Much of the information we convey is not contained in the words we use, but in the way those words are expressed (Gobl & Chasaide, 2003).

Facial expressions are perhaps the most obvious emotional indicators (Horstmann, 2003). We can tell a good deal about a person's emotional state by observing whether that person is laughing, crying, smiling, or frowning. Many facial expressions are innate, not learned (Ekman, 1994; Goldsmith, 2002). Children who are born deaf and blind use the same facial expressions as do other children to express the same emotions. One study for example, showed that adults are quite adept at interpreting infant nonverbal communications, such as whether they are looking at a new or familiar object, just by observing their facial expressions (Camras et al., 2002). Charles Darwin first advanced the idea that most animals share a common pattern of muscular facial movements. For example, dogs, tigers, and humans all bare their teeth in rage. Darwin also observed that expressive behaviors serve a basic biological as well as social function. Darwin's notion that emotions have an evolutionary history and can be traced across cultures as part of our biological heritage laid the groundwork for many modern investigations of emotional expression (Conrad, 2004; Izard, 1992, 1994). (See **Figure 8–12**.) Psychologists who take an evolutionary approach believe that facial expressions served an adaptive function, enabling our ancestors to compete successfully for status, to win mates, and to defend themselves (Plutchik , 2002; Tooby & Cosmides, 1990, 2005).

Recent studies suggest that some patients with severe depressive disorder may also have an impaired ability to accurately judge another person's facial expression of emotion; and that this impairment contributes to their difficulty in interpersonal functioning (Surguladze et al., 2004).

BODY LANGUAGE, PERSONAL SPACE, AND GESTURES

How can posture and personal space communicate emotion?

Body language is another way that we communicate messages nonverbally. How we hold our back, for example, communicates a great deal. When we are relaxed, we tend to stretch back into a chair; when we are tense, we sit more stiffly with our feet together.

The distance we maintain between ourselves and others is called *personal space*. This distance varies depending on the nature of the activity and the emotions felt. If someone stands closer to you than is customary, that proximity may indicate either anger or affection; if farther away than usual, it may indicate fear or dislike. The normal conversing distance between people varies from culture to culture. Two Swedes conversing would ordinarily stand much farther apart than would two Arabs or Greeks.

Figure 8–12
People throughout the world use the "brow-raise" greeting when a friend approaches.
Source: Eibl–Eibesfeldt, 1972.

When having a conversation, most people of middle-Eastern descent stand closer to one another than most Americans do. In our society, two men would not usually stand as close together as these two Arabs unless they were very aggressively arguing with each other (a baseball player heatedly arguing with an umpire, for example).

ON THE CUTTING EDGE

HOW THE BRAIN READS THE FACE

Scientists know that activity in brain circuits involving the amygdala is critical for the release of emotions (Schafe & LeDoux, 2002; P. Shaw et al., 2005). The amygdala may also be critical for our ability to correctly interpret facial expressions. Adolphs and colleagues (Adolphs, Tranel, Damasio, & Damasio 1994) reported the remarkable case of a 30-year-old woman (S. M.) with a rare disease that caused nearly complete destruction of the amygdala. Although S. M. could correctly identify photographs of familiar faces with 100% accuracy, and easily learned to recognize new faces, she had great difficulty recognizing fear and discriminating between different emotions, such as happiness and surprise. Other research also has shown that people with amygdala damage have trouble "reading faces" (Adolphs, Baron-Cohen, & Tranel, 2002; Adolphs & Tranel, 2003). Indeed, some researchers have suggested that abnormalities in the brain circuits associated with the amygdala can, in some cases, make it difficult for people to perceive threat accurately and that, in turn, can lead to unprovoked violence and aggression (R. J. Davidson, Putnam, & Larson, 2000; S. J. Lee, Miller, & Moon, 2004).

Explicit acts, of course, can also serve as nonverbal clues to emotions. A slammed door may tell us that the person who just left the room is angry. If friends drop in for a visit and you invite them into your living room, you are probably less at ease with them than with friends who generally sit down with you at the kitchen table. Gestures, such as a slap on the back or an embrace, can also indicate feelings. Whether people shake your hand briefly or for a long time, firmly or limply, tells you something about how they feel about you.

You can see from this discussion that nonverbal communication of emotions is important. However, a word of caution is needed here. Although nonverbal behavior may offer a clue to a person's feelings, it is not an *infallible* clue. Laughing and crying can sound alike, yet crying may signal sorrow, joy, anger, or nostalgia—or that you are slicing an onion. Moreover, as with verbal reports, people sometimes "say" things nonverbally that they do not mean. We all have done things thoughtlessly—turned our backs, frowned when thinking about something else, or laughed at the wrong time—that have given offense because our actions were interpreted as an expression of an emotion that we were not, in fact, feeling.

Also, many of us overestimate our ability to interpret nonverbal cues. For example, in one study of several hundred "professional lie catchers," including members of the Secret Service, government lie detector experts, judges, police officers, and psychiatrists, every group except for the psychiatrists rated themselves above average in their ability to tell whether another person was lying. Only the Secret Service agents managed to identify the liars at a better-than-chance rate (Ekman & O'Sullivan, 1991). Similar results have been obtained with other groups of people (Frank, 2006). In part, the reason seems to be that many behaviors that might seem to be associated with lying (such as avoiding eye contact, rapid blinking, or shrugs) are not in fact associated with lying; and other behaviors that are associated with lying (such as tenseness and fidgeting) also occur frequently when people are not lying (DePaulo et al., 2003). Thus, even the best nonverbal cues only indicate that a person *may* be lying.

GENDER AND EMOTION

Are men less emotional than women?

Men are often said to be less emotional than women. But do men feel less emotion, or are they simply less likely to express the emotions they feel? And are there some emotions that men are more likely than women to express?

Research sheds some light on these issues. In one study, when men and women saw depictions of people in distress, the men showed little emotion, but the women expressed feelings of concern (Eisenberg & Lennon, 1983). However, physiological measures of emotional arousal (such as heart rate and blood pressure) showed that the men in the study were actually just as affected as the women were. The men simply inhibited the expression of their emotions, whereas the women were more open about their feelings. Emotions such as sympathy, sadness, empathy, and distress are often considered "unmanly," and traditionally, in Western culture, boys are trained from an early age to suppress those emotions in public (L. Brody & Hall, 2000). The fact that men are less likely than women to seek help in dealing with emotional issues (Komiya, Good, & Sherrod, 2000) is probably a result of this early training. In addition, women tend to have stronger emotional reactions to self-generated thoughts and memories (R. Carter, 1998). (See **Figure 8–13**.)

Men and women are also likely to react with very different emotions to the same situation. For example, being betrayed or criticized by another person will elicit anger in males, whereas females are more likely to feel hurt, sad, or disappointed (L. Brody & Hall, 2000; A. H. Fischer, Rodriguez-Mosquera, van-Vianen, & Manstead, 2004). And, when men get angry, they generally turn their anger outward, against other people and against the situation in which they find themselves. Women are more likely to see themselves as the source of the problem and to turn their anger inward, against themselves. These gender-specific reactions are consistent with the fact that men are four times more likely than women to become violent in the face of life crises; women, by contrast, are much more likely to become depressed.

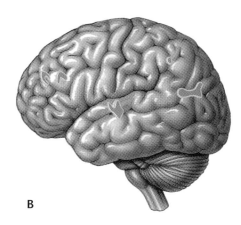

A

B

Figure 8–13
Emotion and brain activity in men and women.
When asked to think of something sad, women (A) generate more activity in their brains than men (B).

Source: Carter, 1998, p. 100. Shading added.

Mind–Body Holding Anger In

People who frequently feel anger and hostility may be at a serious health risk if they don't allow themselves to express and learn to regulate their anger (Carrère, Mittmann, Woodin, Tabares, & Yoshimoto, 2005). In a study that tracked a group of women over 18 years, researchers found that those scoring high on hostility were three times more likely to die during the course of the study than those who scored low (Julius, Harburg, Cottington, & Johnson, 1986). However, this higher level of risk applied only to participants who said they got angry in many situations but did not vent their anger. Other participants who reported frequent bouts of anger, which they expressed, were in the same low-risk group as those who said they rarely or never felt angry. ●●

Men and women also differ in their ability to interpret nonverbal cues of emotion. For example, women and young girls are more skilled than men or young boys at decoding the facial expressions, body cues, and tones of voice of others (Bosacki & Moore, 2004; Grunwald et al., 1999). How can we explain these differences? One possibility is that because women tend to be the primary caregivers for preverbal infants, they need to become more attuned than men to the subtleties of emotional expressions. Some psychologists have even suggested that this skill may be genetically programmed into females. Consistent with this evolutionary perspective, research has shown that male and female infants express and self-regulate emotions differently (McClure, 2000; M. K. Weinberg, Tronick, Cohn, & Olson, 1999).

Another explanation of gender differences in emotional sensitivity is based on the relative power of women and men. Because women historically have occupied less powerful positions, they may have felt the need to become acutely attuned to the emotional displays of others, particularly those in more powerful positions (namely, men). This idea is supported by evidence that, regardless of gender, followers are more sensitive to the emotions of leaders than vice versa (Aries, 2006; Hall, Bernieri, & Carney, 2006).

CULTURE AND EMOTION

How can culture influence the way we express emotion?

Does where we live affect what we feel? And if so, why? For psychologists, the key issue is how cultures help shape emotional experiences.

Among nonverbal channels of communication, facial expressions seem to communicate the most specific information. Hand gestures or posture can communicate general emotional states (e.g., feeling bad), but the complexity of the muscles in the face allows facial expressions to communicate very specific feelings (e.g., feeling sad, angry, or fearful). Some researchers have argued that across cultures, peoples, and societies, the face looks the same whenever certain emotions are expressed; this phenomenon is known as the *universalist* position. Charles Darwin subscribed to this view, arguing that as part of our common evolutionary heritage, people use the same expressions to convey the same emotions. In contrast, other researchers support the *culture-learning* position, which holds that members of a culture learn the appropriate facial expressions for emotions (Marsh, Elfenbein & Ambady, 2003). These expressions, then, can differ greatly from one culture to the next. Which view is more accurate?

As we saw earlier, Ekman and his colleagues have concluded from cross-cultural studies that at least six emotions are accompanied by universal facial expressions: happiness, sadness, anger, surprise, fear, and disgust. Carroll Izard (1980) conducted similar studies in England, Germany, Switzerland, France, Sweden, Greece, and Japan with similar results. These studies seem to support the universalist position: Regardless of culture, people tended to agree on which emotions others were expressing facially. However, this research does not completely rule out the culture-learning view. Because the participants were all members of developed countries that likely had been exposed to one another through

Can you identify the emotions being expressed by this man from New Guinea? The finding that U.S. college students could recognize the emotional expressions of people who had been largely isolated from Western cultures—and vice versa—lent support to the *universalist* position of facial expression.

Source: From P. Ekman and W. V. Friesen, *Unmasking the Face,* Englewood Cliffs, NJ, Prentice-Hall, 1975, p. 27.

movies, magazines, and tourism, they might simply have become familiar with the facial expressions seen in other cultures. A stronger test was needed that reduced or eliminated this possibility.

Such a test was made possible by the discovery of several contemporary cultures that had been totally isolated from Western culture for most of their existence. Members of the Fore and the Dani cultures of New Guinea, for example, had their first contact with anthropologists only a few years before Ekman's research took place. They provided a nearly perfect opportunity to test the universalist/culture-learning debate. If members of these cultures gave the same interpretation of facial expressions and produced the same expressions on their own faces as did people in Western cultures, there would be much stronger evidence for the universality of facial expressions of emotion. Ekman and his colleagues presented members of the Fore culture with three photographs of people from outside their culture and asked them to point to the picture that represented how they would feel in a certain situation. For example, if a participant was told "Your child has died, and you feel very sad," he or she would have the opportunity to choose which of the three pictures most closely corresponded to sadness. The results indicated very high rates of agreement on facial expressions of emotions (Ekman & Friesen, 1971; Ekman, Sorenson, & Friesen, 1969). Moreover, when photographs of the Fore and Dani posing the primary emotions were shown to college students in the United States, the same high agreement was found (Ekman & Friesen, 1975). This finding suggests that at least some emotional expressions are inborn.

If this is true, why are people so often confused about the emotions being expressed by people in other cultures? It turns out that the answer is not simple. Part of the explanation involves **display rules** (Ekman & Friesen, 1975). Display rules concern the circumstances under which it is appropriate for people to show emotion. Display rules differ substantially from culture to culture (Matsumoto & Kupperbusch, 2001). In a study of Japanese and

display rules Culture-specific rules that govern how, when, and why expressions of emotion are appropriate.

American college students, the participants watched graphic films of surgical procedures, either by themselves or in the presence of an experimenter. The students' facial expressions were secretly videotaped as they viewed the films. The results showed that when the students were by themselves, both the Japanese and the Americans showed facial expressions of disgust, as expected. But when the participants watched the films in the presence of an experimenter, the two groups displayed different responses. American students continued to show disgust on their faces, but the Japanese students showed facial expressions that were more neutral, even somewhat pleasant (Ekman, Friesen, & Ellsworth, 1972). Why the sudden switch? The answer in this case appears to lie in the different display rules of the two cultures. The Japanese norm says, "Don't display strong negative emotion in the presence of a respected elder" (in this case, the experimenter). Americans typically don't honor this display rule; hence, they expressed their true emotions whether they were alone or with someone else.

However, display rules don't tell the whole story. In a comprehensive review of the literature, Elfenbein and Ambady (2002, 2003) have demonstrated that differences in language, familiarity, majority or minority status within a culture, cultural learning, expressive style, and a number of other factors may also account for the fact that "we understand emotions more accurately when they are expressed by members of our own cultural or subcultural group" (p. 228). Since research indicates that learning to correctly identify emotions of people from a different culture contributes to intercultural adjustment (Yoo, Matsumoto, & LeRoux, 2006), further research in this area is important as the nations of the world become increasingly multicultural.

CHECK YOUR UNDERSTANDING

1. Cultural differences, particularly _____, influence how we experience emotion.
2. Two important nonverbal cues to emotions are _____ _____ and _____ _____.
3. Men tend to interpret the source of their anger to be in their _____.
4. Research shows that some _____ _____ are recognized universally.
5. _____ _____ are the cultural circumstances under which it is appropriate to show emotions on the face.
6. _____ Overt behavior is an infallible clue to emotions. Is this statement true (T) or false (F)?

Answers: 1. language. 2. facial expression, body language 3. environment. 4. facial expressions 5. Display rules. 6. (F).

APPLY YOUR UNDERSTANDING

1. Which of the following would probably be best at "reading" nonverbal emotional cues?
   a. a young man
   b. an older woman
   c. an older man
   d. They would all be equally accurate since gender is not related to the ability to understand nonverbal cues to emotion.
2. You are studying gender differences in emotion. You show men and women various films of people in distress. On the basis of what you have read in this chapter, you would predict that the men will show _____ amount of physiological arousal, and _____ emotional expression as the women.
   a. the same; the same
   b. the same; less
   c. a greater; less
   d. a smaller; less

Answers: 1. b. 2. b.

KEY TERMS

CHAPTER REVIEW

Perspectives on Motivation

How can you use intrinsic and extrinsic motivation to help you succeed in college? The idea that motivation is based on **instincts** was popular in the early 20th century but since has fallen out of favor. Human motivation has also been viewed as an effort toward **drive reduction** and **homeostasis**, or balance in the body. Another perspective, reflected in **arousal theory**, suggests behavior stems from a desire to maintain an optimum level of arousal. Motivational inducements or incentives can originate from within (**intrinsic motivation**) or from outside (**extrinsic motivation**) the person. The effects of intrinsic motivation are greater and longer-lasting.

Abraham Maslow suggested human motives can be arranged in a **hierarchy of needs**, with primitive ones based on physical needs positioned at the bottom and higher ones such as self-esteem positioned toward the top. Maslow believed that the higher motives don't emerge until the more basic ones have been met, but recent research challenges his view.

Hunger and Thirst

Why do people usually get hungry at mealtime? How can external cues influence our desire to eat? How can the culture in which you were raised in influence your desire to eat? Hunger is regulated by several centers within the brain. These centers are stimulated by receptors that monitor blood levels of **glucose**, fats, and carbohydrates as well as the hormones **leptin** and **ghrelin**. Hunger is also stimulated by **incentives** such as cooking aromas and by emotional, cultural, and social factors.

How do people suffering from anorexia nervosa tend to view their bodies? Eating disorders, particularly **anorexia nervosa** and **bulimia nervosa**, are more prevalent among females than among males. They are characterized by extreme preoccupation with body image and weight. Another food-related problem, obesity, affects millions of Americans. Obesity has complex causes and negative consequences particularly for obese children, who are likely to have health problems as adults.

Sex

How is the sex drive different from other primary drives? Sex is a primary drive that gives rise to reproductive behavior essential for the survival of the species.

How well do we understand the biology of the sex drive? Although hormones such as **testosterone** are involved in human sexual responses, they don't play as dominant a role as they do in some other species. In humans, the brain exerts a powerful influence on the sex drive as well. The human **sexual response cycle**, which differs somewhat for males and females, has four stages—excitement, plateau, orgasm, and resolution.

How does culture influence sexual behavior? Experience and learning affect preferences for sexually arousing stimuli. What is sexually attractive is also influenced by culture. Research suggests a more conservative pattern of sexual behavior in the United States than is portrayed in popular media.

What are the arguments for and against a biological explanation of homosexuality? People with a heterosexual orientation are sexually attracted to members of the opposite sex; those with a homosexual orientation are sexually attracted to members of their own sex. It is likely that both biological and environmental factors play a role in explaining homosexuality.

Other Important Motives

How are stimulus motives different from primary drives? Stimulus motives are less obviously associated with the survival of the organism or the species, although they often help humans adapt to their environments. **Stimulus motives**, such as the urge to explore and manipulate things, are associated with obtaining information about the world.

What motives cause people to explore and change their environment? A gap in understanding may stimulate curiosity, motivating us to explore and, often, to change our environment.

Is the human need for contact universal? Another important stimulus motive in humans and other primates is to seek various forms of tactile stimulation. The importance of contact has been demonstrated in nonhuman animal studies as well as in premature human infants.

Is aggression a biological response or a learned one? Any behavior intended to inflict physical or psychological harm on others is an act of **aggression**. Some psychologists see aggression as an innate drive in humans that must be channeled to constructive ends, but others see it more as a learned response that is greatly influenced by modeling, norms, and values. Aggression differs markedly across cultures, supporting the latter view. Males generally are more inclined than females to strike out at others and commit acts of violence. This gender difference probably stems from an interaction of nature and nurture.

Is being highly competitive important to high achievement? People who display a desire to excel, to overcome obstacles, and to accomplish difficult things well and quickly score high in **achievement motive**. Although hard work and a strong desire to master challenges both contribute to achievement, excessive competitiveness toward others can actually interfere with achievement.

How do psychologists explain the human need to be with other people? The **affiliation motive**, or need to be with other people, is especially pronounced when we feel threatened or anxious. Affiliation with others in this situation can counteract fear and bolster spirits.

Emotions

How many basic emotions are there? Are there basic emotions that all people experience regardless of their culture? Robert Plutchik's circular classification system for **emotions** encompasses eight basic emotions. But not all cultures categorize emotions this way. Some lack a word for emotion; others describe feelings as physical sensations. Cross-cultural research by Paul Ekman argues for the universality of at least six emotions—happiness, surprise, sadness, fear, disgust, and anger. Many psychologists add *love* to this list.

What is the relationship among emotions, biological reactions, and thoughts? According to the **James–Lange theory**, environmental stimuli can cause physiological changes; and emotions then arise from our awareness of those changes. In contrast, the **Cannon–Bard theory** holds that emotions and bodily responses occur simultaneously. A third perspective, the **cognitive theory** of emotion, contends that our perceptions and judgments of situations are essential to our emotional experiences. Without these cog-

nitions we would have no idea how to label our feelings. Not everyone agrees with this view, however, because emotions sometimes seem to arise too quickly to depend on mental evaluations. Counter to the cognitive view, C. E. Izard argues that certain inborn facial expressions and body postures are automatically triggered in emotion-arousing situations and are then "read" by the brain as particular feelings.

Communicating Emotion

What is the most obvious signal of emotion? What role can voice and facial expression play in expressing emotion? People express emotions verbally through words, tone of voice, exclamations, and other sounds. Facial expressions are the most obvious nonverbal indicators of emotion.

How can posture and personal space communicate emotion? Other indicators involve body language—our posture, the way we move, our preferred personal distance from others when talking to them, our degree of eye contact. Explicit acts, such as slamming a door, express emotions, too. People vary in their skill at reading these nonverbal cues.

Are men less emotional than women? Research confirms some gender differences in expressing and perceiving emotions. For instance, when confronted with a person in distress, women are more likely than men to express emotion, even though the levels of physiological arousal are the same for the two sexes. Also, being betrayed or criticized elicits more anger in men, versus more disappointment and hurt in women. Women are generally better than men at reading other people's emotions: decoding facial expressions, body cues, and tones of voice. This skill may be sharpened by their role as caretakers of infants and their traditional subordinate status to men.

How can culture influence the way we express emotion? Regardless of a person's cultural background, the facial expressions associated with certain basic emotions appear to be universal. This finding contradicts the culture-learning view, which suggests facial expressions of emotion are learned within a particular culture. This is not to say that there are no cultural differences in emotional expression, however. Overlaying the universal expression of certain emotions are culturally varying **display rules** that govern when it is appropriate to show emotion—to whom, by whom, and under what circumstances. Other forms of nonverbal communication of emotion vary more from culture to culture than facial expressions do.

9 Life-Span Development

OVERVIEW

ernita Lee was 18 and unmarried in 1954 when she gave birth to a daughter, attended only by a midwife in her mother's rundown Mississippi farmhouse. The baby's father, Vernon, was not seriously involved with Vernita, who continued to live with her mother, Hattie Mae. Four years later Vernita moved to Milwaukee, where she heard that young Black women could earn good money working as maids. Her daughter remained with Hattie Mae, helping to tend the pigs and chickens and hauling water from the well to the house, which lacked indoor plumbing. Without neighborhood friends to play with, the child entertained herself by talking to the animals, delighting in making speeches to the cows. Extremely gifted in language and encouraged by her grandmother, who highly valued education, she learned to read and write at the age of 3. Because of her remarkable ability to memorize passages from the Bible, she soon began delivering inspirational speeches in church. "Jesus rose on Easter Day, Hallelujah, Hallelujah," the preschooler confidently began as she addressed her first Sunday congregation, earning her the nickname "Little Preacher."

But the precocious child's life took a turn for the worse when she went to Milwaukee to live with her mother in a shabby rooming house. Vernita did not share Hattie Mae's devotion to education; and she belittled her daughter's deep love of books. Neglected and often inadequately supervised, the girl was raped by a 19-year-old cousin when she was only 9 years old. Terrified, she kept her dark secret, only to become sexually abused by a procession of other men, including an uncle and some of her mother's boyfriends. Soon she blamed herself for what was happening to her. She also began to lie, steal, and run away. Vernita tried but failed to have her placed in a home for delinquent teenagers. Instead, the now pregnant 14-year-old girl went to live with her father, Vernon, in Nashville, Tennessee.

The move to Nashville was a blessing. After the baby was born prematurely and died soon after birth, Vernon was able to provide his troubled daughter with the love, stability, and discipline she needed to turn her life around. He and his wife Zelma encouraged her to study hard and cultivate her talent for public speaking. Winning a speech contest earned her a 4-year scholarship to college. Other contest victories followed, capturing the attention of staff at a local radio station, who offered her a job as a newscaster even before she had graduated from high school. In college, CBS in Nashville hired her to anchor the evening news. She then moved to Baltimore and continued her TV career, hosting a popular morning talk show. Six years later, she landed a similar job in Chicago. Audiences loved her personal touch and the way she often shared her innermost thoughts and feelings. Within a year the show had a new name. Rather than "A.M. Chicago," now it was "The Oprah Winfrey Show."

The study of how and why people change over the course of the life span is called **developmental psychology**. Because virtually everything about a person changes over the life span, developmental psychology includes all the other topics that psychologists study, such as thinking, language, intelligence, emotions, and social behavior. But developmental psychologists focus only on the changes that occur as people grow older. Developmental psychologists are interested not just in celebrities like Oprah whose lives have undergone a transformation. They also want to learn about the common changes in thought, emotion, and behavior that we all experience throughout life's stages—from conception and prenatal development; to infancy, childhood, and adolescence; to middle and late adulthood. In addition, researchers want to understand individual differences in development. To what extent and for what reasons has your own development differed from that of your friends or your siblings? And why does the course of a person's development sometimes change direction markedly, as Oprah's did? These are some of the fascinating topics we explore in this chapter.

Enduring Issues and Methods in Developmental Psychology

What are some of the limitations of the methods used to study development?

In trying to understand both the "what" and the "why" of human development, psychologists focus on three of the enduring issues we introduced in , Chapter 1, "The Science of Psychology":

1. **Individual characteristics versus shared human traits (diversity-universality)** Although human development is characterized by many common patterns, each person's development is also unique. Oprah Winfrey's life illustrates this well. Like other women, she progressed through the stages of childhood, adolescence, and adulthood; she embarked on a

developmental psychology The study of the changes that occur in people from birth through old age.

How does Oprah Winfrey's life illustrate several key issues in developmental psychology?

career, developed a number of close friendships, and dealt with the normal challenges of growing up to become a mature adult. These are all common developmental milestones. Yet in other ways, Oprah's development was not like everyone else's. Not every woman is born into such a poor family, lacks neighborhood friends, survives sexual assault as a child, or achieves such professional heights. This combination of shared and distinctive elements is common to human development. We all take essentially the same developmental journey, but each of us travels a different road and experiences events in different ways.

2. **Stability versus change (stability-change)** Human development is characterized by major life transitions *and* by continuities with the past. Again, Oprah Winfrey's life is an excellent example. The move to Milwaukee to live with her mother was certainly a major turning point in her development, as was her subsequent move to Nashville to live with her father. And yet with all the changes that these transitions brought, she still had a connection with the person she had been before. We still see many of the qualities displayed as a young child in Mississippi.

3. **Heredity versus environment (nature-nurture)** This issue is central to developmental psychology. Human development can be explained by a combination of biological forces and environmental experiences. These two elements constantly interact to shape human growth. What made Oprah Winfrey into the person she has become? She was gifted in language, but that gift might have gone undeveloped if her grandmother had not encouraged literacy at a very early age and if her father and his wife had not encouraged her to study hard and cultivate her talent for public speaking. How different might she have been had she been born into a different family or chosen a different life's work?

These three major issues will surface often in this chapter as we journey through the human life course. As developmental psychologists study growth and change across the life span, they use the same research methods used by psychologists in other specialized areas: naturalistic observations, correlational studies, and experiments. (See Chapter 1, "The Science of Psychology".) But because developmental psychologists are interested in processes of change over time, they use these methods in three special types of studies: cross-sectional, longitudinal, and biographical. The advantages and disadvantages of these three types are listed in the "Summary Table: **Advantages and Disadvantages of Different Types of Developmental Research Methods**."

SUMMARY TABLE

ADVANTAGES AND DISADVANTAGES OF DIFFERENT TYPES OF DEVELOPMENTAL RESEARCH METHODS

Method	Procedure	Advantages	Disadvantages
Cross-sectional	Studies development by observing people of different ages at the same point in time	• Inexpensive • Takes relatively little time to complete • Avoids high attrition rate (dropout of participants from study)	• Different age groups are not necessarily very much alike • Differences across age groups may be due to cohort differences rather than age
Longitudinal	Studies development by observing the same people at two or more times as they grow older	• Generates detailed information about individuals • Allows for the study of developmental change in great detail • Eliminates cohort differences	• Expensive and time consuming • Potential for high attrition rate—participants may drop out over a long period of time • Differences over time may be due to differences in assessment tools rather than age
Biographical or retrospective	Studies development by interviewing people about past experiences	• Generates rich detail about one individual's life • Allows for in-depth study of one individual	• Individual's recall often untrustworthy • Can be very time consuming and expensive

In a **cross-sectional study**, researchers examine developmental change by observing or testing people of different ages at the same time. For example, they might study the development of logical thought by testing a group of 6-year-olds, a group of 9-year-olds, and a group of 12-year-olds, looking for differences among the age groups. However, one problem with cross-sectional studies is that they don't distinguish age differences from **cohort** differences. A cohort is a group of people born during the same period of history: All Americans born in 1940, for example, form a cohort. Cohort differences stem from the fact that individuals were born and grew up during different historical times. If we found that 40-year-olds were able to solve harder math problems than 80-year-olds, we wouldn't know whether this difference was due to better cognitive ability in younger people (an age difference) or to better math education 40 years ago than 80 years ago (a cohort difference).

Longitudinal studies address this problem by testing the same people two or more times as they grow older. For instance, researchers who are interested in the development of logical thought might begin their study by testing a group of 6-year-olds, then wait 3 years and test the same children again at age 9, then wait another 3 years to test them again at age 12. One problem with longitudinal studies, however, is that they don't distinguish age differences from differences that arise from improved assessment or measurement tools. For example, researchers retesting a cohort at age 9 might have access to a more sensitive measure of logical thought than they did when they tested that cohort at age 6. So if they found significant improvement in logical thought over this 3-year period, they wouldn't know to what extent it reflected the advance in age and to what extent it reflected the more sensitive measuring tool.

Another drawback to a longitudinal study is that it takes considerable time even when investigating childhood alone. When studying the entire course of adulthood, a longitudinal study can take 50 years or more. To avoid the huge expense of such a long study, researchers have devised a third way of studying adulthood: the **biographical** (or **retrospective) study**. With this approach, the researcher might start with some 70-year-olds and pursue their lives backward. That is, the researchers would try to reconstruct their subjects' past by interviewing them and consulting various other sources. Biographical data are less trustworthy than either longitudinal or cross-sectional data, because people's recollections of the past may be inaccurate.

Prenatal Development

Why can an organism or another substance cause devastating effects at one point in prenatal development but not at others?

During the earliest period of **prenatal development**—the stage of development from conception to birth—the fertilized egg divides, embarking on the process that will transform it, in just nine months, from a one-celled organism into a complex human being. The dividing cells form a hollow ball, which implants itself in the uterine wall. Two weeks after conception, the cells begin to specialize: Some will form the baby's internal organs, others will form muscles and bones, and still others will form the skin and the nervous system. No longer an undifferentiated mass of cells, the developing organism is now called an **embryo**.

The embryo stage ends three months after conception, when the *fetal stage* begins. At this point, although it is only 1 inch long, the **fetus** roughly resembles a human being, with arms and legs, a large head, and a heart that has begun to beat. Although it can already move various parts of its body, another month is likely to pass before the mother feels those movements.

An organ called the *placenta* nourishes the embryo and the fetus. Within the placenta, the mother's blood vessels transmit nutritive substances to the embryo or fetus, and carry waste products away from it. Although the mother's blood never actually mingles with that of her unborn child, toxic agents that she eats, drinks, or inhales (known as **teratogens**)

cross-sectional study A method of studying developmental changes by comparing people of different ages at about the same time.

cohort A group of people born during the same period in historical time.

longitudinal studies A method of studying developmental changes by evaluating the same people at different points in their lives.

biographical (or retrospective) study A method of studying developmental changes by reconstructing a person's past through interviews and inferring the effects of past events on current behaviors.

prenatal development Development from conception to birth.

embryo A developing human between 2 weeks and 3 months after conception.

fetus A developing human between 3 months after conception and birth.

teratogens Toxic substances such as alcohol or nicotine that cross the placenta and may result in birth defects.

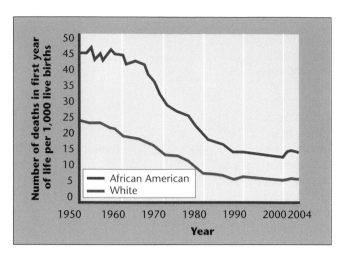

Figure 9–1

Mortality rates for White and African American infants.

Source: National Center for Health Statistics, 1995 (through 1990); *www.BlackHealthCare.com, 2000* (for 1991–1996); Centers for Disease Control (for 2000); Kochanek, K. D., Murphy, S. L., Anderson, R. N., & Scott, C. (2004). Deaths: Final data for 2002. *National Vital Statistics Reports, 53*(5), 1–115 (for 2002); Miniño, A. M., Heron, M., & Smith, B. L. (2006). Deaths: Preliminary data for 2004. Retrieved June 8, 2006, from *http://www.cdc.gov/ nchs/products/pubs/pubd/ hestats/prelimdeaths04/preliminarydeaths04.htm* (for 2003–2004).

Children born with fetal alcohol syndrome often exhibit facial deformities, heart defects, stunted growth, and cognitive impairments that can last throughout life. The syndrome is entirely preventable, but not curable.

are capable of crossing the placenta and compromising the baby's development (Newland & Rasmussen, 2003; Roy, Seidler, & Slotkin, 2002; Wass, Simmons, Thomas, & Riley, 2002). Diseases can also cross the placenta and infect the fetus, often with disastrous results.

There is a **critical period** during development when many substances are most likely to have a major effect on the fetus. At other times, the same substance may have no effect at all. For example, if a woman contracts rubella during the first 3 months of pregnancy, the effects can range from death of the fetus to a child who is born deaf. If she gets rubella during the final 3 months of pregnancy, however, severe damage to the fetus is unlikely, because the critical period for the formation of major body parts has passed.

Pregnancy is most likely to have a favorable outcome when the mother gets good nutrition and good medical care, and when she avoids exposure to substances that could be harmful to her baby, including alcohol and nicotine. Alcohol is the drug most often abused by pregnant women, and with devastating consequences (K. T. Lee, Mattson, & Riley, 2004; Riley et al., 2003). Pregnant women who consume large amounts of alcohol risk giving birth to a child with **fetal alcohol syndrome (FAS)**, a condition characterized by facial deformities, heart defects, stunted growth, and cognitive impairments (Caley, Kramer, & Robinson, 2005; McBee, 2005). Even smaller amounts of alcohol can cause neurological problems (I. Y. Choi, Allan, & Cunningham, 2005,). For that reason, doctors recommend that pregnant women and those who are trying to become pregnant abstain from drinking alcohol altogether.

Pregnant women are also wise not to smoke. Smoking restricts the oxygen supply to the fetus, slows its breathing, and disrupts the regular rhythm of the fetal heartbeat (Zeskind & Gingras, 2006). These changes are associated with a significantly increased risk of miscarriage (Ness et al., 1999). In the United States alone, smoking may cause over 100,000 miscarriages per year. Babies of mothers who smoke are also more likely to suffer low birth weight, setting the stage for other developmental problems (DiFranza & Lew, 1995; Visscher, Feder, Burns, Brady, & Bray, 2003).

The mother's level of psychological stress during pregnancy and the way she copes with it also appear to be related to the health of a newborn (Huizink, Mulder, & Buitelaar, 2004). In, one study (Rini, Dunkel-Schetter, Wadhwa, & Sandman, 1999), researchers found the risks of prematurity and low birth weight were higher in mothers with low self-esteem who felt pessimistic, stressed, and anxious during pregnancy.

Differences in access to good nutrition and health care help explain why the infant death rate in theUnited States is over twice as high for African Americans as it is for Whites. (See **Figure 9–1**.) A much higher percentage of African Americans live in poverty; and it is much harder for poor pregnant women to get proper nutrition and to see a doctor regularly (Giscombé & Lobel, 2005; Roussy, 2000).

CHECK YOUR UNDERSTANDING

Match each of the following terms with the appropriate definition:

1. ____ fetus
2. ____ prenatal development
3. ____ teratogens
4. ____ embryo
5. ____ critical periods
6. ____ placenta

a. substances that cross the placenta, causing birth defects

b. times at which harmful agents can do major damage to the fetus

c. the fertilized egg, two weeks after conception

d. the developing organism, after three months

e. the period from conception to birth

f. the organ that nourishes the fetus

Answers: 1. d, 2. e, 3. a, 4. c, 5. b, 6. f.

APPLY YOUR UNDERSTANDING

1. Sue has just discovered that she is pregnant. She asks you whether you think it would be all right if she drinks a beer or two with her friends at the end of the week. Based on what you have read in this chapter, which of the following would be the most appropriate reply?

   a. "Not during the first three months of pregnancy, and no more than one drink a week thereafter."

   b. "Not during the last six months of pregnancy, but it would be okay prior to that."

   c. "Avoid alcohol at all times during pregnancy."

   d. "Only one drink a week, and then only if you get good nutrition and good medical care."

2. Mary Jane is pregnant and a heavy smoker. If her baby has a health problem, it is most likely to

   a. have mental retardation.

   b. have a low birth weight.

   c. be blind.

   d. be prone to disease.

Answers: 1. c. 2. b.

The Newborn

How competent are newborns?

Research has disproved the old idea that **neonates**, or newborn babies, do nothing but eat, sleep, and cry, while remaining oblivious to the world. True, newborns can sleep up to 20 hours a day, but when awake they are much more aware and competent than they may seem at first glance.

REFLEXES

What early reflexes enable newborns to respond to their environment?

Newborns come equipped with a number of useful reflexes. Many of these reflexes, such as those that control breathing, are essential to life outside the uterus. Some enable babies to nurse. The baby's tendency to turn his or her head toward anything that touches the cheek, called the *rooting reflex*, helps the baby find the mother's nipple. The *sucking reflex* is the tendency to suck on anything that enters the mouth; and the *swallowing reflex* enables the baby to swallow milk and other liquids without choking.

Other reflexes have purposes that are less obvious. The *grasping reflex* is the tendency to cling vigorously to an adult's finger or to any other object placed in the baby's hands. The *stepping reflex* refers to the fact that very young babies take what looks like walking steps if they are held upright with their feet just touching a flat surface. These two reflexes normally disappear after 2 or 3 months, reemerging later as voluntary grasping (at around 5 months of age) and real walking (at the end of the first year).

Infants are also capable of imitating the facial expressions of adults (B. Bower, 2003). If an adult opens his or her mouth or sticks out his or her tongue, newborn babies often respond by opening their mouths or sticking out their tongues (Meltzoff & Moore, 1989; Slater, 2002). When this ability to imitate was first noted in newborns, psychologists were incredulous. How could babies carry out such complex responses when they have no idea how their own face looks, much less how to make specific facial expressions? It now appears that this early imitation is only a primitive reflex, like the grasping and stepping reflexes.

Almost all newborns respond to the human face, the human voice, and the human touch. This behavior improves their chances of survival. After all, babies are totally dependent on the people who take care of them, so it is essential that their social relationships get

critical period A time when certain internal and external influences have a major effect on development; at other periods, the same influences will have little or no effect.

fetal alcohol syndrome (FAS) A disorder that occurs in children of women who drink alcohol during pregnancy; this disorder is characterized by facial deformities, heart defects, stunted growth, and cognitive impairments.

neonates Newborn babies.

off to a good start. From the very beginning, they have a means of communicating their needs: They can cry. And very soon—in only about 6 weeks—they have an even better method of communication, one that serves as a thank you to the people who are working so hard to keep them happy: They can smile.

TEMPERAMENT

Is your temperament the same as when you were a newborn?

We may be tempted to talk about babies as if they are all the same, but babies display individual differences in **temperament** (Gartstein & Rothbart, 2003; Silberg et al., 2005). Some cry much more than others; some are much more active. Some babies love to be cuddled; others seem to wriggle uncomfortably when held. Some are highly reactive to stimuli around them, whereas others are quite placid no matter what they see or hear.

Some evidence suggests, however, that differences in temperament also may be due to prenatal influences. In particular, maternal stress produces reliable changes in heartbeat and movement in the fetus; these, in turn, are correlated with the child's temperament (Gutteling, de Weerth, Willemsen-Swinkels, Huizink, Mulder, & Visser, 2005). Some psychologists believe that the mix of hormones in the womb may be as important as the genes that the child inherits in determining temperament (Azar, 1997; DiPietro, Hodgson, Costigan, & Johnson, 1996; Huizink et al., 2002).

Regardless of what initially causes a baby's temperament, it often remains quite stable over time (Rothbart, Derryberry, & Hershey, 2000). In one study that asked mothers to describe their children's temperaments, characteristics such as degree of irritability, flexibility, and persistence were all relatively stable from infancy through age 8 (Pedlow, Sanson, Prior, & Oberklaid, 1993). Other studies have found that fussy or difficult infants are likely to become "problem children" who are aggressive and have difficulties in school (Guérin, 1994; Persson-Blennow & McNeil, 1988). As we've noted, longitudinal studies have shown that most shy infants continue to be relatively shy and inhibited, just as most uninhibited infants remained relatively outgoing and bold (Kagan, & Snidman, 2004).

A combination of biological and environmental factors generally contributes to this stability in behavior. For instance, if a newborn has an innate predisposition to cry often and react negatively to things, the parents may find themselves tired, frustrated, and often angry. These reactions in the parents may serve to reinforce the baby's difficult behaviors, and so they tend to endure. However, even if children are born with a particular temperament, they need not have that temperament for life. Each child's predispositions interact with his or her experiences, and how the child turns out is the result of that interaction (Kagan, 1994; Karrass & Braungart–Rieker, 2003; Maccoby, 2000; Rothbart, Ellis, & Posner, 2004; Saudino, 2005).

If they are raised in a compatible environment, easy, uninhibited babies will most likely grow to be outgoing children and adults.

Diversity–Universality   Different From Birth

In a classic study of infant temperament, Alexander Thomas and Stella Chess (1977) identified three types of babies: "easy," "difficult," and "slow to warm up."

- "Easy" babies are good natured and adaptable, easy to care for and to please.
- "Difficult" babies are moody and intense, with strong, negative reactions to new people and situations.
- "Slow to warm up" babies are relatively inactive and slow to respond to new things; when they do react, their reactions are mild.

To these three types, Jerome Kagan and his associates (Kagan, Reznick, Snidman, Gibbons, & Johnson, 1988; Kagan & Snidman, 1991) have added a fourth: the "shy child."

temperament Characteristic patterns of emotional reactions and emotional self-regulation.

Shy children are timid and inhibited, fearful of anything new or strange. Their nervous systems react to stimuli in a characteristically hypersensitive way (Kagan, 1994). Kagan found interesting differences in the frequency with which various behaviors related to temperament appear in babies from different cultures. He and his colleagues have speculated that such differences may be due in large part to the effects of different gene pools and genetic predispositions (Kagan, Arcus, & Snidman, 1993). Additional evidence to support the notion that temperament is largely biologically based and stable comes from neuroimaging studies showing that the amygdala (see Figure 2–9) of shy infants overreacts (compared with infants who are less shy and inhibited) when the shy infants are presented with a novel stimulus or situation, a response that continues into adolescence (C. E. Schwartz, Christopher, Shin, Kagan, & Rauch, 2003; C. E. Schwartz, Wright et al., 2003). ●●

PERCEPTUAL ABILITIES

Which senses are the most developed at birth, and which are the least developed?

Newborns can see, hear, and understand far more than previous generations gave them credit for. Their senses work fairly well at birth and rapidly improve to near-adult levels. Neonates begin to absorb and process information from the outside world as soon as they enter it—in some cases, even before.

VISION Unlike puppies and kittens, human babies are born with their eyes open and functioning, even though the world looks a bit fuzzy to them at first. They see most clearly when faces or objects are only 8 to 10 inches away from them. Visual acuity (the clarity of vision) improves rapidly, however, and so does the ability to focus on objects at different distances. By 6 or 8 months of age, babies can see almost as well as the average college student, though their visual system takes another 3 or 4 years to develop fully (Maurer & Maurer, 1988).

Even very young babies already have visual preferences. They would rather look at a new picture or pattern than one they have seen many times before. If given a choice between two pictures or patterns, both of which are new to them, they generally prefer the one with the clearer contrasts and simpler patterns. As babies get older and their vision improves, they prefer more and more complex patterns, perhaps reflecting their need for an increasingly complex environment (Acredolo & Hake, 1982; Fantz, Fagan, & Miranda, 1975; Slater, 2000).

In general, infants find human faces and voices particularly interesting (Flavell, 1999; Turati, 2004). They not only like to look at another person's face, but they also will follow the other person's gaze. For example, when presented with a human face depicted as looking straight ahead, or sometimes to the left or right, infants as young as 2 days old notice the direction of the adult's gaze and shift their gaze accordingly (Farroni, Massaccesi, Pividori, & Johnson, 2004). Newborns also prefer to look at their own mother rather than at a stranger (Bushnell, 2003). Because they see the mother so often, they acquire sets of different images of her (from various angles and so on). This visual familiarity makes the mother preferred.

DEPTH PERCEPTION Depth perception is the ability to see the world in three dimensions, with some objects nearer, others farther away. Although researchers have been unable to find evidence of depth perception in babies younger than 4 months (Aslin & Smith, 1988), the ability to see the world in three dimensions is well developed by the time a baby learns to crawl, between 6 and 12 months of age.

This finding was demonstrated in a classic experiment using a device called a *visual cliff* (Walk & Gibson, 1961). Researchers divided a table into three parts. The center was a solid runway, raised above the rest of the table by about an inch. On one side of this runway was a solid surface decorated in a checkerboard pattern and covered with a sheet of clear glass. The other side was also covered with a thick sheet of clear glass, but on this side—the visual cliff— the checkerboard surface was not directly under the glass, but 40 inches below it. An infant of crawling age was placed on the center runway, and the mother stood on one side or the other, encouraging the baby to crawl toward her across the glass. All of the 6- to 14-month-old infants tested refused to crawl across the visual cliff, even though they were perfectly willing to

When placed on a visual cliff, babies of crawling age (about 6 to 14 months) will not cross the deep side, even to reach their mothers. This classic experiment tells us that by the time they can crawl, babies can also perceive depth.

cross the "shallow" side of the table. When the "deep" side separated the baby from the mother, some of the infants cried; others peered down at the surface below the glass or patted the glass with their hands. Their behaviors clearly showed that they could perceive depth.

OTHER SENSES Even before babies are born, their ears are in working order (Fernald, 2001; Haihui, Zhengping, & Xing, 2005). Fetuses can hear sounds and will startle at a sudden, loud noise in the uterine environment. After birth, babies show signs that they remember sounds they heard in the womb. For example, immediately after birth, newborns prefer the sound of their mother's voice to that of an unfamiliar female voice (Kisilevsky et al., 2003). Babies also are born with the ability to tell the direction of a sound. They show this by turning their heads toward its source (Morrongiello, Fenwick, Hillier, & Chance, 1994).

Infants are particularly tuned in to the sounds of human speech (T. M. Hernandez, Aldridge, & Bower, 2000). One-month-olds can distinguish among similar speech sounds such as "pa-pa-pa" and "ba-ba-ba" (Eimas & Tartter, 1979). In some ways, young infants are even better at distinguishing speech sounds than are older children and adults. As children grow older, they often lose their ability to hear the difference between two very similar speech sounds that are not distinguished in their native language (Werker & Desjardins, 1995). For example, young Japanese infants have no trouble hearing the difference between "ra" and "la," sounds that are not distinguished in the Japanese language. By the time they are 1 year old, however, Japanese infants can no longer tell these two sounds apart (Werker, 1989).

With regard to taste and smell, newborns have clear-cut likes and dislikes. They like sweet flavors, a preference that persists through childhood. Babies only a few hours old will show pleasure at the taste of sweetened water but will screw up their faces in disgust at the taste of lemon juice (Rosenstein & Oster, 2005).

As infants grow older, their perceptions of the world become keener and more meaningful. Two factors are important in this development. One is physical maturation of the sense organs and the nervous system; the other is gaining experience in the world.

CHECK YOUR UNDERSTANDING

1. What are the four types of temperament?
2. Indicate whether each of the following statements is true (T) or false (F):
   a. ____ A newborn baby's ability to imitate facial expressions is best thought of as a reflex.
   b. ____ Newborns prefer to look at their mothers more than at strangers.
   c. ____ A young infant may be better at distinguishing speech sounds than an older child.
   d. ____ The visual cliff is used to determine which visual stimuli babies prefer.

Answers: 1. easy, difficult, slow to warm up, shy. 2. a (T), b (T), c (T), d (F).

APPLY YOUR UNDERSTANDING

1. You show a 6-month-old baby a checkerboard pattern with big, bright, red and white squares. The baby seems fascinated and stares at the pattern for a long time but eventually turns her attention to other things. You then show her two patterns: the familiar checkerboard and a new pattern. Which pattern is she likely to look at more?
   a. the familiar checkerboard
   b. the new pattern
   c. There should be no difference since 6-month-olds do not have visual preferences.
   d. There should be no difference since 6-month-olds cannot yet see patterns.
2. Baby John is moody and intense; he reacts to new people and new situations both negatively and strongly. In contrast, Baby Michael is relatively inactive and quiet; he reacts only mildly to new situations. John's temperament is _____ and Michael's is _____
   a. slow to warm up; easy
   b. shy; slow to warm up
   c. difficult; shy
   d. difficult; slow to warm up

Answers: 1. b. 2. d.

Infancy and Childhood

What kinds of developmental changes occur during infancy and childhood?

During the first dozen or so years of life, a helpless baby becomes a competent member of society. Many important kinds of developments occur during these early years. Here we discuss physical and motor changes as well as cognitive and social ones.

NEUROLOGICAL DEVELOPMENT

How does the human brain change during infancy and early childhood?

The human brain changes dramatically during infancy and early childhood. As noted in Chapter 2, "The Biological Basis of Behavior," infants are born with approximately 100 billion neurons, though the number of connections between neurons immediately after birth is relatively small. During the first 2 years of life however, dendrites begin to bloom and branch out; and the number of interconnections between neurons increases dramatically (Huttenlocher, 1999). The developing nervous system also sees the rapid growth of myelin sheaths, the fatty covering that encases many neurons to provide insulation and increase the speed of conduction (see Figure 2–1). With this rapid growth in the number of connections and speed, the developing brain has an enhanced potential to respond to new and varied experiences, which in turn, further increases the number of connections between neurons.

As the number of interconnections between neurons increases during early childhood, the density of synaptic connections in the brain also swells dramatically. Recall from Chapter 2, synapses are the areas where neurons communicate with one another. Synaptic growth is particularly prominent in the prefrontal cortex, which is involved in reasoning and self-regulation (Thompson-Schill, Bedny, & Goldberg, 2005) as well as the visual and auditory areas of the cortex. (See **Figure 9–2**.) The growth in the number of synaptic connections between neurons in these portions of the brain is rapid during infancy, but in the 3rd year of life there is actually a decrease in both the number and density of synaptic

Figure 9–2

Synaptic density in the human brain from infancy to adulthood.
Note the dramatic increase and pruning in synaptic density over time in the vision, hearing, and reasoning centers of the brain.

Source: Huttenlocher and Debholkar,"Regional Differences in the Synaptogenesis in the Human Cerebral Cortex," *Journal of Comparative Neurology, 387*. Copyright John Wiley & Sons, Inc.

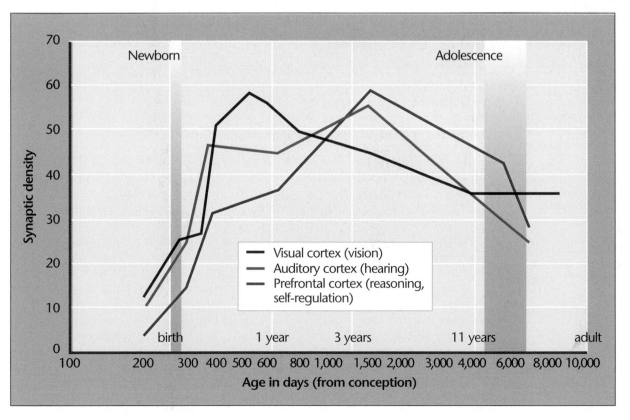

connections. This decrease appears to result from a natural process in which neurons that are stimulated and used grow stronger and more complex, while those that are unused are replaced or "pruned" away (Huttenlocher, 2002a).

These patterns of neurological growth, complexity, and reorganization provide a striking example of how nature and nurture work together, underscoring the importance of early and varied stimulation during development (Huttenlocher, 2002b; Shahin, Roberts, & Trainor, 2004). Indeed, as noted in Chapter 2 (see **Figure 2–5**), a lack of stimulation during this early period of development can negatively impact the growth of neurons and the number of connections between them, adversely affecting development.

PHYSICAL DEVELOPMENT

Do children grow at a steady pace?

During the first year of life, the average baby grows 10 inches and gains 15 pounds. By 4 months, birth weight has doubled and by the first birthday, birth weight has tripled. During the 2nd year, physical growth slows considerably. Rapid increases in height and weight will not occur again until early adolescence.

An infant's growth does not occur in the smooth, continuous fashion depicted in growth charts. Rather, growth takes place in fits and starts (Lampl, Veidhuis, & Johnson, 1992). When babies are measured daily over their first 21 months, most show no growth 90% of the time, but when they do grow, they do so rapidly—sometimes startlingly so. Incredible though it may sound, some children gain as much as 1 inch in height overnight!

Marked changes in body proportions accompany changes in a baby's size. During the first 2 years after birth, children have heads that are large relative to their bodies as the brain undergoes rapid growth. A child's brain reaches three-quarters of its adult size by about the age of 2, at which point head growth slows down, and the body does most of the growing. Head growth is virtually complete by age 10, but the body continues to grow for several more years. (See **Figure 9–3**.)

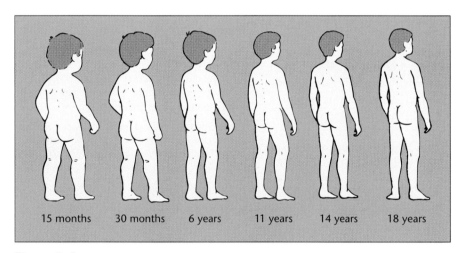

| 15 months | 30 months | 6 years | 11 years | 14 years | 18 years |

Figure 9–3

Body proportions at various ages.
Young children are top heavy: They have large heads and small bodies. As they get older, the body and legs become longer, and the head is proportionately smaller.

Source: From Bayley, *Individual Patterns of Development.* Copyright (c) 1956 by the Society for Research in Child Development. Adapted with permission.

MOTOR DEVELOPMENT

Is walking at an early age a sign of future athletic ability?

Motor development refers to the acquisition of skills involving movement, such as grasping, crawling, and walking. Much early motor development consists of substituting voluntary actions for reflexes. The newborn grasping and stepping reflexes, for instance, give way to voluntary grasping and walking in the older baby (Gallahue & Ozmun, 2006).

The *average ages* at which such skills are achieved are called *developmental norms.* By about 9 months, for example, the average infant can stand up while holding onto something. Crawling occurs, on average, at 10 months, and walking occurs at about 1 year. However, some normal infants develop much faster than average, whereas others develop more slowly. A baby who is 3 or 4 months behind schedule may be perfectly normal, and one who is 3 or 4 months ahead is not necessarily destined to become a star athlete. To some extent, parents can accelerate the acquisition of motor skills in children by providing them with ample training, encouragement, and practice. Differences in these factors seem to account for most of the cross-cultural differences in the average age at which children reach certain milestones in motor development (Hopkins & Westra, 1990; Nixon-Cave, 2001).

Motor development proceeds in a *proximodistal* fashion—that is, from nearest the center of the body (proximal) to farthest from the center (distal). For example, the infant

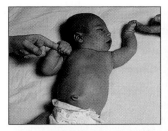

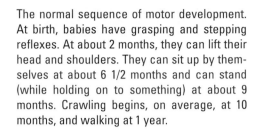

The normal sequence of motor development. At birth, babies have grasping and stepping reflexes. At about 2 months, they can lift their head and shoulders. They can sit up by themselves at about 6 1/2 months and can stand (while holding on to something) at about 9 months. Crawling begins, on average, at 10 months, and walking at 1 year.

initially has much greater control over gross arm movements than over movements of the fingers. Babies start batting at nearby objects as early as 1 month, but they cannot reach accurately until they are about 4 months old. It takes them another month or two before they are consistently successful in grasping objects (von Hofsten & Fazel-Zandy, 1984). At first, they grasp with the whole hand, but by the end of the first year, they can pick up a tiny object with the thumb and forefinger.

Maturation refers to biological processes that unfold as a person grows older and that contribute to orderly sequences of developmental changes, such as the progression from crawling to toddling to walking. Psychologists used to believe that maturation of the central nervous system largely accounted for many of the changes in early motor skills—that environment and experience played only a minor part in their emergence. But this view has been changing (Goodway, Crowe, & Ward, 2003; Thelen, 1995). Many researchers now see early motor development as arising from a combination of factors both within and outside the child. The child plays an active part in the process by exploring, discovering, and selecting solutions to the demands of new tasks. A baby who is learning to crawl, for example, must figure out how to position the body with belly off the ground and to coordinate arm and leg movements to maintain balance while managing to proceed forward (Bertenthal, Campos, & Kermoian, 1994). What doesn't work must be discarded or adapted; what does work must be remembered and called on for future use. This process is a far cry from seeing the baby as one day starting to crawl simply because he or she has reached the point of maturational "readiness."

As coordination improves, children learn to run, skip, and climb. At 3 and 4, they begin to use their hands for increasingly complex tasks, learning how to put on mittens and shoes, then grappling with buttons, zippers, shoelaces, and pencils. Gradually, through a combination of practice and the physical maturation of the body and the brain, they acquire increasingly complex motor abilities, such as bike riding, rollerblading, and swimming. By the age of about 11, some children begin to be highly skilled at such tasks (Gallahue & Ozmun, 2006).

maturation An automatic biological unfolding of development in an organism as a function of the passage of time.

SUMMARY TABLE

PIAGET'S STAGES OF COGNITIVE DEVELOPMENT

Stage	Approximate age	Key features
Sensory-motor	0–2 years	Object permanence Mental representations
Preoperational	2–7 years	Representational thought Fantasy play Symbolic gestures Egocentrism
Concrete-operational	7–11 years	Conservation Complex classification
Formal-operational	Adolescence-adulthood	Abstract and hypothetical thought

COGNITIVE DEVELOPMENT

How does a child's ability to reason change over time?

The most influential theorist in the area of cognitive development was the Swiss psychologist Jean Piaget (1896–1980). Piaget observed and studied children, including his own three. He watched them play games, solve problems, and perform everyday tasks; and he asked them questions and devised tests to learn how they thought. As a result of his observations, Piaget believed that cognitive development is a way of adapting to the environment. In Piaget's view, children are intrinsically motivated to explore and understand things. As they do so, according to Piaget, they progress through four basic stages of cognitive development. These are outlined in the "Summary Table."

SENSORY-MOTOR STAGE (BIRTH TO 2 YEARS) According to Piaget, babies spend the first 2 years of life in the **sensory-motor stage** of development. They start out by simply applying the skills with which they were born—primarily sucking and grasping—to a broad range of activities. Young babies delight in taking things into their mouths—their mother's breast, their own thumb, or anything else within reach. Similarly, young babies will grasp a rattle reflexively. When they eventually realize that the noise comes from the rattle, they begin to shake everything they can get hold of in an effort to reproduce the sound. Eventually, they distinguish between things that make noise and things that do not. In this way, infants begin to organize their experiences, fitting them into rudimentary categories such as "suckable" and "not suckable," "noise making," and "not noise making."

Another important outcome of the sensory-motor stage, according to Piaget, is the development of **object permanence**, an awareness that objects continue to exist even when out of sight. For a newborn child, objects that disappear simply cease to exist—"out of sight, out of mind." But as children gain experience with the world, they develop a sense of object permanence. By the time they are 18 to 24 months old, they can even imagine the movement of an object that they do not actually see move. This last skill depends on the ability to form **mental representations** of objects and to manipulate those representations in their heads. This is a major achievement of the late sensory-motor stage.

By the end of the sensory-motor stage, toddlers have also developed a capacity for self-recognition—that is, they are able to recognize the child in the mirror as "myself." In one famous study, mothers put a dab of red paint on their child's nose while pretending to wipe the child's face. Then each child was placed in front of a mirror. Babies under 1 year of age stared in fascination at the red-nosed baby in the mirror; some of them even reached out to touch the nose's reflection. But babies between 21 and 24 months reached up and touched their own reddened noses, thereby showing that they knew the red-nosed baby in the mirror was "me" (Bard, Todd, Bernier, Love, & Leavens, 2006; Brooks-Gunn & Lewis, 1984).

sensory-motor stage In Piaget's theory, the stage of cognitive development between birth and 2 years of age in which the individual develops object permanence and acquires the ability to form mental representations.

object permanence The concept that things continue to exist even when they are out of sight.

mental representations Mental images or symbols (such as words) used to think about or remember an object, a person, or an event.

PREOPERATIONAL STAGE (2 TO 7 YEARS) When children enter the **preoperational stage** of cognitive development, their thought is still tightly bound to their physical and perceptual experiences. But their increasing ability to use mental representations lays the groundwork for the development of language—using words as symbols to represent events and to describe, remember, and reason about experiences. (We will say much more about language development shortly.) Representational thought also lays the groundwork for two other hallmarks of this stage—engaging in *fantasy play* (a cardboard box becomes a castle) and using *symbolic gestures* (slashing the air with an imaginary sword to slay an imaginary dragon).

In Piaget's famous experiment, the child has to judge which glass holds more liquid: the tall, thin one or the short, wide one. Although both glasses hold the same amount, children in the preoperational stage say that the taller glass holds more, since they focus their attention on only one thing—the height of the column of liquid.

Although children of this age have made advances over sensory-motor thought, in many ways they don't yet think as do older children and adults. For example, preschool children are **egocentric**. They have difficulty seeing things from another person's point of view or putting themselves in someone else's place. An illustration of egocentric behavior can sometimes be seen during the game of hide-and-seek, when young children cover their own eyes to prevent others from seeing them.

Children of this age are also easily misled by appearances. They tend to concentrate on the most outstanding aspect of a display or an event, ignoring everything else. In a famous experiment, Piaget showed preoperational children two identical glasses, filled to the same level with juice. The children were asked which glass held more juice, and they replied (correctly) that both had the same amount. Then Piaget poured the juice from one glass into a taller, narrower glass. (See the accompanying photo.) Again the children were asked which glass held more juice. They looked at the two glasses, saw that the level of the juice in the tall, narrow one was much higher, and then replied that the narrow glass had more. According to Piaget, children at this stage cannot consider the past (Piaget simply poured all the juice from one container into another) or the future (if he poured it back again, the levels of juice would be identical). Nor can they consider a container's height and width at the same time. Thus, they can't understand how an increase in one dimension (height) might be offset by a decrease in another dimension (width).

CONCRETE-OPERATIONAL STAGE (7 TO 11 YEARS) During the **concrete-operational stage**, children become more flexible in their thinking. They learn to consider more than one dimension of a problem at a time and to look at a situation from someone else's viewpoint. This is the age at which they become able to grasp **principles of conservation**, such as the idea that the volume of a liquid stays the same regardless of the size and shape of the container into which it is poured. Other related conservation concepts have to do with number, length, area, and mass. All involve an understanding that basic amounts remain constant despite superficial changes in appearance, which can always be reversed.

Another accomplishment of this stage is the ability to grasp complex classification schemes such as those involving superordinate and subordinate classes. For instance, if you show a preschooler four toy dogs and two toy cats and ask whether there are more dogs or more animals, the child will almost always answer "more dogs." It is not until age 7 or 8 that children are able to think about objects as being simultaneously members of two classes, one more inclusive than the other. Yet even well into the elementary school years, children's thinking is still very much stuck in the "here and now." Often, they are unable to solve problems without concrete reference points that they can handle or imagine handling.

FORMAL-OPERATIONAL STAGE (ADOLESCENCE THROUGH ADULTHOOD) This limitation is overcome in the **formal-operational stage** of cognitive development, often reached during adolescence. Youngsters at this stage can think in abstract terms. They can formulate hypotheses, test them mentally, and accept or reject them according to the outcome of these mental experiments. Therefore, they are capable of going beyond the here and now to understand things in terms of cause and effect, to consider possibilities as well as realities, and to develop and use general rules, principles, and theories.

preoperational stage In Piaget's theory, the stage of cognitive development between 2 and 7 years of age in which the individual becomes able to use mental representations and language to describe, remember, and reason about the world, though only in an egocentric fashion.

egocentric Unable to see things from another's point of view.

concrete-operational stage In Piaget's theory, the stage of cognitive development between 7 and 11 years of age in which the individual can attend to more than one thing at a time and understand someone else's point of view, though thinking is limited to concrete matters.

principles of conservation The concept that the quantity of a substance is not altered by reversible changes in its appearance.

formal-operational stage In Piaget's theory, the stage of cognitive development beginning about 11 years of age in which the individual becomes capable of abstract thought.

CRITICISMS OF PIAGET'S THEORY Piaget's work has produced a great deal of controversy (Shayer, 2003). Many question his assumption that there are distinct stages in cognitive development that always progress in an orderly, sequential way, and that a child must pass through one stage before entering the next (Brainerd, 1978; L. Siegel, 1993). Some see cognitive development as a more gradual process, resulting from the slow acquisition of experience and practice rather than the abrupt emergence of distinctly higher levels of ability (Courage & Howe, 2002; Paris & Weissberg, 1986).

Piaget's theory has also sparked criticism for assuming that young infants understand very little about the world, such as the permanence of objects in it (Gopnik, Meltzoff, & Kuhl, 1999; Kiss, 2001; Meltzoff & Gopnik, 1997). When young babies are allowed to reveal their understanding of object permanence without being required to conduct a search for a missing object, they often seem to know perfectly well that objects continue to exist when hidden by other objects (Baillargeon, 1994). They also show other quite sophisticated knowledge of the world that Piaget thought they lacked, such as a rudimentary grasp of numbers (Wynn, 1995). At older ages, too, milestone cognitive achievements seem to be reached much sooner than Piaget believed (Gopnik, 1996).

Other critics have argued that Piaget underplayed the importance of social interaction in cognitive development. For instance, the influential Russian psychologist Lev Vygotsky contended that people who are more advanced in their thinking provide opportunities for cognitive growth for children with whom they interact (Harreé, 2000; Vygotsky, 1978). These learning experiences greatly depend on a society's culture, another factor that Piaget ignored (M. Siegal, 2003).

Despite these criticisms, Piaget's theory provides a useful schematic road map of cognitive development. Moreover, Piaget profoundly impacted our understanding with his observation that children play an active role in the learning process, his description of qualitative changes in the way children think at various ages, and his emphasis on "readiness to learn."

MORAL DEVELOPMENT

How do gender and ethnic background affect moral development?

One of the important changes in thinking that occurs during childhood and adolescence is the development of moral reasoning. Lawrence Kohlberg (1979, 1981) studied this kind of development by telling his participants stories that illustrate complex moral issues. The "Heinz dilemma" is the best known of these stories:

> In Europe, a woman was near death from cancer. One drug might save her, a form of radium that a druggist in the same town had recently discovered. The druggist was charging $2,000, ten times what the drug cost him to make. The sick woman's husband, Heinz, went to everyone he knew to borrow the money, but he could only get together about half of what it cost. He told the druggist that his wife was dying and asked him to sell it cheaper or let him pay later. But the druggist said, "No." The husband got desperate and broke into the man's store to steal the drug for his wife (Kohlberg, 1969, p. 379).

The children and adolescents who heard this story were asked, "Should the husband have done that? Why?"

On the basis of his participants' replies to these questions (particularly the second one, "Why?"), Kohlberg theorized that moral reasoning develops in stages, much like Piaget's account of cognitive development:

- *Preconventional level* Preadolescent children are at what Kohlberg called the preconventional level of moral reasoning: They tend to interpret behavior in terms of its concrete consequences. Younger children at this level base their judgments of "right" and "wrong" behavior on whether it is rewarded or punished. Somewhat older children, still at this level, guide their moral choices on the basis of what satisfies needs, particularly their own.
- *Conventional level* With the arrival of adolescence and the shift to formal-operational thought, the stage is set for progression to the second level of moral reasoning, the con-

ventional level. At this level, the adolescent at first defines right behavior as that which pleases or helps others and is approved by them. Around midadolescence, there is a further shift toward considering various abstract social virtues, such as being a "good citizen" and respecting authority. Both forms of conventional moral reasoning require an ability to think about such abstract values as "duty" and "social order," to consider the intentions that lie behind behavior, and to put oneself in the "other person's shoes."

- *Postconventional level* The third level of moral reasoning, the postconventional level, requires a still more abstract form of thought. This level is marked by an emphasis on abstract principles such as justice, liberty, and equality. Personal and strongly felt moral standards become the guideposts for deciding what is right and wrong. Whether these decisions correspond to the rules and laws of a particular society at a particular time is irrelevant. For the first time, people may become aware of discrepancies between what they judge to be moral and what society has determined to be legal.

Kohlberg's views have been criticized on several counts. First, research indicates that many people in our society, adults as well as adolescents, never progress beyond the conventional level of moral reasoning (Conger & Petersen, 1991). Does this finding mean that these people are morally "underdeveloped," as Kohlberg's theory implies?

Second, Kohlberg's theory does not take account of cultural differences in moral values (Nucci, 2002). Kohlberg put considerations of "justice" at the highest level of moral reasoning. In Nepal, however, researchers discovered that a group of adolescent Buddhist monks placed the highest moral value on alleviating suffering and showing compassion, concepts that have no place in Kohlberg's scheme of moral development (Huebner, Garrod, & Snarey, 1990).

Third, Kohlberg's theory has been criticized as sexist. Kohlberg found that boys usually scored higher than girls on his test of moral development. According to Carol Gilligan (1982, 1992), this was the case because boys are more inclined to base their moral judgments on the abstract concept of justice, whereas girls tend to base theirs more on the criteria of caring about other people and the importance of maintaining personal relationships. In Gilligan's view, there is no valid reason to assume that one of these perspectives is morally superior to the other. Subsequent research on Gilligan's theory of sex differences in moral reasoning has been mixed (J. L. Murray, Feuerstein, & Adams, 2006). In addition, other research has found that gender differences in moral thinking tend to diminish in adulthood (L. D. Cohn, 1991). However, concerns about gender bias in Kohlberg's theory still remain.

More recent research on moral development has moved in the direction of broadening Kohlberg's focus on changes in moral reasoning. These researchers are interested in the factors that influence moral choices in everyday life, and the extent to which those choices are actually put into action. In other words, they want to understand moral behavior as much as moral thinking (Tappan, 2006).

LANGUAGE DEVELOPMENT

How does a child develop language skills?

The development of language follows a predictable pattern. At about 2 months of age, an infant begins to *coo* (a nondescript word for nondescript sounds). In another month or two, the infant enters the **babbling** stage and starts to repeat sounds such as *da* or even meaningless sounds that developmental psychologists refer to as "grunts"; these sounds are the building blocks for later language development. A few months later, the infant may string together the same sound, as in *dadadada*. Finally, the baby will form combinations of different sounds, as in *dabamaga* (Masataka, 2003).

Even deaf babies with deaf parents who communicate with sign language engage in a form of babbling. Like hearing infants, these babies begin to babble before they are 10 months old—but they babble with their hands! Just as hearing infants utter sounds over and over, deaf babies make repetitive movements of their hands, like those of sign language (G. Morgan, 2005).

Gradually, an infant's babbling takes on certain features of adult language. At about age 4 to 6 months, the infant's vocalizations begin to show signs of *intonation*, the rising and lowering of

babbling A baby's vocalizations, consisting of repetition of consonant–vowel combinations.

From 12 to 24 months, babies typically point at and name, although not always correctly, whatever object interests them.

pitch that allows adults to distinguish, for example, between questions ("You're tired?") and statements ("You're tired."). Also around this time, babies learn the basic sounds of their native language and can distinguish them from the sounds of other languages (Cheour et al., 1998). By 6 months, they may recognize commonly used words, such as their own names and the words *mommy* and *daddy* (Bochner & Jones, 2003).

By around their first birthday, babies begin to use intonation to indicate commands and questions. At about the same age, they show signs of understanding what is said to them, and they begin not only to imitate what others say but also to use sounds to get attention. Vocalization also becomes more and more communicative and socially directed. Caregivers facilitate this process by speaking to their babies in what is called *infant-directed speech*. The parents speak slowly and use simple sentences, a higher pitched voice, repetition, and exaggerated intonations—all of which engage babies' attention and help them to distinguish the sounds of their language (Hampson & Nelson, 1993).

All this preparation leads up to the first word at about 12 months, usually *dada*. During the next 6 to 8 months, children build a vocabulary of one-word sentences called **holophrases**: "Up!"; "Out!"; "More!" Children may also use compound words such as *awgone* [all gone]. To these holophrases, they add words used to address people—*Bye-bye* is a favorite—and a few exclamations, such as *Ouch!*

In the 2nd year of life, children begin to distinguish between themselves and others. Possessive words become a big part of the vocabulary: [The shoes are] "Daddy's." But the overwhelming passion of children from 12 to 24 months old is naming. With little or no prompting, they will name virtually everything they see, though not always correctly! Children at this age are fascinated by objects. If they don't know the name of an object, they will simply invent one or use another word that is almost correct. Feedback from parents ("No, that's not a dog, it's a cow") enhances vocabulary and helps children understand what names can and cannot be assigned to classes of things ("dog" is not used for big four-legged animals that live on farms and moo rather than bark).

During the 3rd year of life, children begin to form two- and three-word sentences such as "See Daddy," "Baby cry," "My ball," and "Dog go woof woof." Recordings of mother–child conversations show that children from 24 to 36 months old noticeably omit auxiliary verbs and verb endings ([Can] "I have that?"; "I [am] eat[ing] it up"), as well as prepositions and articles ("It [is] time [for] Sarah [to] take [a] nap") (Bochner & Jones, 2003). Apparently, children this age seize on the most important parts of speech—those that contain the most meaning.

After 3 years of age, children begin to fill in their sentences ("Nick school" becomes "Nick goes to school"), and language production increases dramatically. Children start to use the past tense as well as the present. Sometimes they *overregularize* the past tense, by applying the regular form when an irregular one is called for (saying "Alex goed" instead of "Alex went," for example). Such mistakes are signs that the child has implicitly grasped the basic rules of language (G. F. Marcus, 1996). Preschoolers also ask more questions and learn to employ "Why?" effectively (sometimes monotonously so). By the age of 5 or 6, most children have a vocabulary of over 2,500 words and can construct sentences of 6 to 8 words.

THEORIES OF LANGUAGE DEVELOPMENT Children readily pick up the vocabulary of their native language, as well as the complex rules for putting words together into sentences. Two very different theories explain how language develops. B. F. Skinner (1957) believed that parents and other people listen to the infant's cooing and babbling and reinforce those sounds that most resemble adult speech. If the infant says something that sounds like *mama*, mommy reinforces this behavior with smiles and attention. As children get older, the things they say must sound more and more like adult speech in order to be reinforced. Children who call the wrong person "mama" are less likely to receive a smile; they are

holophrases One-word sentences commonly used by children under 2 years of age.

praised only when they use the word appropriately. Skinner believed that an understanding of grammar, word construction, and so on are acquired in much the same way.

Most psychologists and linguists now believe that learning alone cannot explain the speed, accuracy, and originality with which children learn to use language (Chomsky, 1986; Jenkins, 2000; Pinker, 1994, 1999). Noam Chomsky (1965, 1986) has been the most influential critic of the notion that children must be *taught* language. Instead, he argues that children are born with a **language acquisition device**, an internal mechanism that is "wired into" the human brain, facilitating language learning and making it universal (Werker & Tees, 2005). This language acquisition device is like an internal "map" of language: All the child has to do is to fill in the blanks with information supplied by the environment. An American child fills in the blanks with English words, a Mexican child with Spanish words, and so on. A more recent theory advanced by Steven Pinker (1994, 1999, 2002) holds that, to a large extent, evolutionary forces may have shaped language, providing humans with what he calls a *language instinct*. (See "On the Cutting Edge: The Evolution of Language From a Neuroscientific Perspective".)

language acquisition device A hypothetical neural mechanism for acquiring language that is presumed to be "wired into" all humans.

ON THE CUTTING EDGE

THE EVOLUTION OF LANGUAGE FROM A NEUROSCIENTIFIC PERSPECTIVE

Steven Pinker, a cognitive neuroscientist at MIT, has put forth a provocative new theory about the evolution and nature of human language (Pinker, 1994, 1999, 2002; Pinker & Jackendoff, 2005). Drawing extensively from the fields of linguistics, evolutionary psychology, and neurolinguistics, Pinker constructs a convincing case that language should not be viewed as a "cultural artifact"—in other words, it is not simply something we learn, like chess or badminton; nor is it simply a set of symbols linked to universal grammar or language structures (Chomsky, 1986). Instead, Pinker argues that language is "a distinct piece of the biological makeup of our brains." He contends, ". . . people know how to talk in more or less the sense that spiders know how to spin webs." Just as a spider spins a web without any special education or aptitude, language develops spontaneously in a child, without formal education or conscious awareness of its underlying complexity. Following Darwin, he describes language as an "instinct to acquire an art," much like song learning in birds.

According to Pinker, the language instinct is a biological adaptation designed for communication. Breaking from the tradition of linguists such as Whorf, who saw thought as dependent on language, or Chomsky, who saw language as dependent on thought, Pinker conceptualizes language as a distinct and independent cognitive ability that he calls the *language instinct*. From an evolutionary perspective, Pinker argues that the language centers in the brain, including Broca's and Wernicke's areas, have evolved what he terms *adapted computational modules* that specialize in processing linguistic information. These language modules evolved to perform a specific task, just as the visual area of the occipital lobe evolved specialized cells that respond to specific features of the visual world (see Chapter 2, "The Biological Basis of Behavior").

As evidence for this view, Pinker points out that even in newborns, the language centers of the brain display a unique sensitivity to speech sounds (Stromswold, 1995). Moreover, Pinker sees these adapted language modules as independent of other forms of symbolic processing. Although the average 3-year-old has a good grasp of syntax, demonstrating competence with linguistic symbols, she is generally incompetent at recognizing other types of symbols, such as religious symbols or traffic signs.

The language instinct, like other instincts, evolved through natural selection, taking the form of an innate circuitry in the brain that uses complex computational rules to perceive, organize, and transmit information. It is because of this adapted circuitry, for instance, that humans are predisposed to attach meaning to words, a process that cognitive neuroscientists recognize as exceedingly complex (G. A. Miller, 1999). According to Pinker, this circuitry also guides the language acquisition process, which enables children to attend to minor but important differences in the pronunciation of words, such as *talk* and *talks*, when they listen to adult speech (Pinker, 1999). This is important because only by focusing on the relevant aspects of speech could a child ever master the grammatical rules of a language. Research with Tamarin monkeys suggests that attending to certain properties of speech may be a characteristic of other primates as well (Ramus, Hauser, Miller, Morris, & Mehler, 2000).

Not everyone agrees with Pinker's position (Fitch, Hauser, & Chomsky, 2005; Karmiloff-Smith, 2002; MacWhinney, 1999; Sampson, 1999). Critics are quick to point out that research has not yet identified any of the specific neural circuits or adapted computational modules that Pinker describes. Also, other theories, based more on learning than on instinct, can just as easily explain many aspects of human language. Quite possibly, advances in neuroimagining (see Chapter 2, "The Biological Basis of Behavior") or behavior genetics (Enard et al., 2002) will soon shed more light on this debate by providing a clearer picture of exactly how the brain processes linguistic information.

Approximately 10 million students in U.S. schools have a first language other than English. Researchers and educators debate the best way to help these students achieve in school.

But the environment must do more for children than provide words to fill in the blanks in their internal map of language (Miranda, 2006). Without the social stimulus of talking to people, children are slow to pick up words and grammatical rules (Hoff, 2006). Babies reared in institutions, without smiling adults around to reward their efforts, babble like other children but take much longer to begin talking than do children reared in families (R. Brown, 1958). Studies have also shown that reading to young children helps them develop their language skills (Weigel, Martin, & Bennett, 2006).

The importance of the social environment to language development was documented in a study by Betty Hart and Todd Risley (1995). Over a 3-year period, these researchers studied the linguistic environment provided in the homes of preschool youngsters. They found that both the quality and quantity of language experiences varied with the educational level of the parents. For example, the most-educated parents directed over three times as many words to their children as did the least-educated parents. The well-educated parents also did more explaining, asked more questions, and provided more feedback. The best-educated parents were also far more likely to give positive feedback, such as, "That's right" or "Good." The least-educated parents were more likely to comment negatively about a child's behavior (saying, "No" or "Stop that") than to comment positively. These differences in environment predicted differences in academic achievement years later, especially in language skills.

BILINGUALISM AND SUCCESS IN SCHOOL Almost 10 million school-aged children in the United States have a primary language other than English. How can we maximize the academic success of such children? Should they be taught only in English, or should at least some of their classes be taught in their primary language? One report on bilingual education in New York City showed that students who take most of their classes in English learn English better than those who are taught some subjects in their primary language. Also, students from groups that place a high value on learning English—such as Russian, Korean, and Chinese immigrants—pass through bilingual classes much faster than students from groups that place a lower value on English literacy (Dillon, 1994).

SOCIAL DEVELOPMENT

How can parents help their children to become both securely attached and independent?

Learning to interact with others is an important aspect of development in childhood. Early in life, children's most important relationships are with their parents and other caregivers. But by the time they are 3 years old, their important relationships have usually expanded to include siblings, playmates, and other adults outside the family. Their social world expands further when they start school. As we will see, social development involves both ongoing relationships and new or changing ones.

PARENT–CHILD RELATIONSHIPS IN INFANCY: DEVELOPMENT OF ATTACHMENT Young animals of many species follow their mothers around because of **imprinting**. Shortly after they are born or hatched, they form a strong bond to the first moving object they see. In nature, this object is most often the mother, the first source of nurturance and protection. But in laboratory experiments, certain species of animals, such as geese, have been hatched in incubators and have imprinted on decoys, mechanical toys, and even human beings (H. S. Hoffman & DePaulo, 1977; Lorenz, 1935). These goslings faithfully follow their human "mother," showing no interest whatever in adult females of their own species.

Konrad Lorenz discovered that goslings will follow the first moving object they see, regardless of whether it is their mother, a mechanical toy, or a human. Here, Lorenz is trailed by ducklings who have imprinted on him.

Human newborns do not imprint on first-seen moving objects, but they do gradually form an **attachment**, or emotional bond, to the people who take care of them (regardless of the caregiver's gender). As we saw in Chapter 8, "Motivation and Emotion," classic studies of baby monkeys suggest that the sense of security engendered by physical contact and closeness is one important root of attachment (Harlow, 1958; Harlow & Zimmerman, 1959).

In humans, of course, this attachment is built on many hours of interaction during which baby and parent come to form a close relationship. Signs of attachment are evident by the age of 6 months or even earlier. The baby will react with smiles and coos at the caregiver's appearance and with whimpers and doleful looks when the caregiver goes away. At around 7 months, attachment behavior becomes more intense. The infant will reach out to be picked up by the caregiver, and will cling to the caregiver, especially when tired, frightened, or hurt. The baby will also begin to display **stranger anxiety**, often reacting with loud wails at even the friendliest approach by an unfamiliar person. If separated from the caregiver even for a few minutes in an unfamiliar place, the baby will usually become quite upset. Stranger anxiety usually begins around 7 months, reaching its peak at 12 months, and then declines during the 2nd year of life.

Parents are often puzzled by this new behavior in their previously nonchalant infants, but it is perfectly normal. In fact, anxiety over separation from the mother indicates that the infant has developed a sense of "person permanence" along with a sense of object permanence. For 5-month-olds, it's still "out of sight, out of mind" when Mom or Dad leaves the room, but for 9-month-olds, the memory of their parent lingers, and they announce at the top of their lungs that they want Mommy or Daddy to come back!

Ideally, infants learn in their first year of life that their primary caregivers can be counted on to be there when needed. Psychologist Erik Erikson (1902–1994) called this result the development of *basic trust*. (See the "Summary Table: **Erikson's Eight Psychosocial Stages, with Corresponding Freudian Stage Indicated**"; we will address this in greater detail in Chapter 10, "Personality.") If babies' needs are generally met, they come to acquire this view. They develop faith in other people and also in themselves. They see the world as a secure, dependable place and have optimism about the future. In contrast, babies whose needs are not usually met, perhaps because of an unresponsive or often-absent caregiver, develop what Erikson referred to as *mistrust*. They grow to be fearful and overly anxious about their own security. This view is supported by research showing that children who grow up in well-adjusted families generally form stronger attachments to their parents than do children who grow up in strife-filled families (Frosch, Mangelsdorf, & McHale, 2000).

As infants develop basic trust, they are freed from preoccupation with the availability of the caregiver. They come to discover that there are other things of interest in the world. Cautiously at first, then more boldly, they venture away from the caregiver to investigate

imprinting The tendency in certain species to follow the first moving thing (usually its mother) it sees after it is born or hatched.

attachment Emotional bond that develops in the first year of life that makes human babies cling to their caregivers for safety and comfort.

stranger anxiety Fear of unfamiliar people which usually emerges around 7 months, reaching its peak at 12 months and declining during the second year.

SUMMARY TABLE

ERIKSON'S EIGHT PSYCHOSOCIAL STAGES, WITH CORRESPONDING FREUDIAN STAGE INDICATED

Stage	Age	Challenge	Freudian Psychosexual Stage
Trust vs. mistrust	Birth to 1 year	Developing a sense that the world is safe and good	Oral
Autonomy vs. shame and doubt	1 to 3 years	Realizing that one is an independent person with the ability to make decisions	Anal
Initiative vs. guilt	3 to 6 years	Developing a willingness to try new things and to handle failure	Phallic
Industry vs. inferiority	6 years to adolescence	Learning competence in basic skills and to cooperate with others	Latency
Identity vs. identity confusion	Adolescence	Developing a coherent, integrated sense of inner self	Genital
Intimacy vs. isolation	Young adulthood	Establishing ties to another in a trusting, loving relationship	
Generativity vs. stagnation	Middle adulthood	Finding meaning in career, family, and community via productive work	
Ego integrity vs. despair	Late life	Viewing one's life as satisfactory and worth living	

According to Erik Erikson, children around age 2 are struggling to establish autonomy from their parents.

objects and other people around them. This exploration is a first indication of children's developing **autonomy**, or a sense of independence. Autonomy and attachment may seem to be opposites, but they are actually closely related. The child who has formed a secure attachment to a caregiver can explore the environment without fear. Such a child knows that the caregiver will be there when really needed, and so the caregiver serves as a "secure base" from which to venture forth (Ainsworth, 1977).

Children who are insecurely attached to their mothers are less likely to explore an unfamiliar environment, even when their mother is present. Moreover, if left in a strange place, most young children will cry and refuse to be comforted, but the insecurely attached child is more likely to continue crying even after the mother returns, either pushing her away angrily or ignoring her altogether. In contrast, a securely attached 12-month-old is more likely to rush to the returning mother for a hug and words of reassurance and then happily begin to play again (Ainsworth, Blehar, Waters, & Wall, 1978).

The importance of secure attachment early in life is evident for many years afterward. For example, studies of children from 1 through 6 years of age have shown that those who formed a secure attachment to their mothers by the age of 12 months later tended to be more at ease with other children, more interested in exploring new toys, and more enthusiastic and persistent when presented with new tasks (Weinfield, Whaley, & Egeland, 2004). Some research indicates the impact of not forming secure attachments during early childhood may also persist into the adult years, increasing the risk for substance abuse (Thorberg & Lyvers, 2006), violence and criminal behavior (Levy & Orlans, 2004), loneliness (Wiseman, Mayseless, & Sharabany, 2006), and even a decreased sense of happiness and well-being (Love & Murdock, 2004).

At about 2 years of age, children begin to assert their growing independence, becoming very negative when interfered with by parents. They refuse everything: getting dressed ("No!"), going to sleep ("No!"), using the potty ("No!"). The usual outcome of these first declarations of independence is that the parents begin to discipline the child. Children are told they have to eat and go to bed at a particular time, they must not pull the cat's tail or kick their sister, and they must respect other people's rights. The conflict between the parents' need for peace and order and the child's desire for autonomy often creates difficulties. But it is an essential first step in **socialization**, the process by which children learn the behaviors and attitudes appropriate to their family and their culture.

Erikson saw two possible outcomes of this early conflict: *autonomy versus shame and doubt.* If a toddler fails to acquire a sense of independence and separateness from others, self-doubt may take root. The child may begin to question his or her own ability to act effectively in the world. If parents and other adults belittle a toddler's efforts, the child may also begin to feel ashamed. The need for both autonomy and socialization can be met if parents allow the child a reasonable amount of independence, while insisting that the child follow certain rules.

PARENT–CHILD RELATIONSHIPS IN CHILDHOOD As children grow older, their social worlds expand. They play with siblings and friends, they go off to nursery school or day care, and they eventually enter kindergarten. Erikson saw the stage between ages 3 and 6 as one of growing initiative, surrounded by a potential for guilt (*initiative versus guilt*). Children of this age become increasingly involved in independent efforts to accomplish goals—making plans, undertaking projects, mastering new skills—from bike riding to table setting to drawing, painting, and writing simple words. Parental encouragement of these initiatives leads to a sense of joy in taking on new tasks. But if children are repeatedly criticized and scolded for things they do wrong, they may develop strong feelings of unworthiness, resentment, and guilt. In Erikson's view, avoiding these negative feelings is the major challenge of this stage.

The effect of parenting style on a child's outlook and behavior has been the subject of extensive research. For example, Diana Baumrind (1972, 1991, 1996) identified four basic parenting styles:

- *Authoritarian* parents, who control their children's behavior rigidly and insist on unquestioning obedience. Authoritarian parents are likely to produce children who generally have poor communication skills and are moody, withdrawn, and distrustful.

autonomy Sense of independence; a desire not to be controlled by others.

socialization Process by which children learn the behaviors and attitudes appropriate to their family and culture.

- *Permissive-indifferent* parents exert too little control, failing to set limits on their children's behavior. They are also neglectful and inattentive, providing little emotional support to their children. The children of permissive-indifferent parents tend to be overly dependent and lacking in social skills and self-control.
- *Permissive-indulgent* parents are very supportive of their children, but fail to set appropriate limits on their behavior. The children of permissive-indulgent parents tend to be immature, disrespectful, impulsive, and out of control.
- *Authoritative* parents, according to Baumrind, represent the most successful parenting style. Authoritative parents provide firm structure and guidance without being overly controlling. They listen to their children's opinions and give explanations for their decisions, but it is clear that they are the ones who make and enforce the rules. Parents who use this approach are most likely to have children who are self-reliant and socially responsible. Moreover, the positive effects of authoritative parenting have been demonstrated across different ethnic groups (Querido, Warner, & Eyberg, 2002).

Although many studies show a relationship between parental behavior and child development, be cautious when drawing conclusions about cause and effect from these data. First, parents do not determine the parent–child relationship on their own. Children also affect it (W. A. Collins, Maccoby, Steinberg, Hetherington, & Bornstein, 2000). Parents do not act the same way toward every child in the family (even though they may try to), because each child is a different individual. A thoughtful, responsible child is more likely to elicit authoritative parenting, whereas an impulsive child who is difficult to reason with is more likely to elicit an authoritarian style. For instance, children with conduct disorders meet with controlling responses from a great many adults, even from those who do not behave toward their own children in a controlling way (S. G. O'Leary, 1995). Thus, children influence the behavior of their caregivers at the same time that the caregivers are influencing them.

So far we have seen that parents can have a profound effect on the development of their children. In the next section, we will examine the extent to which peers also influence development.

RELATIONSHIPS WITH OTHER CHILDREN At a very early age, infants begin to show an interest in other children, but the social skills required to play with them develop only gradually (Pellegrini & Galda, 1994). Among the first peers that most children encounter are their siblings. The quality of sibling relationships can have a major impact, especially on how children learn to relate to other peers. Once children enter school, peer influences outside the family increase greatly. Now they are under a great deal of pressure to be part of a **peer group** of friends. In peer groups, children learn many valuable things, such as how to engage in cooperative activities aimed at collective goals and how to negotiate the social roles of leader and follower (Barber, Stone, Hunt, & Eccles, 2005; Rubin, Coplan, Chen, & McKinnon, 1994). Inability to get along well with classmates has long-lasting consequences. Children whose classmates dislike them are more likely to drop out of school, engage in criminal behavior, and become mentally ill. This tendency is particularly true of children who are disliked because they are overly aggressive (Hymel, Vaillancourt, McDougall, & Renshaw, 2002).

When young children engage in *parallel play*, each plays alone, but near the other.

As children get older, they develop a deeper understanding of the meaning of friendship (Rubin et al., 1994). For preschoolers, a friend is simply "someone I play with," but around age 7, children begin to realize that friends "do things" for one another. At this still egocentric age, however, friends are defined largely as people who "do things for *me*." Later, at about age 9, children come to understand that friendship is a two-way street and that, although friends do things for us, we are also expected to do things for them. During these early years, friendships often come and go at dizzying speed; they endure only as long as needs are being met. It is not until late childhood or early adolescence that friendship is viewed as a stable and continuing social relationship requiring mutual support, trust, and confidence (J. Dunn, Cutting, & Fisher, 2002.

Successfully making friends is one of the tasks that Erikson saw as centrally important to children between the ages of 7 and 11, the stage of *industry versus inferiority*. At this age, children must master many increasingly difficult skills, social interaction with peers being

peer group A network of same-aged friends and acquaintances who give one another emotional and social support.

only one of them. Others have to do with mastering academic skills at school, meeting growing responsibilities placed on them at home, and learning to do various tasks that they will need as independent-living adults. In Erikson's view, if children become stifled in their efforts to prepare themselves for the adult world, they may conclude that they are inadequate or inferior and lose faith in their power to become self-sufficient. Those whose industry is rewarded develop a sense of competence and self-assurance.

NON-SHARED ENVIRONMENTS Most developmental psychologists believe that peer influence is just one example of a much broader class of environmental factors called the **non-shared environment** (Plomin, 1999; Rose et al., 2003; Turkheimer & Waldron, 2000). Even children who grow up in the same home, with the same parents are likely to have very different day-to-day human relationships, and this nonshared environment can have a significant effect on their development. "The message is not that family experiences are unimportant," concludes one review of the research. Instead, the crucial environmental influences that shape personality development are "specific to each child, rather than general to an entire family" (Plomin & Rende, 1991, p. 180).

Children in dual-career families are especially likely to have non-shared environments since they usually spend a sizable portion of their waking hours in childcare settings, which are not usually the same for all their siblings. In the United States, for example, over half of the children between birth and the third grade spend some time being regularly cared for by persons other than their parents (America's Children: Key National Indicators of Well-Being, 2000).

Some researchers have expressed concern that being entrusted to caregivers outside the immediate family may interfere with the development of secure attachments and put children at greater risk for emotional maladjustment (Barglow, Vaughn, & Molitor, 1987; Belsky & Rovine, 1988). But according to the findings of one large-scale longitudinal study (NICHD Early Child Care Research Network, 1997), placing a baby in full-time day care even in the first few months of life doesn't in itself undermine attachment. Working parents and their babies still have ample opportunity to engage in the daily give-and-take of positive feelings on which secure attachments are built. Day care however, can be a negative factor, if working parents generally provide insensitive and unresponsive care. Such behavior is, in itself, associated with insecure attachment, but these babies are even *more* likely to form an insecure attachment if they also experience extensive day care, especially poor-quality care or changing day-care arrangements.

One conclusion, then, is that *quality of care counts* (Brobert, Wessels, Lamb, & Hwang, 1997; Scarr, 1999; Votruba-Drzl, Coley, & Chase-Lansdale, 2004). A secure, affectionate, stimulating environment is likely to produce children who are healthy, outgoing, and ready to learn, just as an environment that encourages fears and doubts is likely to stunt development. Research shows, for example, that children of working mothers who are placed in a quality day care, even at very early ages, are no more likely to develop behavior problems or have problems with their self-esteem than children reared at home (E. Harvey, 1999).

Some research shows clear benefits for the children of mothers who work, even if the children are still very young. For example, the children of employed mothers tend to be more independent and self-confident and to have less stereotyped views of males and females (Clarke-Stewart, Christian, & Fitzgerald, 1994). We discuss next how children learn gender stereotypes.

SEX-ROLE DEVELOPMENT

When do children learn about their gender?

By about age 3, both boys and girls have developed a **gender identity**—that is, a little girl knows that she is a girl, and a little boy knows that he is a boy. At this point, however, children have little understanding of what that means. A 3-year-old boy might think that he could grow up to be a mommy or that if you put a dress on him and a bow in his hair, he will turn into a girl. By the age of 4 or 5, most children know that gender depends on what kind of genitals a person has (Bem, 1989). They have also acquired **gender constancy**, the realization that gender cannot be changed.

non-shared environment The unique aspects of the environment that are experienced differently by siblings, even though they are reared in the same family.

gender identity A little girl's knowledge that she is a girl, and a little boy's knowledge that he is a boy.

gender constancy The realization that gender does not change with age.

At quite a young age, children also start to acquire **gender-role awareness**, a knowledge of what behaviors are expected of males and of females in their society (T. Lewin, 1996). As a result, they develop **gender stereotypes**, or oversimplified beliefs about what the "typical" male and female are like (Sinnott, 1994; Steele, 2003). Girls are supposed to be clean, neat, and careful, whereas boys are supposed to like rough, noisy, physical play; women are kind, caring, and emotional, whereas men are strong, dominant, and aggressive. There is much consistency across cultures regarding the gender stereotypes that children develop (J. E. Williams & Best, 1990). This is the case partly because gender roles tend to be similar in many different cultures and because gender stereotypes tend to "match" the tasks thought appropriate for the sexes.

At the same time that children acquire gender-role awareness and gender stereotypes, they also develop their own **sex-typed behavior**: Girls play with dolls, and boys play with trucks; girls put on pretty clothes and fuss with their hair, and boys run around and wrestle with each other. Although the behavioral differences between boys and girls are minimal in infancy, quite major differences tend to develop as children grow older (Prior, Smart, Sanson, & Oberklaid, 1993). Boys become more active and physically aggressive, and tend to play in larger groups. Girls talk more, shove less, and tend to interact in pairs. If aggression is displayed among girls, it is more likely to take the form of spiteful words and threats of social isolation (L. M. Brown , 2005; Zuger, 1998). Of course, there are some active, physically aggressive girls and some quiet, polite boys, but they are not in the majority. The source of such sex-typed behavior is a matter of considerable debate.

By school age, boys and girls tend to play by the rules of sex-typed behavior. Typically, girls play nonaggressive games, in pairs or small groups, whereas boys prefer more active group games.

ENDURING ISSUES

Nature–Nurture   Sex-Typed Behavior

Because gender-related differences in styles of interaction appear very early in development (even before the age of 3), Eleanor Maccoby, a specialist in this area, believes that they are at least partly biological in origin. In addition to the influence of genes, some evidence suggests that prenatal exposure to hormones plays a part (Collaer & Hines, 1995). But Maccoby thinks that biologically based differences are small at first and later become exaggerated because of the different kinds of socialization experienced by boys and girls. She suggests that a lot of gender-typical behavior is the product of children playing with others of their sex (Maccoby, 1998). Undoubtedly, popular culture—especially as portrayed on television—also influences the norms of gender-appropriate behavior that develop in children's peer groups. And parents, too, can sometimes add input, especially during critical transitions in the child's life when parents feel it is important to behave in more sex-stereotyped ways (Fagot, 1994). The end result is substantial sex-typed behavior by middle childhood. Research on this topic continues, but the growing consensus is that both biology and experience contribute to gender differences in behavior (Collaer & Hines, 1995; W. A. Collins et al., 2000). ●●

TELEVISION AND CHILDREN

Is watching TV a good or bad influence on the development of children?

On average, American children spend 4 hours a day watching television (American Academy of Pediatrics, 2006). Not surprisingly, psychologists, educators, and parents are very concerned about the influence TV may have on children (Funk, Baldacci, Pasold, & Baumgardner, 2004). Indeed, the American Academy of Pediatrics (1999) recommends that children under the age of 2 should not watch television at all and that older children should not have television sets in their bedrooms.

One concern is the violence that pervades much TV entertainment. Children who watch 2 hours of TV daily will see about 8,000 murders and 100,000 other acts of violence by the time they leave elementary school (Kunkel et al., 1996). Even Saturday-morning cartoons average more than 20 acts of violence per hour (Seppa, 1997). Does witnessing this violence

gender-role awareness Knowledge of what behavior is appropriate for each gender.

gender stereotypes General beliefs about characteristics that men and women are presumed to have.

sex-typed behavior Socially prescribed ways of behaving that differ for boys and girls.

Studies confirm that watching television is associated with aggressive behavior in children, but only if the content of the shows is violent.

make children more aggressive, and if so, does TV violence account, at least in part, for the rapid rise in violent crime among adolescents? According to C. A. Anderson et al. (2003), the answer appears to be "yes." The authors of this comprehensive review of the research point out that the effects of media violence can extend well into adulthood even for people who are not highly aggressive. Finally, although media violence affects some people more than others, the authors conclude no one is exempt from its deleterious effects.

Watching too much television can also lead to a variety of sleep disturbances in children, including night wakings, daytime sleepiness, increased anxiety at bedtime, shortened sleep duration, and difficulty falling asleep (Van den Bulck, 2004). Children who watch television before bedtime or who have a television in their bedroom appear to be at the greatest risk (Owens et al., 1999).

In addition, every moment spent watching TV takes time away from such activities as chatting with friends or playing board games and sports, which may be more beneficial. In that connection, obesity in children has been correlated with the amount of time spent watching TV (Vandewater, Shim, & Caplovitz, 2004).

Nonetheless, children can learn worthwhile things from watching television (D. R. Anderson, 1998; J. C. Wright et al., 1999). In one long-term study, the TV viewing habits of 5-year-olds were monitored by parents and recorded by electronic devices. Years later, high school records showed the more time these children had spent viewing such educational programs as *Sesame Street* and *Mr. Rogers*, the higher their high school grades were. In contrast, same-age children who watched a lot of noneducational and violent programming had comparatively lower high school grades than their peers (D. R. Anderson, Huston, Wright, & Collins, 1998). However, these data are correlational and leave open the question of cause and effect. Somewhat stronger evidence comes from a study in which 12- to 18-month-old babies learned new words by hearing them used on a TV show, making TV a kind of "talking picture book" for them (Lemish & Rice, 1986). In addition, the content of some children's shows has been shown to promote good health and nutrition (Calvert & Cocking, 1992).

To summarize, television can be a significant influence on children's development. It presents both "good" and "bad" models for them to copy; and it provides vast amounts of information. Television's ultimate influence may depend as much on what children watch as on how much they watch.

THINKING CRITICALLY ABOUT . . .

Television's Effects

Unless you are a rare exception, you watched a great deal of television when you were growing up. Consider the effects this may have had on you:

1. Do you think you would be very different now if there had been no television in your home when you were growing up? If so, in what ways do you think you would be different?

2. What kinds of things did you miss out on as a result of TV viewing? How would you have spent your time differently had you not had a TV to watch?

3. Will your own (or future) children be better off without TV in the house? How would you determine whether in fact this is so?

CHECK YOUR UNDERSTANDING

1. Early motor development in children (acquiring and refining the abilities to grasp, crawl, walk, and so forth) can best be explained
    a. entirely by biological maturation of the muscles and nervous system.
    b. by a combination of factors both within and outside the child.
2. List, in order, Piaget's four stages of cognitive development.
3. Match each phase of childhood with its major challenge, according to Erik Erikson's theory.

    ___ infancy   a. industry versus inferiority
    ___ toddlerhood   b. trust versus mistrust
    ___ preschool years   c. autonomy versus shame and doubt
    ___ elementary school years   d. initiative versus guilt

Answers: 1. b. 2. sensory-motor, preoperational, concrete-operational, formal-operational. 3. infancy: b; toddlerhood: c; preschool years: d; elementary school years: a.

APPLY YOUR UNDERSTANDING

1. At age 10 months, a child watches a red ball roll under a chair, but fails to search for it. At 2 years, the same child watches the same event, but now searches systematically for the ball. What change most likely accounts for the different reactions?

   a. The 10-month-old lacks depth perception.

   b. The 10-month-old does not yet understand the principle of conservation.

   c. The 2-year-old has acquired a sense of object permanence.

   d. All of the above are equally likely explanations.

2. Three preschoolers of different ages are sitting in a room watching a playful puppy. Child 1 exclaims, "I play puppy tail." Child 2 reaches for the dog and cries out, "Gimme!" Child 3 asks, "Who left the puppy here?" On the basis of your knowledge of language development, which child is most likely to be the youngest and which is most likely to be the oldest?

   a. Child 3 is youngest, child 1 is oldest.

   b. Child 3 is youngest, child 2 is oldest.

   c. Child 2 is youngest, child 3 is oldest.

   d. Child 1 is youngest, child 3 is oldest.

Answers: 1. c. 2. c.

Adolescence

Is adolescence characterized only by physical change?

Adolescence is the period of life roughly between ages 10 and 20, when a person is transformed from a child into an adult. This period involves not just the physical changes of a maturing body, but also many cognitive and social-emotional changes.

PHYSICAL CHANGES

What are the consequences of going through puberty early or late?

A series of dramatic physical milestones ushers in adolescence. The most obvious is the **growth spurt**, a rapid increase in height and weight that begins, on average, at about age $10\frac{1}{2}$ in girls and $12\frac{1}{2}$ in boys, and reaches its peak at ages 12 and 14, respectively. Typical adolescents attain their adult height about six years after the start of the growth spurt.

Teenagers are acutely aware of the changes taking place in their bodies. Many become anxious about whether they are the "right" shape or size and obsessively compare themselves with the models and actors they see on television and in magazines. Because few adolescents can match these ideals, it is not surprising that when asked what they most dislike about themselves, physical appearance is mentioned most often (Altabe & Thompson, 1994; Rathus, 2006). These concerns can lead to serious eating disorders, as we saw in Chapter 8, "Motivation and Emotion."

In both sexes, changes also occur in the face. The chin and nose become more prominent; and the lips get fuller. Increases in the size of oil glands in the skin can contribute to acne; sweat glands produce a more odorous secretion. The heart, lungs, and digestive system all expand.

SEXUAL DEVELOPMENT The visible signs of **puberty**—the onset of sexual maturation—occurs in a different sequence for boys and girls. In boys, the initial sign is growth of the testes. This starts, on average, at around $11\frac{1}{2}$, about a year before the beginning of the growth spurt in height. Along with the growth spurt comes enlargement of the penis. Development of pubic hair takes a little longer, followed by development of facial hair. Deepening of the voice is one of the last noticeable changes of male maturation.

growth spurt A rapid increase in height and weight that occurs during adolescence.

puberty The onset of sexual maturation, with accompanying physical development.

In females, the beginning of the growth spurt is typically the first sign of approaching puberty. Shortly thereafter, the breasts begin to develop; pubic hair appears around the same time. **Menarche**, the first menstrual period, occurs about a year or so later—at age 12 ½ for the average American girl (S. E. Anderson, Dallal, & Must, 2003). The timing of menarche is affected by health and nutrition, with heavier girls maturing earlier than thinner ones. Smoking and drinking alcohol also are associated with early menarche (Danielle, Rose, Viken, & Kaprio, 2000; Graber, 2003).

The onset of menstruation does not necessarily mean that a girl is biologically capable of becoming a mother. It is uncommon (though not unheard of) for a girl to become pregnant during her first few menstrual cycles. Female fertility increases gradually during the first year after menarche. The same is true of male fertility. Boys achieve their first ejaculation at an average age of 13½, often during sleep. First ejaculations contain relatively few sperm (Tanner, 1978). Nevertheless, adolescents are capable of producing babies long before they are mature enough to take care of them.

Psychologists used to believe that the beginnings of sexual attraction and desire in young people coincided with the physical changes of puberty, but recent research may be changing this view. Hundreds of case histories tend to put the first stirrings of sexual interest in the fourth and fifth grades. The cause may be increases in an adrenal sex hormone that begin at age 6 and reach a critical level around age 10 (McClintock & Herdt, 1996). Other pubertal hormones may also begin their rise much earlier than we formerly knew (Marano, 1997). If so, the onset of the obvious physical changes that we now call puberty may actually be more of an ending to a process than a start.

As the students in this middle-school group show, the age at which adolescents reach sexual maturity varies widely. Differences can lead to problems for teenagers of both sexes.

EARLY AND LATE DEVELOPERS Individuals differ greatly in the age at which they go through the changes of puberty. Some 12-year-old girls and 14-year-old boys still look like children, whereas others their age already look like young women and men (Weichold, Silbereisen, & Schmitt-Rodermund, 2003). Among boys, early maturing has psychological advantages. Boys who mature earlier do better in sports and in social activities and receive greater respect from their peers. For girls, early maturation appears to be a mixed blessing. Although an early maturing girl may be admired by other girls, she may feel self-conscious and often dissatisfied with her developing body (Ohring, Graber, & Brooks-Gunn 2002). Early maturing girls are also more likely to be exposed to drugs and alcohol in high school than later maturing girls (Lanza & Collins, 2002).

ADOLESCENT SEXUAL ACTIVITY Achieving the capacity to reproduce is probably the single most important development in adolescence. But sexuality is a confusing issue for adolescents in the United States. Fifty years ago, young people were expected to postpone expressing their sexual needs until they were responsible, married adults. Since then, major changes have occurred in sexual customs. Three fourths of all males and more than half of all females between the ages of 15 and 19 have had intercourse; the average age for first intercourse is 16 for boys and 17 for girls (Stodghill, 1998).

Boys and girls tend to view their early sexual behavior in significantly different ways (T. Lewin, 1994). Fewer high school girls (46%) than boys (65%) report feeling good about their sexual experiences. Similarly, more girls (65%) than boys (48%) say that they should have waited until they were older before having sex.

TEENAGE PREGNANCY AND CHILDBEARING The United States still has the highest teen birth rate in the industrialized world: nearly seven times the rate in France and 13 times the rate in Japan (UNICEF, 2001). One reason for this may be ignorance of basic facts concerning reproduction (M. L. Guthrie & Bates, 2003). In countries such as Norway, Sweden, and the Netherlands, which have extensive programs of sex education, teenage pregnancy rates are much lower. Another explanation for some unwanted teenage pregnancies may be the adolescent tendency to believe that "nothing bad will happen to me." This sense of invulnerability, in the absence of sex education, may blind some teenagers to the possibility of pregnancy (Quadrel, Prouadrel, Fischoff, & Davis, 1993).

menarche First menstrual period.

Whatever the causes of unmarried teenage pregnancy and teen childbearing, its consequences can be devastating. The entire future of a young unmarried mother is in jeopardy, particularly if she has no parental support or is living in poverty. She is less likely to graduate from high school, less likely to improve her economic status, and less likely to get married and stay married than a girl who postpones childbearing (Coley & Chase-Lansdale, 1998). The babies of teen mothers are apt to suffer too. They are more likely to be of low birth weight, which is associated with learning disabilities and later academic problems, childhood illnesses, and neurological problems (Furstenberg, Brooks-Gunn, & Chase-Lansdale, 1989; K. A. Moore, Morrison, & Greene, 1997). In addition, children of teenage mothers are more likely to be neglected and abused than are children of older mothers (Coley & Chase-Lansdale, 1998; Goerge & Lee, 1997).

COGNITIVE CHANGES

What are two common fallacies that characterize adolescent thinking?

Just as bodies mature during adolescence, so do patterns of thought. Piaget (1969) saw the cognitive advances of adolescence as an increased ability to reason abstractly, called *formal-operational thought* (see "Summary Table: **Piaget's Stages of Cognitive Development**" on page 318.). Adolescents can understand and manipulate abstract concepts, speculate about alternative possibilities, and reason in hypothetical terms. This process allows them to debate such problematic issues as abortion, sexual behavior, and AIDS. Of course, not all adolescents reach the stage of formal operations; and many of those who do, fail to apply formal-operational thinking to the everyday problems they face (Flavell, Miller, & Miller, 2002). Younger adolescents especially are unlikely to be objective about matters concerning themselves and lack a deep understanding of the difficulties involved in moral judgments.

Moreover, in those who do achieve formal-operational thinking, this advance has its hazards, among them overconfidence in new mental abilities and a tendency to place too much importance on one's own thoughts. Some adolescents also fail to realize that not everyone thinks the way they do and that other people may hold different views. Piaget called these tendencies the "egocentrism of formal operations" (Piaget, 1967).

David Elkind (1968, 1969) used Piaget's notion of adolescent egocentrism to account for two fallacies of thought in this age group. The first is the **imaginary audience**—the tendency of teenagers to feel they are constantly being observed by others and that people are always judging their appearance and behavior. This feeling of being perpetually "onstage" may be the source of much self-consciousness, concern about personal appearance, and showing off in adolescence (Bell & Bromnick, 2003).

The other fallacy of adolescent thinking is the **personal fable**—adolescents' unrealistic sense of their own uniqueness. For instance, a teenager might insist that others couldn't possibly understand his or her love for a peer because that love is so unique and special. This view is related to the feeling of invulnerability mentioned earlier. Many teenagers believe that they are so different from other people that they won't be touched by the negative things that happen to others. This feeling of invulnerability is consistent with the reckless risk taking among people in this age group (J. Arnett, 1991; Korinek, 2003).

PERSONALITY AND SOCIAL DEVELOPMENT

What important tasks do adolescents face in their personal and social lives?

Adolescents are eager to establish independence from their parents, but simultaneously fear the responsibilities of adulthood. They see they have many important tasks and decisions ahead of them. Particularly in a technologically advanced society, this period of development is bound to involve some stress.

HOW "STORMY AND STRESSFUL" IS ADOLESCENCE? Early in the 20th century, many people saw adolescence as a time of great instability and strong emotions. For example, G. Stanley Hall (1904), one of the first developmental psychologists, portrayed adolescence as a period of "storm and stress," fraught with suffering, passion, and rebellion against adult

imaginary audience Elkind's term for adolescents' delusion that they are constantly being observed by others.

personal fable Elkind's term for adolescents' delusion that they are unique, very important, and invulnerable.

authority. Recent research, however, suggests that the storm-and-stress view greatly exaggerates the experiences of most teenagers (J. J. Arnett, 1999). The great majority of adolescents do not describe their lives as rent by turmoil and chaos (Eccles et al., 1993). Most manage to keep stress in check, experience little disruption in their everyday lives, and generally develop more positively than is commonly believed (Bronfenbrenner, 1986; Galambos & Leadbeater, 2002). For instance, a cross-cultural study of adolescents from 10 countries, including the United State, found that over 75% had healthy self-images, were generally happy, and valued the time they spent at school and at work (Offer, Ostrov, Howard, & Atkinson, 1988).

Adolescence is inevitably accompanied by some difficult stress related to school, family, and peers. However, research indicates that effective parenting and secure attachments to parents during adolescence are just as effective as during early childhood in helping adolescents cope during difficult times (Galambos, Barker, & Almeida, 2003).

FORMING AN IDENTITY To make the transition from dependence on parents to dependence on oneself, the adolescent must develop a stable sense of self. This process is called **identity formation**, a term derived from Erik Erikson's theory, which sees the major challenge of this stage of life as *identity versus role confusion* (Côté, 2006; Erikson, 1968). The overwhelming question for the young person becomes "Who am I?" In Erikson's view, the answer comes by integrating a number of different roles—say, talented math student, athlete, and artist, or political liberal and aspiring architect—into a coherent whole that "fits" comfortably. Failure to form this coherent sense of identity leads to confusion about roles.

James Marcia (1980) believes that finding an identity requires a period of intense self-exploration called an **identity crisis**. He recognizes four possible outcomes of this process. One is *identity achievement*. Adolescents who have reached this status have passed through the identity crisis and succeeded in making personal choices about their beliefs and goals. They are comfortable with those choices because the choices are their own. In contrast are adolescents who have taken the path of *identity foreclosure*. In prematurely settling on an identity chosen for them by others, they have become what those others want them to be without ever going through an identity crisis. Other adolescents are in *moratorium* regarding the choice of an identity. They are in the process of actively exploring various role options, but they have not yet committed to any of them. Finally, some teens experience *identity diffusion:* They avoid considering role options in any conscious way. Some who are dissatisfied with this condition but are unable to start a search to "find themselves" resort to escapist activities such as drug or alcohol abuse. Of course, any given adolescent's identity status can change over time as the person matures or even regresses. Some evidence suggests that identity development varies by social class or ethnic background. For instance, teens from poor families are often less likely to experience a period of identity moratorium, probably because financial constraints make it harder for them to explore many different role options (Forthun, Montgomery, & Bell, 2006; C. Levine, 2003).

RELATIONSHIPS WITH PEERS For most adolescents, the peer group provides a network of social and emotional support that enables both greater independence from adults and the search for personal identity. But peer relationships change during the adolescent years. Friendship groups in early adolescence tend to be small unisex groups, called **cliques**, of three to nine members. Especially among girls, these unisex friendships increasingly deepen and become more mutually self-disclosing as the teens develop the cognitive abilities better to understand themselves and one another (Holmbeck, 1994). Then, in mid-adolescence, unisex cliques generally give way to mixed-sex groups. These, in turn, are usually replaced by groups consisting of couples. At first, adolescents tend to have short-term heterosexual relationships within the group that fulfill short-term needs without exacting the commitment of "going steady" (Sorensen, 1973). Such relationships do not demand love and can dissolve overnight. But between the ages of 16 and 19, most adolescents settle into more stable dating patterns.

RELATIONSHIPS WITH PARENTS While they are still searching for their own identity, striving toward independence, and learning to think through the long-term consequences of their actions, adolescents require guidance and structure from adults, especially from their parents. In their struggle for independence, adolescents question everything and test

identity formation Erickson's term for the development of a stable sense of self necessary to make the transition from dependence on others to dependence on oneself.

identity crisis A period of intense self-examination and decision making; part of the process of identity formation.

cliques Groups of adolescents with similar interests and strong mutual attachment.

every rule. Unlike young children who believe that their parents know everything and are all-powerful and good, adolescents are all too aware of their parents' shortcomings. It takes many years for adolescents to see their mothers and fathers as real people with their own needs and strengths as well as weaknesses (Smollar & Youniss, 1989). In fact, many college graduates are surprised to come home and find how much smarter their parents have become during the previous 4 years!

The low point of parent–child relationships generally occurs in early adolescence, when the physical changes of puberty are occurring. Then the warmth of the parent–child relationship ebbs and conflict rises. Warm and caring relationships with adults outside the home, such as those at school or at a supervised community center, are valuable to adolescents during this period (Eccles et al., 1993). However, conflicts with parents tend to be over minor issues and are usually not intense (Holmbeck, 1994). In only a small minority of families does the relationship between parents and children markedly deteriorate in adolescence (Paikoff & Brooks-Gunn, 1991).

"Is everything all right, Jeffrey? You never call me 'dude' anymore."

Source: © *The New Yorker Collection*, 1997. Leo Cullum from *www.cartoonbank.com*. All Rights Reserved.

SOME PROBLEMS OF ADOLESCENCE

What are some major problems faced by adolescents in our society?

Adolescence is a time of experimentation and risk taking, whether with sex, drugs, hair color, body piercing, or various kinds of rule breaking (R. M. Lerner & Galambos, 1998). It is also a time when certain kinds of developmental problems are apt to arise, especially problems that have to do with self-perceptions, feelings about the self, and negative emotions in general.

DECLINES IN SELF-ESTEEM We saw earlier that adolescents are especially likely to be dissatisfied with their appearance. Satisfaction with one's appearance tends to be tied to satisfaction with oneself. Thus, adolescents who are least satisfied with their physical appearance tend also to have low self-esteem (Altabe & Thompson, 1994). Since adolescent girls are especially likely to be dissatisfied with their appearance, and because perceived attractiveness and self-esteem are more closely related for females than for males (Allgood–Merten, Lewinsohn, & Hops, 1990), it is no surprise that adolescent girls have significantly lower self-esteem than do adolescent boys for whom there is little or no decline in self-esteem during adolescence (Kling, Hyde, Showers, & Buswell, 1999). However, some research shows that although both boys and girls feel less competent in math and language-related subjects as they grow older, boys experience steeper declines than do girls. By the 12th grade, girls see themselves as significantly more competent in those areas than do boys (Jacobs, Lanza, Osgood, Eccles, & Wigfield, 2002).

DEPRESSION AND SUICIDE The rate of suicide among adolescents has increased more than 600% since 1950, though there are signs that since the mid-1990s, it has begun to decrease, at least among males. Suicide is the third leading cause of death among adolescents, after accidents and homicides (American Academy of Child & Adolescent Psychiatry, 2004; National Mental Health Association, 2006). Although successful suicide is much more common in males than in females, twice as many females *attempt* suicide (National Adolescent Health Information Center, 2004).

Research shows that suicidal behavior (thoughts and attempts) in adolescents is often linked to other psychological problems, such as depression, drug abuse, and disruptive behaviors (Andrews & Lewinsohn, 1992; Studer, 2000), though not to risk-taking behaviors (C. Stanton, Spirito, Donaldson, & Doergers, 2003). One study of more than 1,700 adolescents revealed that a set of related factors puts an adolescent at higher-than-average risk for attempting suicide. Among these are being female, thinking about suicide, having a mental disorder (such as depression), and having a poorly educated father who is absent from the home. A history of physical or sexual abuse and poor family communication skills are also associated with suicide and suicide attempts. Although these data allow us to identify people at risk, it is hard to tell which higher-than-average risk adolescents will actually attempt suicide. For example, depression in and of itself rarely leads to suicide: Although 3% of adolescents suffer severe depression at any one time, the suicide rate among adolescents is less than .01% (National Adolescent Health Information Center, 2004). Apparently, a combination of depression and other risk factors makes suicide more likely, but exactly which factors are most important and what kinds of intervention might reduce adolescent suicides are still unclear (B. M. Wagner, 1997).

YOUTH VIOLENCE In April 1999, two teen-aged boys opened fire on their classmates at Columbine High School in Littleton, Colorado. Armed with sawed-off shotguns, a semiautomatic rifle, and a semiautomatic pistol, they killed 12 fellow students and a teacher, and wounded 23 others before killing themselves.

Why did this happen? What causes children as young as 11 to kill other people and, equally often, to kill themselves? Although it is tempting to look for simple answers to these questions, the causes of youth violence are quite complex (Heckel & Shumaker, 2001).

Biology definitely plays a role, although its influence is certain to be much more complex than simply identifying a "murderer gene." More likely the genetic component, if any, is related to a lack of compassion or an inability to control strong emotions. Apart from genetics, the constant interplay between the brain and the environment actually "rewires" the brain, sometimes with disastrous effects (Niehoff, 1999). Research suggests that repeated stress during the first 3 years of life may give rise to a steady flow of "stress chemicals," with two consequences. First, the normal "fight or flight" response may go on "hair-trigger alert," which can result in impulsive aggression. Alternatively, the person may become unresponsive and unfeeling, leading in turn to a lack of empathy and an unresponsiveness to punishment (Perry & Pollard, 1998; Read, Perry, Moskowitz, & Connolly, 2001). Other research has found that early trauma may cause a brain structure to become hyperactive, causing obsession with a single thought (such as violence) at the same time the prefrontal cortex becomes less able to control impulsive behavior (Amen, Stubblefield, Carmicheal, & Thisted, 1996; Schmahl, Vermetten, Elzinga, & Bremmer, 2004).

Environment also plays a role. Most psychologists believe that the "gun culture" in which most of the youthful murderers were raised is an important factor, along with the relatively easy availability of guns (Bushman & Baumeister, 1998; Cooke, 2004). Most youthful killers have had extensive experience with guns.

Severe neglect or rejection contribute as well. All of the young killers have indicated that they felt isolated from their family and from girls, outcast and abandoned by those who should have loved them. In turn, this condition led to feelings of powerlessness and injustice (M. R. Leary, Kowalski, Smith, & Phillips, 2003). In other cases, the youths lacked adult supervision and support, often having no real attachment to even one loving and reliable adult (Garbarino, 1999).

What are the warning signs that might alert family and friends to potential violence? Lack of social connection, masking emotions, withdrawal (being habitually secretive and antisocial), silence, rage, increased lying, trouble with friends, hypervigilance, and cruelty toward other children and animals—these factors should all be a cause for concern. This is especially true if they are exhibited by a boy who comes from a family with a history of criminal violence, who has been abused, who belongs to a gang, who abuses drugs or alcohol, who has previously been arrested, or who has experienced problems at school (Leschied & Cummings, 2002).

THINKING CRITICALLY ABOUT . . .

Kids Who Kill

1. After reading the review of the preceding research on youth violence, have your opinions about what causes school-aged children to kill their classmates been changed? In what way?

2. What steps would you recommend to reduce the incidence of tragedies like the one that occurred at Columbine High School? Be specific.

3. In almost all instances, the schoolchildren who commit these violent crimes are middle-class White children living in rural or suburban communities. Why do you think this is the case?

CHECK YOUR UNDERSTANDING

1. The most obvious indication that adolescence is starting is a rapid increase in height and weight, known as the _____ _____. This is combined with a series of physical changes leading to sexual maturation, the onset of which is called _____.

2. Erikson's view of the major challenge in adolescence is one of _____ versus _____.

3. List the four identity statuses described by James Marcia.

4. True (T) or false (F): The most difficult time in the relationship between a teenager and parents is usually in late adolescence, when the young person is anxious to leave the family "nest."

Answers: 1. growth spurt; puberty. 2. identity; role confusion. 3. identity achievement, identity foreclosure, identity moratorium, identity diffusion. 4. (F).

APPLY YOUR UNDERSTANDING

1. Beth is 14 years old. In the last year or two, she has begun to enjoy debating complex issues such as human rights, poverty, and justice. Which of the following is most likely to be true?

    a. Beth has become capable of formal-operational thought.

    b. Beth is experiencing identity foreclosure.

    c. Beth is experiencing identity diffusion.

    d. Beth's thinking demonstrates adolescent egocentrism.

2. Your adolescent brother is very self-conscious. He feels that he is constantly being observed by others who are judging him on his appearance and his behavior. As a result, he is overly concerned about his behavior and often shows off. You recognize this as a common characteristic of teenagers that is known as

    a. ___ the personal fable.

    b. ___ egocentric distortion.

    c. ___ role confusion.

    d. ___ the imaginary audience.

Answers: 1. a. 2. d.

Adulthood

Does personality change during adulthood?

During adulthood, development is much less predictable than that during adolescence, in that it is much more a function of decisions, circumstances and, even, luck. Although developmental milestones do not occur at particular ages, certain experiences and changes eventually occur in nearly every adult's life; and most adults try to fulfill certain needs, including nurturing partnerships and satisfying work.

LOVE, PARTNERSHIPS AND PARENTING

What factors are important in forming satisfying relationships in adulthood?

Nearly all adults form a long-term, loving partnership with another adult at some point in their lives. Such a partnership can happen at any stage in the life course, but it is especially common in young adulthood. According to Erik Erikson, the major challenge of young adulthood is *intimacy versus isolation*. Failure to form an intimate partnership with someone else can cause a young adult to feel painfully lonely and incomplete. Erikson believed that a person is not ready to commit to an intimate relationship until he or she has developed a firm sense of personal identity, the task of the preceding stage of life.

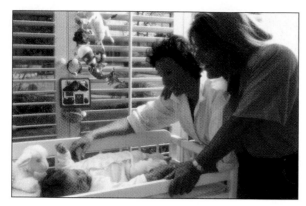

Like heterosexuals in successful relationships, gays in loving partnerships share decision making, trust, respect, and appreciation.

FORMING PARTNERSHIPS Almost 90% of Americans eventually get married (U.S. Bureau of the Census, 2002a), but those who marry are waiting longer to do so. For example, in 1970, the median age of an American woman marrying for the first time was 20.8 years; this increased to 25.3 years by 2002. Similarly, for American men, the median age for first marriages was 23.2 years in 1970, increasing to 26.9 years by 2002 (U.S. Bureau of the Census, 2002b). This postponement of marriage is even greater among African Americans than among Whites (Benokraitis, 2004).

Although heterosexual marriage is still the statistical norm in the United States, other types of partnerships exist. Cohabiting relationships are one example, though most such relationships last no longer than two years (Doyle, 2004). Contrary to popular belief, the greatest recent increase in cohabitation is not among the very young but, rather, among older adults. In fact, more than 1.2 million people over age 50 are currently cohabiting outside of marriage in America (S. L. Brown, Bulanda, & Lee, 2005). Among elderly widows and widowers, cohabitation is increasingly seen as a way of enjoying a life together without financial complications and tax penalties.

Homosexual couples are another example of nontraditional intimate partnerships. Studies show that most gays and lesbians seek the same loving, committed, and meaningful partnerships as their heterosexual counterparts (Kurdek, 2005; Peplau & Cochran, 1990). Moreover, successful homosexual relationships share the same characteristics as successful heterosexual ones: high levels of mutual trust, respect, and appreciation; shared decision making; good communication; and good conflict-resolution skills (Kurdek; 2005; Laird, 2003). (See Applying Psychology: "Resolving Conflicts in Intimate Relationships.")

PARENTHOOD For most parents, loving and being loved by their children is an unparalleled source of fulfillment. However, the birth of the first child is also a major turning point in a couple's relationship, one that requires many adjustments. Romance and fun often give way to duty and obligations. Since young children demand a lot of time and energy, parents may be left with little time or energy for each other.

Parenthood may also heighten conflicts between pursuit of careers and responsibilities at home. This outcome is especially likely among women who have had an active career outside the home. They may be torn between feelings of loss and resentment at the prospect of leaving their job, and anxiety or guilt over the idea of continuing to work. This conflict is added to the usual worries about being an adequate wife and mother (Warner, 2005.) It is no wonder that women feel the need for their partner's cooperation more strongly during this period of life than men do (Kendall-Tackett, 2001). Contemporary fathers spend more time with their children than their fathers did, but mothers still bear the greater responsibility for both child rearing and housework.

Although homosexual couples as a group believe more strongly in equally dividing household duties than heterosexual couples do, homosexuals tend to make an exception when it comes to child rearing. After the arrival of a child (through adoption or artificial insemination), child-care responsibilities tend to fall more heavily on one member of a homosexual couple, whereas the other spends more time in paid employment (C. J. Patterson, 1995; Peplau & Beals, 2004).

Given the demands of child rearing, it isn't surprising that marital satisfaction tends to decline after the arrival of the first child (Ruble, Fleming, Hackel, & Stangor, 1988). (See **Figure 9–4**). But once children leave home, many parents experience renewed satisfaction in their relationship as a couple. Rather than lamenting over their "empty nests," many women experience an increase in positive mood and well-being (Dennerstein, Dudley, & Guthrie, 2002;

Figure 9–4

Marital satisfaction.
This graph shows when married people are most and least content with their marriage, on a scale of 1 (very unhappy) to 7 (very happy).

Source: American Sociological Association; adapted from *USA Today,* August 12, 1997, p. D1.

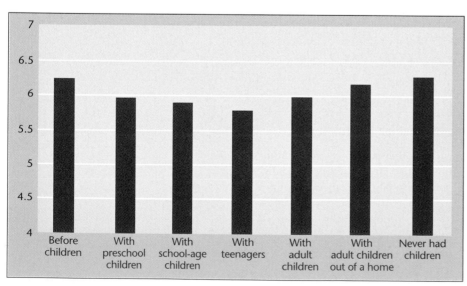

APPLYING PSYCHOLOGY

RESOLVING CONFLICTS IN INTIMATE RELATIONSHIPS

Even the closest, most loving couples have disagreements. People, after all, have different desires, approaches, priorities, and viewpoints. For those reasons, conflict is inevitable in every intimate relationship. But conflict does not necessarily mean destructive forms of fighting. Conflict can be resolved constructively. Constructive fighting can actually bring people closer together in search of mutually satisfactory solutions.

Psychologists suggest a number of steps that lead to constructive conflict resolution:

1. *Carefully choose the time and place for an argument.* If you air a grievance at an inappropriate time, you can expect an unsatisfactory outcome. Try not to begin a major disagreement while your partner is in the middle of an important task or is ready to fall asleep after a long, tiring day.

2. *Be a good listener.* Don't go on the defensive as soon as your partner brings up a concern or complaint. Listen carefully without interrupting. Try to understand your partner's point of view. Listening calmly, without anger, will help to get the discussion off to a good start. Don't let your body give nonverbal cues that contradict good listening. For instance, don't continue to do chores or watch television while your partner is speaking. Don't shrug your shoulders or roll your eyes as if discounting your partner's view.

3. *Give feedback regarding your understanding of the other person's grievance.* Restate what your partner has told you in your own words. Help clarify and avoid misunderstandings by asking questions. For instance, if a wife says she is fed up with the amount of time her husband spends watching television sports, he might respond by saying, "I know you don't like me watching sports a lot, but do you expect me to stop entirely?"

4. *Be candid. Level with your partner about your feelings.* Say what you really think. If you are angry, don't make your partner guess your feelings by being silent or showing anger indirectly. But being candid does not mean being hurtful. Don't engage in counterproductive tactics such as name calling, sarcasm, mockery, or insults.

5. *Use "I" rather than "you" statements.* For instance, if you're angry with your partner for being late, say, "I've been really worried and upset for the last hour," rather than "You're a whole hour late!" "You" statements sound like accusations and tend to put people on the defensive. "I" statements sound more like efforts to communicate feelings in nonjudgmental ways.

6. *Focus on behavior, not on the person.* For example, focus on your partner's lateness as a problem. Don't accuse your partner of being thoughtless and self-centered.

7. *Don't overstate the frequency of a problem or overgeneralize about it.* Don't tell your partner that he's always late or that she's exactly like her mother.

8. *Focus on a limited number of specific issues.* Don't overwhelm your partner with a barrage of grievances. Stick to current concerns of high priority. Don't dredge up a long list of complaints from the past.

9. *Don't find scapegoats for every grievance against you.* We all tend to explain away our shortcomings by blaming them on circumstances or on other people. Take responsibility for your actions and encourage your partner to do the same.

10. *Suggest specific, relevant changes to solve a problem.* Both participants in the conflict should propose at least one possible solution. A proposed solution should be reasonable and consider the other person's viewpoint as well as your own.

11. *Be open to compromise.* Settling disputes successfully often involves negotiation. Both people must be willing to give in a little. Don't back your partner into a corner by making an ultimatum. Partners need to be willing to change themselves to some extent in response to each other's feelings. This willingness is the essence of being in an intimate relationship.

12. *Don't think in terms of winner and loser.* A competitive approach to conflict resolution doesn't work in intimate relationships. Strive for solutions that are satisfactory to both parties. Think of each other as allies attacking a mutual problem. In this way, your relationship will become stronger.

Owen, 2005). For the first time in years, the husband and wife can be alone together and enjoy one another's company (Lauer & Lauer, 1999; Orbuch, House, Mero, & Webster, 1996).

ENDING A RELATIONSHIP Intimate relationships frequently end. Although this is the case for all types of couples—married and unmarried, heterosexual and homosexual—most of the research on ending relationships has focused on married, heterosexual couples. The U.S. divorce rate has risen substantially since the 1960s, as it has in many other developed nations (T. Lewin, 1995). Although the divorce rate appears to have stabilized, it has stabilized at quite a high level. Almost half of American marriages eventually end in divorce (U.S. Bureau of the Census, 2002a).

Rarely is the decision to separate a mutual one. Most often, one partner takes the initiative in ending the relationship after a long period of slowly increasing unhappiness. Making the decision does not necessarily bring relief. In the short term, it often brings turmoil, animosity, and apprehension. However, in the longer term, friendships between divorced mothers often grow very strong which, in turn, helps them to cope more effectively with divorce (Albeck & Kaydare, 2002).

Divorce can have serious and far-reaching effects on children—especially on their school performance, self-esteem, gender-role development, emotional adjustment, relationships with others, and attitudes toward marriage (W. A. Collins et al., 2000; S. M. Greene, Anderson, Doyle, & Riedelbach, 2006). And children who have been involved in multiple divorces are placed at an even greater risk (Kurdek, Fine, & Sinclair, 1995). Children adapt more successfully to divorce when they have good support systems, when the divorcing parents maintain a good relationship, and when sufficient financial resources are made available to them. The effects of divorce also vary with the children themselves: Those who have easygoing temperaments and who were generally well behaved before the divorce usually have an easier time adjusting (Hetherington, Bridges, & Insabella, 1998; Storksen, Roysamb, & Holmen, 2006).

THE WORLD OF WORK

What are the satisfactions and stresses of adult work?

For many young people, the period from the late teens through the early twenties is crucial because it sets the stage for much of adult life. The educational achievements and training obtained during these transitional years often establish the foundation that will shape the income and occupational status for the remainder of adult life (J. J. Arnett, 2000).

Three or four generations ago, choosing a career was not an issue for most young adults. Men followed in their fathers' footsteps or took whatever apprenticeships were available in their communities. Most women were occupied in child care, housework, and helping with the family farm or business; or they pursued such "female" careers as secretarial work, nursing, and teaching. Modern, career choices are far more numerous for both men and women. In 2002, for example, women made up over 46% of the labor force in the United States and accounted for approximately 30% of full-time employed physicians and lawyers (U.S. Department of Labor, 2004). (See **Figure 9–5**.) Of employed women, 74% worked full-time; the rest worked part-time. The largest percentage of employed women (38%) worked in management, professional, and related occupations, while 35% worked in sales and office occupations.

DUAL-CAREER FAMILIES Over the last 50 years, the percentage of women in the paid labor force has increased dramatically from 35% in 1955 to 60% in 2003 (U.S. Bureau of the Census, 2005). The change is even greater for married women (29% to 61%) (Engemann & Owyang, 2006). This increasing role of women as economic providers is a worldwide trend (Elloy & Mackie, 2002).

As we noted earlier, balancing the demands of career and family is a problem in many families, especially for women (Ajay, 2004; Caplan, 2003). Even when the wife has a full-time job outside the home, she is likely to end up doing far more than half of the housework and child care. She is also likely to be aware of this imbalance and to resent it. The "double shift"—one at paid work outside the home and another at unpaid household labor—is the common experience of millions of women throughout the world. True equality—the hopeful goal of the dual-career movement—has yet to be achieved (Viers & Prouty, 2001).

Despite the pressures associated with the double shift, most women report increases in self-esteem when they have a paid job (Elliott, 1996). They also tend to experience less anxiety and depression than childless working women

Figure 9–5

Percentage of selected jobs filled by women in the United States, 1950–2000.
This graph shows the percentage of each job filled by women. The figures in parentheses indicate women's earnings as a percentage of men's in the given field.

Source: Copyright © 2000 Rodger Doyle. Reprinted with permission.

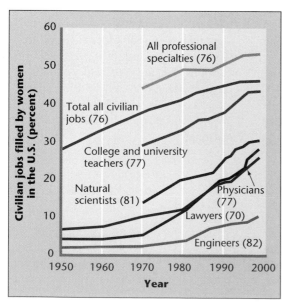

do (R. C. Barnett, Brennan, & Marshall, 1994). The vast majority say that they would continue to work even if they didn't need the money (P. Schwartz, 1994). Those women most apt to feel stressed by a double shift are those who do not find satisfaction in their various roles (R. C. Barnett et al., 1994).

COGNITIVE CHANGES

In what ways do adults think differently than adolescents?

Only recently have researchers begun to explore the ways in which adult and adolescent thinking differ. Nonetheless, a few conclusions have begun to emerge. Although adolescents are able to test alternatives and to arrive at what they see as the "correct" solution to a problem, adults gradually come to realize that there isn't a single correct solution to every problem—there may, in fact, be no correct solution, or there may be several. Adolescents rely on authorities to tell them what is "true," but adults realize that "truth" often varies according to the situation and one's viewpoint. Adults are also more practical: They know that a solution to a problem must be realistic as well as reasonable. No doubt these changes in adult thinking derive from greater experience of the world. Dealing with the kinds of complex problems that arise in adult life requires moving away from the literal, formal, and somewhat rigid thinking of adolescence and young adulthood (G. Goldstein, 2004).

Most measurable cognitive changes during adulthood do not simply involve a rise or fall in general ability. Instead, for most people, such cognitive skills as vocabulary and verbal memory increase steadily through the 6th decade of life. Other cognitive skills, such as reasoning and spatial orientation generally peak during the 40s, falling off only slightly with increasing age. Perceptual speed (the ability to make quick and accurate visual discriminations) and the ability to perform mathematical computations show the largest decrease with age, with the former beginning to decline as early as age 25, and the latter starting to decline around age 40 (Schaie & Willis, 2001; Willis & Shaie, 1999).

And just as physical exercise is necessary for optimal physical development, so mental exercise is necessary for optimal cognitive development. Although some decline in cognitive skills is inevitable as people age, the decline can be minimized if people stay mentally active (Wilson et al., 2003).

MIDLIFE

What are the changes and challenges of midlife?

Psychological health generally improves in adulthood. And adolescents with better psychological health tend to improve even further in adulthood (C. J. Jones & Meredith, 2000; Shiner, Masten, & Roberts, 2003). Both men and women tend to become less self-centered and develop better coping skills with age (Neugarten, 1977). One longitudinal study found that people are more sympathetic, giving, productive, and dependable at 45 than they were at 20 (Block, 1971). Another found that people in their middle years feel an increasing commitment to and responsibility for others, develop new ways of adapting, and are more comfortable in interpersonal relationships (Vaillant, 1977). Such findings suggest that the majority of people are successfully meeting what Erik Erikson saw as the major challenge of middle adulthood: *generativity versus stagnation*. Generativity refers to the ability to continue being productive and creative, especially in ways that guide and encourage future generations. For those who fail to achieve this state, life becomes a drab and meaningless routine, and the person feels stagnant and bored.

Feelings of boredom and stagnation in middle adulthood may be part of what is called a **midlife crisis**. The person in midlife crisis feels painfully unfulfilled and ready for a radical, abrupt shift in career, personal relationships, or lifestyle. Research shows, however, that the midlife crisis is not typical; most people do not make sudden dramatic changes in their lives in midadulthood (Martino, 1995; M. E. Lachman, 2004). In one study, in fact, only about 10%

Erik Erikson suggested that a major goal in middle adulthood is to achieve a sense of generativity, or doing something to help future generations.

midlife crisis A time when adults discover they no longer feel fulfilled in their jobs or personal lives and attempt to make a decisive shift in career or lifestyle.

reported experiencing a midlife crisis (Brim, 1999). Furthermore, a large-scale study found that the majority of middle-aged adults reported lower levels of anxiety and worry than young adults, and generally felt positively about their lives. Daniel Levinson, who studied personality development in men and women throughout their adulthood (Levinson, 1978, 1986, 1987), preferred the term **midlife transition** for the period when people tend to take stock of their lives. Many of the men and women in his studies, confronted with the first signs of aging, began to think about the finite nature of life. They realized that they may never accomplish all that they had hoped to do, and they questioned the value of some of the things they had accomplished so far, wondering how meaningful they were. As a result, some gradually reset their life priorities, establishing new goals based on their new insights.

ENDURING ISSUES

Stability–Change   The "Change of Life"

A decline in reproductive function occurs during middle age both in men and in women. In women, the amount of estrogen produced by the ovaries drops sharply at around age 45, although the exact age varies considerably. Breasts, genital tissues, and the uterus begin to shrink; and menstrual periods become irregular and then cease altogether at around age 50. The cessation of menstruation is called **menopause**.

The hormonal changes that accompany menopause often cause certain physical symptoms; the most noticeable are "hot flashes." Some women also may experience serious thinning of the bones, making them more vulnerable to fractures. Although both conditions can be alleviated by hormone replacement therapy (HRT) in the form of a pill or a skin patch prescribed by a physician, recent studies have shown that taking hormones to reduce the symptoms of menopause may also place women at a higher risk for heart disease and breast cancer (Rymer, Wilson, & Ballard, 2003). Since the severity of menopausal symptoms varies, as do the risk factors associated with these diseases, it is important for women to weigh the costs and benefits of HRT carefully with a physician.

Experts disagree about whether a "male menopause" exists. Men never experience as severe a drop in testosterone as women do with estrogen. Instead, studies have found a more gradual decline—perhaps 30% to 40%—in testosterone in men between the ages of 48 and 70 (J. E. Brody, 2004; Crooks & Bauer, 2002). Recent evidence also confirms that with increasing age, male fertility slowly decreases as well (W. C. L. Ford et al., 2000). ●●

midlife transition According to Levinson, a process whereby adults assess the past and formulate new goals for the future.

menopause The time in a woman's life when menstruation ceases.

CHECK YOUR UNDERSTANDING

1. According to Erik Erikson, the major challenge of young adulthood is _____ versus _____, whereas the major challenge of middle adulthood is _____ versus _____.

2. The cessation of menstruation in middle-age women is called _____.

Answers: 1. intimacy, isolation; generativity, stagnation. 2. menopause.

APPLY YOUR UNDERSTANDING

1. If you were to poll a group of older couples, you would expect to find that most of them say that their marital satisfaction

   a. has steadily decreased over the years.

   b. has not changed over the years.

   c. declined during the child-rearing years, but has increased since then.

   d. has steadily increased over the years.

2. Imagine that you survey a large group of women who have full-time jobs outside the home as well as families (the so-called "double shift"). Compared with women who do not have paying jobs outside the home, what would you expect to find about this group of dual-career women?

a. They are more likely to be anxious and depressed.

b. They are more likely to have higher self-esteem.

c. They are more likely to say they wouldn't work if they didn't need the money.

d. Both (a) and (c) are correct.

Answers: 1. c. 2. b.

Late Adulthood

What factors are related to life expectancy?

Older adults constitute the fastest-growing segments of the U.S. population. Indeed, during the 20th century, the percentage of Americans over 65 more than tripled; and those over 85 now represent the fastest-growing segment of the population (National Institute on Aging, 2006). In the 2000 census, 35 million Americans were over age 65 (U.S. Bureau of the Census, 2001); by the year 2030, there may be more than 70 million in this age group. This dramatic rise stems from the aging of the large baby-boom generation, coupled with increases in life expectancy due primarily to better health care and nutrition. (See **Figure 9–6**.)

However, a sizable gender gap exists in life expectancy. The average American woman today enjoys a life span that is 5.2 years longer than that of the average American man, but that difference has been shrinking since 1980 as the life expectancy of males increases more rapidly than that of females (Miniño, Heron, & Smith, 2006). The reasons for this gender gap are still unclear, but likely factors include differences in hormones, exposure to stress, health-related behaviors (Moeller-Leimkuehler, 2003), and genetic makeup.

There is also a gap in life expectancy between Whites and African Americans in the United States, although that gap also is closing. The average White American child born today is likely to live 5 years longer than the average African American child (Miniño, Heron, & Smith, 2006). This difference seems to stem largely from socioeconomic disparities.

Because older adults are becoming an increasingly visible part of American society, it is important to understand their development. Unfortunately, our views of older adults are often heavily colored by myths. For example, many people believe that most are lonely, poor, and troubled by ill health. Even health-care professionals sometimes assume that it is natural for elderly people to feel ill. As a result, symptoms considered treatable in younger people are sometimes interpreted as inevitable signs of decay in elderly people and, thus, frequently go untreated. The false belief that "senility" is inevitable in old age is another damaging myth, as is the belief that most older adults are helpless and dependent on their families for care and financial support. All the research on late adulthood contradicts these stereotypes. Increasingly, people age 65 and over are healthy, productive, and able (D. M. Cutler, 2001; Manton & Gu, 2001).

Figure 9–6
Population age structure, 2000.
The U.S. population will continue to age over the next several decades, as the huge baby-boom generation matures.

Source: U.S. Census Bureau. Retrieved June 8, 2006, from *http://www.census.gov/cgi-bin/ipc/idbpyrs.pl?cty=US&out=s&ymax=250*.

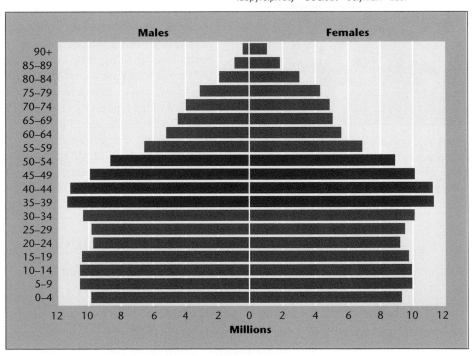

PHYSICAL CHANGES

Why does the body deteriorate with age?

Despite describing themselves as being in poor physical condition, most people in midlife have few serious illnesses. However, in middle adulthood and continuing through late adulthood, physical appearance changes, as does the functioning of every organ in the body. The hair thins and turns white or gray. The skin wrinkles. Bones become more fragile. Muscles lose power; and joints stiffen or deteriorate. Circulation slows, blood pressure rises, and because the lungs hold less oxygen, the older adult has less energy. Body shape and posture change; and the reproductive organs atrophy. Difficulties in falling asleep and staying asleep become more common; and reaction times are slower. Vision, hearing, and the sense of smell all become less acute (Cavanaugh & Blanchard-Fields, 2005). Most people are at first unaware of these changes, which occur gradually.

It is curious that we do not yet know why physical aging happens (DiGiovanna, 1999). There are several theories:

- *Genetics.* One theory is that genes may program our cells eventually to deteriorate and die. According to this theory of aging, the body is genetically directed to age and deteriorate just as maturation shapes early growth and development. The role of inheritance in aging is supported by a recent finding of a gene that appears to be related to exceptional longevity (Puca et al., 2001).
- *Telomeres.* According to a second theory, *telomeres* (special protective structures located on chromosomal tips) become shorter with each replication (Saretzki & Zglinicki, 2002). After about 100 replications, the size of the telomeres has been reduced so significantly that cells are no longer capable of precise replication. Some research indicates that telomeres may also be shortened by increased stress (Epel et al., 2006).
- *Free Radicals.* The recent and widely accepted *free radical theory* of aging contends that unstable oxygen molecules ricochet within cells and damage the cellular components (including DNA) over time, causing them to age (De la Fuente, 2002). Damage from the continued bombardment of oxygen molecules may lead to the wide range of disorders accompanying aging, including arthritis, cancer, and cognitive decline (Berr, 2002; J. A. Knight, 2000; Leborgne, Maziere & Andrejak, 2002; E. G. McGeer, Klegeris, & McGeer, 2005).

Whatever the ultimate explanation for physical decline, many factors affect adults' physical well-being. Among these are things they can control—particularly, diet, exercise, health care, smoking, drug use, and overexposure to sun. Attitudes and interests also matter. People who have a continuing sense of usefulness, who maintain old ties, investigate new ideas, take up new activities, and feel in control of their lives have the lowest rates of disease and the highest survival rates (Butler, Lewis, & Sunderland, 1998.) Indeed, in a survey of 2,724 people age 25 to 74, older adults reported experiencing more positive emotions than did younger adults during the previous month (Mroczek & Kolarz, 1998). So there's a good deal of truth in the saying, "You're only as old as you feel." In fact, psychologists are starting to use functional or psychological age, instead of chronological age, to predict an older adult's adaptability to life's demands.

Although physical changes are inevitable during late adulthood, how people respond to these changes has a major effect on their quality of life.

SOCIAL DEVELOPMENT

What kind of lifestyle and sex life can be expected after age 65?

Far from being weak and dependent, most men and women over age 65 live apart from their children and outside nursing homes; and most are very satisfied with their autonomous lifestyles. The ability to live independently and take enjoyment from everyday situations is an important predictor of satisfaction among the elderly (Rioux, 2005). Moreover, those who remain physically and mentally active, travel, exercise, and attend meetings are more likely to report being happier and more satisfied with their lives than those who stay at home (George, 2001).

Still, gradual social changes do take place in late adulthood. In general, older people interact with fewer people and perform fewer social roles. Behavior becomes less influenced by social rules and expectations than it was earlier in life. Most older people step back and assess life, realize there is a limit to their capacity for social involvement, and learn to live comfortably with those restrictions. This process does not necessarily entail a psychological "disengagement" from the social world, as some researchers have contended. Instead, older people may simply make sensible choices that suit their more limited time frames and physical capabilities (Carstensen, 1995).

RETIREMENT In late adulthood, most people retire from paid employment. Individual reactions to this major change vary widely, partly because society has no clear idea of what retirees are supposed to do (Schlossberg, 2004). Should they sit in rocking chairs and watch life go by, or should they play golf, become foster grandparents, and study Greek? The advantage to this lack of clear social expectations is that older adults have the flexibility to structure their retirement as they please. Men and women often go about this process differently. Men generally see retirement as a time to slow down and do less, whereas women often view it as a time to learn new things and explore new possibilities (Helgesen, 1998). This difference can cause obvious problems for retired couples.

Of course, the nature and quality of retired life depend in part on financial status. If retirement means a major decline in a person's standard of living, that person will be less eager to retire and will lead a more limited life after retirement. Another factor in people's attitudes toward retirement is their feelings about work. People who are fulfilled by their jobs are usually less interested in retiring than people whose jobs are unrewarding (Atchley, 1982). Similarly, people who have very ambitious, hard-driving personalities tend to want to stay at work longer than those who are more relaxed.

SEXUAL BEHAVIOR A common misconception is that elderly people have outlived their sexuality. This myth reflects our stereotypes. To the extent that we see them as physically unattractive and frail, we find it difficult to believe that they are sexually active. Although the sexual response of older people is slower and they are less sexually active than younger people, the majority can enjoy sex and have orgasms. One survey revealed that 37% of married people over age 60 have sex at least once a week, 20% have sex outdoors, and 17% swim in the nude (Woodward & Springen, 1992). Another study of people age 65 to 97 found that about half the men still viewed sex as important; and slightly over half of those in committed relationships were satisfied with the quality of their sex lives (Clements, 1996).

"Then it's moved and seconded that the compulsory retirement age be advanced to ninety-five."

Source: © *The New Yorker Collection*, 1963. Peter Arno from *www.cartoonbank.com*. All Rights Reserved.

COGNITIVE CHANGES

Is memory loss inevitable in old age?

Healthy people who remain intellectually active maintain a high level of mental functioning in old age (Schaie, 1984; Shimamura, Berry, Mangels, Rusting, & Jurica, 1995). Far from the common myth that the brain cells of elderly people are rapidly dying, brain size shrinks an average of only about 10% between the ages of 20 and 70 (Peters, 2005). For a sizable number of older adults, therefore, cognitive abilities remain largely intact. Since the aging mind works a little more slowly (Deary & Der, 2005), certain types of memories are a little more difficult to store and retrieve (Bopp & Verhaeghen, 2005) and the ability to process and attend to information does gradually decline (S.-C. Li, 2002). For the most part, however, these changes do not interfere significantly with the ability to enjoy an active, independent life. Moreover, older adults who stay both mentally and physically active generally experience significantly less cognitive decline than those who do not (Bosma, vanBoxtel, Ponds, Houx, & Jolles, 2003; Colcombe & Kramer, 2003; Vaillant, 2003). Training and practice on cognitive tasks can also help greatly reduce the decline in cognitive performance in

Because people with Alzheimer's disease suffer memory loss, signs can remind them to perform ordinary activities.

later adulthood (Guenther, Schaefer, Holzner, & Kemmler, 2003; Saczynski, Willis, & Schaie, 2002), though the benefits of training are often limited only to the skills that are practiced (Kramer & Willis, 2002).

ALZHEIMER'S DISEASE For people suffering from **Alzheimer's disease**, the picture is quite different. They forget the names of their children or are unable to find their way home from the store. Some even fail to recognize their lifelong partners. Named for the German neurologist Alois Alzheimer, the disease causes brain changes resulting in the progressive loss of the ability to communicate and reason.

For many years, Alzheimer's disease was considered rare and was diagnosed only in people under age 60 who developed symptoms of memory loss and confusion. But now Alzheimer's is recognized as a common disorder in older people formerly described as "senile." According to current estimates, about 10% of adults over age 65 and nearly half of adults over age 85 suffer from Alzheimer's disease (Alzheimer's Association, 2006). Risk factors include having a genetic predisposition (Lleo, Berezovska, Growdon, & Hyman, 2004), having a family history of *dementia* (a general decline in physical and cognitive abilities), having Down syndrome or Parkinson's disease, having been born to a woman over age 40, and suffering a head trauma (especially one that caused unconsciousness) (Mayo Foundation for Medical Education and Research, 2005b). In addition, people who are not active (both physically and intellectually) during their middle years increase their risk for developing Alzheimer's disease (Friedland et al., 2001; Vaillant, 2003; Wilson & Bennett, 2003).

Alzheimer's usually begins with minor memory losses, such as difficulty in recalling words and names or in remembering where something was placed. As it progresses—a process that may take anywhere from 2 to 20 years—personality changes are also likely. First, people may become emotionally withdrawn or flat. Later, they may suffer from delusions, such as thinking that relatives are stealing from them. These people become confused and may not know where they are or what time of day it is. Eventually, they lose the ability to speak, to care for themselves, and to recognize family members. If they do not die of other causes, Alzheimer's will eventually be fatal (Wolfson et al., 2001).

Early diagnosis of Alzheimer's disease is usually based on questions that healthy people can answer easily, but that are troublesome to those in the early stages of the disease (Petersen et al., 2001; Solomon et al., 1998). There is no known cure, but breakthroughs in research are occurring so fast that a drug to slow the progress of the disorder or even a vaccine to prevent it may be developed in the near future (Mayo Foundation for Medical Education and Research, 2005a).

FACING THE END OF LIFE

How well do most elderly people cope with the end of life?

Fear of death is seldom a central concern for people in later adulthood. In fact, such fear seems to be a greater problem in young adulthood or in middle age, when the first awareness of mortality coincides with a greater interest in living (Tomer, 2000).

But elderly people do have some major fears associated with dying. They fear the pain, indignity, and depersonalization that they might experience during a terminal illness, as well as the possibility of dying alone. They also worry about burdening their relatives with the expenses of their hospitalization or nursing care. Sometimes, too, relatives are not able to provide much support for the elderly as they decline, either because they live too far away or because they may be unable to cope either with the pain of watching a loved one die or with their own fears of mortality (Kübler-Ross, 1975).

STAGES OF DYING In her classic work, the late psychiatrist Elisabeth Kübler-Ross (1926–2004), interviewed more than 200 dying people of all ages to try to understand death's psychological aspects. From these interviews, she described a sequence of five stages people pass through as they react to their own impending death (Kübler-Ross, 1969):

Alzheimer's disease A neurological disorder, most commonly found in late adulthood, characterized by progressive losses in memory and cognition and by changes in personality.

1. **Denial**–The person denies the diagnosis, refuses to believe that death is approaching, insists that an error has been made, and seeks other, more acceptable opinions or alternatives.
2. **Anger**–The person now accepts the reality of the situation but expresses envy and resentment toward those who will live to fulfill a plan or dream. The question becomes "Why me?" Anger may be directed at the doctor or directed randomly. The patience and understanding of other people are particularly important at this stage.
3. **Bargaining**–The person desperately tries to buy time, negotiating with doctors, family members, clergy, and God in a healthy attempt to cope with the realization of death.
4. **Depression**–As bargaining fails and time is running out, the person may succumb to depression, lamenting failures and mistakes that can no longer be corrected.
5. **Acceptance**–Tired and weak, the person at last enters a state of "quiet expectation," submitting to fate.

According to Kübler-Ross, Americans have a greater problem coping with death than people in some other cultures. She observed that some cultures are *death affirming*. For example, the Trukese of Micronesia start preparing for death at age 40. Alaskan Indians also begin preparing for death at an early age and the whole community participates in the process. In contrast, American culture is *death denying:* "We are reluctant to reveal our age; we spend fortunes to hide our wrinkles; we prefer to send our old people to nursing homes" (1975, p. 28). We also shelter children from knowledge of death and dying. By trying to protect them from these unpleasant realities, however, we may actually make them more fearful of death.

Some observers have found fault with Kübler-Ross's model of dying (K. Wright, 2003). Most of the criticisms have focused on her methodology. She studied only a relatively small sample of people and provided little information about how they were selected and how often they were interviewed. Also, all her patients were suffering from cancer. Does her model apply as well to people dying from other causes? Finally, some critics question the universality of her model. Death itself is universal, but reactions to dying may differ greatly from one culture to another.

Despite these legitimate questions, there is nearly universal agreement that Kübler-Ross deserves credit for pioneering the study of the transitions that people undergo during the dying process. She was the first to investigate an area long considered taboo; and her research has made dying a more "understandable" experience, perhaps one that is easier to deal with.

WIDOWHOOD The death of one's spouse may be the most severe challenge of late adulthood. Especially if the death was unexpected, people respond to such a loss with initial disbelief, followed by numbness. Only later is the full impact of the loss felt, which can be severe (Kübler-Ross, 2005). The incidence of depression rises significantly following the death of a spouse (Bonanno, Wortman, & Nesse, 2004; Nakao, Kashiwagi, & Yano, 2005). One long-term study revealed that older widows and widowers had a higher incidence of dying within 6 months after the death of their spouse than other married persons of their age. Moreover, this death rate was much higher for widowers than for widows and for people between the age of 55 and 70 than for those over age 70. After this initial 6-month period however, the mortality rate of both the men and the women fell gradually to a more normal level (Impens, 2005).

For somewhat different reasons, then, the burden of widowhood is heavy for both men and women (Feinson, 1986; Wilcox et al., 2003). Perhaps because they are not as used to taking care of themselves, men seem to suffer more than women from the loss of a mate. But because women have a longer life expectancy, there are many more widows than widowers. Thus, men have a better chance of remarrying. More than half the women over 65 are widowed, of whom half will live another 15 years without remarrying.

CHECK YOUR UNDERSTANDING

1. Indicate whether the following statements are true (T) or false (F):

   a. ___ The average man lives as long as the average woman.

   b. ___ The physical changes of aging inevitably become incapacitating.

   c. ___ Most elderly people are dependent on their adult children.

   d. ___ Healthy people who remain intellectually involved maintain a high level of mental functioning in old age.

2. List the five stages of dying described by Elisabeth Kübler-Ross.

Answers: 1. a (F); b (F); c (F); d (T). 2. Denial, anger, bargaining, depression, acceptance.

APPLY YOUR UNDERSTANDING

1. Elisabeth Kübler-Ross notes that Americans "are reluctant to reveal our age; we spend fortunes to hide our wrinkles; we prefer to send our old people to nursing homes." She suggests that this is because American culture is

   a. death affirming.

   b. death denying.

   c. moratorial.

   d. foreclosed.

2. You are having a discussion about cognitive changes in late adulthood, during which people make the claims that follow. Based on what you have learned in this chapter, you agree with all of them EXCEPT

   a. "If you are healthy and remain intellectually active, you are likely to maintain a high level of mental functioning in old age."

   b. "As you get older, it will become more difficult to process and attend to information."

   c. "If you practice mental tasks, you can help to minimize the decline in those skills."

   d. "As you get older, you will become increasingly confused, gradually lose the ability to speak, and eventually be unable to recognize friends and family."

Answers: 1. b. 2. d.

KEY TERMS

Enduring Issues and Methods in Developmental Psychology

developmental psychology, *p. 307*

cross-sectional studies, *p. 309*

cohort, *p. 309*

longitudinal study, *p. 309*

biographical (or retrospective study), *p. 309*

Prenatal Development

prenatal development, *p. 309*

embryo, *p. 309*

fetus, *p. 309*

teratogens, *p. 309*

critical period, *p. 310*

fetal alcohol syndrome (FAS), *p. 311*

The Newborn

neonates, *p. 311*

temperament, *p. 312*

Infancy and Childhood

maturation, *p. 317*

sensory-motor stage, *p. 318*

object permanence, *p. 318*

mental representations, *p. 318*

preoperational stage, *p. 319*

egocentric, *p. 319*

concrete-operational stage, *p. 319*

principles of conservation, *p. 319*

formal-operational stage, *p. 319*

babbling, *p. 321*

holophrases, *p. 322*

language acquisition device, *p. 323*

imprinting, *p. 325*

attachment, *p. 325*

stranger anxiety, *p. 325*

autonomy, *p. 326*

socialization, *p. 326*

peer group, *p. 327*

non-shared environment, *p. 328*

gender identity, *p. 328*

gender constancy, *p. 328*

gender-role awareness, *p. 329*

gender stereotypes, *p. 329*

sex-typed behavior, *p. 329*

Adolescence

growth spurt, *p. 331*

puberty, *p. 331*

menarche, *p. 332*

imaginary audience, *p. 333*

personal fable, *p. 333*

identity formation, *p. 334*

identity crisis, *p. 334*

cliques, *p. 334*

Adulthood

midlife crisis, *p. 341*

midlife transition, *p. 342*

menopause, *p. 342*

Late Adulthood

Alzheimer's disease, *p. 346*

CHAPTER REVIEW

Enduring Issues and Methods in Developmental Psychology

What are some of the limitations of the methods used to study development? **Cross-sectional studies** involve studying different age groups of people at the same time, whereas **longitudinal studies** involve the same group of individuals at different times in their lives. Longitudinal studies are more time consuming, but do account for **cohort** differences in the typical experiences of members of different generations. **Biographical**, or **retrospective**, **studies** involve reconstructing a person's past through interviews.

Prenatal Development

Why can an organism or another substance cause devastating effects at one point in prenatal development but not at others? The period of development from conception to birth is called **prenatal development**. During this time, **teratogens**—disease-producing organisms or potentially harmful substances, such as drugs—can pass through the placenta and cause irreparable harm to the **embryo** or **fetus**. This harm is greatest if the drug or other substance is introduced at the same time that some major developmental process is occurring. If the same substance is introduced outside this **critical period**, little or even no harm may result. Pregnant women who consume alcohol may give birth to a child with **fetal alcohol syndrome (FAS)**.

The Newborn

How competent are newborns? Although **neonates** (newborn babies) appear helpless, they are much more competent and aware than they seem. Newborns see and hear, are capable of reflexive behavior, and are distinctly unique in their underlying temperaments.

What early reflexes enable newborns to respond to their environment? Reflexes that help babies breathe and nurse are critical to survival. For instance, the *rooting reflex* causes newborns, when touched on the cheek, to turn their head in that direction and locate a nipple with their mouths. Nursing is further facilitated by the *sucking reflex*, which causes newborns to suck on anything placed in their mouth, and the *swallowing reflex*, which enables them to swallow liquids without choking.

Is your temperament the same as it was when you were a newborn? Babies are born with individual differences in personality, or **temperament** differences. Often a baby's temperament remains quite stable over time due to a combination of genetic and environmental influences, but stability in temperament is not inevitable. Your own temperament may be both similar to and different from the temperament you displayed as a newborn.

Which senses are the most developed at birth, and which are the least developed? All of a baby's senses are functioning at birth: sight, hearing, taste, smell, and touch. Newborns seem particularly adept at discriminating speech sounds, suggesting their hearing is quite keen. Their least developed sense is probably vision, which takes 6 to 8 months to become as good as the average college student's.

Infancy and Childhood

What kinds of developmental changes occur during infancy and childhood? During the first dozen years of life, a helpless infant becomes a competent older child. This transformation encompasses many important kinds of changes, including physical, motor, cognitive, and social developments.

How does the human brain change during infancy and early childhood? During the first 3 years of life, there are rapid increases in the number of connections between neurons in the brain, the speed of conduction between neurons, and the density of synaptic connections. Beginning in the 3rd year of life, both the number and density of synaptic connections decreases markedly as unused neurons are removed.

Do children grow at a steady pace? Growth of the body is most rapid during the first year, with the average baby growing approximately 10 inches and gaining about 15 pounds. It then slows down considerably until early adolescence. When growth does occur, it happens suddenly—almost overnight—rather than through small, steady changes.

Is walking at an early age a sign of future athletic ability? Babies tend to reach the major milestones in early motor development at broadly similar ages. The average ages are called *developmental norms.* Those who are somewhat ahead of their peers are not necessarily destined for athletic greatness. Motor development that is slower or faster than the norm tells us little or nothing about a child's future characteristics. **Maturation**, the biological process that leads to developmental changes, also is shaped by experiences with the environment.

How does a child's ability to reason change over time? According to Swiss psychologist Jean Piaget, children undergo qualitative cognitive changes as they grow older. During the **sensory-motor stage** (birth to age 2), children acquire **object permanence**, the understanding that things continue to exist even when they are out of sight. In the **preoperational stage** (ages 2 to 7), they become increasingly adept at using **mental representations**; and language assumes an important role in describing, remembering, and reasoning about the world. They are **egocentric** in that they have difficulty appreciating others' viewpoints. Children in the **concrete-operational stage** (ages 7 to 11) are able to pay attention to more than one factor at a time, grasp **principles of conservation**, and can understand someone else's point of view. Finally, in the **formal-operational stage** (adolescence through adulthood), teenagers acquire the ability to think abstractly and test ideas mentally using logic. Not all psychologists agree with Piaget's theory, however.

How do gender and ethnic background affect moral development? Lawrence Kohlberg's stage theory of cognition focused exclusively on moral thinking. He proposed that children at different levels of moral reasoning base their moral choices on different factors: first, a concern about physical consequences, next, a concern about what other people think, and finally a concern about abstract principles. One problem with this view is that it doesn't consider how cultural values (associated with being female, African American, Japanese, and so on) may affect the moral development.

How does a child develop language skills? Language begins with cooing and progresses to **babbling**, the repetition of speech-like sounds. The first word is usually uttered at 12 months. During the next 6 to 8 months, children build a vocabulary of one-word sentences called **holophrases**. Chomsky proposed that children are born with a **language acquisition device**, an innate mechanism that enables them to build a vocabulary, master the rules of grammar, and form intelligible sentences.

How can parents help their children to become both securely attached and independent? Developing a sense of independence is just one of the tasks that children face in their social development. During the toddler period, a growing awareness of being a separate person makes developing some **autonomy** from parents a very important issue. Parents can encourage independence in their children by allowing them to make choices and do things on their own within a framework of reasonable and consistently enforced limits. Another major task during this period is forming a secure **attachment**, or emotional bond, with other people. Young animals of many species form a strong bond to the first moving object they see, a process known as **imprinting**. In contrast, human newborns only gradually form emotional bonds with their caregivers. Some of the other important tasks during infancy and early childhood include overcoming **stranger anxiety,** trusting other people (infancy), learning to take initiative in tackling new tasks (the preschool years), and mastering some of the many skills that will be needed in adulthood (middle and later childhood). Parenting style affects children's behavior and self-image. The most successful parenting style is authoritative, in which parents provide firm guidance but are willing to listen to the child's opinions. However, parents do not act the same way toward every child in the family because children are different from each other and elicit different parental responses. The **nonshared environment** refers to the unique aspects of the environment that are experienced differently by siblings even though they are reared in the same family.

Socialization, the process by which children learn their cultures' behaviors and attitudes, is an important task of childhood. As children get older, they develop a deeper understanding of the meaning of friendship and come under the influence of a **peer group**.

When do children learn about their gender? By age 3, a child has developed a **gender identity**, a girl's knowledge that she is a girl and a boy's knowledge the he is a boy. But children of this age have little idea of what it means to be a particular gender. By 4 or 5, most children develop **gender constancy**, the realization that gender depends on what kind of genitals one has and cannot be changed. Children develop **sex-typed behavior**, or behavior appropriate to their gender, through a process of **gender-role awareness** and the formation of **gender stereotypes** reflected in their culture.

Is watching TV a good or bad influence on the development of children? Watching television can be worthwhile when programs have educational context and provide positive role models. However, TV also reduces the time children could spend on other positive activities. When it contains aggressive content and negative role models, it can encourage aggressive behavior and can perhaps contribute to the decline in academic skills, especially reading.

Adolescence

Is adolescence characterized only by physical change? The **growth spurt** is a rapid increase in height and weight that begins, on average, at about age 10-1/2 in girls and 12-1/2 in boys, and reaches its peak at age 12 in girls and 14 in boys. These physical changes of adolescence are just part of the transformation that occurs during this period. The child turns into an adult, not only physically, but also cognitively, socially, and emotionally.

What are the consequences of going through puberty early or late? Signs of **puberty**—the onset of sexual maturation–begins around 11-1/2 in boys. In girls, **menarche**, the first menstrual period, occurs at 12-1/2 for the average American girl. But individuals vary widely in when they go through puberty. Very early maturing girls like the admiration they get from other girls, but dislike the embarrassing sexual attention given to them by boys. Boys who mature early do better in sports and in social activities and receive greater respect from their peers.

What are two common fallacies that characterize adolescent thinking? In terms of cognitive development, teenagers often reach the level of *formal-operational thought*, in which they can reason abstractly and speculate about alternatives. These newfound abilities may make them overconfident that their own ideas are right, turning adolescence into a time of cognitive egocentrism. Frequent focus on the self may also make teens prone to feeling constantly watched and judged by others, a phenomenon called the **imaginary audience**. In addition, adolescents may think of themselves as so unique as to be untouched by the negative things that happen to other people. This **personal fable** may encourage them to take needless risks.

What important tasks do adolescents face in their personal and social lives? **Identity formation** is the process in which a person develops a stable sense of self. Identity formation usually follows an intense period of self-exploration called an **identity crisis**. In Erik Erikson's theory, *identity versus role confusion* is the major challenge of this period. Most adolescents rely on a peer group for social and emotional support, often rigidly conforming to the values of their friends. From small unisex **cliques** in early adolescence, friendship groups change to mixed-sex groups in which short-lived romantic interests are common. Later, stable dating patterns emerge. Parent–child relationships may become temporarily rocky during adolescence as teenagers become aware of their parents' faults and question parental rules.

What are some major problems among adolescents in our society? Developmental problems often emerge for the first time during adolescence. A sizable number of adolescents think about committing suicide; a much smaller number attempt it; however, suicide is the third leading cause of death among adolescents. Statistics reflect a common decline in self-esteem during adolescence, especially among girls.

Adulthood

Does personality change during adulthood? Reaching developmental milestones in adulthood is much less predictable than in earlier years; it is much more a function of the individual's decisions, circumstances, and even luck. Still, certain experiences and changes eventually take place and nearly every adult tries to fulfill certain needs.

What factors are important in forming satisfying relationships in adulthood? Almost every adult forms a long-term loving partnership with at least one other adult at some point in life. According to Erik Erikson, the task of finding intimacy versus being isolated and lonely is especially important during young adulthood. Erikson believed that people are not ready for love until they have formed a firm sense of identity.

What are the satisfactions and stresses of adult work? The vast majority of adults are moderately or highly satisfied with their jobs and would continue to work even if they didn't need to do so for financial reasons. Balancing the demands of job and family is often difficult, however, especially for women, because they tend to have most of the responsibility for housework and child care. Yet despite this stress of a "double shift," a job outside the home is a positive, self-esteem–boosting factor in most women's lives.

In what ways do adults think differently than adolescents? An adult's thinking is more flexible and practical than that of an adolescent. Whereas adolescents search for the one "correct" solution to a problem, adults realize that there may be several "right" solutions—or none at all. Adults also place less faith in authority than adolescents do.

What are the changes and challenges of midlife? Certain broad patterns of personality change occur in adulthood. As people grow older, they tend to become less self-centered and more comfortable in interpersonal relationships. They also develop better coping skills and new ways of adapting. By middle age, many adults feel an increasing commitment to, and responsibility for, others. This suggests that many adults are successfully meeting what Erik Erikson saw as the major challenge of middle adulthood: *generativity* (the ability to continue being productive and creative, especially in ways that guide and encourage future generations) *versus stagnation* (a sense of boredom or lack of fulfillment, sometimes called a **midlife crisis**). Most adults, however, do not experience dramatic upheaval in their middle years, so this period may be better thought of as one of **midlife transition**.

What is menopause, and what changes accompany it? Middle adulthood brings a decline in the functioning of the reproductive organs. In women, this is marked by **menopause**, the cessation of menstruation, accompanied by a sharp drop in estrogen levels. Although hormone-replacement therapy can alleviate some negative symptoms (such as thinning bones and "hot flashes"), it is associated with cancer and heart risks; thus, women should seek medical advice and supervision. Men experience a slower decline in testosterone levels.

Late Adulthood

What factors are related to life expectancy? Over the past century, life expectancy in America has increased mainly because of improved health care and nutrition. There is, however, a sizable gender gap, with women living an average of 5.2 years longer than men. There is also a sizable racial gap, with White Americans living an average of 5 years longer than Blacks.

Why does the body deteriorate with age? The physical changes of late adulthood affect outward appearance and the functioning of every organ. We don't yet know why these changes happen. Perhaps our genes program cells to eventually deteriorate and die, or perhaps genetic instructions simply degrade over time. Another possible explanation is that body parts wear out after repeated use, with environmental toxins contributing to the wearing-out process. Whatever the reason, physical aging is inevitable, although it can be slowed by a healthy lifestyle.

What kind of lifestyle and sex life can be expected after 65? Most older adults have an independent lifestyle and engage in activities that interest them. Although their sexual responses may be slowed, most continue to enjoy sex beyond the seventies. Still, gradual social changes occur in late adulthood. Older adults start to interact with fewer people and perform fewer social roles. They may also become less influenced by social rules and expectations. Realizing that there is a limit to the capacity for social involvement, they learn to live with some restrictions.

Is memory loss inevitable in old age? The aging mind works a little more slowly and certain kinds of memories are more difficult to store and retrieve, but these changes are generally not extensive enough to interfere with most everyday tasks. Healthy older adults who engage in intellectually stimulating activities usually maintain a high level of mental functioning, unless they develop a condition such as **Alzheimer's disease,** a progressive neurological condition characterized by losses of memory and cognition and changes in personality.

How well do most elderly people cope with the end of life? Most elderly people fear death less than younger people fear it. They do fear the pain, indignity, depersonalization, and loneliness associated with a terminal illness. They also worry about becoming a financial burden to their families. The death of a spouse may be the most severe challenge that the elderly face. Kübler-Ross described a sequence of five stages that people go through when they are dying: *denial, anger, bargaining, depression,* and *acceptance*.

10 Personality

OVERVIEW

Enduring Issues in Personality

Studying Personality

Psychodynamic Theories
- Sigmund Freud
- Carl Jung
- Alfred Adler
- Karen Horney
- Erik Erikson
- A Psychodynamic View of Jaylene Smith
- Evaluating Psychodynamic Theories

Humanistic Personality Theories
- Carl Rogers
- A Humanistic View of Jaylene Smith
- Evaluating Humanistic Theories

Trait Theories
- The Big Five
- A Trait View of Jaylene Smith
- Evaluating Trait Theories

Cognitive–Social Learning Theories
- Expectancies, Self-Efficacy, and Locus of Control

- A Cognitive–Social Learning View of Jaylene Smith
- Evaluating Cognitive–Social Learning Theories

Personality Assessment
- The Personal Interview
- Direct Observation
- Objective Tests
- Projective Tests

Thirty-year-old Jaylene Smith is a talented physician who meets with a psychologist because she is troubled by certain aspects of her social life. Acquaintances describe Jay in glowing terms, saying she is highly motivated, intelligent, attractive, and charming. But Jay feels terribly insecure and anxious. When the psychologist asked her to pick out some self-descriptive adjectives, she selected "introverted," "shy," "inadequate," and "unhappy."

Jay was the firstborn in a family of two boys and one girl. Her father is a quiet, gentle medical researcher. His work often allowed him to study at home, so he had extensive contact with his children when they were young. He loved all his children, but clearly favored Jay. His ambitions and goals for her were extremely high; and as she matured, he responded to her every need and demand almost immediately and with full conviction. Their relationship remains as close today as it was during Jay's childhood.

Jay's mother worked long hours away from home as a store manager and consequently saw her children primarily at night and on an occasional free weekend. When she came home, Mrs. Smith was tired and had little energy for "nonessential" interactions with her children. She had always been career oriented, but she experienced considerable conflict and frustration trying to reconcile her roles as mother, housekeeper, and financial provider. Mrs. Smith was usually amiable toward all her children but tended to argue more with Jay, until the bickering subsided when Jay was about 6 or 7 years of age. Today, their relationship is cordial but lacks the closeness apparent between Jay and Dr. Smith. Interactions between Dr. and Mrs. Smith were sometimes marred by stormy outbursts over seemingly trivial matters. These episodes were always followed by periods of mutual silence lasting for days.

Jay was very jealous of her first brother, born when she was 2 years old. Her parents recall that Jay sometimes staged temper tantrums when the new infant demanded and received a lot of attention (especially from Mrs. Smith). The temper tantrums intensified when Jay's second brother was born, just 1 year later. As time passed, the brothers formed an alliance to try to undermine Jay's supreme position with their father. Jay only became closer to her father, and her relationships with her brothers were marked by greater-than-average jealousy and rivalry from early childhood to the present.

Throughout elementary, junior high, and high school, Jay was popular and did well academically. Early on, she decided on a career in medicine. Yet, off and on between the ages of 8 and 17, she had strong feelings of loneliness, depression, insecurity, and confusion—feelings common enough during this age period, but stronger than in most youngsters and very distressing to Jay.

Jay's college days were a period of great personal growth, but several unsuccessful romantic involvements caused her much pain. The failure to achieve a stable and long-lasting relationship persisted after college and troubled Jay greatly. Although even-tempered in most circumstances, Jay often had an explosive fit of anger that ended each important romantic relationship that she had. "What is wrong with me?" she would ask herself. "Why do I find it impossible to maintain a serious relationship for any length of time?"

In medical school, her conflicts crept into her consciousness periodically: "I don't deserve to be a doctor"; "I won't pass my exams"; "Who am I, and what do I want from life?"

How can we describe and understand Jaylene Smith's personality? How did she become who she is? Why does she feel insecure and uncertain despite her obvious success? Why do her friends see her as charming and attractive, though she describes herself as introverted and inadequate? These are the kinds of questions that personality psychologists are likely to ask about Jay—and the kinds of questions we will try to answer in this chapter.

ENDURING ISSUES IN PERSONALITY ●●

As we explore the topic of personality in this chapter, the enduring issues that interest psychologists emerge at several points. The very concept of personality implies that our behavior differs in significant ways from that of other people (diversity–universality). In addition, our behavior reflects our personality as opposed to the situations in which we find ourselves (person–situation). We will also assess the extent to which personality is a result of inheritance, rather than a reflection of life experiences (nature–nurture). Finally, we will consider the extent to which personality changes as we grow older (stability–change).

Studying Personality

What do psychologists mean when they talk about personality?

Many psychologists define **personality** as an individual's unique pattern of thoughts, feelings, and behaviors that persists over time and across situations. Notice that there are two important parts to this definition. On the one hand, personality refers to *unique differences*—those aspects that distinguish a person from everyone else. On the other hand, the definition asserts that personality is relatively *stable* and *enduring*—that these unique differences persist through time and across situations. If you could view yourself at various ages in home movies or videos, you might notice that certain characteristics are always evident. Maybe you are a natural "actor," always showing off for the camera; or perhaps you are a director type who, at age 4 as well as at age 14, was telling the camera operator what to do. Because we expect people's personalities to be relatively consistent, we tend to suspect something is wrong with a person when that is not the case.

Psychologists vary in their approach to the study of personality. Some set out to identify the most important characteristics of personality, whereas others seek to understand why there are differences in personality. Among the latter group, some consider the family to be the most important factor in personality development, whereas others emphasize the importance of influences outside the family. Still others see personality as the product of how we think about ourselves and our experiences. In this chapter, we explore representative theories of these various approaches. We see how each theoretical paradigm sheds light on the personality of Jaylene Smith. Finally, we will evaluate the strengths and weaknesses of each approach and will see how psychologists go about assessing personality.

Psychodynamic Theories

What ideas do all psychodynamic theories have in common?

Psychodynamic theories see behavior as the product of internal psychological forces that often operate outside our conscious awareness. Freud drew on the physics of his day to coin the term *psychodynamics*: As thermodynamics is the study of heat and mechanical energy and the way that one may be transformed into the other, psychodynamics is the study of psychic energy and the way that it is transformed and expressed in behavior. Psychodynamic theorists disagreed among themselves about the exact nature of this psychic energy. Some, like Freud, traced it to sexual and aggressive urges; other, saw it as rooted in the individual's struggle to deal with dependency. But all psychodynamic theorists share the sense that unconscious processes primarily determine personality and can best be understood within the context of life-span development.

Some aspects of psychodynamic theory, especially Freud's views of female sexuality, are out of date. The following five propositions, however, are central to all psychodynamic theories and have withstood the tests of time (Huprich & Keaschuk, 2006; Westen, 1998):

1. Much of mental life is unconscious; as a result, people may behave in ways that they themselves do not understand.
2. Mental processes (such as emotions, motivations, and thoughts) operate in parallel and thus may lead to conflicting feelings.
3. Not only do stable personality patterns begin to form in childhood, but early experiences also strongly affect personality development.
4. Our mental representations of ourselves, of others, and of our relationships tend to guide our interactions with other people.
5. Personality development involves learning to regulate sexual and aggressive feelings as well as becoming socially interdependent rather than dependent.

personality An individual's unique pattern of thoughts, feelings, and behaviors that persists over time and across situations.

psychodynamic theories Personality theories contending that behavior results from psychological forces that interact within the individual, often outside conscious awareness.

SIGMUND FREUD

When Freud proposed that sexual instinct is the basis of behavior, how was he defining "sexual instinct?"

To this day, Sigmund Freud (1856–1939) is the best known and most influential of the psycho-dynamic theorists (Solms, 2004). As we saw in Chapter 1 "The Science of Psychology", Freud created an entirely new perspective on the study of human behavior. Up to his time, the field of psychology had focused on consciousness—that is, on those thoughts and feelings of which we are aware. In a radical departure, Freud stressed the **unconscious**—the ideas, thoughts, and feelings of which we are *not* normally aware. Freud's ideas form the basis of **psychoanalysis**, a term that refers both to his theory of personality and to the form of therapy that he invented.

According to Freud, human behavior is based on unconscious instincts, or drives. Some instincts are aggressive and destructive; others, such as hunger, thirst, self-preservation, and sex, are necessary to the survival of the individual and the species. Freud used the term *sexual instincts* to refer not just to erotic sexuality, but also to the desire for virtually any form of pleasure. In this broad sense, Freud regarded the sexual instinct as the most critical factor in the development of personality.

HOW PERSONALITY IS STRUCTURED Freud theorized that personality is formed around three structures: the *id*, the *ego*, and the *superego*. The **id** is the only structure present at birth and is completely unconscious. (See **Figure 10–1**.) Consisting of all the unconscious urges and desires that continually seek expression, it operates according to the **pleasure principle**—that is, it tries to obtain immediate pleasure and to avoid pain. As soon as an instinct arises, the id seeks to gratify it. Because the id is not in contact with the real world, however, it has only two ways of obtaining gratification. One way is by reflex actions, such as coughing, which immediately relieve unpleasant sensations. The other is through fantasy, or *wish fulfillment*: A person forms a mental image of an object or a situation that partially satisfies the instinct and relieves the uncomfortable feeling. This kind of thought occurs most often in dreams and daydreams, but it may take other forms. For instance, if someone insults you and you spend the next half hour imagining clever retorts, you are engaging in wish fulfillment.

unconscious In Freud's theory, all the ideas, thoughts, and feelings of which we are not and normally cannot become aware.

psychoanalysis The theory of personality Freud developed, as well as the form of therapy he invented.

id In Freud's theory of personality, the collection of unconscious urges and desires that continually seek expression.

pleasure principle According to Freud, the way in which the id seeks immediate gratification of an instinct.

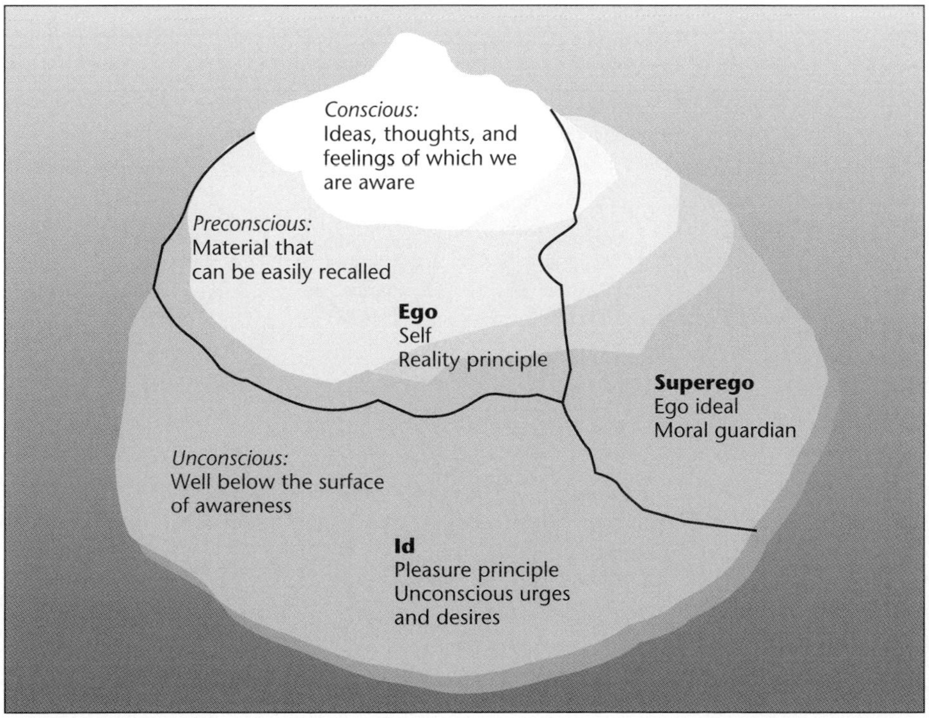

Figure 10–1

The structural relationship formed by the id, ego, and superego.
Freud's conception of personality is often de-picted as an iceberg to illustrate how the vast workings of the mind occur beneath its surface. Notice that the ego is partly conscious, partly unconscious, and partly preconscious; it derives knowledge of the external world through the senses. The superego also works at all three levels. But the id is an entirely unconscious structure.

Source: Adapted from *New Introductory Lectures on Psychoanalysis*, by Sigmund Freud, 1933, New York: Carlton House.

ego Freud's term for the part of the personality that mediates between environmental demands (reality), conscience (superego), and instinctual needs (id); now often used as a synonym for "self."

reality principle According to Freud, the way in which the ego seeks to satisfy instinctual demands safely and effectively in the real world.

superego According to Freud, the social and parental standards the individual has internalized; the conscience and the ego ideal.

ego ideal The part of the superego that consists of standards of what one would like to be.

Mental images of this kind provide fleeting relief, but they cannot fully satisfy most needs. For example, just thinking about being with someone you love is a poor substitute for actually being with that person. Therefore, the id by itself is not very effective at gratifying instincts. It must link to reality if it is to relieve its discomfort. The id's link to reality is the ego.

Freud conceived of the **ego** as the psychic mechanism that controls all thinking and reasoning activities. The ego operates partly consciously, partly *preconsciously*, and partly unconsciously. ("Preconscious" refers to material that is not currently in awareness but can easily be recalled.) The ego learns about the external world through the senses and sees to the satisfaction of the id's drives in the external world. But instead of acting according to the pleasure principle, the ego operates by the **reality principle**: By means of intelligent reasoning, the ego tries to delay satisfying the id's desires until it can do so safely and successfully. For example, if you are thirsty, your ego will attempt to determine how effectively and safely to quench your thirst. (See **Figure 10–2**.)

A personality consisting only of ego and id would be completely selfish. It would behave effectively, but unsociably. Fully adult behavior is governed not only by reality, but also by the individual's conscience or by the moral standards developed through interaction with parents and society. Freud called this moral watchdog the **superego**.

The superego is not present at birth. In fact, young children are amoral and do whatever is pleasurable. As we mature, however, we adopt as our own the judgments of our parents about what is "good" and "bad." In time, the external restraint applied by our parents gives way to our own internal self-restraint. The superego, eventually acting as our conscience, takes over the task of observing and guiding the ego, just as the parents once observed and guided the child. Like the ego, it works at the conscious, preconscious, and unconscious levels.

According to Freud, the superego also compares the ego's actions with an **ego ideal** of perfection and then rewards or punishes the ego accordingly. Unfortunately, the superego is sometimes too harsh in its judgments. An artist dominated by such a punishing superego, for example, may realize the impossibility of ever equaling Rembrandt and so give up painting in despair.

Ideally, our id, ego, and superego work in harmony, with the ego satisfying the demands of the id in a reasonable, moral manner that is approved by the superego. We are then free to love and hate and to express our emotions sensibly and without guilt. When our id is dominant, our instincts are unbridled and we are likely to endanger both ourselves

Figure 10–2

How Freud conceived the workings of the pleasure and reality principles.

Note that according to the reality principle, the ego uses rational thought to postpone the gratification of the id until its desires can be satisfied safely.

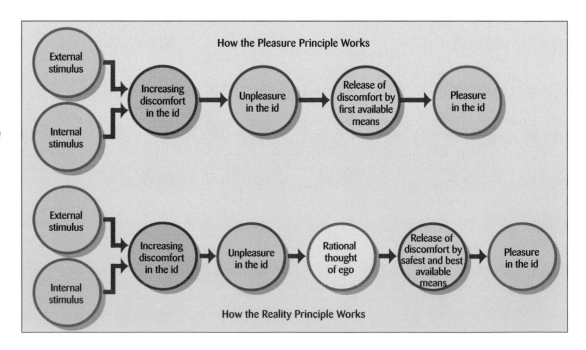

and society. When our superego dominates, our behavior is checked too tightly and we are inclined to judge ourselves too harshly or too quickly, impairing our ability to act on our own behalf and enjoy ourselves.

HOW PERSONALITY DEVELOPS Freud's theory of personality development focuses on the way in which we satisfy the sexual instinct during the course of life. Freud thought of this instinct as a craving for sensual pleasure of all kinds, calling the energy generated by the sexual instinct **libido**. As infants mature, their libido becomes focused on various sensitive parts of the body during sequential stages of development. According to Freud, children's experiences at each of these stages stamp their personality with tendencies that endure into adulthood. If a child is deprived of pleasure (or allowed too much gratification) from the part of the body that dominates a certain stage, some sexual energy may remain permanently tied to that part of the body, instead of moving on in normal sequence to give the individual a fully integrated personality. This is called **fixation** and, as we shall see, Freud believed that it leads to immature forms of sexuality and to certain characteristic personality traits. Let's look more closely at the psychosexual stages that Freud identified and their presumed relationship to personality development.

In the **oral stage** (birth to 18 months), infants, who depend completely on other people to satisfy their needs, relieve sexual tension by sucking and swallowing; when their baby teeth come in, they obtain oral pleasure from chewing and biting. According to Freud, infants who receive too much oral gratification at this stage grow into overly optimistic and dependent adults; those who receive too little may turn into pessimistic and hostile people later in life. Fixation at this stage is linked to such personality characteristics as lack of confidence, gullibility, sarcasm, and argumentativeness.

During the **anal stage** (roughly 18 months to 3½ years), the primary source of sexual pleasure shifts from the mouth to the anus. Just about the time children begin to derive pleasure from holding in and excreting feces, toilet training takes place, and they must learn to regulate this new pleasure. In Freud's view, if parents are too strict in toilet training, some children throw temper tantrums and may live in self-destructive ways as adults. Others become obstinate, stingy, and excessively orderly. If parents are too lenient, their children may become messy, unorganized, and sloppy.

When children reach the **phallic stage** (after age 3), they discover their genitals and develop a marked attachment to the parent of the opposite sex while becoming jealous of the same-sex parent. In boys, Freud called this the **Oedipus complex**, after the character in Greek mythology who killed his father and married his mother. Girls go through a corresponding **Electra complex**, involving possessive love for their father and jealousy toward their mother. Most children eventually resolve these conflicts by identifying with the parent of the same sex. However, Freud contended that fixation at this stage leads to vanity and egotism in adult life, with men boasting of their sexual prowess and treating women with contempt, and with women becoming flirtatious and promiscuous. Phallic fixation may also prompt feelings of low self-esteem, shyness, and worthlessness.

At the end of the phallic period, Freud believed, children lose interest in sexual behavior and enter a **latency period**. During this period, which begins around the age of 5 or 6 and lasts until age 12 or 13, boys play with boys, girls play with girls, and neither sex takes much interest in the other.

At puberty, the individual enters the last psychosexual stage, the **genital stage**. At this time, sexual impulses reawaken and unfulfilled desires from infancy and childhood are satisfied. Ideally, the quest for immediate gratification of these desires yields to mature sexuality, in which postponed gratification, a sense of responsibility, and caring for others all play a part.

Freud is certainly not without his critics. Feminists have assailed Freud's male-centered, phallic view of personality development, especially because he also hypothesized that all little girls feel inferior because they do not have a penis. Many people now see *penis envy* as much less central to female personality development than Freud thought (E. K. Dahl, 1996; C. Hall, 2005). In fact, the whole notion that male and female personality development proceeds along similar lines is being challenged. If this is the case, then the unique developmental tasks encountered by girls may leave them with important skills and abilities that were overlooked or minimized in Freud's theory.

libido According to Freud, the energy generated by the sexual instinct.

fixation According to Freud, a partial or complete halt at some point in the individual's psychosexual development.

oral stage First stage in Freud's theory of personality development, in which the infant's erotic feelings center on the mouth, lips, and tongue.

anal stage Second stage in Freud's theory of personality development, in which a child's erotic feelings center on the anus and on elimination.

phallic stage Third stage in Freud's theory of personality development, in which erotic feelings center on the genitals.

Oedipus complex and Electra complex According to Freud, a child's sexual attachment to the parent of the opposite sex and jealousy toward the parent of the same sex; generally occurs in the phallic stage.

latency period In Freud's theory of personality, a period in which the child appears to have no interest in the other sex; occurs after the phallic stage.

genital stage In Freud's theory of personality development, the final stage of normal adult sexual development, which is usually marked by mature sexuality.

What would Hilary Clinton and Condoleeza Rice say about the Freudian notion that penis envy is central to girls' development? These famous, well respected public figures embody the new female stereotype of the accomplished, assertive, intellectual, powerful modern woman.

Moreover, Freud's beliefs, particularly his emphasis on sexuality, were not completely endorsed even by members of his own psychoanalytic school. Carl Jung and Alfred Adler, two early associates of Freud, eventually broke with him and formulated their own psychodynamic theories of personality. Jung expanded the scope of the unconscious well beyond the selfish satisfactions of the id. Adler believed that human beings have positive—and conscious—goals that guide their behavior. Other psychodynamic theorists put greater emphasis on the ego and its attempts to gain mastery over the world. These neo-Freudians, principally Karen Horney and Erik Erikson, also focused more on the influence of social interaction on personality.

CARL JUNG

How did Carl Jung's view of the unconscious differ from that of Freud?

Carl Jung (1875–1961) agreed with many of Freud's tenets, including his emphasis on the role of the unconscious in human behavior, but he expanded the role of the unconscious. Jung contended that libido represents *all* life forces, not just the sexual ones. And where Freud viewed the id as a "cauldron of seething excitations" that the ego has to control, Jung saw the unconscious as the ego's source of strength and vitality. He also believed that the unconscious consists of the personal unconscious and the collective unconscious. The **personal unconscious** includes our repressed thoughts, forgotten experiences, and undeveloped ideas, which may enter consciousness if an incident or a sensation triggers their recall.

ENDURING ISSUES

Diversity–Universality   Universal Human Archetypes

The **collective unconscious**, Jung's most original concept, comprises memories and behavior patterns that are inherited from past generations and therefore are shared by all humans. Just as the human body is the product of millions of years of evolution, so too, according to Jung, is the human mind. Over millennia, it has developed "thought forms," or collective memories, of experiences that people have had in common since prehistoric times. He called these thought forms **archetypes**. Archetypes appear in our thoughts as mental images. Because all people have mothers, for example, the archetype of "mother" is

personal unconscious In Jung's theory of personality, one of the two levels of the unconscious; it contains the individual's repressed thoughts, forgotten experiences, and undeveloped ideas.

collective unconscious In Jung's theory of personality, the level of the unconscious that is inherited and common to all members of a species.

archetypes In Jung's theory of personality, thought forms common to all human beings, stored in the collective unconscious.

persona According to Jung, our public self, the mask we wear to represent ourselves to others.

universally associated with the image of one's own mother, with Mother Earth, and with a protective presence.

Jung felt that specific archetypes play special roles in shaping personality. The **persona** (an archetype whose meaning stems from the Latin word for "mask") is the element of our personality that we project to other people—a shell that grows around our inner self. For some people, the public self so predominates that they lose touch with their inner feelings, leading to personality maladjustments. ●●

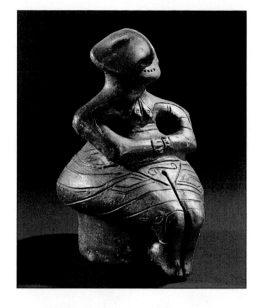

According to Carl Jung, we all inherit from our ancestors collective memories or "thought forms" that people have had in common since the dawn of human evolution. The image of a motherlike figure with protective, embracing arms is one such primordial thought form that stems from the important, nurturing role of women throughout human history. This thought form is depicted here in this Bulgarian clay figure of a goddess that dates back some six or seven thousand years.

A contemporary representation from U.S. culture of the Jungian archetype of the Wise Old Man can be seen in Albus Dumbeledore (from the movies based on J. K. Rowling's *Harry Potter* series), Yoda (from the *Star Wars* films), and Mr. Miyagi (from the *Karate Kid* movies). Although these literary and theatrical images are not universally associated with the archetype, they are one culture's way of capturing and expressing it.

extraverts According to Jung, people who usually focus on social life and the external world instead of on their internal experience.

introverts According to Jung, people who usually focus on their own thoughts and feelings.

compensation According to Adler, the person's effort to overcome imagined or real personal weaknesses.

inferiority complex In Adler's theory, the fixation on feelings of personal inferiority that results in emotional and social paralysis.

Brooke Ellison graduated with honors from Harvard despite being paralyzed from the neck down after an accident (see Chapter 1.) She illustrates what Alfred Adler referred to as *compensation*.

"I'm only a good dane."

Source: © 2000, Mike Twohy from, *www.cartoonbank. com.* All Rights Reserved.

Jung also divided people into two general attitude types—introverts and extraverts. **Extraverts** turn their attention to the external world. They are "joiners" who take an active interest in other people and in the events going on around them. **Introverts** are more caught up in their own private worlds. They tend to be unsociable and lack confidence in dealing with other people. Everyone, Jung felt, possesses some aspects of both attitude types, but one is usually dominant.

Jung further divided people into *rational individuals*, who regulate their actions by thinking and feeling, and *irrational individuals*, who base their actions on perceptions, whether through the senses (sensation) or through unconscious processes (intuition). Most people exhibit all four psychological functions: thinking, feeling, sensing, and intuiting. Jung felt, however, that one or more of these functions is usually dominant. Thus, the thinking person is rational and logical, and decides on the basis of facts. The feeling person is sensitive to his or her surroundings, acts tactfully, and has a balanced sense of values. The sensing type relies primarily on surface perceptions and rarely uses imagination or deeper understanding. And the intuitive type sees beyond obvious solutions and facts to consider future possibilities.

While Freud emphasized the primacy of the sexual instincts, Jung stressed people's rational and spiritual qualities. And while Freud considered development to be shaped in childhood, Jung thought that psychic development comes to fruition only during middle age. Jung brought a sense of historical continuity to his theories, tracing the roots of human personality back through our ancestral past; yet he also contended that a person moves constantly toward self-realization—toward blending all parts of the personality into a harmonious whole. Nonetheless, many psychologists have somewhat neglected Jung's ideas (Addison, 2005; Neher, 1996) for two reasons: first, because Jung broke with Freud, and second, because of the symbolism and mysticism that characterize his theories. Recently, however, his concept of archetypes has been "rediscovered" by those interested in the power of myth (Ellens, 2002; Nuttall, 2002).

ALFRED ADLER

What did Alfred Adler believe was the major determinant of personality?

Alfred Adler (1870–1937) disagreed sharply with Freud's concept of the conflict between the selfish id and the morality-based superego. To Adler, people possess innate positive motives and they strive for personal and social perfection. One of his earliest theories grew out of personal experience: As a child, Adler was frail and almost died of pneumonia at the age of 5. This early brush with death led him to believe that personality develops through the individual's attempt to overcome physical weaknesses, an effort he called **compensation**. The blind person (who, like 21-time Grammy Award winner Stevie Wonder, cultivates particularly acute auditory abilities) and the disabled child (who, like Brooke Ellison in Chapter 1, surmounts the disability and attains extraordinary levels of achievement) exemplify Adler's theory of compensation.

Adler later modified and broadened his views, contending that people seek to overcome *feelings* of inferiority that may or may not have a basis in reality. He thought that such feelings often spark positive development and personal growth. Still, some people become so fixated on their feelings of inferiority that they become paralyzed and develop what Adler called an **inferiority complex**.

Even later in his life, Adler again shifted his theoretical emphasis in a more positive direction when he concluded that strivings for superiority and perfection are more important to personality development than overcoming feelings of inferiority. He suggested that people strive both for personal perfection and for the perfection of the society to which they belong. In the course of doing so, they set important goals for themselves that guide their behavior.

Unlike Freud, Adler believed that individuals are not controlled by their environment; instead, he contended that we have the capacity to master our own fate. The emphasis Adler placed on positive, socially constructive goals and on striving for perfection is in marked contrast to Freud's pessimistic vision of the selfish person locked into eternal conflict with society. Because of this emphasis, Adler has been hailed by many psychologists as the father of humanistic psychology (Cain, 2002), a topic we will explore in greater depth later in this chapter.

KAREN HORNEY

What major contributions did Karen Horney make to the psychodynamic perspective?

Karen Horney (1885–1952), another psychodynamic personality theorist greatly indebted to Freud, nevertheless took issue with some of his most prominent ideas, especially his analysis of women and his emphasis on sexual instincts. Based on her experience as a practicing therapist in Germany and the United States, Horney concluded that environmental and social factors are the most important influences in shaping personality; and among these, the most pivotal are the human relationships we experience as children.

In Horney's view, Freud overemphasized the sex drive, resulting in a distorted picture of human relationships. Horney believed that sexuality does figure in the development of personality, but nonsexual factors—such as the need for a sense of basic security and the person's response to real or imagined threats—play an even larger role. For example, all people share the need to feel loved and nurtured by their parents, regardless of any sexual feelings they might have about them. Conversely, parents' protective feelings toward their children emerge not only from biological forces but also from the value that society places on the nurturance of children.

For Horney, *anxiety*—an individual's reaction to real or imagined dangers—is a powerful motivating force. Whereas Freud believed that anxiety usually emerges from sexual conflicts, Horney stressed that feelings of anxiety also originate in a variety of nonsexual contexts. In childhood, anxiety arises because children depend on adults for their very survival. Insecure about receiving continued nurturance and protection, children develop inner protections, or defenses, that provide both satisfaction and security. They experience more anxiety when those defenses are threatened.

Anxious adults, according to Horney (1937), adopt one of three coping strategies, or **neurotic trends**, that help them deal with emotional problems and ensure safety, albeit at the expense of personal independence: moving toward people (submission), moving against people (aggression), and moving away from people (detachment). Each person's characteristic reliance on one or another of these strategies is reflected in his or her patterns of behavior, or personality type. The *submissive* type is an individual who has an overriding need to give in or submit to others and feels safe only when receiving their protection and guidance. This behavior is neurotic, according to Horney, because the resultant friendliness is superficial and masks feelings of aggression and anxiety. In contrast, the *aggressive* type masks his or her submissive feelings and relates to others in a hostile and domineering manner. The aggressive type, however, is also hiding basic feelings of insecurity and anxiety. Finally, the *detached* type copes with basic anxiety by withdrawing from other people. This person seems to be saying, "If I withdraw, nothing can hurt me."

Well-adjusted people also experience anxiety and threats to their basic security, but because their childhood environment enabled them to satisfy their basic emotional needs, they were able to develop without becoming trapped in neurotic lifestyles.

Karen Horney, a psychotherapist during the first half of the 20th century, disagreed with Freud's emphasis on sexual instincts. She considered environmental and social factors, especially the relationships we have as children, to be the most important influences on personality.

ENDURING ISSUES

Stability–Change   Is Biology Destiny?

Horney's conviction that cultural forces are far more important than biological ones had a profound effect on her views of human development. For example, she believed that adults can continue to develop and change throughout life. Because biology is not destiny, adults can come to understand the source of their basic anxiety and try to eliminate neurotic

neurotic trends Horney's term for irrational strategies for coping with emotional problems and minimizing anxiety.

anxiety. Horney's belief (and that of other psychodynamic thinkers) in the possibility of change through self-understanding also relates to the mind–body question. Psychodynamic therapies, which involve delving into past experiences and hidden motives, rely on the premise that destructive thought patterns and behaviors can change through mental effort only.

Horney also opened the way to a more constructive and optimistic understanding of male and female personality. She emphasized that culture, rather than anatomy, determines many of the characteristics that differentiate women from men, and pointed out that those cultural forces can be changed. For example, if women feel dissatisfied with their gender or men are overly aggressive, the explanation is likely to be found in their social status and social roles, not in their anatomy; fortunately, social status and social roles can be changed. Indeed, she was a forerunner of contemporary thinkers, in particular feminist theorists, who believe that we can change culture and society and, in the process, transform human relationships (Gilman, 2001). ●●

ERIK ERIKSON

Erikson's theory focused less on unconscious conflict and more on what factors?

Erik Erikson (1902–1994), a psychodynamic theorist who studied with Freud in Vienna and was psychoanalyzed by Freud's daughter, Anna, took a socially oriented view of personality development. Erikson agreed with much of Freud's thinking on sexual development and the influence of libidinal needs on personality. But also important for Erikson was the quality of parent–child relationships, because the family constitutes the child's first brush with society. Only if children feel competent and valuable, in their own eyes and in society's view, will they develop a secure sense of identity. In this way, Erikson shifted the focus of Freud's personality theory to ego development. Recent studies of Erikson's concepts of identity, intimacy, and generativity have reaffirmed the importance of these central ideas to personality development (Astalis, 2005; Azarow, 2003; Weigert & Gecas, 2005).

In the previous chapter, we examined how some aspects of Erikson's theory have been incorporated in the contemporary view of human development. Presented in the following list is a brief description of Erikson's eight stages of personality development. According to Erikson, success at each stage depends on the person's adjustments in previous stages:

1. **Trust versus mistrust.** During the 1st year of life, babies are torn between trusting and not trusting their parents. If their needs are generally met, infants come to trust the environment and themselves. This process leads to faith in the predictability of the environment and optimism about the future. Frustrated infants become suspicious, fearful, and overly concerned with security.

2. **Autonomy versus shame and doubt.** During their first three years, as physical development proceeds, children gain increasing autonomy and begin to explore their surroundings. They learn to walk, hold onto things, and control their excretory functions. If the child repeatedly fails to master these skills, self-doubt may take root. One response to self-doubt is the practice of abiding compulsively by fixed routines. At the other extreme is the hostile rejection of all controls, both internal and external. If parents and other adults belittle a child's efforts, the child may also begin to feel shame and may acquire a lasting sense of inferiority.

3. **Initiative versus guilt.** Between the ages of 3 and 6, children become increasingly active, undertaking new projects, manipulating things in the environment, making plans, and conquering new challenges. Parental support and encouragement for these initiatives lead to a sense of joy in exercising initiative and taking on new challenges. However, if the child is scolded for these initiatives, strong feelings of guilt, unworthiness, and resentment may take hold and persist.

4. **Industry versus inferiority.** During the next six or seven years, children encounter a new set of expectations at home and at school. They must learn the skills needed to become well-rounded adults, including personal care, productive work, and indepen-

Erik Erikson, another psychodynamic theorist, also stressed the importance of parent–child relationships for shaping personality. His eight-stage theory of personality development is still influential today.

dent social living. If children are stifled in their efforts to become part of the adult world, they may conclude that they are inadequate, mediocre, or inferior, and may lose faith in their power to become self-sufficient.

5. **Identity versus role confusion.** At puberty, childhood ends and the responsibilities of adulthood loom just ahead. The critical problem at this stage is to find one's identity. In Erikson's view, identity is achieved by integrating a number of roles—student, sister or brother, friend, and so on—into a coherent pattern that gives the young person a sense of inner continuity or identity. Failure to forge an identity leads to role confusion and despair.

	Erikson's stages of personality development							
Stage	**1**	**2**	**3**	**4**	**5**	**6**	**7**	**8**
Oral	Basic trust vs. mistrust							
Anal		Autonomy vs. shame, doubt						
Phallic			Initiative vs. guilt					
Latency				Industry vs. inferiority				
Genital					Identity vs. role confusion			
Young adulthood						Intimacy vs. isolation		
Adulthood							Generativity vs. stagnation	
Maturity								Ego integrity vs. despair

(vertical axis label: Freud's stages of personality development)

Figure 10–3

Erikson's eight stages of personality development.

Each stage involves its own developmental crisis, whose resolution is crucial to adjustment in successive stages. The first five of the eight stages correspond to Freud's stages of personality development.

Source: Childhood and Society, by Erik H. Erikson. Copyright © 1950, 1963 by W. W. Norton & Company, Inc. Renewed © 1978, 1991 by Erik H. Erikson. Used with permission of W. W. Norton & Company, Inc.

6. **Intimacy versus isolation.** During young adulthood, men and women must resolve a critical new issue: the question of intimacy. To love someone else, Erikson argued, we must have resolved our earlier crises successfully and feel secure in our own identities. To form an intimate relationship, lovers must be trusting, autonomous, and capable of initiative, and they must exhibit other hallmarks of maturity. Failure at intimacy brings a painful sense of loneliness and the feeling of being incomplete.

7. **Generativity versus stagnation.** During middle adulthood, roughly between the ages of 25 and 60, the challenge is to remain productive and creative in all aspects of one's life. People who have successfully negotiated the six earlier stages are likely to find meaning and joy in all the major activities of life—career, family, and community. For others, life becomes a drab routine, and they feel dull and resentful.

8. **Integrity versus despair.** With the onset of old age, people must try to come to terms with their approaching death. For some, this is a period of despair at the loss of former roles, such as employee and parent. Yet, according to Erikson, this stage also represents an opportunity to attain full selfhood. By this, he meant an acceptance of one's life, a sense that it is complete and satisfactory. People who have gained full maturity by resolving the conflicts in all the earlier stages possess the integrity to face death with a minimum of fear.

Figure 10–3 shows how the first five of Erikson's eight stages of personality development correspond to Freud's stages of personality development.

A PSYCHODYNAMIC VIEW OF JAYLENE SMITH

How would a psychodynamic theorist view the personality of Jaylene Smith?

According to Freud, personality characteristics such as insecurity, introversion, and feelings of inadequacy and worthlessness often arise from fixation at the phallic stage of development. Thus, had Freud been Jaylene's therapist, he would probably have concluded that Jay has not yet effectively resolved her Electra complex. Working from this premise, he would have hypothesized that Jay's relationship with her father was either very distant and unsatisfying or unusually close and gratifying. We know, of course, that it was the latter.

In all likelihood, Freud would also have asserted that at around age 5 or 6, Jay had become aware that she could not actually marry her father and do away with her mother, as he would say she wished to do. This possibility might account for the fact that fights between Jay and her mother subsided when Jay was about 6 or 7 years of age. Moreover, we know that shortly there-after, Jay began to experience "strong feelings of loneliness, depression, insecurity, and confu-sion." Clearly, something important happened in Jay's life when she was 6 or 7.

Finally, the continued coolness of Jay's relationship with her mother and the unusual closeness with her father would probably have confirmed Freud's suspicion that Jay has still not satisfactorily resolved her Electra complex. Freud would have predicted that Jay would have problems making the progression to mature sexual relationships with other men. Jay, of course, is very much aware that she has problems relating to men, at least when these re-lationships get "serious."

And what does Erikson's theory tell us about Jaylene Smith's personality? Recall that for Erikson, one's success in dealing with later developmental crises depends on how effectively one has resolved earlier crises. Because Jay is having great difficulty in dealing with intimacy (Stage 6), he would have suggested that she is still struggling with problems from earlier de-velopmental stages. Erikson would have looked for the source of these problems in the quali-ty of Jay's relationship with others. We know that her mother subtly communicated her own frustration and dissatisfaction to her children and spent little time on "nonessential" interac-tions with them. These feelings and behavior patterns would not have instilled in a child the kind of basic trust and sense of security that Erikson believed are essential to the first stage of development. In addition, her relationship with her mother and brothers continued to be less than fully satisfactory. It is not surprising, then, that Jay had some difficulty working through subsequent developmental crises. Although she developed a close and caring relationship with her father, Jay was surely aware that his affection partly depended on her fulfilling the dreams, ambitions, and goals that he had for her.

THINKING CRITICALLY ABOUT . . .

Psychoanalysis

Freud's original theory was based on case studies of his patients; and the literature on psychoanalysis consists mainly of case studies—descriptions of individual cases of psychopathology, probable causes, and their treatment. Today, however, psychological science depends increasingly on experimental evidence and biologi-cal explanations for mental phenomena. Review the five basic concepts of psycho-dynamic theory described by Westen on page 354 and think about what kinds of evidence might convince you that they are indeed correct. What evidence would lead you to conclude that they are not in fact correct?

EVALUATING PSYCHODYNAMIC THEORIES

How do modern psychologists view the contributions and limitations of the psychodynamic perspective?

Freud's emphasis on the fact that we are not always—or even often—aware of the real causes of our behavior has fundamentally changed the way people view themselves and others. Freud's ideas have also had a lasting impact on history, literature, and the arts (Krugler, 2004). Yet, Freud was a product of his time and place. Critics who contend his theory reflects a sexist view of women have pointed out that he was apparently unable to imagine a connection between his female patients' sense of inferiority and their subor-dinate position in society. Psychodynamic views have also been criticized as lacking a scientific basis in that they are based largely on retrospective (backward-looking) ac-counts of a limited sample of individuals who have sought treatment, rather than on re-search with "healthy" individuals.

Although it is often difficult to translate psychodynamic personality theories into hy-potheses that can be tested experimentally (Cloninger, 2003; Holt, 2003), Freud's theory has received limited confirmation from research (Leichsenring, 2005). For example, people with eating disorders often have oral personalities (J. Perry, Silvera, & Rosenvinge, 2002). Orally fixated people generally eat and drink too much, tend to mention oral images when inter-preting inkblot tests, and also seem to depend heavily on others, as Freud predicted (Fisher & Greenberg, 1985). Moreover, research confirms an association between specific personality types in childhood and later development of psychological problems. For example, a child with an inhibited temperament is more likely to develop social anxiety disorder as an adult (Gladstone, Parker, Mitchell, Wilhelm, & Malhi, 2005). The effectiveness of psychoanalysis as a therapy has also been cited as evidence in support of Freud's theories (Leichsenring,

2005). Still, as we shall see in Chapter 13, "Therapies," psychoanalysis does not seem to be any more or less effective than therapies based on other theories (J. A. Carter, 2006).

Freud's theories have clearly expanded our understanding of personality, or they would not still be so vigorously debated today, more than 100 years after he proposed them. Whatever their merit as science, psychodynamic theories attempt to explain the root causes of all human behavior. The sheer magnitude of this undertaking helps to account for their lasting attractiveness.

CHECK YOUR UNDERSTANDING

Match the following Jungian terms with the appropriate definition.

1. persona
2. collective unconscious
3. archetype

a. typical mental image or mythical representation
b. memories and behavior patterns inherited from past generations
c. aspect of the personality by which one is known to other people

4. According to Alfred Adler, a person with a fixation on or belief in a negative characteristic has an _____. They may try to overcome their perceived weakness through _____.

5. Horney believed that _____ is a stronger source of emotional disturbance than sexual urges.

Answers: 1. c. 2. b. 3. a. 4. inferiority complex; compensation. 5. anxiety.

APPLY YOUR UNDERSTANDING

1. An angry parent imagines hitting a child for misbehaving, but decides instead to discuss the misbehavior with the child and to point out why the behavior was wrong. After hearing the child's explanation for the behavior, the parent feels guilty for having been so angry. The parent's anger and fantasy are the result of the _____; the decision to discuss the problem is the result of the _____, and the guilt derives from the _____.

   a. ego; superego; id
   b. id; ego; superego
   c. ego; id; superego
   d. id; superego; ego

2. John is an adolescent. According to Erikson, the major challenge he faces is _____, which will be followed in young adulthood by the crisis of _____.

   a. intimacy vs. isolation; integrity vs. despair
   b. intimacy vs. isolation; industry vs. inferiority
   c. identity vs. role confusion; intimacy vs. isolation
   d. identity vs. role confusion; integrity vs. despair
   e. identity vs. role confusion; initiative vs. guilt

Answers: 1. b. 2. c.

Humanistic Personality Theories

What are the major ways that humanistic personality theory differs from psychodynamic theories?

Freud believed that personality grows out of the resolution of unconscious conflicts and developmental crises. Many of his followers—including some who modified his theory and others who broke away from his circle—also embraced this basic viewpoint. But in the

humanistic personality theory Any personality theory that asserts the fundamental goodness of people and their striving toward higher levels of functioning.

actualizing tendency According to Rogers, the drive of every organism to fulfill its biological potential and become what it is inherently capable of becoming.

self-actualizing tendency According to Rogers, the drive of human beings to fulfill their self-concepts, or the images they have of themselves.

fully functioning person According to Rogers, an individual whose self-concept closely resembles his or her inborn capacities or potentials.

unconditional positive regard In Rogers's theory, the full acceptance and love of another person regardless of his or her behavior.

conditional positive regard In Rogers's theory, acceptance and love that are dependent on another's behaving in certain ways and on fulfilling certain conditions.

theory of Alfred Adler, we glimpsed a very different view of human nature. Adler focused on forces that contribute to positive growth and a move toward personal perfection. For these reasons, Adler is sometimes called the first *humanistic* personality theorist.

Humanistic personality theory emphasizes that we are positively motivated and progress toward higher levels of functioning—in other words, that there is more to human existence than dealing with hidden conflicts. Humanistic psychologists believe that life is a process of opening ourselves to the world around us and experiencing joy in living. They stress people's potential for growth and change as well as the ways they experience their lives right now, rather than dwelling on how they felt or acted in the past. This approach holds all of us personally responsible for our own lives. Finally, humanists also believe that given reasonable life conditions, people will develop in desirable directions (Cloninger, 2003; Criswell, 2003). Adler's concept of striving for perfection laid the groundwork for later humanistic personality theorists such as Abraham Maslow and Carl Rogers. We discussed Maslow's theory of the hierarchy of needs leading to self-actualization in Chapter 8, "Motivation and Emotion." We now turn to Rogers's theory of self-actualization.

CARL ROGERS

According to Rogers, how can thinking of yourself as self-assured help you to become so?

One of the most prominent humanistic theorists, Carl Rogers (1902–1987), contended that men and women develop their personalities in the service of positive goals. According to Rogers, every organism is born with certain innate capacities, capabilities, or potentialities— "a sort of genetic blueprint, to which substance is added as life progresses" (Maddi, 1989, p. 102). The goal of life, Rogers believed, is to fulfill this genetic blueprint, to become the best of whatever each of us is inherently capable of becoming. Rogers called this biological push toward fulfillment the **actualizing tendency**. Although Rogers maintained that the actualizing tendency characterizes all organisms—plants, animals, and humans—he noted that human beings also form images of themselves, or *self-concepts*. Just as we try to fulfill our inborn biological potential, so, too, we attempt to fulfill our self-concept, our conscious sense of who we are and what we want to do with our lives. Rogers called this striving the **self-actualizing tendency**. If you think of yourself as "intelligent" and "athletic," for example, you will strive to live up to those images of yourself.

When our self-concept is closely matched with our inborn capacities, we are likely to become what Rogers called a **fully functioning person**. Such people are self-directed: They decide for themselves what it is they wish to do and to become, even though their choices may not always be sound ones. They are not unduly swayed by other people's expectations for them. Fully functioning people are also open to experience—to their own feelings as well as to the world and other people around them—and thus find themselves "increasingly willing to be, with greater accuracy and depth, that self which [they] most truly [are]" (Rogers, 1961, pp. 175–176).

According to Rogers, people tend to become more fully functioning if they are brought up with **unconditional positive regard**, or the experience of being treated with warmth, respect, acceptance, and love regardless of their own feelings, attitudes, and behaviors.

But often parents and other adults offer children what Rogers called **conditional positive regard**: They value and accept only certain aspects of the child. The acceptance, warmth, and love that the child receives from others then depend on the child's behaving in certain ways and fulfilling certain conditions. In the process, self-concept comes to resemble the inborn capacity less and less, and the child's life deviates from the genetic blueprint.

When people lose sight of their inborn potential, they become constricted, rigid, and defensive. They feel threatened and anxious, and experience considerable discomfort and uneasiness. Because their lives are directed toward what other people want and value, they are unlikely to experience much real satisfaction in life. At some point, they may realize that they don't really know who they are or what they want.

This parent is showing warmth and love to her child. Carl Rogers believed that people become more fully functioning if parents provide *unconditional positive regard* by showing warmth, respect, love, and acceptance of all of their children's feelings, attitudes, and behaviors.

A HUMANISTIC VIEW OF JAYLENE SMITH

How would humanistic theorists view the development of Jaylene Smith's personality?

Humanistic personality theory would focus on the discrepancy between Jay's self-concept and her inborn capacities. For example, Rogers would point out that Jay is intelligent and achievement-oriented but nevertheless feels that she doesn't "deserve to be a doctor," worries about whether she will ever be "truly happy," and remembers that when she was 13, she never was able to be herself and really express her feelings, even with a good friend. Her unhappiness, fearfulness, loneliness, insecurity, and other dissatisfactions similarly stem from Jay's inability to become what she "most truly is." Rogers would suspect that other people in Jay's life made acceptance and love conditional on her living up to their ideas of what she should become. We know that for most of her life, Jay's father was her primary source of positive regard. Very possibly, he conditioned his love for Jay on her living up to his goals for her.

EVALUATING HUMANISTIC THEORIES

What have humanistic theories contributed to our understanding of personality?

The central tenet of most humanistic personality theories—that the overriding purpose of the human condition is to realize one's potential—is difficult if not impossible to verify scientifically. The resulting lack of scientific evidence and rigor is one of the major criticisms of these theories. In addition, some critics claim that humanistic theories present an overly optimistic view of human beings and fail to take into account the evil in human nature. Others contend that the humanistic view fosters self-centeredness and narcissism, and reflects Western values of individual achievement rather than universal human potential.

Nonetheless, Maslow and especially Rogers did attempt to test some aspects of their theories scientifically. For example, Rogers studied the discrepancy between the way people perceived themselves and the way they ideally wanted to be. He discovered that people whose real selves differed considerably from their *ideal* selves were more likely to be unhappy and dissatisfied.

CHECK YOUR UNDERSTANDING

Indicate whether the following are true (T) or false (F).

1. _____ Humanistic personality theory emphasizes that we are motivated by conflicts, whereas psychodynamic personality theory emphasizes positive strivings.
2. _____ The goal of life, Rogers believed, is to become the best person that we can inherently become.
3. _____ Our self-concept is our inborn biological potential.
4. _____ When people lose sight of their inborn potential, they are unlikely to experience much satisfaction.

Answers: 1. (F). 2. (T). 3. (F). 4. (T).

APPLY YOUR UNDERSTANDING

1. Barbara was brought up with unconditional positive regard. According to Rogers, she is likely to
   a. be vain and narcissistic.
   b. feel she is valued regardless of her attitudes and behavior.
   c. have self-concepts that do not correspond very closely to her inborn capacities.
   d. Both (b) and (c) are true.

2. Your friend has always known that she wants to be a doctor. When you ask her how she knows that, she says, "That's just who I am. It's what I want to do with my life." Rogers calls the push toward fulfilling this sense of who she is

  a. being fully functioning.

  b. engaging in a compensatory process.

  c. expressing a high need for achievement.

  d. the self-actualizing tendency.

Answers: 1. b. 2. d.

Trait Theories

What is the key focus of trait theories?

The personality theories that we have examined so far all emphasize early childhood experiences; and all attempt to explain the varieties of human personality. Other personality theorists focus on the present, describing the ways in which already-developed adult personalities differ from one another. These *trait theorists* assert that people differ according to the degree to which they possess certain **personality traits**, such as dependency, anxiety, aggressiveness, and sociability.

We infer a trait from how a person behaves. If someone consistently throws parties, goes to great lengths to make friends, and travels in groups, we might safely conclude that this person possesses a high degree of sociability. Our language has many words that describe personality traits. Gordon Allport, along with his colleague H. S. Odbert (1936), found nearly 18,000 dictionary entries that might refer to personality traits.

Only about 2,800 of the words on Allport and Odbert's list concern the kinds of stable or enduring characteristics that most psychologists would call personality traits; and when synonyms and near-synonyms are removed, the number of possible personality traits drops to around 200—which is still a formidable list. Psychologist Raymond Cattell (1965), using a statistical technique called **factor analysis,** found that those 200 traits tend to cluster in groups. Thus, a person who is described as persevering or determined is also likely to be thought of as responsible, ordered, attentive, and stable and probably would not be described as frivolous, neglectful, and changeable. On the basis of extensive research, Cattell originally concluded that just 16 traits account for the complexity of human personality; later he suggested that it might be necessary to add another 7 traits to the list (Cattell & Kline, 1977).

Other theorists thought that Cattell used too many traits to describe personality. Eysenck (1976) argued that personality could be reduced to three basic dimensions: *emotional stability*, *introversion–extraversion*, and *psychoticism*. According to Eysenck, *emotional stability* refers to how well a person controls emotions. On a continuum, individuals at one end of this trait would be seen as poised, calm, and composed, whereas people at the other end might be described as anxious, nervous, and excitable. *Introversion–extraversion* refers to the degree to which a person is inwardly or outwardly oriented. At one end of this dimension would be the socially outgoing, talkative, and affectionate people, known as *extraverts*. *Introverts*—generally described as reserved, silent, shy, and socially withdrawn—would be at the other extreme. Eysenck used the term *psychoticism* to describe people characterized by insensitivity and uncooperativeness at one end and warmth, tenderness, and helpfulness at the other end.

ENDURING ISSUES

Nature–Nurture   Is Personality Inherited?

For Allport, traits—or "dispositions," as he called them—are literally encoded in the nervous system as structures that guide consistent behavior across a wide variety of situations. Allport also believed that while traits describe behaviors that are common to many people, each individual personality comprises a unique constellation of traits. While few

---

personality traits Dimensions or characteristics on which people differ in distinctive ways.

factor analysis A statistical technique that identifies groups of related objects; it was used by Cattell to identify clusters of traits.

psychologists today would deny the influence of the environment in shaping personality, recent evidence substantiating the importance of genetic factors to the development of specific personality traits supports Allport's hunch that at least some personality traits are encoded biologically (Krueger & Markon, 2002). ●●

THE BIG FIVE

What five basic traits describe most differences in personality?

As listed in Table 10–1, contemporary trait theorists have boiled down personality traits to five basic dimensions: *extraversion, agreeableness, conscientiousness, emotional stability,* and *culture* (P. T. Costa & McCrae, 2006; Wiggins, 1996). There is a growing consensus today that these **Big Five** personality dimensions, also known as the *five-factor model,* capture the most salient dimensions of human personality (P. T. Costa & McCrae, 2006; De Raad, 1998; Wiggins, 1996), although there is some disagreement about whether the fifth dimension should be called "culture" or "openness to experience" or "intellect." Recently, each of the Big Five traits has been shown to have at least six *facets,* or components, as shown in Table 10–1 (Jang, Livesey, McCrae, Angleitner, & Riemann, 1998). The 30 identified facets are not an exhaustive listing of all aspects of personality; rather, they represent a broad sample of important traits (P. T. Costa & McCrae, 2006; Paunonen & Ashton, 2001).

table 10–1 THE "BIG FIVE" DIMENSIONS OF PERSONALITY	
Traits	**Facets of Each Big Five Trait**
Extraversion	Warmth, gregariousness, assertiveness, activity, excitement seeking, positive emotions
Agreeableness	Trust, straightforwardness, altruism, compliance, modesty, tender mindedness
Conscientiousness/Dependability	Competence, order, dutifulness, achievement-striving, self-discipline, deliberation
Emotional Stability	Anxiety, hostility, depression, self-consciousness, impulsiveness, vulnerability
Openness to Experience/Culture/Intellect	Fantasy, aesthetics, feelings, actions, ideas, values

Source: Adapted from Jang, K. L., Livesley, W. J., McCrae, R. R., Angleitner, A., & Riemann, R. (1998). Heritability of facet-level traits in a cross-cultural twin sample: Support for a hierarchical model of personality. *Journal of Personality and Social Psychology,* 74, 1556–1565. Table 3, p. 1560. Copyright © 1998 by the American Psychological Association. Adapted with permission.

One survey of the literature found that the Big Five dimensions of personality may have some important real-world applications—particularly as they relate to employment decisions (Bentley-Reed, 2006; Guohua & Jili. 2005). For example, one study (Conte & Gintoft, 2005) found that the dimensions of extraversion and conscientiousness were reliable predictors of performance in sales. In another study, the measures of agreeableness and emotional stability predicted performance for employees in customer service positions (McDaniel & Frei, 1994). The Big Five personality traits have also been shown to be useful in predicting the job performance of police officers (Schneider, 2002). In addition, research has shown that absenteeism in the workplace is related to the conscientiousness, extraversion, and neuroticism scales (Conte & Jacobs, 2003). Thus, the Big Five dimensions of personality show promise as reliable predictors of job performance, especially when other criteria (such as technical skills and experience) are also considered (Conte & Gintoft, 2005; Hogan, Hogan, & Roberts, 1996).

The Big Five personality traits have also proved useful in describing and predicting behavior across a wide range of age groups and social settings. For instance, one nine-year longitudinal study of grade-school children demonstrated the validity and consistency of the Big Five personality traits throughout childhood (Asendorpf & Van-Aken, 2003). In another study, the Big Five reliably predicted alcohol consumption and grade point average among college students (Paunonen, 2003).

ARE THE BIG FIVE PERSONALITY TRAITS UNIVERSAL?

Most studies of the Big Five have been conducted in the United States. Would the same five personality dimensions be evident in other cultures? The answer appears to be yes. P. T. Costa and McCrae (1992) developed a test to measure the Big Five personality dimensions that has since been translated into numerous languages including German, Portuguese, Hebrew, Chinese, Korean, and Japanese.

Source: © Tee and Charles Addams Foundation

Big Five Five traits or basic dimensions currently considered to be of central importance in describing personality.

This person would probably rate high on the Big Five trait of extraversion. Researchers have found that the Big Five can be used to describe the personalities of people in many parts of the world.

McCrae and Costa (1997) then compared the results from the various questionnaires in an effort to determine whether the same Big Five personality dimensions would emerge. The results from the six foreign cultures were virtually identical to the data from American samples: The Big Five personality dimensions were clearly evident. As the authors noted, "The structure found in American volunteers was replicated in Japanese undergraduates and Israeli job applicants. A model of personality rooted in English-language trait adjectives could be meaningfully applied not only in a closely related language like German, but also in such utterly distinct languages as Chinese and Korean" (p. 514). Other researchers have reached the same conclusions using quite different techniques (Salgado, Moscoso & Lado, 2003; J. E. Williams, Satterwhite, & Saiz, 1998).

Surprisingly, many of these same personality traits apparently exist in a number of species besides humans. Studies have found that the Big Five, with the two added factors of dominance and activity, could be used to rate and describe personality characteristics in species including gorillas, chimpanzees, rhesus and vervet monkeys, hyenas, dogs, cats, and pigs (Gosling & John, 1999; King, Weiss, & Farmer, 2005)! These data clearly suggest that there is some kind of common genetic basis for the Big Five personality traits that cuts across cultures and species (see "On the Cutting Edge: The Genetic Basis of Personality Traits").

ON THE CUTTING EDGE

THE GENETIC BASIS OF PERSONALITY TRAITS

Recent evidence shows that not only the Big Five but also many of their individual facets are strongly influenced by heredity (W. Johnson, & Krueger, 2004; Livesley, Jang, & Vernon, 2003). Although some early theorists (Eysenck, 1947) suggested that physiological mechanisms underlie basic personality traits, only recently has solid evidence from twin studies begun to support this idea (Luciano, Wainwright, Wright, & Martin, 2006; Jang, Livesley, McCrae, Angleitner, & Riemann, 1998; Lensvelt-Mulders & Hettema, 2001; Plomin, 1994).

Behavior genetic studies rely strongly on twin studies to tease apart the relative contribution of heredity and environment. For example, Jang and colleagues (1998, 2002) tested almost 1,000 sets of twins from Germany and Canada on the 30 facets of the Big Five. They concluded that genetic effects accounted for a substantial portion of the differences between people's scores on 26 of the 30 facet scales. In addition, the genetic and environmental influences were similar for the Canadian and German samples. In other words, genes seem to affect personality, and they seem to do so to the same extent in at least two different cultures.

Other investigators have had similar results. In a twin study, researchers found that the Big Five dimensions are all substantially *heritable,* and to an equal degree (Loehlin, McCrae, Costa, & John, 1998). Another group found the following estimates of heritability for the Big Five traits: neuroticism, 41%; extraversion, 53%; openness, 61%; agreeableness, 41%; and conscientiousness, 44% (Jang, Livesley, & Vernon, 1996).

Researchers have also confirmed that genetic factors play a significant role in shaping abnormal and dysfunctional personality traits. In one study comparing 128 pairs of identical and fraternal twins on both normal and abnormal personality traits, the influence of genetic factors was found to slightly outweigh the influence of the environment. In addition, the pattern of genetic and environmental influence was similar for both the abnormal traits and the normal ones (Markon, Krueger, Bouchard, & Gottesman, 2002). Other studies have confirmed that genetic factors also contribute to the personality traits that predispose individuals toward alcohol abuse (Mustanski, Viken, Kaprio, & Rose, 2003), eating disorders (Klump, McGue, & Iacono, 2002), depression,

marijuana dependence, and antisocial personality disorder (Fu et al, 2002).

What are the implications of these findings? There are several, although it is important to keep in mind that saying a particular trait such as extraversion has a genetic component does *not* mean that researchers have found a *gene* for extraversion. Nor are they likely to, because genes represent a code for specific proteins, not complex personality traits. It does mean, however, that the Big Five traits and their facets may be hardwired into the human species rather than being cultural artifacts. It also most likely means that complex traits such as extraversion are influenced by many different genes, not just one. That would explain why individual traits are normally distributed throughout the population, such as the physical traits of eye color or hair type, instead of forming distinct types. Many genes—perhaps thousands of them—surely work in combination to account for such complex traits. Though the precise role that genes play in personality is still far from clear, most psychologists would agree that biological factors contribute significantly to the development of most personality traits (Livesley et al., 2003).

A TRAIT VIEW OF JAYLENE SMITH

How would trait theorists describe Jaylene Smith's personality?

A psychologist working from the trait perspective would infer certain traits from Jay's behavior. Since Jay chose at an early age to become a doctor, did well academically year after year, and graduated first in her medical-school class, it seems reasonable to infer a trait of determination or persistence to account for her behavior. Taking the Big Five perspective, it seems that Jaylene's personality is high in conscientiousness but perhaps low in emotional stability and extraversion. These relatively few traits account for a great deal of Jay's behavior, and they also provide a thumbnail sketch of what Jay is like.

THINKING CRITICALLY ABOUT . . .

Cultural Universals

Is it fair to conclude that the Big Five are in fact universal traits? To answer this question, think about the following questions:

- What types of cultures have so far been studied? What do all of these cultures have in common? What types of cultures have not been studied?

- How would researchers determine whether the Big Five traits are in fact the most important ones in the cultures they have studied? Might other, equally important, traits not be measured? Did the researchers explore what personality traits are important in various cultures or simply confirm that people in a variety of cultures recognize the Big Five traits?

- What do we have to know in order to say that something is universal?

EVALUATING TRAIT THEORIES

What major contributions have trait theories made to our understanding of personality?

Traits are the language that we commonly use to describe other people, such as when we say someone is shy or insecure or arrogant. Thus, the trait view of personality has considerable common-sense appeal. Moreover, it is scientifically easier to study personality traits than to study such things as self-actualization and unconscious motives. But trait theories have several shortcomings (P. T. Costa & McCrae, 2006; Maher & Gottesman, 2005). First, they are primarily descriptive: They seek to describe the basic dimensions of personality, but they generally do not try to explain causes (Funder, 1995). As you can see from the trait view of Jaylene Smith, trait theory tells us little about why she is the way she is.

In addition, some critics argue that it is dangerous to reduce human complexity to just a few traits (Mischel & Shoda, 1995). Moreover, although the Big Five model is well supported by research, some disagreement remains among psychologists about whether a five-factor model is the best way to describe the basic traits of personality (De Raad, 2000; Lubinski, 2000; Mershon & Gorsuch, 1988).

 ENDURING ISSUES

Stability–Change   How Stable is Personality Over Time?

Some psychologists question whether traits describe and predict behavior very well over time. Are "agreeable" people at age 20 still agreeable at age 60? As we saw in Chapter 9, "Life-Span Development," numerous research studies have shown that temperament remains quite stable over time. Similarly, the Big Five dimensions of personality show considerable stability during early childhood and appear to be "essentially fixed by age 30" (McCrae & Costa, 1994, p. 173; Asendorpf & Van-Aken, 2003). Though to some extent adults can vary their behavior to fit the situations in which they find themselves, in general it seems that when it comes to personality traits, "You can't teach old dogs new tricks." ●●

The issue of consistency in human behavior has long intrigued personality theorists who are interested in the interaction of personality traits with social environment. In their view, behavior is a product of the person *and* the situation (Mischel, Shoda, & Mendoza-Denton, 2002). That interaction, the blending of the self and the social, is the focus of cognitive–social learning theorists, whom we will consider next.

CHECK YOUR UNDERSTANDING

1. Eysenck stated that personality could be reduced to three basic dimensions: _____, _____ and _____.

2. There is evidence that suggests that personality is almost entirely due to environmental factors. Is this statement true (T) or false (F)?

Answers: 1. emotional stability, introversion–extraversion, psychoticism. 2. F.

APPLY YOUR UNDERSTANDING

1. Peter is competent, self-disciplined, responsible, and well organized. In terms of the Big Five model of personality, he is high in
   a. agreeableness.
   b. conscientiousness.
   c. emotional stability.
   d. intellect.

2. Sherry is warm, assertive, energetic, and enthusiastic. According to the Big Five model of personality, she is high in
   a. extraversion.
   b. agreeableness.
   c. emotional stability.
   d. openness to experience.

Answers: 1. b. 2. a.

Cognitive–Social Learning Theories

How do personal and situational factors combine to shape behavior?

In contrast to personality trait theories, **cognitive–social learning theories** hold that people internally organize their expectancies and values to guide their own behavior. This set of personal standards is unique to each one of us, growing out of our own life history. Our behavior is the product of the interaction of cognitions (how we think about a situation and how we view our behavior in that situation), learning and past experiences (including reinforcement, punishment, and modeling), and the immediate environment.

EXPECTANCIES, SELF-EFFICACY, AND LOCUS OF CONTROL

How does locus of control affect self-efficacy?

Albert Bandura (1977, 1986, 1997) asserts that people evaluate a situation according to certain internal **expectancies**, such as personal preferences, and this evaluation affects their behavior. Environmental feedback that follows the actual behavior, in turn, influences future expectancies. These experience-based expectancies lead people to conduct themselves according to unique **performance standards**, individually determined measures of excellence by which they judge their own behavior. Those who succeed in meeting their own internal performance standards develop an attitude that Bandura calls **self-efficacy** (Bandura & Locke, 2003). For example, two young women trying a video game for the first time may experience the situation quite differently, even if their scores are similarly low. One with a high sense of self-efficacy may find the experience fun and be eager to gain the skills necessary to go on to the next level, whereas the one with a lower sense of self-efficacy may

cognitive–social learning theories Personality theories that view behavior as the product of the interaction of cognitions, learning and past experiences, and the immediate environment.

expectancies In Bandura's view, what a person anticipates in a situation or as a result of behaving in certain ways.

performance standards In Bandura's theory, standards that people develop to rate the adequacy of their own behavior in a variety of situations.

self-efficacy According to Bandura, the expectancy that one's efforts will be successful.

be disheartened by getting a low score, assume she will never be any good at video games, and never play again. Similarly, a person with high self-efficacy who interprets math problems as opportunities to succeed will approach the math SAT with a different expectancy than someone who sees math problems as opportunities to fail.

In our example, the two young women approach the experience with different expectancies. To Rotter (1954), **locus of control** is a prevalent expectancy, or cognitive strategy, by which people evaluate situations. People with an *internal locus* of control are convinced they can control their own fate. They believe that through hard work, skill, and training, they can find reinforcements and avoid punishments. People with an *external locus* of control do not believe they control their fate. Instead, they are convinced that chance, luck, and the behavior of others determine their destiny and that they are helpless to change the course of their lives.

Both Bandura and Rotter have tried to combine personal variables (such as expectancies) with situational variables in an effort to understand the complexities of human behavior. Both theorists believe that expectancies become part of a person's *explanatory style*, which, in turn, greatly influences behavior. Explanatory style, for example, separates optimists from pessimists. It is what causes two beginners who get the same score on a video game to respond so differently.

General expectancies or explanatory styles, such as optimism or pessimism, can have a significant effect on behavior. As studies have shown, a pessimistic explanatory style negatively impacts physical health, academic and career achievement and many aspects of mental health including depression and anxiety disorders. Conversely, having a positive explanatory style appears to serve as a "protective factor" enhancing an individual's experience of well-being (Bennett & Elliott, 2005; Wise & Rosqvist, 2006).

In a now-famous study, researchers tracked 99 students from the Harvard graduation classes of 1939 to 1944. The men were interviewed about their experiences and underwent physical checkups every five years. When researchers analyzed the men's interviews for signs of pessimism or optimism, they found that the explanatory style demonstrated in those interviews predicted the state of an individual's health decades later. Those men who were optimists at age 25 tended to be healthier at age 65, whereas the health of the pessimists had begun to deteriorate at about age 45 (C. Peterson, Vaillant, & Seligman, 1988). Although the reasons for these findings are not yet clear, a separate investigation that used a checklist about health habits found that the pessimists in this study were less careful about their health than were optimists. They tended to smoke and drink more and reported twice as many colds and visits to doctors. Another study looked at insurance agents in their first two years on the job (Seligman & Schulman, 1986). Explanatory style predicted which agents would become excellent agents and which would quit the company (three-fourths of all agents quit within three years). Optimists sold 37% more insurance than pessimists in the first two years and persisted through the difficulties of the job.

HOW CONSISTENT ARE WE? We have seen that trait theorists tend to believe that behavior is relatively consistent across situations. "Agreeable" people tend to be agreeable in most situations all the time. In contrast, cognitive–social learning theorists view personality as the relatively stable cognitive processes that underlie behavior that is a product of the person and the situation: At any time, our actions are influenced by the people around us, and by the way we think we are supposed to behave in a given situation. According to this latter view, although underlying personality is relatively stable, behavior is likely to be more inconsistent than consistent from one situation to another.

If behavior is relatively inconsistent across situations, why does it *appear* to be more consistent than it actually is? Why is the trait view of personality so compelling? One explanation is that, since we see a person only in those situations that tend to elicit the same behavior, we tend to assume that they are consistent across a wide range of situations. Moreover, there is considerable evidence that people need to find consistency and stability even in the face of inconsistency and unpredictability. We therefore see consistency in the behavior of others even when there is none (Mischel, 2003; Mischel & Shoda, 1995).

According to cognitive–social learning theorists, people who meet their own internal standards of performance develop a sense of self-efficacy, a confidence that they can meet their goals.

locus of control According to Rotter, an expectancy about whether reinforcement is under internal or external control.

A COGNITIVE–SOCIAL LEARNING VIEW OF JAYLENE SMITH

How would cognitive–social learning theorists describe the factors that shaped Jaylene Smith's personality?

Jaylene may have *learned* to be shy and introverted because she was rewarded for spending much time by herself studying. Her father probably encouraged her devotion to her studies; certainly she earned the respect of her teachers. Moreover, long hours of studying helped her to avoid the discomfort that she felt being around other people for long periods. Reinforcement may also have shaped Jay's self-discipline and her need to achieve academically.

In addition, at least some aspects of Jaylene's personality were formed by watching her parents and brothers and by learning subtle lessons from these family interactions. Her aggressive behavior with boyfriends, for example, may have grown out of seeing her parents fight. As a young child, she may have observed that some people deal with conflict by means of outbursts. Moreover, as Bandura's concept of self-efficacy would predict, Jay surely noticed that her father, a successful medical researcher, enjoyed and prospered in both his career and his family life, whereas her mother's two jobs as homemaker and store manager left her frustrated and tired. This contrast may have contributed to Jay's interest in medicine and to mixed feelings about establishing a close relationship that might lead to marriage.

EVALUATING COGNITIVE–SOCIAL LEARNING THEORIES

What contributions have cognitive–social learning theories made to our understanding of personality, and what are their limitations?

Cognitive–social learning theories of personality seem to have great potential. They put mental processes back at the center of personality, and they focus on conscious behavior and experience. We can define and scientifically study the key concepts of these theories, such as self-efficacy and locus of control; that is not true of the key concepts of psychodynamic and humanistic theories. Moreover, cognitive–social learning theories help explain why people behave inconsistently, an area in which trait approaches fall short. Cognitive–social learning theories of personality have also spawned useful therapies that help people recognize and change a negative sense of self-efficacy or explanatory style. In particular, as we will see in Chapter 13, "Therapies," these therapies have helped people overcome depression. Self-efficacy theory has also been embraced by management theorists because of its practical implications for work performance. Many studies, conducted over more than 20 years, have shown a positive correlation between self-efficacy and performance in workplaces, schools, and clinical settings.

It is still too early to say how well cognitive–social learning theories account for the complexity of human personality. Some critics point out that hindsight allows us to explain any behavior as the product of certain cognitions, but that doesn't mean those cognitions were the *causes*—or at least the sole causes—of the behavior. Just as psychologists disagree on their views of personality, psychologists also disagree on the best way to measure or assess personality, the topic we turn to next.

CHECK YOUR UNDERSTANDING

1. In Bandura's view, the belief that people can control their own fate is known as _____-_____.

2. According to cognitive–social learning theorists, _____ _____ is what separates optimists from pessimists.

Answers: 1. self-efficacy. 2. explanatory style.

APPLY YOUR UNDERSTANDING

1. Rey Ramos grew up in the South Bronx, an urban ghetto where young males are more likely to go to jail than they are to graduate from high school. He said, "My father always said you can't change anything; destiny has everything written for you. But, I rebelled against that, and I told him I was going to make my own destiny." According to cognitive–social learning theories of personality, which of the following is most descriptive of Rey?

   a. He has an internal locus of control.
   b. He has a low sense of self-efficacy.
   c. He is compensating for feelings of inferiority.
   d. He has an external locus of control.

2. You introduce a friend to a new video game. On her first try, she doesn't do well but she says, "This is fun. I have to climb that ladder more quickly to escape the bombs. Let me try again!" According to Bandura, her optimism reflects

   a. positive internal expectancies.
   b. environmental feedback.
   c. external locus of control.
   d. a low sense of self-efficacy.

Answers: 1. a. 2. a.

Personality Assessment

How do psychologists measure personality?

In some ways, testing personality is much like testing intelligence. In both cases, we are trying to measure something intangible and invisible. And in both cases, a "good test" is one that is both *reliable* and *valid*: It gives dependable and consistent results, and it measures what it claims to measure. (See Chapter 7, "Cognition and Mental Abilities.") But there are special difficulties in measuring personality.

Because personality reflects *characteristic* behavior, we are not interested in someone's *best* behavior. We are interested in *typical* behavior—how a person usually behaves in ordinary situations. Further complicating the measurement process, such factors as fatigue, a desire to impress the examiner, and fear of being tested can profoundly affect a person's behavior in a personality-assessment situation. For the intricate task of measuring personality, psychologists use four basic tools: the personal interview, direct observation of behavior, objective tests, and projective tests. The tools most closely associated with each of the major theories of personality are shown in the "Summary Table: Theories of Personality" and are discussed next.

SUMMARY TABLE

THEORIES OF PERSONALITY

Theory	Roots of Personality	Methods of Assessing
Psychodynamic	Unconscious thoughts, feelings, motives, and conflicts; repressed problems from early childhood.	Projective tests, personal interviews.
Humanistic	A drive toward personal growth and higher levels of functioning.	Objective tests, personal interviews.
Trait	Relatively permanent dispositions within the individual that cause the person to think, feel, and act in characteristic ways.	Objective tests.
Social Learning	Determined by past reinforcement and punishment as well as by observing what happens to other people.	Interviews, objective tests, observations.

THE PERSONAL INTERVIEW

What are the purposes of structured and unstructured interviews?

An interview is a conversation with a purpose: to obtain information from the person being interviewed. Interviews are often used in clinical settings to learn, for example, why someone is seeking treatment and to help diagnose the person's problem. Such interviews are generally *unstructured*—that is, the interviewer asks the client questions about any issues that arise and asks follow-up questions whenever appropriate. The interviewer may also pay attention to the person's manner of speaking, poise, or tenseness when certain topics are raised. The most effective interviewers are warm, interested in what the respondent has to say, calm, relaxed, and confident (Feshbach & Weiner, 1982; Fowler & Perry, 2005).

When conducting systematic research on personality, investigators more often rely on the *structured* interview (van-Iddekinge, Raymark, Eidson, & Attenweiler, 2004). In these interviews, the order and content of the questions are fixed; and the interviewer adheres to the set format. Although less personal, this kind of interview allows the interviewer to obtain comparable information from everyone interviewed. Generally speaking, structured interviews elicit information about sensitive topics that might not come up in an unstructured interview.

DIRECT OBSERVATION

What are the advantages and limits of the observational method?

Another way to find out how a person usually behaves is to observe that person's actions in everyday situations over a long period. Behaviorists and social learning theorists prefer this method of assessing personality because it allows them to see how situation and environment influence behavior and to note a range of behaviors.

In *direct observation*, observers watch people's behavior firsthand. Systematic observation allows psychologists to look at aspects of personality (e.g., traits, moods, or motives) as they are expressed in real life (Ozer & Reise, 1994). Ideally, the observers' unbiased accounts of the subjects' behavior paint an accurate picture of that behavior, but an observer runs the risk of misinterpreting the true meaning of an act. For example, the observer may think that children are being hostile when they are merely protecting themselves from the class bully. An expensive and time-consuming method of research, direct observation may also yield faulty results if, as noted earlier, the presence of the observer affects people's behavior.

OBJECTIVE TESTS

Why are objective tests preferred by trait theorists?

To avoid depending on the skills of an interviewer or the interpretive abilities of an observer in assessing personality, psychologists devised **objective tests**, or personality inventories. Generally, these are written tests that are administered and scored according to a standard procedure. The tests are usually constructed so that the person merely chooses a "yes" or "no" response, or selects one answer among many choices. Objective tests are the most widely used tools for assessing personality, but they have two serious drawbacks. First, they rely entirely on self-report. If people do not know themselves well, cannot be entirely objective about themselves, or want to paint a particular picture of themselves, self-report questionnaire results have limited usefulness (Bagby & Marshall, 2005; Marshall, De Fruyt, Rolland, & Bagby, 2005). In fact, some research indicates that peers who know you well often do a better job characterizing you than you do yourself (Funder, 1995). Second, if people have previously taken personality questionnaires, their familiarity with the test format may affect their responses to it. This is a particular problem with college students, who are likely to participate in many research studies that rely on personality inventories (Council, 1993). (See "Applying Psychology: Evaluating Your Personality.")

objective tests Personality tests that are administered and scored in a standard way.

APPLYING PSYCHOLOGY

EVALUATING YOUR PERSONALITY

The following scales provide a way for you to assess your own personality on the Big Five personality traits. It will examine the extent to which others agree with your assessment, the extent to which your behavior is consistent across a range of situations, and the extent to which your personality has been stable over time. The adjectives correspond to the six facets for each of the Big Five traits. (See **Table 10–1**.)

For each of the adjectives, indicate the extent to which you think it applies to you. If you write your answers on a separate sheet of paper, you can then ask others to do the same and compare their answers to your own. Friends, close relatives, and others who know you well are likely to provide the most useful information. You also might try to get ratings from people who see you in different situations—perhaps some people who see you only in class, some who see you only in informal social situations, and others who have known you for a very long time in a wide variety of situations. That will give you an opportunity to see the extent to which different situations cause you to behave in different ways; in turn, this could lead others, who see you only in those situations, to conclude that your *personality* is different than perhaps it really is.

You might also fill out the form, or have others fill it out, as you were in the past, and compare that with how you are today. It would be interesting to speculate on the reasons for any significant changes over time.

Use the following scales to rate yourself on each adjective:

1: Very true of me
2: Often true of me
3: Sometimes true of me
4: Seldom true of me
5: Almost never true of me

Extraversion

Outgoing	1	2	3	4	5
Sociable	1	2	3	4	5
Forceful	1	2	3	4	5
Energetic	1	2	3	4	5
Adventurous	1	2	3	4	5
Enthusiastic	1	2	3	4	5

Agreeableness

Forgiving	1	2	3	4	5
Not demanding	1	2	3	4	5
Warm	1	2	3	4	5
Not stubborn	1	2	3	4	5
Modest	1	2	3	4	5
Sympathetic	1	2	3	4	5

Conscientiousness

Efficient	1	2	3	4	5
Organized	1	2	3	4	5
Responsible	1	2	3	4	5
Thorough	1	2	3	4	5
Self-disciplined	1	2	3	4	5
Deliberate	1	2	3	4	5

Emotional Stability

Tense	1	2	3	4	5
Irritable	1	2	3	4	5
Depressed	1	2	3	4	5
Self-conscious	1	2	3	4	5
Moody	1	2	3	4	5
Not self-confident	1	2	3	4	5

Openness

Curious	1	2	3	4	5
Imaginative	1	2	3	4	5
Artistic	1	2	3	4	5
Wide interests	1	2	3	4	5
Excitable	1	2	3	4	5
Unconventional	1	2	3	4	5

Because of their interest in accurately measuring personality traits, trait theorists favor objective tests. Cattell, for example, developed a 374-question personality test called the **Sixteen Personality Factor Questionnaire**. As to be expected, the 16PF (as it is usually called) provides scores on each of the 16 traits originally identified by Cattell. More recently, objective tests such as the **NEO-PI-R** have been developed to assess the Big Five major personality traits (P. T. Costa & McCrae, 2006). The NEO-PI-R divides each of the Big Five traits into six facets and yields scores for each facet and each trait. For each of over 200 questions, the test taker indicates to what degree he or she disagrees with the statement made. The primary use of the test is to assess the personality of a normal adult, although recent studies suggest it may also prove useful in some clinical settings (Sanderson & Clarkin, 2002).

The most widely used and thoroughly researched objective personality test, however, is the **Minnesota Multiphasic Personality Inventory (MMPI-2)** (Dorfman & Leonard, 2001). Originally developed as an aid in diagnosing psychiatric disorders, the MMPI-2 remains in use as a means of effectively distinguishing among the varied types (Egger, Delsing, & DeMey, 2003) and detecting *malingering*, or faking a psychiatric disorder (Kucharski, Johnsen, & Procell, 2004). Respondents are asked to answer "true," "false," or "cannot say" to such questions as "Once in a while I put off until tomorrow what I ought to do today,"

Sixteen Personality Factor Questionnaire Objective personality test created by Cattell that provides scores on the 16 traits he identified.

NEO-PI-R An objective personality test designed to assess the Big Five personality traits.

Minnesota Multiphasic Personality Inventory (MMPI-2) The most widely used objective personality test, originally intended for psychiatric diagnosis.

table 10–2		THE 10 CLINICAL SCALES OF THE MMPI-2
Clinical Scale	**Symbol**	**Description**
Hypochondriasis	Hs	Excessive concern with physical health and bodily function, somatic complaints, chronic weakness
Depression	D	Unhappiness, loss of energy, pessimism, lack of self-confidence, hopelessness, feeling of futility
Hysteria	Hy	Reacts to stress with physical symptoms such as blindness or paralysis; lacks insights about motives and feelings
Psychopathic Deviation	Pd	Disregard for rules, laws, ethics, and moral conduct; impulsiveness, rebellious toward authority figures, may engage in lying, stealing and cheating
Masculinity-Femininity	Mf	Adherence to nontraditional gender traits, or rejection of the typical gender role
Paranoia	Pa	Suspiciousness, particularly in the area of interpersonal relations, guarded, moralistic, and rigid; overly responsive to criticism
Psychasthenia	Pt	Obsessiveness and compulsiveness, unreasonable fears, anxious, tense, and high-strung
Schizophrenia	Sc	Detachment from reality, often accompanied by hallucinations, delusions, and bizarre thought processes; often confused, disorganized
Hypomania	Ma	Elevated mood, accelerated speech, flight of ideas, overactivity, energetic, and talkative
Social Introversion	Si	Shy, insecure, and uncomfortable in social situations; timid, reserved, often described by others as cold and distant

"At times I feel like swearing," and "There are people who are trying to steal my thoughts and ideas." Some of the items repeat very similar thoughts in different words: For example, "I tire easily" and "I feel weak all over much of the time." This redundancy provides a check on the possibility of false or inconsistent answers.

Researchers have derived several personality scales from this test, including ratings for masculinity–femininity, depression, and hypochondriasis. These elements of the MMPI-2 are highly regarded as useful tools for differentiating among psychiatric populations (Anastasi & Urbina, 1997). The MMPI-2 is also used to differentiate among more normal personality dimensions, such as extraversion–introversion and assertiveness, but with less success.

PROJECTIVE TESTS

What do projective tests try to measure?

projective tests Personality tests, such as the Rorschach inkblot test, consisting of ambiguous or unstructured material.

Owing to their belief that people are often unaware of the determinants of their behavior, psychodynamic theorists tend to discount self-report–based objective personality tests. Instead, they prefer **projective tests** of personality. Most projective tests consist of simple ambiguous stimuli that can elicit an unlimited number of responses. After looking at an essentially meaningless graphic image or at a vague picture, the test taker explains what the material means. Alternatively, the person may be asked to complete a sentence fragment, such as "When I see myself in the mirror, I . . ." The tests offer no clues regarding the "best way" to interpret the material or to complete the sentence.

Projective tests have several advantages. Because they are flexible and can even be treated as games or puzzles, people can take them in a relaxed atmosphere, without the tension and

THINKING CRITICALLY ABOUT . . .

Projective Tests

Critics of projective tests say that it is the clinician whose personality is actually revealed by the tests, because the clinician's report is itself an interpretation of an ambiguous stimulus (the client's verbal response).

1. Do you agree or disagree? Why?

2. How might this potential source of error be reduced?

3. What are the real or potential advantages to using projective tests?

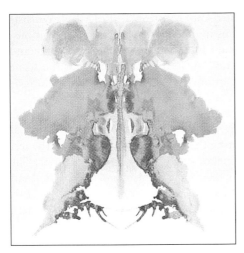

Figure 10–4
Inkblots used in the Rorschach projective test.

self-consciousness that sometimes accompany objective tests. Often, the patient doesn't even know the true purpose of the test, so responses are less likely to be faked. Some psychologists believe that the projective test can uncover unconscious thoughts and fantasies, such as latent sexual or family problems. In any event, the accuracy and usefulness of projective tests depend largely on the skill of the examiner in eliciting and interpreting responses.

The **Rorschach test** is the best known and one of the most frequently used projective personality tests (Weiner, 2006). It is named for Hermann Rorschach, a Swiss psychiatrist who in 1921 published the results of his research on interpreting inkblots as a key to personality. (See **Figure 10–4**.) Each inkblot design is printed on a separate card and is unique in form, color, shading, and white space. People are asked to specify what they see in each blot. Test instructions are minimal, so people's responses will be completely their own. After interpreting all the blots, the person goes over the cards again with the examiner and explains which part of each blot prompted each response. There are different methods of interpreting a person's responses to the blots on the Rorschach test, some of which produce more valid results than others (Exner, 1996; Masling, 2002; Viglione & Taylor, 2003). The MMPI-2 appears to be more valid than the Rorschach (Garb, Florio, & Grove, 1998).

Rorschach test A projective test composed of ambiguous inkblots; the way people interpret the blots is thought to reveal aspects of their personality.

Figure 10–5
A sample item from the Thematic Apperception Test (TAT).
In the photo, the person is making up a story to explain the scene in the painting. The examiner then interprets and evaluates the person's story for what it reveals about her personality.

Source: Reprinted by permission of the publishers from Henry A. Murray, *Thematic Apperception Test*, Plate 12F, Cambridge, Mass.: Harvard University Press, Copyright © 1943 by the President and Fellows of Harvard College, © 1971 by Henry A. Murray.

Thematic Apperception Test (TAT)
A projective test composed of ambiguous pictures about which a person is asked to write a complete story.

Somewhat more demanding is the **Thematic Apperception Test (TAT)**. It consists of 20 cards picturing one or more human figures in deliberately ambiguous situations. (See Figure 10–5; W. G. Morgan, 2002.) A person is shown the cards one by one and asked to write a complete story about each picture, including what led up to the scene depicted, what the characters are doing at that moment, what their thoughts and feelings are, and what the outcome will be.

Although various scoring systems have been devised for the TAT (Aranow, Weiss, & Rezikoff, 2001), examiners usually interpret the stories in the light of their personal knowledge of the storyteller. One key in evaluating the TAT is determining who the test taker identifies with—the story's hero or heroine, or one of the minor characters. The examiner then determines what the attitudes and feelings of the character reveal about the storyteller. The examiner also assesses each story for content, language, originality, organization, consistency, and recurring themes such as the need for affection, repeated failure, or parental domination.

Both the Rorschach and the TAT may open up a conversation between a clinician and a patient who is reluctant or unable to talk about personal problems. Both tests may also provide insight into motives, events, or feelings of which the person is unaware. However, because projective tests are often not administered in a standard fashion, their validity and reliability, especially in cross-cultural settings, have been called into question (Hofer & Chasiotis, 2004; Wierzbicki, 1993). As a result, their use has declined since the 1970s. Still, when interpreted by a skilled examiner, these tests can offer insight into a person's attitudes and feelings.

CHECK YOUR UNDERSTANDING

1. _____ tests require people to fill out questionnaires, which are then scored according to a standardized procedure.

2. In _____ tests of personality, people are shown ambiguous stimuli and asked to describe them or to make up a story about them.

Answers: 1. objective. 2. projective.

APPLY YOUR UNDERSTANDING

1. You are consulting a psychologist who asks you to take a personality test. She shows you pictures of people and asks you to write a complete story about each picture. The test is most likely the

   a. Minnesota Multiphasic Personality Inventory.

   b. Rorschach Test.

   c. Thematic Apperception Test.

   d. NEO-PI-R.

2. "They are often not administered in a standard fashion, they are seldom scored objectively, but when interpreted by a skilled examiner, they can provide insight into a person." To what does this quotation most likely refer?

   a. structured interviews

   b. objective personality tests

   c. projective personality tests

   d. the NEO-PI-R and the MMPI-2

Answers: 1. c. 2. c.

KEY TERMS

CHAPTER REVIEW

Studying Personality

What do psychologists mean when they talk about personality? **Personality** refers to an individual's unique pattern of thoughts, feelings, and behaviors that persists over time and across situations. Key to this definition is the concept of distinctive differences among individuals and the concept of personality's stability and endurance.

Psychodynamic Theories

What ideas do all psychodynamic theories have in common? **Psychodynamic theories** of personality consider behavior to be the transformation and expression of psychic energy within the individual. Often these psychological dynamics are **unconscious** processes.

When Freud proposed that the sexual instinct is the basis of behavior, how was he defining "sexual instinct"? According to Freud, personality is made of three structures. The **id**, the only personality structure present at birth operates in the unconsciousness according to the **pleasure principle**. The **ego**, operating at the conscious level according to the **reality principle**, controls all conscious thinking and reasoning. And, the **superego**, which acts as the moral guardian or conscience helping the person function in society by comparing the ego's actions with the **ego ideal** of perfection. Freud used the term *sexual instinct* to refer to the desire for virtually any form of pleasure. As infants mature, their **libido,** or energy generated by the sexual instinct, becomes focused on sensitive parts of the body. A **fixation** occurs if a child is deprived of or receives too much pleasure from the part of the body that dominates one of the five developmental stages—**oral, anal, phallic, latency,** and **genital.** During the phallic stage, strong attachment to the parent of the opposite sex and jealousy of the parent of the same sex is termed the **Oedipus complex** in boys and the **Electra complex** in girls. Next the child enters the latency period, characterized by a lack of interest in sexual behavior. Finally, at puberty, the individual enters the genital stage of mature sexuality.

How did Carl Jung's view of the unconscious differ from that of Freud? Freud saw the id as a "cauldron of seething excitations," whereas Jung viewed the unconscious as the ego's source of strength. Jung believed that the unconscious consisted of the **personal unconscious**, encompassing an individual's repressed thoughts, forgotten experiences, and undeveloped ideas; and the **collective unconscious**, a subterranean river of memories and behavior patterns flowing to us from previous generations. Certain universal thought forms, called **archetypes**, give rise to mental images or mythological representations and play a special role in shaping personality. Jung used the term *persona* to describe that part of personality by which we are known to other people, like a mask we put on to go out in public.

What did Alfred Adler believe was the major determinant of personality? Adler believed that people possess innate positive motives and strive toward personal and social perfection. He originally proposed that the principal determinant of personality was the individual's attempt to **compensate** for actual physical weakness, but he later modified his theory to stress the importance of *feelings* of inferiority, whether or not those feelings are justified. Adler concluded that strivings for superiority and perfection, both in one's own life and in the society in which one lives, are crucial to personality development.

What major contributions did Karen Horney make to the psychodynamic perspective? For Horney, *anxiety*—a person's reaction to real or imagined dangers or threats—is a stronger motivating force than the sexual drive, or libido. Anxious adults adopt one of three coping strategies, or **neurotic trends**—moving toward people (submission), moving against people (aggression), and moving away from people (detachment). By emphasizing that culture and not anatomy determines many of the personality traits that differentiate women from men and that culture can be changed, Horney became a forerunner of feminist psychology.

Erikson's theory focused less on unconscious conflict and more on what factors? Erikson argued that the quality of the parent–child relationship affects the development of personality because, out of this interaction, the child either feels competent and valuable and is able to form a secure sense of identity or feels incompetent and worthless and fails to build a secure identity. Erikson proposed that each person moves through eight stages of development, each involving a more successful versus a less successful adjustment.

How would a psychodynamic theorist view the personality of Jaylene Smith? Freud would probably conclude that Jay had not successfully resolved her Electra complex. Erikson might suggest that Jay has problems achieving intimacy (Stage 6) because she had failed to develop satisfactory relations with other people earlier in her life.

How do modern psychologists view the contributions and limitations of the psychodynamic perspective? Psychodynamic theories have had a profound impact on the way we view ourselves and others, but some of Freud's theories have been criticized as unscientific and culture bound, based on the anecdotal accounts of troubled individuals. As a therapy, **psychoanalysis** has been shown to be beneficial in some cases but no more so than are other therapies.

Humanistic Personality Theories

What are the major ways that humanistic personality theory differs from psychodynamic theories? Freud and many of his followers believed that personality grows out of the resolution of unconscious conflicts and developmental crises from the past. **Humanistic personality theory** emphasizes that we are positively motivated and progress toward higher levels of functioning; and it stresses people's potential for growth and change in the present.

According to Rogers, how can thinking of yourself as self-assured help you to become so? Rogers contended that every person is born with certain innate potentials and the **actualizing tendency** to realize our biological potential as well as our conscious sense of who we are. A **fully functioning person** is one whose self-concept closely matches the person's inborn capabilities, and is encouraged when a child is raised in an atmosphere characterized by **unconditional positive regard**.

How would humanistic theorists view the development of Jaylene Smith's personality? Humanistic theorists would focus on the difference between Jay's self-concept and her actual capacities. Her inability to become what she "most truly is" would account for her anxiety, loneliness, and general dissatisfaction.

Rogers would suspect that throughout Jay's life, acceptance and love came from satisfying other people's ideas of what she should become.

What have humanistic theories contributed to our understanding of personality? There is a lack of scientifically derived evidence for humanistic theories of personality. In addition, these theories are criticized for taking too rosy a view of human nature, for fostering self-centeredness, and for reflecting Western values of individual achievement.

Trait Theories

What is the key focus of trait theories? Trait theorists reject the notion that there are just a few distinct personality types. Instead, they insist that each person possesses a unique constellation of fundamental **personality traits**, which can be inferred from how the person behaves.

What five basic traits describe most differences in personality? Recent research suggests that there may be just five overarching and universal personality traits: extraversion, agreeableness, conscientiousness, emotional stability, and openness to experience (also called culture or intellect). Research shows these traits have some real world applications and are strongly influenced by heredity.

How would trait theorists describe Jaylene Smith's personality? Trait theorists would probably ascribe Jaylene's high achievements to the traits of determination or persistence. Sincerity, motivation, intelligence, anxiety, and introversion would also describe Jay. In terms of Big Five factors, she would be considered high in conscientiousness, but low in emotional stability and extraversion.

What major contributions have trait theorists made to our understanding of personality? Trait theories are primarily descriptive and provide a way of classifying personalities, but they do not explain why someone's personality developed as it did. Unlike psychodynamic and humanistic theories, however, trait theories are relatively easy to test experimentally, and research confirms the value of the five-factor model, referred to as the "**Big Five**," in pinpointing personality. Also, although most personality theories assume that behavior is consistent across situations and over a lifetime, a number of psychologists believe that situational variables have a significant effect on behavior.

Cognitive–Social Learning Theories

How do personal and situational factors combine to shape behavior? **Cognitive–social learning theories** of personality view behavior as the product of the interaction of cognitions, learning and past experiences, and the immediate environment.

How does one's locus of control affect self-efficacy? Albert Bandura maintains that certain internal **expectancies** determine how a person evaluates a situation and that this evaluation has an effect on the person's behavior. These expectancies prompt people to conduct themselves according to unique **performance standards**, individually determined measures of excellence by which they judge their behavior. According to Rotter, people with an internal **locus of control**—one type of expectancy—believe that they can control their own fate through their actions. Those who succeed in meeting their own internal performance standards develop an attitude that Bandura calls **self-efficacy**.

How would cognitive–social learning theorists describe the factors that shaped Jaylene Smith's personality? These theorists would assert that Jaylene learned to be shy because she was rewarded for the many hours she spent alone studying. Reinforcement would also have shaped her self-discipline and high need to achieve. By watching her parents, Jay could have learned to respond to conflicts with aggressive outbursts.

What contributions have cognitive–social learning theories made to our understanding of personality, and what are their limitations? Cognitive–social learning theories avoid the narrowness of trait theories, as well as the reliance on case studies and anecdotal evidence that weakens psychodynamic and humanistic theories. They also explain why people behave inconsistently, an area where the trait theories fall short. Cognitive-social learning theories have also spawned therapies that have been effectively used to treat depression.

Personality Assessment

How do psychologists measure personality? Psychologists use four different methods to assess personality: the personal interview, direct observation of behavior, **objective tests**, and **projective tests**. Factors such as a desire to impress the examiner, fatigue, and fear of being tested can profoundly affect the reliability and validity of such tests.

What are the purposes of structured and unstructured interviews? During an unstructured interview, the interviewer asks questions about any issues that arise and poses follow-up questions where appropriate. In a structured interview, the order and the content of the questions are fixed, and the interviewer does not deviate from the format. Structured interviews are more likely to be used for systematic research on personality because they elicit comparable information from all interviewees.

What are the advantages and limits of the observational method? Direct observation of a person over a period of time, which enables researchers to assess how situation and environment influence behavior, has the advantage of not relying on people's self-reported behavior. However, the observer runs the risk of misinterpreting the meaning of a given behavior.

Why are objective tests preferred by trait theorists? Objective tests ask respondents to answer "yes–no" questions about their own behavior and thoughts. Cattell's **Sixteen Personality Factor Questionnaire (16PF)** provides scores on 16 basic personality traits, whereas the **NEO-PI-R** reports scores for each of the Big Five traits and their associated facets. The **Minnesota Multiphasic Personality Inventory (MMPI-2)**, originally developed as an aid to diagnose mental disorders, includes questions that measure the truthfulness of a person's response.

What do projective tests try to measure? Psychodynamic theorists, who believe that much behavior is determined by unconscious processes, tend to discount tests that rely on self-reports. They are more likely to use projective tests consisting of ambiguous stimuli that can elicit an unlimited number of interpretations based on these unconscious processes. Two such tests are the **Rorschach Test** and the **Thematic Apperception Test (TAT)**.

11 Stress and Health Psychology

OVERVIEW

Enduring Issues in Stress and Health Psychology

Sources of Stress
- Change
- Everyday Hassles
- Self-Imposed Stress
- Stress and Individual Differences

Coping with Stress
- Direct Coping
- Defensive Coping
- Socioeconomic and Gender Differences in Coping with Stress

How Stress Affects Health
- Stress and Heart Disease
- Stress and the Immune System

Staying Healthy
- Reduce Stress
- Adopt a Healthy Lifestyle

Extreme Stress
- Sources of Extreme Stress
- Posttraumatic Stress Disorder

The Well-Adjusted Person

Blake Miller joined the Marines at age 18 because he heard it was a free way to get certified in auto body repair. Soon he was in Iraq, assigned to spotting the pickup trucks that insurgents use to launch attacks. This war—with its mined roads, suicide bombers, persistent threat of ambush, and children sometimes used as decoys—began to take its psychological toll on Blake. There was no place where he could feel confidently safe. His cigarette consumption increased to $5\frac{1}{2}$ packs a day.

Things became much worse when Blake's unit was sent to invade the rebel stronghold of Fallujah. Pinned down on a rooftop, he was under constant fire throughout an entire day and night. As the sun rose, American tanks finally arrived, bombarding the building sheltering Blake's attackers. The thunderous roar of the tank artillery caused one of Blake's ears to bleed and become deaf. In an instant some 40 insurgents were crushed in the rubble; but the nightmare was not over. There was the time Blake barely escaped a rain of bullets in an ambush, hurling himself through a broken door in the nick of time. But the worst part of Blake's war experiences was training his rifle on a fellow human being and squeezing the trigger (story based on Stannard, 2006).

The psychological wounds that Blake returned home with festered. He was uncharacteristically quiet and easy to anger, with a hair-trigger tendency to go on the defensive. A loud bang would send him spinning into a combat crouch with an imaginary rifle raised to his shoulder. While asleep at night his arm would encircle his wife's neck and tighten into a strangle hold. Nightmares about the war caused him to awaken drenched in sweat. When looking out a window one day he was sure he was seeing the body of a dead Iraqi lying on the ground.

After Blake physically assaulted a sailor who whistled in a way that resembled a rocket-propelled grenade, military doctors diagnosed him with posttraumatic stress disorder (PTSD), in which a person who has suffered a highly traumatic experience repeatedly relives it in all its terror. The person may also be irritable, depressed, anxious, and hypervigilant, just as Blake was. Given the severity of his disorder, the Marines honorably discharged Blake and he began to receive disability benefits (Stannard, 2006). He became one of the estimated 100,000 new American combat veterans who will suffer psychologically as a result of their war experiences (Guthrie, 2005).

PTSD is an extreme manifestation of **stress**—the body's reaction to a difficult situation that disrupts a person's normal functioning and state of well-being. Because difficult situations are common in everyday life, so, too, is stress. We are all familiar with the knotted stomach, pounding heart, or anxious feelings when our car breaks down in traffic, when our computer crashes before we have backed up data, when we are late and ensnarled in a traffic jam, or when we're under pressure to meet deadlines. Whenever people feel threatened physically or psychologically, when they wonder if they can cope with the demands of their environment, and when their heart pounds and their stomach feels queasy, they are experiencing stress. But stress isn't always "bad"; it can have positive as well as negative consequences. Indeed, most people would be bored with an existence that held no challenges or surprises. Moreover, stress may stimulate effort and spark creativity. Even when a situation is hopeless and a happy ending is impossible, people often report that they have grown, acquired new coping skills and resources, and perhaps experienced a spiritual or religious transformation as a result of stress (Folkman & Moskowitz, 2000).

But experiencing too much stress over too long a period can contribute to physical problems as well as psychological ones (Tosevski & Milovancevic, 2006). **Health psychology** focuses on how the mind and body interact. Specifically, health psychologists seek to understand how psychological factors influence wellness and illness. Numerous studies have found that people suffering from acute or chronic stress may be more vulnerable to everything from the common cold to an increased risk for heart disease (S. Cohen et al., 1998; Heinz et al., 2003; Spiegel & Kato, 1996; Thornton, 2005). As you will learn, new research is uncovering the biological mechanisms that link stress to lowered immunity and poor health. The challenge for health psychologists is to find ways to facilitate **adjustment** to stress, to prevent stress from becoming physically and emotionally debilitating, and to *promote* healthy behavior and well-being (Baum, Revenson, & Singer, 2001).

We begin this chapter by looking at common sources of stress and why some people are more vulnerable to stress than others. We then examine strategies for coping with stress. Next we turn to how acute or chronic stress can sometimes make people more susceptible to physical illness by weakening their immune system. The challenge, which we take up in the sections that follow, is to find ways to reduce stress and promote good health and a sense of well-being. This is even possible for those who have suffered extreme stress, as Blake Miller did.

Much of the stress we experience in our lives arises not from major traumas but from small everyday hassles such as traffic jams, petty arguments, and equipment that fails when we need it most.

---

pressure A feeling that one must speed up, intensify, or change the direction of one's behavior or live up to a higher standard of performance.

frustration The feeling that occurs when a person is prevented from reaching a goal.

conflict Simultaneous existence of incompatible demands, opportunities, needs, or goals.

they might usually be able to tolerate (Cross, 2003). In the end, both major and minor events are stressful, since they lead to feelings of pressure, frustration, and conflict.

PRESSURE Pressure occurs when we feel forced to speed up, intensify, or shift direction in our behavior, or when we feel compelled to meet a higher standard of performance. Pressure on the job or in school is a familiar example. Psychologists who study the effects of corporate "downsizing," which requires that production levels are maintained with fewer workers, often find that these workers report increased stress and depression, increased injuries on the job, and lower job satisfaction (N. Crawford, 2002). This pressure also contributes to poor job performance (Clay, 1999; Kaminski, 1999). In our private lives, trying to live up to social and cultural norms about what we *should* be doing, as well as our family's and friends' expectations, also adds pressure.

As our highways have become more congested, incidents of aggressive driving—popularly known as "road rage"—have become more common and more dangerous. One survey found that 9 in 10 drivers had been threatened by speeding, tailgating, failure to yield right of way, lane changes without signaling, weaving, cutting in, and rude, provocative gestures and comments during the previous year. Psychologist Leon James (L. James & Nahl, 2000), who has studied driving patterns for more than a decade, views road rage as a behavioral syndrome that is rooted in exaggerated forms of cultural norms, especially our annoyance with delays and winner-take-all view of competition. What surprises James is how many aggressive drivers are "ordinary people" with no history of violence, and how many considered themselves to be victims of inconsiderate drivers.

FRUSTRATION Frustration occurs when a person is prevented from reaching a goal because something or someone stands in the way. *Delays* are annoying because our culture puts great stock in the value of time. *Lack of resources* is frustrating to those who cannot afford the new cars or lavish vacations they desire. *Losses*, such as the end of a love affair or a cherished friendship, cause frustration because they often make us feel helpless, unimportant, or worthless. *Failure* generates intense frustration—and accompanying guilt—in our competitive society. We imagine that if we had done things differently, we might have succeeded; thus, we usually feel personally responsible for our setbacks and tend to assume that others blame us for not trying harder or being smarter. *Discrimination* also frustrates us: Being denied opportunities or recognition simply because of one's sex, age, religion, or skin color is extremely frustrating.

CONFLICT Of all life's troubles, conflict is probably the most common. A boy does not want to go to his aunt's for dinner, but neither does he want to listen to his parents complain if he stays home. A student finds that both the required courses she wanted to take this semester are given at the same hours on the same days. **Conflict** arises when we face two or more incompatible demands, opportunities, needs, or goals. We can never completely resolve conflict. We must either give up some of our goals, modify some of them, delay our pursuit of some of them, or resign ourselves to not attaining all of our goals. Whatever we do, we are bound to experience some frustration, thereby adding to the stressfulness of conflicts.

In the 1930s, Kurt Lewin described two opposite tendencies of conflict: approach and

---

THINKING CRITICALLY ABOUT . . .

Road Rage and You

One of the techniques Professor James uses in his research is to ask people to tape record their experiences and feelings (a technique called "self-witnessing") when they are driving in traffic. At first he was shocked by how often ordinarily polite, considerate people became intolerant and antisocial when they got behind the wheel—what he calls a "Jekyll and Hyde effect." Try tape recording your thoughts as you drive (and be honest); ask several friends to do the same. Do you find James' "Jekyll and Hyde effect"?

There are three main theories of road rage:

- The *crowding* hypothesis: More cars →more traffic →more frustration →more stress →more anger →more hostility →more violence.

- The *cultural* hypothesis: Americans learn aggressive and dangerous driving patterns as children, by watching their parents and other adults behind the wheel, and by viewing risky driving in movies and television commercials.

- The *displacement* hypothesis: People are more likely to lose their tempers while driving if they have suffered recent blows to their self-esteem, and seek to recoup their sense of worth by winning battles on the road.

Which theory do you find most convincing? Why? How might you go about determining which has the most merit?

SUMMARY TABLE

TYPES OF CONFLICT

Type of Conflict	Nature of Conflict
Approach/approach	You are attracted to two incompatible goals at the same time.
Avoidance/avoidance	Repelled by two undesirable alternatives at the same time, you are inclined to escape, although other factors often prevent such an escape.
Approach/avoidance	You are both repelled by, and attracted to, the same goal.

avoidance. When something attracts us, we want to approach it; when something frightens us, we try to avoid it. Lewin (1935) showed how different combinations of these tendencies create three basic types of conflict: approach/approach conflict, avoidance/avoidance conflict, and approach/avoidance conflict. (See the **Summary Table** "Types of Conflict.")

Approach/approach conflict occurs when a person is simultaneously attracted to two appealing goals. Being accepted for admission at two equally desirable colleges or universities is an example. The stress that occurs in approach/approach conflict is that in choosing one desirable option, we must give up the other.

The reverse is **avoidance/avoidance conflict**, in which we confront two undesirable or threatening possibilities, neither of which has any positive attributes. When faced with an avoidance/avoidance conflict, people usually try to escape the situation altogether. If escape is impossible, their coping method depends on how threatening each alternative is. Most often, they vacillate between choosing one threat or the other, like a baseball player's being caught in a rundown between first and second base. In no-exit situations, people sometimes simply wait for events to resolve their conflict for them.

An **approach/avoidance conflict**, in which a person is both attracted to and repelled by the same goal, is the most common form of conflict. The closer we come to a goal with good and bad features, the stronger grow our desires both to approach and to avoid, but the tendency to avoid increases more rapidly than the tendency to approach. In an approach/avoidance conflict, therefore, we approach the goal until we reach the point at which the tendency to approach equals the tendency to avoid the goal. Afraid to go any closer, we stop and vacillate, making no choice at all, until the situation changes. Can you think of examples of these three types of conflict in your own life?

SELF-IMPOSED STRESS

How do we create stress?

So far, we have considered external sources of stress. Sometimes, however, people create problems for themselves quite apart from stressful events in their environment. Some psychologists argue that many people carry around a set of irrational, self-defeating beliefs that add unnecessarily to the normal stresses of living (A. Ellis & Harper, 1975; Timofeev, 1993). For example, some people believe that "it is essential to be loved or approved by almost everyone for everything I do." For such people, any sign of disapproval will be a source of considerable stress. Others believe that "I must be competent, adequate, and successful at everything I do." For them, the slightest sign of failure or inadequacy means that they are worthless human beings. Still other people believe that "it is disastrous if everything doesn't go the way I would like." These people feel upset, miserable, and unhappy when things don't go perfectly. As we describe in Chapter 12, "Psychological Disorders," self-defeating thoughts like these can contribute to depression (Beck, 1984, 2002).

approach/approach conflict According to Lewin, the result of simultaneous attraction to two appealing possibilities, neither of which has any negative qualities.

avoidance/avoidance conflict According to Lewin, the result of facing a choice between two undesirable possibilities, neither of which has any positive qualities.

approach/avoidance conflict According to Lewin, the result of being simultaneously attracted to and repelled by the same goal.

STRESS AND INDIVIDUAL DIFFERENCES

Do people who are resistant to stress share certain traits?

Just as some people create more stress for themselves than others do, some people cope well with major life stresses, whereas others are thrown by even minor problems. What accounts for these differences? How much stress we experience depends partly on the way we interpret our situation (Suzuki, 2006). Self-confident people who feel capable of coping with life will feel less stress in a given situation than will those who lack self-assurance (Kessler, Price, & Wortman, 1985). Also, seeing a challenging situation as an opportunity for success rather than for failure is typically associated with positive emotions such as eagerness, excitement, and confidence (Bouckenooghe, Buelens, Fontaine, & Vanderheyden, 2005; Folkman & Moskovitz, 2000). For example, students who know they can study when they have to and who have done well on exams in the past tend to be calmer the night before an important test than students who have done poorly on previous exams. Thus some stressors can promote positive change (Linley & Joseph, 2004; Park & Fenster, 2004).

People's overall view of the world is also related to how well they can cope with stress. *Optimists,* who tend to appraise events as challenges rather than threats, are generally better able to cope with stressful events than are *pessimists,* who are more likely to dwell on failure (C. Peterson, 2000). Similarly, people with an *internal locus of control* see themselves as being able to affect their situations while those with an *external locus of control* are more likely to appraise events negatively (Ryan & Deci, 2000) (see Chapter 10, "Personality," for a discussion of locus of control).

HARDINESS AND RESILIENCE People with a trait we call *hardiness* tolerate stress exceptionally well or seem to thrive on it (Kobasa, 1979; Maddi, 2006). They also feel that they control their own destinies and are confident about being able to cope with change (Kessler, Price, & Wortman, 1985; S. E. Taylor, 2003). Conversely, individuals who have little confidence that they can master new situations and can exercise control over events feel powerless and apathetic (C. Peterson, Maier, & Seligman, 1993b). (Recall our discussion of learned helplessness in Chapter 5, "Learning.") Even when change offers new opportunities for taking charge of their situation, they remain passive.

Psychologists are also interested in *resilience*: the ability to "bounce back," recovering one's self-confidence, good spirits, and hopeful attitude after extreme or prolonged stress (Beasley, Thompson, & Davidson, 2003; Bonanno, Galea, Bucciarelli, & Vlahov, 2006). Resilience may partially explain why some children who grow up in adverse circumstances (such as extreme poverty, dangerous neighborhoods, abusive parents, or exposure to drugs and alcohol) become well-adjusted adults, whereas others remain troubled—and frequently get into trouble—throughout their lives (Bonanno, 2004; Feinauer, Hilton, & Callahan, 2003; Leifer, Kilbane, & Kalick, 2004). Research following high-risk children into adulthood suggests mentoring programs can foster resilience. Examples of these are Big Brother/Big Sister (in which an adult volunteer is paired with an "at-risk" child) and after-school programs that offer a range of activities (Brown, cited in Huang, 1998; Clauss & Caroline, 2003).

Why do some children living in adverse conditions remain troubled throughout their lives, while more resilient children in the same circumstances become well-adjusted adults? Here, the children of migrant workers in Beijing, China, play in front of their ramshackle housing.

CHECK YOUR UNDERSTANDING

Indicate whether the following statements are true (T) or false (F):

1. _____ Change that results from "good" events, like marriage or job promotion, does not produce stress.
2. _____ Stressful events almost always involve changes in our lives.
3. _____ Big events in life are always much more stressful than everyday hassles.
4. _____ Optimists are generally better able to cope with stress than are pessimists.

Answers: 1. (F); 2. (T); 3. (F) 4. (T).

APPLY YOUR UNDERSTANDING

1. Bob wants to go to graduate school in pharmacology, but he is very concerned about the intense studying that will be required to complete the curriculum. Bob is faced with a(n)
   a. offensive/defensive coping dilemma.
   b. direct/defensive coping dilemma.
   c. avoidance/avoidance conflict.
   d. approach/avoidance conflict.
2. LaShondra is a caterer. She has just finished the prep work for a 15-person dinner that is scheduled for 7:30 P.M. that night. At 4:00 P.M., the client calls to tell her that there will actually be 30 people, and they need to start dinner at 7:00 P.M. instead of 7:30 P.M. LaShondra feels stressed because this call creates
   a. frustration.
   b. pressure.
   c. self-imposed stress.
   d. conflict.

Answers: 1. d. 2. b.

Coping With Stress

What is the difference between direct coping and defensive coping?

Whatever its source, stress requires that we cope—that is, it requires us to make cognitive and behavioral efforts to manage psychological stress (Lazarus, 1993). There are many different ways of coping with stress (E. A. Skinner, Edge, Altman, & Sherwood, 2003), but two general types of adjustment stand out: direct coping and defensive coping.

DIRECT COPING

What are three strategies that deal directly with stress?

Direct coping refers to intentional efforts to change an uncomfortable situation. Direct coping tends to be problem oriented and to focus on the immediate issue. (See "Applying Psychology: Coping with Stress at College.") When we are threatened, frustrated, or in conflict, we have three basic choices for coping directly: *confrontation, compromise,* or *withdrawal*.

Consider the case of a woman who has worked hard at her job for years, but has not been promoted. She learns that she has not advanced due to her stated unwillingness to temporarily move to a branch office in another part of the country to acquire more experience. Her unwillingness to move stands between her and her goal of advancing in her career. She has several choices, which we will explore.

APPLYING PSYCHOLOGY

COPING WITH STRESS AT COLLEGE

It is 2 weeks before finals, and you must write two papers and study for four exams. You are very worried. You are not alone. There are many techniques you can teach yourself to help cope with the pressures of college life.

1. Plan ahead, do not procrastinate, and get things done well before deadlines. Start work on large projects well in advance.
2. Exercise; do whatever activity you enjoy.
3. Listen to your favorite music, watch a television show, or go to a movie as a study break.
4. Talk to other people.
5. Meditate or use other relaxation techniques.
6. Seek out a stress-reduction workshop. Many colleges and universities offer these.

One very effective technique is to make a list of *everything* you have to do, right down to doing the laundry, getting birthday cards for family and friends, and so on. Then mark the highest-priority tasks—the ones that *really* have to be done first or those that will take a long time. Use your available time to work on *only* those tasks. Cross off high-priority tasks as they are done, add new tasks as they arrive, and continually adjust the priorities so that the most critical tasks are always marked.

This technique serves various purposes. It removes the fear that you'll forget something important, because everything is on a single sheet of paper. It helps you realize that things are not as overwhelming as they might otherwise seem. (The list is finite, and there are probably only a few things that truly are high-priority tasks.) It lets you focus your energy on the most important tasks and makes it easy to avoid spending time on less important things that might drift into your attention. Finally, it assures you that you are doing everything possible to do the most important things in your life, and if you don't manage to do them all, you can truly say, "There's no way I could have done any better; it simply wasn't possible in the time available." Actually, that will seldom be the case. Usually the highest priority tasks get done and the lower priority tasks simply wait, often for weeks or months, after which you wonder how important they really are if they always come out on the bottom of the totem pole.

CONFRONTATION Acknowledging that there is a problem for which a solution must be found, attacking the problem head-on and pushing resolutely toward the goal is called **confrontation**. The hallmark of the "confrontational style" is making intense efforts to cope with stress and to accomplish one's aims. Doing so may involve learning skills, enlisting other people's help, or just trying harder. Or it may require steps to change either oneself or the situation. The woman who wants to advance her career might decide that if she wants to move up in the company, she will have to relocate. Or she might challenge the assumption that working at the branch office would give her the kind of experience that her supervisor thinks she needs. She might try to persuade her boss that even though she has never worked in a branch office, she nevertheless has acquired enough experience to handle a better job in the main office. Or she might remind her supervisor of the company's stated goal of promoting more women to top-level positions.

Confrontation may also include expressions of anger. Anger may be effective, especially if we really have been treated unfairly and if we express our anger with restraint instead of exploding in rage.

COMPROMISE **Compromise** is one of the most common and effective ways of coping directly with conflict or frustration. We often recognize that we cannot have everything we want and that we cannot expect others to do just what we would like them to do. In such cases, we may decide to settle for less than we originally sought. The woman may agree to take a less desirable position that doesn't require branch office experience, or she may strike a bargain to go to the branch office for a shorter time.

WITHDRAWAL In some circumstances, the most effective way of coping with stress is to withdraw from the situation. An amusement park patron who is overcome by anxiety just looking at a roller coaster may simply move on to a less threatening ride or may even leave the park. The woman whose promotion depends on temporarily relocating might just quit her job and join another company.

When we realize that our adversary is more powerful than we are, that there is no way we can effectively modify ourselves or the situation, that there is no possible compromise,

confrontation Acknowledging a stressful situation directly and attempting to find a solution to the problem or to attain the difficult goal.

compromise Deciding on a more realistic solution or goal when an ideal solution or goal is not practical.

and that any form of aggression would be self-destructive, **withdrawal** is a positive and realistic response. In seemingly hopeless situations, such as submarine and mining disasters, few people panic (Mawson, 2005). Believing that there is nothing they can do to save themselves, they often simply give up. If a situation is hopeless, resignation may be the most effective way of coping with it.

Perhaps the greatest danger of coping by withdrawal is that the person will come to avoid all similar situations. The person who grew extremely anxious looking at the roller coaster may refuse to go to an amusement park or a carnival again. The woman who did not want to take a job at her company's branch office may not only quit her present job, but may leave without even looking for a new one. In such cases, coping by withdrawal can become maladaptive avoidance. Moreover, people who have given up on a situation are in a poor position to take advantage of an effective solution if one should come along.

Withdrawal, in whatever form, is a mixed blessing. Although it can be an effective method of coping, it has built-in dangers. The same characteristic tends to be true of defensive coping, to which we now turn.

DEFENSIVE COPING

What are the major ways of coping defensively?

Thus far, we have discussed coping with stress that arises from recognizable sources. But there are times when we either cannot identify or cannot deal directly with the source of our stress. For example, you return to a parking lot to discover that your car has been damaged. In other cases, a problem is so emotionally threatening that it cannot be faced directly: Perhaps someone close to you is terminally ill, or after 4 years of hard work, you have failed to gain admission to medical school and may have to abandon your plan to become a doctor.

In such situations, people may turn to **defense mechanisms** as a way of coping. Defense mechanisms are techniques for *deceiving* oneself about the causes of a stressful situation to reduce pressure, frustration, conflict, and anxiety. The self-deceptive nature of such adjustments led Freud to conclude that they are entirely unconscious, but not all psychologists agree that they always spring from unconscious conflicts over which we have little or no control. Often we realize that we are pushing something out of our memory or are otherwise deceiving ourselves. For example, all of us have blown up at someone when we *knew* we were really angry at someone else. Whether defense mechanisms operate consciously or unconsciously, they provide a means of coping with stress that might otherwise be unbearable. (See **Summary Table:** Defense Mechanisms.")

DENIAL Denial is the refusal to acknowledge a painful or threatening reality. Although denial is a positive response in some situations, it clearly is not in other situations. Frequent drug users who insist that they are merely "experimenting" with drugs are using denial. So are students who consciously expect an exam to be easy and to earn high grades even though they haven't studied, but they unconsciously expect to fail.

REPRESSION The most common mechanism for blocking out painful feelings and memories is **repression**, a form of forgetting to exclude painful thoughts from consciousness. Soldiers who break down in the field often block out the memory of the experiences that led to their collapse (P. Brown, van der Hart, & Graafland, 1999). Many psychologists believe that repression is a symptom that the person is struggling against impulses (such as aggression) that conflict with conscious values. For example, most of us were taught in childhood that violence and aggression are wrong. This conflict between our feelings and our values can create stress, and one way of coping defensively with that stress is to repress our feelings—to completely block out any awareness of our underlying anger and hostility.

Denial and repression are the most basic defense mechanisms. In denial, we block out situations that we can't handle; in repression, we block out unacceptable impulses or thoughts. These psychic strategies form the basis for several other defensive ways of coping.

PROJECTION If a problem cannot be denied or completely repressed, we may be able to distort its nature so that we can handle it more easily through **projection**: the attribution of one's repressed motives, ideas, or feelings onto others. We do not want to acknowledge feelings

withdrawal Avoiding a situation when other forms of coping are not practical.

defense mechanisms Self-deceptive techniques for reducing stress, including denial, repression, projection, identification, regression, intellectualization, reaction formation, displacement, and sublimation.

denial Refusal to acknowledge a painful or threatening reality.

repression Excluding uncomfortable thoughts, feelings, and desires from consciousness.

projection Attributing one's repressed motives, feelings, or wishes to others.

SUMMARY TABLE

DEFENSE MECHANISMS

Defense Mechanism	Process	Example
Denial	Refusing to acknowledge a painful or threatening reality.	Ray, whose best friend has just been killed in a car accident, insists that it is a case of mistaken identity and that his friend is still alive.
Repression	Excluding uncomfortable thoughts from consciousness.	Lisa, whose grandmother died of breast cancer, is at higher-than-average risk for developing breast cancer herself; still, she routinely forgets to get a mammogram.
Projection	Attributing one's repressed motives, feelings, or wishes to others.	Marilyn is unfairly passed over for a promotion; she denies that she is angry about this situation but is certain that her supervisor is angry with her.
Identification	Taking on the characteristics of someone else to avoid feeling inadequate.	Anthony, uncertain of his own attractiveness, takes on the dress and mannerisms of a popular teacher.
Regression	Reverting to childlike behavior and defenses.	Furious because his plan to reorganize his division has been rejected, Bob throws a tantrum.
Intellectualization	Thinking abstractly about stressful problems as a way of detaching oneself from them.	After learning that she has not been asked to a classmate's costume party, Tina coolly discusses the ways in which social cliques form and the ways that they serve to regulate and control school life.
Reaction formation	Expression of exaggerated ideas and emotions that are the opposite of one's repressed beliefs or feelings.	At work, Michael loudly professes that he would never take advantage of a rival employee, though his harassing behavior indicates quite the opposite.
Displacement	Shifting repressed motives from an original object to a substitute object.	Nelson is infuriated at his instructor's unreasonable request that he rewrite his term paper, but he is afraid to say anything for fear that he will make the instructor angry; so he comes home and yells at his housemates for telling him what to do.
Sublimation	Redirecting repressed motives and feelings into more socially acceptable channels.	The child of parents who never paid attention to him, Bill is running for public office.

as our own, thus we ascribe feelings to someone else and locate the source of our conflict outside ourselves. A corporate executive who feels guilty about the way he rose to power may project his own ruthless ambition onto his colleagues. He simply is doing his job, he believes, whereas his associates are all crassly ambitious and consumed with power.

IDENTIFICATION The reverse of projection is **identification**: taking on the characteristics of someone else, so that we can vicariously share in that person's triumphs and overcome feeling inadequate. The admired person's actions, that is, become a substitute for our own. A parent with unfulfilled career ambitions may share emotionally in a son's or daughter's professional success. When the child is promoted, the parent may feel personally triumphant. Identification is often used as a form of self-defense in situations in which a person feels utterly helpless, for example, in a hostage situation. To survive, victims sometimes seek to please their captors and may identify with them as a way of defensively coping with unbearable and inescapable stress. This is called the "Stockholm Syndrome" (Cassidy, 2002), after four Swedes who were held captive in a bank vault for nearly a week, but upon release, defended their captors.

REGRESSION People under stress may revert to childlike behavior through a process called **regression**. Why do people regress? Some psychologists say that it is because an adult cannot stand feeling helpless. Children, on the other hand, feel helpless and dependent every day, so becoming more childlike can make total dependency or helplessness more bearable. Regression is sometimes used as a manipulative strategy, too, albeit an

identification Taking on the characteristics of someone else to avoid feeling incompetent.

regression Reverting to childlike behavior and defenses.

immature and inappropriate one. Adults who cry or throw temper tantrums when their arguments fail may expect those around them to react sympathetically, as their parents did when they were children.

INTELLECTUALIZATION **Intellectualization** is a subtle form of denial in which we detach ourselves from our feelings about our problems by analyzing them intellectually and thinking of them almost as if they concerned other people. Parents who start out intending to discuss their child's difficulties in a new school and then find themselves engaged in a sophisticated discussion of educational philosophy may be intellectualizing a very upsetting situation. They appear to be dealing with their problems, but in fact they are not, because they have cut themselves off from their disturbing emotions.

REACTION FORMATION The term **reaction formation** refers to a behavioral form of denial in which people express, with exaggerated intensity, ideas and emotions that are the opposite of their own. *Exaggeration* is the clue to this behavior. The woman who extravagantly praises a rival may be covering up jealousy over her opponent's success. Reaction formation may also be a way of convincing ourselves that our motives are pure. The man who feels ambivalent about being a father may devote a disproportionate amount of time to his children in an attempt to prove to *himself* that he is a good father.

DISPLACEMENT **Displacement** involves the redirection of repressed motives and emotions from their original objects to substitute objects. The man who has always wanted to be a father may feel inadequate when he learns that he cannot have children. As a result, he may become extremely attached to a pet or to a niece or nephew. In another example of displacement, the woman who must smile and agree with her boss all day may come home and yell at her husband or children.

SUBLIMATION **Sublimation** refers to transforming repressed motives or feelings into more socially acceptable forms. Aggressiveness, for instance, might be channeled into competitiveness in business or sports. A strong and persistent desire for attention might be transformed into an interest in acting or politics. From the Freudian perspective, sublimation is not only necessary but also desirable. People who can transform their sexual and aggressive drives into more socially acceptable forms are clearly better off, for they are able at least partially to gratify instinctual drives with relatively little anxiety and guilt. Moreover, society benefits from the energy and effort that such people channel into the arts, literature, science, and other socially useful activities (T. Adams, 2004).

Does defensive coping mean that a person is immature, unstable, or on the edge of a "breakdown"? Is direct coping adaptive, and is defensive coping maladaptive? Not necessarily (Cramer, 2000; Rhodewalt, & Vohs, 2005). In some cases of prolonged and severe stress, lower level defenses may not only contribute to our overall ability to adjust but also may even become essential to survival. Defenses can also be adaptive for coping with more serious problems. In the short run, especially if there are few other options, defenses may reduce anxiety and thus allow for the highest possible level of adaptation. Over the long run, however, defenses can hinder successful adjustment. Defense mechanisms are maladaptive when they interfere with a person's ability to deal directly with a problem or when they create more problems than they solve.

intellectualization Thinking abstractly about stressful problems as a way of detaching oneself from them.

reaction formation Expression of exaggerated ideas and emotions that are the opposite of one's repressed beliefs or feelings.

displacement Shifting repressed motives and emotions from an original object to a substitute object.

sublimation Redirecting repressed motives and feelings into more socially acceptable channels.

The defense mechanism of sublimation occurs when people redirect their repressed motives into socially acceptable channels. For instance, a person interested in starting fires may become a firefighter as a way to redirect such urges.

ENDURING ISSUES

Person–Situation   Coping Strategies

Individuals use various coping strategies in different combinations and in different ways to deal with stressful events. It is tempting to conclude that styles of coping, like personality, reside within the individual. Yet, a good deal of research indicates that how much stress people encounter and how they cope depend to a significant degree on the environment in which they live (Almeida, 2005; S. E. Taylor & Repetti, 1997). ●●

SOCIOECONOMIC AND GENDER DIFFERENCES IN COPING WITH STRESS

Who experiences the most stress?

Consider the impact of socioeconomic status on stress and coping. In poor neighborhoods, addressing even the basic tasks of living is stressful. Housing is often substandard and crowded; there are fewer stores, and they offer lower quality goods; crime and unemployment rates are likely to be high; and schools have lower teacher–student ratios, high staff turnover, and more part-time teachers. In short, poor people have to deal with more stress than people who are financially secure (N. Adler et al., 1994; G. W. Evans & English, 2002; Gutman, McLoyd, & Tokoyawa, 2005). Moreover, some data indicate that people in low-income groups cope less effectively with stress and that, as a result, stressful events have a stronger impact on their emotional lives (Hammack, Robinson, Crawford, & Li, 2004). People in lower income groups are significantly more depressed, anxious, hopeless, and hostile. As we will see, those negative emotions are associated with worse physical and mental health (Gallo & Matthews, 2003). Psychologists have offered possible explanations for these data. People in lower socioeconomic classes often have fewer means for coping with

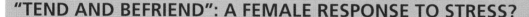

ON THE CUTTING EDGE

"TEND AND BEFRIEND": A FEMALE RESPONSE TO STRESS?

Imagine that two families are walking down a dark street and notice that a suspicious stranger is following them. Both the mothers and the fathers in this group are likely to experience the same symptoms of stress. But do they react in the same way? Or do the men turn to confront the stranger while the women gather the youngsters together and reassure their children and each other that everything will be all right? A new line of research suggests that females and males—across species—respond to stress in different ways as a result of evolutionary adaptation (S. E. Taylor et al., 2000; Volpe, 2004).

When a student casually mentioned that most studies of stress in animals were carried out with male rats, psychologist Shelley E. Taylor and her colleagues reviewed several hundred previous studies of stress in rodents, monkeys, and humans. In studies of humans, only 17% of the subjects were female. The researchers also found that females didn't fit the standard pattern. Rather, danger evokes a *"tend-and-befriend"* response in females, who tend their young and seek contact and support from others, especially other females. For example, women coming home from a bad day at work spend time

with their children or call a friend; men tend to withdraw or get into arguments. This might also help to explain why females are less likely than males to be physically aggressive.

The tend-and-befriend response may be linked to the hormone oxytocin, which is also produced during childbirth and nursing and linked to maternal behavior and social affiliation. Research shows that oxytocin makes rats and humans calmer, more social, and less fearful. Under stress, both males and females secrete oxytocin, but the male hormone testosterone seems to reduce its effect, whereas the female hormone estrogen amplifies it. These hormonal differences might explain why men have higher rates of stress-related health problems than women do, and why the "classic" symptoms of heart attack—such as pain radiating down the arm—are more common in men than women experiencing heart attacks, who are more likely to experience shortness of breath (Goode, 2000c).

Dr. Taylor and her colleagues explain sex differences in response to stress in evolutionary terms. Long ago, when our ancestors were hunter–gatherers who did not build permanent villages,

predators—perhaps including human competitors—were a constant danger. Under those environmental conditions, it was adaptive for men to confront danger (by fighting) or to divert an enemy (by fleeing) while women guarded the children. Taylor argues that this adaptation became "hardwired" and remains with us today. Other psychologists (Eagly & Wood, 1999; Pitman, 2003) are quick to point out that the difference could just as likely be the result of learning and cultural conditioning. As Pavlov demonstrated, physiological responses (whether salivation or hormone production) can be altered through conditioning (see Chapter 5, "Learning"). So, does an inborn physiological response to stress cause females to seek and provide comfort? Or does a culturally conditioned seek-and-provide-comfort response stimulate physiological changes?

For her part, Taylor thinks the most important message of this research is that people respond to stress in different ways. Most studies of stress looked at lone male subjects. Perhaps in group situations males, too, have a tend-and-befriend response to stress. Proving or disproving this hypothesis will require additional research.

hardship and stress (Gallo & Matthews, 2003). Low-income people also have fewer people to turn to and fewer community resources to draw on for support during stressful times (Ghate & Hazel, 2002). These factors help explain why stress often takes a greater toll on people in lower socioeconomic classes.

Are there gender differences in coping with stress? At present, the answer seems to be "yes"—at least under some circumstances. One study of the victims of Hurricane Andrew found that although men and women were affected equally when stress was measured physiologically, women reported experiencing more stress than men (T. Adler, 1993). In another study of 300 dual-income couples, women and men felt equally stressed by the state of their marriage, their jobs, and how well their children were doing. However, the women in this study experienced greater stress than men when problems developed in long-term relationships, largely because they were more committed to their personal and professional relationships than the men were (R. C. Barnett, Brennan, & Marshall, 1994). Women and men also appear to respond differently to the stress caused by an automobile accident, with woman experiencing more stress both immediately after the accident and several months later (Bryant & Harvey, 2003). Some research indicates that when faced with equally stressful situations, men and women generally use quite similar coping strategies (L. S. Porter & Stone, 1995). However other research suggests the opposite—that in at least some circumstances, men and women use rather different coping strategies (Anshel, Porter, & Quek, 1998; Bellman, Forster, Still, & Cooper, 2003; Narayanan, Shanker, & Spector, 1999; Ptacek, Smith, & Dodge, 1994). For example, studies (Hussong, 2003; Nolen-Hoeksema, 1999) have found that when men are down or depressed, they are more likely than women to turn to alcohol; when women are blue, sad, or mad, they are more likely to ruminate about the problem, revisiting negative emotions and the events that led up to them in their minds (see "On the Cutting Edge: Tend and Befriend: A Female Response to Stress?").

CHECK YOUR UNDERSTANDING

1. There are two general types of coping: _____ and _____.
2. Confronting problems, compromising, or withdrawing from the situation entirely are all forms of _____ coping.
3. _____ coping is a means of dealing with situations that people feel unable to resolve.

Answers: 1. direct, defensive. 2. direct. 3. Defensive.

APPLY YOUR UNDERSTANDING

1. You're approaching a deadline by which a project must be finished. Your stress level rises when you realize that it will be nearly impossible to meet the deadline. Which of the following is NOT one of your choices for coping directly with the stressful situation?
   a. trying harder and enlisting the help of others
   b. denying that you will be unable to finish the project on time
   c. admitting defeat and withdrawing from the situation
   d. working out an arrangement through which you submit part of the project on time and get additional time for submitting the rest of it
2. Bill is very frustrated because he did quite poorly on several midterm exams. After returning from an especially difficult exam, he yells at his roommate for leaving clothes strewn around the floor. Bill's reaction is most likely the result of which defense mechanism?
   a. projection
   b. reaction formation
   c. sublimation
   d. displacement

Answers: 1. b. 2. d.

Evidence appears to show that the chronic anger and hostility associated with Type A behavior can predict heart disease.

Type A personalities were evaluated, subjected to harassment or criticism, or playing video games, their heart rate and blood pressure were much higher than those of Type B personalities under the same circumstances (Griffiths & Dancaster, 1995; Lyness, 1993). Both high heart rate and high blood pressure are known to contribute to CHD.

Other studies maintain that the link between Type A behavior and CHD is less direct—that the tendency toward Type A behavior may influence people to engage in behaviors, such as smoking or overeating, that directly contribute to heart disease (K. A. Matthews, 1988; M. Woodward, Oliphant, Lowe, & Tunstall-Pedoe, 2003). On the basis of the preponderance of evidence, however, it seems clear that *chronic anger* and *hostility* (both components of Type A behavior) do indeed predict heart disease (Mohan, 2006; R. B. Williams, 2001). For example, people who scored high on an anger scale were 2.5 times more likely to have heart attacks or sudden cardiac deaths than their calmer peers (J. C. Williams et al., 2000). Counseling designed to diminish the intensity of time urgency and hostility in patients with Type A behavior has been moderately successful in reducing the incidence of CHD (M. Friedman et al., 1996; Kop, 2005).

Depression, too, appears to increase the risk of heart disease and premature death (McCabe, Schneiderman, Field, & Wellens, 2000; Rugulies, 2002; Schwartzman & Glaus, 2000). In fact, recent studies have identified a third personality type that incorporates the precise elements of depression that are most predictive of heart disease. Called *Type D*, or *Distressed Personality*, it is characterized by depression, negative emotions, and social inhibition. The type D personality is linked to heart disease because when stressed, people with a Type D personality produce excessive amounts of cortisol, which damages the heart and blood vessels over time (Denollet, 2005; Habra, Linden, & Anderson, 2003; Sher, 2004). Because long-term stress increases the likelihood of developing CHD, reducing stress has become part of the treatment used to slow the progress of hardening of the arteries, which can lead to a heart attack. A very low-fat diet and stress-management techniques, such as yoga and deep relaxation, have been effective in treating this disease (Ornish, Scherwitz, Billings, Gould, Merritt, Sparler, et al., 1998).

STRESS AND THE IMMUNE SYSTEM

Why do so many students get sick during finals?

Scientists have long suspected that stress also affects the functioning of the immune system. Recall that the immune system is strongly affected by hormones and signals from the brain. The field of **psychoneuroimmunology (PNI)** studies the interaction between stress on the one hand and immune, endocrine, and nervous system activity on the other (Azar, 1999; Dougall & Baum, 2004; Stowell, McGuire, Robles, & Kiecolt-Glaser, 2003). To the extent that stress disrupts the functioning of the immune system, it can impair health (S. Cohen & Herbert, 1996). Chronic stress—from caring for an elderly parent, living in poverty, depression (Kiecolt-Glaser & Glaser, R. 2002; Oltmanns & Emery, 1998), or even living with a spouse with cancer (Mortimer, Sephton, Kimerling, Butler, Bernstein, & Spiegel, 2005)—has been linked to suppressed functioning of the immune system (Irwin, 2002).

THINKING CRITICALLY ABOUT . . .

"Genes Lie Behind Only About 30% of Cancers Studied"*

Stop, *look away from this book, and repeat what you just read.* Was your first impression that genes cause one-third of cancers? The headline is worded so that your eyes might register: **Genes Lie Behind 30% of Cancers**. Given the emphasis on genes in media reports of science, your mind-set may lead to selective perception of genetic causes. Now consider the scientific study behind this headline.

According to a report in the *New England Journal of Medicine*, the chances of developing cancer are largely determined by lifestyle, not inheritance (Lichtenstein et al., 2000). In one of the largest studies of its kind, researchers analyzed longitudinal data on 44,788 pairs of Scandinavian twins born between 1870 and 1958. The data revealed that 10,803 of these individuals developed cancers. Even when one identical twin developed cancer, the chances that the other twin got the same cancer was very low. In contrast to what you may have believed from the newspaper headline, the authors concluded "that the overwhelming contributor to the causation of cancer in the populations of twins that we studied was the environment" (p. 80).

- How much confidence do you have in this report? Why?
- If this report is correct, what can you do to reduce the risk that you will develop cancer?
- Should someone with a family history of cancer ignore his or her heredity? Ask a doctor whether to have periodic tests so that, if they inherited a predisposition toward developing cancer, the cancer will be detected early? Undergo genetic tests, if and when these are available?

*Headline from the *Los Angeles Times*, July 11, 2000, p. 1A.

Increased stress may make us more susceptible to influenza (Tseng, Padgett, Dhabhar, Engler, & Sheridan, 2005) and upper respiratory infections, such as the common cold (S. Cohen, 1996; S. Cohen et al., 2002). For example, volunteers who reported being under severe stress and who had experienced two or more major stressful events during the previous year were more likely to develop a cold when they were exposed to a cold virus (S. Cohen, Tyrrell, & Smith, 1991). A control group of volunteers who reported lower levels of stress were less likely to develop cold symptoms even though they were equally exposed to the virus. People who report experiencing a lot of positive emotions (for example, happiness, pleasure, or relaxation) are also less likely to develop colds when exposed to the virus than those who report a lot of negative emotions (for example, anxiety, hostility, or depression) (S. Cohen, Doyle, Turner, Alper, & Skoner, 2003a).

Psychoneuroimmunologists have also established a possible relationship between stress and cancer (Herberman, 2002). Stress does not cause cancer, but it apparently impairs the immune system so that cancerous cells are better able to establish themselves and spread throughout the body. Current animal research is focused on finding the exact cellular mechanisms that link stress to cancer (Herberman, 2002; Quan et al., 1999).

Establishing a direct link between stress and cancer in humans is more difficult. For obvious reasons, researchers cannot conduct similar experiments with human participants. Some early research showed a correlation between stress and incidence of cancer (McKenna, Zevon, Corn, & Rounds, 1999; A. O'Leary, 1990), but more recent research has not confirmed these findings (Maunsell, Brisson, Mondor, Verreault, & Deschenes, 2001). In addition, several new cancer drugs work by boosting the immune system, although even this does not necessarily mean that damage to the immune system makes people more vulnerable to cancer (Azar, 1999). Thus, the jury is still out on whether stress contributes to cancer in humans (Reiche, Morimoto, & Nunes, 2005).

Regardless, many medical practitioners agree that psychologists can also play a vital role in improving the quality of life for cancer patients (P. A. McGuire, 1999; Rabasca, 1999a; J. E. Smith, Richardson, & Hoffman, 2005). For example, women faced with the diagnosis of late-stage breast cancer understandably experience high levels of depression and mental stress. Many physicians now routinely recommend that their breast-cancer patients attend group therapy sessions, which are effective in reducing depression, mental stress, hostility, insomnia, and the perception of pain (Giese-Davis et al., 2002; Goodwin et al., 2001; Quesnel, Savard, Simard, Ivers, & Morin, 2003; Spiegel, 1995). Some initial reports also showed that breast-cancer patients who attended group therapy sessions actually had an increased survival rate (Spiegel & Moore, 1997), although more recent investigations have not supported this claim (DeAngelis, 2002; Edelman, Lemon, Bell, & Kidman, 1999; Goodwin et al., 2001).

Staying Healthy

What two key areas can people control to help themselves stay healthy?

Stress may be part of life, but there are proven ways to reduce the negative impact of stress on your body and your health. The best method, not surprisingly, is to reduce stress. A healthy lifestyle can also prepare you to cope with the unavoidable stress in your life.

REDUCE STRESS

What steps can people take to reduce stress?

Scientists do not have a simple explanation for the common cold, much less cancer. But they do have advice on how to reduce stress and stay healthy.

CALM DOWN *Exercise* is a good beginning. Running, walking, biking, swimming, or other aerobic exercise lowers your resting heart rate and blood pressure, so that your body does not react as strongly to stress and recovers more quickly. As we discuss later, exercise is also part of a healthy lifestyle. Moreover, numerous studies show that people who exercise

psychoneuroimmunology (PNI) A new field that studies the interaction between stress on the one hand and immune, endocrine, and nervous system activity on the other.

regularly and are physically fit have higher self-esteem than those who do not; are less likely to feel anxious, depressed, or irritable; and have fewer aches and pains, as well as fewer colds (Annesi, 2005; Biddle, 2000; Sonstroem, 1997).

Relaxation training is another stress buster. A number of studies indicate that relaxation techniques lower stress (Pothier, 2002) and improve immune functioning (Andersen, Kiecolt-Glaser, & Glaser, 1994; Antoni, 2003). Relaxation is more than flopping on the couch with the TV zapper, however. Healthful physical relaxation requires lying quietly and alternately tensing and relaxing every voluntary muscle in your body—from your head to your toes—to learn how to recognize muscle tension, as well as to learn how to relax your body. Breathing exercises can have the same effect: If you are tense, deep, rhythmic breathing is difficult, but learning to do so relieves bodily tension. (See also Chapter 4, "States of Consciousness," for a discussion of meditation, and Chapter 5, "Learning," for a discussion of biofeedback, both of which can be useful in relaxing and reducing stress.)

REACH OUT A strong network of friends and family who provide *social support* can help to maintain good health (S. Cohen, Doyle, Turner, Alper, & Skoner, 2003b; Karademas, 2006; Uchino, 2004). Exactly why the presence of a strong social support system is related to health is not fully understood. Some researchers contend that social support may directly affect our response to stress and health by producing physiological changes in endocrine, cardiac, and immune functioning (Uchino, Uno, & Holt-Lunstad, 1999). Whatever the underlying mechanism, most people can remember times when other people made a difference in their lives by giving them good advice (informational support), helping them to feel better about themselves (emotional support), providing assistance with chores and responsibilities or financial help (tangible support), or simply by "hanging out" with them (belonging support) (Uchino, Uno, & Holt-Lunstad, 1999).

Not all relationships are alike, however. Knowing a lot of people or having a partner may or may not be a stress buffer; what matters are the characteristics of friends and partners and the quality of the relationships (Hartup & Stevens, 1999). For example, studies have found that married couples who argue in a hostile way—criticizing, belittling, and insulting one another—have suppressed immune function compared with couples who interact in more constructive ways—listening to one another's points of view, seeking common ground and compromise, as well as using humor to break up tension (Kiecolt-Glaser, Malarkey, Chee, Newton, & Cacioppo, 1993; Kiecolt-Glaser, Bane, Glaser, & Malarkey, 2003).

RELIGION AND ALTRUISM Health psychologists are also investigating the role religion may play in reducing stress and bolstering health (Freedland, 2004; Joseph, Linley, & Maltby, 2006; W. R. Miller & Thoresen, 2003; Rabin & Koenig, 2002; K. Siegel, Anderman, & Schrimshaw, 2001). For example, research has found that elderly people who pray or attend religious services regularly enjoy better health and markedly lower rates of depression than those who do not (Koenig, McCullough, & Larson, 2000). Other studies have shown that having a religious commitment may also help to moderate high blood pressure and hypertension (Levin & Vanderpool, 1989; Wilkins, 2005).

It is unclear why there is an association between health and religion (Contrada et al., 2004). One explanation holds that religion provides a system of social support that includes caring friends and opportunities for close personal interactions. As previously described, a strong network of social support can reduce stress in a variety of ways, and in turn, reduced stress is associated with better health (Uchino et al., 1996, 1999). Other possible explanations are that regular attendance at religious services encourages people to help others, which in turn increases feelings of personal control and reduces feelings of depression; that frequent attendance at religious services increases positive emotions; and that most religions encourage healthy lifestyles (L. H. Powell, Shababi, & Thoresen, 2003).

Altruism—reaching out and giving to others because this brings *you* pleasure—is one of the more effective ways to reduce stress (Vaillant, 2000). Caring for others tends to take our minds off our own problems, to make us realize that there are others who are worse off than we are, and to foster the feeling that we're involved in something larger than our own small slice of life (R. S. Allen, Haley, & Roff, 2006; Folkman, Chesney, & Christopher-Richards, 1994). Altruism is a component of most religions, suggesting that altruism and religious commitment may have something in common that helps to reduce stress. Altruism may also channel loss, grief, or anger into constructive action. An example is *Mothers Against Drunk Driving* (MADD), an organization founded by a mother whose child was killed by a drunken driver.

LEARN TO COPE EFFECTIVELY How you appraise events in your environment—and how you appraise your ability to cope with potentially unsettling, unpredictable events—can minimize or maximize stress and its impact on health.

Proactive coping is the psychological term for anticipating stressful events and taking advance steps to avoid them or to minimize their impact (Aspinwall & Taylor, 1997; Greenglass, 2002). Proactive coping does not mean "expect the worst"; constant vigilance actually increases stress and may damage health. Rather, proactive coping means (as in the Boy Scout motto), "Be prepared." This may include accumulating resources (time, money, social support, and information), recognizing potential stress in advance, and making realistic plans. For example, a recent widower anticipates that his first Christmas without his late wife will be lonely and makes plans to spend the holidays with friends. A woman who is moving to a new city knows the transition may be stressful. She finds out as much as she can about her new location before she moves—whether her friends have friends there, where she can participate in activities she enjoys (such as taking classes in drawing or karate), places and groups or organizations where she might meet people who share her interests (a house of worship, the best jazz clubs, the local animal shelter), and so on.

In many cases, you cannot change or escape stressful circumstances, but you can change the way you think about things. *Positive reappraisal* helps people to make the best of a tense or painful situation. A low grade can be seen as a warning sign, not a catastrophe, a job you hate provides information on what you really want in your career; instead of brooding about a nasty remark from your sister, ask what does this tell you about *her?* Positive reappraisal does not require you to become a "Pollyanna" (the heroine of a novel who was optimistic to the point of being ridiculous). Rather, it requires finding new meaning in a situation, or finding a perspective or insight that you had overlooked. After his partner died, one HIV caregiver told researchers, "What his death did was snap a certain value into my behavior, which is, 'Listen, you don't know how long you've got. You've just lost another one. Spend more time with the people who mean something to you'" (S. E. Taylor, Kemeny, Reed, Bower, & Gruenwald, 2000, p. 105).

One of the most effective, stress-relieving forms of reappraisal is *humor*. As Shakespeare so aptly put it in *The Winter's Tale*: "A merry heart goes all the day/ Your sad tires in a mile" (*Act IV, Scene 3*). Journalist Norman Cousins (1981) attributed his recovery from a life-threatening disease to regular "doses" of laughter. Watching classic comic films, he believed, reduced both his pain and the inflammation in his tissues. He wrote:

> What was significant about the laughter . . . was not just the fact that it provides internal exercise for a person flat on his or her back—a form of jogging for the innards—but that it creates a mood in which the other positive emotions can be put to work, too. In short, it helps make it possible for good things to happen (pp. 145–146).

Some health psychologists agree that a healthy body and a sense of humor go hand in hand (J. E. Myers & Sweeney, 2006; Salovey, Rothman, Detweiler, & Steward, 2000; Vaillant, 2000), while others believe that more research is needed before any firm conclusions can be drawn (R. A. Martin, 2002). Most are in agreement, however, that doing what we can to maintain a healthy body helps us both reduce and cope with stress.

ADOPT A HEALTHY LIFESTYLE

What are the elements of a healthy lifestyle?

While learning how to avoid and cope with stress is important, the *positive psychology* movement (see Chapter 1, "The Science of Psychology") has prompted many health psychologists to explore other ways to promote good health by adopting a healthier lifestyle. Developing healthy habits—like eating a well-balanced diet, getting regular exercise, not smoking, and avoiding high-risk behaviors—are all important to maintaining health (H. S. Friedman, 2002).

Soldiers who have been in combat, such as the ones who served in Iraq, are at risk for developing posttraumatic stress disorder.

posttraumatic stress disorder (PTSD)
Psychological disorder characterized by episodes of anxiety, sleeplessness, and nightmares resulting from some disturbing past event.

POSTTRAUMATIC STRESS DISORDER

Severely stressful events can cause a psychological disorder known as **posttraumatic stress disorder (PTSD)**. Dramatic nightmares in which the victim reexperiences the terrifying event exactly as it happened are common. So are daytime flashbacks, in which the victim relives the trauma. Often, victims of PTSD withdraw from social life and from job and family responsibilities (Kashdan, Julian, Merritt, & Uswatte, 2006). PTSD can set in immediately after a traumatic event or within a short time afterwards. But sometimes, months or years may go by in which the victim seems to have recovered from the experience, and then, without warning, psychological symptoms reappear, then may disappear only to recur repeatedly (Corales, 2005).

The experiences of soldiers have heightened interest in PTSD. For example, more than one-third of the soldiers who served in Vietnam experienced PTSD at some point afterward (E. J. Ozer, Best, Lipsey, & Weiss, 2003). Many veterans of World War II, who are now old men, still have nightmares from which they awake sweating and shaking. The memories of combat continue to torment them after more than half a century (Port, Engdahl, & Frazier, 2001). Recently, therapists have begun to observe a new phenomenon: Veterans who seemed to be healthy and well adjusted throughout their postwar lives suddenly develop symptoms of PTSD when they retire and enter their "golden years" (Sleek, 1998; van Achterberg, Rohrbaugh, & Southwick, 2001).

Soldiers are not the only victims of war. Indeed, during the 20th century, civilian deaths outnumbered military deaths in most wars. Yet only in the last decade—especially following the tragedy of the September 11 terrorist attacks on the World Trade Center and the devastation of New Orleans by Hurricane Katrina—have medical researchers begun to investigate the psychological and physiological effects of war, tragedy, and terrorism on civilian survivors. For many, the immediate response following a traumatic event is one of shock and denial. Shock leaves victims feeling stunned, confused, and in some cases, temporarily numb. Denial often causes them to be unwilling to acknowledge the impact and emotional intensity of the event. After the initial shock passes, individual reactions to trauma vary considerably, but commonly include: heightened emotionality, irritability, nervousness, difficulty concentrating, changes in sleep patterns, physical symptoms such as nausea, headaches, chest pain, and even depression. Some civilians also experience long-lasting and severe problems, such as exhaustion, hatred, mistrust, and the symptoms of PTSD (Gurwitch, Sitterle, Young, & Pfefferbaum, 2002; Mollica, 2000).

ENDURING ISSUES

Diversity–Universality   Reactions to Severe Stress

Not everyone who is exposed to severely stressful events (such as heavy combat or childhood sexual abuse) develops PTSD. Although more than half of the American population is exposed to a severely traumatic event at some time, less than 10% will develop symptoms of PTSD (E. J. Ozer et al., 2003). Individual characteristics—including gender, personality, a family history of mental disorders, prior exposure to trauma, substance abuse among relatives, and even preexisting neurological disorders—appear to predispose some people to PTSD more than others (Najavits, 2004; Parslow, Jorm, & Christensen, 2006; Post et al, 2003; Rabasca, 1999b). Both men and women who have a history of emotional problems are more likely to experience severe trauma and to develop PTSD as a consequence of trauma. Not surprisingly, people who may already be under extreme stress (perhaps caused by a health problem or interpersonal difficulties) prior to experiencing a traumatic event are at greatest risk (M. Heinrichs et al., 2005; S. Lipsky, Field, Caetano, & Larkin, 2005).

Some psychologists have found that following a significant trauma, a few particularly stable individuals experience a *positive* form of personal growth called *posttraumatic growth* (Calhoun & Tedeschi, 2001). In the rare instances where posttraumatic growth occurs, it appears to emerge largely from an individual's struggle to reconcile their loss through religious or existential understanding. When it does occur, posttraumatic growth is more likely to be seen in young adults than in older people (S. Powell, Rosner, Butollo, Tedeschi, & Calhoun, 2003). ●●

Recovery from posttraumatic stress disorder is strongly related to the amount of emotional support survivors receive from family, friends, and community. Treatment consists of helping those who have experienced severe trauma to come to terms with their terrifying memories. Immediate treatment near the site of the trauma coupled with the expectation that the individual will return to everyday life is often effective. Reliving the traumatic event in a safe setting is also crucial to successful treatment (Jaycox, Zoellner, & Foa, 2002). This helps desensitize people to the traumatic memories haunting them (Oltmanns & Emery, 2006).

THINKING CRITICALLY ABOUT . . .

Posttraumatic Stress

1. Obviously, war is not the only cause of extreme stress and trauma. Do you think an individual's response to a personal attack, such as a rape, is similar to or different from that caused by serving in combat?

2. What might you do to help a friend recover from a significant personal trauma? How could you find out about counseling and other resources to provide further help?

CHECK YOUR UNDERSTANDING

Is each of the following statements true (T) or false (F)?

1. ___ If people who are bereaved following the death of a spouse or child have not recovered by the end of 1 year, this outcome indicates that they are coping abnormally.

2. ___ Catastrophes—including floods, earthquakes, violent storms, fires, and plane crashes—produce different psychological reactions than do other kinds of stressful events.

3. ___ Most children whose parents divorce experience serious and long-term problems.

4. ___ Posttraumatic stress disorder can appear months or even years after a traumatic event.

Answers: 1. (F), 2. (F), 3. (F), 4. (T).

APPLY YOUR UNDERSTANDING

1. Your friend Patrick has just survived a traumatic event. Which of the following would you LEAST expect to observe?
   a. difficulty sleeping, frequent nightmares
   b. physical symptoms, such as nausea and headaches
   c. irritability, rapid mood changes, and nervousness
   d. a healthy appetite and increased interest in food and eating

2. As you try to help Patrick begin to recover from the traumatic event, which of the following would be most beneficial?
   a. Encourage him to get over it as quickly as possible and move on with his life.
   b. Suggest that he change jobs and move to a new location so he can "start over."
   c. Listen supportively without probing.
   d. Encourage him to describe the details of the event so he won't go into denial.

Answers: 1. d. 2. c.

The Well-Adjusted Person

What qualities describe a well-adjusted person?

We noted at the beginning of the chapter that adjustment is any effort to cope with stress. Psychologists disagree, however, about what constitutes *good* adjustment. Some think it is the ability to live according to social norms. Thus, a woman who grows up in a small town, attends college, teaches for a year or two, and then settles down to a peaceful family life might be considered well adjusted because she is living by the predominant values of her community.

Other psychologists disagree strongly with this view. They argue that society is not always right. Thus, if we accept its standards blindly, we renounce the right to make individual judgments. For instance, one view from feminist psychology (O'Leary & Bhaju, 2006) argues that well-adjusted people enjoy the difficulties and ambiguities of life, treating them as challenges to be overcome. Such people are aware of their strengths and weaknesses; this awareness empowers them to live in harmony with their inner selves. For example, although aging involves declining health and decreased mobility, successful aging also involves the opportunity for psychological growth and maturation. The idea that adversity may serve as an impetus for psychological growth is also consistent with the positive psychology movement.

We may also evaluate adjustment by using specific criteria, such as the following, to judge an action:

1. Does the action realistically meet the demands of the situation, or does it simply postpone resolving the problem?
2. Does the action meet the individual's needs?
3. Is the action compatible with the well-being of others?

Abraham Maslow, whose hierarchy of needs was discussed in Chapter 8, "Motivation and Emotion," believed that well-adjusted people attempt to "actualize" themselves. That is, they live in a way that enhances their own growth and fulfillment, regardless of what others might think. According to Maslow, well-adjusted people are unconventional and creative thinkers, perceive people and events realistically, and set goals for themselves. They also tend to form deep, close relationships with a few chosen individuals.

As we have seen, there are many standards for judging whether an individual is well adjusted. A person deemed well adjusted by one standard might not be considered well adjusted by other standards. The same principle holds true when we try to specify what behaviors are "abnormal"—the topic of the next chapter.

THINKING CRITICALLY ABOUT . . .

Who is Well Adjusted?

Write down the names of three individuals whom you consider well adjusted. Take some time before you answer. Include one person whom you know only distantly, perhaps someone you read about.

- What personal qualities set these individuals apart?
- Describe an action or situation that impressed you.
- What do these people have in common? What are their individual distinctions?

CHECK YOUR UNDERSTANDING

1. The well-adjusted person has learned to balance
   a. conformity and nonconformity.
   b. self-control and spontaneity.
   c. flexibility and structure.
   d. all of the above.

Answer: 1. d.

APPLY YOUR UNDERSTANDING

1. Your roommate is attempting to deal with a particularly stressful set of events in her life. You wonder whether she is coping well or whether there is cause for concern. Which of the following criteria would be LEAST useful in making that judgment?

   a. Whether her behavior is realistically meeting the demands of the situation.

   b. Whether she is doing what society says people should do in these kinds of situations.

   c. Whether her behavior is interfering with the well-being of others around her.

   d. Whether her actions are effectively meeting her needs.

2. Mary lives in a way that enhances her own growth and fulfillment regardless of what others think. In many ways, she is unconventional, is a creative thinker, and has close relationships with only a few chosen individuals. According to Maslow, Mary is most likely

   a. a well-adjusted, self-actualizing person.

   b. engaging in positive reappraisal.

   c. a Type A personality.

   d. making excessive use of intellectualization.

Answers: 1. b. 2. a.

KEY TERMS

stress, *p. 386*
health psychology, *p. 386*
adjustment, *p. 386*

Sources of Stress

stressor, *p. 386*
pressure, *p. 388*
frustration, *p. 388*
conflict, *p. 388*
approach/approach
  conflict, *p. 389*

avoidance/avoidance conflict,
  p. 389
approach/avoidance conflict,
  p. 389

Coping with Stress

confrontation, *p. 392*
compromise, *p. 392*
withdrawal, *p. 393*
defense mechanisms, *p. 393*

denial, *p. 393*
repression, *p. 393*
projection, *p. 393*
identification, *p. 394*
regression, *p. 394*
intellectualization, *p. 395*
reaction formation, *p. 395*
displacement, *p. 395*
sublimation, *p. 395*

How Stress Affects Health

general adaptation syndrome
  (GAS), *p. 398*
psychoneuroimmunology
  (PNI), *p. 401*

Extreme Stress

posttraumatic stress disorder
  (PTSD), *p. 408*

CHAPTER REVIEW

Sources of Stress

What are stressors? We experience **stress** when we are faced with a tense or threatening situation that requires us to change or adapt our behavior (a **stressor**). Life-and-death situations, like war and natural disasters, are inherently stressful. Even events that are usually viewed as positive, like a wedding or a job promotion, can be stressful, because they require change, adaptation, and **adjustment**. How we adjust to the stress affects our health, since prolonged or severe stress can contribute to physical and psychological disorders. **Health psychologists** try to find ways to prevent stress from becoming debilitating and to promote healthy behaviors.

Why is change so stressful for most people? Because most people strongly desire order in their lives, any good or bad event involving change will be experienced as stressful.

How can everyday hassles contribute to stress? Day-to-day petty annoyances and irritations can be as stressful as major life events, because these seemingly minor incidents give rise to feelings of pressure, frustration, conflict, and anxiety.

When we experience **pressure** from either internal or external forces, we feel forced to intensify our efforts or to perform at higher levels. Internal forces include trying to live up to social and cultural norms as well as family and peer expectations.

We feel frustrated when someone or something stands between us and our goal. Five basic sources of **frustration** are delays, lack of resources, losses, failure, and discrimination.

Conflict arises when we are faced with two or more incompatible demands, opportunities, needs, or goals. With **approach/approach conflict**, a person must either choose between two attractive but incompatible goals or opportunities, or modify them so as to take some advantage of both. With **avoidance/avoidance conflict**, a person must choose between two undesirable or threatening possibilities. If escape is impossible, the person may often vacillate between the two possibilities. With **approach/avoidance conflict**, a person is both attracted to and repelled by the same goal or opportunity. Because the desire to approach and the desire to avoid the goal both grow stronger as the person in this dilemma nears the goal, eventually the tendency to approach equals the tendency to avoid. The person then vacillates finally making a decision or until the situation changes.

How do we create stress? Sometimes we subject ourselves to stress by internalizing a set of irrational, self-defeating beliefs that add unnecessarily to the normal stresses of living.

Do people who are resistant to stress share certain traits? People who cope well with stress tend to be self-confident and optimistic. With their internal locus of control, they also see themselves as being able to affect their situations. Stress-resistant people share a trait called *hardiness*—a tendency to experience difficult demands as challenging rather than threatening. *Resilience*, the ability to bounce back after a stressful event, is also related to positive adjustment.

Coping with Stress

What is the difference between direct coping and defensive coping? People generally adjust to stress in one of two ways: *Direct coping* describes any action people take to change an uncomfortable situation, whereas *defensive coping* denotes the various ways people convince themselves—through a form of self-deception—that they are not really threatened or do not really want something they cannot get.

What are three strategies that deal directly with stress? When we confront a stressful situation and admit to ourselves that there is a problem that needs to be solved, we may learn new skills, enlist other people's aid, or try harder to reach our goal. **Confrontation** may also include expressions of anger. **Compromise** usually requires adjusting expectations or desires; the conflict is resolved by settling for less than what was originally sought. Sometimes the most effective way of coping with a stressful situation is to distance oneself from it. The danger of **withdrawal,** however, is that it may become a maladaptive habit.

What are the major ways of coping defensively? When a stressful situation arises and there is little that can be done to deal with it directly, people often turn to **defense mechanisms** as a way of coping. Defense mechanisms are ways of deceiving ourselves about the causes of stressful events, thus reducing conflict, frustration, pressure, and anxiety. **Denial** is the refusal to acknowledge a painful or threatening reality. **Repression** is the blocking out of unacceptable thoughts or impulses from consciousness. When we cannot deny or repress a particular problem, we might resort to **projection**—attributing our repressed motives or feelings to others, thereby locating the source of our conflict outside ourselves. **Identification** may occur when people feel completely powerless. People who adopt this technique take on others' characteristics to gain a sense of control or adequacy. People under severe stress sometimes revert to childlike behavior, called **regression**. Because adults can't stand feeling helpless, becoming more childlike can make total

dependency or helplessness more tolerable. A subtle form of denial is seen in **intellectualization**, when people emotionally distance themselves from a particularly disturbing situation. **Reaction formation** refers to a behavioral form of denial in which people express with exaggerated intensity ideas and emotions that are the opposite of their own. Through **displacement**, repressed motives and feelings are redirected from their original objects to substitute objects. **Sublimation** involves transforming repressed emotions into more socially accepted forms. Defensive coping can help us adjust to difficult circumstances, but it can also lead to maladaptive behavior if it interferes with our ability to deal constructively with a difficult situation.

Who experiences the most stress? How people handle stress is determined to a significant degree by the environment in which they live. People in low-income groups often experience more stress and have fewer personal and community resources to draw on for support as well as fewer coping strategies. Men and women may cope differently with stress.

How Stress Affects Health

What long-lasting effects of stress do we need to be concerned with? Physiologist Hans Selye contended that people react to physical and psychological stress in three stages. In Stage 1 (*alarm reaction*) of the **general adaptation syndrome (GAS),** the body recognizes that it must fight off some physical or psychological danger, resulting in quickened respiration and heart rate, increased sensitivity and alertness, and a highly charged emotional state—a physical adaptation that augments our coping resources and helps us to regain self-control. If direct or defensive coping mechanisms fail to reduce the stress, we progress to Stage 2 (*resistance stage*), during which physical symptoms of strain appear as we intensify our efforts to cope both directly and defensively. If these attempts to regain psychological equilibrium fail, psychological disorganization rages out of control until we reach Stage 3 (*exhaustion*). During this phase, we use increasingly ineffective defense mechanisms to bring the stress under control. At this point, some people lose touch with reality, whereas others show signs of "burnout," such as shorter attention spans, irritability, procrastination, and general apathy.

How is Type A behavior related to heart disease? Stress is known to be an important factor in chemical changes in the body leading to the development of coronary heart disease (CHD). Research has demonstrated that the type A behavior pattern—characterized by impatience, hostility, urgency, competitiveness, and striving—predicts CHD.

Why do so many students get sick during finals? Stress—such as that experienced by students during examination periods—can suppress the functioning of the immune system, the focus of the relatively new field of **psychoneuroimmunology** (PNI). Stress can also increase one's susceptibility to the common cold, and it appears to be linked to the development of some forms of cancer.

Staying Healthy

What two key areas can people control to help themselves stay healthy? We can reduce the negative impact of stress on our health by trying to reduce stress and by maintaining a healthy lifestyle, which equips the body to cope with stress that is unavoidable.

What steps can people take to reduce stress? Exercising regularly and learning to relax reduce the body's responses to stress. Having a strong network of social support is also related to healthier adjustment. Religious and altruistic people also typically experience less stress, although the mechanism involved is not clear. Finally, people can take steps to minimize the impact of stressful events (proactive coping), by making the best of difficult situations (positive reappraisal), and by maintaining a sense of humor.

What are the elements of a healthy lifestyle? The *positive psychology* movement has prompted many psychologists to promote good health by adopting a healthier lifestyle. Eating a well-balanced diet, getting regular exercise, not smoking, and avoiding high-risk behaviors are all important to maintaining health.

Extreme Stress

How does extreme stress differ from everyday stress? People experiencing extreme stress cannot continue their everyday life as they did before the stress and, in some cases, they never fully recover.

What are some sources of extreme stress, and what impact do they have? Extreme stress derives from a number of sources, including unemployment, divorce and separation, bereavement, combat, and natural catastrophes. One of the impediments to effective coping occurs when a grieving person feels compelled to adjust in socially prescribed ways that do not provide effective relief.

What experiences can lead to posttraumatic stress disorder? Extreme traumas may result in **posttraumatic stress disorder (PTSD)**, a disabling emotional disorder whose symptoms include daytime flashbacks, social and occupational withdrawal, sleeplessness, and nightmares. Combat veterans and people with a history of emotional problems are especially vulnerable to PTSD.

The Well-Adjusted Person

What qualities describe a well-adjusted person? Psychologists disagree on what constitutes good adjustment. Some believe that well-adjusted people live according to social norms. Others disagree, arguing that well-adjusted people enjoy overcoming challenging situations and that this ability leads to growth and self-fulfillment. Finally, some psychologists use specific criteria to evaluate a person's ability to adjust, such as how well the adjustment solves the problem and satisfies both personal needs and the needs of others.

12 Psychological Disorders

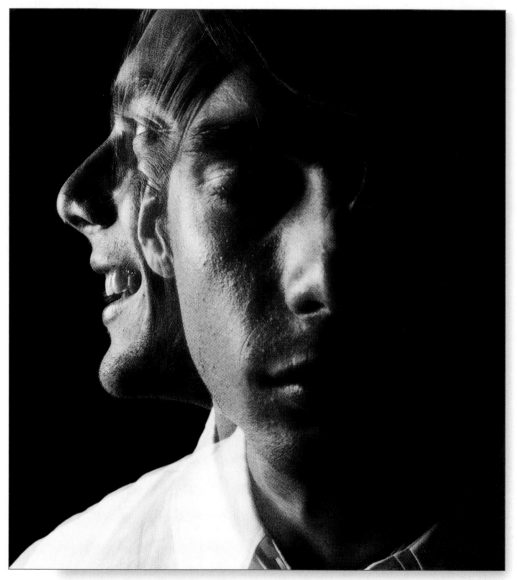

OVERVIEW

Jack was a very successful chemical engineer known for the meticulous accuracy of his work. But Jack also had a "little quirk." He constantly felt compelled to double-, triple-, and even quadruple-check things to assure himself that they were done properly. For instance, when leaving his apartment in the morning, he occasionally got as far as the garage—but invariably he would go back to make certain that the door was securely locked and the stove, lights, and other appliances were all turned off. Going on a vacation was particularly difficult for him because his checking routine was so exhaustive and time consuming. Yet Jack insisted that he would never want to give up this chronic checking. Doing so, he said, would make him "much too nervous."

For Claudia, every day was more than just a bad-hair day. She was always in utter despair over how "hideous" her hair looked. She perceived some parts of it to be too long, and others to be too short. In her eyes, one area would look much too "poofy," while another area would look far too flat. Claudia got up early each morning just to work on her hair. For about 2 hours she would wash it, dry it, brush it, comb it, curl it, straighten it, and snip away infinitesimal amounts with an expensive pair of hair-cutting scissors. But she was never satisfied with the results. Not even trips to the most expensive salons could make her feel content about her hair. She declared that virtually every day was ruined because her hair looked so bad. Claudia said that she desperately wanted to stop focusing on her hair, but for some reason she just couldn't.

Jonathan was a 22-year-old auto mechanic whom everyone described as a loner. He seldom engaged in conversation and seemed lost in his own private world. At work, the other mechanics took to whistling sharply whenever they wanted to get his attention. Jonathan also had a "strange look" on his face that could make customers feel uncomfortable. But his oddest behavior was his assertion that he sometimes had the distinct feeling his dead mother was standing next to him, watching what he did. Although Jonathan realized that his mother was not really there, he nevertheless felt reassured by the illusion of her presence. He took great care not to look or reach toward the spot where he felt his mother was, because doing so inevitably made the feeling go away.

Cases adapted from J. S. Nevis, S. A. Rathus, & B. Green (2005). *Abnormal Psychology in a Changing World* (5th ed.) Upper Saddle River, NJ: Prentice Hall.

ENDURING ISSUES IN PSYCHOLOGICAL DISORDERS ●●

As we explore psychological disorders in this chapter, we will again encounter some of the enduring issues that interest psychologists. A recurring topic is the relationship between genetics, neurotransmitters and behavior disorders (mind–body). We will also see that many psychological disorders arise because a vulnerable person encounters a particularly stressful environment (person–situation). As you read the chapter, think about how you would answer the question "What is normal?" and how the answer to that question has changed over time and differs even today across cultures (diversity–universality). Consider also whether a young person with a psychological disorder is likely to suffer from it later in life and, conversely, whether a well-adjusted young person is immune to psychological disorders later in life (stability–change).

Perspectives on Psychological Disorders

How does a mental health professional define a psychological disorder?

When is a person's behavior abnormal? This is not always easy to determine. There is no doubt about the abnormality of a man who dresses in flowing robes and accosts pedestrians on the street, claiming to be Jesus Christ, or a woman who dons an aluminum-foil helmet to prevent space aliens from "stealing" her thoughts. But other instances of abnormal behavior aren't always so clear. What about the three people we have just described? All of them exhibit unusual behavior. But does their behavior deserve to be labeled "abnormal"? Do any of them have a genuine psychological disorder?

The answer depends in part on the perspective you take. As Table 12–1 summarizes, society, the individual, and the mental health professional all adopt different perspectives when distinguishing abnormal behavior from normal behavior. Society's main standard of

table 12–1	PERSPECTIVES ON PSYCHOLOGICAL DISORDERS	
	Standards/Values	**Measures**
Society	Orderly world in which people assume responsibility for their assigned social roles (e.g., breadwinner, parent), conform to prevailing mores, and meet situational requirements.	Observations of behavior, extent to which a person fulfills society's expectations and measures up to prevailing standards.
Individual	Happiness, gratification of needs.	Subjective perceptions of self-esteem, acceptance, and well-being.
Mental health professional	Sound personality structure characterized by growth, development, autonomy, environmental mastery, ability to cope with stress, adaptation.	Clinical judgment, aided by behavioral observations and psychological tests of such variables as self-concept; sense of identity; balance of psychic forces; unified outlook on life; resistance to stress; self-regulation; the ability to cope with reality; the absence of mental and behavioral symptoms; adequacy in interpersonal relationships.

Source: H. H. Strupp and S. W. Hadley (1977). A tripartite model of mental health and therapeutic outcomes with special reference to negative effects on psychotherapy. *American Psychologist, 32,* 187–196. Copyright © 1977 by the American Psychological Association. Adapted by permission of the authors.

abnormality is whether the behavior fails to conform to prevailing ideas about what is socially expected of people. In contrast, when individuals assess the abnormality of their own behavior, their main criterion is whether that behavior fosters a sense of unhappiness and lack of well-being. Mental health professionals take still another perspective. They assess abnormality chiefly by looking for maladaptive *personality traits, psychological discomfort* regarding a particular behavior, and evidence that the behavior is preventing the person from *functioning well in life.*

These three approaches to identifying abnormal behavior are not always in agreement. For example, of the three people previously described, only Claudia considers her own behavior to be a genuine problem that is undermining her happiness and sense of well-being. In contrast to Claudia, Jack is not really bothered by his compulsive behavior (in fact, he sees it as a way of relieving anxiety); and Jonathan is not only content with being a loner, but he also experiences great comfort from the illusion of his dead mother's presence. But now suppose we shift our focus and adopt society's perspective. In this case, we must include Jonathan on our list of those whose behavior is abnormal. His self-imposed isolation and talk of sensing his mother's ghost violate social expectations of how people should think and act. Society would not consider Jonathan normal. Neither would a mental health professional. In fact, from the perspective of a mental health professional, all three of these cases show evidence of a psychological disorder. The people involved may not always be distressed by their own behavior, but that behavior is impairing their ability to function well in everyday settings or in social relationships. The point is that there is no hard and fast rule as to what constitutes abnormal behavior. Distinguishing between normal and abnormal behavior always depends on the perspective taken.

Identifying behavior as abnormal is also a matter of degree. To understand why, imagine that each of our three cases is slightly less extreme. Jack is still prone to double-checking, but he doesn't check over and over again. Claudia still spends much time on her hair, but she doesn't do so constantly and not with such chronic dissatisfaction. As for Jonathan, he only occasionally withdraws from social contact; and he has had the sense of his dead mother's presence just twice over the last three years. In these less severe situations, a mental health professional would not be so ready to diagnose a mental disorder. Clearly, great care must be taken when separating mental health and mental illness into two *qualitatively* different categories. It is often more accurate to think of mental illness as simply being *quantitatively* different from normal behavior—that is, different in degree. The line between one and the other is often somewhat arbitrary. Cases are always much easier to judge when they fall at the extreme end of a dimension than when they fall near the "dividing line."

HISTORICAL VIEWS OF PSYCHOLOGICAL DISORDERS

How has the view of psychological disorders changed over time?

The place and times also contribute to how we define mental disorders. Thousands of years ago, mysterious behaviors were probably attributed to supernatural powers; and madness was a sign that spirits had possessed a person. As late as the 18th century, the emotionally disturbed person was thought to be a witch or to be possessed by the devil. Exorcisms, ranging from the mild to the hair raising, were performed, and many people endured horrifying tortures. Some people were even burned at the stake.

By the late Middle Ages, there was a move away from viewing the mentally ill as witches and possessed by demons, and they were increasingly confined to public and private asylums. Even though these institutions were founded with good intentions, most were little more than prisons. In the worst cases, inmates were chained down and deprived of food, light, or air in order to "cure" them.

Little was done to ensure humane standards in mental institutions until 1793, when Philippe Pinel (1745–1826) became director of the Bicêtre Hospital in Paris. Under his direction, patients were released from their chains and allowed to move about the hospital grounds, rooms were made more comfortable and sanitary, and questionable and violent medical treatments were abandoned (J. C. Harris, 2003). Pinel's reforms were soon followed by similar efforts in England and, somewhat later, in the United States where Dorothea Dix (1802–1887), a schoolteacher from Boston, led a nationwide campaign for the humane treatment of mentally ill people. Under her influence, the few existing asylums in the United States were gradually turned into hospitals.

The basic reason for the failed—and sometimes abusive—treatment of mentally disturbed people throughout history has been the lack of understanding of the nature and causes of psychological disorders. Although our knowledge is still inadequate, important advances in understanding abnormal behavior can be traced to the late 19th and early 20th centuries, when three influential but conflicting models of abnormal behavior emerged: the biological model, the psychoanalytic model, and the cognitive–behavioral model.

In the 17th century, French physicians tried various devices to cure their patients of "fantasy and folly."

THE BIOLOGICAL MODEL

How can biology influence the development of psychological disorders?

The **biological model** holds that psychological disorders are caused by physiological malfunctions—for example, of the nervous system or the endocrine glands—often stemming from hereditary factors. As we shall see, evidence is growing in support of the biological model of mental illness. Moreover, advances in the new interdisciplinary field of *neuroscience* leaves little doubt that our understanding of the role of biological factors in mental illness will continue to expand. (See "On the Cutting Edge: The Neuroscience Revolution.")

THE PSYCHOANALYTIC MODEL

What did Freud and his followers believe was the underlying cause of psychological disorders?

Freud and his followers developed the **psychoanalytic model** during the late 19th and early 20th centuries. (See Chapter 10, "Personality.") According to this model, behavior disorders

biological model View that psychological disorders have a biochemical or physiological basis.

psychoanalytic model View that psychological disorders result from unconscious internal conflicts.

ON THE CUTTING EDGE

THE NEUROSCIENCE REVOLUTION

Throughout this text we have shown how human behavior, thought, and emotion can be linked with the brain processes that govern them. In this chapter, too, we explore how current advances in neuroscience have increased our understanding of psychological disorders. This new interdisciplinary field is providing exciting insights into the nature and causes of psychological disorders. It brings together research from such diverse disciplines as psychobiology, neurology, neurochemistry, neuroendocrinology, psychiatry, psychology, neurosurgery, neuroimaging, and neuropharmacology.

For instance, new neuroimaging techniques have enabled researchers to pinpoint regions of the brain involved in such disorders as schizophrenia (S. A. Chance, Esiri, & Timothy, 2003; Yotsutsuji et al., 2003) and antisocial personality (Birbaumer et al., 2005; Pridmore, Chambers, & McArthur, 2005). By unraveling the complex chemical interactions that take place at the synapse, neurochemists have spawned advances in neuropharmacology leading to the development of promising new psychoactive drugs (see Chapter 14, "Therapies"). Many of these advances are also linked to the field of behavior genetics, which is continually increasing our understanding of the role of specific genes in the development of complex disorders such as schizophrenia (Gerber et al., 2003; Horiuchi et al., 2006; Tang et al., 2006) and autism (Kuehn, 2006; Nurmi et al., 2003).

Although recent neuroscientific breakthroughs are indeed remarkable, to date no neuroimaging technique can clearly and definitively differentiate among various mental disorders (Sarason & Sarason, 1999; Callicott, 2003). And despite the availability of an increasing number of medications to alleviate the symptoms of some mental disorders, most drugs can only control—rather than cure—abnormal behavior. There is also some concern that advances in identifying the underlying neurological structures and mechanisms associated with mental illnesses may interfere with the recognition of equally important psychological causes of abnormal behavior (Widiger & Sankis, 2000). Despite this concern, the integration of neuroscientific research and traditional psychological approaches to understanding behavior is taking place at an increasingly rapid pace (Lacy & Hughes, 2006; Westen, 2005). As neuroscientists continue to explore the complex neurological processes involved in human behavior, our understanding of psychological disorders will, no doubt, increase.

are symbolic expressions of unconscious conflicts, which can usually be traced to childhood. For example, a man who behaves violently toward women may be unconsciously expressing rage at his mother for being unaffectionate toward him during his childhood. The psychoanalytic model argues that in order to resolve their problems effectively, people must become aware that the source of their problems lies in their childhood and infancy.

Although Freud and his followers profoundly influenced both the mental health disciplines and Western culture, only weak and scattered scientific evidence supports their psychoanalytic theories about the causes and effective treatment of mental disorders.

THE COGNITIVE–BEHAVIORAL MODEL

According to the cognitive–behavioral model, what causes abnormal behavior?

A third model of abnormal behavior grew out of 20th-century research on learning and cognition. The **cognitive–behavioral model** suggests that psychological disorders, like all behavior, result from learning. From this perspective, fear, anxiety, sexual deviations, and other maladaptive behaviors are learned—and they can be unlearned.

The cognitive–behavioral model stresses both internal and external learning processes in the development and treatment of psychological disorders. For example, a bright student who believes that he is academically inferior to his classmates and can't perform well on a test may not put much effort into studying. Naturally, he performs poorly, and his poor test score both punishes his minimal efforts and confirms his belief that he is academically inferior. This student is caught up in a vicious cycle (Albano & Barlow, 1996). A cognitive–behavior therapist might try to modify both the young man's dysfunctional studying behavior and his inaccurate and maladaptive cognitive processes.

cognitive–behavioral model View that psychological disorders result from learning maladaptive ways of thinking and behaving.

The cognitive–behavioral model has led to innovations in the treatment of psychological disorders, but the model has been criticized for its limited perspective, especially its emphasis on environmental causes and treatments.

THE DIATHESIS–STRESS MODEL AND SYSTEMS THEORY

Why do some people with a family history of a psychological disorder develop the disorder, whereas other family members do not?

Each of the three major theories is useful in explaining the causes of certain types of disorders. The most exciting recent developments, however, emphasize integration of the various theoretical models to discover specific causes and specific treatments for different mental disorders.

One promising integrative approach is seen in the **diathesis–stress model** (McKeever & Huff, 2003; Schmidt, Polak, & Spooner, 2005). This model suggests that a biological predisposition called a **diathesis** must combine with a stressful circumstance before the predisposition to a mental disorder is manifested (Zuckerman, 1999). According to this model, some people are biologically prone to developing a particular disorder under stress, whereas others are not.

The **systems approach**, also known as the *biopsychosocial model*, examines how biological risks, psychological stresses, and social pressures and expectations combine to produce psychological disorders (Weston, 2005). According to this model, emotional problems are "lifestyle diseases" that, much like heart disease and many other physical illnesses, result from a combination of risk factors and stresses. Just as heart disease can result from a combination of genetic predisposition, personality styles, poor health habits (such as smoking), and stress, psychological problems result from several risk factors that influence one another. In this chapter, we follow the systems approach in examining the causes and treatments of abnormal behavior.

ENDURING ISSUES

Mind–Body Causes of Mental Disorders

Throughout this chapter, as we discuss what is known about the causes of psychological disorders, you will see that biological and psychological factors are intimately connected. For example, there is strong evidence for a genetic component in some personality disorders as well as in schizophrenia. However, not everyone who inherits these factors develops a personality disorder or becomes schizophrenic. Our current state of knowledge allows us to pinpoint certain causative factors for certain conditions, but it does not allow us to completely differentiate biological and psychological factors. ●●

THE PREVALENCE OF PSYCHOLOGICAL DISORDERS

How common are mental disorders?

How common are psychological disorders in the United States? Are they increasing or decreasing over time? Are some population groups more prone to these disorders than others? These questions interest psychologists and public-health experts, who are concerned with both the prevalence and the incidence of mental health problems. *Prevalence* refers to the frequency with which a given disorder occurs at a given time. If there were 100 cases of depression in a population of 1,000, the prevalence of depression would be 10%. The *incidence* of a disorder refers to the number of new cases that arise in a given period. If there were 10 new cases of depression in a population of 1,000 in a single year, the incidence would be 1% per year.

The American Psychiatric Association funded an ambitious and wide-ranging study of the prevalence of psychological disorders, which involved interviewing more than 20,000

The cognitive–behavioral view of mental disorders suggests that people can learn—and unlearn—thinking patterns that affect their lives unfavorably. For example, an athlete who is convinced she will not win may not practice as hard as she should and end up "defeating herself."

diathesis–stress model View that people biologically predisposed to a mental disorder (those with a certain diathesis) will tend to exhibit that disorder when particularly affected by stress.

diathesis Biological predisposition.

systems approach View that biological, psychological, and social risk factors combine to produce psychological disorders. Also known as the biopsychosocial model of psychological disorders.

people around the country. The results were surprising: 15% of the population was found to be experiencing a clinically significant mental disorder, and 6% was experiencing a significant substance abuse disorder (Narrow, Rae, Robins, & Regier, 2001). The most common mental disorders were anxiety disorders, followed by phobias and mood disorders. (All of these are described in detail later in this chapter.) Schizophrenia, a severe mental disorder that often involves hospitalization, was found to afflict 1% of the population, or over 2 million people. Substance abuse problems were found in 6% of the population, with abuse of alcohol being three times more prevalent than abuse of all other drugs combined.

More recently, diagnostic interviews with more than 60,000 people in 14 countries around the world showed that over a 1-year period, the prevalence of moderate or serious psychological disorders varied widely from 12% of the population in the Americas to 7% in Europe, 6% in the Middle East and Africa, and just 4% in Asia (World Health Organization [WHO] World Mental Health Survey Consortium, 2004).

MENTAL ILLNESS AND THE LAW

Is there a difference between being "mentally ill" and being "insane"?

Particularly horrifying crimes—assassinations of public figures, mass murders, and serial murders, for instance—have often been attributed to mental disturbance, because it seems to many people that anyone who could commit such crimes must be "crazy." But to the legal system, this presents a problem: If a person is truly "crazy," are we justified in holding him or her responsible for criminal acts? The legal answer to this question is a qualified yes. A mentally ill person is responsible for his or her crimes unless he or she is determined to be *insane*. What's the difference between being "mentally ill" and being "insane"? **Insanity** is a legal term, not a psychological one. It is typically applied to defendants who were so mentally disturbed when they committed their offense that they either lacked substantial capacity to appreciate the criminality of their actions (to know right from wrong) or to conform to the requirements of the law (to control their behavior).

When a defendant is suspected of being mentally disturbed or legally insane, another important question must be answered before that person is brought to trial: Is the person able to understand the charges against him or her and to participate in a defense in court? This issue is known as *competency* to stand trial. The person is examined by a court-appointed expert and, if found to be incompetent, is sent to a mental institution, often for an indefinite period. If judged to be competent, the person is required to stand trial.

CLASSIFYING ABNORMAL BEHAVIOR

Why is it useful to have a manual of psychological disorders?

For nearly 40 years, the American Psychiatric Association (APA) has issued a manual describing and classifying the various kinds of psychological disorders. This publication, the *Diagnostic and Statistical Manual of Mental Disorders* (*DSM*), has been revised four times. The fourth edition, text revision *DSM-IV-TR* (American Psychiatric Association, 2000), was coordinated with the 10th edition of the World Health Organization's *International Classification of Diseases*.

The *DSM-IV-TR* provides a complete list of mental disorders, with each category painstakingly defined in terms of significant behavior patterns so that diagnoses based on it will be reliable (see Table 12–2). Although the manual provides careful descriptions of symptoms of different disorders to improve consistent diagnosis, it is generally silent on cause and treatment. The DSM has gained increasing acceptance because its detailed criteria for diagnosing mental disorders have made diagnosis much more reliable. Today, it is the most widely used classification of psychological disorders. In the remainder of this chapter, we will explore some of the key categories in greater detail.

insanity Legal term applied to defendants who do not know right from wrong or are unable to control their behavior.

table 12–2 DIAGNOSTIC CATEGORIES OF DSM-IV-RT

Category	Example
Disorders Usually First Diagnosed in Infancy, Childhood, or Adolescence	Mental retardation, learning disorders, autistic disorder, attention-deficit/hyperactivity disorder.
Delirium, Dementia, and Amnestic and Other Cognitive Disorders	Delirium, dementia of the Alzheimer's type, amnestic disorder.
Mental Disorders Due to a General Medical Condition	Psychotic disorder due to epilepsy.
Substance-Related Disorders	Alcohol dependence, cocaine dependence, nicotine dependence.
Schizophrenia and Other Psychotic Disorders	Schizophrenia, schizoaffective disorder, delusional disorder.
Mood Disorders	Major depressive disorder, dysthymic disorder, bipolar disorder.
Anxiety Disorders	Panic disorder with agoraphobia, social phobia, obsessive-compulsive disorder, post-traumatic stress disorder, generalized anxiety disorder.
Somatoform Disorders	Somatization disorder, conversion disorder, hypochondriasis.
Factitious Disorders	Factitious disorder with predominantly physical signs and symptoms.
Dissociative Disorders	Dissociative amnesia, dissociative fugue, dissociative identity disorder, depersonalization disorder.
Sexual and Gender-Identity Disorders	Hypoactive sexual desire disorder, male erectile disorder, female orgasmic disorder, vaginismus.
Eating Disorders	Anorexia nervosa, bulimia nervosa.
Sleep Disorders	Primary insomnia, narcolepsy, sleep terror disorder.
Impulse-Control Disorders	Kleptomania, pyromania, pathological gambling.
Adjustment Disorders	Adjustment disorder with depressed mood, adjustment disorder with conduct disturbance.
Personality Disorders	Antisocial personality disorder, borderline personality disorder, narcissistic personality disorder, dependent personality disorder.

CHECK YOUR UNDERSTANDING

1. It is likely that people in early societies believed that _____ forces caused abnormal behavior.
2. There is growing evidence that _____ factors are involved in mental disorders as diverse as schizophrenia, depression, and anxiety.
3. _____ is a legal term that is not the same thing as mental illness.

Indicate whether the following statements are true (T) or false (F):

4. The line separating normal from abnormal behavior is somewhat arbitrary.
5. About two-thirds of Americans are suffering from one or more serious mental disorders at any given time.
6. The cognitive view of mental disorders suggests that they arise from unconscious conflicts, often rooted in childhood.

Answers: 1. supernatural. 2. genetic. 3. Insanity. 4. (T). 5. (F). 6. (F).

APPLY YOUR UNDERSTANDING

1. You are talking to a friend whose behavior has you concerned. She says, "Look, I'm happy, I feel good about myself, and I think things are going well." Which viewpoint on mental health is reflected in her statement?

   a. society's view

   b. the individual's view

   c. the mental health professional's view

   d. Both (b) and (c) are true.

cognitive distortions An illogical and maladaptive response to early negative life events that leads to feelings of incompetence and unworthiness that are reactivated whenever a new situation arises that resembles the original events.

PSYCHOLOGICAL FACTORS Although a number of psychological factors are thought to play a role in causing severe depression, in recent years, researchers have focused on the contribution of maladaptive **cognitive distortions**. According to Aaron Beck (1967, 1976, 1984), during childhood and adolescence, some people undergo wrenching experiences such as the loss of a parent, severe difficulties in gaining parental or social approval, or humiliating criticism from teachers and other adults. One response to such experience is to develop a negative self-concept—a feeling of incompetence or unworthiness that has little to do with reality, but that is maintained by a distorted and illogical interpretation of real events. When a new situation arises that resembles the situation under which the self-concept was learned, these same feelings of worthlessness and incompetence may be activated, resulting in depression.

Although critics point out that these negative responses may be the result of depression rather than its cause (Hammen, 1985), considerable research supports Beck's view of depression (Alloy, Abramson, & Francis, 1999; Alloy, Abramson, Whitehouse, et al., 1999; Kwon & Oei, 2003). Therapy based on Beck's theories has proven quite successful in treating depression. (See Chapter 13, "Therapies.")

SOCIAL FACTORS Many social factors have been linked with mood disorders, particularly difficulties in interpersonal relationships. In fact, some theorists have suggested that the link between depression and troubled relationships explains the fact that depression is two to three times more prevalent in women than in men (National Alliance on Mental Illness, 2003), because women tend to be more relationship oriented than men are in our society (Gilligan, 1982; Pinhas, Weaver, Bryden, Ghabbour, & Toner, 2002). Yet, not every person who experiences a troubled relationship becomes depressed. As the systems approach would predict, it appears that a genetic predisposition or cognitive distortion is necessary before a distressing close relationship or other significant life stressor will result in a mood disorder.

ENDURING ISSUES

Person–Situation   The Chicken or the Egg?

It is sometimes difficult to tease apart the relative contribution of the person's biological or cognitive tendencies and the social situation. People with certain depression-prone genetic or cognitive tendencies may be more likely than others to encounter stressful life events by virtue of their personality and behavior. For example, studies show that depressed people tend to evoke anxiety and even hostility in others, partly because they require more emotional support than people feel comfortable giving. As a result, people tend to avoid those who are depressed, and this shunning can intensify the depression. In short, depression-prone and depressed people may become trapped in a vicious circle that is at least partly of their own creation (Coyne & Whiffen, 1995; Pettit & Joiner, 2006). ●●

CHECK YOUR UNDERSTANDING

Indicate whether the following statements are true (T) or false (F):

1. _____ People with a mood disorder always alternate between the extremes of euphoria and sadness.
2. _____ More men attempt suicide, but more women actually kill themselves.
3. _____ Most psychologists now believe that mood disorders result from a combination of risk factors.
4. _____ Mania is the most common mood disorder.

Answers: 1. (F), 2. (F), 3. (T), 4. (F).

APPLY YOUR UNDERSTANDING

1. Bob is "down in the dumps" most of the time. He is having a difficult time dealing with any criticism he receives at work or at home. Most days he feels that he is a failure, despite the fact that he is successful in his job and his family is happy. Although he participates in various activities outside the home, he finds no joy in anything. He says he is constantly tired, but he has trouble sleeping. It is most likely that Bob is suffering from

   a. clinical depression.

   b. generalized anxiety disorder.

   c. depersonalization disorder.

   d. somatoform disorder.

2. Mary almost seems to be two different people. At times, she is hyperactive and talks nonstop. (sometimes so fast that nobody can understand her). At those times, her friends say she is "bouncing off the walls." But then she changes: She becomes terribly sad, loses interest in eating, spends much of her time in bed, and rarely says a word. It is most likely that Mary is suffering from

   a. dissociative identity disorder.

   b. depression.

   c. bipolar disorder.

   d. schizophrenia.

Answers: 1. a. 2. c.

Anxiety Disorders

How does an anxiety disorder differ from ordinary anxiety?

All of us are afraid from time to time, but we usually know why we are fearful. Our fear is caused by something appropriate and identifiable, and it passes with time. In the case of **anxiety disorders**, however, either the person does not know why he or she is afraid, or the anxiety is inappropriate to the circumstances. In either case, the person's fear and anxiety just don't seem to make sense.

As we noted earlier in this chapter, surveys have found that anxiety disorders are more common than any other form of mental disorder (Narrow, Rae, Robins, & Regier, 2001). Anxiety disorders can be subdivided into several diagnostic categories, including specific phobias, panic disorder, and other anxiety disorders, such as generalized anxiety disorder, obsessive–compulsive disorder, and disorders caused by specific traumatic events.

SPECIFIC PHOBIAS

Into what three categories are phobias usually grouped?

A **specific phobia** is an intense, paralyzing fear of something that perhaps should be feared, but the fear is excessive and unreasonable. In fact, the fear in a specific phobia is so great that it leads the person to avoid routine or adaptive activities and thus interferes with life functioning. For example, it is appropriate to be a bit fearful as an airplane takes off or lands, but people with a phobia about flying refuse to get on or even go near an airplane. Other common phobias focus on animals, heights, closed places, blood, needles, and injury. About 10% of people in the United States suffer from at least one specific phobia.

Most people feel some mild fear or uncertainty in many social situations, but when these fears interfere significantly with life functioning, they are considered to be **social phobias**. Intense fear of public speaking is a common form of social phobia. In other cases, simply talking with people or eating in public causes such severe anxiety that the phobic person will go to great lengths to avoid these situations.

Agoraphobia is much more debilitating than social phobia. This term comes from Greek and Latin words that literally mean "fear of the marketplace," but the disorder typically involves multiple, intense fears, such as the fear of being alone, of being in public places from which escape might be difficult, of being in crowds, of traveling in an automobile, or of

anxiety disorders Disorders in which anxiety is a characteristic feature or the avoidance of anxiety seems to motivate abnormal behavior.

specific phobia Anxiety disorder characterized by an intense, paralyzing fear of something.

social phobias Anxiety disorders characterized by excessive, inappropriate fears connected with social situations or performances in front of other people.

agoraphobia An anxiety disorder that involves multiple, intense fears of crowds, public places, and other situations that require separation from a source of security such as the home.

dissociative disorders Disorders in which some aspect of the personality seems separated from the rest.

dissociative amnesia A disorder characterized by loss of memory for past events without organic cause.

dissociative fugue A disorder that involves flight from home and the assumption of a new identity with amnesia for past identity and events.

dissociative identity disorder (Also called multiple personality disorder.) Disorder characterized by the separation of the personality into two or more distinct personalities.

APPLY YOUR UNDERSTANDING

1. Bob is concerned about a few warts that have appeared on his arms. His doctor says that they are just warts and are not a concern, but Bob believes they are cancerous and that he will die from them. He consults another doctor and then another, both of whom tell him they are just normal warts, but he remains convinced they are cancerous and he is going to die. It appears that Bob is suffering from

   a. hypochondriasis.

   b. a psychosomatic disorder.

   c. a somatoform disorder.

   d. a phobia.

2. John is a writer, but work on his latest novel has come to a halt because he has lost all feeling in his arm and his hand. His doctor can find no physical cause for his problem; however, there is no question that he no longer has feeling in his arm and that he can no longer hold a pencil or type on a keyboard. It seems likely that John is suffering from

   a. body dysmorphic disorder.

   b. hypochondriasis.

   c. conversion disorder.

   d. dissociative disorder.

Answers: 1. a. 2. c.

When she was found by a Florida park ranger, Jane Doe was suffering from amnesia. She could not recall her name, her past, or how to read and write. She never regained her memory of the past.

Dissociative Disorders

What do dissociative disorders have in common?

Dissociative disorders are among the most puzzling forms of mental disorders, both to the observer and to the sufferer. *Dissociation* means that part of an individual's personality appears to be separated from the rest. The disorder usually involves memory loss and a complete, though generally temporary, change in identity. Rarely, several distinct personalities appear in one person.

Loss of memory without an organic cause can occur as a reaction to an extremely stressful event or period. During World War II, for example, some hospitalized soldiers could not recall what their names were, where they lived, where they were born, or how they came to be in battle. But war and its horrors are not the only causes of **dissociative amnesia**. The person who betrays a friend in a business deal or the victim of rape may also forget, selectively, what has happened. Total amnesia, in which people forget everything, is rare, despite its popularity in novels and films. Sometimes an amnesia victim leaves home and assumes an entirely new identity; this phenomenon, known as **dissociative fugue**, is also very unusual.

In **dissociative identity disorder**, commonly known as *multiple personality disorder*, several distinct personalities emerge at different times. Although this dramatic disorder has been the subject of popular fiction and films, most psychologists believe it to be rare, although in recent years, the number of cases appears to be increasing (Eich, Macaulay, Loewenstein, & Dihle, 1997). In the true multiple personality, the various personalities are distinct people with their own names, identities, memories, mannerisms, speaking voices, and even IQs. Sometimes the personalities are so separate that they don't know they inhabit a body with other "people." At other times, the personalities do know of the existence of other "people" and even make disparaging remarks about them. Typically, the personalities contrast sharply with one another, as if each one represents different aspects of the same person—one being the more socially acceptable, "nice" side of the person and the other being the darker, more uninhibited or "evil" side.

The origins of dissociative identity disorder are still not understood (Dell, 2006). One theory suggests that it develops as a response to childhood abuse. The child learns to cope with abuse by a process of dissociation—by having the abuse, in effect, happen to "someone else," that is, to a personality who is not conscious most of the time (Putnam, Guroff, Silberman, Barban, & Post, 1986). The fact that one or more of the multiple personalities in almost every case is a child (even when the patient is an adult) seems to support this idea, and clinicians report a history of child abuse in more than three-quarters of their cases of dissociative identity disorder (C. A. Ross, Norton, & Wozney, 1989).

Other clinicians suggest that dissociative identity disorder is not a real disorder at all, but an elaborate kind of role playing—faked in the beginning and then perhaps genuinely believed by the patient (Lilienfeld & Lynn, 2003; Mersky, 1992; Rieber, 1998). Some intriguing biological data show that in at least some patients, however, the various personalities have different blood pressure readings, different responses to medication, different allergies, different vision problems (necessitating a different pair of glasses for each personality), and different handedness—all of which would be difficult to feign. Each personality may also exhibit distinctly different brain-wave patterns (Dell'Osso, 2003; Putnam, 1984).

A far less dramatic (and much more common) dissociative disorder is **depersonalization disorder**, in which the person suddenly feels changed or different in a strange way. Some people feel that they have left their bodies, whereas others find that their actions have suddenly become mechanical or dreamlike. This kind of feeling is especially common during adolescence and young adulthood, when our sense of ourselves and our interactions with others change rapidly. Only when the sense of depersonalization becomes a long-term or chronic problem or when the alienation impairs normal social functioning can this be classified as a dissociative disorder (American Psychological Association, 2000).

Dissociative disorders, like conversion disorders, seem to involve some kind of unconscious processes. Trauma is one important psychological factor in the onset of amnesia and fugue and appears to play a role in the development of dissociative identity disorder (Oltmanns & Emery, 2006). The loss of memory is real in amnesia, fugue, and in many cases of multiple personality disorder. Patients often lack awareness of their own memory loss and cannot overcome memory impairments despite their desire and effort to do so. Biological factors may also play a role. Dissociation and amnesia are commonly associated with aging and disorders such as Alzheimer's disease; and dissociative experiences are a common consequence of the ingestion of drugs such as LSD. Nevertheless, all of these observations are only leads in the mystery of what causes dissociative disorders.

depersonalization disorder A dissociative disorder whose essential feature is that the person suddenly feels changed or different in a strange way.

CHECK YOUR UNDERSTANDING

1. _____ _____ usually involve memory loss and a complete—though generally temporary—change in identity.

2. Clinicians report a history of _____ _____ in over three-quarters of their cases of dissociative identity disorder.

3. Dissociative disorders, like conversion disorders, seem to involve _____ processes.

Answers: 1. dissociative disorders. 2. child abuse. 3. unconscious.

APPLY YOUR UNDERSTANDING

1. A person who was being interrogated by the police confessed on tape to having committed several murders. When the alleged killer was brought to trial, his lawyers agreed that the voice on the tape belonged to their client. But they asserted that the person who confessed was another personality that lived inside the body of their client. In other words, they claimed that their client was suffering from

   a. depersonalization disorder.

   b. dissociative identity disorder.

   c. conversion disorder.

   d. body dysmorphic disorder.

Repeated use of nonhuman objects, such as shoes, underwear, or leather goods, as the preferred or exclusive method of achieving sexual excitement is known as fetishism.

voyeurism Desire to watch others having sexual relations or to spy on nude people.

exhibitionism Compulsion to expose one's genitals in public to achieve sexual arousal.

frotteurism Compulsion to achieve sexual arousal by touching or rubbing against a nonconsenting person in public situations.

transvestic fetishism Wearing the clothes of the opposite sex to achieve sexual gratification.

sexual sadism Obtaining sexual gratification from humiliating or physically harming a sex partner.

sexual masochism Inability to enjoy sex without accompanying emotional or physical pain.

pedophilia Desire to have sexual relations with children as the preferred or exclusive method of achieving sexual excitement.

gender-identity disorders Disorders that involve the desire to become, or the insistence that one really is, a member of the other biological sex.

gender-identity disorder in children Rejection of one's biological gender in childhood, along with the clothing and behavior that society considers appropriate to that gender.

preferred or exclusive method of achieving sexual excitement—is considered a sexual disorder. Fetishes are typically articles of women's clothing or items made out of rubber or leather (Mason, 1997). Most people who practice fetishism are male, and the fetish frequently begins during adolescence (Fagan, Lehne, Strand, & Berlin, 2005). Fetishes may derive from unusual learning experiences: As their sexual drive develops during adolescence, some boys learn to associate arousal with inanimate objects, perhaps as a result of early sexual exploration while masturbating or because of difficulties in social relationships (Bertolini, 2001).

Other unconventional patterns of sexual behavior are **voyeurism**, watching other people have sex or spying on people who are nude; achieving arousal by **exhibitionism**, the exposure of one's genitals in inappropriate situations, such as to strangers; **frotteurism**, achieving sexual arousal by touching or rubbing against a nonconsenting person in situations like a crowded subway car; and **transvestic fetishism**, wearing clothes of the opposite sex for sexual excitement and gratification. **Sexual sadism** ties sexual pleasure to aggression. To attain sexual gratification, sadists humiliate or physically harm sex partners. **Sexual masochism** is the inability to enjoy sex without accompanying emotional or physical pain. Sexual sadists and masochists sometimes engage in mutually consenting sex, but at times sadistic acts are inflicted on unconsenting partners.

One of the most serious paraphilias is **pedophilia**, which according to *DSM-IV-TR* is defined as engaging in sexual activity with a child, generally under the age of 13. Child sexual abuse is shockingly common in the United States; and the abuser usually is someone close to the child, rather than a stranger.

Pedophiles are almost invariably men under age 40 (Barbaree & Seto, 1997). Although there is no single cause of pedophilia, some of the most common explanations are that pedophiles cannot adjust to the adult sexual role and have been interested exclusively in children as sex objects since adolescence; they turn to children as sexual objects in response to stress in adult relationships in which they feel inadequate; or they have records of unstable social adjustment and generally commit sexual offenses against children in response to a temporary aggressive mood. Studies also indicate that the majority of pedophiles have histories of sexual frustration and failure, tend to perceive themselves as immature, and are rather dependent, unassertive, lonely, and insecure (L. J. Cohen & Galynker, 2002).

Gender-identity disorders involve the desire to become—or the insistence that one really is—a member of the other sex. Some little boys, for example, want to be girls instead. They may reject boys' clothing, desire to wear their sisters' clothes, and play only with girls and with toys that are considered "girls' toys." Similarly, some girls wear boys' clothing and play only with boys and "boys' toys." When such children are uncomfortable being a male or a female and are unwilling to accept themselves as such, the diagnosis is **gender-identity disorder in children** (Zucker, 2005).

The causes of gender-identity disorders are not known. Both animal research and the fact that these disorders are often apparent from early childhood suggest that biological factors, such as prenatal hormonal imbalances, are major contributors. Family dynamics and learning experiences, however, may also be contributing factors.

CHECK YOUR UNDERSTANDING

Match each of the following terms with the appropriate description:

1. _____ pedophilia
2. _____ gender-identity disorder
3. _____ female sexual arousal disorder
4. _____ paraphilias

a. The inability for a woman to become sexually excited or to reach orgasm.

b. Involve the use of unconventional sex objects or situations to obtain sexual arousal.

c. Recurrent, intense sexually arousing fantasies, sexual urges, or behaviors involving sexual activity with a prepubescent child.

d. The desire to become—or the insistence that one really is—a member of the other biological sex.

Answers: 1. c. 2. d. 3. a. 4. b.

APPLY YOUR UNDERSTANDING

1. Viagra and similar drugs have become best sellers because they provide temporary relief from
   a. erectile disorder.
   b. paraphilias.
   c. generalized anxiety disorder.
   d. body dysmorphic disorder.

2. A man is arrested for stealing women's underwear from clotheslines and adding them to the large collection he has hidden in his home. He says that he finds the clothing sexually exciting. It would appear that he is suffering from
   a. erectile disorder.
   b. gender-identity disorder.
   c. pedophilia.
   d. fetishism.

Answers: 1. a. 2. d.

Personality Disorders

Which personality disorder creates the most significant problems for society?

As we discussed in Chapter 10, "Personality", is the individual's unique and enduring pattern of thoughts, feelings, and behavior. We saw that despite having certain characteristic views of the world and ways of doing things, people normally can adjust their behavior to fit different situations. But some people, starting at some point early in life, develop inflexible and maladaptive ways of thinking and behaving that are so exaggerated and rigid that they cause serious distress to themselves or problems to others. People with such **personality disorders** range from harmless eccentrics to cold-blooded killers. A personality disorder may also coexist with one of the other problems already discussed in this chapter; someone with a personality disorder may also become depressed, develop sexual problems, and so on.

One group of personality disorders, **schizoid personality disorder**, is characterized by odd or eccentric behavior. People with this disorder lack the ability or desire to form social relationships and have no warm or tender feelings for others. Such loners cannot express their feelings and appear cold, distant, and unfeeling. Moreover, they often seem vague, absentminded, indecisive, or "in a fog." Because their withdrawal is so complete, persons with schizoid personality disorder seldom marry and may have trouble holding jobs that require them to work with or relate to others (American Psychological Association, 2000).

People with **paranoid personality disorder** also appear to be odd. Although they often see themselves as rational and objective, they are guarded, secretive, devious, scheming, and argumentative. They are suspicious and mistrustful even when there is no reason to be; they are hypersensitive to any possible threat or trick; and they refuse to accept blame or criticism even when it is deserved.

A cluster of personality disorders characterized by anxious or fearful behavior includes dependent personality disorder and avoidant personality disorder. People with **dependent personality disorder** are unable to make decisions on their own or to do things independently. Rather, they rely on parents, a spouse, friends, or others to make the major choices in their lives and usually are extremely unhappy being alone. Their underlying fear seems to be that they will be rejected or abandoned by important people in their lives. In **avoidant personality disorder**, the person is timid, anxious, and fearful of rejection. It is not surprising that this social anxiety leads to isolation, but unlike the schizoid type, the person with avoidant personality disorder *wants* to have close relationships with others.

personality disorders Disorders in which inflexible and maladaptive ways of thinking and behaving learned early in life cause distress to the person or conflicts with others.

schizoid personality disorder Personality disorder in which a person is withdrawn and lacks feelings for others.

paranoid personality disorder Personality disorder in which the person is inappropriately suspicious and mistrustful of others.

dependent personality disorder Personality disorder in which the person is unable to make choices and decisions independently and cannot tolerate being alone.

avoidant personality disorder Personality disorder in which the person's fears of rejection by others lead to social isolation.

narcissistic personality disorder Personality disorder in which the person has an exaggerated sense of self-importance and needs constant admiration.

borderline personality disorder Personality disorder characterized by marked instability in self-image, mood, and interpersonal relationships.

antisocial personality disorder Personality disorder that involves a pattern of violent, criminal, or unethical and exploitative behavior and an inability to feel affection for others.

Another cluster of personality disorders is characterized by dramatic, emotional, or erratic behavior. People with **narcissistic personality disorder**, for example, display a grandiose sense of self-importance and a preoccupation with fantasies of unlimited success. Such people believe that they are extraordinary, need constant attention and admiration, display a sense of entitlement, and tend to exploit others. They are given to envy and arrogance, and they lack the ability to really care for anyone else (American Psychological Association, 2000).

Borderline personality disorder is characterized by marked instability in self-image, mood, and interpersonal relationships. People with this personality disorder tend to act impulsively and, often, self-destructively. They feel uncomfortable being alone and often manipulate self-destructive impulses in an effort to control or solidify their personal relationships.

Borderline personality disorder is common and serious. The available evidence indicates that although it runs in families, genetics do not seem to play an important role in its development (Oltmanns & Emery, 2006). Instead, studies point to the influence of dysfunctional relationships with parents, including a marked lack of supervision, frequent exposure to domestic violence, and physical and sexual abuse (Helgeland & Torgersen, 2004; Schmahl, Vermetten, Elzinga, & Bremner, 2004).

One of the most widely studied personality disorders is **antisocial personality disorder**. People who exhibit this disorder lie, steal, cheat, and show little or no sense of responsibility, although they often seem intelligent and charming at first. The "con man" exemplifies many of the features of the antisocial personality, as does the person who compulsively cheats business partners, because she or he knows their weak points. Antisocial personalities rarely show any anxiety or guilt about their behavior. Indeed, they are likely to blame society or their victims for the antisocial actions that they themselves commit. As you might suspect, people with antisocial personality disorder are responsible for a good deal of crime and violence.

Approximately 3% of American men and less than 1% of American women suffer from antisocial personality disorder. It is not surprising that prison inmates show high rates of personality disorder: One study identified it in 50% of the populations of two prisons (Hare, 1983). Not all people with antisocial personality disorder are convicted criminals, however. Many manipulate others for their own gain while avoiding the criminal justice system.

Antisocial personality disorder seems to result from a combination of biological predisposition, difficult life experiences, and an unhealthy social environment (Gabbard, 2005; Moffitt, Caspi, & Rutter, 2006). Some findings suggest that heredity is a risk factor for the later development of antisocial behavior (Fu et al., 2002; Lyons et al., 1995). Impulsive violence and aggression have also been linked with abnormal levels of certain neurotransmitters (Virkkunen, 1983). Although none of this research is definitive, the weight of evidence suggests that some people with antisocial personalities are less responsive to stress and thus are more likely to engage in thrill-seeking behaviors, such as gambling and substance abuse, which may be harmful to themselves or others (Pietrzak & Petry, 2005; Patrick, 1994). Because they respond less emotionally to stress, punishment does not affect them as it does other people (Hare, 1993). Another intriguing explanation for the cause of antisocial personality disorder is that it arises as a consequence of damage to the prefrontal region of the brain during infancy (S. W. Anderson, Bechara, Damasio, Tranel, & Damasio, 1999; A. R. Damasio & Anderson, 2003).

Some psychologists believe that emotional deprivation in early childhood predisposes people to antisocial personality disorder. The child for whom no one cares, say psychologists, cares for no one. Respect for others is the basis of our social code, but when you cannot see things from another person's perspective, behavior "rules" seem like nothing more than an assertion of adult power to be defied.

THINKING CRITICALLY ABOUT . . .

Causation

We have offered a number of different theories about the cause of antisocial personality disorder, all supported by research. Think about each of these theories and try to answer the following questions:

- To what extent do the different perspectives conflict? To what extent do they support one another?

- What kind of evidence—what kinds of research studies—is offered in support of each theory?

- Which theory would be most useful from a clinical, or treatment, point of view? Which would be most likely to spawn further research?

- Why do different theoretical perspectives exist?

Family influences may also prevent the normal learning of rules of conduct in the preschool and school years. A child who has been rejected by one or both parents is not likely to develop adequate social skills or appropriate social behavior. Further, the high incidence of antisocial behavior in people with an antisocial parent suggests that antisocial behavior may be partly learned and partly inherited. Once serious misbehavior begins in childhood, there is an almost predictable progression: The child's conduct leads to rejection by peers and failure in school, followed by affiliation with other children who have behavior problems. By late childhood or adolescence, the deviant patterns that will later show up as a full-blown antisocial personality disorder are well established (J. Hill, 2003; Levy & Orlans, 2004).

Cognitive theorists emphasize that in addition to the failure to learn rules and develop self-control, moral development may be arrested in children who are emotionally rejected and inadequately disciplined (Soyguet & Tuerkcapar, 2001). For example, between the ages of about 7 and 11, all children are likely to respond to unjust treatment by behaving unjustly toward someone else who is vulnerable. At about age 13, when they are better able to reason in abstract terms, most children begin to think more in terms of fairness than vindictiveness, especially if new cognitive skills and moral concepts are reinforced by parents and peers (M. W. Berkowitz & Gibbs, 1983). Some theorists suggest that people with antisocial personality disorder may not have successfully completed this moral transition.

CHECK YOUR UNDERSTANDING

Match the following personality disorders with the appropriate description:

1. _____ schizoid personality disorder
2. _____ paranoid personality disorder
3. _____ dependent personality disorder
4. _____ avoidant personality disorder
5. _____ borderline personality disorder

a. shows instability in self-image, mood, and relationships.
b. is fearful and timid
c. is mistrustful even when there is no reason
d. lacks the ability to form social relationships
e. is unable to make own decisions

Answers: 1. d. 2. c. 3. e. 4. b. 5. a.

APPLY YOUR UNDERSTANDING

1. John represents himself as a stockbroker who specializes in investing the life savings of elderly people, but he never invests the money. Instead, he puts it into his own bank account and then flees the country. When he is caught and asked how he feels about financially destroying elderly people, he explains, "Hey, if they were stupid enough to give me their money, they deserved what they got." John is most likely suffering from _____ personality disorder.

   a. dependent
   b. avoidant
   c. antisocial
   d. borderline

2. Jennifer is a graduate student who believes that her thesis will completely change the way that scientists view the universe. She believes that she is the only person intelligent enough to have come up with the thesis, that she is not sufficiently appreciated by other students and faculty, and that nobody on her thesis committee is sufficiently knowledgeable to judge its merits. Assuming that her thesis is not, in fact, revolutionary, it would appear that Jennifer is suffering from _____ personality disorder.

   a. paranoid
   b. narcissistic
   c. borderline
   d. antisocial

Answers: 1. c. 2. b.

schizophrenic disorders Severe disorders in which there are disturbances of thoughts, communications, and emotions, including delusions and hallucinations.

psychotic (psychosis) Behavior characterized by a loss of touch with reality.

hallucinations Sensory experiences in the absence of external stimulation.

delusions False beliefs about reality that have no basis in fact.

disorganized schizophrenia Schizophrenic disorder in which bizarre and childlike behaviors are common.

catatonic schizophrenia Schizophrenic disorder in which disturbed motor behavior is prominent.

paranoid schizophrenia Schizophrenic disorder marked by extreme suspiciousness and complex, bizarre delusions.

Schizophrenic Disorders

How is schizophrenia different from multiple-personality disorder?

A common misconception is that *schizophrenia* means "split personality." But, as we have seen, split personality (or multiple personality) is actually a dissociative identity disorder. The misunderstanding comes from the fact that the root *schizo* derives from the Greek verb meaning "to split." What is split in schizophrenia is not so much personality as the connections among thoughts.

Schizophrenic disorders are severe conditions marked by disordered thoughts and communications, inappropriate emotions, and bizarre behavior that lasts for months or even years. People with schizophrenia are out of touch with reality, which is to say that they are **psychotic**.

People with schizophrenia often suffer from **hallucinations**, false sensory perceptions that usually take the form of hearing voices that are not really there. (Visual, tactile, or olfactory hallucinations are more likely to indicate substance abuse or organic brain damage.) They also frequently have **delusions**—false beliefs about reality with no factual basis—that distort their relationships with their surroundings and with other people. Typically, these delusions are *paranoid*: People with schizophrenia often believe that someone is out to harm them. They may think that a doctor wishes to kill them or that they are receiving radio messages from aliens invading from outer space. They often regard their own bodies—as well as the outside world—as hostile and alien. Because their world is utterly different from reality, people with schizophrenia usually cannot live a normal life unless they are successfully treated with medication. (See Chapter 13, "Therapies.") Often, they are unable to communicate with others, since their words are incoherent when they speak. The following case illustrates some of the major characteristics of schizophrenia:

> For many years [a 35-year-old widow] has heard voices, which insult her and cast suspicion on her chastity. . . . The voices are very distinct, and in her opinion, they must be carried by telescope or a machine from her home. Her thoughts are dictated to her; she is obliged to think them, and hears them repeated after her. She . . . has all kinds of uncomfortable sensations in her body, to which something is "done." In particular, her "mother parts" are turned inside out, and people send a pain through her back, lay ice water on her heart, squeeze her neck, injure her spine, and violate her. There are also hallucinations of sight—black figures and the altered appearance of people—but these are far less frequent (Spitzer et al., 2002, pp. 491–492).

There are actually several kinds of schizophrenic disorders, which have different characteristic symptoms. We will consider them next.

TYPES OF SCHIZOPHRENIC DISORDERS

Disorganized schizophrenia includes some of the more bizarre symptoms of schizophrenia, such as giggling, grimacing, and frantic gesturing. People suffering from disorganized schizophrenia show a childish disregard for social conventions and may urinate or defecate at inappropriate times. They are active, but aimless, and they are often given to incoherent conversations.

In **catatonic schizophrenia**, motor activity is severely disturbed. People in this state may remain immobile, mute, and impassive. They may behave in a robotlike fashion when ordered to move, and they may even let doctors put their arms and legs into uncomfortable positions that they maintain for hours. At the opposite extreme, they may become excessively excited, talking and shouting continuously.

Paranoid schizophrenia is marked by extreme suspiciousness and complex delusions. People with paranoid schizophrenia may believe themselves to be Napoleon or the Virgin Mary, or they may insist that Russian spies with laser guns are constantly on their trail because they have learned some great secret. As they are less likely to be incoherent or to look or act "crazy," these people can appear more "normal" than people with other schizophrenic disorders when their delusions are compatible with everyday life. They may, however, become hostile or aggressive toward anyone who questions their thinking or delusions. Note that this disorder is far more severe than paranoid personality disorder, which does not involve bizarre delusions or loss of touch with reality.

Finally, **undifferentiated schizophrenia** is the classification developed for people who have several of the characteristic symptoms of schizophrenia—such as delusions, hallucinations, or incoherence—yet do not show the typical symptoms of any other subtype of the disorder.

undifferentiated schizophrenia Schizophrenic disorder in which there are clear schizophrenic symptoms that do not meet the criteria for another subtype of the disorder.

CAUSES OF SCHIZOPHRENIA

Because schizophrenia is a very serious disorder, considerable research has been directed at trying to discover its causes (R. W. Heinrichs, 2001; Williamson, 2006). Many studies indicate that schizophrenia has a genetic component (Gerber et al., 2003; Gottesman, 1991; Hashimoto et al., 2003). People with schizophrenia are more likely than other people to have children with schizophrenia, even when those children have lived with adoptive parents since early in life. If one identical twin suffers from schizophrenia, the chances are almost 50% that the other twin will also develop this disorder. In fraternal twins, if one twin has schizophrenia, the chances are only about 17% that the other twin will develop it as well.

Recent research suggests that the biological predisposition to schizophrenia may involve the faulty regulation of the neurotransmitters dopamine and glutamate in the central nervous system (Goff & Coyle, 2001; Javitt & Coyle, 2004; Koh et al., 2003). Some research also indicates that pathology in various structures of the brain may influence the onset of schizophrenia (S. A. Chance, Esiri, & Timothy, 2003; Flashman & Green, 2004; van Elst & Trimble, 2003; Weiss et al., 2004; Yotsutsuji et al., 2003). Other studies link schizophrenia to some form of early prenatal disturbance (Bresnahan, Schaefer, Brown, & Susser, 2005). Nevertheless, scientists have found only average differences in brain structure and chemistry between schizophrenic and healthy people (Noga, Bartley, Jones, Torrey, & Weinberger, 1996). As yet, no laboratory tests can diagnose schizophrenia on the basis of brain abnormalities. In fact, studies of identical twins in which only one suffers from schizophrenia have sometimes found more evidence of brain abnormalities in the well twin than in the sick twin.

Studies of identical twins have also been used to identify the importance of environment in causing schizophrenia. Because identical twins are genetically identical and because half of the identical twins of people with schizophrenia do not develop schizophrenia themselves, this severe and puzzling disorder cannot be caused by genetic factors alone. Environmental factors—ranging from disturbed family relations to taking drugs to biological damage that may occur at any age, even before birth—must also figure in determining whether a person will develop schizophrenia. Recall that systems theory would predict that environment and experience can increase or decrease the effects of any inherited tendency. Consequently, identical twins afflicted with psychological disorders will show different degrees of functioning.

Finally, although quite different in emphasis, the various explanations for schizophrenic disorders are not mutually exclusive. Genetic factors are universally acknowledged, but many theorists believe that only a combination of biological, psychological, and social factors produces schizophrenia (K. Dean, Bramon, & Murray, 2003). According to systems theory, genetic factors predispose some people to schizophrenia; and family interaction and life stress activate the predisposition.

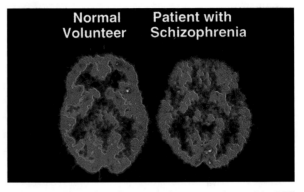

Neuroimaging techniques, such as this PET scan, often reveal important differences between the brains of people with schizophrenia and normal volunteers. Still, neuroimaging does not provide a decisive diagnostic test for schizophrenia.

THINKING CRITICALLY ABOUT . . .

Genius and Mental Disorders

Jean-Jacques Rousseau allegedly was paranoid. Mozart composed his *Requiem* while under the delusion that he was being poisoned. Van Gogh cut off his ear and sent it to a prostitute. Schopenhauer, Chopin, and John Stuart Mill were depressed. Robert Burns and Lord Byron apparently were alcoholics. Virginia Woolf suffered from bipolar disorder through her entire adult life.

- Do you think that creative people in general are more likely than others to suffer from psychological problems? What leads you to believe as you do?

- What evidence would you need to have in order to answer this question in a scientific way?

CHECK YOUR UNDERSTANDING

Indicate whether the following statements are true (T) or false (F):

1. _____ Schizophrenia is almost the same thing as multiple personality disorder.

2. _____ Psychotic symptoms, or loss of contact with reality, are indicators that a person suffers from disorders other than schizophrenia.

3. _____ Studies indicate that a biological predisposition to schizophrenia may be inherited.

4. _____ Laboratory tests can be used to diagnose schizophrenia on the basis of brain abnormalities.

Answers: 1. (F), 2. (F), 3. (T), 4. (F).

APPLY YOUR UNDERSTANDING

1. The book *A Beautiful Mind* is about John Nash, a mathematical genius. In young adulthood, he became convinced that people were spying on him and hunting him down. He searched for secret codes in numbers, sent bizarre postcards to friends, and made no sense when he spoke. On the basis of this description, it seems most likely that he was suffering from

   a. disorganized schizophrenia.

   b. catatonic schizophrenia.

   c. undifferentiated schizophrenia.

   d. paranoid schizophrenia.

2. Your roommate asks you what the difference is between "hallucinations" and "delusions." You tell her

   a. hallucinations involve false beliefs, while delusions involve false sensory perceptions.

   b. hallucinations occur primarily in schizophrenic disorders, while delusions occur primarily in dissociative disorders.

   c. hallucinations involve false sensory perceptions, while delusions involve false beliefs.

   d. there is no difference; those are just two words for the same thing.

Answers: 1. d. 2. c.

Childhood Disorders

Why do stimulants appear to slow down hyperactive children and adults?

Children may suffer from conditions already discussed in this chapter—for example, depression and anxiety disorders. But other disorders are either characteristic of children or are first evident in childhood. The *DSM-IV-TR* contains a long list of disorders usually first diagnosed in infancy, childhood, or adolescence. Two of these disorders are attention-deficit hyperactivity disorder and autistic disorder.

Attention-deficit hyperactivity disorder (ADHD) was once known simply as *hyperactivity*. The new name reflects the fact that children with the disorder typically have trouble focusing their attention in the sustained way that other children do. Instead, they are easily distracted, often fidgety and impulsive, and almost constantly in motion. Many theorists believe that this disorder—which affects 3 to 5% of all school-age children and is much more common in boys than girls—is present at birth, but becomes a serious problem only after the child starts school. The class setting demands that children sit quietly, pay attention as instructed, follow directions, and inhibit urges to yell and run around. The child with ADHD simply cannot conform to these demands.

We do not yet know what causes ADHD, but considerable evidence indicates biological factors play an important role (Nigg, 2005). Neuroimagining studies, for example, reveal

attention-deficit hyperactivity disorder (ADHD) A childhood disorder characterized by inattention, impulsiveness, and hyperactivity.

individuals with ADHD display altered brain functioning when presented with tasks that require shifting attention. The deficiency appears to involve the frontal lobe (see Chapter 2, "The Biological Basis of Behavior"), which normally recruits appropriate regions of the brain to solve a problem. In people with ADHD, however, the frontal lobe sometimes activates brain centers unrelated to solving a problem (Konrad, Neufang, Hanisch, Fink, & Herpertz-Dahlmann, 2006; Mulas et al 2006).

Family interaction and other social experiences may be more important in preventing the disorder than in causing it (C. Johnston & Ohan, 2005). That is, some exceptionally competent parents and patient, tolerant teachers may be able to teach "difficult" children to conform to the demands of schooling. Although some psychologists train the parents of children with ADHD in these management skills, the most frequent treatment for these children is a type of drug known as a **psychostimulant**. Psychostimulants do not work by "slowing down" hyperactive children; rather, they appear to increase the children's ability to focus their attention so that they can attend to the task at hand, which decreases their hyperactivity and improves their academic performance (Duesenberg, 2006; Gimpel et al., 2005). Unfortunately, psychostimulants often produce only short-term benefits; and their use and possible overuse in treating ADHD children is controversial (LeFever, Arcona, & Antonuccio, 2003).

A very different and profoundly serious disorder that usually becomes evident in the first few years of life is **autistic disorder**. Autistic children fail to form normal attachments to parents, remaining distant and withdrawn into their own separate worlds. As infants, they may even show distress at being picked up or held. As they grow older, they typically do not speak, or they develop a peculiar speech pattern called *echolalia*, in which they repeat the words said to them. Autistic children typically show strange motor behavior, such as repeating body movements endlessly or walking constantly on tiptoe. They don't play as normal children do; they are not at all social and may use toys in odd ways, constantly spinning the wheels on a toy truck or tearing paper into strips. Autistic children often display the symptoms of retardation (LaMalfa, Lassi, Bertelli, Salvini, & Placidi, 2004), but it is hard to test their mental ability because they generally don't talk. The disorder lasts into adulthood in the great majority of cases.

In recent years, autistic disorder has come to be viewed as just one dimension of a much broader range of developmental disorders known as **autistic spectrum disorder (ASD)** (Dawson & Toth, 2006; Simpson et al., 2005). Individuals with disorders in the autistic spectrum display symptoms that are similar to those seen in autistic disorder, but the severity of the symptoms is often quite reduced. For example, high functioning children with a form of ASD known as *Asperger syndrome* may show difficulty interacting with other people, but may have little or no problem with speech or intellectual development.

One explanation for the inability of individuals within the autistic spectrum to develop normal patterns of social interaction holds they may not understand or correctly interpret others' thoughts and feelings. This *theory of mind* explanation argues that because they do not realize other people may have different thoughts, emotions, and attitudes than their own, they often have problems communicating with and relating socially to them (Attwood, 2005; Papp, 2006). For example a child with Asperger syndrome may not understand why others do not know the answer to a question they know the answer to, or why they may take a point of view different from their own. This failure to comprehend another person's point of view or opinion is often a source of frustration leading to inappropriate social responses.

THINKING CRITICALLY ABOUT . . .

ADHD

When ADHD was first conceptualized at the turn of the 20th century, the estimated prevalence was not more than 1%. Recent estimates of prevalence in the United States however, are greater than 4% for males and almost 2% for females (Cuffe, Moore, & McKeown, 2005). What do you think accounts for this dramatic rise? Is it a true change in incidence, perhaps resulting from environmental or biological changes that affect children's functioning? Or is it an artifact of changing social expectations of children?

- In the United States, prevalence in boys is estimated at more than 4%, compared with less than 1% in Britain (Jacobson, 1999). What do you think could account for this difference? What research evidence would you need to know whether your theory is correct?

- Researchers claim that play and physical activity are basic needs of young mammals, similar to the need for food and fluids (Panksepp, Siviy, & Normansell, 1984; Vanderschuren, Niesink, & Van Ree, 1997). Could what we call ADHD be a normal variation of this need? In other words, is it possible that many children diagnosed with ADHD merely have an increased need for play? How might you go about collecting evidence to determine if your view is correct?

---

psychostimulant Drugs that increase ability to focus attention in people with ADHD.

autistic disorder A childhood disorder characterized by lack of social instincts and strange motor behavior.

autistic spectrum disorder (ASD) A range of disorders involving varying degrees of impairment in communication skills, social interactions, and restricted, repetitive, and stereotyped patterns of behavior.

We don't know what causes autism, although most theorists believe that it results almost entirely from biological conditions (Goode, 2004). Some causes of mental retardation, such as fragile X syndrome (see Chapter 7, "Cognition and Mental Abilities"), also seem to increase the risk of autistic disorder. Recent evidence suggests that genetics also play a strong role in causing the disorder (J. A. Lamb, Moore, Bailey, & Monaco, 2000; Nurmi et al., 2003; Rodier, 2000; Rutter, 2005), though no specific gene or chromosome responsible for autistic disorder has yet been identified (Shastry, 2005).

CHECK YOUR UNDERSTANDING

Indicate whether the following statements are true (T) or false (F):

1. ___ ADHD is much more common in boys than in girls.
2. ___ Psychostimulants work by "slowing down" hyperactive children.
3. ___ Most theorists believe that autistic disorder results almost entirely from biological conditions.

Answers: 1. (T). 2. (F). 3. (T).

APPLY YOUR UNDERSTANDING

1. Marie is a 7-year-old who is easily distracted and who has great difficulty concentrating. While reading or studying, her attention will often be drawn to events going on elsewhere. She is fidgety, impulsive, and never seems to stop moving. She finds it almost impossible to sit quietly, pay attention, and follow directions. Marie is most likely suffering from
   a. attention-deficit hyperactivity disorder.
   b. autistic disorder.
   c. echolalia.
   d. disorganized personality disorder.

2. Harry is a child who is usually distant and withdrawn. He doesn't seem to form attachments with anyone, even his parents. He plays by himself. He rarely talks; when he does, it is usually to repeat what someone else just said to him. It is most likely that Harry is suffering from
   a. attention-deficit hyperactivity disorder.
   b. autistic disorder.
   c. bipolar disorder.
   d. disorganized personality disorder.

Answers: 1. a. 2. b.

Gender and Cultural Differences in Psychological Disorders

What are the differences between men and women in psychological disorders?

GENDER DIFFERENCES

For the most part, men and women are similar with respect to mental disorders, but differences do exist. Many studies have concluded that women have a higher rate of psychological disorders than men do, but this is an oversimplification (Cosgrove & Riddle, 2004; Hartung & Widiger, 1998; Klose & Jacobi, 2004). We do know that more women than men are *treated* for mental disorders. But this cannot be taken to mean that more women than men have mental disorders, for in our society, it is much more acceptable for women to discuss their emotional difficulties and to seek professional help openly. It may be that mental disorders are equally common among men—or even more common—but that men do not so readily show up in therapists' offices and therefore are not counted in the studies (H. Lerman, 1996).

Moreover, mental disorders for which there seems to be a strong biological component, such as bipolar disorder and schizophrenia, are distributed fairly equally between the sexes. Differences tend to be found for those disorders *without* a strong biological component—that is, disorders in which learning and experience play a more important role. For example, men are more likely than women to suffer from substance abuse and antisocial personality disorder. Women, on the other hand, are more likely to suffer from depression, agoraphobia, simple phobia, obsessive–compulsive disorder, and somatization disorder (Craske, 2003; Douglas, Moffitt, Dar, McGee, & Silva, 1995). These tendencies, coupled with the fact that gender differences observed in the United States are not always seen in other cultures (Culbertson, 1997), suggest that socialization plays a part in developing a disorder: When men display abnormal behavior, it is more likely to take the forms of drinking too much and acting aggressively; when women display abnormal behavior, they are more likely to become fearful, passive, hopeless, and "sick" (Basow, 1986; Mabery, 2002).

One commonly reported difference between the sexes concerns marital status. Men who are separated, divorced, or who have never married have a higher incidence of mental disorders than do either women of the same marital status or married men. But married women have higher rates than married men. What accounts for the apparent fact that marriage is psychologically less beneficial for women than for men?

Here, too, socialization appears to play a role. For women, marriage, family relationships, and child rearing are likely to be more stressful than they are for men (Erickson, 2005; Stolzenberg & Waite, 2005). For men, marriage and family provide a haven; for women, they are a demanding job. In addition, women are more likely than men to be the victims of incest, rape, and marital battering. As one researcher has commented, "for women, the U.S. family is a violent institution" (Koss, 1990, p. 376).

For some married women, employment outside the home seems to provide the kind of psychological benefits that marriage apparently provides for many men. However, these benefits are likely to be realized only if the woman freely chooses to work, has a satisfying job, receives support from family and friends, and is able to set up stable child-care arrangements (R. C. Barnett, 2005; R. C. Barnett & Hyde, 2001; L. Hoffman, 1989). For women who enter the workforce because they have to rather than because they want to, whose work is routine or demeaning, or who are responsible for all domestic duties as well as their outside jobs, economic pressures and the stress of performing two demanding roles can be additional risk factors for psychological disorder.

We saw in Chapter 11 that the effects of stress are proportional to the extent that a person feels alienated, powerless, and helpless. Alienation, powerlessness, and helplessness are more prevalent in women than in men. These factors are especially common among minority women, so it is not surprising that the prevalence of psychological disorders is greater among them than among other women (Laganà & Sosa, 2004). In addition, these factors play an especially important role in anxiety disorders and depression—precisely those disorders experienced most often by women (M. Byrne, Carr, & Clark, 2004; Kessler et al., 1994). The rate of depression among women is twice that of men, a difference that is usually ascribed to the more negative and stressful aspects of women's lives, including lower incomes and the experiences of bias and physical and sexual abuse (American Psychological Association, 2006; Blehar & Keita, 2003).

In summary, women do seem to have higher rates of anxiety disorders and depression than men do; and they are more likely than men to seek professional help for their problems. However, greater stress, due in part to socialization and lower status rather than psychological weakness, apparently accounts for this statistic. Marriage and family life,

More women than men in the United States seek help for mental disorders, but this may not mean mental disorders are more prevalent in women. Women are more likely than men to seek help for a variety of problems, physical and mental.

13 Therapies

OVERVIEW

Mike Wallace is widely known as a hard-hitting investigative reporter on the weekly TV newsmagazine *60 Minutes*. His tenacious interviewing style is legendary. A framed newspaper clipping on his office wall declares that the words "Mike Wallace is here" are the four most dreaded words in the English language. Given his tough-minded reputation and years of award-winning success, Wallace is hardly the kind of person who others might imagine as prone to depression. But bouts of clinical depression are exactly what Wallace has suffered during the past 20 years.

The problem began in 1984 when Wallace and his employer, CBS News, were defending themselves against a $120 million libel suit in connection with a *60 Minutes* story on the Vietnam War. The daily courtroom accusations that Wallace was a liar and a fraud began to eat away at his self-confidence. He lost his powers of concentration. He couldn't sleep at night. In the morning, he found it very difficult to get out of bed. He felt physically and emotionally exhausted and began to think about suicide. Finally, in a state of collapse, he checked himself into a hospital, where he was diagnosed with clinical depression.

At first, Wallace felt ashamed about making his condition public. He didn't want people to know of his vulnerability, viewing it as a sign of personal weakness. In the United States, this reaction is fairly common among men with depression, who often perceive it as an unmasculine social stigma. Many avoid seeking therapy, even though depression is in fact a very treatable disorder. People who fail to get treatment, however, may remain incapacitated for many weeks or months.

But Wallace was luckier than most. He was placed on the antidepressant drug Ludiomil; and at the same time, he began frequent psychotherapy sessions. The drug helped to correct the chemical imbalance in his brain, while the therapist encouraged him to see that his situation was actually far less hopeless than he imagined. He gradually came to acknowledge that even if he lost the lawsuit, his life would certainly not be over. Wallace also had the support of two close friends who had suffered similar episodes of depression. As a result of this therapeutic mix, Wallace's depression began to lift and his life returned to normal. Although he has had some relapses since that time, mild drug treatment and occasional psychotherapy continue to keep his depression in check today.

Having learned about a wide range of psychological disorders in Chapter 12, "Psychological Disorders", you are probably curious about the kinds of treatments available for them. Mike Wallace's treatment for depression, a combination of medication and **psychotherapy**, exemplifies the help that is available. This chapter describes a broad variety of treatments that mental health professionals provide. We begin with a category collectively known as insight therapies.

ENDURING ISSUES IN THERAPIES ●●

The underlying assumption behind providing therapy for psychological disorders is the belief that people are capable of changing (stability–change). Throughout this chapter are many opportunities to think about whether people suffering from psychological disorders can change significantly and whether they can change even without therapeutic intervention. In the discussion of biological treatments for psychological disorders we will again encounter the issue of mind–body. Finally, the enduring issue of diversity–universality will arise again when we discuss the challenges therapists face when treating people from cultures other than their own.

Insight Therapies

What do insight therapies have in common?

Several of the individual psychotherapies used both in private practice and in institutions fall under the heading of **insight therapies**. Although the details of various insight therapies differ, their common goal is to give people a better awareness and understanding of their feelings, motivations, and actions in the hope that this will lead to better adjustment (Milton, Polmear, & Fabricius, 2004; Person, Cooper, & Gabbard, 2005). In this section, we consider three major insight therapies: psychoanalysis, client-centered therapy, and Gestalt therapy.

psychotherapy The use of psychological techniques to treat personality and behavior disorders.

insight therapies A variety of individual psychotherapies designed to give people a better awareness and understanding of their feelings, motivations, and actions in the hope that this will help them to adjust.

systematic desensitization A behavioral technique for reducing a person's fear and anxiety by gradually associating a new response (relaxation) with stimuli that have been causing the fear and anxiety.

that all behavior, both normal and abnormal, is learned (Tryon, 2000). People suffering from hypochondriasis *learn* that they get attention when they are sick; people with paranoid personalities *learn* to be suspicious of others. Behavior therapists also assume that maladaptive behaviors *are* the problem, not symptoms of deeper underlying causes. If behavior therapists can teach people to behave in more appropriate ways, they believe that they have cured the problem. The therapist does not need to know exactly how or why a client learned to behave abnormally in the first place. The job of the therapist is simply to teach the person new, more satisfying ways of behaving on the basis of scientifically studied principles of learning, such as classical conditioning, operant conditioning, and modeling.

THERAPIES BASED ON CLASSICAL CONDITIONING

How can classical conditioning be used as the basis of treatment?

As we saw in Chapter 5, "Learning," *classical conditioning* involves the repeated pairing of a neutral stimulus with one that evokes a certain reflex response. Eventually, the formerly neutral stimulus alone comes to elicit the same response. The approach is one of learned stimulus-response associations. Several variations on classical conditioning have been used to treat psychological problems.

DESENSITIZATION, EXTINCTION, AND FLOODING Systematic desensitization, a method for gradually reducing fear and anxiety, is one of the oldest behavior therapy techniques (J. Wolpe, 1990). The method works by gradually associating a new response (relaxation) with stimuli that have been causing anxiety. For example, an aspiring politician might seek therapy because he is anxious about speaking to crowds. The therapist explores the kinds of crowds that are most threatening: Is an audience of 500 worse than one of 50? Is it harder to speak to men than it is to women? Is there more anxiety facing strangers than a roomful of friends? From this information the therapist develops a *hierarchy of fears*—a list of situations from the least to the most anxiety provoking. The therapist then teaches the client how to relax, including both mental and physical techniques of relaxation. Once the person has mastered deep relaxation, she or he begins work at the bottom of the hierarchy of fears. The person is told to relax while imagining the least threatening situation on the list, then the next most threatening, and so on, until the most fear-arousing one is reached and the client can still remain calm.

The clients in these photographs are overcoming a simple phobia: fear of snakes. After practicing a technique of deep relaxation, clients in desensitization therapy work from the bottom of their hierarchy of fears up to the situation that provokes the greatest fear or anxiety. Here, clients progress from handling rubber snakes (top left) to viewing live snakes through a window (top center) and finally to handling live snakes. This procedure can also be conducted vicariously in the therapist's office, where clients combine relaxation techniques with imagining anxiety-provoking scenes.

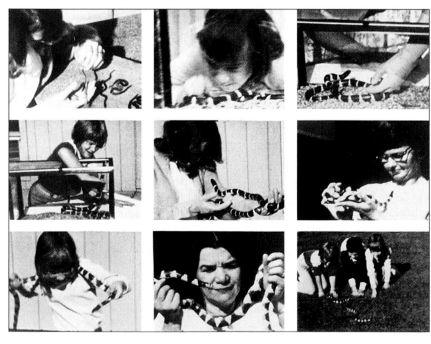

Numerous studies show that systematic desensitization helps many people overcome their fears and phobias (Hazel, 2005; D. W. McNeil & Zvolensky, 2000; C. Wang & Chen, 2000). The key to its success may not be the learning of a new conditioned relaxation response, but rather the *extinction* of the old fear response through mere exposure. Recall from Chapter 5, "Learning," that in classical conditioning, extinction occurs when the learned, conditioned stimulus is repeatedly presented without the unconditioned stimulus following it. Thus, if a person repeatedly imagines a frightening situation without actually encountering danger, the fear associated with that situation should gradually decline.

Desensitization is most effective when clients gradually confront their fears in the real world rather than merely in their imaginations. People who are deathly afraid of flying, for example, might first simply drive to an airport. When they are able to do this without anxiety, they may move on to walking near a plane on the ground. When they can do that calmly, they may go inside a stationary plane. Eventually they may take a short flight. This common-sense approach of working step-by-step through a hierarchy of fears in real life is probably familiar to you. For example, folk wisdom says that if you fall off a horse, the best way to get over your fear of riding is to get right back on the horse and continue to ride until the fear is gone.

The technique of *flooding* is a less familiar and more frightening method of desensitization. It involves full-intensity exposure to a feared stimulus for a prolonged period of time (Pollard, 2000; J. Wolpe, 1990). For example, someone with a powerful fear of snakes might be forced to handle dozens of snakes, or someone with an overwhelming fear of spiders might be forced to stroke a tarantula and allow it to crawl up an arm. If you think that flooding is an unnecessarily harsh method, remember how debilitating many untreated anxiety disorders can be to a person. (See Chapter 12.)

AVERSIVE CONDITIONING Another classical conditioning technique is **aversive conditioning**, in which pain and discomfort are associated with the behavior that the client wants to unlearn. Aversive conditioning has been used with limited success to treat alcoholism, obesity, smoking, and some psychosexual disorders. For example, the taste and smell of alcohol are sometimes paired with drug-induced nausea and vomiting. Before long, clients feel sick just seeing a bottle of liquor. A follow-up study of nearly 800 people who completed alcohol-aversion treatment found that 63% had maintained continuous abstinence for at least 12 months (S. L. Johnson, 2003; Wiens & Menustik, 1983). The long-term effectiveness of this technique has been questioned. When the punishment no longer follows, the undesired behavior may reemerge. In addition, aversive conditioning is a controversial technique because of its unpleasant nature.

THERAPIES BASED ON OPERANT CONDITIONING

How could "behavior contracting" change an undesirable behavior?

In *operant conditioning*, a person learns to behave in a certain way because that behavior is reinforced, or rewarded. One therapy based on the principle of reinforcement is called **behavior contracting**. The therapist and the client agree on behavioral goals and on the reinforcement that the client will receive when he or she reaches those goals. These goals and reinforcements are often written in a contract that binds both the client and the therapist, as if by legal agreement. For instance, a contract to help a person stop smoking might read as follows: "For each day that I smoke fewer than 20 cigarettes, I will earn 30 minutes of time to go bowling. For each day that I exceed the goal, I will lose 30 minutes from the time that I have accumulated." Behavior contracting has also been used effectively in schools to assist students with emotional and behavior difficulties. Contracts specify which negative behaviors (such as aggressiveness or disruptiveness) will be followed by penalties, and which positive behaviors (such as completing class work on time or classroom participation) will be followed by rewards (Ruth, 1996).

Another therapy based on operant conditioning is called the **token economy**. Token economies are usually used in schools and hospitals, where controlled conditions are most feasible (Boniecki & Moore, 2003; Comaty, Stasio, & Advokat, 2001). People are rewarded with tokens or points for behaviors that are considered appropriate and adaptive. The tokens or points can be exchanged for desired items and privileges. On the ward of a mental hospital, for example, improved grooming habits might earn points that can be used to purchase special foods or weekend passes. Token economies have proved effective in modifying the behavior of people who are resistant to other forms of treatment, such as those with chronic schizophrenia (Dickerson, Tenhula, & Green-Paden, 2005; Kopelowicz, Liberman, & Zarate, 2002). The positive changes in behavior, however, do not always generalize to everyday life outside the hospital or clinic, where adaptive behavior is not always reinforced and maladaptive behavior is not always punished.

aversive conditioning Behavioral therapy techniques aimed at eliminating undesirable behavior patterns by teaching the person to associate them with pain and discomfort.

behavior contracting Form of operant conditioning therapy in which the client and therapist set behavioral goals and agree on reinforcements that the client will receive on reaching those goals.

token economy An operant conditioning therapy in which people earn tokens (reinforcers) for desired behaviors and exchange them for desired items or privileges.

THERAPIES BASED ON MODELING

What are some therapeutic uses of modeling?

Modeling—the process of learning a behavior by watching someone else perform it—can also be used to treat problem behaviors. In a now classic demonstration of modeling, Albert Bandura and colleagues helped people to overcome a snake phobia by showing films in which models confronted snakes and gradually moved closer and closer to them (Bandura, Blanchard, & Ritter, 1969). Modeling techniques have also been successfully used as part of job training programs (P. J. Taylor, Russ-Eft, & Chan, 2005) and have been used extensively with people with mental retardation to teach job and independent living skills (Matson, Smalls, Hampff, Smiroldo, & Anderson, 1998; Sundel, 1991).

CHECK YOUR UNDERSTANDING

1. The therapeutic use of rewards to encourage desired behavior is based on a form of learning called _____ _____.
2. When client and therapist agree on a written set of behavioral goals, as well as a specific schedule of reinforcement when each goal is met, they are using a technique called _____ _____.
3. Some therapy involves learning desired behaviors by watching others perform those actions, which is also known as _____.
4. A _____ _____ is an operant conditioning technique whereby people earn some tangible item for desired behavior, which can then be exchanged for more basic rewards and privileges.
5. The technique of _____ involves intense and prolonged exposure to something feared.

Answers: 1. operant conditioning. 2. behavior contracting. 3. modeling. 4. token economy. 5. flooding.

APPLY YOUR UNDERSTANDING

1. Maria is in an alcoholism treatment program in which she must take a pill every morning. If she drinks alcohol during the day, she immediately feels nauseous. This treatment is an example of
   a. transference.
   b. flooding.
   c. aversive conditioning.
   d. desensitization.
2. Robert is about to start a new job in a tall building; and he is deathly afraid of riding in elevators. He sees a therapist who first teaches him how to relax. Once he has mastered that skill, the therapist asks him to relax while imagining that he is entering the office building. Once he can do that without feeling anxious, the therapist asks him to relax while imagining standing in front of the elevator doors, and so on until Robert can completely relax while imagining riding in elevators. This therapeutic technique is known as
   a. transference.
   b. desensitization.
   c. behavior contracting.
   d. flooding.

Answers: 1. c. 2. b.

modeling A behavior therapy in which the person learns desired behaviors by watching others perform those behaviors.

Cognitive Therapies

How can people overcome irrational and self-defeating beliefs about themselves?

Cognitive therapies are based on the belief that if people can change their distorted ideas about themselves and the world, they can also change their problem behaviors and make their lives more enjoyable (Bleijenberg, Prins, & Bazelmans, 2003). The task facing cognitive therapists is to identify erroneous ways of thinking and to correct them. This focus on learning new ways of thinking shares many similarities with behavior therapies, which also focus on learning. In fact, many professionals consider themselves to be *cognitive–behavior therapists*—therapists who combine both cognitive and behavior therapies (J. H. Wright, Basco, & Thase, 2005). Three popular forms of cognitive therapy are stress-inoculation therapy, rational–emotive therapy, and Aaron Beck's cognitive approach.

STRESS-INOCULATION THERAPY

How can self-talk help us deal with difficult situations?

As we go about our lives, we talk to ourselves constantly—proposing courses of action, commenting on our performance, expressing wishes, and so on. **Stress-inoculation therapy** makes use of this self-talk to help people cope with stressful situations. The client is taught to suppress any negative, anxiety-evoking thoughts and to replace them with positive, "coping" thoughts. Take a student with exam anxiety who faces every test telling herself, "Oh no, another test. I'm so nervous. I'm sure I won't think calmly enough to remember the answers. If only I'd studied more. If I don't get through this course, I'll never graduate!" This pattern of thought is highly dysfunctional because it only makes anxiety worse. With the help of a cognitive therapist, the student learns a new pattern of self-talk: "I studied hard for this exam, and I know the material well. I looked at the textbook last night and reviewed my notes. I should be able to do well. If some questions are hard, they won't all be, and even if it's tough, my whole grade doesn't depend on just one test." Then the person tries out the new strategy in a real situation, ideally one of only moderate stress (like a short quiz). Finally, the person is ready to use the strategy in a more stressful situation, like a final exam (Sheehy & Horan, 2004). Stress-inoculation therapy works by turning the client's thought patterns into a kind of vaccine against stress-induced anxiety.

According to cognitive therapists, the confidence this person is showing stems from the positive thoughts she has about herself. Stress-inoculation therapy helps replace negative, anxiety-evoking thoughts with confident self-talk.

RATIONAL–EMOTIVE THERAPY

What irrational beliefs do many people hold?

Another type of cognitive therapy, **rational–emotive therapy (RET)**, developed by Albert Ellis (1973, 2001), is based on the view that most people in need of therapy hold a set of irrational and self-defeating beliefs (Macavei, 2005; Overholser, 2003). They believe that they should be competent at *everything*, liked by *everyone, always* treated fairly, quick to find solutions to *every* problem, and so forth. Such beliefs involve absolutes—"musts" and "shoulds"—that allow for no exceptions, making no room for mistakes. When people with such irrational beliefs come up against real-life struggles, they often experience excessive psychological distress. For example, when a college student who believes that he must be liked by everyone isn't invited to join a certain fraternity, he may view the rejection as a catastrophe and become deeply depressed rather than just feeling disappointed.

Rational–emotive therapists confront such dysfunctional beliefs vigorously, using a variety of techniques, including persuasion, challenge, commands, and theoretical arguments (A. Ellis & MacLaren, 1998). Studies have shown that RET often does enable people to reinterpret their negative beliefs and experiences in a more positive light, decreasing the likelihood of becoming depressed (Blatt, Zuroff, Quinlan, & Pilkonis, 1996; Bruder et al., 1997).

cognitive therapies Psychotherapies that emphasize changing clients' perceptions of their life situation as a way of modifying their behavior.

stress-inoculation therapy A type of cognitive therapy that trains clients to cope with stressful situations by learning a more useful pattern of self-talk.

rational–emotive therapy (RET) A directive cognitive therapy based on the idea that clients' psychological distress is caused by irrational and self-defeating beliefs and that the therapist's job is to challenge such dysfunctional beliefs.

BECK'S COGNITIVE THERAPY

How can cognitive therapy be used to combat depression?

One of the most important and promising forms of cognitive therapy for treating depression is known simply as **cognitive therapy** (J. Cahill et al., 2003). Sometimes it is referred to as "Beck's cognitive therapy," after Aaron Beck who developed it (1967), to avoid confusion with the broader category of cognitive therapies.

Beck believes that depression results from inappropriately self-critical patterns of thought about the self. Such people have unrealistic expectations, magnify their failures, make sweeping negative generalizations about themselves from little evidence, notice only negative feedback from the outside world, and interpret anything less than total success as failure. This negative chain of thinking may often spiral downward from small setbacks, until the person concludes that he or she is worthless. According to Beck, the downward spiral of negative, distorted thoughts is at the heart of depression. For instance, Mike Wallace's depression was triggered, in part, when he started to pay attention to negative feedback during the lawsuit against him.

Beck's assumptions about the cause of depression are very similar to those underlying RET, but the style of treatment differs considerably. Cognitive therapists are much less challenging and confrontational than rational–emotive therapists (Dozois, Frewen, & Covin, 2006). Instead, they try to help clients examine each dysfunctional thought in a supportive, but objectively scientific manner ("Are you *sure* your whole life will be totally ruined if you break up with Frank? What is your evidence for that? Didn't you once tell me how happy you were *before* you met him?"). Like RET, Beck's cognitive therapy tries to lead the person to more realistic and flexible ways of thinking.

CHECK YOUR UNDERSTANDING

1. Developing new ways of thinking that lead to more adaptive behavior lies at the heart of all _____ therapies.

2. An important form of cognitive therapy used to combat depression was developed by Aaron _____.

3. The immediate focus in cognitive therapies is to help clients change their behaviors. Is this statement true (T) or false (F)?

Answers: 1. cognitive. 2. Beck. 3. (F).

APPLY YOUR UNDERSTANDING

1. Larry has difficulty following his boss's directions. Whenever his boss asks him to do something, Larry panics. Larry enters a stress-inoculation program. Which is most likely to be the first step in this program?
   a. Have Larry volunteer to do a task for his boss.
   b. Show Larry a film in which employees are asked to do tasks and they perform well.
   c. Ask Larry what he says to himself when his boss asks him to perform a task.
   d. Ask Larry how he felt when he was a child and his mother asked him to do something.

2. Sarah rushes a sorority but isn't invited to join. She has great difficulty accepting this fact and as a consequence she becomes deeply depressed. She sees a therapist who vigorously challenges and confronts her in an effort to show her that her depression comes from an irrational, self-defeating belief that she must be liked and accepted by everyone. This therapist is most likely engaging in
   a. rational–emotive therapy.
   b. stress-inoculation therapy.
   c. flooding.
   d. desensitization therapy.

Answers: 1. c. 2. a.

cognitive therapy Therapy that depends on identifying and changing inappropriately negative and self-critical patterns of thought.

Group Therapies

What are some advantages of group therapies?

Some therapists believe that treating several people simultaneously is preferable to treating each alone. Such **group therapy** allows both client and therapist to see how the person acts around others. If a person is painfully anxious and tongue-tied, chronically self-critical, or hostile and aggressive, these tendencies will show up quickly in a group.

Group therapies have other advantages, too. A good group offers social support, a feeling that one is not the only person in the world with problems. Group members can also help one another learn useful new behaviors (how to express feelings, how to disagree without antagonizing others). Interactions in a group can lead people toward insights into their own behavior, such as why they are so defensive or feel compelled to complain constantly. Finally, because group therapy consists of several clients "sharing" a therapist, it is less expensive than individual therapy (Fejr, 2003; N. Morrison, 2001).

There are many kinds of group therapy. Some groups follow the general outlines of the therapies we have already mentioned. Others are oriented toward a very specific goal, such as stopping smoking, drinking, or overeating. Some have a single, but more open-ended goal—for example, a happier family or romantic relationship. The *self-help group* is a particularly popular form of group therapy today.

Group therapy can help to identify problems that a person has when interacting with other people. The group also offers social support, helping people to feel less alone with their problems.

FAMILY THERAPY

Who is the client in family therapy?

Family therapy is another form of group therapy (Lebow, 2006; Snow, Crethar, & Robey, 2005). Family therapists believe that if one person in the family is having problems, it is often a signal that the entire family needs assistance. Therefore, it would be a mistake to treat a client without making an attempt to meet the person's parents, spouse, and children. Family therapists do not try to reshape the personalities of family members (Gurman & Kniskern, 1991). Instead, the primary goals of family therapy are improving family communication, encouraging family members to become more empathetic, getting them to share responsibilities, and reducing conflict within the family. To achieve these goals, all family members must believe that they will benefit from changes in their behavior.

Although family therapy is especially appropriate when there are problems between husband and wife or parents and children, it is increasingly used when only one family member has a clear psychological disorder, such as schizophrenia, agoraphobia, or in some cases, depression (Keitner, Archambault, Ryan, & Miller, 2003; Mueser, 2006). The goal of treatment in these circumstances is to help the mentally healthy members of the family cope more effectively with the impact of the disorder on the family unit. The improved coping of the well-adjusted family members may in turn help the troubled person. Family therapy is also called for when a person's progress in individual therapy is slowed by the family (often because other family members have trouble adjusting to that person's improvement).

Unfortunately, not all families benefit from family therapy. Sometimes the problems are too entrenched. In the other cases, important family members may be absent or unwilling to cooperate. In still others, one family member monopolizes sessions, making it hard for anyone else's views to be heard. In all these cases, a different therapeutic approach is needed.

COUPLE THERAPY

What are some techniques used in couple therapy?

A third form of group therapy is **couple therapy**, which is designed to assist partners who are having difficulties with their relationship. In the past, this therapy was generally called *marital*

group therapy Type of psychotherapy in which clients meet regularly to interact and help one another achieve insight into their feelings and behavior.

family therapy A form of group therapy that sees the family as at least partly responsible for the individual's problems and that seeks to change all family members' behaviors to the benefit of the family unit as well as the troubled individual.

therapy, but the term "couple therapy" is considered more appropriate today because it captures the broad range of partners who may seek help (Lebow, 2006; Sheras & Koch-Sheras, 2006).

Most couple therapists concentrate on improving patterns of communication and mutual expectations. In *empathy training*, for example, each member of the couple is taught to share inner feelings and to listen to and understand the partner's feelings before responding to them. This technique requires that people spend more time listening, trying to grasp what is really being said, and less time in self-defensive rebuttal. Other couple therapists use behavioral techniques. For example, a couple might be helped to develop a schedule for exchanging specific caring actions, such as helping with chores around the house, making time to share a special meal together, or remembering special occasions with a gift or card. This approach may not sound very romantic, but proponents say it can break a cycle of dissatisfaction and hostility in a relationship, and hence, it is an important step in the right direction (N. B. Epstein, 2004). Couple therapy for both partners is generally more effective than therapy for only one of them (S. M. Johnson, 2003).

SELF-HELP GROUPS

Why are self-help groups so popular?

Because an estimated 40 million Americans suffer some kind of psychological problem (Narrow, Rae, Robins, & Regier, 2001) and because the cost of individual treatment can be so high, more and more people faced with life crises are turning to low-cost self-help groups. Most groups are small, local gatherings of people who share a common problem or predicament and who provide mutual assistance. Alcoholics Anonymous is perhaps the best-known self-help group, but self-help groups are available for virtually every life problem.

Do these self-help groups work? In many cases, they apparently do. Alcoholics Anonymous has developed a reputation for helping people cope with alcoholism. Most group members express strong support for their groups, and studies have demonstrated that they can indeed be effective (Galanter, Hayden, Castañeda, & Franco, 2005; Kurtz, 2004; McKellar, Stewart, & Humphreys, 2003; Ouimette et al., 2001).

Such groups also help to prevent more serious psychological disorders by reaching out to people who are near the limits of their ability to cope with stress. The social support they offer is particularly important in an age when divorce, geographic mobility, and other factors have reduced the ability of the family to comfort people. A list of some self-help organizations is included in Applying Psychology: "How to Find Help."

CHECK YOUR UNDERSTANDING

1. Which of the following is an advantage of group therapy?
   a. The client has the experience of interacting with other people in a therapeutic setting.
   b. It often reveals a client's problems more quickly than individual therapy.
   c. It can be cheaper than individual therapy.
   d. All of the above.

Answers: 1. d.

APPLY YOUR UNDERSTANDING

1. You are talking to a clinical psychologist who explains that, in her view, it is a mistake to try to treat a client's problems in a vacuum. Quite often, well-adjusted members of a family can help the client cope more effectively. Other times, the client's progress is slowed due to other people in the family. She is most likely a
   a. self-help therapist.
   b. family therapist.
   c. proximity therapist.
   d. social-attribution therapist.

couple therapy A form of group therapy intended to help troubled partners improve their problems of communication and interaction.

2. Imagine that you believe most problems between partners arise because they don't share their inner feelings and they don't truly listen to and try to understand each other. You meet with them together and teach them to spend more time listening to the other person and trying to understand what the other person is really saying. Your beliefs are closest to which of the following kinds of therapists?

   a. Gestalt therapists.

   b. rational–emotive therapists.

   c. family therapists.

   d. couple therapists.

Answers: 1. b. 2. d.

APPLYING PSYCHOLOGY

HOW TO FIND HELP

The attitude that seeking help for psychological problems is a sign that you are "crazy" or "not strong enough" to help yourself is very common in our society. But the fact is that millions of people are helped by psychological counseling and therapy every year. These people include business executives, artists, sports heroes, celebrities, and students. Therapy is a common, useful aid in coping with daily life.

College is a time of stress and anxiety for many people. The pressure of work, the competition for grades, the exposure to many different kinds of people with unfamiliar views, the tension of relating to peers—all these factors take a psychological toll, especially for students away from home for the first time. Most colleges and universities have their own counseling services, and many of them are as sophisticated as the best clinics in the country. Most communities also have mental health programs. As an aid to a potential search for the right counseling service, we include here a list of some of the available resources for people who would like the advice of a mental health professional. Many of these services have national offices that will provide you with local branches and the appropriate people to contact in your area.

For Alcohol and Drug Abuse
National Clearinghouse for Alcohol and Drug Information
Rockville, MD (301) 468–2600

General Service Board
Alcoholics Anonymous, Inc.
New York, NY (212) 870-3400

For Friends or Relatives of Those With an Alcohol Problem
Al-Anon Family Groups
Virginia Beach, VA
(888) 4alanon (meeting information)
(757) 563-1600 (personal assistance)
Web site: www.al-anon.alateen.org

National Association for Children of Alcoholics
Rockville, MD
(301) 468-0985

For Depression and Suicide
Mental Health Counseling Hotline
New York, NY
(212) 734-5876

Heartbeat (for survivors of suicides)
Colorado Springs, CO
(719) 596-2575

For Sexual and Sex-Related Problems
Sex Information and Education Council of the United States (SIECUS)
New York, NY
(212) 819-9770

National Organization for Women
Legislative Office
Washington, DC
(202) 331-0066

For Physical Abuse
Child Abuse Listening and Mediation (CALM)
Santa Barbara, CA
(805) 965-2376

For Help in Selecting a Therapist
National Mental Health Consumer Self-Help Clearinghouse
(215) 751-1810

For General Information on Mental Health and Counseling
The National Alliance for the Mentally Ill
Arlington, VA
(703) 524-7600

The National Mental Health Association
Alexandria, VA
(703) 684–7722

The American Psychiatric Association
Washington, DC
(703) 907-7300

The American Psychological Association
Washington, DC
(202) 336-5500

The National Institute of Mental Health
Rockville, MD
(301) 443-4513

Effectiveness of Psychotherapy

How much better off is a person who receives psychotherapy than one who gets no treatment at all?

We have noted that some psychotherapies are generally effective, but how much better are they than no treatment at all? Researchers have found that roughly twice as many people (two-thirds) improve with formal therapy than with no treatment at all (Borkovec & Costello, 1993; M. J. Lambert, 2001; M. J. Lambert, Shapiro, & Bergin, 1986). Furthermore, many people who do not receive formal therapy get therapeutic help from friends, clergy, physicians, and teachers. Thus, the recovery rate for people who receive *no* therapeutic help at all is quite possibly even less than one-third. Other studies concur on psychotherapy's effectiveness (Hartmann & Zepf, 2003; M. J. Lambert & Archer, 2006; Leichsenring & Leibing, 2003), although its value appears to be related to a number of other factors. For instance, psychotherapy works best for relatively mild psychological problems (Kopta, Howard, Lowry, & Beutler, 1994) and seems to provide the greatest benefits to people who really *want* to change (Orlinsky & Howard, 1994).

Finally, one very extensive study designed to evaluate the effectiveness of psychotherapy was reported by *Consumer Reports*. Largely under the direction of psychologist Martin E. P. Seligman (1995), this investigation surveyed 180,000 *Consumer Reports* subscribers on everything from automobiles to mental health. Approximately 7,000 people from the total sample responded to the mental health section of the questionnaire that assessed satisfaction and improvement in people who had received psychotherapy, with the following results.

First, the vast majority of respondents reported significant overall improvement after therapy (M. E. P. Seligman, 1995). Second, there was no difference in the overall improvement score among people who had received therapy alone and those who had combined psychotherapy with medication. Third, no differences were found between the various forms of psychotherapy. Fourth, no differences in effectiveness were indicated between psychologists, psychiatrists, and social workers, although marriage counselors were seen as less effective. And fifth, people who had received long-term therapy reported more improvement than those who had received short-term therapy. This last result, one of the most striking findings of the study, is illustrated in **Figure 13–1**.

The *Consumer Reports* study lacked the scientific rigor of more traditional investigations designed to assess psychotherapeutic efficacy (Jacobson & Christensen, 1996; M. E. P. Seligman, 1995, 1996). For example, it did not use a control group to assess change in people who did not receive therapy. Nevertheless, it provides broad support for the idea that psychotherapy does work. Exactly why no differences were found between the various forms of psychotherapy is the topic of the next section. (See "Thinking Critically About: Survey Results.")

THINKING CRITICALLY ABOUT . . .

Survey Results

The text states that the *Consumer Reports* study lacked the scientific rigor of more traditional investigations. Think about the following questions:

- How were the respondents selected? How does that compare to the way in which scientific surveys select respondents (see Chapter 1, "The Science of Psychology")?

- How did the study determine whether the respondents had improved?

- How would a psychologist conduct a more scientific study of the effectiveness of psychotherapy? What variables would need to be defined? How would the participants be chosen? What ethical issues might need to be considered?

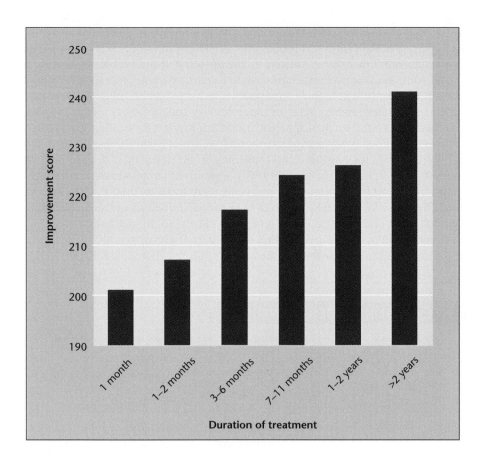

Figure 13–1
Duration of therapy and improvement.
One of the most dramatic results of the *Consumer Reports* (1995) study on the effectiveness of psychotherapy was the strong relationship between reported improvement and the duration of therapy.

Source: Adapted from Seligman, M. E. P. (1995). The effectiveness of psychotherapy: The *Consumer Reports* study. *American Psychologist, 50,* 965–974. Copyright © 1995 by the American Psychological Association. Adapted with permission.

WHICH TYPE OF THERAPY IS BEST FOR WHICH DISORDER?

Another important question is whether some forms of psychotherapy are more effective than others (Lyddon & Jones, 2001). Is behavior therapy, for example, more effective than insight therapy? In general, the answer seems to be "not much" (J. A. Carter, 2006; Hanna, 2002; Wampold et al., 1997). Most of the benefits of treatment seem to come from being in *some* kind of therapy, regardless of the particular type.

As we have seen, the various forms of psychotherapy are based on very different views about what causes mental disorders and, at least on the surface, approach the treatment of mental disorders in different ways. Why, then, is there no difference in their effectiveness? To answer this question, some psychologists have focused their attention on what the various forms of psychotherapy have in common, rather than emphasizing their differences (J. A. Carter, 2006; Roberts, Kewman, Mercer, & Hovell, 1993):

1. All forms of psychotherapy provide people with an *explanation for their problems*. Along with this explanation often comes a new perspective, providing people with specific actions to help them cope more effectively.
2. Most forms of psychotherapy offer people *hope*. Because most people who seek therapy have low self-esteem and feel demoralized and depressed, hope and the expectation for improvement increase their feelings of self-worth.
3. All major types of psychotherapy engage the client in a *therapeutic alliance* with a therapist. Although their therapeutic approaches may differ, effective therapists are warm, empathetic, and caring people who understand the importance of establishing a strong emotional bond with their clients that is built on mutual respect and understanding (Norcross, 2002; Wampold, 2001).

Together, these nonspecific factors common to all forms of psychotherapy appear, at least in part, to explain why most people who receive any form of therapy show some benefits as compared with those who receive no therapeutic help at all (D. N. Klein et al., 2003).

Still, some kinds of psychotherapy seem to be particularly appropriate for certain people and problems. Insight therapy, for example, seems to be best suited to people seeking profound self-understanding, relief of inner conflict and anxiety, or better relationships with others. Behavior therapy is apparently most appropriate for treating specific anxieties or other well-defined behavioral problems, such as sexual dysfunctions. Family therapy is generally more effective than individual counseling for the treatment of drug abuse (Liddle & Rowe, 2002; M. D. Stanton & Shadish, 1997). Cognitive therapies have been shown to be effective treatments for depression (Kopta, Lueger, Saunders, & Howard, 1999; Leahy, 2004; Merrill, Tolbert, & Wade, 2003;) and seem to be promising treatments for anxiety disorders as well (Dugas et al., 2003; Howard, 1999). The trend in psychotherapy is toward **eclecticism**—that is, toward a recognition of the value of a broad treatment package, rather than commitment to a single form of therapy (J. A. Carter, 2006; Slife & Reber, 2001).

CHECK YOUR UNDERSTANDING

1. There is a trend among psychotherapists to combine treatment techniques in what is called _____.
2. Most researchers agree that psychotherapy helps about _____–_____ of the people treated.
3. Psychotherapy works best for relatively _____ disorders, as compared with _____ ones.

Answers: 1. eclecticism. 2. two-thirds. 3. mild, severe.

APPLY YOUR UNDERSTANDING

1. Your friend is experiencing anxiety attacks, but doesn't want to see a therapist because "they don't do any good." Which of the following replies most accurately reflects what you have learned about the effectiveness of therapy?
   a. "You're right. Psychotherapy is no better than no treatment at all."
   b. "Actually, even just initiating therapy has a beneficial effect compared with doing nothing."
   c. "You're at least twice as likely to improve if you see a therapist than if you don't."
   d. "Therapy could help you, but you'd have to stick with it for at least a year before it has any effect."
2. John is suffering from moderate depression. Which of the following therapies is most likely to help him?
   a. insight therapy.
   b. cognitive therapy.
   c. behavioral contracting.
   d. group therapy.

Answers: 1. c. 2. b.

eclecticism Psychotherapeutic approach that recognizes the value of a broad treatment package over a rigid commitment to one particular form of therapy.

biological treatments A group of approaches, including medication, electroconvulsive therapy, and psychosurgery, that are sometimes used to treat psychological disorders in conjunction with, or instead of, psychotherapy.

Biological Treatments

What are biological treatments, and who can provide them?

Biological treatments—a group of approaches including medication, electroconvulsive therapy, and psychosurgery—may be used to treat psychological disorders in addition to, or instead of, psychotherapy. Clients and therapists opt for biological treatments for several reasons. First, some people are too agitated, disoriented, or unresponsive to be helped by psychotherapy. Second, biological treatment is virtually always used for disorders with a strong biological component. Third, biological treatment is often used for people who are dangerous to themselves and to others.

Traditionally, the only mental health professionals licensed to offer biological treatments were psychiatrists, who are physicians. But as we noted in Chapter 1, "The Science of Psychology," some states now permit specially trained psychologists to prescribe drugs. Therapists without such training often work with physicians who prescribe medication for their clients. In many cases where biological treatments are used, psychotherapy is also recommended. For example, medication and psychotherapy used together, as Mike Wallace has done, work better for treating major depression and for preventing a recurrence than either treatment used alone (M. B. Keller et al., 2000; Reynolds et al., 1999).

DRUG THERAPIES

What are some of the drugs used to treat psychological disorders?

Medication is frequently and effectively used to treat a number of different psychological problems. (See Table 13–1.) In fact, Prozac, a drug used to treat depression, today is one of the best selling of all prescribed medications. Two major reasons for the widespread use of drug therapies today are the development of several very effective psychoactive medications and the fact that drug therapies can cost less than psychotherapy. Critics suggest, however, that another reason is our society's "pill mentality," or belief that we can take a medicine to fix any problem.

ANTIPSYCHOTIC DRUGS Before the mid-1950s, drugs were not widely used to treat psychological disorders, because the only available sedatives induced sleep as well as calm. Then the major tranquilizers *reserpine* and the *phenothiazines* were introduced. In addition to alleviating anxiety and aggression, both drugs reduce psychotic symptoms, such as hallucinations and delusions; for that reason, they are called **antipsychotic drugs**. Antipsychotic drugs are prescribed primarily for very severe psychological disorders, particularly schizophrenia. They are very effective for treating schizophrenia's "positive symptoms," like hallucinations, but less effective for the "negative symptoms," like social withdrawal.

table 13–1	MAJOR TYPES OF PSYCHOACTIVE MEDICATIONS	
Therapeutic Use	**Chemical Structure***	**Trade Name***
Antipsychotics	Phenothiazines	Thorazine, Therazine, Olanzapine, Risperdal, Clozapine
Antidepressants	Tricyclics	Elavil
	MAO inhibitors	Nardil
	SSRIs	Paxil, Prozac, Zoloft
	SNRI	Effexor
Psychostimulants	Amphetamines	Dexedrine
	Other	Ritalin, Adderall
Antiseizure	Carbamazepine	Tegretol
Antianxiety	Benzodiazepines	Valium
Sedatives	Barbiturates	
Antipanic	Tricyclics	Tofranil
Antiobsessional	Tricyclics	Anafranil

*The chemical structures and especially the trade names listed in this table are representative examples, rather than an exhaustive list, of the many kinds of medications available for the specific therapeutic use.
Source: Klerman et al., 1994 (adapted and updated).

antipsychotic drugs Drugs used to treat very severe psychological disorders, particularly schizophrenia.

The most widely prescribed antipsychotic drugs are known as *neuroleptics,* which work by blocking the brain's receptors for dopamine, a major neurotransmitter. Research indicates the effectiveness of a neuroleptic is directly related to its ability to block these receptors (Leuner & Müller, 2006; Oltmanns & Emery, 2006). The success of antipsychotic drugs in treating schizophrenia supports the notion that schizophrenia is linked in some way to an excess of this neurotransmitter in the brain. (See Chapter 12, "Psychological Disorders.")

Antipsychotic medications sometimes have dramatic effects. People who take them can go from being perpetually frightened, angry, confused, and plagued by auditory and visual hallucinations to being totally free of such symptoms. These drugs do not, however, cure schizophrenia; they only alleviate the symptoms while the person is taking the drug. Therefore, most people with schizophrenia must take antipsychotics for years—perhaps for the rest of their lives (Mueser & Glynn, 1995; Oltmanns & Emery, 2006). This can lead to discomfort because antipsychotic drugs can also have a number of undesirable side effects (H. Y. Lane et al., 2006; Roh, Ahn, & Nam, 2006). Blurred vision, weight gain, and constipation are among the common complaints, as are temporary neurological impairments such as muscular rigidity or tremors. A very serious potential side effect is *tardive dyskinesia,* a permanent disturbance of motor control, particularly of the face (uncontrollable smacking of the lips, for instance), which can be only partially alleviated with other drugs (Eberhard, Lindström, & Levander, 2006). The risk of tardive dyskinesia increases with the length of time that antipsychotics are taken.

Another problem is that antipsychotics are of little value in treating the problems of social adjustment that people with schizophrenia face outside an institutional setting. Because many discharged people fail to take their medications, relapse is common. The relapse rate can be reduced if drug therapy is effectively combined with psychotherapy.

ENDURING ISSUES

Mind–Body   Combining Drugs and Psychotherapy

As we have seen, for some disorders a combination of drugs and psychotherapy works better than either approach used alone. This underscores the fact that the relationship between mind and body is highly complex. The causes of depression have not yet been fully determined, but they will probably be found to include a mixture of genetic predisposition, chemical changes in the brain, and life situation (see Chapter 12, "Psychological Disorders"). ●●

ANTIDEPRESSANT DRUGS A second group of drugs, known as antidepressants, is used to combat depression like that experienced by Mike Wallace. Until the end of the 1980s, there were only two main types of antidepressant drugs (both named for their chemical properties): *monoamine oxidase inhibitors (MAO inhibitors)* and *tricyclics.* Both drugs work by increasing the concentration of the neurotransmitters serotonin and norepinephrine in the brain (McKim, 2007; Szabo, 2003). Both are effective for most people with serious depression, but both produce a number of serious and troublesome side effects.

In 1988, Prozac (fluoxetine) came onto the market. This drug works by reducing the uptake of serotonin in the nervous system, thus increasing the amount of serotonin active in the brain at any given moment. (See **Figure 13–2.**) For this reason, Prozac is part of a group of psychoactive drugs known as *selective serotonin reuptake inhibitors (SSRIs).* (See Chapter 2, "The Biological Basis of Behavior.") Today, a number of second-generation SSRIs are available to treat depression, including *Paxil* (paroxetine), *Zoloft* (sertraline), and *Effexor* (venlafaxine HCl). In addition to increasing serotonin, Effexor also raises the levels of norepinephrine in the brain, so owing to its dual action it is technically known as an *SNRI* (serotonin and norepinephrine reuptake inhibitor). For many patients, correcting the imbalance in these chemicals in the brain reduces their symptoms of depression and also relieves the associated symptoms of anxiety. Moreover, because these drugs have fewer side effects than do MAO inhibitors or tricyclics (Nemeroff & Schatzberg, 2002), they have been heralded in the popular media as "wonder drugs" for the treatment of depression.

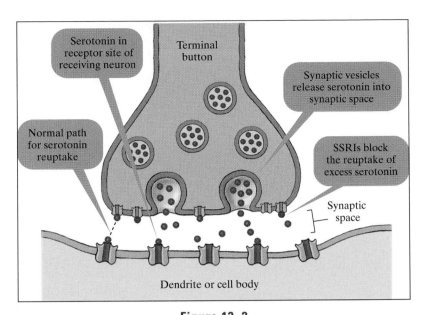

Today, antidepressant drugs are not only used to treat depression, but also have shown promise in treating generalized anxiety disorder, panic disorder, obsessive–compulsive disorder, social phobia, and posttraumatic stress disorder (Bourin, 2003; Donnelly, 2003; Shelton & Hollon, 2000). Antidepressant drugs like the SSRIs do not work for everyone, however. At least a quarter of the patients with major depressive disorder do not respond to antidepressant drugs (Shelton & Hollon, 2000). Moreover, for some patients, these drugs produce unpleasant side effects, including nausea, insomnia, headaches, anxiety, and impaired sexual functioning. They can also cause severe withdrawal symptoms in patients who abruptly stop taking them (Balon, 2002; Clayton, McGarvey, Abouesh, & Pinkerton, 2001).

LITHIUM Bipolar disorder, or manic depression, is frequently treated with lithium carbonate. Lithium is not a drug, but a naturally occurring salt that helps level out the wild and unpredictable mood swings of manic depression. It is effective in treating bipolar disorder in approximately 75% of cases (Gnanadesikan, Freeman, & Gelenberg, 2003). We do not know exactly how lithium works, but recent studies with mice indicate that it may act to stabilize the levels of specific neurotransmitters (Dixon & Hokin, 1998) or alter the receptivity of specific synapses (G. Chen & Manji, 2006). Unfortunately, some people with bipolar disorder stop taking lithium when their symptoms improve—against the advice of their physicians; this leads to a relatively high relapse rate (Gershon & Soares, 1997; M. Pope & Scott, 2003).

OTHER MEDICATIONS Several other medications can be used to alleviate the symptoms of various psychological problems. (See **Table 13–1**.) *Psychostimulants*, for example, heighten alertness and arousal. Some psychostimulants, such as Ritalin, are commonly used to treat children with attention-deficit hyperactivity disorder (Adesman, 2000). In these cases, they have a calming, rather than a stimulating effect. As with the antidepressants, some professionals worry that psychostimulants are being overused, especially with young children (Rey & Sawyer, 2003). *Antianxiety medications*, such as Valium, are commonly prescribed as well. Quickly producing a sense of calm and mild euphoria, they are often used to reduce general tension and stress. Because they are potentially addictive, however, they must be used with caution. Another class of drugs, the *sedatives*, produce both calm and drowsiness, and they are used to treat agitation or to induce sleep. These drugs, too, can become addictive.

Figure 13–2
How do the SSRIs work?
Antidepressants like Prozac, Paxil, and Zoloft belong to a class of drugs called SSRIs (selective serotonin reuptake inhibitors). These drugs reduce the symptoms of depression by blocking the reabsorption (or reuptake) of serotonin in the synaptic space between neurons. The increased availability of serotonin to bind to receptor sites on the receiving neuron is thought to be responsible for the ability of these drugs to relieve the symptoms of depression.

ELECTROCONVULSIVE THERAPY

How is modern electroconvulsive therapy different from that of the past?

Electroconvulsive therapy (ECT) is most often used for cases of prolonged and severe depression that do not respond to other forms of treatment (Birkenhaeger, Pluijms, & Lucius, 2003; Olfson, Marcus, Sackeim, Thompson, & Pincus, 1998). The technique involves briefly passing a mild electric current through the brain or, more recently, through only one of its hemispheres (S. G. Thomas & Kellner, 2003). Treatment normally consists of 10 or fewer sessions of ECT.

No one knows exactly why ECT works, but its effectiveness has been clearly demonstrated. In addition, the fatality rate for ECT is markedly lower than for people taking antidepressant drugs (Henry, Alexander, & Sener, 1995). Still, ECT has many critics and its use remains controversial (Krystal, Holsinger, Weiner, & Coffey, 2000). Side effects include brief confusion, disorientation, and memory impairment, though research suggests that unilateral ECT produces fewer side effects and is only slightly less effective than the traditional method (Bajbouj et al., 2006; Diaz, 1997). In view of the side effects, ECT is usually considered a "last-resort" treatment after all other methods have failed.

electroconvulsive therapy (ECT) Biological therapy in which a mild electrical current is passed through the brain for a short period, often producing convulsions and temporary coma; used to treat severe, prolonged depression.

psychosurgery Brain surgery performed to change a person's behavior and emotional state; a biological therapy rarely used today.

PSYCHOSURGERY

What is psychosurgery, and how is it used today?

Psychosurgery refers to brain surgery performed to change a person's behavior and emotional state. This is a drastic step, especially because the effects of psychosurgery are difficult to predict. In a *prefrontal lobotomy*, the frontal lobes of the brain are severed from the deeper centers beneath them. The assumption is that in extremely disturbed people, the frontal lobes intensify emotional impulses from the lower brain centers (chiefly, the thalamus and hypothalamus). Unfortunately, lobotomies can work with one person and fail completely with another—possibly producing permanent, undesirable side effects, such as the inability to inhibit impulses or a near-total absence of feeling.

Prefrontal lobotomies are rarely performed today. In fact, very few psychosurgical procedures are done, except as desperate attempts to control such conditions as intractable psychoses, Parkinson's disease, epilepsy that does not respond to other treatments (see Chapter 2, "Biological Bases of Behavior"), severe obsessive–compulsive disorders, and pain in a terminal illness (S. W. Anderson & Booker, 2006; Weingarten & Cummings, 2001).

In this chapter, you have seen the sometimes bewildering variety of treatments that mental health professionals provide. The Summary Table: "Major Perspectives on Therapy" captures the key characteristics of psychological and biological mental health treatments.

SUMMARY TABLE

MAJOR PERSPECTIVES ON THERAPY

Type of Therapy	Cause of Disorder	Goal	Techniques
Insight therapies			
Psychoanalysis	Unconscious conflicts and motives; repressed problems from childhood.	To bring unconscious thoughts and feeling to consciousness; to gain insight.	Free association, dream analysis, interpretation, transference.
Client-centered therapy	Experiences of conditional positive regard.	To help people become fully functioning by opening them up to all of their experiences.	Regarding clients with unconditional positive regard.
Gestalt therapy	Lack of wholeness in the personality.	To get people to "own their feelings" and to awaken to sensory experience in order to become whole.	Active rather than passive talk; empty chair techniques, encounter groups.
Behavior therapies	Reinforcement for maladaptive behavior.	To learn new and more adaptive behavior patterns.	Classical conditioning (systematic desensitization, extinction, flooding); aversive conditioning (behavior contracting, token economies); modeling.
Cognitive therapies	Misconceptions; negative, self-defeating thinking.	To identify erroneous ways of thinking and to correct them.	Rational–emotive therapy; stress-inoculation therapy; Beck's cognitive therapy.
Group therapies	Personal problems are often interpersonal problems.	To develop insight into one's personality and behavior by interacting with others in the group.	Group interaction and mutual support; family therapy; couple therapy; self-help therapy.
Biological treatments	Physiological imbalance or malfunction.	To eliminate symptoms; prevent recurrence.	Drugs, electroconvulsive therapy, psychosurgery.

CHECK YOUR UNDERSTANDING

1. Traditionally, the only mental health professionals licensed to provide drug therapy were _____.

2. Bipolar disorder (also called manic–depressive illness) is often treated with _____.

3. Which of the following is true of psychosurgery?

   a. It never produces undesirable side effects.

   b. It is useless in controlling pain.

   c. It is widely used today.

   d. Its effects are hard to predict.

4. Although it is considered effective in treating depression, electroconvulsive therapy (ECT) is considered a treatment of last resort because of its potential negative side effects. Is this statement true (T) or false (F)?

Match the following antidepressant medications with the neurotransmitter(s) that each is believed to influence. They may be more than one answer for each medication.

5. ___ monoamine oxidase inhibitors

6. ___ tricyclics

7. ___ SSRIs

   a. norepinephrine

   b. serotonin

   c. epinephrine

Answers: 1. psychiatrists. 2. lithium. 3. d. 4. (T). 5. a and b. 6. a and b. 7. b.

APPLY YOUR UNDERSTANDING

1. Blue Haven is a (fictional) state mental hospital where five therapists are responsible for hundreds of patients. These patients are often violent. The therapy most likely to be used here is

   a. psychoanalysis.

   b. biological therapy.

   c. cognitive therapy.

   d. client-centered therapy.

2. Brian is suffering from schizophrenia. Which of the following biological treatments is most likely to be effective in reducing or eliminating his symptoms?

   a. any drug, such as a phenothiazine, that blocks the brain's receptors for dopamine.

   b. selective serotonin reuptake inhibitors (SSRIs), such as Paxil and Prozac.

   c. lithium carbonate.

   d. electroconvulsive therapy.

Answers: 1. b. 2. a.

Institutionalization and Its Alternatives

How were people with severe psychological disorders cared for in the past?

For persons with severe mental illness, hospitalization has been the treatment of choice in the United States for the past 150 years. Several different kinds of hospitals offer such care. General hospitals admit many affected people, usually for short-term stays until they can be released to their families or to other institutional care. Private hospitals—some nonprofit and some for profit—offer services to people with adequate insurance. Veterans Administration hospitals admit veterans with psychological disorders.

When most people think of "mental hospitals," however, large, state-run institutions come to mind. These public hospitals, many with beds for thousands of patients, were often built in rural areas in the 19th century. The idea was that a country setting would calm patients and help to restore their mental health. Despite the good intentions behind

Lacking adequate funding and staff, mental hospitals frequently were crowded and failed to provide adequate treatment to their residents.

deinstitutionalization Policy of treating people with severe psychological disorders in the larger community or in small residential centers such as halfway houses, rather than in large public hospitals.

the establishment of these hospitals, in general they have not provided adequate care or therapy for their residents. Perpetually underfunded and understaffed, state hospitals have often been little more than warehouses for victims of serious mental illness who were unwanted by their families. Except for new arrivals, who were often intensively treated in the hope of quickly discharging them, patients received little therapy besides drugs; and most spent their days watching television or staring into space. Under these conditions, many patients became completely apathetic and accepted a permanent "sick role."

The development of effective drug therapies starting in the 1950s led to a number of changes in state hospitals (Shorter, 1997). First, people who were agitated could now be sedated with drugs. Although the drugs often produced lethargy, this was considered an improvement over the use of physical restraints. The second major, and more lasting, result of the new drug therapies was the widespread release of people with severe psychological disorders back into the community—a policy called **deinstitutionalization**. As we will discuss in the next section, this created new problems for patients and for society.

DEINSTITUTIONALIZATION

What problems have resulted from deinstitutionalization?

The advent of antipsychotic drugs in the 1950s created a favorable climate for deinstitutionalization. The practice of placing people in smaller, more humane facilities or returning them under medication to care within the community intensified during the 1960s and 1970s. By 1975, 600 regional mental health centers accounted for 1.6 million cases of outpatient care.

In recent years, however, deinstitutionalization has created serious problems (H. R. Lamb & Weinberger, 2001). Discharged people often find poorly funded community mental health centers—or none at all. Many are not prepared to live in the community and they receive little guidance in coping with the mechanics of daily life. Those who return home can become a burden to their families, especially when follow-up care is inadequate. The quality of such residential centers as halfway houses can vary, with many providing poor care and minimal contact with the outside world. Insufficient sheltered housing forces many former patients into nonpsychiatric facilities—often rooming houses located in dirty, unsafe, isolated neighborhoods. The patients are further burdened by the social stigma of mental illness, which may be the largest single obstacle to their rehabilitation. Moreover, although outpatient care is presumed to be a well-established national mental health policy objective, health insurance typically discourages outpatient care by requiring substantial copayments and limiting the number of treatment visits.

The full effects of deinstitutionalization are unknown; few studies have followed discharged patients, who are difficult to keep track of for long periods. But it is obvious that deinstitutionalization, though a worthy ideal, has had dire effects on patients and society. Many released patients have been unable to obtain follow-up care or housing and are incapable of looking after their own needs. Consequently, many have ended up literally on the streets. Without supervision, they have stopped taking the drugs that made their release possible in the first place and their psychotic symptoms have returned. Perhaps one of the most tragic outcomes of the deinstitutionalization movement is the increase in the suicide rate among deinstitutionalized patients (Goldney, 2003). Every major U.S. city now has a population of homeless mentally ill men and women living in makeshift shelters or sleeping in doorways, bus stations, parks, and other public spaces (Drury, 2003). Surveys indicate that nearly 40% of homeless people are mentally ill (Burt et al., 1999). Obviously, providing adequate mental health care to the homeless presents many challenges (Bhui, Shanahan, & Harding, 2006).

This situation is tragic not only for the mentally ill homeless, who are easy prey for criminals, but for society as well. The public finds their constant presence unpleasant; and compassion for them is waning to the point of pressuring public officials to "get them off the street." Most mental health professionals now agree that many chronically ill patients should not be released to live "in the community" without better planning, more funding, more community support, and readily available short-term rehospitalization for those who require it.

Beginning in the 1950s and 1960s, the policy of deinstitutionalization led to the release of many individuals, who, without proper follow-up care, ended up living on the streets. Although not all homeless people are mentally ill, estimates suggest that nearly 40% of homeless persons suffer from some type of mental disorder.

ALTERNATIVE FORMS OF TREATMENT

Are there any alternatives to deinstitutionalization other than rehospitalizing patients?

For several decades, Charles Kiesler (1934–2002) argued for a shift from the focus on institutionalization to forms of treatment that avoid hospitalization altogether (Kiesler & Simpkins, 1993). Kiesler (1982b) examined 10 controlled studies in which seriously disturbed people were randomly assigned either to hospitals or to an alternative program. The alternative programs took many forms: training patients living at home to cope with daily activities; assigning patients to a small, homelike facility in which staff and residents share responsibility for residential life; placing patients in a hostel, offering therapy and crisis intervention; providing family-crisis therapy and day care treatment; providing visits from public-health nurses combined with medication; and offering intensive outpatient counseling combined with medication. All of these alternatives involved daily professional contact and skillful preparation of the community to receive the patients. Even though the hospitals to which some people in these studies were assigned provided very good patient care—probably substantially above average for institutions in the United States—9 out of the 10 studies found that the outcome was more positive for alternative treatments than for the more expensive hospitalization. Moreover, the people who received alternative care were less likely to undergo hospitalization later, thus suggesting that hospitalizing those with mental illness is a self-perpetuating process. Many such people "could be treated in alternative settings more effectively and less expensively," Kiesler concluded (1982a, p. 358).

PREVENTION

What is the difference between primary, secondary, and tertiary prevention?

Yet another approach to managing mental illness is trying to prevent it in the first place. This requires finding and eliminating the conditions that cause or contribute to mental disorders and substituting conditions that foster well-being. Prevention takes three forms: primary, secondary, and tertiary.

Primary prevention refers to efforts to improve the overall environment so that new cases of mental disorders do not develop. Family planning and genetic counseling are two examples of primary prevention programs. They assist prospective parents to think through such questions as how many children to have and when. They also provide testing to diagnose genetic defects in embryos, and they direct parents to treatments, including fetal surgery, that may be able to alleviate those defects before the baby is born. Other primary prevention programs aim at increasing personal and social competencies in a wide variety of groups. For example, there are programs designed to help mothers encourage problem-solving skills in their children and programs to enhance competence and adjustment among elderly persons. Current campaigns to educate young people about drugs, alcohol abuse, violence, and date rape are other examples of primary prevention (Schinke & Schwinn, 2005; Foxcroft, Ireland, Lister, Lowe, & Breen, 2003; Reppucci, Woolard, & Fried, 1999).

Secondary prevention involves identifying groups at high risk for mental disorders— for example, abused children, people who have recently divorced, those who have been laid off from their jobs, and victims of terrorist incidents. The main thrust of secondary prevention is *intervention* with such high-risk groups—that is, detecting maladaptive behavior early and treating it promptly. One form of intervention is *crisis intervention*, which includes such programs as suicide hotlines (R. K. James & Gilliland, 2001). Another is the establishment of short-term crisis facilities at which a therapist can provide face-to-face counseling and support, although so far there is no evidence that such "psychological first aid" is effective (McNally, Bryant, & Ehlers, 2003).

The main objective of **tertiary prevention** is to help people adjust to community life after release from a mental hospital. For example, hospitals often grant passes to encourage people to leave the institution for short periods of time before their release. Other tertiary prevention measures are halfway houses, where people find support and skills training during the period of transition between hospitalization and full integration into the community, and

primary prevention Techniques and programs to improve the social environment so that new cases of mental disorders do not develop.

secondary prevention Programs to identify groups that are at high risk for mental disorders and to detect maladaptive behavior in these groups and treat it promptly.

tertiary prevention Programs to help people adjust to community life after release from a mental hospital.

Suicide hotlines and other crisis intervention programs are secondary prevention measures designed to serve individuals and groups at high risk for mental disorders.

THINKING CRITICALLY ABOUT . . .

Access to Mental Health Care

A friend feels overwhelmed by sadness, has lost interest in most activities, and is exhibiting other depressive symptoms. He comes to you for advice. How likely would you be to suggest that your friend seek psychotherapy or drug treatment? Think about the following questions:

- Would you seek therapy yourself in a similar situation?
- What would you think of a friend who you knew was seeing a therapist?
- Would your friend be able to obtain therapy services? Would he be able to afford these kinds of services?
- Do you think that mental illness and physical illness are equivalent and should be treated the same by insurance companies?

nighttime and outpatient programs that provide supportive therapy while people live at home and hold down full-time jobs. Tertiary prevention also includes efforts to educate the community that the person will reenter.

Preventing behavior disorders has been the ideal of the mental health community since at least 1970, when the final report of the Joint Commission on Mental Health of Children called for a new focus on prevention in mental health work. Ironically, because preventive programs are usually long range and indirect, they are often the first mental health programs to be eliminated in times of economic hardship. Such cuts, predicated on cost effectiveness, exemplify the old adage about being penny wise and pound foolish.

CHECK YOUR UNDERSTANDING

1. The practice of treating severely mentally ill people in large, state-run facilities is known as _____.

2. Many people released from mental hospitals have ended up homeless and on the streets. Is this statement true (T) or false (F)?

3. The development of effective antipsychotic drugs and the establishment of a network of community mental health centers starting in the 1950s led to _____, which increased throughout the 1960s and 1970s, and continues today.

Answers: 1. institutionalization. 2. (T) 3. deinstitutionalization.

APPLY YOUR UNDERSTANDING

1. Harold argues that institutionalizing people suffering from serious mental illnesses is not only the most effective way to treat them, but also the least expensive. On the basis of what you have learned in this chapter, which of the following would be the most appropriate reply?

    a. "Mental institutions are indeed the least expensive form of treatment, but they are also the least effective treatment option."

    b. "You're right. Mental institutions are both the least expensive form of treatment and the most effective treatment option."

    c. "Actually, mental institutions are not only the most expensive form of treatment, they are also the least effective treatment option."

    d. "Actually, mental institutions are the most expensive form of treatment, but they are the most effective treatment option."

2. Your community is especially aware of the importance of preventing psychological disorders. So far, financial support has been provided for family planning, genetic counseling, increasing competence among the elderly, and educational programs aimed at reducing the use of drugs and acts of violence. From this description, it is clear that your community is putting its emphasis on

    a. primary prevention efforts.

    b. secondary prevention efforts.

    c. tertiary prevention efforts.

Answers: 1. c. 2. a.

Client Diversity and Treatment

Do particular groups of people require special treatment approaches for psychological problems?

A major topic of this book is human diversity, the wide range of differences that exist in human beings. Although we all share certain basic human characteristics as individuals and as groups, we also have our own distinctive traits and ways of responding to the world. Do such human differences affect the treatment of psychological problems? Two areas that researchers have explored to answer this question are gender differences and cultural differences.

GENDER AND TREATMENT

How can gender stereotypes be avoided in treatment?

In Chapter 12, "Psychological Disorders," we saw that there are significant gender differences in the prevalence of many psychological disorders. In part, this is because women have traditionally been more willing than men to admit that they have psychological problems and need help to solve them (S. V. Cochran & Rabinowitz, 2003; Addis & Mahalik, 2003). Moreover, psychotherapy is more socially accepted for women than for men (Mirkin, Suyemoto, & Okun, 2005). However, in recent years, the number of males willing to seek psychotherapy and counseling has increased (Pollack & Levant, 1998). Researchers attribute this growth to the changing roles of men in today's society: Men are increasingly expected to provide emotional as well as financial support for their families.

If gender differences exist in the prevalence of psychological disorders, are there gender differences in their treatment as well? In most respects, the treatment given to women is the same as that given to men, a fact that has become somewhat controversial in recent years (Ogrodniczuk, Piper, & Joyce, 2004; Ogrodniczuk & Staats, 2002). Because most therapists are male and most vocational and rehabilitation programs are male oriented, some critics of "equal treatment" have claimed that women in therapy are often encouraged to adopt traditional, male-oriented views of what is "normal" or "appropriate." For instance, male therapists tend to urge women to adapt or conform passively to their surroundings. They also tend to be insufficiently sensitive to the fact that much of the stress that women experience comes from trying to cope with a world in which they are not treated equally (L. S. Brown & Ballou, 1992). For all these reasons, there has been an increase recently in the number of "feminist therapists." These therapists help their female clients to become aware of the extent to which their problems derive from external controls and inappropriate sex roles, to become more conscious of and attentive to their own needs and goals, and to develop a sense of pride in their womanhood, rather than passively accepting or identifying with the status quo. In addition, the American Psychological Association (1978) has established a detailed set of guidelines regarding treatment of women in psychotherapy.

Because most traditional therapeutic programs are male oriented, many female clients seek out female therapists who are more sensitive to their situation.

CULTURE AND TREATMENT

How can a therapist interact appropriately with clients from different cultures?

When a client and a therapist come from different cultural backgrounds or belong to different racial or ethnic groups, misunderstandings can arise in therapy.

ENDURING ISSUES

Diversity–Universality   On Being Culture Bound

Imagine the following scenario: As a Native American client is interviewed by a psychologist, the client stares at the floor. He answers questions politely, but during the entire consultation, he looks away continually, never meeting the doctor's eye. This body language

Many African American clients are more comfortable dealing with a therapist of the same racial background.

might lead the psychologist to suppose that the man is depressed or has low self-esteem—unless, that is, the psychologist knows that in the person's culture, avoiding eye contact is a sign of respect.

This example shows how culture bound are our ideas of what constitutes normal behavior. When psychotherapist and client come from different cultures, misunderstandings of speech, body language, and customs are almost inevitable (Cardemil & Battle, 2003; Helms & Cook, 1999). Even when client and therapist are of the same nationality and speak the same language, there can be striking differences if they belong to different racial and ethnic groups (Casas, 1995). Some Black people, for example, are wary of confiding in a White therapist—so much so that their wariness is sometimes mistaken for paranoia. In addition, Black patients also perceive Black therapists as being more understanding and accepting of their problems than White therapists are (V. L. S. Thompson & Alexander, 2006). For this reason, many Black people seek out a Black therapist, a tendency that is becoming more common as larger numbers of Black middle-class people enter therapy (Diala et al., 2000; Snowden & Yamada, 2005). ●●

One of the challenges for U.S. therapists in recent years has been to treat immigrants, many of whom have fled such horrifying circumstances at home that they arrive in the United States exhibiting PTSD (Paunovic & Oest, 2001). These refugees must overcome not only the effects of past trauma, but also the new stresses of settling in a strange country, which often include separation from their families, ignorance of the English language, and inability to practice their traditional occupations. Therapists in such circumstances must learn something of their clients' culture. Often they have to conduct interviews through an interpreter—hardly an ideal circumstance for therapy.

Therapists need to recognize that some disorders that afflict people from other cultures may not exist in Western culture at all. For example, as we saw in Chapter 12, "Psychological Disorders," *taijin kyofusho* (roughly translated as "fear of people") involves a morbid fear that one's body or actions may be offensive to others. Because this disorder is rarely seen outside Japan, American therapists require specialized training to identify it.

Ultimately, however, the best solution to the difficulties of serving a multicultural population is to train therapists of many different backgrounds so that members of ethnic, cultural, and racial minorities can choose therapists of their own group if they wish to do so (Bernal & Castro, 1994). Research has shown that psychotherapy is more likely to be effective when the client and the therapist share a similar cultural background (Gibson & Mitchell, 2003; Pedersen & Carey, 2003).

Similarly, efforts aimed at preventing mental illness in society must also be sensitive to cultural diversity. Many intervention programs have proven unsuccessful because they failed to take into account the appropriate cultural norms and values of the group being served (Reppucci et al., 1999). To be effective, treatment and prevention approaches must reflect the beliefs and cultural practices of the person's ethnic group.

CHECK YOUR UNDERSTANDING

Indicate whether the following statements are true (T) or false (F):

1. ____ Men are more likely to be in psychotherapy than women.
2. ____ Our ideas about what constitutes normal behavior are culture bound.
3. ____ Trained mental health professionals rarely misinterpret the body language of a client from another culture.

Answers: 1. (F). 2. (T). 3. (F).

APPLY YOUR UNDERSTANDING

1. An immigrant from the Middle East who speaks very little English seeks assistance from an American psychotherapist who only speaks English. Which of the following problems may interfere with the therapeutic process?

   a. misunderstanding body language

   b. the therapist's lack of familiarity with the cultural norms and values of the immigrant's home country

   c. need for an interpreter

   d. all of the above

2. Preventing and treating psychological disorders is especially challenging in a society such as ours, which has a culturally diverse population. Which of the following is NOT a constructive way of dealing with this challenge?

   a. Therapists need to recognize that some disorders that afflict people from other cultures may not exist in Western culture at all.

   b. Therapists from many different backgrounds need to receive training so that people who wish to do so can be treated by a therapist who shares their cultural background.

   c. Clients should be treated by therapists who represent the dominant culture so that they can best adapt to their new environment.

   d. Intervention programs need to take into account the cultural norms and values of the group being served.

Answers: 1. d. 2. c.

KEY TERMS

psychotherapy, *p. 451*

Insight Therapies
insight therapies, *p. 451*
psychoanalysis, *p. 452*
free association, *p. 452*
transference, *p. 452*
insight, *p. 452*
client-centered (or person-centered) therapy, *p. 454*
Gestalt therapy, *p. 455*
short-term psychodynamic therapy, *p. 456*

Behavior Therapies
behavior therapies, *p. 457*
systematic desensitization, *p. 458*
aversive conditioning, *p. 459*
behavior contracting, *p. 459*
token economy, *p. 459*
modeling, *p. 460*

Cognitive Therapies
cognitive therapies, *p. 461*
stress-inoculation therapy, *p. 461*
rational–emotive therapy (RET), *p. 461*
cognitive therapy, *p. 462*

Group Therapies
group therapy, *p. 463*
family therapy, *p. 463*
couple therapy, *p. 464*

Effectiveness of Psychotherapy
eclecticism, *p. 468*

Biological Treatments
biological treatments, *p. 468*
antipsychotic drugs, *p. 469*

electroconvulsive therapy (ECT), *p. 471*
psychosurgery, *p. 472*

Institutionalization and Its Alternatives
deinstitutionalization, *p. 474*
primary prevention, *p. 475*
secondary prevention, *p. 475*
tertiary prevention, *p. 475*

CHAPTER REVIEW

Insight Therapies

What do insight therapies have in common? The various types of **insight therapy** share the common goal of providing people with better awareness and understanding of their feelings, motivations, and actions to foster better adjustment. Among these are psychoanalysis, client-centered therapy, and Gestalt therapy.

How does "free association" in psychoanalysis help a person to become aware of hidden feelings? **Psychoanalysis** is based on the belief that psychological problems stem from feelings and conflicts repressed during childhood. These repressed feelings can be revealed through **free association**, a process in which the client discloses whatever thoughts or fantasies come to mind without inhibition. As therapy progresses, the analyst takes a more active interpretive role.

Why did Carl Rogers call his approach to therapy "client centered"? Carl Rogers believed treatment for psychological problems should be based on the client's view of the world rather than that of the therapist. The therapist's most important task in his approach, called **client-centered** or **person-centered therapy**, is to provide unconditional positive regard for clients so they will learn to accept themselves.

How is Gestalt therapy different from psychoanalysis? **Gestalt therapy**, which grew out of the work of Fritz Perls, helps people become more aware of their feelings and thus more genuine. Unlike Freud, who sat quietly out of sight while his clients dredged up memories from the past, the Gestalt therapist confronts the patient, emphasizes the present, and focuses on the *whole* person.

What are some recent developments in insight therapies? Contemporary insight therapists are more actively involved than traditional psychoanalysts, offering clients direct guidance and feedback. An especially significant development is the trend toward **short-term psychodynamic therapy**, in which the course of treatment is time limited and oriented toward current life situations and relationships, rather than childhood traumas.

Behavior Therapies

What do behaviorists believe should be the focus of psychotherapy? **Behavior therapies** are based on the belief that all behavior is learned and that people can be taught more satisfying ways of behaving. To behaviorists, maladaptive behaviors are the focus of psychotherapy, rather than the deeper underlying conflicts that presumably are causing them.

How can classical conditioning be used as the basis of treatment? When new conditioned responses are evoked to old stimuli, classical conditioning principles are being used as a basis for treatment. One therapeutic example is **systematic desensitization**, in which people learn to remain in a deeply relaxed state while confronting feared situations. *Flooding,* which exposes phobic people to feared situations at full intensity for a prolonged period, is a harsh but effective method of desensitization. In **aversive conditioning**, the goal is to eliminate undesirable behavior by associating it with pain and discomfort.

How could "behavior contracting" change an undesirable behavior? Therapies based on operant conditioning encourage or discourage behaviors by reinforcing or punishing them. In **behavior contracting**, client and therapist agree on certain behavioral goals and on the reinforcement that the client will receive on reaching them. In the **token economy** technique, tokens that can be exchanged for rewards are used for positive reinforcement of adaptive behaviors.

What are some therapeutic uses of modeling? In **modeling**, a person learns new behaviors by watching others perform them. Modeling has been used to teach fearless behaviors to phobic people and job skills to mentally retarded people.

Cognitive Therapies

How can people overcome irrational and self-defeating beliefs about themselves? **Cognitive therapies** focus not so much on maladaptive behaviors as on maladaptive ways of thinking. By changing people's distorted, self-defeating ideas about themselves and the world, cognitive therapies help to encourage better coping skills and adjustment.

How can self-talk help us to deal with difficult situations? The things we say to ourselves as we go about our daily lives can encourage either success or failure, a self-confident outlook or

acute anxiety. With **stress-inoculation therapy,** clients learn how to use self-talk to "coach" themselves through stressful situations.

What irrational beliefs do many people hold? **Rational–emotive therapy (RET)** is based on the idea that emotional problems derive from a set of irrational and self-defeating beliefs that people hold about themselves and the world. They think in terms of absolutes—they must be liked by *everyone*, be competent at *everything, always* be treated fairly, *never* be stymied by a problem. The therapist vigorously challenges these dysfunctional beliefs, enabling clients to reinterpret their experiences in a more positive light.

How can cognitive therapy be used to combat depression? Aaron Beck believes that depression results from thought patterns that are strongly and inappropriately self-critical. Like RET but in a less confrontational manner, Beck's **cognitive therapy** tries to help such people think more objectively and positively about themselves and their life situations.

Group Therapies

What are some advantages of group therapies? **Group therapies** are based on the idea that psychological problems are at least partly interpersonal and are therefore best approached in a group. Group therapies offer a circle of support for clients, shared insights into problems, and the opportunity to obtain psychotherapy at a lower cost. Among the many different kinds of group therapy are self-help groups, family therapy, and couple therapy.

Who is the client in family therapy? **Family therapy** is based on the belief that a person's psychological problems often signal family problems. Therefore, the therapist treats the entire family, rather than just the troubled individual, with the primary goals being to improve communication and empathy and to reduce family conflict.

What are some techniques used in couple therapy? **Couple therapy** concentrates on improving patterns of communication and interaction between partners. Like family therapy, it attempts to change relationships, rather than individuals. Empathy training and scheduled exchanges of rewards are two of the techniques used to improve relationships.

Why are self-help groups so popular? Owing to the high cost of private psychotherapy, low-cost self-help groups have become increasingly popular. In such groups as Alcoholics Anonymous, people share their concerns and feelings with others who are experiencing similar problems.

Effectiveness of Psychotherapy

How much better off is a person who receives psychotherapy than one who gets no treatment at all? Formal psychotherapy helps about two-thirds of the people treated. Although there is some debate over how many untreated people also recover, the consensus is that those who get therapy are generally better off than those who don't.

Which type of therapy is best for which disorder? Although each kind of therapy works better for some problems than for others, most treatment benefits derive from the therapeutic experience, regardless of the therapist's particular perspective. All therapies provide an explanation of problems, hope, and an alliance with a caring, supportive person. The general trend in psychotherapy is toward **eclecticism**, the use of whatever treatment works best for a particular problem.

Biological Treatments

What are biological treatments, and who can provide them? **Biological treatments**—including medication, electroconvulsive therapy, and psychosurgery—are sometimes used when people are too agitated or disoriented to respond to psychotherapy, when there is a strong biological component to the psychological disorder, and when people are dangerous to themselves and others. Medication, especially, is very often used in conjunction with psychotherapy. Traditionally, psychiatrists (who are also physicians) were the only mental health professionals licensed to offer biological treatments. However, some states now extend that privilege to specially trained clinical psychologists.

What are some of the drugs used to treat psychological disorders? Drugs are the most common form of biological therapy. **Antipsychotic drugs** are valuable in treating schizophrenia. They do not cure the disorder, but they reduce its symptoms, although side effects can be severe. Antidepressant drugs alleviate depression, though some also have unpleasant side effects. Many other types of medications are used to treat psychological disorders, including antimanic and antianxiety drugs, sedatives, and psychostimulants for children with attention-deficit hyperactivity disorder.

How is modern electroconvulsive therapy different from that of the past? **Electroconvulsive therapy (ECT)** is used for cases of severe depression that do not respond to other treatments. An electric current briefly passed through the brain of the patient. Newer forms of ECT are given to only one side of the brain.

What is psychosurgery, and how is it used today? **Psychosurgery** is brain surgery performed to change a person's behavior and emotional state. It is rarely used today, and then only as a last, desperate measure on people who have severe and intractable problems and don't respond to any other form of treatment.

Institutionalization and Its Alternatives

How were people with severe psychological disorders cared for in the past? For 150 years, institutionalization in large mental hospitals was the most common approach. Patients with serious mental disorders were given shelter and some degree of treatment, but a great many never recovered enough to be released. With the advent of antipsychotic drugs in the 1950s, a trend began toward **deinstitutionalization,** in which people with serious mental disorders were integrated back into the community.

What problems have resulted from deinstitutionalization? Poorly funded community mental health centers and other support services have proved inadequate to the task of caring for previously institutionalized patients with mental disorders. Many patients stopped taking their medication, became psychotic, and ended up homeless on the streets where they remain. Thus, although the concept of deinstitutionalization may have been a good idea in principle, in practice it has failed for many patients and for society.

Are there any alternatives to deinstitutionalization other than rehospitalizing patients? Alternatives to rehospitalization include living at home with adequate supports provided to all family members; living in small, homelike facilities in which residents and staff share responsibilities; living in hostels with therapy and crisis intervention provided; and receiving intensive outpatient counseling or frequent visits from public health nurses. Most alternative treatments involve daily professional contact and skillful preparation of the family and community. Most studies have found more positive outcomes for alternative treatments than for hospitalization.

What is the difference between primary, secondary, and tertiary prevention? Prevention refers to efforts to reduce the incidence of mental illness before it arises. **Primary prevention** consists of improving the social environment through assistance to parents, education, and family planning. **Secondary prevention** involves identifying high-risk groups and intervening to direct service to them. **Tertiary prevention** involves helping hospitalized patients return to the community and educating that community to prepare for their return.

Client Diversity and Treatment

Are there particular groups of people who may require special approaches in the treatment of psychological problems? Given that human beings differ as much as they do, it isn't surprising that a one-size-fits-all concept isn't always appropriate in the treatment of psychological problems. In recent years, the special needs of women and people from other cultures have particularly occupied the attention of mental health professionals.

How can gender stereotypes be avoided in treatment? Women are more likely than men to be in psychotherapy, and they are more likely to be given psychoactive medication. Because, in traditional therapy, women are often expected to conform to gender stereotypes in order to be pronounced "well," many women have turned to "feminist therapists." The American Psychological Association has issued guidelines to ensure that women receive treatment that is not tied to traditional ideas about appropriate behavior for the sexes.

How can a therapist interact appropriately with clients from different cultures? When a client and therapist come from different cultural backgrounds or belong to different racial or ethnic groups, misunderstandings can arise in therapy. Therapists must recognize that cultural differences exist in the nature of the psychological disorders that affect people. Treatment and prevention must be tailored to the beliefs and cultural practices of the person's ethnic group.

14 Social Psychology

On September 12, 2001, the day after the terrorist attacks on the Pentagon and the World Trade Center, Sher Singh, a telecommunications consultant from Virginia, managed to catch a train home from Boston where he had been on a business trip. "With the horrific images of the terrorist attacks still fresh in my mind," Sher Singh recalls, "I was particularly anxious to get home to my family" (S. J. B. Singh, 2002, p. 1). Singh was very much like any other shocked and sorrowful American on that day—except for one small difference: As a member of the Sikh religion, Singh, unlike most Americans, wore a full beard and a turban.

The train made a scheduled stop in Providence, Rhode Island, about an hour outside of Boston. But oddly, the stop dragged on for a very long time. Singh began to wonder what was wrong. A conductor walking through the coaches announced that the train had mechanical trouble. However, when passengers from neighboring coaches began to disembark and line up on the platform, Singh became suspicious that this was not the true story. He didn't have long to speculate about the genuine cause of the problem, because suddenly law-enforcement officers burst into his coach and pulled him off the train at gunpoint. They were searching for four Arab men who had evaded authorities in a Boston hotel. A Sikh, however, is not an Arab. A Sikh belongs to a Hindu sect that comes from India, not the Middle East.

On the station platform, Singh was abruptly handcuffed and asked about his citizenship. Assurances that he was a U.S. citizen did not satisfy the officers. They asked him if he had a weapon. Singh informed them that, as a de-

Police never apologized for arresting Sher Singh as a terrorist after the September 11, 2001, attacks in the United States.

vout Sikh, he is required to carry a miniature ceremonial sword. They promptly arrested Singh and pushed him through a crowd of onlookers to a waiting police car. According to news reports, as Singh passed by, some teenagers shouted, "Let's kill him!" while a woman yelled, "Burn in Hell!"

As a terrorist suspect, Singh was photographed, fingerprinted, and strip-searched. He was held in custody at police headquarters until 9:00 P.M. While he was jailed, news media nationwide had displayed a photo of him side by side with a photo of Osama bin Laden. Although all charges against Sher Singh were eventually dropped, he never received an apology from the law-enforcement officers involved.

How could this blatant case of mistaken identity have happened? Why were police so convinced that Sher Singh could be a fugitive terrorist? Researchers who specialize in the field of social psychology help provide some answers. **Social psychology** is the scientific study of how people's thoughts, feelings, and behaviors are influenced by the behaviors and characteristics of other people, whether these behaviors and characteristics are real, imagined, or inferred. Sher Singh was clearly a victim of imagined and inferred characteristics formed on the basis of his ethnic appearance. As you read about the findings of social psychologists in this chapter, you will discover that Singh's experience is far from unique. Every day, we all make judgments concerning other people that are often based on very little "real" evidence. The process by which we form such impressions, whether accurate or not, is part of a fascinating area of social psychology known as *social cognition*. We turn to this topic first.

ENDURING ISSUES IN SOCIAL PSYCHOLOGY ●●

A key issue throughout this chapter is the extent to which a particular behavior reflects personal characteristics like attitudes and values, versus situational ones like the behavior of others and social expectations (person–situation). And especially prominent in this chapter is the extent to which there are differences in social behavior among people in different cultures (individuality–universality).

social psychology The scientific study of the ways in which the thoughts, feelings, and behaviors of one individual are influenced by the real, imagined, or inferred behavior or characteristics of other people.

Social Cognition

What do forming impressions, explaining others' behavior, and experiencing interpersonal attraction have in common?

Part of the process of being influenced by other people involves organizing and interpreting information about them to form first impressions, to try to understand their behavior, and to determine to what extent we are attracted to them. This collecting and assessing of information about other people is called **social cognition**. Social cognition is a major area of interest to social psychologists.

FORMING IMPRESSIONS

How do we form first impressions of people?

Forming first impressions of people is more complex than you may think. You must direct your attention to various aspects of the person's appearance and behavior and then make a rapid assessment of what those characteristics mean. How do you complete this process? What cues do you interpret? How accurate are your impressions? The concept of *schemata*, which we first encountered in Chapter 5, "Memory," helps to answer these questions.

SCHEMATA When we meet someone for the first time, we notice a number of things about that person—clothes, gestures, manner of speaking, body build, and facial features. We then draw on these cues to fit the person into a category. No matter how little information we have or how contradictory it is, no matter how many times our initial impressions have been wrong, we still categorize people after meeting them only briefly. Associated with each category is a *schema*—an organized set of beliefs and expectations based on past experience that is presumed to apply to all members of that category (Aronson, Wilson, & Akert, 2005). *Schemata* (the plural of schema) influence the information we notice and remember. They also help us flesh out our impressions as we peg people into categories. For example, if a woman is wearing a white coat and has a stethoscope around her neck, you could reasonably categorize her as a doctor. Associated with this category is a schema of various beliefs and expectations: highly trained professional, knowledgeable about diseases and their cures, qualified to prescribe medication, and so on. By applying this schema, you expect that this particular woman has these traits.

Over time, as we continue to interact with people, we add new information about them to our mental files. Our later experiences, however, generally do not influence us nearly so much as our earliest impressions. This phenomenon is called the **primacy effect**. For example, if you already like a new acquaintance, you may excuse something that annoys you later. Conversely, if someone makes an early *bad* impression, subsequent evidence of that person's good qualities will do little to change your feelings.

Schemata and the primacy effect reflect a desire to lessen our mental effort. Humans have been called "cognitive misers" (Fiske & Taylor, 1991; Madon, 1999). Instead of exerting ourselves to interpret every detail that we learn about a person, we are stingy with our mental efforts. Nevertheless, if we are specifically warned to beware of first impressions, or if we are encouraged to interpret information about others slowly and carefully, the primacy effect can be weakened or even eliminated (Stewart, 1965). Generally, speaking, however, once we have formed an impression about someone, we do not exert the mental effort to change it, even if that impression was formed by jumping to conclusions or through prejudice (Fiske, 1995).

Schemata can sometimes lead us astray, luring us into "seeing" things about a person that we don't actually observe. For instance, most of have an *introvert* schema that includes the traits of shyness, quietness, and preoccupation with one's own thoughts. If we notice that Melissa is shy, we are likely to categorize her as an introvert. Later, we may "remember" that she also seemed preoccupied with her own thoughts. In other words, thinking of Melissa as an introvert saves us the trouble of taking into account all the subtle shadings of

social cognition Knowledge and understanding concerning the social world and the people in it (including oneself).

primacy effect The fact that early information about someone weighs more heavily than later information in influencing one's impression of that person.

her personality. But this kind of thinking can easily lead to errors if we attribute to Melissa qualities that belong to the schema, but not to her.

Schemata can even help us create the behavior we expect from other people. In a classic study, pairs of participants played a competitive game (M. Snyder & Swann, 1978). The researchers told one member of each pair that his or her partner was either hostile or friendly. The players who were led to believe that their partner was hostile behaved differently toward that partner than did the players led to believe that their partner was friendly. In turn, those treated as hostile actually began to display hostility. In fact, these people continued to show hostility later, when they were paired with new players who had no expectations about them at all. The expectation of hostility seemed to produce actual aggressiveness, and this behavior persisted. When we bring about expected behavior in another person in this way, our impression becomes a **self-fulfilling prophecy**.

Considerable scientific research has shown how teacher expectations can take the form of a self-fulfilling prophecy and can influence student performance in the classroom (M. Harris & Rosenthal, 1985; Osborne, 1997; Rosenthal, 2002b; Trouilloud, Sarrazin, Bressoux, Bressoux, & Bois, 2006). That finding has been named the *Pygmalion effect*, after the mythical sculptor who created the statue of a woman and then brought it to life. Although the research does not suggest that high teacher expectations can turn an "F" student into an "A" student, it does show that both high and low expectations can exert a powerful influence on student achievement. One study, for example, compared the performance of "at risk" ninth-grade students who had been assigned to regular classrooms with that of students assigned to experimental classrooms that received a year-long intervention aimed at increasing teachers' expectations. After 1 year, the students in the experimental classrooms had higher grades in English and history than the students who were not in the intervention classrooms. Two years later, the experimental students were less likely to drop out of high school (Weinstein et al., 1991).

STEREOTYPES Just as schemata shape our impressions of others, so do stereotypes. As a set of characteristics presumed to be shared by all members of a social category, a **stereotype** is actually a special kind of schema—one that is simplistic, very strongly held, and not necessarily based on firsthand experience. A stereotype can involve almost any distinguishing personal attribute, such as age, sex, race, occupation, place of residence, or membership in a certain group. As Sher Singh learned after the terrorist attacks of September 11, 2001, many Americans developed a stereotype suggesting that all males who "looked" like they were from the Middle East were potential terrorists.

When our first impression of a person is governed by a stereotype, we tend to infer things about that person solely on the basis of some key distinguishing feature and to ignore facts that are inconsistent with the stereotype, no matter how apparent they are. As a result, we may perceive things about the person selectively or inaccurately, thereby perpetuating our initial stereotype. For example, once you have categorized someone as male or female, you may rely more on your stereotype of that gender than on your own observations of how the person acts. Because women are traditionally stereotyped as more emotional and submissive whereas men are stereotyped as more rational and assertive, you may come to see these traits in men and women more than they really exist (Firestone, Firestone, & Catlett, 2006). Recent studies (Castelli, Macrae, Zogmaister, & Arcuri, 2004; Macrae & Bodenhausen, 2000) indicate that sorting people into categories is not automatic or inevitable. People are more likely to apply stereotyped schemata in a chance encounter than in a structured, task-oriented situation (such as a classroom or the office); more likely to pay attention to individual signals than to stereotypes when they are pursuing a goal; and consciously, or unconsciously, to suppress stereotypes that violate social norms. For example, a man who has operated according to stereotyped schemata may expect women in gender-typed roles, such as a nurse or secretary or his wife, to be warm and gentle. However, he may not necessarily have the same expectations toward women at work or those in other professional roles (as lawyer, executive, or telephone repair person, for example).

Suppose you are a new teacher entering this classroom on the first day of school in September. Do you have any expectations about children of any ethnic or racial groups that might lead to a self-fulfilling prophecy?

self-fulfilling prophecy The process in which a person's expectation about another elicits behavior from the second person that confirms the expectation.

stereotype A set of characteristics presumed to be shared by all members of a social category.

Person–Situation   Interpreting Behavior

The study of attribution, or how people explain their own and other people's behavior, focuses on when and why people interpret behavior as reflecting personal traits or social situations. Suppose you run into a friend at the supermarket. You greet him warmly, but he barely acknowledges you, mumbles "Hi," and walks away. You feel snubbed and try to figure out why he acted like that. Did he behave that way because of something in the situation? Perhaps you did something that offended him; perhaps he was having no luck finding the groceries he wanted; or perhaps someone had just blocked his way by leaving a cart in the middle of an aisle. Or did something within him, some personal trait such as moodiness or arrogance, prompt him to behave that way? ●●

ATTRIBUTION

How do we decide why people act as they do?

EXPLAINING BEHAVIOR Social interaction is filled with occasions that invite us to make judgments about the causes of behavior. When something unexpected or unpleasant occurs, we wonder about it and try to understand it. Social psychologists' observations about how we go about attributing causes to behavior form the basis of **attribution theory**.

An early attribution theorist, Fritz Heider (1958), argued that we attribute behavior to either internal or external causes, but not both. Thus, we might conclude that a classmate's lateness was caused by his laziness (a personal factor, or an internal attribution) *or* by traffic congestion (a situational factor, or an external attribution).

How do we decide whether to attribute a given behavior to internal or external causes? According to another influential attribution theorist, Harold Kelley (Kelley, 1967, 1973), we rely on three kinds of information about the behavior: distinctiveness, consistency, and consensus. For example, if your instructor asks you to stay briefly after class so that she can talk with you, you will probably try to figure out what lies behind her request by asking yourself three questions.

First, how *distinctive* is the instructor's request? Does she often ask students to stay and talk (low distinctiveness) or is such a request unusual (high distinctiveness)? If she often asks students to speak with her, you will probably conclude that she has personal reasons for talking with you. But if her request is highly distinctive, you will probably conclude that something about you, not her, underlies her request.

Second, how *consistent* is the instructor's behavior? Does she regularly ask you to stay and talk (high consistency), or is this a first for you (low consistency)? If she has consistently made this request of you before, you will probably guess that this occasion is like those others. But if her request is inconsistent with past behavior, you will probably wonder whether some particular event—perhaps something you said in class—motivated her to request a private conference.

Finally, what degree of *consensus* among teachers exists regarding this behavior? Do your other instructors ask you to stay and talk with them (high consensus), or is this instructor unique in making such a request (low consensus)? If it is common for your instructors to ask to speak with you, this instructor's request is probably due to some external factor. But if she is the only instructor ever to ask to speak privately with you, it must be something about this particular person—an internal motive or a concern—that accounts for her behavior (Iacobucci & McGill, 1990).

If you conclude that the instructor has her own reasons for wanting to speak with you, you may feel mildly curious for the remainder of class until you can find out what she wants. But if you think external factors—like your own actions—have prompted her request, you may worry about whether you are in trouble and nervously wait for the end of class.

BIASES Unfortunately, the causal attributions we make are often vulnerable to *biases*. For instance, imagine that you are at a party and you see an acquaintance, Ted, walk across the

---

attribution theory The theory that addresses the question of how people make judgments about the causes of behavior.

room carrying several plates of food and a drink. As he approaches his chair, Ted spills food on himself. You may attribute the spill to Ted's personal characteristics—he is clumsy. Ted, however, is likely to make a very different attribution. He will likely attribute the spill to an external factor—he was carrying too many other things. Your explanation for this behavior reflects the **fundamental attribution error**—the tendency to attribute others' behavior to causes within themselves (Aronson, Wilson, & Akert, 2005; R. A. Smith & Weber, 2005).

The fundamental attribution error is part of the *actor–observer bias*—the tendency to explain the behavior of others as caused by internal factors, while attributing *one's own* behavior to *external* forces (Gordon & Kaplar, 2002; Hansen, Kimble, & Biers, 2001). Thus, Ted, the actor, attributed his own behavior to an external source, whereas you, the observer, attributed the behavior to an internal one. For example, during World War II, some Europeans risked their own safety to help Jewish refugees who were being persecuted in Nazi-occupied Europe. From the perspective of an observer, we tend to attribute this behavior to personal qualities. Indeed, Robert Goodkind, chairman of the foundation that honored the rescuers, called for parents to "inculcate in our children the values of altruism and moral courage as exemplified by the rescuers." Clearly, Goodkind was making an internal attribution for the heroic behavior. The rescuers themselves, however, attribute their actions to external factors. One said, "We didn't feel like rescuers at all. We were just ordinary students doing what we had to do." (Lipman, 1991).

Did this accident happen because of poor driving or because the driver swerved to avoid a child in the street? The fundamental attribution error says that we are more likely to attribute behavior to internal causes, such as poor driving, rather than situational factors, such as a child in the street.

A related class of biases is called **defensive attribution**. These types of attributions occur when we are motivated to present ourselves well, either to impress others or to feel good about ourselves (Aronson, Wilson, & Akert, 2005; Gyekye & Salminen, 2006). One example of a defensive attribution is the *self-serving bias*, which is a tendency to attribute our successes to our personal attributes while chalking up our failures to external forces beyond our control (Sedikides, Campbell, Reeder, & Elliot, 1998; R. A. Smith & Weber, 2005). Students do this all the time. They tend to regard exams on which they do well as good indicators of their abilities and exams on which they do poorly as bad indicators (R. A. Smith, 2005). Similarly, teachers are more likely to assume responsibility for students' successes than for their failures (R. A. Smith, 2005). In one survey of more than 800,000 high school seniors, less than 1% said they were below average in "ability to get along with others," while more than half said they were in the top 10%. In another survey, less than 80% of the respondents said that Mother Teresa was likely to go to heaven, though 87% said that they themselves were likely to do so (Shermer, 2004).

A second type of defensive attribution comes from thinking that people get what they deserve: Bad things happen to bad people, and good things happen to good people. This is called the **just-world hypothesis** (Aronson, Wilson, & Akert, 2005; Blader & Tyler, 2002; M. J. Lerner, 1980). When misfortune strikes someone, we often jump to the conclusion that the person deserved it, rather than giving full weight to situational factors that may have been responsible. Why do we behave this way? One reason is that doing so gives us the comforting illusion that such a thing could never happen to us. By reassigning the blame for a terrible misfortune from a chance event (something that could happen to us) to the victim's own negligence (a trait that *we*, of course, do not share), we delude ourselves into believing that we could never suffer such a fate (Dalbert, 2001).

ATTRIBUTION ACROSS CULTURES Historically, most of the research on attribution theory has been conducted in Western cultures. Do the basic principles of attribution theory apply to people in other cultures as well? The answer appears to be "not always." Some recent research has observed the self-serving bias among people from Eastern collectivist cultures like Japan (Sedikides, Gaertner, & Toguchi, 2003; Kudo & Numazaki, 2003), while other research has not. In one study, Japanese students studying in the United States usually explained failure as a lack of effort (an internal attribution) and attributed their successes to the assistance that they received from others (an external attribution) (Kashima & Triandis, 1986). This process is the reverse of the self-serving bias. Similarly, the fundamental attribution error may not be universal. In some other cultures, people are much less likely to attribute behavior to internal personal characteristics; they place more emphasis on the role

fundamental attribution error The tendency of people to overemphasize personal causes for other people's behavior and to underemphasize personal causes for their own behavior.

defensive attribution The tendency to attribute our successes to our own efforts or qualities and our failures to external factors.

just-world hypothesis Attribution error based on the assumption that bad things happen to bad people and good things happen to good people.

proximity How close two people live to each other.

of external, situational factors in explaining both their own behavior and that of others (Menon, Morris, Chiu, & Hong, 1998; Triandis, 2001). In general, members of Eastern collectivist cultures are particularly likely to attribute both their own and other people's behavior to external, rather than internal, factors (I. Choi, Nisbett, & Norenzayan, 1999; I. Choi, Dalal, Kim-Prieto, & Park, 2003).

INTERPERSONAL ATTRACTION

Do "birds of a feather flock together," or do "opposites attract"?

A third aspect of social cognition involves interpersonal attraction. When people meet, what determines whether they will like each other? This is the subject of much speculation and even mystification, with popular explanations running the gamut from fate to compatible astrological signs. Romantics believe that irresistible forces propel them toward an inevitable meeting with their beloved, but social psychologists take a more hardheaded view. They have found that attraction and the tendency to like someone else are closely linked to such factors as *proximity*, *physical attractiveness*, *similarity*, *exchange*, and *intimacy*.

PROXIMITY Proximity is usually the most important factor in determining attraction (Aronson, Wilson, & Akert, 2005; Brehm, 2002). The closer two people live to each other, the more likely they are to interact; the more frequent their interaction, the more they will tend to like each other. Conversely, two people separated by considerable geographic distance are not likely to run into each other and thus have little chance to develop a mutual attraction. The proximity effect has less to do with simple convenience than with the security and comfort we feel with people and things that have become familiar. Familiar people are predictable and safe—thus more likable (Bornstein, 1989).

PHYSICAL ATTRACTIVENESS Physical attractiveness can powerfully influence the conclusions that we reach about a person's character. We actually give attractive people credit for more than their beauty. We presume them to be more intelligent, interesting, happy, kind, sensitive, moral, and successful than people who are not perceived as attractive. They are also thought to make better spouses and to be more sexually responsive (Dion, 1972; Feingold, 1992; S. Katz, 2003; Zuckerman, Miyake, & Elkin, 1995).

Not only do we tend to credit physically attractive people with a wealth of positive qualities, but we also tend to like them more than we do less attractive people. One reason is that physical attractiveness itself is generally considered a positive attribute (Baron & Byrne, 1991). We often perceive beauty as a valuable asset that can be exchanged for other things in social interactions. We may also believe that beauty has a "radiating effect"—that the glow of a companion's good looks enhances our own public image (Kernis & Wheeler, 1981; Sekides, Olsen, & Reis, 1993).

Wonderful or just beautiful? Physically attractive people are often perceived to have a host of other attractive qualities. The movie *Shrek 2* used this premise for humor by presenting the handsome Prince Charming as a villain.

Our preoccupation with physical attractiveness has material consequences. Research has found that mothers of more attractive infants tend to show their children more affection and to play with them more often than mothers of unattractive infants (Langlois, Ritter, Casey, & Sawin, 1995). Even in hospitals, premature infants rated as more attractive by attending nurses thrived better and gained weight faster than those judged as less attractive, presumably because they receive more nurturing (Badr & Abdallah, 2001). Attractive children are more likely to be treated leniently by teachers (M. McCall, 1997), and attractive adults are generally judged to be more productive by their employers (Hosoda, Stone, & Coats, 2003).

In general, we tend to give good-looking people the benefit of the doubt: If they don't live up to our expectations during the first encounter, we give them a second chance, ask for or accept a second date, or seek further opportunities for interaction. These reactions can give attractive people substantial advantages in life and can lead to self-fulfilling prophecies. Physically attractive people may come to think of themselves as good or lovable because they are continually treated as if they are. Conversely, unattractive people may begin to see themselves as bad or unlovable because they have always been regarded that way—even as children. (See "On the Cutting Edge: Beauty and Privilege.")

SIMILARITY Attractiveness isn't everything. In the abstract, people might prefer extremely attractive individuals, but in reality they usually choose friends and partners who are close to their own level of attractiveness (J. H. Harvey & Pauwells, 1999). Similarity—of attitudes, interests, values, backgrounds, and beliefs, as well as looks—underlies much interpersonal attraction (AhYun, 2002; Buss, 1985; Sano, 2002; Tan & Singh, 1995). When we know that someone shares our attitudes and interests, we tend to have more positive feelings toward that person. For example, voters are more attracted to and are more likely to vote for a candidate with whom they share similar attitudes (Quist & Crano, 2003). In addition, the higher the proportion of attitudes that two people share, the stronger the attraction between them (Byrne, 1997).

We value similarity because it is important to us to have others agree with our choices and beliefs. By comparing our opinions with those of other people, we clarify our understanding of and reduce our uncertainty about social situations. Finding that others agree with us strengthens our convictions and boosts our self-esteem.

If similarity is such a critical determinant of attraction, what about the notion that opposites attract? Aren't people sometimes attracted to others who are completely different from them? Extensive research has failed to confirm this notion. In long-term relationships,

ON THE CUTTING EDGE

BEAUTY AND PRIVILEGE

Poets and philosophers have been fascinated by beauty for centuries. With rare exceptions, the heroes and heroines of ancient myths and contemporary Hollywood fables are physically attractive—and the villains homely and deformed. Yet our culture includes age-old maxims that hold beauty either is not, or should not be, a significant factor in our judgments of, and behavior toward, other people. Judith Langlois and her colleagues (Langlois et al., 2000) conducted an extensive review and analysis of scientific studies relevant to three of our proverbs.

"Never judge a book by its cover."

Many researchers have found that evaluations and treatment of attractive people are significantly more favorable than those of unattractive people (Griffin & Langlois, 2006; Hosoda, Stone, & Coats, 2003; Langlois et al., 2000). Moreover, these judgments are not confined to first impressions: People who know an individual well attribute more positive traits to cute children and beautiful or handsome adults.

"Beauty is only skin-deep."

Here again, the scientific evidence contradicts the proverb. Compared with unattractive children, attractive children are more positive toward other people, better adjusted, and display greater intelligence. And so it is for adults: Attractive men and women tend to have other positive traits as well, such as occupational success, being liked, enjoying better health, being self-confident, being a better teacher, and even being slightly more intelligent (L. A. Jackson, Hunter, & Hodge, 1995; Langlois et al., 2000; Riniolo, Johnson, Sherman, & Misso, 2006).

"Beauty is in the eye of the beholder."

In other words, judgments of attractiveness are subjective and variable; different people have different ideas about who is or is not beautiful. Langlois and her colleagues found that this, too, is a myth. In general, people agree when rating the attractiveness of others. People who are seen by others as handsome or pretty know they are viewed as being nice looking

(D. K. Marcus & Miller, 2003). In addition, people from different cultures and ethnic groups generally agree as to who is or is not beautiful. Even young infants prefer the same faces as adults (Rubenstein, Kalakanis, & Langlois, 1999). This cross-cultural, cross-ethnic agreement suggests the possibility of a universal standard of beauty (Rhodes, 2006).

What kind of face do people see as beautiful? Researchers have found that, across cultures, both sexes prefer "ultra-feminine" female faces with a soft, somewhat girlish look (Angier, 1998; Perret et al., 1998), and both sexes also preferred feminine-looking men!

Scientific studies have not resolved the mysteries of beauty and perhaps never will. But the evidence does indicate that our culture's maxims are myths: "Beauty is more than just in the eye of the beholder; people do judge and treat others with whom they interact based on attractiveness; and, perhaps most surprisingly, beauty is more than just skin-deep" (Langlois et al., 2000, p. 404).

exchange The concept that relationships are based on trading rewards among partners.

equity Fairness of exchange achieved when each partner in the relationship receives the same proportion of outcomes to investments.

where attraction plays an especially important role, people overwhelmingly prefer to associate with people who are similar to themselves (Buss, 1985; McPherson, Smith-Lovin, & Cook, 2001).

In some cases in which people's attraction seems to be founded on their lack of similarity, their critical qualities are not so much opposites as they are complements. Complementary traits are needs or skills that complete or balance each other (Dryer & Horowitz, 1997; S. Hendrick & Hendrick, 1992). For example, a person who likes to care for and fuss over others will be most compatible with a mate who enjoys receiving such attention. Complementarity almost always occurs between people who share similar goals and values and are willing to adapt to each other. True opposites are unlikely even to meet each other, much less interact long enough to achieve such compatibility.

EXCHANGE According to the *reward theory of attraction*, we tend to like people who make us feel rewarded and appreciated. The relationship between attraction and rewards is subtle and complex. For example, Aronson's gain–loss theory of attraction (2003) suggests that *increases* in rewarding behavior influence attractiveness more than constant rewarding behavior does. Say that you were to meet and talk with someone at three successive parties, and during these conversations, that person's behavior toward you changed from polite indifference to overt flattery. You would be inclined to like this person more than if she or he had immediately started to praise you during the first conversation and kept up the stream of praise each time you met. The reverse also holds true: We tend to dislike people whose opinion of us changes from good to bad even more than we dislike those who consistently display a low opinion of us.

The reward theory of attraction is based on the concept of **exchange**. In social interactions, people make exchanges. For example, you may agree to help a friend paint his apartment if he prepares dinner for you. Every exchange involves both rewards (you get a free dinner; he gets his apartment painted) and costs. (You have to paint first; he then has to cook you dinner.)

Exchanges work only insofar as they are fair or equitable. A relationship is based on **equity** when both individuals receive equally from each other (Walster, Walster, & Berscheid, 1978; Van Yperen & Buunk, 1990). As long as both parties find their interactions more rewarding than costly, and continue to feel the relationship is equitable, their exchanges are likely to continue (Cook & Rice, 2003; Takeuchi, 2000; Van Yperen & Buunk, 1990). When exchanges are consistently unfair, the one who reaps fewer rewards feels cheated; and the one who gains is apt to feel guilty. This result may undermine the mutual attraction that once drew the two people together.

INTIMACY When does liking someone become something more? *Intimacy* is the quality of genuine closeness to and trust in another person. People become closer and stay closer through a continuing reciprocal pattern where each person tries to know the other and allows the other to know him or her (J. H. Harvey & Pauwells, 1999). When people communicate, they do more than just interact—they share deep-rooted feelings and ideas. When you are first getting to know someone, you communicate about "safe," superficial topics like the weather, sports, or shared activities. As you get to know each other better over time, your conversation progresses to more personal subjects: your personal experiences, memories, hopes and fears, goals and failures (I. Altman & Taylor, 1973).

Intimate communication is based on the process of *self-disclosure* (Laurenceau, Barrett, & Pietromonaco, 2004). As you talk with friends, you disclose or reveal personal experiences and opinions that you might conceal from strangers. Because self-disclosure is possible only when you trust the listener, you will

THINKING CRITICALLY ABOUT . . .

Intimacy and the Internet

Many of the studies of interpersonal attraction were conducted before the advent of new Internet technologies.

- What impact (if any) has e-mail, instant messaging, online networking communities like Facebook, and dating services like match.com had on close relationships?

- Do these new technology tools make it easier to maintain long-distance relationships? Influence attributions? Encourage self-disclosure with intimates and/or strangers? Subtly shape social cognition in other ways?

- Suppose you were conducting a survey to collect data on these questions. What would you ask your participants? How might you determine whether their self-reports are accurate?

seek—and usually receive—a reciprocal disclosure to keep the conversation balanced. For example, after telling your roommate about something that embarrassed you, you may expect him or her to reveal a similar episode; you might even ask directly, "Has anything like that ever happened to you?" Such reciprocal intimacy keeps you "even" and makes your relationship more emotionally satisfying (Sprecher & Hendrick, 2004). The pacing of disclosure is important. If you "jump levels" by revealing too much too soon—or to someone who is not ready to make a reciprocal personal response—the other person will probably retreat, and communication will go no further.

Self-disclosure—revealing personal experiences and opinions—is essential to all close relationships.

CHECK YOUR UNDERSTANDING

1. Associated with the many categories into which we "peg" people are sets of beliefs and expectations called _____ that are assumed to apply to all members of a category. When these are quite simplistic, but deeply held, they are often referred to as _____.

2. When the first information we receive about a person weighs more heavily in forming an impression than later information does, we are experiencing the _____ effect.

3. The tendency to attribute the behavior of others to internal causes and one's own behavior to external causes is called the _____ _____ _____.

4. The belief that people must deserve the bad things that happen to them reflects the _____-_____ _____.

5. The tendency to attribute the behavior of others to personal characteristics is the _____-_____ bias.

6. Which of the following is a basis for interpersonal attraction? (There can be more than one correct answer.)

   a. proximity

   b. similarity

   c. exchange

   d. attraction of true opposites

   e. all of the above

Answers: 1. schemata, stereotypes. 2. primacy. 3. fundamental attribution error. 4. just-world hypothesis. 5. actor observer. 6. a, b, and c.

APPLY YOUR UNDERSTANDING

1. You meet someone at a party who is outgoing, entertaining, and has a great sense of humor. A week later, your paths cross again, but this time the person seems very shy, withdrawn, and humorless. Most likely, your impression of this person after the second meeting is that he or she

   a. is actually shy, withdrawn and humorless, despite your initial impression.

   b. is actually outgoing and entertaining but was just having a bad day.

   c. is low in self-monitoring.

   d. Both (b) and (c) are correct.

2. Your roommate tells you she did really well on her history midterm exam because she studied hard and "knew the material cold." But she says she did poorly on her psychology midterm because the exam was unfair and full of ambiguous questions. On the basis of what you have learned in this portion of the chapter, this may be an example of

   a. defensive attribution.

   b. the primacy effect.

   c. the ultimate attribution error.

   d. the just-world effect.

Answers: 1. b. 2. a.

Attitudes

Why are attitudes important?

The phrase "I don't like his attitude" is a telling one. People are often told to "change your attitude" or make an "attitude adjustment." An **attitude** is a relatively stable organization of beliefs, feelings, and tendencies toward something or someone—called an *attitude object*. Attitudes are important mainly because they often influence our behavior. Discrimination, for example, is often caused by prejudiced attitudes. Psychologists wonder how attitudes are formed and study how they can be changed.

THE NATURE OF ATTITUDES

What are the three major components of attitudes?

An attitude has three major components: *evaluative beliefs* about the object, *feelings* about the object, and *behavior tendencies* toward the object. Beliefs include facts, opinions, and our general knowledge. Feelings encompass love, hate, like, dislike, and similar sentiments. Behavior tendencies refer to our inclinations to act in certain ways toward the object—to approach it, avoid it, and so on. For example, our attitude toward a political candidate includes our beliefs about the candidate's qualifications and positions on crucial issues and our expectations about how the candidate will vote on those issues. We also have feelings about the candidate—like or dislike, trust or mistrust. And because of these beliefs and feelings, we are inclined to behave in certain ways toward the candidate—to vote for or against the candidate, to contribute time or money to the candidate's campaign, to make a point of attending or staying away from rallies for the candidate, and so forth.

As we will see shortly, these three aspects of an attitude are often consistent with one another. For example, if we have positive feelings toward something, we tend to have positive beliefs about it and to behave positively toward it. This tendency does not mean, however, that our every action will accurately reflect our attitudes. For example, our feelings about going to dentists are often negative, yet most of us make an annual visit anyway. Let's look more closely at the relationship between attitudes and behavior.

ATTITUDES AND BEHAVIOR The relationship between attitudes and behavior is not always straightforward (Albarracín, Zanna, Johnson, & Kumkale, 2005). Variables such as the strength of the attitude, how easily it comes to mind, how noticeable a particular attitude is in a given situation, and how relevant the attitude is to the particular behavior in question help to determine whether a person will act in accordance with an attitude.

Personality traits are also important (Rowatt, Franklin, & Cotton, 2005). Some people consistently match their actions to their attitudes, while others have a tendency to override their own attitudes in order to behave properly in a given situation. As a result, attitudes predict behavior better for some people than for others. People who rate highly on **self-monitoring** are especially likely to override their attitudes to behave in accordance with others' expectations (Jawahar, 2001; O. Klein, Snyder, & Livingston, 2004). Before speaking or acting, those who score high in self-monitoring observe the situation for clues about how they should react. Then they try to meet those "demands," rather than behave according to their own beliefs or sentiments. In contrast, those who score low in self-monitoring express and act on their attitudes with great consistency, showing little regard for situational clues or constraints. Let's say both of these types are at a dinner party where they both disagree with the politics of a fellow dinner guest. The former may keep her thoughts to herself in an effort to be polite and agreeable, whereas the latter might dispute the speaker openly, even though doing so might disrupt the social occasion (M. Snyder, 1987).

ATTITUDE DEVELOPMENT How do we acquire our attitudes? Where do they come from? Many of our most basic attitudes derive from early, direct personal experience (Jaccard & Blanton, 2005). Children are rewarded with smiles and encouragement when they please their parents, and they are punished through disapproval when they displease them. These

---

attitude Relatively stable organization of beliefs, feelings, and behavior tendencies directed toward something or someone— the attitude object.

self-monitoring The tendency for an individual to observe the situation for cues about how to react.

early experiences give children enduring attitudes. Attitudes are also formed by imitation. Children mimic the behavior of their parents and peers, acquiring attitudes even when no one is deliberately trying to shape them.

But parents are not the only source of attitudes. Teachers, friends, and even famous people are also important in shaping our attitudes. New fraternity or sorority members, for example, may model their behavior and attitudes on upper-class members. A student who idolizes a teacher may adopt many of the teacher's attitudes toward controversial subjects, even if they run counter to attitudes of parents or friends.

The mass media, particularly television, also have a great impact on attitude formation. (This is why having his photo televised with the label of terrorist suspect was particularly devastating for Sher Singh.) Television bombards us with messages—not merely through its news and entertainment, but also through commercials. Without experience of their own against which to measure the merit of these messages, children are particularly susceptible to the influence of television on their attitudes.

Children may learn prejudice from their parents or from other adults, but attitudes can be changed.

PREJUDICE AND DISCRIMINATION

How does a person develop a prejudice toward someone else?

Although the terms *prejudice* and *discrimination* are often used interchangeably, they actually refer to different concepts. **Prejudice**—an attitude—is an unfair, intolerant, or unfavorable view of a group of people. **Discrimination**—a behavior—is an unfair act or a series of acts directed against an entire group of people or individual members of that group. To discriminate is to treat an entire class of people in an unfair way.

ENDURING ISSUES

Person–Situation   Does Discrimination Reflect Prejudice?

Prejudice and discrimination do not always occur together. It is possible to be prejudiced against a particular group without openly behaving in a hostile or discriminatory manner toward its members. Discrimination, the expression of prejudice, is determined by a variety of factors. Some of these encourage suppressing prejudice and others encourage or justify expression (Crandall & Eshleman, 2003). A prejudiced storeowner may smile at an African American customer, for example, to disguise opinions that could hurt his business. Likewise, many institutional practices can be discriminatory even though they are not based on prejudice. For example, regulations establishing a minimum height requirement for police officers may discriminate against women and certain ethnic groups whose average height falls below the arbitrary standard, even though the regulations do not stem from sexist or racist attitudes. ●●

PREJUDICE Like attitudes, prejudice has three components: beliefs, feelings, and behavioral tendencies. Prejudicial beliefs are virtually always negative stereotypes; and, as mentioned earlier, reliance on stereotypes can lead to erroneous thinking about other people. When a prejudiced White employer interviews an African American, for example, the employer may attribute to the job candidate all the traits associated with the employer's African American stereotype. In so doing, qualities of the candidate that do not match the stereotype are likely to be ignored or quickly forgotten. For example, the employer whose stereotype includes the belief that African Americans are lazy may belittle the candidate's hard-earned college degree by thinking, "I never heard of that college. It must be an easy school."

prejudice An unfair, intolerant, or unfavorable attitude toward a group of people.

discrimination An unfair act or series of acts taken toward an entire group of people or individual members of that group.

This thinking, which is similar to the fundamental attribution error, is known as the *ultimate attribution error*. This refers to the tendency for a person with stereotyped beliefs about a particular group of people to make internal attributions for their shortcomings and external attributions for their successes. In the preceding example, the employer is making an external attribution (an easy school) for the college success of the African American job seeker. The other side of the ultimate attribution error is to make internal attributions for the failures of people who belong to groups we dislike. For instance, many White Americans believe that lower average incomes among Black Americans as compared with White Americans are due to lack of ability or low motivation (P. J. Henry, Reyna, & Weiner, 2004).

Along with stereotyped beliefs, prejudiced attitudes are usually marked by strong emotions, such as dislike, fear, hatred, or loathing. For example, on learning that a person whom they like is a homosexual, heterosexuals may suddenly view the person as undesirable, sick, a sinner, or a pervert (See Herek, 2000).

SOURCES OF PREJUDICE Many theories attempt to sort out the causes and sources of prejudice. According to the **frustration–aggression theory**, prejudice is the result of people's frustrations (Allport, 1954; E. R. Smith & Mackie, 2005). As we saw in Chapter 8, "Motivation and Emotion," under some circumstances frustration can spill over into anger and hostility. People who feel exploited and oppressed often cannot vent their anger against an identifiable or proper target, so they displace their hostility onto those even "lower" on the social scale than themselves. The result is prejudice and discrimination. The people who are the victims of this displaced aggression, or *scapegoats,* are blamed for the problems of the times.

After the 2001 terrorist attacks in the United States, many Arabs, Muslims, and even people who looked Middle Eastern, became scapegoats for some Americans' frustration about the violence. Recall the experiences of Sher Singh, whom we described at the start of this chapter. African Americans have long been scapegoats for the economic frustrations of some lower-income White Americans who feel powerless to improve their own condition. However, Latin Americans, Asian Americans, Jewish Americans, and women are also scapegoated—at times by African Americans. Like kindness, greed, and all other human qualities, prejudice is not restricted to a particular race, religion, gender, or ethnic group.

Another theory locates the source of prejudice in a bigoted or an **authoritarian personality** (Adorno, Frenkel-Brunswick, Levinson, & Sanford, 1950; Altemeyer, 2004). Authoritarian people tend to be rigidly conventional. They favor following the rules and abiding by tradition and are hostile to those who defy social norms. They respect and submit to authority and are preoccupied with power and toughness. Looking at the world through a lens of rigid categories, they are cynical about human nature, fearing, suspecting, and rejecting all groups other than those to which they belong. Prejudice is only one expression of their suspicious, mistrusting views (Jost & Sidanius, 2004). Returning to our opening vignette, Sher Singh's turban may have been a symbol of difference that led to authoritarian responses from some police officers and bystanders.

Cognitive sources of prejudice also exist (Cornelis & Van Hiel, 2006). As we saw earlier, people are "cognitive misers" who try to simplify and organize their social thinking as much as possible. Too much simplification—*oversimplification*—leads to erroneous thinking, stereotypes, prejudice, and discrimination. For example, a stereotyped view of women as indecisive or weak will prejudice an employer against hiring a qualified woman as a manager. Belief in a just world—where people get what they deserve and deserve what they get—also oversimplifies one's view of the victims of prejudice as somehow "deserving" their plight. This may be why people watching Sher Singh's arrest jumped to the conclusion that he was a terrorist who "deserved" arrest.

In addition, prejudice and discrimination may originate in people's attempts to conform. If we associate with people who express prejudices, we are more likely to go along with their ideas than to resist them. The pressures of social conformity help to explain why children quickly absorb the prejudices of their parents and playmates long before they have formed their own beliefs and opinions on the basis of experience. Peer pressure often makes it "cool" or acceptable to express certain biases rather than to behave tolerantly toward members of other social groups. Conformity may have been why no one among a largely hostile crowd came forward to question Sher Singh's arrest.

---

frustration–aggression theory The theory that, under certain circumstances, people who are frustrated in their goals turn their anger away from the proper, powerful target and toward another, less powerful target that is safer to attack.

authoritarian personality A personality pattern characterized by rigid conventionality, exaggerated respect for authority, and hostility toward those who defy society's norms.

Racism is the belief that members of certain racial or ethnic groups are *innately* inferior. Racists believe that intelligence, industry, morality, and other valued traits are biologically determined and therefore cannot be changed. Racism leads to *either–or* thinking: Either you are one of "us," or you are one of "them." An *in-group* is any group of people who feels a sense of solidarity and exclusivity in relation to nonmembers. An *out-group*, in contrast, is a group of people who are outside this boundary and are viewed as competitors, enemies, or different and unworthy of respect. These terms can be applied to opposing sports teams, rival gangs, and political parties, or to entire nations, regions, religions, and ethnic or racial groups. According to the *in-group bias*, members see themselves not just as different, but also as superior to members of out-groups. In extreme cases, members of an in-group may see members of an out-group as less than human and feel hatred that may lead to violence, civil war, and even genocide. The people shouting at Sher Singh as he was led from the train may have been expressing this view of him as a member of an out-group.

Signs like this were common in the South before the civil rights movement.

The most blatant forms of racism in the United States have declined during the past several decades. For example, 9 out of 10 Whites say that they would vote for a Black president. But racism still exists in subtle forms. For example, many Whites say that they approve of interracial marriage, but would be "uncomfortable" if someone in their family married an African American. Moreover, unlike their parents, Generation-Xers (those born between 1965 and 1980) tend to support school integration—yet are not in favor of affirmative action in employment settings (Andolina & Mayer, 2003). Thus, it is not surprising that Blacks and Whites have different views of how Blacks are treated in our society. In one survey of 1,000 Americans shortly after hurricane Katrina hit the Gulf Coast, 66% of African Americans said that the government's response would have been faster if most victims had been White; only 26% of White Americans agreed. Only 19% of African Americans, compared to 41% of White Americans, felt that the federal government's response was good or excellent. When asked about people who "took things from businesses and homes" during the flooding, 57% of African Americans said they were ordinary people trying to survive; only 38% of White Americans agreed. (Pew Research Center for the People and the Press, 2005).

STRATEGIES FOR REDUCING PREJUDICE AND DISCRIMINATION How can we use our knowledge of prejudice, stereotypes, and discrimination to reduce prejudice and its expression? Three strategies appear promising: recategorization, controlled processing, and improving contact between groups. (See "Applying Psychology: Ethnic Conflict and Violence," for a discussion of how these strategies can be used to reduce ethnic conflict.)

- **Recategorization.** When we recategorize, we try to expand our schema of a particular group—such as viewing people from different races or genders as sharing similar qualities. These more inclusive schemata become superordinate categories. For instance, both Catholics and Protestants in the United States tend to view themselves as Christians, rather than as separate competing groups (as has occurred in Northern Ireland). If people can create such superordinate categories, they can often reduce stereotypes and prejudice (Dovidio, Gaertner, Hodson, Houlette, & Johnson, 2005).
- **Controlled Processing.** Some researchers believe that we all learn cultural stereotypes, so the primary difference between someone who is prejudiced and someone who is not is the ability to suppress prejudiced beliefs through controlled processing (W. A. Cunningham, Johnson, Raye, Gatenby, & Gore, 2004; K. L. Dion, 2003). We can train ourselves to be more "mindful" of people who differ from us. For example, to reduce children's prejudice toward people with disabilities, children could be shown slides of handicapped people and be asked to imagine how difficult it might be for such individuals to open a door or drive a car.
- **Improving group contact.** Finally, we can reduce prejudice and tensions between groups by bringing them together (K. McClelland & Linnander, 2006; Pettigrew, 1998). This was one of the intentions of the famous 1954 U.S. Supreme Court's decision in *Brown v. Board of Education* of Topeka, Kansas, which mandated that public

racism Prejudice and discrimination directed at a particular racial group.

THINKING CRITICALLY ABOUT . . .

Ethnic Conflict and Violence

1. Can you think of some examples of propaganda in this country that promote prejudice toward racial and ethnic groups? How can you distinguish "propaganda" from factual information?

2. Using the procedures described here to reduce ethnic hostility and violence, design a program to reduce ethnic conflict in a troubled inner city high school. How could you tell whether your program was effective?

schools become racially integrated. Intergroup contact alone is not enough, however (D. M. Taylor & Moghaddam, 1994). It can work to undermine prejudicial attitudes if certain conditions are met:

1. *Group members must have equal status.* When African Americans and Whites were first integrated in the army and in public housing, they had relatively equal status, so prejudice between them was greatly reduced (Wernet, Follman, Magueja, & Moore-Chambers, 2003). School desegregation has been less than successful because the structure of our school system tends to reward the economic and academic advantages of White children, giving them an edge over many African American schoolchildren (E. G. Cohen, 1984; Schofield, 1997).

2. *People need to have one-on-one contact with members of the other group.* Simply putting students with differing racial and ethnic backgrounds together in a classroom does not change attitudes. Personal contact, like that which occurs among friends at lunch and after school, is more effective.

3. *Members of the two groups must cooperate rather than compete.* Perhaps because it provides the personal contact, as well as common ground and equal status, working together to achieve a goal helps to break down prejudice. (Wernet, Follman, Magueja, & Moore-Chambers, 2003).

4. *Social norms should encourage intergroup contact.* In many cases, school desegregation took place in a highly charged atmosphere. Busloads of African American children arrived at their new schools only to face the protests of angry White parents. These conditions did not promote genuine intergroup contact. In situations in which contact is encouraged by social norms, prejudiced attitudes are less likely.

In all of these suggestions, the primary focus is on changing behavior, not on changing attitudes directly. But changing behavior is often a first step toward changing attitudes. This is not to say that attitude change follows automatically. Attitudes can be difficult to budge because they are often so deeply rooted. Completely eliminating deeply held attitudes, then, can be very difficult. That is why social psychologists have concentrated so much effort on techniques that encourage attitude change. In the next section, we examine some of the major findings in the psychological research on attitude change.

One of the best antidotes to prejudice is contact among people of different racial groups. Working on class projects together, for example, can help children to overcome negative stereotypes about others.

CHANGING ATTITUDES

What factors encourage someone to change an attitude?

A man watching television on Sunday afternoon ignores scores of beer commercials, but listens to a friend who recommends a particular brand. A political speech convinces one woman to change her vote in favor of the candidate, but leaves her next-door neighbor determined to vote against him. Why would a personal recommendation have greater persuasive power than an expensively produced television commercial? How can two people with similar initial views derive completely different messages from the same speech? What makes one attempt to change attitudes fail and another succeed? Are some people more resistant to attitude change than others are?

THE PROCESS OF PERSUASION The first step in persuasion is to seize and retain the audience's attention (Albarracín, 2002). To be persuaded, you must first pay attention to the message; then you must comprehend it; finally, you must accept it as convincing (Perloff, 2003).

APPLYING PSYCHOLOGY

ETHNIC CONFLICT AND VIOLENCE

Since the end of the Cold War, interethnic conflict has become the dominant form of war (Mays, Bullock, Rosenzweig, & Wessells, 1998; Rouhana & Bar-Tal, 1998). Bosnia, Croatia, East Timor, Russia, Turkey, Iraq, Ireland, Israel, Sri Lanka . . . the list of countries torn by ethnic conflict is long; and civilian deaths continue to increase by the thousands. As coalition forces entered Iraq in 2003, they had to cope with eruptions of interethnic violence between the Arabs and the Kurds, Turkomans, and Assyrians. In Iraq alone, ethnic violence during the previous decade was responsible for tens of thousands of civilian deaths (Human Rights Watch, 2003). Why does such conflict arise, and why is it so difficult to resolve?

Ethnic conflict has no single cause. In part, it ". . . is often rooted in histories of colonialism, ethnocentrism, racism, political oppression, human rights abuses, social injustice, poverty, and environmental degradation" (Mays et al., 1998, p. 737; Pederson, 2002; Toft, 2003). But these structural problems are only part of the story, determining primarily who fights whom. The rest of the story is found in psychological processes such as intense group loyalty, personal and social identity, shared memories, polarization and deep-rooted prejudice, and societal beliefs (Cairns & Darby, 1998; Tindale, Munier, Wasserman, & Smith, 2002). In other words, structural problems don't have the same effect when people are not prepared to hate and fear others. This hate and fear largely determine the extent to which ethnic conflict becomes violent (Des Forges, 1995; M. H. Ross, 1993; D. N. Smith, 1998).

What are some of the psychological forces at work?

- *Propaganda* causes opponents to be painted in the most negative fashion possible, thus perpetuating racism, prejudice, and stereotypes. In Rwanda, for example, Tutsis (who were almost exterminated by the resulting

Conflict among different ethnic groups has led to many years of violence in Iraq.

violence with Hutus) for years were falsely accused in the mass media of having committed horrible crimes and of plotting the mass murder of Hutus (D. N. Smith, 1998).

- When ethnic violence is protracted, *shared collective memories* become filled with instances of violence, hostility, and victimization. Prejudices are thus reinforced, and people increasingly come to view the conflict as inevitable and their differences as irreconcilable (Rouhana & Bar-Tal, 1998).

- *Personal and social identity* can also contribute. Because group memberships contribute to self-image, if your group is maligned or threatened, then by extension you also are personally maligned and threatened. If you are unable to leave the group, you are pressured to defend it to enhance your own feelings of self-esteem (Cairns & Darby, 1998). In this way, what starts out as ethnic conflict quickly becomes a highly personal threat.

- Finally, widespread *societal beliefs* about the conflict and the parties to the conflict also play a role in prolonged ethnic conflicts. Four especially important societal beliefs are "Our goals are just," "The opponent has no legitimacy," "We can do no wrong," and "We are the victims" (Rouhana & Bar-Tal, 1998). These societal beliefs "provide a common social prism through which society members view the conflict. Once formed, they become incorporated into an ethos and are reflected in the group's language, stereotypes, images, myths, and collective memories" (Rouhana & Bar-Tal, 1998, p. 765). The result is a form of "cognitive freezing" in which people selectively seek out and process information in a way that perpetuates the societal beliefs. This cognitive freezing heightens fear, anger, and hatred—the emotions that are the basis of ethnic violence.

(continued on p. 498)

Because conflict and violence stem partly from psychological processes, attempts to build peace cannot address only structural problems. Attempts to redistribute resources more equitably, to reduce oppression and victimization, and to increase social justice are essential, but they will succeed only if attention is also given to important psychological processes. Concerted efforts must be made to increase tolerance and improve intergroup relations while also developing new, nonviolent means for resolving conflicts (Mays et al., 1998; D. N. Smith, 1998). The strategies of recategorization, controlled processing, and contact between groups have helped reduce ethnic conflict in some countries (D. N. Smith, 1998). But cognitive changes must also be made: Societal beliefs must be changed, and new beliefs must be developed that are more consistent with conflict resolution and peaceful relationships. In addition, multidisciplinary techniques must be developed if programs are to be fully effective in addressing conflicts in different cultures. As one group of experts put it, "It is both risky and ethnocentric to assume that methods developed in Western contexts can be applied directly in different cultures and contexts. Research on different cultural beliefs and practices and their implications for ethnopolitical conflict analysis and prevention is essential if the field of psychology is going to be successful in its contributions" (Mays et al., 1998, p. 739).

As competition has stiffened, advertisers have become increasingly creative in catching your attention (Clay, 2002). For example, ads that arouse emotions, especially feelings that make you want to act, can be memorable and thus persuasive (DeSteno & Braverman, 2002; Engel, Black, & Miniard, 1986). Humor, too, is an effective way to keep you watching or reading an ad that you would otherwise ignore (M. Conway & Dube, 2002; C. Scott, Klein, & Bryant, 1990). Other ads "hook" the audience by involving them in a narrative. A commercial might open with a dramatic scene or situation—for example, two people seemingly "meant" for each other but not yet making eye contact—and the viewer stays tuned to find out what happens. Some commercials even feature recurring characters and story lines so that each new commercial in the series is really the latest installment in a soap opera. Even annoying ads can still be effective in capturing attention, because people tend to notice them when they appear (Aaker & Bruzzone, 1985).

With so many clever strategies focused on seizing and holding your attention, how can you shield yourself from unwanted influences and resist persuasive appeals? Start by reminding yourself that these are deliberate attempts to influence you and to change your behavior. Research shows that to a great extent, "forewarned is forearmed" (W. Wood & Quinn, 2003). Another strategy for resisting persuasion is to analyze ads to identify which attention-getting strategies are at work. Make a game of deciphering the advertisers' "code" instead of falling for the ad's appeal. In addition, raise your standards for the kinds of messages that are worthy of your attention and commitment.

THE COMMUNICATION MODEL The second and third steps in persuasion—comprehending and then accepting the message—are influenced by both the message itself and the way in which it is presented. The *communication model* of persuasion spotlights four key elements to achieve these goals: the source, the message itself, the medium of communication, and characteristics of the audience. Persuaders manipulate each of these factors in the hopes of changing your attitudes.

The effectiveness of a persuasive message first depends on its *source*, the author or communicator who appeals to the audience to accept the message. Credibility makes a big difference, at least initially (Ito, 2002; Jain & Posavac, 2001). For example, we are less likely to change our attitude about the oil industry's antipollution efforts if the president of a major refining company tells us about them than if we hear the same information from an impartial commission appointed to study the situation. However, over a period of time, the message may nonetheless be influential. Apparently we are inclined to forget the source, while remembering the content. Not surprisingly, this is known as the *sleeper effect* (Kumkale & Albarracín, 2004).

For an ad to affect our behavior, it must first attract our attention. This one also generates fear, which can sometimes be effective.

Source: © MADD. Used by permission.

The credibility of the source is also important (Ehigie & Shenge, 2000; Putrevu, 2005), especially when we are not inclined to pay attention to the message (Petty & Cacioppo, 1986a). But in cases in which we have some interest in the message, the message itself plays the greater role in determining whether we change our attitudes (Petty & Cacioppo, 1986b). Researchers have discovered that we frequently tune out messages that simply contradict our own point of view. The more effective you are at generating counterarguments, the less likely you are to be persuaded by opposing arguments (Jacks & Cameron, 2003). Thus, messages are generally more successful when they present both sides of an argument and when they present novel arguments, rather than when they rehash old standbys, heard many times before. A two-sided presentation generally makes the speaker seem less biased and thus enhances credibility. We have greater respect and trust for a communicator who acknowledges that there is another side to a controversial issue. Messages that create fear sometimes work well, too (Cochrane & Quester, 2005; Dillard & Anderson, 2004), for example in convincing people to stop smoking (D. W. Dahl, Frankenberger, & Manchanda, 2003; K. H. Smith & Stutts, 2003), or to drive safely (Shehryar & David, 2005). But if a message generates too much fear, it has the potential to turn off the audience and be ignored (Worchel, Cooper, Goethals, & Olson, 1999).

When it comes to choosing an effective *medium* of persuasion, written documentation is best suited to making people understand complex arguments, whereas videotapes or live presentations are more effective with an audience that already grasps the gist of an argument (Chaiken & Eagly, 1976). Most effective, however, are face-to-face appeals or the lessons of our own experience. Salespeople who sell products door to door rely on the power of personal contact.

The most critical factors in changing attitudes—and the most difficult to control—have to do with the *audience*. Attitudes are most resistant to change if (1) the audience has a strong commitment to its present attitudes, (2) those attitudes are shared by others, and (3) the attitudes were instilled during early childhood by a pivotal group such as the family. The *discrepancy* between the content of the message and the present attitudes of the audience also affects how well the message will be received. Up to a point, the greater the difference between the two, the greater the likelihood of attitude change, as long as the person delivering the message is considered an expert on the topic. If the discrepancy is too great, however, the *audience* may reject the new information altogether, even though it comes from an expert.

Finally, certain personal characteristics make some people more susceptible to attitude change than others. People with low self-esteem are more easily influenced, especially when the message is complex and hard to understand. Highly intelligent people tend to resist persuasion because they can think of counterarguments more easily.

COGNITIVE DISSONANCE THEORY One of the more fascinating approaches to understanding the process of attitude change is the theory of **cognitive dissonance**, developed by Leon Festinger (J. Cooper, Mirabile, & Scher, 2005; Festinger, 1957; B. J. Friedman, 2000). Cognitive dissonance exists whenever a person has two contradictory cognitions, or beliefs, at the same time. "I am a considerate and loyal friend" is one cognition; "Yesterday I repeated some juicy gossip I heard about my friend Chris" is another cognition. These two cognitions are dissonant—each one implies the opposite of the other. According to Festinger, cognitive dissonance creates unpleasant psychological tension, which motivates us to try to resolve the dissonance in some way.

Sometimes changing one's attitude is the easiest way to reduce the discomfort of dissonance. I cannot easily change the fact that I have repeated gossip about a friend; therefore, it is easier to change my attitude toward my friend. If I conclude that Chris is not really a friend but simply an acquaintance, then my new attitude now fits my behavior—spreading gossip about someone who is *not* a friend does not contradict the fact that I am loyal and considerate to those who *are* my friends. Similarly, one way to reduce the discomfort or guilt associated with cheating in school is to show support for other students who engage in academic dishonesty (Storch & Storch, 2003).

Discrepant behavior that contradicts an attitude does not necessarily bring about attitude change, however, because there are other ways a person can reduce cognitive dissonance. One alternative is to *increase the number of consonant elements*—that is, the thoughts that are consistent with one another. For example, I might recall the many times I defended Chris when others were critical of him. Now my repeating a little bit of gossip seems less at

cognitive dissonance Perceived inconsistency between two cognitions.

odds with my attitude toward Chris as a friend. Another option is to reduce the importance of one or both dissonant cognitions. For instance, I could tell myself, "The person I repeated the gossip to was Terry, who doesn't really know Chris very well. Terry doesn't care and won't repeat it. It was no big deal, and Chris shouldn't be upset about it." By reducing the significance of my disloyal action, I reduce the dissonance that I experience and so make it less necessary to change my attitude toward Chris.

But why would someone engage in behavior that goes against an attitude in the first place? One answer is that cognitive dissonance is a natural part of everyday life. Simply choosing between two or more desirable alternatives leads inevitably to dissonance. Suppose you are in the market for a computer, but can't decide between a Dell™ and a Macintosh. If you choose one, all of its bad features and all the good aspects of the other contribute to dissonance. After you have bought one of the computers, you can reduce the dissonance by changing your attitude: You might decide that the other keyboard wasn't "quite right" and that some of the "bad" features of the computer you bought aren't so bad after all.

You may also engage in behavior at odds with an attitude because you are enticed to do so. Perhaps someone offers you a small bribe or reward: "I will pay you 25 cents just to try my product." Curiously, the larger the reward, the smaller the change in attitude that is likely to result. When rewards are large, dissonance is at a minimum, and attitude change is small, if it happens at all. Apparently, when people are convinced that there is a good reason to do something that goes against their beliefs ("I'll try almost anything in exchange for a large cash incentive"), they experience little dissonance, and their attitudes are not likely to shift, even though their behavior may change for a time. If the reward is small, however—just barely enough to induce behavior that conflicts with one's attitude—dissonance will be great, maximizing the chances of attitude change: "I only got 25 cents to try this product, so it couldn't have been the money that attracted me. I must really like this product after all." The trick is to induce the behavior that goes against an attitude, while leaving people feeling personally responsible for the dissonant act. In that way, they are more likely to change their attitudes than if they feel they were blatantly induced to act in a way that contradicted their beliefs.

In the final analysis, the most effective means of changing attitudes—especially important attitudes, behaviors, or lifestyle choices—may be self-persuasion (Aronson, 2003; Gordijn, Postmes, & de Vries, 2001). In contrast to traditional, direct techniques of persuasion, people are put in situations in which they are motivated to persuade themselves to change their attitudes or behavior. For example, many educators hoped that school integration would reduce racial prejudices. But often the reverse proved true: Although they attended the same schools and classes, African American and White children tended to "self-segregate." When children were assigned to small, culturally diverse study groups, in which they were forced to cooperate, attitudes changed—albeit slowly. Insults and put-downs, often ethnically based, decreased. Having learned both to teach and to listen to "others," students emerged from the experience with fewer group stereotypes and greater appreciation of individual differences. This outcome, in turn, made them less likely to stereotype others. In a nutshell, working with diverse individuals who did not fit preconceived notions made it difficult to maintain prejudice, because of cognitive dissonance.

THINKING CRITICALLY ABOUT . . .

Attitudes Toward Smoking

Most adolescents and young adults are well aware of the dangers of smoking cigarettes. Nonetheless a significant number of those same people smoke regularly. Based on what you have read concerning attitude change, how would you go about changing people's attitudes toward smoking? For each technique you would use, explain why you think it would be effective. How would you demonstrate whether your program was having the desired effect?

CHECK YOUR UNDERSTANDING

1. A(n) _____ is a fairly stable organization of beliefs, feelings, and behavioral tendencies directed toward some object, such as a person or group.
2. Are the following statements true (T) or false (F)?
   a. ___ The best way to predict behavior is to measure attitudes.
   b. ___ Prejudice is the act of treating someone unfairly.

c. ___ Messages are more persuasive when they present both sides of an argument.

d. ___ A person who has two contradictory beliefs at the same time is experiencing cognitive dissonance.

3. The message that most likely will result in a change in attitude is one with

a. high fear from a highly credible source.

b. high fear from a moderately credible source.

c. moderate fear from a highly credible source.

d. moderate fear from a moderately credible source.

Answers: 1. attitude. 2. a. (F); b. (F); c. (T); d. (T). 3. c.

APPLY YOUR UNDERSTANDING

1. You are asked to advise an elementary school on ways to reduce prejudice in an integrated third grade classroom. On the basis of what you have read, which of the following is most likely to be effective?

a. Seating Black and White children alternately around the drawing table.

b. Talking to the group regularly about the unfairness of prejudice and discrimination.

c. Holding frequent competitions to see whether the Black students or the White students perform classroom work better.

d. Assigning pairs consisting of one Black student and one White student to do interdependent parts of homework assignments.

2. Two people listen to a discussion on why our government should increase defense spending. John has never really thought much about the issue, while Jane has participated in marches and demonstrations against increased defense spending. Which person is LESS likely to change their attitude about defense spending?

a. Jane

b. John

c. Both are equally likely to change their attitudes.

Answers: 1. d. 2. a.

Social Influence

What are some areas in which the power of social influence is highly apparent?

In social psychology, **social influence** refers to the process by which others—individually or collectively—affect our perceptions, attitudes, and actions (Nowak, Vallacher, & Miller, 2003; Petty, Wegener, & Fabrigar, 1997). In the previous section, we examined one form of social influence: attitude change. Next, we'll focus on how the presence or actions of others can control behavior without regard to underlying attitudes.

CULTURAL INFLUENCES

How does your culture influence how you dress or what you eat?

Culture exerts an enormous influence on our attitudes and behavior, and culture is itself a creation of people. As such, culture is a major form of social influence. Consider for a moment the many aspects of day-to-day living that are derived from culture:

1. **Culture dictates how you dress.** A Saudi woman covers her face before venturing outside her home; a North American woman freely displays her face, arms, and legs; and women in some other societies roam completely naked.

social influence The process by which others individually or collectively affect one's perceptions, attitudes, and actions.

cultural truisms Beliefs that most members of a society accept as self-evidently true.

norm A shared idea or expectation about how to behave.

conformity Voluntarily yielding to social norms, even at the expense of one's preferences.

2. **Culture specifies what you eat—and what you do not eat.** Americans do not eat dog meat, the Chinese eat no cheese, and the Hindus refuse to eat beef. Culture further guides *how* you eat: with a fork, chopsticks, or your bare hands.
3. **People from different cultures seek different amounts of personal space.** Latin Americans, French people, and Arabs get closer to one another in most face-to-face interactions than do Americans, British, or Swedes.

To some extent, culture influences us through formal instruction. For example, your parents might have reminded you from time to time that certain actions are considered "normal" or the "right way" to behave. But more often, we learn cultural lessons through modeling and imitation. One result of such learning is the unquestioning acceptance of **cultural truisms**—beliefs or values that most members of a society accept as self-evident (Aronson, Wilson, & Akert, 2005; Maio & Olson, 1998). We are rewarded (reinforced) for doing as our companions and fellow citizens do in most situations—for going along with the crowd. This social learning process is one of the chief mechanisms by which a culture transmits its central lessons and values.

In the course of comparing and adapting our own behavior to that of others, we learn the norms of our culture. A **norm** is a culturally shared idea or expectation about how to behave (Aronson, Wilson, & Akert, 2005; Cialdini & Trost, 1998). As in the preceding examples, norms are often steeped in tradition and strengthened by habit. Cultures seem strange to us if their norms are very different from our own. It is tempting to conclude that *different* means "wrong," simply because unfamiliar patterns of behavior can make us feel uncomfortable. To transcend our differences and get along better with people from other cultures, we must find ways to overcome such discomfort.

One technique for understanding other cultures is the *cultural assimilator*, a strategy for perceiving the norms and values of another group (Kempt, 2000). This technique teaches by example, asking students to explain why a member of another culture has behaved in a particular way. For example, why do the members of a Japanese grade school class silently follow their teacher single file through a park on a lovely spring day? Are they afraid of being punished for disorderly conduct if they do otherwise? Are they naturally placid and compliant? Once you understand that Japanese children are raised to value the needs and feelings of others over their own selfish concerns, their orderly, obedient behavior seems much less perplexing. Cultural assimilators encourage us to remain open-minded about others' norms and values by challenging such cultural truisms as "Our way is the right way."

CONFORMITY

What increases the likelihood that someone will conform?

Why do Japanese schoolchildren behave in such an orderly way? How does your answer compare with the discussion of cultural influences?

Accepting cultural norms should not be confused with conformity. For instance, millions of Americans drink coffee in the morning, but not because they are conforming. They drink coffee because they like and desire it. **Conformity**, in contrast, implies a conflict between an individual and a group that is resolved when individual preferences or beliefs yield to the norms or expectations of the larger group.

Since the early 1950s, when Solomon Asch conducted the first systematic study of the subject, conformity has been a major topic of research in social psychology. Asch demonstrated in a series of experiments that under some circumstances, people will conform to group pressures even if this action forces them to deny obvious physical evidence. His studies ostensibly tested visual judgment by asking people to view cards with several lines of differing lengths; then, people were asked to choose the card with the line most similar to the line on a comparison card. (See **Figure 14–1.**) The lines were deliberately drawn so that the comparison was obvious and the correct choice was clear. All but one of the participants were confederates of the experimenter. On certain trials, these confederates deliberately gave the same wrong answer. This procedure put the lone dissenter on the spot: Should he conform to what he knew to be a wrong decision and agree with the group, thereby denying the evidence of his own eyes, or should he disagree with the group, thereby risking the social consequences of nonconformity?

Overall, participants conformed on about 35% of the trials. There were large individual differences, however; and in subsequent research, experimenters discovered that two sets of factors influence the likelihood that a person will conform: characteristics of the situation and characteristics of the person.

The *size* of the group is one situational factor that has been studied extensively (R. Bond, 2005). Asch (1951) found that the likelihood of conformity increased with group size until four confederates were present. After that point, the number of others made no difference to the frequency of conformity.

Another important situational factor is the degree of *unanimity* in the group. If just one confederate broke the perfect agreement of the majority by giving the correct answer, conformity among participants in the Asch experiments fell from an average of 35% to about 25% (Asch, 1956). Apparently, having just one "ally" eases the pressure to conform. The ally does not even have to share the person's viewpoint—just breaking the unanimity of the majority is enough to reduce conformity (V. L. Allen & Levine, 1971).

The *nature of the task* is still another situational variable that affects conformity. For instance, conformity has been shown to vary with the difficulty and ambiguity of a task. When the task is difficult or poorly defined, conformity tends to be higher (Blake, Helson, & Mouton, 1956). In an ambiguous situation, people are less sure of their own opinion and more willing to conform to the majority view.

Personal characteristics also influence conforming behavior. The more a person is attracted to the group, expects to interact with its members in the future, holds a position of relatively low status, and does not feel completely accepted by the group, the more that person tends to conform. The fear of rejection apparently motivates conformity when a person scores high on one or more of these factors.

CONFORMITY ACROSS CULTURES A Chinese proverb states that "if one finger is sore, the whole hand will hurt." In a collectivist culture such as China, community and harmony are very important. Although members of all societies show a tendency to conform, you might suspect that members of collectivist cultures conform more frequently to the will of a group than do members of noncollectivist cultures. Psychologists who have studied this question have used tests similar to those used by Asch in his experiments. They have found that levels of conformity in collectivist cultures are in fact frequently higher than those found by Asch (H. Jung, 2006). In collectivist societies as diverse as Fiji, Zaire, Hong Kong, Lebanon, Zimbabwe, Kuwait, Japan, and Brazil, conformity rates ranged from 25% to 51% (P. B. Smith & Bond, 1994).

ENDURING ISSUES

Individuality–Universality   Social Influence Across Cultures

Given these somewhat conflicting data, what conclusion can we reach about the universality of social influence? The fact that rates of conformity in the Asch situation were relatively high across a variety of cultures suggests that there may be some kind of universal conformity norm. But the fact that conformity was often especially high within collectivist societies suggests that the tendency toward conformity is heightened or lessened by a specific cultural context. As psychologists gain a better understanding of the differences among cultures, the answers to the questions, "What is universal about social influence?" and "What is culturally determined?" should become clearer. ●●

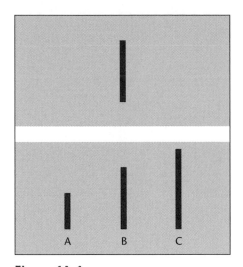

Figure 14–1
Asch's experiment on conformity.
In Asch's experiment on conformity, participants were shown a comparison card like the top one and asked to indicate which of the three lines on the bottom card was the most similar. Participants frequently chose the wrong line in order to conform to the group choice.

COMPLIANCE

How could a salesperson increase a customer's compliance in buying a product?

Conformity is a response to pressure exerted by norms that are generally left unstated. In contrast, **compliance** is a change of behavior in response to an explicitly stated request. One technique for inducing compliance is the so-called *foot-in-the-door effect* (Rodafinos, Vucevic, & Sideridis, 2005). Every salesperson knows that the moment a prospect allows the sales pitch to begin, the chances of making a sale improve greatly. The same effect operates in other areas of life: Once people have granted a small request, they are more likely to comply with a larger one.

In the most famous study of this phenomenon, Freedman and Fraser (1966) approached certain residents of Palo Alto, California, posing as members of a committee for safe driving. They asked residents to place a large, ugly sign reading "Drive Carefully" in their front yards. Only 17% agreed to do so. Then other residents were asked to sign a petition calling for more safe-driving laws. When these same people were later asked to place the ugly "Drive Carefully" sign in their yards, an amazing 55% agreed. Compliance with the first small request more than tripled the rate of compliance with the larger request.

Why does the foot-in-the-door technique work so well? One possible explanation is that agreeing to the token act (signing the petition) realigns the person's self-perception with that of someone who more strongly favors the cause. When presented with the larger request, the person then feels obligated to comply (Cialdini & Trost, 1998).

Another strategy commonly used by salespeople is the *lowball procedure* (Cialdini & Trost, 1998; Guéguen, Pascual, & Dagot, 2002). The first step is to induce a person to agree to do something. The second step is to raise the cost of compliance. Among new-car dealers, lowballing works like this: The dealer persuades the customer to buy a new car by reducing the price well below that offered by competitors. Once the customer has agreed to buy the car, however, the terms of the sale shift abruptly (for example, the trade-in value promised by the used-car manager is cut); in the end, the car is more costly than it would be at other dealerships. Despite the added costs, many customers follow through on their commitment to buy. Although the original inducement was the low price (the "lowball" that the salesperson originally pitched), once committed, the buyer remains committed to the now pricier car.

Under certain circumstances, a person who has refused to comply with one request may be more likely to comply with a second. For example, if saying no to the first request made you feel guilty, you may say yes to something else. This phenomenon has been dubbed the *door-in-the-face effect* (Cialdini, 1995; Rodafinos, Vucevic, & Sideridis, 2005). In one study, researchers approached students and asked them to make an unreasonably large commitment: Would they counsel delinquent youths at a detention center for two years? Nearly everyone declined, thus effectively "slamming the door" in the researcher's face. But when later asked to make a much smaller commitment—supervising children during a trip to the zoo—many of the same students quickly agreed. The door-in-the-face effect may work because people interpret the smaller request as a concession and feel pressured to comply.

OBEDIENCE

How does the "power of the situation" affect obedience?

Compliance is agreement to change behavior in response to a request. **Obedience** is compliance with a command. Like compliance, it is a response to an explicit message; in this case, however, the message is a direct order, generally from a person in authority, such as a police officer, principal, or parent, who can back up the command with some sort of force if necessary. Obedience embodies social influence in its most direct and powerful form.

Several of the studies by Stanley Milgram mentioned in Chapter 1, "The Science of Psychology" showed how far many people will go to obey someone in authority (Milgram, 1963; Blass, 2002; P. Meyer, 2003). People who agreed to participate in what they believed

compliance Change of behavior in response to an explicit request from another person or group.

obedience Change of behavior in response to a command from another person, typically an authority figure.

was a learning experiment administered what they thought were severe electrical shocks to the "learners." Milgram's research has been replicated in different cultures and with both male and female participants (P. B. Smith & Bond, 1999). What factors influence the degree to which people will do what they are told? Studies in which people were asked to put a dime in a parking meter by people wearing uniforms show that one important factor is the amount of power vested in the person giving the orders. People obeyed a guard whose uniform looked like that of a police officer more often than they obeyed a man dressed either as a milkman or as a civilian. Another factor is surveillance. If we are ordered to do something and then left alone, we are less likely to obey than if we are being watched, especially if the act seems unethical to us. Milgram, for instance, found that his "teachers" were less willing to give severe shocks when the experimenter was out of the room.

Milgram's experiments revealed other factors that influence a person's willingness to follow orders. When the victim was in the same room as the "teacher," obedience dropped sharply. When another "teacher" was present, who refused to give shocks, obedience also dropped. But when responsibility for an act was shared, so that the person was only one of many doing it, the degree of obedience was much greater.

Why do people willingly obey an authority figure, even if doing so means violating their own principles? Milgram (1974) suggested that people come to see themselves as the agents of *another* person's wishes and therefore as not responsible for the obedient actions or their consequences. Once this shift in self-perception has occurred, obedience follows, because in their own minds, they have relinquished control of their actions. For example, you may recall that in the aftermath of the Abu Ghraib prison scandal, the enlisted personnel who were photographed abusing prisoners insisted that they did so only on orders from higher authorities.

An alternative explanation is that perhaps obedient participants do not succumb to situational forces, but rather fail to *perceive* the situation correctly (Nissani, 1990). Thus, in Milgram's study, the participants began with the belief that the experiment would be safe and that the experimenter would be trustworthy. The real emotional struggle for the obedient participants, then, may not have been in deciding whether to obey malevolent orders, but in recognizing that a trusted authority figure proved to be treacherous.

Nazi concentration camps are a shocking example of the extremes to which people will go to obey orders. How do you explain the behaviors of the people who ran these camps?

CHECK YOUR UNDERSTANDING

1. A _____ is a shared idea or expectation about how to behave.

2. Many people are more likely to comply with a smaller request after they have refused a larger one. This is called the _____ effect.

3. Are the following statements true (T) or false (F)?

   a. ____ Research shows that compliance is often higher in collectivist cultures than in noncollectivist ones.

   b. ____ Many people are willing to obey an authority figure, even if doing so means violating their own principles.

   c. ____ Solomon Asch found that people were much more likely to conform in groups of four or more people.

   d. ____ A person is more likely to conform to the group when the group's task is ambiguous or difficult than when it is easy and clear.

Answers: 1. norm. 2. door-in-the-face. 3. a. (T), b. (T), c. (F), d. (T).

APPLY YOUR UNDERSTANDING

1. You answer the telephone and hear the caller say, "Good morning. My name is _____ and I'm calling on behalf of XYZ. How are you today?" Right away you know this caller is using which of the following social influence techniques?

   a. the lowball technique

   b. the assimilator technique

   c. the foot-in-the-door technique

   d. the door-in-the-face technique

2. You would like to say something in class. You raise your hand and wait to be recognized, even though the teacher has not told you to do so. This is an example of

   a. compliance.

   b. conformity.

   c. obedience.

Answers: 1. c. 2. b.

Social Action

Do we behave differently when other people are present?

The various kinds of social influence we have just discussed may take place even when no one else is physically present. We refrain from playing our stereo at full volume when our neighbors are sleeping, comply with jury notices received in the mail, and obey traffic signals even when no one is on the road to enforce them. We now turn to processes that *do* depend on the presence of others. Specifically, we examine processes that occur when people interact one on one and in groups. One of these social actions is called *deindividuation*.

DEINDIVIDUATION

What negative outcomes can result from deindividuation?

We have seen several cases of social influence in which people act differently in the presence of others from the way they would if they were alone. The most striking and frightening instance of this phenomenon is *mob behavior*. Some well-known violent examples of mob behavior are the beatings and lynchings of African Americans, the looting that sometimes accompanies urban rioting, and the wanton destruction of property that mars otherwise peaceful protests and demonstrations. One reason for mob behavior is that people can lose their personal sense of responsibility in a group, especially in a group subjected to intense pressures and anxiety. This process is called **deindividuation**, because people respond not as individuals, but as anonymous parts of a larger group. In general, the more anonymous that people feel in a group, the less responsible that they feel as individuals (Aronson, Wilson, & Akert, 2005). Perhaps feelings of anonymity emboldened people to yell hate-filled comments at Sher Singh as he was led away under arrest.

But deindividuation only partly explains mob behavior. Another contributing factor is that, in a group, one dominant and persuasive person can convince people to act through a *snowball effect*: If the persuader convinces just a few people, those few will convince others, who will convince still others, and the group becomes an unthinking mob. Moreover, large groups provide *protection*. Anonymity makes it difficult to press charges. If 2, or even 10, people start smashing windows, they will probably be arrested. If a thousand people do so, very few of them will be caught or punished.

deindividuation A loss of personal sense of responsibility in a group.

HELPING BEHAVIOR

What factors make us more inclined to help a person in need?

Research on deindividuation seems to support the unfortunate—and inaccurate—notion that when people get together, they become more destructive and irresponsible than they would be individually. But human society depends on people's willingness to work together and help one another. In fact, instances of cooperation and mutual assistance are just as abundant as examples of human conflict and hostility. We need only to recall the behavior of people all over the United States in the aftermath of the September 11, 2001, terrorist attacks on the World Trade Center and the Pentagon to find hundreds of examples of people working together and helping each other (Ballie, 2001). If, as we saw in Chapter 8, "Motivation and Emotion," our willingness to harm others is influenced by social forces, so is our willingness to help others.

After natural disasters like hurricane Katrina, which swept New Orleans in 2005, strangers often reach out to help each other with physical and financial support.

What are some of the social forces that can promote helping behavior? One is perceived self-interest. We offer our boss a ride home from the office because we know that our next promotion depends on how much she likes us. We volunteer to feed a neighbor's cat while he is away because we want him to do the same for us. But when helpful actions are not linked to such personal gain, they are considered **altruistic behavior** (Batson & Powell, 2003). A person who acts in an altruistic way does not expect any recognition or reward in return, except perhaps the good feeling that comes from helping someone in need. For example, many altruistic acts are directed toward strangers in the form of anonymous charitable donations, as is often demonstrated in the aftermath of a natural disaster.

Under what conditions is helping behavior most likely to occur? Like other things that social psychologists study, helping is influenced by two sets of factors: those in the situation and those in the individual.

The most important situational variable is the *presence of other people*. In a phenomenon called the **bystander effect**, the likelihood that a person will help someone else in trouble *decreases* as the number of bystanders present increases (Clarkson, 1996; Chekroun & Brauer, 2002). In one experiment, people filling out a questionnaire heard a taped "emergency" in the next room, complete with a crash and screams. Of those who were alone, 70% offered help to the unseen female victim, but of those who waited with a companion—a stranger who did nothing to help—only 7% offered help (Latané & Rodin, 1969).

Another key aspect of the situation is its *ambiguity*. Any factors that make it harder for others to recognize a genuine emergency reduce the probability of altruistic actions (R. D. Clark & Word, 1974; Jex, Adams, & Bachrach, 2003). The *personal characteristics* of bystanders also affect helping behavior. Not all bystanders are equally likely to help a stranger. Increasing the amount of personal responsibility that one person feels for another boosts the likelihood that help will be extended (Moriarty, 1975; Ting & Piliavin, 2000). The amount of *empathy* that we feel toward another person affects our willingness to help, too (Batson, Ahmad, Lishner, & Tsang, 2002; Batson & Ahmad, 2001). *Mood* also makes a difference: A person in a good mood is more likely to help another in need than is someone who is in a neutral or bad mood (Salovey, Mayer, & Rosenhan, 1991; Aronson, Wilson, & Akert, 2005). In addition, helping behavior is more likely to come from people who are not shy or fear negative evaluation for helping (Karakashian, Walter, Christopher, & Lucas, 2006). Finally, when others are watching, people who score high on the need for approval are more likely to help than are low scorers (Jonas, Schimel, Greenberg, & Pyszczynski, 2002; Satow, 1975).

HELPING BEHAVIOR ACROSS CULTURES People often assume that there is a "helping personality" or a set of traits that determines who is helpful and who is not. This is unlikely. Several conditions, both individual and situational, combine to determine when help will be offered. Similarly, it is doubtful that there is such a thing as a "helpful culture"—that is,

altruistic behavior Helping behavior that is not linked to personal gain.

bystander effect The tendency for an individual's helpfulness in an emergency to decrease as the number of passive bystanders increases.

THINKING CRITICALLY ABOUT . . .

Helping Someone in Distress

On August 18, 1999, 24-year-old Kevin Heisinger was on his way home to Illinois from the University of Michigan. In the bathroom of a bus station, he was attacked and beaten to death. Several people were within earshot and heard his cries for help, but none of them helped him or called the police. One person saw him lying on the floor in a pool of blood, but he did nothing. Another person saw him struggling to breathe, but he also walked away. Eventually, a 12-year-old boy called for help. The police arrived in less than 20 seconds, but it was too late to save Kevin's life.

- What factors might have contributed to the unwillingness of people to help Kevin during and after the beating?

- One commentator writing for *The Detroit News* said, "Have our souls been this coarsened, this deadened, by the daily barrage of real and imaginary violence? Or have some of us become like a couple of the contestants on that summer television hit, *Survivor,* so consumed with winning our own pot of gold that we really don't care how we treat others?" (DeRamus, 2000). To what extent do you think the failure of bystanders to help was due to personal characteristics?

- Do your answers to the questions above shed light on the question of why a 12-year-old was the only person to call for help?

a society, nation, or group whose members are invariably "more helpful" than those of other groups. Psychologists have instead focused on the cultural factors that make helping more or less likely to take place.

Individualism–collectivism is an important dimension in this area: It seems plausible that members of individualist cultures feel less obligated to help other people than do members of collectivist cultures. A study using Indian and American participants investigated this possibility (J. G. Miller, Bersoff, & Harwood, 1990). Participants were presented with helping scenarios involving either a stranger, a friend, or a close relative whose need was either minor, moderate, or extreme. There were no cultural differences in cases of extreme need; members of both cultures reported being equally willing to help. But the two groups differed in cases of minor needs. Almost three times as many Indians (from a collectivist culture) as Americans (from an individualist culture) felt obligated to help in a scenario involving a close friend or a stranger asking for minor assistance. Even within collectivist cultures, however, the prediction of when help will be offered can be problematic (Triandis, 1994, 2001). Some members of collectivist societies are reluctant to offer help to anyone outside their in-group. They are therefore less likely to help strangers. Other cultures treat a stranger as a member of their group until that person's exact status can be determined.

GROUPS AND DECISION MAKING

How is making a decision in a group different from making a decision on your own?

There is a tendency in American society to turn important decisions over to groups. In the business world, key decisions are often made around a conference table rather than behind one person's desk. In politics, major policy decisions are seldom vested in just one person. Groups of advisers, cabinet officers, committee members, or aides meet to deliberate and forge a course of action. In the courts, a defendant may request a trial by jury, and for some serious crimes, jury trial is required by law. The nine-member U.S. Supreme Court renders group decisions on legal issues affecting the entire nation.

Many people trust these group decisions more than decisions made by individuals. Yet, the dynamics of social interaction within groups sometimes conspire to make group decisions *less* sound than those made by someone acting alone. Social psychologists are intrigued by how this outcome happens.

POLARIZATION IN GROUP DECISION MAKING People often assume that an individual acting alone is more likely to take risks than a group considering the same issue. This assumption remained unchallenged until the early 1960s. At that time, James Stoner (1961) designed an experiment to test the idea. He asked participants individually to counsel imaginary people who had to choose between a risky, but potentially rewarding course of action and a conservative, but less rewarding alternative. Next, the participants met in small groups to discuss each decision until they reached unanimous agreement. Surprisingly, the groups consistently recommended a riskier course of action than the people working alone did. This phenomenon is known as the **risky shift**.

The risky shift is simply one aspect of a more general group phenomenon called **polarization**—the tendency for people to become more extreme in their attitudes as a

risky shift Greater willingness of a group than an individual to take substantial risks.

polarization Shift in attitudes by members of a group toward more extreme positions than the ones held before group discussion.

result of group discussion. Polarization begins when group members discover during discussion that they share views to a greater degree than they realized. Then, in an effort to be seen in a positive light by the others, at least some group members become strong advocates for what is potentially the dominant sentiment in the group. Arguments leaning toward one extreme or the other not only reassure people that their initial attitudes are correct, but they also intensify those attitudes so that the group as a whole becomes more extreme in its position (J. H. Liu & Latane, 1998). So, if you want a group decision to be made in a cautious, conservative direction, you should be certain that the members of the group hold cautious and conservative views in the first place. Otherwise, the group decision may polarize in the opposite direction.

THE EFFECTIVENESS OF GROUPS "Two heads are better than one" reflects the common assumption that members of a group will pool their abilities and arrive at a better decision than will individuals working alone. In fact, groups are more effective than individuals only under certain circumstances (Turner, 2001). For one thing, their success depends on the task they face. If the requirements of the task match the skills of the group members, the group is likely to be more effective than any single individual.

Groups can make decisions and perform tasks very effectively under the right conditions.

Even if task and personnel are perfectly matched, however, the ways in which group members *interact* may reduce the group's efficiency. For example, high-status individuals tend to exert more influence in groups, so if they do not possess the best problem-solving skills, group decisions may suffer (Lovaglia, Mannix, Samuelson, Sell, & Wilson, 2005). Another factor affecting group interaction and effectiveness is group size. The larger the group, the more likely it is to include someone who has the skills needed to solve a difficult problem. On the other hand, it is much harder to coordinate the activities of a large group. In addition, large groups may be more likely to encourage *social loafing*, the tendency of group members to exert less individual effort on the assumption that others in the group will do the work (J. A. Miller, 2002). Finally, the quality of group decision making also depends on the *cohesiveness* of a group. When the people in a group like one another and feel committed to the goals of the group, cohesiveness is high. Under these conditions, members may work hard for the group, spurred by high morale. But cohesiveness can undermine the quality of group decision making. If the group succumbs to *groupthink*, according to Irving Janis (1982, 1989), strong pressure to conform prevents its members from criticizing the emerging group consensus (Henningsen, Henningsen, & Eden, 2006). In such a group, amiability and morale supersede judgment. Members with doubts may hesitate to express them. The result may be disastrous decisions—such as the Bay of Pigs invasion, the Watergate burglary and cover-up, or the ill-fated *Columbia* and *Challenger* space flights (Kruglanski, 1986; Raven, 1998; Vaughn, 1996).

LEADERSHIP

What makes a great leader?

Every group has a leader, but how do group leaders come to the fore? For many years, the predominant answer was the **great-person theory**, which states that leaders are extraordinary people who assume positions of influence and then shape events around them. In this view, people like George Washington, Winston Churchill, and Nelson Mandela were "born leaders"—who would have led any nation at any time in history.

Most historians and psychologists now regard this theory as naive, because it ignores social and economic factors. An alternative theory holds that leadership emerges when the right person is in the right place at the right time. For instance, in the late 1950s and early 1960s, Dr. Martin Luther King, Jr., rose to lead the Black civil rights movement. Dr. King was clearly a "great person"—intelligent, dynamic, eloquent, and highly motivated. Yet, had the times not been right (for instance, had he lived 30 years earlier), it is doubtful that he would have been as successful as he was.

Recently, social scientists have argued that there is more to leadership than either the great-person theory or the right-place-at-the-right-time theory implies. Rather, the

great-person theory The theory that leadership is a result of personal qualities and traits that qualify one to lead others.

One theory of leadership holds that the particularly effective leader is the right person in the right place at the right time. For the American civil rights movement, Martin Luther King, Jr., was such a leader.

leader's traits, certain aspects of the situation in which the group finds itself, and the response of the group and the leader to each other are all important considerations (Bennis, Spreitzer, & Cummings, 2001). Fred Fiedler's *contingency theory* of leader effectiveness is based on such a transactional view of leadership (Fiedler, 1993, 2002).

According to Fiedler's theory, personal characteristics are important to the success of a leader. One kind of leader is *task oriented*, concerned with doing the task well—even at the expense of worsening relationships among group members. Other leaders are *relationship oriented*, concerned with maintaining group cohesiveness and harmony. Which style is most effective depends on three sets of situational factors. One is the nature of the task (whether it is clearly structured or ambiguous). The second consideration is the relationship between leader and group (whether the leader has good or bad personal relations with the group members). The third consideration is the leader's ability to exercise great or little power over the group.

Fiedler has shown that if conditions are either very favorable (good leader–member relations, structured tasks, high leader power) or very unfavorable (poor leader–member relations, unstructured task, low leader power) for the leader, the most effective leader is the one who is task oriented. However, when conditions within the group are only moderately favorable for the leader, the most effective leader is one who is concerned about maintaining good interpersonal relations.

The contingency view of leadership, which has received a great deal of support from research conducted in the laboratory as well as in real-life settings, clearly indicates that there is no such thing as an ideal leader for all situations (Ayman et al., 1998; DeYoung, 2005; Graen & Hui, 2001; Hughes, Ginnett, & Curphy, 1998). "Except perhaps for the unusual case," Fiedler states, "it is simply not meaningful to speak of an effective or of an ineffective leader; we can only speak of a leader who tends to be effective in one situation and ineffective in another" (Fiedler, 1967, p. 261). We discuss contingency theories of leadership in greater detail in Appendix B, "Psychology Applied to Work."

LEADERSHIP ACROSS CULTURES The distinction between task-oriented and relationship-oriented leaders seems to be a main operating principle in most work groups in the United States. Someone who is explicitly appointed as a manager or crew chief is charged with making sure that the job gets done, whereas someone else usually emerges informally to act as the relationship-oriented specialist who tells jokes, remembers everyone's birthday, smoothes disputes, and generally maintains morale. In the Western world, this division of leadership often operates in informal social groups as well. Yet, it is not the only approach to leadership. Consider a collectivist culture that values cooperation and interdependence among group members. In such an environment, it is unlikely that individuals would emerge to serve specific functions within a group. Although one member may be named "the manager," there is less need for individuals to have clearly defined roles as "this type of leader" or "that type of leader." All members see themselves as working together to accomplish the group's goals.

Leadership in American businesses has undergone a transformation through the introduction of a management style that has proven successful in Japan and other Eastern collectivist cultures (J. W. Dean & Evans, 1994; McFarland, Senn, & Childress, 1993). This approach emphasizes decision-making input from all group members, small work teams that promote close cooperation, and a leadership style in which managers receive much the same treatment as any other employee. In the West, it is not uncommon for executives to have their own parking spaces, dining facilities, and fitness and social clubs, as well as separate offices and independent schedules. Most Japanese executives consider this privileged style of management very strange. In many Eastern cultures, managers and executives share the same facilities as their workers, hunt for parking spaces like everyone else, and eat and work side by side with their employees. It is interesting that the Japanese model has effectively combined the two leadership approaches—task oriented and relationship oriented—into a single overall style. By being a part of the group, the leader can simultaneously work toward and direct the group's goals, while also contributing to the group's morale and social climate.

WOMEN IN LEADERSHIP POSITIONS Just as leadership styles differ across cultures, research has shown that the leadership styles of men and women can also vary considerably. In one five-year study of 2,482 managers in more than 400 organizations, female and male coworkers said that women make better managers than men (Kass, 1999). The reason seems to be that female managers have added such traditionally "masculine" task-oriented traits as decisiveness, planning, and setting standards to such "feminine" relationship-oriented assets as communication, feedback, and empowering other employees, whereas male managers still rely on an autocratic style that emphasizes individual competition and achievement (Eagly, 2003). For example, one review concluded that, in contrast to the directive and task-oriented leadership style common among men, women tend to have a more democratic, collaborative, and interpersonally oriented style of managing employees (V. E. O'Leary & Flanagan, 2001). Moreover, a woman's more collaborate style of leadership is often able to overcome any preconceived resistance to their leadership (Lips, 2002).

Another large-scale review of 45 studies of gender and leadership found women's leadership styles are generally more effective than traditional male leadership styles (Eagly, Johannesen-Schmidt, & van-Engen, 2003). This review found that female leaders are generally more effective than male leaders at winning acceptance for their ideas and instilling self-confidence in their employees (Lips, 2002). Results like these have prompted some experts to call for specialized women-only leadership training programs, to assist women in developing their full feminine leadership potential independent of male influence (Vinnicombe & Singh, 2003).

KEY TERMS

social psychology, *p. 483*

Social Cognition

social cognition, *p. 484*
primacy effect, *p. 484*
self-fulfilling prophecy, *p. 485*
stereotype, *p. 485*
attribution theory, *p. 486*
fundamental attribution
  error, *p. 487*
defensive attribution, *p. 487*

just-world
  hypothesis, *p. 487*
proximity, *p. 488*
exchange, *p. 490*
equity, *p. 490*

Attitudes

attitude, *p. 492*
self-monitoring, *p. 492*
prejudice, *p. 493*
discrimination, *p. 493*

frustration–aggression
  theory, *p. 494*
authoritarian personality, *p. 494*
racism, *p. 495*
cognitive dissonance, *p. 499*

Social Influence

social influence, *p. 501*
cultural truisms, *p. 502*
norm, *p. 502*
conformity, *p. 502*

compliance, *p. 504*
obedience, *p. 504*

Social Action

deindividuation, *p. 506*
altruistic behavior, *p. 507*
bystander effect, *p. 508*
risky shift, *p. 508*
polarization, *p. 508*
great-person theory, *p. 509*

CHAPTER REVIEW

Social Cognition

What do forming impressions, explaining others' behavior, and experiencing interpersonal attraction have in common? Forming impressions, explaining others' behavior, and experiencing interpersonal attraction are all examples of **social cognition**, the process of taking in and assessing information about other people. It is one way in which we are influenced by others' thoughts, feelings, and behaviors.

How do we form first impressions of people? When forming impressions of others, we rely on *schemata,* or sets of expectations and beliefs about categories of people. Impressions are also affected by the order in which information is acquired. First impressions are the strongest (the **primacy effect**), probably because we prefer not to subsequently expend more cognitive effort to analyze or change them. This same preference also encourages us to form impressions

by using simplistic, but strongly held schemata called **stereotypes**. First impressions can also bring about the behavior we expect from other people, a process known as **self-fulfilling prophecy**.

How do we decide why people act as they do? **Attribution theory** holds that people seek to understand human behavior by attributing it either to internal or external causes. Perceptual biases can lead to the **fundamental attribution error**, in which we overemphasize others' personal traits in attributing causes to their behavior. **Defensive attribution** motivates us to explain our own actions in ways that protect our self-esteem. *Self-serving bias* refers to our tendency to attribute our successes to internal factors and our failures to external ones. The **just-world hypothesis** may lead us to blame the victim when bad things happen to other people.

Do "birds of a feather flock together" or do "opposites attract"? People who are similar in attitudes, interests, backgrounds, and values tend to like one another. **Proximity** also promotes liking. The more we are in contact with certain people, the more we tend to like them. We also tend to like people who make us feel appreciated and rewarded, an idea based on the concept of **exchange**. Exchanges work only insofar as they are fair or equitable. A relationship is based on **equity** when both individuals receive equally from each other. Most people also tend to like physically attractive people, as well as attributing to them, correctly or not, many positive personal characteristics.

Attitudes

Why are attitudes important? An **attitude** is a relatively stable organization of beliefs, feelings, and tendencies toward an *attitude object*. Attitudes are important because they often influence behavior.

What are the three major components of attitudes? The three major components of attitudes are (1) evaluative beliefs about the attitude object, (2) feelings about that object, and (3) behavioral tendencies toward it. These three components are very often (but not always) consistent with one another.

How does a person develop a prejudice toward someone else? **Prejudice** is an unfair negative attitude directed toward a group and its members, whereas **discrimination** is unfair behavior based on prejudice. One explanation of prejudice is the **frustration–aggression theory**, which states that people who feel exploited and oppressed displace their hostility toward the powerful onto *scapegoats*—people who are "lower" on the social scale than they are. Another theory links prejudice to the **authoritarian personality**, a rigidly conventional and bigoted type marked by exaggerated respect for authority and hostility toward those who defy society's norms. A third theory proposes a cognitive source of prejudice—oversimplified or stereotyped thinking about categories of people. Finally, conformity to the prejudices of one's social group can help to explain prejudice. Three strategies for reducing prejudice appear to be especially promising: recategorization (expanding our schema of a particular group), controlled processing (training ourselves to be mindful of people who differ from us), and improving contact between groups.

What factors encourage someone to change an attitude? Attitudes may be changed when new actions, beliefs, or perceptions contradict preexisting attitudes, called **cognitive dissonance**. Attitudes can also change in response to efforts at persuasion. The first step in persuasion is to get the audience's attention. Then the task is to get the audience to comprehend and accept the message. According to the *communication model*, persuasion is a function of the source, the message itself, the medium of communication, and the characteristics of the audience. The most effective means of changing attitudes—especially important attitudes, behaviors, or lifestyle choices—may be *self-persuasion*.

Social Influence

What are some areas in which the power of social influence is highly apparent? **Social influence** is the process by which people's perceptions, attitudes, and actions are affected by others' behavior and characteristics. The power of social influence is especially apparent in the study of cultural influences and of conformity, compliance, and obedience.

How does your culture influence how you dress or what you eat? The culture in which you are immersed has an enormous influence on your thoughts and actions. Culture dictates differences in diet, dress, and personal space. One result of this is the unquestioning acceptance of **cultural truisms**—beliefs or values that most members of a society accept as self-evident. Eating pizza, shunning rattlesnake meat, dressing in jeans instead of a loincloth, and feeling uncomfortable when others stand very close to you when they speak are all results of culture. As we adapt our behavior to that of others, we learn the **norms** of our culture, as well as its beliefs and values.

What increases the likelihood that someone will conform? Voluntarily yielding one's preferences, beliefs, or judgments to those of a larger group is called **conformity**. Research by Solomon Asch and others has shown that characteristics of both the situation and the person influence the likelihood of conforming. Cultural influences on the tendency to conform also exist, with people in collectivist cultures often being more prone to conformity than those in noncollectivist ones.

How could a salesperson increase a customer's compliance in buying a product? **Compliance** is a change in behavior in response to someone's explicit request.. One technique to encourage compliance is the *foot-in-the-door approach*, or getting people to go along with a small request to make them more likely to comply with a larger one. Another technique is the *lowball procedure*: initially offering a low price to win commitment, and then gradually escalating the cost. Also effective is the *door-in-the-face tactic*, or initially making an unreasonable request that is bound to be turned down but will perhaps generate enough guilt to foster compliance with another request.

How does the "power of the situation" affect obedience? Classic research by Stanley Milgram showed that many people were willing to obey orders to administer harmful shocks to other people. This **obedience** to an authority figure was more likely when certain situational factors were present. For example, people found it harder to disobey when the authority figure issuing the order was nearby. They were also more likely to obey the command when the person being given the shock was some distance from them. According to Milgram, obedience is brought on by the constraints of the situation.

Social Action

Do we behave differently when other people are present? Conformity, compliance, and obedience may take place even when no one else is physically present, but other processes of social influence depend on the presence of others.

What negative outcomes can result from deindividuation? Immersion in a large, anonymous group may lead to **deindividuation**, the loss of a sense of personal responsibility for one's actions. Deindividuation can sometimes lead to violence or other forms of irresponsible behavior. The greater the sense of anonymity, the more this effect occurs.

What factors make us more inclined to help a person in need? Helping someone in need without expectation of a reward is called

altruistic behavior. Altruism is influenced by situational factors such as the presence of other people. According to the **bystander effect**, a person is less apt to offer assistance when other potential helpers are present. Conversely, being the only person to spot someone in trouble tends to encourage helping. Also encouraging helping are an unambiguous emergency situation and certain personal characteristics, such as empathy for the victim and being in a good mood.

How is making a decision in a group different from making a decision on your own? Research on the **risky shift** and the broader phenomenon of group **polarization** shows that group decision making actually increases tendencies toward extreme solutions, encouraging members to lean toward either greater risk or greater caution. People deliberating in groups may also display *social loafing*, or a tendency to exert less effort on the assumption that others will do most of the work. And in very cohesive groups, there is a tendency toward *groupthink*, an unwillingness to criticize the emerging group consensus even when it seems misguided.

What makes a great leader? According to the **great-person theory**, leadership is a function of personal traits that qualify one to lead others. An alternative theory attributes leadership to being in the right place at the right time. According to the transactional view, traits of the leader and traits of the group interact with certain aspects of the situation to determine what kind of leader will come to the fore. Fred Fiedler's *contingency theory* focused on two contrasting leadership styles: task oriented and relationship oriented. The effectiveness of each style depends on the nature of the task, the relationship of the leader with group members, and the leader's power over the group.

The task-oriented leadership style typical of American businesses is being transformed through the introduction of a management style that emphasizes small work teams and input from all members of the group. Recent research indicates that women in leadership positions tend to have a more democratic, collaborative, and interpersonally oriented style of managing employees than do men in similar positions.

APPENDIX A: Measurement and Statistical Methods

Overview

Most of the experiments described in this book involve measuring one or more variables and then analyzing the data statistically. The design and scoring of all the tests we have discussed are also based on statistical methods. **Statistics** is a branch of mathematics that provides techniques for sorting out quantitative facts and ways of drawing conclusions from them. Statistics let us organize and describe data quickly, guide the conclusions we draw, and help us make inferences.

Statistical analysis is essential to conducting an experiment or designing a test, but statistics can only handle numbers—groups of them. To use statistics, the psychologist first must measure things—count and express them in quantities.

Scales of Measurement

No matter what we are measuring—height, noise, intelligence, attitudes—we have to use a scale. The data we want to collect determine the scale we will use and, in turn, the scale we use helps determine the conclusions we can draw from our data.

NOMINAL SCALES A **nominal scale** is a set of arbitrarily named or numbered categories. If we decide to classify a group of people by the color of their eyes, we are using a nominal scale. We can count how many people have blue, green, or brown eyes, and so on, but we cannot say that one group has more or less eye color than the other. The colors are simply different. Since a nominal scale is more of a way of classifying than of measuring, it is the least informative kind of scale. If we want to compare our data more precisely, we will have to use a scale that tells us more.

ORDINAL SCALES If we list horses in the order in which they finish a race, we are using an ordinal scale. On an **ordinal scale**, data are ranked from first to last according to some criterion. An ordinal scale tells the order, but nothing about the distances between what is ranked first and second or ninth and tenth. It does not tell us how much faster the winning horse ran than the horses that placed or showed. If a person ranks her preferences for various kinds of soup—pea soup first, then tomato, then onion, and so on—we know what soup she likes most and what soup she likes least, but we have no idea how much better she likes tomato than onion, or if pea soup is far more favored than either one of them.

Since we do not know the distances between the items ranked on an ordinal scale, we cannot add or subtract ordinal data. If mathematical operations are necessary, we need a still more informative scale.

INTERVAL SCALES An **interval scale** is often compared to a ruler that has been broken off at the bottom—it only goes from, say, $5\text{-}1/2$ to 12. The intervals between 6 and 7, 7 and 8, 8 and 9, and so forth are equal, but there is no zero. A Fahrenheit or centigrade thermometer is an interval scale—even though a certain degree registered on such thermometer specifies a certain state of cold or heat, there is no such thing as the absence of temperature. One day is never twice as hot as another; it is only so many equal degrees hotter.

An interval scale tells us how many equal-size units one thing lies above or below another thing of the same kind, but it does not tell us how many times bigger, smaller, taller, or fatter one thing is than another. An intelligence test cannot tell us that one person is three times as intelligent as another, only that he or she scored so many points above or below someone else.

RATIO SCALES We can only say that a measurement is two times as long as another or three times as high when we use a **ratio scale**, one that has a true zero. For instance, if we measure the snowfall in a certain area over several winters, we can say that six times as much snow fell during the winter in which we measured a total of 12 feet as during a winter in which only 2 feet fell. This scale has a zero—there can be no snow.

Measurements of Central Tendency

Usually, when we measure a number of instances of anything—from the popularity of TV shows to the weights of 8-year-old boys to the number of times a person's optic nerve fires in response to electrical stimulation—we get a distribution of measurements that range from smallest to largest or lowest to highest. The measurements will usually cluster around some value near the middle. This value is the **central tendency** of the distribution of the measurements.

Suppose, for example, you want to keep 10 children busy tossing rings around a bottle. You give them three rings to toss each turn, the game has six rounds, and each player scores one point every time he or she gets the ring around the neck of the bottle. The highest possible score is 18. The distribution of scores might end up like this: 11, 8, 13, 6, 12, 10, 16, 9, 12, 3.

What could you quickly say about the ring-tossing talent of the group? First, you could arrange the scores from lowest to highest: 3, 6, 8, 9, 10, 11, 12, 12, 13, and 16. In this order, the central tendency of the distribution of scores becomes clear. Many of the scores cluster around the values between 8 and 12. There are three ways to describe the central tendency of a distribution. We usually refer to all three as the *average*.

The arithmetical average is called the **mean**—the sum of all the scores in the group divided by the number of scores. If you add up all the scores and divide by 10, the total number of scores in this group of ring tossers, you find that the mean for the group is 10.

The **median** is the point that divides a distribution in half—50 % of the scores fall above the median, and 50 % fall below. In the ring-tossing scores, five scores fall at 10 or below, five at 11 or above. The median is thus halfway between 10 and 11, which is 10.5.

The point at which the largest number of scores occurs is called the **mode**. In our example, the mode is 12. More people scored 12 than any other.

DIFFERENCES AMONG THE MEAN, MEDIAN, AND MODE

If we take many measurements of anything, we are likely to get a distribution of scores in which the mean, median, and mode are all about the same—the score that occurs most often (the mode) will also be the point that half the scores are below and half above (the median). And the same point will be the arithmetical average (the mean). This is not always true, of course, and small samples rarely come out so symmetrically. In these cases, we often have to decide which of the three measures of central tendency—the mean, the median, or mode—will tell us what we want to know.

statistics A branch of mathematics that psychologists use to organize and analyze data.

nominal scale A set of categories for classifying objects.

ordinal scale Scale indicating order or relative position of items according to some criterion.

interval scale Scale with equal distances between the points or values, but without a true zero.

ratio scale Scale with equal distances between the points or values and with a true zero.

central tendency Tendency of scores to congregate around some middle value.

mean Arithmetical average calculated by dividing a sum of values by the total number of cases.

median Point that divides a set of scores in half.

mode Point at which the largest number of scores occurs.

For example, a shopkeeper wants to know the general incomes of passersby so he can stock the right merchandise. He might conduct a rough survey by standing outside his store for a few days from 12:00 to 2:00 and asking every tenth person who walks by to check a card showing the general range of his or her income. Suppose most of the people checked the ranges between $25,000 and $60,000 a year. However, a couple of the people made a lot of money—one checked $100,000–$150,000 and the other checked the $250,000-or-above box. The mean for the set of income figures would be pushed higher by those two large figures and would not really tell the shopkeeper what he wants to know about his potential customers. In this case, he would be wiser to use the median or the mode.

Suppose instead of meeting two people whose incomes were so great, he noticed that people from two distinct income groups walked by his store—several people checked the box for $25,000–$35,000, and several others checked $50,000–$60,000. The shopkeeper would find that his distribution was bimodal. It has two modes—$30,000 and $55,000. This might be more useful to him than the mean, which could lead him to think his customers were a unit with an average income of about $40,000.

Another way of approaching a set of scores is to arrange them into a **frequency distribution**—that is, to select a set of intervals and count how many scores fall into each interval. A frequency distribution is useful for large groups of numbers; it puts the number of individual scores into more manageable groups.

Suppose a psychologist tests memory. She asks 50 college students to learn 18 nonsense syllables, then records how many syllables each student can recall two hours later. She arranges her raw scores from lowest to highest in a rank distribution:

2	6	8	10	11	14
3	7	9	10	12	14
4	7	9	10	12	15
4	7	9	10	12	16
5	7	9	10	13	17
5	7	9	11	13	
6	8	9	11	13	
6	8	9	11	13	
6	8	10	11	13	

The scores range from 2 to 17, but 50 individual scores are too cumbersome to work with. So she chooses a set of two-point intervals and tallies the number of scores in each interval:

Interval	Tally	Frequency
1–2		1
3–4		3
5–6		6
7–8		9
9–10		13
11–12		8
13–14		7
15–16		2
17–18		1

frequency distribution A count of the number of scores that fall within each of a series of intervals.

frequency histogram Type of bar graph that shows frequency distributions.

frequency polygon Type of line graph that shows frequency distributions.

Now she can tell at a glance what the results of her experiment were. Most of the students had scores near the middle of the range, and very few had scores in the high or low intervals. She can see these results even better if she uses the frequency distribution to construct a bar graph—a **frequency histogram**. Marking the intervals along the horizontal axis and the frequencies along the vertical axis would give her the graph shown in **Figure A–1**. Another way is to construct a **frequency polygon**, a line graph. A frequency polygon drawn from the same

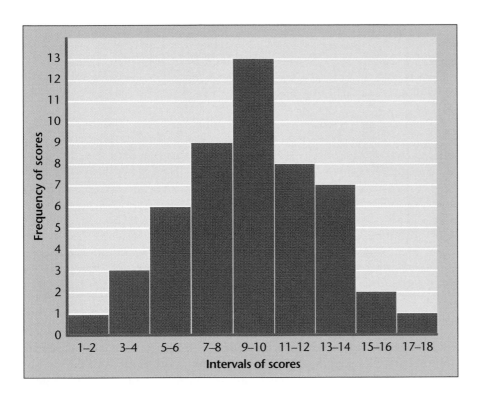

Figure A–1
A frequency histogram for a memory experiment.
The bars indicate the frequency of scores within each interval.

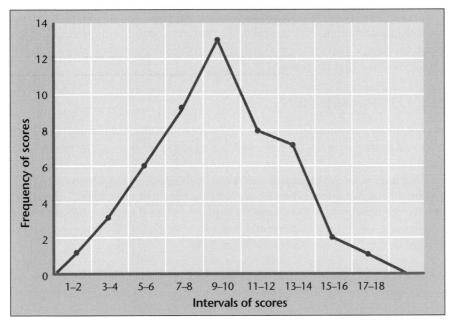

Figure A–2
A frequency polygon drawn from data used in Figure A–1.
The dots, representing the frequency of scores in each interval, are connected by straight lines.

set of data is shown in **Figure A–2**. Note that the figure is not a smooth curve, since the points are connected by straight lines. With many scores, however, and with small intervals, the angles would smooth out, and the figure would resemble a rounded curve.

The Normal Curve

Ordinarily, if we take enough measurements of almost anything, we get a *normal distribution*. Tossing coins is a favorite example of statisticians. If you tossed 10 coins into the air 1,000 times and recorded the heads and tails on each toss, your tabulations would reveal a normal distribution. Five heads and five tails would be the most frequent, followed by four heads/ six tails and six heads/six tails, and so on down to the rare all heads or all tails.

Figure A-3
A normal curve.
This curve is based on measurements of the heights of 1,000 adult males.

Source: From Hill, 1966.

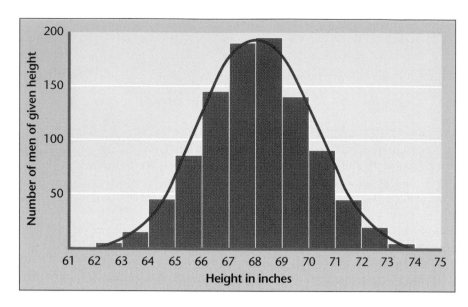

Figure A-4
A skewed distribution.
Most of the scores are gathered at the high end of the distribution, causing the hump to shift to the right. Since the tail on the left is longer, we say that the curve is skewed to the left. Note that the *mean, median,* and *mode* are different.

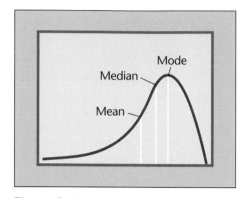

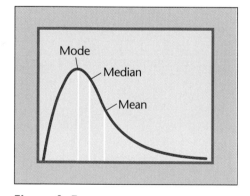

Figure A-5
In this distribution, most of the scores are gathered at the low end, so the curve is skewed to the right. The *mean, median,* and *mode* do not coincide.

Plotting a normal distribution on a graph yields a particular kind of frequency polygon, called a **normal curve. Figure A-3** shows data on the heights of 1,000 men. Superimposed over the bars that reflect the actual data is an "ideal" normal curve for the same data. Note that the curve is absolutely symmetrical—the left slope parallels the right slope exactly. Moreover, the mean, median, and mode all fall on the highest point on the curve.

The normal curve is a hypothetical entity. No set of real measurements shows such a smooth gradation from one interval to the next, or so purely symmetrical a shape. But because so many things do approximate the normal curve so closely, the curve is a useful model for much that we measure.

SKEWED DISTRIBUTIONS

If a frequency distribution is asymmetrical—if most of the scores are gathered at either the high end or the low end—the frequency polygon will be skewed. The hump will sit to one side or the other, and one of the curve's tails will be disproportionately long.

If a high school mathematics instructor, for example, gives her students a sixth-grade arithmetic test, we would expect nearly all the scores to be quite high. The frequency polygon would probably look like the one in **Figure A-4**. But if a sixth-grade class were asked to do advanced algebra, the scores would probably be quite low. The frequency polygon would be very similar to the one shown in **Figure A-5**.

Note, too, that the mean, median, and mode fall at different points in a skewed distribution, unlike in the normal curve, where they coincide. Usually, if you know that the mean is greater than the median of a distribution, you can predict that the frequency polygon will be skewed to the right. If the median is greater than the mean, the curve will be skewed to the left.

BIMODAL DISTRIBUTIONS

We have already mentioned a bimodal distribution in our description of the shopkeeper's survey of his customers' incomes. The frequency polygon for a bimodal distribution has two humps—one for each mode. The mean and the median may be the same (**Figure A-6**) or different (**Figure A-7**).

MEASURES OF VARIATION

Sometimes it is not enough to know the distribution of a set of data and what their mean, median, and mode are. Suppose an automotive safety expert feels that too much damage occurs in tail-end accidents because automobile bumpers are not all the same height. It is

normal curve Hypothetical bell-shaped distribution curve that occurs when a normal distribution is plotted as a frequency polygon.

not enough to know what the average height of an automobile bumper is. The safety expert also wants to know about the variation in bumper heights: How much higher is the highest bumper than the mean? How do bumpers of all cars vary from the mean? Are the latest bumpers closer to the same height?

RANGE

The simplest measure of variation is the **range**—the difference between the largest and smallest measurements. Perhaps the safety expert measured the bumpers of 1,000 cars 2 years ago and found that the highest bumper was 18 inches from the ground, the lowest only 12 inches from the ground. The range was thus 6 inches—18 minus 12. This year the highest bumper is still 18 inches high, the lowest still 12 inches from the ground. The range is still 6 inches. Moreover, our safety expert finds that the means of the two distributions are the same—15 inches off the ground. But look at the two frequency polygons in **Figure A–8**—there is still something the expert needs to know, since the measurements cluster around the mean in drastically different ways. To find out how the measurements are distributed around the mean, our safety expert has to turn to a slightly more complicated measure of variation—the standard deviation.

THE STANDARD DEVIATION

The **standard deviation,** in a single number, tells us much about how the scores in any frequency distribution are dispersed around the mean. Calculating the standard deviation is one of the most useful and widely employed statistical tools.

To find the standard deviation of a set of scores, we first find the mean. Then we take the first score in the distribution, subtract it from the mean, square the difference, and jot it down in a column to be added up later. We do the same for all the scores in the distribution. Then we add up the column of squared differences, divide the total by the number of scores in the distribution, and find the square root of that number. **Figure A–9** shows the calculation of the standard deviation for a small distribution of scores.

In a normal distribution, however peaked or flattened the curve, about 68 % of the scores fall between one standard deviation above the mean and one standard deviation below the mean (see **Figure A–10**). Another 27 % fall between one standard deviation and two standard deviations on either side of the mean, and 4 percent more between the second and third standard deviations on either side. Overall, then, more than 99 % of the scores fall between three standard deviations above and three standard deviations below the mean. This makes the standard deviation useful for comparing two different normal distributions.

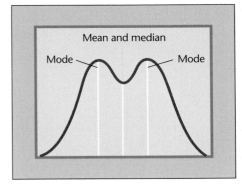

Figure A–6
A bimodal distribution in which the *mean* and the *median* are the same.

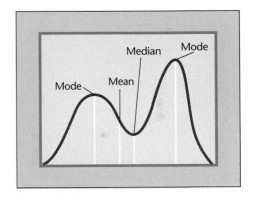

Figure A–7
In this bimodal distribution, the *mean* and the *median* are different.

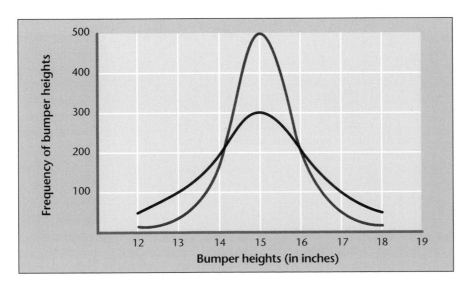

Figure A–8
Frequency polygons for two sets of measurements of automobile bumper heights.
Both are normal curves, and in each distribution the *mean, median,* and *mode* are 15. But the variation from the mean is different, causing one curve to be flattened and the other to be much more sharply peaked.

---

range Difference between the largest and smallest measurements in a distribution.

standard deviation Statistical measure of variability in a group of scores or other values.

Figure A–9

Step-by-step calculation of the *standard deviation* for a group of 10 scores with a mean of 7.

Number of scores = 10		Mean = 7
Scores	Difference from mean	Difference squared
4	7 – 4 = 3	$3^2 = 9$
5	7 – 5 = 2	$2^2 = 4$
6	7 – 6 = 1	$1^2 = 1$
6	7 – 6 = 1	$1^2 = 1$
7	7 – 7 = 0	$0^2 = 0$
7	7 – 7 = 0	$0^2 = 0$
8	7 – 8 = – 1	$-1^2 = 1$
8	7 – 8 = – 1	$-1^2 = 1$
9	7 – 9 = – 2	$-2^2 = 4$
10	7 – 10 = – 3	$-3^2 = 9$

Sum of squares = 30

÷

Number of scores = 10

Variance = 3

Standard deviation = $\sqrt{3}$ = 1.73

Figure A–10

A normal curve, divided to show the percentage of scores that fall within each *standard deviation* from the *mean*.

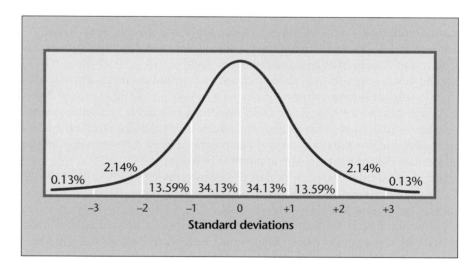

Now let us see what the standard deviation can tell our automotive safety expert about the variations from the mean in the two sets of data. The standard deviation for the cars measured two years ago is about 1.4. A car with a bumper height of 16.4 is one standard deviation above the mean of 15; one with a bumper height of 13.6 is one standard deviation below the mean. Since the engineer knows that the data fall into a normal distribution, he can figure that about 68 % of the 1,000 cars he measured will fall somewhere between these two heights: 680 cars will have bumpers between 13.6 and 16.4 inches high. For the more recent set of data, the standard deviation is just slightly less than 1. A car with a bumper height of about 14 inches is one standard deviation below the mean; a car with a bumper height of about 16 is one standard deviation above the mean. Thus, in this distribution, 680 cars have bumpers between 14 and 16 inches high. This tells the safety expert that car bumpers are becoming more similar, although the range of heights is still the same (6 inches), and the mean height of bumpers is still 15.

Measures of Correlation

Measures of central tendency and measures of variation can be used to describe a single set of measurements—like the children's ring-tossing scores—or to compare two or more sets of measurements—like the two sets of bumper heights. Sometimes, however, we need to know if two sets of measurements are in any way associated with each other—if they are correlated. Is parental IQ related to children's IQ? Does the need for achievement relate to the need for power? Is watching violence on TV related to aggressive behavior?

One fast way to determine whether two variables are correlated is to draw a **scatter plot.** We assign one variable (X) to the horizontal axis of a graph, the other variable (Y) to the vertical axis. Then we plot a person's score on one characteristic along the horizontal axis and his or her score on the second characteristic along the vertical axis. Where the two scores intersect, we draw a dot. When several scores have been plotted in this way, the pattern of dots tells whether the two characteristics are in any way correlated with each other.

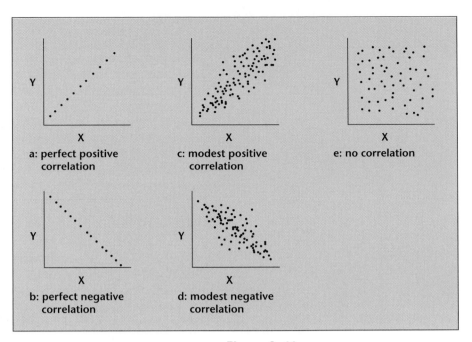

If the dots on a scatter plot form a straight line running between the lower-left-hand corner and the upper-right-hand corner, as they do in **Figure A–11a**, we have a perfect positive correlation—a high score on one of the characteristics is always associated with a high score on the other one. A straight line running between the upper-left-hand corner and the lower-right-hand corner, as in **Figure A–11b**, is the sign of a perfect negative correlation—a high score on one of the characteristics is always associated with a low score on the other one. If the pattern formed by the dots is cigar shaped in either of these directions, as in **Figures A–11c and d,** we have a modest correlation—the two characteristics are related but not highly correlated. If the dots spread out over the whole graph, forming a circle or a random pattern, as they do in **Figure A–11e**, there is no correlation between the two characteristics.

A scatter plot can give us a general idea if a correlation exists and how strong it is. To describe the relation between two variables more precisely, we need a **correlation coefficient**—a statistical measure of the degree to which two variables are associated. The correlation coefficient tells us the degree of association between two sets of matched scores—that is, to what extent high or low scores on one variable tend to be associated with high or low scores on another variable. It also provides an estimate of how well we can predict from a person's score on one characteristic how high he or she will score on another characteristic. If we know, for example, that a test of mechanical ability is highly correlated with success in engineering courses, we could predict that success on the test would also mean success as an engineering major.

Correlation coefficients can run from $+1.0$ to -1.0. The highest possible value $(+1.0)$ indicates a perfect positive correlation—high scores on one variable are always and systematically related to high scores on a second variable. The lowest possible value (-1.0) means a perfect negative correlation—high scores on one variable are always and regularly related to low scores on the second variable. In life, most things are far from perfect, so most correlation coefficients fall somewhere between $+1.0$ and -1.0. A correlation smaller than $\pm.20$ is considered very low, from $\pm.20$ to $\pm.40$ is low, from $\pm.40$ to $\pm.60$ is moderate, from $\pm.60$ to $\pm.80$ is high, and from $\pm.80$ to ±1.0 is very high. A correlation of zero indicates that there is no correlation between two sets of scores—no regular relation between them at all.

Correlation tells us nothing about causality. If we found a high positive correlation between participation in elections and income levels, for example, we still could not say that being wealthy made people vote or that voting made people wealthy. We would still not know which came first, or whether some third variable explained both income levels and voting behavior. Correlation only tells us that we have found some association between scores on two specified characteristics.

Figure A–11
Scatter plots provide a picture of the strength and direction of a correlation.

scatter plot Diagram showing the association between scores on two variables.

correlation coefficient Statistical measure of the strength of association between two variables.

Using Statistics to Make Predictions

Behind the use of statistics is the hope that we can generalize from our results and use them to predict behavior. We hope, for example, that we can use the record of how well a group of rats run through a maze today to predict how another group of rats will do tomorrow, that we can use a person's scores on a sales aptitude test to predict how well he or she will sell life insurance, that we can measure the attitudes of a relatively small group of people about pollution control to indicate what the attitudes of the whole country are.

First we have to determine whether our measurements are representative and whether we can have confidence in them. In Chapter 1, "The Science of Psychology", we discussed this problem when we considered the problem of proper sampling.

PROBABILITY

Errors based on inadequate sampling procedures are somebody's fault. Other kinds of errors occur randomly. In the simplest kind of experiment, a psychologist will gather a representative sample, split it randomly into two groups, and then apply some experimental manipulation to one of the groups. Afterward, the psychologist will measure both groups and determine whether the experimental group's score is now different from the score of the control group. But even if there is a large difference between the scores of the two groups, it may still be wrong to attribute the difference to the manipulation. Random effects might influence the results and introduce error.

Statistics give the psychologist many ways to determine precisely whether the difference between the two groups is really significant, whether something other than chance produced the results, and whether the same results would be obtained with different subjects. These probabilities are expressed as measures of **significance**. If the psychologist computes the significance level for the results as .05, he or she knows that there are 19 chances out of 20 that the results are not due to chance. But there is still 1 chance in 20—or a .05 likelihood—that the results are due to chance. A .01 significance level would mean that there is only 1 chance in 100 that the results are due to chance.

Using Meta-Analysis in Psychological Research

In several places in this text, we have presented findings from reviews of psychological research in which a research team has summarized a wide selection of literature on a topic in order to reach some conclusions on that topic. There are several crucial decisions to be made in such a process: Which research reports should be included? How should the information be summarized? What questions might be answered after all the available information is gathered?

Traditionally, psychologists reviewing the literature in a particular area relied on the *box-score method* to reach conclusions. That is, after collecting all the relevant research reports, the researcher simply counted the number supporting one conclusion or the other, much like keeping track of the scoring in nine innings of a baseball game (hence the term *box score*). For example, if there were 200 studies of gender differences in aggressive behavior, researchers might find that 120 of them showed that males were more aggressive than females, 40 showed the opposite pattern, and 40 showed no evidence of gender differences. On the basis of these box scores, the reviewer might conclude that males are more likely than females to act aggressively.

Today researchers tend to rely on a more sophisticated strategy known as **meta-analysis.** Meta-analysis provides a way of statistically combining the results of individual research studies to reach an overall conclusion. In a single experiment, each participant contributes data to help the researcher reach a conclusion. In a meta-analysis, each published study contributes data to help the reviewer reach a conclusion, as **Figure A–12** illustrates. Rather than relying on the raw data of individual participants, meta-analysis treats the results of

significance Probability that results obtained were due to chance.

meta-analysis A statistical procedure for combining the results of several studies so the strength, consistency, and direction of the effect can be estimated.

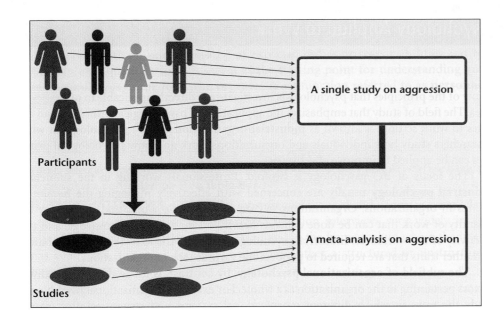

Figure A–12
Meta-Analysis.
Meta-analysis enables researchers to combine the results of individual studies to reach an overall conclusion.

entire studies as its raw data. Meta-analysts begin by collecting all available research reports that are relevant to the question at hand. Next they statistically transform these results into a common scale for comparison. That way differences in sample size (one study might have used 50 participants, another 500), in the magnitude of an effect (one study might have found a small difference, another a more substantial one), and in experimental procedures (which might vary from study to study) can be examined using the same methods.

The key element in this process is its statistical basis. Rather than keeping a tally of "yeas" and "nays," meta-analysis allows the reviewer to determine both the strength and the consistency of a research conclusion. For example, instead of simply concluding that there were more studies that found a particular gender difference, the reviewer might determine that the genders differ by $^6/_{10}$ s of a percentage point, or that across all the studies the findings are highly variable.

Meta-analysis has proved to be a valuable tool for psychologists interested in reaching conclusions about a particular research topic. By systematically examining patterns of evidence across individual studies whose conclusions vary, psychologists are able to gain a clearer understanding of the findings and their implications.

In a *structured job interview,* all job applicants are asked the same questions, usually in a fixed order by the same individual or team of interviewers. The chosen questions, which are usually derived from the job analysis, pertain directly to the applicant's ability to perform the tasks of the job. In a structured interview, the applicant's responses usually are scored, often numerically, using a consistent scoring scheme. In contrast, an *unstructured job interview* typically has no fixed format and the questions asked may vary widely from person to person. Furthermore, in unstructured interviews there usually is no specified method of scoring applicants' responses. Most often an overall rating or ranking is assigned to each applicant based on the interviewer's subjective impression and judgment.

Compared to scores from unstructured interviews, scores from structured interviews are more highly correlated with measures of subsequent job performance (see **Table B–1**). In other words, structured interviews have higher *criterion-related validity,* sometimes called *predictive validity* (see Chapter 7, "Cognition and Mental Abilities," for a discussion of validity).

Whether structured or unstructured, employment interviews also provide an opportunity to talk about the nature of the job. By giving applicants a realistic picture of the demands of a job, employers can help them determine whether the job will be a good match to their expectations.

EMPLOYMENT TESTS. Interviews are time-consuming and relatively expensive. When there are many more applicants than can be hired, organizations often rely on objective, paper-and-pencil tests as a first step in screening applicants. And since most such tests are scored objectively, the possibility of bias in favor of applicants whom managers personally like or who are similar to them is greatly reduced (Stanley, 2004).

Industrial psychologists use a wide variety of employment tests. Some measure cognitive abilities, while others measure personality characteristics. Research has shown that both types of tests are excellent predictors of job performance (Barrick & Mount, 1991; Ree, Earles, & Teachout, 1994; F. L. Schmidt & Hunter, 1998). However, tests of cognitive abilities have the highest overall predictive validity and the lowest cost (F. L. Schmidt & Hunter, 2004). Tests of cognitive ability, for the most part, measure general intelligence or general mental ability (see Chapter 7, "Cognition and Mental Abilities"). As one I/O psychologist put it, "If we could know only one attribute of a job candidate upon which to base a prediction, we would want an assessment of intelligence" (Muchinsky, 2006, p. 103).

Unlike tests of general mental ability, which have correct and incorrect answers, objective tests of personality generally include self-descriptive statements about personal preferences ("I would rather go to a baseball game than read a book") and typical behaviors ("I am able to set clear goals and work effectively to achieve them"). In recent years, most I/O researchers have used the *Five Factor Model* of personality to explore the relationship between personality and job performance. See Chapter 10, "Personality," for a discussion of personality tests and of the Five Factor model.) Of the five major personality traits, conscientiousness is tied most closely to job performance. **Conscientiousness** refers to a person's ability to finish projects that are started, to attend to detail without becoming absorbed by it, and to care enough about the quality of work that it is not compromised by inattention or lack of effort. Although the other four major personality traits (emotional stability, agreeableness, openness to experience, and extraversion) may be related to job performance in some settings (Hogan & Holland, 2003), conscientiousness is a valid predictor of job performance in all jobs (Barrick & Mount, 1991; Barrick, Mount, & Judge, 2001; W. S. Dunn, Mount, & Barrick, 1995). Furthermore, conscientiousness is not significantly correlated with general mental ability. Therefore, using both a test of general mental ability and a test of conscientiousness typically results in a better, more accurate prediction of future job performance than is possible from either test alone (Schmidt & Hunter, 2004).

Other employment tests, known as **integrity tests**, predict negative or counterproductive behavior. These tests include questions that measure three of the five factors linked to counterproductive behavior: *conscientiousness, agreeableness,* and *emotional stability*

---

conscientiousness A person's ability to finish projects that are started, to attend to detail without becoming absorbed by it, and to care enough about the quality of work that it is not compromised by inattention or lack of effort.

integrity tests Paper-and-pencil tests that predict the likelihood that a job applicant will engage in counterproductive behavior in the workplace.

(Schmidt & Hunter, 2004). By identifying applicants who score low on these three dimensions, integrity tests can help employers screen out potentially difficult employees before they are hired.

MEASURES OF PREVIOUS PERFORMANCE. One of the long-standing dictums in psychology is this: *The best predictor of future performance is past performance.* In an organizational context, this means that, in general, high performers in previous positions will most likely perform at a high level in future positions as well. Thus, personnel selection specialists often pay particular attention to job applicants' previous work histories. One method of accomplishing this is by requiring each applicant to provide a prior job history as well as general personal information (such as name, phone number, and so forth). Applications are the most frequently used method of selection (Schultz & Schultz, 1998).

Personnel selection specialists also check references to assess an applicant's previous job performance. Job applicants can be required to provide contact data for their former work supervisors. However, many employers are reluctant to comment on the quality of a previous employee's work, since any negative information preventing the employee from securing a new job could result in a costly lawsuit (Fishman, 2005).

Finally, job applicants can be asked to demonstrate content knowledge of the sought-after job or to actually perform the skills relevant to it. The predictive validity of job knowledge and work sample tests is very high, although they are only useful if job applicants are applying for jobs like those they have performed in the past.

ASSESSMENT CENTERS. High-level management positions call for skills that are difficult to evaluate using traditional selection methods (Jansen & Stoop, 2001). In these cases, several applicants may be put into a simulated and highly structured group setting, or **assessment center**. The typical assessment center evaluation lasts two days, involves several group exercises and the administration of a variety of ability and personality tests, and includes a lengthy, detailed, structured interview (Gaugler, Rosenthal, Thornton, & Benson, 1987). The ability of assessment centers to predict the long-term performance of individuals in upper management is reasonably good.

Is it possible to use just a few selection methods with good results? Industrial psychologists have investigated this question, concluding that the most effective combination generally includes a test of general mental ability along with either a structured interview or a test of conscientiousness (Schmidt & Hunter, 2004).

Measuring Performance on the Job

Evaluating employee job performance is important for a variety of reasons. Most obviously, organizations depend on high levels of employee performance to maximize their productivity and profitability. But effective evaluation of performance also improves the quality of organizational decisions, including pay raises, promotions, and terminations. It helps employees understand how well they are doing their jobs; and can encourage worker loyalty toward the organization (Murphy & Cleveland, 1995). Finally, formal performance appraisals also can provide a legally defensible rationale for terminating an employee.

Formal methods of evaluating performance, called **performance appraisal systems**, have as their overriding goal the unbiased assessment of the quantity and quality of work contributed by each individual. Several methods of performance appraisal have been devised, each of which is appropriate for different kinds of work.

When productivity can be measured directly, an **objective performance appraisal** is usually used. *Objective* methods are based on *quantitative* measurement, such as counting the number of goods produced, the number of pieces assembled, or the dollars of product sold. However, most jobs do not involve work that can be measured objectively. For example, teachers, managers, nurses, and many other employees do important work that cannot be "counted." For these types of jobs, *subjective* measures of performance

assessment center Method used to select high-level managers that places applicants in a simulated and highly structured group setting where they are given personnel tests and extensive interviews, and they engage in various role-playing activities.

performance appraisal systems Formal methods used to assess the quantity and quality of work contributed by each individual within an organization.

objective performance appraisal Method of performance appraisal based on quantitative measurement of the amount of work done.

Figure B–1

Example of a BARS Performance Evaluation.

Source: From *Psychology of Work Behavior*, rev. ed., by F. J. Landy and D. A Trumbo. © 1980, Reprinted with permission from Brooks/ Cole, a division of Thomson Learning Inc.

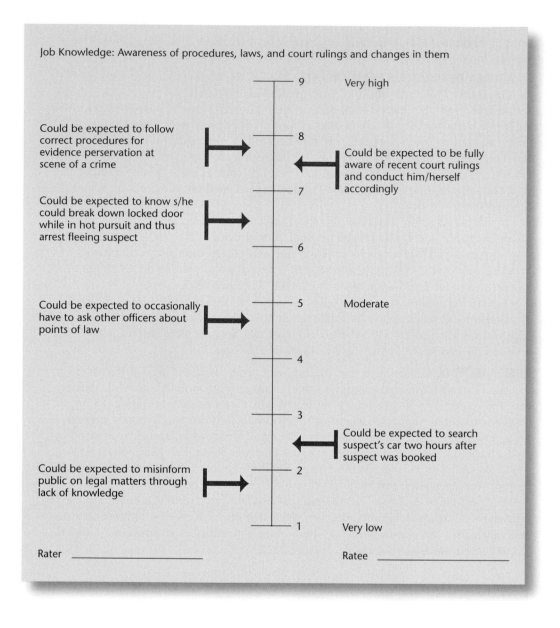

Job Knowledge: Awareness of procedures, laws, and court rulings and changes in them

9 — Very high

Could be expected to follow correct procedures for evidence perservation at scene of a crime → 8

Could be expected to be fully aware of recent court rulings and conduct him/herself accordingly ←

7

Could be expected to know s/he could break down locked door while in hot pursuit and thus arrest fleeing suspect →

6

Could be expected to occasionally have to ask other officers about points of law → 5 — Moderate

4

3

Could be expected to search suspect's car two hours after suspect was booked ←

Could be expected to misinform public on legal matters through lack of knowledge → 2

1 — Very low

Rater _____   Ratee _____

must be used. **Subjective performance appraisal** methods rely on *judgments* about the *quality* of an employee's work. Subjective methods are used extensively throughout all types of organizations.

One of the greatest challenges in creating a fair, unbiased performance appraisal system is to identify exactly what is expected of workers. Carefully written job analysis-based descriptions help personnel psychologists identify the important tasks the job entails. They serve as a good starting point for the development of a performance evaluation system that is clear and relatively free from error.

Generally speaking, evaluations based on *behaviors*, rather than on attitudes or intentions, are less prone to error. Behaviors are observable; therefore evaluators need to rely less on subjective judgments. One commonly used performance appraisal method is the **behaviorally anchored ratings scale (BARS)**. A BARS system first identifies specific behaviors that are associated with high performance, average performance, and substandard performance for the job being evaluated. These behaviors are then arranged into a rating scale (See **Figure B–1**). When evaluators use a BARS scale to rate a particular employee, that employee's typical behavior is compared to the positive and negative incidents identified on the scale. The result is a performance rating that reflects the job-related behaviors that the employee characteristically displays in his or her work.

subjective performance appraisal
Performance appraisal that relies on judgments about the quality of an employee's work.

behaviorally anchored ratings scale (BARS)
Performance appraisal that matches employee behavior to specific behaviors associated with high, average, and poor performance.

Issues of Fairness in Employment

In the past, both in the United States and abroad, some companies have refused to hire employees based on their gender, age, race, or religious beliefs (Brinkley, 1999). Today, most industrialized nations have developed legislation to guard against discriminatory employment practices. In 1964, the United States Congress enacted the **Civil Rights Act of 1964**, a sweeping set of laws and regulations aimed at protecting the rights of individuals and groups who had historically experienced discrimination because they were women or belonged to certain racial, ethnic, or religious groups. The overarching purpose of these laws, and others that have followed, has been to create a society that is fair to all individuals, regardless of their background and beliefs. The Civil Rights Act includes an array of provisions that define and prohibit discriminatory practices in all walks of life. Title VII of this act expressly prohibits discrimination against employees because of their race, color, religion, sex, or national origin.

In the years since the Civil Rights Act was passed, the scope and number of groups protected by the Civil Rights Act has expanded. Citizens over the age of 40, pregnant women, and people with physical or mental disabilities are now protected against discrimination under federal law. And in some cities and states, civil rights have been extended to members of groups beyond those protected under federal law. For example, in certain areas there are now laws that prohibit discrimination on the basis of sexual orientation, thereby protecting the rights of gay men and lesbian women. Although federal laws currently do not include sexual orientation as a category protected under federal statute, considerable debate on this issue is sure to come.

Behavior Within Organizations

Industrial/organizational psychologists are concerned not only with selecting employees, evaluating their performance, and ensuring that they are treated fairly. They also are involved in preparing workers to perform to the best of their ability and in creating an organizational environment that motivates them to do just that.

TRAINING EMPLOYEES

The first step in developing an employee training program is to determine the need for training by means of a three-step process (Landy & Conte, 2004; Ostroff & Ford, 1989). First, an *organizational analysis* is done in which the company's goals are examined and problems are identified. Next, for problems that lend themselves to training-based solutions, a *task analysis* is performed. Task analysis identifies which job tasks can be addressed through training. It also determines the knowledge (K), skills (S), abilities (A), and other characteristics (O) required to perform those tasks successfully. Finally, a *person analysis* is conducted which examines the knowledge, skills, and current performance of workers to determine which ones need additional training.

Where discrepancies exist between tasks required on the job and skill levels of workers, training programs can be designed to teach workers the necessary skills, behaviors, or attitudes that will allow them to perform job tasks at an acceptable level. Once training is complete, an assessment of training outcomes should be performed, so managers can evaluate which training needs have been successfully addressed, and which remain (Alliger & Janak, 1989; I. L. Goldstein & Ford, 2002).

Depending on the type of skills or attitudes that the organization wishes to address, several methods of training are available. When specific, job-related skills need to be learned, on-the-job, vestibule, or simulation training methods are often used.

ON-THE-JOB TRAINING. One of the most common methods of teaching new workers the skills they need to perform their job is **on-the-job training**, in which the trainee learns new

---

Civil Rights Act of 1964 A sweeping set of laws and regulations aimed at protecting the rights of people despite their gender, age, race, or religious beliefs.

on-the-job training Teaching employees a new job by actually performing the job.

job tasks while actually performing the job. For example, an assistant chef may have worked in several restaurants before coming to work at a new job, but may be unfamiliar with how the current employer wants food to be plated and sauced. Through on-the-job training, the new assistant chef can be given step-by-step instructions and can be shown by an experienced employee exactly how these tasks are to be performed.

There are many advantages associated with on-the-job training. Foremost among these is that employees learn the new skills required for the job on the very equipment they are to use when performing their work. On-the-job training also conserves the organization's resources, since it usually minimizes costs for training equipment and supplies. However, it also has some disadvantages. For example, productivity usually declines during the training period because learning each new task slows performance. Moreover, coworkers functioning as trainers usually cannot instruct trainees and perform their own jobs at the same time, leading to further declines in productivity. Finally, experienced employees do not always make skilled trainers: A highly competent worker may not necessarily have the skills to effectively train a new employee (Riggio, 2003).

One of the oldest on-the-job training programs is referred to *apprenticeship*, which is still used extensively in the crafts and trades. Many jobs associated with apprentice training programs are in heavily unionized occupations; plumbers, carpenters, electricians, and equipment operators in all types of manufacturing industries often learn their skills through apprenticeship training. Today, more than 30,000 apprentice programs exist in the United States involving nearly a half-million trainees, called *apprentices* (U.S. Department of Labor, 2006). Apprentices go through a formal and extensive program of on-the-job training, which includes both instruction and supervision by a skilled worker in the field.

Another type of on-the-job training is **job rotation**, in which workers are trained to perform all jobs in a particular supervisory unit. For example, in an assembly unit in which five different workers each perform a specific part of the assembly of a machine, each worker would learn each of the five jobs involved. Job rotation programs provide organizations an effective way of staffing jobs that have high turnover, since workers are already trained to take over the job of a person who quits (Riggio, 2003). Oftentimes, job rotation is part of the training that supervisors receive. Because supervisors need to understand how each of the jobs in their unit is performed, job rotation can be used to help them develop a better understanding of procedures throughout their work division. Research suggests that supervisors who are rotated through several jobs are more apt to remain with a company than those who receive no such training (Grensing-Pophal, 2005; Pooley, 2005).

VESTIBULE AND SIMULATION TRAINING. When new job skills cannot be learned while performing the actual job, an alternative approach is vestibule training. **Vestibule training** allows employees to learn job tasks at work stations similar to those used in production in a training facility, rather than on the actual production floor.

In other cases, *training simulators* are used. For example, flight simulators are used to teach pilots how to fly. Flight simulators operate like real airplanes, with fully-equipped cockpits and pitch-and-roll machines that move the simulator to replicate the actual movements of an aircraft. From the pilot's perspective, the only major difference between flying a simulator versus a real airplane is that the simulator doesn't actually leave the ground.

Computer-based simulations can provide yet another vehicle for some types of training needs. Today, computer-based simulations are being used to train firefighters, medical personnel, and heavy equipment operators, as well as workers in many other jobs (J. P. Bliss, Scerbo, Schmidt, & Thompson, 2006; Construction Equipment, 2006; Foundry Management and Technology, 2006; J. M. Smith 2006). Because computer-based training often provides a cost-effective and safe way to provide training, its use is increasing in a wide variety of training applications.

CHANGING ATTITUDES IN THE WORKPLACE. Sometimes organizations wish to develop their workforce in terms of attitudes and interpersonal behaviors. Cultural diversity training and sexual harassment training are two examples of such training.

job rotation Training workers to perform a variety of jobs.

vestibule training Teaching employees new techniques and behaviors in a simulated workplace.

cultural diversity training Teaching employees to adjust their attitudes and actions so they can work effectively as part of a diverse workforce.

Cultural diversity training is used to help workers adapt their actions and attitudes so they can work effectively in a multicultural work environment. The U.S. workplace broadly reflects the population overall, and that population is becoming much more diverse. For example, of all new additions to the workforce in the decade of the 1990s, nearly half (45%) were non-White and nearly two-thirds were women. In response to increasing workplace diversity, a growing trend exists among organizations to offer programs in cultural diversity training. One goal of such training is to create an atmosphere that is fair and nondiscriminatory for all employees; failing to do so puts companies at risk for lawsuits filed under antidiscrimination laws such as The Civil Rights Acts of 1964 and 1991. Cultural diversity training also alerts workers to how their actions may be offensive to others and helps them learn to work cooperatively with coworkers who represent different cultures or gender. Another goal of diversity training is to better capture "the benefits in creativity and problem-solving capabilities that a diverse workforce provides" (Chrobot-Mason & Quinones, 2002). When workers are able to appreciate and embrace the various points of view expressed in a diverse work environment, productivity is enhanced. Finally, the ever-increasing globalization of the workplace means that increasing numbers of employees take assignments abroad, which in turn leads to a need for cultural-diversity training (Speitzer, McCall, & Mahoney, 1997). For these reasons, most industrial/organizational psychologists predict that this type of training will become even more important in the future (Bhawuk & Brislin, 2000).

Most organizations also offer employee training that is aimed at reducing sexual harassment in the workplace. **Sexual harassment** can take several forms. *Quid pro quo* (Latin for "this for that") harassment is defined as behavior in which sexual favors are solicited in return for favorable treatment. An example of quid pro quo harassment might involve a manager offering a salary increase or a promotion to a subordinate in exchange for sexual attention. Sexual harassment also exists when managers or coworkers create a *hostile work environment*, perhaps by telling sexist jokes, posting nude "pin-up" photos in lockers, or teasing of a sexual nature. The goals of sexual-harassment-prevention training parallel those of cultural-diversity training: to protect the organization from lawsuits and to create an environment where every worker is able to perform to his or her maximum level of creativity, effort, and productivity.

MOTIVATING EMPLOYEES

Another means of improving workforce productivity involves motivating workers to give their best effort. Over the years, a variety of theories have been proposed to explain why workers work and what factors motivate them to give their best performance. (See Chapter 8, "Motivation and Emotion.") One way of understanding how these theories approach the topic of motivation is to categorize them into groups (Donovan, 2001).

COGNITIVE THEORIES OF MOTIVATION. Rather than emphasizing inherent individual differences among workers (skills), cognitive-based theories of motivation emphasize how workers think about their jobs and how that in turn affects their attitudes and behaviors on the job. Three cognitive views that have received considerable attention from I/O psychologists are equity theory, expectancy theory, and goal-setting theory.

Equity theory holds that relative to coworkers, employees monitor the amount of effort they expend on the job and the rewards that they receive for this effort. In the simplest case, equity theory predicts that when workers believe they are expending equal amounts of effort, they should benefit from equal levels of reward. Motivation, then, depends on the worker's sense of fairness, or *equity*. When employees are either over- or under-rewarded relative to their coworkers, their motivation suffers and they will adjust the quality or quantity of work they produce correspondingly.

Expectancy theory also emphasizes the cognitive processes workers use in evaluating their level of effort and the rewards they receive. However, in expectancy theory the comparison made is not how our own effort and rewards compare to those of others, but

sexual harassment Soliciting sexual favors in exchange for favorable treatment, or creating a hostile work environment.

equity theory Theory that worker motivation depends on the relationship between personal effort expended and rewards received when compared to that of other workers.

expectancy theory Theory that worker motivation depends on the expectation that by working hard they will achieve valued rewards.

rather how we view the connection between our own behavior and the likelihood of attaining desired rewards. According to expectancy theory, employees are aware of the goals or rewards they wish to attain through their work, and they are aware of how their behavior on the job is connected with attaining those rewards. Based on their assessment of the value of the rewards they seek and of the degree to which they expect they can attain those rewards by working harder, they will expend the corresponding amount of effort on the job (Van Eerde & Thierry, 1996; Vroom, 1964). For example, if workers attach high value to a promotion and if they believe that through hard work they will be promoted, this expectancy will motivate them to perform. Conversely, if the rewards offered on the job are not perceived by workers to be valuable, or if workers do not believe that their efforts will result in the attainment of valued rewards, motivation will diminish and effort will not be expended.

A similar set of assumptions is advanced by **goal-setting theory**, which emphasizes the impact on motivation of clearly articulated goals. According to this theory, when workers believe that their efforts on the job will lead to the attainment of previously set, clearly stated goals, they will be highly motivated toward meeting those goals (Locke & Latham, 2002). Many people apply goal-setting theory in their own lives. For example, a student may work extra hours at a second part-time job to buy a car or pay the rent. The keys in goal-setting theory are to identify appropriate, attainable goals and to clearly communicate to workers what they need to do to reach those goals.

REINFORCEMENT THEORY. Some motivational theories focus less on how workers think about their jobs and more on the outcomes associated with an employee's work. **Reinforcement theory**, which is based on the principles of operant conditioning (see Chapter 5, "Learning"), has been used to explain how workers can be motivated toward high levels of performance.

According to this theory, when work behavior is followed by positive outcomes (reinforcements), that behavior will be maintained and strengthened; when work behavior is punished, that behavior will decrease. An example of reinforcement theory in a production setting is the *piece-rate system* of compensation. In a piece-rate system, workers are paid according to the number of "pieces" they assemble. Thus, a worker who builds 25 pieces in a day will be paid more than one who builds only 20 pieces. Sales commission systems, where sales agents are paid a percentage of the price of the products they sell, is another compensation system based on reinforcement theory.

Research indicates that reinforcement can indeed increase workplace productivity. One study that examined the effect of reinforcement-based performance systems over a span of 20 years showed a 17% improvement in productivity (Stajkovic & Luthans, 1997). In a more recent study, more than 90% of organizations experienced sustainable improvements in worker productivity through reinforcement (Komaki, 2003). Moreover, when workers are paid according to their performance, their sense of autonomy and control over their work is also enhanced (Eisenberger, Rhoades, & Cameron, 1999).

However, there are some potential pitfalls associated with the use of reinforcement. For example, when workers are paid according to their own individual successes, they may be reluctant to participate in activities that require cooperation with others. In fact, "pay-for-performance" systems can encourage competitive behavior which, at the extreme, may involve sabotage of coworkers' efforts and an overall decline in workplace productivity. Placing workers in highly stressful, competitive work environments poses yet another issue to consider when evaluating the desirability of reinforcement-based motivational approaches.

Organizational Culture

All of the topics discussed thus far—job analysis, personnel selection and performance evaluation, fair employment practices, and employee training and motivation—occur in the context of a particular organization. Organizations have their own **corporate (organizational) culture**, which refers to the formal and informal rules, procedures, and expectations that define an organization's values, attitudes, beliefs, and customs. In that

---

goal-setting theory Theory that worker motivation requires clearly stated goals and a belief that good job performance will lead to the attainment of these goals.

reinforcement theory Theory that work behavior that is followed by positive outcomes will be maintained and repeated.

corporate (organizational) culture The formal and informal rules, procedures, and expectations that define the values, attitudes, beliefs, and customs of an organization.

organizations sometimes differ dramatically from each other, they are characterized by their own unique organizational culture.

As jobs have become more complex, technology has continued to explode, and worker expectations have changed, many organizations have adopted a "team-based" approach to work.

TEAMS AND TEAMWORK

The basic idea behind work teams is that productivity is enhanced when several people collaborate to solve organizational problems. Teams are particularly effective when problems must be solved by the workers themselves. A good team generally outperforms individual work efforts in tasks that require experience, judgment, and multiple skills (Salas, Stagl, & Burke, 2004). Moreover, research suggests that people who work in teams are more satisfied with their work and are more productive (Glassop, 2002).

Depending somewhat on the goals of an organization, there are many different ways that work teams can be organized and several different functions they can perform (Sunstrom, DeMeuse, & Futrell, 1990). As one example, workers on a team may be trained to perform all jobs in their unit (a technique discussed earlier under *job rotation*) and then regularly exchange jobs. This rotation of jobs helps to keeps their skills sharp and also helps to relieve the boredom of performing the same job over and over, day after day.

Team-based approaches have been gaining popularity (Borman, Ilgen, & Klimoski, 2003). Three factors appear to underlie this trend. First, businesses exist within a complex, information-rich culture in which no employee can know or master everything needed to run a successful enterprise. Second, the modern workforce is better educated and thus better prepared to perform complex decision-making functions. Furthermore, workers at every organizational level expect to find challenge in their work; and most are unwilling to work at repetitive, intellectually empty tasks. Finally, the work performed in modern organizations has itself changed. Most jobs no longer consist of performing the same set of simple repetitive tasks; rather, they involve flexible approaches to rapidly changing technologies and business climates (Muchinsky, 2006).

A discussion of team approaches to organizational structure and operation raises the question of leadership. Although workers within a group team are interdependent and share responsibilities, team success also depends on effective leadership.

LEADERSHIP

As we saw in Chapter 14, "Social Psychology," several theories of leadership have emerged to explain why some individuals become leaders and others do not. Contingency theories are based on the assumption that leadership is the product of both the characteristics of the leader and those of the worker and the workplace.

An important aspect of contingency theories is that there is no specific set of traits, skills, abilities, or attitudes that will guarantee leadership success. On the contrary, to be effective, the leader's characteristics must match the demands of the situation. Consequently, a person who is very effective as a leader in one setting may not be effective in another. This situation is often observed in sales-based organizations that promote managers from within. There is no certainty that someone who is an outstanding leader in one division of a company will be effective if transferred to a different division or promoted to a higher level of management. Similarly, a person who forms a small start-up company and leads it effectively during its formative years may not be the best person to lead the company when it has hundreds or thousands of employees and multiple offices worldwide.

Certain leadership characteristics do seem to generalize across different types of organizational settings. For example, leaders who are *charismatic*, who exude confidence and have a vision that followers can relate to, are oftentimes effective in a wide array of settings

(Yukl, 2002). They are also especially effective in motivating the productivity of work teams (R. T. Keller, 2006). Charismatic leaders, who in some organizations are called "transformational leaders," seem to inspire higher levels of job satisfaction in employees as well (Judge & Bono, 2000). Leaders who establish clear expectations for how work is to be performed are also generally effective in a wide range of situations (R. T. Keller, 2006).

Organizational Attitudes

Effective leadership contributes to organizational productivity in many ways. For example, a leader can have a significant effect on the attitudes that workers develop about their jobs and the organizations for which they work. Among the attitudes that organizational psychologists are most interested in are the degree to which workers derive satisfaction from their jobs and the extent to which they develop a sense of trust in the organization and an appreciation that its processes and procedures are fair.

JOB SATISFACTION

Organizational psychologists are interested in job satisfaction because it is linked to many important organizational variables. Perhaps the most closely studied relationship is that between job satisfaction and job performance. Intuitively it seems that workers who are satisfied with their jobs will perform at higher levels than those who are unhappy in their work. However, hundreds of research studies have shown that job satisfaction is, at best, only moderately linked to job performance (Judge, Thoresen, Bono, & Patton, 2001). Nevertheless, most employees want satisfying jobs and so most employers seek to create a workplace that contributes to job satisfaction.

The amount of pleasure employees derive from their jobs is determined in large part by the extent to which they feel that their expectations about their jobs are met (Hulin & Judge, 2003). When expectations are met or exceeded, levels of job satisfaction are generally high. However, there is a limit to what employers can do to increase job satisfaction since it is also affected by employee age, length of employment, overall health, personal motivation, marital status, and leisure activities (Schultz & Schultz, 1998).

ORGANIZATIONAL JUSTICE

In recent years, I/O psychologists have become interested in the extent to which employees perceive fairness and justice in the workplace. Such topics often are referred to as issues of **organizational justice**. One aspect of organizational justice is employees' perceptions that what they receive in recognition is appropriate for what they contribute to the organization. Most employees expect that when they work hard and contribute positively to the productivity of the organization, they will receive appropriate rewards.

Another aspect of organizational justice involves the extent to which the policies and procedures used within the organization are responsive to the feelings of employees. For example, if an organization needs to eliminate a position within a unit, advance notification about the reasons why the position must be terminated, the criteria for deciding which position will be affected, the timeline for making the change, and an appeal process for workers to voice their concerns all contribute to perceived fairness in the workplace.

Finally, organizational justice is high when organizations show concern for workers as individuals. When a manager sends a get-well card to a subordinate following a surgery or attends the wedding of a worker in the unit he supervises, such actions contribute to a feeling of organizational justice.

organizational justice Degree to which employees perceive fairness in the workplace.

Research clearly demonstrates that all three forms of organizational justice contribute to employees' perceptions of fairness in the workplace (Colquitt, Conlon, Wesson, Porter, & Ng, 2001). When workers perceive that rewards are distributed fairly, that rules and procedures are just and are enforced without favoritism, and that they are valued and respected by the organization and its leaders, organizational justice is enhanced. When workers are treated fairly, job satisfaction, commitment, and productivity increase, and negative workplace behaviors, such as absenteeism and sabotage, decline (Simons & Roberson, 2003). Research on the topic of organizational justice is likely to continue as I/O psychologists work to better understand how to enhance workplace productivity while maintaining a positive environment.

Glossary

Absolute threshold The least amount of energy that can be detected as a stimulation 50% of the time.

Achievement motive The need to excel, to overcome obstacles.

Actualizing tendency According to Rogers, the drive of every organism to fulfill its biological potential and become what it is inherently capable of becoming.

Adaptation An adjustment of the senses to the level of stimulation they are receiving.

Additive color mixing The process of mixing lights of different wavelengths to create new hues.

Adjustment Any effort to cope with stress.

Adoption studies Research carried out on children, adopted at birth by parents not related to them, to determine the relative influence of heredity and environment on human behavior.

Adrenal glands Two endocrine glands located just above the kidneys.

Aerial perspective Monocular cue to distance and depth based on the fact that more distant objects are likely to appear hazy and blurred.

Afferent neurons Neurons that carry messages from sense organs to the spinal cord or brain.

Affiliation motive The need to be with others.

Afterimage Sense experience that occurs after a visual stimulus has been removed.

Aggression Behavior aimed at doing harm to others; also, the motive to behave aggressively.

Agoraphobia An anxiety disorder that involves multiple, intense fears of crowds, public places, and other situations that require separation from a source of security such as the home.

Alcohol Depressant that is the intoxicating ingredient in whiskey, beer, wine, and other fermented or distilled liquors.

Algorithm A step-by-step method of problem solving that guarantees a correct solution.

All-or-none law Principle that the action potential in a neuron does not vary in strength; either the neuron fires at full strength, or it does not fire at all.

Altered states of consciousness Mental states that differ noticeably from normal waking consciousness.

Altruistic behavior Helping behavior that is not linked to personal gain.

Alzheimer's disease A neurological disorder, most commonly found in late adulthood, characterized by progressive losses in memory and cognition and by changes in personality.

Amphetamines Stimulant drugs that initially produce "rushes" of euphoria often followed by sudden "crashes" and, sometimes, severe depression.

Amplitude The magnitude of a wave; in sound, the primary determinant of loudness.

Anal stage Second stage in Freud's theory of personality development, in which a child's erotic feelings center on the anus and on elimination.

Anorexia nervosa A serious eating disorder that is associated with an intense fear of weight gain and a distorted body image.

Antipsychotic drugs Drugs used to treat very severe psychological disorders, particularly schizophrenia.

Antisocial personality disorder Personality disorder that involves a pattern of violent, criminal, or unethical and exploitative behavior and an inability to feel affection for others.

Anxiety disorders Disorders in which anxiety is a characteristic feature or the avoidance of anxiety seems to motivate abnormal behavior.

Aphasias Impairments of the ability to use (expressive aphasia) or understand (receptive aphasia) language that usually results from brain damage.

Apnea Sleep disorder characterized by breathing difficulty during the night and feelings of exhaustion during the day.

Approach/approach conflict According to Lewin, the result of simultaneous attraction to two appealing possibilities, neither of which has any negative qualities.

Approach/avoidance conflict According to Lewin, the result of being simultaneously attracted to and repelled by the same goal.

Archetypes In Jung's theory of personality, thought forms common to all human beings, stored in the collective unconscious.

Arousal theory Theory of motivation that proposes that organisms seek an optimal level of arousal.

Assessment center Method used to select high-level managers that places applicants in a simulated and highly structured group setting where they are given personnel tests and extensive interviews, and they engage in various role-playing activities.

Association areas Areas of the cerebral cortex where incoming messages from the separate senses are combined into meaningful impressions and outgoing messages from the motor areas are integrated.

Attachment Emotional bond that develops in the first year of life that makes human babies cling to their caregivers for safety and comfort.

Attention The selection of some incoming information for further processing.

Attention-deficit hyperactivity disorder (ADHD) A childhood disorder characterized by inattention, impulsiveness, and hyperactivity.

Attitude Relatively stable organization of beliefs, feelings, and behavior tendencies directed toward something or someone—the attitude object.

Attribution theory The theory that addresses the question of how people make judgments about the causes of behavior.

Auditory nerve The bundle of axons that carries signals from each ear to the brain.

Authoritarian personality A personality pattern characterized by rigid conventionality, exaggerated respect for authority, and hostility toward those who defy society's norms.

Autistic disorder A childhood disorder characterized by lack of social instincts and strange motor behavior.

Autistic spectrum disorder (ASD) A range of disorders involving varying degrees of impairment in communication skills, social interactions, and restricted, repetitive, and stereotyped patterns of behavior.

Autokinetic illusion The perception that a stationary object is actually moving.

Autonomic nervous system The part of the peripheral nervous system that carries messages between the central nervous system and the internal organs.

Autonomy Sense of independence; a desire not to be controlled by others.

Availability A heuristic by which a judgment or decision is based on information that is most easily retrieved from memory.

Aversive conditioning Behavioral therapy techniques aimed at eliminating undesirable behavior patterns by teaching the person to associate them with pain and discomfort.

Avoidance training Learning a desirable behavior to prevent the occurrence of something unpleasant, such as punishment.

Avoidance/avoidance conflict According to Lewin, the result of facing a choice between two undesirable possibilities, neither of which has any positive qualities.

Avoidant personality disorder Personality disorder in which the person's fears of rejection by others lead to social isolation.

Axon Single long fiber extending from the cell body; it carries outgoing messages.

Babbling A baby's vocalizations, consisting of repetition of consonant–vowel combinations.

Barbiturates Potentially deadly depressants, first used for their sedative and anticonvulsant properties, now used only to treat such conditions as epilepsy and arthritis.

Basilar membrane Vibrating membrane in the cochlea of the inner ear; it contains sense receptors for sound.

Behavior contracting Form of operant conditioning therapy in which the client and therapist set behavioral goals and agree on reinforcements that the client will receive on reaching those goals.

Behavior genetics Study of the relationship between heredity and behavior.

Behavior therapies Therapeutic approaches that are based on the belief that all behavior, normal and abnormal, is learned, and that the objective of therapy is to teach people new, more satisfying ways of behaving.

Behaviorally anchored ratings scale (BARS) Performance appraisal that matches employee behavior to specific behaviors associated with high, average, and poor performance.

Behaviorism School of psychology that studies only observable and measurable behavior.

Big Five Five traits or basic dimensions currently considered to be of central importance in describing personality.

Binaural cues Cues to sound location that involve both ears working together.

Binocular cues Visual cues requiring the use of both eyes.

Biofeedback A technique that uses monitoring devices to provide precise information about internal physiological processes, such as heart rate or blood pressure, to teach people to gain voluntary control over these functions.

Biographical (or retrospective) study   A method of studying developmental changes by reconstructing a person's past through interviews and inferring the effects of past events on current behaviors.

Biological model   View that psychological disorders have a biochemical or physiological basis.

Biological treatments   A group of approaches, including medication, electroconvulsive therapy, and psychosurgery, that are sometimes used to treat psychological disorders in conjunction with, or instead of, psychotherapy.

Biopsychosocial theory   The theory that the interaction of biological, psychological, and cultural factors influences the intensity and duration of pain.

Bipolar cells   Neurons that have only one axon and one dendrite; in the eye, these neurons connect the receptors on the retina to the ganglion cells.

Bipolar disorder   A mood disorder in which periods of mania and depression alternate, sometimes with periods of normal mood intervening.

Blind spot   The place on the retina where the axons of all the ganglion cells leave the eye and where there are no receptors.

Blocking   A process whereby prior conditioning prevents conditioning to a second stimulus even when the two stimuli are presented simultaneously.

Body dysmorphic disorder   A somatoform disorder in which a person becomes so preoccupied with his or her imagined ugliness that normal life is impossible.

Body mass index (BMI)   A numerical index calculated from a person's height and weight that is used to indicate health status and predict disease risk.

Borderline personality disorder   Personality disorder characterized by marked instability in self-image, mood, and interpersonal relationships.

Brainstorming   A problem-solving strategy in which an individual or a group produces numerous ideas and evaluates them only after all ideas have been collected.

Brightness   The nearness of a color to white as opposed to black.

Brightness constancy   The perception of brightness as the same, even though the amount of light reaching the retina changes.

Bulimia nervosa   An eating disorder characterized by binges of eating followed by self-induced vomiting.

Bystander effect   The tendency for an individual's helpfulness in an emergency to decrease as the number of passive bystanders increases.

Cannon–Bard theory   States that the experience of emotion occurs simultaneously with biological changes.

Case study   Intensive description and analysis of a single individual or just a few individuals.

Catatonic schizophrenia   Schizophrenic disorder in which disturbed motor behavior is prominent.

Central nervous system (CNS)   Division of the nervous system that consists of the brain and spinal cord.

Central tendency   Tendency of scores to congregate around some middle value.

Cerebellum   Structure in the hindbrain that controls certain reflexes and coordinates the body's movements.

Cerebral cortex   The outer surface of the two cerebral hemispheres that regulates most complex behavior.

Childhood amnesia   The difficulty adults have remembering experiences from their first two years of life.

Chromosomes   Pairs of threadlike bodies within the cell nucleus that contain the genes.

Chunking   The grouping of information into meaningful units for easier handling by short-term memory.

Circadian rhythm   A regular biological rhythm with a period of approximately 24 hours.

Civil Rights Act of 1964   A sweeping set of laws and regulations aimed at protecting the rights of people despite their gender, age, race, or religious beliefs.

Classical (or Pavlovian) conditioning   The type of learning in which a response naturally elicited by one stimulus comes to be elicited by a different, formerly neutral, stimulus.

Client-centered (or person-centered) therapy   Nondirectional form of therapy developed by Carl Rogers that calls for unconditional positive regard of the client by the therapist with the goal of helping the client become fully functioning.

Cliques   Groups of adolescents with similar interests and strong mutual attachment.

Cocaine   Drug derived from the coca plant that, although producing a sense of euphoria by stimulating the sympathetic nervous system, also leads to anxiety, depression, and addictive cravings.

Cochlea   Part of the inner ear containing fluid that vibrates, which in turn causes the basilar membrane to vibrate.

Cognition   The processes whereby we acquire and use knowledge.

Cognitive dissonance   Perceived inconsistency between two cognitions.

Cognitive distortions   An illogical and maladaptive response to early negative life events that leads to feelings of incompetence and unworthiness that are reactivated whenever a new situation arises that resembles the original events.

Cognitive learning   Learning that depends on mental processes that are not directly observable.

Cognitive map   A learned mental image of a spatial environment that may be called on to solve problems when stimuli in the environment change.

Cognitive psychology   School of psychology devoted to the study of mental processes in the broadest sense.

Cognitive theory   States that emotional experience depends on one's perception or judgment of a situation.

Cognitive therapies   Psychotherapies that emphasize changing clients' perceptions of their life situation as a way of modifying their behavior.

Cognitive therapy   Therapy that depends on identifying and changing inappropriately negative and self-critical patterns of thought.

Cognitive–behavioral model   View that psychological disorders result from learning maladaptive ways of thinking and behaving.

Cognitive–social learning theories   Personality theories that view behavior as the product of the interaction of cognitions, learning and past experiences, and the immediate environment.

Cohort   A group of people born during the same period in historical time.

Collective unconscious   In Jung's theory of personality, the level of the unconscious that is inherited and common to all members of a species.

Color blindness   Partial or total inability to perceive hues.

Color constancy   An inclination to perceive familiar objects as retaining their color despite changes in sensory information.

Compensation   According to Adler, the person's effort to overcome imagined or real personal weaknesses.

Compensatory model   A rational decision-making model in which choices are systematically evaluated on various criteria.

Compliance   Change of behavior in response to an explicit request from another person or group.

Compromise   Deciding on a more realistic solution or goal when an ideal solution or goal is not practical.

Concepts   Mental categories for classifying objects, people, or experiences.

Concrete-operational stage   In Piaget's theory, the stage of cognitive development between 7 and 11 years of age in which the individual can attend to more than one thing at a time and understand someone else's point of view, though thinking is limited to concrete matters.

Conditional positive regard   In Rogers's theory, acceptance and love that are dependent on another's behaving in certain ways and on fulfilling certain conditions.

Conditioned response (CR)   After conditioning, the response an organism produces when a conditioned stimulus is presented.

Conditioned stimulus (CS)   An originally neutral stimulus that is paired with an unconditioned stimulus and eventually produces the desired response in an organism when presented alone.

Conditioned taste aversion   Conditioned avoidance of certain foods even if there is only one pairing of conditioned and unconditioned stimuli.

Cones   Receptor cells in the retina responsible for color vision.

Confirmation bias   The tendency to look for evidence in support of a belief and to ignore evidence that would disprove a belief.

Conflict   Simultaneous existence of incompatible demands, opportunities, needs, or goals.

Conformity   Voluntarily yielding to social norms, even at the expense of one's preferences.

Confrontation   Acknowledging a stressful situation directly and attempting to find a solution to the problem or to attain the difficult goal.

Conscientiousness   A person's ability to finish projects that are started, to attend to detail without becoming absorbed by it, and to care enough about the quality of work that it is not compromised by inattention or lack of effort.

Consciousness   Our awareness of various cognitive processes, such as sleeping, dreaming, concentrating, and making decisions.

Content validity   Refers to a test's having an adequate sample of questions measuring the skills or knowledge it is supposed to measure.

Contingency   A reliable "if–then" relationship between two events, such as a CS and a US.

Control group   In a controlled experiment, the group not subjected to a change in the independent variable; used for comparison with the experimental group.

Convergence   A visual depth cue that comes from muscles controlling eye movement as the eyes turn inward to view a nearby stimulus.

Convergent thinking   Thinking that is directed toward one correct solution to a problem.

Conversion disorders   Somatoform disorders in which a dramatic specific disability has no physical cause but instead seems related to psychological problems.

Cornea   The transparent protective coating over the front part of the eye.

Corporate (organizational) culture   The formal and informal rules, procedures, and expectations that define the values, attitudes, beliefs, and customs of an organization.

Corpus callosum   A thick band of nerve fibers connecting the left and right cerebral hemispheres.

Correlation coefficient   Statistical measure of the strength of association between two variables.

Correlation coefficients   Statistical measures of the degree of association between two variables.

Correlational research   Research technique based on the naturally occurring relationship between two or more variables.

Counterfactual thinking   Thinking about alternative realities and things that never happened.

Couple therapy   A form of group therapy intended to help troubled partners improve their problems of communication and interaction.

Creativity   The ability to produce novel and socially valued ideas or objects.

Criterion-related validity   Validity of a test as measured by a comparison of the test score and independent measures of what the test is designed to measure.

Critical period   A time when certain internal and external influences have a major effect on development; at other periods, the same influences will have little or no effect.

Cross-cultural research   Research involving the exploration of the extent to which people differ from one culture to another.

Cross-sectional study   A method of studying developmental changes by comparing people of different ages at about the same time.

Cultural diversity training   Teaching employees to adjust their attitudes and actions so they can work effectively as part of a diverse workforce.

Cultural truisms   Beliefs that most members of a society accept as self-evidently true.

Culture   The tangible goods and the values, attitudes, behaviors, and beliefs that are passed from one generation to another.

Culture-fair tests   Intelligence tests designed to eliminate cultural bias by minimizing skills and values that vary from one culture to another.

Dark adaptation   Increased sensitivity of rods and cones in darkness.

Daydreams   Apparently effortless shifts in attention away from the here and now into a private world of make-believe.

Decay theory   A theory that argues that the passage of time causes forgetting.

Decibel   Unit of measurement for the loudness of sounds.

Defense mechanisms   Self-deceptive techniques for reducing stress, including denial, repression, projection, identification, regression, intellectualization, reaction formation, displacement, and sublimation.

Defensive attribution   The tendency to attribute our successes to our own efforts or qualities and our failures to external factors.

Deindividuation   A loss of personal sense of responsibility in a group.

Deinstitutionalization   Policy of treating people with severe psychological disorders in the larger community or in small residential centers such as halfway houses, rather than in large public hospitals.

Delusions   False beliefs about reality that have no basis in fact.

Dendrites   Short fibers that branch out from the cell body and pick up incoming messages.

Denial   Refusal to acknowledge a painful or threatening reality.

Deoxyribonucleic acid (DNA)   Complex molecule in a double-helix configuration that is the main ingredient of chromosomes and genes and that forms the code for all genetic information.

Dependent personality disorder   Personality disorder in which the person is unable to make choices and decisions independently and cannot tolerate being alone.

Dependent variable   In an experiment, the variable that is measured to see how it is changed by manipulations in the independent variable.

Depersonalization disorder   A dissociative disorder whose essential feature is that the person suddenly feels changed or different in a strange way.

Depressants   Chemicals that slow down behavior or cognitive processes.

Depression   A mood disorder characterized by overwhelming feelings of sadness, lack of interest in activities, and perhaps excessive guilt or feelings of worthlessness.

Desensitization therapy   A conditioning technique designed to gradually reduce anxiety about a particular object or situation.

Developmental psychology   The study of the changes that occur in people from birth through old age.

Diathesis   Biological predisposition.

Diathesis–stress model   View that people biologically predisposed to a mental disorder (those with a certain diathesis) will tend to exhibit that disorder when particularly affected by stress.

Dichromats   People (and animals) that are blind to either red–green or yellow–blue.

Difference threshold or just-noticeable difference (jnd)   The smallest change in stimulation that can be detected 50% of the time.

Discrimination   An unfair act or series of acts taken toward an entire group of people or individual members of that group.

Disorganized schizophrenia   Schizophrenic disorder in which bizarre and childlike behaviors are common.

Displacement   Shifting repressed motives and emotions from an original object to a substitute object.

Display rules   Culture-specific rules that govern how, when, and why expressions of emotion are appropriate.

Dissociative amnesia   A disorder characterized by loss of memory for past events without organic cause.

Dissociative disorders   Disorders in which some aspect of the personality seems separated from the rest.

Dissociative fugue   A disorder that involves flight from home and the assumption of a new identity with amnesia for past identity and events.

Dissociative identity disorder   (Also called multiple personality disorder.) Disorder characterized by the separation of the personality into two or more distinct personalities.

Divergent thinking   Thinking that meets the criteria of originality, inventiveness, and flexibility.

Dominant gene   Member of a gene pair that controls the appearance of a certain trait.

Double-blind procedure   Experimental design useful in studies of the effects of drugs, in which neither the subject nor the researcher knows at the time of administration which subjects are receiving an active drug and which are receiving an inactive substance.

Dreams   Vivid visual and auditory experiences that occur primarily during REM periods of sleep.

Drive   State of tension or arousal that motivates behavior.

Drive-reduction theory   States that motivated behavior is aimed at reducing a state of bodily tension or arousal and returning the organism to homeostasis.

Eclecticism   Psychotherapeutic approach that recognizes the value of a broad treatment package over a rigid commitment to one particular form of therapy.

Efferent neurons   Neurons that carry messages from the spinal cord or brain to the muscles and glands.

Ego   Freud's term for the part of the personality that mediates between environmental demands (reality), conscience (superego), and instinctual needs (id); now often used as a synonym for "self."

Ego ideal   The part of the superego that consists of standards of what one would like to be.

Egocentric   Unable to see things from another's point of view.

Eidetic imagery   The ability to reproduce unusually sharp and detailed images of something one has seen.

Elaborative rehearsal   The linking of new information in short-term memory to familiar material stored in long-term memory.

Electroconvulsive therapy (ECT)   Biological therapy in which a mild electrical current is passed through the brain for a short period, often producing convulsions and temporary coma; used to treat severe, prolonged depression.

Elevation   Monocular cue to distance and depth based on the fact that the higher on the horizontal plane an object is, the farther away it appears.

Embryo   A developing human between 2 weeks and 3 months after conception.

Emotion   Feeling, such as fear, joy, or surprise, that underlies behavior.

Emotional intelligence   According to Goleman, a form of intelligence that refers to how effectively people perceive and understand their own emotions and the emotions of others, and can regulate and manage their emotional behavior.

Emotional memories   Learned emotional responses to various stimuli.

Endocrine glands   Glands of the endocrine system that release hormones into the bloodstream.

Episodic memories   The portion of long-term memory that stores personally experienced events.

Equity   Fairness of exchange achieved when each partner in the relationship receives the same proportion of outcomes to investments.

Equity theory   Theory that worker motivation depends on the relationship between personal effort expended and rewards received when compared to that of other workers.

Erectile disorder (or erectile dysfunction) (ED)   The inability of a man to achieve or maintain an erection.

Ethnicity   A common cultural heritage—including religion, language, or ancestry—that is shared by a group of individuals.

Evolutionary psychology   An approach to, and subfield of, psychology that is concerned with the evolutionary origins of behaviors and mental processes, their adaptive value, and the purposes they continue to serve.

Evolutionary psychology   A subfield of psychology concerned with the origins of behaviors and mental processes, their adaptive value, and the purposes they continue to serve.

Exchange   The concept that relationships are based on trading rewards among partners.

Exhibitionism   Compulsion to expose one's genitals in public to achieve sexual arousal.

Expectancies   In Bandura's view, what a person anticipates in a situation or as a result of behaving in certain ways.

Expectancy theory   Theory that worker motivation depends on the expectation that by working hard they will achieve valued rewards.

Experimental group   In a controlled experiment, the group subjected to a change in the independent variable.

Experimental method   Research technique in which an investigator deliberately manipulates selected events or circumstances and then measures the effects of those manipulations on subsequent behavior.

Experimenter bias   Expectations by the experimenter that might influence the results of an experiment or its interpretation.

Explicit memory   Memory for information that we can readily express in words and are aware of having; these memories can be intentionally retrieved from memory.

Extinction   A decrease in the strength or frequency, or stopping, of a learned response because of failure to continue pairing the US and CS (classical conditioning) or withholding of reinforcement (operant conditioning).

Extraverts   According to Jung, people who usually focus on social life and the external world instead of on their internal experience.

Extrinsic motivation   A desire to perform a behavior to obtain an external reward or avoid punishment.

Factor analysis   A statistical technique that identifies groups of related objects; it was used by Cattell to identify clusters of traits.

Family studies   Studies of heritability in humans based on the assumption that if genes influence a certain trait, close relatives should be more similar on that trait than distant relatives.

Family therapy   A form of group therapy that sees the family as at least partly responsible for the individual's problems and that seeks to change all family members' behaviors to the benefit of the family unit as well as the troubled individual.

Feature detectors   Specialized brain cells that only respond to particular elements in the visual field such as movement or lines of specific orientation.

Female sexual arousal disorder   The inability of a woman to become sexually aroused or to reach orgasm.

Feminist theory   Feminist theories offer a wide variety of views on the social roles of women and men, the problems and rewards of those roles, and prescriptions for changing those roles.

Fetal alcohol syndrome (FAS)   A disorder that occurs in children of women who drink alcohol during pregnancy; this disorder is characterized by facial deformities, heart defects, stunted growth, and cognitive impairments.

Fetishism   A paraphilia in which a nonhuman object is the preferred or exclusive method of achieving sexual excitement.

Fetus   A developing human between 3 months after conception and birth.

Fixation   According to Freud, a partial or complete halt at some point in the individual's psychosexual development.

Fixed-interval schedule   A reinforcement schedule in which the correct response is reinforced after a fixed length of time since the last reinforcement.

Fixed-ratio schedule   A reinforcement schedule in which the correct response is reinforced after a fixed number of correct responses.

Flashbulb memory   A vivid memory of a certain event and the incidents surrounding it even after a long time has passed.

Formal-operational stage   In Piaget's theory, the stage of cognitive development beginning about 11 years of age in which the individual becomes capable of abstract thought.

Fovea   The area of the retina that is the center of the visual field.

Framing   The perspective from which we interpret information before making a decision.

Fraternal twins   Twins developed from two separate fertilized ova and therefore different in genetic makeup.

Free association   A psychoanalytic technique that encourages the person to talk without inhibition about whatever thoughts or fantasies come to mind.

Frequency   The number of cycles per second in a wave; in sound, the primary determinant of pitch.

Frequency distribution   A count of the number of scores that fall within each of a series of intervals.

Frequency histogram   Type of bar graph that shows frequency distributions.

Frequency polygon   Type of line graph that shows frequency distributions.

Frequency theory   Theory that pitch is determined by the frequency with which hair cells in the cochlea fire.

Frontal lobe   Part of the cerebral cortex that is responsible for voluntary movement; it is also important for attention, goal-directed behavior, and appropriate emotional experiences.

Frotteurism   Compulsion to achieve sexual arousal by touching or rubbing against a nonconsenting person in public situations.

Frustration   The feeling that occurs when a person is prevented from reaching a goal.

Frustration–aggression theory   The theory that, under certain circumstances, people who are frustrated in their goals turn their anger away from the proper, powerful target and toward another, less powerful target that is safer to attack.

Fully functioning person   According to Rogers, an individual whose self-concept closely resembles his or her inborn capacities or potentials.

Functional fixedness   The tendency to perceive only a limited number of uses for an object, thus interfering with the process of problem solving.

Functional job analysis   A method for identifying the procedures and processes that workers must use in the performance of the job.

Functionalist theory   Theory of mental life and behavior that is concerned with how an organism uses its perceptual abilities to function in its environment.

Fundamental attribution error   The tendency of people to overemphasize personal causes for other people's behavior and to underemphasize personal causes for their own behavior.

Ganglion cells   Neurons that connect the bipolar cells in the eyes to the brain.

Gate-control theory   The theory that a "neurological gate" in the spinal cord controls the transmission of pain messages to the brain.

Gender   The psychological and social meanings attached to being biologically male or female.

Gender constancy   The realization that gender does not change with age.

Gender identity   A little girl's knowledge that she is a girl, and a little boy's knowledge that he is a boy.

Gender stereotypes   General beliefs about characteristics that men and women are presumed to have.

Gender-identity disorder in children   Rejection of one's biological gender in childhood, along with the clothing and behavior that society considers appropriate to that gender.

Gender-identity disorders   Disorders that involve the desire to become, or the insistence that one really is, a member of the other biological sex.

Gender-role awareness   Knowledge of what behavior is appropriate for each gender.

General adaptation syndrome (GAS)   According to Selye, the three stages the body passes through as it adapts to stress: alarm reaction, resistance, and exhaustion.

Generalized anxiety disorder   An anxiety disorder characterized by prolonged vague but intense fears that are not attached to any particular object or circumstance.

Genes   Elements that control the transmission of traits; they are found on the chromosomes.

Genetics   Study of how traits are transmitted from one generation to the next.

Genital stage   In Freud's theory of personality development, the final stage of normal adult sexual development, which is usually marked by mature sexuality.

Genotype   An organism's entire unique genetic makeup.

Gestalt psychology   School of psychology that studies how people perceive and experience objects as whole patterns.

Gestalt therapy   An insight therapy that emphasizes the wholeness of the personality and attempts to reawaken people to their emotions and sensations in the present.

Ghrelin   A hormone produced in the stomach and small intestines that increases appetite.

Giftedness   Refers to superior IQ combined with demonstrated or potential ability in such areas as academic aptitude, creativity, and leadership.

Glial cells (or glia)   Cells that insulate and support neurons by holding them together, provide nourishment and remove waste products, prevent harmful substances from passing into the brain, and form the myelin sheath.

Glucose   A simple sugar used by the body for energy.

Goal-setting theory   Theory that worker motivation requires clearly stated goals and a belief that good job performance will lead to the attainment of these goals.

Golgi tendon organs   Receptors that sense movement of the tendons, which connect muscle to bone.

Gonads   The reproductive glands—testes in males and ovaries in females.

Graded potential   A shift in the electrical charge in a tiny area of a neuron.

Grammar   The language rules that determine how sounds and words can be combined and used to communicate meaning within a language.

Great-person theory   The theory that leadership is a result of personal qualities and traits that qualify one to lead others.

Group tests   Written intelligence tests administered by one examiner to many people at one time.

Group therapy   Type of psychotherapy in which clients meet regularly to interact and help one another achieve insight into their feelings and behavior.

Growth spurt   A rapid increase in height and weight that occurs during adolescence.

Hallucinations   Sensory experiences in the absence of external stimulation.

Hallucinogens   Any of a number of drugs, such as LSD and mescaline, that distort visual and auditory perception.

Health psychology   A subfield of psychology concerned with the relationship between psychological factors and physical health and illness.

Hertz (Hz)   Cycles per second; unit of measurement for the frequency of sound waves.

Heuristics   Rules of thumb that help in simplifying and solving problems, although they do not guarantee a correct solution.

Hierarchy of needs   A theory of motivation advanced by Maslow holding that higher order motives involving social and personal growth only emerge after lower level motives related to survival have been satisfied.

Higher order conditioning   Conditioning based on previous learning; the conditioned stimulus serves as an unconditioned stimulus for further training.

Hill climbing   A heuristic, problem-solving strategy in which each step moves you progressively closer to the final goal.

Hindbrain   Area containing the medulla, pons, and cerebellum.

Hindsight bias   The tendency to see outcomes as inevitable and predictable after we know the outcome.

Holophrases   One-word sentences commonly used by children under 2 years of age.

Homeostasis   State of balance and stability in which the organism functions effectively.

Hormones   Chemical substances released by the endocrine glands; they help regulate bodily activities.

Hues   The aspects of color that correspond to names such as red, green, and blue.

Human genome   The full complement of genes within a human cell.

Humanistic personality theory   Any personality theory that asserts the fundamental goodness of people and their striving toward higher levels of functioning.

Humanistic psychology   School of psychology that emphasizes nonverbal experience and altered states of consciousness as a means of realizing one's full human potential.

Hypnosis   Trancelike state in which a person responds readily to suggestions.

Hypochondriasis   A somatoform disorder in which a person interprets insignificant symptoms as signs of serious illness in the absence of any organic evidence of such illness.

Hypothalamus   Forebrain region that governs motivation and emotional responses.

Hypotheses   Specific, testable predictions derived from a theory.

Id   In Freud's theory of personality, the collection of unconscious urges and desires that continually seek expression.

Identical twins   Twins developed from a single fertilized ovum and therefore identical in genetic makeup at the time of conception.

Identification   Taking on the characteristics of someone else to avoid feeling incompetent.

Identity crisis   A period of intense self-examination and decision making; part of the process of identity formation.

Identity formation   Erickson's term for the development of a stable sense of self necessary to make the transition from dependence on others to dependence on oneself.

Image   A mental representation of a sensory experience.

Imaginary audience   Elkind's term for adolescents' delusion that they are constantly being observed by others.

Implicit memory   Memory for information that we cannot readily express in words and may not be aware of having; these memories cannot be intentionally retrieved from memory.

Imprinting   The tendency in certain species to follow the first moving thing (usually its mother) it sees after it is born or hatched.

Incentive   External stimulus that prompts goal-directed behavior.

Independent variable   In an experiment, the variable that is manipulated to test its effects on the other, dependent variables.

Industrial psychology   Subfield of industrial/organizational psychology concerned with effectively managing human resources.

Industrial/organizational (I/O) psychology   The study of how individuals and organizations work and how psychological principles can be used to improve organizational effectiveness.

Inferiority complex   In Adler's theory, the fixation on feelings of personal inferiority that results in emotional and social paralysis.

Information-processing model   A computerlike model used to describe the way humans encode, store, and retrieve information.

Insanity   Legal term applied to defendants who do not know right from wrong or are unable to control their behavior.

Insight   Learning that occurs rapidly as a result of understanding all the elements of a problem.

Insight   Awareness of previously unconscious feelings and memories and how they influence present feelings and behavior.

Insight therapies   A variety of individual psychotherapies designed to give people a better awareness and understanding of their feelings, motivations, and actions in the hope that this will help them to adjust.

Insomnia   Sleep disorder characterized by difficulty in falling asleep or remaining asleep throughout the night.

Instincts   Inborn, inflexible, goal-directed behaviors that is characteristic of an entire species.

Integrity tests   Paper-and-pencil tests that predict the likelihood that a job applicant will engage in counterproductive behavior in the workplace.

Intellectualization   Thinking abstractly about stressful problems as a way of detaching oneself from them.

Intelligence   A general term referring to the ability or abilities involved in learning and adaptive behavior.

Intelligence quotient (IQ)   A numerical value given to intelligence that is determined from the scores on an intelligence test on the basis of a score of 100 for average intelligence.

Intermittent pairing   Pairing the conditioned stimulus and the unconditioned stimulus on only a portion of the learning trials.

Interneurons (or association neurons)   Neurons that carry messages from one neuron to another.

Interposition   Monocular distance cue in which one object, by partly blocking a second object, is perceived as being closer.

Interval scale   Scale with equal distances between the points or values, but without a true zero.

Intrinsic motivation   A desire to perform a behavior that stems from the enjoyment derived from the behavior itself.

Introverts   According to Jung, people who usually focus on their own thoughts and feelings.

Ions   Electrically charged particles found both inside and outside the neuron.

Iris   The colored part of the eye that regulates the size of the pupil.

James–Lange theory   States that stimuli cause physiological changes in our bodies, and emotions result from those physiological changes.

Job analysis   Identifying the various tasks required by a job and the human qualifications that are required to perform that job.

Job rotation   Training workers to perform a variety of jobs.

Just-world hypothesis   Attribution error based on the assumption that bad things happen to bad people and good things happen to good people.

Kinesthetic senses   Senses of muscle movement, posture, and strain on muscles and joints.

KSAO system of job analysis   A method for identifying the knowledge, skills, abilities, and other human characteristics that are required for the job.

Language   A flexible system of communication that uses sounds, rules, gestures, or symbols to convey information.

Language acquisition device   A hypothetical neural mechanism for acquiring language that is presumed to be "wired into" all humans.

Latency period   In Freud's theory of personality, a period in which the child appears to have no interest in the other sex; occurs after the phallic stage.

Latent learning   Learning that is not immediately reflected in a behavior change.

Law of effect (principle of reinforcement)   Thorndike's theory that behavior consistently rewarded will be "stamped in" as learned behavior, and behavior that brings about discomfort will be "stamped out."

Learned helplessness   Failure to take steps to avoid or escape from an unpleasant or aversive stimulus that occurs as a result of previous exposure to unavoidable painful stimuli.

Learning   The process by which experience or practice results in a relatively permanent change in behavior or potential behavior.

Learning set   The ability to become increasingly more effective in solving problems as more problems are solved.

Lens   The transparent part of the eye behind the pupil that focuses light onto the retina.

Leptin   A hormone released by fat cells that reduces appetite.

Libido   According to Freud, the energy generated by the sexual instinct.

Light adaptation   Decreased sensitivity of rods and cones in bright light.

Limbic system   Ring of structures that plays a role in learning and emotional behavior.

Linear perspective   Monocular cue to distance and depth based on the fact that two parallel lines seem to come together at the horizon.

Linguistic determinism   The belief that thought and experience are determined by language.

Linguistic relativity hypothesis   Whorf's idea that patterns of thinking are determined by the specific language one speaks.

Locus of control   According to Rotter, an expectancy about whether reinforcement is under internal or external control.

Longitudinal studies   A method of studying developmental changes by evaluating the same people at different points in their lives.

Long-term memory (LTM)   The portion of memory that is more or less permanent, corresponding to everything we "know."

Long-term potentiation (LTP)   A long-lasting change in the structure or function of a synapse that increases the efficiency of neural transmission and is thought to be related to how information is stored by neurons.

Lysergic acid diethylamide (LSD)   Hallucinogenic or "psychedelic" drug that produces hallucinations and delusions similar to those occurring in a psychotic state.

Mania   A mood disorder characterized by euphoric states, extreme physical activity, excessive talkativeness, distractedness, and sometimes grandiosity.

Marijuana   A mild hallucinogen that produces a "high" often characterized by feelings of euphoria, a sense of well-being, and swings in mood from gaiety to relaxation; may also cause feelings of anxiety and paranoia.

Maturation   An automatic biological unfolding of development in an organism as a function of the passage of time.

Mean   Arithmetical average calculated by dividing a sum of values by the total number of cases.

Means-end analysis   A heuristic strategy that aims to reduce the discrepancy between the current situation and the desired goal at a number of intermediate points.

Median   Point that divides a set of scores in half.

Meditation   Any of the various methods of concentration, reflection, or focusing of thoughts undertaken to suppress the activity of the sympathetic nervous system.

Medulla   Structure in the hindbrain that controls essential life support functions including breathing, heart rate and blood pressure.

Memory   The ability to remember the things that we have experienced, imagined, and learned.

Menarche   First menstrual period.

Menopause   The time in a woman's life when menstruation ceases.

Mental representations   Mental images or symbols (such as words) used to think about or remember an object, a person, or an event.

Mental retardation   Condition of significantly subaverage intelligence combined with deficiencies in adaptive behavior.

Mental set   The tendency to perceive and to approach problems in certain ways.

Meta-analysis   A statistical procedure for combining the results of several studies so the strength, consistency, and direction of the effect can be estimated.

Midbrain   Region between the hindbrain and the forebrain; it is important for hearing and sight, and it is one of several places in the brain where pain is registered.

Midlife crisis   A time when adults discover they no longer feel fulfilled in their jobs or personal lives and attempt to make a decisive shift in career or lifestyle.

Midlife transition   According to Levinson, a process whereby adults assess the past and formulate new goals for the future.

Minnesota Multiphasic Personality Inventory (MMPI-2)   The most widely used objective personality test, originally intended for psychiatric diagnosis.

Mnemonics   Techniques that make material easier to remember.

Mnemonists   People with highly developed memory skills.

Mode   Point at which the largest number of scores occurs.

Modeling   A behavior therapy in which the person learns desired behaviors by watching others perform those behaviors.

Monaural cues   Cues to sound location that require just one ear.

Monochromats   Organisms that are totally color blind.

Monocular cues   Visual cues requiring the use of one eye.

Mood disorders   Disturbances in mood or prolonged emotional state.

Morphemes   The smallest meaningful units of speech, such as simple words, prefixes, and suffixes.

Motion parallax   Monocular distance cue in which objects closer than the point of visual focus seem to move in the direction opposite to the viewer's moving head, and objects beyond the focus point appear to move in the same direction as the viewer's head.

Motive   Specific need or desire, such as hunger, thirst, or achievement, that prompts goal-directed behavior.

Motor (or efferent) neurons   Neurons that carry messages from the spinal cord or brain to the muscles and glands.

Myelin sheath   White fatty covering found on some axons.

Narcissistic personality disorder   Personality disorder in which the person has an exaggerated sense of self-importance and needs constant admiration.

Narcolepsy   Hereditary sleep disorder characterized by sudden nodding off during the day and sudden loss of muscle tone following moments of emotional excitement.

Natural selection   The mechanism proposed by Darwin in his theory of evolution, which states that organisms best adapted to their environment tend to survive, transmitting their genetic characteristics to succeeding generations, whereas organisms with less adaptive characteristics tend to vanish from the earth.

Naturalistic observation   Research method involving the systematic study of animal or human behavior in natural settings rather than in the laboratory.

Negative reinforcers   Events whose reduction or termination increases the likelihood that ongoing behavior will recur.

Neonates   Newborn babies.

NEO-PI-R   An objective personality test designed to assess the Big Five personality traits.

Nerve (or tract)   Group of axons bundled together.

Neural impulse (or action potential)   The firing of a nerve cell.

Neural plasticity   The ability of the brain to change in response to experience.

Neurofeedback   A biofeedback technique that monitors brain waves with the use of an EEG to teach people to gain voluntary control over their brain wave activity.

Neurogenesis   The growth of new neurons.

Neurons   Individual cells that are the smallest unit of the nervous system.

Neuroscience   The study of the brain and the nervous system.

Neurotic trends   Horney's term for irrational strategies for coping with emotional problems and minimizing anxiety.

Neurotransmitters   Chemicals released by the synaptic vesicles that travel across the synaptic space and affect adjacent neurons.

Night terrors   Frightening, often terrifying dreams that occur during NREM sleep from which a person is difficult to awaken and doesn't remember the content.

Nightmares   Frightening dreams that occur during REM sleep and are remembered.

Nominal scale   A set of categories for classifying objects.

Non-REM (NREM) sleep   Non-rapid-eye-movement stages of sleep that alternate with REM stages during the sleep cycle.

Non-shared environment   The unique aspects of the environment that are experienced differently by siblings, even though they are reared in the same family.

Norm   A shared idea or expectation about how to behave.

Normal curve   Hypothetical bell-shaped distribution curve that occurs when a normal distribution is plotted as a frequency polygon.

Obedience   Change of behavior in response to a command from another person, typically an authority figure.

Object permanence   The concept that things continue to exist even when they are out of sight.

Objective performance appraisal   Method of performance appraisal based on quantitative measurement of the amount of work done.

Objective tests   Personality tests that are administered and scored in a standard way.

Observational (or vicarious) learning   Learning by observing other people's behavior.

Observer bias   Expectations or biases of the observer that might distort or influence his or her interpretation of what was actually observed.

Obsessive–compulsive disorder (OCD)   An anxiety disorder in which a person feels driven to think disturbing thoughts or to perform senseless rituals.

Occipital lobe   Part of the cerebral hemisphere that receives and interprets visual information.

Oedipus complex and Electra complex   According to Freud, a child's sexual attachment to the parent of the opposite sex and jealousy toward the parent of the same sex; generally occurs in the phallic stage.

Olfactory bulb   The smell center in the brain.

On-the-job training   Teaching employees a new job by actually performing the job.

Operant (or instrumental) conditioning   The type of learning in which behaviors are emitted (in the presence of specific stimuli) to earn rewards or avoid punishments.

Operant behaviors   Behaviors designed to operate on the environment in a way that will gain something desired or avoid something unpleasant.

Opiates   Drugs, such as opium and heroin, derived from the opium poppy, that dull the senses and induce feelings of euphoria, well-being, and relaxation. Synthetic drugs resembling opium derivatives are also classified as opiates.

Opponent-process theory   Theory of color vision that holds that three sets of color receptors (yellow–blue, red–green, black–white) respond to determine the color you experience.

Optic chiasm   The point near the base of the brain where some fibers in the optic nerve from each eye cross to the other side of the brain.

Optic nerve   The bundle of axons of ganglion cells that carries neural messages from each eye to the brain.

Oral stage   First stage in Freud's theory of personality development, in which the infant's erotic feelings center on the mouth, lips, and tongue.

Ordinal scale   Scale indicating order or relative position of items according to some criterion.

Organ of Corti   Structure on the surface of the basilar membrane that contains the receptor cells for hearing.

Organizational justice   Degree to which employees perceive fairness in the workplace.

Organizational psychology   Subfield of industrial/organizational psychology that focuses on the organization as a whole, rather than on the individuals who work within it.

Orgasmic disorders   Inability to reach orgasm in a person able to experience sexual desire and maintain arousal.

Oval window   Membrane across the opening between the middle ear and inner ear that conducts vibrations to the cochlea.

Overtones   Tones that result from sound waves that are multiples of the basic tone; primary determinant of timbre.

Pancreas   Organ lying between the stomach and small intestine; it secretes insulin and glucagon to regulate blood-sugar levels.

Panic disorder   An anxiety disorder characterized by recurrent panic attacks in which the person suddenly experiences intense fear or terror without any reasonable cause.

Paranoid personality disorder   Personality disorder in which the person is inappropriately suspicious and mistrustful of others.

Paranoid schizophrenia   Schizophrenic disorder marked by extreme suspiciousness and complex, bizarre delusions.

Paraphilias   Sexual disorders in which unconventional objects or situations cause sexual arousal.

Parasympathetic division   Branch of the autonomic nervous system; it calms and relaxes the body.

Parathyroids   Four tiny glands embedded in the thyroid.

Parietal lobe   Part of the cerebral cortex that receives sensory information from throughout the body.

Participants   Individuals whose reactions or responses are observed in an experiment.

Pedophilia   Desire to have sexual relations with children as the preferred or exclusive method of achieving sexual excitement.

Peer group   A network of same-aged friends and acquaintances who give one another emotional and social support.

Perception   The brain's interpretation of sensory information so as to give it meaning.

Perceptual constancy   A tendency to perceive objects as stable and unchanging despite changes in sensory stimulation.

Performance appraisal systems   Formal methods used to assess the quantity and quality of work contributed by each individual within an organization.

Performance standards   In Bandura's theory, standards that people develop to rate the adequacy of their own behavior in a variety of situations.

Performance tests   Intelligence tests that minimize the use of language.

Peripheral nervous system (PNS)   Division of the nervous system that connects the central nervous system to the rest of the body.

Persona   According to Jung, our public self, the mask we wear to represent ourselves to others.

Personal fable   Elkind's term for adolescents' delusion that they are unique, very important, and invulnerable.

Personal unconscious   In Jung's theory of personality, one of the two levels of the unconscious; it contains the individual's repressed thoughts, forgotten experiences, and undeveloped ideas.

Personality   An individual's unique pattern of thoughts, feelings, and behaviors that persists over time and across situations.

Personality disorders   Disorders in which inflexible and maladaptive ways of thinking and behaving learned early in life cause distress to the person or conflicts with others.

Personality traits   Dimensions or characteristics on which people differ in distinctive ways.

Personnel selection   The process of selecting from a pool of job applicants those who will be hired to perform a job.

Phallic stage   Third stage in Freud's theory of personality development, in which erotic feelings center on the genitals.

Phenotype   The characteristics of an organism; determined by both genetics and experience.

Pheromones   Chemicals that communicate information to other organisms through smell.

Phi phenomenon   Apparent movement caused by flashing lights in sequence, as on theater marquees.

Phonemes   The basic sounds that make up any language.

Pineal gland   A gland located roughly in the center of the brain that appears to regulate activity levels over the course of a day.

Pitch   Auditory experience corresponding primarily to frequency of sound vibrations, resulting in a higher or lower tone.

Pituitary gland   Gland located on the underside of the brain; it produces the largest number of the body's hormones.

Place theory   Theory that pitch is determined by the location of greatest vibration on the basilar membrane.

Placebo   Chemically inactive substance used for comparison with active drugs in experiments on the effects of drugs.

Placebo effect   Pain relief that occurs when a person believes a pill or procedure will reduce pain. The actual cause of the relief seems to come from endorphins.

Pleasure principle   According to Freud, the way in which the id seeks immediate gratification of an instinct.

Polarization   The condition of a neuron when the inside is negatively charged relative to the outside; for example, when the neuron is at rest.

Polarization   Shift in attitudes by members of a group toward more extreme positions than the ones held before group discussion.

Polygenic inheritance   Process by which several genes interact to produce a certain trait; responsible for our most important traits.

Pons   Structure in the midbrain that regulates sleep and wake cycles.

Positive psychology   An emerging field of psychology that focuses on positive experiences, including subjective well-being, self-determination, the relationship between positive emotions and physical health, and the factors that allow individuals, communities, and societies to flourish.

Positive reinforcers   Events whose presence increases the likelihood that ongoing behavior will recur.

Posttraumatic stress disorder (PTSD)   Psychological disorder characterized by episodes of anxiety, sleeplessness, and nightmares resulting from some disturbing past event.

Prejudice   An unfair, intolerant, or unfavorable attitude toward a group of people.

Premature ejaculation   Inability of man to inhibit orgasm as long as desired.

Prenatal development   Development from conception to birth.

Preoperational stage   In Piaget's theory, the stage of cognitive development between 2 and 7 years of age in which the individual becomes able to use mental representations and language to describe, remember, and reason about the world, though only in an egocentric fashion.

Preparedness   A biological readiness to learn certain associations because of their survival advantages.

Pressure   A feeling that one must speed up, intensify, or change the direction of one's behavior or live up to a higher standard of performance.

Primacy effect   The fact that early information about someone weighs more heavily than later information in influencing one's impression of that person.

Primary drives   Unlearned drive, such as hunger, that are based on a physiological state.

Primary motor cortex   The section of the frontal lobe responsible for voluntary movement.

Primary prevention   Techniques and programs to improve the social environment so that new cases of mental disorders do not develop.

Primary reinforcers   Reinforcers that are rewarding in themselves, such as food, water, or sex.

Primary somatosensory cortex   Area of the parietal lobe where messages from the sense receptors are registered.

Principles of conservation   The concept that the quantity of a substance is not altered by reversible changes in its appearance.

Proactive interference   The process by which information already in memory interferes with new information.

Problem representation   The first step in solving a problem; it involves interpreting or defining the problem.

Procedural memories   The portion of long-term memory that stores information relating to skills, habits, and other perceptual-motor tasks.

Projection   Attributing one's repressed motives, feelings, or wishes to others.

Projective tests   Personality tests, such as the Rorschach inkblot test, consisting of ambiguous or unstructured material.

Prototype (or model)   According to Rosch, a mental model containing the most typical features of a concept.

Proximity   How close two people live to each other.

Psychoactive drugs   Chemical substances that change moods and perceptions.

Psychoanalysis   The theory of personality Freud developed, as well as the form of therapy he invented.

Psychoanalysis   The theory of personality Freud developed as well as the form of therapy he invented.

Psychoanalytic model   View that psychological disorders result from unconscious internal conflicts.

Psychobiology   The area of psychology that focuses on the biological foundations of behavior and mental processes.

Psychodynamic theories   Personality theories contending that behavior results from psychological factors that interact within the individual, often outside conscious awareness.

Psychodynamic theories   Personality theories contending that behavior results from psychological forces that interact within the individual, often outside conscious awareness.

Psychology   The scientific study of behavior and mental processes.

Psychoneuroimmunology (PNI)   A new field that studies the interaction between stress on the one hand and immune, endocrine, and nervous system activity on the other.

Psychosomatic disorder   A disorder in which there is real physical illness that is largely caused by psychological factors such as stress and anxiety.

Psychostimulant   Drugs that increase ability to focus attention in people with ADHD.

Psychosurgery   Brain surgery performed to change a person's behavior and emotional state; a biological therapy rarely used today.

Psychotherapy   The use of psychological techniques to treat personality and behavior disorders.

Psychotic (psychosis)   Behavior characterized by a loss of touch with reality.

Puberty   The onset of sexual maturation, with accompanying physical development.

Punishers   Stimuli that follows a behavior and decreases the likelihood that the behavior will be repeated.

Punishment   Any event whose presence decreases the likelihood that ongoing behavior will recur.

Pupil   A small opening in the iris through which light enters the eye.

Race   A subpopulation of a species, defined according to an identifiable characteristic (that is, geographic location, skin color, hair texture, genes, facial features, and so forth).

Racism   Prejudice and discrimination directed at a particular racial group.

Random sample   Sample in which each potential participant has an equal chance of being selected.

Range   Difference between the largest and smallest measurements in a distribution.

Rapid-eye movement (REM) or paradoxical sleep   Sleep stage characterized by rapid-eye movements and increased dreaming.

Ratio scale   Scale with equal distances between the points or values and with a true zero.

Rational–emotive therapy (RET)   A directive cognitive therapy based on the idea that clients' psychological distress is caused by irrational and self-defeating beliefs and that the therapist's job is to challenge such dysfunctional beliefs.

Reaction formation   Expression of exaggerated ideas and emotions that are the opposite of one's repressed beliefs or feelings.

Reality principle   According to Freud, the way in which the ego seeks to satisfy instinctual demands safely and effectively in the real world.

Receptor cell   A specialized cell that responds to a particular type of energy.

Receptor sites   Locations on a receptor neuron into which a specific neurotransmitter fits like a key into a lock.

Recessive gene   Member of a gene pair that can control the appearance of a certain trait only if it is paired with another recessive gene.

Regression   Reverting to childlike behavior and defenses.

Reinforcement theory   Theory that work behavior that is followed by positive outcomes will be maintained and repeated.

Reinforcers   A stimuli that follows a behavior and increases the likelihood that the behavior will be repeated.

Reliability   Ability of a test to produce consistent and stable scores.

Representative sample   Sample carefully chosen so that the characteristics of the participants correspond closely to the characteristics of the larger population.

Representativeness   A heuristic by which a new situation is judged on the basis of its resemblance to a stereotypical model.

Repression   Excluding uncomfortable thoughts, feelings, and desires from consciousness.

Response generalization   Giving a response that is somewhat different from the response originally learned to that stimulus.

Resting potential   Electrical charge across a neuron membrane resulting from more positive ions concentrated on the outside and more negative ions on the inside.

Reticular formation (RF)   Network of neurons in the hindbrain, the midbrain, and part of the forebrain, whose primary function is to alert and arouse the higher parts of the brain.

Retina   The lining of the eye containing receptor cells that are sensitive to light.

Retinal disparity   Binocular distance cue based on the difference between the images cast on the two retinas when both eyes are focused on the same object.

Retroactive interference   The process by which new information interferes with information already in memory.

Retrograde amnesia   The inability to recall events preceding an accident or injury, but without loss of earlier memory.

Risky shift   Greater willingness of a group than an individual to take substantial risks.

Rods   Receptor cells in the retina responsible for night vision and perception of brightness.

Rorschach test   A projective test composed of ambiguous inkblots; the way people interpret the blots is thought to reveal aspects of their personality.

Rote rehearsal   Retaining information in memory simply by repeating it over and over.

Sample   A subgroup of a population.

Saturation   The vividness or richness of a hue.

Scatter plot   Diagram showing the association between scores on two variables.

Schedule of reinforcement   In operant conditioning, the rule for determining when and how often reinforcers will be delivered.

Schema   (skee-mah; plural: schemata) A set of beliefs or expectations about something that is based on past experience.

Schizoid personality disorder   Personality disorder in which a person is withdrawn and lacks feelings for others.

Schizophrenic disorders   Severe disorders in which there are disturbances of thoughts, communications, and emotions, including delusions and hallucinations.

Scientific method   An approach to knowledge that relies on collecting data, generating a theory to explain the data, producing testable hypotheses based on the theory, and testing those hypotheses empirically.

Secondary drives   Learned drives, such as ambition, that are not based on a physiological state.

Secondary prevention   Programs to identify groups that are at high risk for mental disorders and to detect maladaptive behavior in these groups and treat it promptly.

Secondary reinforcers   Reinforcers whose value is acquired through association with other primary or secondary reinforcers.

Selection studies   Studies that estimate the heritability of a trait by breeding animals with other animals that have the same trait.

Self-actualizing tendency   According to Rogers, the drive of human beings to fulfill their self-concepts, or the images they have of themselves.

Self-efficacy   According to Bandura, the expectancy that one's efforts will be successful.

Self-fulfilling prophecy   The process in which a person's expectation about another elicits behavior from the second person that confirms the expectation.

Self-monitoring   The tendency for an individual to observe the situation for cues about how to react.

Semantic memories   The portion of long-term memory that stores general facts and information.

Sensation   The experience of sensory stimulation.

Sensory (or afferent) neurons   Neurons that carry messages from sense organs to the spinal cord or brain.

Sensory registers   Entry points for raw information from the senses.

Sensory-motor stage   In Piaget's theory, the stage of cognitive development between birth and 2 years of age in which the individual develops object permanence and acquires the ability to form mental representations.

Serial position effect   The finding that when asked to recall a list of unrelated items, performance is better for the items at the beginning and end of the list.

Set point theory   A theory that our bodies are genetically predisposed to maintaining a certain weight by changing our metabolic rate and activity level in response to caloric intake.

Sex-typed behavior   Socially prescribed ways of behaving that differ for boys and girls.

Sexual desire disorders   Disorders in which the person lacks sexual interest or has an active distaste for sex.

Sexual dysfunction   Loss or impairment of the ordinary physical responses of sexual function.

Sexual harassment   Soliciting sexual favors in exchange for favorable treatment, or creating a hostile work environment.

Sexual masochism   Inability to enjoy sex without accompanying emotional or physical pain.

Sexual orientation   Refers to the direction of one's sexual interest toward members of the same sex, the other sex, or both sexes.

Sexual orientation   Refers to the direction of one's sexual interest toward members of the same sex, the other sex, or both sexes.

Sexual response cycle   The typical sequence of events, including excitement, plateau, orgasm, and resolution, characterizing sexual response in males and females.

Sexual sadism   Obtaining sexual gratification from humiliating or physically harming a sex partner.

Shadowing   Monocular cue to distance and depth based on the fact that shadows often appear on the parts of objects that are more distant.

Shape constancy   A tendency to see an object as the same shape no matter what angle it is viewed from.

Shaping   Reinforcing successive approximations to a desired behavior.

Short-term memory (STM)   Working memory; briefly stores and processes selected information from the sensory registers.

Short-term psychodynamic therapy   Insight therapy that is time limited and focused on trying to help clients correct the immediate problems in their lives.

Significance   Probability that results obtained were due to chance.

Signs   Stereotyped communications about an animal's current state.

Sixteen Personality Factor Questionnaire   Objective personality test created by Cattell that provides scores on the 16 traits he identified.

Size constancy   The perception of an object as the same size regardless of the distance from which it is viewed.

Skinner box   A box often used in operant conditioning of animals; it limits the available responses and thus increases the likelihood that the desired response will occur.

Social cognition   Knowledge and understanding concerning the social world and the people in it (including oneself).

Social influence   The process by which others individually or collectively affect one's perceptions, attitudes, and actions.

Social learning theorists   Psychologists whose view of learning emphasizes the ability to learn by observing a model or receiving instructions, without firsthand experience by the learner.

Social phobias   Anxiety disorders characterized by excessive, inappropriate fears connected with social situations or performances in front of other people.

Social psychology   The scientific study of the ways in which the thoughts, feelings, and behaviors of one individual are influenced by the real, imagined, or inferred behavior or characteristics of other people.

Socialization   Process by which children learn the behaviors and attitudes appropriate to their family and culture.

Somatic nervous system   The part of the peripheral nervous system that carries messages from the senses to the central nervous system and between the central nervous system and the skeletal muscles.

Somatization disorder   A somatoform disorder characterized by recurrent vague somatic complaints without a physical cause.

Somatoform disorders   Disorders in which there is an apparent physical illness for which there is no organic basis.

Sound   A psychological experience created by the brain in response to changes in air pressure that are received by the auditory system.

Sound waves   Changes in pressure caused when molecules of air or fluid collide with one another and then move apart again.

Specific phobia   Anxiety disorder characterized by an intense, paralyzing fear of something.

Spinal cord   Complex cable of neurons that runs down the spine, connecting the brain to most of the rest of the body.

Split-half reliability   A method of determining test reliability by dividing the test into two parts and checking the agreement of scores on both parts.

Spontaneous recovery   The reappearance of an extinguished response after the passage of time, without training.

Standard deviation   Statistical measure of variability in a group of scores or other values.

Statistics   A branch of mathematics that psychologists use to organize and analyze data.

Stereoscopic vision   Combination of two retinal images to give a three-dimensional perceptual experience.

Stereotype   A set of characteristics presumed to be shared by all members of a social category.

Stimulants   Drugs, including amphetamines and cocaine, that stimulate the sympathetic nervous system and produce feelings of optimism and boundless energy.

Stimulus control   Control of conditioned responses by cues or stimuli in the environment.

Stimulus discrimination   Learning to respond to only one stimulus and to inhibit the response to all other stimuli.

Stimulus generalization   The transfer of a learned response to different but similar stimuli.

Stimulus motives   Unlearned motives, such as curiosity or contact, that prompts us to explore or change the world around us.

Strain studies   Studies of the heritability of behavioral traits using animals that have been inbred to produce strains that are genetically similar to one another.

Stranger anxiety   Fear of unfamiliar people which usually emerges around 7 months, reaching its peak at 12 months and declining during the second year.

Stress   A state of psychological tension or strain.

Stress-inoculation therapy   A type of cognitive therapy that trains clients to cope with stressful situations by learning a more useful pattern of self-talk.

Stressor   Any environmental demand that creates a state of tension or threat and requires change or adaptation.

Stretch receptors   Receptors that sense muscle stretch and contraction.

Stroboscopic motion   Apparent movement that results from flashing a series of still pictures in rapid succession, as in a motion picture.

Structuralism   School of psychology that stresses the basic units of experience and the combinations in which they occur.

Subgoals   Intermediate, more manageable goals used in one heuristic strategy to make it easier to reach the final goal.

Subjective performance appraisal   Performance appraisal that relies on judgments about the quality of an employee's work.

Sublimation   Redirecting repressed motives and feelings into more socially acceptable channels.

Substance abuse   A pattern of drug use that diminishes the ability to fulfill responsibilities at home, work, or school that results in repeated use of a drug in dangerous situations or that leads to legal difficulties related to drug use.

Substance dependence   A pattern of compulsive drug taking that results in tolerance, withdrawal symptoms, or other specific symptoms for at least a year.

Subtractive color mixing   The process of mixing pigments, each of which absorbs some wavelengths of light and reflects others.

Superego   According to Freud, the social and parental standards the individual has internalized; the conscience and the ego ideal.

Suprachiasmatic nucleus (SCN)   A cluster of neurons in the hypothalamus that receives input from the retina regarding light and dark cycles and is involved in regulating the biological clock.

Survey research   Research technique in which questionnaires or interviews are administered to a selected group of people.

Sympathetic division   Branch of the autonomic nervous system; it prepares the body for quick action in an emergency.

Synapse   Area composed of the axon terminal of one neuron, the synaptic space, and the dendrite or cell body of the next neuron.

Synaptic space (or synaptic cleft)   Tiny gap between the axon terminal of one neuron and the dendrites or cell body of the next neuron.

Synaptic vesicles   Tiny sacs in a terminal button that release chemicals into the synapse.

Systematic desensitization   A behavioral technique for reducing a person's fear and anxiety by gradually associating a new response (relaxation) with stimuli that have been causing the fear and anxiety.

Systems approach   View that biological, psychological, and social risk factors combine to produce psychological disorders. Also known as the biopsychosocial model of psychological disorders.

Taste buds   Structures on the tongue that contain the receptor cells for taste.

Temperament   Characteristic patterns of emotional reactions and emotional self–regulation.

Temporal lobe   Part of the cerebral hemisphere that helps regulate hearing, balance and equilibrium, and certain emotions and motivations.

Teratogens   Toxic substances such as alcohol or nicotine that cross the placenta and may result in birth defects.

Terminal button (or synaptic knob)   Structure at the end of an axon terminal branch.

Tertiary prevention   Programs to help people adjust to community life after release from a mental hospital.

Testosterone   The primary male sex hormone.

Texture gradient   Monocular cue to distance and depth based on the fact that objects seen at greater distances appear to be smoother and less textured.

Thalamus   Forebrain region that relays and translates incoming messages from the sense receptors, except those for smell.

Thematic Apperception Test (TAT)   A projective test composed of ambiguous pictures about which a person is asked to write a complete story.

Theory   Systematic explanation of a phenomenon; it organizes known facts, allows us to predict new facts, and permits us to exercise a degree of control over the phenomenon.

Theory of multiple intelligences   Howard Gardner's theory that there is not one intelligence, but rather many intelligences, each of which is relatively independent of the others.

Threshold of excitation   The level an impulse must exceed to cause a neuron to fire.

Thyroid gland   Endocrine gland located below the voice box; it produces the hormone thyroxin.

Timbre   The quality or texture of sound; caused by overtones.

Tip-of-the-tongue phenomenon (or TOT)   Knowing a word, but not being able to immediately recall it.

Token economy   An operant conditioning therapy in which people earn tokens (reinforcers) for desired behaviors and exchange them for desired items or privileges.

Transduction   The conversion of physical energy into coded neural signals.

Transference   The client's carrying over to the analyst feelings held toward childhood authority figures.

Transvestic fetishism   Wearing the clothes of the opposite sex to achieve sexual gratification.

Triarchic theory of intelligence   Sternberg's theory that intelligence involves mental skills (analytical intelligence), insight and creative adaptability (creative intelligence), and environmental responsiveness (practical intelligence).

Trichromatic (or three-color) theory   The theory of color vision that holds that all color perception derives from three different color receptors in the retina (usually red, green, and blue receptors).

Trichromats   People (and animals) that have normal color vision.

Twin studies   Studies of identical and fraternal twins to determine the relative influence of heredity and environment on human behavior.

Unconditional positive regard   In Rogers's theory, the full acceptance and love of another person regardless of his or her behavior.

Unconditioned response (UR)   A response that takes place in an organism whenever an unconditioned stimulus occurs.

Unconditioned stimulus (US)   A stimulus that invariably causes an organism to respond in a specific way.

Unconscious   In Freud's theory, all the ideas, thoughts, and feelings of which we are not and normally cannot become aware.

Undifferentiated schizophrenia   Schizophrenic disorder in which there are clear schizophrenic symptoms that do not meet the criteria for another subtype of the disorder.

Vaginismus   Involuntary muscle spasms in the outer part of the vagina that make intercourse impossible.

Validity   Ability of a test to measure what it has been designed to measure.

Variable-interval schedule   A reinforcement schedule in which the correct response is reinforced after varying lengths of time following the last reinforcement.

Variable-ratio schedule   A reinforcement schedule in which a varying number of correct responses must occur before reinforcement is presented.

Vestibular senses   The senses of equilibrium and body position in space.

Vestibule training   Teaching employees new techniques and behaviors in a simulated workplace.

Vicarious reinforcement (or punishment)   Reinforcement or punishment experienced by models that affects the willingness of others to perform the behaviors they learned by observing those models.

Visual acuity   The ability to distinguish fine details visually.

Volley principle   Refinement of frequency theory; it suggests that receptors in the ear fire in sequence, with one group responding, then a second, then a third, and so on, so that the complete pattern of firing corresponds to the frequency of the sound wave.

Voyeurism   Desire to watch others having sexual relations or to spy on nude people.

Waking consciousness   Mental state that encompasses the thoughts, feelings, and perceptions that occur when we are awake and reasonably alert.

Wavelengths   The different energies represented in the electromagnetic spectrum.

Weber's law   The principle that the jnd for any given sense is a constant fraction or proportion of the stimulation being judged.

Wechsler Adult Intelligence Scale—Third Edition (WAIS-III)   An individual intelligence test developed especially for adults; measures both verbal and performance abilities.

Wechsler Intelligence Scale for Children—Third Edition (WISC-III)   An individual intelligence test developed especially for school-aged children; measures verbal and performance abilities and also yields an overall IQ score.

Withdrawal   Avoiding a situation when other forms of coping are not practical.

Working backward   A heuristic strategy in which one works backward from the desired goal to the given conditions.

Yerkes–Dodson law   States that there is an optimal level of arousal for the best performance of any task; the more complex the task, the lower the level of arousal that can be tolerated before performance deteriorates.

References

Aaker, D. A., & Bruzzone, D. E. (1985). Causes of irritation in advertising. *Journal of Marketing, 49*, 47–57.

Abbar, M., Courtet, P., Bellivier, F., Leboyer, M., Boulenger, J. P., Castelhau, D., et al. (2001). Suicide attempts and the tryptophan hydroxylase gene. *Molecular Psychiatry, 6*, 268–273.

Abdel, H. T. K. (2003). Exercise and diet in obesity treatment: An integrative system dynamics perspective. *Medicine and science in sports and exercise, 35*, 400–413.

Abramov, I., & Gordon, J. (1994). Color appearance: On seeing red or yellow, or green, or blue. *Annual Review of Psychology, 45*, 451–485.

Abramson, C. I., & Aquino, I. S. (2002). Behavioral studies of learning in the Africanized honey bee (*Apis mellifera L.*). *Brain, Behavior, and Evolution, 59*, 68–86.

Accreditation Council for Graduate Medical Education. (2003). The ACGME's approach to limit resident duty hours: The common standards and activities to promote adherence. Retrieved March 15, 2006 from http://www.acgme.org/acWebsite/dutyHours/dh_dhSummary.pdf

Achter, J. A., Lubinski, D., & Benbow, C. P. (1996). Multipotentiality among intellectually gifted: "It was never there and already it's vanishing." *Journal of Counseling Psychology, 43*, 65–76.

Ackerman, D. (1995). *A natural history of the senses*. New York: Vintage.

Ackerman, J. (2004, January–February). Untangling the brain: The search for the causes and cures of dyslexia. *Yale Alumni Magazine*, 47–55.

Acredolo, L. P., & Hake, J. L. (1982). Infant perception. In B. B. Wolman (Ed.), *Handbook of developmental psychology* (pp. 244–283). Englewood Cliffs, NJ: Prentice Hall.

Adams, J. L. (1980). *Conceptual blockbusting: A guide to better ideas* (2nd ed.). New York: Norton.

Adams, K., & Johnson-Greene, D. (1995, August). *PET and neuropsychological performance among chronic alcoholics*. Paper presented at the annual meeting of the American Psychological Assoc., New York.

Adams, T. (2004). Art: Sublimation or symptom. *British Journal of Psychotherapy, 20*, 563–566.

Addis, M. E., & Mahalik, J. R. (2003). Men, masculinity, and the contexts of help seeking. *American Psychologist, 58*, 5–14.

Addison, A. (2005). The first formal reaction to C. G. Jung's departure from psychoanalysis: Sandor Ferenczi's review of *Symbols of Transformation*. *Journal of Analytical Psychology, 50*, 551–552.

Addolorato, G., Leggio, L., Abenavoli, L., & Gasbarrini, G. (2005). Neurobiochemical and clinical aspects of craving in alcohol addiction: A review. *Addictive Behaviors, 30*, 1209–1224.

Adelson, R. (2002). Figure this: Deciding what's figure, what's ground. *Monitor on Psychology, 33*, 44–45.

Adesman, A. (2000, April). Does my child need Ritalin? *Newsweek*, p. 81.

Adler, N., Boyce, T., Chesney, M. A., Cohen, S., Folkman, S., Kahn, R. I., et al. (1994). Socioeconomic status and health. The challenge of the gradient. *American Psychologist, 49*, 15–24.

Adler, T. (1993, July). Men and women affected by stress, but differently. *APA Monitor*, pp. 8–9.

Adolphs, R., Baron-Cohen, S., & Tranel, D. (2002). Impaired recognition of social emotions following amygdala damage. *Journal of Cognitive Neuroscience, 14*, 1264–1274.

Adolphs, R., & Tranel, D. (2003). Amygdala damage impairs emotion recognition from scenes only when they contain facial expressions. *Neuropsychologia, 41*, 1281–1289.

Adolphs, R., Tranel, D., Damasio, H., & Damasio, A. (1994). Impaired recognition of emotion in facial expressions following bilateral damage to the human amygdala. *Nature, 372*, 669–672.

Adorno, T. W., Frenkel-Brunswick, E., Levinson, D. J., & Sanford, R. N. (1950). *The authoritarian personality*. New York: Harper & Row.

Aeschleman, S. R., Rosen, C. C., & Williams, M. R. (2003). The effect of noncontingent negative and positive reinforcement operations on the acquisition of superstitious behaviors. *Behavioural Processes, 61*, 37–45.

AhYun, K. (2002). Similarity and attraction. In M. Allen & R. W. Raymond (Eds.), *Interpersonal communication research: Advances through meta-analysis. LEA's communication series* (pp. 145–167). Mahwah, NJ: Lawrence Earlbaum.

Aiken, L. R., & Groth-Marnat, G. (2005). *Psychological testing and assessment* (12th ed.). Boston: Allyn & Bacon.

Ainsworth, M. D. (1977). Attachment theory and its utility in cross-cultural research. In P. H. Leiderman, S. R. Tulkin, & A. Rosenfields (Eds.), *Culture and infancy: Variation in the human experience*. New York: Academic Press.

Ainsworth, M. D. (1989). Attachments beyond infancy. *American Psychologist, 44*, 709–716.

Ainsworth, M. D., Blehar, M. C., Waters, E., & Wall, S. (1978). *Patterns of attachment*. New York: Halstead.

Ajay C. (2004). *Putting children first: How low-wage working mothers manage child care*. New York: Russell Sage Foundation.

Al Dawi, S., Dorvlo, A. S. S., Burke, D. T., Al, B. S., Martin, R. G., & Al Ismaily, S. (2002). Presence and severity of anorexia and bulimia among male and female Omani and non-Omani adolescents. *Journal of the American Academy of Child and Adolescent Psychiatry, 41*, 1124–1130.

Albano, A. M., & Barlow, D. H. (1996). Breaking the vicious cycle: Cognitive-behavioral group treatment for socially anxious youth. In E. D. Hibbs & P. S. Jensen (Eds.), *Psychosocial treatments for child and adolescent disorders: Empirically based strategies for clinical practice* (pp. 43–62). Washington, DC: American Psychological Assoc.

Albarracín, D. (2002). Cognition in persuasion: An analysis of information processing in response to persuasive communications. In M. P. Zanna (Ed.), *Advances in experimental social psychology* (Vol. 34, pp. 61–130). San Diego, CA: Academic Press

Albarracín, D., Zanna, M. P., Johnson, B. T., & Kumkale, G. T. (2005). Attitudes: Introduction and scope. In D. Albarracín, B. T. Johnson, & M. P. Zanna (Eds.), *The handbook of attitudes* (pp. 3–19). Mahwah, NJ: Erlbaum.

Albeck, S., & Kaydar, D. (2002). Divorced mothers: Their network of friends, pre- and post-divorce. *Journal of Divorce and Remarriage, 36*, 111–138.

Alexander, C. N., Robinson, P., & Rainforth, N. (1994). Treating and preventing alcohol, nicotine, and drug abuse through Transcendental Meditation: A review and statistical meta-analysis. [Special issue] *Alcoholism Treatment Quarterly, 11*(1–2), 13–87.

Allen, L. S., & Gorski, R. A. (1992). Sexual orientation and size of the anterior commissure in the human brain. *Proceedings of the National Academy of Sciences, 89*, 7199–7202.

Allen, R. S., Haley, W. E., & Roff, L. L. (2006). Responding to the needs of caregivers near the end of life: Enhancing benefits and minimizing burdens. In J. L. Werth, Jr. & D. Blevins (Eds.), *Psychosocial issues near the end of life: A resource for professional care providers* (pp. 183–201). Washington, DC: American Psychological Assoc.

Allen, V. L., & Levine, J. M. (1971). Social support and conformity: The role of independent assessment of reality. *Journal of Experimental Social Psychology, 7*, 48–58.

Allgood-Merten, B., Lewinsohn, P. M., & Hops, H. (1990). Sex differences and adolescent depression. *Journal of Abnormal Psychology, 99*, 55–63.

Alliger, G. M., & Janak, E. A. (1989). Kirkpatrick's levels of training criteria: Thirty years later. *Personnel Psychology, 42*, 331–342.

Alloy, L. B., Abramson, L. Y., & Francis, E. L. (1999). Do negative cognitive styles confer vulnerability to depression? *Current Directions in Psychological Science, 8*, 128–132.

Alloy, L. B., Abramson, L. Y., Whitehouse, W. G., Hogan, M. E., Tashman, N. A., Steinberg, D. L., et al. (1999). Depressogenic cognitive styles: Predictive validity, information processing and personality characteristics, and developmental origins. *Behaviour Research and Therapy, 37*, 503–531.

Allport, G. W., & Odbert, H. S. (1936). Trait-names: A psycholexical study. *Psychological Monographs, 47*(1, Whole No. 211).

Almeida, D. M. (2005). Resilience and vulnerability to daily stressors assessed via diary methods. *Current Directions in Psychological Science, 14*, 64–68.

Almer, E. (2000, April 22). On-line therapy: An arm's-length approach. *New York Times*, pp. A1, A11.

Almgren, G., Guest, A., Immerwahr, G., & Spittel, M. (2002). Joblessness, family disruption, and violent death in Chicago, 1970–90. *Social Forces, 76*, 1465–1493.

Altabe, M. N., & Thompson, J. K. (1994). Body image. In V. A. Ramachandran (Ed.), *Encyclopedia of human behavior* (Vol. 1, pp. 407–414). San Diego, CA: Academic Press.

Altemeyer, B. (2004). Highly dominating, highly authoritarian personalities. *Journal of Social Psychology, 144*, 421–447.

Altman, I., & Taylor, D. A. (1973). *Social penetration: The development of interpersonal relationships*. New York: Holt, Rinehart & Winston.

Alvarez, N. (1998). Barbiturates in the treatment of epilepsy in people with intellectual disability. *Journal of Intellectual Disability Research, 42*, 16–23.

Alzheimer's Association. (2006). *Statistics about Alzheimer's disease*. Retrieved May 11, 2006 from http://www.alz.org/AboutAD/statistics.asp

Amedi, A., Merabet, L. B., Bermpohl, F., & Pascual-Leone, A. (2005). The occipital cortex in the blind: Lessons about plasticity and vision. *Current Directions in Psychological Science, 14*, 306–311.

Amen, D. G., Stubblefield, M., Carmichael, B., & Thisted, R. (1996). Brain SPECT findings and aggressiveness. *Annals of Clinical Psychiatry, 8*(3), 129–137.

American Academy of Child & Adolescent Psychiatry. (2004). *Facts for families, #10: Teen suicide*. Washington, DC: American Academy of Child & Adolescent Psychiatry. Retrieved May 11, 2006, from http://www.aacap.org/publications/factsfam/suicide.htm

American Academy of Pediatrics. (1999, August 2). *AAP discourages television for very young children*. Press release.

American Academy of Pediatrics. (2006). *Television and the family*. Retrieved June 8, 2006, from http://www.aap.org/family/tv1.htm

American Psychiatric Association (APA). (1994). *Diagnostic and statistical manual of mental disorders* (4th ed.). Washington, DC: Author.

American Psychiatric Association. (2000). *Diagnostic and statistical manual of mental disorders* (4th ed., Text Revision). Arlington, VA: American Psychiatric Pub.

American Psychological Association. (1978). Guidelines for therapy with women. *American Psychologist, 33*, 1122–1123.

American Psychological Association. (1992). *Ethical principles of psychologists and code of conduct*. Washington. DC: Author.

American Psychological Association. (2000, November). Facts & figures. *Monitor on Psychology, 31*, 10.

American Psychological Association. (2003). *Ethical principles of psychologists and code of conduct*. Retrieved January 29, 2006, from http://www.apa.org/ethics/code2002.html#intro

American Psychological Association. (2005). New definition: Hypnosis. Retrieved March 4, 2006 from http://www.apa.org/divisions/div30/define_hypnosis.html

American Psychological Association. (2006). *Briefing sheet: Women and depression*. Washington, DC: Public Policy Office, American Psychological Association. Retrieved July 13, 2006, from http://www.apa.org/ppo/issues/pwomenanddepress.html

America's Children: Key National Indicators of Well-Being. (2000). A report from the National Maternal and Child Health Clearinghouse. Retrieved November 10, 2000, from the http://childstats.gov

Anastasi, A., & Urbina, S. (1997). *Psychological testing* (7th ed.). Upper Saddle River, NJ: Prentice Hall.

Andersen, B. L., Kiecolt-Glaser, J. K., & Glaser, R. (1994). A biobehavioral model of cancer stress and disease course. *American Psychologist, 49*, 389–404.

Anderson, C. A. (1997). Effects of violent movies and trait hostility on hostile feelings and aggressive thoughts. *Aggressive Behavior, 23*, 161–178.

Anderson, C. A., Berkowitz, L., Donnerstein, E., Huesmann, L. R., Johnson, J. D., Linz, D., et al. (2003). The influence of media violence on youth. *Psychological Science in the Public Interest, 4*, 81–110.

Anderson, C. A., Gentile, D. A., & Buckley, K. E. (2006). Violent video game effects on children and adolescents: Further developments and tests of the general aggression model. Retrieved March 9, 2006, from http://www.psychologymatters.org/videogames.html

Anderson, D. R. (1998). Educational television is not an oxymoron. *Annals of Public Policy Research, 557*, 24–38.

Anderson, D. R., Huston, A. C., Wright, J. C., & Collins, P. A. (1998). Initial findings on the long term impact of *Sesame Street* and educational television for children: The Recontact Study. In R. Noll & M. Price (Eds.), *A communications cornucopia: Markle Foundation essays on information policy* (pp. 279–296). Washington, DC: Brookings Institution.

Anderson, N. B., & Nickerson, K. J. (2005). Genes, race, and psychology in the genome era: An introduction. *American Psychologist, 60*, 5–8.

Anderson, S. E., Dallal, G. E., & Must, A. (2003). Relative weight and race influence average age at menarche: Results from two nationally representative surveys of US girls studied 25 years apart. *Pediatrics, 111*, 844–850.

Anderson, S. W., Bechara, A., Damasio, H., Tranel, D., & Damasio, A. R. (1999). Impairment of social and moral behavior related to early damage in human prefrontal cortex. *Nature Neuroscience, 2*, 1032–1037.

Anderson, S. W., & Booker, M. B. (2006). Cognitive behavioral therapy versus psychosurgery for refractory obsessive-compulsive disorder. *Journal of Neuropsychiatry & Clinical Neurosciences, 18*, 129.

Andolina, M. W., & Mayer, J. D. (2003). Demographic shifts and racial attitudes: How tolerant are whites in the most diverse generation? *Social Science Journal, 40,* 19–31.

Andreou, G., Krommydas, G., Gourgoulianis, K. I., Karapetsas, A., U., & Molyvdas, P. A. (2002). Handedness, asthma, and allergic disorders: Is there an association? *Psychology, Health & Medicine, 7,* 53–60.

Andrews, J. A., & Lewinsohn, P. M. (1992). Suicidal attempts among older adolescents: Prevalence and co-occurrence with psychiatric disorders. *Journal of the American Academy of Child and Adolescent Psychiatry, 31,* 655–662.

Ang, R. P., & Woo, A. (2003). Influence of sensation seeking boys' psychosocial adjustment. *North American Journal of Psychology, 5,* 121–136.

Angier, N. (1995, June 20). Does testosterone equal aggression? Maybe not. *New York Times,* p. 1.

Angier, N. (1998, September 1). Nothing becomes a man more than a woman's face. *New York Times,* p. B9.

Annesi, J. J. (2005). Changes in depressed mood associated with 10 weeks of moderate cardiovascular exercise in formerly sedentary adults. *Psychological Reports, 96,* 855–862.

Anshel, M. H., Porter, A., & Quek, J-J. (1998). Coping with acute stress in sports as a function of gender: An exploratory study. *Journal of Sport Behavior, 21,* 363–376.

Anthony, J. C., & Helzer, J. E. (2002). Epidemiology of drug dependence. In M. T. Tsuang & M. Tohen (Eds.), *Textbook in psychiatric epidemiology* (2nd ed., pp. 479–561). New York: Wiley-Liss.

Antoni, M. H. (2003). Stress management and psychoneuroimmunology in HIV Infection. *CNS Spectrums, 8,* 40–51.

Aranow, E., Weiss, K. A., & Rezikoff, M. (2001). *A practical guide to the Thematic Apperception Test: The TAT in clinical practice.* Philadelphia: Brunner-Routledge.

Archer, J. (1996). Sex differences in social behavior: Are the social role and evolutionary explanations compatible? *American Psychologist, 51*(9), 909–917.

Archer, J., & Côté, S. (2005). Sex differences in aggressive behavior: A developmental and evolutionary perspective. In R. E. Tremblay, W. W. Hartup, & J. Archer (Eds.), *Developmental origins of aggression* (pp. 425–443). New York: Guilford.

Aries, E. (2006). Sex differences in interaction: A reexamination. In K. Dindia & D. J. Canary (Eds.), *Sex differences and similarities in communication* (2nd ed., pp. 21–36). Mahwah, NJ: Erlbaum.

Arnaut, G. L. Y. (2006). Sensation seeking, risk taking, and fearlessness. In J. C. Thomas, D. L. Segal, & M. Hersen (Eds.), *Comprehensive handbook of personality and psychopathology, Vol. 1: Personality and everyday functioning* (pp. 322–341). Hoboken, NJ: John Wiley & Sons.

Arnedt, J., T., Owens, J., Crouch, M., Stahl, J., & Carskadon, M. A. (2005). Neurobehavioral performance of residents after heavy night call vs. after alcohol ingestion. *Journal of the American Medical Association, 294,* 1025–1033.

Arnett, J. (1991, April). *Sensation seeking and egocentrism as factors in reckless behaviors among a college-age sample.* Paper presented at the meeting of the Society for Research in Child Development, Seattle, WA.

Arnett, J. J. (1999). Adolescent storm and stress, reconsidered. *American Psychologist, 54,* 317–326.

Arnett, J. J. (2000). Emerging adulthood: A theory of development from the late teens through the twenties. *American Psychologist, 55,* 469–480.

Aronson, E. (2003). *The social animal* (9th ed.). New York: Worth.

Aronson, E., Wilson, T. D., & Akert, R. M. (2005). *Social Psychology* (5th ed.). Upper Saddle River, NJ: Prentice Hall.

Arrigo, J. M., & Pezdek, K. (1997). Lessons from the study of psychogenic amnesia. *Current Directions in Psychological Science, 6,* 148–152.

Arsenio, W. F. (2004). The stability of young children's physical aggression: Relations with child care, gender, and aggression subtypes. *Monographs of the Society for Research in Child Development, 69,* 130–143.

Asch, S. E. (1951). Effects of group pressure upon the modification and distortion of judgments. In H. Guetzkow (Ed.), *Groups, leadership, and men.* Pittsburgh: Carnegie Press.

Asch, S. E. (1956). Studies of independence and conformity: I. A minority of one against a unanimous majority. *Psychological Monographs, 70*(9, Whole No. 416).

Asendorpf, J. B., & Van-Aken, M. A. G. (2003). Validity of Big Five personality judgements in childhood: A 9 year longitudinal study. *European Journal of Personality, 17,* 1–17.

Ashcraft, M. H. (2006). *Cognition* (4th ed). Upper Saddle River, NJ: Prentice Hall.

Ashley, R. (1975, October 17). The other side of LSD. *New York Times Magazine,* pp. 40ff.

Aslin, R. N., & Smith, L. B. (1988). Perceptual development. *Annual Review of Psychology, 39,* 435–473.

Aspinwall, L. G., & Taylor, S. E. (1997). A stitch in time: Self-regulation and proactive coping. *Psychological Bulletin, 121,* 417–436.

Astalis, P. (2005). Locating identity: The influence of Erik H. Erikson on society and the social construction of adolescence. *Dissertation Abstracts International: Section B: The Sciences and Engineering, 66,* 2323.

Aston, R. (1972). Barbiturates, alcohol and tranquilizers. In S. J. Mule & H. Brill (Eds.), *The chemical and biological aspects of drug dependence.* Cleveland, OH: CRC Press.

Astur, R. S., Taylor, L. B., Marnelak, A. N., Philpott, L., & Sutherland, R. J. (2002). Humans with hippocampus damage display severe spatial memory impairments in a virtual Morris water task. *Behavioural Brain Research, 132,* 77–84.

Atchley, R. C. (1982). Retirement as a social institution. *Annual Review of Sociology, 8,* 263–287.

Attwood, T. (2005). Theory of mind and Asperger's syndrome. In L. J. Baker & L. A. Welkowitz (Eds.), *Asperger's syndrome: Intervening in schools, clinics, and communities,* (pp. 11–41). Mahwah, NJ: Erlbaum.

Austin, E. J., Saklofske, D. H., Huang, S. H. S., & McKenney, D. (2004). Measurement of trait emotional intelligence: Testing and cross-validating a modified version of Schutte et al.'s (1998) measure. *Personality and Individual Differences, 36,* 555–562.

Auvergne, R., Lere, C., El-Bahh, B., Arthaud, S., Lespinet, V., Rougier, A., et al. (2002). Delayed kindling epileptogenesis and increased neurogenesis in adult rats housed in an enriched environment. *Brain Research, 954,* 277–285.

Aveleyra, E., Carranza-Lira, S., Ulloa-Aguirre, A., & Ostrosky-Solís, F. (2005). Cognitive effects of hormone therapy in early postmenopausal women. *International Journal of Psychology, 40,* 314–323.

Aviles, F., Earleywine, M., Pollock, V., Stratton, J., & Miller, N. (2005). Alcohol's effect on triggered displaced aggression. *Psychology of Addictive Behaviors, 19,* 108–111.

Ayman, R., Chemers, M. M., Fiedler, F., Romano, R., Vecchio, R. P., & Zaccaro, S. J. (1998). Contingency model. In F. Dansereau & F. J. Yammarino (Eds.), *Leadership: The multiple-level approaches: Classical and new wave monographs in organizational behavior and industrial relations* (Vol. 24, pp. 73–143). Stamford, CT: JAI Press.

Azar, B. (1997, December). Maternal emotions may influence fetal behaviors. *APA Monitor,* 17.

Azar, B. (1999, March). "Decade of Behavior" moves forward. *APA Monitor,* 16.

Azarow, J. A. (2003). Generativity and well-being: An investigation of the Eriksonian hypothesis (Erik Erikson). *Dissertation Abstracts International: Section B: The Sciences and Engineering, 64,* 1932.

Babkoff, H., Caspy, T., Mikulincer, M., & Sing, H. C. (1991). Monotonic and rhythmic influences: A challenge for sleep deprivation research. *Psychological Bulletin, 109,* 411–428.

Back-Madruga, C., Boone, K. B., Chang, L., Grob, C. S., Lee, A., Nations, H., et al. (2003). Neuropsychological effects of 3,4-methylenedioxymethamphetamine (MDMA or Ecstasy) in recreational users. *Clinical Neuropsychologist, 17,* 446–459.

Baddeley, A. D. (1986). *Working memory.* New York: Clarendon Press/Oxford University Press.

Baddeley, A. D. (1987). Amnesia. In R. L. Gregory & O. L. Zangwill (Eds.), *The Oxford companion to the mind* (pp. 20–22). New York: Oxford Univ. Press.

Baddeley, A. D. (1994). The magical number seven: Still magic after all these years? *Psychological Review, 101,* 353–356.

Baddeley, A. D. (2002). Is working memory still working? *European Psychologist, 7,* 85–97.

Baddeley, A. D., & Hitch, G. J. (1994). Developments in the concept of working memory. *Neuropsychology, 6,* 485–493.

Badner, J. A. (2003). The genetics of bipolar disorder. In B. Geller & M. DelBello (Eds.), *Bipolar disorder in childhood and early adolescence* (pp. 247–254). New York: Guilford.

Badr, L. K., & Abdallah, B. (2001). Physical attractiveness of premature infants affects outcome at discharge from NICU. *Infant Behavior and Development, 24,* 129–133.

Bagby, R. M., & Marshall, M. B. (2005). Assessing response bias with the MCMI modifying indices. In R. J. Craig (Ed.), *New directions in interpreting the Millon^{TM} Clinical Multiaxial Inventory-III (MCMI-III^{TM})* (pp. 227–247). Hoboken, NJ: John Wiley & Sons.

Bagemihl, B. (2000). *Biological exuberance: Animal homosexuality and natural diversity.* New York: St. Martin's Press.

Bahrick, H. P. (1984). Semantic memory in permastore: Fifty years of memory for Spanish learned in school. *Journal of Experimental Psychology: General, 113,* 1–31.

Bahrick, H. P., Bahrick, P. O., & Wittlinger, R. P. (1974, December). Those unforgettable high school days. *Psychology Today,* pp. 50–56.

Baillargeon, R. (1994). How do infants learn about the physical world? *Current Directions in Psychological Science, 3,* 133–140.

Bajbouj, M., Lang, U. E., Niehaus, L., Hellen, F. E., Heuser, I., & Neu, P. (2006). Effects of right unilateral electroconvulsive therapy on motor cortical excitability in depressive patients. *Journal of Psychiatric Research, 40,* 322–327.

Baker, A., & Dawe, S. (2005). Amphetamine use and co-occurring psychological problems: Review of the literature and implications for treatment. *Australian Psychologist, 40,* 88–95.

Baldwin, D. (2006). Serotonin noradrenaline reuptake inhibitors: A new generation of treatment for anxiety disorders. *International Journal of Psychiatry in Clinical Practice, 10,* 12–15.

Balfour, M. E. (2004). Sexual behavior causes activation and functional alterations of mesolimbic systems: Neurobiology of motivation and reward. *Dissertation Abstracts International: Section B: The Sciences and Engineering, 64,* 4789.

Ball, D. (2004). Genetic approaches to alcohol dependence. *British Journal of Psychiatry, 185,* 449–451.

Ballie, R. (2001). Teen drinking more dangerous than previously thought. *Monitor on Psychology, 32,* 12.

Balon, R. (2002). Emotional blunting, sexual dysfunction, and SSRIs. *International Journal of Neuropsychopharmacology, 5,* 415–416.

Banaji, M. R., & Hardin, C. D. (1996). Automatic stereotyping. *Psychological Science, 7,* 136–141.

Bandura, A. (1962). Social learning through imitation. In M. R. Jones (Ed.), *Nebraska Symposium on Motivation* (pp. 211–274). Lincoln: Univ. of Nebraska Press.

Bandura, A. (1965). Influence of models' reinforcement contingencies on the acquisition of imitative responses. *Journal of Personality and Social Psychology, 1,* 589–595.

Bandura, A. (1973). *Aggression: A social learning analysis.* Englewood Cliffs, NJ: Prentice Hall.

Bandura, A. (1977). *Social learning theory.* Englewood Cliffs, NJ: Prentice Hall.

Bandura, A. (1986). *Social foundations of thought and action: A social cognitive theory.* Englewood Cliffs, NJ: Prentice Hall.

Bandura, A. (1997). *Self-efficacy: The exercise of control.* New York: Freeman.

Bandura, A. (2004). Model of causality in social learning theory. In A. Freeman, M. J. Mahoney, P. DeVito, & D. Martin (Eds.), *Cognition and psychotherapy* (2nd ed.) (pp. 25–44). New York: Springer.

Bandura, A., Blanchard, E. B., & Ritter, B. (1969). Relative efficacy of desensitization and modeling approaches for inducing behavioral, affective, and attitudinal changes. *Journal of Personality and Social Psychology, 13,* 173–199.

Bandura, A., & Locke, E. A. (2003). Negative self-efficacy and goal effects revisited. *Journal of Applied Psychology, 8,* 87–99.

Banich, M. T. (1998). Integration of information between the cerebral hemispheres. *Current Directions in Psychological Science, 7,* 32–37.

Barbaree, H. E., & Marshall, W. L. (1991). The role of male sexual arousal in rape: Six models. *Journal of Consulting and Clinical Psychology, 59,* 621–630.

Barbaree, H. E., & Seto, M. C. (1997). Pedophilia: Assessment and treatment. In D. R. Laws & W. T. O'Donohue (Eds.), *Sexual Deviance: Theory, assessment and treatment* (pp. 175–193). New York: Guilford.

Barber, B. L., Stone, M. R., Hunt, J. E., & Eccles, J. S. (2005). Benefits of activity participation: The roles of identity affirmation and peer group norm sharing. In J. S. Mahoney, R. W. Larson, & J. S. Eccles (Eds.), *Organized activities as contexts of development: Extracurricular activities, after-school and community programs* (pp. 185–210). Mahwah, NJ: Erlbaum.

Bard, K. A., Todd, B. K., Bernier, C., Love, J., & Leavens, D. (2006). Self-awareness in human and chimpanzee infants: What is measured and what is meant by the mark and mirror test? *Infancy, 9,* 191–219.

Barglow, P., Vaughn, B. E., & Molitor, N. (1987). Effects of maternal absence due to employment on the quality of infant-mother attachment in a low-risk sample. *Child Development, 58,* 945–954.

Barinaga, M. (2000, March 3). Asilomar revisited: Lessons for today. *Science, 287,* 1584–1585.

Barnett, J. E., & Scheetz, K. (2003). Technological advances and telehealth: Ethics, law, and the practice of psychotherapy. *Psychotherapy: Theory, Research, Practice, Training, 40,* 86–93.

Barnett, R. C. (2005). Dual-earner couples: Good/bad for her and/or him? In D. F. Halpern & S. E. Murphy(Eds.), *From work-family balance to work-family interaction: Changing the metaphor* (pp. 151–171). Mahwah, NJ: Erlbaum.

Barnett, R. C., Brennan, R. T., & Marshall, N. L. (1994). Gender and the relationship between parent role quality and psychological distress: A study of men and women in dual-earner couples. *Journal of Family Issues, 15,* 229–252.

Barnett, R. C., & Hyde, J. S. (2001). Women, men, work, and family. *American Psychologist, 56,* 781–796.

Barnett, W. S. (1998). Long-term effects on cognitive development and school success. In W. S. Barnett & S. S. Boocock (Eds.), *Early care and education for children in poverty* (pp. 11–44). Albany, NY: State Univ. of New York Press.

Bar-On, R., Handley, R., & Fund, S. (2006). The impact of emotional intelligence on performance. In V. U. Druskat, F. Sala, & G. Mount (Eds.), *Linking emotional intelligence and performance at work: Current research evidence with individuals and groups* (pp. 3–19). Mahwah, NJ: Erlbaum.

Bar-On, R., & Parker, J. D. A. (Eds.) (2000). *The handbook of emotional intelligence: Theory, development, assessment, and application at home, school, and in the workplace.* San Francisco: Jossey-Bass.

Baron, R. A., & Byrne, D. (1991). *Social psychology: Understanding human interaction* (6th ed.). Boston: Allyn & Bacon.

Barret, G. V., & Depinet, R. L. (1991). A reconsideration of testing for competence rather than for intelligence. *American Psychologist, 46,* 1012–1024.

Barrick, M. R., & Mount, M. K. (1991). The Big Five personality dimensions and job performance: A meta-analysis. *Personnel Psychology, 44,* 1–26.

Barrick, M. R., Mount, M. K., & Judge, T. A. (2001). Personality and performance at the beginning of the next millennium: What do we know and where do we go? *International Journal of Selection and Assessment, 9,* 9–30.

Barron, F., & Harrington, D. M. (1981). Creativity, intelligence, and personality. *Annual Review of Psychology, 32,* 439–476.

Bartlett, F. C. (1932). *Remembering: A study in experimental and social psychology.* New York: Macmillan.

Bartoshuk, L. M., & Beauchamp, G. K. (1994). Chemical senses. *Annual Review of Psychology, 45,* 419–449.

Baruss, I. (2003). *Alterations of consciousness : An empirical analysis for social scientists.* Washington, DC: American Psychological Assoc.

Basow, S. A. (1986). *Gender stereotypes: Traditions and alternatives* (2nd ed.). Pacific Grove, CA: Brooks/Cole.

Batson, C. D., & Ahmad, N. (2001). Empathy-induced altruism in a prisoner's dilemma II: What if the target of empathy has defected? *European Journal of Social Psychology, 31,* 25–36.

Batson, C. D., Ahmad, N., Lishner, D. A., & Tsang, J. (2002). Empathy and altruism. In C. R. Snyder & S. J. Lopez (Eds.), *Handbook of positive psychology* (pp. 485–498). New York, NY: Oxford Univ. Press.

Batson, C. D., & Powell, A. A. (2003). Altruism and prosocial behahavior. In T. Millon & M. J. Lerner (Eds.), *Handbook of psychology: Vol. 5, Personality and social psychology* (pp. 463–484). New York: John Wiley & Sons.

Battro, A. M. (2000). *Half a brain is enough: The story of Nico.* New York: Cambridge Univ. Press.

Bauer, P. J. (1996). What do infants recall of their lives? Memory for specific events by one- to two-year-olds. *American Psychologist, 51,* 29–41.

Baum, A., Revenson, T. A., & Singer, J. E. (2001). *Handbook of health psychology.* Mahwah, NJ: Erlbaum.

Baumeister, A. A., & Baumeister, A. A. (2000). Mental retardation: Causes and effects. In M. Hersen & R. T. Ammerman (Eds.), *Advanced abnormal child psychology* (2nd. ed.) (pp. 327–355). Mahwah, NJ: Erlbaum.

Baumeister, R. F., & Leary, M. R. (2000). The need to belong: Desire for interpersonal attachments as a fundamental human motivation. In E. T. Higgins & A. W. Kruglanski (Eds.), *Motivational science: Social and personality perspectives* (pp. 24–49). New York: Psychology Press.

Baumrind, D. (1972). Socialization and instrumental competence in young children. In W. W. Hartup (Ed.), *The young child: Reviews of research* (Vol. 2). Washington, DC: National Association for the Education of Young Children.

Baumrind, D. (1991). Parenting styles and adolescent development. In J. Brooks-Gunn, R. Lerner, & A. C. Petersen (Eds.), *The encyclopedia of adolescence* (Vol. 2, pp. 746–758). New York: Garland.

Baumrind, D. (1996). The discipline controversy revisited. *Family Relations: Journal of Applied Family and Child Studies, 45,* 405–414.

Baumrind, D. (2001, August). *Does causally relevant research support a blanket injunction against disciplinary spanking by parents?* Paper presented at the annual meeting of the American Psychological Association, San Francisco.

Baumrind, D., Larzelere, R. E., & Cowan, P. A. (2002). Ordinary physical punishment: Is it harmful? Comment on Gershoff (2002). *Psychological Bulletin, 128,* 580–589.

Bayley, N. (1956). Individual patterns of development. *Child Development, 27,* 45–74.

Beasley, M., Thompson, T., & Davidson, J. (2003). Resilience in response to life stress: The effects of coping style and cognitive hardiness. *Personality and Individual Differences, 34,* 77–95.

Beauregard, M., Lévesque, J., & Bourgouin, P. (2001). Neural correlates of conscious self-regulation of emotion. *Journal of Neuroscience, 21,* 6993–7000.

Bechara, A., Damasio, H., Tranel, D., & Damasio, A. R. (1997, February 28). Deciding advantageously before knowing the advantageous strategy. *Science, 275,* 1293–1295.

Beck, A. T. (1967). *Depression: Clinical, experimental and theoretical aspects.* New York: Harper (Hoeber).

Beck, A. T. (1976). *Cognitive therapy and emotional disorders.* New York: International Universities Press.

Beck, A. T. (1984). Cognition and therapy. *Archives of General Psychiatry, 41,* 1112–1114.

Beck, A. T. (2002). Cognitive models of depression. In R. L Leahy & T. E. Dowd (Eds.), *Clinical advances in cognitive psychotherapy: Theory and Application* (pp. 29–61). New York: Springer.

Beck, J. G. (1995). Hypoactive sexual desire disorder: An overview. *Journal of Consulting and Clinical Psychology, 63,* 919–927.

Bédard, J., & Chi, M. T. H. (1992). Expertise. *Current Directions in Psychological Science, 1,* 135–139.

Beecher, H. K. (1972). The placebo effect as a nonspecific force surrounding disease and the treatment of disease. In R. Jansen, W. D. Kerdel, A. Herz, C. Steichele, J. P. Payne, & R. A. P. Burt (Eds.), *Pain, basic principles, pharmacology, and therapy.* Stuttgart: Thieme.

Beirne-Smith, M., Patton, J., & Ittenbach, R. (1994). *Mental retardation* (4th ed.). New York: Macmillan.

Bell, J. H., & Bromnick, R. D. (2003). The social reality of the imaginary audience: A ground theory approach. *Adolescence, 38,* 205–219.

Bellman, S., Forster, N., Still, L., & Cooper, C. L. (2003). Gender differences in the use of social support as a moderator of occupational stress. *Stress and Health: Journal of the International Society for the Investigation of Stress, 19,* 45–58.

Belsky, J., & Rovine, M. (1988). Nonmaternal care in the first year of life and infant parent attachment security. *Child Development, 59,* 157–167.

Bem, S. L. (1989). Genital knowledge and gender constancy in preschool children. *Child Development, 60,* 649–662.

Beniczky, S., Keri, S., Voeroes, E., Ungurean, A., Benedek, G., Janka, Z., et al. (2002). Complex hallucinations following occipital lobe damage. *European Journal of Neurology, 9,* 175–176.

Benjamin, L. T., Jr. (2000). The psychology laboratory at the turn of the 20th century. *American Psychologist, 55,* 318–321.

Bennett, K. K., & Elliott, M. (2005). Pessimistic explanatory style and cardiac health: What is the relation and the mechanism that links them? *Basic and Applied Social Psychology, 27,* 239–248.

Bennett, M. D., Jr., & Miller, D. B. (2006). An exploratory study of the urban hassles index: A contextually relevant measure of chronic multidimensional urban stressors. *Research on Social Work Practice, 16,* 305–314.

Bennis, W., Spreitzer, G. M., & Cummings, T. G. (Eds.) (2001). *The future of leadership: Today's top leadership thinkers speak to tomorrow's leaders.* San Francisco: Jossey-Bass.

Benokraitis, N. V. (2004). *Marriages and families: Changes, choices, and constraints* (5th ed.). Upper Saddle River, NJ: Prentice Hall.

Benson, E. (2002). Pheromones, in context. *Monitor on Psychology, 33,* 46–48.

Benson, E. (2003). Intelligent intelligence testing. *Monitor on Psychology, 34,* 48–58.

Bentley-Reed, L. L. (2006). The Big Five personality traits as tools for retention of Florida e 9-1-1 telecommunicators. *Dissertation Abstracts International Section A: Humanities and Social Sciences, 66,* 2629.

Benton, D., & Roberts, G. (1988). Effect of vitamin and mineral supplementation on intelligence of a sample of schoolchildren. *Lancet, 1,* 14–144.

Benton, T. R., Ross, D. F., Bradshaw, E., Thomas, W. M., & Bradshaw, G. S. (2006). Eyewitness memory is still not common sense: Comparing jurors, judges and law enforcement to eyewitness experts. *Applied Cognitive Psychology, 20,* 115–129.

BenTovim, D. I. (2003). Eating disorders: Outcome, prevention and treatment of eating disorders. *Current Opinion in Psychiatry, 16,* 65–69.

Berg, S. J., & Wynne-Edwards, K. E. (2001). Changes in testosterone, cortisol, estradiol levels in men becoming fathers. *Mayo Clinic Proceedings, 76,* 582–592.

Bergeron, N., & Schneider, B. H. (2005). Explaining cross-national differences in peer-directed aggression: A quantitative synthesis. *Aggressive Behavior, 31,* 116–137.

Bering, J. M., & Shackelford, T. K. (2005). Evolutionary psychology and false confession. *American Psychologist, 60,* 1037–1038.

Berkowitz, L., & Harmon-Jones, E. (2004). Toward an understanding of the determinants of anger. *Emotion, 4,* 107–130.

Berkowitz, M. W., & Gibbs, J. C. (1983). Measuring the developmental features of moral discussion. *Merrill-Palmer Quarterly, 29,* 399–410.

Bernal, M. E., & Castro, F. G. (1994). Are clinical psychologists prepared for service and research with ethnic minorities? *American Psychologist, 49,* 797–805.

Bernhard, F., & Penton-Voak, I. (2002). The evolutionary psychology of facial attractiveness. *Current Directions in Psychological Science, 11,* 154–158.

Berr, C. (2002). Oxidative stress and cognitive impairment in the elderly. *Journal of Nutrition, Health and Aging, 6,* 261–266.

Bertenthal, B. I., Campos, J. J., & Kermoian, R. (1994). An epigenetic perspective on the development of self-produced locomotion and its consequences. *Current Directions in Psychological Science, 3,* 140–145.

Bertolini, M. (2001). Central masturbatory fantasy, fetish and transitional phenomenon. In M. Bertolini & A. Giannakoulas (Eds.), *Squiggles and spaces: Revisiting the work of D. W. Winnicott,* (Vol. 1, pp. 210–217). London: Whurr.

Betancourt, H., & López, S. R. (1993). The study of culture, ethnicity, and race in American psychology. *American Psychologist, 48,* 629–637.

Bettencourt, B. A., & Miller, N. (1996). Gender differences in aggression as a function of provocation: A meta-analysis. *Psychological Bulletin, 119,* 422–427.

Bhawuk, D. P., & Brislin, R. W. (2000). Cross-cultural training: A review. *Applied Psychology: An International Review, 49,* 162–191.

Bhui, K., Shanahan, L., & Harding, G. (2006). Homelessness and mental Illness: A literature review and a qualitative study of perceptions of the adequacy of care. *International Journal of Social Psychiatry, 52,* 152–165.

Biassoni, E. C., Serra, M. R., Richter, U., Joekes, S., Yacci, M., Carignani, J. A., et al. (2005). Recreational noise exposure and its effects on the hearing of adolescents. Part II: Development of hearing disorders. *International Journal of Audiology, 44,* 74–85.

Biddle, S. (2000). Exercise, emotions, and mental health. In Y. Hanin (Ed.), *Emotions in sport* (pp. 267–291). Champaign, IL: Human Kinetics.

Biesmeijer, J. C., & Seeley, T. D. (2005). The use of waggle dance information by honey bees throughout their foraging careers. *Behavioral Ecology and Sociobiology, 59,* 133–142.

Bilkey, D. K., & Clearwater, J. M. (2005). The dynamic nature of spatial encoding in the hippocampus. *Behavioral Neuroscience, 119,* 1533–1545

Birbaumer, N., Veit, R., Lotze, M., Erb, M., Hermann, C., Grodd, W., et al. (2005). Deficient fear conditioning in psychopathy: A functional magnetic resonance imaging study. *Archives of General Psychiatry, 62,* 799–805.

Birkenhaeger, T. K., Pluijms, E. M., & Lucius, S. A. P. (2003). ECT response in delusional versus non-delusional depressed inpatients. *Journal of Affective Disorders, 74,* 191–195.

Birmingham, C. L., Su, J., Hlynsky, J. A., Goldner, E. M., & Gao, M. (2005). The mortality rate from anorexia nervosa. *International Journal of Eating Disorders, 38,* 143–146.

Bjorklund, D. F. (2003). Evolutionary psychology from a developmental systems perspective: Comment on Lickliter and Honeycutt (2003). *Psychological Bulletin, 129,* 836–841.

Bjornson, C. R. R., Rietze, R. L., Reynolds, B. A., Magli, M. C., & Vescovi, A. L. (1999, January 22). Turning brain into blood: A hematopoietic fate adopted by adult neural stem cells in vivo. *Science, 283,* 534–537.

Blader, S. L., & Tyler, T. R. (2002). Justice and empathy: What motivates people to help others? In M. Ross & M. D. T. Miller (Eds.), *The justice motive in everyday life* (pp. 226–250). New York: Cambridge Univ. Press.

Blagrove, M., & Akehurst, L. (2000). Effects of sleep loss on confidence-accuracy relationships for reasoning and eyewitness memory. *Journal of Experimental Psychology: Applied, 6,* 59–73.

Blagrove, M., & Akehurst, L. (2001). Personality and the modulation of effects of sleep loss on mood and cognition. *Personality and Individual Differences, 30,* 819–828.

Blake, R. R., Helson, H., & Mouton, J. (1956). The generality of conformity behavior as a function of factual anchorage, difficulty of task and amount of social pressure. *Journal of Personality, 25,* 294–305.

Blanchard, E. B., Appelbaum, K. A., Radnitz, C. L., Morrill, B., Michultka, D., Kirsch, C., et al. (1990). A controlled evaluation of thermal biofeedback and thermal biofeedback combined with cognitive therapy in the treatment of vascular headache. *Journal of Consulting & Clinical Psychology, 58,* 216–224.

Blass, T. (2002). Perpetrator behavior as destructive obedience: An evaluation of Stanley Milgram's perspective, the most influential social-psychological approach to the Holocaust. In L. S. Newman & R. Erber (Eds.), *Understanding genocide: The social psychology of the Holocaust* (pp. 91–109). London: Oxford Univ. Press.

Blatt, S. J., Zuroff, D. C., Quinlan, D. M., & Pilkonis, P. (1996). Interpersonal factors in brief treatment of depression: Further analysis of the NIMH Treatment of Depression Collaborative Research Program. *Journal of Consulting and Clinical Psychology, 64,* 162–171.

Blehar, M. C., & Keita, G. P. (2003). Women and depression: A millennial perspective. *Journal of Affective Disorders, 74,* 1–4.

Bleijenberg, G., Prins, J., & Bazelmans, E. (2003). Cognitive–behavioral therapies. In L. A. Jason & P. A. Fennell (Eds.), *Handbook of chronic fatigue syndrome* (pp. 493–526). New York: John Wiley & Sons.

Bliss, J. P., Scerbo, M. W., Schmidt, E. A., & Thompson, S. N. (2006). The efficacy of a medical virtual reality simulator for training phlebotomy. *Human Factors, 48,* 72–84.

Bliss, T., Collingridge, G., & Morris R. (2004). *Long-term potentiation: Enhancing neuroscience for 30 years.* Oxford, UK: Oxford Univ. Press.

Block, J. (1971). *Lives through time.* Berkeley, CA: Bancroft.

Blood, A. J., & Zatorre, R. J. (2001). Intensely pleasurable responses to music correlate with activity in brain regions implicated in reward and emotion. *Proceedings from the National Academy of Sciences, USA, 98,* 11818–11823.

Blum, J. M. (1979). *Pseudoscience and mental ability: The origins and fallacies of the IQ controversy.* New York: Monthly Review Press.

Blumberg, M. S., & Wasserman, E. A. (1995). Animal mind and the argument from design. *American Psychologist, 50,* 133–144.

Blumenthal, A. L. (1975). A reappraisal of Wilhelm Wundt. *American Psychologist, 30,* 1081–1088.

Blundell, J. E., & Halford, J. C. G. (1998). Serotonin and appetite regulation: Implications for the pharmacological treatment of obesity. *CNS Drugs, 9,* 473–495.

Bochner, S., & Jones, J. (2003). *Child language development: Learning to talk.* London: Whurr.

Boelte, S., Uhlig, N., & Poustka, F. (2002). The savant syndrome: A review. *Zeitschrift fuer Klinische Psychologie und Psycholtherapie: Forschung und Praxis, 31,* 291–297.

Bohart, A. C., & Greening, T. (2001). Humanistic psychology and positive psychology. *American Psychologist, 56,* 81–82.

Bolhuis J. J., & Giraldeau, L.-A. (Eds.) (2005). *The behavior of animals: Mechanisms, function and evolution.* Malden, MA: Blackwell.

Bolton, D., Eley, T. C., & O'Connor, T. G. (2006). Prevalence and genetic and environmental influences on anxiety disorders in 6-year-old twins. *Psychological Medicine, 36,* 335–344.

Bonanno, G. A. (2004). Loss, trauma, and human resilience: Have we underestimated the human capacity to thrive after extremely aversive events? *American Psychologist, 59,* 20–28.

Bonanno, G. A., Galea, S., Bucciarelli, A., & Vlahov, D. (2006). Psychological resilience after disaster. *Psychological Science, 17,* 181–186.

Bonanno, G. A., Wortman, C. B., & Nesse R. M. (2004). Prospective patterns of resilience and maladjustment during widowhood. *Psychology and Aging, 19,* 260–271.

Bond, C. F., Pitre, U., & Van Leeuwen, M. D. (1991). Encoding operations and the next-in-line effect. *Personality and Social Psychology Bulletin, 17,* 435–141.

Bond, R. (2005). Group size and conformity. *Group Processes & Intergroup Relations, 8,* 331–354.

Bonham, V. L. (2001). Race, ethnicity, and pain treatment: striving to understand the causes and solutions to the disparities in pain treatment. *Journal of Law and Medical Ethics, 29,* 52–68.

Boniecki, K., & Moore, S. (2003). Breaking the silence: Using a token economy to reinforce classroom participation. *Teaching of Psychology, 30,* 224–227.

Bonvillian, J. D., & Patterson, F. G. P. (1997). Sign language acquisition and the development of meaning in a lowland gorilla. In C. Mandell & A. McCabe (Eds.), *The problem of meaning: Behavioral and Cognitive Perspectives* (pp. 181–219). Amsterdam, Netherlands: North-Holland/Elsevier Science.

Bopp, K. L., & Verhaeghen, P. (2005). Aging and verbal memory span: A meta-analysis. *Journals of Gerontology: Series B: Psychological Sciences and Social Sciences, 60B,* P223–P233.

Borkovec, T. D., & Costello, E. (1993). Efficacy of applied relaxation and cognitive-behavioral therapy in the treatment of generalized anxiety disorder. *Journal of Consulting and Clinical Psychology, 61,* 611–619.

Borman, W. C., Ilgen, D. R., & Klimoski, R. J. (2003). *Industrial and organizational psychology.* New York: Wiley.

Bornstein, R. F. (1989). Exposure and affect: Overview and meta-analysis of research, 1968–1987. *Psychological Reports, 106,* 265–289.

Bornstein, R. F., & Masling, J. M. (Eds.). (1998). *Empirical studies of the therapeutic hour. Empirical studies of psychoanalytic theories* (Vol. 8). Washington, DC: American Psychological Assoc.

Bosacki, S. L., & Moore, C. (2004). Preschoolers' understanding of simple and complex emotions: Links with gender and language. *Sex Roles, 50,* 659–675.

Bosma, H., vanBoxtel, M. P. J., Ponds, R. W. H. M., Houx, P. J. H., & Jolles, J. (2003). Education and age-related cognitive decline: The contribution of mental workload. *Educational Gerontology, 29,* 165–173.

Bosworth, R. G., & Dobkins, K. R. (1999). Left-hemisphere dominance for motion processing in deaf signers. *Psychological Science, 10,* 256–262.

Bottini, G., Karnath, H. O., Vallar, G., Sterzi, R., Frith, C. D., Frackowiak, R. S. J., et al. (2001). Cerebral representations for egocentric space: Functional-anatomical evidence from caloric vestibular stimulation and neck vibration. *Brain: A Journal of Neurology, 124,* 1182–1196.

Bouchard, T. J., Jr. (1984). Twins reared together and apart: What they tell us about human diversity. In S. W. Fox (Ed.), *Individuality and determinism* (pp. 147–178). New York: Plenum.

Bouchard, T. J., Jr. (1996). IQ similarity in twins reared apart: Findings and responses to critics. In R. J. Sternberg & E. Grigorenko (Eds.), *Intelligence: Heredity and environment* (pp. 126–160). New York: Cambridge Univ. Press.

Bouchard, T. J., Jr., Lykken, D. T., McGue, M., Segal, N. L., & Tellegren, A. (1990, October 12). Sources of human psychological differences: The Minnesota study of twins reared apart. *Science, 250,* 223–228.

Bouckenooghe, D., Buelens, M., Fontaine, J., & Vanderheyden, K. (2005). The prediction of stress by values and value conflict. *Journal of Psychology: Interdisciplinary and Applied, 139,* 369–382.

Bourgois, P. (1999). Participant observation study of indirect paraphernalia sharing/HIV risk in a network of heroin injectors. Community Epidemiology Work Group Publications, National Institute on Drug Abuse (NIDA). Retrieved October 3, 2006, from www.drugabuse.gov/about/organization/cewg/ethno.html

Bourin, M. (2003). Use of paroxetine for the treatment of depression and anxiety disorders in the elderly: A review. *Human Psychopharmacology, 18,* 185–190.

Bouton, M. E. (1993). Context, time and memory retrieval in the interference paradigms of Pavlovian conditioning. *Psychological Bulletin, 114*, 80–99.

Bouton, M. E. (1994). Context, ambiguity and classical conditioning. *Current Directions in Psychological Science, 3*, 49–52.

Bouton, M. E. (2002). Context, ambiguity, and unlearning: Sources of relapse after behavioral extinction. *Biological Psychiatry, 51*, 976–986.

Bovbjerg, D. H. (2003). Conditioning, cancer, and immune regulation. *Brain, Behavior and Immunity, 17* [Special issue: *Biological mechanisms of psychosocial effects on disease: Implications for cancer control*], S58–S61.

Bowden, E. M., & Jung-Beeman, M. (2003). Aha! Insight experience correlates with solution activation in the right hemisphere. *Psychonomic Bulletin and Review, 10*, 730–737.

Bower, B. (2003a, April 19). Words get in the way: Talk is cheap, but it can tax your memory. *Science News*, 250–251.

Bower, B. (2003b, May 24). Repeat after me: Imitation is the sincerest form of perception. *Science News*, 330–332.

Bower, B. (2006, February 11). Self-serve brains: Personal identity veers to the right hemisphere. *Science News*, 90–92.

Bower, G. H., & Mann, T. (1992). Improving recall by recoding interfering material at the time of recall. *Journal of Experimental Psychology: Learning, Memory, and Cognition, 18*, 1310–1320.

Bower, G. H., & Sivers, H. (1998). Cognitive impact of traumatic events. *Development & Psychopathology, 10*, 625–653.

Bower, J. M., & Parsons, L. M. (2003). Rethinking the "lesser brain." *Scientific American, 282*(2), 50–57.

Boyer, J. L., Harrison, S., & Ro, T. (2005) Unconscious processing of orientation and color without primary visual cortex. *Proceedings of the National Academy of Sciences of the United States of America, 102*, 16875–16879.

Boysen, S. T., & Himes, G. T. (1999). Current issues and emerging theories in animal cognition. *Annual Review of Psychology, 50*, 683–705.

Bradley, R., Conklin, C. Z., & Westen, D. (2005). The borderline personality diagnosis in adolescents: Gender differences and subtypes. *Journal of Child Psychology and Psychiatry, 46*, 1006–1019.

Brainerd, C. J. (1978). The stage question in cognitive-developmental theory. *Behavioral and Brain Sciences, 2*, 172–213.

Brainerd, C. J., & Reyna, V. F. (1998). When things that were never experienced are easier to "remember" than things that were. *Psychological Science, 9*, 484–489.

Brannon, E. M., & Terrace, H. S. (1998, October 23). Ordering of the numerosities 1–9 by monkeys. *Science, 282*, 746–749.

Braun, A. R., Balkin, T. J., Wesensten, N. J., Gwadry, F., Varga, M., Baldwin, P., et al. (1998, January 2). Dissociated pattern of activity in visual cortices and their projections during human rapid eye movement sleep. *Science, 279*, 91–95.

Brehm, S. S. (2002). *Intimate relationships* (3rd ed.). New York: McGraw-Hill.

Bremner, J. D. (2001). Hypotheses and controversies related to effects of stress on the hippocampus: An argument for stress-induced damage to the hippocampus in patients with posttraumatic stress disorder. *Hippocampus, 11*, 75–81.

Bremner, J. D., & Marmar, C. R. (Eds.). (1998). *Trauma, memory and dissociation*. Washington, DC: American Psychiatric Press.

Brenner, M. H. (1973). *Mental illness and the economy*. Cambridge, MA: Harvard Univ. Press.

Brenner, M. H. (1979). Influence of the social environment on psychopathology: The historic perspective. In J. E. Barrett (Ed.), *Stress and mental disorder*. New York: Raven.

Bresnahan, M., Schaefer, C. A., Brown, A. S., & Susser, E. S. (2005). Prenatal determinants of schizophrenia: What we have learned thus far? *Epidemiologiae Psichiatria Sociale, 14*, 194–197.

Bressan, R. A., & Crippa, J. A. (2005). The role of dopamine in reward and pleasure behaviour—Review of data from preclinical research. *Acta Psychiatrica Scandinavica, 111*, 14–21.

Brewer, J. B., Zhao, Z., Desmond, J. E., Glover, G. H., & Gabriel, J. D. E. (1998, August 21). Making memories: Brain activity that predicts how well visual experience will be remembered. *Science, 281*, 1185–1187.

Brewer, R. D., & Swahn, M. H. (2005). Binge drinking and violence. *JAMA: Journal of the American Medical Association, 294*, 616–617.

Brim, O. (1999). *The McArthur Foundation study of midlife development*. Vero Beach, FL: The McArthur Foundation.

Brinkley, A. (1999). *American history: A survey* (10th ed.). New York: McGraw-Hill.

Broadbent, D. E. (1958). *Perception and communication*. New York: Pergamon.

Brobert, A. G., Wessels, H., Lamb, M. E., & Hwang, C. P. (1997). Effects of day care on the development of cognitive abilities in 8-year-olds: A longitudinal study. *Developmental Psychology, 33*, 62–69.

Brodsky, S. L. (1999). *The expert expert witness: More maxims and guidelines for testifying in court*. Washington, DC: American Psychological Assoc.

Brody, J. E. (2004, February 24). Age-fighting hormones put men at risk, too. *New York Times*, p. D7.

Brody, L., & Hall, J. (2000). Gender, emotion, and expression. In M. Lewis & J. Haviland-Jones (Eds.), *Handbook of emotions* (2nd ed., pp. 338–349). New York: Guilford.

Brody, N. (2000). Intelligence. In A. Kazdin, (Ed.), *Encyclopedia of psychology* (Vol. 4, pp. 318 -324). Washington, DC: American Psychological Assoc.

Bronfenbrenner, U. (1986). Ecology of the family as a context for human development: Research perspectives. *Developmental Psychology, 22*, 723–742.

Brooks, D. C., Bowker, J. L., Anderson, J. E., & Palmatier, M. I. (2003). Impact of brief or extended extinction of a taste aversion on inhibitory associations: Evidence from summation, retardation and preference tests. *Learning and Behavior, 31*, 69–84.

Brooks-Gunn, J., & Lewis, M. (1984). The development of early visual self-recognition. *Developmental Review, 4*, 215–239.

Brown, L. M. (2005). *Girlfighting: Betrayal and rejection among girls*. New York: New York Univ. Press.

Brown, L. S., & Ballou, M. (1992). *Personality and psychopathology: Feminists reappraisals*. New York: Guilford.

Brown, N. R. (2005). On the prevalence of event clusters in autobiographical memory. *Social Cognition, 23*, 35–69.

Brown, N. R., & Schopflocher, D. (1998). Event clusters: An organization of personal events in autobiographical memory. *Psychological Science, 9*, 470–475.

Brown, P., van der Hart, O., & Graafland, M. (1999). Trauma-induced dissociative amnesia in World War I combat soldiers. II. Treatment dimensions. *Australian and New Zealand Journal of Psychiatry, 33*, 392–398.

Brown, P. L., & Jenkins, H. M. (1968). Autoshaping of the pigeon's key peck. *Journal of Experimental and Analytical Behavior, 11*, 1–8.

Brown, R. (1958). *Words and things*. New York: Free Press/Macmillan.

Brown, R., & McNeill, D. (1966). The "tip of the tongue phenomenon." *Journal of Verbal Learning and Verbal Behavior, 8,* 325–337.

Brown, S. L., Bulanda, J. R., & Lee, G. R. (2005). The significance of nonmarital cohabitation: Marital status and mental health benefits among middle-aged and older adults. *Journals of Gerontology: Series B: Psychological Sciences and Social Sciences, 60,* S21–S29.

Bruch, H. (2001). *The golden cage: The enigma of anorexia nervosa.* Cambridge, MA: Harvard Univ. Press.

Bruder, G. E., Stewart, M. W., Mercier, M. A., Agosti, V., Leite, P., Donovan, S., et al. (1997). Outcome of cognitive-behavioral therapy for depression: Relation to hemispheric dominance for verbal processing. *Journal of Abnormal Psychology, 106,* 138–144.

Bruner, J. (2005). Cultural psychology and its functions. *Constructivism in the Human Sciences, 10,* 53–63.

Bryant, R. A., & Harvey, A. G. (2003). Gender differences in the relationship between acute stress disorder and posttraumatic stress disorder following motor vehicle accidents. *Australian and New Zealand Journal of Psychiatry, 37,* 226–229.

Bryden, P. J., Bruyn, J., Fletcher, P. (2005). Handedness and health: An examination of the association between different handedness classifications and health disorders. *Laterality: Asymmetries of Body, Brain and Cognition, 10,* 429–440.

Bubka, A., & Bonato, F. (2003), Optokinetic drum tilt hastens the onset of vection-induced motion sickness. *Aviation, Space, and Environmental Medicine, 74,* 315–319.

Buck, L., & Axel, R. (1991). A novel multigene family may encode odorant receptors: A molecular basis for odor recognition. *Cell, 65,* 175–187.

Buist, C. M. (2002). Reducing essential hypertension in the elderly using biofeedback assisted self-regulatory training. *Dissertation Abstracts International: Section B: The Sciences and Engineering, 63,* 516.

Buklina, S. B. (2005). The corpus callosum, interhemisphere interactions, and the function of the right hemisphere of the brain. *Neuroscience and Behavioral Physiology, 35,* 473–480.

Bulik, C. M., Reba, L., Siega-Riz, A.-M., & Reichborn-Kjennerud, T. (2005). Anorexia nervosa: Definition, epidemiology, and cycle of risk. *International Journal of Eating Disorders, 37,* S2–S9.

Bulik, C. M., Sullivan, P. F., & Kendler, K. S. (2003). Genetic and environmental contributions to obesity and binge eating. *International Journal of Eating Disorders, 33,* 293–298.

Bulik, C. M., Sullivan, P. F., Tozzi, F., Furberg, H., Lichtenstein, P., & Pedersen, N. L. (2006). Prevalence, heritability, and prospective risk factors for anorexia nervosa. *Archives of General Psychiatry, 63,* 305–312.

Buller, D. J. (2005). Evolutionary psychology: The emperor's new paradigm. *Trends in Cognitive Sciences, 9,* 277–283.

Burch, S. (2004). Capturing a movement: Sign language preservation. *Sign Language Studies, 4,* 293–304.

Bursik, K. (1998). Moving beyond gender differences: Gender role comparisons of manifest dream content. *Sex Roles, 38,* 203–214.

Burt, M. R., Aron, L. Y., Douglas, T., Valente, J., Lee, E., & Iwen, B. (1999). Homelessness: Programs and the people they serve. Retrieved September 18, 2003, from http://www.urban.org/UploadedPDF/homelessness.pdf

Buscemi, N., Vandermeer, B., Hooton, N., Pandya, R., Tjosvold, L., Hartling, L., et al. (2006). Efficacy and safety of exogenous melatonin for secondary sleep disorders and sleep disorders accompanying sleep restriction: meta-analysis. *British Medical Journal, 332,* 385–393.

Bushman, B. J. (2002). Does venting anger feed or extinguish the flame? Catharsis rumination, distraction, anger and aggressive responding. *Personality and Social Psychology Bulletin, 28,* 724–731.

Bushman, B. J., & Baumeister, R. F. (1998). Threatened egotism, narcissism, self-esteem, and direct and displaced aggression: Does self-love or self-hate lead to violence? *Journal of Personality & Social Psychology, 75,* 219–229.

Bushman, B. J., Baumeister, R. F., & Stack, A. D. (1999). Catharsis, aggression, and persuasive influence: Self-fulfilling or self-defeating prophecies? *Journal of Personality and Social Psychology, 76,* 367–376.

Bushnell, I. W. R. (2003). Newborn face recognition. In O. Pascalis & A. Slater (Eds.), *The development of face processing in infancy and early childhood: Current perspectives* (pp. 41–53). Hauppauge, NY: Nova Science.

Buss, D. M. (1985). Human mate selection. *American Scientist, 73,* 47–51.

Buss, D. M. (1990). The evolution of anxiety and social exclusion. *Journal of Social and Clinical Psychology, 9,* 196–210.

Buss, D. M. (1991). Evolutionary personality psychology. *Annual Review of Psychology, 42,* 459–491.

Buss, D. M. (2000a). The evolution of happiness. *American Psychologist, 55,* 15–23.

Buss, D. M. (2000b). *The dangerous passion: Why jealousy is as necessary as love and sex.* New York: Free Press.

Buss, D. M. (2004). *Evolutionary psychology: The new science of the mind* (2nd ed.). Boston: Pearson Education.

Buss, D. M. (2005). *The handbook of evolutionary psychology.* Hoboken, NJ: John Wiley & Sons.

Buss, D. M., & Reeve, H. K. (2003). Evolutionary psychology and developmental dynamics: Comment on Lickliter and Honeycutt (2003). *Psychological Bulletin, 129,* 848–853.

Butler, R. N., & Lewis, M. I., & Sunderland, T. (1998). *Aging and mental health: Positive psychosocial and biomedical approaches* (5th ed.). Boston: Allyn & Bacon.

Butnik, S. M. (2005). Neurofeedback in adolescents and adults with Attention Deficit Hyperactivity Disorder. *Journal of Clinical Psychology, 61,* 621–625.

Byne, W. (1994). The biological evidence challenged. *Scientific American, 270*(5), 50–55.

Byrne, D. (1997). An overview (and underview) of research and theory within the attraction paradigm. *Journal of Social and Personal Relationships, 14,* 417–431.

Byrne, M., Carr, A., & Clark, M. (2004). Power in relationships of women with depression. *Journal of Family Therapy, 26,* 407–429.

Byrne, R. W. (2002). *Evolutionary psychology and primate cognition.* Cambridge, Mass: MIT Press.

Cabeza, R., & Nyberg, L. (2000). Imaging cognition II: An empirical review of 275 PET and fMRI studies. *Journal of Cognitive Neuroscience, 12,* 1–47.

Cacioppo, J. T., & Berntson, G. G. (2005). *Social neuroscience: Key readings.* New York: Psychology Press.

Cacioppo, J. T., & Gardner, W. L. (1999). Emotion. *Annual Review of Psychology, 50,* 191–214.

Cacioppo, J. T., Hawkley, L. C., Berntson, G. G., Ernst, J. M., Gibbs, A. C., Strickgold, R., et al. (2002). Do lonely days invade the nights? Potential social modulation of sleep efficiency. *Psychological Science, 13,* 384–387.

Cahill, J., Barkham, M., Hardy, G., Rees, A., Shapiro, D. A., Stiles, W. B., et al. (2003). Outcomes of patients completing and not completing cognitive therapy for depression. *British Journal of Clinical Psychology, 42,* 133–143.

Cahill, L., & Alkire, M. T. (2003). Epinephrine enhancement of human memory consolidation: Interaction with arousal at encoding. *Neurobiology of Learning and Memory, 79,* 194–198.

Cahill, L., & McGaugh, J. L. (1998). Mechanisms of emotional arousal and lasting declarative memory. *Trends in Neurosciences, 21,* 294–299.

Cahn, B. R., & Polich, J. (2006). Meditation states and traits: EEG, ERP, and neuroimaging studies. *Psychological Bulletin, 132,* 180–211

Cain, D. J. (2002). Defining characteristics, history, and evolution of humanistic psychotherapies. In D. J. Cain (Ed.), *Humanistic psychotherapies: Handbook of research and practice* (pp. 3–54). Washington, DC: American Psychological Assoc.

Cairns, E., & Darby, J. (1998). The conflict in Northern Ireland: Causes, consequences, and controls. *American Psychologist, 53,* 754–760.

Caley, L. M., Kramer, C., & Robinson, L. (2005). Fetal alcohol spectrum disorder. *Journal of School Nursing, 21,* 139–146.

Calhoun, L. G., & Tedeschi, R. G. (2001). Posttraumatic growth: The positive lessons of loss. In R. A. Neimeyer (Ed.), *Meaning reconstruction & the experience of loss* (pp. 157–172). Washington, DC: American Psychological Assoc.

Califano, J. A., Jr. (1999, August 24). White-Line Fever: What an older and wiser George W. should do. *Washington Post,* p. A17.

Califano, J. A., Jr. (2000, March). *It's the substance abuse, stupid!* Opening remarks. National Center on Addiction and Substance Abuse (CASA) at Columbia University. Retrieved September 15, 2000, from http://www.casacolumbia.org

Callahan, R. (2000, January 13). Tall Polish men have tall kids, study says. *Charlotte Observer,* p. 12A.

Callicott, J. H. (2003). An expanded role for functional neuroimaging in schizophrenia. *Current Opinions in Neurobiology, 13,* 256–260.

Calvert, S., & Cocking, R. (1992). Health promotion through mass media. *Journal of Applied Developmental Psychology, 13,* 143–149.

Cambras, T., López, L., & Arias, J. L. (2005). Quantitative changes in neuronal and glial cells in the suprachiasmatic nucleus as a function of the lighting conditions during weaning. *Developmental Brain Research, 157,* 27–33.

Cameron, J., Banko, K. M., & Pierce, W. D. (2001). Pervasive negative effects of rewards on intrinsic motivation: The myth continues. *The Behavior Analyst, 24,* 1–44.

Camperio-Ciani A., Corna, F., & Capiluppi C. (2004). Evidence for maternally inherited factors favouring male homosexuality and promoting female fecundity. *Proceedings of the Royal Society of London B., 271,* 2217–21.

Campo, P., Maestú, F., Capilla, A., Fernández, S., Fernández, A., & Ortiz, T. (2005). Activity in human medial temporal lobe associated with encoding process in spatial working memory revealed by magnetoencephalography. *European Journal of Neuroscience, 21,* 1741–1748.

Camras, L., Meng, Z., Ujiie, T., Dharamsi, S., Myake, K., Oster, H., et al. (2002). Observing emotion in infants: Facial expression, body behavior, and rater judgments of responses to an expectancy-violating event. *Emotion, 2,* 179–193.

Cannon, W. B. (1929). *Bodily changes in pain, hunger, fear, and rage,* (Rev. ed.) New York: D. Appleton and Co.

Caplan, P. J. (2003). Balancing career and family. In M. J. Prinstein & M. D. Patterson (Eds.), *The portable mentor: Expert guide to a successful career in psychology* (pp. 45–54). New York: Kluwer Academic/Plenum.

Caporael, L. R. (2001). Evolutionary psychology: Toward a unifying theory and a hybrid science. *Annual Review of Psychology, 52,* 607–628.

Capron, C., & Duyme, M. (1989). Assessment of effects of socioeconomic status on IQ in a full cross-fostering study. *Nature (London), 340,* 552–554.

Cardemil, E. V., & Battle, C. L. (2003). Guess who's coming to therapy? Getting comfortable with conversations about race and ethnicity in psychotherapy. *Professional Psychology: Research and Practice, 34,* 278–286.

Cardena, E., Butler, L. D., & Spiegel, D. (2003). Stress disorders. In G. Stricker & T. A. Widiger (Eds.), *Handbook of psychology: Vol. 8, Clinical psychology* (pp. 229–249). New York: John Wiley & Sons.

Carello, C., & Turvey, M. T. (2004). Physics and psychology of the muscle sense. *Current Directions in Psychological Science, 13,* 25–28.

Carlson, N. R. (2000). *Physiology of behavior* (7th ed.). Boston: Allyn & Bacon.

Carmona, F. J., Sanz, L. J., & Marin, D. (2002). Type-A behaviour pattern and coronary heart disease. *Psiquis: Revista de Psiquiatria, Psicologia Medica y Psicosomatica, 23,* 22–30.

Carnagey, N. L., & Anderson, C. A. (2005). The effect of reward and punishment in violent video games in aggressive affect, cognition, and behavior. *Psychological Science, 16,* 882–889.

Carpenter, S. (2001). Research confirms the virtue of "sleeping on it." *Monitor on Psychology, 32,* 49–51.

Carpenter, S. K. (2005). Some neglected contributions of Wilhelm Wundt to the psychology of memory. *Psychological Reports, 97,* 63–73.

Carr, D., & Friedman, M. A. (2005). Is obesity stigmatizing? Body weight, perceived discrimination, and psychological well-being in the United States. *Journal of Health and Social Behavior, 46,* 244–259.

Carr, L., Lacoboni, M., Dubeau, M., Mazziotta, J. C., & Lenzi, G. L. (2005). Neural mechanisms of empathy in humans: A relay from neural systems for imitation to limbic areas. In J. T. Cacioppo & G. G. Berntson (Eds.), *Social neuroscience: Key readings* (pp. 143–152). New York: Psychology Press.

Carr, M., Borkowski, J. G., & Maxwell, S. E. (1991). Motivational components of underachievement. *Developmental Psychology, 27,* 108–118.

Carrére, S., Mittmann, A., Woodin, E., Tabares, A., & Yoshimoto, D. (2005). Anger dysregulation, depressive symptoms, and health in married women and men. *Nursing Research, 54,* 184–192.

Carskadon, M. A. (2002). Risks of driving while sleepy in adolescents and young adults. In M. A. Carskadon (Ed.), *Adolescent sleep patterns: Biological, social, and psychological influences* (pp. 148–158). New York: Cambridge Univ. Press.

Carskadon, M. A., Acebo, C., & Jenni, O. G. (2004). Regulation of adolescent sleep: Implications for behavior. In D. E. Ronald & L. P. Spear (Eds.), *Adolescent brain development: Vulnerabilities and opportunities* (pp. 276–292). New York: New York Academy of Sciences.

Carskadon, M. A., & Dement, W. C. (1982). Nocturnal determinants of daytime sleepiness. *Sleep, 5*(Suppl. 2), 73–81.

Carson, R. C., & Butcher, J. N. (1992). *Abnormal psychology and modern life.* New York: HarperCollins.

Carstensen, L. (1995). Evidence for a life-span theory of socioemotional selectivity. *Current Directions in Psychological Science, 4,* 151–156.

Carter, J. A. (2006). Theoretical pluralism and technical eclecticism. In C. D. Goodheart, A. E. Kazdin, & R. J. Sternberg (Eds.), *Evidence-based psychotherapy: Where practice and research meet* (pp. 63–79). Washington, DC: American Psychological Assoc.

Carter, R. (1998). *Mapping the mind.* Berkeley, CA: Univ. of California Press.

Carter, T., Hardy, C. A., & Hardy, J. C. (2001). Latin vocabulary acquisition: An experiment using information processing techniques of chunking and imagery. *Journal of Instructional Psychology, 28,* 225–228.

Cartwright, J. (2000). *Evolution and human behavior: Darwinian perspectives on human nature.* Cambridge, MA: MIT Press.

Cartwright, R. D. (1996). Dreams and adaptation to divorce. In D. Barrett (Ed.), *Trauma and dreams* (pp. 179–185). Cambridge, MA: Harvard Univ. Press.

Casas, J. M. (1995). Counseling and psychotherapy with racial/ethnic minority groups in theory and practice. In B. Bongar & L. E. Beutler (Eds.), *Comprehensive handbook of psychotherapy* (pp. 311–335). New York: Oxford Univ. Press.

Caspi, O., & Burleson, K. O. (2005). Methodological challenges in meditation research. *Advances in Mind-Body Medicine, 21,* 4–11.

Cassidy, J. P. (2002). The Stockholm Syndrome, battered woman syndrome and the cult personality: An integrative approach. *Dissertation Abstracts International: Section B: The Sciences and Engineering, 62,* 5366.

Castelli, L., Macrae, C. N., Zogmaister, C., & Arcuri, L. (2004). A tale of two primes: Contextual limits on stereotype activation. *Social Cognition, 22,* 233–247.

Cattell, R. B. (1965). *The scientific analysis of personality.* Baltimore: Penguin.

Cattell, R. B., & Kline, P. (1977). *The specific analysis of personality and motivation.* New York: Academic Press.

Cauli, O., & Morelli, M. (2005). Caffeine and the dopaminergic system. *Behavioural Pharmacology, 16,* 63–77.

Cavanaugh, J. C., & Blanchard-Fields, F. (2005). *Adult development and aging* (5th ed.). Belmont, CA: Wadsworth.

Ceci, S. J., & Williams, W. M. (1997). Schooling, intelligence, and income. *American Psychologist, 52,* 1051–1058.

Cemalcilar, Z., Canbeyli, R., & Sunar, D. (2003). Learned helplessness, therapy, and personality traits: An experimental study. *Journal of Social Psychology, 143,* 65–81.

Centers for Disease Control. (2006). Deaths: Final data for 2003. *National Vital Statistics Reports, 54*(13). Retrieved July 11, 2006, from http://www.cdc.gov/nchs/data/nvsr/nvsr54/nvsr54_13.pdf

Cerri, M. M. (2005). Recovered memory: Historical and theoretical foundations of the debate. *Dissertation Abstracts International: Section B: The Sciences and Engineering, 65,* 4820.

Chafee, M. V., Crowe, D. A., Averbeck, B. B., & Georgopoulos, A. P. (2005). Neural correlates of spatial judgement during object construction in parietal cortex. *Cerebral Cortex, 15,* 1393–1413.

Chaiken, S., & Eagly, A. H. (1976). Communication modality as a determinant of message persuasiveness and message comprehensibility. *Journal of Personality and Social Psychology, 34,* 605–614.

Chance, P. (1992). The rewards of learning. *Phi Delta Kappan, 73,* 200–207.

Chance, S. A., Esiri, M. M., & Timothy, J. C. (2003). Ventricular enlargement in schizophrenia: A primary change in the temporal lobe? *Schizophrenia Research, 62,* 123–131.

Chang, A. (2006, January 5). The scent of a woman–lost. Retrieved May 10, 2006, from http://www.jenniferboyer.com/AnosmiaNews4.html

Chang, E. C., & Sanna, L. J. (2003). Experience of life hassles and psychological adjustment among adolescents: Does it make a difference if one is optimistic or pessimistic? *Personality and Individual Differences, 34,* 867–879.

Check, E. (2005). The rocky road to success. *Nature, 437,* 185–186.

Chekroun, P., & Brauer, M. (2002). The bystander effect and social control behavior: The effect of the presence of others on people's reactions to norm violations. *European Journal of Social Psychology, 32,* 853–866.

Chen, G., & Manji, H. K. (2006). The extracellular signal-regulated kinase pathway: An emerging promising target for mood stabilizers. *Current Opinion in Psychiatry, 19,* 313–323.

Chen, J-Q., & Gardner, H. (2005). Assessment based on multiple-intelligences theory. In D. P. Flanagan & P. L. Harrison (Eds.), *Contemporary intellectual assessment: Theories, tests, and issues* (pp. 77–102). New York: Guilford.

Chen, P., Goldberg, D. E., Kolb, B., Lanser, M., & Benowitz, L. I. (2002). Inosine induces axonal rewiring and improves behavioral outcome after stroke. *Proceedings of the National Academy of Sciences USA, 99,* 9031–9036.

Cheour, M., Ceponiene, R., Lehtokoski, A., Luuk, A., Allik, J., Alho, K., et al. (1998). Development of language-specific phoneme representations in the infant brain. *Nature Neuroscience, 1,* 351–353.

Cherlin, A. (1992). *Marriage, divorce, remarriage.* Boston, MA: Harvard Univ. Press.

Cherniss, C., & Goleman, D. (2001). *The emotionally intelligent workplace.* San Francisco: Jossey-Bass.

Cherry, C. (1966). *On human communication: A review, a survey, and a criticism* (2nd ed.). Cambridge, MA: MIT Press.

Chervin, R. D., Killion, J. E., Archbold, K. H., & Ruzicka, D. L. (2003). Conduct problems and symptoms of sleep disorders in children. *Journal of the American Academy of Child and Adolescent Psychiatry, 42,* 201–208.

Chester, J. A., Lumeng, L., Li, T. K., & Grahame, N. J. (2003). High and low alcohol preferring mice show differences in conditioned taste aversion to alcohol. *Alcoholism: Clinical and Experimental Research, 27,* 12–18.

Cheung, S. W., Nagarajan, S. S., & Schreiner, C. E. (2005). Plasticity in primary auditory cortex of monkeys with altered vocal production. *Journal of Neuroscience, 25,* 2490–2503.

Chipman, S. F., Krantz, D. H., & Silver, R. (1992). Mathematics anxiety and science careers among able bodied college women. *Psychological Science, 5,* 292–295.

Choi, I., Dalal, R., Kim-Prieto, C., & Park, H. (2003). Culture and judgment of causal relevance. *Journal of Personality and Social Psychology, 84,* 46–59.

Choi, I., Nisbett, R. E., & Norenzayan, A. (1999). Casual attribution across cultures: Variation and universality. *Psychological Bulletin, 125,* 47–63.

Choi, I. Y., Allan, A. M., & Cunningham, L. A. (2005). Moderate fetal alcohol exposure impairs the neurogenic response to an enriched environment in adult mice. *Alcoholism: Clinical and Experimental Research, 29,* 2053–2062.

Choi, J., & Silverman, I. (2003). Processes underlying sex differences in route-learning strategies in children and adolescents. *Personality and Individual Differences, 34,* 113–1166.

Choi, W. S., Pierce, J. P., Gilpin, E. A., Farkas, A. J., & Berry, C. C. (1997). Which adolescent experimenters progress to established smoking in the United States. *American Journal of Preventive Medicine, 13,* 385–391.

Chomsky, N. (1957). *Syntactic structures.* The Hague: Mouton.

Chomsky, N. (1965). *Aspects of the theory of syntax.* Cambridge, MA: MIT Press.

Chomsky, N. (1986). *Knowledge of language: It's nature, origins and use.* New York: Praeger.

Chomsky, N., Place, U., & Schoneberger, T. (2000). The Chomsky–Place correspondence 1993–1994. *Analysis of Verbal Behavior, 17,* 7–38.

Christie, C. (2003). *Gender and language: Towards a feminist pragmatics.* Edinburgh, Scotland: Edinburgh Univ. Press.

Chrobot-Mason, D., & Quinones, M. A. (2002). Training for a diverse workplace. In K. Kraiger (Ed.), *Creating, implementing, and managing effective training and development* (pp. 117–159). San Francisco: Jossey-Bass.

Chuang, Y. C. (2002). Sex differences in mate selection preference and sexual strategy: Tests for evolutionary hypotheses. *Chinese Journal of Psychology, 44*, 75–93.

Chwalisz, K., Diener, E., & Gallagher, D. (1988). Autonomic arousal feedback and emotional experience: Evidence from the spinal cord injured. *Journal of Personality and Social Psychology, 54*, 820–828.

Cialdini, R. B. (1995). Principles and techniques of social influence. In A. Tesser (Ed.), *Advanced social psychology* (pp. 257–282). New York: McGraw-Hill.

Cialdini, R. B., & Trost, M. (1998). Social influence: Social norms, conformity, and compliance. In D. Gilbert, S. T. Fiske, & G. Lindzey (Eds.), *Handbook of social psychology* (4th ed., Vol. 2, pp. 151–192). Boston: McGraw-Hill.

Cicchetti, D., & Toth, S. L. (1998). The development of depression in children and adolescents. *American Psychologist, 53*, 221–241.

Clapham, M. M.(2004). The convergent validity of the Torrance Tests of Creative Thinking and Creativity Interest Inventories. *Educational and Psychological Measurement, 64*, 828–841.

Clark, G. M. (1998). Research advances for cochlear implants. *Auris Nasus Larynx, 25*, 73–87.

Clark, R. D., & Word, L. E. (1974). Where is the apathetic bystander? Situational characteristics of the emergency. *Journal of Personality and Social Psychology, 29*, 279–287.

Clarke-Stewart, K. A., Christian, P. G., & Fitzgerald, L. M. (1994). *Children at home and in day care*. Hillsdale, NJ: Erlbaum.

Clarkson, P. (1996). *To act or not to act: That is the question*. London: Whurr.

Clauss, E., & Caroline, C. C. (2003). Promoting ecologic health resilience for minority youth: Enhancing health care access through the school health center. *Psychology in the Schools, 40*, 265–278.

Clay, R. A. (1999, January). "Lean production" may also be a lean toward injuries. *APA Monitor*, p. 26.

Clay, R. A. (2002, October). Advertising as science. *Monitor on Psychology, 33*, 38–41.

Clayton, A. H., McGarvey, E. L., Abouesh, A. L., & Pinkerton, R. C. (2001). Substitution of an SSRI with bupropion sustained release following SSRI-induced sexual dysfunction. *Journal of Clinical Psychiatry, 62*, 185–190.

Clements, M. (1996, March). Sex after 65. *Parade Magazine*, 4–5, 7.

Cloninger, S. C. (2003). *Theories of personality: Understanding persons* (4th ed.). Englewood Cliffs, NJ: Prentice Hall.

Cocchini, G., Logie, R. H., Sala, S. D., MacPherson, S. E., & Baddeley, A. D. (2002). Concurrent performance of two memory tasks: Evidence for domain-specific working memory systems. *Memory and Cognition, 30*, 1086–1095.

Cochran, S. D., & Mays, V. M. (2006). Estimating prevalence of mental and substance using disorders among lesbians and gay men from existing national health data. In A. M. Omoto & H. S. Kurtzman (Eds.), *Sexual orientation and mental health: Examining identity and development in lesbian, gay, and bisexual people* (pp. 143–165). Washington, DC: American Psychological Assoc.

Cochran, S. V., & Rabinowitz, F. E. (2003). Gender-sensitive recommendations for assessment and treatment of depression in men. *Professional Psychology: Research and Practice, 34*, 132–140.

Cochrane, L., & Quester, P. (2005). Fear in advertising: The influence of consumers' product involvement and culture. *Journal of International Consumer Marketing, 17*, 7–32.

Cohen, E. G. (1984). The desegregated school: Problems in status, power and interethnic climate. In N. Miller & M. B. Brewer (Eds.), *Groups in contact: The psychology of desegregation* (pp. 77–96). New York: Academic Press.

Cohen, L. J., & Galynker, I. I. (2002). Clinical features of pedophilia and implications for treatment. *Journal of Psychiatric Practice, 8*, 276–289.

Cohen, S. (1996). Psychological stress, immunity, and upper respiratory infections. *Current Directions in Psychological Science, 5*, 86–88.

Cohen, S., Doyle, W. J., Turner, R. B., Alper, C. M., & Skoner, D. P. (2003a). Emotional styles and susceptibility to the common cold. *Psychosomatic Medicine, 65*, 652–657.

Cohen, S., Doyle, W. J., Turner, R. B., Alper, C. M., & Skoner, D. P. (2003b). Sociability and susceptibility to the common cold. *Psychological Science, 14*, 389–396.

Cohen, S., Frank, E., Doyle, W. J., Skoner, D. P., Rabin, B. S., & Gwaltney, J. M., Jr. (1998). Types of stressors that increase susceptibility to the common cold in healthy adults. *Health Psychology, 17*, 214–223.

Cohen, S., Hamrick, N., Rodriguez, M. S., Feldman, P. J., Rabin, B. S., & Manuck, S. B. (2002). Reactivity and vulnerability to stress-associated risk for upper respiratory illness. *Psychosomatic Medicine, 64*, 302–310.

Cohen, S., & Herbert, T. B. (1996). Health psychology: Psychological factors and physical disease from the perspective of human psychoneuroimmunology. *Annual Review of Psychology, 47*, 113–142.

Cohen, S., Tyrrell, D. A., & Smith, A. P. (1991). Psychological stress and susceptibility to the common cold. *New England Journal of Medicine, 325*, 606–612.

Cohn, L. D. (1991). Sex differences in the course of personality development: A meta-analysis. *Psychological Bulletin, 109*, 252–266.

Colcombe, S., & Kramer, A. F. (2003). Fitness effects on the cognitive function of older adults: A meta-analytic study. *Psychological Science, 14*, 125–130.

Coleman, J., Glaros, A., & Morris, C. G. (1987). *Contemporary psychology and effective behavior* (6th ed.). Glenview, IL: Scott Foresman.

Coleman, L. J., & Cross, T. L. (2001). *Gifted: Is it a state of being or an application of abilities?* Waco, TX: Prufrock Press.

Coley, R. L., & Chase-Lansdale, L. (1998). Adolescent pregnancy and parenthood: Recent evidence and future directions. *American Psychologist, 53*, 152–166.

Collaer, M. L., & Hines, M. (1995). Human behavioral sex differences: A role for gonadal hormones during early development? *Psychological Bulletin, 118*, 55–107.

Collett, T. S., & Graham, P. (2004). Animal navigation: Path integration, visual landmarks and cognitive Maps. *Current Biology, 14*, R475–R477.

Collins, W. A., Maccoby, E. E., Steinberg, L., Hetherington, E. M., & Bornstein, M. H. (2000). Contemporary research on parenting: The case for nature and nurture. *American Psychologist, 55*, 218–232.

Collins, W. A., Maccoby, E. E., Steinberg, L., Hetherington, E. M., & Bornstein, M. H. (2001). Toward nature WITH nurture. *American Psychologist, 56*, 171–172.

Colquitt, J. A., Conlon, D. E., Wesson, M. J., Porter, C. O., & Ng, K. Y. (2001). Justice at the millennium: A meta-analytic review of 25 years of organizational justice research. *Journal of Applied Psychology, 86*, 425–445.

Comaty, J. E., Stasio, M., & Advokat, C. (2001). Analysis of outcome variables of a token economy system in a state psychiatric hospital: A program evaluation. *Research in Developmental Disabilities, 22*, 233–253.

Comstock, G., & Scharrer, E. (1999). *Television: What's on, who's watching, and what it means*. San Diego, CA: Academic Press.

Confino, A., & Fritzsche, P. (2002). *The work of memory: New directions in the study of German society and culture.* Champaign, IL: Univ. of Illinois Press.

Conger, J. J., & Petersen, A. C. (1991). *Adolescence and youth* (4th ed.). New York: HarperCollins.

Conrad, R. (2004). "[A]s if she defied the world in her joyousness": Rereading Darwin on emotion and emotional development. *Human Development, 47,* 40–65.

Conroy, J. W. (1996). The small ICF/MR program: Dimensions of quality and cost. *Mental Retardation, 34,* 13–26.

Construction Equipment. (2006). Train operators with a PC-based simulator. *Construction Equipment, 10,* 23.

Conte, J. J., & Jacobs, R. R. (2003). Validity evidence linking polychronicity and Big Five personality dimensions to absence, lateness, and supervisory performance ratings. *Human Performance, 16,* 107–129.

Conte, J. M., & Gintoft, J. N. (2005). Polychronicity, Big Five personality dimensions, and sales performance. *Human Performance, 18,* 427–444.

Contrada, R. J., Idler, E. L., Goyal, T. M., Cather, C., Rafalson, L., & Drause, T. J. (2004). Why not find out whether religious beliefs predict surgical outcomes? If they do, why not find out why? Reply to Freedland (2004). *Health Psychology, 23,* 243–246.

Conway, A. R. A., Cowan, N., & Bunting, M. F. (2001). The cocktail party phenomenon revisited: The importance of working memory capacity. *Psychonomic Bulletin and Review, 8,* 331–335.

Conway, M., & Dube, L. (2002). Humor in persuasion on threatening topics: Effectiveness is a function of audience sex role orientation. *Personality and Social Psychology Bulletin, 28,* 863–873.

Conway, M. A. (1996). Failures of autobiographical remembering. In D. Hermann, C. McEvoy, C. Hertzog, P. Hertel, & M. K. Johnson (Eds.), *Basic and applied memory research: Theory in context.* Mahwah, NJ: Erlbaum.

Cook, K. S., & Rice, E. (2003). Social exchange theory. In J. Delamater (Ed.), *Handbook of social psychology. Handbooks of sociology and social research,* (pp. 53–76). New York: Kluwer Academic/Plenum.

Cooke, C. A. (2004). Young people's attitudes towards guns in America, Great Britain and Western Australia. *Aggressive Behavior, 30,* 93–104.

Cooper, J., Mirabile, R., & Scher, S. J. (2005). Actions and attitudes: The theory of cognitive dissonance. In T. C. Brock & M. C. Green (Eds.), *Persuasion: Psychological insights and perspectives* (2nd ed., pp. 63–79). Thousand Oaks, CA: Sage.

Corales, T. A. (2005). *Focus on posttraumatic stress disorder research.* Hauppauge, NY: Nova Science.

Corballis, M. C. (2003). From mouth to hand: Gesture, speech, and the evolution of right-handedness. *Behavioral and Brain Sciences, 26,* 199–260.

Coren, S., Porac, C., & Ward, L. M. (1984). *Sensation and perception* (2nd ed.). Orlando, FL: Academic Press.

Cornelis, I., & Van Hiel, A. (2006). The impact of cognitive styles on authoritarianism based conservatism and racism. *Basic and Applied Social Psychology, 28,* 37–50.

Cornelius, R. R. (1996). *The science of emotion: Research and tradition in the psychology of emotions.* Upper Saddle River, NJ: Prentice Hall.

Cosgrove, L., & Riddle, B. (2004). Gender bias and sex distribution of mental disorders in the *DSM-IV-TR.* In P. J. Caplan & L. Cosgrove (Eds.), *Bias in psychiatric diagnosis* (pp. 127–140). Lanham, MD: Jason Aronson.

Cosmides, L., & Tooby, J. (2000). Evolutionary psychology and the emotions. In M. Lewis & J. M. Haviland-Jones (Eds.), *Handbook of Emotions* (2nd ed., pp. 91–115). New York: Guilford.

Cosmides, L., Tooby, J., & Barkow, J. (1992). *The adapted mind: Evolutionary psychology and the generation of culture.* New York: Oxford.

Costa, A., Peppe, A., Dell'Agnello, G., Carlesimo, G., Murri, L., Bonuccelli, U., et al. (2003). Dopaminergic modulation of visual-spatial working memory in Parkinson's disease. *Dementia and Geriatric Cognitive Disorders, 15,* 55–66.

Costa, P. T., Jr., & McCrae, R. R. (1992). *Revised NEO Personality Inventory (NEO-PI-R) and NEO Five-Factor Inventory (NEO-FFI) professional manual.* Odessa, FL: Psychological Assessment Resources.

Costa, P. T., Jr., & McCrae, R. R. (2006). Trait and factor theories. In J. C. Thomas, D. L. Segal, L. Daniel, & M. Hersen (Eds.), *Comprehensive handbook of personality and psychopathology, Vol. 1: Personality and everyday functioning* (pp. 96–114). Hoboken, NJ: John Wiley & Sons.

Côté, J. E. (2006). Emerging adulthood as an institutionalized moratorium: Risks and benefits to identity formation. In J. J. Arnett & J. L. Tanner (Eds.), *Emerging adults in America: Coming of age in the 21st century* (pp. 85–116). Washington, DC: American Psychological Assoc.

Council, J. R. (1993). Context effects in personality research. *Current Directions, 2,* 31–34.

Courage, M. L., & Howe, M. L. (2002). From infant to child: The dynamics of cognitive change in the second year of life. *Psychological Bulletin, 128,* 250–277.

Cousins, N. (1981). *Anatomy of an illness as perceived by the patient.* New York: Bantam.

Cowan, N. (1988). Evolving conceptions of memory storage, selective attention, and their mutual constraints within the human information-processing system. *Psychological Bulletin, 104,* 163–191.

Cowan, N., Elliott, E. M., Saults, J. S., Morey, C. C., Mattox, S., Hismjatullina, A., et al. (2005). On the capacity of attention: Its estimation and its role in working memory and cognitive aptitudes. *Cognitive Psychology, 51,* 42–100.

Craik, F. I. M. (2002). Levels of processing: Past, present . . . and future? *Memory, 10,* 305–318.

Craik, F. I. M., & Lockhart, R. S. (1972). Levels of processing: A framework for memory research. *Journal of Verbal Learning and Verbal Behavior, 11,* 671–684.

Craik, F. I. M., Moroz, T. M., Moscovitch, M., Stuss, D. T., Winocur, G., Tulving, E., et al. (1999). In search of the self: A positron emission tomography study. *Psychological Science, 10,* 26–34.

Cramer, P. (2000). Defense mechanisms in psychology today: Further processes for adaptation. *American Psychologist, 55,* 637–646.

Crandall, C. S., & Eshleman, A. (2003). A justification-suppression model of the expression and experience of prejudice. *Psychological Bulletin, 129,* 414–446.

Craske, M. G. (2003). *Origins of phobias and anxiety disorders: Why more women than men?* Oxford, UK: Elsevier.

Crawford, C. B. (2003). A prolegomenon for a viable evolutionary psychology—The myth and the reality: Comment on Lickliter and Honeycutt (2003). *Psychological Bulletin, 129,* 854–857.

Crawford, N. (2002, June). Employees' longer working hours linked to family conflict, stress-related health problems. *Monitor on Psychology,* p. 17.

Creed, P. A., & Klisch, J. (2005). Future outlook and financial strain: Testing the personal agency and latent deprivation models of unemployment and well-being. *Journal of Occupational Health Psychology, 10,* 251–260.

Crick, F., & Mitchison, G. (1995). REM sleep and neural nets. *Behavioural Brain Research* [Special Issue: *The function of sleep*], 69, 147–155.

Crinion, J. T., Lambon-Ralph, M. A., & Warburton, E. A. (2003). Temporal lobe regions engaged during normal speech comprehension. *Brain: A Journal of Neurology, 126*, 1193–1201.

Criswell, E. (2003). A challenge to humanistic psychology in the 21st century. *Journal of Humanistic Psychology, 43*, 42–52.

Cronan, T. A., Walen, H. R., & Cruz, S. G. (1994). The effects of community-based literacy training on Head Start parents. *Journal of Community Psychology, 22*, 248–258.

Crooks, R., & Bauer, K. (2002). *Our sexuality* (8th ed.). Belmont CA: Wadsworth.

Cross, M. R. (2003). The relationship between trauma history, daily hassles, and physical symptoms. *Dissertation Abstracts International: Section B: The Sciences and Engineering, 63*, 4364.

Crosscope-Happel, C. (2005). Male anorexia nervosa: An exploratory study. *Dissertation Abstracts International: Section A: Humanities and Social Sciences, 65.*

Cross-Mellor, S. K., Kavaliers, M., & Ossenkopp, K. P. (2004). Comparing immune activation (lipopolysaccharide) and toxin (lithium chloride)-induced gustatory conditioning: Lipopolysaccharide produces conditioned taste avoidance but not aversion. *Behavioural Brain Research, 148*, 11–19.

Crovitz, H. F., & Schiffman, H. (1974). Frequency of episodic memories as a function of their age. *Bulletin of the Psychonomic Society, 4*, 517–518.

Crow, T. J. (2004). Auditory hallucinations as primary disorders of syntax: An evolutionary theory of the origins of language. *Cognitive Neuropsychiatry, 9*, 125–145.

Crowther, J., Kichler, J., Shewood, N., & Kuhnert, M. (2002). The role of familial factors in bulimia nervosa. *Eating Disorders: The Journal of Treatment & Prevention. 10*, 141–151.

Crutchfield, R. A. (1955). Conformity and character. *American Psychologist, 10*, 191–198.

Csikszentmihalyi, M., Rathunde, K., & Whalen, S. (1993). *Talented teenagers: The roots of success and failure.* New York: Cambridge Univ. Press.

Cuffe, S. P., Moore, C. G., & McKeown, R. E. (2005). Prevalence and correlates of ADHD symptoms in the National Health Interview Survey. *Journal of Attention Disorders, 9*, 392–401.

Culbertson, F. M. (1997). Depression and gender: An international review. *American Psychologist, 52*, 25–31.

Cunningham, J. E. C. (2003). Neuropsychology, genetic liability, and psychotic symptoms in those at high risk of schizophrenia. *Journal of Abnormal Psychology, 112*, 38–48.

Cunningham, W. A., Johnson, M. K., Raye, C. L., Gatenby, J. C., & Gore, J. C. (2004). Separable neural components in the processing of black and white faces. *Psychological Science, 15*, 806–813.

Curtin, J. S. (2004). *Suicide in Japan: Part Eleven—Comparing international rates of suicide.* Japanese Institute of Global Communications. Retrieved July 11, 2006, from http://www.glocom.org/special_topics/social_trends/20040818_trends_s79/index.html

Cutler, D. M. (2001). The reduction in disability among the elderly. *Proc. Natl. Acad. Sci., USA, 98*, 6546–6547.

Cutler, W. B., Friedmann, E., & McCoy, N. L. (1998). Pheromonal influences on sociosexual behavior in men. *Archives of Sexual Behavior, 27*, 1–13.

D'Augelli, A. R. (2006). Developmental and contextual factors and mental health among lesbian, gay, and bisexual youths. In A. M. Omoto & H. S. Kurtzman (Eds.), *Sexual orientation and mental health: Examining identity and development in lesbian, gay, and bisexual people* (pp. 37–53). Washington, DC: American Psychological Assoc.

D'Esposito, M., Zarahn, E., & Aguirre, G. K. (1999). Event-related functional MRI: Implications for cognitive psychology. *Psychological Bulletin, 125*, 155–164.

D'Silva, M. U., Grant-Harrington, N., Palmgreen, P., Donohew, L., & Pugzles-Lorch, E. (2001). Drug use prevention for the high sensation seeker: The role of alternative activities. *Substance Use and Misuse, 36*, 373–385.

Dahl, D. W., Frankenberger, K. D., & Manchanda, R. V. (2003). Does it pay to shock? Reactions to shocking and nonshocking advertising content among university students. *Journal of Advertising Research, 43*, 268–280.

Dahl, E. K. (1996). The concept of penis envy revisited: A child analyst listens to adult women. *Psychoanalytic Study of the Child, 51*, 303–325.

Dalbert, C. (2001). *The justice motive as a personal resource: Dealing with challenges and critical life events.* New York: Kluwer Academic/Plenum.

Daley, T. C., Whaley, S. E., Sigman, M. D., Espinosa, M. P., & Neumann, C. (2003). IQ on the rise: The Flynn Effect in rural Kenyan children. *Psychological Science, 14*, 215–219.

Dalton, P., Doolittle, N., & Breslin, P. A. S. (2002). Gender-specific induction of enhanced sensitivity to odors. *Nature Neuroscience, 5*, 199–200.

Damas, A. (2002). A factorial invariance analysis of intellectual abilities in children across different age and cultural groups using the Wechsler Intelligence Scale for Children. *Dissertation Abstracts International: Section B: The Sciences and Engineering, 62*, 4832.

Damasio, A. R. (1999). *The feeling of what happens: Body and emotion in the making of consciousness.* New York: Harcourt.

Damasio, A. R. (2003). *Looking for Spinoza: Joy, sorrow, and the feeling brain.* New York: Harcourt.

Damasio, A. R., & Anderson, S. W. (2003). The frontal lobes. In K. M. Heilman & E. Valenstein (Eds.), *Clinical neuropsychology* (4th ed., pp. 404–446). New York: Oxford Univ. Press.

Damasio, H., Grabowski, T. F. R., Galaburda, A. M., & Damasio, A. R. (2005). The return of Phineas Gage: Clues about the brain from the skull of a famous patient. In J. T. Cacioppo & G. G. Berntson (Eds.), *Social neuroscience: Key readings* (pp. 21–28). New York: Psychology Press.

Damasio, H., Grabowski, T. J., Tranel, D., Hichawa, R. D., & Damasio, A. R. (1996). A neural basis for lexical retrieval. *Nature, 380*, 499–505.

Danielle, D. M., Rose, R. J., Viken, R. J., & Kaprio, J. (2000). Pubertal timing and substance use: Associations between and within families across late adolescence. *Developmental Psychology, 36*, 180–189.

Darwin, C. R. (1859). *On the origin of species.* London: John Murray.

Davidson, P. S. R., & Glisky, E. L. (2002). Is flashbulb memory a special instance of source memory? Evidence from older adults. *Memory, 10*, 99–111.

Davidson, R. J. (1992). Emotion and affective style: Hemispheric substrates. *Psychological Science, 3*, 39–43.

Davidson, R. J., Jackson, D. C., & Kalin, N. H. (2000). Emotion, plasticity, context, and regulation: Perspectives from affective neuroscience. *Psychological Bulletin, 126*, 890–909.

Davidson, R. J., Kabat-Zinn, J., Schumacher, J., Rosenkranz, M., Muller, D., Santorelli, S. F., et al. (2003). Alterations in brain and immune function produced by mindfulness meditation. *Psychosomatic Medicine, 65*, 564–570.

Davidson, R. J., Putnam, K. M., & Larson, C. L. (2000, July 28). Dysfunction in the neural circuitry of emotion regulation—A possible prelude to violence. *Science, 289*, 591–594.

Davies, M., Stankov, L., & Roberts, R. D. (1998). Emotional intelligence: In search of an elusive construct. *Journal of Personality and Social Psychology, 75*, 989–1015.

Davis, C. G., Wortman, C. B., Lehman, D. R., & Silver, R. C. (2000). Searching for meaning in loss: Are clinical assumptions correct? *Death Studies, 24*, 497–540.

Daw, J. (2002). New Mexico becomes first state to gain Rx privileges. *Monitor on Psychology, 33*, 24–25.

Dawson, G., & Toth, K. (2006). Autism spectrum disorders. In D. Cicchetti & D. J. Cohen (Eds.), *Developmental psychopathology, Vol 3: Risk, disorder, and adaptation* (2nd ed., pp. 317–357). Hoboken, NJ: John Wiley & Sons.

De la Fuente, M. (2002). Effects of antioxidants on the immune system aging. *European Journal of Clinical Nutrition, 56*(Suppl. 3), S5–8.

De Raad, B. (1998). Five big, Big Five issues: Rationale, content, structure, status, and crosscultural assessment. *European Psychologist, 3*, 113–124.

De Raad, B. (2000). *The Big Five personality factors: The psycholexical approach to personality.* Ashland, OH: Hogrefe & Huber.

Dean, J. W., Jr., & Evans, J. R. (1994). *Total quality: Management, organization, and strategy.* St. Paul, MN: West.

Dean, K., Bramon, E., & Murray, R. M. (2003). The causes of schizophrenia: Neurodevelopment and other risk factors. *Journal of Psychiatric Practice, 9*, 442–454.

DeAngelis, T. (2002, June). How do mind–body interventions affect breast cancer? *Monitor on Psychology*, 51–53.

Deary, I. J., & Der, G. (2005). Reaction time, age, and cognitive ability: Longitudinal findings from age 16 to 63 years in representative population samples. *Aging, Neuropsychology, and Cognition, 12*, 187–215.

deCharms, R. C., Maeda, F., Glover, G. H., Ludlow, D., Pauly, J. M., Soneji, D., et al. (2005). Control over brain activation and pain learned by using real-time functional MRI. *Proceedings of the National Academy of Sciences of the United States of America, 102*, 18626–18631.

Deci, E. L., Koestner, R., & Ryan, R. M. (1999). A meta-analytic review of experiments examining the effects of extrinsic rewards on intrinsic motivation. *Psychological Bulletin, 125*, 627–668.

Deci, E. L., Koestner, R., & Ryan, R. M. (2001). Extrinsic rewards and intrinsic motivation in education: Reconsidered once again. *Review of Educational Research, 71*, 1–27.

de-l'Etoile, S. K. (2002). The effect of musical mood induction procedure on mood state-dependent word retrieval. *Journal of Music Therapy, 39*, 145–160.

Dell, P. F. (2006). A new model of dissociative identity disorder. *Psychiatric Clinics of North America, 29*, 1–26.

Dell'Osso, M. C. (2003). A historical discussion of the neuropsychological correlates in dissociative identity disorder. *Dissertation Abstracts International: Section B: The Sciences and Engineering, 63*, 5510.

Dement, W. C. (1974). *Some must watch while some must sleep.* San Francisco: Freeman.

Denmark, F., Rabinowitz, V., & Sechzer, J. (2000). *Engendering psychology: Bringing women into focus.* Boston: Allyn & Bacon.

Dennerstein, L., Dudley, E., & Guthrie, J. (2002). Empty nest or revolving door? A prospective study of women's quality of life in midlife during the phase of children leaving and re-entering the home. *Psychological Medicine, 32*, 545–550.

Denollet, J. (2005). DS14: standard assessment of negative affectivity, social inhibition, and Type D personality. *Psychosomatic Medicine, 67*, 89–97.

DePaulo, B. M., Lindsay, J. J., Malone, B. E., Muhlenbruck, L., Charlton, K., & Cooper, H. (2003). Cues to deception. *Psychological Bulletin, 129*, 74–118.

Derman, T., & Szabo, C. P. (2006). Why do individuals with anorexia die? A case of sudden death. *International Journal of Eating Disorders, 39*, 260–262.

Derry, F. A., Dinsmore, W. W., Fraser, M., Gardner, B. P., Glass, C. A., Maytom, M. C., et al. (1998). Efficacy and safety of oral sildenafil (Viagra) in men with erectile dysfunction caused by spinal cord injury. *Neurology, 51*, 1629–1633.

Des Forges, A. L. (1995). The ideology of genocide. *Issue, 23*(2), 44–47.

Dess, N. K., & Foltin, R. W. (2005). The ethics cascade. In C. K. Akins, S. Panicker, & C. L. Cunningham (Eds.), *Laboratory animals in research and teaching: Ethics, care, and methods* (pp. 31–39). Washington, DC: American Psychological Assoc.

DeSteno, D., & Braverman, J. (2002). Emotion and persuasion: Thoughts on the role of emotional intelligence. In L. F. Barrett & P. Salovey, *The wisdom in feeling: Psychological processes in emotional intelligence* (pp. 191–210). New York: Guilford.

DeWaal, F. B. M. (1999). The end of nature versus nurture. *Scientific American, 281*(12), 94–99.

DeYoung, R. (2005). Contingency theories of leadership. In N. Borkowski (Ed.), *Organizational behavior in health care* (pp. 187–208). Boston: Jones & Bartlett.

Dhami, M. K. (2003). Psychological models of professional decision making. *Psychological Science, 14*, 175–180.

Diala, C., Muntaner, C., Walrath, C., Nickerson, K., LaVeist, T. A., & Leaf, P. J. (2000). Racial differences in attitudes toward professional mental health care and in the use of services. *American Journal of Orthopsychiatry, 70*, 455–464.

Diamond, J. (1994). Race without color. *Discover, 15*, 82–92.

Diaz, J. (1997). *How drugs influence behavior: Neuro-behavioral approach.* Upper Saddle River, NJ: Prentice Hall.

Dickerson, F. B., Tenhula, W. N., & Green-Paden, L. D. (2005). The token economy for schizophrenia: Review of the literature and recommendations for future research. *Schizophrenia Research, 75*, 405–416.

Diehm, R., & Armatas, C. (2004). Surfing: An avenue for socially acceptable risk-taking, satisfying needs for sensation seeking and experience seeking. *Personality and Individual Differences, 36*, 663–677.

Dieter, J., Field, T., Hernandez, R. M., Emory, E. K., & Redzepi, M. (2003). Stable preterm infants gain more weight and sleep less after five days of massage therapy. *Journal of Pediatric Psychology, 28*, 403–411.

DiFranza, J. R., & Lew, R. A. (1995). Effect of maternal cigarette smoking on pregnancy complications and sudden infant death syndrome. *Journal of Family Practice, 40*, 385–394.

DiGiovanna, A. G. (1999). *Human aging: Biological perspectives* (2nd ed.). New York: McGraw-Hill.

Dijksterhuis, A., Aarts, H., & Smith, P. K. (2005). The power of the subliminal: On subliminal persuasion and other potential applications. In R. R. Hassin, J. S. Uleman, & J. A. Bargh (Eds.), *The new unconscious* (pp. 77–106). New York: Oxford Univ. Press.

DiLalla, L. F. (2004). Behavioral genetics: Background, current research, and goals for the future. In L. F DiLalla (Ed.), *Behavior genetics principles: Perspectives in development, personality, and psychopathology* (pp. 3–15). Washington, DC: American Psychological Assoc.

Dill, K. E., Gentile, D. A., Richter, W. A., & Dill, J. C. (2005) Violence, sex, race, and age in popular video games: A content analysis. In E. Cole & J. H. Daniel (Eds.), *Featuring females: Feminist analyses of the media* (pp. 115–130). Washington, DC: American Psychological Assoc.

Dillard, J. P., & Anderson, J. W. (2004). The role of fear in persuasion. *Psychology & Marketing, 21*, 909–926.

Dillon, S. (1994, October 21). Bilingual education effort is flawed, study indicates. *New York Times*, p. A20.

Dion, K. K. (1972). Physical attractiveness and evaluations of children's transgressions. *Journal of Personality and Social Psychology, 24*, 285–290.

Dion, K. L. (2003). Prejudice, racism, and discrimination. In T. Millon & M. Lerner (Eds.), *Handbook of psychology: Vol. 5, Personality and social psychology* (pp. 507–536). Hoboken, NJ: John Wiley & Sons.

DiPietro, J. A., Hodgson, D. M., Costigan, K. A., & Johnson, T. R. (1996). Fetal antecedents of infant temperament. *Child Development, 67*, 2568–2583.

Dixon, J. F., & Hokin, L. E. (1998). Lithium acutely inhibits and chronically upregulates and stabilizes glutamate uptake by presynaptic nerve endings in mouse cerebral cortex. *Proceedings of the National Academy of Sciences, 95*, 8363–8368.

Dobson, J. L. (2004). The relationship of personal and contextual differences to grief distress and personal growth. *Dissertation Abstracts International: Section B: The Sciences and Engineering, 64*, 4611

Domhoff, G. W. (1996). *Finding meaning in dreams: A quantitative approach.* New York: Plenum.

Domhoff, G. W. (2003). A critique of traditional dream theories. In G. W. Domhoff (Ed.), *The scientific study of dreams: Neural networks, cognitive development, and content analysis* (pp. 135–170). Washington, DC: American Psychological Assoc.

Domhoff, G. W. (2005). The content of dreams: Methodologic and theoretical implications. In M. H. Kryger, T. Roth, & W. C. Dement (Eds.), *Principles and Practies of Sleep Medicine* (4th ed., pp. 522–534). Philadelphia: Saunders.

Donatelle, R. J. (2004). *Access to health* (8th ed.). Englewood Cliffs, NJ: Prentice Hall.

Donley, M. P., Schulkin, J., & Rosen, J. B. (2005). Glucocorticoid receptor antagonism in the basolateral amygdala and ventral hippocampus interferes with long-term memory of contextual fear. *Behavioural Brain Research, 164*, 197–205.

Donnelly, C. L. (2003). Pharmacologic treatment approaches for children and adolescents with posttraumatic stress disorder. *Child and Adolescent Psychiatric Clinics of North America, 12*, 251–269.

Doré, R., Wagner, S., & Doré, I. (2002). From mainstreaming to inclusion: A transformation of service delivery. In R. L. Schalock, P. C. Baker, & M. D. Croser (Eds.), *Embarking on a new century: Mental retardation at the end of the 20th century* (pp. 185–201). Washington, DC: American Assoc. on Mental Retardation.

Dorfman, W. I., & Leonard, S. (2001). The Minnesota Multiphasic Personality Inventory-2 (MMPI-2). In W. I. Dorfman & M. Hersen (Eds.), *Understanding psychological assessment: Perspectives on individual differences* (pp. 145–171). Dordrecht, Netherlands: Kluwer.

Doty, R. L. (1989). Influence of age and age-related diseases on olfactory function. *Annals of the New York Academy of Sciences, 561*, 76–86.

Doty, R. L. (2001). Olfaction. *Annual Review of Psychology, 52*, 423–452.

Dougall, A. L., & Baum, A. (2004). Psychoneuroimmunology and trauma. In P. P. Schnurr & B. L. Green (Eds.), *Trauma and health: Physical health consequences of exposure to extreme stress.* (pp. 129–155). Washington, DC: American Psychological Assoc.

Douglas, H. M., Moffitt, T. E., Dar, R., McGee, R., & Silva, P. (1995). Obsessive-compulsive disorder in a birth cohort of 18-year-olds: Prevalence and predictors. *Journal of the American Academy of Child and Adolescent Psychiatry, 34*, 1424–1429.

Dovidio, J. F., Gaertner, S. L., Hodson, G., Houlette, M. A., & Johnson, K. M. (2005). Social inclusion and exclusion: Recategorization and the perception of intergroup boundaries. In D. Abrams, M. A. Hogg, & J. M. Marques (Eds.), *The social psychology of inclusion and exclusion* (pp. 245–264). New York: Psychology Press.

Doyle, R. (2004). Living together. *Scientific American, 290*(1), 28.

Doyon, J., & Benali, H. (2005). Reorganization and plasticity in the adult brain during learning of motor skills. *Current Opinion in Neurobiology, 15*, 161–167.

Dozois, D. J. A., Frewen, P. A., & Covin, R. (2006). Cognitive theories. In J. C. Thomas, D. L. Segal, & M. Hersen (Eds.), *Comprehensive handbook of personality and psychopathology, Vol. 1: Personality and everyday functioning* (pp. 173–191). Hoboken, NJ: John Wiley & Sons.

Drury, L. J. (2003). Community care for people who are homeless and mentally ill. *Journal of Health Care for the Poor and Underserved, 14*, 194–207.

Druskat, V. U., Sala, F., & Mount, G. (2006). *Linking emotional intelligence and performance at work: Current research evidence with individuals and groups.* Mahwah, NJ: Erlbaum.

Dryer, D. C., & Horowitz, L. M. (1997). When do opposites attract? Interpersonal complementarity versus similarity. *Journal of Personality and Social Psychology, 72*(3), 592–603.

Du, L., Faludi, G., Palkovits, M., Demeter, E., Bakish, D., Lapierre, Y. D., et al. (1999). Frequency of long allele in serotonin transporter gene is increased in depressed suicide victims. *Biological Psychiatry, 46*, 196–201.

Dubner, R., & Gold, M. (1998, December). *The neurobiology of pain.* Paper presented at the National Academy of Sciences colloquium, Irvine, CA.

Dubois, B., & Levy, R. (2004). Cognition, behavior and the frontal lobes. *International Psychogeriatrics, 16*, 379–387.

Duckworth, A. L., Steen, T. A., & Seligman, M. E. P. (2005). Positive psychology in clinical practice. *Annual Review of Clinical Psychology, 1*, 629–651.

Duesenberg, D. (2006). ADHD: Diagnosis and current treatment options to improve functional outcomes. In T. K. Parthasarathy (Ed.), *An introduction to auditory processing disorders in children* (pp. 187–201). Mahwah, NJ: Erlbaum.

Dugas, M. J., Ladouceur, R., Leger, E., Freeston, M. H., Langolis, F., Provencher, M. D., et al. (2003). Group cognitive behavioral therapy for generalized anxiety disorder: Treatment outcome and long-term follow-up. *Journal of Consulting and Clinical Psychology, 71*, 821–825.

Duncan, J., Seitz, R. J., Kolodny, J., Bor, D., Herzog, H., Ahmed, A., et al. (2000, July 21). A neural basis for general intelligence. *Science, 285*, 457–460.

Duncan, T. G., & McKeachie, W. J. (2005). The making of the Motivated Strategies for Learning Questionnaire. *Educational Psychologist, 40*, 117–128.

Dunn, J., Cutting, A., & Fisher, N. (2002). Old friends, new friends: Predictors of children's perspective on their friends at school. *Child Development 73*, 621–635.

Dunn, W. S., Mount, M. K., & Barrick, M. R. (1995). Relative importance of personality and general mental ability in managers' judgments of applicant qualifications. *Journal of Applied Psychology, 80*, 500–509.

Durex Global Sex Survey (2005). Retrieved April 13, 2006, from http://www.durex.com/cm/gss2005result.pdf

Eachus, P. (2004). Using the brief sensation seeking scale (BSSS) to predict holiday preferences. *Personality and Individual Differences, 36*, 141–153.

Eacott, M. J. (1999). Memory for the events of early childhood. *Current Directions in Psychological Science, 8,* 46–48.

Eagly, A. H. (2003). The rise of female leaders. *Zeitschrift-fur-Sozialpsychologie, 34,* 123–132.

Eagly, A. H., & Carli, L. L. (1981). Sex of researchers and sex-typed communications as determinants of sex differences in influenceability: A meta-analysis of social influence studies. *Psychological Bulletin, 90,* 1–20.

Eagly, A. H., Johannesen-Schmidt, M. C., & van-Engen, M. L. (2003). Transformational, transactional, and laissez-faire leadership styles: A meta analysis comparing women and men. *Psychological Bulletin, 129,* 569–591.

Eagly, A. H., & Steffen, V. J. (1986). Gender and aggressive behavior: A meta-analytic review of the social psychological literature. *Psychological Bulletin, 100,* 309–330.

Eberhard, J., Lindström, E., & Levander, S. (2006). Tardive dyskinesia and antipsychotics: A 5-year longitudinal study of frequency, correlates and course. *International Clinical Psychopharmacology, 21,* 35–42.

Edelman, S., Lemon, J., Bell, D. R., & Kidman, A. D. (1999). Effects of group CBT on the survival time of patients with metastatic breast cancer. *Psycho-Oncology, 8,* 474–481.

Edery, H. G., & Nachson, I. (2004). Distinctiveness in flashbulb memory: Comparative analysis of five terrorist attacks. *Memory, 12,* 147–157.

Edwards, R. (2004). ABC of smoking cessation: The problem of tobacco smoking. *British Medical Journal, 328,* 217–219.

Egeth, H., & Lamy, D. (2003). Attention. In A. F. Healy & R. W. Proctor (Eds.), *Handbook of Psychology: Vol. 4, Experimental Psychology* (pp. 269–292). New York: John Wiley & Sons.

Egger, J. I. M., Delsing, P. A. M., & DeMey, H. R. A. (2003). Differential diagnosis using the MMPI-2: Goldberg's index revisited. *European Psychiatry, 18,* 409–411.

Eggermont, J. J., & Roberts, L. E. (2004). The neuroscience of tinnitus. *Trends in Neurosciences, 27,* 676–682.

Ehigie, B. O., & Shenge, N. A. (2000). Psychological strategies in managing television commercial efficacy. *IFE Psychologia: An International Journal, 9,* 115–122.

Eibl-Eibesfeldt, I. (1972). *Love and hate.* New York: Holt, Rinehart & Winston.

Eich, E., Macaulay, D., Loewenstein, R. J., & Dihle, P. H. (1997). Memory, amnesia, and dissociative identity disorder. *Psychological Science, 8,* 417–422.

Eichenbaum, H., & Cohen, N. J. (2001). *From conditioning to conscious recollection: Memory systems of the brain.* New York: Oxford Univ. Press.

Eichenbaum, H., & Fortin, N. (2003). Episodic memory and the hippocampus: It's about time. *Current Directions in Psychological Science, 12,* 53–57.

Eimas, P. D., & Tartter, V. C. (1979). The development of speech perception. In H. W. Reese & L. P. Lipsitt (Eds.), *Advances in child development and behavior* (Vol. 13). New York: Academic Press.

Eisenberg, N., & Lennon, R. (1983). Sex differences in empathy and related capacities. *Psychological Bulletin, 94,* 100–131.

Eisenberger, R., & Cameron, J. (1996). Detrimental effects of reward. *American Psychologist, 51,* 1153–1166.

Eisenberger, R., & Rhoades, L. (2001). Incremental effects of reward on creativity. *Journal of Personality and Social Psychology, 81,* 728–741.

Eisenberger, R., Rhoades, L., & Cameron, J. (1999). Does pay for performance increase or decrease perceived self-determination and intrinsic motivation, *Journal of Personality and Social Psychology, 77,* 1026–1040.

Eisenberger, R., & Shanock, L. (2003). Rewards, intrinsic motivation, and creativity: A case study of conceptual and methodological isolation. *Creativity Research Journal, 15,* 121–130.

Ekman, P. (1994). Strong evidence for universals in facial expressions: A reply to Russell's mistaken critique. *Psychological Bulletin, 115,* 268–287.

Ekman, P. (2003). *Emotions revealed: Recognizing faces and feelings to improve communication and emotional life.* New York: Henry Holt.

Ekman, P., & Davidson, R. J. (1993). Voluntary smiling changes regional brain activity. *Psychological Science, 4,* 342–345.

Ekman, P., & Friesen, W. V. (1971). Constants across cultures in the face and emotion. *Journal of Personality and Social Psychology, 17,* 124–129.

Ekman, P., & Friesen, W. V. (1975). *Unmasking the face.* Englewood Cliffs, NJ: Prentice Hall.

Ekman, P., Friesen, W. V., & Ellsworth, P. (1972). *Emotion in the human face.* Elmsford, NY: Pergamon.

Ekman, P., Friesen, W. V., O'Sullivan, M., Chan, A., Diacoyanni-Tarlatzis, I., Heider, K., et al. (1987). Universals and cultural differences in the judgments of facial expressions of emotion. *Journal of Personality and Social Psychology, 53,* 712–717.

Ekman, P., & O'Sullivan, M. (1991). Who can catch a liar? *American Psychologist, 46,* 913–920.

Ekman, P., Sorenson, E. R., & Friesen, W. V. (1969). Pancultural elements in facial displays of emotion. *Science, 164,* 86–88.

El-Ad, B., & Lavie, P. (2005). Effect of sleep apnea on cognition and mood. *International Review of Psychiatry, 17,* 277–282.

Elbert, T., Pantev, C., Wienbruch, C., Rockstroh, B., & Taub, E. (1995, October 13). Increased cortical representation of the fingers of the left hand in string players. *Science, 270,* 305–307.

Eley, T. C., Lichenstein, P., & Stevenson, J. (1999). Sex differences in the etiology of aggressive and nonaggressive antisocial behavior: Results from two twin studies. *Child Development, 70,* 155–168.

Eley, T. C., & Stevenson, J. (1999). Exploring the covariation between anxiety and depression symptoms: A genetic analysis of the effects of age and sex. *Journal of Child Psychology & Psychiatry & Allied Disciplines, 40,* 1273–1282.

Elfenbein, H. A., & Ambady, N. (2002). On the universality and cultural specificity of emotion recognition: A meta-analysis. *Psychological Bulletin, 128,* 203–235.

Elfenbein, H. A., & Ambady, N. (2003). Universals and cultural differences in recognizing emotions. *Current Directions in Psychological Science, 12,* 159–164.

Elkind, D. (1968). Cognitive development in adolescence. In J. F. Adams (Ed.), *Understanding adolescence.* Boston: Allyn & Bacon.

Elkind, D. (1969). Egocentrism in adolescence. In R. W. Grinder (Ed.), *Studies in adolescence* (2nd ed.). New York: Macmillan.

Ellens, J. H. (2002). Psychological legitimization of violence by religious archetypes. In C. E. Stout (Ed.), *The psychology of terrorism: Theoretical understandings and perspectives,* Vol. III. *Psychological dimensions to war and peace* (pp. 149–162). Westport, CT: Praeger/Greenwood.

Elliott, M. E. (1996). Impact of work, family, and welfare receipt on women's self-esteem in young adulthood. *Social Psychology Quarterly, 59,* 80–95.

Ellis, A. (1973). *Humanistic psychotherapy: The rational emotive approach.* New York: Julian.

Ellis, A. (2001). *Overcoming destructive beliefs, feelings, and behaviors: New directions for Rational Emotive Behavior Therapy.* Amherst, NY: Prometheus.

Ellis, A., & Harper, R. A. (1975). *A new guide to rational living*. North Hollywood, CA: Wilshire.

Ellis, A., & MacLaren, C. (1998). *Rational emotive behavior therapy: A therapist's guide*. San Luis Obispo, CA: Impact.

Ellis, L., & Coontz, P. D. (1990). Androgens, brain functioning, and criminality: The neurohormonal foundations of antisociality. In L. Ellis & H. Hoffman (Eds.), *Crime in biological, social, and moral contexts* (pp. 36–49). New York: Praeger.

Ellis, L., Robb, B., & Burke, D. (2005). Sexual orientation in United States and Canadian college students. *Archives of Sexual Behavior, 34*, 569–581.

Ellison, B., & Ellison, J. (2001). *Miracles happen: One mother, one daughter, one journey*. New York: Hyperion.

Elloy, D. F., & Mackie, B. (2002). Overload and work-family conflict among Australian dual-career families: Moderating effects of support. *Psychological Reports, 91*, 907–913.

Ellsworth, P. C. (2002). Appraisal processes in emotion. In R. R. Davidson, K. R. Scherer, & H. H. Goldsmith (Eds.), *Handbook of affective science* (pp. 233–248). New York: Oxford Univ. Press.

Else-Quest, N. M., Hyde, J. S., & Goldsmith, H. H. (2006). Gender differences in temperament: A meta-analysis. *Psychological Bulletin, 132*, 33–72.

Elzinga, B. M., & Bremner, J. D. (2002). Are the neural substrates of memory the final common pathway in posttraumatic stress disorder (PTSD)? *Journal of Affective Disorders, 70*, 1–17.

Enard, W., Przeworski, M., Fisher, S. E., Lai, C. S., Wiebe, V., Kitano, T., et al. (2002). Molecular evolution of FOXP2, a gene involved in speech and language. *Nature, 418*, 869–872.

Engel, J. F., Black, R. D., & Miniard, P. C. (1986). *Consumer behavior*. Chicago: Dryden.

Engemann, K. M., & Owyang, M. T. (2006, April). Social changes lead married women into labor force. *The Regional Economist*, 10–11.

Engle, R. W. (2002). Working memory capacity as executive attention. *Current Directions in Psychological Science, 11*, 19–23.

Enns, C. Z., & Sinacore, A. L. (2005). *Teaching and social justice: Integrating multicultural and feminist theories in the classroom*. Washington, DC: American Psychological Assoc.

Enoch G. (1998). NIAAA director's statement before the House Committee on Appropriations Subcommittee on Labor, Health and Human Services, Education and Related Agencies, March 19, 1998. Retrieved February 26, 2006 from http://www.niaaa.nih.gov/AboutNIAAA/CongressionalInformation/Testimony/1998-03-19.htm

Epel, E. S., Lin, J., Wilhelm, F. H., Wolkowitz, O. M., Cawthon, R., Adler, N. E., et al. (2006). Cell aging in relation to stress arousal and cardiovascular disease risk factors. *Psychoneuroendocrinology, 31*, 277–287.

Epstein, N. B. (2004). Cognitive-behavioral therapy with couples: Theoretical and empirical status. In R. L. Leahy (Ed.), *Contemporary cognitive therapy: Theory, research, and practice* (pp. 367–388). New York, NY: Guilford.

Epstein, R., Kirshnit, C. E., Lanza, R. P., & Rubin, L. C. (1984). "Insight" in the pigeon: Antecedents and determinants of an intelligent performance. *Nature (London), 308*, 61–62.

Erdley, C. A., & D'Agostino, P. R. (1988). Cognitive and affective components of automatic priming effects. *Journal of Personality and Social Psychology, 54*, 741–747.

Erickson, R. J. (2005). Why emotion work matters: Sex, gender, and the division of household labor. *Journal of Marriage and Family, 67*, 337–351.

Ericsson, K. A., & Charness, N. (1994). Expert performance. *American Psychologist, 49*, 725–747.

Ericsson, K. A., & Chase, W. G. (1982). Exceptional memory. *American Scientist, 70*, 607–615.

Ericsson, K. A., Chase, W. G., & Faloon, S. (1980). Acquisition of a memory skill. *Science, 208*, 1181–1182.

Erikson, E. H. (1968). *Identity: Youth in crisis*. New York: Norton.

Esposito, M. D., Zarahn, E., & Aguirre, G. K. (1999). Event-related functional MRI: Implications for cognitive psychology. *Psychological Bulletin, 125*, 155–164.

Esterson, A. (2002). The myth of Freud's ostracism by the medical community in 1896–1905: Jeffrey Masson's assault on truth. *History of Psychology, 5*, 115–134.

Evans, G. W., & English, K. (2002). The environment of poverty: Multiple stressor exposure, psychophysiological stress, and socioemotional adjustment. *Child Development, 73*, 1238–1248.

Evans, G. W., & Stecker, R. (2004). Motivational consequences of environmental stress. *Journal of Environmental Psychology, 24*, 143–165.

Evans, R. B. (1999, December). A century of psychology. *APA Monitor*, pp. 14–30.

Everett, C. A., Livingston, S. E., & Bowen, L. E. (2005). Separation, divorce, and remarriage. In R. H. Coombs (Ed.), *Family therapy review: Preparing for comprehensive and licensing examinations* (pp. 257–275). Mahwah, NJ: Erlbaum.

Everly, G. S., & Lating, J. M. (2004). Neurologic desensitization in the treatment of posttraumatic stress. In G. S. Everly & J. M. Lating (Eds.) *Personality guided therapy for posttraumatic stress disorder* (pp. 161–176). Washington, DC: American Psychological Assoc.

Evers, A. W., Kraaimaat, F. W., Geenen, R., Jacobs, J. W., & Bijlsma, J. W. (2003). Pain coping and social support as predictors of long-term functional disability and pain in early rheumatoid arthritis. *Behaviour Research and Therapy, 41*, 1295–310.

Exner, J. E. (1996). A comment on "the comprehensive system for the Rorschach: A critical examination." *Psychological Science, 7*, 11–13.

Eyer, J. (1977). Prosperity as a cause of death. *International Journal of Health Services, 7*, 125–150.

Eysenck, H. J. (1947). *Dimensions of personality*. London: Routledge & Kegan Paul.

Eysenck, H. J. (1976). *The measurement of personality*. Baltimore, MD: Univ. Park.

Fadiga, L., Fogassi, L., Pavesi, G., & Rizzolatti, G. (1995). Motor facilitation during action observation: A magnetic stimulation study. *Journal of Neurophysiology, 73*, 2608–2611.

Fagan, P. J., Lehne, G., Strand, J. G., & Berlin, F. S. (2005). Paraphilias. In G. O. Beck & J. Holmes (Eds.), *Oxford textbook of psychotherapy* (pp. 213–225). New York: Oxford Univ. Press.

Fagot, B. I. (1994). Parenting. In V. A. Ramachandran (Ed.), *Encyclopedia of human behavior* (Vol. 3, pp. 411–419). San Diego, CA: Academic Press.

Fairbrother, N., & Rachman, S. (2006). PTSD in victims of sexual assault: Test of a major component of the Ehlers-Clark theory. *Journal of Behavior Therapy and Experimental Psychiatry, 37*, 74–93.

Fairburn, C. G., & Brownell, K. D. (2002). *Eating disorders and obesity: A comprehensive handbook* (2d ed.) London: Guildford.

Fairburn, C. G., Cooper, Z., & Shafran, R. (2003). Cognitive behaviour therapy for eating disorders: A transdiagnostic theory and treatment. *Behaviour Research and Therapy, 41,* 509–528.

Faith, M. S. (2005). Development and modification of child food preferences and eating patterns: Behavior genetics strategies. *International Journal of Obesity, 29,* 549–556.

Fan, J. B., & Sklar, P. (2005). Meta-analysis reveals association between serotonin transporter gene STin2 VNTR polymorphism and schizophrenia. *Molecular Psychiatry, 10,* 928–938.

Fantz, R. L., Fagan, J. F., & Miranda, S. B. (1975). Early visual selectivity. In L. B. Cohen & P. Salapatek (Eds.), *Infant perception: From sensation to cognition* (Vol. 1). New York: Academic Press.

Farroni, T., Massaccesi, S., Pividori, D., & Johnson, M. (2004). Gaze following in newborns. *Infancy, 5,* 39–60.

Farthing, C. W. (1992). *The psychology of consciousness.* Englewood Cliffs, NJ: Prentice Hall.

Favaro, A., Tenconi, E., & Santonastaso, P. (2006). Perinatal factors and the risk of developing anorexia nervosa and bulimia nervosa. *Archives of General Psychiatry, 63,* 82–88.

Featherstone, R. E., Fleming, A. S., & Ivy, G. O. (2000). Plasticity in the maternal circuit: Effects of experience and partum condition on brain astrocyte number in female rats. *Behavioral Neuroscience, 114,* 158–172.

Federal Bureau of Investigation. (2005). *Crime in the United States: 2004. Uniform Crime Reports.* Washington, DC: Government Printing Office.

Feeney, B. C., & Cassidy, J. (2003). Reconstructive memory related to adolescent-parent conflict interactions: The influence of attachment-related representations on immediate perceptions and changes in perceptions over time. *Journal of Personality and Social Psychology, 85,* 945–955.

Fehr, B. (1994). Prototype-based assessment of laypeople's views of love. *Personal Relationships, 1,* 309–331.

Feinauer, L., Hilton, H. G., & Callahan, E. H. (2003). Hardiness as a moderator of shame associated with childhood sexual abuse. *American Journal of Family Therapy, 31,* 65–78.

Feinberg, T. D., & Keenan, J. P. (2005). Where in the brain is the self? *Consciousness and Cognition, 14,* 647–790.

Feingold, A. (1992). Good-looking people are not what we think. *Psychological Bulletin, 111,* 304–341.

Feinson, M. C. (1986). Aging widows and widowers: Are there mental health differences? *International Journal of Aging and Human Development, 23,* 244–255.

Fejr. S. S. (2003). *Introduction to group therapy: A practical guide* (2nd ed.). New York: Haworth.

Feldhusen, J. F., & Goh, B. E. (1995). Assessing and accessing creativity: An integrative review of theory, research, and development. *Creativity Research Journal, 8,* 231–247.

Feldman, R. S., Salzinger, S., Rosario, M., Alvarado, L., Caraballo, L., & Hammer, M. (1995). Parent, teacher, and peer ratings of physically abused and nonmaltreated children's behavior. *Journal of Abnormal Child Psychology, 23*(3), 317–334.

Ferguson, M. J., Bargh, J. A., & Nayak, D. A. (2005). After-affects: How automatic evaluations influence the interpretation of subsequent, unrelated stimuli. *Journal of Experimental Social Psychology, 41,* 182–191.

Fernald, A. (2001). Hearing, listening, and understanding: Auditory development in infancy. In G. Bremner & A. Fogel (Eds.), *Blackwell handbook of infant development. Handbooks of developmental psychology* (pp. 35–70). Malden, MA: Blackwell.

Feshbach, S., & Weiner, B. (1982). *Personality.* Lexington, MA: D. C. Heath.

Festinger, L. (1957). *A theory of cognitive dissonance.* Evanston, IL: Row, Peterson.

Fiedler, F. E. (1967). *A theory of leadership effectiveness.* New York: McGraw-Hill.

Fiedler, F. E. (1993). The leadership situation and the black box contingency theories. In M. Chemers & R. Ayman (Eds.), *Leadership theory and research: Perspective and directions* (pp. 1–28). San Diego, CA: Academic Press.

Fiedler, F. E. (2002). The curious role of cognitive resources in leadership. In R. E. Riggio & S. E. Murphy (Eds.), *Multiple intelligences and leadership. LEA's organization and management series* (pp. 91–104). Mahwah, NJ: Erlbaum.

Field, T. M. (1986). Interventions for premature infants. *Journal of Pediatrics, 109,* 183–191.

Field, T. M. (2001). *Touch.* Cambridge, MA: MIT Press.

Finger, T. E., Danilova, V., Barrows, J., Bartel, D. L., Vigers, A. J., Stone, et al. (2005, December 2). ATP signaling is crucial for communication from taste buds to gustatory nerves. *Science, 310,* 1495–1499.

Fiore, S. M., & Schooler, J. W. (2002). How did you get here from there? Verbal overshadowing of spatial mental models. *Applied Cognitive Psychology, 16,* 897–910.

Firestone, R. W., Firestone, L. A., & Catlett, J. (2006). Men, women, and sexual stereotypes. In R. W. Firestone, L. A. Firestone, & J. Catlett (Eds.), *Sex and love in intimate relationships* (pp. 75–109). Washington, DC: American Psychological Assoc.

Fischer, A. H., Rodriguez–Mosquera, P. M., van-Vianen, A. E. M., & Manstead, A. S. R. (2004). Gender and culture differences in emotion. *Emotion, 4,* 87–94.

Fischetti, M. (2003). To hear again. *Scientific American, 288*(6), *82*–83.

Fischhoff, B., & Downs, J. (1997). Accentuate the relevant. *Psychological Science, 8,* 154–158.

Fischman, J. (1985, September). Mapping the mind. *Psychology Today,* 18–19.

Fisher, S., & Greenberg, R. P. (1985). *The scientific credibility of Freud's theories and therapy.* New York: Columbia Univ. Press.

Fishman, N. (2005, June 13). Risky business: Making hiring decisions without background checks can lead to costly mistakes. *Nation's Restaurant News, 13,* 12. Retrieved October 3, 2006, from http://findarticles.com/ p/articles/mi_m3190/is_24_39/ai_n14697040).

Fiske, S. T., & Taylor, S. E. (1991). *Social cognition* (2nd ed.). New York: McGraw-Hill.

Fitch, W. T., Hauser, M. D., & Chomsky, N. (2005). The evolution of the language faculty: Clarifications and implications. *Cognition, 97,* 179–210.

Fitzgerald, S. (1999, October 11). "Brain exercise" under scrutiny to aid attention deficit. *Charlotte Observer,* p. 12E.

Flannery, R. B. (2002). Treating learned helplessness in the elderly dementia patient: Preliminary inquiry. *American Journal of Alzheimer's Disease and Other Dementias, 17,* 345–349.

Flashman, L. A., & Green, M. F. (2004). Review of cognition and brain structure in schizophrenia: Profiles, longitudinal course, and effects of treatment. *Psychiatric Clinics of North America, 27,* 1–18.

Flavell, J. H. (1999). Cognitive development: Children's knowledge about the mind. *Annual Review of Psychology, 50,* 21–45.

Flavell, J. H., Miller, P. H., & Miller, S. A. (2002). *Cognitive development* (4th ed.). Upper Saddle River, NJ: Prentice Hall.

Flieller, A. (1999). Comparison of the development of formal thought in adolescent cohorts aged 10–15 years. *Developmental Psychology, 35,* 1048–1058.

Flier, J. S., & Maratos-Flier, E. (1998). Obesity and the hypothalamus: Novel peptides for new pathways. *Cell, 92,* 437–440.

Flor, H., Elbert, T., Knecht, S., Wienbruch, C., & Pantev, C. (1995). Phantom-limb pain as a perceptual correlate of cortical reorganization following arm amputation. *Nature, 375,* 482–484.

Flynn, J. R. (1984). The mean IQ of Americans: Massive gains 1932 to 1978. *Psychological Bulletin, 95,* 29–51.

Flynn, J. R. (1987). Massive IQ gains in 14 nations: What IQ tests really measure. *Psychological Bulletin, 101,* 171–191.

Flynn, J. R. (1999). Searching for justice: The discovery of IQ gains over time. *American Psychologist, 54,* 5–20.

Foley, D. L., Neale, M. C., & Kendler, K. S. (2000). Does intra-uterine growth discordance predict differential risk for adult psychiatric disorder in a population-based sample of monozygotic twins? *Psychiatric Genetics, 10,* 1–8.

Folkman, S., Chesney, M. A., & Christopher-Richards, A. (1994). Stress and coping in partners of men with AIDS. *Psychiatric Clinics of North America, 17,* 33–55.

Folkman, S., & Moskowitz, S. T. (2000). Positive affect and the other side of coping. *American Psychologist, 55,* 647–654.

Ford, B. D. (1993). Emergenesis: An alternative and a confound. *American Psychologist, 48,* 1294.

Ford, W. C. L., North, K., Taylor, H., Farrow, A., Hull, M. G. R., & Golding, J. (2000). Increasing paternal age is associated with delayed conception in a large population of fertile couples: Evidence for declining fecundity in older men. *Human Reproduction, 15,* 1703–1708.

Forthun, L. F., Montgomery, M. J., & Bell, N. J. (2006). Identity formation in a relational context: A person-centered analysis of troubled youth. *Identity, 6,* 141–167.

Foundry Management and Technology. (2006). Fire extinguisher training simulator. *Foundry Management and Technology, 1334,* 22.

Fowler, J. C., & Perry, J. C. (2005). Clinical tasks of the dynamic interview. *Psychiatry: Interpersonal and Biological Processes, 68,* 316–336.

Foxcroft, D. R., Ireland, D., Lister, S. D. J., Lowe, G., & Breen, R. (2003). Longer-term primary prevention for alcohol misuse in young people: A systematic review. *Addiction, 98,* 397–411.

Frank, M. G. (2006). Research methods in detecting deception research. In J. A. Harrigan, R. Rosenthal, & K. R. Scherer (Eds.), *The new handbook of methods in nonverbal behavior research* (pp. 341–368). New York: Oxford Univ. Press.

Fredrickson, P., Boules, M., Lin, S. C., & Richelson, E. (2005). Neurobiologic basis of nicotine addiction and psychostimulant abuse: A role for neurotensin? *Psychiatric Clinics of North America, 28,* 737–751.

Freedland, K. E. (2004). Religious beliefs shorten hospital stays? Psychology works in mysterious ways: Comment on Contrada et al. (2004). *Health Psychology, 23,* 239–242.

Freedman, J. L., & Fraser, S. C. (1966). Compliance without pressure: The foot-in-the-door technique. *Journal of Personality and Social Psychology, 4,* 195–202.

Freeman, W., Brebner, K., Lynch, W., Patel, K., Robertson, D., Roberts, D. C., et al. (2002). Changes in rat frontal cortex gene expression following chronic cocaine. *Molecular Brain Research, 104,* 11–20.

Freud, S. (1900). The interpretation of dreams. In J. Strachey (Ed.), *The standard edition of the complete psychological works of Sigmund Freud* (Vol. 5). London: Hogarth.

Fridberger, A., de Monvel, J. B., Zheng, J., Hu, N., Zou, Y., Ren., T., et al. (2004). Organ of corti potentials and the motion of the basilar membrane. *Journal of Neuroscience, 24,* 10057–10063.

Friedland, R. P., Fritsch, T., Smyth, K. A., Koss, E., Lerner, A. J., Chen, C. H., et al. (2001). Patients with Alzheimer's disease have reduced activities in midlife compared with healthy control-group members. *Proc. Natl. Acad. Sci, USA, 98,* 3440–3445.

Friedman, B. J. (2000). An historical review of the life and works of an important man: Leon Festinger. *Dissertation Abstracts International: Section B: The Sciences and Engineering, 61,* 2816.

Friedman, H. S. (2002). *Health Psychology* (2nd ed.) Upper Saddle River, NJ: Prentice Hall.

Friedman, M., Breall, W. S., Goodwin, M. L., Sparagon, B. J., Ghandour, G., & Fleischmann, N. (1996). Effect of Type A behavioral counseling on frequency of episodes of silent myocardial ischemia in coronary patients. *American Heart Journal, 132,* 933–937.

Friedman, M., & Rosenman, R. H. (1959). Association of specific overt behavior patterns with blood and cardiovascular findings: Blood cholesterol level, blood clotting time, incidence of arcus senilis and clinical coronary artery disease. *JAMA, Journal of the American Medical Association, 169,* 1286–1296.

Frijda, N. H., Markam, S., & Sato, K. (1995). Emotions and emotion words. In J. A. Russell, J-M. Fernàndez-Dols, A. S. R. Manstead, & J. C. Wellenkamp (Eds.), *Everyday conceptions of emotion: An introduction to the psychology, anthropology and linguistics of emotion* (pp. 121–143). New York: Kluwer Academic/Plenum.

Froelich, L., & Hoyer, S. (2002). The etiological and pathogenetic heterogeneity of Alzheimer's disease. *Nervenarzi, 73,* 422–427.

Froh, J. J. (2004). The history of positive psychology: Truth be told. *NYS Psychologist, 16,* 18–20.

Frosch, C. A., Mangelsdorf, S. C., & McHale, J. L. (2000). Marital behavior and the security of preschooler–parent attachment relationships. *Journal of Family Psychology, 14,* 144–161.

Fu, Q., Heath, A. C., Bucholz, K. K., Nelson, E., Goldberg, J., Lyons, M. J., et al. (2002). Shared genetic risk of major depression, alcohol dependence, and marijuana dependence: Contribution of antisocial personality disorder in men. *Archives of General Psychiatry, 59,* 1125–1132.

Fuchs, T., Birbaumer, N., Lutzenberger, W., Gruzelier, J. H., & Kaiser, J. (2003). Neurofeedback treatment for attention-deficit/hyperactivity disorder in children: A comparison with methylphenidate. *Applied Psychophysiology and Biofeedback, 28,* 1–12.

Fujimoto, Y., & Härtel, C. E. J. (2004). Culturally specific prejudices: Interpersonal prejudices of individualists and intergroup prejudices of collectivists. *Cross Cultural Management, 11,* 54–69.

Funder, D. C. (1995). On the accuracy of personality judgment: A realistic approach. *Psychological Review, 102*(4), 652–670.

Funk, J. B., Baldacci, H., Pasold, T., & Baumgardner, J. (2004). Violence exposure in real-life, video games, television, movies, and the Internet: Is there desensitization? *Journal of Adolescence, 27,* 23–39.

Furnham, A., McClelland, A., & Omer, L. (2003). A cross-cultural comparison of ratings of perceived fecundity and sexual attractiveness as a function of body weight and waist-to-hip ratio. *Psychology, Health and Medicine, 8,* 219–230.

Furstenberg, F. F., Jr., Brooks-Gunn, J., & Chase-Lansdale, L. (1989). Teenaged pregnancy and childbearing. *American Psychologist, 44,* 313–320.

Gabbard, G. O. (2005). Mind, brain, and personality disorders. *American Journal of Psychiatry, 162,* 648–655.

Gable, S. L., & Haidt, J. (2005). What (and why) is positive psychology? *Review of General Psychology, 9 (Special issue: Positive Psychology)*, 103–110.

Gabrieli, J. D. E. (1998). Cognitive neuroscience of human memory. *Annual Review of Psychology, 49*, 87–115.

Gage, F. H. (2000, February 25). Mammalian neural stem cells. *Science, 287*, 1433–1438.

Gage, F. H. (2003). Brain, repair yourself. *Scientific American, 289*(3), 46–53.

Galambos, N., Barker, E., & Almeida, D. (2003). Parents do matter: Trajectories of change in externalizing and internalizing problems in early adolescence. *Child Development, 74*, 578–594.

Galambos, N. L., & Leadbeater, B. J. (2002). Transitions in adolescent research. In W. W. Hartup & R. K. Silbereisen (Eds.), *Growing points in developmental science: An introduction*, (pp. 287–306). Philadelphia: Psychology Press.

Galanter, M., Hayden, F., Castañeda, R., & Franco, H. (2005). Group therapy, self-help groups, and network therapy. In R. J. Frances, S. I. Miller, & A. H. Mack (Eds.), *Clinical textbook of addictive disorders* (3rd ed., pp. 502–527). New York: Guilford.

Galef, B. G. (1993). Functions of social learning about food: A causal analysis of effects of diet novelty on preference transmission. *Animal Behaviour, 46*, 257–265.

Galef, B. G. Jr., & Whiskin, E, E. (2004). Effects of environmental stability and demonstrator age on social learning of food preferences by young Norway rats. *Animal Behaviour, 68*, 897–902.

Gallahue, D. L., & Ozmun, J. C. (2006). Motor development in young children. In B. Spodek & O. N. Saracho (Eds.), *Handbook of research on the education of young children* (2nd ed., pp. 105–120). Mahwah, NJ: Erlbaum.

Gallo, L. C., & Matthews, K. A. (2003). Understanding the association between socioeconomic status and physical health: Do negative emotions play a role? *Psychological Bulletin, 129*, 10–51.

Gallup, G. G., Jr. (1985). Do minds exist in species other than our own? *Neuroscience and Biobehavioral Reviews, 9*, 631–641.

Gallup, G. G., Jr. (1998). Self-awareness and the evolution of social intelligence. *Behavioural Processes, 42*, 239–247.

Gandhi, N., Depauw, K. P., Dolny, D. G., & Freson, T. (2002). Effect of an exercise program on quality of life of women with fibromyalgia. *Women and Therapy, 25*, 91–103.

Garb, H. N., Florio, C. M., & Grove, W. M. (1998). The validity of the Rorschach and the Minnesota Multiphasic Personality Inventory: Results from meta-analysis. *Psychological Science, 9*, 402–404.

Garbarino, J. (1999). *Lost boys: Why our sons turn violent and how we can save them.* New York: Free Press.

Garber, H., & Heber, R. (1982). Modification of predicted cognitive development in high risk children through early intervention. In D. K. Detterman & R. J. Sternberg (Eds.), *How and how much can intelligence be increased?* (pp. 121–137). Norwood, NJ: Ablex.

Gardner, H. (1983). *Frames of mind: The theory of multiple intelligences.* New York: Basic Books.

Gardner, H. (2004). *Frames of mind: The theory of multiple intelligences.* New York: Basic Books.

Garlick, D. (2003). Integrating brain science with intelligence research. *Current Directions in Psychological Science, 12*, 185–189.

Garner, D. M., & Magana, C. (2006). Cognitive vulnerability to anorexia vervosa. In L. B. Alloy & J. H. Riskind (Eds.), *Cognitive vulnerability to emotional disorders* (pp. 365–403). Mahwah, NJ: Erlbaum.

Garnets, L. K. (2002). Sexual orientation in perspective. *Cultural Diversity and Ethnic Minority Psychology, 8*, 115–129.

Garry, M., & Polaschek, D. L. L. (2000). Imagination and memory. *Current Directions in Psychological Science, 9*, 6–10.

Gartstein, M. A., & Rothbart, M. K. (2003). Studying infant temperament via the revised infant behavior questionnaire. *Infant Behavior and Development, 26*, 64–86.

Gates, L., Clarke, J. R., Stokes, A., Somorjai, R., Jarmasz, M., Vandorpe, R., et al. (2004). Neuroanatomy of coprolalia in Tourette syndrome using functional magnetic resonance imaging. *Progress in Neuro Psychopharmacology and Biological Psychiatry, 28*, 397–400.

Gatewood, R. D., & Field, H. S. (1998). *Human resource selection.* Fort Worth, TX: Harcourt College Publishers.

Gathchel, R. J., & Oordt, M. S. (2003). Insomnia. In R. J. Gathchel & M. S. Oordt (Eds.), *Clinical health psychology and primary care: Practical advice and clinical guidance for successful collaboration* (pp. 135–148). Washington, DC: American Psychological Assoc.

Gaugler, B. B., Rosenthal, D. B., Thornton, G. C., & Bentson, C. (1987). Meta-analysis of assessment center validity. *Journal of Applied Psychology, 72*, 493–511.

Gazzaniga, M. S. (2005a). Cerebral specialization and interhemispheric communication: Does the corpus callosum enable the human condition? *Brain: A Journal of Neurology, 123*, 1293–1326.

Gazzaniga, M. S. (2005b). Forty-five years of split-brain research and still going strong. *Nature Reviews Neuroscience, 6*, 653–659.

Gécz, J., & Mulley, J. (2000). Genes for cognitive function: Developments on the X. *Genome Research, 10*, 157–163.

Geen, R. G. (1998). Aggression and antisocial behavior. In D. Gilbert, S. T. Fiske, & G. Lindzey (Eds.), *Handbook of social psychology* (4th ed., Vol. 2, pp. 317–356). Boston: McGraw-Hill

Gehring, J. (2001, April 4). U.S. seen as losing edge on education measures. *Education Week.* Retrieved October 4, 2006, from http://www.ecs.org/clearinghouse/25/19/2519.htm

George, L. K. (2001). The social psychology of health. In R. H. Binstock & L. K. George (Eds.), *Handbook of the psychology of aging* (5th ed., pp. 213–237). San Diego: Academic Press.

George, S., Rogers, R. D., & Duka, T. (2005). The acute effect of alcohol on decision making in social drinkers. *Psychopharmacology, 182*, 160–169.

Gerber, D. J., Hall, D., Miyakawa, T., Demars, S., Gogos, J. A., Karayiorgou, M., et al. (2003). Evidence for association of schizophrenia with genetic variation in 8p21.3 gene, PPP3ccc, encoding the calcineurin gamma subunit. *Proceedings of the National Academy of Sciences, 100*, 8993–8998.

Gerkens, D. (2005). Are recovered memories accurate? *Dissertation Abstracts International: Section B: The Sciences and Engineering, 66*, 2321.

Gernsbacher, M. A., & Kaschak, M. P. (2003). Neuroimaging studies of language production and comprehension. *Annual Review of Psychology, 54*, 91–114.

Gershoff, E. T. (2002). Corporal punishment by parents and associated child behaviors and experiences: A meta-analytic and theoretical review. *Psychological Bulletin, 128*, 539–579.

Gershon, S., & Soares, J. C. (1997). Current therapeutic profile of lithium. *Archives of General Psychiatry, 54*, 16–20.

Getzels, J. W. (1975). Problem finding and the inventiveness of solutions. *Journal of Creative Behavior, 9*, 12–18.

Getzels, J. W., & Jackson, P. (1962). *Creativity and intelligence.* New York: Wiley.

Ghate, D., & Hazel, N. (2002). *Parenting in poor environments: Stress, support and coping.* New York: Jessica Kingsley Publishers.

Gibson, R. L., & Mitchell, M. (2003). *Introduction to counseling and guidance* (6th ed.). Upper Saddle River, NJ: Prentice Hall.

Giese-Davis, J., Koopman, C., Butler, L. D., Classen, C., Cordova, M., Fobair, P., et al. (2002). Change in emotion-regulation strategy for women with metastic breast cancer following supportive-expressive group therapy. *Journal of Consulting and Clinical Psychology, 70,* 916–925.

Gila, A., Castro, J., & Cesena, J. (2005). Anorexia nervosa in male adolescents: Body image, eating attitudes and psychological traits. *Journal of Adolescent Health, 36,* 221–226.

Gilhooly, K. J., & Murphy, P. (2005). Differentiating insight from non-insight problems. *Thinking & Reasoning, 11,* 279–302.

Gilligan, C. (1982). *In a different voice: Psychological theory and women's development.* Cambridge, MA: Harvard Univ. Press.

Gilligan, C. (1992, August). *Joining the resistance: Girls' development in adolescence.* Paper presented at the meeting of the American Psychological Association, Montreal, Canada.

Gilman, S. L. (2001). Karen Horney, M. D., 1885–1952. *American Journal of Psychiatry, 158,* 1205.

Gilovich, T. (1991). *How we know what isn't so: The fallibility of human reason in everyday life.* New York: Free Press.

Gimpel, G. A., Collett, B. R., Veeder, M. A., Gifford, J. A., Sneddon, P., Bushman, B., et al. (2005). Effects of stimulant medication on cognitive performance of children with ADHD. *Clinical Pediatrics, 44,* 405–411.

Giovanni, B. (2003). Language, mind, and culture: From linguistic relativity to representational modularity. In M. Mack & M. T. Banich (Eds.), *Mind, brain, and language: Multidisciplinary perspectives* (pp. 23–59). Mahwah, NJ: Erlbaum.

Giscombé, C. L., & Lobel, M. (2005). Explaining disproportionately high rates of adverse birth outcomes among African Americans: The impact of stress, racism, and related factors in pregnancy. *Psychological Bulletin, 131,* 662–683.

Glassop, L. I. (2002). The organizational benefits of teams. *Human Relations, 55,* 225–250.

Gladstone, G. L., Parker, G. B., Mitchell, P. B., Wilhelm, K. A., & Malhi, G. S. (2005). Relationship between self-reported childhood behavioral inhibition and lifetime anxiety disorders in a clinical sample. *Depression and Anxiety, 22,* 103–113.

Gleaves, D. H., Miller, K. J., Williams, T. L., & Summers, S. A. (2000). Eating disorders: An overview. In K. J. Miller & J. S. Mizes (Eds.), *Comparative treatments for eating disorders* (pp. 1–49). New York: Springer.

Gleaves, D. H., Smith, S. M., Butler, L. D., & Spiegel, D. (2004). False and recovered memories in the laboratory and clinic: A review of experimental and clinical evidence. *Clinical Psychology: Science and Practice, 11,* 3–28.

Glidden, L. M. (Ed.) (2004). *International review of research in mental retardation (Vol. 29).* San Diego, CA: Elsevier.

Gnanadesikan, M., Freeman, M. P., & Gelenberg, A. J. (2003). Alternatives to lithium and divalproex in the maintenance treatment of bipolar disorder. *Bipolar Disorders, 5,* 203–216.

Gobet, F. (2005). Chunking models of expertise: Implications for education. *Applied Cognitive Psychology, 19,* 183–204.

Gobet, F. L., Peter, C. R., Croker, S., Cheng, P., Jones, G., Oliver, I., et al. (2001). Chunking mechanisms in human learning. *Trends in Cognitive Sciences, 5,* 236–243.

Gobl, C., & Chasaide, A. N. (2003). The role of voice quality in communicating emotion, mood, and attitude. *Speech Communication, 40,* 189–212.

Goddard, A. W., Mason, G. F., Rothman, D. L., Behar, K. L., Petroff, O. A. C., & Krystal, J. H. (2004). Family psychopathology and magnitude of reductions in occipital cortex GABA levels in panic disorder. *Neuropsychopharmacology, 29,* 639–640.

Goerge, R. M., & Lee, B. J. (1997). Abuse and neglect of the children. In R. A. Maynard (Ed.), *Kids having kids: Economic costs and social consequences of teen pregnancy* (pp. 205–230). Washington, DC: Urban Institute Press.

Goff, D. C., & Coyle, J. T. (2001). The emerging role of glutamate in the pathophysiology and treatment of schizophrenia. *American Journal of Psychiatry, 158,* 1367–1377.

Gold, P. E. (2003). Acetylcholine modulation of neural systems involved in learning and memory. *Neurobiology of Learning and Memory, 80,* 194–210.

Gold, P. E., & Greenough, W. T. (2001). *Memory consolidation: Essays in honor of James L. McGaugh.* Washington, DC: American Psychological Assoc.

Goldberg, E. (2001). *The executive brain: Frontal lobes and the civilized mind.* New York: Oxford Univ. Press.

Goldberg, T. E., & Weinberger, D. R. (2004). Genes and the parsing of cognitive processes. *Trends in Cognitive Sciences, 8,* 325–335.

Goldman, W., McCulloch, J., Cuffel, B., Zarin, D., Suarez, A., & Burns, B. (1998). Outpatient utilization patterns of integrated and split psychotherapy and pharmacotherapy for depression. *Psychiatric Services, 49,* 477–482.

Goldney, R. D. (2003). Deinstitutionalization and suicide. *Crisis, 24,* 39–40.

Goldsmith, H. H. (2002). Genetics of emotional development. In R. J. Davidson, K. R. Scherer, & H. H. Goldsmith (Eds.), *Handbook of affective sciences.* New York: Oxford Univ. Press.

Goldstein, E. B. (1999). *Sensation and perception* (5th ed.). Pacific Grove, CA: Brooks/Cole.

Goldstein, G. (2004). Abstract reasoning and problem solving in adults. In G. Goldstein, S. R. Beers, & M. Hersen (Eds.), *Comprehensive handbook of psychological assessment, Vol. 1: Intellectual and neuropsychological assessment* (pp. 293–308). Hoboken, NJ: John Wiley & Sons.

Goldstein, I. L., & Ford, J. K. (2002). *Training in organizations* (4th ed.). Belmont, CA: Wadsworth.

Goleman, D. (1997). *Emotional intelligence.* New York: Bantam.

Goleman, D., Boyatzis, R., & McKee, A. (2002). *Primal leadership: Realizing the power of emotional intelligence.* Boston: Harvard Business School Press.

Gonsalkorale, W. M., Miller, V., Afzal, A., & Whorwell, P. J. (2003). Long term benefits of hypnotherapy for irritable bowel syndrome. *Gut, 52,* 1623–9.

Goodall, J. (1971). *In the shadow of man.* New York: Dell.

Goode, E. (2000a, August 8). How culture molds habits of thought. *New York Times,* pp. D1, D4.

Goode, E. (2000b, March 14). Human nature: born or made? *New York Times,* pp. F1, F9.

Goode, E. (2000c, May 19). Scientists find a particularly female response to stress. *New York Times.* Available on-line at: http://query.nytimes.com/gst/fullpage.html?sec=health&res=9B04E1D8153AF93AA25756C0A9669C8B63.

Goode, E. (2004, February 24). Lifting the veils of autism, one by one. *New York Times,* pp. D1, D4.

Goodway, J. D., Crowe, H., & Ward, P. (2003). Effects of motor skill instruction on fundamental motor skill development. *Adapted Physical Activity Quarterly, 20,* 298–314.

Goodwin, P. J., Leszcz, M., Ennis, M., Koopmans, J., Vincent, L., Guther, H., et al. (2001). The effect of group psychosocial support on survival in metastatic breast cancer. *New England Journal of Medicine, 345,* 1719–1726.

Gopnik, A. (1996). The post-Piaget era. *Psychological Science, 7*(4), 221–225.

Gopnik, A., Meltzoff, A. N., & Kuhl, P. (1999). *The scientist in the crib: Minds, brains and how children learn.* New York: William Morrow.

Gordijn, E. H., Postmes, T., & de Vries, N. K. (2001). Devil's advocate or advocate of oneself: Effects of numerical support on pro- and counterattitudinal self-persuasion. *Personality and Social Psychology Bulletin, 27,* 395–407.

Gordis, E. (1996). Alcohol research: At the cutting edge. *Archives of General Psychiatry, 53,* 199–201.

Gordon, A. K., & Kaplar, M. E. (2002). A new technique for demonstrating the actor-observer bias. *Teaching of Psychology, 29,* 301–303.

Gosling, S. D., & John, O. P. (1999). Personality dimensions in nonhuman animals: A cross-species review. *Current Directions in Psychological Science, 8,* 69–75.

Gottesman, I. I. (1991). *Schizophrenia genesis: The origins of madness.* New York: Freeman.

Gouzoulis-Mayfrank, E., Daumann, J., Tuchtenhagen, F., Pelz, S., Becker, S., Kunert, et al. (2000). Impaired cognitive performance in drug free users of recreational Ecstasy (MDMA). *Journal of Neurology, Neurosurgery and Psychiatry, 68,* 719–725.

Graber, J. S. (2003). Puberty in context. In C. Hayward (Ed.), *Gender differences at puberty* (pp. 307–325). New York: Cambridge Univ, Press.

Grady, C. L., McIntosh, A. R., & Craik, F. I. M. (2003). Age-related differences in the functional connectivity of the hippocampus during memory encoding. *Hippocampus, 13,* 572–586.

Graen, G. B., & Hui, C. (2001). Approaches to leadership: Toward a complete contingency model of face-to-face leadership. In M. Erez & U. Kleinbeck (Eds.), *Work motivation in the context of a globalizing economy* (pp. 211–225). Mahwah, NJ: Erlbaum.

Grafton, S. T., Mazziotta, J. C., Presty, S., Friston, K. J., Frackowiak, R. S., J., & Phelps, M. E. (1992). Functional anatomy of human procedural learning determined with regional cerebral blood flow and PET. *Journal of Neuroscience, 12,* 2542–2548.

Graham, S. (1992). Most of the subjects were white and middle class. *American Psychologist, 47,* 629–639.

Grandchamp, N., & Schenk, F. (2006). Adaptive changes in a radial maze task: Efficient selection of baited arms with reduced foraging in senescent hooded rats. *Behavioural Brain Research, 168,* 161–166.

Grandey, A. A. (2000). Emotional regulation in the workplace: A new way to conceptualize emotional labor. *Journal of Occupational Health Psychology, 5,* 95–110.

Grant, J. E., Kim, S. W., & Eckert, E. D. (2002). Body dysmorphic disorder in patients with anorexia nervosa: Prevalence, clinical features and delusionality of body image. *International Journal of Eating Disorders, 32,* 291–300.

Gray, J. R., Braver, T. S., & Raichle, M. E. (2002). Integration of emotion and cognition in the lateral prefrontal cortex. *Proceedings of the National Academy of Sciences of the United States of America, 99,* 4115–4120.

Gray, P. B., Kahlenberg, S. M., Barrett, E. S., Lipson, S. F., & Ellison, P. T. (2002). Marriage and fatherhood are associated with lower testosterone in males. *Evolution and Human Behavior, 23,* 193–201.

Green, J. P., & Lynn, S. J. (2000). Hypnosis and suggestion-based approaches to smoking cessation: An examination of the evidence. *International Journal of Clinical & Experimental Hypnosis* [Special Issue: *The status of hypnosis as an empirically validated clinical intervention*], *48,* 195–224.

Greene, J., & Haidt, J. (2002). How (and where) does moral judgment work? *Trends in Cognitive Sciences, 6,* 517–523.

Greene, R. L. (1987). Effects of maintenance rehearsal on human memory. *Psychological Bulletin, 102,* 403–413.

Greene, S. M., Anderson, E. R., Doyle, E. A., & Riedelbach, H. (2006). Divorce. In G. G. Bear & K. M Minke (Eds.), *Children's needs III: Development, prevention, and intervention* (pp. 745–757). Washington, DC: National Association of School Psychologists.

Greenfield, P. M. (1998). The cultural evolution of IQ. In U. Neisser (Ed.), *The rising curve: Long-term gains in IQ and related measures* (pp. 81–123). Washington, DC: American Psychological Assoc.

Greenglass, E. R. (2002). Proactive coping and quality of life management. In E. Frydenber (Ed.), *Beyond coping: Meeting goals, visions, and challenges* (pp. 37–62). New York: Oxford Univ. Press.

Greenwald, A. G. (1992). New Look 3: Unconscious cognition reclaimed. *American Psychologist, 47,* 766–779.

Greenwald, A. G., Spangenberg, E. R., Pratkanis, A. R., & Eskenazi, J. (1991). Double-blind tests of subliminal self-help audiotapes. *Psychological Science, 2,* 119–122.

Gregory, R. J. (2004). *Psychological testing: History, principles, and applications.* Needham Heights, MA: Allyn & Bacon.

Gregory, R. L. (1970). *The intelligent eye.* London: Weidenfeld

Grekin, E. R., Sher, K. J., & Larkins, J. M. (2004). The role of behavioral undercontrol in the relation between alcohol use and partner aggression. *Journal of Studies on Alcohol, 65,* 658–662.

Grensing-Pophal, L. (2005). Job rotation. *Credit Union Management, 28,* 50–53.

Griffin, A. M., & Langlois, J. H. (2006). Stereotype directionality and attractiveness stereotyping: Is beauty good or is ugly bad? *Social Cognition, 24,* 187–206.

Griffiths, M. D., & Dancaster, I. (1995). The effect of Type A personality on physiological arousal while playing computer games. *Addictive Behaviors, 120,* 543–548.

Gruber, H. E., & Wallace, D. B. (2001). Creative work: The case of Charles Darwin. *American Psychologist, 56,* 346–349.

Grunwald, I. S., Borod, J. C., Obler, L. K., Erhan, H. M., Pick, L. H., Welkowitz, J., et al. (1999). The effects of age and gender on the perception of lexical emotion. *Applied Neuropsychology, 6,* 226–238.

Gruzelier, J. (2005). Altered states of consciousness and hypnosis in the twenty-first century: Comment. *Contemporary Hypnosis, 22,* 1–7.

Guéguen, N., Pascual, A., & Dagot, L. (2002). Low-ball and compliance to a request: An application in a field setting. *Psychological Reports, 91,* 81–84.

Guenther, V. K., Schaefer, P., Holzner, B. J., & Kemmler, G. W. (2003). Long-term improvements in cognitive performance through computer-assisted cognitive training: A pilot study in a residential home for older people. *Aging and Mental Health, 7,* 200–206.

Guérin, D. (1994, August). *Fussy infants at risk.* Paper presented at the meeting of the American Psychological Association, Los Angeles.

Guohua, R., & Jiliang, L. (2005). The advance in correlation research between Big Five personality dimensions and job performance. *Psychological Science* (China), *28,* 406–408.

Gurman, A. S., & Kniskern, D. P. (1991). *Handbook of family therapy* (Vol. 2). Philadelphia: Brunner/Mazel.

Gurwitch, R. H., Sitterle, K. A., Young, B. H., & Pfefferbaum, B. (2002). The aftermath of terrorism. In A. M. La Greca & W. K. Silverman (Eds.), *Helping children cope with disasters and terrorism* (pp. 327–357). Washington, DC: American Psychological Assoc.

Guthrie, J. (2005, January 17). Iraq war vets fight an enemy at home. Experts say up to 30% may need psychiatric care. *San Francisco Chronicle.* Retrieved June 28, 2006 from http://sfgate.com/cgi-bin/article.cgi?file=/c/a/2005/01/17/MNG24ARHTU1.DTL

Guthrie, M. L., & Bates, L. W. (2003). Sex education sources and attitudes toward sexual precautions across a decade. *Psychological Reports, 92,* 581–592.

Guthrie, R. (1976). *Even the rat was white.* New York: Harper & Row.

Gutman, L. M., McLoyd, V. C., & Tokoyawa, T. (2005). Financial strain, neighborhood stress, parenting behaviors, and adolescent adjustment in urban African American families. *Journal of Research on Adolescence, 15,* 425–449.

Gutteling, B. M., de Weerth, C., Willemsen-Swinkels, S. H., Huizink, A. C., Mulder, E. J. H., Visser, G. H. A., et al. (2005). The effects of prenatal stress on temperament and problem behavior of 27-month-old toddlers. *European Child & Adolescent Psychiatry, 14,* 41–51.

Gyekye, S. A., & Salminen, S. (2006). The self-defensive attribution hypothesis in the work environment: Co-workers' perspectives. *Safety Science, 44,* 157–168.

Haber, R. N. (1969). Eidetic images. *Scientific American, 220*(4), 36–44.

Haberlandt, K. (1997). *Cognitive psychology.* Boston: Allyn & Bacon.

Habra, M. E., Linden, W., & Anderson, J. C. (2003). Type D personality is related to cardiovascular and neuroendocrine reactivity to acute stress. *Journal of Psychosomatic Research, 55,* 235–245.

Hadjikhani, N., & Tootell, R. B. H. (2000). Projection of rods and cones within human visual cortex. *Human Brain Mapping, 9,* 55–63.

Hagemann, D., Hewig, J., Naumann, E., Seifert, J., & Bartussek, D. (2005). Resting brain asymmetry and affective reactivity: Aggregated data support the right-hemisphere hypothesis. *Journal of Individual Differences, 26,* 139–154.

Hagerman, R. J., & Hagerman, P. J. (2002). Fragile X syndrome. In P. Howlin & O. Udwin, (Eds.), *Outcomes in neurodevelopmental and genetic disorders. Cambridge child and adolescent psychiatry* (pp. 198–219). New York: Cambridge Univ. Press.

Haier, R. J. (1993). Cerebral glucose metabolism and intelligence. In P. A. Vernon (Ed.), *Biological approaches to the study of human intelligence* (pp. 317–332). Norwood, NJ: Ablex.

Haier, R. J. (2003). Brain imaging studies of intelligence: Individual differences and neurobiology. In R. J. Sternberg & J. Lautrey (Eds.), *Models of intelligence: International perspectives* (pp. 18–193). Washington, DC: American Psychological Association.

Haihui, Y., Zhengping, W., & Xing, X. (2005). The responses of term fetuses to different acoustic stimulations. *Acta Psychologica Sinica, 37,* 62–66.

Halbreich, U., & Karkun, S. (2006). Cross-cultural and social diversity of prevalence of postpartum depression and depressive symptoms. *Journal of Affective Disorders, 91,* 97–111.

Hall, C. (2005). A 21st century view of female genital anxiety. *Psychoanalytic Social Work, 12,* 37–49.

Hall, C. C. I. (1997). Cultural malpractice: The growing obsolescence of psychology with the changing U.S. population. *American Psychologist, 52,* 642–651.

Hall, G. S. (1904). *Adolescence: Its psychology and its relations to physiology, anthropology, sex, crime, religion and education* (Vol. 1). New York: Appleton-Century-Crofts.

Hall, J. A., Bernieri, F. J., & Carney, D. R. (2006). Nonverbal behavior and interpersonal sensitivity. In J. A. Harrigan, R. Rosenthal, & K. R. Scherer (Eds.), *The new handbook of methods in nonverbal behavior research* (pp. 237–281). New York: Oxford Univ. Press.

Hall, W. G., Arnold, H. M., & Myers, K. P. (2000). The acquisition of an appetite. *Psychological Science, 11,* 101–105.

Hallschmid, M., Benedict, C., Born, J., Fehm, H.-L., & Kern, W. (2004). Manipulating central nervous mechanisms of food intake and body weight regulation by intranasal administration of neuropeptides in man. *Physiology & Behavior, 83,* 55–64.

Halpern, D. F. (1992). *Sex differences in cognitive abilities* (2nd ed.). Hillsdale, NJ: Erlbaum.

Halpern, D. F. (1997). Sex differences in intelligence: Implications for education. *American Psychologist, 52,* 1091–1102.

Hamann, S. B., Ely, T. D., Hoffman, J. M., & Kilts, C. D. (2002). Ecstasy and agony: Activation of the human amygdala in positive and negative emotion. *Psychological Science, 13,* 135–141.

Hamberger, M. J., & Seidel, W. T. (2003). Auditory and visual naming tests: Normative and patient data for accuracy, response time, and tip-of-the-tongue. *Journal of the International Neuropsychological Society, 9,* 479–489.

Hamilton, A. (1999, May 24). On the virtual couch. *Time,* p. 71.

Hamilton, S. P., Slager, S. L., de Leon, A. B., Heiman, G. A., Klein, D. F., Hodge, S. E., et al. (2004). Evidence for genetic linkage between a polymorphism in the Adenosine 2A receptor and panic disorder. *Neuropsychopharmacology, 29,* 558–565.

Hammack, P. L. (2005). The life course development of human sexual orientation: An integrative paradigm. *Human Development, 48,* 267–290.

Hammack, P. L., Robinson, W. L., Crawford, I., & Li, S. T. (2004). Poverty and depressed mood among urban African-American adolescents: A family stress perspective. *Journal of Child and Family Studies, 13,* 309–323.

Hammen, C. L. (1985). Predicting depression: A cognitive-behavioral perspective. In P. Kendall (Ed.), *Advances in cognitive-behavioral research and therapy* (Vol. 4, pp. 29–71). New York: Academic Press.

Hammen, C. L., Gitlin, M., & Altshuler, L. (2000). Predictors of work adjustment in bipolar I patients. A naturalistic longitudinal follow-up. *Journal of Consulting & Clinical Psychology, 68,* 220–225.

Hampson, J., & Nelson, K. (1993). The relation of maternal language to variation in rate and style of language acquisition. *Journal of Child Language, 20,* 313–342.

Haney, M., Hart, C. L., Vosburg, S. K., Nasser, J., Bennett, A., Zubaran, C., et al. (2004). Marijuana withdrawal in humans: Effects of oral THC or divalproex. *Neuropsychopharmacology, 29,* 158–170.

Hanna, F. J. (2002). *Therapy with difficult clients: Using the precursors model to awaken change.* Washington, DC: American Psychological Assoc.

Hansen, E. M., Kimble, C. E., & Biers, D. W. (2001). Actors and observers: Divergent attributions of constrained unfriendly behavior. *Social Behavior and Personality, 29,* 87–104.

Hare, R. D. (1983). Diagnosis of antisocial personality disorder in two prison populations. *American Journal of Psychiatry, 140,* 887–890.

Hare, R. D. (1993). *Without conscience: The disturbing world of the psychopaths among us.* New York: Pocket Books.

Harley, H. E., Roitblat, H. L., & Nachtigall, P. E. (1996). Object representation in the bottlenose dolphin (*Tursiops truncatus*): Integration of visual and echoic information. *Journal of Experimental Psychology and Animal Behavior Process, 22,* 164–174.

Harlow, H. F. (1949). The formation of learning sets. *Psychological Review, 56,* 51–65.

Harlow, H. F. (1958). The nature of love. *American Psychologist, 13,* 673–685.

Harlow, H. F., & Zimmerman, R. R. (1959). Affectional responses in the infant monkey. *Science, 130,* 421–432.

Haro, R., & Drucker-Colín, R. (2004). A two-year study on the effects of nicotine and its withdrawal on mood and sleep. *Pharmacopsychiatry, 37,* 221–227.

Harreé, R. (2000). Piaget's "sociological studies." *New Ideas in Psychology, 18,* 135–138.

Harrell, R. F., Woodyard, E., & Gates, A. I. (1955). *The effect of mother's diet on the intelligence of the offspring.* New York: Teacher's College, Columbia Bureau of Publications.

Harris, J. C. (2003). Pinel delivering the insane. *Archives of General Psychiatry, 60,* 552.

Harris, M., & Rosenthal, R. (1985). Mediation of the interpersonal expectancy effect: A taxonomy of expectancy situations. In P. Blanck (Ed.), *Interpersonal expectations: Theory, research, and application* (pp. 350–378). New York: Cambridge Univ. Press.

Hart, B., & Risley, T. R. (1995). *Meaningful differences in the everyday experience of young American children.* Baltimore: Brookes.

Hart, N. (1985). *The sociology of health and illness.* London: Causeway.

Hartmann, S., & Zepf, S. (2003). Effectiveness of psychotherapy in Germany: A replication of the *Consumer Reports* study. *Psychotherapy Research, 13,* 235–242.

Hartung, C. M., & Widiger, T. A. (1998). Gender differences in the diagnosis of mental disorders: Conclusions and controversies of *DSM-IV. Psychological Bulletin, 123,* 260–278.

Hartup, W. W., & Stevens, N. (1999). Friendships and adaptation across the life span. *Current Directions in Psychological Science, 8,* 76–79.

Harvey, E. (1999). Short-term and long-term effects of early parental employment on children of the National Longitudinal Survey of Youth. *Developmental Psychology, 35,* 445–459.

Harvey, J. H., & Pauwells, B. G. (1999). Recent developments in close-relationships theory. *Current Directions in Psychological Science, 8,* 93–95.

Harvey, R. J. (1991). Job analysis. In M. D. Dunnette & L. M. Hough (Eds.), *Handbook of industrial and organizational psychology* (2nd ed., Vol. 2, pp. 71–163). Palo Alto, CA: Consulting Psychologists Press.

Hashimoto, T., Volk, D. W., Eggan, S. M., Mirnics, K., Pierri, J. N., Sun, Z., et al. (2003). Gene expression deficits in a subclass of GABA neurons in the prefrontal cortex of subjects with schizophrenia. *Journal of Neuroscience, 16,* 6315–6326.

Haskell, I. O. (2003). Explaining regional variation in rates of aggression: Are differences accounted for by the southern culture of violence? *Dissertation Abstracts International: Section B: The Sciences and Engineering, 64,* 463.

Hasson, D., Arnetz, B., Jelveus, L., & Edelstam, B. (2004). A randomized clinical trial of the treatment effects of massage compared to relaxation tape recordings on diffuse long-term pain. *Psychotherapy and Psychosomatics, 73,* 17–24.

Hayden, E. P., & Nurnberger, J. I., Jr. (2006). Molecular genetics of bipolar disorder. *Genes, Brain & Behavior, 5,* 85–95.

Haykin, S., & Chen, Z. (2006). The cocktail party problem. *Neural Computation, 17,* 1875–1902.

Hayne, H. (2004). Infant memory development: Implications for childhood amnesia. *Developmental Review, 24,* 33–73.

Hayslip, B., Jr., & Peveto, C. A. (2005). *Cultural changes in attitudes toward death, dying, and bereavement.* New York: Springer.

Hazel, M. T. (2005). Visualization and systematic desensitization: Interventions for habituating and sensitizing patterns of public speaking anxiety. *Dissertation Abstracts International Section A: Humanities and Social Sciences, 66,* 30.

Head Start Bureau (2006). Head Start program fact sheet. Retrieved May 11, 2006 from http://www.acf.hhs.gov/programs/hsb/research/2006.htm

Heath, K. M., & Gant, L. M. (2005). Evolution, culture, and the processes of learning and memory. *International Journal of Cognitive Technology, 10,* 12–14.

Hebb, D. O. (1955). Drives and the CNS (conceptual nervous system). *Psychological Review, 62,* 243–254.

Heber, R., Garber, H., Harrington, S., & Hoffman, C. (1972). *Rehabilitation of families at risk for mental retardation.* Madison: Univ. of Wisconsin, Rehabilitation Research and Training Center in Mental Retardation.

Heckel, R. V., & Shumaker, D. M. (2001). *Children who murder: A psychological perspective.* Westport, CT: Praeger.

Hedges, L. V., & Nowell, A. (1995, July 7). Sex differences in mental test scores, variability, and numbers of high-scoring individuals. *Science, 269,* 41–45.

Heider, E. R., & Oliver, D. C. (1972). The structure of the color space in naming and memory in two languages. *Cognitive Psychology, 3,* 337–354.

Heider, F. (1958). *The psychology of interpersonal relations.* New York: Wiley.

Heinrichs, M., Wagner, D., Schoch, W., Soravia, L. M., Hellhammer, D. H., & Ehlert, U. (2005). Predicting posttraumatic stress symptoms from pretraumatic risk factors: A 2-year prospective follow-up study in firefighters. *American Journal of Psychiatry, 162,* 2276–2286.

Heinrichs, R. W. (2001). *In search of madness: Schizophrenia and neuroscience.* New York: Oxford Univ. Press.

Heinz, A., Hermann, D., Smolka, M. N., Rieks, M., Graef, K. J., Poehlau, D., et al. (2003). Effects of acute psychological stress on adhesion molecules interleukins and sex hormones: Implications for coronary heart disease. *Psychopharmacology, 165,* 111–117.

Heinzel, A., Bermpohl, F., Niese, R., Pfennig, A., Pascual-Leone, A., Schlaug, G., et al. (2005). How do we modulate our emotions? Parametric fMRI reveals cortical midline structures as regions specifically involved in the processing of emotional valences. *Cognitive Brain Research, 25,* 348–358.

Hekkanen, S. T., & McEvoy, C. (2005). Source monitoring in eyewitness memory: Implicit associations, suggestions, and episodic traces. *Memory & Cognition, 33,* 759–769.

Helgeland, M. I., & Torgersen, S. (2004). Developmental antecedents of borderline personality disorder. *Comprehensive Psychiatry, 45,* 138–147.

Helgesen, S. (1998). *Everyday revolutionaries: Working women and the transformation of American life.* New York: Doubleday.

Hellige, J. B. (1993). *Hemispheric asymmetry: What's right and what's left.* Cambridge, MA: Harvard Univ. Press.

Helmreich, R., & Spence, J. (1978). The Work and Family Orientation Questionnaire: An objective instrument to assess components of achievement motivation and scientific attainment. *Personality and Social Psychology Bulletin, 4,* 222–226.

Helms, J. E., & Cook, D. A. (1999). *Using race and culture in counseling and psychotherapy: Theory and process.* Needham Heights, MA: Allyn & Bacon.

Hendrick, C., & Hendrick, S. S. (2003). Romantic love: Measuring Cupid's arrow. In S. J. Lopez & C. R. Snyder (Eds.), *Positive psychological assessment:*

A handbook of models and measures (pp. 235–249). Washington, DC: American Psychological Assoc.

Hendrick, S., & Hendrick, C. (1992). *Liking, loving and relating* (2nd ed.). Pacific Grove, CA: Brooks/Cole.

Henkel, L. A., Franklin, N., & Johnson, M. K. (2000). Cross-modal source monitoring confusions between perceived and imagined events. *Journal of Experimental Psychology: Learning, Memory, & Cognition, 26*, 321–335.

Henningsen, D. D., Henningsen, M. L. M., & Eden, J. (2006). Examining the symptoms of groupthink and retrospective sensemaking. *Small Group Research, 37*, 36–64.

Henry, J. A., Alexander, C. A., & Sener, E. K. (1995). Relative mortality from overdose of antidepressants. *British Medical Journal, 310*, 221–224.

Henry, P. J., Reyna, C., & Weiner, B. (2004). Hate welfare but help the poor: How the attributional content of stereotypes explains the paradox of reactions to the destitute in America. *Journal of Applied Social Psychology, 34*, 34–58.

Herberman, R. B. (2002). Stress, natural killer cells, and cancer. In H. G. Koenig & H. J. Cohen (Eds.), *The link between religion and health: Psychoneuroimmunology and faith factor* (pp. 69–83). London: Oxford Univ. Press.

Herek, G. M. (2000). The psychology of sexual prejudice. *Current Directions in Psychological Science, 9*, 19–22.

Herek, G. M. (2002). Gender gaps in public opinion about lesbians and gay men. *Public Opinion Quarterly 66*, 40–66.

Herman, C. P., Roth, D. A., & Polivy, J. (2003). Effects of the presence of others on food intake: A normative interpretation. *Psychological Bulletin, 129*, 873–886.

Herman, L. M. (2002). Exploring the cognitive world of the bottlenose dolphin. In M. Bekoff, C. Allen, & G. M. Burghardt (Eds.), *The cognitive animal: Empirical and theoretical perspectives on animal cognition* (pp. 275–283). Cambridge, MA: MIT Press.

Hermann, B. P., Seidenberg, M., Sears, L., Hansen, R., Bayless, K., Rutecki, P., et al. (2004). Cerebellar atrophy in temporal lobe epilepsy affects procedural memory. *Neurology, 63*, 2129–2131.

Hermann, C., & Blanchard, E. B. (2002). Biofeedback in the treatment of headache and other childhood pain. *Applied Psychophysiology and Biofeedback, 27*, 143–162.

Hernandez, A., & Sachs-Ericsson, N. (2006). Ethnic differences in pain reports and the moderating role of depression in a community sample of Hispanic and Caucasian participants with serious health problems. *Psychosomatic Medicine, 68*, 121–128.

Hernandez, T. M., Aldridge, M. A., & Bower, T. G. R. (2000). Structural and experiential factors in newborns' preference for speech sounds. *Developmental Science, 3*, 46–49.

Herrnstein, R. J., & Murray, C. (1994). *The bell curve.* New York: Free Press.

Hersher, L. (Ed.). (1970). *Four psychotherapies.* New York: Appleton-Century-Crofts.

Herzog, H. A. (2005). Dealing with the animal research controversy. In C. K. Akins, S. Panicker, & C. L. Cunningham (Eds.), *Laboratory animals in research and teaching: Ethics, care, and methods* (pp. 9–29). Washington, DC: American Psychological Assoc.

Hetherington, E. M., Bridges, M., & Insabella, G. M. (1998). What matters? What does not? Five perspectives on the association between marital transitions and children's adjustment. *American Psychologist, 53*, 167–184.

Heyes, C. M., Jaldow, E., & Dawson, G. R. (1993). Observational extinction: Observation of nonreinforced responding reduces resistance to extinction in rats. *Animal Learning & Behavior, 21*, 221–225.

Hidehiro W., & Makoto M. (2006). Classical conditioning of activities of salivary neurones in the cockroach. *Journal of Experimental Biology 209*, 766–779.

Highstein, S. M., & Thatch, W. T. (Eds.) (2002). *The cerebellum: Recent developments in cerebellar research.* New York: New York Academy of Sciences.

Hildebrandt, H., Brokate, B., Eling, P., & Lanz, M. (2004). Response shifting and inhibition, but not working memory, are impaired after long-term heavy alcohol consumption. *Neuropsychology, 18*, 203–211.

Hill, C. E., Zack, J. S., Wonnell, T. L., Hoffman, M. A., Rochlen, A. B., Goldberg, J. L., et al. (2000). Structured brief therapy with a focus on dreams or loss for clients with troubling dreams and recent loss. *Journal of Counseling Psychology, 47*, 90–101.

Hill, J. (2003). Early identification of individuals at risk for antisocial personality disorder. *British Journal of Psychiatry, 182*(Suppl. 44), s11-s14.

Hines, M. (2004). *Brain gender.* New York: Oxford Univ. Press.

Hingson, R., Heeren, T., Winter, M., & Wechsler, H. (2005). Magnitude of alcohol-related mortality and morbidity among U.S. college students ages 18–24: Changes from 1998 to 2001. *Annual Review of Public Health 26*, 259–279.

Hinton, E. C., Parkinson, J. A., Holland, A. J., Arana, F. S., Roberts, A. C., & Owen, A. M. (2004). Neural contributions to the motivational control of appetite in humans. *European Journal of Neuroscience, 20*, 1411–1418.

Hochschild, A., & Machung, A. (1989). *The second shift: Working parents and the revolution at home.* New York: Viking.

Hofer, J., & Chasiotis, A. (2004). Methodological considerations of applying a TAT-type picture-story test in cross-cultural research. *Journal of Cross Cultural Psychology, 35*, 224–241.

Hoff, E. (2006). How social contexts support and shape language development. *Developmental Review, 26*, 55–88.

Hoffman, H. S., & DePaulo, P. (1977). Behavioral control by an imprinting stimulus. *American Scientist, 65*, 58–66.

Hoffman, R. E., Hawkins, K. A., Gueorguieva, R., Boutros, N. N., Rachid, F., Carroll, K., et al. (2003). Transcranial magnetic stimulation of left temporoparietal cortex and medication-resistant auditory hallucinations. *Archives of General Psychiatry, 60*, 49–56.

Hoffrage, U., Hertwig, R., & Gigerenzer, G. (2000). Hindsight bias: A by-product of knowledge updating? *Journal of Experimental Psychology: Learning, Memory & Cognition, 26*, 566–581.

Hoffrage, U., & Pohl, R. F. (2003). Research on hindsight bias: A rich past, a productive present, and a challenging future. *Memory, 11*, 329–335.

Hofmann, S. G., Moscovitch, D. A., & Heinrichs, N. (2004). Evolutionary mechanisms of fear and anxiety. In P. Gilbert (Ed.), *Evolutionary theory and cognitive therapy* (pp. 119–136). New York: Springer.

Hogan, R., Hogan, J., & Roberts, B. W. (1996). Personality measurement and employment decisions: Questions and answers. *American Psychologist, 51*(5), 469–477.

Hogan, J., & Holland, B. (2003). Using theory to evaluate personality and job-performance relations: A socioanalytic perspective. *Journal of Applied Psychology, 88*, 100–112.

Holdstock, J. S. (2005). The role of the human medial temporal lobe in object recognition and object discrimination. *Quarterly Journal of Experimental Psychology B: Comparative and Physiological Psychology, 58*, 326–339.

Hollis, K. L. (1997). Contemporary research on Pavlovian conditioning: A "new" functional analysis. *American Psychologist, 52*, 956–965.

Holmbeck, G. N. (1994). Adolescence. In V. A. Ramachandran (Ed.) *Encyclopedia of human behavior* (Vol. 1, pp. 17–28). San Diego, CA: Academic Press.

Holt, R. R. (2003). New directions for basic psychoanalytic research: Implications from the work of Benjamin Rubinstein. *Psychoanalytic Psychology, 20,* 195–213.

Holtkamp, K., Hebeband, J., Mika, C., Grzella, I., Heer, M., Heussen, N., et al. (2003). The effect of therapeutically induced weight gain on plasma leptin levels in patients with anorexia nervosa. *Journal of Psychiatric Research, 37,* 165–169.

Holtzman, S., Newth, S., & Delongis, A. (2004). The role of social support in coping with daily pain among patients with rheumatoid arthritis. *Journal of Health Psychology, 9,* 677–695.

Honeybourne, C., Matchett, G., & Davey, G. C. (1993). Expectancy models of laboratory preparedness effects: A UCS-expectancy bias in phylogenetic and ontogenetic fear-relevant stimuli. *Behavior Therapy, 24,* 253–264.

Hopkins, B., & Westra, T. (1990). Motor development, maternal expectation, and the role of handling. *Infant Behavior and Development, 13,* 117–122.

Hopkins, W. D., Cantalupo, C., Freeman, H., Russell, J., Kachin, M., & Nelson, E. (2005a). Chimpanzees are right-handed when recording bouts of hand use. *Laterality: Asymmetries of Body, Brain and Cognition, 10,* 121–130.

Hopkins, W. D., Russell, J., Freeman, H., Buehler, N., Reynolds, E., & Schapiro, S. J. (2005b). The distribution and development of handedness for manual gestures in captive chimpanzees (*Pan troglodytes*). *Psychological Science, 16,* 487–493.

Horiuchi, Y., Arai, M., & Niizato, K. (2006). A polymorphism in the PDLIM5 gene associated with gene expression and schizophrenia. *Biological Psychiatry, 59,* 434–439.

Horner, V., & Whiten, A. (2005). Imitation and emulation switching in chimpanzees (*Pan troglodytes*) and children (*Homo sapiens*). *Animal Cognition, 8,* 164–181.

Horney, K. (1937). *The neurotic personality of our time.* New York: Norton.

Horstmann, G. (2003). What do facial expressions convey: Feeling states, behavioral intentions, or action requests? *Emotion, 3,* 150–166.

Hosoda, M., Stone, R. E., & Coats, G. (2003). The effects of physical attractiveness on job-related outcomes: A meta-analysis of experimental studies. *Personnel Psychology, 56,* 431–462.

Howard, R. C. (1999). Treatment of anxiety disorders: Does specialty training help? *Professional Psychology: Research & Practice, 30,* 470–473.

Howe, M. L. (2003). Memories from the cradle. *Current Directions in Psychological Science, 12,* 62–65.

Howe, M. L., & Courage, M. (1993). On resolving the enigma of infantile amnesia. *Psychological Bulletin, 113,* 305–326.

Hsu, L. K. (1996). Epidemiology of the eating disorder. *Psychiatric Clinics of North America, 19*(4), 681–700.

Huang, T. (1998, February 3). Weathering the storms. *Charlotte Observer,* pp. 1–2E.

Hubel, D. H. (1963). The visual cortex of the brain. *Scientific American, 209*(5), 54–62.

Hubel, D. H., & Wiesel, T. N. (1959). Receptive fields of single neurons in the cat's striate cortex. *Journal of Physiology, 148,* 574–591.

Hubel, D. H., & Wiesel, T. N. (1979). Brain mechanisms of vision. *Scientific American, 241*(3), 150–162.

Hudson, J. A., & Sheffield, E. G. (1998). Deja vu all over again: Effects of reenactment on toddlers' event memory. *Child Development, 69,* 51–67.

Huebner, A. M., Garrod, A., & Snarey, J. (1990). *Moral development in Tibetan Buddhist monks: A cross-cultural study of adolescents and young adults in Nepal.* Paper presented at the meeting of the Society for Research in Adolescence, Atlanta, GA.

Hulin, C. L., & Judge, T. A. (2003). Job attitudes. In W. C. Borman, D. R. Ilgen, & R. J. Klimoski (Eds.), *Handbook of psychology*: Vol. 12, Industrial and organizational psychology (pp. 255–276). Hoboken, NJ: Wiley.

Huffman, C. J., Matthews, T. D., & Gagne, P. E. (2001). The role of part-set cuing in the recall of chess positions: Influence of chunking in memory. *North American Journal of Psychology, 3,* 535–542.

Hughes, R. L., Ginnett, R. C., & Curphy, G. J. (1998). Contingency theories of leadership. In G. R. Hickman (Ed.), *Leading organizations: Perspectives for a new era* (pp. 141–157). Thousand Oaks, CA: Sage.

Huizink, A. C., Mulder, E. J. H., & Buitelaar, J. K. (2004). Prenatal stress and risks of psychopathology: Specific effects or induction of general susceptibility? *Psychological Bulletin, 130,* 115–142.

Huizink, A. C., Robles, de M., Pascale, G., Mulder, E. J. H., Visser, G. H. A., & Buitelaar, J. K. (2002). Psychological measures of prenatal stress as predictors of infant temperament. *Journal of the American Academy of Child and Adolescent Psychiatry, 41,* 1078–1085.

Human Rights Watch, (2003). *Iraq: Impending inter-ethnic violence in Kirkuk.* New York, NY. Retrieved September 6, 2003 at http://hrw.org/english/docs/2003/03/28/iraq5450.htm

Hunt, M. (1994). *The story of psychology.* New York: Anchor/Random House.

Hunt, R. R., & Ellis, H. (2003). *Fundamentals of cognitive psychology.* New York: McGraw-Hill.

Huprich, S. K., & Keaschuk, R. A. (2006). Psychodynamic psychotherapy. In F. Andrasik, (Ed.), *Comprehensive handbook of personality and psychopathology: Adult Psychopathology* (Vol. 2, pp. 469–486). Hoboken, NJ: John Wiley & Sons.

Hussong, A. M. (2003). Further refining the stress-coping model of alcohol involvement. *Addictive Behaviors, 28,* 1515–1522.

Hutchison, K. E., Stallings, M., McGeary, J., & Bryan, A. (2004). Population stratification in the candidate gene study: Fatal threat or red herring? *Psychological Bulletin, 130,* 66–79.

Hutschemaekers, G. J. M., & van de Vijver, F. J. R. (1989). Economic recessions and neurotic problems: The Netherlands 1930–1985. In R. Veenhoven & A. Hagenaars (Eds.), *Did the crisis really hurt? Effects of the 1980–1982 economic recession on satisfaction, mental health and mortality.* Rotterdam: Universitaire Pers Rotterdam.

Hutsler, J. J. (2003). The specialized structure of human language cortex: Pyramidal cell size asymmetries within auditory and language-associated regions of the temporal lobes. *Brain and Language, 86,* 226–242.

Huttenlocher, P. R. (1999) Dendritic synaptic development in human cerebral cortex: Time course and critical periods. *Developmental Neuropsychology, 16,* 347–349.

Huttenlocher, P. R. (2002a). Morphometric study of human cerebral cortex development. In M. H. Johnson, Y. Munakata, & R. O. Gilmore (Eds.), *Brain development and cognition: A reader* (2nd ed., pp. 117–128). Malden, MA: Blackwell.

Huttenlocher, P. R. (2002b). *Neural plasticity: The effects of environment on the development of the cerebral cortex.* Cambridge, MA: Harvard Univ. Press.

Hyde, J. S. (1984). Children's understanding of sexist language. *Developmental Psychology, 20,* 697–706.

Hyde, J. S. (1986). Gender differences in aggression. In. J. S. Hyde, & M. C. Linn (Eds.), *The psychology of gender differences: Advances through meta-analysis* (pp. 51–66). Baltimore: Johns Hopkins Univ. Press.

Hyde, J. S. (2005a). The gender similarities hypothesis. *American Psychologist, 60*, 581–592.

Hyde, J. S. (2005b). The genetics of sexual orientation. In J. S. Hyde (Ed.) *Biological substrates of human sexuality* (pp. 9–20). Washington, DC: American Psychological Assoc.

Hyde, J. S., Fennema, E., & Lamon, S. J. (1990). Gender differences in mathematics performance: A meta-analysis. *Psychological Bulletin, 107*, 139–155.

Hyde, J. S., & Linn, M. C. (1988). Gender differences in verbal ability: A meta-analysis. *Psychological Bulletin, 104*, 53–69.

Hyde, J. S., & Mezulis, A. H. (2002). Gender differences research: Issues and critique. In J. Worrell (Ed.), *Encyclopedia of women and gender*. San Diego: Academic Press.

Hyman, I. E., Husband, T. H., & Billings, F. J. (1995). False memories of childhood experiences. *Applied Cognitive Psychology, 9*, 181–197.

Hymel, S., Vaillancourt, T., McDougall, P., & Renshaw, P. D. (2002). Peer acceptance and rejection in childhood. In P. K. Smith & C. H. Hart (Eds.), *Blackwell handbook of childhood social development* (pp. 265–284). Malden, MA: Blackwell.

Iacobucci, D., & McGill, A. L. (1990). Analysis of attribution data: Theory testing and effects estimation. *Journal of Personality and Social Psychology, 59*, 426–441.

Impens, A. J. (2005). Bereavement related mortality among older adults. *Dissertation Abstracts International: Section B: The Sciences and Engineering, 66*, 846.

Imrie, R. (1999, September 3). $850,000 awarded in repressed-memory case. *Charlotte Observer*, p. 8A.

Inaba, A., Thoits, P. A., Ueno, K., Gove, W. R., Evenson, R. J., & Sloan, M. (2005). Depression in the United States and Japan: Gender, marital status, and SES patterns. *Social Science & Medicine, 61*, 2280–2292.

Inciardi, J. A., & Harrison, L. D. (1998). *Heroin in the age of crack cocaine*. Thousand Oaks, CA: Sage.

Inciardi, J. A., Surratt, H. L., & Saum, C. A. (1997). *Cocaine-exposed infants: Social, legal, and public health issues*. Thousand Oaks, CA: Sage.

Inhoff, A. W., Connine, C., Eiter, B., Radach, R., & Heller, D. (2004). Phonological representation of words in working memory during sentence reading. *Psychonomic Bulletin & Review, 11*, 320–325.

Irwin, M. (2002). Psychoneuroimmunology of depression: Clinical implications. *Brain, Behavior and Immunity, 16*, 1–16.

Irwin, M. R., Cole, J. C., & Nicassio, P. M. (2006). Comparative meta-analysis of behavioral interventions for insomnia and their efficacy in middle-aged adults and in older adults 55+ years of age. *Health Psychology, 25*, 3–14.

Ito, K. (2002). Additivity of heuristic and systematic processing persuasion: Effects of source credibility, argument quality, and issue involvement. *Japanese Journal of Experimental Social Psychology, 41*, 137–146.

Iwamasa, G. Y., & Smith, S. K. (1996). Ethnic diversity in behavioral psychology: A review of the literature. *Behavioral Modification, 20*, 45–59.

Izard, C. E. (1971). *The face of emotion*. New York: Appleton-Century-Crofts.

Izard, C. E. (1980). Cross-cultural perspectives on emotion and emotion communication. In H. C. Triandis & W. J. Lonner (Eds.), *Handbook of cross-cultural psychology* (Vol. 3, pp. 185–220). Boston: Allyn & Bacon.

Izard, C. E. (1992). Basic emotions, relations among emotions, and emotion-cognition relations. *Psychological Review, 99*, 561–565.

Izard, C. E. (1994). Innate and universal facial expressions: Evidence from developmental and cross-cultural research. *Psychological Bulletin, 115*, 288–299.

Jaakkola, K., Fellner, W., Erb, L., Rodriguez, M., & Guarino, E. (2005). Understanding of the concept of numerically 'less' by bottlenose dolphins (*Tursiops truncatus*). *Journal of Comparative Psychology, 119*, 296–303.

Jaccard, J., & Blanton, H. (2005). The origins and structure of behavior: Conceptualizing behavior in attitude research. In D. Albarracín, B. T. Johnson, & M. P. Zanna (Eds.), *The handbook of attitudes* (pp. 125–171). Mahwah, NJ: Erlbaum.

Jacks, J. Z., & Cameron, K. A. (2003). Strategies for resisting persuasion. *Basic and Applied Social Psychology, 25*, 145–161.

Jackson, D. C., Mueller, C. J., Dolski, I., Dalton, K. M., Nitschke, J. B., Urry, H. L., et al. (2003). Now you feel it, now you don't: Frontal brain electrical asymmetry and individual differences in emotion regulation. *Psychological Science, 14*, 612–617.

Jackson, L. A., Hunter, J. E., & Hodge, C. N. (1995). Physical attractiveness and intellectual competence: A meta-analytic review. *Social Psychology Quarterly, 58*, 108–122.

Jackson, O. (2004). Episodic memory in the brain: Association, recognition, and prediction. *Dissertation Abstracts International: Section B: The Sciences and Engineering, 64*, 4647.

Jacobi, C., Hayward, C., de Zwaan, M., Kraemer, H. C., & Agras, W. S. (2004). Coming to terms with risk factors for eating disorders: Application of risk terminology and suggestions for a general taxonomy. *Psychological Bulletin, 130*, 19–65.

Jacobs, J. E., Lanza, S., Osgood, D. W., Eccles, J. S., & Wigfield, A. (2002). Changes in children's self-competence and values: Gender and domain differences across grades one through twelve. *Child Development, 73*, 509–527.

Jacobs, W. J., & Nadel, L. (1998). Neurobiology of reconstructed memory. *Psychology, Public Policy, & Law, 4*, 1110–1134.

Jacobsen, P. B., Bovbjerg, D. H., Schwartz, M. D., & Andrykowski, M. A. (1994). Formation of food aversions in patients receiving repeated infusions of chemotherapy. *Behaviour Research & Therapy, 38*, 739–748.

Jacobson, K. (1999, November). *In search of a "normal" student: Six months in a British classroom*. Paper presented at the annual meeting of the American Anthropological Association, Chicago, IL.

Jacobson, N. S., & Christensen, A. (1996). Studying the effectiveness of psychotherapy: How well can clinical trials do the job? *American Psychologist, 51*, 1031–1039.

Jain, S., & Posavac, S. S. (2001). Prepurchase attribute verifiability, source credibility, and persuasion. *Journal of Consumer Psychology, 11*, 169–180.

James, L., & Nahl, D. (2000). *Road rage and aggressive driving: Steering clear of highway warfare*. Amherst, NY: Prometheus.

James, L. C., Folen, R. A., & Earles, J. (2001). Behavioral telehealth applications in the treatment of obese soldiers. A feasibility project and a report on preliminary findings. *Military Psychology, 13*, 177–186.

James, R. K., & Gilliland, B. E. (2001). *Crisis intervention strategies* (4th ed.). Pacific Grove, CA: Brooks/Cole.

James, W. (1890). *The principles of psychology*. New York: Holt.

Jamison, R. N., & Virts, K. L. (1990). The influence of family support on chronic pain. *Behaviour Research and Therapy, 28*, 283–287.

Jang, K. L., Livesley, W. J., Angleitner, A., Riemann, R., & Vernon, P. A. (2002). Genetic and environmental influences on the convariance of facets defining the domains of the five-factor model of personality. *Personality and Individual Differences, 33*, 83–101.

Jang, K. L., Livesley, W. J., McCrae, R. R., Angleitner, A., & Riemann, R. (1998). Heritability of facet-level traits in a cross-cultural twin sample: Support for a hierarchical model of personality. *Journal of Personality and Social Psychology, 74*, 1556–1565.

Jang, K. L., Livesley, W. J., & Vernon, P. A. (1996). Heritability of the Big Five personality dimensions and their facets: A twin study. *Journal of Personality, 64*, 577–591.

Janis, I. L. (1982). *Groupthink: Psychological studies of policy decisions and fiascoes* (2nd ed.). Boston: Houghton Mifflin.

Janis, I. L. (1989). *Crucial decisions: Leadership in policymaking and crisis management*. New York: Free Press.

Janofsky, M. (1994, December 13). Survey reports more drug use by teenagers. *New York Times*, p. A1.

Janos, P. M., & Robinson, N. M. (1985). Psychosocial development in intellectually gifted children. In F. D. Horowitz & M. O'Brien (Eds.), *Gifted and talented: Developmental perspectives* (pp. 149–195). Washington, DC: American Psychological Assoc.

Jansen, P. G. W., & Stoop, B. A. M. (2001). The dynamics of assessment center validity: Results of a 7-year study. *Journal of Applied Psychology, 86*, 741–753.

Janssen, S. M. J., Chessa, A. G., & Murre, J. M. J. (2005). The reminiscence bump in autobiographical memory: Effects of age, gender, education, and culture. *Memory, 13*, 658–668.

Javitt, D. C., & Coyle, J. T. (2004). Decoding schizophrenia. *Scientific American, 290*(1), 48–55.

Jawahar, I. M. (2001). Attitudes, self-monitoring, and appraisal behaviors. *Journal of Applied Psychology, 86*, 875–883.

Jaycox, L. H., Zoellner, L., & Foa, E. B. (2002). Cognitive-behavior therapy for PTSD in rape survivors. *Journal of Clinical Psychology, 58*, 891–906.

Jemmott, J. B., III, Jemmott, L. S., Fong, G. T., & McCaffree, K. (2002). Reducing HIC risk-associated sexual behavior among African-American adolescents: Testing the generality of intervention effects. *American Journal of Community Psychology, 27*, 161–187.

Jenkins, L. (2000). *Biolinguistics*. New York: Cambridge Univ. Press.

Jex, S. M., Adams, G. A., & Bachrach, D. G. (2003). The impact of situational constraints, role stressors, and commitment on employee altruism. *Journal of Occupational Health Psychology, 8*, 171–180.

Johansson, M., & Arlinger, S. D. (2003). Prevalence of hearing impairment in a population in Sweden. *International Journal of Audiology, 42*, 18–28.

Johnson, A. (2003). Procedural memory and skill acquisition. In A. F. Healy & R. W. Proctor (Eds.), *Handbook of Psychology: Vol. 4, Experimental Psychology*, (pp. 499–523). New York: John Wiley & Sons.

Johnson, C. (2002). Obesity, weight management, and self-esteem. In T. A. Wadden & A. J. Stunkard, *Handbook of obesity treatment* (pp. 480–493). New York: Guilford.

Johnson, D. M., & Erneling, C. A. (Eds.). (1997). *The future of the cognitive revolution*. New York: Oxford Univ. Press.

Johnson, J. L., Kalaw, C., Lovato, C. Y., Baillie, L., & Chambers, N. A. (2004). Crossing the line: Adolescents' experiences of controlling their tobacco use. *Qualitative Health Research, 14*, 1276–1291.

Johnson, P. J. (2003). Obesity is America's greatest threat, Surgeon General says. *Orlando Sentinel: Knight Ridder News Features*. Retrieved June 6, 2003, from http://www.defeatdiabetes.org/Articles/obesity2030123.htm

Johnson, S. L. (2003). *Therapist's guide to substance abuse intervention*. San Diego, CA: Academic Press.

Johnson, S. M. (2003). Couples therapy research: Status and directions. In G. P. Sholevar (Ed.), *Textbook of family and couples therapy: Clinical applications* (pp. 797–814). Washington, DC: American Psychiatric Publishing.

Johnson, W., Bouchard, T. J., Jr., Segal, N. L., & Samuel, J. (2005). General intelligence and reading performance in adults: Is the genetic factor structure the same as for children? *Personality and Individual Differences, 38*, 1413–1428.

Johnson, W., & Krueger, R. F. (2004). Genetic and environmental structure of adjectives describing the domains of the Big Five model of personality: A nationwide US twin study. *Journal of Research in Personality, 38*, 448–472.

Johnston, C., & Ohan, J. L. (2005). The importance of parental attributions in families of children with attention-deficit/hyperactivity and disruptive behavior disorders. *Clinical Child and Family Psychology Review, 8*, 167–182.

Johnston, L. D., O'Malley, P. M., Bachman, J. G., & Schulenberg, J. E. (2005). Monitoring the Future national results on adolescent drug use: Overview of key findings, 2004. (NIH Publication No. 05-5726). Bethesda, MD: National Institute on Drug Abuse. Retrieved March 12, 2006 from http://www.drugabuse.gov/PDF/overview2004.pdf

Jonas, E., Schimel, J., Greenberg, J., & Pyszczynski, T. (2002). The Scrooge Effect: Evidence that mortality salience increases prosocial attitudes and behavior. *Personality and Social Psychology Bulletin, 28*, 1342–1353.

Jones, C. J., & Meredith, W. (2000). Developmental paths of psychological health from early adolescence to later adulthood. *Psychology & Aging, 15*, 351–360.

Jones, L. W., Sinclair, R. C., & Courneya, K. S. (2003). The effects of source credibility and message framing on exercise intentions, behaviors and attitudes: An integration of the elaboration likelihood model and prospect theory. *Journal of Applied Social Psychology, 33*, 179–196.

Jones, M. C. (1924). Elimination of children's fears. *Journal of Experimental Psychology, 7*, 381–390.

Jonides, J., Lacey, S. C., & Nee, D. E. (2005). Processes of working memory in mind and brain. *Current Directions in Psychological Science, 14*, 2–5.

Joseph, S., Linley, P. A., & Maltby, J. (2006). Editorial: Positive psychology, religion, and spirituality. *Mental Health, Religion & Culture, 9*, 209–212.

Jost, J. T., & Sidanius, J. (2004). The authoritarian personality and the organization of attitudes. In R. Brown (Ed.), *Political psychology: Key readings* (pp. 39–68). New York: Psychology Press.

Judge, T. A., & Bono, J. E. (2000). Five-factor model of personality and transformational leadership. *Journal of Applied Psychology, 85*, 751–765.

Judge, T. A., Thoresen, C. J., Bono, J. E., & Patton, G. K. (2001). The job satisfaction-job performance relationship: A qualitative and quantitative review. *Psychological Bulletin, 127*, 376–407.

Juliano, L. M., & Griffiths, R. R. (2004). A critical review of caffeine withdrawal: Empirical validation of symptoms and signs, incidence, severity, and associated features. *Psychopharmacology, 176*, 1–29.

Jung, H. (2006). Assessing the influence of cultural values on consumer susceptibility to social pressure for conformity: Self-image enhancing motivations vs. information searching motivation. In L. R. Kahle & C. H. Kim (Eds.), *Creating images and the psychology of marketing communication* (pp. 309–329). Mahwah, NJ: Erlbaum.

Kadotani, H., Kadotani, T., Young, T., Peppard, P. E., Finn, L., Colrain, I. M., et al. (2001). Association between apolipoprotein E C 4 and sleep-disordered breathing in adults. *Journal of the American Medical Association, 285*, 2888–2890.

Kagan, J. (1994, October 5). The realistic view of biology and behavior. *Chronicle of Higher Education*, p. A64.

Kagan, J., Arcus, D., & Snidman, N. (1993). The idea of temperament: Where do we go from here? In R. Plomin & G. E. McClearn (Eds.), *Nature, nurture, and psychology* (pp. 197–210). Washington, DC: American Psychological Assoc.

Kagan, J., Reznick, J. S., Snidman, N., Gibbons, J., & Johnson, M. O. (1988). Childhood derivatives of inhibition and lack of inhibition to the unfamiliar. *Child Development, 59*, 1580–1589.

Kagan, J., & Snidman, N. (1991). Infant predictors of inhibited and uninhibited profiles. *Psychological Science, 2*, 40–44.

Kagan, J., & Snidman, N. (2004). *The long shadow of temperament*. Cambridge, MA: Belknap/Harvard Univ. Press.

Kagitcibasi, C. (1997). Individualism and collectivism. In J. W. Berry, Y. H. Poortinga, & J. Kirpatrick (Eds.), *Person, self, and experience: Exploring pacific ethnopsychologies* (pp. 3–32). Berkeley: Univ. of California Press.

Kahneman, D., & Tversky, A. (1996). On the reality of cognitive illusions. *Psychological Review, 103*, 582–591.

Kalat, J. W. (2001). *Biological psychology* (7th ed.). Belmont, CA: Wadsworth/Thomson Learning.

Kalat, J. W. (2003). *Biological psychology* (8th ed.). Belmont, CA: Wadsworth.

Kamin, L. J. (1969). Selective association and conditioning. In N. J. Mackintosh & W. K. Honig (Eds.), *Fundamental issues in associative learning* (pp. 42–64). Halifax, Nova Scotia: Dalhousie Univ. Press.

Kaminski, M. (1999). *The team concept: A worker-centered alternative to lean production*. APA Public Interest Directorate. Retrieved December 3, 2006, from http://www.apa.org/pi/wpo/niosh/abstract22.html

Kanaya, T. (2004). Age differences in IQ trends: Unpacking the Flynn effect. *Dissertation Abstracts International: Section B: The Sciences and Engineering, Vol. 65*, 1051.

Kandel, E. R. (2001). The molecular biology of memory storage: A dialogue between genes and synapses. *Science, 294*, 1030–1038.

Karademas, E. C. (2006). Self-efficacy, social support and well-being. The mediating role of optimism. *Personality and Individual Differences, 40*, 1281–1290.

Karakashian, L. M., Walter, M. I., Christopher, A. N., & Lucas, T. (2006). Fear of negative evaluation affects helping behavior: The bystander effect revisited. *North American Journal of Psychology, 8*, 13–32.

Karch, S. B. (2006). *A brief history of cocaine* (2nd ed.) Philadelphia: Taylor & Francis.

Karmiloff-Smith, A. (2002). Elementary, my dear Watson, the clue is in the genes. Or is it? *The Psychologist, 15*, 608–611.

Karrass, J., & Braungart-Rieker, J. M. (2003). Parenting and temperament as interacting agents in early language development. *Parenting: Science and Practice, 3*, 235–259.

Kashdan, T. B., & Fincham, F. D. (2002). "Facilitating creativity by regulating curiosity": Comment. *American Psychologist, 57*, 373–374.

Kashdan, T. B., Julian, T., Merritt, K., & Uswatte, G. (2006). Social anxiety and posttraumatic stress in combat veterans: Relations to well-being and character strengths. *Behaviour Research and Therapy, 44*, 561–583.

Kashima, Y., & Triandis, H. C. (1986). The self-serving bias in attributions as a coping strategy: A cross-cultural study. *Journal of Cross-Cultural Psychology, 17*, 83–98.

Kass, S. (1999, September). Employees perceive women as better managers than men, finds five-year study. *APA Monitor*, p. 6.

Kassin, S. M., Tubb, V. A., Hosch, H. M., & Memon, A. (2001). On the 'general acceptance' of eyewitness testimony research: a new survey of the experts. *American Psychologist, 50*, 405–416.

Kathuria, S., Gaetani, S., Fegley, D., Valino, F., Duranti, A., Tontini, A., et al. (2003). Modulation of anxiety through blockade of anadamide hydrolysis. *Nature Medicine, 9*, 76–81.

Kato, K., & Pedersen, N. L. (2005). Personality and coping: A study of twins reared apart and twins reared together. *Behavior Genetics, 35*, 147–158.

Kato, T. (2001). Molecular genetics of bipolar disorder. *Neuroscience Research, 40*, 105–113.

Katz, R., & McGuffin, P. (1993). The genetics of affective disorders. In D. Fowles (Ed.), *Progress in experimental personality and psychopathology research*. New York: Springer.

Katz, S. (2003). Physical appearance: The importance of being beautiful. In J. M. Henslin (Ed.), *Down to earth sociology: Introductory readings* (12th ed., pp. 313–320). New York: Free Press.

Kavale, K. A. (2002). Mainstreaming to full inclusion: From orthogenesis to pathogenesis of an idea. *International Journal of Disability, Development and Education, 49*, 201–214.

Kawai, N., & Matsuzawa, T. (2000). Cognition: Numerical memory span in a chimpanzee. *Nature, 403*, 39–40.

Keel, P. K., Heatherton, T. F., Dorer, D. J., Joiner, T. E., & Zalta, A. K. (2006). Point prevalence of bulimia nervosa in 1982, 1992, and 2002. *Psychological Medicine, 36*, 119–127.

Keel, P. K., & Klump, K. L. (2003). Are eating disorders culture-bound syndromes? Implications for conceptualizing their etiology. *Psychological Bulletin, 129*, 747–769.

Keilhoff, G., Bernstein, H. G., Becker, A., Grecksch, G., & Wolf, G. (2004). Increased neurogenesis in a rat ketamine model of schizophrenia. *Biological Psychiatry, 56*, 317–322.

Keitner, G. I., Archambault, R., Ryan, C. E., & Miller, I. W., (2003). Family therapy and chronic depression. *Journal of Clinical Psychology, 59*, 873–884.

Kelemen, W. L., & Creeley, C. E. (2003). State-dependent memory effects using caffeine and placebo do not extend to metamemory. *Journal of General Psychology, 130*, 70–86.

Keller, A., & Vosshall, L. B. (2004). A psychophysical test of the vibration theory of olfaction. *Nature Neuroscience, 7*, 337–338.

Keller, M. B., McCullough, J. P., Klein, D. N., Arnow, B., Dunner, D. L., Gelenberg, A. J., et al. (2000). A comparison of Nefazodone, the cognitive behavioral-analysis system of psychotherapy, and their combination for the treatment of chronic depression. *New England Journal of Medicine, 342*, 1462–1470.

Keller, R. T. (2006). Transformational leadership, initiating structure, and substitutes for leadership: A longitudinal study of research and development project team performance. *Journal of Applied Psychology, 91*, 202–210.

Kelley, H. H. (1967). Attribution theory in social psychology. In D. Levine (Ed.), *Nebraska Symposium on Motivation* (Vol. 15, pp. 192–238). Lincoln: Univ. of Nebraska Press.

Kelley, H. H. (1973). The process of causal attribution. *American Psychologist, 28*, 107–128.

Kelsoe, J. (2004). Genomics and the Human Genome Project: Implications for psychiatry. *International Review of Psychiatry 16*, 294–300.

Kempt, H. (2000). Culture assimilator training for students with limited English proficiency at the University of Mississippi intensive English program. *Dissertation Abstracts International Section A: Humanities and Social Sciences, 60*, 2773.

Kendall-Tackett, K. A. (2001). *The hidden feelings of motherhood: Coping with stress, depression, and burnout*. Oakland, CA: New Harbinger.

Kendler, K. S., Myers, J. M., O'Neill, F. A., Martin, R., Murphy, B., MacLean, C. J., et al. (2000). Clinical features of schizophrenia and linkage to chromosomes 5q, 6p, 8p, and 10p in the Irish study of high-density schizophrenia families. *American Journal of Psychiatry, 157*, 402–408.

Kendler, K. S., Thornton, L. M., & Pedersen, N. L. (2000). Tobacco consumption in Swedish twins reared apart and reared together. *Archives of General Psychiatry, 57*, 886–892.

Keppel, B. (2002). Kenneth B. Clark in patterns of American culture. *American Psychologist, 57*, 29–37.

Kernis, M. H., & Wheeler, L. (1981). Beautiful friends and ugly strangers: Radiation and contrast effects in perception of same-sex pairs. *Personality and Social Psychology Bulletin, 7*, 617–620.

Kessler, R. C., Berglund, P., Demler, O., Jin, R., Koretz, D., Merikangas, K. R., et al. (2003). The epidemiology of major depressive disorder: Results from the National Comorbidity Survey Replication (NCS-R). *Journal of the American Medical Association, 289*, 3095–3105.

Kessler, R. C., Price, R. H., & Wortman, C. B. (1985). Social factors in psychopathology: Stress, social support, and coping processes. *Annual Review of Psychology, 36*, 531–572.

Keverne, E. B. (2004). Importance of olfactory and vomeronasal systems for male sexual function. *Physiology & Behavior, 83*, 177–187.

Kiecolt-Glaser, J. K., Bane, C., Glaser, R., & Malarkey, W. B. (2003). Love, marriage, and divorce: Newlyweds' stress hormones foreshadow relationship changes. *Journal of Consulting and Clinical Psychology, 71*, 176–188.

Kiecolt-Glaser, J. K., & Glaser, R. (2002). Depression and immune function: Central pathways to morbidity and mortality. *Journal of Psychosomatic Research, 53*, 873–876.

Kiecolt-Glaser, J. K., Malarkey, W. B., Chee, M., Newton, T., & Cacioppo, J. T. (1993). Negative behavior during marital conflict is associated with immunological down-regulation. *Psychosomatic Medicine, 55*, 395–409.

Kiesler, C. A. (1982a). Mental hospitals and alternative care: Noninstitutionalization as a potential public policy for mental patients. *American Psychologist, 37*, 349–360.

Kiesler, C. A. (1982b). Public and professional myths about mental hospitalization: An empirical reassessment of policy-related beliefs. *American Psychologist, 37*, 1323–1339.

Kiesler, C. A., & Simpkins, C. G. (1993). *The unnoticed majority in psychiatric inpatient care*. New York: Plenum.

Kihara, T., & Shimohama, S. (2004). Alzheimer's disease and acetylcholine receptors. *Acta Neurobiologiae Experimentalis, 64*, 99–105.

Kihlström, J. F. (1999). The psychological unconscious. In L. A. Pervin & O. P. John (Eds.), *Handbook of personality: Theory and research* (2nd ed., pp. 424–442). New York: Guilford.

Kihlström, J. F. (2005). Is hypnosis an altered state of consciousness or what?: Comment. *Contemporary Hypnosis, 22*, 34–38.

Kihlström, J. F., Mulvaney, S., Tobias, B. A., & Tobis, I. P. (2000). The emotional unconscious. In E. Eich, J. F. Kihlstrom, G. H. Bower, J. P. Forgas, & P. Niedenthal (Eds.), *Cognition and emotion* (pp. 30–86). New York: Oxford Univ. Press.

Kileny, P. R., Zwolan, T. A., & Ashbaugh, C. (2001). The influence of age at implantation on performance with a cochlear implant in children. *Otology and Neurotology, 22*, 42–46.

Kim, S. A., Kim, J. W., Song, J. Y., Park, S., Lee, H. J., & Chung, J. H. (2004). Association of polymorphisms in nicotinic acetylcholine receptor α-sub-4 sub-unit gene (CHRNA4), μ-opioid receptor gene (OPRM1), and ethanol-metabolizing enzyme genes with alcoholism in Korean patients. *Alcohol, 34*, 115–120.

Kimura, D., & Hampson, E. (1994). Cognitive pattern in men and women is influenced by fluctuations in sex hormones. *Current Directions in Psychological Science, 3*, 57–61.

King, J. E., Weiss, A., & Farmer, K. H. (2005). A chimpanzee (*Pan troglodytes*) analogue of cross-national generalization of personality structure: Zoological parks and an African sanctuary. *Journal of Personality, 73*, 389–410.

Kingstone, A., Enns, J. T., Mangun, G. R., & Gazzaniga, M. S. (1995). Right-hemisphere memory superiority: Studies of a split-brain patient. *Psychological Science, 6*, 118–121.

Kinnunen, L. H., Moltz, H., Metz, J., & Cooper, M. (2004). Differential brain activation in exclusively homosexual and heterosexual men produced by the selective serotonin reuptake inhibitor, fluoxetine. *Brain Research, 1024*, 251–254.

Kinsey, A. C., Pomeroy, W. B., & Martin, C. E. (1948). *Sexual behavior in the human male*. Philadelphia: Saunders.

Kinsey, A. C., Pomeroy, W. B., Martin, C. E., & Gebhard, P. H. (1953). *Sexual behavior in the human female*. Philadelphia: Saunders.

Kinsley, C., & Lambert, K. G. (2006). The maternal brain. *Scientific American, 294*(1), 72–79.

Kirilly, E., Benko, A., Ferrington, L., Ando, R. D., Kelly, P. A. T., & Bagdy, G. (2006). Acute and long-term effects of a single dose of MDMA on aggression in Dark Agouti rats. *International Journal of Neuropsychopharmacology, 9*, 63–76.

Kirsch, I., & Braffman, W. (2001). Imaginative suggestibility and hypnotizability. *Current Directions in Psychological Science, 10*, 57–60.

Kirschenbaum, H., & Jourdan, A. (2005). The current status of Carl Rogers and the person-centered approach. *Psychotherapy: Theory, Research, Practice, Training, 42*, 37–51.

Kisilevsky, B., Hains, S., Lee, K., Xie, X., Huang, H., Ye, H., et al. (2003). Effects of experience on fetal voice recognition. *Psychological Science, 14*, 220–224.

Kiss, S. (2001). The formation of the object concept during ontogeny. *Pszichológia: Az MTA Pszichológiai Intézetenek folyóirata, 21*, 249–267.

Kissell, J. L. (2002). The human genome project: A Pandora's Box. *Journal of Systemic Therapies, 21*, 19–29.

Kitayama, S., Duffy, S., Kawamura, T., & Larsen, J. T. (2003). Perceiving an object and its context in different cultures: A cultural look at New Look. *Psychological Science, 14*, 201–206.

Kite, M. E., Russo, N. F., Brehm, S. S., Fouad, N. A., Hall, C. C., Hyde, J. S., et al. (2001). Women psychologists in academe. *American Psychologist, 56*, 1080–1098.

Kleim, J. A., Vij, K., Ballard, D. H., & Greenough, W. T. (1997). Learning-dependent synaptic modifications in the cerebellar cortex of the adult rat persist for at least four weeks. *Journal of Neuroscience, 17*, 717–721.

Klein, D. N., Schwartz, J. E., Santiago, N. J., Vivian, D., Vocisano, C., Castonguay, L. G., et al. (2003). Therapeutic alliance in depression treatment: Controlling for prior change and patient characteristics. *Journal of Consulting and Clinical Psychology, 71*, 997–1006.

Klein, G. S. (1951). The personal world through perception. In R. R. Blake & G. V. Ramsey (Eds.), *Perception: An approach to personality* (pp. 328–355). New York: Ronald Press.

Klein, O., Snyder, M., & Livingston, R. W. (2004). Prejudice on the stage: Self-monitoring and the public expression of group attitudes. *British Journal of Social Psychology, 43*, 299–314.

Klerman, G. L., Weissman, M. M., Markowitz, J. C., Glick, I., Wilner, P. J., Mason, B., et al. (1994). Medication and psychotherapy. In A. E. Bergin & S. L. Garfield (Eds.), *Handbook of psychotherapy and behavior change* (4th ed., pp. 734–782). New York: Wiley.

Kling, K. C., Hyde, J. S., Showers, C. J., & Buswell, B. N. (1999). Gender differences in self-esteem: A meta-analysis. *Psychological Bulletin, 125*, 470–500.

Klose, M., & Jacobi, F. (2004). Can gender differences in the prevalence of mental disorders be explained by sociodemographic factors? *Archives of Women's Mental Health, 7*, 133–148.

Kluckhohn, C. (1949). *Mirror for man: The relation of anthropology to modern life.* New York: Whittlesey House.

Klump, K. L., McGue, M., & Iacono, W. G. (2002). Genetic relationships between personality and eating attitudes and behaviors. *Journal of Abnormal Psychology, 111*, 380–389.

Knecht, S., Dräger, B., Deppe, M., Bobe, L., Lohmann, H., & Flöel, A., et al. (2000). Handedness and hemispheric language dominance in healthy humans. *Brain: A Journal of Neurology, 123*, 2512–2518.

Knickmeyer, R. C., Wheelwright, S., Taylor, K., Raggatt, P., Hackett, G., & Baron-Cohen, S. (2005). Gender-typed play and amniotic testosterone. *Developmental Psychology, 41*, 517–528.

Knight, G. P., Fabes, R. A., & Higgins, D. A. (1996). Concerns about drawing causal inferences from meta-analyses: An example in the study of gender differences in aggression. *Psychological Bulletin, 119*(3), 410–421.

Knight, J. A. (2000). The biochemistry of aging. *Advances in Clinical Chemistry, 35*, 1–62.

Kobasa, S. C. (1979). Stressful life events, personality, and health: An inquiry into hardiness. *Journal of Personality and Social Psychology, 37*, 1–11.

Kochanek, K. D., & Smith, B. L. (2004). Deaths: Preliminary data for 2002. *National vital statistics report, 52*(13), 1–7. Retrieved May 10, 2006 from: http://www.cdc.gov/nchs/data/nvsr/nvsr52/nvsr52_13.pdf

Koenig, H. G., McCullough, M. E., & Larson, D. B. (2000). *Handbook of religion and health.* New York: Oxford Univ. Press.

Koh, P. O., Bergson, C., Undie, A., S., Goldman, R., Patricia, S., & Lidow, M. S. (2003). Up regulation of D1 dopamine receptor interacting protein, calcyon, in patients with schizophrenia. *Archives of General Psychiatry, 60*, 311–319.

Kohlberg, L. (1969). Stage and sequence: The cognitive–developmental approach to socialization. In D. A. Goslin (Ed.), *Handbook of socialization theory and research.* Chicago: Rand McNally.

Kohlberg, L. (1979). *The meaning and measurement of moral development* (Clark Lectures). Worcester, MA: Clark Univ.

Kohlberg, L. (1981). *The philosophy of moral development* (Vol. 1). San Francisco: Harper & Row.

Kohn, A. (1993). *Punished by rewards.* Boston: Houghton Mifflin.

Kokaia, Z., & Lindvall, O. (2003). Neurogenesis after ischaemic brain insults. *Current Opinion in Neurobiology, 13*,. 127–132.

Kolb, B., Gibb, R., & Robinson, T. E. (2003). Brain plasticity and behavior. *Current Directions in Psychological Science, 12*, 1–5.

Kolb, H. (2003). How the retina works. *American Scientist, 91*, 28–35.

Kolchakian, M. R., & Hill, C. E. (2002). Dream interpretation with heterosexual dating couples. *Dreaming: Journal of the Association For the Study of Dreams, 12*, 1–16.

Komaki, J. L. (2003). Reinforcement theory at work: Enhancing and explaining what employees do. In L. W. Porter, G. A. Bigley, & R. M Steers (Eds.), *Motivation and work behavior* (7th ed., pp. 95–112). Boston: McGraw-Hill Irwin.

Komiya, N., Good, G. E., & Sherrod, N. B. (2000). Emotional openness as a predictor of college students' attitudes toward seeking psychological help. *Journal of Counseling Psychology, 47*, 138–143.

Kong, J., Gollub, R. L., Rosman, I. S., Webb, J. M., Vangel, M. G., Kirsch, I., et al. (2006). Brain activity associated with expectancy-enhanced placebo analgesia as measured. *The Journal of Neuroscience, 26*, 381–388.

Konrad, K., Neufang, S., Hanisch, C., Fink, G. R., & Herpertz-Dahlmann, B. (2006). Dysfunctional attentional networks in children with attention deficit/hyperactivity disorder: Evidence from an event-related functional magnetic resonance imaging study. *Biological Psychiatry, 59*, 643–651.

Konradi, C., Eaton, M., MacDonald, M. L., Walsh, J., Benes, F. M., & Heckers, S. (2004). Molecular evidence for mitochondrial dysfunction in bipolar disorder. *Archives of General Psychiatry, 61*, 300–308.

Kop, W. J. (2005). Psychological interventions in patients with coronary heart disease. In L. C. James & R. A. Folen (Eds.), *The primary care consultant: The next frontier for psychologists in hospitals and clinics* (pp. 61–81). Washington, DC: American Psychological Assoc.

Kopelowicz, A., Liberman, R. P., & Zarate, R. (2002). Psychosocial treatments for schizophrenia. In P. E. Nathan & J. M. Gorman (Eds.), *A guide to treatments that work* (2nd ed., pp. 201–228). London: Oxford Univ. Press.

Kopta, S. M., Howard, K. I., Lowry, J. L., & Beutler, L. E. (1994). Patterns of symptomatic recovery in psychotherapy. *Journal of Consulting and Clinical Psychology, 62*, 1009–1016.

Kopta, S. M., Lueger, R. J., Saunders, S. M., & Howard, K. I. (1999). Individual psychotherapy outcome and process research: Challenges leading to greater turmoil or a positive transition? *Annual Review of Psychology, 50*, 441–469.

Koriat, A., Goldsmith, M., & Pansky, A. (2000). Toward a psychology of memory accuracy. *Annual Review of Psychology, 51*, 481–537.

Korinek, K. E. (2003). Separation individuation, risk-taking behavior, social support, and personal fable: An exploratory study of integrated understanding of early adolescence and adolescent behavior. *Dissertation Abstracts International: Section B: The Sciences and Engineering, 64*, 967.

Koss, M. P. (1990). Violence against women. *American Psychologist, 45*, 374–380.

Kosslyn, S. M. (2002). Einstein's mental images: The role visual, spatial, and motoric representations. In A. M. Galaburda, S. M. Kosslyn, & C. Yves (Eds.), *The languages of the brain* (pp. 271–287). Cambridge, MA: Harvard Univ. Press.

Kovas, Y., Harlaar, N., Petrill, S. A., & Plomin, R. (2005). "Generalist genes" and mathematics in 7-year-old twins. *Intelligence, 33*, 473–489.

Koyama, T., McHaffie, J. G., Laurienti, P. J., & Coghill, R. C. (2005). The subjective experience of pain: Where expectations become reality. *Proceedings of the National Academy of Sciences of the United States of America, 102*, 12950–12955.

Kramer, A. F., & Willis, S. L. (2002). Enhancing the cognitive vitality of older adults. *Current Directions in Psychological Science, 11*, 173–176.

Krasne, F. B., & Glanzman, D. L. (1995). What we can learn from invertebrate learning. *Annual Review of Psychology, 46*, 585–624.

Kraut, R., & Kiesler, S. (2003). The social impact of Internet use. *Psychological Science Agenda, 16* (4), 11–14.

Kraut, R., Kiesler, S., Boneva, B., Cummings, J. N., Helgeson, V., & Crawford, A. M. (2002). Internet paradox revisited. *Journal of Social Issues, 58*(1), 49–74.

Kraut, R., Patterson, M., Lundmark, V., Kiesler, S., Mukopadhyay, T., & Scherlis, W. (1998). Internet paradox: A social technology that reduces social involvement and psychological well-being? *American Psychologist, 53,* 1017–1031.

Krebs, D. L. (2003). Fictions and fact about evolutionary approaches to human behavior: Comment on Lickliter and Honeycutt (2003). *Psychological Bulletin, 129,* 842–847.

Kreiman, G., Koch, C., & Fried, I. (2000). Imagery neurons in the human brain. *Nature, 408,* 357–361.

Kringlen, E. (1981). *Stress and coronary heart disease. Twin research 3: Epidemiological and clinical studies.* New York: Alan R. Liss.

Kropp, P., Siniatchkin, M., & Gerber, W.-D. (2005). On the pathophysiology of migraine—Links for 'empirically based treatment' with neurofeedback. *Applied Psychophysiology and Biofeedback, 27,* 203–213.

Kroska, A. (2003). Investigating gender differences in the meaning of household chores and child care. *Journal of Marriage and Family, 65,* 456–473.

Krosnick, J. A. (1999). Survey research. *Annual Review of Psychology, 50,* 537–567.

Krueger, R. F., & Markon, K. E. (2002). Behavior genetic perspectives on clinical personality assessment. In J. N. Butcher (Ed.), *Clinical personality assessment: Practical approaches* (2nd ed., pp. 40–55). London: Oxford Univ. Press.

Kruglanski, A. W. (1986, August). Freeze-think and the Challenger. *Psychology Today,* pp. 48–49.

Kugler, P. (2004). Reading psychoanalysis: Freud, Rank, Ferenczi, Groddeck. *Journal of Analytical Psychology, 49,* 271–274.

Krupinski, E., Nypaver, M., Poropatich, R., Ellis, D., Safwat, R., & Sapci, H. (2002). Clinical applications in telemedicine/telehealth. *Telemedicine Journal and eHealth, 8,* 13–34.

Kruschke, J. K. (2003). Attention in learning. *Current Directions in Psychological Science, 12,* 171–175.

Krützen, M., Mann, J., Meithaus, M. R., Connor, R. C., Bejder, L., & Sherwin, W. B. (2005). Cultural transmission of tool use in bottlenose dolphins. *Proceedings of the National Academy of Sciences, 95,* 8939–8943.

Krystal, A. D., Holsinger, T., Weiner, R. D., & Coffey, C. E. (2000). Prediction of the utility of a switch from unilateral to bilateral ECT in the elderly using treatment 2 ictal EEG indices. *Journal of ECT, 16,* 327–337.

Kübler-Ross, E. (1969). *On death and dying.* New York: Macmillan.

Kübler-Ross, E. (1975). *Death: The final stage of growth.* Englewood Cliffs, NJ: Prentice Hall.

Kübler-Ross, E. (2005). *On grief and grieving.* New York: Scribner.

Kucharski, L. T., Johnsen, D., & Procell, S. (2004). The utility of the MMPI-2 infrequency psychopathology F(p) and the revised infrequency psychopathology scales in the detection of malingering. *American Journal of Forensic Psychology, 22,* 33–40.

Kudo, E., & Numazaki, M. (2003). Explicit and direct self-serving bias in Japan. Reexamination of self-serving bias for success and failure. *Journal of Cross-Cultural Psychology, 34,* 511–521.

Kuehn, B. M. (2006). Studies probe autism anatomy, genetics. *Journal of the American Medical Association, 295,* 19–20.

Kumar, C. T. S., Mohan, R., & Ranjith, G. (2006). Characteristics of high intent suicide attempters admitted to a general hospital. *Journal of Affective Disorders, 91,* 77–81.

Kumar, K. G., & Ali, M. H. (2003). Meditation—A harbinger of subjective well-being. *Journal of Personality and Clinical Studies, 19,* 93–102.

Kumkale, G. T., & Albarracín, D. (2004). The sleeper effect: A meta-analytic review. *Psychological Bulletin, 130,* 143–172.

Kuncel, N. R., Hezlett, S. A., & Ones, D. S. (2004). Academic performance, career potential, creativity, and job performance: Can one construct predict them all? *Journal of Personality and Social Psychology, 86,* 148–161.

Kunkel, D., Wilson, B. J., Linz, D., Potter, J., Donnerstein, E., Smith, S. L., et al. (1996). *The national television violence study.* Studio City, CA: Mediascope.

Kurdek, L. A. (2005). What do we know about gay and lesbian couples? *Current Directions in Psychological Science, 14,* 251–254.

Kurdek, L. A., Fine, M. A., & Sinclair, R. J. (1995). School adjustment in sixth graders: Parenting transitions, family climate, and peer norm effects. *Child Development, 66,* 430–445.

Kurtz, L. D. (2004). Support and self-help groups. In C. D. Garvin, L. M. Gutiérrez, & M. J. Galinsky (Eds.), *Handbook of social work with groups* (pp. 139–159). New York: Guilford.

Kwantes, C. T., Bergeron, S., & Kaushal, R. (2005). Applying social psychology to diversity. In F. W. Schneider, J. A. Gruman, & L. M. Coutts (Eds.), *Applied social psychology: Understanding and addressing social and practical problems* (pp. 331–354). Thousand Oaks, CA: Sage.

Kwon, S. M., & Oei, T. P. S. (2003). Cognitive change processes in a group cognitive behavior therapy of depression. *Journal of Behavior Therapy and Experimental Psychiatry, 34,* 73–85.

Lachman, M. E. (2004). Development in midlife. *Annual Review of Psychology, 55,* 305–331.

Lachman, S. J. (1984, August). *Processes in visual misperception: Illusions for highly structured stimulus material.* Paper presented at the 92nd annual convention of the American Psychological Association, Toronto, Canada.

Lachman, S. J. (1996). Processes in perception: Psychological transformations of highly structured stimulus material. *Perceptual and Motor Skills, 83,* 411–418.

Lacy, T. J., & Hughes, J. D. (2006). A systems approach to behavioral neurobiology: Integrating psychodynamics and neuroscience in a psychiatric curriculum. *Journal of the American Academy of Psychoanalysis and Dynamic Psychiatry, 34,* 43–74.

Ladd, P. (2003). *Understanding deaf culture: In search of deafhood.* Clevedon, UK: Multilingual Matters.

Laganà, L., & Sosa, G. (2004). Depression among ethnically diverse older women: The role of demographic and cognitive factors. *Educational Gerontology, 30,* 801–820.

Laird, J. (2003). Lesbian and gay families. In F. Walsh (Ed.), *Normal family processes: Growing diversity and complexity* (3rd ed., pp. 176–209). New York: Guilford.

Lal, S. (2002). Giving children security. *American Psychologist, 57,* 20–28.

LaMalfa, G., Lassi, S., Bertelli, M., Salvini, R., & Placidi, G. F. (2004). Autism and intellectual disability: A study of prevalence on a sample of the Italian population. *Journal of Intellectual Disability Research, 48,* 262–267.

Lamb, H. R., & Weinberger, L. E. (2001). *Deinstitutionalization: Promise and problems.* San Francisco: Jossey-Bass.

Lamb, J. A., Moore, J., Bailey, A., & Monaco, A. P. (2000). Autism: Recent molecular genetic advances. *Human Molecular Genetics, 9,* 861–868.

Lamberg, L. (1998). New drug for erectile dysfunction boon for many, "viagravation" for some. *JAMA: Medical News & Perspectives, 280,* 867–871

Lambert, M. J. (2001). The effectiveness of psychotherapy: What a century of research tells us about the effects of treatment. *Psychotherapeutically speaking—Updates from the Division of Psychotherapy.* Washington, DC: American Psychological Assoc.

Lambert, M. J., & Archer, A. (2006). Research findings on the effects of psychotherapy and their implications for practice. In C. D. Goodheart, A. E. Kazdin, & R. J. Sternberg (Eds.), *Evidence-based psychotherapy: Where practice and research meet* (pp. 111–130). Washington, DC: American Psychological Association.

Lambert, M. J., Shapiro, D. A., & Bergin, A. E. (1986). The effectiveness of psychotherapy. In S. L. Garfield & A. E. Bergin (Eds.), *Handbook of psychotherapy and behavior change* (3rd ed., pp. 157–212). New York: Wiley.

Lambert, W. W., Solomon, R. L., & Watson, P. D. (1949). Reinforcement and extinction as factors in size estimation. *Journal of Experimental Psychology, 39*, 637–641.

Lampl, M., Veidhuis, J. D., & Johnson, M. L. (1992, October 30). Saltation and stasis: A model of human growth. *Science, 258*, 801–803.

Landrigan, C. P. (2005). Sliding down the bell curve: Effects of 24-hour work shifts on physicians' cognition and performance." *Sleep, 28*(11),1351–1353.

Landrigan, C. P., Rothschild, J. M., Cronin, J. W., Kaushal, R., Burdick, E., Katz, J. T., et al. (2004). Effect of reducing interns' work hours on serious medical errors in intensive care units. *New England Journal of Medicine, 351*, 1838–1848.

Landy, F. J. (1987). *Psychology: The science of people.* Englewood Cliffs, NJ: Prentice Hall.

Landy, F. J., & Conte, J. M. (2004). *Work in the 21st century.* New York: McGraw-Hill.

Landy, F. J., & Trumbo, D. (1976). *A psychology of work behavior.* Homewood, IL: Dorsey.

Lane, H. Y., Liu, Y. C., Huang, C. L., Chang, Y. C., Wu, P. L., Lu, C. T., et al. (2006). Risperidone-related weight gain: Genetic and nongenetic predictors. *Journal of Clinical Psychopharmacology, 26*, 128–134.

Lane, S. D., Cherek, D. R., Lieving, L. M., & Tcheremissine, O. V. (2005). Marijuana effects on human forgetting functions. *Journal of the Experimental Analysis of Behavior, 83*, 67–83.

Lange, K., Williams, L. M., Young, A. W., Bullmore, E. T., Brammer, M. J., Williams, S. C. R., et al. (2003). Task instructions modulate neural responses to fearful facial expressions. *Biological Psychiatry, 53*, 226–232.

Lange, T., Perras, B., Fehm, H. L., & Born, J. (2003). Sleep enhances the human antibody response to hepatitis A vaccination. *Psychosomatic Medicine, 65*, 831–835.

Langens, T. A., & Schmalt, H. D. (2002). Emotional consequences of positive daydreaming: The moderating role of fear of failure. *Personality and Social Psychology Bulletin, 28*, 1725–1735.

Langlois, J. H., Kalakanis, L., Rubinstein, A. J., Larson, A., Hallam, M., & Smoot, M. (2000). Maxims of myths of beauty? A meta-analytic and theoretical review. *Psychological Bulletin, 126*, 390–423.

Langlois, J. H., Ritter, J. M., Casey, R. J., & Sawin, D. B. (1995). Infant attractiveness predicts maternal behaviors and attitudes. *Developmental Psychology, 31*, 464–472.

Lansford, J. E., Chang, L., Dodge, K. A., Malone, P. S., Oburu, P., Palmérus, K., et al. (2005). Physical discipline and children's adjustment: Cultural normativeness as a moderator. *Child Development, 76*, 1234–1246.

Lantz, M. S., Buchalter, E. N., & McBee, L. (1997). The wellness group: A novel intervention for coping with disruptive behavior in elderly nursing home residents. *Gerontologist, 37*, 551–556.

Lanza, S., & Collins, L. (2002). Pubertal timing and the onset of substance use in females during early adolescence. *Prevention Science, 3*, 69–82.

Larzelere, R. E. (2000). Child outcomes of nonabusive and customary physical punishment by parents: An updated literature review. *Clinical Child and Family Psychology Review, 3*, 199–221.

Lasiuk, G. C., & Hegadoren, K. M. (2006). Posttraumatic stress disorder Part I: Historical development of the concept. *Perspectives in Psychiatric Care, 42*, 13–20.

Latané, B., & Rodin, J. (1969). A lady in distress: Inhibiting effects of friends and strangers on bystander intervention. *Journal of Experimental Social Psychology, 5*, 189–202.

Lauer, J. C., & Lauer, R. H. (1999). *How to survive and thrive in an empty nest.* Oakland, CA: New Harbinger.

Laumann, E. O., Gagnon, J. H., Michael, R. T., & Michaels, S. (1994). *The social organization of sexuality: Sexual practices in the United States.* Chicago: Univ. of Chicago Press.

Laungani, P. (2004). Counseling and therapy in a multi-cultural setting. *Counselling Psychology Quarterly, 17*, 195–207.

Laurenceau, J. P., Barrett, L. F., & Pietromonaco, P. R. (2004). Intimacy as an interpersonal process: The importance of self-disclosure, partner disclosure, and perceived partner responsiveness in interpersonal exchanges. In H. T. Reis & C. E. Rusbult (Eds.), *Close relationships: Key readings* (pp. 199–211). Philadelphia: Taylor & Francis.

Lawrence, C. J., Lott, I., & Haier, R. J. (2005). Neurobiology of autism, mental retardation, and Down syndrome: What can we learn about intelligence? In C. Stough (Ed.), *Neurobiology of exceptionality* (pp. 125–142). New York: Kluwer/Plenum.

Layton, B., & Krikorian, R. (2002). Memory mechanisms in posttraumatic stress disorder. *Journal of Neuropsychiatry and Clinical Neurosciences, 14*, 254–261.

Lazarus, R. S. (1981, July). Little hassles can be hazardous to health. *Psychology Today*, 58–62.

Lazarus, R. S. (1991a). Cognition and motivation in emotion. *American Psychologist, 46*, 352–367.

Lazarus, R. S. (1991b). Progress on a cognitive-motivational-relational theory of emotion. *American Psychologist, 46*, 819–834.

Lazarus, R. S. (1991c). *Emotion and adaptation.* New York: Oxford Univ. Press.

Lazarus, R. S. (1993). From psychological stress to the emotions: A history of changing outlooks. *Annual Review of Psychology, 44*, 1–21.

Lazer, D. (2004). *DNA and the criminal justice system: The technology of justice.* Cambridge, MA: MIT Press.

Leahy, R. L. (2004). *Contemporary cognitive therapy: Theory, research, and practice.* New York: Guilford.

Leary, M. R., Kowalski, R. M., Smith, L., & Phillips, S. (2003). Teasing, rejection, and violence: Case studies of the school shootings. *Aggressive Behavior, 29*, 202–214.

Leary, W. E. (1990, January 25). Risk of hearing loss is growing, panel says. *New York Times*, Sec. B.

LeBoeuf, R. A., & Shafir, E. (2003). Deep thoughts and shallow frames on the susceptibility to framing effects. *Journal of Behavioral Decision Making, 16*, 77–92.

Leborgne, L., Maziere, J. C., & Andrejak, M. (2002). Oxidative stress, atherogenesis, and cardiovascular risk factors. *Arch. Mal. Coeur Vaiss, 95*, 805–814.

Lebow, J. L. (2006). Integrative couple therapy. In G. Stricker & J. Gold (Eds.), *A casebook of psychotherapy integration* (pp. 211–223). Washington, DC: American Psychological Assoc.

Leccese, A. P. (1991). *Drugs and society.* Englewood Cliffs, NJ: Prentice Hall.

Lee, K. T., Mattson, S. N., & Riley, E. P. (2004). Classifying children with heavy prenatal alcohol exposure using measures of attention. *Journal of the International Neuropsychological Society, 10,* 271–277.

Lee, S., Chan, Y. Y. L., & Hsu, L. K. G. (2003). The intermediate term outcome of Chinese patients with anorexia nervosa in Hong Kong. *American Journal of Psychiatry, 160,* 967–972.

Lee, S. J., Miller, H. A., & Moon, J. (2004). Exploring the forensic use of the emotional recognition test (ERT). *International Journal of Offender Therapy and Comparative Criminology, 48,* 644–682.

LeFever, G. B., Arcona, A. P., & Antonuccio, D. O. (2003). ADHD among American schoolchildren: Evidence of overdiagnosis and overuse of medication. *Scientific Review of Mental Health Practice, 2,* 49–60.

Leichsenring, F. (2005). Are psychodynamic and psychoanalytic therapies effective?: A review of empirical data. *International Journal of Psychoanalysis, 86,* 841–868.

Leichsenring, F., & Leibing, E. (2003). The effectiveness of psychodynamic therapy and cognitive behavior therapy in the treatment of personality disorders: A meta-analysis. *American Journal of Psychiatry, 160,* 1223–1232.

Leifer, M., Kilbane, T., & Kalick, S. (2004). Vulnerability or resilience to intergenerational sexual abuse: The role of maternal factors. *Child Maltreatment: Journal of the American Professional Society on the Abuse of Children, 9,* 78–91.

Leit, R. A., Gray, J. J., & Pope, H. G. (2002). The media's representation of the ideal male body: A cause for muscle dysmorphia? *International Journal of Eating Disorders, 31,* 334–338.

Leitenberg, H., & Henning, K. (1995). Sexual fantasy. *Psychological Bulletin, 117,* 469–496.

Lemish, D., & Rice, M. L. (1986). Television as a talking picture book: A prop for language acquisition. *Journal of Child Language, 13,* 251–274.

Lensvelt-Mulders, G., & Hettema, J. (2001). Analysis of genetic influences on the consistency and variability of the Big Five across different stressful situations. *European Journal of Personality, 15,* 355–371.

Leonardo, E. D., & Hen, R. (2006). Genetics of affective and anxiety disorders. *Annual Review of Psychology, 57,* 117–137.

Lerman, C., Caporaso, N. D., Audrain, J., Main, D., Bowman, E. D., Lockshin, B., et al. (1999). Evidence suggesting the role of specific genetic factors in cigarette smoking. *Health Psychology, 18,* 14–20.

Lerman, H. (1996). *Gender bias in the diagnostic classification of mental disorders.* New York: Basic Books.

Lerner, M. J. (1980). *The belief in a just world: A fundamental delusion.* New York: Plenum.

Lerner, R. M., & Galambos, N. L. (1998). Adolescent development: Challenges and opportunities for research, programs and policies. *Annual Review of Psychology, 49,* 413–446.

Leroy, P., Dessolin, S., Villageois, P., Moon, B. C., Friedman, J. M., Ailhaud, G., et al. (1996). Expression of ob gene in adipose cells. Regulation by insulin. *Journal of Biological Chemistry, 271,* 2365–2368.

Leschied, A. W., & Cummings, A. L. (2002). Youth violence: An overview of predictors, counseling interventions, and future directions. *Canadian Journal of Counseling, 36,* 256–264.

Leuner, K., & Müller, W. E. (2006). The complexity of the dopaminergic synapses and their modulation by antipsychotics. *Pharmacopsychiatry, 39*(Suppl. 1), S15–20.

LeVay, S. (1991, November 1). A difference in hypothalamic structure between heterosexual and homosexual men. *Science, 253,* 1034–1038.

LeVay, S., & Hamer, D. H. (1994). Evidence for a biological influence in male homosexuality. *Scientific American, 270*(5), 44–49.

Levenson, R. W. (1992). Autonomic nervous system differences among emotions. *Psychological Science, 3,* 23–27.

Levin, F. R., McDowell, D., Evans, S. M., Nunes, E., Akerele, E., Donovan, S., et al. (2004). Pharmacotherapy for marijuana dependence: A double-blind, placebo-controlled pilot study of divalproex sodium. *American Journal on Addictions, 13,* 21–32.

Levin, J. S., & Vanderpool, H. Y. (1989). Is religion therapeutically significant for hypertension? *Social Science and Medicine, 29,* 69–78.

Levine, C. (2003). Introduction: Structure, development, and identity formation. *Identity, 3,* 191–195.

Levine, E. L., Sistrunk, F., McNutt, K. J., & Gael, S. (1988). Exploring job analysis systems in selected organizations: A description of process and outcomes. *Journal of Business and Psychology, 3,* 3–21.

Levine, S. B. (2006). The PDE-5 inhibitors and psychiatry. *Journal of Psychiatric Practice, 12,* 46–49.

Levinson, D. J. (1978). *The seasons of a man's life.* New York: Knopf.

Levinson, D. J. (1986). A conception of adult development. *American Psychologist, 41,* 3–13.

Levinson, D. J. (1987). *The seasons of a woman's life.* New York: Knopf.

Levy, T. M., & Orlans, M. (2004). Attachment disorder, antisocial personality, and violence. *Annals of the American Psychotherapy Association, 7,* 18–23.

Lewin, K. A. (1935). *A dynamic theory of personality* (K. E. Zener & D. K. Adams, trans.). New York: McGraw-Hill.

Lewin, T. (1994, May 18). Boys are more comfortable with sex than girls are, survey finds. *New York Times,* p. A10.

Lewin, T. (1995, May 30). The decay of families is global study says. *New York Times,* p. A5.

Lewin, T. (1996, March 27). Americans are firmly attached to traditional roles for sexes, poll finds. *New York Times,* p. A12.

Lewy, A. J., Ahmed, S., Latham, J. J., & Sack R. (1992). Melatonin shifts human circadian rhythms according to a phase-response curve. *Chronobiology International 9,* 380–392.

Li, S-C. (2002). Connecting the many levels and facets of cognitive aging. *Current Directions in Psychological Science, 11,* 38–43.

Li, Y., & Hou, Y. (2005). Burnout, stress and depression. *Psychological Science* (China), *28,* 972–974.

Liang, K. C. (2001). Epinephrine modulation of memory: Amygdala activation and regulation of long-term memory storage. In P. E. Gold, & W. T. Greenough (Eds.), *Memory consolidation: Essays in honor of James L. McGaugh* (pp. 165–183). Washington, DC: American Psychological Assoc.

Lichtenstein, E. (1999). Nicotine Anonymous: Community resource and research implications. *Psychology of Addictive Behaviors, 13,* 60–68.

Lichtenstein, K. L., Wilson, N. M., & Johnson, C. T. (2000). Psychological treatment of secondary insomnia. *Psychology & Aging, 15,* 232–240.

Lickliter, R., & Honeycutt, H. (2003a). Developmental dynamics: Toward a biologically plausible evolutionary psychology. *Psychological Bulletin, 129,* 819–835.

Lickliter, R., & Honeycutt, H. (2003b). Developmental dynamics and contemporary evolutionary psychology: Status quo or irreconcilable views? Reply to Bjorklund (2003), Krebs (2003), Buss and Reeve (2003), Crawford (2003), and Tooby et al. (2003). *Psychological Bulletin, 129,* 866–872.

Liddle, H. A., & Rowe, C. L. (2002). Multidimensional family therapy for adolescent drug abuse: Making the case for a developmental-contextual, family-based intervention. In D. W. Brook & H. I. Spitz (Eds.), *The group therapy of substance abuse* (pp. 275–291). New York: Haworth.

Liggett, D. R. (2000). *Sport hypnosis*. Champaign, IL: Human Kinetics.

Lightdale, J. R., & Prentice, D. A. (1994). Rethinking sex differences in aggression: Aggressive behavior in the absence of social roles. *Personality and Social Psychology Bulletin, 20*, 34–44.

Lilienfeld, S. O., & Lynn, S. J. (2003). Dissociative identity disorder: Multiple personalities, multiple controversies. In S. O. Lilienfeld & S. J. Lynn (Eds.), *Science and pseudoscience in clinical psychology* (pp. 109–142). New York: Guilford.

Lincoln, D. S. (2004). Human genome: End of the beginning. *Nature 431*, 915–916.

Lipman, S. (1991). *Laughter in Hell: The use of humor during the Holocaust.* Northvale, NJ: J. Aronson.

Lippa, R. R. (2005). *Gender, nature, and nurture* (2nd ed.). Mahwah, NJ: Erlbaum.

Lips, H. M. (2002). *A new psychology of women: Gender, culture,* and *ethnicity* (2nd ed.). New York: McGraw-Hill.

Lipsky, D. K., & Gartner, A. (1996). Inclusive education and school restructuring. In W. Stainback & S. Stainback (Eds.), *Controversial issues confronting special education: Divergent perspectives* (pp. 3–15). Baltimore: Brookes.

Lipsky, S., Field, C. A., Caetano, R., & Larkin, G. L. (2005). Posttraumatic stress disorder symptomatology and comorbid depressive symptoms among abused women referred from emergency department care. *Violence and Victims, 20*, 645–659.

Litman, J. A., Collins, R. P., & Spielberger, C. D. (2005). The nature and measurement of sensory curiosity. *Personality and Individual Differences, 39*, 1123–1133.

Little, K. Y., Krowlewski, D. M., Zhang, L., & Cassin, B. J. (2003). Loss of striatal vesicular monoamine transporter protein (VMAT2) in human cocaine users. *American Journal of Psychiatry, 160*, 47–55.

Liu, C., Weaver, D. R., Jin, X., Shearman, I. P., Pieschl, R. I., Gribkoff, V. K., et al. (1997). Molecular dissection of two distinct actions of melatonin on the suprachiasmatic circadian clock. *Neuron, 19*, 99–102.

Liu, I. C., Blacker, D. L., Xu, R., Fitzmaurice, G., Tsuang, M. T., & Lyons, M. J. (2004). Genetic and environmental contributions to age of onset of alcohol dependence symptoms in male twins. *Addiction, 99*, 1403–1409.

Liu, J. H., & Latane, B. (1998). Extremitization of attitudes: Does thought-and-discussion-induced polarization cumulate? *Basic and Applied Social Psychology, 20*, 103–110.

Liu, X. (2004). Sleep and adolescent suicidal behavior. *Sleep: Journal of Sleep and Sleep Disorders Research, 27*, 1351–1358.

Livesley, W. J., Jang, K. L., & Vernon P. A. (2003). Genetic basis of personality structure. In T. Millon & M. J. Lerner, (Eds.), *Handbook of psychology: Vol. 5, Personality and social psychology* (pp. 59–83). New York: John Wiley & Sons.

Lleo, A., Berezovska, O., Growdon, J. H., & Hyman, B. T. (2004). Clinical, pathological, and biochemical spectrum of Alzheimer disease associated with PS-1 mutations. *American Journal of Geriatric Psychiatry, 12*, 146–156.

Loehlin, J. C., Horn, J. M., & Willerman, L. (1997). Heredity, environment, and IQ in the Texas adoption study. In R. J. Sternberg & E. Grigorenko (Eds.), *Intelligence: Heredity and environment*. New York: Cambridge Univ. Press.

Loehlin, J. C., McCrae, R. R., Costa, P. T., & John, O. P. (1998). Heritability of common and measure-specific components of the Big Five personality traits. *Journal of Research in Personality, 32*, 431–453.

Loewenstein, G. (1994). The psychology of curiosity: A review and reinterpretation. *Psychological Bulletin, 116*, 75–98.

Loftus, E. F. (1993). Psychologists in the eyewitness world. *American Psychologist, 48*, 550–552.

Loftus, E. F. (1997). Repressed memory accusations: Devastated families and devastated patients. *Applied Cognitive Psychology, 11*, 25–30.

Loftus, E. F., Coan, J. A., & Pickrell, J. E. (1996). Manufacturing false memories using bits of reality. In L. Reder (Ed.), *Implicit memory and metacognition* (pp. 195–220). Mahwah, NJ: Erlbaum.

Loftus, E. F., & Hoffman, H. G. (1989). Misinformation and memory: The creation of new memories. *Journal of Experimental Psychology: General, 118*, 100–114.

Loftus, E. F., & Palmer, J. C. (1974). Reconstruction of automobile destruction: An example of the interaction between language and memory. *Journal of Verbal Learning and Verbal Behavior, 13*, 585–589.

Loftus, E. F., & Pickrell, J. E. (1995). The formation of false memories. *Psychiatric Annals, 25*, 720–725.

Logue, A. W. (2000). Self-control and health behavior. In W. K. Bickel & R. E. Vuchinich (Eds.), *Reframing health behavior change with behavioral economics* (pp. 167–192). Mahwah, NJ: Erlbaum.

Logue, A. W., Ophir, I., & Strauss, K. E. (1981). The acquisition of taste aversions in humans. *Behavior Research and Therapy, 19*, 319–333.

Long, J. E. (2005). Power to prescribe: The debate over prescription privileges for psychologists and the legal issues implicated. *Law & Psychology Review, 29*, 243–260.

Lonner, W. J. (2005). The psychological study of culture: Issues and questions of enduring importance. In W. Friedlmeier, P. Chakkarath, & B. Schwarz (Eds.), *Culture and human development: The importance of cross-cultural research for the social sciences* (pp. 9–29). Hove, UK Psychology Press/Erlbaum.

Lonsdorf, E. V. (2005). Sex differences in the development of termite-fishing skills in wild chimpanzees (*Pan troglodytes schweinfurthii*) of Gombe National Park, Tanzania. *Animal Behaviour, 70*, 673–683.

López, S. R., & Guarnaccia, P. J. J. (2000). Cultural psychopathology: Uncovering the social world of mental illness. *Annual Review of Psychology, 51*, 571–598.

Lorenz, K. (1935). Der Kumpan inder Umwelt des Vogels. *Journal of Ornithology, 83*, 137–213, 289–413.

Lorenz, K. (1968). *On aggression*. New York: Harcourt.

Louie, T. A., Curren, M. T., & Harich, K. R. (2000). "I knew we could win": Hindsight bias for favorable and unfavorable decision outcomes. *Journal of Applied Psychology, 85*, 264–272.

Lovaglia, M., Mannix, E. A., Samuelson, C. D., Sell, J., & Wilson, R. K. (2005). Conflict, power, and status in groups. In M. S. Poole, & A. B. Hollingshead (Eds.), *Theories of small groups: Interdisciplinary perspectives* (pp. 139–184). Thousand Oaks, CA: Sage.

Love, K. M., & Murdock, T. B. (2004). Attachment to parents and psychological well-being: An examination of young adult college students in intact families and stepfamilies. *Journal of Family Psychology, 18*, 600–608.

Lovibond, P. F., Siddle, D. A., & Bond, N. W. (1993). Resistance to extinction of fear-relevant stimuli: Preparedness or selective sensitization? *Journal of Experimental Psychology: General, 122*, 449–461.

Lubinski, D. (2000). Scientific and social significance of assessing individual differences: "Sinking shafts at a few critical points." *Annual Review of Psychology, 51*, 405–444.

Lubinski, D., & Benbow, C. P. (2000). States of excellence. *American Psychologist, 55*, 137–150.

Lucas, R. E. (2005). Time does not heal all wounds: A longitudinal study of reaction and adaptation to divorce. *Psychological Science, 16*, 945–950.

Luciano, M., Wainwright, M. A., Wright, M. J., & Martin, N. G. (2006). The heritability of conscientiousness facets and their relationship to IQ and academic achievement. *Personality and Individual Differences, 40*, 1189–1199.

Lundström, J. N., Goncalves, M., Esteves, F., & Olsson, M. J. (2003). Psychological effects of subthreshold exposure to the putative human pheromone 4,16-androstadien-3-one. *Hormones and Behavior, 44*, 395–401.

Lundström, J. N., & Olsson, M. J. (2005). Subthreshold amounts of social odorant affect mood, but not behavior, in heterosexual women when tested by a male, but not a female, experimenter. *Biological Psychology, 70*, 197–204.

Luria, A. R. (1968). *The mind of a mnemonist* (L. Solotaroff, Trans.). New York: Basic Books.

Luria, A. R., & Solotaroff, L. (1987). *The mind of a mnemonist: A little book about a vast memory*. Cambridge, MA: Harvard Univ. Press.

Lyddon, W. J., & Jones, J. V. (2001). Empirically supported treatments: An introduction. In W. J. Lyddon & J. V. Jones (Eds.), *Empirically supported cognitive therapies: Current and future applications* (pp. 1–12). New York: Springer.

Lyness, S. A. (1993). Predictors of differences between Type A and B individuals in heart rate and blood pressure reactivity. *Psychological Bulletin, 114*, 266–295.

Lynn, R. (1989). Positive correlation between height, head size and IQ: A nutrition theory of the secular increases in intelligence. *British Journal of Educational Psychology, 59*, 372–377.

Lynn, S. J., Fassler, O., & Knox, J. (2005). Hypnosis and the altered state debate: Something more or nothing more? Comment. *Contemporary Hypnosis, 22*, 39–45.

Lynn, S. J., & Kirsch, I. (2006a). Anxiety disorders. In S. J. Lynn & I. Kirsch (Eds.), *Essentials of clinical hypnosis: An evidence-based approach* (pp. 135–157). Washington, DC: American Psychological Assoc.

Lynn, S. J., & Kirsch, I. (2006b). Posttraumatic Stress Disorder. In S. J. Lynn, & I. Kirsch (Eds.), *Essentials of clinical hypnosis: An evidence-based approach* (pp. 159–173). Washington, DC: American Psychological Assoc.

Lynn, S. J., & Kirsch, I. (2006c). Questions and controversies. In S. J. Lynn, & I. Kirsch, (Eds.), *Essentials of clinical hypnosis: An evidence-based approach* (197–213). Washington, DC: American Psychological Assoc.

Lynn, S. J., & Kirsch, I. (2006d). Smoking cessation. In S. J. Lynn, & I. Kirsch (Eds.), *Essentials of clinical hypnosis: An evidence-based approach* (pp. 79–98). Washington, DC: American Psychological Assoc.

Lynn, S. J., Kirsch, I., & Koby, D. G. (2006). Pain management, behavioral medicine, and dentistry with Danielle G. Koby. In S. J. Lynn, & I. Kirsch (Eds.), *Essentials of clinical hypnosis: An evidence-based approach* (pp. 175–196). Washington, DC: American Psychological Assoc.

Lyons, M. J., True, W. R., Eisen, S. A., Goldberg, J., Meyer, J. M., Faraone, S. V., et al. (1995). Differential heritability of adult and juvenile antisocial traits. *Archives of General Psychiatry, 52*, 906–915.

Lyubomirsky, S., & Ross, L. (1999). Changes in attractiveness of elected, rejected and precluded alternatives: A comparison of happy and unhappy individuals. *Journal of Personality and Social Psychology, 76*, 988–1007.

Ma, D. J. (2004). Wedding planning: Brides' engagement stress and social support. *Dissertation Abstracts International: Section B: The Sciences and Engineering, 65*, 2101.

Maas, J. (1998). *Power sleep: The revolutionary program that prepares your mind for peak performance.* New York: Villard.

Mabery, D. L. (2002). Gender differences in the relationship between depression, internalizing/externalizing problems, and personality styles in adolescents. *Dissertation Abstracts International: Section B: The Sciences and Engineering, 63*, 3014.

Macavei, B. (2005). The role of irrational beliefs in the rational emotive behavior theory of depression. *Journal of Cognitive and Behavioral Psychotherapies, 5*, 73–81.

Maccoby, E. E. (1998). *The two sexes: Growing up apart, coming together.* Cambridge, MA: Belknap.

Maccoby, E. E. (2000). Parenting and its effects on children: On reading and misreading behavior genetics. *Annual Review of Psychology, 51*, 1–27.

MacDonald, T. K., MacDonald, G., Zanna, M. P., & Fong, G. (2000). Alcohol, sexual arousal and intentions to use condoms in young men: Applying alcohol myopia theory to risky sexual behavior. *Health Psychology, 19*, 290–298.

Mackavey, W. R., Malley, J. E., & Stewart, A. J. (1991). Remembering autobiographically consequential experiences: Content analysis of psychologists' accounts of their lives. *Psychology and Aging, 6*, 50–59.

Mackey, S. (2005). The strain in pain lies mainly in the brain. Retrieved March 22, 2006 from http://paincenter.stanford.edu/research/

MacLeod, D. I. A. (1978). Visual sensitivity. *Annual Review of Psychology, 29*, 613–645.

Macmillan, M. (2000). *An odd kind of fame: Stories of Phineas Gage.* Cambridge, MA: MIT Press.

Macrae, C. N., & Bodenhausen, G. V. (2000). Social cognition: Thinking categorically about others. *Annual Review of Psychology, 51*, 93–120.

MacWhinney, B. (1999). *The emergence of language.* Mahwah, NJ: Erlbaum.

MacWhinney, B. (2005). Language evolution and human development. In B. J. Ellis & D. F. Bjorklund (Eds.), *Origins of the social mind: Evolutionary psychology and child development* (pp. 383–410). New York: Guilford.

Maddi, S. R. (1989). *Personality theories: A comparative approach* (5th ed.). Homewood, IL: Dorsey.

Maddi, S. R. (2006). Hardiness: The courage to be resilient. In J. C. Thomas, D. L. Segal, & M. Hersen (Eds.), *Comprehensive handbook of personality and psychopathology: Vol. 1, Personality and everyday functioning* (pp. 306–321). Hoboken, NJ: John Wiley & Sons.

Madon, S. J. (1999). The best guess model of stereotyping: Information seekers versus cognitive misers. *Dissertation Abstracts International: Section B: The Sciences and Engineering, 59*, 6517.

Magaletta, P. R., Fagan, T. J., & Peyrot, M. F. (2000). Telehealth in the federal bureau of prisons: Inmates' perceptions. *Professional Psychology: Research & Practice, 31*, 497–502.

Maher, B. A., & Gottesman, I. I. (2005). Deconstructing, reconstructing, preserving Paul E. Meehl's legacy of construct validity. *Psychological Assessment, 17*, 415–422.

Maio, G. R., & Olson, J. M. (1998). Values as truisms: Evidence and implications. *Journal of Personality and Social Psychology, 74*, 294–311.

Maisto, A. A., & Hughes, E. (1995). Adaptation to group home living for adults with mental retardation as a function of previous residential placement. *Journal of Intellectual Disability Research, 39*, 15–18.

Maj, M. (2003). The effect of lithium in bipolar disorder: A review of recent research evidence. *Bipolar Disorders, 5*, 180–188.

Maloney, M. P., & Ward, M. P. (1976). *Psychological assessment: A conceptual approach.* New York: Academic Press.

Manalo, E., (2002). Uses of mnemonics in educational settings: A brief review of selected research. *Psychologia: An International Journal of Psychology in the Orient, 45*, 69–79.

Manger, T. A., & Motta, R. W. (2005). The impact of an exercise program on posttraumatic stress disorder, anxiety, and depression. *International Journal of Emergency Mental Health, 7*, 49–57.

Mann, K., Ackermann, K., Croissant, B., Mundle, G., Nakovics, H., & Diehl, A. (2005). Neuroimaging of gender differences in alcohol dependence: Are women more vulnerable? *Alcoholism: Clinical and Experimental Research, 29*, 896–901.

Mann, T., Sherman, D., & Updegraff, J. (2004). Dispositional motivations and message framing: A test of the congruency hypothesis in college students. *Health Psychology, 23*, 330–334.

Manns, J. R., Hopkins, R. O., & Squire, L. R. (2003). Semantic memory and the human hippocampus. *Neuron, 38*, 127–133.

Manto, M. U., & Jacquy, J. (2002). Alcohol toxicity in the cerebellum: Clinical aspects. In M. U. Manto & M. Pandolfo (Eds.), *The cerebellum and its disorders* (pp. 336–341). New York: Cambridge Univ. Press.

Manton, K. G., & Gu, X. (2001). Changes in the prevalence of chronic disability in the United States black and nonblack population above age 65 from 1982 to 1999. *Proc. Natl. Acad. Sci, USA, 98*, 6354–6359.

Maquet, P., Laureys, S., Peigneus, P., Fuchs, S., Petiau, C., Phips, C., et al. (2000). Experience-dependent changes in cerebral activation during human REM sleep. *Nature: Neuroscience, 3*, 831–836.

Marano, H. E. (1997, July 1). Puberty may start at 6 as hormones surge. *New York Times*, pp. C1, C6.

Maranto, C. L., & Stenoien, A. F. (2000). Weight discrimination: A multidisciplinary analysis. *Employee Responsibilities and Rights Journal, 12*, 9–24.

Marcia, J. E. (1980). Identity in adolescence. In J. Adelson (Ed.), *Handbook of adolescent psychology* (pp. 159–187). New York: Wiley.

Marcus, D. K., & Miller, R. S. (2003). Sex differences in judgments of physical attractiveness: A social relations analysis. *Personality and Social Psychology Bulletin, 29*, 325–335.

Marcus, G. F. (1996). Why do children say "breaked"? *Current Directions in Psychological Science, 5*, 81–85.

Marcus, S. M., Young, E. A., Kerber, K. B., Kornstein, S., Farabaugh, A. H., Mitchell, J., et al. (2005). Gender differences in depression: Findings from the STAR*D study. *Journal of Affective Disorders, 87*, 141–150.

Marinelli, L., & Mayer, A. (2003). *Dreaming by the book: Freud's the interpretation of dreams and the history of the psychoanalytic movement.* New York: Other Press.

Mark, A. (2003). Inattentional blindness: Looking without seeing. *Current Directions in Psychological Science, 12*, 180–184.

Markon, K. E., Krueger, R. F., Bouchard, T. J., Jr., & Gottesman, I. I. (2002). Normal and abnormal personality traits: Evidence for genetic and environmental relationships in the Minnesota Study of Twins Reared Apart. *Journal of Personality, 70*, 661–693.

Markovic, B. M., Dimitrijevic, M., & Jankovic, B. D. (1993). Immunomodulation by conditioning: Recent developments. *International Journal of Neuroscience, 71*, 231–249.

Marks, L. S., Duda, C., Dorey, F. J., Macairan, M. L., & Santos, P. B. (1999). Treatment of erectile dysfunction with sildenafil. *Urology, 53*, 19–24.

Marsh, A., Elfenbein, H., & Ambady, N. (2003). Nonverbal "accents": Cultural differences in facial expressions of emotion. *Psychological Science, 14*, 373–376.

Marshall, M. B., De Fruyt, F., Rolland, J.-P., & Bagby, R. M. (2005). Socially desirable responding and the factorial stability of the NEO PI-R. *Psychological Assessment, 17*, 379–384.

Martin, R. A. (2002). Is laughter the best medicine? Humor, laughter, and physical health. *Current Directions in Psychological Science, 11*, 216–220.

Martin, S., (2001). Substance abuse is nation's No. 1 health problem, but there is hope. *Monitor on Psychology, 32*, 10.

Martino, A. (1995, February 5). Mid-life usually brings positive change, not crisis. *Ann Arbor News*.

Masataka, N. (2003). *The onset of language.* New York: Cambridge Univ. Press.

Maslach, C., & Leiter, M. P. (1997). *The truth about burnout.* San Francisco: Jossey-Bass.

Masling, J. (2002). How do I score thee? Let me count the ways. Or some different methods of categorizing Rorschach responses. *Journal of Personality Assessment, 79*, 399–421.

Maslow, A. H. (1954). *Motivation and personality.* New York: Harper & Row.

Mason, F. L. (1997). Fetishism: Psychopathology and theory. In D. R. Laws & W. T. O'Donohue (Eds.), *Handbook of sexual deviance: Theory and application* (pp. 75–91). New York: Guilford.

Masters, W. H., & Johnson, V. E. (1966). *Human sexual response.* Boston: Little, Brown.

Mather, M., Shafir, E., & Johnson, M. (2000). Misremembrance of options past: Source monitoring and choice. *Psychological Science, 11*, 132–138.

Matre, D., Casey, K. L., & Knardahl, S. (2006). Placebo-induced changes in spinal cord pain processing. *Journal of Neuroscience, 26*, 559–563.

Matson, J. L., Smalls, Y., Hampff, A., Smiroldo, B. B., & Anderson, S. J. (1998). Acomparison of behavioral techniques to teach functional independent-living skills to individuals with severe and profound mental retardation. *Behavior Modification, 22*, 298–306.

Matsumoto, D. (1996). *Culture and psychology.* Pacific Grove, CA: Brooks/Cole.

Matsumoto, D. (2000). *Culture and psychology: People around the world* (2nd ed.). Belmont, CA: Wadsworth/Thomson Learning.

Matsumoto, D., & Kupperbusch, C. (2001). Idiocentric and allocentric differences in emotional expression, experience, and the coherence between expression and experience. *Asian Journal of Social Psychology, 4*, 113–131.

Matta, M. A. (2002). Parental corporal punishment as a predictor of child maladjustment: Race and parental responsiveness as potential moderators. *Dissertation Abstracts International: Section B: The Sciences and Engineering, 63*, 2091.

Matthews, G., Zeidner, M., & Roberts, R. D. (2002). *Emotional intelligence: Science and myth.* Cambridge, MA: MIT Press.

Matthews, K. A. (1988). Coronary heart disease and Type A behaviors: Update on and alternative to the Booth-Kewley and Friedman (1987) quantitative review. *Psychological Bulletin, 104*, 373–380.

Maunsell, E., Brisson, J., Mondor, M., Verreault, R., & Deschenes, L. (2001). Stressful life events and survival after breast cancer. *Psychosomatic Medicine, 63*, 306–315.

Maurer, D., & Maurer, C. (1988). *The world of the newborn.* New York: Basic Books.

Mawson, A. R. (2005). Understanding mass panic and other collective responses to threat and disaster. *Psychiatry: Interpersonal and Biological Processes, 68*, 95–113.

Mayer, J. D., & Geher, G. (1996). Emotional intelligence and the identification of emotion. *Intelligence, 22*, 89–113.

Mayne, T. J., & Bonanno, G. A. (Eds.) (2001). *Emotions: Current issues and future directions.* New York: Guilford.

Mayo Foundation for Medical Education and Research. (2005a). *Alzheimer's disease: Prevention.* Retrieved May 11, 2006 from http://www.mayoclinic.com/health/alzheimers-disease/DS00161/DSECTION=8

Mayo Foundation for Medical Education and Research. (2005b). *Alzheimer's disease: Risk factors.* Retrieved May 11, 2006 from http://www.mayoclinic.com/health/alzheimers-disease/DS00161/DSECTION=4

Mays, V. M., Bullock, M., Rosenzweig, M. R., & Wessells, M. (1998). Ethnic conflict: Global challenges and psychological perspectives. *American Psychologist, 53,* 737–742.

Mazzoni, G. A. L., Lombardo, P., Malvagia, S., & Loftus, E. F. (1999). Dream interpretation and false beliefs. *Professional Psychology: Research & Practice, 30,* 45–50.

Mazzoni, G. A. L., & Memon, A. (2003). Imagination can create false autobiographical memories. *Psychological Science, 14,* 186–188.

McBee, C. H. (2005). Fetal alcohol syndrome and other drug use during pregnancy. *Journal of Applied Rehabilitation Counseling, 36,* 43–44.

McBurney, D. H., & Collings, V. B. (1984). *Introduction to sensation/ perception* (2nd ed.). Englewood Cliffs, NJ: Prentice Hall.

McCabe, P. M., Schneiderman, N., Field, T., & Wellens, A. R. (2000). *Stress, coping, and cardiovascular disease.* Mahwah, NJ: Erlbaum.

McCall, M. (1997). Physical attractiveness and access to alcohol: What is beautiful does not get carded. *Journal of Applied Social Psychology, 27,* 453–462.

McCann, I. L., & Holmes, D. S. (1984). Influence of aerobic exercise on depression. *Journal of Personality and Social Psychology, 46,* 1142–1147.

McClelland, D. C., & Atkinson, J. W. (1948). The projective expression of needs: I. The effect of different intensities of the hunger drive on perception. *Journal of Psychology, 25,* 205–222.

McClelland, K., & Linnander, E. (2006). The role of contact and information in racial attitude change among white college students. *Sociological Inquiry, 76,* 81–115.

McClintock, M. K. (1999). Reproductive biology. Pheromones and regulation of ovulation. *Nature, 401,* 232–233.

McClintock, M. K., & Herdt, G. (1996). Rethinking puberty: The development of sexual attraction. *Current Directions in Psychological Science, 5,* 178–183.

McCloskey, M., & Egeth, H. E. (1983). Eyewitness identification: What can a psychologist tell a jury? *American Psychologist, 38,* 550–563.

McClure, E. B. (2000). A meta-analytic review of sex differences in facial expression processing and their development in infants, children, and adolescents. *Psychological Bulletin, 126,* 424–453

McCoy, N. L., & Pitino, L. (2002). Pheromonal influences on sociosexual behavior in young women. *Physiology & Behavior, 75,* 367–375.

McCrae, R. R., & Costa, P. T., Jr. (1994). The stability of personality: Observations and evaluations. *Current Directions in Psychological Science, 3,* 173–175.

McCrae, R. R., & Costa, P. T., Jr. (1997). Personality trait structure as a human universal. *American Psychologist, 52,* 509–516.

McDaniel, M. A., & Frei, R. L. (1994). Validity of customer service measures in personnel selection: A review of criterion and construct evidence. (Cited in Hogan, R., Hogan, J., & Roberts, B. W. [1996]. Personality measurement and employment decisions: Questions and answers. *American Psychologist, 51,* 469–477.)

McDonald, J. W. (1999). Repairing the damaged spinal cord. *Scientific American, 281*(3), 65–73.

McElhatton, P. R., Bateman, D. N., Evans, C., Pughe, K. R., & Thomas, S. H. L. (1999). Congenital anomalies after prenatal Ecstasy exposure. *Lancet, 354,* 1441–1442.

McFadden, D. (2002). Masculinization effects in the auditory system. *Archives of Sexual Behavior, 31,* 99–111.

McFarland, L. J., Senn, L. E., & Childress, J. R. (1993). *21st century leadership: Dialogues with 100 top leaders.* Los Angeles: Leadership Press.

McGeer, E. G., Klegeris, A., & McGeer, P. L. (2005). Inflammation, the complement system and the diseases of aging. *Neurobiology of Aging, 26,* S94–S97.

McGeer, P. L., & McGeer, E. G. (1980). Chemistry of mood and emotion. *Annual Review of Psychology, 31,* 273–307.

McGlynn, R. P., McGurk, D., Effland, V. S., Johll, N. L., & Harding, D. J. (2004). Brainstorming and task performance in groups constrained by evidence. *Organizational Behavior and Human Decision Processes, 93,* 75–87.

McGuffin, P., Katz, R., Watkins, S., & Rutherford, J. (1996). A hospital-based twin register of the heritability of *DSM-IV* unipolar depression. *Archives of General Psychiatry, 53,* 129–136.

McGuire, M. T., Wing, R. R., Klem, M. L., Lang, W., & Hill, J. O. (1999). What predicts weight regain in a group of successful weight losers? *Journal of Consulting & Clinical Psychology, 67,* 177–185.

McGuire, P. A. (1999, June 6). Psychology and medicine connecting in the war over cancer. *APA Monitor,* pp. 8–9.

McIntyre, C. K., Marriott, L. K., & Gold, P. E. (2003). Cooperation between memory systems: Acetylcholine release in the amygdala correlates positively with performance on a hippocampus-dependent task. *Behavioral Neuroscience, 117,* 320–326.

McKeever, V. M., & Huff, M. E. (2003). A diathesis-stress model of posttraumatic stress disorder: Ecological, biological, and residual stress pathways. *Review of General Psychology, 7,* 237–250.

McKellar, J., Stewart, E., & Humphreys, K. (2003). Alcoholics Anonymous involvement and positive alcohol-related outcomes: Cause, consequence, or just a correlate? A prospective 2-year study of 2,319 alcohol-dependent men. *Journal of Consulting and Clinical Psychology 71,* 302–308.

McKenna, M. C., Zevon, M. A., Corn, B., & Rounds, J. (1999). Psychosocial factors and the development of breast cancer: A meta-analysis. *Health Psychology, 18,* 520–531.

McKim, W. A. (2007). *Drugs and behavior: An introduction to behavioral pharmacology* (6th ed.). Upper Saddle River, NJ: Prentice Hall.

McMillan, T. M., Robertson, I. H., & Wilson, B. A. (1999). Neurogenesis after brain injury: Implications for neurorehabilitation. *Neuropsychological Rehabilitation, 9,* 129–133.

McNally, R. J. (2003a). Experimental approaches to the recovered memory controversy. In M. F. Lenzenweger & J. M. Hooley (Eds.), *Principles of experimental psychopathology: Essays in honor of Brendan A. Maher* (pp. 269–277). Washington, DC: American Psychological Assoc.

McNally, R. J. (2003b). Recovering memories of trauma: A view from the laboratory. *Current Directions in Psychological Science, 12,* 32–35.

McNally, R. J., Bryant, R. A., & Ehlers, A. (2003). Does early psychological intervention promote recovery from posttraumatic stress? *Psychological Science in the Public Interest, 4,* 45–79.

McNamara, H. J., Long, J. B., & Wike, E. L. (1956). Learning without response under two conditions of external cues. *Journal of Comparative and Physiological Psychology, 49,* 477–480.

McNamara, P. (2004). *An evolutionary psychology of sleep and dreams.* Westport, CT: Praeger/ Greenwood.

McNeil, B. J., Pauker, S. G., Sox, H. C., Jr., & Tversky, A. (1982). On the elicitation of preferences for alternative therapies. *New England Journal of Medicine, 306,* 1259–1262.

McNeil, D. W., & Zvolensky, M. J. (2000). Systematic desensitization. In A. E. Kazdin (Ed.), *Encyclopedia of psychology,* (Vol. 7, pp. 533–535). Washington, DC: American Psychological Assoc.

McPherson, J. M., Smith-Lovin, L., & Cook, J. M. (2001). Birds of a feather: Homophily in social networks. *Annual Review of Sociology, 27,* 415–444.

Mead, M. (1935). *Sex and temperament in three primitive societies.* New York: Morrow.

Mednick, S. A. (1962). The associative basis of creativity. *Psychological Review, 69,* 220–232.

Mednick, S. C., Nakayama, K., Cantero, J. L., Atienza, M., Levin, A. A., Pathak, N., et al. (2002). The restorative effect of naps on perceptual deterioration. *Nature Neuroscience, 5,* 677–681.

Melcher, D. (2006). Accumulation and persistence of memory for natural scenes. *Journal of Vision, 6,* 8–17.

Meltzoff, A. N., & Gopnik, A. (1997). *Words, thoughts and theories.* Boston, MA: MIT Press.

Meltzoff, A. N., & Moore, M. K. (1989). Imitation in newborn infants: Exploring the range of gestures imitated and the underlying mechanisms. *Developmental Psychology, 25,* 954–962.

Melzack, R. (1980). Psychological aspects of pain. In J. J. Bonica (Ed.), *Pain.* New York: Raven.

Melzack, R., & Katz, J. (2004). The gate control theory: Reaching for the brain. In T. Hadjistavropoulos, & K. Craig, (Eds.), *Pain: Psychological perspectives* (pp. 13–34). Mahwah, NJ: Erlbaum.

Mendez, B., & Martha, M. (2001). Changes in parental sense of competence and attitudes in low-income Head Start parents as a result of participation in a Parent Education Workshop. *Dissertation Abstracts International: Section B: The Sciences and Engineering, 62,* 2976.

Menon, T., Morris, M. W., Chiu, C. Y., & Hong, Y. Y. (1998). *Culture and the perceived autonomy of individuals and groups: American attributions to personal dispositions and Confucian attributions to group.* Unpublished manuscript, Stanford Univ.

Merrick, J., Aspler, S., & Schwarz, G. (2005). Phenylalanine-restricted diet should be life long. A case report on long term follow-up of an adolescent with untreated phenylketonuria. *International Journal of Adolescent Medicine and Health, 15,* 165–168.

Merrill, K. A., Tolbert, V. E., & Wade, W. A. (2003). Effectiveness of cognitive therapy for depression in a community mental health center: A benchmarking study. *Journal of Consulting and Clinical Psychology, 71,* 404–409.

Mershon, B., & Gorsuch, R. L. (1988). Number of factors in the personality sphere: Does increase in factors increase predictability of real-life criteria? *Journal of Personality and Social Psychology, 55,* 675–680.

Mersky, H. (1992). The manufacture of personalities: The production of multiple personality disorder. *British Journal of Psychiatry, 160,* 327–340.

Meston, C. M., & Frohlich, M. A. (2000). The neurobiology of sexual function. *Archives of General Psychiatry, 57,* 1012–1030.

Meuret, A. E., Wilhelm, F. H., & Roth, W. T. (2004). Respiratory feedback for treating panic disorder. *Journal of Clinical Psychology, 60,* 197–207.

Meyer, G. J., Finn, S. E., Eyde, L. D., Kay, G. G., Moreland, K. L., Dies, R. R., et al. (2001). Psychological testing and psychological assessment: A review of evidence and issues. *American Psychologist, 56,* 128–165.

Meyer, P. (2003). Conformity and group pressure: If Hitler asked you to electrocute a stranger would you? Probably. In J. M. Henslin (Ed.), *Down to earth sociology: Introductory readings* (12th ed., pp. 253–260). New York: Free Press.

Meyers, L. (2005). Psychologists back increased parity, prescriptive authority and professional access. *Monitor on Psychology, 36,* 42.

Michael, R. T., Gagnon, J. H., Laumann, E. O., & Kolata, G. (1994). *Sex in America.* Boston: Little, Brown.

Milgram, S. (1963). Behavioral study of obedience. *Journal of Abnormal and Social Psychology, 67,* 371–378.

Milgram, S. (1974). *Obedience to authority: An experimental view.* New York: Harper & Row.

Miller, G. (2000). *The mating mind: Why our ancestors scribbled on cave walls.* New York: Doubleday.

Miller, G. A. (1999). On knowing a word. *Annual Review of Psychology, 50,* 1–19.

Miller, G. E., & Cohen, S. (2001). Psychological interventions and the immune system: A meta-analytic review and critique. *Health Psychology, 20,* 47–63.

Miller, J. A. (2002). Individual motivation loss in group settings: An exploratory study of the social-loafing phenomenon. *Dissertation Abstracts International Section A: Humanities and Social Sciences, 62,* 2972.

Miller, J. G., Bersoff, D. M., & Harwood, R. L. (1990). Perceptions of social responsibilities in India and the United States: Moral imperatives or personal decisions? *Journal of Personality and Social Psychology, 58,* 33–47.

Miller, L. K. (1999). The savant syndrome: Intellectual impairment and exceptional skill. *Psychological Bulletin, 125,* 31–46.

Miller, L. K. (2005). What the savant syndrome can tell us about the nature and nurture of talent. *Journal for the Education of the Gifted, 28,* 361–373.

Miller, T. Q., Turner, C. W., Tindale, R. S., Posavac, E. J., & Dugoni, B. L. (1991). Reasons for the trend toward null findings in research on Type A behavior. *Psychological Bulletin, 110,* 469–485.

Miller, T. W., Miller, J. M., Kraus, R. F., Kaak, O., Sprang, R., & Veltkamp, L. J. (2003). Telehealth: A clinical application model for rural consultation. *Consulting Psychology Journal: Practice and Research, 55,* 119–127.

Miller, W. R., & Thoresen, C. E. (2003). Spirituality, religion, and health: An emerging research field. *American Psychologist, 58,* 24–35.

Milner, B. (1959). The memory defect in bilateral hippocampal lesions. *Psychiatric Research Reports, 11,* 43–52.

Milner, B., Corkin, S., & Teuber, H. H. (1968). Further analysis of the hippocampal amnesic syndrome: 14-year follow-up study of H. M. *Neuropsychologia, 6,* 215–234.

Milos, G., Spindler, A., Ruggiero, G., Klaghofer, R., & Schnyder, U. (2002). Comorbidity of obsessive-compulsive disorders and duration of eating disorders. *International Journal of Eating Disorders, 31,* 284–289.

Milton, J., Polmear, C., & Fabricius, J. (2004). *A short introduction to psychoanalysis.* London: SAGE.

Milton, J., & Wiseman, R. (1999). Does psi exist? Lack of replication of an anomalous process of information transfer. *Psychological Bulletin, 125,* 387–391.

Milton, J., & Wiseman, R. (2002). A response to Storm and Ertel (2002). *Journal of Parapsychology, 66,* 183–185.

Mindell, J. A., & Owens, J. A. (2003). *A clinical guide to pediatric sleep: Diagnosis and management of sleep problems in children and adolescents.* Philadelphia: Lippincott Williams & Wilkins.

Mineka, S., & Oehman, A. (2002). Phobias and preparedness: The selective, autonomic, and encapsulated nature of fear. *Biological Psychiatry*, 51, 927–937.

Miniño, A. M., Heron, M., & Smith, B. L. (2006). Deaths: Preliminary data for 2004. Retrieved June 8, 2006, from http://www.cdc.gov/nchs/products/pubs/pubd/hestats/prelimdeaths04/preliminarydeaths04.htm

Minor, T. R., & Hunter A. M. (2002). Stressor controllability and learned helplessness research in the United States: Sensitization and fatigue processes. *Integrative Physiological and Behavioral Science*, 37, 44–58.

Minton, H. L. (2002). Psychology and gender at the turn of the century. *American Psychologist*, 55, 613–615.

Mintun, M. A., Sheline, Y. I., Moerlein, S. M., Vlassenko, A. G., Huang, Y., & Snyder, A. Z. (2004). Decreased hippocampal 5-HT2A receptor binding in major depressive disorder: In vivo measurement with [18F]altanserin positron emission tomography. *Biological Psychiatry*, 55, 217–224.

Miranda, G. E. (2006). Unequal childhoods: Class, race, and family life. *Children and Youth Services Review*, 28, 96–99.

Mirescu, C., Peters, J. D., & Gould, E. (2004). Early life experience alters response of adult neurogenesis to stress. *Nature Neuroscience*, 7, 841–846.

Mirkin, M. P., Suyemoto, K. L., & Okun, B. F. (Eds.). (2005). *Psychotherapy with women: Exploring diverse contexts and identities.* New York: Guilford.

Mischel, W. (2003). Challenging the traditional personality psychology paradigm. In R. J. Sternberg (Ed.), *Psychologists defying the crowd: Stories of those who battled the establishment and won* (pp. 139–156). Washington, DC: American Psychological Assoc.

Mischel, W., & Shoda, Y. (1995). A cognitive-affective system theory of personality: Reconceptualizing situations, dispositions, dynamics, and invariance in personality structure. *Psychological Review*, 102, 246–268.

Mischel, W., Shoda, Y., & Mendoza-Denton, R. (2002). Situation-behavior profiles as a locus of consistency in personality. *Current Directions in Psychological Science*, 11, 50–54.

Mistry, J., & Rogoff, B. (1994). Remembering in cultural context. In W. W. Lonner & R. Malpass (Eds.), *Psychology and culture* (pp. 139–144). Boston: Allyn & Bacon.

Modesto-Lowe, V., & Fritz, E. M. (2005). The opioidergic-alcohol link: Implications for treatment. *CNS Drugs*, 19, 693–707.

Mody, R. R., & Smith, M. J. (2006). Smoking status and health-related quality of life: Findings from the 2001 Behavioral Risk Factor Surveillance System data. *American Journal of Health Promotion*, 20, 251–258.

Moeller-Lemkuehler, A. M. (2003). The gender gap in suicide and premature death or: Why are men so vulnerable? *European Archives of Psychiatry and Clinical Neuroscience*, 253, 1–8.

Moffitt, T. E. (2005). The new look of behavioral genetics in developmental psychopathology: Gene-environment interplay in antisocial behaviors. *Psychological Bulletin*, 131, 533–554.

Moffitt, T. E., Caspi, A., & Rutter, M. (2006). Measured gene-environment interactions in psychopathology: Concepts, research strategies, and implications for research, interventions, and public understanding of genetics. *Perspectives on Psychological Science*, 1, 5–26.

Mohan, J. (2006). Cardiac psychology. *Journal of the Indian Academy of Applied Psychology*, 3, 214–220.

Mohapel, P., Leanza, G., Kokaia, M., & Lindvall, O. (2005). Forebrain acetylcholine regulates adult hippocampal neurogenesis and learning. *Neurobiology of Aging*, 26, 939–946.

Mohl, A. S. (2006). Growing up male: Is violence, crime and war endemic to the male gender? *Journal of Psychohistory*, 33, 270–289.

Monastra, V. J., Monastra, D. M., & George, S. (2002). The effects of stimulant therapy, EEG biofeedback, and parenting style on the primary symptoms of attention-deficit hyperactivity disorder. *Applied Psychophysiology and Biofeedback*, 27, 231–249.

Monteleone, P., DiLieto, A., Castaldo, E., & Maj, M. (2004). Leptin functioning in eating disorders. *CNS Spectrums*, 9, 523–529.

Monti, M. R., & Sabbadini, A. (2005). New interpretative styles: Progress or contamination? Psychoanalysis and phenomenological psychopathology. *International Journal of Psychoanalysis*, 86, 1011–1032.

Moore, J. (2005). Some historical and conceptual background to the development of B. F. Skinner's "Radical Behaviorism"—Part 1. *Journal of Mind and Behavior*, 26, 65–94.

Moore, K. A., Morrison, D. R., & Greene, A. D. (1997). Effects on the children born to adolescent mothers. In R. A. Maynard (Ed.), *Kids having kids: Economic costs and social consequences of teen pregnancy* (pp. 145–180). Washington, DC: Urban Institute Press.

Moore, R. Y. (1999, June 25). A clock for the ages. *Science*, 284, 2102–2103.

Morgan, G. (2005). The resilience of language: What gesture creation in deaf children can tell us about how all children learn language. *Journal of Child Language*, 32, 925–928.

Morgan, M. (1999). Sensory perception: Supernormal hearing in the blind? *Current Biology*, 9, R53–R54.

Morgan, W. G. (2002). Origin and history of the earliest thematic apperception test pictures. *Journal of Personality Assessment*, 79, 422–445.

Moriarty, T. (1975). Crime, commitment and the responsive bystander: Two field experiments. *Journal of Personality and Social Psychology*, 31, 370–376.

Moriconi, C. B. (2004). A systemic treatment program of mindfulness meditation for fibromyalgia patients and their partners. *Dissertation Abstracts International: Section B: The Sciences and Engineering*, 64, 5228.

Morin, C. M., Bastien, C. H., Brink, D., & Brown, T. R. (2003). Adverse effects of temazepam in older adults with chronic insomnia. *Human Psychopharmacology Clinical and Experimental*, 18, 75–82.

Morrison, N. (2001). Group cognitive therapy: Treatment of choice or suboptimal option? *Behavioural and Cognitive Psychotherapy*, 29, 311–332.

Morrison, R. G. (2005). Thinking in working memory. In K. J. Holyoak & R. G. Morrison (Eds.), *The Cambridge handbook of thinking and reasoning* (pp. 457–473). New York: Cambridge Univ. Press.

Morrone, A. S., & Pintrich, P. R. (2006). Achievement motivation. In G. G. Bear & K. M. Minke (Eds.), *Children's needs III: Development, prevention, and intervention* (pp. 431–442). Washington, DC: National Assoc. of School Psychologists.

Morrongiello, B. A., Fenwick, K. D., Hillier, L., & Chance, G. (1994). Sound localization in newborn human infants. *Developmental Psychobiology*, 27, 519–538.

Mortimer, J. S. B., Sephton, S. E., Kimerling, R., Butler, L., Bernstein, A. S., & Spiegel, D. (2005). Chronic stress, depression and immunity in spouses of metastatic breast cancer patients. *Clinical Psychologist*, 9, 59–63.

Moyer, C. A., Rounds, J., & Hannum, J. W. (2004). A meta-analysis of massage therapy research. *Psychological Bulletin*, 130, 3–18.

Mroczek, D. K., & Kolarz, C. M. (1998). The effect of age on positive and negative affect: A developmental perspective on happiness. *Journal of Personality and Social Psychology*, 75, 1333–1349.

Mucci, A., Galderisi, S., Bucci, P., Tresca, E., Forte, A., Koenig, T., et al. (2005). Hemispheric lateralization patterns and psychotic experiences in healthy subjects. *Psychiatry Research: Neuroimaging*, 139, 141–154.

Muchinsky, P. M. (2006). *Psychology applied to work* (8th Ed.). Belmont, CA: Thomson Wadsworth.

Mueser, K. T. (2006). Family intervention for schizophrenia. In L. VandeCreek (Ed.), *Innovations in clinical practice: Focus on adults* (pp. 219–233). Sarasota, FL: Professional Resource Press/Professional Resource Exchange, Inc.

Mueser, K. T., & Glynn, S. M. (1995). *Behavioral family therapy for psychiatric disorders*. Boston: Allyn & Bacon.

Mulas, F., Capilla, A., Fernàndez, S., Etchepareborda, M. C., Campo, P., Maestú, F., et al. (2006). Shifting-related brain magnetic activity in attention-deficit/hyperactivity disorder. *Biological Psychiatry, 59*, 373–379.

Mumford, M. D., & Gustafson, S. B. (1988). Creativity syndrome: Integration, application, and innovation. *Psychological Bulletin, 103*, 27–43.

Muris, P., Merckelbach, H., Gadet, B., & Moulaert, V. (2000). Fears, worries, and scary dreams in 4- to 12-year-old children: Their content, developmental pattern, and origins. *Journal of Clinical Child Psychology, 29*, 43–52.

Murphy, K. R., & Cleveland, J. N. (1995). *Understanding performance appraisal: Social, organizational, and goal-based perspectives.* Thousand Oaks, CA: Sage.

Murray, B. (2002). More students blend business and psychology. *Monitor on Psychology, 33*, 34–35.

Murray, H. A. (1938). *Explorations in personality*. New York: Oxford Univ. Press.

Murray, J. L., Feuerstein, A. N., & Adams, D. C. (2006). Gender differences in moral reasoning and university student views on juvenile justice. *Journal of College and Character, 2*. Retrieved May 10, 2006, from http://www.collegevalues.org/articles.cfm?a=1&id=617

Mussweiler, T., & Englich, B. (2005). Subliminal anchoring: Judgmental consequences and underlying mechanisms. *Organizational Behavior and Human Decision Processes, 98*, 133–143.

Mustanski, B. S., Viken, R. J., Kaprio, J., & Rose, R. J. (2003). Genetic influences on the association between personality risk factors and alcohol use and abuse. *Journal of Abnormal Psychology, 112*, 282–289.

Muth, E. R., Stern, R. M., Uijtdehaage, S. H. J., & Koch, K. L. (1994). Effects of Asian ancestry on susceptibility to vection-induced motion sickness. In J. Z. Chen & R. W. McCallum (Eds.), *Electrogastrography: Principles and applications* (pp. 227–233). New York: Raven.

Myers, G. (2002). Symbolic animals and the developing self. *Anthrozoos, 15*, 19–36.

Myers, J. E., & Sweeney T. J. (2006). *Counseling for wellness: Theory, research, and practice.* Alexandria, VA: American Counseling Assoc.

Naglieri, J. A., & Kaufman, J. C. (2001). Understanding intelligence, giftedness, and creativity using PASS theory. *Roeper Review, 23*, 151–156.

Nairne, J. S. (2003). Sensory and working memory. In A. F. Healy & R. W. Proctor (Eds.), *Handbook of Psychology: Vol. 4, Experimental Psychology*, (pp. 423–444). New York: John Wiley & Sons.

Najavits, L. (2004). Assessment of trauma, PTSD, and substance use disorder: A practical guide. In J. Wilson & T. M. Keane (Eds.), *Assessing psychological trauma and PTSD* (2nd ed., pp. 466–491). New York: Guilford.

Nakao, M., Kashiwagi, M., & Yano, E. (2005). Alexithymia and grief reactions in bereaved Japanese women. *Death Studies, 29*, 423–433.

Narayanan, L., Shanker, M., & Spector, P. E. (1999). Stress in the workplace: A comparison of gender and occupations. *Journal of Organizational Behavior, 20*, 63–73.

Narrow, W. E., Rae, D. S., Robins, L. N., & Regier D. A. (2001). Revised prevalence estimates of mental disorders in the United States: Using a clinical significance criterion to reconcile 2 survey estimates. *Archives of General Psychiatry, 59*, 115–123.

Nash, M. R. (2001). The truth and the hype of hypnosis. *Scientific American, 285*(1), 47–54.

Nash, M. R. (2004). Salient findings: Pivotal reviews and research on hypnosis, soma, and cognition. *International Journal of Clinical and Experimental Hypnosis, 52*, 82–88.

National Adolescent Health Information Center. (2004). *Fact Sheet on Suicide: Adolescents & Young Adults.* San Francisco, CA: Author, Univ. of California, San Francisco.

National Advisory Mental Health Council. (1995). Basic behavioral science research for mental health: A national investment: Emotion and motivation. *American Psychologist, 50*(10), 838–845.

National Alliance on Mental Illness. (2003). About mental illness: Women and depression. Retrieved June 12, 2006, from http://www.nami.org/ Template.cfm?Section=By_Illness&template=/ContentManagement/ContentDisplay.cfm&ContentID=17627

National Clearing House on Child Abuse and Neglect (2006). *Child Maltreatment 2004.* Retrieved May 1, 2006, from http://www.acf.hhs.gov/programs/cb/pubs/cm04/index.htm

National Household Survey on Drug Abuse. (1998). *Summary of findings from the 1998 National Household Survey on Drug Abuse.* Retrieved October 5, 2006, from http://www.oas.samhsa.gov/NHSDA/ 98MF.pdf

National Institute of Mental Health. (2000). *Suicide facts.* Washington, DC. Retrieved October 5, 2006, from http://www.nimh.nih.gov/suicideprevention/suifact.cfm

National Institute of Neurological Disorders and Stroke. (2003). *Brain basics: Understanding sleep.* Retrieved October 5, 2006, from http://www.ninds.nih.gov/disorders/brain_basics/understanding_sleep.htm

National Institute on Aging. (2006). The impact of Alzheimer's disease. Retrieved May 11, 2006 from http://www.nia.nih.gov/Alzheimers/Publications/UnravelingTheMystery/ImpactOfAlzheimerIll.htm

National Institute on Alcohol Abuse and Alcoholism. (2003). Does alcohol affect women differently? Retrieved February 26, 2006, from http://www.niaaa.nih.gov/FAQs/General-English/FAQs16.htm

National Institute on Drug Abuse. (2004a). *NIDA InfoFacts: Marijuana.* Retrieved March 16, 2006, from http://www.nida.nih.gov/Infofacts/marijuana.html

National Institute on Drug Abuse. (2004b). *NIDA InfoFacts: Marijuana: Facts parents need to know.* Retrieved March 16, 2006, from http://www.nida.nih.gov/MarijBroch/MarijparentsN.html

National Institute on Drug Abuse. (2005a). *NIDA InfoFacts: Methamphetamine.* Retrieved March 16, 2006, from http://www.nida.nih.gov/Infofacts/methamphetamine.html

National Institute on Drug Abuse (2005b). What is the scope of heroin use in the United States. Retrieved February 26, 2006, from http://www.nida.nih.gov/ResearchReports/Heroin/heroin2.html#scope

National Mental Health Association. (2006). *Suicide: Teen Suicide.* Alexandria, VA: National Mental Health Association. Retrieved May 11, 2006, from http://www.nmha.org/infoctr/factsheets/82.cfm

National Science Foundation. (2001). *Characteristics of recent science and engineering graduates: 2001.* Arlington, VA: National Science Foundation, Division of Science Resources Statistics.

National Science Foundation. (2002). *Women, minorities, and persons with disabilities in science and engineering: 2002.* Arlington, VA: National Science Foundation, Division of Science Resources Statistics.

National Sleep Foundation. (2005). Sleepwalking. Retrieved March 15, 2005 from http://www.sleepfoundation.org/sleeptionary/index.php?id=22

Navarro, J. F., & Maldonado, E. (2004). Effects of acute, subchronic, and intermittent MDMA ("Ecstasy") administration on agonistic interactions between male mice. *Aggressive Behavior, 30*, 71–83.

Neal, A., & Turner, S. M. (1991). Anxiety disorders research with African Americans: Current status. *Psychological Bulletin, 109*, 400–410.

Neath, I. (1993). Contextual and distinctive processes and the serial position function. *Journal of Memory and Language, 32*, 820–840.

Neath, I., Brown, G. D. A., Poirier, M., & Fortin, C. (2005). Short-term and working memory: Past, progress, and prospects. *Memory, 13*, 225–235.

Neher, A. (1991). Maslow's theory of motivation: A critique. *Journal of Humanistic Psychology, 31*, 89–112.

Neisser, U. (1982). *Memory observed: Remembering in natural contexts.* San Francisco: Freeman.

Neisser, U. (1998). Introduction: Rising test scores and what they mean. In U. Neisser (Ed.), *The rising curve: Long-term gains in IQ and related measures* (pp. 3–22). Washington, DC: American Psychological Assoc.

Neisser, U., Boodoo, G., Bouchard, T. J., Jr., Boykin, A. W., Brody, N., Ceci, S. J., et al. (1996). Intelligence: Knowns and unknowns. *American Psychologist, 51*, 77–101.

Nekisha, E. L., Gerald, D. W, Hsiao-ye, Y., & Michael, E. H. (2005). Surveillance report #73, Apparent per capita alcohol consumption: National, State, and Regional trends, 1977–2003. *National Institute on Alcohol Abuse and Alcoholism,Division of Epidemiology and Prevention Research.* Retrieved February 26, 2006 from http://pubs.niaaa.nih.gov/publications/surveillance73/CONS03.htm#fig1

Nelson, C. A., Monk, C. S., Lin, J., Carver, L. C., Thomas, K. M., & Truwit, C. L. (2000). Functional neuroanatomy of spatial working memory in children. *Developmental Psychology, 36*, 109–116.

Nelson, D. L. (1994). Implicit memory. In D. E. Morris & M. Gruneberg (Eds.), *Theoretical aspects of memory* (pp. 130–167). London: Routledge.

Nelson, K., & Fivush, R. (2004). The emergence of autobiographical memory: A social cultural developmental theory. *Psychological Review, 111*, 486–511.

Nelson, S., Lerner, E., Needlman, R., Salvator, M. A., & Singer, L. T. (2004). Cocaine, anemia, and neurodevelopmental outcomes in children: A longitudinal study. *Journal of Developmental and Behavioral Pediatrics, 25*, 1–9.

Nemeroff, C. B., & Schatzberg, A. F. (2002). Pharmacological treatments for unipolar depression. In P. Nathan & J. M. Gorman (Eds.), *A guide to treatments that work* (2nd ed., pp. 212–225). New York: Oxford Univ. Press.

Ness, R. B., Grisso, J. A., Hirschinger, N., Markovic, N., Shaw, L. M., Kay, N. L., et al. (1999). Cocaine and tobacco use and the risk of spontaneous abortion. *New England Journal of Medicine, 340*, 333–339.

Nesse, R. M. (2000). Is depression an adaptation? *Archives of General Psychiatry, 57*, 14–20.

Nestler, E. J., & Malenka, R. C. (2004). The addicted brain. *Scientific American, 290*(3), 78–85.

Neubauer, A. C. (2000). Physiological approaches to human intelligence: A review. *Psychologische Beitrage, 42*, 161–173.

Neugarten, B. L. (1977). Personality and aging. In I. Birren & K. W. Schaie (Eds.), *Handbook of the psychology of aging* (pp. 626–649). New York: Van Nostrand.

Neuschatz, J. S., Preston, E. L., Burkett, A. D., Lampinen, J. M., Neuschatz, J. S., Fairless, A. H., et al. (2005). The effects of post-identification feedback and age on retrospective eyewitness memory. *Applied Cognitive Psychology, 19*, 435–453.

Newcombe, N. S., Drummey, A. B., Fox, N. A., Lie, E., & Ottinger-Alberts, W. O. (2000). Remembering early childhood: How much, how, and why (or why not). *Current Directions in Psychological Science, 9*, 55–58.

Newland, M. C., & Rasmussen, E. B. (2003). Behavior in adulthood and during aging is affected by contaminant exposure in utero. *Current Directions in Psychological Science, 12*, 212–217.

Nickerson, R. S. (1998). Confirmation bias: A ubiquitous phenomenon in many guises. *Review of General Psychology, 2*, 175–220.

Nickerson, R. S., & Adams, M. J. (1979). Long-term memory for a common object. *Cognitive Psychology, 11*, 287–307.

Niehoff, D. (1999). *The biology of violence (How understanding the brain, behavior, and environment can break the vicious circle of aggression).* New York: Free Press.

Nigg, J. T. (2005). Neuropsychologic theory and findings in attention-deficit/hyperactivity disorder: The state of the field and salient challenges for the coming decade. *Biological Psychiatry, 57*, 1424–1435.

Nisbett, R. E., & Norenzayan, A. (2002). Culture and cognition. In H. Pashler & D. Medin (Eds.), *Steven's handbook of experimental psychology* (3rd Ed.): *Vol. 2. Memory and cognitive processes* (pp. 561–597). New York: John Wiley & Sons.

Nisbett, R. E., Peng, K., Choi, I., & Norenzayan, A. (2001). Culture and systems of thought: Holistic versus analytic cognition. *Psychological Review, 108*, 291–310.

Nishimura, Y., Nishimura, T., Hattori, H., Hattori, C., Yonekura, A., & Suzuki, K. (2003). Obesity and obstructive sleep apnea syndrome. *Acta Oto Laryngologica, 123*, 22–24

Nissani, M. (1990). A cognitive reinterpretation of Stanley Milgram's observations on obedience to authority. *American Psychologist, 45*, 1384–1385.

Nixon, N. L., & Doody, G. A. (2005). Official psychiatric morbidity and the incidence of schizophrenia 1881–1994. *Psychological Medicine, 35*, 1145–1153.

Nixon, S. J. (1999). Neurocognitive performance in alcoholics: Is polysubstance abuse important? *Psychological Science, 10*, 181–185.

Nixon-Cave, K. A. (2001). Influence of cultural/ethnic beliefs and behaviors and family environment on the motor development of infants 12–18 months of age in three ethnic groups: African-American, Hispanic/Latino and Anglo-European. *Dissertation Abstracts International: Section B: The Sciences and Engineering, 6*, 2519.

Noël, X., Paternot, J., Van der Linden, M., Sferrazza, R., Verhas, M., Hanak, C., et al. (2001). Correlation between inhibition, working memory and delimited frontal area blood flow measured by ^{99m}Tc-Bicisate SPECT in alcohol-dependent patients. *Alcohol and Alcoholism, 36*, 556–563.

Noga, J. T., Bartley, A. J., Jones, D. W., Torrey, E. F., & Weinberger, D. R. (1996). Cortical gyral anatomy and gross brain dimensions in monozygotic twins discordant for schizophrenia. *Schizophrenia Research, 22*(1), 27–40.

Nolen-Hoeksema, S. (1999, October). Men and women handle negative situations differently, study suggests. *APA Monitor.*

Norcross, J. C. (2002). *Psychotherapeutic relationships that work.* New York: Oxford Univ. Press.

Novak, C. M., & Albers, H. E. (2002). N-Methyl-D-aspartate microinjected into the suprachiasmatic nucleus mimics the phase-shifting effects of light in the diurnal Nile grass rat. *Brain Research, 951*, 255–263.

Novak, M. A. (1991, July). "Psychologists care deeply" about animals. *APA Monitor*, p. 4.

Novick, L. R., & Sherman, S. J. (2003). On the nature of insight solutions: Evidence from skill differences in anagram solution. *Quarterly Journal of Experimental Psychology: Human Experimental Psychology, 56A,* 351–382.

Nowak, A., Vallacher, R. R., & Miller, M. E. (2003). Social influence and group dynamics. In T. Millon & M. J. Lerner (Eds.), *Handbook of psychology: Vol. 5, Personality and social psychology* (pp. 383–417). New York: John Wiley & Sons.

Nowakowski, R. S., & Hayes, N. L. (2004). Quantitative analysis of fetal and adult neurogenesis: Regulation of neuron number. In M. S. Gazzaniga (Ed.), *The cognitive neurosciences* (3rd ed.) (pp. 149–159*)*. Cambridge, MA: MIT Press.

Nower, L., Derevensky, J. L., & Gupta, R. (2004). The relationship of impulsivity, sensation seeking, coping, and substance use in youth gamblers. *Psychology of Additive Behaviors, 18,* 49–55.

Nucci, L. P. (2002). The development of moral reasoning. In U. Goswami (Ed.), *Blackwell handbook of childhood cognitive development* (pp. 303–325). Malden, MA: Blackwell.

Nunokawa, K. (2001). Interactions between subgoals and understanding of problem situations in mathematical problem solving. *Journal of Mathematical Behavior, 20,* 187–205.

Nurmi, E. L., Amin, T., Olson, L. M., Jacobs, M. M., McCauley, J. L., Lam, A. Y., et al. (2003). Dense linkage disequilibrium mapping in the 15q11-q13 maternal expression domain yields evidence for association in autism. *Molecular Psychiatry, 8,* 624–634.

Nuttall, J. (2002). Archetypes and architecture: The coniunctio of Canary Wharf. *Psychodynamic Practice: Individuals, Groups and Organizations, 8,* 33–53.

Nyberg, L., Marklund, P., Persson, J., Cabeza, R., Forkstarn, C., Petersson, K. M., et al. (2003). Common prefrontal activations during working memory, episodic memory, and semantic memory. *Neuropsychologia, 41,* 371–377.

Oberman, L. M., Hubbard, E. M., McCleery, J. P., Altschuler, E. L., Ramachandran, V. S., & Pineda, J. A. (2005). EEG evidence for mirror neuron dysfunction in autism spectrum disorders. *Cognitive Brain Research, 24,* 190–198.

O'Brien, K. M., & Vincent, N. K. (2003). Psychiatric comorbidity in anorexia and bulimia nervosa: Nature, prevalence and causal relationships. *Clinical Psychology Review, 23,* 57–74.

O'Brien, E. M., & Mindell, J. A. (2005). Sleep and risk-taking behavior in adolescents. *Behavioral Sleep Medicine, 3,* 113–133.

O'Callahan, M., Andrews, A. M., & Krantz, D. S. (2003). Coronary heart disease and hypertension. In A. M. Nezu & C. M. Nezu (Eds.), *Handbook of psychology: Vol. 9, Health psychology* (pp. 339–364). New York: John Wiley & Sons.

O'Connor, P. J. (2006). Trends in spinal cord injury. *Accident Analysis & Prevention, 38,* 71–77.

O'Connor, T. G., McGuire, S., Reiss, D., Hetherington, E. M., & Plomin, R. (1998). Co-occurrence of depressive symptoms and antisocial behavior in adolescence: A common genetic liability. *Journal of Abnormal Psychology, 107,* 27–37.

O'Hara, R., Schröder, C. M., Bloss, C. B., Bailey, A., Alyeshmerni, A. M., Mumenthaler, A. M. et al. (2005). Hormone replacement therapy and longitudinal cognitive performance in postmenopausal women. *American Journal of Geriatric Psychiatry, 13,* 1107–1110.

O'Leary, A. (1990). Stress, emotion, and human immune function. *Psychological Bulletin, 108,* 363–382.

O'Leary, D. S., Block, R. I., Turner, B. M., Koeppel, J., Magnotta, V. A., Ponto, L. B., et al. (2003). Marijuana alters the human cerebellar clock. *Neuroreport: For Rapid Communication of Neuroscience Research, 14,* 1145–1151.

O'Leary, S. G. (1995). Parental discipline mistakes. *Current Directions in Psychological Science, 4,* 11–14.

O'Leary, V. E., & Flanagan, E. H. (2001). Leadership. In J. Worell (Ed.), *Encyclopedia of gender.* (Vol. 2, pp. 245–257). San Diego, CA: Academic Press.

O'Leary, V. E., & Bhaju, J. (2006). Resilience and empowerment. In J. Worell & C. D. Goodheart (Eds.), *Handbook of girls' and women's psychological health: Gender and well-being across the life span* (pp. 157–165). New York: Oxford Univ. Press.

Ocampo, C., Prieto, L. R., Whittlesey, V., Connor, J., Janco-Gidley, J., Mannix, S., et al. (2003). Diversity research in *Teaching of Psychology*: Summary and recommendations. *Teaching of Psychology, 30,* 5–18.

Occhionero, M. (2004). Mental processes and the brain during dreams. *Dreaming, 14,* 54–64.

Offer, D., Ostrov, E., Howard, K. I., & Atkinson, R. (1988). *The teenage world: Adolescents' self-image in ten countries.* New York: Plenum.

Ogawa, S., Lubahn, D., Korach, K., & Pfaff, D. (1997). Behavioral effects of estrogen receptor gene disruption in male mice. *Proceedings of the National Academy of Sciences of the U.S.A., 94,* 1476.

Ogrodniczuk, J. S., Piper, W. E., & Joyce, A. S. (2004). Differences in men's and women's responses to short-term group psychotherapy. *Psychotherapy Research, 14,* 231–243.

Ogrodniczuk, J. S., & Staats, H. (2002). Psychotherapy and gender: Do men and women require different treatments? *Zeitschrift fuer Psychosomatische Medizin und Psychotherapie, 48,* 270–285.

Ohring, R., Graber, J., & Brooks-Gunn, J. (2002). Girl's recurrent and concurrent body dissatisfaction: Correlates and consequences over 8 years. *International Journal of Eating Disorders, 31,* 404–415.

Olds, M. E., & Forbes, J. L. (1981). The central basis of motivation: Intracranial self-stimulation studies. *Annual Review of Psychology, 32,* 523–574.

Olfson, M., Marcus, S. C., Druss, B., & Pincus, H. A. (2002). National trends in the use of outpatient psychotherapy. *American Journal of Psychiatry, 19,* 1914–1920.

Olfson, M., Marcus, S., Sackeim, H. A., Thompson, J., & Pincus, H. A. (1998). Use of ECT for the inpatient treatment of recurrent major depression. *American Journal of Psychiatry, 155,* 22–29.

Olney, J. W., Wozniak, D. F., Farber, N. B., Jevtovic-Todorovic, V., & Bittigau, I. C. (2002). The enigma of fetal alcohol neurotoxicity. *Annals of Medicine, 34,* 109–119.

Olson, M. V., & Varki, A. (2003). Sequencing the chimpanzee genome: insights into human evolution and disease. *Nature Review Genetics, 4,* 20–8.

Oltmanns, T. F., & Emery, R. E. (1998). *Abnormal psychology* (2nd ed.). Upper Saddle River, NJ: Prentice Hall.

Oltmanns, T. F., & Emery, R. E. (2006). *Abnormal psychology* (5th ed.). Upper Saddle River, NJ: Prentice Hall.

Olton, D. S., & Noonberg, A. R. (1980). *Biofeedback: Clinical applications in behavioral science.* Englewood Cliffs, NJ: Prentice Hall.

Olzewski-Kubilius, P. (2003). Gifted education programs and procedures. In W. M. Reynolds & G. E. Miller (Eds.), *Handbook of psychology: Vol. 7, Educational psychology* (pp. 487–510). New York: John Wiley & Sons.

Omi, M., & Winant, H. (1994). *Racial formation in the United States: From the 1960s to the 1990s* (2nd ed). New York: Routledge.

Onyskiw, J. E. (2000). Processes underlying children's responses to witnessing physical aggression in their families. *Dissertation Abstracts International: Section B: The Sciences and Engineering, 61*, 1620.

Orbuch, T. L., House, J. S., Mero, R. P., & Webster, P. S. (1996). Marital quality over the life course. *Social Psychology Quarterly, 59*, 162–171.

Orlinsky, D. E., & Howard, K. I. (1994). Unity and diversity among psychotherapies: A comparative perspective. In B. Bonger & L. E. Beutler (Eds.), *Foundations of psychotherapy: Theory, research, and practice* (pp. 3–23). New York: Basic Books.

Ornish, D., Scherwitz, L. W., Billings, J. H., Gould, K. L, Merritt, T. A. Sparler, S., et al. (1998). Intensive lifestyle changes for reversal of coronary heart disease. *Journal of the American Medical Association, 280*, 2001–2007.

Ortiz, S. O., & Dynda, A. M. (2005). Use of intelligence tests with culturally and linguistically diverse populations. In D. P. Flanagan & P. L. Harrison (Eds.), *Contemporary intellectual assessment: Theories, tests, and issues* (pp. 545–556). New York: Guilford.

Osborne, J. W. (1997). Race and academic disidentification. *Journal of Educational Psychology, 89*, 728–735.

Ostroff, C., & Ford, J. K. (1989). Assessing training needs: Critical levels of analysis. In I. L. Goldstein & Associates (Eds.), *Training and development in organizations* (pp. 25–62). San Francisco: Jossey-Bass.

Ostrov, J. M., & Keating, C. F. (2004). Gender differences in preschool aggression during free play and structured interactions: An observational study. *Social Development, 13*, 255–277.

Otmani, S., Pebayle, T., Roge, J., & Muzet, A. (2005). Effect of driving duration and partial sleep deprivation on subsequent alertness and performance of car drivers. *Physiology & Behavior, 84*, 715–724.

Ouimette, P., Humphreys, K., Moos, R. H., Finney, J. W., Cronkite, R., & Federman, B. (2001). Self-help group participation among substance use disorder patients with posttraumatic stress disorder. *Journal of Substance Abuse Treatment, 20*, 25–32.

Overholser, J. C. (2003). Rational–emotive behavior therapy: An interview with Albert Ellis. *Journal of Contemporary Psychotherapy, 33*, 187–204.

Overmier, J. B. (2002). On learned helplessness. *Integrative Physiological and Behavioral Science, 37*, 4–8.

Owen, C. J. (2005). The empty nest transition: The relationship between attachment style and women's use of this period as a time for growth and change. *Dissertation Abstracts International: Section B: The Sciences and Engineering, 65*, 3747.

Owens, J., Maxim R., McGuinn, M., Nobile, C., Msall, M., & Alario, A. (1999). Television-viewing habits and sleep disturbance in school children. *Pediatrics, 104*, 27.

Ozer, D. J., & Reise, S. P. (1994). Personality assessment. *Annual Review of Psychology, 45*, 357–388.

Ozer, E. J., Best, S. R., Lipsey, T. L., & Weiss, D. S. (2003). Predictors of posttraumatic stress disorder and symptoms in adults: A meta-analysis. *Psychological Bulletin, 2003*, 52–73.

Padhi, K. (2005). Pain and psychological approaches to its management—The gate control theory of pain. *Social Science International, 21*, 121–130.

Paikoff, R. L., & Brooks-Gunn, J. (1991). Do parent–child relationships change during puberty? *Psychological Bulletin, 110*, 47–66.

Paivio, A. (1986). *Mental representations: A dual coding approach.* New York: Oxford Univ. Press.

Palmer, J. (2003). ESP in the Ganzfeld: Analysis of a debate. *Journal of Consciousness Studies, 10* [Special issue: Parapsychology], 51–68.

Palomares, N. A.(2004). Gender schematicity, gender identity salience, and gender-linked language use. *Human Communication Research, 30*, 556–588.

Panksepp, J. (2005). Affective consciousness: Core emotional feelings in animals and humans. *Consciousness and Cognition: An International Journal, 14*, 30–80.

Panksepp, J., Siviy, S., & Normansell, L. A. (1984). The psychology of play: Theoretical and methodological perspectives. *Neuroscience and Biobehavioral Reviews, 8*, 465–492.

Papassotiropoulos, A., Luetjohann, D., Bagli, M., Locatelli, S., Jessen, F., Buschfort, R., et al. (2002). 24S-hydroxycholesterol in cerebrospinal fluid is elevated in early stages of dementia. *Journal of Psychiatric Research, 36*, 27–32.

Papp, S. (2006). A relevance-theoretic account of the development and deficits of theory of mind in normally developing children and individuals with autism. *Theory and Psychology, 16*, 141–161.

Pare, D., Collins, D. R., & Guillaume, P. J. (2002). Amygdala oscillations and the consolidation of emotional memories. *Trends in Cognitive Sciences, 6*, 306–314.

Paris, S. G., & Weissberg, J. A. (1986). Young children's remembering in different contexts: A reinterpretation of Istomina's study. *Child Development, 57*, 1123–1129.

Park-Gates, S. L. (2002). Effects of group interactive brainstorming on creativity. *Dissertation Abstracts International: Section A: Humanities and Social Science, 62*, 2363.

Parks, J. B., & Roberton, M. A. (2004). Explaining age and gender effects on attitudes toward sexist language. *Journal of Language and Social Psychology, 24*, 401–411.

Parr, L. A. (2003). Case study 10A. Emotional recognition by chimpanzees. In F. B. M. de Waal & P. L. Tyack (Eds.), *Animal social complexity: Intelligence, culture, and individualized societies* (pp. 288–292). Cambridge, MA: Harvard Univ. Press.

Parslow, R. A., Jorm, A. F., & Christensen, H. (2006). Associations of pretrauma attributes and trauma exposure with screening positive for PTSD: Analysis of a community-based study of 2085 young adults. *Psychological Medicine, 36*, 387–395.

Pate, W. E. II (2001, April). *Analyses of data from Graduate Study in Psychology: 1999–2000.* Washington: American Psychological Assoc.

Patenaude, A. F. (2005). Genetics and social change. In A. F. Patenaude (Ed.), *Genetic testing for cancer: Psychological approaches for helping patients and families* (pp. 267–276). Washington, DC: American Psychological Assoc.

Patenaude, A. F., Guttmacher, A. E., & Collins, F. S. (2002). Genetic testing and psychology: New roles, new responsibilities. *American Psychologist, 5*, 271–282.

Patrick, C. J. (1994). Emotion and psychopathy: Startling new insights. *Psychophysiology, 31*, 319–330.

Patterson, C. J. (1995). Families of the baby boom: Parents' division of labor and children's adjustment. [Special issue: *Sexual orientation and human development*]. *Developmental Psychology, 31*, 115–123.

Patterson, C. J. (2000). Family relationships of lesbians and gay men. *Journal of Marriage and the Family, 62*, 1052–1069.

Patterson, D. R., & Jensen, M. P. (2003). Hypnosis and clinical pain. *Psychological Bulletin, 129*, 495–521.

Patterson, D. R., & Ptacek, J. T. (1997). Baseline pain as a moderator of hypnotic analgesia for burn injury treatment. *Journal of Consulting & Clinical Psychology, 65*, 60–67.

Patterson, F. G. (1981). *The education of Koko.* New York: Holt, Rinehart & Winston.

Patterson, F. G., & Cohn, R. H. (1990). Language acquisition by a lowland gorilla: Koko's first ten years of vocabulary development. *Word, 41*, 97–143.

Paul, T., Schroeter, K., Dahme, B., & Nutzinger, D. (2002). Self-injurious behavior in women with eating disorders. *American Journal of Psychiatry, 15*, 408–411.

Paunonen, S. V. (2003). Big Five factors of personality and replicated predictions of behavior. *Journal of Personality and Social Psychology, 84*, 411–422.

Paunonen, S. V., & Ashton, M. C. (2001). Big Five factors and facets and the prediction of behavior. *Journal of Personality and Social Psychology, 81*, 524–539.

Paunovic, N., & Oest, L. G. (2001). Cognitive behavior therapy versus exposure therapy in the treatment of PTSD in refugees. *Behaviour Research and Therapy, 39*, 1183–1197.

Pavlov, I. P. (1927). *Conditional reflexes* (G. V. Anrep, trans.). London: Oxford Univ. Press.

Payne, J. D., Jackson, E. D., Ryan, L., Hoscheidt, S., Jacobs, W. J., & Nadel, L. (2006). The impact of stress on neutral and emotional aspects of episodic memory. *Memory, 14*, 1–16.

Payne, J. D., & Nadel, L. (2004). Sleep, dreams, and memory consolidation: The role of the stress hormone cortisol. *Learning & Memory, 11*, 671–678.

Pechnick, R. N., & Ungerleider, J. T. (2004). Hallucinogens. In M. Galanter & D. Herbert (Eds.), *The American Psychiatric Publishing textbook of substance abuse treatment* (3rd ed., pp. 199–209). Washington, DC: American Psychiatric Publishing.

Peck, J. S., LeGoff, D. B., Ahmed, I., & Goebert, D. (2004). Cognitive effects of exogenous melatonin administration in elderly persons: A pilot study. *American Journal of Geriatric Psychiatry, 12*, 432–436.

Pedersen, P. B., & Carey, J. C. (2003). *Multicultural counseling in schools* (2nd ed.). Boston: Allyn & Bacon.

Pederson, D. (2002). Political violence, ethnic conflict, and contemporary wars: Broad implications for health and social well-being. *Social Science and Medicine, 55*, 175–190.

Pedlow, R., Sanson, A., Prior, M., & Oberklaid, F. (1993). Stability of maternally reported temperament from infancy to 8 years. *Developmental Psychology, 29*, 998–1007.

Pegna, A. J., Khateb, A., & Lazeyras, F. (2005). Discriminating emotional faces without primary visual cortices involves the right amygdala. *Nature Neuroscience, 8*, 24–25.

Pellegrini, A. D., & Galda, L. (1994). Play. In V. A. Ramachandran (Ed.) *Encyclopedia of human behavior* (Vol. 3, pp. 535–543). San Diego, CA: Academic Press.

Pelletier, S., & Dorval, M. (2004). Predictive genetic testing raises new professional challenges for psychologists. *Canadian Psychology, 45*, 16–30.

Peng, K., & Nisbett, R. E. (1999). Culture, dialectics, and reasoning about contradiction. *American Psychologist, 54*, 741–754.

Peplau, L. A. (2003). Human sexuality: How do men and women differ? *Current Directions in Psychological Science, 12*, 37–40.

Peplau, L. A., & Beals, K. P. (2004). The family lives of lesbians and gay men. In A. L. Vangelisti (Ed.), *Handbook of family communication* (pp. 233–248). Mahwah, NJ: Erlbaum.

Peplau, L. A., & Cochran, S. D. (1990). A relationship perspective on homosexuality. In D. P. McWhirter, S. A. Sanders, & J. M. Reinisch (Eds.), *Homosexuality/heterosexuality: The Kinsey scale and current research.* New York: Oxford Univ. Press.

Pepperberg, I. M. (2000). *The Alex studies: Cognitive and communicative abilities of gray parrots.* Cambridge, MA: Harvard Univ. Press.

Pepperberg, I. M. (2002). Cognitive and communicative abilities of grey parrots. In M. Bekoff & C. Allen (Eds.), *The cognitive animal: Empirical and theoretical perspectives on animal cognition* (pp. 247–253). Cambridge, MA: MIT Press.

Pepperberg, I. M. (2006). Grey parrot (*Psittacus erithacus*) numerical abilities: Addition and further experiments on a zero-like concept. *Journal of Comparative Psychology, 120*, 1–11.

Perkins, S. (2005, May 14). Learning to listen: How some invertebrates evolved biological sonar. *Science News*, 314–316.

Perloff, R. M. (2003). *The dynamics of persuasion: Communication and attitudes in the 21st century* (2nd ed.). Mahwah, NJ: Erlbaum.

Perret, D. I., Lee, K. J., Penton-Voak, I., Rowland, D., Yoshikawa, S., Burt, D. M., et al., (1998). Effects of sexual dimorphism on facial attractiveness. *Nature, 394*, 884.

Perry, B. D., & Pollard, R. (1998). Homeostasis, stress, trauma, and adaptation: A neurodevelopmental view of childhood trauma. *Child Adolescent Psychiatric Clinics of North America, 7*, 33–51.

Perry, D. G., Perry, L. C., & Weiss, R. J. (1989). Sex differences in the consequences that children anticipate for aggression. *Developmental Psychology, 25*, 312–319.

Perry, J., Silvera, D., & Rosenvinge, J. H. (2002). Are oral, obsessive, and hysterical personality traits related to disturbed eating patterns? A general population study of 6,313 men and women. *Journal of Personality Assessment, 78*, 405–416.

Persky, H. (1983). Psychosexual effects of hormones. *Medical Aspects of Human Sexuality, 17*, 74–101.

Person, E. S., Cooper, A., & Gabbard, G. O. (2005). *Textbook of psychoanalysis.* Washington, DC: American Psychiatric Publishing.

Persson-Blennow, I., & McNeil, T. F. (1988). Frequencies and stability of temperament types in childhood. *Journal of the American Academy of Child and Adolescent Psychiatry, 27*, 619–622.

Pert, C. B., & Snyder, S. H. (1973). The opiate receptor: Demonstration in nervous tissue. *Science, 179*, 1011–1014.

Peters, R. (2005). Ageing and the brain. *Postgraduate Medical Journal, 82*, 84–88.

Petersen, R. C., Stevens, J. C., Ganguli, M., Tangalos, E. G., Cummings, J. L., & DeKosky, S. T. (2001). Practice parameter: Early detection of dementia: Mild cognitive impairment (an evidence-based review.) *Neurology, 56*, 1133–1142.

Peterson, C. (2000). The future of optimism. *American Psychologist, 55*, 44–55.

Peterson, C., & Bossio, L. M. (1989). Learned helplessness. In R. C. Curtis (Ed.), *Self-Defeating Behaviors: Experimental Research, Clinical Impressions, and Practical Implications* (pp. 235–257). New York: Plenum.

Peterson, C., Maier, S. F., & Seligman, M. E. P. (1993a). Explanatory style and helplessness. *Social Behavior and Personality, 20*, 1–14.

Peterson, C., Maier, S. F., & Seligman, M. E. P. (1993b). *Learned helplessness: A theory for the age of personal control.* New York: Oxford Univ. Press.

Peterson, C., Vaillant, G. E., & Seligman, M. E. P. (1988). Explanatory style as a risk factor for illness. *Cognitive Therapy and Research, 12*, 119–132.

Peterson, L. R., & Peterson, M. J. (1959). Short-term retention of individual verbal items. *Journal of Experimental Psychology, 58*, 193–198.

Pettigrew, T. F. (1998). Intergroup contact theory. *Annual Review of Psychology, 49,* 65–85.

Pettit, J. W., & Joiner, T. E. (2006). Interpersonal conflict avoidance. In J. W. Pettit & J. T. Joiner (Eds.), *Chronic depression: Interpersonal sources, therapeutic solutions* (pp. 73–84). Washington, DC: American Psychological Assoc.

Petty, R. E., & Cacioppo, J. T. (1986a). The elaboration likelihood model of persuasion. In L. Berkowitz (Ed.), *Advances in experimental social psychology* (Vol. 19, pp. 123–205). Orlando, FL: Academic Press.

Petty, R. E., & Cacioppo, J. T. (1986b). *Communication and persuasion: Central and peripheral routes to attitude change.* New York: Springer-Verlag.

Petty, R. E., Wegener, D. T., & Fabrigar, L. R. (1997). Attitudes and attitude change. *Annual Review of Psychology, 48,* 609–647.

Pew Research Center for the People and the Press. (2002, September 5). *One year later: New Yorkers more troubled, Washingtonians more on edge.* Retrieved July 13, 2004, from http://people-press.org/reports/display.php3?PageID=632

Pew Research Center for the People and the Press. (2005). *Huge racial divide over Katrina and its consequences.* Washington, DC. Retrieved August 1, 2006, from http://people-press.org/reports/pdf/255.pdf

Phelps, J. A., Davis, J. O., & Schartz, K. M. (1997). Nature, nurture, and twin research strategies. *Current Directions in Psychological Science, 6,* 117–121.

Philip, P., Taillard, J., Sagaspe, P., Valtat, C., Sanchez, O., Moore, N., et al., (2004). Age, performance and sleep deprivation. *Journal of Sleep Research, 13,* 105–110.

Piaget, J. (1967). *Six psychological studies.* New York: Random House.

Piaget, J. (1969). The intellectual development of the adolescent. In G. Caplan & S. Lebovici (Eds.), *Adolescence: Psychosocial perspectives.* New York: Basic Books.

Pickren, W. E. (2004). Between the cup of principle and the lip of practice: Ethnic minorities and American psychology, 1966–1980. *History of Psychology, 7,* 45–64.

Piefke, M., Weiss, P. H., & Markowitsch, H. J. (2005). Gender differences in the functional neuroanatomy of emotional episodic autobiographical memory. *Human Brain Mapping, 24,* 313–324.

Pietrzak, R. H., & Petry, N. M. (2005). Antisocial personality disorder is associated with increased severity of gambling, medical, drug and psychiatric problems among treatment-seeking pathological gamblers. *Addiction, 100,* 1183–1193.

Pinhas, L., Weaver, H., Bryden, P., Ghabbour, N., & Toner, B. (2002). Gender-role conflict and suicidal behaviour in adolescent girls. *Canadian Journal of Psychiatry, 47,* 473–476.

Pinker, S. (1994). *The language instinct: How the mind creates language.* New York: HarperCollins.

Pinker, S. (1997). *How the mind works.* New York: Norton.

Pinker, S. (1999). *Words and rules: The ingredients of language.* New York: Basic Books.

Pinker, S. (2002). *The blank slate: The modern denial of human nature.* New York: Viking.

Pinker, S., & Jackendoff, R. (2005). The faculty of language: What's special about it? *Cognition, 95,* 201–236.

Pinto, S., Thobois, S., Costes, N., Le Bars, D., Benabid, A. L., Broussolle, E., et al. (2004). Subthalamic nucleus stimulation and dysarthria in Parkinson's disease: A PET study. *Brain: A Journal of Neurology, 127,* 602–615.

Piomelli, D. (2001). Cannabinoid activity curtails cocaine craving. *Nature Medicine, 7,* 1099–1100.

Pirkle, E. C., & Richter, L. (2006). Personality, attitudinal and behavioral risk profiles of young female binge drinkers and smokers. *Journal of Adolescent Health, 38,* 44–54.

Pitman, G. E. (2003). Evolution, but no revolution. The "tend and befriend" theory of stress and coping. *Psychology of Women Quarterly, 27,* 194–195.

Plomin, R. (1994). *Genetics and experience: The interplay between nature and nurture.* Thousand Oaks, CA: Sage.

Plomin, R. (1997). Identifying genes for cognitive abilities and disabilities. In R. J. Sternberg & E. Grigorenko (Eds.), *Intelligence: Heredity and environment.* New York: Cambridge Univ. Press.

Plomin, R. (1999). Parents and personality. *Contemporary Psychology, 44,* 269–271.

Plomin, R., & Asbury, K. (2005). Nature and nurture: Genetic and environmental influences on behavior. *Annals of the American Academy of Political and Social Science, 600,* 86–98.

Plomin, R., Defries, J. C., Craig, I. W., & McGuffin, P. (2003). Behavioral genomics. In R. Plomin & J. C. Defries (Eds.). *Behavioral genetics in the postgenomic era* (pp. 531–540). Washington, DC: American Psychological Assoc.

Plomin, R., DeFries, J. C., & McClearn, G. E. (1990). *Behavioral genetics: A primer* (2nd ed.). New York: Freeman.

Plomin, R., & Rende, R. (1991). Human behavioral genetics. *Annual Review of Psychology, 42,* 161–190.

Plomin, R., & Spinath, F. M. (2004). Intelligence: Genetics, genes, and genomics. *Journal of Personality and Social Psychology, 86,* 112–129.

Plutchik, R. (1980). *Emotion: A psychoevolutionary synthesis.* New York: Harper & Row.

Plutchik, R. (1994). *The psychology and biology of emotion.* New York: Harper-Collins.

Plutchik, R. (2002). *Emotions and life: Perspectives for psychology, biology, and evolution.* Washington, DC: American Psychological Assoc.

Pogarsky, G., & Piquero, A. R. (2003). Can punishment encourage offending? Investigating the "resetting" effect. *Journal of Research in Crime and Delinquency, 40,* 95–120.

Pohl, R. F., Schwarz, S., Sczesny, S., & Stahlberg, D. (2003). Hindsight bias in gustatory judgements. *Experimental Psychology, 50,* 107–115.

Pollack, W. S., & Levant, R. F. (1998). *New psychotherapy for men.* New York: Wiley.

Pollard, C. A. (2000). Flooding. In A. E. Kazdin (Ed.), *Encyclopedia of Psychology,* (Vol. 3, pp. 377–379). Washington, DC: American Psychological Assoc.

Pooley, E. (2005). Job rotation. *Canadian Business, 78,* 109.

Pope, C. G., Pope, H. G., & Menard, W. (2005). Clinical features of muscle dysmorphia among males with body dysmorphic disorder. *Body Image, 2,* 395–400.

Pope, H. G. (2000). *The Adonis complex: The secret crisis of male obsession.* New York: Free Press.

Pope, M., & Scott, J. (2003). Do clinicians understand why individuals stop taking lithium? *Journal of Affective Disorders, 74,* 287–291.

Porkka-Heiskanen, T., Strecker, R. E., Thakkar, M., Bjˉrkum, A. A., Greene, R. W., & McCarley, R. W. (1997, May 23). Adenosine: A mediator of the sleep-inducing effects of prolonged wakefulness. *Science, 276,* 1265–1268.

Port, C. L., Engdahl, B., & Frazier, P. (2001). A longitudinal and retrospective study of PTSD among older prisoners of war. *American Journal of Psychiatry, 158,* 1474–1479.

Porter, L. S., & Stone, A. A. (1995). Are there really gender differences in coping? A reconsideration of previous results from a daily study. *Journal of Social and Clinical Psychology, 14*, 184–202.

Post, R. M., Leverich, G. S., Weiss, S. R. B., Zhang, L-X., Xing, G., Li, H., et al. (2003). Psychosocial stressors as predisposing factors to affective illness and PTSD: Potential neurobiological mechanisms and theoretical implications. In D. Cicchetti & E. Walker (Eds.), *Neurodevelopmental mechanisms in psychopathology* (pp. 491–525). New York: Cambridge Univ. Press.

Pothier, P. K. T. (2002). Effect of relaxation on neuro-immune responses of persons undergoing chemotherapy. *Dissertation Abstracts International: Section B: The Sciences and Engineering, 62*, 4471.

Powell, L. H., Shababi, L., & Thoresen, C. E. (2003). Religion and spirituality: Linkages to physical health. *American Psychologist, 58*, 36–52.

Powell, S., Rosner, R., Butollo, W., Tedeschi, R. G., & Calhoun, L. G. (2003). Posttraumatic growth after a war: A study with former refugees and displaced people in Sarajevo. *Journal of Clinical Psychology, 59*, 71–83.

Powers, R. S., & Reiser, C. (2005). Gender and self-perceptions of social power. *Social Behavior and Personality, 33*, 553–568.

Premack, D. (1971, May 21). Language in chimpanzee? *Science, 172*, 808–822.

Premack, D. (1976). *Intelligence in ape and man.* Hillsdale, NJ: Erlbaum.

Prickaerts, J., Koopmans, G., Blokland, A., & Scheepens, A. (2004). Learning and adult neurogenesis: Survival with or without proliferation? *Neurobiology of Learning and Memory, 81*, 1–11.

Pridmore, S., Chambers, A., & McArthur, M. (2005). Neuroimaging in psychopathy. *Australian and New Zealand Journal of Psychiatry, 39*, 856–865.

Prinz, J. J. (2005). Emotions, embodiment, and awareness. In L. F. Barrett, P. M. Niedenthal, & P. Winkielman (Eds.), *Emotion and consciousness* (pp. 363–383). New York: Guilford.

Prior, M., Smart, D., Sanson, A., & Obeklaid, F. (1993). Sex differences in psychological adjustment from infancy to 8 years. *Journal of the American Academy of Child and Adolescent Psychiatry, 32*, 291–304.

Ptacek, J. T., Smith R. E., & Dodge, K. L. (1994). Gender differences in coping with stress: When stressor and appraisals do not differ. *Personality and Social Psychology Bulletin, 20*, 421–430.

Puca, A. A., Daly, M. J., Brewster, S. J., Matise, T. C., Barrett, J., Shea-Drinkwater, M., et al. (2001). A genome-wide scan for linkages to human exceptional longevity identifies a locus on chromosome 4. *Proceedings of the National Academy of Sciences, USA, 98*, 10505–10508.

Putnam, F. W. (1984). The psychophysiological investigation of multiple personality: A review. *Psychiatric Clinics of North America, 7*, 31–39.

Putnam, F. W., Guroff, J. J., Silberman, E. D., Barban, L., & Post, R. M. (1986). The clinical phenomenology of multiple personality disorder: Review of 100 recent cases. *Journal of Clinical Psychology, 47*, 285–293.

Putrevu, S. (2005). Differences in readers' response towards advertising versus publicity. *Psychological Reports, 96*, 207–212.

Pych, J. C., Chang, Q., & Colon-Rivera, C. (2005). Acetylcholine release in the hippocampus and striatum during place and response training. *Learning & Memory, 12*, 564–572.

Quadrel, M. J., Prouadrel, Fischoff, B., & Davis, W. (1993). Adolescent (In)vulnerability. *American Psychologist, 2*, 102–116.

Quan, N., Zhang, Z. B., Demetrikopoulos, M. K., Kitson, R. P., Chambers, W. H., Goldfarb, R. H., et al. (1999). Evidence for involvement of B lymphocytes in the surveillance of lung metastases in the rat. *Cancer Research, 59*, 1080–1089.

Querido, J., Warner, T., & Eyberg, S. (2002). Parenting styles and child behavior in African American families of preschool children. *Journal of Clinical Child and Adolescent Psychology, 31*, 272–277.

Quesnel, C., Savard, J., Simard, S., Ivers, H., & Morin, C. M. (2003). Efficacy of cognitive-behavioral therapy for insomnia in women treated for nonmetastatic breast cancer. *Journal of Consulting and Clinical Psychology, 71*, 189–200.

Quist, R. M., & Crano, W. D. (2003). Assumed policy similarity and voter preference. *Journal of Social Psychology, 143*, 149–162.

Rabasca, L. (1999a, June). Improving life for the survivors of cancer. *APA Monitor*, pp. 28–29.

Rabasca, L. (1999b, November). Is it depression? Or could it be a mild traumatic brain injury? *APA Monitor*, pp. 27–28.

Rabasca, L. (2000a, March). Lessons in diversity [and] helping American Indians earn psychology degrees. *Monitor on Psychology, 31*, 50–53.

Rabasca, L. (2000b, April). Self-help sites: A blessing or a bane? *Monitor on Psychology, 31*, 28–30.

Rabasca, L. (2000c, April). Taking telehealth to the next step. *Monitor on Psychology, 31*, 36–37.

Rabasca, L. (2000d, April). Taking time and space out of service delivery. *Monitor on Psychology, 31*, 40–41.

Rabin, B. S., & Koenig, H. G. (2002). Immune, neuroendocrine, and religious measures. In H. G. Koenig & H. J. Cohen (Eds.), *The link between religion and health: Psychoneuroimmunology and the faith factor* (pp. 197–249). London: Oxford Univ. Press.

Rahman, Q., & Wilson, G. (2003). Born gay? The psychobiology of human sexual orientation. *Personality & Individual Differences, 34*, 1387–1382.

Rainer, G., & Miller, E. K. (2002). Timecourse of object-related neural activity in the primate prefrontal cortex during a short-term memory task. *European Journal of Neuroscience, 15*, 1244–1254.

Rajan, R., Clement, J. P., & Bhalla, U. S. (2006, February 3). Rats smell in stereo. *Science, 311*, 666–670.

Ramachandran, V. S. (2005). Mirror neurons and imitation learning as the driving force behind "the great leap forward" in human evolution. Retrieved March 8, 2006 from http://www.edge.org/documents/archive/edge69.html

Ramey, C. T., Ramey, S. L., & Lanzi, R. G. (2001). Intelligence and experience. In R. J. Sternberg & E. L. Grigorenko (Eds.), *Environmental effects on cognitive abilities* (pp. 83–115). Mahwah, NJ: Erlbaum.

Ramey, S. L. (1999). Head Start and preschool education: Toward continued improvement. *American Psychologist, 54*, 344–346.

Ramus, F., Hauser, M. D., Miller, C., Morris, D., & Mehler, J. (2000, April 14). Language discrimination by human newborns and by cotton-top Tamarin monkeys. *Science, 288*, 349–351.

Rapoport, M. J., McCullagh, S., Streiner, D., & Feinstein, A. (2003). The clinical significance of major depression following mild traumatic brain injury. *Psychosomatics: Journal of Consultation Liaison Psychiatry, 44*, 31–37.

Rapp, M. A., Schnaider-Beeri, M., Grossman, H. T., Sano, M., Perl, D. P., Purohit, D. P., et al. (2006). Increased hippocampal plaques and tangles in patients with Alzheimer disease with a lifetime history of major depression. *Archives of General Psychiatry, 63*, 161–167.

Rasika, S., Alvarez-Buylla, A., & Nottebohm, F. (1999). BDNF mediates the effects of testosterone on the survival of new neurons in an adult brain. *Neuron, 22*, 53–62.

Rathus, S. A. (2006). *Childhood and adolescence: Voyages in development.* Belmont CA: Wadsworth.

Rau, H., Buehrer, M., & Weitkunat, R. (2003). Biofeedback of R-wave-to-pulse interval normalizes blood pressure. *Applied Psychophysiology and Biofeedback, 28*, 37–46.

Raven, B. H. (1998). Groupthink: Bay of Pigs and Watergate reconsidered. *Organizational Behavior and Human Decision Processes, 73*, 352–361.

Ravussin, E., Pratley, R. E., Maffei, M., Wang, H., Friedman, J. M., Bennett, P. H., et al. (1997). Relatively low plasma leptin concentrations precede weight gain in Pima Indians. *Nature Medicine, 3*, 238–240.

Rayman, P., & Bluestone, B. (1982). *The private and social response to job loss: A metropolitan study*. Final report of research sponsored by the Center for Work and Mental Health, National Institute of Mental Health.

Read, J., Perry, B. D., Moskowitz, A., & Connolly, J. (2001). The contribution of early traumatic events to schizophrenia in some patients: A traumagenic neurodevelopmental model. *Psychiatry: Interpersonal and Biological Processes, 64*, 319–345.

Redelmeier, D. A., & Tversky, A. (2004). On the belief that arthritis pain is related to the weather. In E. Shafir (Ed.), *Preference, belief, and similarity: Selected writings by Amos Tversky* (pp. 377–381). Cambridge, MA: MIT Press.

Ree, M. J., & Earles, J. A. (1992). Intelligence is the best predictor of job performance. *Current Directions in Psychological Science, 1*, 86–89.

Ree, M. J., Earles, J. A., & Teachout, M. S. (1994). Predicting job performance: Not much more than g. *Journal of Applied Psychology, 79*, 518–524.

Reed, S. K. (2003). *Cognition: Theory and applications* (6th ed.). Belmont, CA: Wadsworth.

Refinetti, R. (2000). *The clocks within us.* Boca Raton, FL: CRC Press.

Reiche, E. M. V., Morimoto, H. K., & Nunes, S. O. V. (2005). Stress and depression-induced immune dysfunction: Implications for the development and progression of cancer. *International Review of Psychiatry, 17*, 515–527.

Reinisch, J. M., & Sanders, S. A. (1982). Early barbiturate exposure: The brain, sexually dimorphic behavior and learning. *Neuroscience and Biobehavioral Reviews, 6*, 311–319.

Reinisch, J. M., Ziemba-Davis, M., & Sanders, S. A. (1991). Hormonal contributions to sexually dimorphic behavioral development in humans. *Psychoneuroendocrinology, 16*, 213–278.

Reiss, S. (2005). Extrinsic and intrinsic motivation at 30: Unresolved scientific issues. *Behavior Analyst, 28*, 1–14.

Renner, M. J., & Mackin, R. S. (1998). A life stress instrument for classroom use. *Teaching of Psychology, 25*, 46–48.

Renner, M. J., & Mackin, R. S. (2002). A life stress instrument for classroom use. In R. A. Griggs (Ed.), *Handbook for teaching introductory psychology* (Vol. 3, pp. 236–238). Mahwah, NJ: Erlbaum.

Renzulli, J. S. (1978). What makes giftedness? Reexamining a definition. *Phi Delta Kappan, 60*, 180–184, 216.

Reppucci, N. D., Woolard, J. L., & Fried, C. S. (1999). Social, community and preventive interventions. *Annual Review of Psychology, 50*, 387–418

Rescorla, R. A. (1966). Predictability and number of pairings in Pavlovian fear conditioning. *Psychonomic Science, 4*, 383–384.

Rescorla, R. A. (1967). Pavlovian conditioning and its proper control procedures. *Psychological Review, 74*, 71–80.

Rescorla, R. A. (1988). Pavlovian conditioning: It's not what you think. *American Psychologist, 43*, 151–160.

Resing, W. C., & Nijland, M. I. (2002). Are children becoming more intelligent? Twenty-five years' research using the Leiden Diagnostic Test. *Kind-en-Adolescent, 23*, 42–49.

Reuter-Lorenz, P. A., & Miller, A. C. (1998). The cognitive neuroscience of human laterality: Lessons from the bisected brain. *Current Directions in Psychological Science, 7*, 15–20.

Rey, J. M., & Sawyer, M. G. (2003). Are psychostimulant drugs being used appropriately to treat child and adolescent disorders? *British Journal of Psychiatry, 182*, 284–286.

Reyna, V. F., & Titcomb, A. L. (1997). Constraints on the suggestibility of eye-witness testimony: A fuzzy-trace theory analysis. In D. G. Payne & F. G. Conrad (Eds.), *Intersections in basic and applied memory research* (pp. 27–55). Mahwah, NJ: Erlbaum.

Reynolds, C. F., Frank, E., Perel, J. M., Imber, S. D., Cornes, C., Miller, M. D., et al. (1999). Nortriptyline and interpersonal psychotherapy as maintenance therapies for recurrent major depression. *Journal of the American Medical Association, 281*, 39–45.

Rhodes, G. (2006). The evolutionary psychology of facial beauty. *Annual Review of Psychology, 57*, 199–226

Rhodewalt, F., & Vohs, K. D. (2005). Defensive strategies, motivation, and the self: A self-regulatory process view. In A. J. Elliot & C. S. Dweck (Eds.), *Handbook of competence and motivation* (pp. 548–565). New York: Guilford.

Rhue, J. W., Lynn, S. J., & Kirsch, I. (1993). *Handbook of clinical hypnosis.* Washington, DC: American Psychological Assoc.

Ricaurte, G. A., Yuan, J., Hatzidimitriou, G., Cord, B. J., & McCann, U. D. (2003). Severe dopaminergic neurotoxicity in primates after a common recreational dose regime of MDMA ("Ecstasy"): Retraction. *Science, 301*, 1479.

Riccio, D. C., Millin, P. M., & Gisquet-Verrier, P. (2003). Retrograde amnesia: Forgetting back. *Current Directions in Psychological Science, 12*, 41–44.

Richards, J., Encel, J., & Shute, R. (2003). The emotional and behavioural adjustment of intellectually gifted adolescents: A multidimensional, multi-informant approach. *High Ability Studies, 14*, 153–164.

Rieber, R. W. (1998, August). *Hypnosis, false memory and multiple personality: A trinity of affinity*. Paper presented at the annual meeting of the American Psychological Association, San Francisco.

Riggio, R. E. (2003). *Introduction to industrial/organizational psychology* (4th ed.). Upper Saddle River, NJ: Prentice Hall.

Riley, E. P., Guerri, C., Calhoun, F., Charness, M. E., Foroud, T. M., Li, T. K., et al. (2003). Prenatal alcohol exposure: Advancing knowledge through international collaborations. *Alcoholism: Clinical and Experimental Research, 27*, 118–135.

Rilling, M. (2000). John Watson's paradoxical struggle to explain Freud. *American Psychologist, 55*, 301–312.

Rini, C. K., Dunkel-Schetter, C., Wadhwa, P. D., & Sandman, C. A. (1999). Psychological adaptation and birth outcomes: The role of personal resources, stress, and sociocultural context in pregnancy. *Health Psychology, 18*, 333–345.

Riniolo, T. C., Johnson, K. C., Sherman, T. R., & Misso, J. A. (2006). Hot or not: Do professors perceived as physically attractive receive higher student evaluations? *Journal of General Psychology, 133*, 19–35.

Rioux, L. (2005). The well-being of aging people living in their own homes. *Journal of Environmental Psychology, 25*, 231–243.

Rizzolatti, G. (2005). The mirror neuron system and imitation. In S. Hurley & N. Chater (Eds.), *Perspectives on imitation: From neuroscience to social science: Vol. 1: Mechanisms of imitation and imitation in animals* (pp. 55–76). Cambridge, MA: MIT Press.

Rizzolatti, G., & Craighero, L. (2004). The Mirror-Neuron System. *Annual Review of Neuroscience, 27*, 169–192.

Rizzolatti, G., Fadiga, L., Fogassi, L., & Gallese, V. (2002). From mirror neurons to imitation: Facts and speculations. In A. Meltzoff & W. Prinz (Eds.), *The imitative mind: Development, evolution, and brain bases* (pp. 247–266). New York: Cambridge Univ. Press.

Rizzolatti, G., Gallese, V., & Keysers, C. (2004). A unifying view of the basis of social cognition. *Trends in Cognitive Sciences, 8,* 396–403.

Roberson, D., Davies, I., & Jules, D. (2000). Color categories are not universal: Replications and new evidence from a stone-age culture. *Journal of Experimental Psychology: General, 129,* 369–398.

Roberts, A. H., Kewman, D. G., Mercer, L., & Hovell, M. (1993). The power of nonspecific effects in healing: Implications for psychosocial and biological treatments. *Clinical Psychology Review, 13,* 375–391.

Robins, L. N., & Regier, D. A. (1991). *Psychiatric disorders in America: The Epidemiologic Catchment Area Study.* New York: Free Press.

Robins, R. W., Gosling, S. D., & Craik, K. H. (1999). An empirical analysis of trends in psychology. *American Psychologist, 54,* 117–128.

Robinson, A., & Clinkenbeard, P. R. (1998). Giftedness: An exceptionality examined. *Annual Review of Psychology, 49,* 117–139.

Rodafinos, A., Vucevic, A., & Sideridis, G. D. (2005). The effectiveness of compliance techniques: Foot in the door versus door in the face. *Journal of Social Psychology, 145,* 237–239.

Rodier, P. M. (2000). The early origins of autism. *Scientific American, 282*(2), 56–63.

Roese, N. J. (1997). Counterfactual thinking. *Psychological Bulletin, 121,* 133–148.

Rofe, Y. (1984). Stress and affiliation: A utility theory. *Psychological Review, 91,* 251–268.

Rofe, Y., Hoffman, M., & Lewin, I. (1985). Patient affiliation in major illness. *Psychological Medicine, 15,* 895–896.

Rogers, C. R. (1961). *On becoming a person: A therapist's view of psychotherapy.* Boston: Houghton Mifflin.

Roh, S., Ahn, D. H., & Nam, J. H. (2006). Cardiomyopathy associated with clozapine. *Experimental and Clinical Psychopharmacology, 14,* 94–98.

Roitblat, H. L., Penner, R. H., & Nachtigall, P. E. (1990). Matching-to-sample by an echolocating dolphin (*Tursiops truncatus*). *Journal of Experimental Psychology: Animal Behavior Processes, 16,* 85–95.

Rolls, E. T. (2000). Memory systems in the brain. *Annual Review of Psychology, 51,* 599–630.

Rolls, E. T., Tovee, M. J., & Panzeri, S. (1999). The neurophysiology of backward visual masking: Information analysis. *Journal of Cognitive Neuroscience, 11,* 335–346.

Roncadin, C., Guger, S., Archibald, J., Barnes, M., & Dennis, M. (2004). Working memory after mild, moderate, or severe childhood closed head injury. *Developmental Neuropsychology, 25,* 21–36.

Roper, R., & Shewan, D. (2002). Compliance and eyewitness testimony: Do eyewitnesses comply with misleading "expert pressure" during investigative interviewing. *Legal and Criminological Psychology, 7,* 155–163.

Rosch, E. H. (1973). Natural categories. *Cognitive Psychology, 4,* 328–350.

Rosch, E. H. (1978). Principles of categorization. In E. H. Rosch & B. B. Lloyd (Eds.), *Cognition and categorization* (pp. 27–48). Hillsdale, NJ: Erlbaum.

Rosch, E. H. (1998). Principles of categorization. In A. M. Collens & E. E. Smith (Eds.), *Readings in cognitive science: A perspective from psychology and artificial intelligence* (pp. 312–322). San Mateo, CA: Morgan Kaufman.

Rosch, E. H. (2002). Principles of categorization. In D. J. Levitin (Ed.), *Foundations of Cognitive Psychology: Core Readings* (pp. 251–270). Cambridge, MA: MIT Press.

Rose, R. J., Viken, R. J., Dick, D. M., Bates, J. E., Pulkkinen, L., & Kaprio, J. (2003). It *does* take a village: Nonfamilial environments and children's behavior. *Psychological Science, 14,* 273–277.

Rosengren, A., Hawken, S., 'unpuu, S., Sliwa, K., Zubaid, M., Almahmeed, W. A., et al. (2004). Association of psychosocial risk factors with risk of acute myocardial infarction in 11,119 cases and 13,648 controls from 52 countries (the INTERHEART study): Case-control study. *Lancet, 364,* 953–962.

Rosenstein, D., & Oster, H. (2005). Differential facial responses to four basic tastes in newborns. In P. Ekman & E. Rosenberg (Eds.), *What the face reveals: Basic and applied studies of spontaneous expression using the facial action coding system (FACS)* (2nd ed., pp. 302–327). New York: Oxford Univ. Press.

Rosenthal, R. (2002a). Covert communications in classrooms, clinics, courtrooms, and cubicles. *American Psychologist, 57,* 839–849.

Rosenthal, R. (2002b). The Pygmalion effect and its mediating mechanisms. In J. Aronson (Ed.), *Improving academic achievement: Impact of psychological factors on education* (pp. 25–36). San Diego, CA: Academic Press.

Rosenvinge, J. H., Borgen, J. S., & Boerresen, R. (1999). The prevalence and psychological correlates of anorexia nervosa, bulimia nervosa and binge eating among 15-year-old students: A controlled epidemiological study. *European Eating Disorders Review, 7,* 382–391.

Rosenzweig, M. R. (1984). Experience, memory, and the brain. *American Psychologist, 39,* 365–376.

Rosenzweig, M. R. (1996). Aspects of the search for neural mechanisms of memory. *Annual Review of Psychology, 47,* 1–32.

Rosenzweig, M. R., Breedlove, S. M., & Watson, N. V. (2005). *Biological psychology: An introduction to behavioral and cognitive neuroscience* (4th ed.). Sunderland, MA: Sinauer.

Rosenzweig, M. R., & Leiman, A. L. (1982). *Physiological psychology.* Lexington, MA: Heath.

Ross, C. A., Norton, G. R., & Wozney, K. (1989). Multiple personality disorder: An analysis of 236 cases. *Canadian Journal of Psychiatry, 34,* 413–418.

Ross, M. H. (1993). *The culture of conflict.* New Haven, CT: Yale Univ. Press.

Ross, P. (2003). Mind readers. *Scientific American, 289*(3), 74–77.

Ross, P. E. (2004). Draining the language out of color. *Scientific American, 290*(4), 46–47.

Rossiter, T. (2002). Neurofeedback for AD/HD: A ratio feedback case study and tutorial. *Journal of Neurotherapy, 6,* 9–35.

Rotenberg, V. S. (2004). The peculiarity of the right-hemisphere function in depression: Solving paradoxes. *Progress in Neuro Psychopharmacology and Biological Psychiatry, 28,* 1–13.

Roth, B. (2004). *Separate roads to feminism: Black, chicana, and white feminist movements in America's second wave.* New York: Cambridge Univ. Press.

Rothbart, M. K., Derryberry, D., & Hershey, K. (2000). Stability of temperament in childhood: Laboratory infant assessment to parent report at seven years. In V. J. Molfese & D. L. Molfese (Eds.), *Temperament and personality development across the life span* (pp. 85–119). Mahwah, NJ: Erlbaum.

Rothbart, M. K., Ellis, L. K., & Posner, M. I. (2004). Temperament and self-regulation. In R. F. Baumeister & K. D. Vohs (Eds.), *Handbook of self-regulation: Research, theory, and applications* (pp. 357–370). New York: Guilford.

Rothblum, E. D, Brand, P. A., Miller, C. T., & Oetjen, H. A. (1990). The relationship between obesity, employment discrimination, and employment-related victimization. *Journal of Vocational Behavior, 37*, 251–266.

Rottenstreich, Y., & Tversky, A. (1997). Unpacking, repacking, and anchoring: Advances in support theory. *Psychological Review, 104*, 406–415.

Rotter, J. B. (1954). *Social learning and clinical psychology.* Englewood Cliffs, NJ: Prentice Hall.

Rouhana, N. N., & Bar-Tal, D. (1998). Psychological dynamics of intractable ethnonational conflicts: The Israeli-Palestinian case. *American Psychologist, 53*, 761–770.

Roussy, J. M. (2000). How poverty shapes women's experiences of health during pregnancy: A grounded theory study. *Dissertation Abstracts International: Section B: The Sciences and Engineering, 60*, 3205.

Rowatt, W. C., Franklin, L. M., & Cotton, M. (2005). Patterns and personality correlates of implicit and explicit attitudes toward Christians and Muslims. *Journal for the Scientific Study of Religion, 44*, 29–43.

Rowe, C. J. (1998). Aggression and violence in sports. *Psychiatric Annals, 28*, 265–269.

Rowe, D. C. (2001). The nurture assumption persists. *American Psychologist, 56*, 168–169.

Rowe, D. C., & Rodgers, J. L. (2002). Expanding variance and the case of historical changes in IQ means: A critique of Dickens and Flynn (2001). *Psychological Review, 109*, 79–763.

Rowland, N. E. (2002). Thirst and water-salt appetite. In H. Pashier & R. Gallistel (Eds.), *Steven's handbook of experimental psychology: Vol. 3, Learning, motivation, and emotion* (3rd ed., pp. 669–707). New York: John Wiley & Sons.

Roy, T. S., Seidler, F. J., & Slotkin, T. A. (2002). Prenatal nicotine exposure evokes alterations of cell structure in hippocampus and somatosensory cortex. *Journal of Pharmacology and Experimental Therapeutics, 300*, 124–133.

Rubenstein, A. J., Kalakanis, L., & Langlois, J. H. (1999). Infant preferences for attractive faces: A cognitive explanation. *Developmental Psychology, 35*, 848–855.

Rubin, K. H., Coplan, R. J., Chen, X., & McKinnon, J. E. (1994). Peer relationships and influences in childhood. In V. S. Ramachandran (Ed.), *Encyclopedia of human behavior* (Vol. 3, pp. 431–439). San Diego, CA: Academic Press.

Ruble, D. N., Fleming, A. S., Hackel, L. S., & Stangor, C. (1988). Changes in the marital relationship during the transition to first time motherhood: Effects of violated expectations concerning division of household labor. *Journal of Personality and Social Psychology, 55*, 78–87.

Ruffin, C. L. (1993). Stress and health: Little hasslers vs. major life events. *Australian Psychologist, 28*, 201–208.

Rugulies, R. (2002). Depression as a predictor for coronary heart disease: A review and meta-analysis. *American Journal of Preventive Medicine, 23*, 51–61.

Ruifang, G., & Danling, P. (2005). A review of studies on the brain plasticity. *Psychological Science, 28*, 409–411.

Rule, R. R. (2001). Modulation of the orienting response by prefrontal cortex. *Dissertation Abstracts International: Section B: The Sciences and Engineering, 61*, 3894.

Rumbaugh, D. M. (1977). *Language learning by a chimpanzee.* New York: Academic Press.

Rumbaugh, D. M., & Savage-Rumbaugh, E. S. (1978). Chimpanzee language research: Status and potential. *Behavior Research Methods and Instrumentation, 10*, 119–131.

Runco, M. A. (2004). Creativity. *Annual Review of Psychology, 55*, 657–687.

Rushton, J. P., & Bons, T. A. (2005). Mate choice and friendship in twins: Evidence for genetic similarity. *Psychological Science, 16*, 555–559.

Russell, J. (2004). Management of anorexia nervosa revisited: Early intervention can help—but some cases still need tertiary inpatient care. *British Medical Journal, 328*, 479–480.

Russell, J. A. (1991). Culture and the categorization of emotions. *Psychological Bulletin, 110*, 426–450.

Russell, S. T. (2006). Substance use and abuse and mental health among sexual-minority youths. In A. M. Omoto & H. S. Kurtzman (Eds.), *Sexual orientation and mental health: Examining identity and development in lesbian, gay, and bisexual people* (pp. 13–35). Washington, DC: American Psychological Assoc.

Rust, J. O., & Wallace, M. A. (2004). Adaptive Behavior Assessment System (2nd ed.). *Journal of Psychoeducational Assessment, 22*, 367–373.

Ruth, W. (1996). Goal setting and behavior contracting for students with emotional and behavioral difficulties: Analysis of daily, weekly, and total goal attainment. *Psychology in the Schools, 33*, 153–158.

Ruttan, L. A., & Heinrichs, R. W. (2003). Depression and neurocognitive functioning in mild traumatic brain injury patients referred for assessment. *Journal of Clinical and Experimental Neuropsychology, 25*, 407–419.

Rutter, M. (1997). Nature-nurture integration: An example of antisocial behavior. *American Psychologist, 52*, 390–398.

Rutter, M. (2005). Genetic influences and autism. In F. R. Volkmar, R. Paul, A. Klin, & D. Cohen (Eds.), *Handbook of autism and pervasive developmental disorders, Vol. 1: Diagnosis, development, neurobiology, and behavior* (3rd ed., pp. 425–452). Hoboken, NJ: John Wiley & Sons.

Ryan, R. M., & Deci, E. L. (2000). Self-determination theory and the facilitation of intrinsic motivation, social development, and well-being. *American Psychologist, 55*, 68–78.

Rymer, J., Wilson, R., & Ballard, K. (2003). Making decisions about hormone replacement therapy. *British Medical Journal, 326*, 322–326.

Rynes, S. L., Gerhart, B., & Parks, L. (2005). Personnel psychology: Performance evaluation and pay for performance. *Annual Review of Psychology, 56*, 571–600.

Saade, S., Balleine, Bernard, W., & Minor, T. R. (2003). The L-type calcium channel blocker nimodipine mitigates "learned helplessness" in rats. *Pharmacology, Biochemistry and Behavior, 74*, 269–278.

Sabini, J., & Silver, M. (2005). Ekman's basic emotions: Why not love and jealousy? *Cognition & Emotion, 19*, 693–712.

Sack, R. L., Brandes, R. W., Kendall, A. R., & Lewy, A. J. (2001). Entrainment of free-running circadian rhythms by melatonin in blind people. *The New England Journal of Medicine, 343*, 1070–1077.

Sacks, O. (2000). *Seeing voices: A journey into the world of the deaf.* New York: Vintage.

Saczynski, J. S., Willis, S. L., & Schaie, K. W. (2002). Strategy use in reasoning training with older adults. *Aging, Neuropsychology, and Cognition, 9*, 48–60.

Sadeh, A., Raviv, A., & Gruber, R. (2000). Sleep patterns and sleep disruptions in school-age children. *Developmental Psychology, 36*, 291–301.

Sadoski, M. (2005). A dual coding view of vocabulary learning. *Reading & Writing Quarterly: Overcoming Learning Difficulties, 21*, 221–238.

Sadoski, M., & Paivio, A. (2001). *Imagery and text: A dual coding theory of reading and writing.* Mahwah, NJ: Erlbaum.

Safdar, S., & Lay, C. H. (2003). The relations of immigrant-specific and immigrant-nonspecific daily hassles to distress controlling for psychological adjustment and cultural competence. *Journal of Applied Social Psychology, 33*, 299–320.

Saint-Amour, D., Lepore, F., Lassonde, M., & Guillemot, J. P. (2004). Effective binocular integration at the midline requires the corpus callosum. *Neuropsychologia, 43*, 164–174.

Salas, E., Stagl, K. C., & Burke, C. S. (2004). 25 years of team effectiveness in organizations: Research, themes, and emerging needs. In C. L. Cooper & I. T. Robertson (Eds.), *International review of industrial and organizational psychology 2004* (Vol. 19, pp. 47–91). West Sussex, UK Wiley.

Salgado, J. F., Moscoso, S., & Lado, M. (2003). Evidence of cross-cultural invariance of the Big Five personality dimensions in work settings. *European Journal of Personality, 1* (Suppl. 1), S67–S76.

Salovey, P. (2006). Epilogue: The agenda for future research. In V. U. Druskat, F. Sala, & G. Mount (Eds.), *Linking emotional intelligence and performance at work: Current research evidence with individuals and groups* (pp. 267–272). Mahwah, NJ: Erlbaum.

Salovey, P., Mayer, J. D., Caruso, D., & Lopes, P. N. (2003). Measuring emotional intelligence as a set of abilities with the Mayer–Salovey–Caruso Emotional Intelligence test. In S. J. Lopez & C. R. Snyder (Eds.), *Positive psychological assessment: A handbook of models and measures* (pp. 251–265). Washington, DC: American Psychological Assoc.

Salovey, P., Mayer, J. D., & Rosenhan, D. L. (1991). Mood behavior. In M. S. Clark (Ed.), *Review of personality and social psychology: Prosocial behavior* (Vol. 12, pp. 215–237). Newbury Park, CA: Sage.

Salovey, P., Rothman, A. J., Detweiler, J. B., & Steward, W. T. (2000). Emotional states and physical health. *American Psychologist, 55*, 110–121.

Sanderson, C., & Clarkin, J. F. (2002). Further use of the NEO-PI-R personality dimensions in differential treatment planning. In P. T. Costa, Jr., & T. A. Widiger (Eds.), *Personality disorders and the five-factor model of personality* (2nd ed., pp. 351–375). Washington, DC: American Psychological Assoc.

Sanford, R. N. (1937). The effects of abstinence from food upon imaginal processes: A further experiment. *Journal of Psychology, 3*, 145–159.

Sano, D. L. (2002). Attitude similarity and marital satisfaction in long-term African American and Caucasian marriages. *Dissertation Abstracts International Section A: Humanities and Social Sciences, 62*, 289.

Saper, C. B., Scammell, T. E., & Lu, J. (2005). Hypothalamic regulation of sleep and circadian rhythms. *Nature, 437*, 1257–1263.

Saporta, I., & Halpern, J. J. (2002). Being different can hurt: Effects of deviation from physical norms on lawyers' salaries. *Industrial Relations: A Journal of Economy and Society, 41*, 442–466.

Sarason, I. G., & Sarason, B. R. (1999). *Abnormal psychology: The problem of maladaptive behavior.* Upper Saddle River, NJ: Prentice Hall.

Saretzki, G., & Zglinicki, T. (2002). Replicative aging, telomeres, and oxidative stress. In D. Harman (Ed.), *Increasing healthy life span: Conventional measures and slowing the innate aging precess. Annals of the New York Academy of Science* (Vol. 959, pp. 24–29). New York: New York Academy of Sciences.

Sarlo, M., Palomba, D., & Buodo, G. (2005). Blood pressure changes highlight gender differences in emotional reactivity to arousing pictures. *Biological Psychology, 70*, 188–196.

Sarter, M., Berntson, G. G., & Cacioppo, J. T. (1996). Brain imaging and cognitive neuroscience: Toward strong inference in attributing function to structure. *American Psychologist, 51*, 13–21.

Sarwer, D. B., Allison, K. C., & Berkowitz, R. I. (2004). Obesity: Assessment and treatment. In L. J. Hass (Ed.), *Handbook of primary care psychology* (pp. 435–453). New York: Oxford Univ. Press.

Satcher, D. (2000). Mental health: A report of the Surgeon General—Executive summary. *Professional Psychology: Research and Practice, 31*, 5–13.

Satow, K. K. (1975). Social approval and helping. *Journal of Experimental Social Psychology, 11*, 501–509.

Sattler, J. M. (1992). *Assessment of children* (3rd ed.). San Diego, CA: Jerome M. Sattler.

Sattler, J. M. (2005). *Assessment of children: Behavioral and clinical applications* (5th ed.). La Mesa, CA: Jerome M. Sattler.

Saudino, K. J. (2005). Special article: Behavioral genetics and child temperament. *Journal of Developmental & Behavioral Pediatrics, 26*, 214–223.

Savage-Rumbaugh, E. S., & Fields, W. M. (2000). Linguistic, cultural and cognitive capacities of bonobos (*Pan paniscus*). *Culture and Psychology, 6*, 131–153.

Savage-Rumbaugh, S., & Lewin, R. (1994). *Kanzi: The ape at the brink of the human mind.* New York: Wiley.

Save, E., & Poucet, B. (2005). Piloting. In I. Q. Whishaw & B. Kolb (Eds.), *The behavior of the laboratory rat: A handbook with tests* (pp. 392–400). New York: Oxford Univ. Press.

Savic, I., Berglund, H., & Lindstrom, P. (2005). Brain response to putative pheromones in homosexual men. *Proceedings of the National Academy of Sciences of the United States of America, 102*, 7356–7361.

Scammell, T. E. (2003) The neurobiology, diagnosis, and treatment of narcolepsy. *Annals of Neurology, 53*, 154–166.

Scarr, S. (1999). Freedom of choice for poor families. *American Psychologist, 54*, 144–145.

Scarr, S., & Weinberg, R. (1983). The Minnesota Adoption Study: Genetic differences and malleability. *Child Development, 54*, 260–267.

Schachter, S., & Singer, J. (1962). Cognitive, social, and physiological determinants of emotional state. *Psychological Review, 69*, 379–399.

Schachter, S., & Singer, J. E. (2001). Cognitive, social, and psychological determinants of emotional state. In. G. W. Parrott (Ed.), *Emotions in social psychology: Essential readings* (pp. 76–93). Philadelphia: Psychology Press.

Schacter, D. L. (1999). The seven sins of memory: Insights from psychology and cognitive neuroscience. *American Psychologist, 54*, 182–203.

Schacter, D. L., Norman, K. A., & Koutstaal, W. (1998). The cognitive neuroscience of constructive memory. *Annual Review of Psychology, 49*, 289–318.

Schafe, G. E., & LeDoux, J. E. (2002). Emotional plasticity. In H. Pashler & R. Gallistel (Eds.), *Steven's handbook of experimental psychology: Vol. 3, Learning, motivation, and emotion* (3rd ed., pp. 535–561). New York: John Wiley & Sons.

Schaie, K. W. (1984). Midlife influences upon intellectual functioning in old age. *International Journal of Behavioral Development, 7*, 463–478.

Schaie, K. W., & Willis, S. L. (2001). *Adult development and aging* (5th ed.). Upper Saddle River, NJ: Prentice Hall.

Scheibel, R. S., & Levin, H. S. (2004). Working memory and the functional anatomy of the frontal lobes. *Cortex, 40*, 218–219.

Scherer, K. R., Schorr, A., & Johnstone, T. (Eds.) (2001). *Appraisal processes in emotion: Theory, methods, research.* New York: Oxford Univ. Press.

Schick, S., & Glantz, S. (2005). Scientific analysis of second-hand smoke by the tobacco industry, 1929–1972. *Nicotine & Tobacco Research, 7*, 591–612.

Schiffman, S. S. (1997). Taste and smell losses in normal aging and disease. *Journal of the American Medical Association, 278*, 1357–1352.

Schimmack, U., & Crites, S. L., Jr. (2005). The structure of affect. In D. Albarracín, B. T. Johnson, & M. P. Zanna (Eds.), *The handbook of attitudes* (pp. 397–435). Mahwah, NJ: Erlbaum.

Schinke, S., & Schwinn, T. (2005). Gender-specific computer-based intervention for preventing drug abuse among girls. *American Journal of Drug and Alcohol Abuse, 31,* 609–616.

Schlossberg, M. K (2004). *Retire smart, retire happy: Finding your true path in life.* Washington, DC: American Psychological Assoc.

Schmahl, C. G., Vermetten, E., Elzinga, B. M., & Bremmer, J. D. (2004). A positron emission tomography study of memories of childhood abuse in borderline personality disorder. *Biological Psychiatry, 55,* 759–765.

Schmid, D. A., Held, K., Ising, M., Uhr, M., Weikel, J. C., & Steiger, A. (2005). Ghrelin stimulates appetite, imagination of food, GH, ACTH, and cortisol, but does not affect leptin in normal controls. *Neuropsychopharmacology, 30,* 1187–1192.

Schmidt, F. L., & Hunter, J. (2004). General mental ability in the world of work: Occupational attainment and job performance. *Journal of Personality and Social Psychology, 86,* 162–173.

Schmidt, F. L., & Hunter, J. E. (1998). The validity and utility of selection methods in personnel psychology: Practical and theoretical implications of 85 years of research findings, *Psychological Bulletin, 124,* 262–274.

Schmidt, L. A., Polak, C. P., & Spooner, A. L. (2005). Biological and environmental contributions to childhood shyness: A diathesis-stress model. In W. R. Crozier & L. E. Alden (Eds.), *The essential handbook of social anxiety for clinicians* (pp. 33–55). New York: John Wiley & Sons.

Schmidt, S. R. (2004). Autobiographical memories for the September 11th attacks: Reconstructive errors and emotional impairment of memory. *Memory & Cognition, 32,* 443–454.

Schmolck, H., Buffalo, E. A., & Squire, L. R. (2000). Memory distortions develop over time: Recollections of the O. J. Simpson trial verdict after 15 months and 32 months. *Psychological Science, 11,* 29–45.

Schneider, B. M. (2002). Using the Big-Five personality factors in the Minnesota Multiphasic Personality Inventory, California Psychological Inventory, and Inwald Personality Inventory to predict police performance. *Dissertation Abstracts International: Section B: The Sciences and Engineering, 63,* 2098.

Schoenthaler, S. J., Amos, S. P., Eysenck, H. J., Peritz, E., & Yudkin, J. (1991). Controlled trial of vitamin-mineral supplementation: Effects on intelligence and performance. *Personality and Individual Differences, 12,* 251–362.

Schofield, J. W. (1997). School desegregation 40 years after Brown v. Board of Education: Looking forward and looking backward. In D. Johnson (Ed.), *Minorities and girls in school: Effects on achievement and performance* (pp. 1–36). Thousand Oaks, CA: Sage.

Scholey, A. B., Bosworth, J. A. J., & Dimitrakaki, V. (1999). The effects of exposure to human pheromones on mood and attraction. *Proceedings of the British Psychological Society, 7*(1), 77.

Schooler, C. (1998). Environmental complexity and the Flynn effect. In U. Neisser (Ed.), *The rising curve: Long-term gains in IQ and related measures* (pp. 67–79). Washington, DC: American Psychological Assoc.

Schopp, L., Johnstone, B., & Merrell, D. (2000). Telehealth and neuropsychological assessment: New opportunities for psychologists. *Professional Psychology: Research & Practice, 13,* 179–183.

Schultz, D. P., & Schultz, S. E. (1998). *Psychology and work today: An introduction to industrial and organizational psychology* (7th ed.). Upper Saddle River, NJ: Prentice Hall.

Schunk, D. H. (2005). Self-regulated learning: The educational legacy of Paul R. Pintrich. *Educational Psychologist, 40,* 85–94.

Schwartz, B. (1989). *Psychology of learning and behavior* (3rd ed.). New York: Norton.

Schwartz, B. (2000). Self-determination: The tyranny of freedom. *American Psychologist, 55,* 79–88.

Schwartz, B. L. (2002). *Tip-of-the-tongue states: Phenomenology, mechanism, and lexical retrieval.* Mahwah, NJ: Erlbaum.

Schwartz, B. L., & Frazier, L. D. (2005). Tip-of-the-tongue states and aging: Contrasting psycholinguistic and metacognitive perspectives. *Journal of General Psychology, 132,* 377–391.

Schwartz, C. E., Christopher, I. W., Shin, L. M., Kagan, J., & Rauch, S. L. (2003). Inhibited and uninhibited infants "grown up": Adult amygdalar response to novelty. *Science, 300,* 1952–1953.

Schwartz, C. E., Wright, C. I., Shin, L. M., Kagan, J., Whalen, P. J., McMullin, K. G., et al. (2003). Differential amygdalar response to novel versus newly familiar neutral faces: A functional MRI probe developed for studying inhibited temperament. *Biological Psychiatry, 53,* 854–862.

Schwartz, P. (1994, November 17). Some people with multiple roles are blessedly stressed. *New York Times.*

Schwartzman, J. B., & Glaus, K. D. (2000). Depression and coronary heart disease in women: Implications for clinical practice and research. *Professional Psychology: Research & Practice, 31,* 48–57.

Schwarz, N., & Vaughn, L. A. (2002). The availability heuristic revisited: Ease of recall and content of recall as distinct sources of information. In T. Gilovich & D. Griffin (Eds.), *Heuristics and biases: The psychology of intuitive judgment* (pp. 103–119). New York: Cambridge Univ. Press.

Scott, C., Klein, D. M., & Bryant, J. (1990). Consumer response to humor in advertising: A series of field studies using behavioral observation. *Journal of Consumer Research, 16,* 498–501.

Scott, J. P. R., McNaughton, L. R., & Polman, R. C. J. (2006). Effects of sleep deprivation and exercise on cognitive, motor performance and mood. *Physiology & Behavior, 87,* 396–408.

Sedikides, C., Gaertner, L., & Toguchi, Y. (2003). Pancultural self-enhancement. *Journal of Personality and Social Psychology, 84,* 60–79.

Seeley, R. J., & Schwartz, J. C. (1997). The regulation of energy balance: Peripheral hormonal signals and hypothalamic neuropeptides. *Current Directions in Psychological Science, 6,* 39–44.

Segall, M. H., Lonner, W. J., & Berry, J. W. (1998). Cross-cultural psychology as a scholarly discipline: On the flowering of culture in behavioral research. *American Psychologist, 53,* 1011–1110.

Segerstrom, S. C., & Miller, G. E. (2004). Psychological stress and the human immune system: A meta-analytic study of 30 years of inquiry. *Psychological Bulletin, 130,* 601–630.

Segura, S., & McCloy, R. (2003). Counterfactual thinking in everyday life situations: Temporal order effects and social norms. *Psicologica, 24,* 1–15.

Sekides, C., Olsen, L., & Reis, H. T. (1993). Relationships as natural categories. *Journal of Personality and Social Psychology, 64,* 71–82.

Seligman, J., Rogers, P., & Annin, P. (1994, May 2). The pressure to lose. *Newsweek,* pp. 60, 62.

Seligman, M. E. P. (1971). Phobias and preparedness. *Behavior Therapy, 2,* 307–320

Seligman, M. E. P. (1995). The effectiveness of psychotherapy: The *Consumer Reports* study. *American Psychologist, 50,* 965–974.

Seligman, M. E. P. (1996). Science as an ally of practice. *American Psychologist, 51,* 1072–1079.

Seligman, M. E. P., & Csikzentmihalyi, M. (2000). Positive psychology. *American Psychologist, 55,* 5–14.

Seligman, M. E. P., & Maier, S. F. (1967). Failure to escape traumatic shock. *Journal of Experimental Psychology, 74,* 1–9.

Seligman, M. E. P., & Schulman, P. (1986). Explanatory styles as a predictor of productivity and quitting among life insurance sales agents. *Journal of Personality and Social Psychology, 50,* 832–838.

Seligman, M. E. P., Steen, T. A., & Park, N. (2005). Positive psychology progress: Empirical validation of interventions. *American Psychologist, 60,* 410–421.

Selye, H. (1956). *The stress of life.* New York: McGraw-Hill.

Selye, H. (1976). *The stress of life* (rev. ed.). New York: McGraw-Hill.

Seppa, N. (1997, June). Children's TV remains steeped in violence. *APA Monitor,* p. 36.

Serdula, M. K., Brewer, R. D., Gillespie, C., Denny, C. H., & Mokdad, A. (2004). Trends in alcohol use and binge drinking, 1985–1999: Results of a multistate survey. *American Journal of Preventive Medicine, 26,* 294–298.

Sewards, T. V., & Sewards, M. A. (2003). Representations of motivational drives in mesial cortex, medial thalamus, hypothalamus and midbrain. *Brain Research Bulletin, 61,* 25–49.

Shader, R. I. (2003). Obsessions and compulsions and obsessive-compulsive disorder. In R. I. Shader (Ed.), *Manual of psychiatric therapeutics* (3rd ed., pp. 73–80). Philadelphia: Lippincott Williams & Wilkins.

Shaffer, J. B. P. (1978). *Humanistic psychology.* Upper Saddle River, NJ: Pearson Education.

Shah, K. R., Eisen, S. A., Xian, H., & Potenza, M. N. (2005). Genetic studies of pathological gambling: A review of methodology and analyses of data from the Vietnam era twin registry. *Journal of Gambling Studies, 21,* 179–203.

Shahin, A., Roberts, L. E., & Trainor, L. J. (2004). Enhancement of auditory cortical development by musical experience in children. *Neuroreport: For Rapid Communication of Neuroscience Research, 15,* 1917–1921.

Shallop, J. K., Jin, S. H., Driscoll, C. L. W., & Tribisar, R. J. (2004). Characteristics of electrically evoked potentials in patients with auditory neuropathy/auditory dys-synchrony. *International Journal of Audiology, 43,* S22–S27.

Shankman, S. A., Tenke, C. E., Bruder, G. E., Durbin, C. E., Hayden, E. P., & Klein, D. N. (2005). Low positive emotionality in young children: Association with EEG asymmetry. *Development and Psychopathology, 17,* 85–98.

Shapiro, T. F. (2002). Suggestibility in children's eyewitness testimony: Cognitive and social influences. *Dissertation Abstracts International: Section B: The Sciences and Engineering, 63,* 2086.

Shastry, B. S. (2005). Recent advances in the genetics of autism spectrum disorders: A minireview. *British Journal of Developmental Disabilities, 51,* 129–142.

Shaw, P., Bramham, J., Lawrence, E. J., Morris, R., Baron-Cohen, S., & David, A. S. (2005). Differential effects of lesions of the amygdala and prefrontal cortex on recognizing facial expressions of complex emotions. *Journal of Cognitive Neuroscience, 17,* 1410–1419.

Shaw, P., Greenstein, D., Lerch, L., Slasen, R., Lenroot, N., & Gogtay, A., et al., (2006). Intellectual ability and cortical development in children and adolescents. *Nature, 440,* 676–679.

Shaw, P. J., Cirelli, C., Greenspan, R. J., & Tononi, G. (2000, March 10). Correlates of sleep and waking in *Drosophila melanogaster. Science, 287,* 1834–1837.

Shayer, M. (2003). Not just Piaget; not just Vygotsky, and certainly not Vygotsky as an alternative to Piaget. *Learning and Instruction, 13,* 465–485.

Shaywitz, S. E., Shaywitz, B. A., Pugh, K. R., Fulbright, R. K., Constable, R. T., Mencl, W. E., et al. (1998). Functional disruption in the organization of the brain for reading in dyslexia. *Neurobiology, 95,* 2636–2641.

Sheehy, R., & Horan, J. J. (2004). Effects of stress inoculation training for 1st-year law students. *International Journal of Stress Management, 11,* 41–55.

Shehryar, O. H., & David M. (2005). A terror management perspective on the persuasiveness of fear appeals. *Journal of Consumer Psychology, 15,* 275–287.

Sheldon, K. M., & King, L. (2001). Why positive psychology is necessary. *American Psychologist, 56,* 216–217.

Shelton R. C., & Hollon, S. D. (2000). Antidepressants. In A. Kazdin (Ed.), *Encyclopedia of psychology* (Vol. 1, pp. 196–200). Washington, DC: American Psychological Assoc.

Sher, L. (2004). Type D personality, cortisol and cardiac disease. *Australian and New Zealand Journal of Psychiatry, 38,* 652–653.

Sheras, P. L., & Koch-Sheras, P. R. (2006). Redefining couple: Shifting the paradigm. In P. L. Sheras & P. R. Koch-Sheras (Eds.), *Couple power therapy: Building commitment, cooperation, communication, and community in relationships* (pp. 19–39). Washington, DC: American Psychological Assoc.

Sherman, R. A. (1996). *Unraveling the mysteries of phantom limb sensations.* New York: Plenum.

Shermer, M. (2004). The enchanted glass. *Scientific American, 290*(5), 46.

Shermer, M. (2005). Turn me on, dead man. *Scientific American, 292*(5), p. 37.

Shimamura, A. P., Berry, J. M., Mangels, J. A., Rusting, C. L., & Jurica, P. J. (1995). Memory and cognitive abilities in university professors: Evidence for successful aging. *Psychological Science, 6,* 271–277.

Shiner, R. L., Masten, A. S., & Roberts, J. M. (2003). Childhood personality foreshadows adult personality and life outcomes two decades later. *Journal of Personality, 71,* 1145–1170.

Shorter, E. (1997). *A history of psychiatry: From the era of the asylum to the age of Prozac.* New York: Wiley.

Shum, M. (1998). The role of temporal landmarks in autobiographical memory processes. *Psychological Bulletin, 124,* 423–442.

Shumake, J., & Gonzalez-Lima, F. (2003). Brain systems underlying susceptibility to helplessness and depression. *Behavioral and Cognitive Neuroscience Reviews, 2,* 198–221.

Siegal, M. (2003). Cognitive development. In A. Slater & G. Bremner (Eds.), *An introduction to developmental psychology* (pp. 189–210). Malden, MA: Blackwell.

Siegel, J. M. (2005). Clues to the functions of mammalian sleep. *Nature, 437,* 1264–1271.

Siegel, K., Anderman, S. J., & Schrimshaw, E. W. (2001). Religion and coping with health stress. *Psychology and Health, 16,* 631–653.

Siegel, L. (1993). Amazing new discovery: Piaget was wrong. *Canadian Psychology, 34,* 239–245.

Siegel, S. (2005). Drug tolerance, drug addiction, and drug anticipation. *Current Directions in Psychological Science, 14,* 296–300.

Siegert, R. J., & Ward, T. (2002). Evolutionary psychology: Origins and criticisms. *Australian Psychologist, 37,* 20–29.

Sigman, M. D. (2000). Determinants of intelligence: Nutrition and intelligence. In A. E. Kazdin (Ed.), *Encyclopedia of psychology:* (Vol. 2, pp. 501–502). Washington, DC: American Psychological Assoc.

Silberg, J. L., & Bulik, C. M. (2005). The developmental association between eating disorders symptoms and symptoms of depression and anxiety in juvenile twin girls. *Journal of Child Psychology and Psychiatry, 46,* 1317–1326.

Silberg, J. L., San Miguel, V. F., Murrelle, E. L., Prom, E., Bates, J. E., Canino, G., et al. (2005). Genetic and environmental influences on temperament in the first year of life: The Puerto Rico infant twin study (PRINTS). *Twin Research and Human Genetics, 8,* 328–336.

Silver, H., Goodman, C., Isakov, V., Knoll, G., & Modai, I. (2005). A double-blind, cross-over comparison of the effects of amantadine or placebo on visuomotor and cognitive function in medicated schizophrenia patients. *International Clinical Psychopharmacology, 20,* 319–326.

Simcock, G., & Hayne, H. (2002). Breaking the barrier? Children fail to translate their preverbal memories into language. *Psychological Science, 13,* 225–231.

Simon, H. A. (1974, February 8). How big is a chunk? *Science, 165,* 482–488.

Simons, T., & Roberson, Q. (2003). Why managers should care about fairness: The effects of aggregate justice perceptions on organizational outcomes. *Journal of Applied Psychology, 88,* 432–443.

Simpson, R. L., de Boer-Ott, S. R., Griswold, D. E., Myles, B. S., Byrd, S. E., Ganz, J. B., et al. (2005). *Autism spectrum disorders: Interventions and treatments for children and youth.* London: Corwin.

Sinclair, M., & Ashkanasy, N. M. (2005). Intuition: Myth or a decision-making tool? *Management Learning, 36,* 353–370.

Singer, J. L. (1975). *The inner world of daydreaming.* New York: Harper Colophon.

Singer, J. L. (2006). *Imagery in psychotherapy.* Washington DC: American Psychological Assoc.

Singh, D. (1993) Adaptive significance of female physical attractiveness: Role of waist-to-hip ratio. *Journal of Personality and Social Psychology, 65,* 293–307.

Singh, S. J. B. (2002, March 19). "I was wrongly accused of being a terrorist." *The Progressive.* Retrieved October 6, 2006, from http://progressive.org/media_1611

Singular, S. (1982, October). A memory for all seasonings. *Psychology Today,* pp. 54–63.

Sinnott, J. D. (1994). Sex roles. In V. A. Ramachandran (Ed.), *Encyclopedia of human behavior* (Vol. 4, pp. 151–158). San Diego, CA: Academic Press.

Skaalvik, E. M., & Rankin, R. J. (1994). Gender differences in mathematics and verbal achievement, self-perception and motivation. *British Journal of Educational Psychology, 64,* 419–428.

Skeels, H. M. (1938). Mental development of children in foster homes. *Journal of Consulting Psychology, 2,* 33–43.

Skeels, H. M. (1942). The study of the effects of differential stimulation on mentally retarded children: A follow-up report. *American Journal of Mental Deficiencies, 46,* 340–350.

Skeels, H. M. (1966). Adult status of children with contrasting early life experiences. *Monographs of the Society for Research in Child Development, 31*(3), 1–65.

Skinner, B. F. (1938). *The behavior of organisms.* New York: Appleton-Century-Crofts.

Skinner, B. F. (1948). *Science and human behavior.* New York: Macmillan.

Skinner, B. F. (1953). Some contributions of an experimental analysis of behavior to psychology as a whole. *American Psychologist, 8,* 69–78.

Skinner, B. F. (1957). *Verbal behavior.* Englewood Cliffs, NJ: Prentice Hall.

Skinner, B. F. (1987). Whatever happened to psychology as the science of behavior? *American Psychologist, 42,* 780–786.

Skinner, B. F. (1989). The origins of cognitive thought. *American Psychologist, 44,* 13–18.

Skinner, B. F. (1990). Can psychology be a science of mind? *American Psychologist, 45,* 1206–1210.

Skinner, E. A., Edge, K., Altman, J., & Sherwood, H. (2003). Searching for the structure of coping: A review and critique of category systems for classifying ways of coping. *Psychological Bulletin, 129,* 216–269.

Slater, A. (2000). Visual perception in the young infant. Early organization and rapid learning. In D. Muir & A. Slater (Eds.), *Infant development: Essential readings in developmental psychology* (pp. 9–116). Malden, MA: Blackwell.

Slater, A. (2002). Visual perception in the newborn infant: Issues and debates. *Intellectica, 34,* 57–76.

Sleek, S. (1998, May). Older vets just now feeling pain of war. *APA Monitor,* pp. 1, 28.

Sleek, S. (1999, February). Programs aim to attract minorities to psychology. *APA Monitor,* p. 47.

Slessareva, E., & Muraven, M. (2004). Sensitivity to punishment and self-control: The mediating role of emotion. *Personality and Individual Differences, 36,* 307–319.

Slife, B. D., & Reber, J. S. (2001). Eclecticism in psychotherapy: Is it really the best substitute for traditional theories? In B. D. Slife & R. N. Wiliams (Eds.), *Critical issues in psychotherapy: Translating new ideas into practice* (pp. 213–233). Thousand Oaks, CA: Sage.

Smith, C. T., Nixon, M. R., & Nader, R. S. (2004). Posttraining increases in REM sleep intensity implicate REM sleep in memory processing and provide a biological marker of learning potential. *Learning & Memory, 11,* 714–719.

Smith, D. (2001). Impairment on the job. *Monitor on Psychology, 32,* 52–53.

Smith, D. E., Roberts, J., Gage, F. H., & Tuszynski, M. H. (1999). Age-associated neuronal atrophy occurs in the primate brain and is reversible by growth factor gene therapy. *Proceedings of the National Academy of Sciences, 96,* 10893–10898.

Smith, D. N. (1998). The psychocultural roots of genocide: Legitimacy and crisis in Rwanda. *American Psychologist, 53,* 743–753.

Smith, E. R., & Mackie, D. M. (2005). Aggression, hatred, and other emotions. In J. F. Dovidio, P. Glick, & L. A. Rudman (Eds.), *On the nature of prejudice: Fifty years after Allport* (pp. 361–376). Malden, MA: Blackwell.

Smith, J. E., Richardson, J., & Hoffman, C. (2005). Mindfulness-based stress reduction as supportive therapy in cancer care: Systematic review. *Journal of Advanced Nursing, 52,* 315–327.

Smith, J. M. (2006). Mobile training unit: A cost-effective live fire option. *Fire Engineering, 159,* 133–134.

Smith, K. H., & Stutts, M. A. (2003). Effects of short-term cosmetic versus long-term health fear appeals in anti-smoking advertisements on the smoking behaviour of adolescents. *Journal of Consumer Behaviour, 3,* 157–177.

Smith, M. T., & Perlis, M. L. (2006). Who is a candidate for cognitive-behavioral therapy for insomnia? *Health Psychology, 25,* 15–19.

Smith, P. B., & Bond, M. H. (1994). *Social psychology across cultures: Analysis and perspectives.* Boston: Allyn & Bacon.

Smith, P. B., & Bond, M. H. (1999). *Social psychology across cultures: Analysis and perspectives* (2nd ed.). Boston: Allyn & Bacon.

Smith, R. A. (2005). The classroom as a social psychology laboratory. *Journal of Social & Clinical Psychology, 24,* [Special issue: *Dispelling the fable of "Those who can, do, and those who can't, teach:" The (social and clinical) psychology of instruction*], 62–71.

Smith, R. A., & Weber, A. L. (2005). Applying social psychology in everyday life. In F. W. Schneider, J. A. Gruman, & L. M. Coutts (Eds.), *Applied social psychology: Understanding and addressing social and practical problems* (pp. 75–99). Thousand Oaks, CA: Sage.

Smith, S. M., Gleaves, D. H., Pierce, B. H., Williams, T. L., Gilliland, T. R., & Gerkens, D. R. (2003). Eliciting and comparing false and recovered memories: An experimental approach. *Applied Cognitive Psychology, 17,* 251–279.

Smithson, H., & Mollon, J. (2006). Do masks terminate the icon? *Quarterly Journal of Experimental Psychology, 59,* 150–160.

Smits, J. A. J., O'Cleirigh, C. M., & Otto, M. W. (2006). Panic and agoraphobia. In F. Andrasik (Ed.), *Comprehensive handbook of personality and psychopathology: Vol. 2, Adult psychopathology* (pp. 121–137). Hoboken, NJ: John Wiley & Sons.

Smollar, J., & Youniss, J. (1989). Transformations in adolescents' perceptions of parents. *International Journal of Behavioral Development, 12,* 71–84.

Snow, K., Crethar, H. C., & Robey, P. (2005). Theories of family therapy (Part I). In R. H. Coombs (Ed.), *Family therapy review: Preparing for comprehensive and licensing examinations* (pp. 117–141). Mahwah, NJ: Erlbaum.

Snowden, L. R., & Yamada, A.-M. (2005). Cultural differences in access to care. *Annual Review of Clinical Psychology, 1,* 143–166.

Snyder, M. (1987). *Public appearances/private realities: The psychology of self-monitoring.* New York: Freeman.

Snyder, M., & Swann, W. B., Jr. (1978). Behavioral confirmation in social interaction: From social perception to social reality. *Journal of Experimental Social Psychology, 14,* 148–162.

Solms, M. (2003). Dreaming and REM sleep are controlled by different brain mechanisms. In E. F. Pace-Schott, M. Soms, M. Blagrove, & S. Harnad (Eds.), *Sleep and dreaming: Scientific advances and reconsiderations* (pp. 51–58). New York: Cambridge Univ. Press.

Solms, M. (2004). Freud returns. *Scientific American, 290*(5), 82–88.

Solomon, P. R., Hirschoff, A., Kelly, B., Relin, M., Brush, M., DeVeaux, R. D., et al. (1998). A 7 minute neurocognitive screening battery highly sensitive to Alzheimer's disease. *Archives of Neurology, 55,* 349–355.

Solomon, S. G., Lee, B. B., White, A. J. R., Rüttiger, L., & Martin, P. R. (2005). Chromatic organization of ganglion cell receptive rields in the peripheral retina. *Journal of Neuroscience, 25,* 4527–4539.

Somer, E. (2002). Maladaptive daydreaming: A qualitative inquiry. *Journal of Contemporary Psychotherapy, 32,* 197–212.

Sommers-Flanagan, R., Sommers-Flanagan, J., & Davis, B. (1993). What's happening on music television? A gender role content analysis. *Sex Roles, 28,* 745–754.

Sonstroem, R. J. (1997). Physical activity and self-esteem. In W. P. Morgan (Ed.), *Physical activity and mental health* (pp. 127–143). Philadelphia: Taylor & Francis.

Sorensen, R. C. (1973). *Adolescent sexuality in contemporary America.* New York: World.

Sotres, J. F. C., Velasquez, C. B., & Cruz, M. L. V. (2002). Profile of emotional intelligence: Construction, validity and reliability. *Salud Mental, 25,* 50–60.

Soussignan, R. (2002). Duchenne smile, emotional experience, and autonomic reactivity: A test of the facial feedback hypothesis. *Emotion, 2,* 52–74.

Sowell, E. R., Thompson, P. M., Welcome, S. E., Henkenius, A. L., Toga, A. W., & Peterson, B. S. (2003). Cortical abnormalities in children and adolescents with attention-deficit hyperactivity disorder. *Lancet, 362,* 1699–1707.

Soyguet, G., & Tuerkcapar, H. (2001). Assessment of interpersonal schema patterns in antisocial personality disorder: A cognitive interpersonal perspective. *Turk Psikoloji Dergisi, 16,* 55–69.

Spanos, N. P. (1996). *Multiple identities and false memories.* Washington, DC: American Psychological Assoc.

Spanos, N. P., Burgess, C. A., Burgess, M. F., Samuels, C., & Blois, W. O. (1997). *Creating false memories of infancy with hypnotic and nonhypnotic procedures.* Unpublished manuscript, Carlton Univ., Ottawa, Canada.

Spehar, B., & Gillam, B. (2002). Modal completion in the Poggendorff illusion: Support for the depth-processing theory. *Psychological Science, 13,* 306–312.

Speitzer, G. M., McCall, M. M., & Mahoney, J. D. (1997). Early identification of international executive potential. *Journal of Applied Psychology, 82,* 6–29.

Spelke, E. S. (2005). Sex differences in intrinsic aptitude for mathematics and science? A Critical Review. *American Psychologist, 60,* 950–958.

Sperling, G. (1960). The information available in brief visual presentations. *Psychological Monographs, 74,* 1–29.

Sperry, R. W. (1964). The great cerebral commissure. *Scientific American, 210*(1), 42–52.

Sperry, R. W. (1968). Hemisphere disconnection and unity in conscious awareness. *American Psychologist, 23,* 723–733.

Sperry, R. W. (1970). *Perception in the absence of neocortical commissures. In perception and its disorders* (Res. Publ. A.R.N.M.D., Vol. 48). New York: The Association for Research in Nervous and Mental Disease.

Sperry, R. W. (1988). Psychology's mentalists paradigm and the religion/science tension. *American Psychologist, 43,* 607–613.

Sperry, R. W. (1995). The future of psychology. *American Psychologist, 5*(7), 505–506.

Spiegel, D. (1995). Essentials of psychotherapeutic intervention for cancer patients. *Support Care Cancer, 3,* 252–256.

Spiegel, D., & Kato, P. M. (1996). Psychological influences on cancer incidence and progression. *Harvard Review of Psychiatry, 4,* 10–26.

Spinath, F. M., Harlaar, N., Ronald, A., & Plomin, R. (2004). Substantial genetic influence on mild mental impairment in early childhood. *American Journal of Mental Retardation, 109,* 34–43.

Spitzer, R. L., Gibbon, M., Skodol, A. E., Williams, J. B. W., & First, M. B. (2002). *DSM-IV-TR Casebook.* Washington, DC: American Psychiatric Publishing.

Spoendlin, H. H., & Schrott, A. (1989). Analysis of the human auditory nerve. *Hearing Research, 43,* 25–38.

Sprecher, S., & Hendrick, S. S. (2004). Self-disclosure in intimate relationships: Associations with individual and relationship characteristics over time. *Journal of Social & Clinical Psychology, 23,* 857–877.

Squier, L. H., & Domhoff, G. W. (1998). The presentation of dreaming and dreams in introductory psychology textbooks: A critical examination with suggestions for textbook authors and course instructors. *Dreaming: Journal of the Association for the Study of Dreams, 8,* 149–168.

Squire, L. R., & Kandel, E. R. (1999). *Memory: From mind to molecules.* New York: Scientific American Library.

Stajkovic, A. D., & Luthans, F. (1997). Business ethics across cultures: A social cognitive model. *Journal of World Business, 32,* 17–34.

Stamm, B. H. (2003). Bridging the rural-urban divide with telehealth and telemedicine. In B. H. Stamm (Ed.), *Rural behavioral health care: An interdisciplinary guide* (pp. 145–155). Washington, DC: American Psychological Assoc.

Stancliffe, R. J. (1997). Community residence size, staff presence and choice. *Mental Retardation, 35,* 1–9.

Stanley, T. L. (2004). The wisdom of employment testing. *Supervision, 65,* 11–13.

Stannard, M. B. (2006, January 29). The war within. *San Francisco Chronicle.* Retrieved June 28, 2006 from http://www.sfgate.com/cgi-bin/article.cgi?f=/c/a/2006/01/29/MNGMHGVCEV1.DTL

Stansfeld, S., & Fuhrer, R. (2002). Social relations and coronary heart disease. In S. A. Stansfeld & M. G. Marmot (Eds.), *Stress and the heart: Psychosocial pathways to coronary heart disease* (pp. 72–85). Williston, VT: BMJ Books.

Stanton, C., Spirito, A., Donaldson, D., & Doergers, J. (2003). Risk taking behavior and adolescent suicide attempts. *Suicide and Life Threatening Behavior, 33,* 74–79.

Stanton, M. D., & Shadish, W. R. (1997). Outcome, attrition, and family-couples treatment for drug abuse: A meta-analysis and review of the controlled, comparative studies. *Psychological Bulletin, 122,* 170–191.

Steele, J. (2000). Handedness in past human populations: Skeletal markers. *Laterality 5,* 193–220.

Steele, J. (2003). Children's gender stereotypes about math: The role of stereotype stratification. *Journal of Applied Social Psychology, 33,* 2587–2606.

Stein, J. (2002, November 4). The new politics of pot. *Time,* pp. 56–66.

Stein, M., Herman, D. S., Trisvan, E., Pirraglia, P., Engler, P., & Anderson, B. J. (2005). Alcohol use and sexual risk behavior among human immunodeficiency virus-positive alcoholism persons. *Clinical and Experimental Research, 29,* 837–843.

Steinke, W. R. (2003). Perception and recognition of music and song following right hemisphere stroke: A case study. *Dissertation Abstracts International: Section B: The Sciences and Engineering, 63,* 4948.

Stelmack, R. M., Knott, V., & Beauchamp, C. M. (2003). Intelligence and neural transmission time: A brain stem auditory evoked potential analysis. *Personality and Individual Differences, 34,* 97–107.

Stern, K., & McClintock, M. K. (1998, March 12). Regulation of ovulation by human pheromones. *Nature, 392,* 177.

Stern, L. (1985). *The structures and strategies of human memory.* Homewood, IL: Dorsey.

Stern, R. M., & Koch, K. L. (1996). Motion sickness and differential susceptibility. *Current Directions in Psychological Science, 5,* 115–120.

Sternberg, R. J. (1986). *Intelligence applied.* Orlando, FL: Harcourt Brace Jovanovich.

Sternberg, R. J. (2001). What is the common thread of creativity? Its dialectical relation to intelligence and wisdom. *American Psychologist, 56,* 360–362.

Sternberg, R. J. (2003). Intelligence. In D. K. Freedheim (Ed.), *Handbook of psychology: Vol. 1, History of psychology* (pp. 135–156). New York: John Wiley & Sons.

Sternberg, R. J., & Grigorenko, E. L. (2001). *Environmental effects on cognitive abilities.* Mahwah, NJ: Erlbaum.

Sternberg, R. J., Lautrey, J., & Lubart, T. I. (2003). Brain imaging studies of intelligence: Individual differences and neurobiology. In R. J. Haier (Ed.), *Models of intelligence: International perspectives* (pp. 185–193). Washington, DC: American Psychological Assoc.

Stevenson, H. W. (1992). Learning from Asian schools. *Scientific American, 265*(6), 70–76.

Stevenson, H. W. (1993). Why Asian students still outdistance Americans. *Educational Leadership,* 63–65.

Stevenson, H. W., Chen, C., & Lee, S.-Y. (1993, January 1). Mathematics achievement of Chinese, Japanese, and American children: Ten years later. *Science, 259,* 53–58.

Stevenson, H. W., Lee, S., & Mu, X. (2000). Successful achievement in mathematics: China and the United States. In F. M. van Lieshout & P. G. Heymans (Eds.), *Developing talent across the life span* (pp. 167–183). Philadelphia: Psychology Press.

Stevenson, H. W., Lee, S.-Y., & Stigler, J. W. (1986, February 14). Mathematics achievment of Chinese, Japanese, and American children. *Science, 231,* 693–697.

Stewart, R. H. (1965). Effect of continuous responding on the order effect in personality impression formation. *Journal of Personality and Social Psychology, 1,* 161–165.

Stock, M. B., & Smythe, P. M. (1963). Does undernutrition during infancy inhibit brain growth and subsequent intellectual development? *Archives of Disorders in Childhood, 38,* 546–552.

Stodghill, R. (1998, June 15). Where'd you learn that? *Time,* 52–59.

Stokes, P. D. (2006). *Creativity from constraints: The psychology of breakthrough.* New York: Springer.

Stolzenberg, R. M., & Waite, L. J. (2005). Effects of marriage, divorce, and widowhood on health. In S. M. Bianchi, L. M. Casper, & B. R. King (Eds.), *Work, family, health, and well-being* (pp. 361–377). Mahwah, NJ: Erlbaum.

Stoner, J. A. F. (1961). *A comparison of individual and group decisions involving risk.* Unpublished master's thesis, School of Industrial Management, MIT.

Storch, E. A., & Storch, J. B. (2003). Academic dishonesty and attitudes towards academic dishonest acts: Support for cognitive dissonance theory. *Psychological Reports, 92,* 174–176.

Storksen, I., Roysamb, E., & Holmen, T. L. (2006). Adolescent adjustment and well-being: Effects of parental divorce and distress. *Scandinavian Journal of Psychology, 47,* 75–84.

Storm, L., & Ertel, S. (2001). Does psi exist? Comments on Milton and Wiseman's (1999) meta-mnalysis of Ganzfeld research. *Psychological Bulletin, 12,* 424–433.

Stowell, J. R., McGuire, L., Robles, T., Glaser, R., & Kiecolt-Glaser, J. K. (2003). Psychoneuroimmunology. In. A. M. Nezu & C. M. Nezu (Eds.), *Handbook of psychology: Vol. 9, Health psychology,* (pp. 75–95). New York: John Wiley & Sons.

Straton, D. (2004). Guilt and PTSD. *Australian and New Zealand Journal of Psychiatry, 38,* 269–270.

Strecker, R. R., Morairty, S., Thakkar, M. M., Porkka-Heiskanen, T., Basheer, R., Dauphin, L. J., et al. (2002). Adenosinergic modulation of basal forebrain and preoptic/anterior hypothalamic neuronal activity in the control of behavioral state. *Behavioural Brain Research, 115,* 183–204.

Streeter, S. A., & McBurney, D. H. (2003). Waist-hip ratio and attractiveness. New evidence and a critique of a "critical test". *Evolution and Human Behaviour, 24,* 88–98

Strickland, B. R. (2000). Misassumptions, misadventures, and the misuse of psychology. *American Psychologist, 55,* 331–338.

Strollo, P. J., Jr., & Davé, N. B. (2005). Sleep apnea. In D. J. Buysse (Ed.), *Sleep disorders and psychiatry* (pp. 77–105). Washington, DC: American Psychiatric Publishing.

Stromswold, K. (1995). The cognitive and neural bases of language acquisition. In M. S. Gazzaniga (Ed.), *The cognitive neurosciences* (pp. 855–870). Cambridge, MA: MIT Press.

Studer, J. R. (2000). Adolescent suicide: Aggression turned inward. In D. S. Sandhu & C. B. Aspy (Eds.), *Violence in American schools: A practical guide for counselors* (pp. 269–284). Alexandria, VA: American Counseling Assoc.

Stumpf, H., & Stanley, J. C. (1998). Stability and change in gender-related differences on the college board advanced placement and achievement tests. *Current Directions in Psychological Research, 7,* 192–196.

Stylianou, D. A. (2002). On the interaction of visualization and analysis: The negotiation of a visual representation in expert problem solving. *Journal of Mathematical Behavior, 21,* 303–317.

Subotnik, R. F., & Arnold, K. D. (1994). *Beyond Terman: Contemporary longitudinal studies of giftedness and talent*. Norwood, NJ: Ablex.

Suhr, J. A. (2002). Malingering, coaching, and the serial position effect. *Archives of Clinical Neuropsychology, 17,* 69–77.

Sullivan, E. V., Rosenbloom, M. J., Lim, K. O., & Pfefferbaum, A. (2000). Longitudinal changes in cognition, gait, and balance in abstinent and relapsed alcoholic men: Relationships to changes in brain structure. *Neuropsychology, 14,* 178–188.

Sullivan, M. (2004). Exaggerated pain behavior: By what standard? *Clinical Journal of Pain, 20,* 433–439.

Sumnall, H. R., Jerome, L., Doblin, R., & Mithoefer, M. C. (2004). Response to Parrott, A. C., Buchanan T., Heffernan, T. M., Scholey, A., Ling, J., & Rodgers, J. (2003): Parkinson's disorder, psychomotor problems and dopaminergic neurotoxicity in recreational Ecstasy/MDMA users. *Psychopharmacology, 167,* 449–450.

Sumova, A., Saladek, M., Jac, M., & Illnervoa, H. (2002). The circadian rhythm of Per1 gene product in rat's suprachiasmatic nucleus and its modulation by seasonal changes in daylight. *Brain Research, 947,* 260–270.

Sundel, S. S. (1991). The effects of videotaped modeling on the acquisition, performance, and generalization of job-related social skills in adults with mental retardation living in group homes. *Dissertation Abstracts International, 51,* 2522.

Sunstrom, E., DeMeuse, K., & Futrell, D. (1990). Work teams: Applications and effectiveness. *American Psychologist, 31,* 120–133.

Surguladze, S. A., Young, A. W., Senior, C., Brebion, G., Travis, M. J., & Phillips, M. L. (2004). Recognition accuracy and response bias to happy and sad facial expressions in patients with major depression. *Neuropsychology, 18,* 212–218.

Susser, E., Sprecher, E., & Yarnitsky, D. (1999). Paradoxical heat sensation in healthy subjects: Peripherally conducted by A or C fibres? *Brain: A Journal of Neurology, 122,* 239–246.

Suzuki, S. (2006). Investigation of the cognitive process in selection of stress coping behavior. *Japanese Journal of Psychology, 76,* 527–533.

Swaab, D. F., & Hoffman, M. A. (1995). Sexual differentiation of the human hypothalamus in relation to gender and sexual orientation. *Trends in Neuroscience, 18,* 264–270.

Symons, C. S., & Johnson, B. T. (1997). The self-reference effect in memory: A meta-analysis. *Psychological Bulletin, 121,* 371–394.

Szabo, S. T. (2003). Interactions between serotonergic and noradrenergic systems: Their involvement in antidepressant treatment of anxiety and affective disorders. *Dissertation Abstracts International: Section B: The Sciences and Engineering, 64,* 1642.

Szatkowska, I., Grabowska, A., & Szymanska, O. (2001). Evidence for involvement of ventro-medial prefrontal cortex in a short-term storage of visual images. *Neuroreport: for Rapid Communication of Neuroscience Research, 12,* 1187–1190.

Szucs, R. P., Frankel, P. S., McMahon, L. R., & Cunningham, K. A. (2005). Relationship of cocaine-induced c-Fos expression to behaviors and the role of serotonin 5-HT2A receptors in cocaine-induced c-Fos expression. *Behavioral Neuroscience, 119,* 1173–1183.

Takami, S., Getchell, M. L., Chen, Y., Monti-Bloch, L., & Berliner, D. L. (1993). Vomeronasal epithelial cells of the adult human express neuron-specific molecules. *Neuro Report, 4,* 374–378.

Takeuchi, S. A. (2000). If I don't look good, you don't look good? Toward a new matching theory of interpersonal attraction based on the behavioral and the social exchange principles. *Dissertation Abstracts International Section A: Humanities and Social Sciences, 60,* 4198.

Talarico, J. M., & Rubin, D. C. (2003). Confidence, not consistency, characterizes flashbulb memories. *Psychological Science, 14,* 455–461.

Tamminga, C. A., & Vogel, M. (2005). Images in neuroscience: The cerebellum. *American Journal of Psychiatry, 162,* 1253.

Tan, D. T. Y., & Singh, R. (1995). Attitudes and attraction: A developmental study of the similarity-attraction and dissimilarity-repulsion hypotheses. *Personality and Social Psychology Bulletin, 21,* 975–986.

Tanaka, J. W., Curran, T., & Sheinberg, D. L. (2005). The training and transfer of real-world perceptual expertise. *Psychological Science, 16,* 145–151.

Tang, R. Q., Zhao, X. Z., Shi, Y. Y., Tang, W., Gu, N. F., Feng, G. Y., et al. (2006). Family-based association study of Epsin 4 and schizophrenia. *Molecular Psychiatry, 11,* 395–399.

Tanner, J. M. (1978). *Foetus into man: Physical growth from conception to maturity*. Cambridge, MA: Harvard Univ. Press.

Tapert, S. F., & Schweinsburg, A. D. (2005). The human adolescent brain and alcohol use disorders. In M. Galanter (Ed.), *Recent developments in alcoholism: Volume 17. Alcohol problems in adolescents and young adults* (pp. 177–197). New York: Kluwer/ Plenum.

Tappan, M. B. (2006). Mediated moralities: Sociocultural approaches to moral development. In M. Killen & J. G. Smetana (Eds.), *Handbook of moral development* (pp. 351–374). Mahwah, NJ: Erlbaum.

Taufiq, A. M., Fujii, S., Yamazaki, Y., Sasaki, H., Kaneko, K., Li, J., et al. (2005). Involvement of IP3 receptors in LTP and LTD induction in guinea pig hippocampal CA1 neurons. *Learning & Memory, 12,* 594–600.

Taylor, D. M., & Moghaddam, F. M. (1994). *Theories of intergroup relations: International social psychological perspectives*. Westport, CT: Praeger.

Taylor, P. J., Russ-Eft, D. F., & Chan, D. W. L. (2005). A meta-analytic review of behavior modeling training. *Journal of Applied Psychology, 90,* 692–709.

Taylor, S. E. (2003). *Health Psychology* (5th ed.) New York: McGraw-Hill.

Taylor, S. E., Klein, L. C., Lewis, B. P., Gruenewald, T. L., Gurung, R. A. R., & Updegraff, J. A. (2000). Biobehavioral responses to stress in females: Tend-and-befriend, not fight-or-flight. *Psychological Review, 107,* 411–429.

Taylor, S. E., Pham, L. B., Rivkin, I. D., & Armor, D. A. (1998). Harnessing the imagination: Mental simulation, self-regulation, and coping. *American Psychologist, 53,* 429–439.

Taylor, S. E., & Repetti, R. L. (1997). Health psychology: What is an unhealthy environment and how does it get under the skin? *Annual Review of Psychology, 48,* 411–447.

Teasdale, T. W., & Owen, D. R. (2005). A long-term rise and recent decline in intelligence test performance: The Flynn effect in reverse. *Personality and Individual Differences, 39,* 837–843.

Terman, L. M. (1925). *Mental and physical traits of a thousand gifted children: Genetic studies of genius* (Vol. 1). Stanford, CA: Stanford Univ. Press.

Terrace, H. S., Son, L. K., & Brannon, E. M. (2003). Serial expertise of rhesus macaques. *Psychological Science, 14,* 66–73.

Terry, W. S. (2005). Serial position effects in recall of television commercials. *Journal of General Psychology, 132,* 151–163.

Testa, M., Livingston, J. A., & Collins, R. L. (2000). The role of women's alcohol consumption in evaluation of vulnerability to sexual aggression. *Experimental & Clinical Psychopharmacology, 8,* 185–191.

Thakkar, M. M., Winston, S., & McCarley, R. W. (2003). A-sub-1 receptor and adenosinergic homeostatic regulation of sleep-wakefulness: Effects of antisense to the A-sub-1 receptor in the cholinergic basal forebrain. *Journal of Neuroscience, 23,* 4278–4287.

Thelen, E. (1995). Motor development: A new synthesis. *American Psychologist, 50,* 79–95.

Thierry, K. L., & Spence, M. J. (2002). Source-monitoring training facilitates preschoolers' eyewitness memory performance. *Developmental Psychology, 38,* 428–437.

Thierry, N., Willeit, M., Praschak-Rieder, N., Zill, P., Hornik, K., Neumeister, A., et al. (2004). Serotonin transporter promoter gene polymorphic region (5-HTTLPR) and personality in female patients with seasonal affective disorder and in healthy controls. *European Neuropsychopharmacology, 14,* 53–58.

Thiffault, P., & Bergeron, J. (2003). Fatigue and individual differences in monotonous simulated driving. *Personality and Individual Differences, 34,* 159–176.

Thomas, A., & Chess, S. (1977). *Temperament and development.* New York: Brunner/Mazel.

Thomas, S. G., & Kellner, C. H. (2003). Remission of major depression and obsessive-compulsive disorder after a single unilateral ECT. *Journal of ECT, 19,* 50–51.

Thompson, C. P., Cowan, T. M., & Frieman, J. (1993). *Memory search by a memorist.* Hillsdale, NJ: Erlbaum.

Thompson, M. P., & Kingree, J. B. (2006). The roles of victim and perpetrator alcohol use in intimate partner violence outcomes. *Journal of Interpersonal Violence, 21,* 163–177.

Thompson, P. M., Hayashi, K. M., Zubicaray, G. D., Janke, A. L., Rose, S. E., Semple, J., et al. (2003). Dynamics of gray matter loss in Alzheimer's disease. *The Journal of Neuroscience, 23,* 994.

Thompson, P. M., Vidal, C., Giedd, J. N., Gochman, P., Blumnethal, J., Nicolson, R., et al. (2001). Mapping adolescent brain changes reveals dynamic wave accelerated gray matter loss in very early-onset schizophrenia. *Proceedings from the National Academy of Sciences, USA, 98,* 11650–11655.

Thompson, V. L. S., & Alexander, H. (2006). Therapists' race and African American clients' reactions to therapy. *Educational Publishing Foundation, 43,* 99–110.

Thompson-Schill, S. L, Bedny, M., Goldberg, R. F. (2005). The frontal lobes and the regulation of mental activity. *Current Opinion in Neurobiology, 15,* 219–224.

Thorberg, F. A., & Lyvers, M. (2006). Attachment, fear of intimacy and differentiation of self among clients in substance disorder treatment facilities. *Addictive Behaviors, 31,* 732–737.

Thorndike, E. L. (1898). Animal intelligence. *Psychological Review Monograph, 2*(4, Whole No. 8).

Thorne, F., Neave, N., Scholey, A., Moss, M., & Fink, B. (2002). Effects of putative male pheromones on female ratings of male attractiveness: Influence of oral contraceptives and the menstrual cycle. *Neuroendocrinology Letters, 23,* 291–297.

Thorne, F., Scholey, A. B., & Neave, N. (2000). Love is in the air? Effects of pheromones, oral contraceptive use and menstrual cycle phase on attraction. *Proceeding of the British Psychological Society, 8,* 49.

Thornhill, R., & Gangestad, S. W. (1999). The scent of symmetry: A human sex pheromone that signals fitness. *Evolution and Human Behavior, 20,* 175–201.

Thornton, L. M. (2005). Stress and immunity in a longitudinal study of breast cancer patients. *Dissertation Abstracts International: Section B: The Sciences and Engineering, 66,* 2843.

Thurstone, L. L. (1938). Primary mental abilities. *Psychometric Monographs,* 1.

Tilleczek, K. C., & Hine, D. W. (2006). The meaning of smoking as health and social risk in adolescence. *Journal of Adolescence, 29,* 273–287.

Timofeev, M. I. (1993). Irrational beliefs and conflict-handling orientations. *Journal of Rational-Emotive & Cognitive Behavior Therapy, 11,* 109–119.

Tindale, R. S., Munier, C., Wasserman, M., & Smith, C. M. (2002). Group processes and the holocaust. In L. S. Newman & R. Erber (Eds.), *Understanding genocide: The social psychology of the Holocaust* (pp. 143–161). New York: Oxford Univ. Press.

Ting, J., & Piliavin, J. A. (2000). Altruism in comparative international perspective. In J. Phillips, B. Chapman, & D. Stevens (Eds.), *Between state and market: Essays on charities law and policy in Canada* (pp. 51–105). Montreal and Kingston, Ontario, Canada: McGill-Queens Univ. Press.

Toft, M. D. (2003). *The geography of ethnic violence: Identity, interests, and the indivisibility of territory.* Princeton, NJ: Princeton Univ. Press.

Toga, A. W., & Thompson, P. M. (2003). Mapping brain asymmetry. *Nature Reviews Neuroscience, 4,* 37–48.

Tolman, E. C., & Honzik, C. H. (1930). Introduction and removal of reward, and maze performance in rats. University of California Publications in *Psychology, 4,* 257–275.

Tomer, A. (Ed.) (2000). *Death attitudes and the older adult: Theories, concepts, and applications.* Philadelphia: Brunner-Routledge.

Tooby, J., & Cosmides, L. (1990). The past explains the present: Emotional adaptations and the structure of ancestral environments. *Ethology and Sociobiology, 10,* 29–50.

Tooby, J., & Cosmides, L. (2005). Conceptual foundations of evolutionary psychology. In D. M. Buss (Ed.), *The handbook of evolutionary psychology* (pp. 5–67). Hoboken, NJ: John Wiley and Sons.

Tooby, J., Cosmides, L., & Barrett, H. C. (2003). The second law of thermodynamics is the first law of psychology: Evolutionary developmental psychology and the theory of tandem, coordinated inheritances: Comment on Lickliter and Honeycutt (2003). *Psychological Bulletin, 129,* 858–865.

Tosevski, D. L., Milovancevic, M. P. (2006). Stressful life events and physical health. *Current Opinion in Psychiatry, 19,* 184–189.

Tourangeau, R., Rips., J. L., & Rasinski, K. (2000). *Stalking the cognitive measurement error.* New York: Cambridge Univ. Press.

Travis, J. (2003, October 11). Visionary research: Scientists delve into the evolution of color vision in primates. *Science News,* 234–236.

Travis, J. (2004a, February 14). Code breakers: Scientists tease out the secrets of proteins that DNA wraps around. *Science News,* 106–107.

Travis, J. (2004b, January 17). Fear not: Scientists are learning how people can unlearn fear. *Science News,* 42–44.

Treaster, J. B. (1994, February 1). Survey finds marijuana use is up in high schools. *New York Times,* p. A1.

Treffert, D. A., & Wallace, G. L. (2002). Islands of genius. *Scientific American, 286*(6), 76–85.

Treisman, A. (2004). Psychological issues in selective attention. In M. S. Gazzaniga (Ed.), *The cognitive neurosciences* (3rd ed.) (pp. 529–544). Cambridge, MA: MIT Press.

Treisman, A. M. (1960). Contextual cues in selective listening. *Quarterly Journal of Experimental Psychology, 12,* 242–248.

Treisman, A. M. (1964). Verbal cues, language and meaning in selective attention. *American Journal of Psychology, 77,* 206–219.

Tremblay, J., & Cohen, J. (2005). Spatial configuration and list learning of proximally cued arms by rats in the enclosed four-arm radial maze. *Learning and Behavior, 33,* 78–89.

Tremblay, R. E., Hartup, W. W., & Archer, J. (Eds.) (2005). *Developmental origins of aggression*. New York: Guilford.

Triandis, H. C. (1994). *Culture and social behavior*. New York: McGraw-Hill.

Triandis, H. C. (2001). Individualism-collectivism and personality. *Journal of Personality, 69,* 907–924.

Trichopoulou, A, Costacou, T., Bamia, C., & Trichopoulos, D. (2003). Adherence to a Mediterranean diet and survival in a Greek population. *The New England Journal of Medicine, 348,* 2599–2608.

Trost, M. R., & Alberts, J. K. (2006). How men and women communicate attraction: An evolutionary view. In K. Dindia, C. Kathryn, & D. J. Canary (Eds.), *Sex differences and similarities in communication* (2nd ed, pp. 317–336). Mahwah, NJ: Erlbaum.

Trouilloud, D., Sarrazin, P., Bressoux, P., Bressoux, P., & Bois, J. (2006). Relation between teachers' early expectations and students' later perceived competence in physical education classes: Autonomy-supportive climate as a moderator. *Journal of Educational Psychology, 98,* 75–86.

Tryon, W. W. (2000). Behavior therapy as applied learning theory. *Behavior Therapist, 23,* 131–133.

Tryon, W. W. (2002). Neural network learning theory: Unifying radical behaviorism and cognitive neuroscience. *Behavior Therapist, 25,* 53–57.

Tseng, R. J., Padgett, D. A., Dhabhar, F. S., Engler, H., & Sheridan, J. F. (2005). Stress-induced modulation of NK activity during influenza viral infection: Role of glucocorticoids and opioids. *Brain, Behavior and Immunity, 19,* 153–164.

Tucker, C. M., & Herman, K. C. (2002). Using culturally sensitive theories and research to meet the academic needs of low-income African American children. *American Psychologist, 57,* 762–773.

Tugade, M. M., & Fredrickson, B. L. (2004). Resilient individuals use positive emotions to bounce back from negative emotional experiences. *Journal of Personality and Social Psychology, 86,* 320–333.

Tulving, E. (2002). Episodic memory: From mind to brain. *Annual Review of Psychology, 53,* 1–25.

Tulving, E. (2005). Episodic memory and autonoesis: Uniquely human? In H. S. Terrace & J. Metcalfe (Eds.), Th*e missing link in cognition: Origins of self-reflective consciousness* (pp. 3–56). New York: Oxford Univ. Press.

Turati, C. (2004). Why faces are not special to newborns: An alternative account of the face preference. *Current Directions in Psychological Science, 13,* 5–8.

Turkeltaub, P. E., Gareau, L., Flowers, D. L., Zeffiro, T. A., & Eden, G. F. (2003). Development of neural mechanisms for reading. *Nature Neuroscience, 6,* 767–773.

Turkheimer, E. (1991). Individual and group differences in adoption studies of IQ. *Psychological Bulletin, 110,* 392–405.

Turkheimer, E., Haley, A., Waldron, M., D'Onofrio, B., & Gottesman, I. I. (2003). Socioeconomic status modifies heritability of IQ in young children. *Psychological Science, 14,* 623–628.

Turkheimer, E., & Waldron, M. (2000). Nonshared environment: A theoretical, methodological, and quantitative review. *Psychological Bulletin, 126,* 78–108.

Turnbull, C. M. (1961). Observations. *American Journal of Psychology, 1,* 304–308.

Turnbull, S., Ward, A., Treasure, J., Jick, H., & Derby, L. (1996). The demand for eating disorder care. An epidemiological study using the general practice research database. *British Journal of Psychiatry, 169,* 705–712.

Turner, M. E. (2001). *Groups at work: Theory and research.* Mahwah, NJ: Erlbaum.

U.S. Department of Labor (2004). Bureau of Statistics. Retrieved April 28, 2006 from: http://www.bls.gov/cps/wlf-databook.htm

U.S. Bureau of the Census. (1990). *Statistical abstract of the United States* (110th ed.). Washington, DC: U.S. Government Printing Office.

U.S. Bureau of the Census. (2001). *The 65 years and over population.* Retrieved May 11, 2006 from http://www.census.gov/prod/2001pubs/c2kbr01-10.pdf

U.S. Bureau of the Census (2002a). *United States Department of Commerce News.* Washington, DC. Retrieved August 23, 2003 from http://www.census.gov/Press-Release/www/2002/cb02-19.html

U.S. Bureau of the Census, (2002b). *Median age at first marriage.* Washington, DC. Retrieved August 23, 2003, from http://www.infoplease.com/ipa/A0005061.html

U.S. Bureau of the Census, (2005). Facts for features: Women's history month. Retrieved June 6, 2006, from http://www.census.gov/Press-Release/www/releases/archives/facts_for_features_special_editions/003897.html

U.S. Department of Labor (2006). *Training: Apprenticeship.* Retrieved June 29, 2006 from http://www.dol.gov/dol/topic/training/apprenticeship.htm

Uchino, B. N. (2004). *Social support and physical health: Understanding the health consequences of relationships.* New Haven, CT: Yale Univ. Press.

Uchino, B. N., Cacioppo, J. T., & Kiecolt-Glaser, J. K. (1996). The relationship between social support and physiological processes: A review with emphasis on underlying mechanisms and implications for health. *Psychological Bulletin, 119,* 488–531.

Uchino, B. N., Uno, D., & Holt-Lunstad, J. (1999). Social support, physiological processes, and health. *Current Directions in Psychological Science, 8,* 145–148.

Uddin, L. Q., Kaplan, J. T., Molnar-Szakacs, I., Zaidel, E., & Iacoboni, M. (2005). Self-face recognition activates a frontoparietal "mirror" network in the right hemisphere: An event-related fMRI study. *Neuroimage, 25,* 926–35.

Ulrich, R., & Azrin, N. (1962). Reflexive fighting in response to aversive stimulation. *Journal of Experimental Analysis of Behavior, 5,* 511–520.

Underwood, M. K. (2003). *Social aggression among girls.* New York: Guilford.

UNICEF. (2001). A league table of teenage births in rich nations. *Innocenti Report Card, 3.*

Vaillant, G. E. (1977). *Adaptation to life.* Boston: Little, Brown.

Vaillant, G. E. (2000). Adaptive mental mechanisms: Their role in positive psychology. *American Psychologist, 55,* 89–98.

Vaillant, G. E. (2003). *Aging well: Surprising guideposts to a happier life from the landmark Harvard Study of Adult Development.* New York: Little, Brown.

Valaki, C., Maestu, F., Ortiz, T., Papanicolaou, A. C., & Simos, P. G. (2004). Contributions of magnetoencephalography to neurolinguistics: Evidence from cross-linguistic studies. *Hellenic Journal of Psychology, 1,* 268–281.

Vallar, G. (2006). Memory systems: The case of phonological short-term memory. A festschrift for Cognitive Neuropsychology. *Cognitive Neuropsychology, 23,* 135–155.

Vallee, B. I. (1998). Alcohol in the Western world. *Scientific American, 278*(6), 80–85.

Valtonen, M., Niskanen, L., Kangas, A., & Koskinen, T. (2005). Effect of melatonin-rich night-time milk on sleep and activity in elderly institutionalized subjects. *Nordic Journal of Psychiatry, 59,* 217–221.

van Achterberg, M. E., Rohrbaugh, R. M., & Southwick, S. M. (2001). Emergence of PTSD in trauma survivors with dementia. *Journal of Clinical Psychiatry, 62,* 206–207.

Van den Bulck, J. (2004). Media use and dreaming: The relationship among television viewing, computer game play, and nightmares or pleasant dreams. *Dreaming, 14,* 43–49.

Van Dongen, H. P. A., Maislin, G., Mullington, J. M., & Dinges, D. F. (2003). The cumulative cost of additional wakefulness: Dose-response effects on neurobehavioral functions and sleep physiology from chronic sleep restriction and total sleep deprivation. *Sleep, 26,* 117–126.

Van Eerde, W., & Thierry, H. (1996). Vroom's expectancy models and work-related criteria: A meta-analysis. *Journal of Applied Psychology, 81,* 575–586.

van Elst, L. T., & Trimble, M. R. (2003). Amygdala pathology in schizophrenia and psychosis of epilepsy. *Current Opinion in Psychiatry, 16,* 321–326.

Van Praag, H., & Gage, F. H. (2002). Stem cell research, part 1: New neurons in the adult brain. *Journal of the American Academy of Child and Adolescent Psychiatry, 41,* 354–356.

Van Praag, H., Zhao, X., & Gage, F. H. (2004). Neurogenesis in the adult mammalian brain. In M. S. Gazzaniga (Ed.), *The cognitive neurosciences* (3rd ed.) (pp. 127–137). Cambridge, MA: MIT Press.

Van Yperen, N. W., & Buunk, B. P. (1990). A longitudinal study of equity and satisfaction in intimate relationships. *European Journal of Social Psychology, 54,* 287–309.

VandenBos, G., & Williams, S. (2000). The Internet versus the telephone: What is telehealth anyway? *Professional Psychology: Research & Practice, 31,* 490–492.

Vanderschuren, L. J., Niesink, R. J., & Van Ree, J. M. (1997). The neurobiology of social play behavior in rats. *Neuroscience and Biobehavioral Reviews, 21,* 309–326.

Vanderwerker, L. C., & Prigerson, H. G. (2004). Social support and technological connectedness as protective factors in bereavement. *Journal of Loss & Trauma, 9,* 45–57.

Vandewater, E. A., Shim, M. S., & Caplovitz, A. G. (2004). Linking obesity and activity level with children's television and video game use. *Journal of Adolescence, 27,* 71–85.

Van-Hooff, J. C., & Golden, S. (2002). Validation of an event-related potential memory assessment procedure: Intentional learning as opposed to simple repetition. *Journal of Psychophysiology, 16,* 12–22.

van-Iddekinge, C. H., Raymark, P. H., Eidson, C. E. Jr., & Attenweiler, W. J. (2004). What do structured selection interviews really measure? The construct validity of behavior description interviews. *Human Performance, 17,* 71–93.

Vastag, B. (2003). Addiction poorly understood by clinicians: Experts say attitudes, lack of knowledge hinder treatment. *Journal of the American Medical Association, 290,* 1299–1303.

Vauclair, J. (1996). *Animal cognition: An introduction to modern comparative psychology.* Cambridge, MA: Harvard Univ. Press.

Vaughn, D. (1996). *The Challenger launch decision: Risky technology, culture, and deviance at NASA.* Chicago, IL: Univ. of Chicago Press.

Vecera, S. P., Vogel, E. K., & Woodman, G. F. (2002). Lower region: A new cue for figure-ground assignment. *Journal of Experimental Psychology: General, 131,* 194–205.

Vermetten, E., & Bremner, J. D. (2002). Circuits and systems in stress: II. Applications to neurobiology and treatment in posttraumatic stress disorder. *Depression and Anxiety, 16,* 14–38.

Vernon, P. A. (Ed.). (1993). *Biological approaches to the study of human intelligence.* Norwood, NJ: Ablex.

Vernon, P. A. (2000). Biological theories. In A. E. Kazdin (Ed.), *Encyclopedia of psychology* (Vol. 5, pp. 145–147). Washington, DC: American Psychological Assoc. and New York: Oxford Univ. Press.

Verona, E., Joiner, T. E., Johnson, F., & Bender, T. W. (2006). Gender specific gene-environment interactions on laboratory-assessed aggression. *Biological Psychology, 71,* 33–41.

Viding, E., Spinath, F. M., Price, T. S., Bishop, D. V. M., Dale, P. S., & Plomin, R. (2004). Genetic and environmental influence on language impairment in 4-year-old same-sex and opposite-sex twins. *Journal of Child Psychology and Psychiatry and Allied Disciplines, 45,* 315–325.

Viers, D., & Prouty, A. M. (2001). We've come a long way? An overview of research of dual-career couples' stressors and strengths. *Journal of Feminist Family Therapy, 13,* 169–190.

Viglione, D. J., & Taylor, N. (2003). Empirical support for interrater reliability of Rorschach comprehensive system coding. *Journal of Clinical Psychology, 59,* 111–121.

Villemure, C., & Bushnell, M. C. (2002). Cognitive modulation of pain: How do attention and emotion influence pain processing? *Pain, 95,* 195–199.

Villemure, C., Slotnick, B. M., & Bushnell, M. C. (2003). Dissociation of attentional and emotional modulation of pain using pleasant and unpleasant odors in humans. *Pain, 106,* 101–108.

Vingerhoets, G., Berckmoes, C., & Stroobant, N. (2003). Cerebral hemodynamics during discrimination of prosodic and semantic emotion in speech studied by transcranial Doppler ultrasonography. *Neuropsychology, 17,* 93–99.

Vinnicombe, S., & Singh, V. (2003). Women-only management training: An essential part of women's leadership development. *Journal of Change Management, 3,* 294–306.

Viñuales-Mas, M., Fernàndez-Aranda, F., Jiménez-Murcia, S., Turón-Gil, V., & Vallejo-Ruiloba, J. (2001). Low self-esteem, restricting eating behavior, and psychopathological variables in anorexia and bulimia nervosa: A study of cases and controls. *Psicología Conductual Revista Internacional de Psicología Clínica de las Salud, 9,* 267–278.

Virkkunen, M. (1983). Insulin secretion during the glucose tolerance test in antisocial personality. *British Journal of Psychiatry, 142,* 598–604.

Visootsak, J., Warren, S. T., & Anido, A. (2005). Fragile X syndrome: An update and review for the primary pediatrician. *Clinical Pediatrics, 44,* 371–381.

Visscher, W. A., Feder, M., Burns, M., Brady, T. M., & Bray, R. M. (2003). The impact of smoking and other substance use by urban women on birthweight of their infants. *Substance Use and Misuse, 38,* 1063–1093.

Visser, P. S., Krosnick, J. A., & Lavrakas, P. J. (2000). Survey research. In T. Harry & C. M. Judd (Eds.), *Handbook of research methods in social and personality psychology* (pp. 223–252). New York: Cambridge Univ. Press.

Volkow, N. D., Wang, G-J., Maynard, L., Jayne, M., Fowler, J. S., & Zhu, W. (2003). Brain dopamine is associated with eating behaviors in humans. *International Journal of Eating Disorders, 33,* 136–142.

Volpe, K. (2004, January). Taylor takes on "fight-or-flight." *APS Observer,* p. 21.

von Hippel, W., Hawkins, C., & Narayan, S. (1994). Personality and perceptual expertise: Individual differences in perceptual identification. *Psychological Science, 5,* 401–406.

von Hofsten, C., & Fazel-Zandy, S. (1984). Development of visually guided hand orientation in reaching. *Journal of Experimental Child Psychology, 38,* 208–219.

Vossel, G., & Rossman, R. (1986). Classical conditioning of electrodermal activity and Maltzman's conception of voluntary orienting responses: A successful replication. *Zeitschrift fuer Experimentelle und Angewandte Psychologie, 33,* 312–328.

Votruba-Drzal, E., Coley, R. L., & Chase-Lansdale, P. L. (2004). Child care and low-income children's development: Direct and moderated effects. *Child Development, 75,* 296–312.

Voyer, D., Voyer, S., & Bryden, M. P. (1995). Magnitude of sex differences in spatial abilities: A meta-analysis and consideration of critical variables. *Psychological Bulletin, 117,* 250–270.

Vroom, V. H. (1964). *Work and motivation.* New York: Wiley.

Vygotsky, L. S. (1978). Mind in society: The development of higher mental processes. Cambridge, MA: Harvard Univ. Press. (Original works published 1930, 1933, and 1935.)

Wadden, T. A., Crerand, C. E., & Brock, J. (2005). Behavioral treatment of obesity. *Psychiatric Clinics of North America, 28,* 151–170.

Wade, G. W. (2004). Regulation of body fat content? *American Journal of Physiology—Regulatory, Integrative and Comparative Physiology, 286,* R14–R15.

Wade, T. D., Bulik, C. M., Neale, M., & Kendler, K. S. (2000). Anorexia nervosa and major depression: Shared genetic and environmental risk factors. *American Journal of Psychiatry, 157,* 469–471.

Wagar, B. M., & Thagard, P. (2004). Spiking Phineas Gage: A neurocomputational theory of cognitive–affective integration in decision making. *Psychological Review, 111,* 67–79.

Wagner, B. M. (1997). Family risk factors for child and adolescent suicidal behavior. *Psychological Bulletin, 121,* 246–298.

Wagner, U., Gais, S., Haider, H., Verleger, R., & Born, J. (2004). Sleep inspires insight. *Nature, 427,* 352–355.

Wahlsten, D. (1999). Single-gene influences on brain and behavior. *Annual Review of Psychology, 50,* 599–624.

Waite, L. J., & Joyner, K. (2001). Emotional satisfaction and physical pleasure in sexual unions: Time horizon, sexual behavior, and sexual exclusivity. *Journal of Marriage & the Family, 63,* 247–264.

Walchle, S. B., & Landman, J. (2003). Effects of counterfactual thought on post-purchase consumer affect. *Psychology and Marketing, 20,* 23–46.

Wald, M. L. (1997, September 11). "Truckers are driving with too little sleep, research shows." *New York Times,* p. A22.

Walk, R. D., & Gibson, E. J. (1961). A comparative and analytical study of visual depth perception. *Psychological Monographs,* No. 75.

Walker, M. P., & Stickgold, R. (2006). Sleep, memory, and plasticity. *Annual Review of Psychology, 57,* 139–166.

Wall, P. D., & Melzack, R. (1996). *The challenge of pain* (2nd ed.). Harmondworth, UK: Penguin.

Wallerstein, J. S., Blakeslee, S., & Lewis, J. (2000). *The unexpected legacy of divorce: Twenty-five year landmark study.* New York: Hyperion.

Walster, E., Walster, G. W., & Berscheid, E. (1978). *Equity: Theory and research.* Boston: Allyn & Bacon.

Waltz, J. A., Knowlton, B. J., Holyoak, K. J., Boone, K. B., Mishkin, F. S., Santos, M. M., et al. (1999). A system for relational reasoning in human prefrontal cortex. *Psychological Science, 10,* 119–125.

Wampold, B. E. (2001). *The great psychotherapy debate: Models, methods, and findings.* Mahwah, NJ: Erlbaum.

Wampold, B. E., Mondin, G. W., Moody, M., Stich, F., Benson, K., & Ahn, H. (1997). A meta-analysis of outcome studies comparing bona fide psychotherapies: Empirically, "all must have prizes." *Psychological Bulletin, 122,* 203–215.

Wang, C., & Chen, W. (2000). The efficacy of behavior therapy in 9 patients with phobia. *Chinese Mental Health Journal, 14,* 351–352.

Wang, Q. (2003). Infantile amnesia reconsidered: A cross-cultural analysis. *Memory, 11,* 65–80.

Wang, Q., & Ross, M. (2005). What we remember and what we tell: The effects of culture and self-priming on memory representations and narratives. *Memory, 13,* 594–606.

Wang, V. O., & Sue, S. (2005). In the eye of the storm: Race and genomics in research and practice. *American Psychologist, 60,* 37–45.

Warner J. (2005). *Perfect madness: Motherhood in the age of anxiety.* New York: Riverhead Books.

Warnock, J. (2002). Female hypoactive sexual desire disorder: Epidemiology, diagnosis and treatment. *CNS Drugs, 16,* 745–753.

Wasik, B. A., Bond, M. A., & Hindman, A. (2006). The effects of a language and literacy intervention on Head Start children and teachers. *Journal of Educational Psychology, 98,* 63–74.

Wass, T. S., Simmons, R. W., Thomas, J. D., & Riley, E. P. (2002). Timing accuracy and variability in children with prenatal exposure to alcohol. *Alcoholism: Clinical and Experimental Research, 26,* 1887–1896.

Watanabe, H., Kobayashi, Y., Sakura, M., Matsumoto, Y., & Mizunami, M. (2003). Classical olfactory conditioning in the cockroach *Periplaneta americana. Zoological* Science, *20,* 1447–1454.

Waters, A. J., Gobet, F., & Leyden, G. (2002). Visuospatial abilities of chess players. *British Journal of Psychology, 93,* 557–565.

Watkins, L. R., & Maier, S. F. (2003). When good pain turns bad. *Current Directions in Psychological Science, 12,* 232–236.

Watson, D. L., & Tharp, R. G. (1997). *Self-directed behavior: Self-modification for personal adjustment* (7th ed.). Pacific Grove, CA: Brooks/Cole.

Watson, J. B. (1913). Psychology as the behaviorist views it. *Psychological Review, 20,* 158–177.

Watson, J. B. (1924). *Behaviorism.* Chicago: Univ. of Chicago Press.

Watson, J. B., & Rayner, R. (1920). Conditioned emotional reactions. *Journal of Experimental Psychology, 3,* 1–14.

Wechsler, H., Dowdall, G. W., Davenport, A., & DeJong, W. (2000). *Binge drinking on college campuses: Results of a national study.* Available online at: www.hsph.harvard.edu/cas

Wedeking, C., Seebeck, T., Bettens, F., & Paepke, A. J. (1995). MHC-dependent mate preferences in humans. *Proceedings of the Royal Society of London, B, 260,* 245–249.

Wegner, D. M., Wenzlaff, R. M., & Kozak, M. (2004). Dream rebound. *Psychological Science, 15,* 232–236.

Weichold, K., Silbereisen, R. K., & Schmitt-Rodermund, E. (2003). Short-term and long-term consequences of early versus late physical maturation in adolescents. In C. Hayward (Ed.), *Gender differences at puberty* (pp. 241–276). New York: Cambridge Univ. Press.

Weigel, D. J., Martin, S. S., & Bennett, K. K. (2006). Contributions of the home literacy environment to preschool-aged children's emerging literacy and language skills. *Early Child Development and Care, 176,* 357–378.

Weigert, A. J., & Gecas, V. (2005). Symbolic interactionist reflections on Erikson, identity, and postmodernism. *Identity, 5,* 161–174.

Weinberg, M. K., Tronick, E. Z., Cohn, J. F., & Olson, K. L. (1999). Gender differences in emotional expressivity and self-regulation during early infancy. *Developmental Psychology, 35,* 175–188.

Weinberg, R. S., & Gould, D. (1999). *Foundations of sport and exercise psychology* (2nd ed.). Champaign, IL: Human Kinetics.

Weiner, I. B. (2006). The Rorschach inkblot method. In R. P. Archer (Ed.), *Forensic uses of clinical assessment instruments* (pp. 181–207). Mahwah, NJ: Erlbaum.

Weinfield, N. S., Whaley, G. J. L., & Egeland, B. (2004). Continuity, discontinuity, and coherence in attachment from infancy to late adolescence: Sequelae of organization and disorganization. *Attachment and Human Development, 6*, 73–97.

Weingarten, S. M., & Cummings, J. L. (2001). Psychosurgery of frontal–subcortical circuits. In D. G. Lichter & J. L. Cummings (Eds.), *Frontal-subcortical circuits in psychiatric and neurological disorders* (pp. 421–435). New York: Guilford.

Weinstein, R. S., Madison, W., & Kuklinski, M. (1995). Raising expectations in schooling: Obstacles and opportunities for change. *American Educational Research Journal, 32*, 121–160.

Weinstein, R. S., Soule, C. R., Collins, F., Cone, J., Melhorn, M., & Simantocci, K. (1991). Expectations and high school change: Teacher-researcher collaboration to prevent school failure. *American Journal of Community Psychology, 19*, 333–402.

Weiss, A. P., Zalesak, M., DeWitt, L., Goff, D., Kunkel, L., & Heckers, S. (2004). Impaired hippocampal function during the detection of novel words in schizophrenia. *Biological Psychiatry, 55*, 668–675.

Weiss, S. J., Wilson, P., & Morrison, D. (2004). Maternal tactile stimulation and the neurodevelopment of low birth weight infants. *Infancy, 5*, 85–107.

Weisse, C. S., Foster, K. K., & Fisher, E. A. (2005). The influence of experimenter gender and race on pain reporting: Does racial or gender concordance matter? *Pain Medicine, 6*, 80–87.

Weissman, D. E., Gordon, D., & Bidar-Sielaff, S. (2002) Fast fact and concept #78: Cultural aspects of pain management. Retrieved February 22, 2006, from http://www.eperc.mcw.edu/fastFact/ff_78.htm

Weisz, J. R., McCarty, C. A., Eastman, K. L., Chaiyasit, W., & Suwanlert, S. (1997). Developmental psychopathology and culture: Ten lessons from Thailand. In S. S. Luthar, J. A. Burack, D. Cicchetti, & J. R. Weisz (Eds.), *Developmental psychopathology: Perspectives on adjustment, risk, and disorder* (pp. 568–592). New York: Cambridge Univ. Press.

Wells, G. L., & Bradfield, A. L. (1998). "Good, you identified the suspect": Feedback to eyewitnesses distorts their reports of the witnessing experience. *Journal of Applied Psychology, 83*, 360–376.

Wells, G. L., & Bradfield, A. L. (1999). Distortions in eyewitnesses' recollections: Can the postidentification-feedback effect be moderated? *Psychological Science, 10*, 138–144.

Wells, G. L., & Olsen, E. A. (2003). Eyewitness testimony. *Annual Review of Psychology, 54*, 277–295.

Werker, J. F. (1989). Becoming a native listener. *American Scientist, 77*, 54–59.

Werker, J. F., & Desjardins, R. N. (1995). Listening to speech in the 1st year of life: Experiential influences on phoneme perception. *Current Directions in Psychological Science, 4*, 76–81.

Werker, J. F., & Tees, R. C. (2005). Speech perception as a window for understanding plasticity and commitment in language systems of the brain. *Developmental Psychobiology, 46*, 233–251.

Wernet, S. P., Follman, C., Magueja, C., & Moore-Chambers, R. (2003). Building bridges and improving racial harmony: An evaluation of the Bridges Across Racial Polarization Program®. In J. J. Stretch, E. M. Burkemper, W. J. Hutchison, & J. Wilson (Eds.), *Practicing social justice* (pp. 63–79). New York: Haworth.

Westen, D. (1998). Unconscious thought, feeling and motivation: The end of a century-long debate. In R. F. Bornstein & J. M. Masling (Eds.), *Empirical perspectives on the psychoanalytic unconscious* (pp. 1–43). Washington, DC: American Psychological Assoc.

Westen, D. (2005). Implications of research in cognitive neuroscience for psychodynamic psychotherapy. In F. O. Gabbard, J. S. Beck, & J. Holmes (Eds.), *Oxford textbook of psychotherapy* (pp. 443–448). New York: Oxford Univ. Press.

Weston, W. W. (2005). Patient-centered medicine: A guide to the biopsychosocial model. *Families, Systems, & Health, 23*, [Special issue: The Current State of the Biopsychosocial Approach], 387–392.

Wetzel, W., Wagner, T., & Balschun, D. (2003). REM sleep enhancement induced by different procedures improves memory retention in rats. *European Journal of Neuroscience, 18*, 2611–2617.

Wheeler, M. A., Stuss, D. T., & Tulving, E. (1997). Toward a theory of episodic memory: The frontal lobes and autonoetic consciousness. *Psychological Bulletin, 121*, 331–354.

White, K. K., & Abrams, L. (2002). Does priming specific syllables during tip-of-the-tongue states facilitate word retrieval in older adults? *Psychology and Aging, 17*, 226–235.

White, M. A., Kohlmaier, J. R., Varnado, S. P., & Williamson, D. A. (2003). Racial/ethnic differences in weight concerns: Protective and risk factors for the development of eating disorders and obesity among adolescent females. *Eating and Weight Disorders, 8*, 20–25.

White, P., & Waghorn, G. (2004). Mental illness and employment status. *Australian and New Zealand Journal of Psychiatry, 38*, 174–175.

Whiten, A., Horner, V., & Marshall-Pescini, S. (2005). Selective imitation in child and chimpanzee: A window on the construal of others' actions. In S. Hurley & N. Chater (Eds.), *Perspectives on imitation: From neuroscience to social science: Vol. 1: Mechanisms of imitation and imitation in animals* (pp. 263–283). Cambridge, MA: MIT Press.

Whorf, B. L. (1956). *Language, thought, and reality*. New York: MIT Press–Wiley.

Wicker, B., Keysers, J., Plailly, J., Royet, J-P., Gallese, V., & Rizzolatti, G. (2003). Both of us disgusted in my insula: The common neural basis of seeing and feeling disgust. *Neuron, 40*, 655–664.

Widiger, T. A., & Sankis, L. M. (2000). Adult psychopathology: Issues and controversies. *Annual Review of Psychology, 51*, 377–404.

Widner, R. L., Otani, H., & Winkelman, S. E. (2005). Tip-of-the-tongue experiences are not merely strong feeling-of-knowing experiences. *Journal of General Psychology, 132*, 392–407.

Wiens, A. N., & Menustik, C. E. (1983). Treatment outcome and patient characteristics in an aversion therapy program for alcoholism. *American Psychologist, 38*, 1089–1096.

Wierzbicki, M. (1993). *Issues in clinical psychology: Subjective versus objective approaches*. Boston: Allyn & Bacon.

Wiggins, J. S. (Ed.). (1996). *The five-factor model of personality: Theoretical perspectives*. New York: Guilford.

Wiggs, C. L., Weisberg, J. M., & Martin, A. (1999). Neural correlates of semantic and episodic memory retrieval. *Neuropsychologia, 37*, 103–118.

Wilcox, S., Evenson, K. R., Aragaki, A., Wassertheil–Smoller, S., Mouton, C. P., & Loevinger, B. L. (2003). The effects of widowhood on physical and mental health, health behaviors, and health outcomes: The Women's Health Initiative. *Health Psychology, 22*, 513–522.

Wilder, B. J., & Bruni, J. (1981). *Seizure disorders: A pharmacological approach to treatment*. New York: Raven.

Wilding, J., & Valentine, E. (1997). *Superior memory*. Hove, England: Psychology Press/Erlbaum.

Wilkins, V. M. (2005). Religion, spirituality, and psychological distress in cardiovascular disease. *Dissertation Abstracts International: Section B: The Sciences and Engineering, 66,* 3430.

Williams, J. C., Paton, C. C., Siegler, I. C., Eigenbrodt, M. L., Nieto, F. J., & Tyroles, H. A. (2000). Anger proneness predicts coronary heart disease risk: Prospective analysis from the atherosclerosis risk in communities (ARIC) study. *Circulation, 101,* 2034–2039.

Williams, J. E., & Best, D. L. (1990). *Sex and psyche: Gender and self viewed cross-culturally.* Newbury Park, CA: Sage.

Williams, J. E., Satterwhite, R. C., & Saiz, J. L. (1998). *The importance of psychological traits: A cross-cultural study.* New York: Plenum.

Williams, R. B. (2001). Hostility (and other psychological risk factors): Effects on health and the potential for successful behavioral approaches to prevention and treatment. In A. Baum, T. A. Revenson, & J. E. Singer (Eds.), *Handbook of health psychology* (pp. 661–688). Mahwah, NJ: Erlbaum.

Williams, S. (2000). How is telehealth being incorporated into psychology practice? *Monitor on Psychology, 31,* 15.

Williamson, P. (2006). *Mind, brain, and schizophrenia.* New York: Oxford Univ. Press.

Willis, S. L., & Schaie, K. W. (1999). Intellectual functioning in midlife. In S. L. Willis & J. D. Reid (Eds.), *Life in the middle: Psychological and social development in middle age* (pp. 233–247). San Diego, CA: Academic Press.

Wilson, R. S., & Bennett, D. A. (2003). Cognitive activity and risk of Alzheimer's disease. *Current Directions in Psychological Science, 12,* 87–91.

Wilson, R. S., Bennett, D. A., Bienias, J. L., de Leon, C. F. M., Morris, M. C., & Evans, D. A. (2003). Cognitive activity and cognitive decline in a biracial community population. *Neurology, 61,* 812–816.

Winerman, L. (2005). The mind's mirror. *Monitor on Psychology, 36,* 48.

Wing, H. (1969). *Conceptual learning and generalization.* Baltimore, MD: Johns Hopkins Univ.

Winn, P. (1995). The lateral hypothalamus and motivated behavior: An old syndrome reassessed and a new perspective gained. *Current Directions in Psychological Science, 4,* 182–187.

Winner, E. (1998). *Psychological aspects of giftedness.* New York: Basic Books.

Winner, E. (2000). The origins and ends of giftedness. *American Psychologist, 55,* 159–169.

Winson, J. (1990). The meaning of dreams. *Scientific American, 263*(11), 94–96.

Winston, A., & Winston, B. (2002). *Handbook of integrated short-term psychotherapy.* Washington, DC: American Psychiatric Assoc.

Wise, D., & Rosqvist, J. (2006). Explanatory style and well-being. In J. C. Thomas, D. L. Segal, & M. Hersen (Eds.), *Comprehensive handbook of personality and psychopathology, Vol. 1: Personality and everyday functioning* (pp. 285–305). Hoboken, NJ: John Wiley & Sons.

Wiseman, H., Mayseless, O., & Sharabany, R. (2006). Why are they lonely? Perceived quality of early relationships with parents, attachment, personality predispositions and loneliness in first-year university students. *Personality and Individual Differences, 40,* 237–248.

Witkin, H. A., Dyk, R. B., Faterson, H. F., Goodenough, D. R., & Karp, S. A. (1962). *Psychological differentiation: Studies of development.* New York: Wiley.

Wolberg, L. R. (1977). *The technique of psychotherapy* (3rd ed.). New York: Grune & Stratton.

Woldt, A. L., & Toman, S. M. (2005). Cultural influences and considerations in gestalt therapy. In S. Fernbacher & D. Plummer (Eds.), *Gestalt therapy: History, theory, and practice* (pp. 117–132). Thousand Oaks, CA: Sage.

Wolfson, C., Wolfson, D. B., Asgharian, M., M'Lan, C. E., Ostbye, T., Rockwood, K., et al. (2001). Reevaluation of the duration of survival after the onset of dementia. *New England Journal of Medicine, 344,* 1111–1116.

Wolpe, J. (1973). *The practice of behavior therapy* (2nd ed.). New York: Pergamon.

Wolpe, J. (1990). *The practice of behavior therapy* (4th ed.). New York: Pergamon.

Wood, W., & Quinn, J. M. (2003). Forewarned and forearmed? Two meta-analytic syntheses of forewarnings of influence appeals. *Psychological Bulletin, 129,* 119–138.

Wood, W., Wong., F. Y., & Chachere, J. G. (1991). Effects of media violence on viewers' aggression in unconstrained social interaction. *Psychological Bulletin, 109,* 371–383.

Woodruff-Pak, D. S. (2001). Insights about learning in Alzheimer's disease from the animal model. In M. E. Carrol & B. J. Overmier (Eds.), *Animal Research and Human Health: Advancing Human Welfare Through Behavioral Science* (pp. 385–406). Washington, DC: American Psychological Association.

Woods, S. C., Schwartz, M. W., Baskin, D. G., & Seeley, R. J. (2000). Food intake and the regulation of body weight. *Annual Review of Psychology, 51,* 255–277.

Woods, S. C., Seeley, R. J., Porte, D., Jr., & Schwartz, M. W. (1998, May 29). Signals that regulate food intake and energy homeostasis. *Science, 280,* 1378–1383.

Woodward, K. L., & Springen, K. (1992, August 22). Better than a gold watch. *Newsweek,* p. 71.

Woodward, M., Oliphant, J., Lowe, G., & Tunstall-Pedoe, H. (2003). Contribution of contemporaneous risk factors to social inequality in coronary heart disease and all causes of mortality. *Preventive Medicine: An International Journal Devoted to Practice and Theory, 36,* 561–568.

Wooffitt, R. (2005). From process to practice: Language, interaction and "flashbulb" memories. In H. Molder, & J. Potter (Eds.), *Conversation and cognition* (pp. 203–225). New York: Cambridge Univ. Press.

Worchel, S., Cooper, J., Goethals, G. R., & Olson, J. (1999). *Social psychology.* Belmont, CA: Wadsworth.

World Health Organization World Mental Health Survey Consortium. (2004). Prevalence, severity, and unmet need for treatment of mental disorders in the World Health Organization World Mental Health Surveys. *Journal of the American Medical Association, 291,* 2581–2590.

Worth, R. (1999, January). Exhaustion that kills—Medical residents suffer chronic sleep deprivation. *Washington Monthly,* pp. 15–20.

Wortman, C. B., & Silver, R. C. (1989). The myths of coping with loss. *Journal of Consulting & Clinical Psychology, 57,* 349–357.

Wright, A. A. (1998). Auditory list memory in rhesus monkeys. *Psychological Science, 9,* 91–98.

Wright, J. C., Anderson, D. R., Huston, A. C., Collins, P. A., Schmitt, K. L., & Linebarger, D. L. (1999). Early viewing of educational television programs: The short- and long-term effects on schooling. *Insights, 2,* 5–8.

Wright, J. H., Basco, M. R., & Thase, M. E. (2005). *Learning cognitive-behavior therapy: An illustrated guide.* Washington, DC: American Psychiatric Publishing.

Wright, K. (2003). Relationships with death: The terminally ill talk about dying. *Journal of Marital and Family Therapy, 29,* 439–454.

Wubbolding, R. E. (2005). The power of belonging. *International Journal of Reality Therapy, 24,* 43–44.

Wyatt, W. J. (1993). Identical twins, emergenesis, and environments. *American Psychologist, 48,* 1294–1295.

Wynn, K. (1995). Infants possess a system of numerical knowledge. *Current Directions in Psychological Science, 4,* 172–177.

Wynne, C. D. L. (2004). The perils of anthropomorphism. *Nature, 428,* 606.

Yaffe, K., Yung, L. L., Zmuda, J., & Cauley, J. (2002). Sex hormones and cognitive function in older men. *Journal of the American Geriatrics Society, 50,* 707–712.

Yaggi, H. K., Concato, J., Kernan, W. N., Lichtman, J. H., Brass, L. M., & Mohsenin, V. (2005). Obstructive sleep apnea as a risk factor for stroke and death. *New England Journal of Medicine, 353,* 2034–2041.

Yamada, M., Murai, T., Sato, W., Namiki, C., Miyamoto, T., & Ohigashi, Y. (2005). Emotion recognition from facial expressions in a temporal lobe epileptic patient with ictal fear. *Neuropsychologia, 43,* 434–441.

Yamamoto, K., & Chimbidis, M. E. (1966). Achievement, intelligence, and creative thinking in fifth grade children: A correlational study. *Merrill-Palmer Quarterly, 12,* 233–241.

Yang, C. C., Chen, H., & Hong, K. (2003). Visualization of large category map for Internet browsing. *Decision Support Systems, 35,* 89–102.

Yang, Q., & Chen, F. (2001). Behavior problems in children with simple obesity. *Chinese Journal of Clinical Psychology, 9,* 273–274.

Yanovski, S. Z., & Yanovski, J. A. (2002). Obesity. *New England Journal of Medicine, 346,* 591–602.

Yi, H., Williams, G. D., & Dufour, M. C. (December 2002). *Surveillance Report #61: Trends in alcohol-related fatal traffic crashes, United States, 1977–2000.* Rockville, MD: National Institute on Alcohol Abuse and Alcoholism, Division of Biometry and Epidemiology.

Yoo, S. H., Matsumoto, D., & LeRoux, J. A. (2006). The influence of emotion recognition and emotion regulation on intercultural adjustment. *International Journal of Intercultural Relations, 30,* 345–363.

Yotsutsuji, T., Saitoh, O., Suzuki, M., Hagino, H., Mori, K., Takahashi, T., et al. (2003). Quantification of lateral ventricular subdivisions in schizophrenia by high-resolution three-dimensional magnetic resonance imaging. *Psychiatry Research: Neuroimaging, 122,* 1–12.

Young, Q. W., Hellawell, D. J., Wan de Wal, C., & Johnson, M. (1996). Facial expression processing after amygdalotomy. *Neuropsychologia, 34,* 31–39.

Yrizarry, N., Matsumoto, D., Imai, C., Kookenm, K., & Takeuchi, S. (2001). Culture and emotion. In L. L. Adler & U. P. Gielen (Eds.), *Cross-cultural topics in psychology* (2nd ed., pp. 131–147). Westport, CT: Praeger/Greenwood.

Yukl, G. A. (2002). *Leadership in organizations.* Upper Saddle River, NJ: Prentice Hall.

Zadra, A., & Donderi, D. C. (2000). Nightmares and bad dreams: Their prevalence and relationship to well-being. *Journal of Abnormal Psychology, 109,* 273–281.

Zajonc, R. B. (1984). On the primacy of affect. *American Psychologist, 39,* 117–129.

Zalsman, G., & Mann, J. J. (2005). Editorial: The neurobiology of suicide in adolescents. An emerging field of research. *International Journal of Adolescent Medicine and Health, 17,* 195–196.

Zaragoza, M. S., Lane, S. M., Ackil, J. K., & Chambers, K. L. (1997). Confusing real and suggested memories: Source monitoring and eyewitness suggestibility. In N. L. Stein, P. A. Ornstein, B. Tversky, & C. Brainerd (Eds.), *Memory for everyday and emotional events* (pp. 401–425). Mahwah, NJ: Erlbaum.

Zaragoza, M. S., & Mitchell, K. J. (1996). Repeated exposure to suggestion and the creation of false memories. *Psychological Science, 7,* 294–300.

Zehr, D. (2000). Portrayals of Wundt and Titchener in introductory psychology texts: A content analysis. *Teaching of Psychology, 27,* 122–123.

Zemlan, F. P., Mulchahey, J. J., Scharf, M. B., Mayleben, D. W., Rosenberg, R., & Lankford, A. (2005). The efficacy and safety of the melatonin agonist β,-methyl-6-chloromelatonin in primary insomnia: A randomized, placebo-controlled, crossover clinical trial. *Journal of Clinical Psychiatry, 66,* 384–390.

Zeskind, P. S., & Gingras, J. L. (2006). Maternal cigarette-smoking during pregnancy disrupts rhythms in fetal heart rate. *Journal of Pediatric Psychology, 31,* 5–14.

Zhang, W. (1995). A study of field-dependent and field-independent cognitive styles of college students. *Psychological Science (China), 18,* 29–33.

Zigler, E. (1998). By what goals should Head Start be assessed? *Children's Services: Social Policy, Research, and Practice, 1,* 5–18.

Zigler, E. (2003). What would draw a basic scientist into Head Start (and why would he never leave? In R. J. Sternberg (Ed.), *Psychologists defying the crowd: Stories of those who battled the establishment and won* (pp. 273–282). Washington, DC: American Psychological Assoc.

Zigler, E., Finn-Stevenson, M., & Hall, N. W. (2002). *The first three years & beyond: Brain development and social policy.* New Haven, CT: Yale Univ. Press.

Zigler, E., & Hodapp, R. M. (1991). Behavioral functioning in individuals with mental retardation. *Annual Review of Psychology, 42,* 29–50.

Zigler, E., & Styfco, S. J. (Eds.). (1993). *Head Start and beyond.* New Haven, CT: Yale Univ. Press.

Zigler, E., & Styfco, S. J. (1994). Head Start: Criticisms in a constructive context. *American Psychologist, 49,* 127–132.

Zigler, E., & Styfco, S. J. (2001). Extended childhood intervention prepares children for school and beyond. *Journal of the American Medical Association, 285,* 2378–2380.

Zimmer, C. (2005, December 13). Children learn by monkey see, monkey do. Chimps don't. *New York Times,* p. D2.

Zimmer-Gembeck, M. J., Geiger, T. C., & Crick, N. R. (2005). Relational and physical aggression, prosocial behavior, and peer relations: Gender moderation and bidirectional associations. *Journal of Early Adolescence, 25,* 421–452.

Zisapel, N. (2001). Circadian rhythm sleep disorders: Pathophysiology and potential approaches to management. *CNS Drugs, 15,* 311–328.

Zonnevylle-Bender, M. J. S., van Goozen, S. H. M., Cohen-Kettenis, P. T., van Elburg, A., de Wildt, M., Stevelmans, E., et al. (2004). Emotional functioning in anorexia nervosa patients: Adolescents compared to adults. *Depression and Anxiety, 19,* 35–42.

Zubenko, G. S., Maher, B. S., Hughes, H. B., Zubenko, W. N., Stiffle, J. S., Kaplan, B. S., et al. (2003). Genome-wide linkage survey for genetic loci that influence the development of depressive disorders in families with recurrent, early-onset, major depression. *American Journal of Medical Genetics Part B: Neuropsychiatric Genetics, 123B,* 1–18.

Zubieta, J., Heitzeg, M. M., Smith, Y. R., Bueller, J. A., Yanjun Xu, K. X., Koeppe, R. A., et al. (2003, February 21). COMT val158met genotype affects -Opioid neurotransmitter responses to a pain stressor. *Science, 299,* 1240–1243.

Zubieta, J.-K., Bueller, J. A., Jackson, L. R., Scott, D. J., Xu, Y., Koeppe, R. A., et al. (2005). Placebo effects mediated by endogenous opioid activity on μ-opioid receptors. *The Journal of Neuroscience, 25,* 7754–7762.

Zucker, K. J. (2005). Gender identity disorder in children and adolescents. *Annual Review of Clinical Psychology, 1,* 467–492.

Zuckerman, M. (1979). *Sensation seeking: Beyond the optimal level of arousal.* Hillsdale, NJ: Erlbaum.

Zuckerman, M. (1994). *Behavioral expressions and biosocial bases of sensation seeking.* New York: Cambridge Univ. Press.

Zuckerman, M. (1999). Diathesis-stress models. In M. Zuckerman (Ed.), *Vulnerability to psychopathology: A biosocial model* (pp. 3–23). Washington, DC: American Psychological Assoc.

Zuckerman, M. (2000). Sensation seeking. In A. Kazdin (Ed.), *Encyclopedia of psychology* (pp. 225–226). Washington, DC: American Psychological Assoc.

Zuckerman, M. (2005). The neurobiology of impulsive sensation seeking: Genetics, brain physiology, biochemistry, and neurology. In C. Stough (Ed.), *Neurobiology of exceptionality* (pp. 31–52). New York: Kluwer/Plenum.

Zuckerman, M., Miyake, K., & Elkin, C. S. (1995). Effects of attractiveness and maturity of face and voice on interpersonal impression. *Journal of Research in Personality, 29,* 253–272.

Zuger, A. (1998, July 28). A fistful of aggression is found among women. *New York Times,* p. B8

Zwislocki, J. J. (1981). Sound analysis in the ear: A history of discoveries. *American Scientist, 245,* 184–192.

Photo Credits

Chapter 1

Opener: Chuck Savage; 3 Matt Stone/Corbis/Sygma; 5 Scott Camazine/Photo Researchers, Inc.; 7 Universal Press Syndicate; 8 right Steve Vidler/SuperStock; 8 middle right Robert Caputo/Stock Boston; 8 left Arvind Garg/Getty Images, Inc–Liaison; 8 middle left Frank Siteman/Index Stock Imagery, Inc.; 9 B. Daemmrich/The Image Works; 13 (T) ZUMA Press, Inc./Keystone Press Agency; 13 (B) Courtesy of the Library of Congress; 14 (T) BILDARCHIV DER OSTERREICHISCHE NATIONALBIBLIOTHEK, WIEN; 14 (B) Getty Images Inc.–Hulton Archive Photos; 15 G. Paul Bishop; 16 Chris J. Johnson/Stock Boston; 19 (T) Bob Mahony/The Image Works; 20 ©Jodi/CORBIS All Rights Reserved; 22 (T) Paul Newman/PhotoEdit Inc.; 22 (B) Jerry Bauer/Carol Gilligan; 23 Bob Daemmrich/Stock Boston; 24 UPI/Corbis/Bettmann; 26 Getty Images, Inc.; 27 Bill Anderson/Photo Researchers, Inc.; 28 Robert Brenner/PhotoEdit Inc.; 34 From the film OBEDIENCE copyright 1965 by Stanley Milgram and distributed by Penn State Media Sales. Permission granted by Alexandra Milgram; 37 Wade Bruton–UNC Charlotte.

Chapter 2

Opener: Scott Camazine/ Photo Researchers, Inc.; 47 E.R. Lewis,Y.Y. Zeevi, T.E. Everhart/ Edwin R. Lewis, Professor Emeritus; 49 Sanders Nicolson/Getty Images Inc.–Stone Allstock; 52 Brad Markel/Getty Images, Inc–Liaison; 55 ©Dan McCoy; 57 Courtesy of the Library of Congress; 63 (T) Richard T. Nowitz/Photo Researchers, Inc.; 63 middle Howard Sochurek/Woodfin Camp & Associates; 63 (B) Catherine Pouedras/Science Photo Library/Photo Researchers, Inc.; 64 Photo Researchers, Inc.; 67 Corbis RF; 71 (T) CNRI/Science Photo Library/Photo Researchers, Inc.; 71 (B) CNRI/Science Photo Library/Science Source/Photo Researchers, Inc.; 73 Jean Claude Revy/Phototake NYC; 74 Getty Images, Inc.; 76 Thomas Wanstall/The Image Works; 84 Joaquin Palting/CORBIS-NY.

Chapter 3

Opener: Bob Daemmrich/The Image Works; 89 Corbis/Bettmann; 90 Don Wong/Science Source/ Photo Researchers, Inc.; 91 E.R. Lewis, Y.Y. Zeevi, F.S. Werblin. Brain Research 15 (1969): 559–562. Scanning Electron microscopy of vertebrate receptors; 95 (T) Pearson Education/PH College; 95 (B) E.R. Lewis, Y.Y. Zeevi, F.S. Werblin. Brain Research 15 (1969): 559–562. Scanning Electron microscopy of vertebrate receptors; 102 Getty Images, Inc.; 104 Greg E. Mathieson/MAI/Landov/Landov LLC; 107 Robbie Jack/ Corbis/Bettmann; 108 Nik Kleinberg/ Stock Boston; 110 Fujifotos/The Image Works; 111 Steve Raymer/ Corbis/Bettmann; 120 Getty Images, Inc.; 117 Pawan Sinha and Tomaso Poggio. Photo ©Dirck Halstead/Gamma Liaison; 119 Paul Griffin/ Stock Boston.

Chapter 4

Opener: Piko/ Photo Researchers, Inc.; 132 Will & Deni McIntyre/ Photo Researchers, Inc.; 133 PhotoDisc/Getty Images; 149 The Granger Collection; 150 www.smokingisugly.com. Reprinted by permission of Christy Turlington; 152 (T) The Granger Collection; 152 (B) Kal Muller/ Woodfin Camp & Associates; 157 Tibor Hirsch/ Photo Researchers, Inc.; 158 Micael Newman/ PhotoEdit Inc.

Chapter 5

Opener: Azzara Steve/ Corbis/Sygma; 166 Joe Sohm/ The Image Works; 167 Tom Bean/ Getty Images Inc.–Stone Allstock; 168 Gregory K. Scott/Photo Researchers, Inc.; 170 Walter Dawn/Photo Researchers, Inc.; 173 Charles Gupton/Corbis/Bettmann; 183 Getty Images, Inc.; 180 David Ball/Corbis/Stock Market; 182 Carroll Seghers/Photo Researchers, Inc.; 188 Library of Congress; 189 Michael Newman/PhotoEdit Inc.; 190 Albert Bandura; 192 Amanda Coakes and Janet Mann.

Chapter 6

Opener: LWA-Sharie Kennedy/CORBIS-NY; 198 Babor Demjen/Stock Boston; 200 Jim Craigmyle/Masterfile Corporation; 201 A. Brucelle/Corbis/Sygma; 205 Jeff Isaac/Photo Researchers, Inc.; 208 Getty Images, Inc.-Photodisc.; 210 Michele Burgess/Corbis/Stock Market; 213 Courtesy of Dr. Hana Damasio, University of Iowa; 215 A. Pakieka/Photo Researchers, Inc.; 218 ©Renee Lynn/CORBIS All Rights Reserved; 221 Carmen Taylor/AP Wide World Photos.

Chapter 7

Opener: Rich LaSalle/Getty Images Inc.–Stone Allstock; 232 Picasso, Pablo (1881–1973). Nude with bunch of irises and mirror. 1934. 162 × 130 cm. ©Copyright Succession Picasso/ARS, NY Photo: R.G. Ojeda. Musee Picasso, Paris, France; 234 Kal Muller/Woodfin Camp & Associates; 237 Michael Nichols/NGS Image Collection; 249 EPA/Jens Wolf /Landov/Landov LLC; 252 Lew Merrim; 257 Jeff Greenberg/Photo Researchers, Inc.; 258 Jacques Chenet/Woodfin Camp & Associates; 260 Charles Gupton/Corbis/Bettmann; 263 James Schnepf/Getty Images, Inc–Liaison.

Chapter 8

Opener: Ellis Herwig/ Stock Boston; 276 James Marshall/ The Image Works; 280 (T) Camermann/ The Image Works; 280 bottom Rob Lewine/ CORBIS- NY; 281 AP Wide World Photos; 286 Michele Burgess; 287 Animals Animals © Jim Tuten; 288 © Fred / CORBIS All Rights Reserved; 289 (T) BARBARA PEACOCK/ Getty Images, Inc.–Taxi; 289 (B) Harlow Primate Laboratory/University of Wisconsin; 290 Getty Images, Inc.; 292 Catherine Ursillo/Photo Researchers, Inc.; 295 left Animals Animals © Zigmund Leszczynski; 295 right ©Michael S. Yamashita/CORBIS; 296 Photos by Peter DaSilva for The New York Times; 299 Robert Azzi/Woodfin Camp & Associates.

Chapter 9

Opener: PhotoDisc/Getty Images; 308 ©Keith/CORBIS All Rights Reserved; 310 ©Ellen B. Senisi; 312 David Young-Wolff/PHOTOEDIT; 314 Mark Richards/PHOTOEDIT; 317 top left Spencer Grant/Getty Images, Inc–Liaison; 317 bottom left Pearson Education/PH College; 317 top middle Lew Merrim/Photo Researchers, Inc.; 317 top right John Eastcott/The Image Works; 317 middle left Myrleen Ferguson Cate/PhotoEdit Inc.; 317 bottom right John Coletti/Stock Boston; 319 Lew Merrim/Photo Researchers, Inc.; 322 D. Greco/The Image Works; 324 (T) GeoStock/Getty Images, Inc.–Photodisc; 324 (B) Nina Leen/Getty Images/Time Life Pictures; 326 Getty Images, Inc.; 327 Will Faller; 329 Getty Images, Inc.; 330 Peter Byron/Photo Researchers, Inc.; 332 Suzanne Arms/The Image Works; 338 Deborah Davis/PhotoEdit Inc.; 341 PhotoDisc/Getty Images; 344 Bob Daemmrich/The Image Works.

Chapter 10

Opener: George Shelley/Masterfile Corporation; 358 left Ron Sachs/CORBIS-NY; 358 right Getty Images, Inc.; 359 top right Erich Lessing/Art Resource, NY; 359 top left Murray Close/Photofest; 359 bottom left LUCASFILM/20TH CENTURY FOX/Picture Desk, Inc./Kobal Collection; 359 bottom right Getty Images, Inc.; 360 (T) Matt Stone/Corbis/Sygma;

361 Corbis/Bettmann; 362 Library of Congress; 366 Jose Louis Pelaez/CORBIS-NY; 370 Lynsey Addario/AP Wide World Photos; 379 (T) Bob Daemmrich/Stock Boston; 379 bottom right Ken Karp/Pearson Education/PH College.

Chapter 11

Opener: Spencer Grant/PhotoEdit Inc.; 386 Grant LeDuc; 388 David W. Hamilton/Getty Images Inc.–Image Bank; 390 Peter Rogers/Getty Images, Inc.–Liaison; 395 Vince Streano/CORBIS-NY; 400 Christopher Bissell/Getty Images Inc.–Stone Allstock; 404 Philip North-Coombes/Getty Images Inc.–Stone Allstock; 407 Lawrence Migdale/Getty Images Inc.–Stone Allstock; 408 Getty Images, Inc.

Chapter 12

Opener: Getty Images, Inc.; 417 Stock Montage, Inc./Historical Pictures Collection; 419 Getty Images, Inc.; 432 Susan Greenwood/Getty Images, Inc.–Liaison; 436 B. Sporre/zefa/Masterfile Corporation; 441 Monte S. Buchsbaum, M.D., Mt. Sinai School of Medicine, New York, NY; 445 Jose Luis Pelaez/CORBIS-NY.

Chapter 13

Opener: Getty Images, Inc.; 452 The Freud Museum/Corbis/Sygma; 454 Michael Rougier/Getty Images/Time Life Pictures; 458 Albert Bandura; 461 Corbis - Comstock Images Royalty Free; 463 Bob Daemmrich/Stock Boston; 474 (T) Eric Roth/Index Stock Imagery, Inc.; 474 (B) Laima E. Druskis/Pearson Education/PH College; 476 M. Antman/The Image Works; 477 Zigy Kaluzny/Getty Images Inc.–Stone Allstock; 478 Spencer Grant/PhotoEdit Inc..

Chapter 14

Opener: Getty Images, Inc.; 483 AP Wide World Photos; 486 David Buffington/Getty Images, Inc.–Photodisc.; 487 PHILLIP HAYSON/Photolibrary.Com; 488 Getty Images, Inc.; 491 Sidney/The Image Works; 493 Ross Taylor/AP Wide World Photos; 495 CORBIS-NY; 496 Richard Hutchings/PhotoEdit Inc.; 497 AP Wide World Photos; 498 ©MADD. Used by pemission; 502 Alain Oddie/PhotoEdit Inc.; 505 Getty Images Inc.–Hulton Archive Photos; 507 AP Wide World Photos; 509 Walter Hodges/Getty Images Inc.–Stone Allstock; 510 William Langley/Getty Images, Inc.–Taxi.

Name Index

Subject Index